P9-AFV-853

THE COLLECTED WORKS OF
SAMUEL TAYLOR COLERIDGE 12

MARGINALIA

General Editor: KATHLEEN COBURN

THE COLLECTED WORKS

1. LECTURES 1795: ON POLITICS AND RELIGION

2. THE WATCHMAN

3. ESSAYS ON HIS TIMES

4. THE FRIEND

5. LECTURES 1808–1819: ON LITERATURE

6. LAY SERMONS

7. BIOGRAPHIA LITERARIA

8. LECTURES 1818–1819: ON THE HISTORY OF PHILOSOPHY

9. AIDS TO REFLECTION

10. ON THE CONSTITUTION OF THE CHURCH AND STATE

11. SHORTER WORKS AND FRAGMENTS

12. MARGINALIA

13. LOGIC

14. TABLE TALK

15. OPUS MAXIMUM

16. POETICAL WORKS

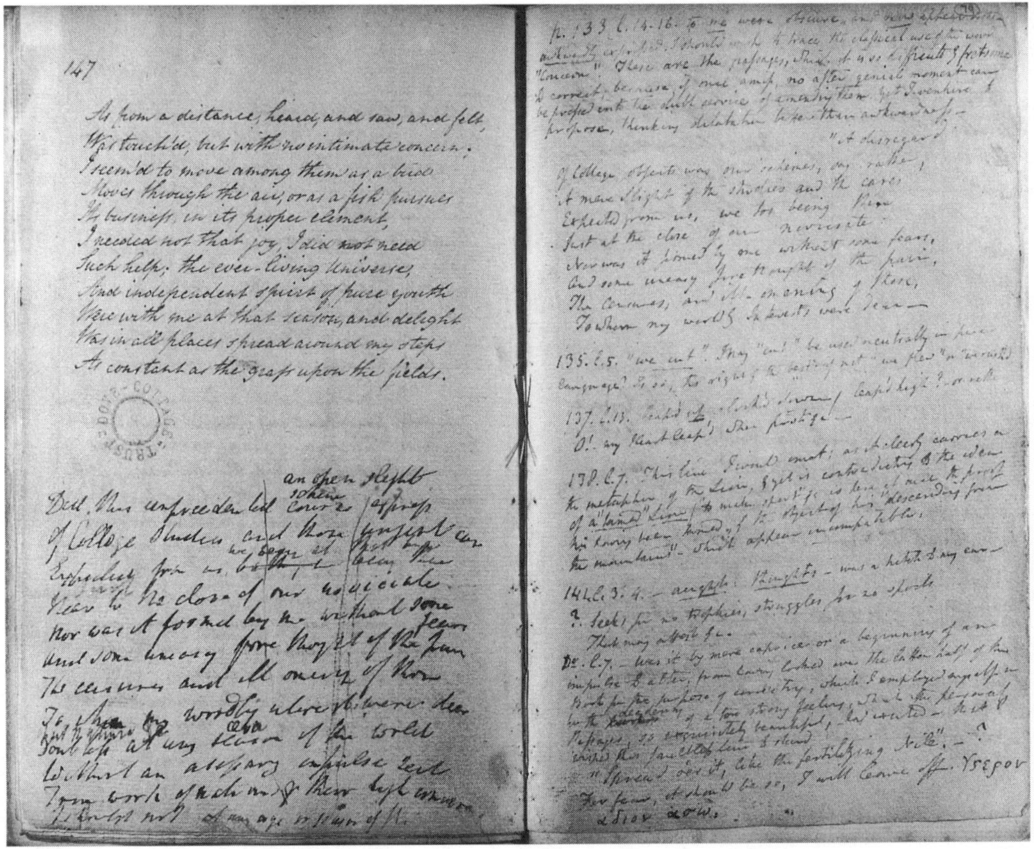

1. Two pages of "Prelude" MS B, containing notes in the hands of SH, WW, and C, respectively. See W. Wordsworth "Prelude" headnote. The Wordsworth Trust; reproduced by kind permission

THE COLLECTED WORKS OF

Samuel Taylor Coleridge

Marginalia

VI

Valckenaer to Zwick

ADDENDA

INDEX

EDITED BY

H. J. Jackson and

George Whalley

BOLLINGEN SERIES LXXV

PRINCETON UNIVERSITY PRESS

This edition of the text by Samuel Taylor Coleridge is
copyright © 2001 by Princeton University Press

The Collected Works, sponsored by Bollingen Foundation, is published in
the United States of America by Princeton University Press,
41 William Street, Princeton, New Jersey 08540
All rights reserved
ISBN 0-691-00495-1
LCC 87-104402

Library of Congress Cataloging-in-Publication Data
(Revised for vol. 3)
Coleridge, Samuel Taylor, 1772–1834.
Marginalia.
(Bollingen series; 75) (The Collected Works
of Samuel Taylor Coleridge; 12)
Includes bibliographical references.
Contents: 1. Abbt to Byfield—2. Camden to Hutton—3. Irving to Oxlee
I. Whalley, George, 1915–1983. II. Title. III. Series. IV. Series: Coleridge,
Samuel Taylor, 1772–1834. Works. 1969; 12.
PR4470.F69 vol. 12 [PR4480] 87-104402
ISBN 0-691-09879-4 (Princeton University Press: v. 1)
ISBN 0-691-09889-1 (Princeton University Press: v. 2)
ISBN 0-691-09954-5 (Princeton University Press: v. 3)

The Collected Works constitutes
the seventy-fifth publication in Bollingen Series

The present work, number 12 of the Collected Works,
is in 6 volumes, this being 12: VI

Princeton University Press books are printed on acid-free paper and meet
the guidelines for permanence and durability of the Committee on
Production Guidelines for Book Longevity of the Council on Library Resources

Printed in the United States of America
1 3 5 7 9 10 8 6 4 2

THIS EDITION
OF THE WORKS OF
SAMUEL TAYLOR COLERIDGE
IS DEDICATED
IN GRATITUDE TO
THE FAMILY EDITORS
IN EACH GENERATION

CONTENTS

VI

LIST OF ILLUSTRATIONS *page* xi
FOREWORD xiii
EDITORIAL PRACTICE: A BRIEF GUIDE xxiii
ABBREVIATIONS xxv
ADDENDA 247
INDEX 337

Marginalia

[† designates a "Lost Book"—a book reported to contain marginal notes in C's hand but which the editor has not been able to find and for which no transcript of marginalia is known to exist.]

Lodewijk Kasper Valckenaer *Diatribe de Aristobulo Judaeo* 3
Sir Harry Vane *A Healing Question Propounded and Resolved* 10
Robert Vaughan *The Life and Opinions of John de Wycliffe* 12
William Vincent *The Greek Verb Analysed* 25
Vindex *The Conduct of the British Government* 28
Virgil *Georgica . . . hexaglotta* 30
Aeneid tr Wordsworth *see* William WORDSWORTH
François Marie Arouet de Voltaire *A Treatise on Toleration* 32
Gerhard Voss *Poeticarum institutionum libri tres* 34
[Edward Gibbon Wakefield] *A Letter from Sydney* 35
John Walker *A Dictionary of the English Language* 38
William Wall *Conference between Two Men* 41
John Benn Walsh, Baron Ormathwaite
On the Present Balance of Parties 44
Popular Opinions on Parliamentary Reform 50

Daniel Waterland
The Importance of the Doctrine of the Holy Trinity 54
A Vindication of Christ's Divinity 73
Alaric Alexander Watts *Poetical Sketches* 94
John Webster *The Displaying of Supposed Witchcraft* 95
Adam Weishaupt
Apologie des Misvergnügens und Uebels 125
Pythagoras† 128
Ueber den Kantischen Anschauungen† 129
Ueber Wahrheit und sittliche Vollkommenheit 130
William Charles Wells *Two Essays* 131
Benjamin Wheeler *Theological Lectures* 134
Whistlecraft *see* FRERE
John Whitaker *The Origin of Arianism Disclosed* 136
Gilbert White *Works, in Natural History* 147
Thomas Whitfield *A Discourse of Liberty of Conscience* 154
Christoph Martin Wieland
Comische Erzählungen 156
Idris 158
Neueste Gedichte 159
Edward Williams *Poems, Lyric and Pastoral* 161
Walter Wilson *Memoirs of the Life and Times of Daniel De Foe* 163
Johann Christoph Wolf *Curae philologicae et criticae* 164
Karl Christian Wolfart *Jahrbücher für den Lebens-Magnetismus* 169
Christian Wolff *Logic* 171
[Christopher Wordsworth]
Six Letters to Granville Sharp 177
"Who Wrote ΕΙΚΩΝ ΒΑΣΙΛΙΚΗ*?" Considered* 184
William Wordsworth
"Benjamin the Waggoner" MS I 187
The Excursion 189
"The Prelude" MS B 194
"Translation of Virgil *Aeneid*" 197
Francis Wrangham
Life of Dr Richard Bentley 216
Scraps 218
Xenophon *Memoirs of Socrates* 222

Thomas Young *A Course of Lectures on Natural Philosophy*† 224
Zeitschrift für spekulative Physik ed Friedrich Wilhelm Joseph von Schelling 225
Henry Augustus Zwick *Calmuc Tartary* 246

ADDENDA
Thomas Amory *The Life of John Buncle* 249
Edwin Atherstone *The Last Days of Herculaneum* 251
John and Michael Banim *Tales by the O'Hara Family* 256
Richard Baxter *Reliquiae Baxterianae* COPY A 257
Joseph Beaumont *Some Observations upon the Apologie of Dr Henry More*† 265
La danse des morts 266
Declaration of Principles 267
Henry Augustus Dillon-Lee *The Life and Opinions of Sir Richard Maltravers* 268
William Godwin *Abbas* 270
John Haslam *Medical Jurisprudence* 285
Johann Gottfried Herder *Verstand und Erfahrung* 290
Immanuel Kant *Vermischte Schriften* COPY D 291
Robert Leighton *The Genuine Works* COPY B 295
Pietro Metastasio *Opere* 320

APPENDIX
Some Mistaken Attributions 331

INDEX to Vols I to VI 337

LIST OF ILLUSTRATIONS

1. Two pages of "Prelude" MS B, containing notes in the hands of SH, WW, and C, respectively *frontispiece*

2. Plate XXV from Andrew Tooke *The Pantheon* (1771) 111

3. Frontispiece portrait of the author from Robert Leighton *The Genuine Works* I (1819) 313

FOREWORD

BUT FOR PRECEDENT and consistency, this Foreword could as well be called an Afterword. Its brief reflections on the experience of editing Coleridge's marginalia are intended to act as a bookend to the "Editor's Introduction" by George Whalley in the first volume of the series, and to offer a different though perfectly compatible perspective.[1]

There is, on the face of it, something inherently absurd about the business of annotating annotations which may themselves be notes to notes. And yet those of us who produce and use this edition are convinced of the value of Coleridge's writings and understand that with the passage of time and the loss of awareness of the original occasion, they will be hard to understand without some glossing. We have had to ask ourselves what sort of note is really necessary, and what sort of note is most useful. Although the answers to these questions vary a bit from one instance to the next, and although the physical uniformity of the thirty-odd volumes of the *Collected Works* conceals some disparity in practice, it is possible to detect general principles at work. Some are—or appear to be—self-evident. Words in languages other than English have to be translated. Names of people, places, and things liable to be unfamiliar to a conventionally-educated reader in the late twentieth century have to be identified (Anna Laetitia Barbauld, then, but not William Wordsworth or Queen Anne). Readers will want to know the sources of direct quotations. All these are matters of common knowledge that Coleridge would have been able to take for granted in a conventionally-educated reader of his own time, and these we have taken as minimal requirements for our annotation. Since this is a scholarly edition, however, we go beyond the minimum and also provide cross-references to the larger body of Coleridge's thought as revealed in his published works, letters, and notebooks; and we make an effort to indicate the sources of his ideas and information. But here begins the slippery slope. How much should a reader be told about a given person, place, or thing; and how far should an editor go in tracing connections? Where do you start, and where do you stop?

[1] I regret that I have not been able to fulfil George Whalley's plans for this volume by including several Appendices that he mentioned—marked books, lost books, etc. Fortunately, other publications are now available to cover most of the ground.

The first general law of editorial annotation, it seems to me, must be, the shorter the better. We all feel so, almost instinctively; it takes decades of academic training to persuade us otherwise. Coleridge himself praised the unobtrusive editorial work of Ralph Winterton as contrasted with "your ponderous Note-makers" (POETAE **1**). Samuel Johnson's Preface to Shakespeare (1765) offers a psychological explanation for this widespread preference: "Particular passages are cleared by notes, but the general effect of the work is weakened. The mind is refrigerated by interruption; the thoughts are diverted from the principal subject; the reader is weary, he suspects not why; and at last he throws away the book which he has too diligently studied." Since marginalia are by nature responsive and already, arguably, distracting enough, notes to marginalia have to be particularly careful about making further demands on the reader's attention. If the editor after many hours has ceased to be a reliable judge of superfluity, a fresher pair of eyes and a more ruthless pair of scissors may have to be brought in.

The second general law is that you must be sure to pitch the notes at a level you can maintain and avoid the seduction of the endless quest, the temptation of becoming expansive about your own hobby-horses, and the desire to put on display all the cul-de-sacs you had to explore before coming to a conclusion. A note that I am particularly proud of is one that took me to ten libraries in four cities and to increasingly rare and technical material in three languages. It reads, "E. F. F. Chladni *Ueber Feuer-Meteore* (Vienna 1819) 412–13."

The third law is not a general law but one that certainly holds true for Coleridge: the immediate source is usually the best, meaning the most satisfying, most complete, most revealing one. Since in his case we have extraordinarily full records of his reading, partly through the marginalia, it is often possible to cite the very book from which he derived the point he is making. If you can get the edition and even the copy that he used, so much the better. The exact source has the unquestionable rightness of the solution to a cryptic crossword. In J. SEDGWICK **14**, for example, Coleridge observes that the author's ad hominem argument against Methodist doctrine—that the Methodists themselves were a lot of scruffy malcontents—could have been used against the early Christians, and that in fact one does encounter such an argument in "Trajan, Pliny, Tacitus, the Antonines, Celsus, Lucian, &c &c." We might have gone trolling through the writings of Trajan, Pliny, and the rest—in fact we did do so—but all these names appear in Chapter 16, entitled "The Conduct of the Roman Government towards the Christians, from the Reign of Nero to that of Constantine", in Edward Gibbon's *Decline and Fall of the Roman*

Empire, a book that Coleridge and his contemporaries knew well. He had no idea of displaying arcane learning and it would be misleading to suggest that he did. A reference to Gibbon is therefore neater and more accurate than a much fuller note might have been.

Similarly, Coleridge's throw-away line, "the adorable Maia (i.e. Delusion) of the Brahmin Theosophers" (VALCKENAER **7**), requires a gloss; but where do you begin? I started with reference books, including some that Coleridge is known to have used, and with a standard source for his information about the Brahmins, and came up with a note that is at once loaded with information and nigglingly tenuous:

> Maia is the name of a minor Greek deity, one of the Pleiades, mother of Hermes, as well as of a Roman fertility or harvest goddess. Both of these are thought to be versions of an earth goddess, the "Great Mother", whose cult originated in Asia Minor. C may mean that their Brahmin equivalent represents the merely phenomenal world, and this interpretation of his remark gains some support from such exercises in comparative mythology as Thomas Maurice *History of Hindostan* (2 vols 1795, 1798), which opens with a Plate representing a female figure called the "Isis Omnia" or "the Indian Isa, and Grecian Ceres", and later described as "universal nature personified" (I [xxxiii]). Maurice also refers to "the Egyptian Isis and Osiris (without doubt the Isa and Eswara of India)" (II 129).

But then one day, looking for something else, I came on a passage in Sir William Jones's essay "On the Gods of Greece, Italy, and India" in *Asiatic Researches* I (1788) 223:

> Hence also the *Indian* MÁYÁ, or, as the word is explained by some *Hindu* scholars, "the first inclination of the Godhead to diversify himself (such is their phrase) by creating worlds," is feigned to be the mother of universal nature, and of all the inferiour Gods . . . but the word MÁYÁ, or *delusion*, has a more subtile and recondite sense in the *Védánta* philosophy, where it signifies the system of *perceptions* . . .

If this was not Coleridge's direct or only source, it is still more useful than the fuzzy formulations of the reference books because it gives us exactly the right wording, and from an eminent and accessible contemporary authority.

Finally, you have to put your faith in your author and give him the benefit of the doubt. For example, Coleridge responds to a point made in an argument about plant chemistry—that plants grown in distilled water contain the same chemical elements "as were found in the ashes of plants that grew in the open"—by affirming the contrary. "Ellis positively denies this, and Davy's experiment with the vetches appears to contradict it" (SCHUBERT *Ansichten* **45**). This statement refers immediately and accurately to Daniel Ellis's *Inquiry into the Changes Induced in Atmos-*

pheric Air, by the Germination of Seeds, the Vegetation of Plants, and the Respiration of Animals (Edinburgh 1807) and *Farther Inquiries* (Edinburgh 1811), the latter of which cites experiments by Humphry Davy published in 1799 and 1807, though Ellis does not specifically mention vetches and indeed they do not appear in the published papers. The indexes to Davy's works do not include the vetch. Coleridge was not a great botanist. It seemed quite likely that Ellis was his only source and that he had simply made a mistake in translating from the Latin to the common name of the plant; alternatively, since he knew Davy personally, that he had heard of the vetch experiment by word of mouth. One further work published by Davy prior to the writing of the note—*Elements of Agricultural Chemistry* (1813)—might have been worth examining (although it had been included in the indexing exercise), but the case that contained it was jammed in the library I was working in, so I couldn't get at it. I returned a year later and found no vetches in the index; no vetches in the text; but in a three-page chart in extremely small print, giving an analysis of the ashes of several states of a dozen or so different plants, the chemical composition of vetches before flowering, vetches in flower, ripe vetches, vetch seeds, and vetches grown in distilled water. I hate to think how many other notes I have let pass for no better reason than a jammed bookcase.

Of course any defence of the editorial process rests ultimately on the value of the text itself. A few of Coleridge's notes were published during his lifetime. He may well have been the first to popularise the term "marginalia" when he allowed a note about Sir Thomas Browne to be published in 1819; certainly it has been strongly associated with him ever since. Many more of his annotations were included in the Victorian editions supervised by his family, and they were gradually absorbed into literary culture and made their way—even into the *OED*. They would not appear really to need defending. But we are ambivalent about notes in books, and it is not only the honest librarian who told me so, who considers Coleridge as having "spoiled other people's books". Marginalia strike many people as a violation—against property or against aesthetics or against the privacy of the reading act. Coleridge anticipated this as he did other charges against him, describing himself, in a note written in 1811 in one of Charles Lamb's books, as having "spoiled" the book "in order to leave a Relic" (BEAUMONT AND FLETCHER COPY A **13**); and again, about 1813, in a copy of Shakespeare, beginning a note with the words, "As Morgan allows me thus to spoil his Book . . ." (SHAKESPEARE COPY A **86**). In 1820 Lamb's famous essay on "The Two Races of Men", weighing gains against losses, claimed that Coleridge's attentions would triple a book's value (*CM—CC*—I cxvi).

Our present sense of the impropriety of writing marginalia, especially in books that are not one's own, has to be seen in historical perspective. When the absolute number of books in circulation and the number likely to belong to any particular individual were much smaller, and when the recollection of manuscript culture was less remote, the combination of printed text and handwritten gloss was less uncommon than it is today. During the eighteenth century, readers wrote in books for a variety of reasons. Student were accustomed to write notes—often just subject-headings—as part of a process of assimilation that also involved the use of notebooks and commonplace books. Owners added notes to books in order to keep them up to date: you could make your own dictionary, for example, go farther and last longer if you supplemented it with examples and evidence from other sources; it was also efficient to have everything in one place instead of having to consult several volumes. Scholars collated their copies of classical works with other editions and schoolboys put translations of hard words directly into their textbooks. Lawyers entered records of new statutes and significant judgments that affected the law into their Coke upon Littleton and other handbooks. Amateur naturalists made notes in their field guides about the incidence of species of birds, butterflies, and plants in their own areas. Readers exercised their wits and displayed their knowingness, as they were meant to do, by filling in the blanks in satires and poems *à clef* with the proper names of the subjects (so that "D— of B—ck—m" would be fleshed out as "Duke of Buckingham"). The devout filled their Bibles and prayer-books with learned commentary and pious meditations. Those who were engaged in controversy carried their arguments into their opponents' margins and end-papers. Coleridge's notes, multifarious and personal as they are, are therefore not out of line with contemporary practice. He was not doing something new; he was doing something ordinary unusually well. By 1820 he had achieved a measure of public recognition as a master in an interesting minor genre.

One of the complaints that is made about the policies of this edition is that it makes Coleridge look like a human library rather than a human being. But to say that is to have lost sight of the reasons for his writing. As George Whalley's Introduction indicates, Coleridge began to annotate books in earnest in his thirties, when he began to annotate for friends. As time went on and his reputation spread, he was increasingly invited to "spoil" other people's books. Indeed close examination shows that nearly all the extant notes, and certainly the ones we think of as the best, were written for a specific audience—Thomas Poole, Charles Lamb, Sara Hutchinson, one of the Morgans or Gillmans, Henry Crabb Robinson, Joseph Henry Green. In this custom too, he is in conformity with his pe-

riod, that is, with the late eighteenth century and the early nineteenth. Writing marginalia had by then become a social act. Annotated books were exchanged as gifts and circulated among friends. To take Johnson's circle as an example, we know that Johnson annotated a book sent him by Hill Boothby so that she could see his views in detail and then return it to him; that Boswell received, even from strangers, annotated copies of his *Life of Johnson*, with suggestions for improvement in the second edition; and that Hester (Thrale) Piozzi made up a magnificent annotated Bible as well as annotated copies of Boswell, to present to special friends.[2] It is not Coleridge's personality alone, but also the conventions of an established social practice, that account for the charm and intimacy of his marginalia.

The stock of Coleridge's notes has risen over time even though their original value as an expression of friendship has been lost sight of. We cannot know what will become of it in future, but the prospect looks hopeful to me. If the Victorians welcomed Coleridge's marginalia because they were curious about him as a troubled celebrity, as well as for the insight he offered into a great range of difficult books, we have additional historical and critical motives. We want to find out as much as we can about his period, and particularly about the cultural conditions he experienced. Coleridge's annotated books, many of the notes unpublished or incomplete till now, offer a huge body of new material to be explored. Textual studies, history of the book, reception theory, and reader response are all academic fields of recent development to which the marginalia could be a godsend. And speaking from my own experience, I can recommend immersion in the marginalia as an education in itself, albeit a rather eccentric one.

As time passes, I find I am increasingly grateful to the marginalia for offering an introduction to—indeed a sort of guided tour of—authors and ideas that I would never have encountered otherwise. (To be honest, some, if I had encountered them, I would probably have done my best to avoid.) Though Coleridge read what everyone else he knew was reading, he also pursued writers such as Emanuel Swedenborg, Heinrich Steffens, and Jakob Boehme, whose works were unpopular or almost unknown in England. He was not put off by either learning or vulgarity. He relished

[2] Samuel Johnson *Letters* ed Bruce Redford (Princeton 1992) I 120; James Boswell *The Principal Corrections and Additions to the First Edition of Mr. Boswell's Life of Johnson* (1793), e.g. 31; James Boswell *The Life of Samuel Johnson LL.D. with Marginal Comments and Markings from Two Copies Annotated by Hester Lynch Thrale Piozzi* ed Edward G. Fletcher (1938), also *The Imperial Family Bible* (Stourbridge 1811), BL shelfmark C 61 f 3.

out-of-the-way older English writers like John Reynolds and Nehemiah Grew. To read them *through* his notes can be a revelation, for he was a tremendously charitable reader. I hope I may have learned something from his generous receptivity.

The passages he comments on are printed here because they prompted the notes in the first place. They merit attention, however, in their own right. Reading through the volumes of the marginalia or dipping into them can be compared to the experience of using Johnson's *Dictionary* (which Coleridge described as "our entertaining *Quotation-book*, but most contemptible *Dictionary*": PASINI **1**). Although Coleridge did not exercise the same level of conscious control that Johnson demonstrated in his selection and editing of passages that were meant to educate the reader while they illustrated the meanings of English words, the marginalia too constitute an anthology of good things chosen by an expert. They have also the same kind of loose coherence as the entries in the *Dictionary*: there's been one mind seizing and acting upon them. And though some texts and some notes may be more inspiring than others, since the extracts are short there are good odds that a little browsing will turn up something useful or enchanting. The word "mussitation", for example, appears in the *OED* and in Johnson, but they hardly prepare you for the way it is used by the translator of Swedenborg's *True Christian Religion*: "It may be proper to inform the unlearned Reader, that Mussitation meaneth the same as Muttering or Whispering, and is therefore a Term very properly applied by the Angels to denote an Art, which consisteth in speaking obscurely and perplexedly on all Subjects, and thereby darkening the Clearness and Plainness of simple genuine Truth."

Reading the marginalia gives us direct experience of a keen mind struggling to absorb, interpret, and (because it's Coleridge) systematise the details of miscellaneous reading—which is a richer and more complex experience than simply taking in the details by our own unconscious processes, whatever they may be. *Editing* the marginalia entails even deeper engagement, with its own rewards and frustrations. In July of 1993, I was high up in the stacks of the Senate House at the University of London working my way volume by volume through the 66 indexes of a scientific periodical running from 1798 to 1820, without much hope of an answer to any of my collected queries, but on the lookout for an American boy with great arithmetical powers (*America*, *Boy*, *Mathematics*); for reports of a Megatherium or Giant Sloth sighted on the banks of the Missouri River (*Megatherium*, *Missouri*, *Monster*); and for an appearance of "Faraday's Microphone" (*Faraday*, *Microphone*) fifty years or more before the microphone is thought to have been invented. As I plodded on in

an almost lifeless state on that especially gloomy day, my eye took in "*Mouse*, suckled by cat"—and I thought with delight how like us they were, Coleridge's contemporaries, how curious about the world around them; how credulous; how fond of prodigies; how humanly serious, and how absurd. Trying to reproduce Coleridge's reading leads far away from the beaten tracks of the late twentieth century but not without profit even to a grasp of our own world. There is something to be said for being able to read cognitive psychology as mediated by Spurzheim and the phrenologists, or the neo-Darwinians through the Erasmus-Darwinians.

It may seem perverse even to consider such a work as the *Marginalia* as a means of education, it being not only out of date but adventitious. And yet many parts of our education are like that, and learning always has its haphazard aspect. The method Coleridge used—marking passages and writing comments in the margin—had been sanctioned for centuries as an *aide-mémoire*, even if the freedom and the length of his notes were rather unusual. Every time Coleridge wrote a note, he subjected a small portion of the text he was reading to close scrutiny. Often there is also a general note on one of the end-papers, summing up his judgment of the work. His procedure reflects the natural process of digestion of books. When he shared his experience with a friend by sending back the annotated book, the friend's experience would in turn be guided by his intervention in a way that seems likewise—in the absence of tutors, telephones, and book clubs—a natural extension of the process. We like to have a way of communicating what we have learnt, which for any competent and independent reader will not be the same as what we have read.

Reconstructing Coleridge's notes in the Bollingen Edition would not have been possible if they had not been treasured by their original owners, collected by his executors, and preserved by great libraries. In this final volume, perhaps because of its miscellaneous character, I have been more conscious than before of this deep background of support, as well as of a need for coordination of energies and resources that makes the editor feel at times, grandiosely, like the director of a movie with scriptwriters, actors, sound personnel, camera crew, wardrobe, distributors, gaffers, best boys and all the rest.

For providing funding and "infrastructure" over the last few years, I am grateful to the University of Toronto, Victoria College, and the Social Sciences and Humanities Research Council of Canada. To the libraries and the private owners holding marginalia, as indicated in the headnotes to entries here, and to Cambridge University Library, the University of London Library, the Wellcome Library in London and the National Library of Medicine in Bethesda, Maryland, I am indebted for un-

failing cooperation and courtesy. I wrote the last of my notes at Magdalen College in Oxford, where they showed me what hospitality can be.

Daniel Roberts and Claudia Strasky, who were post-graduate students at Cambridge at the time, gave valuable assistance with this volume, the first supplying the addenda entries for Herder and Kant, and the second seeking out very rare editions of Weishaupt in German and Swiss libraries. Bruce Graver, of Providence College, allowed me a sneak-preview of his Cornell Edition of Wordworth's translation of Virgil. Desmond Conacher and Eric Csapo, of the Classics Department at Toronto, traced an elusive Greek fragment for me; John Revell, in Near and Middle Eastern Civilizations, sorted out C's Hebrew; Konrad Eisenbichler, of Italian, translated and commented on the METASTASIO addenda. For expert copy-editing and proof-reading, I am especially indebted to Allyson May and the graduate and undergraduate students who worked with her. As before, I have been able to depend on the good advice of colleagues in the edition, particularly Lorna Arnold, John Beer, Jim Engell, Marion Filipiuk, Anthony Harding, and Jim Mays. The benchmark of all editors, Samuel Johnson, observes, "What will the world do, but look on and laugh, when one Scholar dedicates to another?" But for his warning I would dedicate my share of the project now at last completed to Robin Jackson, who was in at the beginning and has quietly but staunchly stayed the course.

Garden Island, Ontario, August 1997 H. J. JACKSON

EDITORIAL PRACTICE: A BRIEF GUIDE

FOR the definition of "marginalia", "textus", and "submarginalia" see *CM* (*CC*) I xxiii–xxvi. For special terms such as "fly-pages", "annex", "ms transcript", "quasi-marginalia", "lost book", and "marked book" see I xxx–xxxii.

All marginalia are transcribed literatim from the original mss, whenever these were available to the editor: cancelled words and phrases are restored; idiosyncratic spellings and obvious misspellings are reproduced without comment; slips of the pen and accidental repetitions are also reproduced, normally with explanation in a textual note. See I xxiii. (When C's notes are published from a transcript in another hand, slips of the pen and cancellations are normally ignored.) A second parenthesis or quotation mark omitted by oversight is supplied by the editor without comment unless the placing of the mark is in doubt. Illegible deletions are omitted.

The annotated books are entered in alphabetical order by author, and within an author-entry in alphabetical order by title. Reference to annotated books within this edition is made by short title (identifiable from the running headlines) to which the serial number of a particular annotation can be attached: e.g. DONNE *Sermons* COPY B **57**. (Bold figures are used only for serial numbers of marginalia.) Editorial footnotes are identified by attaching the number of the footnote indicator to the abbreviated title of the book: e.g. DONNE *Sermons* COPY B **57** n 2. See also I xxix–xxx.

CONVENTIONS USED IN TRANSCRIPTION

[wild]	A reading supplied by the editor when the word has been lost from the ms by cropping or physical damage
[not][a]	A word inserted by the editor to supply an unintentional omission on C's part, or to clarify the sense of an elliptical or ambiguous phrase. The accompanying textual note [a] accounts for the insertion
[? wild]	An uncertain reading
[? wild/world]	Possible alternative readings
[. . .]	An illegible word or phrase
[. . . . .]	A passage of undetermined extent illegible through rubbing or offsetting, or lost by cropping or other physical damage

⟨ ⟩ A word or passage inserted between the lines, or marked for insertion from another part of the page (in which case a textual note is provided). An inserted word or passage is not so marked when it follows immediately upon a cancellation in the ms

ABBREVIATIONS

THE FOLLOWING LIST includes abbreviations used in Vols I to VI of *Marginalia*. Place of publication is London, unless otherwise noted. Special abbreviations that apply only to certain author-entries or book-entries are given in the appropriate headnote.

Allsop	[Thomas Allsop] *Letters, Conversations and Recollections of S. T. Coleridge* (2 vols 1836)
Altick	Richard D. Altick *The Shows of London* (Cambridge MA & London 1978)
AM	S. T. Coleridge *The Rime of the Ancient Mariner*
AP	*Anima Poetae: from the Unpublished Notebooks of S. T. Coleridge* ed. E. H. Coleridge (1895)
AR (1825)	S. T. Coleridge *Aids to Reflection* (1825)
AR (*CC*)	S. T. Coleridge *Aids to Reflection* ed John Beer (London & Princeton 1993) = *CC* IX
A Reg	*The Annual Register* (1758–)
Ashley LC	Thomas J. Wise *The Ashley Library: A Catalogue of Printed Books, Manuscripts and Autograph Letters Collected by Thomas James Wise* (11 vols 1922–36). Coleridge items are principally in Vols I, VIII, X. Items from Wise's collection now in the BM bear the prefix "Ashley" in the press-mark
AV	The "Authorised Version"—or "King James Version"—of the Bible, in modern orthography
B&F	Beaumont and Fletcher
BCP	*The Book of Common Prayer and Administration of the Sacraments and Other Rites and Ceremonies of the Church According to the Use of the Church of England*
BL (1817)	S. T. Coleridge *Biographia Literaria; or Biographical Sketches of My Literary Life and Opinions* (2 vols 1817)
BL (1847)	S. T. Coleridge *Biographia Literaria* ed H. N. and Sara Coleridge (2 vols 1847)
BL (1907)	S. T. Coleridge *Biographia Literaria . . . with His Aesthetical Essays* ed J. Shawcross (2 vols Oxford 1907)

BL (*CC*)	S. T. Coleridge *Biographia Literaria* ed James Engell and W. Jackson Bate (2 vols London & Princeton 1983) = *CC* VII
Bl Mag	*Blackwood's Magazine*
BM	British Library, Reference Division, formerly "British Museum Library"
BMC	*The British Museum Catalogue of Printed Books*
BNPL	*The New York Public Library Bulletin* (New York 1897–)
B Poets	*The Works of the British Poets* ed Robert Anderson (13 vols Edinburgh & London 1792–5; vol 14 1807). The annotated copies are referred to as "ANDERSON"
Bristol LB	George Whalley "The Bristol Library Borrowings of Southey and Coleridge" *Library* IV (Sept 1949) 114–31
B Works	George Berkeley *Works* ed A. A. Luce and T. E. Jessop (9 vols 1948–57)
C	Samuel Taylor Coleridge
C&S	S. T. Coleridge *On the Constitution of the Church and State, According to the Idea of Each* (2nd ed 1830)
C&S (*CC*)	S. T. Coleridge *On the Constitution of the Church and State* ed John Colmer (London & Princeton 1976) = *CC* X
C & SH	George Whalley *Coleridge and Sara Hutchinson and the Asra Poems* (1955)
Carlisle LB	Carlisle Cathedral Library Borrowings 1801–2
Carlyon	Clement Carlyon *Early Years and Late Reflections* (4 vols 1836–58)
C at H	L. E. Watson *Coleridge at Highgate* (London & New York 1925)
CC	*The Collected Works of Samuel Taylor Coleridge* general ed Kathleen Coburn (London & Princeton 1969–)
CCD	J. Robert Barth, S.J. *Coleridge and Christian Doctrine* (Cambridge MA 1969)
C d r V	See Kant *C d r V*
CH	*Coleridge: The Critical Heritage* ed J. R. de J. Jackson (1970)
CIS	S. T. Coleridge *Confessions of an Inquiring Spirit and Some Miscellaneous Pieces* ed H. N. Coleridge (1849)
CL	Charles Lamb
CL	*Collected Letters of Samuel Taylor Coleridge* ed Earl Leslie Griggs (6 vols Oxford & New York 1956–71)

C Life (C)	E. K. Chambers *Samuel Taylor Coleridge* (Oxford 1938)
C Life (G)	James Gillman *The Life of Samuel Taylor Coleridge* (1838)
C Life (H)	Lawrence Hanson *The Life of Samuel Taylor Coleridge: the Early Years* (1938)
C Life (JDC)	James Dykes Campbell *Samuel Taylor Coleridge* (1894)
CM (*CC*)	S. T. Coleridge *Marginalia* ed George Whalley and H. J. Jackson (London & Princeton 1980–) = *CC* XII
CN	*The Notebooks of Samuel Taylor Coleridge* ed Kathleen Coburn (New York, Princeton & London 1957–)
Coffman	Ralph J. Coffman *Coleridge's Library: A Bibliography of Books Owned or Read by Samuel Taylor Coleridge* (Boston 1987)
col(s)	column(s)
C Pantheist	Thomas McFarland *Coleridge and the Pantheist Tradition* (Oxford 1969)
CR (*BCW*)	*Blake, Coleridge, Wordsworth, Lamb, etc. being Selections from the Remains of Henry Crabb Robinson* ed Edith J. Morley (Manchester 1922)
CRB	*Henry Crabb Robinson on Books and Their Writers* ed Edith J. Morley (3 vols 1938)
CRC	*The Correspondence of Henry Crabb Robinson with the Wordsworth Circle* ed Edith J. Morley (2 vols Oxford 1927)
CRD	*Diary, Reminiscences, and Correspondence of Henry Crabb Robinson* ed Thomas Sadler (2 vols 1872)
CR Life	Edith J. Morley *The Life and Times of Henry Crabb Robinson* (1935)
C 17th C	*Coleridge on the Seventeenth Century* ed R. F. Brinkley (Durham NC 1955)
C Talker	R. W. Armour and R. F. Howes *Coleridge the Talker* (1949)
CW	*The Complete Works of S. T. Coleridge* ed W. G. T. Shedd (7 vols New York 1853)
DC	Derwent Coleridge
DCL	Dove Cottage Library, Grasmere
DC SC (1888)	*The Philological Library of . . . Derwent Coleridge* (Sotheby Jul 1888). Marked copy: BM S-C S 956(1)
De Q	Thomas De Quincey
De Q to W	John E. Jordan *De Quincey to Wordsworth. A Biography of a Relationship* (Berkeley & Los Angeles 1962)

De Q Works	*The Collected Writings of Thomas De Quincey* ed David Masson (14 vols Edinburgh 1889–90)
Diels	Hermann Diels *Die Fragmente der Vorsokratiker* ed Walther Kranz (3 vols Zürich 1971)
DNB	*Dictionary of National Biography* (1885–)
Durham LB	Durham Cathedral Library Borrowings 1801
DW	Dorothy Wordsworth
DW (S)	Ernest de Selincourt *Dorothy Wordsworth* (Oxford 1933)
DWJ	*Journals of Dorothy Wordsworth* ed Ernest de Selincourt (2 vols 1941)
DWJ (M)	*Journals of Dorothy Wordsworth. The Alfoxden Journal 1798* [and] *The Grasmere Journals 1800–1803* ed Mary Moorman (Oxford 1971)
D Works	René Descartes *Philosophical Works* tr E. S. Haldane and G. T. Ross (2 vols 1911)
EC	*The English Catalogue of Books (including the original "London" Catalogue* [of 1786 for 1700–86]*) . . . Issued in the United Kingdom . . . 1801–1836* ed R. A. Peddie and Q. Waddington (London 1914)
Ed Rev	*The Edinburgh Review* (Edinburgh & London 1802–1929)
EHC	Ernest Hartley Coleridge
EICHHORN *AT*	J. G. Eichhorn *Einleitung ins Alte Testament* (2nd ed 3 vols Leipzig 1787), the edition C annotated
EICHHORN *NT*	J. G. Eichhorn *Einleitung in das Neue Testament* (3 vols Leipzig 1804–14), the edition C annotated
EOT (*CC*)	S. T. Coleridge *Essays on His Times in "The Morning Post" and "The Courier"* ed David V. Erdman (3 vols London & Princeton 1978) = *CC* III
Farington Diary	Joseph Farington *The Farington Diary* ed James Greig (8 vols 1922–8)
Friend (*CC*)	S. T. Coleridge *The Friend* ed Barbara E. Rooke (2 vols London & Princeton 1969) = *CC* IV
Gillman SC (1843)	*Catalogue of a Valuable Collection of Books, Including the Library of James Gillman, Esq* (Henry Southgate 1843). Marked copies: BM SC Sg 64 (2) and Sg a 53. The Gillman lots were 303–466, 468–501, 504–34: *CM* (*CC*) I clxi n 1
G Mag	*The Gentleman's Magazine* (1731–1907)
Göttingen LB	A. D. Snyder "Books Borrowed by Coleridge from the Library of the University of Göttingen, 1799" *Modern Philology* XXV (1928) 377–80

Graver	William Wordsworth *Translations of Chaucer and Virgil* ed Bruce E. Graver (Ithaca 1998). Includes transcriptions and facsimiles of C's notes to WW's translation of *Aeneid*
Green List	VCL MS 18. A handlist of Coleridge's books prepared by Mrs J. H. Green c 1863
Green SC (1880)	*Catalogue of the Library of Joseph Henry Green . . . Sold by Auction* (Sotheby Jul 1880). Marked copy: BM SC S 805 (1)
Green SC (1884)	*Catalogue of Scarce and Valuable Books, Including a Remarkable Collection of Coleridgeiana* (Scribner & Welford, New York 1884)
Haney	John Louis Haney *A Bibliography of Samuel Taylor Coleridge* (Philadelphia 1903)
Hansard	*The Parliamentary Debates from the Year 1803 to the Present Time* ed T. C. Hansard (41 vols 1812–20)
HC	Hartley Coleridge
HC Essays	*Essays and Marginalia by Hartley Coleridge* ed Derwent Coleridge (2 vols 1851)
HCL	*Letters of Hartley Coleridge* ed Grace Evelyn and Earl Leslie Griggs (Oxford 1936)
HC Poems	*Poems by Hartley Coleridge, with a memoir of his life by his brother* [Derwent Coleridge] (2 vols 1851)
HCR	Henry Crabb Robinson
HD	Humphry Davy
Healey	George Harris Healey *The Cornell Wordsworth Collection* (Ithaca 1957)
HEHL	The Henry E. Huntington Library and Art Gallery, San Marino, CA
Highgate List	Wordsworth LC entries 1186–1299: a handlist in WW's hand of books "Sent to Coleridge" in c 1829
HNC	Henry Nelson Coleridge
H Works	*The Complete Works of William Hazlitt* ed P. P. Howe (12 vols 1930–4)
IS	*Inquiring Spirit: a New Presentation of Coleridge from His Published and Unpublished Prose Writings* ed Kathleen Coburn (London & New York 1951)
JDC	James Dykes Campbell
JHG	Joseph Henry Green
JW	John Wordsworth

JWL	*Letters of John Wordsworth* ed C. H. Ketcham (Ithaca 1969)
Kant *C d r V*	Immanuel Kant *Critik der reinen Vernunft*; B indicates that page references are from the 2nd ed (1787)
Kant *VS*	Immanuel Kant *Vermischte Schriften* (4 vols Halle & Königsberg 1799–1807)
Kemp Smith	*Immanuel Kant's Critique of Pure Reason* tr Norman Kemp Smith (rev ed 1933)
L	*Letters of Samuel Taylor Coleridge* ed E. H. Coleridge (2 vols 1895)
Lamb SC	*Books from the Library of Charles Lamb, Offered for Sale by Bartlett and Welford, New York City* (New York 1848)
L&L	*Coleridge on Logic and Learning* ed Alice D. Snyder (New Haven & London 1929)
LB	William Wordsworth [and S. T. Coleridge] *Lyrical Ballads with Other Poems* (Bristol 1798 &c); the edition referred to indicated by a bracketed date. "*LB*" following a place-name (e.g. *Durham LB* means "Library Borrowing")
LCL	Loeb Classical Library
Lects 1795 (*CC*)	S. T. Coleridge *Lectures 1795: On Politics and Religion* ed Lewis Patton and Peter Mann (London & Princeton 1971) = *CC* I
Lects 1808–1819 (*CC*)	S. T. Coleridge *Lectures 1808–1819: On Literature* ed Reginald A. Foakes (2 vols London & Princeton 1987) = *CC* V
Levere	Trevor H. Levere *Poetry Realized in Nature: Samuel Taylor Coleridge and Early Nineteenth-Century Science* (Cambridge 1981)
LHP (*CC*)	S. T. Coleridge *Lectures 1818–1819: On the History of Philosophy* ed J. R. de J. Jackson (2 vols Princeton 2000) = *CC* VIII
lit	literally
LL	*The Letters of Charles Lamb to Which Are Added Those of His Sister Mary Lamb* ed E. V. Lucas (3 vols 1935)
LL (M)	*The Letters of Charles and Mary Anne Lamb* ed Edwin W. Marrs, Jr (3 vols Ithaca NY 1975–8)
L Life	E. V. Lucas *The Life of Charles Lamb* (1921)
LLP	*Letters from the Lake Poets to Daniel Stuart* [ed Mary Stuart and E. H. Coleridge] (1889)
Logic (*CC*)	S. T. Coleridge *Logic* ed J. R. de J. Jackson (London & Princeton 1981) = *CC* XIII

Lost List	A handlist prepared by George Whalley of books known to have been annotated by C but not located at the time this edition went to press. An incomplete version was published in *Book Collector* XVII (1968) 428–42 and XVIII (1969) 223
LR	*The Literary Remains of Samuel Taylor Coleridge* ed H. N. Coleridge (4 vols 1836–9)
LS	S. T. Coleridge *A Lay Sermon, Addressed to the Higher and Middle Classes, on the Existing Distresses and Discontents* (1817)
LS (1852)	S. T. Coleridge *Lay Sermons. I. The Statesman's Manual. II. Blessed are ye that sow beside all Waters* [i.e. *A Lay Sermon*] ed Derwent Coleridge (1852)
LS (*CC*)	S. T. Coleridge *Lay Sermons* [being *The Statesman's Manual* and *A Lay Sermon*] ed R. J. White (London & Princeton 1972) = *CC* VI
L Works	In *CM* (*CC*) I–II *The Works of Charles and Mary Lamb* ed E. V. Lucas (6 vols 1912); in III–VI (5 vols 1903)
M Chron	*The Morning Chronicle* (1769–1862)
Method	*S. T. Coleridge's Treatise on Method as Published in the Encyclopaedia Metropolitana* ed Alice D. Snyder (1934)
Migne *PG*	*Patrologiae cursus completus . . . series graeca* ed J. P. Migne (162 vols Paris 1857–1912)
Migne *PL*	*Patriologiae cursus completus . . . series latina* ed J. P. Migne (221 vols Paris 1844–64)
Minnow	*Minnow among Tritons: Mrs S. T. Coleridge's Letters to Thomas Poole, 1799–1834* ed Stephen Potter (1934)
Misc C	*Coleridge's Miscellaneous Criticism* ed T. M. Raysor (1936)
M Mag	*The Monthly Magazine* (1796–1843)
M Post	*The Morning Post* (1772–1937)
Mrs C	Sara Coleridge née Fricker (wife of C)
MS Leatherhead	A manuscript formerly in the collection of the Rev Gerard H. B. Coleridge when Vicar of Leatherhead
MW	Mary Wordsworth née Hutchinson (wife of WW)
N	Notebook of Samuel Taylor Coleridge (numbered or lettered) in ms. References are given by folio
N&Q	*Notes and Queries* (1849–)
NEB	*The New English Bible* (Oxford & Cambridge 1964)

NEB Gk	*The Greek New Testament being the text translated in the New English Bible 1961* ed R. V. G. Tasker (Oxford & Cambridge 1964)
NED	S. T. Coleridge *Notes on English Divines* ed Derwent Coleridge (2 vols 1853)
NLS	S. T. Coleridge *Notes and Lectures upon Shakespeare and Some Other Old Poets and Dramatists with Other Literary Remains* ed Sara Coleridge (2 vols 1849)
NT Gk Lex	W. Bauer *A Greek-English Lexicon of the New Testament and Other Early Christian Literature* ed and tr W. F. Arndt and F. W. Gingrich (Chicago & Cambridge 1968)
NTP	*Notes, Theological, Political and Miscellaneous* ed Derwent Coleridge (1853)
NYPL	New York Public Library
ODCC	*The Oxford Dictionary of the Christian Church* ed F. L. Cross (1971)
OED	*The Oxford English Dictionary* (12 vols Oxford 1970) and *Supplement* (4 vols Oxford 1987)
OLD	*Oxford Latin Dictionary* (Oxford 1968–)
Omniana	*Omniana, or Horae otiosiores* ed Robert Southey [with articles by C] (2 vols 1812)
Op Max	"Opus Maximum" MSS in the Huntington Library, San Marino CA; and in VCL
p-d	paste-down. See "Editorial Practice" *CM* (*CC*) I xxx
Peake (1967)	*Peake's Commentary on the Bible* ed Matthew Black and Harold Henry Rowley
Phil Trans RS	*The Philosophical Transactions of the Royal Society* (1665–1821)
P Lects (1949)	*The Philosophical Lectures of Samuel Taylor Coleridge* ed Kathleen Coburn (London & New York 1949)
PML	The Pierpont Morgan Library, New York
PMLA	*Publications of the Modern Language Association of America* (Baltimore 1886–)
Poole	M. E. Sandford *Thomas Poole and His Friends* (2 vols 1888)
Prelude	William Wordsworth *The Prelude: or, Growth of a Poet's Mind* ed Ernest de Selincourt, rev Helen Darbishire (Oxford 1959)
"*Prometheus*"	S. T. Coleridge "On the *Prometheus* of Aeschylus: An Essay . . . read at the Royal Society of Literature, May 18, 1825" as printed in *LR* II 323–59

Proto-*Prometheus*	The ms draft of "*Prometheus*" written c 1821: Duke University
PW (*CC*)	S. T. Coleridge *Poetical Works* ed J. C. C. Mays (3 vols Princeton in preparation) = *CC* XVI
PW (EHC)	*The Complete Poetical Works of Samuel Taylor Coleridge* ed E. H. Coleridge (2 vols Oxford 1912)
PW (JDC)	*The Poetical Works of Samuel Taylor Coleridge* ed J. D. Campbell (1893)
QR	*The Quarterly Review* (1809–1952)
Rees	*Cyclopaedia* ed Abraham Rees (39 vols 1809–19)
RES	*Review of English Studies* (1925–)
RS	Robert Southey
RSV	The [American] Revised Standard Version of the Bible: NT 1946, OT 1952
RV	The Revised Version of the Bible: NT 1881, OT 1885, Apocr 1895
RX	John Livingston Lowes *The Road to Xanadu* (rev ed Boston 1930)
SC	Sara Coleridge (daughter of C, and wife of HNC)
SC Life	Earl Leslie Griggs *Coleridge Fille. A Biography of Sara Coleridge* (Oxford 1940)
SC Memoir	*Memoir and Letters of Sara Coleridge* [ed Edith Coleridge] (2 vols 1873)
SH	Sara Hutchinson
Sh (Arden)	The Arden Edition of the Works of William Shakespeare (London 1899–) (for editorial details see SHAKESPEARE General Note)
Sh C	*Coleridge's Shakespearean Criticism* ed T. M. Raysor (2nd ed 2 vols 1960)
Sh (Reed)	*The Plays of William Shakespeare* ed Isaac Reed (21 vols 1803)
SHL	*The Letters of Sara Hutchinson* ed Kathleen Coburn (London & Toronto 1954)
SL	S. T. Coleridge *Sibylline Leaves* (1817)
S Letters (Curry)	*New Letters of Robert Southey* ed Kenneth Curry (2 vols New York & London 1965)
S Letters (Warter)	*A Selection from the Letters of Robert Southey* ed J. W. Warter (4 vols 1856)

S Life (CS)	*Life and Correspondence of Robert Southey* ed C. C. Southey (6 vols 1849–50)
S Life (Simmons)	Jack Simmons *Southey* (1945)
SM	S. T. Coleridge *The Statesman's Manual: or, The Bible, the Best Guide to Political Skill and Foresight. A Lay-Sermon Addressed to the Higher Classes of Society* (1816)
SM (1852)	S. T. Coleridge *The Statesman's Manual* in *Lay Sermons* ed Derwent Coleridge (1852)
SM (*CC*)	S. T. Coleridge *The Statesman's Manual* in *Lay Sermons* ed R. J. White (London & Princeton 1972) = *CC* VI
Southey SC (1844)	*Catalogue of the Valuable Library of the Late Robert Southey* (Sotheby May 1844). Marked copy: BM S-C S 252 (1)
Spedding	Francis Bacon *Works* ed J. Spedding, R. L. Ellis, and D. D. Heath (11 vols 1857–68)
Studies	*Coleridge: Studies by Several Hands on the Hundredth Anniversary of His Death* ed E. Blunden (1934)
SW	F. W. J. von Schelling *Sämmtliche Werke* ed K. F. A. Schelling (14 vols Stuttgart 1856–61)
SW & F (*CC*)	S. T. Coleridge *Shorter Works and Fragments* ed H. J. Jackson and J. R. de J. Jackson (2 vols London & Princeton 1995) = *CC* XI
TL (1848)	S. T. Coleridge *Hints Towards the Formation of a More Comprehensive Theory of Life* ed Seth B. Watson (1848)
TL (*CC*)	S. T. Coleridge *Hints Towards the Formation of a More Comprehensive Theory of Life*. Pub *SW & F* (*CC*) 481–557
Tooke	John Horne Tooke *Ἔπεα Πτερόεντα, or, The Diversions of Purley* (Vol I 1786, repr 1798; Vol II 1805)
TT	*Table Talk of Samuel Taylor Coleridge* ed H. N. Coleridge (rev ed 1836). Cited by date
TT (*CC*)	*Table Talk of Samuel Taylor Coleridge* ed Carl R. Woodring (London & Princteon 1990) = *CC* XIV
UL	*Unpublished Letters of Samuel Taylor Coleridge* ed Earl Leslie Griggs (2 vols 1932)
V & A	Victoria and Albert Museum
var	*variatim* "variously": used to indicate minor differences from the original in a quoted text
VCL	Victoria College Library, University of Toronto

VS	See Kant *VS*
Watchman (*CC*)	S. T. Coleridge *The Watchman* ed Lewis Patton (London & Princeton 1970) = *CC* II
WL (*E* 2)	*Letters of William and Dorothy Wordsworth; the Early Years* ed Ernest de Selincourt, rev Chester L. Shaver (Oxford 1967)
WL (*L*)	*Letters of William and Dorothy Wordsworth; the Later Years* ed Ernest de Selincourt (3 vols Oxford 1939)
WL (*L* 2)	*Letters of William and Dorothy Wordsworth; the Later Years* ed Ernest de Selincourt, rev Alan G. Hill (4 vols Oxford 1980–88)
WL (*M* 2)	*Letters of William and Dorothy Wordsworth; the Middle Years* ed Ernest de Selincourt, rev Mary Moorman (2 vols Oxford 1969–70)
W Library	Chester L. Shaver and Alice C. Shaver *Wordsworth's Library. A Catalogue Including a List of Books Housed by Wordsworth for Coleridge from c. 1810 to c. 1830* (New York & London 1979)
W Life	Mary Moorman *William Wordsworth: A Biography* (2 vols Oxford 1957–65)
W Mem	Christopher Wordsworth *Memoirs of William Wordsworth* (2 vols 1851)
Wordsworth LC	Wordsworth Library Catalogue. Harvard MS Eng 880. A handlist of books in WW's library at Rydal Mount from c 1823. Serial numbers supplied by George Whalley; see also *W Library*
Wordsworth SC (1859)	*Catalogue of the . . . Library of . . . William Wordsworth* (Preston 1859)
W Prose	*The Prose Works of William Wordsworth* ed W. J. B. Owen and Jane W. Smyser (3 vols Oxford 1974)
WPW	*The Poetical Works of William Wordsworth* ed Ernest de Selincourt and Helen Darbishire (5 vols Oxford 1940–9)
WW	William Wordsworth

MARGINALIA

LODEWIJK KASPER VALCKENAER
1715–1785

Ludovici Caspari Valckenaeri Diatribe de Aristobulo Judaeo; Philosopho Peripatetico Alexandrino. Edidit, praefatus est, et lectionem publicam Petri Wesselingii adjunxit Joannes Luzac. Leyden 1806. 4°.

Bound with OKEN *Erste Ideen zur Theorie des Lichts* and two other works: see TRACTS.

British Library C 44 g 4 (2)

DATE. c 1820–25, like the OKEN? Certainly later than C's first reading of SCHELLING *Ueber die Gottheiten von Samothrace* c 1817 (see **4** n 2 below), and probably after his delivery of the lectures on the history of philosophy in 1819 (**6** nn 2–3 below).

1 half-title

This Book is well worth reading: ~~and~~ but of all books worth reading the most prolix, *lengthy*, & *fall-a-broad*! as far as occurs to the present recollection of S. T. Coleridge.

2 p 56 | § 19

[Valckenaer, discussing Humphrey Hody's account of Demetrius of Phalerum, quotes from Cicero *De Finibus* 5.19:] *Princeps hujus civitatis Phalereus Demetrius, cum patria pulsus esset injuria, ad Ptolemaeum se Regem Alexandriam contulit: qui, cum in hac ipsa philosophia excelleret, Theophrastique esset auditor, multa praeclara in illo calamitoso otio scripsit.* Hoc in loco Cicero quoque materiae, quam tractabat, serviisse videtur. *Cur enim Philosopho literatissimo *calamitosum* illud poterat *otium* videri, quo patriâ quidem exulans, sed ingratâ, vitâque liber negotiosâ, suis ille totus vacare poterat deliciis, affluens per munificentiam Regis amicissimi rebus omnibus ad vitam jucunde transigendam necessariis.

["Demetrius of Phalerum, the ruler of this city, when unjustly banished from his country, repaired to the court of King Ptolemy at Alexandria. Being eminent in the very system of philosophy which we are recommending to you, and a pupil of Theophrastus, he employed the leisure afforded by his disaster in composing a number of excellent treatises." [H. Rackham LCL (1914)] In this passage Cicero seems also to have

made use of the matter that he was discussing.* For how could an eminently learned philosopher think that *leisure disastrous* by which—exiled, it's true, but from an ungrateful country—he was set free from a life of exertion and was able to devote his time to his own favourite pursuits, supplied by the bounty of a friendly monarch with everything necessary for a delightful existence.]

* Ex suo ipsius animo scripsit Cicero, ipse quoque philosophus literatissimus/ heu! quàm acerbe calam~~a~~itosum illi non visum est patriâ quamvis ingratissimâ exulari: utpote qui sub Demetrii nomine ipse proprias fortunas relege~~ba~~rit, Νομοθετης, πολιτικος, functoque omnium fere magistratuum munere splendidus[1]

3 p 57

Hunccine virum, qui libros scripsit περὶ Νόμων, περὶ Πολιτικῆς, *Theophrasti* discipulum, Peripateticorum istius aevi eruditissimum, Alexandriae habitantem, ubi tot Iudaeorum erant millia, hunccine dedecebat desiderium cognoscendarum Legum istius populi veterum, de quibus ante vix fando quid inaudiverat? Non equidem opinor. Quid jam probabilius, quam undique libros in suam conquirenti Bibliothecam Regi Lagidae *Demetrium* fuisse suasorem, ut Leges etiam Iudaeorum sibi Graece curaret converti.

[Was it inappropriate that this man [Demetrius], who had written the books *Of Laws* and *Of Politics*, who was the pupil of Theophrastus, the most learned of the Peripatetics of his time, who lived at Alexandria, where there were so many thousands of Jews, should wish to know about that people's ancient laws, which he had scarcely heard of before? I think not. What is more likely than that Demetrius should have persuaded the king, Ptolamaus Lagis, who was looking everywhere for books for his library, to have the laws of the Jews also translated into Greek?]

Valck: potuisset in exemplum ducere Leges Indorum-Judaicis fere coævas, quas illustrissimus noster Sir W. Jones sibi Anglicè curavit converti.[1]

2[1] "Cicero—he too an eminently learned philosopher—wrote this from his own heart. Alas, how bitterly disastrous he found it to be an exile, though from an ungrateful country; so that he was retelling his own fortunes under Demetrius's name, having himself been a lawgiver, a leader of the state, distinguished in the holding of almost every public office."

3[1] "Valckenaer could have adduced as an example the laws of the Indians almost contemporary with those of the Jews—which our distinguished compatriot Sir William Jones arranged on his own account to have translated into English." C had made notes about the contents of Sir William Jones *Institutes of Hindu Law* (1794) as early as 7 Nov 1796: *CL* I 252.

4 p 64 | § 21

[Valckenaer rejects the theories that Pythagoras, Plato, and others had the use of a Greek translation of the Books of Moses, or were influenced in any way by the Hebrew sacred books.]

Had the genuine Oracles of the Sibyl, so magnificently characterized by Heraclitus in one of the few genuine fragments of his works; or had these works, especially the Book said to have been deposited by him in the Delphic Temple; been preserved to us: we should have some grounds on which ~~this~~ a probable Judgement might have been built.[1]—As it is, I find nothing in Plato that requires us to suppose him acquainted with the Books of Moses, or which may not be sufficiently accounted for by the patriarchal Doctrines *refracted* thro' the Phœnician Pantheism or Theophysy, in the Cabiric Mysteries instituted by Phœnician Navigators in Samothrace.[2]—From the first division of the Cainite Race from the descendants of Seth[3] there existed ~~a~~ two opposite Philosophies—the Cainites as after the Deluge the Race of Ham, or Canaan, de~~duceing~~riving all Personality from a Nature, or impersonal Absolute = το παν, η Νυξ και Χαος;[4] the Sethites e contra[5] originating all things in the primal Personëity, or an Eternal Will co-eternally realizing itself for itself. This co-eternal Act of the Eternal is called the ἀρχὴ or ἐν ἀρχῃ (by St John,[6] who accordingly commences his Good Tidings with the Truth ~~/~~on which all other Good Tidings must be grounded—Εν αρχῃ ην ο Λογος—[7]

S. T. C.

4[1] Plutarch *De Pythiae oraculis* 397A preserves Heraclitus's description of the Sibyl as one who "with frenzied lips . . . uttering words mirthless, unembellished, unperfumed, yet reaches to a thousand years with her voice through the god" (tr Frank Cole Babbitt LCL); C himself comments on a translation of the passage in J. SMITH **5**. Diogenes Laertius 9.5–6 reports that Heraclitus deposited in the temple of Artemis (not at Delphi) "a continuous treatise *On Nature* . . . divided into three discourses, one on the universe, another on politics, and a third on theology" (tr R. D. Hicks LCL).

4[2] For the theory that Phoenician sailors had carried some of the monotheistic beliefs of the Jews into Greece where they formed the basis of the worship of the Cabiri in the Samothracian mysteries see SCHELLING *Ueber die Gottheiten von Samothrace* passim. "Theophysy" or "god-nature" is not in *OED* and appears to be C's coinage: cf BÖHME **136** and n 2.

4[3] Starting with the two surviving sons of Adam and Eve (Seth standing, conventionally, for "the true Church" in BIBLE COPY B **15**), C traces the division and dispersion of religions as well as races. For the traditional idea of the origins of race in the families descended from Shem, Ham, and Japhet, the sons of Noah, see STEFFENS *Geognostisch-geologische Aufsätze* **4** and n 1.

4[4] "The All, Night, and Chaos". C's phrase reflects the content, but not the actual wording, of Hesiod *Works and Days* 11–26.

4[5] "On the other hand".

4[6] The "beginning" or "in the beginning": John 1.1.

4[7] "In the beginning was the Word": John 1.1.

5 p 65 | § 22, footnote 9

Ἀφορμὴν εἰληφότες et ἀφορμηθέντες hinc illinc dicebantur, qui sua partim aliis debebant, sive ex aliorum scriptis derivarant . . .

[The expressions "taking their departure", or "starting" from this or that point, were used of those who owed part of their material to others or derived it from what others had written . . .]

the *Hint*, the *idea* in modern English—the *motivo*, as the Italian Artists say.[1]

6 p 65

[The accusation of Timon of Phlius is quoted, that Plato bought a copy of the work of Timaeus Locrus and plagiarised it.] Multa jecit in Philosophos maledicta *Timon*; objecit hic quidem vera *Platoni:* veteris enim TIMAEI libellus est in manibus . . .

[Timon abused the philosophers often; but his charge against Plato here is true: for the little book of Timaeus, his senior, was in his hands . . .]

Is this quite *certain*? I think otherwise. But ~~were~~ be it so, ⟨yet⟩ where is the proof that Plato meant to conceal in order to appropriate the tract in question? Would he have entitled it *Timæus*?[1]—It must appear presumptuous in an Individual to speak of a *universal* mistake; and yet I can not help thinking that *this* Charge with many others originates in a universal misconception of the *purpose* of Plato's *writings*: which, I am convinced, were intended as *preparations* for Platonism, and by no means containing the same.[2] Plato's Object, I hold, was to avail himself of the Socratic Opinions & those of elder Philosophers, in order to remove errors, unsettle prejudices, & by bringing forward some imperfect anticipations of his own System imperceptibly to lead & fit the favored minds for that interior Doctrine which he did not deem it wise or even holy to *publish*—while the majority of his readers he was content to make men of good sense, useful Citizens and enlightened Statesmen.—Not without

5[1] The evolution (to C's mind, the degeneration) of the meaning of "idea" in English is traced in *BL* ch 5 (*CC*) I 97* (and see n 2). *Motivo*, in aesthetic contexts, means "motif" or "pattern", but also more broadly, as here, the "motive" or initiating impulse.

6[1] Commenting on a notebook entry of 1810, *CN* III 3824n explains that Timaeus Locrus, the chief speaker in Plato's *Timaeus*, may have been an entirely fictional character: the work *On the Soul of the World and Nature* is now generally held to be an abridgement from Plato's dialogue, not a source for it.

6[2] C makes similar assertions in GRAY **5** and in *P Lects* Lect 4 (1949) 163–7—with the comment, in the latter case, that "All great and bold ideas in their first conception . . . are TOO GREAT FOR utterANCE" (166).

design was the Dialogue, 'Ο Φιλοσοφος, that ought to follow the Sophistes & Politicus, left a Desideratum.[3]

7 pp 81-2 | § 26

[Valckenaer states that Eusebius disagrees with Porphyry's statement that the authors of the Orphic hymns supposed Zeus to be the soul of the world. He quotes Eusebius:] ταῦτα δ', ait, ἄντικρυς τὸν ὁρώμενον ὑποφαίνειν ἡγοῦμαι κόσμον, εἰ μή τι καὶ σφαλλομαι, καὶ τὸ ὅλον ἐκ μερῶν συνεστὼς διδάσκει. λέγει δ'οὖν

Πάντα γὰρ ἐν μεγάλου Ζηνὸς τάδε σώματι κεῖται. καὶ τίνα τὰ πάντα διασαφεῖ,

Πῦρ, καὶ ὕδωρ, καὶ γαῖα, καὶ αἰθὴρ.

Paulo post versuum Pater istius *Iovis mentem* vocasse videtur *Eusebio*, et recte videtur, *Aethera*, νοῦν τοῦ Διὸς, εἶναι λέγων τὸν αἰθέρα in his, quae reponit ibidem;

Νοῦς δ'αψευδὴς, βασιλήϊος, ἄφθιτος αἰθὴρ,
Ὧι δὴ πάντα κυκλοῖ καὶ φράζεται·

["These things," he [Eusebius] says, "I suppose to indicate directly the visible world, unless I am somewhat mistaken, and to show us the universe made up of various parts." He [Porphyry] says at all events

For in Zeus' mighty body these all lie

And what "these all" are he clearly states

Fire, water, earth and ether, etc.

A little later in these verses the Father [Porphyry] seems to Eusebius (who is right in thinking so) to call the ether the mind of this Zeus; he adds the statement that the mind of Zeus is the ether in these words, which he repeats in the same passage:

His mind immortal ether, sovereign truth,
Hears and considers all.]

Eusebius is perfectly right in denying the identity of the Orphic Zeus and the God revealed in the O. and N. Testament. Nevertheless, I cannot bring myself to believe that the Mystæ and the Mythic Hymnists[1] meant the *visible* World, *quoad* visible/[2] which is described as his *Body*, ⟨or rather *in* his body.⟩ Most certainly, they did not conceive the Zeus as an *Aggre-*

6[3] "The tradition was that he had written a dialogue entitled 'The Philosopher', but it was admitted that it was never published. The truth is that I believe Plato would have baffled his own purposes had he done so. There he stopped": *P Lects* Lect 4 (1949) 164.

7[1] I.e. the earliest priests and poets in Rome. In T. Fuller *Holy State* **7** C refers to "the first *Thinkers* (= Mystæ)"; for the "Orphic" hymns see Faber **13** n 5.

7[2] "Insofar as it is" visible.

gate, or an accidental ⟨subjective⟩ Unity ⟨(i.e.⟩ subsisting ~~wholly~~ not in the Object itself but wholly in the percipient). I no where find aught in the oldest Orphics, in those fragments, ~~that~~ which have the best pretensions to Genuineness, that makes the Jupiter εκ μερων συνεστωτα/[3] In what precise mode they conceived the World to have been evolved, ~~and~~ or to be ever evolving, out of the Absolute Being, I have not been able to ascertain/. Not improbably, they were content with some indefinite analogy of ~~the~~ an Organic Body, in its relations to the plastic Vis Vitæ.[4]—But then the Organic Body, ⟨μεγάλου Ζήνος Σώμα⟩ was itself, as far as it was a νουμενον,[5] having real being, ~~in a~~ the immediate Product indeed of the organizing Spirit but yet indivisibly *one* therewith—even as the constructive Act of the Geometrician is one with the Diagram in the imagination, which is its immediate Product.—Jupiter, they expressly assert, is the *Life* of the Universe—Zeus, Ζηνος *a* ζαω.[6] But then this Life is not the functional life, the *result* of the Organization, but the Antecedent Unity, as the Principle of Form (= Forma formatrix).[7] Zeus was an absolute Life, Ἓν ὑπεραριθμιον, of which the Whole (τὸ ὅλον ἐκ μερῶν συνεστος[)] was but the Phænomenon[8]—the adorable Maia (i.e. Delusion) of the Brahmin Theosophers.[9] S. T. C.

Neither Eusebius or Valcknaer seem to have seen, that if according to Orpheus the Ether was the Mens Jovis, the *Mens* was the Ether.[10] It is not an Ether in lieu of a Mind—but the Ether is Mind.—Jove's Mind is the true Ether. ο αιθηρ <u>εστι</u> Νους, ο γαρ Νους Διος εστι τον αιθερα.[11] The Ether *is* (hath its true Being in) Mind: for the Divine Mind *is* (constitutes the Being of) the Ether. This double import of the Verb Substantive in

7[3] "Made up of various parts"—adapted from textus.

7[4] "Life-force".

7[5] "The Body of great Zeus" as far as it was a "noumenon"—that is, entirely immaterial.

7[6] "Zeus, Zenos [nominative and genitive of 'Zeus'] *from* zao ['I live']". The suggested etymology (to which C alludes also in LUTHER *Colloquia* **16**) is proposed in Aeschylus *Suppliants* 584 and Plato *Cratylus* 396A, B: *CN* IV 4616n.

7[7] "Formative form".

7[8] The "One beyond number" of which "the whole made up of various parts" (textus) was the material manifestation.

7[9] "Hence also the *Indian* MÁYÁ, or, as the word is explained by some *Hindu* scholars, 'the first inclination of the Godhead to diversify himself (such is their phrase) by creating worlds,' is feigned to be the mother of universal nature, and of all the inferiour Gods . . . but the word MÁYÁ, or *delusion*, has a more subtile and recondite sense in the *Védànta* philosophy, where it signifies the system of *perceptions* . . .": Sir William Jones "On the Gods of Greece, Italy, and India" *Asiatic Researches* I (1788) 223. This point was perhaps a commonplace: cf "a pure illusion, or *Maya*" in DUBOIS **1** textus.

7[10] C alludes again to textus: if the Ether was "the Mind of Jove", the "*Mind*" was the Ether.

7[11] "The ether *is* Mind, for the Divine Mind is the ether."

the *idea* I have endeavored to express by ~~the~~ an accusative case after the second εστι.[12] The Ether is mind: for the divine mind *is*-eth the Ether.—[13]

8 p 130 | Appendix

[The author is discussing the use of the verb προστιθεναι (literally "put to") to mean "shut (a door)":] Verum illa opus est minime; bene habent verba, vertendaque; *januam occludens, Socratis utebantur disciplinâ*, sive *Socratis particeps erat.*

[Indeed there is no need for that [conjecture]; the words are correct, and are to be translated *shutting the door he partook of Socrates' teaching* or *he had his share of Socrates.*]

Precisely, our English Idiom—*put to* the door—for shut the door.—Nay, I have heard "shut to".—

7[12] The second "is" in C's Greek above. For the "Verb Substantive" "to be" see also IRVING *Sermons* **1** n 3, *Logic* (*CC*) 16–19.

7[13] I.e. brings it into being.

HENRY VANE
(SIR HARRY VANE THE YOUNGER)
1613–1662

A Healing Question Propounded and Resolved upon Occasion of the Late Publique and Seasonable Call to Humiliation, in order to Love and Union amongst the Honest Party, and with Desire to apply Balsome to the Wound, before it become Incurable. London 1660. 4°.

In CROMWELLIAN TRACTS.

Not located; marginal note published from MS TRANSCRIPT.

MS TRANSCRIPT. VCL BT 37.

DATE. After mid-1818, when it appears that C acquired the collection of tracts in which this is included: see CROMWELLIAN TRACTS in *CM* (*CC*) II.

1 p 4

For the first of these, that is to say, the Naturall right, which the whole party of Honest men adhearing to this Cause, are by success of their Armes restored unto, fortified in, and may claim as their undeniable priviledge, that righteously cannot be taken from them, nor they debarred from bringing into exercise, it lies in this. They are to have and enjoy the freedom (by way of dutiful compliance and condiscention from all the parts and members of this society) to set up meet persons in the place of Supreme Judicature and Authority amongst them; whereby they may have the use & benefit of the choicest light and wisdom of the Nation, that they are capable to call forth, for the Rule and Government under which they will live; and through the orderly exercise of such become of wisdom and counsel as the Lord in this way shall please to give unto them, to shape and form all subordinate actings and administrations of Rule and Government, so as shall best answere the publique welfare and safety of the whole.

N.B. The Right is unquestionable; the question is, in whom is it vested? Sir H. Vane answers: The Honest Men—i.e. my own party. No [? man], at that time, might do so without absurdity—for he grounds *this* Right in part on the prior Right of conquest, and God's decision on an appeal to arms. But this Judgment has been reversed, and what shall we substitute?

The Nation? Who compose it? The people? Whom do you mean? The majority of convictions, i.e. convinced Understanding? How are these to be collected? Of Wills? What, a right of Might?— *S. T. C.*[a]

1[a] The initials may not be in C's hand

ROBERT VAUGHAN

1795–1868

The Life and Opinions of John de Wycliffe, D.D. Illustrated principally from his unpublished manuscripts; with a preliminary view of the Papal system, and of the state of the Protestant doctrine in Europe, to the commencement of the fourteenth century. 2 vols. London 1828.

Not located; published from William Scott's transcription in *Christian Remembrancer* n.s. VII (1844) 250–5. Scott, who was co-editor of the periodical, was familiar with C's hand from mss at Highgate, where he himself lived after C's death. In an introductory letter, he describes C's habit of writing in books and remarks, that "even the otherwise-sacred pages of the books of the Highgate Society had no immunity; and our periodical sales were sometimes enriched by extra biddings for books more than usually bepencilled. From one of these, the dissenter Vaughan's Life of Wycliffe, in the possession of a friend, I copied what I now send . . ." (250). The text in the *Christian Remembrancer* uses ligatures (œ, æ) in accordance with C's usual practice and presumably following the original ms; they are preserved here as an exception to the convention of expanding the ligatures that appear in printed sources.

DATE. 1830 or later: in **6** C refers to *C&S* (pub Dec 1829) as a published work. On 13 May 1833, C comments on Wycliffe as one whom he knows "from Vaughan and Le Bas, both whose books I like": *TT* (*CC*) I 380 and n 24.

1 I 38 | "Preliminary View" ch 1 § 2

It was not, however, until after the civil establishment of christianity, that the privileged order became distinguished by any peculiar costume. Previous to that important event, much had been done to facilitate the introduction of a law ["of clerical celibacy"] among churchmen, which has since formed the ground of pretensions to an almost unearthly purity; and which by rendering the prosperity of their order the chief solicitude, has contributed much to the increase both of its opulence and power.

One of the great errors of the Protestant polemic divines, but especially those of the Church of England, is that of assigning too late a date to the corruptions of the Latin Church. Laud's party regarded the first five cen-

turies as almost of apostolical authority. Alas! before the year A.D. 200, I could show the germs of every abuse and every false doctrine.[1]

2 I 42

The monastic discipline also, and the celibacy of the clergy, rose into importance amid the increasing corruption of the christian profession, and as the effect of the same causes. In the language of its authors, it was formed principally from the severer maxims of primitive believers, and was designed to preserve to a declining community, the benefit of examples truly christian.

Few things more disgusting than the impudent blank contradictions given by Butler, and sundry Irish papists, to the testimony of Blanco White, on a point so notorious to every man who has for any time resided in Spain, Portugal, Italy, or Sicily.[1] I was, when abroad, in confidential intercourse with the best and most intelligent of the Roman clerisy, secular and religious, and I never met a man who pretended to deny the fact that the obligation of chastity hung very lightly on them; and that if a priest was attentive to his duties in other respects, occasional deviations of this kind found easy absolution.

3 I 102 | § 4

The sacred scriptures, the common property of primitive believers, were a source of instruction which millions of baptized men in succeeding generations never saw . . . . Having supplied to the church those statements of doctrine which were contained in the decrees of councils, or adopted in the established ritual, they [the clergy of the middle ages] were regarded as having performed every thing to be reasonably expected from them, in immediate relation to the people. It is plain also that such was the ignorance of the popular mind, that the statements which were thus allowed to supersede the inspired volume, proved susceptible of almost

1[1] On C's opinion about the early sources of corruption in Christianity, as opposed to the High Church reverence for the "first five centuries", see Jeremy TAYLOR *Worthy Communicant* **1** and n 2.

2[1] In the continuing public debate about Catholic Emancipation in the 1820s, RS's *Book of the Church* (1824) became a focus of controversy, particularly in the warring responses in 1825–6 of the Roman Catholic lawyer Charles Butler and the C of E convert Joseph Blanco White. C annotated several works contributing to this dispute: see BLANCO WHITE and BUTLER. In the present annotation he appeals both to his own Mediterranean experience and to Blanco White's testimony about the sexual laxity of the Roman Catholic clergy, as expressed e.g. in Letter 5 of *Practical and Internal Evidence against Catholicism* (1825) 123–35.

any interpretation which the weakness or the artifice of the individual priest might deem it expedient to suggest.

But these are the effects of Christianity, *in spite of* the papacy, or at all events the papacy notwithstanding. The Church of Christ existed, or Antichrist could not have been throned therein. Mr. Vaughan should have distinguished the good effects of the papacy, *quoad* papacy, *ex. grat.* the facilitation of the settlement of the feudal tribes into the federal unity of a Christendom with international laws. Item, the universality of the Latin as the common language of intellectual commerce, though dearly purchased by the superstition and ignorance of the laity, excluded from the Scriptures, and praying in an unknown tongue. N.B. England derived less benefit and more evil from Rome than any other state.

4 I 150[a] | Ch 2 § 2

[In the crusade against the Albigenses:] The city of Beziers was first captured by the insurgents; and its inhabitants, amounting to many thousands, after a few hours were no more! [Footnote:] The numbers of the slain have been variously determined by catholic writers from 10,000 to 60,000. The half of the latter number is the more probable amount . . .

This frightful massacre itself,[b] under the circumstances of that dark and ferocious age, is less shocking to the moral sense than the reiterated attempts of recent Catholic writers to defend or palliate the atrocity, by keeping up anew the infamous calumnies on the innocent victims. The great objects of our Church at present ought to be, first, the removal of the wall of separation between them and the orthodox dissenters, by explaining the difference between the national clerisy, which ought to include all the three liberal professions as an *ordo civilis ad erudiendos mores institutus*,[1] and the Church, *i.e.* the Christian Church.[2] 2. To promote throughout the continent, especially in France, Germany, and the north of Italy, the commencing reform *in*, not *from*, the Catholic Church, strictly confining their exhortations to two points—the emancipation of the bishops and their sees from all dependency on the Roman Pontiff,—and of the Clergy collectively from the obligation of celibacy. These

4[a] Scott cites I 156—a slip or printer's error

4[b] Here Scott introduces what is evidently an editorial gloss and not part of C's note: "(the crusade against the Albigenses)"

4[1] A "secular order instituted to improve morals": C is describing the role proposed for a "clerisy" such as he describes in *C&S* (*CC*) 46–7, 52–4.

4[2] The distinction between national and universal manifestations of the Church of Christ is also central to *C&S*: see esp *C&S* (*CC*) 113–28.

points attained, all other errors will die away gradually, or become harmless, or at worst, *ineptiæ tolerabiles*.[3]

5 I 187 | Ch 3 § 1

The zeal of Bradwardine, directed thus vigorously toward a reformation of the doctrine of the church, passed over the obnoxious features of its policy and discipline.

There are myriads of Catholics at the present time most anxious for a reform *in* the Catholic Church, who would resolutely oppose a reform *from* it. They perhaps attach too much importance to the unity of the Church,—we too little.

6 I 278[a] | "Life of Wycliffe" ch 2

. . . in the assembly where these questions [of papal authority over secular matters in England] were so ably investigated, it was also affirmed . . . that the canon law on which so much pretension had been founded, was in itself but of humble authority, being rendered superfluous by the christian scriptures, which, considered alone, are described as sufficient to determine every point of moral or religious obligation. The pontiff also, contrasted with the invisible head of the church, is not only described as a mere man and as peccable, but as liable to the guilt of mortal transgression; and considered in the latter state is declared to have forfeited every right to ecclesiastical dominion.

1. That Peter never was bishop of Rome; and that his ever having been at Rome, or in any part of Italy, is a mere tradition, unsupported by any tenable historical evidence easily explained.[1] 2. That if he had been, and had been, in direct contradiction to Paul's Epistle to the Romans, a Roman bishop,[2] it proves nothing in support of the papal pretensions. 3. That the sole pretext, the only plausible ground for the pontificate, is the supposition that it is a necessary condition of the unity of the Catholic

6[a] Scott cites I 288, but there is no appropriate textus on that page. I 278, the last page of ch 2, provides half a blank page to receive a note

4[3] "Tolerable fooleries"—Calvin's phrase, in comment on the English liturgy: see Jeremy TAYLOR *Polemicall Discourses* **9** n 1.

6[1] Cf LACUNZA **56** "the unproved and improbable Tradition . . . of S[t] Peter's having been Bishop of Rome". C makes the same point elsewhere, e.g. FIELD **31**, JURIEU **5**.

6[2] C also mentions Paul's Epistle to the Romans in FIELD **31** as a counterweight to the tradition about Peter's episcopacy (based on Matt 16.18). It is not that Paul denies the tradition but that his not naming Peter at all in references to the congregation at Rome is implicit evidence against it.

Church. But 4. Mede has demonstrated (see my Essay on the Constitution in Church and State) that *à priori*, it is an inept and inadequate means to that end; and that, in fact, it has ever worked in the contrary direction.[3]

7 I 295 | Ch 3

. . . such, in a peculiar degree, was the culture of the mind which led the way to the english reformation. Wycliffe's acquaintance with the compositions of devout men, and especially with the writings of inspired teachers, had contributed to place human nature before him, in all the deformity and ruin of its lapsed condition; and had at the same time, disclosed to him, the moral loveliness of the state in which it first[a] stood, and to which by the influence of the gospel, it may yet be restored.

Still, the elevation of the national character in the inheritable and inherited consciousness of the natives, which still lives and works in the heart of every Englishman, must be taken as an important set-off against the evils of our continental wars.[b]

8 I 311, evidently referring to I 295[a] | **7** textus, at the end

Where is the proof of this? How long did Adam stand? and even during this brief probation he was but a *living* soul, not a life-making spirit. Of this "moral loveliness," the aim and goal of our Christian race, Christ is the only *righteousness*, and in Him alone God loveth the world.

9 II 37 | [ii][a] ch 2

That the gospel was embraced by many of our Celtic ancestors, previous to the close of the first century, is the general testimony of historians; and three centuries intervened before that connexion between the subject provinces of Britain, and the capital of the empire which had led to this diffusion of christianity was dissolved. We have no authority, however,

7[a] The word "first" is italicized in Scott but not in Vaughan; Scott's italics apparently represent C's underlining

7[b] Scott adds what is apparently an editorial gloss: "(in the fourteenth century)"

8[a] Scott cites I 311—an unaccountable error

9[a] The chapter-numbers of the *Life* begin a second series at the beginning of Vol II

6[3] Like C in *C&S* (*CC*) 129–45, Joseph Mede frankly treated the Roman Catholic Church as the church of Antichrist. In Discourse 29 in *Works* (2 vols 1664) I 182–8, for example, he interprets Isa 2.2–4 as a promise of the eventual triumph of the universal Christian Church, but considers the period before the Reformation as an age "overshadowed with the thick darkness of Idolatrous *Antichristianism*" (I 184).

for supposing, that any portion of the sacred writings was possessed by the people of this island during that period, in the vernacular tongue.

The Gothic version by Ulphilas, in the close of the second century, renders the existence of a Celtic translation of parts at least of the Bible (the Psalms, for instance, and St. John's Gospel) not improbable.[1]

10 II 39

In the following century [the eighth], Aldhelm, bishop of Sherborne, and Cuthlac, the celebrated anchoret, are among the authors of Anglo-saxon versions of the Psalter; and the venerable Bede, prefers his claim to the honor of a literal translation of St. John's Gospel. [Vaughan then cites Saxon versions and other vernacular versions down to the tenth century.]

Query. What is the date of the earliest Welsh translation of the Scriptures, or of any integral portion, as the Psalter?[1] An ecclesiastical history of North and South Wales—are there materials for such a work? It could not but be of great interest; and the Welsh genius hath been hitherto eminently antiquarian. I cannot bring myself to believe that the British, Scottish, and Pictish monastic clergy of the fifth to the eighth century were an exception to the zeal for translation. But we must remember, that during this period, when the purer Church of Britain succumbed to the papal domination, the numerous clergy in their vagrant cœnobitic establishments, were men of learning sufficient at least to use the Latin version, which doubtless they rendered and expounded in their itinerary to the people *vivâ voce*:[2] while, except these ministers, few indeed could read.[a] Nevertheless I think it probable that metrical versions and paraphrases did exist, probably may still be discovered, in the Welsh language. How glad I should be to converse with Sharon Turner on this subject![3]

10[a] Scott introduces points of ellipsis here to indicate material omitted from the transcript (possibly no more than an illegible word)

9[1] The surviving sections of the 4th-century (not 2nd-) translation of the Bible into Gothic by bp Ulphilas or Wulfila constitute almost the only record of that language; there does not appear to have been any early Celtic version. In *BL* ch 10 (*CC*) I 207–8, C describes his education in Gothic, at Göttingen in 1799: "From professor TYCHSEN I received as many lessons in the Gothic of Ulphilas as sufficed to make me acquainted with its grammar, and the radical words of most frequent occurrence".

10[1] There does not appear to have been a Welsh Bible, nor even a Welsh NT, before the 16th century.

10[2] "Out loud".

10[3] RS's friend Sharon Turner (1768–1847), historian and philologist, was a champion of early Welsh literature, notably in his *Vindication of the Genuineness of the Antient British Poems of Aneurin, Taliesin, Llywarch Hen, and Merdhin, with Specimens of the Poems* (1803).

11 II 44

[Vaughan quotes Henry Knighton (fl 1363):] ". . . this master John Wycliffe translated it [the gospel] out of latin into english, and thus laid it more open to the laity, and to women who could read, than it had formerly been to the most learned of the clergy . . . . And in this way the gospel pearl is cast abroad, and trodden under foot of swine, and that which was before precious to both clergy and laity, is rendered as it were the common jest of both. The jewel of the church is turned into the sport of the people, and what was hitherto the principal gift of the clergy and divines, is made for ever common to the laity."

Strange power of prejudice on the strongest minds! Even Vico, that profound thinker, lays it down as a rule, that in Jerusalem religion cannot hold its ground, unless by the jealous confinement of its sacred writings to a learned order. Yet Vico, though a Catholic, almost idolized the writings of Bucer and Grotius.[1] But I fear that Vico inwardly regarded the Christian only as one of the various positive religions, the examples of which he quotes.

12 II 48[a]

[Vaughan quotes Wycliffe:] "As the faith of the church is contained in the scriptures, the more these are known in an orthodox sense, the better. . . . the conclusion is abundantly plain, that believers should ascertain for themselves the matters of their faith, by having the scriptures in a language which they fully understand."

12[a] This long note cannot have been written on II 48; it could have been written (with a page-reference) on flyleaves, or through a sequence of pages of the text

11[1] C's first-hand knowledge of Vico dates from 1825, when he borrowed a copy of *Scienza nuova* from de' Prati and wrote, in May, "I am more and more delighted with G. B. Vico": *CL* V 454. He was also reading the *Vita*, Vico's autobiography. Notebook entries made at the time record two points that reappear here. First, in *CN* IV 5204, C expresses his amazement at Vico's decision (mentioned in the *Vita*) to stop reading Grotius *De juri belli et pacis*, much as he admires it, because it is unsuitable reading for a Catholic: C remarks, "Striking instance of the bigot-izing influence of the Romish Superstition—even on the noblest Minds". (Vico does not mention Bucer—for whom see **14**—in either of these works, so C may be using the name to represent Protestant thought in general; or be mistaken; or have drawn on another source of information.) Secondly, in *CN* IV 5207 he takes note of the point made in *Scienza nuova* (3 vols Milan 1816) I 135 that the words for "sacred" and "secret" have the same root: Vico has been explaining that priests in all the ancient nations (he mentions the Jews particularly) kept their sacred books to themselves, excluding not only foreigners but also their own people.

Note.—To *ascertain*, not for the first time to *learn* the truth. In order to this, Christ had founded a *Church*, and by the first spiritually-gifted ministers of this Church, *some* of them instructed by Christ himself while in the flesh, and all by the Spirit, with whom, and in whom, Christ returned to the faithful, as an indwelling Light and Life;—by the first ministers of the Church, I say, who were the fathers and founders of particular churches, the universal (Catholic) essential truths and doctrines of Christ were committed to writing, without withholding of any truth applicable to all times and countries, and binding on all Christians. Now these writings, collectively, form the New Testament, and whatever cannot be *recognised* there cannot be an essential article of faith. But the Scriptures, the great *charter* of the Church, does not supersede the Church; and till we have learnt the *whole scheme* of Christianity from the Church, by her creeds, catechisms, homilies, and according to the constitution of the apostles, the Bible could not but produce erring fancies, perplexities, jarring subjects;—and on the other hand, withdraw the Scriptures, and where is the check on the proceedings and pretensions of the certainly uninspired, and too probably ambitious Churchman? No! learn from the Church, and then in humility, yet freedom of spirit, test it by the Scripture. Note.—The Church doctrines are the bank-notes, the Scripture the bullion, which the notes represent, and which the Bank (*i.e.* the Church) must be always ready to bring forwards when fairly demanded.

Note to this note, by S. T. C.:—[b]

> Nullum simile omnino quadrat—
> Quicquid *simile* est, non est *idem*.[1]

> No simile goes on all fours, or
> Every *simile* necessarily limps.[2]

With this understanding, and so qualified, must the reader take my comparison of the Church doctrine relatively to Scripture as bank-notes to bullion. Now in this respect the simile halts,—that the bullion *may be* subdivided into doubloons, sovereigns, half-sovereigns, or to penny-pieces; and yet, notwithstanding this divisibility, we are assured, by the greater master[c] of the science of trade, our most experienced Ploutono-

12[b] This line may be Scott's
12[c] A slip—C's or Scott's—for the plural "masters"

12[1] "No simile squares with everything—whatever is *like* is not *the same*."
12[2] For C's use of this proverbial formulation see also CHALMERS **5** and n 1, *C&S* (*CC*) 86 and n 3, *Logic* (*CC*) 11 and n 4.

mists, (Rothschild, Ricardo, Lloyd, &c. &c. &c.,)[3] that the trade and commerce of this kingdom could not be carried on without ruinous stops and retardations, for a single week, by a metallic currency, however large! But be this as it may, the bullion of Scripture is not a bullion of this kind. It may be formally, I own, divided into bars = books; ingots = chapters; and coins, *i.e.* verses; but, alas! you might almost as well subdivide an organized body, and expect that the extracted eye would see, the insulated heart remain a heart, as attempt to interpret a text without its context, or that context without reference to the whole scheme. It is in the ὁμοπνευστια,[4] in the one and same divine spirit pervading and modifying all the differences, all the sundry workings of the *human* mind under different lights and different dispensations that the *divinity* of the Bible is manifested. The imperfect humanity must be there, in order, by its diversity and varying nature, to contrast with the *One* breathing in all, and giving to all one and the same direction.

13 II 72[a] | Ch 3

. . . until the middle of the ninth century, the manner in which the body and the blood of Christ are present in the eucharist, was the subject of debate, or rather of a peaceful difference of sentiment among persons holding the chief dignities of the hierarchy. . . . But from that period . . . the advocates of the mysterious dogma, which in the twelfth century, began to be designated transubstantiation, rapidly increased. Its progress, however, was far from being interrupted; and among its opponents, the most distinguished place must be allotted to Berengarius . . .

I have ever regretted that the efforts of our Luther and his followers had not been limited to the reclaiming of the cup for the laity; and that the controversy on the dogma of transubstantiation had not been deferred to a later and calmer period. For hence, as the main source, flowed the bitter waters of strife among the Protestants themselves. Instead of *advancing*[b] Berengarius, Luther *retrograded.* The best that can be said of him

13[a] Scott cites II 52, which has to do with a parliament of 1379
13[b] Here Scott uses points of ellipsis as in **10**

12[3] *OED* does not recognise "Ploutonomists" (experts in the sciences that have to do with wealth), but it does record the spelling "plutonomist", with a first instance in 1851. C's examples are two contemporary bankers and an economist: Nathan Meyer Rothschild (1777–1836), head of the English branch of the great banking family; David Ricardo (1772–1823), economic theorist; and Charles Lloyd (1748–1828), Quaker banker in Birmingham and father of C's onetime pupil Charles Lloyd.

12[4] C translates the word—not classical or NT Greek—himself: "the one and same divine spirit".

is, that he substituted a comparatively harmless for a positively mischievous *nonsense*, while the sacramentary hemlock extinguished the very life of the awful mystery.[1]

14 II 75–6[a]

Our Saxon ancestors were in general sufficiently obedient to the opinions and customs of the papacy, and we may believe that the doctrine of transubstantiation was not unknown, not wholly unapproved, by their spiritual guides. We have, however, the most decisive proof that the dogma so named, formed no part of the national creed in the tenth century. Elfric . . . has adverted in one of his epistles to the elements of the eucharist in a manner which incidentally, but most distinctly, proscribes the doctrine of a "real presence."

Now Berengarius, (see his uncompleted Treatise, edited by Lessing from a MS. in the Wolfenbuttel Library,) Bucer, and the Church Catechism distinctly assert the *real* presence, with and in the spirit of the Gospel (John vi.), and contradistinguish *real* from *phenomenal*, substantive from accidental.[1] The Romish doctors sensualize the doctrine into an idol; while the sacramentaries volatilize it into a metaphor; and, alas! too large a number of our clergy are sacramentaries! Often I have had occasion to mourn the dissonance between the sermon and the service.

14[a] Scott cites II 55

13[1] For the sacramentaries see Jeremy TAYLOR *Worthy Communicant* **4** n 1; also **14** following. Luther's main contribution to the controversy about the eucharist was to substitute the concept of consubstantiation for the Roman Catholic doctrine of transubstantiation, which had been challenged by Berengar of Tours before him, as C notes in LACUNZA **30** and in **14** below. Luther also led the way in the restoration of communion in both kinds to the laity; cf Article 30 in the C of E Articles of Religion.

14[1] The text to which C alludes is perhaps John 6.51, "I am the living bread which came down from heaven: if any man eat of this bread, he shall live for ever: and the bread that I will give is my flesh, which I will give for the life of the world." Lessing's writings include comments upon a ms concerned with transubstantiation by Berengar in the Wolfenbüttel Library; his editor, to C's annoyance, published the comments without the ms: LESSING *Sämmtliche Schriften* **1** n 2, **85** and n 3. In BLANCO WHITE *Preservative* **2**, C proclaimed, "I receive the Eucharist in Bucer's sense"—meaning, as *AR* (*CC*) 338 and n 97 reveal, in the spiritual sense articulated by Martin Bucer (1491–1551) in "Sentencious Sayinges . . . upon the Lordes Supper" appended to STRYPE *Cranmer* 124–33. The C of E Catechism affirms of all the sacraments that they consist of an "outward visible sign" and an "inward spiritual grace", and of the Lord's Supper particularly that in it the body and blood of Christ "are verily and indeed taken and received by the faithful".

15 II 193[a] | Ch 6

[Summarising *The Plowman's Tale*:] The assent of the commonalty, is declared to be necessary to every measure of taxation; but the pope, who obtained his elevation from the emperor, ere long to become his superior, is regarded as viewing the power of the english constitution in the light of a rival authority; and the king and the lords are admonished to bear this in mind, and to prove the shield of the nation against the meditated encroachment of a merciless despotism.

1. The separation of the poor's-rates from the tythes, *i.e.* the reserved nationalty as distinguished from property, or the estates of individuals and families.[1] 2. The confounding the maintenance of the proper *poor* with the maintenance of healthy workmen thrown out of employ by the fluctuations of trade—a compromise entered into in order to make the rate of wages measured by the demand. 3. The extension of this from trade, of which *things* are the proper objects, to agriculture, of which *persons* should be the final end. And, 4. The consequent withdrawing of the poor-laws from the national Church and all Church discipline. These four I regard as the main causes of our national distress and corruption.

16 II 227–8

[On the appointment of Henry Spencer, bishop of Norwich, as champion of the Roman Pope in the crusade against the pope of Avignon:] The bull with which he was entrusted, vested him with extraordinary powers. . . . With respect to the clergy who had become parties to the schism, he was instructed to exert his whole power with a view to deprive them of every cure, honor, and emolument; and it was left to his discretion, to insist on the presence of the most privileged members of the hierarchy, in the camp of the crusaders.

In the eye of a philosopher, the papal hierarchy is the pope. Think, then, of Ireland, and ask whether it is not as fearfully and mischievously active at the present day as it ever was in the age of Wycliffe.

17 II 206, apparently referring to II 239[a]

[Vaughan quotes from Wycliffe's ms "How antichrist and his clerks travail to destroy holy writ":] ". . . the devil, studieth by antichrist, and his

15[a] Scott cites II 192, but see **18** below
17Â[a] Scott cites II 206—the last page of ch 6 and one-third blank; he may have omitted C's page-reference

15[1] "Nationalty" is C's coinage, as he himself announces in *C&S* (*CC*) 35.

false worldly clerks, to destroy holy writ and the belief of christian men, by four accursed methods or false reasonings. 1st, that the Church is of more authority and credence than any gospel; 2nd, that Augustine saith he would not believe in the gospel if the church had not taught him so; 3rd, that no man now alive knoweth which is the gospel, except it be by an approval of the church; 4th, and hence if men say that they believe this to be the gospel of Matthew or John, they do so for no cause but that the church confirmeth it, and teacheth it."

These four "accursed methods" are weakened but not fully answered by Wycliffe, or even by the Protestant divines down to this day.[1] That the papal hierarchy, nor the clergy generally, as a distinct class from the laity, constitute the Church is indeed shown, and ably shown; but not so the question, what, then, *is* the Church?

18 II 259,[a] referring to II 274 | Ch 8

[In his ms "Of Servants and Lords how each should keep his degree", Wycliffe stated:] ". . . that men are charged of God, by St. Peter and St. Paul, to be thus subject to wicked lords; and therefore Christ paid tribute for himself, and his apostles, to the heathen emperors. Yet we read not that he, or any apostle, paid tithes to the wicked high priests, after the time that he began to preach."

With sorrow, I say, a very weak reply. Have we any reason to assert the contrary? But the fact is, that Wycliffe overlooked (and how few since his time have seen!) the distinction between the legal, constitutional, and civil claims of a parson as a member of the national clerisy, and his claims as a minister of the Gospel. Wycliffe erroneously regarded the clergyman in this latter relation exclusively. But had he considered the tythes as a revenue set aside and appropriated to a learned order, say authority, of the nation itself, and independent of, because prior to, the introduction of Christianity, and therefore resting on the same ground as the property of the laity, he would have made no such conclusion, and therefore it is most

18[a] Scott cites I 239, but 259–60, the end of a section and the following blank page, would provide more space; he gives enough of the textus, however, to identify it with confidence

17[1] Vaughan outlines Wycliffe's response II 239–43: "ecclesiastics alone do not constitute the church" (II 240); it is self-interest that leads "the clerks of antichrist" (Wycliffe's phrase) to quote Augustine as in textus; and "the most obscure student of the bible may find in that book a more certain guide to truth, than in the pontiffs or in the wisest of their councils" (II 241).

unfair in his adversaries, to infer from his opinion respecting clerical revenues, a similar opinion as to the rights of the gentry. Wycliffe said no more of the clergy's rights than we say now of the right of placemen, that the rights depend on the competence of the person to the duties.

WILLIAM VINCENT

1739–1815

The Greek Verb Analysed. An Hypothesis. In which the source and structure of the Greek language, and of language in general, is considered. London 1795. 8°.

Victoria College Library (Coleridge Collection)

EHC description of the marginalia in pocket p $^{+}3$, where the book is designated as part of the "Green Bequest"; his transcript of **1** mounted on p $^{-}2$.

DATE. c 1800? The hand looks early, and C mentions having read the work in a letter of Jun 1802: *CL* II 803. His remark about the Trinity in **2**, however, might indicate a date after 1804, when he turned from Unitarian to Trinitarian beliefs.

1 half-title

This work gives proof of Ingenuity, tho' not of exact or extensive Reading; & may usefully be turned over by any one engaged in the simplification or illustration of the Greek & Latin Verbs.—But its Logic is at the freezing point, and its arrangement! no ordinary Κριoz[?o]meter[a1] would suffice to mark its Nadir—. I—never ~~perused~~ noticed such a—here & there, to and fro Skipper~~age~~!—& Jack o' Lanthorn! or a more awkward game of literary Blindsman's Buff.— S. T. C.—[2]

1[a] A hole in the leaf has been repaired, with the loss of one or two characters

1[1] The reading appears to be *Kriozometer*—C using Greek letters at the beginning but putting zed for zeta as he often does—and the context suggests that the word is to mean an instrument for measuring skill at arrangement or order of reasoning; but the root is obscure and there may be more than one letter missing. It is possible that he intended "krinozometer" from *krino* "I arrange".

1[2] Taking a hint from Horne Tooke, Vincent acts on the hypothesis "of the primitive verb ΕΩ as the origin of all terminations in the Greek verb, and the source of all its extensive variety" (7). He assumes (also following Tooke) that nouns came first, verbs being formed by the addition of *eo* or *eimi* as a suffix to nouns, and past tenses all including as a prefix some version of *e*, from the same source. He reduces all conjugations to one, and presents his system as an efficient way of teaching the rudiments of Greek even if the working hypothesis should be proved to be erroneous.

2 p 11

EOMAI, I cause myself to be; that is, in a neuter sense, I am. Explain this by the verb *Exist**, it will appear still more evidently . . . [Footnote *:] Stephens says in his Thesaurus, ΩN, ENS, non EXISTENS. I do not understand him: for though I can render ENS being, and ENS EXISTING, being in existence; I can use them mutually for each other.

a bad symptom of astheny in philosophical penetration and acquirements.[1] Ens = Being, when made manifest to other Beings becomes *existens*, existence—it stands out of itself.[2] Thus before the creation (but for the aweful & profound Doctrine of the Trinity) God would have a Being; but not an *existence*.

3 p 16

[Vincent argues that all Greek verbs may be deduced from ἔω, and illustrates this contention with the example of παύω, "I stop".] Two objections occur to this statement.

1st. That I assume a *person*, which does not exist in any part of the verb I pretend to form. . . . To the first I answer, that the person is always to be found by asking who is the Cause? and therefore I have added it.

A strange answer!—especially when the true reason is so obvious; that ⟨as⟩ the 2nd & 3rd Persons ~~are~~ do exist as part of the verbs of the 2 and 3 Person, the omission therefore becomes a sufficient character of the first; as in the omission of ὁ (the) in Greek is the *character* of "a".—ο ανηρ, ανηρ.[1] Besides, the consciousness of the speaker more vividly supplies the word, "I" to himself, than you, or it.

4 pp 33–5

. . . for the Greek beta* sounded like our English v . . . [Footnote *:] In the work of M. Antoninus Τῶν ἐις ἑαυτὸν, he writes in the first page,

2[1] "Astheny", weakness, is not in *OED* but the original Greek term had been taken over into English as "asthenia" as a medical commonplace.

2[2] C draws attention to the formation of the word from Latin *ex* "out of" and *stare* "to stand".

3[1] "The man; man". Though this is an elementary fact of Greek grammar, C's remark may reflect his awareness of the importance of the issue in theological debates and perhaps specifically his reading of Granville Sharp *Remarks on the Uses of the Definitive Article in the Greek Text of the New Testament* (Durham 1798) and—though later than the earliest likely date for these marginalia—subsequent contributions to the debate that it initiated, particularly *The Doctrine of the Greek Article* (1808) by C's old schoolmate Thomas Middleton, and Christopher Wordsworth's anonymously-published *Six Letters to Granville Sharp* (1802): *CN* III 3275 and n; BIBLE COPY B **102** and n 1, **132** and n 1; *CL* III 69–70; C. WORDSWORTH *Six Letters*.

Ὀυήρος for *Verus*; Βενετιανὸς for *Venetianus*; would not one suppose that a Latin, writing Greek should have known the true pronunciation of V?

If in the age of M. Antoninus the Ϝ had been an allowed or intelligible Letter in Orthography, this argument would have *some* weight; tho' by no means irresistable—for a Roman writing Greek would be desirous to give the *air* of elegant Greek, & would be shy of Letters not familiar to a Greek Eye.—[1] As it is, the argument is wholly without Weight—/ If he had written Delia, Θηλια, we might then reasonably suppose, that the Romans pronounced D as Θ;[2] but where the fashionable Alphabet of one Language has no letter corresponding to a given one of another Language, the Letter substituted must be subject to much caprice; & the classical Look of the Word will most frequently be preferred to the nearest degree of Sound/ of which the French Writers furnish abundant proofs.—

4[1] Scholars disagreed about whether the Greek digamma should be pronounced "v" or "w". C on several occasions proposed "ng". See esp Hartley COLERIDGE **4** and n 1.

4[2] As "th", as in the name C has proposed, *Thelia*.

"VINDEX"

The Conduct of the British Government towards the Church of England in the West India Colonies: in a letter to Viscount Goderich, Secretary of State for the Colonial Department. London 1831. 8°.

Brandeis University: Henry and Hannah Hofheimer Collection

DATE. Presumably 1831, soon after publication.

1 Half-title and title-page, referring to pp [1–3]

A vigorous, eloquent, and for the far greater portion, wise and well-reasoned Remonstrance. My only objection, only important Objection, respects the ambiguity of the word "compatible" and "incompatible" in reference to Christianity.[1] That it is and ever was compatible with the *co-existence* of the Christian Church, is fact of history—but so is ingratitude, gaming &c &c. But surely, ~~it~~ what ~~is~~ may co-exist with the Preaching, is not necessarily consistent with the precepts, and ultimate aims—i.e. with the Spirit, of Christianity. *War* is not forbidden, by the Gospel; but only the Passions, whence alone come Wars among men. Evils, the ultimate tho' perhaps slow & very gradual removal of which, are among the *Objects* of a Religion, cannot be incompatible with its *existence*. But let every remedy be applied ~~to~~ according to its specific Powers—The Gospel is a remedy for Corruptions in the Will ~~and errors in~~ and darkness in the Reason (whence proceed the ⟨only dangerous⟩ errors in the Understanding) of Persons, of Individuals—It was not intended as a *direct* remedy for *Things*—and Institutions, *States* of Society, &c are *Things*—& therefore excluded from a *Spiritual* agency.—Indirectly indeed, and in as much as Causa Causæ Causa Causati,[2] the Gospel no doubt is an antidote to the evil of Slavery, as to the evil of War—of a bribed or a mob-

1[1] This 24-page pamphlet responds to a remark made by Sir George Murray "in the House of Commons, with reference to the existing state of society in the West Indies, that 'Christianity and Slavery were incompatible'" (6). Vindex argues that this statement is "an implicit libel on our Saviour Christ, and an express indictment of our Apostle Paul" (6) since, for example, slavery was a fact of life "within and without the limits of the Roman Empire" (6) during the lifetime of Christ, and yet it is nowhere condemned in the NT.

1[2] "The cause of a cause is the cause of the effect." For the origins of this Scholastic maxim and for C's use of it, see DONNE *Sermons* COPY B **65** n 1, *AR* (*CC*) 267 n 11.

managed Legislature—& what not?—In this one respect only I differ equally from Vindex & from Buxton & his Confreres.[3]—Slavery is compatible with Christianity—& therefore Parliament may protect it, argues Vindex.—

Sl. is utterly incompatible with Christianity—screams B.—and therefore put it down by an Act of Parliament!—

Slavery—i.e. the perversion of a Person into a Thing—is contrary to the Spirit of Christianity ⟨(say I)⟩—& therefore it is the duty of Christians to labor (as far as it is in their power & lies within the sphere of their immediate duties) for its ultimate removal from the Christian World—/ But that an Act of Parliament would be a fit or effectual Means toward this end, I not only do not believe; but I believe the very contrary/ and under these convictions give my conscientious vote for the measures recommended by Vindex as the right substitute for the fiery remedies prescribed by the Anti-slavery Society[4]— S. T. Coleridge

1A p 9, marked with a pencil line in the margin

My Lord, after a patient and anxious scrutiny of the entire body of the Scriptures of the New Testament, I find, as every one of the meanest capacity may find, and as men of the highest capacity have found, that Christ's kingdom was not, nor is, a kingdom of this world; that it revolutionized neither governments nor laws by any direct action; that, with reference to politics, and forms of economy, it was a collateral influence, taking men and things as they were all over the earth, and no otherwise interfering with the customs or regulations of civil governments, than by inculcating the eternal principles of Truth, Justice, and Mercy, in every existing relation of life, and by substituting the rule of Conscience for the spur of Interest or Fear.

1[3] Thomas Fowell Buxton (1786–1845), MP for Weymouth 1818–37, was a prominent member of the Anti-Slavery Society which promoted the argument quoted in n 1. Vindex concedes that the tendency of Christianity is towards the abolition of slavery, but argues that the mission of the Christian Church, and esp of the C of E in the colonies, is not to engage in direct political action but to teach the gospel of Christ. Using the Church to subvert society will, he thinks, undermine the constitution.

1[4] Vindex argues that the Church in the colonies should be spreading the word of the gospel (to the slaves among others) and acting in general as a civilising force, but not attempting to overturn the status quo.

VIRGIL
(PUBLIUS VIRGILIUS MARO)
70–19 B.C.

Georgica Publii Virgilii Maronis Hexaglotta. Georgica Publii Virgilii Maronis in quinque linguas conversa, Hispanicam à Joanne de Guzman; Germanicam—Joanne Henrico Voss; Anglicam—Gulielmo Sotheby; Italicam—Francisco Soave; Gallicam—Jacobo Delille. London 1827. F^{o}.

Victoria College Library (Coleridge Collection)

Signed on half-title preceding title-page: "Edith Coleridge. 1852". A note by EHC describing the volume, in a pocket on p $^{+}$5 (p-d), indicates that it was Edith Coleridge who had it rebound in its present white vellum.

For C's comments on WW's translation of Virgil *Aeneid*, see W. WORDSWORTH "Translation" below.

DATE. 3 Sept 1829 (**1**).

1 half-title

After my decease this splendid Volume presented to me by William Sotheby, Esqre (and not the only Mark of Regard and Kindness that I have received from this accomplished Scholar and truly worthy Man) is to belong, and I hereby give and appropriate it to, my beloved and love-worthy Child, SARA COLERIDGE And I hope and trust, that she will never willingly part with this Volume or alienate the same. ~~And~~ For if she she should marry and should have a Daughter, it is my wish that this Volume should descend to *her*, or (if Sarah have Daughters) to her eldest Daughter—who ~~will~~ is to regard it as a Memento provided by her maternal Grandfather, that her dear Mother's Accomplishments and her unusual Attainments in Ancient and Modern Languages, were not so much nor so justly the Objects of Admiration, as their co-existence in the same Person with so much piety, simplicity and unaffected Meekness—in short, in a mind, character and demeanour so perfectly feminine.

S. T. Coleridge
3 Septr 1829
Grove, Highgate.

N.B. On the very day, that the above was written, Sara Coleridge was married to her Cousin, Henry Nelson Coleridge, at Keswick.[1]

1[1] C's inscription and gift of the vol to his daughter on her wedding-day realise the intention that he had expressed in his letter of thanks to Sotheby in 1827: *CL* VI 691.

FRANÇOIS MARIE AROUET DE VOLTAIRE
1694–1778

A Treatise on Toleration; memorials, letters, &c. relating to persecution; and particularly to the cases of Calas and Sirven. Translated from the French of Mr. de Voltaire, by the Rev. David Williams. London 1779. 8°.

Victoria College Library (Coleridge Collection)

Inscribed on p $^{-}2$ "Frances Cline 1790" with 8 lines of translation from Horace. Bookplates of C. M. Ingleby and Kathleen Coburn on p $^{-}7$ (p-d), squiggle in ink p 16.

DATE. After 1817; possibly Jun 1818. The owner of this copy, Frances Cline, was the mother of JHG. C spent a holiday with Green at his parents' country house in Jun 1818, and sent regards to Mrs Green senior in a letter of 3 Jul: *CL* IV 870.

1 p 97

The high priest interrogated him, and said, "I command thee, by the living God, to tell us if thou art Christ the Son of God." We are not informed, what the high priest meant by the *Son of God*. This expression was sometimes used to signify a just man, as the words *son of Belial* were used to signify a wicked man. The gross minds of the Jews had no idea of a sacred mystery of a Son of God, God himself coming upon earth.

as truly might the Writer have said, that the Whigs in the reign of George the first had no *idea* of the Son of James IInd by divine Right King of England, Scotland &c—when they set a price on his head, as the Pretender.—The writings of of[a] Philo Judæus might have taught Voltaire, that before the Baptism of Jesus a Party existed who held *the Word* a Person in the Deity, Deus alter et idem/[1] contra-distinguished from Personification, Attribute & the like—that this Word was to assume humanity, and be the Messiah—. This Party was held in detestation by the Pales-

1[a] Preposition repeated at the beginning of a new line

1[1] "God the other and the same". C habitually used this phrase to sum up the position of Philo Judaeus (c 30 BC–c AD 40), whose writings on the Logos are often represented as anticipations of Trinitarian doctrine: cf BÖHME **178** and n 1, *SM* (*CC*) 95 and n 3, *C&S* (*CC*) 84* and n 3, *TT* (*CC*) I 34 and n 23.

tine Zelotæ and Miso-romanists[2]—Caiaphas asks Jesus if he were the King of the Jews, in order to alarm *Pilate*—but if he were the Son of the living God in order to excite the hatred of the Zelotæ against him.—

1[2] "Zealots and Haters of the Romans". In EICHHORN *Apocalypse* COPY A **7**, C likens the Zealots—a Jewish party fanatically opposed to Roman rule—to the radicals of the French Revolution.

GERHARD VOSS

1577–1649

Poeticarum institutionum, libri tres. Amsterdam 1647. 4°.

Victoria and Albert Museum: Dyce Collection

Inscribed "T. Bradbury. April 2. 1753." on p $^{-}2$. A stanza from Strozzi and a brief note in Greek and Latin—both in unidentified hands—appear on p $^{-}4$. The initials "S T C" in C's hand on the title-page, with "Sara Coleridge [. . .] 1849 From H.C." There are faint pencil-markings on pt i sigg †3, †† [verso] and pp [3] (where an incorrect p number has been corrected in ink), 6, 16, 22, 25, 53, 67: they do not follow C's usual practices, and it is unlikely that any of them is his.

CONTENTS. (i) Institutionum poeticarum bk 1; (ii) De artis poeticae natura, ac constitutione; (iii) Institutionum poeticarum bk 2; (iv) Institutionum poeticarum bk 3; (v) De imitatione; (vi) Index. They are all separately paginated. Only (i), (ii), and (v) have separate title-pages, all bearing the date 1647.

DATE. Dated by C (**1**): 21 Apr 1803.

1 p $^{-}2$

I looked thro' this book with some attention, April 21, 1803—, and seldom indeed have I read a more thoroughly worthless one.

S. T. Coleridge

EDWARD GIBBON WAKEFIELD

1796–1862

A Letter from Sydney, the principal town of Australasia. Edited by Robert Gouger. Together with the outline of a system of Colonization. London 1829. 12°.

National Library of Australia, Canberra

In a note written in pencil in an unidentified hand on the title-page, "Robert Gouger" is identified as "E. G. Wakefield".

DATE. Apr 1830 (**6**).

1 title-page, pencil

a very clever little Book S. T. C.

2 pp 29–30, pencil, overtraced

. . . there must constantly exist [in a waste country] an urgent need for labour, so long as the territory at the disposal of the people shall remain immense in proportion to their numbers—so long . . . as there shall remain any fertile land not cultivated.

* M[r] Gouger seems to have overlooked the increasing effort of condensation and increased distance from fertile free land. Doubtless, the immense natural and artificial water conveyance with Steam-boats lessen this effect in N. America, but in Australasia it[a] in time become a great obstacle to independent Settling and of course tend to increase the number & diminish the wages of hired Labourers.

3 p 36, pencil, overtraced

It is wonderful, but true, that notwithstanding the great exertions of the abolitionists, the number of slaves owned by Christians is increasing every day. But why should we wonder?

pretty Christians! Sweet Lambs of the Gospel *Fold*. For "Christians" read "christen'd" ~~Folk~~

2[a] For "it will" or "it may"?

4 pp 36–9, pencil, overtraced

I constantly ask myself, whether it be possible to devise any means by which to establish, in a new country, such a proportion between people and land as would render labour plentiful, and not extravagantly dear.

If Man should ever become *generally* sufficiently good, or if the few good & wise should become sufficiently powerful, to make each of a 100 ~~or 500~~ Men submit to that which would produce the largest quantity of power, work and happiness contemplated & weighed *collectively* and independent of the proportions, in which the Sum total was distributed to the several individual Members of this Hundred; yet so as to render it demonstrable that he who of the Hundred came in for the Minimum Dividend received a Sum equal to or greater than the Maximum Prize in the existing Law & System—*then* I doubt not that I could make it evident, that confederacies of Free Labor could be so organized as to admit an inequality of circumstance & leisure (i.e. Comforts and free time) proportional & correspondent to the natural ⟨& acquired⟩ inequalities of the Men—so as to supersede all pretext for Slavery.—But in the present state of things & opinions, I dare not deny that very plausible arguments in favor of a well-regulated Slavery under the jealous superintendance of public Laws might be advanced./ *S. T. C.*

4A p 103, marked with a line in ink

[Wakefield has been calculating "the effect of penal slavery in producing wealth" by imagining different ways in which convict labour might be distributed.] It follows that to domiciliate the criminals of Britain amongst those British subjects not criminal, who reside in Australasia, is unjust and wicked, provided the system be calculated to do the latter and their posterity a great moral injury.

5 p 169

Does it not follow that the government might, by restricting the amount of grants, establish and maintain the most desirable proportion between people and territory?

* *No*, NO[a] NO! Squatting would be the Rage, and before 30 years had elapsed, the number and strength of the Squatters would compel a title from any such Government as could exist in a country so circumstanced!

S. T. C.

5[a] Underlined twice in ms

6 pp 170–1

* . . . what is the inference, but that the price which the American Government requires for waste land is too low for the only purpose that calls for any price at all?

Why, even as it is, the American Gov[nt] find it difficult to maintain their titles against the Squatters: and in very many cases the legal Purchaser is obliged to secure his possession by a Compromise with them. Bush-rangers,[1] and the worst and most ferocious forms of Bewilderment would be among the fruits of such an Attempt. Sic cogitat et credet

S. T. Coleridge[2]
10 April 1830

6A p 181, marked with a pencil line

[Wakefield speculates about the heart's desire of "an Englishman who ardently desires the greatest good of his country":] on the whole, he would, I think, wish for the power to increase the territory of Britain according to the wants of the people.

6B p 181, marked with a pencil line

His sole object would be to put an end to that portion of crime and misery which in Britain is produced by an excess of people [a]in proportion to territory; and he would not care, therefore, whether the increase of territory, having that effect, should take place[b] near to or at a distance from Britain.

6C p 200, final sentence of text, marked with a line in ink

For my part, the Sun which I learned to love in Italy, and Hope, which, if you know how to indulge it, is more grateful than reality, tempt me to remain for the present.

6B[a] Pencil line begins **6B**[b] Pencil line ends

6[1] This term was a recent introduction from Australia. Giving as its first example a quotation from 1817, *OED* defines it as referring to "an escaped convict who took refuge in the Australian 'bush'".

6[2] "So S. T. Coleridge thinks and believes."

JOHN WALKER

1732–1807

A Dictionary of the English Language, answering at once the purposes of rhyming, spelling, and pronouncing. On a plan not hitherto attempted. . . . And for the purposes of poetry is added an index of allowable rhymes. With authorities for their usage from our best authors. London 1775. 8°.

Harvard University (Houghton Library)

Harvard College Library bookplate p ⁻13 (p-d) along with a pencilled account of the vol; typed notice p ⁻12. A few rhyming words that the compiler had not included are written into the vol in pencil, not in C's hand. A letter of c 8 Jan 1821 to L. Neumegen, on an unrelated matter, was once enclosed in the vol but has now been removed from it: *CL* v 135.

This may be the copy of Walker's *Dictionary* which C told Launcelot Wade on 13 Oct 1815 he thought he had lost—"it must have dropt out in the carriage, from the *ram-shackling* state of my Box": *CL* IV 597. C cites Walker as a standard reference-book in the 1809 *Friend* (*CC*) II 191 and again in *BL* (*CC*) II 165; in a notebook entry of 1811–12 (*CN* III 4134 f 168 and n); and in the 1818 "Essays on Method", *Friend* (*CC*) I 469.

DATE. Probably after 1813 (**1** n 2).

1 p ⁻2, cropped

⟨[. . . . .] *routine* plans regarding [. . .] judicious, I have yet seen. The following is the regular Plan of the Dublin Fever Hospital, in which during 10 years 15,164 Patients had been received.[1]—Dr Mills, however, is decidedly an advocate for the German Plan, brought into England by Clutterbuck, of *copious general* BLEEDING—.[2] I think myself that *Courage* is chiefly wanting to adopt the plan—⟩ Contagious Typhus—originates, at least is always aggravated by impure air—especially human Effluvia—

1[1] C appears to be reacting to a proposal made in a medical book or periodical concerned with the treatment of fevers, but no specific text has been identified. (Thomas Mills [n 2] was physician at a fever hospital in Dublin, but the statistics do not come from his book.)

1[2] Thomas Mills, author of *An Essay on the Utility of Bloodletting, in Fever* (1813); and Henry Clutterbuck *Inquiry into the Seat and Nature of Fever* (1807). Mills's book is dedicated to Clutterbuck, for advocating bloodletting as a remedy for fever.

General treatment, applicable to all cases = Cleanliness, Ventilation, plentiful dilution—partial fomentation, friction.

Most important remedies, variable & modifiable according to the symptoms—ranked in the ratio of their importance.

1. Purgatives, on Dr Hamilton's plan—[3]

2. Cold or tepid ablution, when no pulmonary Complaint or manifest predisposition thereto exists.

3. Topical Bleeding.—as from 4 to six Ounces from the Temporal Artery.

4. Antimonial Powders—especialy when there exist pulmonic affections.—⟨The usual Hour of Rest—& critical days—to be preferred as the time for administering them.⟩

5. Yeast, when putrid symptoms appear or threaten—Ditto, Wine—but reluctantly.

6. Emetics.

7. Blisters—But only when the Fever tends to inter- or re-mitt.

8. General Bleeding indicated only[a] the co-existence of pulmonic Disease—in Typhus, [. . .] present relief by the [. . .]

2 pp xxii–xxiii, cropped | Introduction

. . . and *great** is rhymed with *bate*, that it may be distinguished from the sound the Irish are apt to give it as if it spelled *greet*.

* Excellent!—Mr Walker must have been an Irishman. It is noticeable, that certain words have never any strong emphasis layed on them in comparison with some other words ex. gr. [. . . . .] the same meaning with the emphasis. Magnum imo, ingens = Great—nay, vast, huge—. Now these words have sometimes a sound to which no other ~~sound~~ word *exactly* rhymes—but the nearest to "great" is wait, weight—certainly not bāte.

3 p +3, pencil, fifteen lines almost entirely erased

[? Oh! that thy longer . . .
His Ab . . . . . the God]
Oh! Haste the living Love to [? reach]
Thy [? Light . . . . .]
If his [? . . . heavily/heav'nly fare]

1[a] For "only in"?

1[3] James Hamilton *Observations on the Utility and Administration of Purgative Medicines in Several Diseases* (Edinburgh 1805).

[. . . . .]
[? To continual fear . . . . .] Love
[. . . . .]
Thy Absence [. . .] Cause
[. . . . .] I appeal
[. . . . .]
[. . . . .]
[. . . . .]
[. . . . .]
[? . . . froze . . .][1]

3[1] These fragmentary lines do not correspond to any published verse by C, but *Constancy to an Ideal Object* line 14 makes use of the phrase "living Love": *PW* (EHC) I 456.

WILLIAM WALL
1647–1728

A Conference between Two Men that had Doubts about Infant-Baptism. London 1706 etc. 8°.

C's edition has not been identified: title and textus supplied from the 9th ed of 1809.

Not located. Note published in *AR* (1825) 375–6 from the copy lent to the printer: *CL* v 432. In *AR*, for the sake of coherence, C made some revisions to the passage printed as textus. Cf *AR* (*CC*) 380–1.

Wall's work, a pamphlet of about 80 pp, went through 10 eds between 1706 and 1810. In *AR* (1825), C introduces his note at the end of the Aphorisms on Spiritual Religion and immediately before the "Conclusion", with the heading: "*Marginal Note written* (*in* 1816) *by the Editor in his own Copy of Wall's work*". He identifies the book in a note to p 372 (*AR*—*CC*—377*–8*): "Conference between Two Men that had Doubts about Infant Baptism. By W. Wall, Author of the Hist. of Inf. Bapt. and Vicar of Shoreham in Kent. A very sensible little Tract, and written in an excellent spirit: though it failed, I confess, in satisfying my mind as to the existence of any decisive proofs or documents of Infant Baptism having been an Apostolic Usage, or specially intended in any part of the New Testament: though deducible *generally* from many passages, and in perfect according with the *spirit* of the whole."

DATE. C himself dates the note 1816.

1 pp 6–8

[These words are given to A., the Antipaedobaptist, in his dialogue with P. the Paedobaptist.] ". . . that all christians in the world that hold the same fundamentals, ought to make one church, though differing in lesser opinions; and that the sin, the mischief, and danger to the souls of men, that divide into those many sects and parties among us, does (for the most of them) consist not so much in the opinions themselves, as in their dividing and separating for them. . . . I will (because you seem not to have considered this matter so well as some others) refer you to some plain places of scripture, which if you please now to peruse, I will be silent the while. See what our Saviour himself says, *John* x. 16. *John* xvii. 11. And what the primitive christians practised, *Acts* ii. 46. and iv. 32. And what

St. *Paul* says, I *Cor*. i. 10, 11, 12. and 2, 3, 4, also the whole twelfth chapter: *Eph*. ii. 18, *&c*. to the end. Where the Jewish and Gentile christians are shewed to be *one body, one houshold, one temple fitly framed together:* and yet these were of different opinions in several matters. Likewise chap. iii. 6. iv. 1 to 13. *Phil*. ii. 1, 2. where he uses the most solemn adjurations to this purpose. But I would more especially recommend to you the reading of *Gal*. v. 20, 21. *Phil*. iii. 15, 16. The fourteenth chapter to the *Romans*, and part of the fifteenth, to *verse* 7. and also *Rom*. xv. 17. . . . Are they not plain, full, and earnest? Do you find any of the controverted points to be determined by scripture in words nigh so plain or pathetic?"

This and the two following pages are excellent.[1] If I addressed the ministers recently seceded,[2] I would first prove from Scripture and Reason the justness of their doctrines concerning Baptism and Conversion. 2. I would show, that even in respect of the Prayer-book, Homilies, &c. of the Church of England, taken as a whole, their opponents were comparatively as ill off as themselves, if not worse. 3. That the few mistakes or inconvenient phrases of the Baptismal Service did not impose on the conscience the necessity of resigning the pastoral office. 4. That even if they did, this would by no means justify schism from Lay-membership: or else there could be no schism except from an immaculate and infallible Church. Now, as our Articles have declared that no Church is or ever was such, it would follow that there is no such sin as that of Schism—*i.e.* that St. Paul wrote falsely or idly.[3] 5. That the Escape through the Channel of Dissent is from the Frying Pan to the Fire—or to use a less worn and vulgar simile, the Escape of a Leech from a glass-jar of Water into the naked and open Air. But never, never, would I in one breath allow my Church to be fallible, and in the next contend for her absolute freedom from all error—never confine inspiration and perfect truth to the Scriptures, and

1[1] The two following pages pursue the argument in favour of church unity: A. concedes that baptism itself is a fundamental article of faith, "But the parties we speak of do both of them own baptism: They differ only about the age or manner of receiving it."

1[2] I.e. clergymen who had left the C of E on a point of conscience, finding themselves in conflict with the teaching of the Church on infant baptism. It is not clear whether C refers to Baptist congregations of Wall's time or of his own.

1[3] In some of the passages cited in textus in which he writes about the problem of schism, e.g. 1 Cor 1.10–11: "Now I beseech you, brethren, by the name of our Lord Jesus Christ, that ye all speak the same thing, and that there be no divisions among you; but that ye be perfectly joined together in the same mind and in the same judgment. For it hath been declared unto me of you, my brethren, by them which are of the house of Chloe, that there are contentions among you."

then scold for the perfect Truth of each and every word in the Prayer-book. Enough for me, if in my Heart of Hearts, free from all fear of man and all lust of preferment, I believe (as I do) the Church of England to be the *most* Apostolic Church; that its doctrines and ceremonies contain nothing dangerous to Righteousness or Salvation; and that the imperfections in its Liturgy are spots indeed, but spots on the sun, which impede neither its Light nor its Heat, so as to prevent the good seed from growing in a good soil and producing fruits of Redemption.

JOHN BENN WALSH
BARON ORMATHWAITE
1798–1881

On the Present Balance of Parties in the State. 2nd ed. London 1832. 8°.

Bound in PAMPHLETS ON THE REFORM BILL.

British Library C 126 h 15(2)

DATE. 1 Mar 1832 (**1**).

1 p [1], title-page

Mem!/ Agriculture would bear a discipline of which the Manufacturing community are un- —or at least far less, susceptible and the Duties of Government in its widest sense are accordant.[1] The Peasant who labors on the land, should be maintained by the Land, and with *human* comforts. If there are too many, this argues the fault of Government—Rational, dignified, *parental* Colonization ought to have prevented it.—But in fact, it has never occurred. O if the fully or over payed Rioters had been sternly punished, and at the same time the aggrieved, who had been misled, pardoned; ~~but~~ while those of the Districts, as in too many parts of Wiltshire & Dorsetshire, who, tho' ground to the earth by the hard-hearted Farmers, & neglectful Land-owners, had remained quiet, had been protected and righted—how different would the moral impression have been! But the maxims of Trade—just and no less true than necessary within the sphere of Trade—these universalized, and acting on the selfish Superstition of absolute Property, "an unqualified right to do what I like with my own"—have been the disease, & too probably will be the ruin, of Great Britain.

1 March, 1832—

S. T. C.

1[1] C's note may have been prompted by such passages as **5** textus, in which Walsh describes unrest among rural workers, complaining that a Whig government had given in too timidly to "popular demand" (47). Walsh writes to oppose the Reform Bill by setting the current movement in a broader historical context; he argues that by bowing to pressure from the public and the Tories and the radicals, the Whigs had departed from the founding principles of their party and lent support to "those bent on the subversion of the Constitution" (57).

2 p 15

[The Whigs] constantly held forth that every evil of our social state admitted of a prompt, easy remedy by this recurrence to first causes, or, in plain terms, by the dissolution and reconstruction of the existing system. Their tenets had this advantage—that they possessed equal attraction for the mass of the lower orders, and for minds of a visionary and speculative cast.

See *O P Q* (supposed to be Wilks: Junior, the outlawed Ex-Member of Sudbury) in the Morn. Chronicle, which this almost every day correspondence renders *infamous.*[1]

3 p 21

They [the Whig Opposition in the aftermath of the French Revolution] continued to arraign the policy, and to scrutinise the conduct, of the Ministry with equal acuteness, with no mitigated severity, and with a deeper shade of personal animosity. But no one can read the debates, and the history of that period, without perceiving in their tone a consciousness of the difficulty of their situation, and traces of the inconsistencies in which it involved them. At one time they launch out in eloquent praise of the French Revolution; at another, they gently blame, while they palliate its excesses.

See the two Letters to M[r] Fox, at the Court of the First Consul, published in the Morning Post during the peace of Amiens, by S. T. C.—Letter I, in particular.[1]

4 p 40

When, therefore, the Whigs were, in the embarrassed position of affairs, called upon to form a Ministry, they did not bring with them that force of numbers or of opinion which could give it strength. . . . They included in their arrangements the remains of the Canning and Huskisson party, the

2[1] In a series of articles presented as letters from Paris, a correspondent of the pro-reform *Morning Chronicle* identified as O.P.Q. was at this time writing in favour of popular movements taking place on the Continent: see e.g. the *Morning Chronicle* for 8, 9, 11, 28 Feb and 1 Mar 1832. John Benn Walsh was himself the current Member for Sudbury. C correctly identifies the author of the articles as Walsh's predecessor John Wilks Junior (d 1846), who according to *The Times* 27 Mar 1828 had had to flee to the Continent to avoid his creditors. C mentions Wilks's articles of 1831 in *TT* (*CC*) I 242 (and see n 13).

3[1] C's two "Letters" in the *Morning Post* 4 and 9 Nov 1802 characterised Fox in similar terms to those used in textus: *EOT* (*CC*) I 376–90, 391–400.

portion of the former Pittites who were separated by the least wide interval from the most moderate among themselves; but this accession, although valuable as supplying their own deficiency of practical men, was numerically slender.

O if Lord Gray & his Friends had had faith in the Institutions of his Country, never was there a Period in which whatever is highest and best, in rank, wealth, literature, moral worth, piety, was so disposed to rally round and support with love a liberal but firm Ministry![1]

5 pp 43–5

Whether from the apathy and too great leniency of the local magistracy, from embarrassments and demands upon the military force which we are not aware of, or, in effect, from a want of sufficient promptitude and energy in the last days of the Wellington administration, the disturbances in Kent had spread with alarming rapidity over the southern counties. Bands of rioters and marauders traversed the country in every district, defying the authorities, fixing arbitrary scales of wages, forcing the clergy to remit their tithes, breaking machinery, and proceeding to acts of undisguised pillage and robbery.

In a settled and free Government, limited in all directions by Law, and sensitively dependent on Public Opinion, a new or a sudden State of Things, like that of the Kent Incendiaries, must always at first produce a hesitation, a questioning, an apparent want of vigor—and it is not fair to ~~con~~ judge of such a ministry for their measures in the outbreak by the more decisive acts of their Successors. It is as with the first Physicians to a new & unexpected Disease—Their successors come prepared.

But even at the last there was an utter want of true vigor. The disturbances, indeed, were for the time put down; & a few of the Incendiaries hanged, or transported.[1] But what *should* have been done—viz. a detailed examination into the known Rioters in each parish, and their weekly wages & circumstances—this, which in each parish might have been done, would have been equally wise and humane. Then the Nation would have learnt what the *proportions* between the Causes were, viz. impatience under grinding privations; & the evil passions instilled by Cobbet & Co[2]—In a majority of instances the Ringleaders were Men who earned from 25 to 40 shillings a week./

4[1] Charles Grey (1764–1845), 2nd Earl Grey, formed a Whig government in Nov 1830 that eventually succeeded in carrying the cause of Reform.

5[1] Walsh himself makes this point p 45.

5[2] The populist writer William Cobbett (1762–1835) was a particular *bête noire* of C's: see e.g. *TT* (*CC*) II 190 n 1.

Then, then, the Clergy should have been every where awake and active. I have ever thought, that the Scottish Church has an inestimable advantage over ours in their Lay Elders, procuring for the Minister in each parish co-interested Associates. But the best should have been done—the dissenting Ministers affectionately invoked &c &c—

6 p 47

If, in the case of the riots and the special commissions, the Government commenced by showing a determination to vindicate its authority, and to separate itself entirely from the party of the movement, it exhibited the same resolution still more unequivocally in Ireland.* The removal of the Catholic disabilities had not tranquillised that country—had not produced the slightest cessation or abatement of violence in the parties which distracted it.

* Sir J. Walsh does not, or will not, see it, but this is the weakness of the Conservative Party. The unvacillating Tories are without Leader, plans, or internal Organization—& the Leaders of the Party generally, the D. of W., and Sir R. Peele, are *Apostates* on the confessed ground of intimidation. They sacrificed a known Principle to *Fear*—and Gray and Lansdown are only carrying on the same policy, on the same pretence. Nay, there are excuses for the Reform, which there are not for Sir R. Peele.[1]

7 p 78

The truth is (it were vain to deny or conceal it), the stability of British institutions—the framework of British society—the foundations of our national glory and our national pre-eminence, have sustained a shock which even their firm texture may not be able to withstand. . . . We are put again upon proving those first principles of social order—upon defending those fundamental elements of our own constitution, which we thought had received the stamp of sterling value by the universal assent of successive generations of our countrymen. There is no positive convulsion, there is no present calamity; but men's minds are filled with gloomy foreboding and undefined fears. The props and fastenings which sustain and secure the machine of the state seem gradually loosening; its cohesion is greatly relaxed. . . . In our happy country, where peace, order, and internal tranquillity have been established by a long and glorious prescription, men

6[1] C names the leaders of the Tory and Whig parties respectively, i.e. the Duke of Wellington, who had been Prime Minister until Nov 1830, with Sir Robert Peel as his Home Secretary during the last six months of his term in office; and Lord Grey, the current Prime Minister, and the Marquis of Lansdowne, Lord President of the Council.

are ashamed: they fear the ridicule of their hearers in prognosticating such evils as revolution, civil war, and anarchy.

This and the two following pages ~~are~~ contain for *me*, the most momentous and aweful truths, that I have ever had impressed on my mind on any subject not strictly religious!—[1]

8 p 81

Another large portion of the nation waits with anxious expectation till the Ministry themselves, feeling the extremity of the danger, shall retrace their steps.

But I ask Sir J. Walsh, I ask every lover of his Country (and the Constitution *is* his Country)—has the Language of Sir R. Peele—scarcely that of the D. of Wellington—been proportionate to the aweful juncture?—Has it been solemn, decisive? or too & fro, in the *candid* line!—Has there been on the part of the Nobles & Gentry language like this—We are ready to make any Sacrifices of individual interests, that only give A. a larger influence than B.—but O! do not sacrifice the Constitution!—save the Country!—

9 p 83

If the Ministry had consented to abandon some of the most obnoxious clauses in their Bill, these noble Lords were, I believe, prepared to have made, to the preservation of the tranquillity and harmony of the country, a great sacrifice of their own abstract views and convictions.

But Sir J. W.—nor the Quart. Rev.—say[a] a word of that *larger* part of the Peers, but fearfully larger part of the Landed Commons, who support Lord Gray!—Norfolk & the Catholic Party I can understand—and the D. of Sussex I can understand—but for the *rest*![1]

9[a] For "say not"?

7[1] The chapter is entitled "Prospects of the Country". Textus incorporates material from 78–80—all the pages C refers to.

9[1] The "noble Lords" of textus are Lords Harrowby and Wharncliffe, identified on p 82; cf **10**. C expresses surprise at the extent of support for Reform among the Lords, although it was to be expected of the Roman Catholic Duke of Norfolk and of Augustus Frederick, Duke of Sussex (1773–1843)—the latter being well known to hold liberal views in the matters of Roman Catholic Emancipation and parliamentary reform. The Tory *Quarterly Review* had been analysing and opposing the progress of the Reform Bill through the Lords with long essay-reviews, notably one entitled "Progress of Misgovernment" in Jan 1832: *QR* XLVI (1832) 544–622.

10 pp 83–4, incorporating **9** textus

. . . a negotiation was set on foot between the Cabinet and some of the most distinguished and respectable of the Opposition Peers. Lords Harrowby and Wharncliffe . . . agreed to admit an extensive measure of Reform—in short, the present Bill, with modifications. . . . If the Ministry had consented to abandon some of the most obnoxious clauses in their Bill, these noble Lords were, I believe, prepared to have made . . . a great sacrifice of their own abstract views and convictions. . . . by a moderate concession of the extreme principles of their measure, they might have accomplished a Reform, exceeding in amount of change all that the country had ever dreamed of a few months back; they might have carried it without violence through the Upper House.*

* *Might* they? then the Sun of G.B. is set—What! were Lords H. and Wh.[1] prepared to purchase a miserable Reprieve by a *Lie*? by a legislative conservation of principles, which they themselves held false & ruinous?—But the conduct of Lord Gray in this negotiation extinguishes all rational hope of any successful appeal to his Reason—or his Humanity. Otherwise, I would take all the counties & elective Towns in Ireland one by one, & in like manner all the great Towns & Cities, Leeds, Birmingham, &c in England—& for each ask, whom, my Lord! and of *what* class & *character*, do *you* expect that those whom your Bill render the great majority of the Electors, will send up to you?

11 p 87

No observations have led me to believe that the present Government is generally popular. . . . They take their Reform Bill at their hands as a concession to their own irresistible strength . . . but it creates no enthusiasm for its authors. They are watched, on the contrary, with jealous vigilance and some suspicion.

Most true! But early in life I learnt from experience, that there is no baseness of which a sullen *proud* Man may not be guilty—and in this experience I drew the character of Ordonio in the Remorse.[1]—So Lord Gray—but add the baseness of the Submission of the Ministers! & Stanley!!—/[2]

10[1] Harrowby and Wharncliffe, in textus.

11[1] *Remorse* was performed in 1813; but C recalls its original incarnation as *Osorio*, written 1797. The wicked Osorio of the first version was renamed Ordonio in the 1813 version.

11[2] Edward George Geoffrey Smith Stanley (1799–1869), 14th Earl of Derby, was at the time Chief Secretary for Ireland in Grey's Cabinet.

Popular Opinions on Parliamentary Reform, Considered. 4th ed rev. London 1831. 8°.

Bound in PAMPHLETS ON THE REFORM BILL.

British Library C 126 h 15(1)

"S. T. C." label on verso of title-page. One note in ink on p 22, correcting a matter of fact, is not by C.

DATE. Probably 1831, upon publication.

1 p 7 | § 2 "The Sovereignty of the People"

In the physical world, our discoveries of the great secondary causes, or laws, which govern the universe, have been derived from an attentive observation of facts, and the inferences which have been drawn from them. Wherever an uniform operation of nature has been perceived, a general principle has been established, and the mightiest results of science are contained in this generalization of the fruits of our experience.

False in part, and in contradiction to the whole History of great discoveries.[1]

2 p 7 | **1** textus continued

The most powerful minds, in quitting this sure guide, and in entering upon the trackless void of hypothesis and conjecture, have been speedily led into error.*

* Aye, *if* they enter &c—but that they must ~~on h~~ proceed on hypothesis or conjecture, if they seek for truth otherwise than by generalizing the past, is a mere assumption. Whence came the principle, on which the generalization is to be conducted? Alas!—how is a noble cause vindicated on the erroneous principles, the prevalence of which is the main reason of its jeopardy!

1[1] C was inclined to argue that Bacon himself, the supposed father of empirical method in the sciences, had been a Platonist, and that all advances in knowledge depended upon a prior and governing idea: see esp *Friend* (*CC*) I 488–93, and the "Essays on Method" in general, *Friend* (*CC*) I 448–524.

3 pp 8–9

The Sovereignty of the People cannot be established as the true principle of government, simply, because such a Sovereignty never has existed to our knowledge since the creation of man* . . .

* No! no—for in the days of Aristotle a Sovereignty by representatives of the various Interests of the Body Politic had not existed—but because "the Sov. of the People" is *nonsense*, and involves a contradiction—because a People *derives* its unity from the Government (or the State) & that Unity is *real* only where each individual of the 3 or the 30 million yield~~s~~ing the same obedience to the State, all are capable of being contemplated as *one*, as *a* people, *this* or *that* People!

4 p 9

But although it is generally admitted by sane minds that the will of the mass cannot directly govern, the existence of an inherent though dormant right is still stoutly maintained* . . .

* This is good—but does not go ⟨to⟩ the bottom of the error. A Right without a Power is a right to an impossibility, i.e. an absurd Right. Where Nature gives the instinctive Volition, the Will is assuredly followed by the appropriate *Organs*—so the Butting of the Bull Calf predicts the coming Horns. But of all Rights the most whimsical would be the Right to a non-existent Thing, which could only *exist* by the non-exercise or overwhelming of that Right.

5 p 11

I have already read enough to convince myself, that as far[a] the theoretical or speculative principles of Government are concerned, Sir J. W. is always in the right, so far that the notions, he attacks, are gross errors; the principles, he supports, are sacred truths; but that he is not equal to the subject.

6 p 11

I do not see how (whatever practical modification might be introduced) we could avoid drawing this conclusion, that the great end and aim of government should be, upon every measure, to elicit the wishes of the majority of the nation, and to fulfil them. The attempt to establish this form of government is no new experiment.*

5[a] For "as far as"

It has uniformly, except in one very peculiar recent instance, totally failed.

* Aye!—from this place Sir John Walsh steps into ~~its~~ his proper sphere—that of plain good sense, enriched as well as enlightened by Observation, & History.

7 pp 16–17

Perhaps, were England polled, the majority might still be of opinion, that the Sun moved round the Earth. Would they be likely to entertain juster notions upon politics, that most difficult and deceiving of all sciences . . . ?

Excellent![a]

Government—or take any integral part of it, Taxation for instance, is a *Science* as much as Astronomy, tho' we are not yet advanced so far in the former as in the latter. Or was Astronomy no Science before the days of Kepler & Newton? Taxation requires principles, insight into the process, and tendencies of production, the laws of circulation &c &c—a Science of almost infinite complexity—~~Yet~~ We should laugh at the notion of determining an astronomical problem by universal suffrage—& yet *the Mob* are to predetermine the Votes of the Legislature on every Tax!! Sir J. W's illustration is peculiarly happy; and might be carried on into a detail of analogies.

8 pp 19–20 | § 3 "Composition, and Powers of the House of Commons, at Former Periods of our History"

Fortunately for those who believe, that, in spite of a thousand errors, temporary misfortunes, partial retrograde movements, mankind are essentially progressive, who love liberal government . . . because they think that a large mixture of the ingredient of freedom* promotes the development of our highest faculties . . .

* Even this, undeniably true as it is, is yet delusive if given as an independent truth—First of all, Freedom is a vague term—& in its proper sense is the *effect* & fruits of a good government—but here it means a diffusion of *political power*. Now this is good not for itself; but only as far as it[a] the occasion or security of *equal* Law. The *Law* is the true effi-

7[a] This word written in the margin beside the textus, followed by "*"; the note continued in the foot-margin with "*"

8[a] For "it is"

cient Cause of the progression of the social state—. The mode in which the elective franchise is distributed, and even the legislative power is good only as far as it[b] a *means to this end.*—Attained without *them*, they become superfluous—

8[b] For "it is"

DANIEL WATERLAND

1683–1740

The Importance of the Doctrine of the Holy Trinity Asserted, in reply to some late pamphlets. . . . 2nd ed rev. London 1734. 8°.

Bound in mottled leather matching C's copy of Waterland's *Vindication of Christ's Divinity*. The title on the spine of this book mistakenly reads "Waterland's Vindication".

British Library C 43 b 24

DATE. More than one reading, perhaps c 1823 and later. In **7** C expresses the desire to be admitted as a Reader to the British Museum, as he did in 1823 when he was working on the Leighton project that turned into *AR*; in **4** he refers to *AR* as published; **27** and **30** contradict each other in a way that may be accounted for by his having read RHENFERD on the Ebionites in Jul 1827.

1 pp 18–19, pencil | Ch 1

It is the Property of the *divine* Being to be *unsearchable:* And if he were not so, he would not be *divine.** Must we therefore reject the most certain Truths concerning the *Deity*, only because they are *incomprehensible*, when every thing almost belonging to him must be so of course?

* It is strange, that so sound, so admirable a Logician as Waterland, should have thought "unsearchable" & "incomprehensible" synonimous or at least equivalent terms!—& this, tho' Paul hath made it the privilege of the full-grown Christian "to search into the deep things of God himself".—[1]

2 pp 111–15, pencil | Ch 4

The *delivering* over *unto Satan*, seems to have been a Form of Excommunication, declaring the Person reduced to the State of an *Heathen:* And in the *Apostolical* Age, it was accompanied with *supernatural* or miraculous Effects upon the Bodies of the Persons so delivered: δ ?Tho' it may be supposed that such Effects might last beyond the Apostolick Age, be-

1[1] C alludes to 1 Cor 2.10: "But God hath revealed them unto us by his Spirit: for the Spirit searcheth all things, yea, the deep things of God."

cause other *miraculous* Gifts certainly did so. I am well aware of the Disputes which have been among Persons of the best Learning, about the precise Meaning of the Phrase, whether it signified *Excommunication*, or an Appendage to it. I have chosen that Interpretation which appears most probable.

? Suspecting Ananias & Sepphira as an interpolation, I must likewise doubt the truth of this assertion—as tending to destroy the essential Spirituality of Christian Motives and in *my* judgement irreconcilable with our Lord's declaration that his Kingdom was not of this World.[1] Let me be once convinced, that S[t] Paul ~~or~~ with the Elders of an Apostolic Church knowingly & intentionally *appended* a Palsy, or Consumption to the sentence of excommunication, I should know what to say as to the *antichristian* principles of the Romish Inquisition. *S. T. C.*

3 pp 114–15, pencil

*A Man that is an Heretick, after the first and second Admonition, reject; knowing that he that is such, is subverted, and sinneth being condemned of himself.** (Tit. 3. 10, 11)

* This ⟨text⟩ would be among my minor arguments for doubting the Paulinity of the Ep. to Titus.[1] It seems to me to breath the spirit of a later age, & a more established Church *Power*. S. T. C.

4 p 114, pencil

Here the first Question is, who, or what is an *Heretick*? To which I answer in the general, not every one that mistakes in Judgment, tho' in Matters of great *Importance*, in Points *fundamental*, but he that openly *espouses* such fundamental Error. . . . Dr. *Whitby* adds to the Definition, the espousing it *out of Disgust*, *Pride*, *Envy*, or some *worldly Principle*, and *against his Conscience*.

See Aids to Reflection—who lifts it up as a Banner/[1] [a]Every Schismatic

4[a] Here there is a horizontal line and then a change to a sharper pencil; the remainder of the note may belong to a later reading

2[1] For another comment on the case of Ananias and Saphira (Acts 5.1), who conspired to defraud the Apostles but were detected by Peter and died instantly, see Jeremy TAYLOR *Polemicall Discourses* **228** and n 1. "My kingdom is not of this world" is from John 18.36.

3[1] C's doubts about the attribution of this Epistle to Paul seem to have changed over time: see BIBLE COPY B **116** and n 1.

4[1] C refers to his own note about schism and heresy, *AR* (*CC*) 33†, 34 n 4. In it he suggests that "heresy" is derived ultimately from the Greek *airo* "I raise" and "schism"

is not necessarily an Heretic: but every Heretic is virtually a Schismatic. [b]Whitby went too far: Waterland not far enough.[2]

5 pp 117–18, pencil

Admonish *a Man that is an Heretick*; not a Man that is really no Heretick, which would be contumelious and injurious. And if he persists after two Admonitions, then look upon him as αὐτοκατάκριτος, self-condemned, and *reject* him. It is plain enough from the whole Tenor of this Passage, that αὐτοκατάκριτος, whatever it means, does not belong to the Definition of an *Heretick* as such, but to that of an *admonished* and still *obstinate* Heretick.

This surely is making too much of a very plain matter. What was the sentence passed on a Heretic? A public declaration, that he was no longer a member, i.e. of one faith with, the Church. This the Man himself, after two public notices, admits & involves in the very act of persisting—. However confident as to the truth of the doctrine he has held aloft, he cannot after two public admonitions be ignorant, that it is a doctrine contrary to the Articles of his Communion with the Church ⟨that has admonished him:⟩ & in regard of his *Alien*ation from that Communion he is, necessarily, αυτοκατακριτος:[1] tho' in his pride of heart he might say with Diogenes—"And I banish you to Corinth".—[2]

6 p 118, pencil

There is some Error always in *Judgment*, before there is an Error in *Practice*; for Evil, *as Evil*, cannot be chosen.

? Here lurks the fundamental error—viz. Reason, Motive, made the ground of Action.

4[b] Horizontal lines separate the following sentence from surrounding notes

---

from *schizein* "I cut": "[I] should explain *haeresis*, as a wilful raising into public notice, an uplifting (for display) of any particular opinion differing from the established belief of the church at large, and making it a ground of schism, *i.e.* division, from schizein, to cut off". The phrase "who lifts it up as a banner" is an allusion to Isa 13.2, "Lift ye up a banner upon the high mountain". For another note on the meaning of "heresy" see SHERLOCK **10** and n 4.

4[2] Daniel Whitby, commenting on Gal 5.19 in *A Paraphrase and Commentary on the New Testament* (1st ed 1700), q in textus. Waterland does not specify the edition he used.

5[1] *Autokatakritos*, from Tit 3.11, in textus.

5[2] A version of the anecdote recorded by Diogenes Laertius (6.49, tr R. D. Hicks): "Again, when some one reminded him that the people of Sinope had sentenced him to exile, 'And I them,' said he, 'to home-staying.'" Diogenes (the Cynic philosopher) was for a time a slave in Corinth.

7 pp 123–5, pencil

The Sum of his [Whitby's] Answer is, "That *Titus* might have the *discerning of Spirits*, a Gift belonging to those Times: And the Church that was in the Days of the Apostles, could easily know, whether the Doctrines which others taught in Opposition to them, were indeed Doctrines received from the Apostles or not: If they were not, they who taught them must know, they received no such Doctrine from them, and so must be *self- condemned* in teaching it as received from them, or as the Faith once delivered to the Saints.["] Never was there a looser Reply, in so momentous a Cause. For, I. This amounts to saying, that all the Precepts about *admonishing*, *avoiding*, or *excommunicating* of Hereticks, and of Consequence, all the other Precepts about preserving *sound* Doctrine, or *contending* earnestly for the Faith, expired in a great measure as soon as the miraculous Gifts, or Gift of *discerning Spirits* ceased.

I know of no one point in the New Testament, that perplexes me so much as these (so-called) "miraculous Gifts."[1] I feel a *moral* repugnance to the reduction of them to natural & acquired talents ennobled and made energic by the *life* ~~of Faith~~ and convergency of Faith—& yet on no other scheme can I reconcile them with the Idea of Christianity.—or the particular supposed with the general *known* facts. But thank God! it is a question which does not in the least degree *affect* our *faith* or practice. But I mean, if God permit, to go thro' the Middletonian controversy, as soon as I can procure the Loan of the Books, or have health enough to become a Reader at the British Museum/[2]

8 pp 126–7, pencil

And what if after all, *spiritual* Censures (for of such only I am speaking) should happen to fall upon such a Person, he may be in some measure hurt in his *Reputation* by it, and that is all: And possibly hereupon his Errors before *invincible* through Ignorance, may be removed by wholsome

7[1] C quotes textus, which is in turn referring to 1 Cor 12.4–11, esp 10: "To another [is given] the working of miracles; to another prophecy; to another discerning of spirits; to another divers kinds of tongues; to another the interpretation of tongues."

7[2] Conyers Middleton (1683–1750) aroused controversy when he responded to Waterland's attack upon deism in an anonymous *Letter to Dr. Waterland* (1731). He was quickly identified and put on the defensive, publishing three more pamphlets in the dispute 1731–2. In a letter of 9 Sept 1823, C says he has "this morning written to Sir H. Davy to be admitted, as a Reader" at the British Museum: *CL* v 301. Davy, as President of the Royal Society, was *ex officio* a Trustee of the British Museum 1820–6. The Reading Room Registers in the Central Archives of the Museum, however, contain no record of C's having been issued a reader's ticket in this period.

Instruction and *Admonitions*, and so he is befriended in it, and may now come to a covenant Right to Happiness, who before stood only in *unconvenanted Mercy*.

D[r] Waterland is quite in the Right, *so far*; but the penal *Laws*, the *temporal* inflictions—would He have called for the Repeal of *these*?

S. T. C.[a]

Milton saw this Subject with a mastering Eye—saw that the aweful power of Excommunication was degraded and weakened even to impotence by any the least connection with the Law of the State.[1]

9 p 127, pencil

And so these Words of the Apostle carry in them the Force of an Excommunication, with respect to the *Hereticks* there pointed to, and the Force of a Prohibition, with respect to other Christians, who are hereby forbidden to receive such *Hereticks* into their Houses, or to pay them so much as common Civilities. ? This Precept of the Apostle may be further illustrated by his own Practice, recorded by *Irenaeus*, who had the Information at second hand from *Polycarp* a Disciple of St. *John*'s, that St. *John* once meeting with *Cerinthus* at the *Bath*, retired instantly without bathing; for fear, said he, lest the Bath should fall, by reason of *Cerinthus*'s being there, the *Enemy to Truth*.

⟨The⟩ "God speed you![''] of St John's Epistle is a *Spirituality* and no mere *Civility*.[1] If St John knew or suspected that Cerinthus had the Itch, there would have been some sense in the refusal—or rather, some probability in Irenæus's Gossip.

10 pp 128–9, pencil

They [the heretics Cerinthus and Marcion] *corrupted* the *Faith* of Christ, and in effect, *subverted* the *Gospel*. That was enough to render them de-

8[a] Here C has written "^", and continued the note in the foot-margin with "^"

8[1] Milton discusses the power of bishops to excommunicate kings in *Of Reformation Touching Church-Discipline* (1641), but it is more likely that C has in mind his *Treatise of Civil Power in Ecclesiastical Causes* (1659), where he says, for example, "If from such uncertain, or rather such improbable Grounds as these, they endue Magistracy with spiritual Judgment, they may as well invest him in the same spiritual kind with power of utmost Punishment, Excommunication; and then turn Spiritual into Corporal . . .": *Works* ed Birch (2 vols 1738) I 551.

9[1] 2 John 10, 11: "If there come any unto you, and bring not this doctrine, receive him not into your house, neither bid him God speed: For he that biddeth him God speed is partaker of his evil deeds."

testable in the Eyes of all Men who sincerely loved and valued *sound* Faith.

O no! no! not "them." *Error*, quidem, haud verè *Homo* errans, *abhominandus* sit.[1] Be bold in denouncing the Heresy; but slow and timorous in denouncing the erring Brother as a *Heretic*. The unmistakable Passions of a Factionary and a Schismatic, the ostentatious *Display*, the Ambition, and dishonest Arts, of a Sect-founder, must be superinduced on the false doctrine before the *Heresy* makes the *Man* a Heretic—[2]

11 p 129, pencil

The Bishops of *Pergamus* and *Thyatira* are reproved by our Lord for *suffering*, that is, for not ejecting the *Balaamites* or *Nicolaitans*, who taught false Doctrine, relating to the Fundamentals of Christian *Practice*. They taught the Lawfulness of *Fornication*, and of *eating things offered to Idols*. . . . There is not much Difference in the main, between the two Cases; excepting that one is more *gross* and *scandalous*, and shews itself in more *sensible* Effects.

Could W. have been ignorant, that the Nicolaitans were an *imaginary* Sect—a mere rendering in Greek of "the Children of Balaam"—i.e. men of grossly immoral and disorderly Lives?[1] S. T. C.

12 pp 130–3, pencil

. . . the most criminal Circumstance would be the *espousing* and publickly *supporting* such false Persuasion to the Detriment of Religion. For if he who shall break one of the *least moral Commandments*,* and shall *teach Men so*, shall be called *least in the Kingdom of Heaven*, (*Matt*. v. 19.) it must be a very dangerous Experiment for any Man to presume to *teach* any thing contrary to the Gospel of Christ in the *main* Articles of *Faith*, or *Doctrine*, because, the *Christian Life* is nearly concerned in both . . .

A sad misinterpretation of our Lord's words—which had no reference to any moral, i.e. universal, Commandment ⟨*as such*;⟩ but to the *national* In-

10[1] "Let the *Error*, indeed, but not the erring *Man*, be *abominated*."

10[2] This is a point C makes more than once; see esp *BL* ch 7 (*CC*) I 122: ". . . man may perchance determine, *what* is an heresy; but God only can know, *who* is a heretic".

11[1] This long-perpetuated historical blunder, reiterated by Waterland, was exposed by Eichhorn but also earlier—as C points out in EICHHORN *Apocalypse* COPY A **3** (and see n 2) and in *CN* IV 5323—by Cocceius, whose work C also annotated.

stitutes of the Jewish State, as long as that State should be in existence—i.e. till the Heaven = the Government, and the Earth = the People, ~~as~~ or the Governed as a one corpus politicum[1] or Nation, had passed away.[2] Till that time (which was fulfilled under Titus, & more thoroughly ~~by~~ under Hadrian[)], no *Jew* was released from his duties as a Citizen & Subject by his having become a *Christian*.—This text together with the ~~M~~ Command implied in the miracle of the Tribute-money in the Fish's Mouth[3] might be fairly and powerfully adduced against the Quakers in their refusal to pay their Tythes, & whatever Tax, they please to regard as having an unchristian destination. But are they excluded from the K. of H.? i.e. the Christian Church?—No; but they must be considered as weak & injudicious Members.[4]

13 pp 140–1, pencil | Ch 5

. . . it is not owing to any *immoderate* Rigours of the more cautious Divines, if *Infidelity* happens to gain ground, but to the *immoderate* and *extravagant* Concessions of those who are not so careful as they should be, to keep up the ancient Faith in its first Purity and Perfection. Accordingly it may be observed, how the *Unbelievers* caress and compliment those complying Gentlemen who meet them half way, while they are perpetually inveighing against the stiff Divines, as they call them, whom they can make no Advantage of.

Lessing, an honest and frank-hearted Infidel, expresses the same sentiment. As long as a Protestant Divine keeps stiff and steadfast to the Augsburgh Confession, to the full Creed of Melancthon, he is impregnable/ and may bid defiance to Sceptic, & Philosopher. But as soon as he quits the Citadel, the Cossacs are on him.—[1]

14 p 187, pencil

We are *morally* and *indubitably* certain of the Truth of the Doctrine of the Trinity. And tho' we presume not to say, or to think, that we *may not*, or *cannot* misconstrue Scripture, yet we have many and strong Reasons

12[1] "State-body".

12[2] C questions Waterland's interpretation in the context of the preceding verses, Matt 5.17–18, which he reads allegorically in his usual way (cf G. BURNET *History of the Reformation* **1** and n 2, EICHHORN *NT* COPY A **51**): "Think not that I am come to destroy the law, or the prophets: I am not come to destroy, but to fulfil. For verily I say unto you, Till heaven and earth pass, one jot or one tittle shall in no wise pass from the law, till all be fulfilled."

12[3] Matt 17.24–7.

12[4] C's contact with the Quakers and Quakerism is summarised in MORE *Theological Works* **17** n 1.

13[1] This passage has not so far been traced in Lessing, and it may be that the particulars are C's own contribution. C owned sets of Lessing's collected works, literary remains, and letters, and annotated all but the last of them: see LESSING.

to persuade us that in this Instance we *do not*: And therefore it is *infallibly* certain, (as Mr. *Chillingworth* well argues with respect to Christianity in general) that we *ought* firmly to believe it; because *Wisdom* and *Reason* require, that we should *believe* those Things which are by many Degrees *more credible and probable* than the contrary.

Yes! where there are but two positions, *one* of which must be true. But when B is presented to my mind with probability = 5, and C. with probability = equal to 15, I must think that C. is three times more probable than B.—& yet it is possible, that a D may be found which supersedes both.

15 p 230 | Ch 6

The *Creed* of *Jerusalem* preserved by *Cyril*, (the most ancient perhaps of any now extant) is very express for the *Divinity* of God the Son, in these Words:* "And in our Lord Jesus Christ, the only begotten Son of God, *true God* begotten of the Father *before all Ages*; by whom all Things were made."

* I regard this both from its antiquity and from the peculiar character of the Church of Jerusalem, so far removed from the influence of the Pythagoro-platonic Sects of Paganism, the most important and [?~~con~~] convincing facts in the Trinitarian Controversy. S. T. C.

16 p 233

[Waterland quotes "the famous Creed of *Gregory* Bishop of *Neocaesarea*":] "There is *one God*, Father of the living *Word*, the substantial *Wisdom*, and *Power*, and eternal express Image: Perfect Parent of one perfect, Father of the only begotten Son. There is *one Lord*, one of one, God of God, the express Character and Image of the Godhead, the effective *Word*, the *Wisdom* that grasps the System of the Universe, and the *Power* that made every Creature, true Son of the true Father, invisible of invisible, incorruptible of incorruptible, immortal of immortal, and eternal of eternal."

* ? John Ch. 1. v. 18.[a]

* How is this reconcilable with John's Gospel—I. 18.?[1] or with the "*express Image*"? "Invisible" must be taken in the narrowest sense—i.e.

16[a] These first few words are in the margin; the rest of the note is written at the foot of the page

16[1] "No man hath seen God at any time; the only begotten Son, which is in the bosom of the Father, he hath declared him."

to *bodily* eyes. But then the first "Invisible" [? would/could] not mean the same as the second.

17 p 236, pencil

The Creeds of the Church ought most certainly to be interpreted according to the Mind of the *Church*, and not by any After-thoughts of *Hereticks*. For tho' the Scripture, properly, is the Rule for *receiving* any Creed, or any Doctrine, yet it is not the Rule of *Interpretation*; but Words, Phrases and Formularies must be interpreted according to their received Use, and the known Sense of the Compilers and Imposers.

The *truth* of a Creed must be tried by the holy Scriptures; but the *sense* of the Creed by the known sentiments & inferred intention of its Compilers.

18 pp 238–43, pencil

From what has been said, it ought to be admitted as a clear Case, or a ruled Point that the Creeds of the *Church* should be interpreted according to the Mind of the *Church*; and the Mind of the Church is to be learned chiefly from the *Writings* of the *Fathers*. And while we proceed by this Rule, it is manifest that the Antient Creeds, whether of the larger or shorter kind, do express the Doctrine of the Trinity, as commonly received at this Day. The *Roman* Creed for instance, even in its shorter Form, (as it stood in and before the fourth Century) fully expresses the true and proper Divinity of Christ; indirectly, in calling the first Person *Father*, and directly in calling the second Person *only Son*. The very name of *Father*, applied in the Creed to the first Person, intimates the Relation he bears to a *Son*, of the same Nature with him, existing of him, and from him and with him. This is an Observation frequently occurring in the *Post-Nicene* Writers, who derived it from the more early Fathers . . .

The most probable solution in my humble Judgement is, that the so called Apostles' Creed was at first the *preparatory* Confession of the Catechumens, the *admission-ticket*, as it were (Symbolum ad Baptismum) at the Gate of the Church, and gradually augmented as Heresies started up.[1] (The latest of these seems to have consisted in the doubt respecting the

18[1] Waterland had speculated "that some of the *additional* Articles might have been inserted into the Creeds, in the very Age of the *Apostles*, in Opposition to the *Heresies* then breaking out" (227). C was very well versed in the history of the Creeds and his note reflects the standard vocabulary, esp in the use of *symbolum* as meaning "Token" or "Entry-pass" "into Baptism" in the parenthetical phrase. For further discus-

entire *death* of Jesus on the Cross as distinguished from suspended animation—Hence in the sixth Century the clause—"And he descended into Hades" was inserted,[2] i.e. the indissoluble principle of the *Man*, Jesus, was separated from, & left the *dissoluble*, and *subsisted* apart in Scheol,[3] or the abode of separated Souls—but really meaning no more than "vere mortuus est."[4] Jesus was taken from the Cross *dead*, in the very same sense, in which the Baptist was after his Beheading.[)] Nevertheless, well adopted as this Creed was to its purposes, I cannot but regret the high place & precedence which by means of its title & the fable, to which that Title gave rise, has usurped. It has certainly indirectly favored Arianism and Socianianism. S. T. C.

19 pp 252–5, pencil

That St. *John* wrote his *Gospel* with a View to confute *Cerinthus*, among other false Teachers, is attested first by *Irenaeus*, who was a Disciple of *Polycarp*, and who flourished within less than a Century of St. *John*'s Time. . . . *Epiphanius* of the same Time [as Jerome] testifies more than once, that St. *John* wrote against *Cerinthus* and *Ebion*, who had taught that Christ was a mere Man. It is some Confirmation of this, what *Irenaeus* relates of St. *John*'s meeting with *Cerinthus* at the Bath . . . and running from him with Disdain. It shews at least, that St. *John* and he were Contemporaries, and that the Apostle well understood his Principles, and detested them.

I have little trust and no faith in the Gossip and Hear-say Anecdotes of the early Fathers, Irenæus not excepted.[1] "Within a Century of St John's time". Alas! a century in the paucity of writers and of men of education in the Age succeeding the Apostolic must be reckoned more than equal to five Centuries since the use of Printing.—Supposing, however, the truth of the Irenæan Tradition, that the Creed of Cerinthus was what Irenæus states it to have been; & that John at the instance of the Asiatic Bishops wrote his Gospel, as an Antidote to the Cerinthian Heresy—what an overwhelming Argument does not this supply me with, against the

---

sion of these issues see BAXTER *Reliquiae* COPY B **58**, **100**, Jeremy TAYLOR *Polemicall Discourses* **186**, and nn.

18[2] C often makes this point, on the authority esp of John Pearson *An Exposition of the Creed* (12th ed 1641) 225–52: see also LEIGHTON COPY C **47** and n 2, LUTHER *Colloquia* **23** and n 1; and PEARSON.

18[3] For another use of this Hebrew word for a realm of death see BIBLE COPY B **46**.

18[4] "He really died". C interprets the descent into hell by the same phrase in DONNE *Sermons* COPY B **125** (and see n 3), LUTHER *Colloquia* **23**, LEIGHTON COPY C **47**.

19[1] For this incident as related by Irenaeus see **9**.

Apostolicity of the *Christopædia*—both that prefixed to Luke, & that concorporated with Matthew![2] *S. T. C.*

20 pp 257–9, pencil

* IN HIM WAS LIFE, AND THE LIFE WAS THE LIGHT OF MEN. The same *Word* was *Life*, the λογος [word] and ζωὴ [life], Both one. There was no Occasion therefore for subtilly distinguishing the *Word* and *Life* into two *Aeons*, as some did.

* I will not deny the possibility of this interpretation. It may be, nay, it is, fairly deducible from the words of the great Evangelist;[1] but I cannot help thinking, that taken as the primary intention, it degrades this most divine Chapter, which unites in itself the three characters of *sublime*, *profound*, and *pregnant*, alloys its *universality* by a mixture of Times and Accidents.

21 p 258–61, pencil

AND THE LIGHT SHINETH IN DARKNESS AND THE DARKNESS COMETH NOT UPON IT. So I render the Verse, conformable to the rendering of the same *Greek* Verb, καταλαμβάνω, by our Translators, in another place of this same Gospel. The Apostle, as I conceive, in this fifth Verse of his first Chapter, alludes to the prevailing Error of the *Gnostics*, and of all that sort of Men; who had adopted the antient *Magian* Notion of a *good God* and an *evil God*, the first called *Light*, and the other *Darkness:* which two they supposed to be under perpetual Struggles, and *obstructed* by each other.

O sad! sad!—How must the Philosopher have been eclipsed by the shadow of antiquarian erudition, in order that a mind like Waterland's could have sacrificed the profound universal import of "*comprehend*" to an allusion to a worthless dream of heretical nonsense, the mushroom of the Day! Had W. one thought of the relation of his ⟨own⟩ *Understanding* to his *Reason*? But alas! the identification of these two *diversities*!! of how many errors has it been the ground & occasion.[1]

19[2] For the inauthenticity of the narratives of the childhood of Christ (here "*Christopædia*") in Luke 1–2 and in Matt see cross-references collected in SCHLEIERMACHER *Luke* **9** n 2, and for the distinction that C sometimes makes between Christopaedia and *evangelia infantiae* "gospels of the infancy" see BIBLE *NT Apocrypha* **4**, CHILLINGWORTH COPY B **2** n 2. C uses the verb "concorporate" of Matt in this context also in BIBLE *NT Apocrypha* **4**, BLANCO WHITE *Letters* **7**.

20[1] John 1.4, q at beginning of textus.

21[1] For the crucial distinction between Reason and Understanding see LEIGHTON COPY C **12** and nn, *AR* (*CC*) 214–36 and nn.

22 pp 260–1, pencil

AND THE WORD WAS MADE FLESH, became personally united with the Man *Jesus*; AND DWELT AMONG US, resided constantly in the human Nature so assumed. Very emphatical and pointed Expressions, searching to the Root of every Heresy almost of that Time, so far as concerned the Person of Christ: For none of them would admit the *Word made Flesh*, or *God made Man*. Such Sentiments agreed not with their vain Philosophy; they deemed the thing to be *incredible*.

Waterland himself did but dimly see the aweful import of "εγενετο σαρξ"[1]—the mystery of the alien Ground, & the truth that as the *Ground*, such must be the *life*. "He caused himself to *become Flesh*,["] and therein assumed a *mortal* life into his own person, or *unity*—in order in himself to transsubstantiate the corruptible into the incorrupt.

23 pp 265–6, pencil

The Apostle goes on to say, WHOSOEVER SHALL CONFESS THAT JESUS IS THE SON OF GOD, GOD DWELLETH IN HIM, AND HE IN GOD. Where again he manifestly strikes at the *Cerinthian* and *Ebionite* Principles, which allowed not *Jesus* to be the *Son of God*, in any true and proper Sense, such as St. *John* lays down in several Places of his Writings, but particularly in the Entrance to his *Gospel* . . .

I still cannot but feel, that in Waterland's anxiety to shew the anti-heretical force of John's Gospel & Epistles, he has overlooked their Catholicity, their applicability to all countries, at times—the truth independent of all temporary accidents & errors—which Catholicity alone constitutes their claim to Canonicity—i.e. to be *canonical*, *inspired* Writings.

24 pp 266–8, pencil

Hereupon therefore the Apostle, in defence of Christ's real *Humanity*, says, THIS IS HE THAT CAME BY WATER AND BLOOD. What he elsewhere expresses, by his *coming in the Flesh*, here he expresses more emphatically, by his *coming* in, or by, *Water* and *Blood*; alluding to what Christ shed at his *Passion*, as a Proof that he had then a real Body, and was really *Man*, not a Spectre, Phantom, or Apparition, as some Hereticks pretended.

22[1] "Became flesh" or, in AV, "was made flesh" (John 1.14)—a crucial phrase in Trinitarian theology. C glosses it below and discusses it at some length in *AR* (*CC*) 29 (and see n 3), 387*.

Water and blood, i.e. Serum and Crassament, mean simply Blood, the Blood of the animal or carnal Life, which (saith Moses) *is* the Life. Hence "Flesh" is often taken ⟨as,⟩ & indeed *is* a *form* of the Blood—Blood *formed*, organized. Thus B. often includes F. and F. includes B. Flesh and Blood = Blood in its twofold form, or rather formed and formless. "Water and Blood" has therefore two meanings in S[t] John, but which co-incidant in idem—[1]

1. true animal human Blood, & no *celestial Ichor* or Phantom. 2. The whole *sentiently* vital Body, fixed or flowing, the Pipe and the Stream.

For the Ancients, and especially the Jews, had no distinct apprehension of the *nerves*. In the Old Testament *Heart* is used as we use *Head*.[2] "The Fool hath said in his *Heart*["][3]—is in English "The worthless (Vaurien) hath taken it into his *Head*—["] &c.

25 pp 269–72, pencil

The Apostle, having said that the *Spirit is Truth*, or essential Truth, (which was giving him a Title, common to *God the Father* and to *Christ*)* in order to obviate any Misapprehension, or Offence, accounts for what he had said, and reconciles it, by declaring presently, that the *Father* and the *Word*, and the *Spirit*, are all *One*, are equally *Truth* it self: FOR THERE ARE THREE THAT BEAR RECORD IN HEAVEN, THE FATHER, THE WORD, AND THE HOLY SPIRIT; AND THESE THREE ARE ONE. Therefore it was as right to say, that *the Spirit is Truth*, as it might be to say it either of *Father* or *Son*, since they are all *One*.

* In what part of *St John's* Writings?—I would ask Dr Waterland. Aye, or of *St Paul's*, in any text in which "the Father" is used distinctively from "the Son", and not as inclusively of the Son and the Spirit?—

It grieves me to think, that such giant Archaspistæ[1] of the Catholic Faith as Bull and Waterland[2] should have so clung to this intruded Gloss, which in Opulence and continuity of the Evidences, as displayed by their own *Master*-minds, would have *superfluous*[a]—had it not been worse

25[a] For "been *superfluous*"

24[1] "Coincide in the same one". The text in question is 1 John 5.6, q at beginning of textus.

24[2] In HEINROTH **40** and LEIGHTON COPY B **16** C asserts simply that Hebrew uses the word for "heart" where we would expect "head", to refer to the seat of the intellect.

24[3] Ps 14.1, 53.1.

25[1] "Chief shield-bearers", i.e. champions—a term that appears in C's writings as early as 1803 (*CN* I 1565) and that he uses also (sometimes ironically) in CHILLINGWORTH COPY A **1**, IRVING *Sermons* **29** at n 21, LEIGHTON COPY C **13**.

25[2] Waterland consciously defends positions formulated by Bull, and their names are regularly linked to one another by C: see esp SHERLOCK **6** n 5.

than superfluous—viz. senseless in itself and interruptive of the profound sense of the Apostle.[3]

Qy—Whether the *distinct* Hypostasis of the H. Spirit, in the *same* sense as the only-begotten Son is hypostatically distinguished from the Father, was a truth that formed an immediate Object or intention of St John? That it is a Truth implied in, and fairly deducible from, *many* texts both in his Gospel and his Epistles, I do not, indeed, I can not, doubt; But only whether *this* article of our Faith he was commissioned to declare *explicitely*.

26 p 272, pencil[a]

He *is come*, come in the Flesh, and not merely to reside for a time, or occasionally, and to fly off again, but to abide and dwell with Man, cloathed with Humanity.

Incautiously worded, at best.

Compare our Lord's own declaration to his Disciples, that he had dwelt a brief while *with* or *among* them, in order to dwell *in* them permanently.[1]

27 pp 286–96, pencil

It is very observable, that the *Ebionites* rejected three of the *Gospels*, receiving only St. *Matthew*'s (or what they called so) and that curtail'd. They rejected likewise all St. *Paul*'s Writings, reproaching him as an Apostate. How unlikely is it, that *Justin* should own such Reprobates as those were, for Fellow Christians!

I dare avow my belief—or rather I dare not withhold my avowal—that both Bull and Waterland are here hunting on the Trail of an old Blunder or Figment concocted by the gross ignorance of the Gentile Christians and their *Fathers* in all that respect~~ing~~ed Hebrew Literature and the Palestine Christians. I persist in the belief, that tho' a *refuse* of the persecuted

26[a] This note was already on the page when the end of **25** was written around it

25[3] C alludes to a famous textual crux in 1 John 5.7–8, "For there are three that bear record in heaven, the Father, the Word, and the Holy Ghost: and these three are one. And there are three that bear witness in earth, the spirit, and the water, and the blood: and these three agree in one." The passage running from "in heaven" through to "in earth" appears only in late mss and is not generally considered to have been part of the Epistle originally. C says of these words in Hartley COLERIDGE **3**, "They are, doubtless, a marginal Gloss, cited from St Augustine . . . & afterwards slipped into the text".

26[1] John 14.19–20: "Yet a little while, and the world seeth me no more; but ye see me: because I live, ye shall live also. At that day ye shall know that I am in my Father, and ye in me, and I in you."

& from neglect degenerating Jew-Christians may have sunk into the mean carnal notions of their unconverted Brethren respecting the Messiah, yet that no *Sect* of Ebionites ever existed but those whom St Paul travelled to with the Contributions of the Churches, nor any such man as Ebion;[1] unless indeed it was St Barnabas, who in his humility might have so named himself, ~~in providing for~~ while soliciting relief for the distressed Palestine Christians—I am Barnabas, the Beggar/ But I will go further—and confess my belief, that the (so called) Ebionites of the first and second Century, who rejected the Christopædia, and whose Gospel commenced with the Baptism of John, were orthodox apostolic christians, who received Christ as the *Lord*—i.e. as Jehovah manifested in the flesh./[2] As to their rejection of the other Gospels & of Paul's writings, I might ask—Could they *read* them?—But the whole notion rests on an anachronical misconception of the Evangelia.—Every great Mother Church had its own Gospel.—

28 p 288, pencil

It is pleaded, that those Impugners of Christ's *Divinity*, are styled *Men of our Profession*, that is, *Christians*; and therefore he admitted them as Fellow-Christians. To say nothing here of the *truer* reading (*Men of your Nation*)* there is no Consequence in the Argument. The *Ebionites* were *Christians* in a large Sense, Men of *Christian Profession*, nominal Christians; as *Justin* allowed the worst of Hereticks to be: And this is all he could mean by allowing the *Ebionites* to be Christians.

* I agree with Bull in holding "υμετερου" the more probable Reading—& am by means convinced, that the celebrated passage in Josephus is an interpolation.[1] But I do not believe, that such men ever professed themselves *Christians* or were or could have been, baptized.

27[1] C's reading of RHENFERD in Jul 1827 settled the question of the non-existence of Ebion and the Ebionites: see Jeremy TAYLOR *Polemicall Discourses* **197** n 1.

27[2] C directly contradicts this assertion in **30**, attributing the Christopaedia to this very group. Physically, the two notes look as though they were written at the same reading, but it is possible that C's reading of RHENFERD intervened between them.

28[1] In the text and notes of 282–4, Waterland both translates and quotes in Greek a controverted passage from Justin Martyr *Dialogue with Trypho* ch 48 in which Justin appears to say that some "of our Profession", i.e. Christians, conceive of Christ as "a Man born of human Parents". He also approves Bull's conjecture that the text should not read *hemeterou genous* "of our kind" but *hymeterou genous* "of your Nation". He does not mention Josephus. C is presumably recalling Josephus *Jewish Antiquities* 18.3.3, a passage that has been suspected of being an interpolation, and that contains both a reference to Christ as "a wise man, if it be lawful to call him a man" and an account of the rise of Christianity. C considers the passage as he found it discussed in Josephus *Works* ed William Whiston in a notebook entry of 21 Feb 1826, and there

29 p 292, pencil

* *Le Clerc* would appear to doubt, whether the Persons pointed to in *Justin*, really denied Christ's *divine Nature* or no. It is as plain as possible, that they did.

No, NO![a] Le Clerc is no Favorite of mine: and Waterland is a prime Favorite. Nevertheless, in this instance, I too doubt with Le Clerc, & *more* than doubt.[1]

30 pp 298–9, pencil

Irenaeus here lays the Charge upon the fundamental Error of the *Ebionites*, their rejecting Christ's *Divinity*; an Error which they had imbibed from their Countrymen the *Jews*, and brought with them into Christianity. And this was the principal Ground and Reason of their rejecting some of the *Gospels*, particularly St. *John*'s: For they had not yet learned the Art of reconciling the Doctrine of the New Testament with their Principles.

Aye! and to the Ebionites, of whom Irenæus here speaks, & whom I suspect to have been the Judaizing Christians in the mixt Churches as that of Rome, composed at first of a few Gentile Converts with a majority of converted, & gradually reversing this proportion—it is to these I attribute the Ante-baptismal Chapters of Matthew and Luke.[1]

31 pp 338–9, pencil

Justin Martyr, in a *Fragment* produced by Dr. *Grabe*, lays a very particular Stress upon the Article of Christ's *Divinity*, as the Reconciliation of God and Man is nearly concerned in it. The Passage runs thus: "When Man's Nature had contracted Corruption, it was necessary that He who would save it, should do away the Principle of Corruption. But this could not be done without uniting *Life by Nature* [or *essential Life*][a] with the Nature so corrupted, to do away the Corruption, and to immortalize the corrupt Nature ever after. Wherefore it was meet that the *Word* should become incarnate to deliver us from the Death of natural Corruption."

29[a] The first two words are written in the inner margin of the page, the remainder of the note at the top of the page and in the outer margin

31[a] Square brackets in original

---

decides against its authenticity: *CN* IV 5331 and n. His position here is not altogether clear, since "by means" is obscure and might even be a slip for "by no means".

29[1] Jean Leclerc or Joannes Clericus (1657–1736), Arminian theologian and friend of Locke. Waterland refers to his history of the Church on 291.

30[1] I.e. the "Christopædia" which in **27** he says they rejected.

* Here *Justin* asserts, that it was necessary for *essential Life*, (or *Life by Nature*) to be united with human Nature, in order to *save* it: Which is the same as to say, that it was necessary for *God* to become incarnate, in order to save lost Man.

* Waterland has not mastered the *full* force of ἡ κατὰ φύσιν ζωὴ.[1] If indeed he had taken in the *full* force of the whole of this invaluable fragment, he would never have complimented the extract from Irenæus, as saying "much the *same* thing in fuller and stronger words."[2] Compared with the fragment from Justin, it is but the flat common-place Logic of Analogy, so common in the early Fathers. S. T. C.

32 pp 340–1

[Quoting Irenaeus:] "They who make [*Jesus*][a] a mere Man begotten of *Joseph*, remaining under the Bondage of the first Disobedience, are in a dead State, in as much as they are not yet conjoined with the *Word* of God the Father, nor have received *Freedom* by the Son . . ."

non nudè hominem—not a *mere* Man[1]—~~but~~ do I hold Jesus to have been & to be; but a perfect Man and by personal union with the Logos perfect God. That his having an earthly Father might be requisite to his being a perfect Man, I can readily suppose: but why the having an earthly Father should be more incompatible with his perfect ~~Godhead~~ Divinity by personal union with the Logos, than his having an earthly Mother, I can not comprehend! All that John & Paul believed, God forbid! that I should not! S. T. C.

33 p 387, pencil | Ch 7

[Quoting Daniel Whitby *A Treatise of Traditions* (1688–9):] "In such Doctrines as were rejected by the *universal* Church* as *Heresies*, Austin

32[a] Square brackets in original

31[1] In a footnote (337–8), Waterland quotes the Greek original, including this phrase, rendered "*Life by Nature*" in textus.

31[2] C is quoting from 338–9: "*Irenaeus* has said much the same thing with *Justin*, in fuller and stronger Words. After observing that the *Son of God* and *Word of the Father* became *Man*, that he might give *Salvation* to his own Creature, or Workmanship, he proceeds as follows: 'Therefore, as I said before, he united *Man* to *God*: For if it were not *Man* that should overcome the Adversary of *Man*, the Enemy would not have been rightly vanquished; and again, if it were not *God* to give the *Salvation*, we could not be firmly possessed of it: Besides, if Man had not been united to God, he could never have been Partaker of Incorruption. So it was meet that a *Mediator* between God and Man, should bring both together into Amity and Concord by his own Proximity to both; that so he might present Man to God, and notify God to Men.'"

32[1] The phrase in textus translates the Latin, which is provided in a footnote (340) and which C has adapted.

saith truly, that it was sufficient Cause to reject them, because *The Church held the contrary* . . ."

* It would be of use, if some able & wise[a] would explain and vindicate the term "The universal Church" against the plausible tho' sophistical Argument from the existence of the Heretical churches themselves.

34 pp 389–91, pencil

The *Antients* are likewise of Use to us under the same View, against the *Socinians*, who *innovate* in Doctrines of the highest *importance*, teaching things *contrary* to the Faith of all the primitive Churches. . . . It is sufficient Reason for rejecting such *Novelties*, and the *Interpretations* which they are founded upon, that the Christian World, in the best and purest Times, either knew nothing of them, or rejected them.

As excellent means of raising a *presumption* in the mind of the falsehood of Arianism & Socinianism, and thus of preparing the mind for a docile reception of the great IDEA itself, I admit & value the testimonies from the writings of the early Fathers. But, alas! the increasing dimness, ending in the final want, of the *Idea* of this all-truths-including Truth of the Tetractys eternally manifested in the Triad[1]—this, this is the ground & cause of all the main Heresies from Semi-Arianism recalled by Dr S. Clark[2] to the last setting Ray of departing Faith in the necessitarian Psilanthropism of Dr Priestley![3] S. T. C.

35 p $^{+}$1, pencil, referring to p 412 and following

Since that Time, I do not know a warmer or keener Adversary that the *Fathers* have had, than Mons. *Barbeyrac*, Professor of *Civil Law* at *Groningen*, and known to the learned World by his *French* Translations of *Pufendorf* and *Grotius*, and his learned Notes upon both. He attacks

33[a] For "able & wise man", presumably

34[1] C develops his idea that "the Tetractys = Triad is the Divine or Eternal Nature" in BÖHME **172**; cf FLEURY **92**, IRVING *Sermons* **2**, TENNEMANN **127**, and nn.

34[2] C must mean that Samuel Clarke (1675–1729) can be taken to represent "Semi-Arianism". Many of Clarke's contemporaries also held this view. His *Scripture Doctrine of the Trinity* (1712) led him into controversy with Waterland and prompted the latter's *Vindication of Christ's Divinity*, which C also annotated. This note of C's would tend to confirm the reading "Clark" in *CN* III 3749, a note of 1810 referring to "cold moral Essays just *lappelled* & turned up with Christianity".

34[3] As a word for the doctrine that Christ was merely human, "psilanthropism" is one of C's coinages: *OED*. For other uses of the term, and its derivatives, see e.g. CHANNING **2**, LESSING *Sämmtliche Schriften* **60**, LUTHER *Colloquia* **35**.

the *Fathers* principally upon the Head of *Morality* . . . and seems to exert his utmost Endeavours to sink their Reputation for *Sense*, and *Conduct*, and even for *Conscience* too, in some measure, in order to strike them out of all Credit or Authority. . . . In Justice to the *Fathers*, and to *primitive Christianity* struck at through their Sides, it ought to be told, that the learned Civilian . . . has not been careful about the *Facts* upon which he grounds his Censure, but has often taken them upon *Trust* from others, transcribing their Oversights, or *partial* Accounts.

I cannot help thinking, that Waterland's Defence of the Fathers against Barbeyrac[1] is below his great powers, and characteristic vigor of Judgement—It is enough, that the~~y~~ Fathers of the 3 first Centuries were the Lights of their Age—& worthy of all reverence for their good gifts—but it appears to me impossible to deny their *credulity*; ~~and~~ their *ignorance* in the interpretation of the old testament, or their hardihood in asserting the truth of whatever they thought it for the interest of the Church & for the good of Souls, to have believed as true.[2] A whale swallowed Jonas; but a Believer in all the assertions & narrations of Tertullian, and Irenæus would be a more wonder-working Jonas, or John-Ass! For he must have swallowed Whales. *S. T. C.*

36 p [258], last page of Advertisement for "Books printed for W. Innys and R. Manby"

11. A Critical History of the *Athanasian* Creed, representing the Opinion of the Antients and Moderns concerning it: With an Account of the Manuscripts, Versions and Comments, and such other Particulars as are of Moment for the determining the Age, and Author, and Value of it, and the Time of its Reception in the Christian Churches. 4to. 1724.

How could W. the chosen Elisha, Scholar & Compeer of Bishop Bull, have even *tolerated* this blundering Creed of some red-hot Monk, who understood the writings of the great Athanasius, just as much as [? blundering] Sinner Saved, ~~or Dr~~ understood St Paul?—[1]

35[1] Waterland's critique of the work of Jean Barbeyrac (1674–1744) continues to 436.

35[2] For C's opinion of the unreliability of the Church Fathers see Jeremy TAYLOR *Worthy Communicant* **1** and n 2.

36[1] The work advertised is by Waterland. The Athanasian Creed was known not to have been composed by Athanasius personally (Waterland's work makes a case for attributing it to Hilary of Arles), and C often writes of it irritably as a "Pseudo-Athanasian Creed": see SHERLOCK **8** and n 1.

A Vindication of Christ's Divinity: being a defense of some queries, relating to Dr. Clarke's scheme of the H. Trinity, in answer to a clergy-man in the country. . . . 2nd ed rev. Cambridge 1719. 8°.

British Library C 126 d 1

"S. T. C." label on the title-page and John Duke Coleridge's monogram on p $^{-}$6. A note by EHC, dated 15 May 1890, is pasted to $^{-}$6: "These notes with some slight alterations are to be found in the Literary Remains—Vol IV. 221 (1839)." The pencilled crosses appearing in conjunction with C's notes seem to belong to the process of making *LR*, and are not separately recorded.

C may have given or lent this book for a time to JHG; or, just possibly, been made a late gift of it by JHG. In a letter of 28 Oct 1833 C asks him for transcriptions of **4** and other notes, implying that the book was then in Green's possession: *CL* VI 962–3.

DATE. In the 1820s? C must have read this work early in his career: Thomas Methuen (*C Talker* 307) mentions having lent him a copy to annotate in 1815. By 1818 he was recommending it as an indispensable guide in Trinitarian debate: *CL* IV 850. But he appears to have annotated this copy for JHG, and some statements of 1825–30 refer to the book as though it was fresh in his mind: *AR* (*CC*) 313*, *TT* (*CC*) 213.

1 pp $^{-}$7–$^{-}$6, $^{-}$4, $^{-}$2

It would be no easy matter to find a tolerably competent Individual who more venerates the writings of Dr Waterland, than I do & long *have* done. But still, in how many pages do I not find reason to regret, that the total Idea of the 4 = 3 = 1, of the Adorable Tetractys, eternally self-manifested in the Trias, Father, Son and Spirit, was never in its cloudless Unity present to him.[1] Hence both he, & Bishop Bull,[2] too often treat it as a peculiarity of ~~the~~ positive Religion, which is to be cleared of all *Contradiction* to Reason, & then, thus *negatively* qualified, to be actually received by an act of the mere Will/ Stet pro Ratione Voluntas.[3]—Now, I affirm that the Article of the Trinity *is* Religion, *is* Reason, and the universal Formula of all Reason—& that there neither is, nor can be, *any*

1[1] For the tetractys as triad see TENNEMANN **127** n 5. C reiterates this objection to Waterland's case in **21**, **22**, **23**, **46**.

1[2] Waterland had taken up the Trinitarian cause championed by George Bull before him, and C often treats them as a team: cf SHERLOCK **6** n 5.

1[3] "Let Will stand in for Reason": Juvenal *Satires* 6.223.

Reason, any Religion, but what is or is an expansion of the Truth of the Trinity. In short, that all other pretended Religions, Pagan or pseudo-Christian (ex. gr. Sabellian, Arian, Socinian) are in themselves *Atheism*, tho' God forbid, I should call or even think the men so denominated Atheists. I affirm a Heresy often/ but never dare denounce the Holder an *Heretic*.[4] S. T. Coleridge.

On this ground only can it be made comprehensible, how any *honest* & commonly intelligent Man can withstand the proofs & sound ~~logic~~ Logic of Bull & Waterland—that they failed in the first place to present the *Idea* itself of the great Doctrine, which they so ably advocated.—Take *myself*, S. T. C., as a humble Instance—I was never so befooled as to think that that the Author of the 4th Gospel or that St Paul ever ~~were~~ taught the Priestleyian Psilanthropism/[5] or that Unitarianism (presumptuously, nay, absurdly, so called) was the doctrine of the New Testament generally. But during the 16 months of my aberration from the Catholic Faith I ~~presumed~~[a] presumed, that the tenets of the Divinity of Jesus, the Redemption, &c were irrational and that what was contradictory to Reason, could not have been revealed by the *Supreme* Reason. As soon as I discovered, that these doctrines were not only consistent with Reason, but themselves *very Reason*, I returned at once to the literal interpretation of the Scripture—& to the Faith.[6] S. T. C.—

2 p ⁻2, pencil

The Will = the absolute Subjectivity

3 p ⁻2, pencil

Mem. Every Generation has its one or more overrated Men.—Dr Johnson in George the Third's—Dr S. Clark in George the First's—Lord Byron being the ~~Idol~~ [. . .] star now in the Ascendant.[1]

4 title-page verso | sig A3

In all religious and moral use of the word, God, taken absolutely—(i.e. not *a* God or *the* God, but God), a *relativity*, a *distinction* in kind ab aliquo

1[a] The word blotted when C wrote it; he has rewritten the word above the first version

1[4] See WATERLAND *Importance* **10** and n 2.

1[5] I.e. the "mere-manism" of the Unitarian followers of Joseph Priestley. For C's coinage of this word see WATERLAND *Importance* **34** n 3.

1[6] The period in which C's faith was "confined in the trammels of Unitarianism" (BÖHME **10**) lasted from 1794 to about 1802: *BL* ch 10 (*CC*) I 180.

3[1] For the general over-rating of Samuel Johnson see e.g. BARCLAY COPY A **3** ("pilfered brutalities of Wit"); for Byron, *TT* (*CC*) I 61 ("Nothing of Lord Byron's would live"); for Samuel Clarke, WATERLAND *Importance* **34** n 2.

quod non est Deus,[1] is so *essentially* implied, that it ⟨is⟩ a̸ matter of perfect indifference, whether we assert World without God, or make God the World. The one is as truly Atheism as the other. In fact, for all moral and practical purposes they are the same position, differently expressed—whether I say, God is the World, or the World is God, the inevitable conclusion, the Sense and *import*, is—there is no other God than the World, ⟨i.e.⟩ There is no other *meaning* to the term, God. Whatever you may mean by, or choose to believe of the WORLD, that and that alone you mean by or believe of *God*.—Now, I very much question whether in any other sense ~~there is~~ Atheism, i.e. speculative Atheism, is possible—~~and~~ for even in the Lucretian coarsest & crudest scheme of the Epicurean Doctrine a hylozoism, a *potential* life, is clearly implied, and in the celebrated "lene Clinamen" becoming Actual.[2]—Bravadoes articulating breath into a blasphemy of Nonsense, ~~wh~~ to which they themselves ~~are~~ attach no connected meaning, and ~~which~~ the wickedness of which is alone intelligible, there may be but a La Place, a La Grand would & with justice, resent and repel the imputation of a belief in Chance, or a denial of Law, Order, and Self-balancing Life and Power in the World.[3] Their error is, that they make them the proper, underived Attributes *of* the World.—It follows then, that Pantheism = Atheism and that there is no other ~~anteced~~ Atheism ~~other~~ actually existing or speculatively conceivable, but Pantheism/ Now I hold demonstrable, that a consistent Socinianism following its own consequences must come to Pantheism, and in ungodding their Saviour goddify Cats, and Dogs, Fleas and Frogs, &c &c. There is, there can be no medium between the Catholic Faith (Trinitari-

4[1] "From anything that is not God".

4[2] Since only a few fragments exist of Epicurus's great work *On Nature*, Lucretius's *De rerum natura* is a major source of information about his philosophy. One of the innovations in the system was its postulating a "slight swerve", to translate C's phrase, in every atom. (Lucretius 2.292 uses *clinamen* alone.) Cf C's reference to "epicurean *clinamen*" in BAXTER *Reliquiae* COPY B **47**. For hylozoism, the idea that matter is endowed with life or that life is a property of matter, see also DUBOIS **2**.

4[3] Taking it as given that French science was liable to be atheistic, C nevertheless draws attention to the visions of an ordered universe presented by Laplace in his *Traité de mécanique céleste* (5 vols Paris 1799–1825) and *Exposition du système du monde* (2 vols Paris 1796). The second name appears to be a mistake for "Lagrange", i.e. the mathematician Joseph Louis Lagrange (1736–1813), author of *Leçons sur le calcul des fonctions* (Paris 1804). (If so, C's error perhaps arose from his mentally coupling this name with the name of John Landen—1719–90—, as in "Landen's and Le Grange's Analysis of Functions" in *CN* IV 4931 f 101.) Another possibility is Joseph Jérôme Lefrançais de Lalande (1732–1807), French astronomer and mathematician, associated with "the Doctrine of Chances without Mind, or intelligence, or Goodness or the like unphilosophical Trumpery" in *SW & F* (*CC*) 1108.

anism) and *Atheism* disguised in the self-contradictory term, *Pan*theism: for every thing God, and no God are identical positions.

5 p 1 and sig B4v,[a] pencil

I am the Lord, and there is none else; *There is no God besides me*, Isa. 45. 5.

Is there a God besides me? *Yea, there is no God, I know not any*, Is. 44. 8.

I am God and there is none like me;* *Before me there was no god form'd, neither shall there be after me*, Is. 46. 9.

* In all these texts the "*is*" is to be rendered *positively*, *objectively*, & not as [b]a mere connective. The Word is[c]

The Word *is* God—& saith, *I am* the *Lord*; There *is* no God besides me, the Supreme Being, Deitas ⟨objectiva⟩[1] The Father saith *I am* in that I am—Deitas subjectiva.[2]

6 p 2, pencil

The Sum of your Answer to this Query, is, that *the Texts cited from* Isaiah, *in the first Column* [**5** textus], *are spoken of* one Person only, (p. 34) *The Person of the Father*, (p. 39.) *And therefore all other Persons, or Beings* (which you make equivalent) *how divine soever, are necessarily excluded*; *and by Consequence, our Lord Jesus Christ is as much excluded from being* the one Supreme God, *as from being the Person of the Father*, (p. 40).

O most unhappy mistranslation of Hypostasis by Person.[1] The *Word* is the only *Person* of the Deity.

7 p 4, pencil

[Summary, p 5, of detailed points made pp 4–5:] The Sum then is, that by the Texts of the Old Testament, it is not meant only that there is no other *Supreme* God; but absolutely *no Other*: And therefore our blessed

5[a] At the end of "Contents", facing p 1

5[b–c] Bottom of p 1, darker pencil and perhaps added by another hand when C's note was cropped or rubbed away; the last three words will be repeated as the beginning of the text on the facing page

5[1] "⟨Objective⟩ deity".

5[2] "Subjective deity". "I am in that I am" is C's proposed clarification of the "I am that I am" of Exod 3.14, in OMNIANA **2**.

6[1] On this point and the related objection in **31**, see Jeremy TAYLOR *Polemicall Discourses* **198** and n 5.

Lord must either be included and comprehended in the one Supreme God of *Israel*, or be intirely excluded with the other pretended, or nominal, Deities.

Waterland's Argument is absolutely unanswerable by a Worshipper of Christ. The modern ultra-Socinian[1] *cuts* the knot.

8 pp +1–+4, referring to p 42

He is represented *eminently* now as God; and Christ, as *Son of God*; or *Mediator*, or *Messiah*. Christ having before took upon Him that Part, Character, or Office, which since that time has been reserved, in a peculiar manner, to the Father, may be said to have acted in the *Person* of the Father, or *in the Name* of the Father; that is, under the same Character or Capacity, which the Father now chiefly bears with respect to Men.

p. 42. And *why* did not Dr Waterland—why did not his great Predecessor in the glorious Controversy, Bishop Bull—contend for a revisal of our law-established Version of the Bible; but especially of the New Testament?—either the [?~~us~~] unanimous belief and testimony of the 5 or 6 first Centuries, grounded /on the elevated declarations of John, Paul, & the Writer of the Epistle to the Hebrews, were erroneous or at best doubtful—& then why not wipe them off? Why these references to them?—Or else they were (as I believe, & both Bull & Waterland believed) the *very truth*—& then why continue the translation of the Hebrew into English at second hand thro' the Medium of the Septuagint?[1] Have we not adopted the Hebrew word, JEHOVAH? Is not then Κυριος, i.e. Lord, of the Septuagint, a Greek Substitute in countless instances for *Jehovah*?—Why not then restore the *original* Word—and both in the Old Testament religiously render Jehovah by *Jehovah*, & every text of the New Testament referring to the Old by the Hebrew Word in the Text referred to? Had this been done, Socinianism would have been scarcely possible.[2]

Why?—I will tell you WHY!—Because that great Truth, in which is contained all treasures of all possible knowlege, was still *opake* even to Bull & Waterland—because the *Idea* itself—that Idea idearum,[3] the one

7[1] I.e. the Unitarian, who goes "beyond" the Socinians of earlier times.

8[1] For C's awareness of the consequences of commentators' relying on the Greek translation of the Hebrew scriptures, and esp on the hazards of basing translations (such as the Vulgate) on translations, see e.g. BIBLE COPY B **67**, EICHHORN *Apocrypha* **13**, GREW **39**.

8[2] As C observes in Jeremy TAYLOR *Polemicall Discourses* **16** (and see n 9) "Lord" may be used in a secular sense open to Socinian interpretations.

8[3] "Idea of ideas". For this repeated reservation about Waterland's work see **1** and n 1.

substantive Truth which is the *Form*, *Measure*, and Involvent[4] of *all* Truths, was never present to them in its entireness, unity, and transparency!

They most ably vindicated the doctrine of the Trinity, *negatively*, against the charge of positive irrationality. With equal ability they shewed the contradictions, nay, the Absurdities involved in the rejection of the same by a professed Christian. They demonstrated the utter unscriptural and contra-scriptural nature of Arianism, and of Sabellianism & Socinianism—

But the self-evidence of the Truth, as a universal of the Reason, as the Reason itself—as a *Light* which revealed itself by its own essence as Light—this they had not had vouchsafed to them.

9 p 43

As *Son of God*, He was really God: and as *Son* of the Almighty, He was *Almighty*, in his *own right*, as Tertullian expresses it . . .

Strange, how little use has been made of that profound & most pregnant Text, v. 18 of Chapt. 1. of John's Gospel!—[1]

10 226, pencil

The pretence is, that we *equivocate* in talking of eternal Generation . . . . *Generation*, you say, implies *Beginning*; and yet we call it *Eternal*.

All *generation* is necessarily αναρχος,[1] without a dividuous *Beginning* and hence contra-distinct from *Creation*.

11 pp 226–7, pencil

And where then is the Impropriety, or *Equivocation* in the word *Generation*, as used by us? True, it is not the same with Human *Generation*.* But who will pretend that *Human* is to be the measure and standard of all *Generation*?

* Not eodem modo,[1] but so *essentially* the same, that ⟨the Generation of the Son of God⟩ is the *transcendent*, that gives to *Human* Generation its right to be *so*-called. It is in the *most* proper, ⟨the fontal,⟩ sense of the term *Generation*.

8[4] *OED* quotes this note as its only example of "involvent" as a noun.

9[1] "No man hath seen God at any time; the only begotten Son, which is in the bosom of the Father, he hath declared him."

10[1] "Without a beginning"—but the Greek *anarchos* "leaderless" is based on *archos* "leader" and not on *arche* "beginning".

11[1] "By the same means".

12 p 227, pencil

You have not proved that all *Generation* implies Beginning; and what is more, cannot.*

* It would be difficult to *disprove* the contrary. Generation with a *Beginning* not Gen. but creation.

13 p 227, pencil

Mem. The expediency of strictly *pre-defining* every term *negatively*, always—i.e. what is *not* meant—The Positive, what is meant, is to be the Result, the Conclusion.

14 p $^{+}$5 (p-d), evidently referring to pp 226–7 (i.e. **10–13**), pencil

In all important Controversies let the Terms be pre-defined *negatively*—i.e. exclude and preclude all that is *not* meant—~~and~~ and then the *positive* meaning i.e. what *is* meant, will be the Result.—~~when~~ the post-definition, which is at once the Definition and the *Impletion*, the Circumference and the Area.

I admit however that Dr Waterland has done good service in reducing the controversy to the question—Shall we accept the Homoūsian Doctrine?[1] Or reject the Christian Scriptures & the Tradition of the Church, as the Rule of our Faith?

15 pp 228–33, pencil

It is an usual Thing with many (Moralists may account for it) when they meet with a difficulty which They cannot readily answer, immediately to conclude that the Doctrine is False; and to run directly into the opposite Perswasion; not considering that They may meet with much more weighty Objections there, than before; or that They may have reason sufficient to maintain and believe many Things in *Philosophy* or *Divinity*, tho' They cannot answer every Question which may be started, or every Difficulty which may be raised against them.

O if Bull and Waterland had been first Philosophers, and *then* divines, instead of being first *manacled*, or say, *articled* Clerks of a Guild—if the clear free intuition of the Truth had led them to the Article, & not the Ar-

14[1] "Homousios" and "homousian" are alternative forms for "homoousios" and "homoousian", referring to the doctrine that the Son is "of the same substance" as the Father—the great issue of the Trinitarian debate in the early Church. The Articles of the C of E accept "of one substance" (Art 2). For further reflections on the terms of the debate see **27** and **31** below.

ticle to *the defence* of it as not proved to be *false*, how different would have been the result! Now we only feel the inconsistency of *Arianism*, not the *truth* of the doctrine attacked/ Arianism is *confuted*—and so, that I will not reject Orthodoxy for *these* reasons. It *may* still be true. But that it *is* true, because the Arians have hitherto failed to prove its falsehood, is no logical conclusion. The Unitarian may have better luck; or if he fail, the Deist.

16 pp 234–5

I will suppose (without granting) that Creatures may be wise enough to know, ready enough to hear, and able to relieve our wants, at any Distance. I will suppose also, that one Creature may be appointed to bear Rule and have Dominion over many; as some have thought particular *Angels* to preside over such and such Kingdoms or Countries. I will suppose likewise, that it may seem to Human Wisdom very fit and proper that such Creatures as can assist, or have the charge of others, should be respected, *worship'd*, and *adored* by Them. I will suppose also, that we may be so ignorant as not to perceive any great harm, in these Suppositions, from the Nature of the thing, barely and singly considered. *But God's *Thoughts are not our Thoughts:* He has been pleas'd to enter an express *Caveat* and Prohibition in the Case; and has, no doubt, good reason for it.

* i.e, as I would interpret the text[1]—the *Ideas* in and by which God reveals himself to Man, are not the same with, and are not to be judged by, the *Conceptions* which the Human Understanding generalizes from the notices of the *Senses*, common to man & to the Animals (Dog, Elephant, Beaver, &c) endowed with the same Senses. Therefore, I regard this §ph. p. 233, 234. as a specimen of admirable Special Pleading *ad* hominem, in the Court of Eristic Logic; but condemn it, as a wilful Resignation, or temporary self-deposition, of the Reason. I will *not* suppose, what my Reason declares ~~an~~ to be no *position* at all, & therefore an impossible *Sub-position*.[2]

17 pp 235-6

Let us keep to the *Terms* we began with; lest, by the changing of Words, we make a change of *Ideas*,* and alter the very state of the Question.

16[1] Isa 55.8: "For my thoughts are not your thoughts, neither are your ways my ways, saith the Lord."

16[2] A "subposition" or "supposition" being literally something placed *under* a position, something on which it is grounded. C uses "subposition" also in FICHTE *Bestimmung* **7**.

* This misuse, or rather this omnium-gatherum Expansion & consequent extenuation of the word, Idea, and Ideas, may be regarded as a Calamity inflicted by M[r] Lock on the Reigns of W[m] IIIrd, Queen Anne; & the two first Georges.—[1] S. T. C.

18 pp 238–40

Sacrifice was one Instance of Worship required under the Law; and it is said; *He that Sacrificeth unto any God, save unto the Lord only, He shall be utterly destroyed*, Exod. 22. 20. Now suppose any person, considering with Himself that only *absolute* and *soveraign* Sacrifice was *appropriated* to God, by this Law, should have gone and *sacrificed* to other Gods, and have been convicted of it before the Judges: The Apology He must have made for it, I suppose, must have run thus. "Gentlemen, tho' I have sacrificed to other Gods, yet, I hope, you'l observe, that I did it not *absolutely*: I meant not any *absolute* or *supreme* Sacrifice (which is all that the Law forbids) but *relative* and *inferior* only. I regulated my *Intentions* with all imaginable care; and my *esteem* with the most critical Exactness: I *consider'd* the other Gods, whom I sacrificed to, as *inferior* only, and *infinitely* so; reserving all *soveraign* Sacrifice to the *supreme* God of *Israel*.["] This, or the like Apology must, I presume, have brought off the Criminal, with some applause for his Acuteness, if your Principles be true. Either you must allow this; or you must be content to say, that not only *absolute supreme* Sacrifice (if there be any Sense in that Phrase) but *all Sacrifice* was, by the Law, *appropriate* to God only.

How was it possible for an Arian to answer this? But it was impossible: and Arianism was extinguished by Waterland, but in order to the increase of Socinianism—& this, I doubt not, Waterland foresaw. He was too wise a man, to suppose, that the exposure of the folly & falsehood of one *form* of Infidelism, would cure or prevent Infidelity. Enough! that he made it more bare-faced. I might say, bare-*breeched*—for ~~the~~ modern Unitarianism is the *Sansculotterie* of Religion.—[1]

19 p 239

You imagine that Acts of *religious* Worship are to derive their Signification and Quality, from the *intention* and *meaning* of the Worshippers;

17[1] This is a favourite theme: see *BL* ch 5 (*CC*) I 96–8*, TETENS **7** n 1.

18[1] The plebeian supporters of the Revolution in France, said to have been called *sans-culottes* ("without culottes") because they wore trousers rather than the breeches or *culottes* of gentlemen (but the etymology is disputed), were commonly represented in satirical British prints as literally bare-bottomed.

whereas the very reverse of it is the Truth. Their *Meaning* and *Signification* is fix'd and determin'd by God Himself; and therefore we are never to use them with any other meaning, under peril of Profaneness or Idolatry.

truly excellent. Let the Church of E. praise God for her Saints—a more glorious Calendar than Rome can shew!

20 p 251

The Sum then of the case is this: If the Son could be included as being *uncreated*, and very God; as *Creator*, *Sustainer*, *Preserver* of all Things, and one with the Father; then He might be worship'd upon their [the Ante-Nicene Fathers'] Principles, but otherwise could not.

Every where in this invaluable Writer ⟨I have to regret⟩ the absence of all distinct *Idea* of the *I AM*, as *the proper* Attribute of the FATHER: & hence the ignorance of the proper Jehovaism of the Son—& hence while we worship the Son together with the Father, yet that we *pray* to the Father only, thro' the Son.[1]

21 pp 254–5

As to the *Subordination* of Persons in the same Godhead, That is of distinct Consideration; and we may never be able perfectly to comprehend the Relations of the three Persons, *ad intra* [inwardly], amongst themselves;* the ineffable Order and Oeconomy of the ever blessed Co-eternal Trinity.

* Comprehend? No! For how can any Spiritual Truth be *com*prehended? Who can *com*prehend his own Will, or his own Personëity (i.e. his "I") or his own Mind, i.e. his Person, or his own *Life*? But we c~~ou~~an distinctly *app*rehend them.[1]

22 pp 269–71, pencil

From what hath been observed, it may appear sufficiently, that the divine Λογος [Logos] was our King, and our God long before; that He had the

20[1] For Waterland's failure to grasp this idea see also **1** n 1; for the "I AM", **5**; and for the Jehovaism of the Son, **8**.

21[1] The importance of the distinction between "comprehend" and "apprehend"—the former suggesting an act of inclusion, the latter only of recognition—is touched on also in **29** below. In BÖHME **11**, C says, "So far from comprehending it we are not even capable of the preparatory act of *ap*prehension. We cannot even take it up into the mind." In *Logic* (*CC*) 64, "contain" is given as a synonym for "comprehend".

same Claim and Title to religious Worship that the Father Himself had;* only not so distinctly reveal'd . . .

* Here I differ *toto orbe*[1] from W. and say with Luther and Zinzendorf, that before the Baptism of John the Logos alone had been distinctly revealed; & that first in Christ He declared himself as Son, ⟨viz.⟩ the co-eternal only-begotten Son, and thus revealed the Father.[2] Indeed, the want of the *Idea* of the 1 = 3 could alone have prevented Waterland from inferring this from his own Query II.—p. 28 to p. 38 in this Volume—see MSS note at the end of this Book.[3] S. T. C.

23 pp 273–6, pencil

. . . my Argument is still good, that the Son (having been in *the Form of God*, and *God*; *Creator, Preserver* and *Sustainer* of all Things, from the Beginning) had a Right to Worship, even upon *your* Principles . . . long before the commencing of his *Mediatorial Kingdom:* And therefore his Right and Title to Worship was not *founded* upon the *Powers* then supposed to have been given Him . . .

Again, the Want of the *Idea*. The Father *cannot* be revealed except in and thro' the Son, his eternal Exegesis. The contrary position is an *absurdity*. The Supreme Will, indeed, the Absolute Good, knoweth *himself* as the Father; but the Act of Self-Affirmation, the I AM in that I AM,[1] is not a manifestation *ad extra* not an εξηγησις.[2]

22[1] "By a whole world"—i.e. C sees himself as worlds apart from Waterland on this point.

22[2] C outlines this "splendid Conception" of the Moravian leader Count Zinzendorf, from his *Theologischer und dahin einschlagender Bedencken* (Frankfurt & Leipzig 1741), in EICHHORN *Apocrypha* **11**: "the bold Idea, that the Father, Θεος αορατος [God invisible], . . . was unknown to the Jews under the Law & was first revealed by Christ, from whom as by a reflected Light Θεος [God] without the article is named ο πατηρ [the father]". A passage in Luther's sermon on John 1.1 is susceptible of a similar interpretation (tr): "Any attempt to fathom and comprehend such statements with human reason and understanding will avail nothing, for none of this has its source in the reason: that there was a Word in God before the world's creation, and that this Word was God; that, as John says further on, this same Word, the Only-begotten of the Father, full of grace and truth, rested in the Father's bosom or heart and became flesh; and that no one else had ever seen or known God, because the Word, who is God's only-begotten Son, rested in the bosom of the Father and revealed Him to us" (*Works* ed Jaroslav Pelikan and Helmut T. Lehmann—Saint Louis MI 1958–86—XXII 8).

22[3] See **1** and n 1. Waterland's 28–38 contain a part of his response to "Query II" ("*Whether the Texts of the New Testament (in the second column) do not show that He* (Christ) *is not excluded, and therefore must be the same God?*"), specifically, the part that cites several OT texts about God that have traditionally been understood as referring also to the Son.

23[1] See **5** and n 2.

23[2] Not a manifestation "outwards", not an *exegesis*—literally a "leading out from". In John 1.18, q in **9** n 1, this is the verb tr "hath declared".

24 pp 274–6, pencil, marked with a short pencil line in the margin

. . . our Blessed Lord was then first *worship'd*, or *commanded* to be worship'd by us, under that distinct *Title* or *Character*; having before had no other *Title* or *Character* peculiar and *proper* to Himself, but only what was *common* to the Father and Him too.

* *Qy*[a] Rather shall I say, that the Son and the Spirit, the Word and the Wisdom, were alone worshipped because alone revealed under the Law.[1]—See Proverbs, Chapt. 1 and 2.[2]

25 p 275, pencil

[Footnote quotes Bishop Bull:] Profecto admiranda mihi videtur divinarum Personarum in Sacrosanctissima *Triade* οἰκονομία, qua Unaquaeque Persona *distincto* quasi *Titulo* humanum imprimis genus imperio suo divino obstrinxerit, *Titulo* illi respondente etiam *distincta* uniuscujusque imperii *patefactione*. *Patrem* Colimus sub *Titulo Creatoris* hujus Universi, qui & ab ipsa Mundi *Creatione* hominibus *innotuerit*; *Filium* adoramus sub *Titulo Redemptoris* ac *Servatoris* nostri, cujus idcirco divina gloria atque imperium non nisi post peractum in terris humanae *Redemptionis* ac *Salutis* negotium fuerit *patefactum*; *Spiritum* denique *Sanctum* veneramur sub *Titulo Paracleti*, *Illuminatoris*, ac *Sanctificatoris* nostri, cujus adeo divina Majestas demum post descensum ejus in Apostolos primosque Christianos donorum omne genus copiosissima largitione illustrissimum, *clarius emicuerit*. Nimirum tum demum Apostoli, idque ex Christi mandato, Gentes baptizabant in *Plenam atque adunatam Trinitatem* (ut cum *Cypriano* loquar) h.e. in nomine Patris, Filii, & Spiritus Sancti. *Bull. Prim. Trad.* p. 142.

[The oeconomy of the Divine Persons in the most Holy Trinity is to me indeed wonderful; that oeconomy, by which every distinct Person holds mankind obliged to his divine authority, by a distinct title, with which title the distinct revelation of every Person's authority corresponds. We worship the Father under the title of Creator of the Universe, who was also known to man from the Creation of the world: we worship the Son under the title of our Saviour and Redeemer, whose divine glory and authority therefore was not revealed, till he had accomplished the affair of man's salvation and redemption upon earth. Lastly, we worship the Holy Spirit under the title of *Paraclete*, our inlightner and sanctifier, whose divine majesty did then appear more plain after his descent upon the Apostles and first Christians, exceeding illustrious by the most

24[a] This is written on p 274 and marked "* p. 275"; the rest is written on pp 275–6 with "*"

24[1] See **22** for C's view as to the priority of the Logos.

24[2] C offers Prov 1–2 as proof of this revelation, e.g. 2.6, "For the Lord giveth wisdom: out of his mouth cometh knowledge and understanding."

plentiful effusions of all sorts of gifts. Then at last the Apostles, and that by their Lord's command, baptized the nations into the full and united Trinity, (as St Cyprian speaks) i.e. in the name of the *Father, Son, and Holy Ghost*. (Tr Francis Holland, 1725)]

Very plausible, and very eloquent, but only *cum multis granis salis*[1] true.

26 pp 279–83, pencil

He [Christ] meant what He has said, and what the Words literally import; that the Father (whose Honour had been sufficiently secured under the *Jewish* Dispensation,* and could not but be so under the *Christian* also) being as much concern'd for the *Honour* of his *Son*, had been pleased to commit *all Judgment* to Him . . .

* Here again—This contradiction of Waterland to his own principles is continually recurring—yea, and in one place he involves the very Tritheism, of which he was so victorious an Antagonist—viz. that the Father is Jehovah, the Son Jehovah, & the Spirit Jehova—thus making Jehovah either a mere synonime of *God*, whereas he himself rightly renders it, ο ὢν,[1] which S[t] John every where (and S[t] Paul no less) makes the *peculiar* name of the Son, μονογενὴς Υιος, ο ων εν κολπῳ του πατρος[2]—or affirms the same absurdity, as if he had said The Father is the Son, and the Son the Son, & the Holy Ghost the Son; yet there are not *three* Sons but *one* Son.

S. T. C.

N.B. Ο ὢν is the *Verbal Noun* of ὃς ἔστι not of Εγω ΕΙΜΙ.—[3]

27 pp 302–3

* The ομοούσιον [homoousion "of the same substance"] it self might have been spared, at least, out of the *Creeds*, had not a fraudulent abuse of good words brought Matters to that pass, that the *Catholick* Faith was in danger of being lost, even under *Catholick* Language.

* Most especially, the very disputable Rendering of Ὁμοούσιον by *Consubstantial* not only *might* have been spared, but *should* have been su-

25[1] Only "*with many grains of salt*".

26[1] Waterland considers the meaning of *ho on* "Being" at some length, e.g. 153–4, where he explains how Justin took the Logos to be one with *ho on* "in his own proper Person". BIBLE COPY B **119** n 1 comments extensively on theological and philological issues associated with this phrase. In *AR* (*CC*) 313* C expresses considerable doubt "as to the ὁ ὢν, both in this place and in *John* 1.18, being *adequately* rendered by our '*which is*'".

26[2] John 1.18 (var), "the only begotten Son, *which is* in the bosom of the father".

26[3] Of "he who is" not of "I AM".

perseded.[1] Why not as in[a] felt the interest of Science/ in all the physical Sciences, retain the same term in all languages? Why not üsia and homöusial, as well as hypostasis, hypostatic, homogeneous, heterogeneous, &c &c?/ as well as Baptism, Eucharist, Liturgy, Epiphany?

28 p 303, pencil

The Doctor's insinuating from the 300 Texts (which stile the Father *God* absolutely, or the one God) that the Son is not strictly and *essentially* God, not one God with the Father, is a strain'd and remote Inference of his *own*; not warranted by Scripture, nor countenanc'd by Catholick Antiquity; but Contradictory to both.

W. has weakened his own argument by seeming to admit, that in all these 300 texts the Father (i.e. distinctivè) *is* meant.

29 pp 307–8

You are so kind as to allow the *Manner* of the Son's *Derivation*, or Generation, to be *above Comprehension*. The *Eunomians*, your Predecessors in this Controversy, thought (and They thought right) that, in order to support their Cause, it would be necessary to affirm the Nature of God to be *Comprehensible*, or not above Human Comprehension . . .

One can neither assent to, or dissent from, this position of Waterland's without a strict definition of "to *com*prehend["]. The Idea, God, like all other *Ideas*, rightly so called and as contra-distinguished from "Conceptions" is not so properly *above* Comprehension, as *alien* from it.[1] It is = smelling a sound.

30 pp 316–18, pencil

The *Simplicity* of God is another *Mystery*, of which we have some, but a very imperfect, general, and obscure *Idea*. . . . When we come to inquire, whether *all* extension, or *all plurality*, *diversity*, Composition of *Substance* and *Accident*, and the like, be consistent with it, then it is that we discover how *confuse* and *inadequate* our *Ideas* are.

27[a] For "is" or "it"?

27[1] The controversial translation of the Greek *homoousion* into the Latin *consubstantialis* is attributed to Tertullian. For the history of the controversy and of C's consistently deploring "this unhappy, ill-chosen word", see FLEURY **56** and nn 1–3.

29[1] For C's resistance to the use of "comprehend" in this context see **21** and n 1; and for other instances of the distinction between idea and conception, invoked in **30** also, see TENNEMANN **76** n 8.

Surely, the far larger part of these assumed difficulties rests on misapplication either of the *Senses* to the Sense, or of the Sense to the Understanding, or of the Understanding to the Reason—in short, on asking Images where only Theorems can be, or Theorems for Thoughts, (= Conceptions or Notions) or lastly, Conceptions for *Ideas*. S. T. C.

31 p 351, pencil

You would not say that the *Sabellians* held one *Substance*, and the Church *three Substances* (tho' you do say it in effect) because the Thing is notoriously false. But taking advantage of the Ambiguity of the word, *Hypostasis*, sometimes used to signify *Substance*, and sometimes *Person*, you contrive a Fallacy.

And why did not W. lift up his voice against this mischievous abuse of the term Hypostasis, and the perversion of its Latin Rendering *Substantia*, as = Ουσια?/[1] Why ουσια should not have been rendered by Essentia, I cannot conceive. Est is clearly the Contraction of esset, and ens of Essens.—ων, ουσα, ουσια—essens, essentis, essentia.[2]

32 pp 354–5, pencil

* Let me desire you not to give so great a loose to your Fancy, in divine Things: You seem to consider every thing under the Notion of Extension, and sensible Images.

* Very true. The whole delusion of the Anti-trinitarians arises out of this, that they apply the property of imaginable matter, in which ⟨A⟩ *is* (i.e. can only be *imagined*) by exclusion of B, as the universal predicate of all Substantive Being.

33 p 357, pencil

The *Arian* Scheme . . . has many real and great Difficulties; being as well too *high* for some Texts, as too *low* for others; which the *Catholicks*, or *Sabellians* can much better deal with.

The Sabellian and Unitarian seem to differ only in this: that what the

31[1] For C's repeated complaints about the translation of *hypostasis* either as "person" or as equivalent to *ousia* "being" or "essence" see FLEURY **56** and nn 1–3, JURIEU **3** and n 2.

31[2] The Latin *essentia* usually is given as equivalent to Greek *ousia*. The Greek verb εἶναι "to be" having been the root of the Latin *esse* from which *essentia* is derived, C traces a plausible parallel evolution from participle to substantive "being" in the two languages.

Sabellian calls *Union* with, the Unitarians call, full inspiration by, the Divinity.[1]

34 pp 359–60, pencil

It is obvious, at first sight, that the true *Arian* or *Semi-Arian* Scheme . . . can never tolerably support it self, without taking in the *Catholick* Principle of a *Human Soul* to join with the *Word.**

* Here comes one of the consequences of the Cartesian *Dualism*—as if the Σαρξ,[1] the living Body, could *be* without a Soul, or a Human living Body without a Human Soul. Σαρξ is not the Greek for Carrion, nor Σωμα[2] for Carcase/

35 p 371, pencil

Necessary existence is an *essential* Character, and belongs equally to *Father* and *Son:* If That be what you mean by *Self-existence*, then That also belongs to Both.

i.e. subsistent in themselves are F., Son, and Spirit—the Father only has *origin* in himself.

36 pp 412–13, pencil

[Waterland comments on the interpretation of a passage in Athanagoras.] The words οὐχ ὡς γενόμενον [not as created (or as having become)], He [Dr Whitby] construes thus: *Not as eternally generated*, as if He had read γεννώμενον [begotten], supplying ἀϊδίως [eternally] by Imagination. The Sense and Meaning of the word γενόμενον,* signifying *made*, or *created*, is so fix'd and certain in this Author, that no doubt or scruple can be reasonably made of it.

i.e. The only-*begotten* never *became*, but all things became thro' him.

* This is but ⟨one⟩ of 50 instances, in which the true Englishing of γενομενον, εγενετο,[1] &c would have prevented all mistake—*not* ⟨by was⟩ made, but ⟨by⟩ *became*. Thus here—begotten eternally, and not one that *became*—i.e. not having been before.

33[1] For the Sabellians see Jeremy TAYLOR *Polemicall Discourses* **78** n 2.

34[1] "Flesh".

34[2] "Body".

36[1] "[C]reated" or "having become" (textus tr); and "he was made" or "he became". For other instances of C's taking issue with the customary translation of NT *egeneto* see FLEURY **98**, *AR* (*CC*) 29* and n 3.

37 p 412, pencil

He [Dr Whitby] makes a ridiculous Representation of *Tertullian*, as if that Writer believed two *Angels* to be as much *One*, as God the Father and God the Son are. I shall only transcribe the Passage, and trust it with the intelligent Reader. [Footnote quotes Tertullian *Apology* 21.11–12:] Et nos etiam Sermoni atque Rationi, itemque Virtuti, per quae omnia molitum Deum ediximus, propriam Substantiam *Spiritum* inscribimus; cui & *Sermo* insit praenuntianti, & *Ratio* adsit dispanenti, & *Virtus* perficienti. Hunc ex Deo prolatum didicimus, & prolatione generatum, & idcirco Filium Dei & Deum dictum, ex *Unitate Substantiae*, Nam & *Deus Spiritus*.—Ita de *Spiritu Spiritus* & de Deo *Deus*, ut *Lumen* de *Lumine* accensum.

[We, too, to that Word, Reason and Power (by which we said God devised all things) would ascribe Spirit as its proper nature; and in Spirit, giving utterance, we should find Word; with Spirit, ordering and disposing all things, Reason; and over Spirit, achieving all things, Power. This, we have been taught, proceeds from God, begotten in this proceeding from God, and therefore called "Son of God" and "God" because of unity of nature. For God too is spirit. . . . Spirit from Spirit, God from God—as light is lit from light. (Tr T. R. Glover, LCL)]

* How strange and crude the *Realism* of the Christian Faith appears in Tertullian's rugged Latinity!

38 p 414, pencil

He [Thomas Emlyn, in *Dr Bennet's New Theory of the Trinity Examined* (1718)] imagines that the good Father [Irenaeus] supposed the Λόγος, or Word, as such, *passible*. . . . The most that you can espy in [the passages cited] is, that the Λόγος *suffered* in the Flesh . . . . [Waterland quotes several passages from Irenaeus in footnotes, beginning with this one:] Solus vere Magister Dominus noster; & bonus vere Filius Dei, & patiens, verbum Dei Patris Filius Hominis factus. [Our Lord is truly our only master; the Son of God is truly good and suffering, the word of God the Father was made the Son of Man.] *Iren*. I. 3. c. 18. p. 211.

I rather think that by "patiens"[1] Irenæus might refer to the Logos, as the Deitas relativè objectiva ⚹ to the Father, the I AM, as the Deitas relativè ~~obj~~subjectiva.[2] S. T. C.

38[1] "Suffering", in textus.

38[2] "Deity relatively objective, as opposed" to the Father or "deity relatively subjective": cf the use of this opposition in **5**.

39 pp 415–16, pencil

He [Emlyn] represents *Tertullian*, as making the Son, in his highest Capacity, *Ignorant of the Day of Judgment*. Let the Reader see the whole Passage, and compare it with another, four chapters lower; and from thence judge of *Tertullian*'s meaning. [Waterland provides the two passages in a footnote, given here as **40** textus.]

Of the true sense of this Text I still remain in *doubt*,[a] but tho' as zealous & stedfast an Homoūsian as Bull & Waterland themselves, I am inclined to understand it of the Son, *in his highest capacity*; but I would avoid all the inferiorizing consequences by a stricter rendering of the ει μη ο πατηρ. *Mem.* The μονον of the other Gospel is here omitted.[1]

40 pp 494–[495], referring to p 415, pencil

[Footnote:] *Ignorans & Ipse Diem & Horam Ultimam, Soli Patri notam*; disponens Regnum Discipulis, quomodo & sibi dispositum dicit a Patre; habens Potestatem Legiones Angelorum postulandi ad auxilium a Patre si vellet, *Exclamans quod se Deus reliquisset*, in Patris manibus Spiritum ponens. *Tertull. Adv. Prax.* c. 26. p. 516.

Habes ipsum *Exclamantem* in Passione, *Deus Meus, Deus Meus*, ut quid me dereliquisti?—Sed Haec Vox Carnis & Animae, id est, Hominis, non *Sermonis*, nec *Spiritus*, id est, non *Dei*, propterea emissa est, ut impassibilem Deum ostenderet, qui sic Filium dereliquit, dum Hominem ejus tradidit in mortem. *Tertull. adv. Prax.* c. 30. p. 518.

[*Adversus Praxean* §26: . . . and he [the Son] even himself knows not the last day or hour, which is known to the Father alone: and he ordains for his disciples a kingdom even as he says one has been ordained for him by his Father: and he has power to ask his Father for legions of angels to help him, if he wished: and he cries aloud that God has forsaken him, and he places his spirit in the Father's hands . . .

§30: You leave him [Christ] crying aloud at his passion, *My God, my God, why hast thou forsaken me?* . . . But this utterance of flesh and soul (that is, of the manhood), not of the Word and Spirit (that is, not of God), was sent forth with the express purpose of showing the impassibility of God who thus forsook the Son when he delivered his manhood unto death. (Tr Ernest Evans)]

39[a] C wrote the note to this point in the top right-hand corner of the page, then wrote a caret and continued the note in the foot-margin, beginning again with a caret

39[1] C alludes to the phrase "but [i.e. except for] the Father" in the Greek text of Mark 13.32, tr (AV): "But of that day and that hour knoweth no man, no, not the angels which are in heaven, neither the Son, but the Father." The corresponding verse in Matt 24.36 adds μονον "only" (AV) or "alone".

P. 415. The ignorance of the Fathers, & Origen excepted, of the Antenicene Fathers in particular, in all that respects Hebrew Learning & the ⟨N.T.⟩ References to the O.T., is shewn in this so early fantastic misinterpretation grounded on the fact of our Lord's reminding, and as it were "*giving out* aloud" to, John & Mary the 22nd Psalm/ the prediction of his present Sufferings and after Glory![1] But the entire passage in Tertullian, tho' no proof of his Arianism, is full of proofs of his want of insight into the true sense of the Scripture Texts.

41 p 417, pencil

Thus, in regard to the Son's *Ignorance of the Day of Judgment*, it is manifest that the *Father* and *Son* are there spoken of, as of Two Persons; and One as *knowing*, the Other as *not knowing* . . .

No I have said before, I hold this a very unsatisfying Solution of the Text.[1]

42 p 421, pencil

It seems to me, that if there be not Reasons of Conscience obliging a *good* Man to speak out, there are always Reasons of Prudence which should make a *wise* Man hold his Tongue.*

* True, and as happily expressed. But to this, however, the honest judicious Anti-trinitarian must come off i.e. Well, well! I admit, that John & Paul thought differently; but this remains *my* Opinion.

43 pp 427–8

The Doctor's Version [of a text by Athanasius, quoted in a footnote] runs thus: "For He (*the Father*) is the one God, and the only One, and the First. And yet *these Things do not destroy the Divinity of the Son.*" This rendring is flat and low; and neither answers the *intent*, nor *Letter of* the Author. Οὐκ εἰς ἀναίρεσιν, literally, is, *not to exclude the Son*: plainly meaning, not to exclude Him from being the *one God*, and the *only One*, and the *First*, together with the Father.

This passage admits of a somewhat different interpretation than this of Waterland's—and of equal if not greater force, against the Arian Notion—viz. τον οντως οντα distinctively from ο ων[1]—the Ens *omnis* en-

40[1] See Jeremy TAYLOR *Polemicall Discourses* **25** and n 4.

41[1] See **39** and n.

43[1] "That which really is" distinctively from "Being".

titatis, etiam *suæ*[2] = the I Am, the FATHER. [? In] distinction from the Ens Supremum,[3] the Son. It cannot, however, be denied, that in changing the formula of the Tetractys, into the *Trias* by merging the Prothesis in the Thesis, the Identity in the Ipsëity, the Christian Fathers subjected their exposition to many inconveniences.[4]

44 p 432

"It was not God the Creator of the Universe, which then said to *Moses*, that He was the God of *Abraham*, and the God of *Isaac*, and the God of *Jacob*." . . . The unlearned Reader should be told, that what is here said by *Justin*, was in dispute with a *Jew*, who would not acknowledge more *divine* Persons than One. It was *Justin*'s Business to show, that there was a *divine* Person, one who was God of *Abraham*, *Isaac*, and *Jacob*, and was not the *Father*; and therefore there were two *divine* Persons.

~~all~~ At all events, it was a very incautious *expression* on the part of Justin Martyr: tho' his meaning was, doubtless, that which W. gives. The same most improper or at least most inconvenient because equivocal phrase has been interpolated into our Apostles' Creed./[1]

45 p 434

Novation . . . was intent upon . . . explaining and illustrating, as well as He was able, the Union and Communion of *Substance* in Father and Son; and showing how all recurs to one Head and Fountain . . .

See again Mss. p. 428.[1]

46 p 436, pencil

He cites *Gregory Nazianzen*, and translates him thus: "There is but one God; the Son and the Holy Ghost being referred to the one Cause.["] But then He adds a Note, which confounds all: *Namely*, says He, *as being divine Persons by whom the one God, or one Cause and Original of all Things, made and governs the World*. [Waterland quotes the Greek, from Gregory Nazianzen, Orat. 20.7 in a footnote:] *Τηροῖτο δ' ἄν, ὡς ὁ ἐμὸς λόγος, εἷς μὲν Θεὸς, εἰς ἓν αἴτιον καὶ υἱοῦ καὶ πνεύματος ἀναφερομένων· οὐ συντιθεμένων, οὐδὲ συναλειφομένων· καὶ κατὰ τὸ ἕν καὶ

43[2] The "Being of *all beings*, even of *himself*".

43[3] "Supreme Being".

43[4] On the misunderstanding of the tetractys see **1** and n 1.

44[1] I.e. "Maker of heaven and earth". For C's understanding of the evolution of the Creed see Jeremy TAYLOR *Polemicall Discourses* **185** and n 1.

45[1] I.e. **43** above.

ταυτὸ της θεότητος, ἵνα οὕτως ὀνομάσω, κίνημά τε καὶ βούλημα, καὶ τὴν της οὐσίας ταυτότητα.

[One god would be preserved, in my opinion, by referring son and spirit to one cause; and [this] in conformity with, if I may so describe it, the one and same movement and will of the godhead, and the sameness of substance and essence.]

* Another instance of the inconvenience of the Trias compared with the Tetractys.[1]

47 p 488, at the end of the book

Without detraction from the inestimable Service of the Fathers from Tertullian to Augustin, respecting this fundamental Article of the Christian Faith; yet commencing from the 5th Century, I dare claim for the Reformed Church of England the honorable name of the Αρχασπιστης[1] of Trinitarianism, and the foremost Rank among the Churches, Roman or Protestant. The Learned R. Catholic Divines themselves admit this, & make a merit of the reluctance with which they nevertheless admit it, in respect of Bp Bull.[2]

46[1] See **1** n 1.

47[1] "*Archaspistes*" "chief shield-bearer", i.e. defender of the faith. For other applications of this term, some of them ironical, see WATERLAND *Importance* **25** and n 1.

47[2] On 8 Oct 1830, talking about "the essential article of the Filial subordination in the Godhead", C made the same claim—that in their defence of this point, Bull and Waterland had made "the Church of England the classical authority on the subject of the Trinity even in the eyes of the Church of Rome itself": *TT* (*CC*) I 213.

ALARIC ALEXANDER WATTS
1797–1864

Poetical Sketches: The Profession; The Broken Heart, etc. with Stanzas for Music, and other poems. London 1823. 8°.

Victoria College Library (Coleridge Collection)

Inscribed on p ⁻2: "Samuel Taylor Coleridge Esq with the Author's very respectful Compliments". Description of volume by EHC in pocket mounted on p ⁺3 (p-d). Only a few gatherings at the beginning have been cut: pp [vi–vii], 41–8, 49–56, 59–64, 65–72, 83–6, 93–6, 99–102, 105–12, 113–20, 129–36, 139–42, 145–8 remain unopened, and it seems likely that C did not read beyond p 41.

DATE. Nov–Dec 1823? In *CL* v 311 (3 Dec 1823), C wrote to Watts to say that he had received and "in good part" read through the volume. C's remarks on a later edition (1828) are published in *SW & F* (*CC*) 1464–71.

1 p ⁻3, pencil

The Highland & probably Scotch History generally from Malcolm Ceamor (1050) to James VI, a remarkable instance of the contrast of public Acts which the Chronicler almost exclusively records—these full of atrocity—and the Virtues of private or internal Life proved by the long lineal Descents & enthusiastic Love & Fidelity to their patriarchal Chiefs—/[1]

1[1] There is no apparent connection between the contents of the vol and this note. C's reading in Scottish history, esp in Scottish church history—and esp in 1823, when he worked for a while on a biography of Robert Leighton—was fairly extensive. If the generalisations of this note were prompted by any particular text, it has not been identified, though the most likely candidate is Vol I of George Chalmers *Caledonia: or, An Account, Historical and Topographic, of North Britain* (3 vols London 1807–24), which C made some notes from in 1820–1: *CN* IV 4780. Chalmers's table of Scottish kings (I 375), which C noted, includes Malcolm-ceanor (d 1093), whereas other sources that C is known to have used either do not mention Malcolm or give his name in a form less closely resembling C's version.

JOHN WEBSTER
1610–1682

The Displaying of Supposed Witchcraft. Wherein is affirmed that there are many sorts of deceivers and impostors, and divers persons under a passive delusion of melancholy and fancy. But that there is a corporeal league made betwixt the devil and the witch, or that he sucks on the witches body, has carnal copulation, or that witches are turned into cats, dogs, raise tempests, or the like, is utterly denied and disproved. Wherein also is handled, the existence of angels and spirits, the truth of apparitions, the nature of astral and sydereal spirits, the force of charms, and philters; with other abstruse matters. London 1677. F°.

British Library C 126 l 10

Inscribed on the title-page in a 17th-century hand: "hunc librum perlegi" ("this book I have read through"). The Imprimatur, which originally faced the title-page, has been rebound to follow it, thereby dislocating the original pp $^-2/^-1$ to a remounted leaf following title-page and causing the substitution of a blank fly leaf (now pp $^-2/^-1$). On p $^-3$ (p-d) and on the recto of Imprimatur leaf (originally facing p-d), is written in the same hand an index entitled "A Table of Persons, Places and other Things". (Around the first page of this table C has written his note **1**.) Notes in this same hand are written on pp 69, 95–7, 103, 199, 240, 285–6, 309. Throughout the work, passages are marked with a star (not part of C's repertoire of symbols), probably by the same 17th-century owner, and on p 2 a passage is marked with a letter—again not by C.

Inscribed by John Duke Coleridge on recto of Imprimatur leaf: "C" and "Coleridge | Heath's Court | 1892 | This book belonged to S. T. C." The top of the title-page has been cut off, possibly to secure C's autograph signature.

At pp 70/71 a folded sheet of paper watermarked 1813 is tipped in, comprising objections to C's interpretation, and signed "Ch: Aug: Tulk": for the text, see **7** n 7. The marginalia may have been written for Tulk: certainly **47** is addressed to somebody unfamiliar with RS and the Cumberland setting.

MS TRANSCRIPT. VCL BT 21.

DATE. Oct 1819 and later: **3** is dated 27 Oct 1819, and a series of notebook entries of about the same time (*CN* IV 4611, 4618, 4619, 4621, 4622 and nn) comment on the same text. There appear to be two sets of ink notes, the pencil notes being written between: see **51** which refers to RS's *Life of Wesley* (2 vols 1820), and **31** which refers to "the late Mr. J. Kemble"; Kemble died in 1823.

1 p $^{-}$3 (p-d), written in a small space by the beginning of **2**

+ added to
x multiplied into
= equal to
⚹ opposite to
− less by

2 p $^{-}$3 (p-d)[a]

One good thing I have derived from my fondness for Old Books, that I estimate Men and Authors by qualities, that have the same worth & value, or the Contrary, in all ages; but which are more creditable to the Individual in proportion to the weaknesses and ignorance which he partakes of with his Age. Thus: I reverence the excellent good Sense of Webster & the sound Judgement, he displays, in his examination of the supposed Scripture Authority for Witches, all the more for the Helmontian Philosophy and Helmontian Credulity which he shared with his Age & even with the best & wisest of his Contemporaries.[1] The reliance on external testimony is, necessarily, in inverse proportion to the Canons and Measures of a priori Credibility furnished by Science, Scientific Experiment, and Observation guided and enlightened by Principles. Boyle & Webster might have been justified in believing what a very inferior Naturalist or Philosopher ⟨of our Times⟩ would deserve to be laughed at for even inquiring into. ~~the story.~~[2] S. T. Col[eridge][b]

3 p 17 | Ch 1

It hath been common almost in all Ages, not only for the vulgar, but also for the whole rabble of Demonographers and Witchmongers to ascribe those strange and wonderful effects, whether arising from Art or Nature, unto the worst of Gods Creatures, if they did not themselves understand their causes, and to censure the Authors that writ of them, as Conjurers

2[a] C has written his note in the space left by a ms index written in a 17th-century hand
2[b] Paper torn

2[1] Jean Baptiste van Helmont (1577–1644), Flemish physician and chemist. Webster cites him frequently as an authority, e.g. in **13**, **47**, **49** below. In a note of May 1818, C had recorded his dismay at the evidence of van Helmont's credulity and attempted to account for it psychologically as "a specific form of Mania . . . originating in the constant intension of the Mind on an imaginary *End*, associated with an immense variety of Means"; C's source, the *New Method of Chemistry* (1727) attributed to Boerhaave, less charitably described van Helmont as suffering from "distemper'd reveries": *CN* III 4414 and n.

2[2] The chemist Robert Boyle (1627–91), cited in **46**, was contemporary with Webster.

and Magicians, as I have made manifest in my former Instances, and might be further made good and illustrated by the effects of healing by the Weapon-salve, the Sympathetick Powder, the Curing of divers Diseases by Appensions, Amulets, or by Transplantation, and many other most admirable effects both of Art and Nature, which by these self-conceited Ignorants are all thrown upon the Devils back, and he made the Author and effector of them, as though he had a kind of omnipotent power . . .

Webster's ~~Creed~~ Belief will be thought by the Learned, yea and by the Unlearned, and above all by ⟨the⟩ numberless Half-learned of the present day, not less senseless and superstitious, than the Witch-monger Creed which he opposes. I dare confess myself of a different opinion, as far at least, as that I accede to the distinction of Physics into mechanical or mediate, and magical or immediate, agency—not unlike the difference between conducted and radiant Heat. By "immediate" I ~~in~~ do not exclude the possibility of an Intermediate; but mean only that the effect passes from A to b without any known tangible, visible, or ponderable interagent. Thus the Act of the Will on the nerves and muscles of my Arm & Fingers I call "magical" in the original and unsuperstitious use of the term.[1]

S. T. Coleridge, 27 Octr 1819.

4 p 18

Though these men should believe the power of the Devil to be great by his Creation, and not lessened by his Fall (which is doubtful or false) yet can he not exert, or put this power into execution, but when, where, as oft, and in what manner, as God doth send, order, direct, and command him: and could not enter into the herd of Swine, until that Christ had ordered and commanded him; nor to touch *Job* or afflict him either in his goods or body, until that God had given him licence and order with express limitation how far he should proceed, and no further.

The Satan (Circuitor) in the first Chapter of Job is merely the Attorney General, the accusing Angel—who acts only in his assigned Office.[1] The

3[1] C makes the same point in *CN* IV 4621, commenting on a passage further on (p 208, not annotated) in Webster, and saying, "Whatever acts, acts either with or without the sensuous phænomena of Contact—or Quicquid agit, agit vel mechanicè vel magicè [Whatever acts, acts either mechanically or magically]—for such (as I have a 1000 times observed) is the true and original as well as the only philosophical import of the word *magic*.—"

4[1] When God asks Satan in Job 1.7 what he has been doing, he replies that he has come "From going to and fro in the earth"; the Vulgate version is *circuivi terram*. In the Vulgate NT the same verb is used of the Devil (1 Pet 5.8, q in **9** textus), but C more than once makes a point of the difference

derivative Senses, from public Inspector ⟨& Reporter⟩ who goes his Circuits, to Spy/ or Informer; from Accuser to *false* Accuser & (diabolus); and thence to secret and common Enemy (hostis publicus, hostis humani generis, The Tempter ere the accuser of Mankind)[2] follow naturally, but are all of a later date than the composition of the Book of Job—Nor is there any necessity for supposeding the first Chapter, or the *Prologus* of this incomparable drama, or epico-dramatic Poem, to have been added by a later pen-man.[3] S. T. C.

5 p 27, pencil | Ch 2

[Quoting Thomas Ady *A Candle in the Dark* (1656):] "Witchcraft is a Devillish craft of seducing the people for gain, from the knowledge and worship of God, and from his truth, to vain credulity (or believing of lyes) or to the worshipping of Idols." . . . But against this Mr. *Glanvil* and the rest of his opinion will object and say, that it is hard and severe that Cheaters and Impostors should be ranked with Inchanters, and such as converse with Devils and with Idolaters, and that of this it is hard to give a reason.

The Objection is ludicrous: for it takes for granted the very thing denied, viz. converse with the Devil.

6 p 27, pencil

. . . we shall find that the Law was peremptory in point of adultery, which saith: *If a man be found lying with a woman married to an husband, then they shall both of them dye*. Now the act of copulation, as it is an act, is all one with a lawful wife, and with the wife of another man (that is, one generically considered) and yet the one is lawful, as agreeing with Gods Law and Ordinance, and the other is unlawful, sinful, wicked, and therefore to be punished with death, because it is an aberration from the Divine Ordinance, and contrary to the Command of God, who saith, *Thou shalt not commit adultery*.

Webster is quite right. The Caitiffs in question were guilty of High Treason/[1] Would not a General sentence to death an emissary employed in

between the Satan of Job 1 and the Devil or *diabolos*: see esp GREW **25** and n 3, also SWEDENBORG *De coelo* **21**. For Satan as Circuitor in Job see also John SMITH **7** and n 1.

4[2] The Latin means "Public enemy, enemy of humankind". "The Tempter, ere the accuser of Mankind" is Milton *Paradise Lost* IV 10.

4[3] C in general agrees with Eichhorn's account of the Book of Job, and was probably influenced by it: cf EICHHORN *Alte Testament* **51**, GREW **25** n 3, **26** and n 1.

6[1] Adultery has never been considered

tempting his Soldiers to desert to the enemy? And if this were notoriously done by pretended Harpers, Fiddlers, or Jugglers, would he not forbid all such men to come near his Camp, on pain of being shot—& put his law in execution on every such Vagrant whether come to seduce his men or not?

7 pp 69–70 | Ch 5

[Webster tells a story from Johannes Baptista Porta, "a great Naturalist, and a person of competent veracity", of a witch who was observed to anoint herself with an ointment which put her into a deep sleep in which she apparently dreamed of journeys and adventures which she reported, when she woke up, as having really taken place. While insensible she was also severely beaten, but retained afterwards no memory of the incident.]

This of Porta's is not the only well attested instance of the use of the Cataleptic properties of narcotic Ointments and Potions in the Pharmacy of the poor Self-bewitched. They are a traditional Derivati~~on~~ve from Pagan Antiquity (Pocula Circëia &c)[1] and even in the earliest mention of them seem, like most superstitions, to be the cadaver et putrimenta[2] of a defunct Natural Philosophy. In many respects the voluntary confessions of Witches would lead one to suppose that an empirical Animal Magnetism was in play; but there is this characteristic difference, that the magnetized Cataleptic retain no memory of what they said or imagined during their Trance.[3]

Q^y^. Might this difference arise from the Witches remaining unquestioned and unroused, unexcited ab et ad extra[4] during the magnetic torpor? Or by the continuance & sequelæ[5] of the narcotic Influence, so as not to afford any chasm, or abrupt transition into the waking & natural state? That Self-magnetism is in certain conditions, those indeed of the rarest occurrence, possible, has been rendered highly probable, at least. The cases of Behmen, Helmont, Swedenborg, and the assertions of Philo

---

tantamount to treason in Western law. C is exaggerating to make a point about the thinking behind the OT decree.

7[1] "Circeian draught": Cicero *Divinatio in Caecilium* 17.57. C liked to point out the resemblance between such accounts of folk magic and, on the one hand, the effects of animal magnetism or mesmerism in his own day and, on the other, the methods recorded of the holiest of the ancient oracles, e.g. in *P Lects* Lect 2 (1949) 105.

7[2] "Corpse and decaying parts". For C's use of the phrase in a similar context see *SW & F (CC)* 918.

7[3] For C's informed interest in the effects of animal magnetism or mesmerism see e.g. SOUTHEY *Wesley* **27** n 1.

7[4] "From and towards the outside", externally.

7[5] "Those that follow [from it]", consequences.

Judæus of himself, and Porphyry both of Plotinus and of himself might at all events receive a natural solution from the hypothesis.[6] Indeed, the best service which ~~the~~ mesmerism or zoomagnetism has yet done is that it enables us to explain the Oracles & a score other superstitions without recourse either to downright Self-conscious Lying and Imposture on the one side, or to the Devil and his Works on the other—reducing the whole of Dæmonology and Diabolography to Neuro-pathology.[7] S. T. C.—

8 p 73

Have there not been many thousands of true and faithful Martyrs, that have suffered and been condemned in many Ages, in many and several Countries, at many different and distinct times? And some of these have been condemned by such as were called and accounted General Councils, Parliaments, High-Courts of Justice, and other places of great Judicature, before Judges that were accounted wise, grave, and learned, and by Juries of honesty and understanding: were there therefore no true Martyrs, and were they all justly condemned and put to death? or is it absurd to be guilty of such incredulity, as to think and hold, that so many grave and wise Judges, and knowing Juries were deceived, and did unjustly?

To which add, that the will and purpose *were* in many instances malignant and devilish, and the effects on others too often real, tho' through the medium of their own imagination. If I wittingly & maliciously frightened a woman or child to death by optical Tricks, (Phantasmagoria)[1]

7[6] C identifies some of the famous figures whose accounts of supernatural experiences might, he thinks, be honourably explained as a form of "Self-magnetism" or a self-induced trance. For van Helmont see **2** above. Philo is not much given to self-revelation but he does eloquently describe the state of mind of "ecstasy and divine possession" in *Quis rerum divinarum heres* (*Who is the Heir of Divine Things*) 263–5. C annotated works by all the others named, and his notes sometimes raise the possibility of fraud or self-delusion: BÖHME esp **5**, **6**; PLOTINUS (including Porphyry's life of Plotinus) **4**, **5**, **6**; SWEDENBORG esp *De coelo* **4** and n 2. In FLEURY **57** C makes a distinction between Plotinus and Porphyry in this matter, maintaining that "Plotinus by magic intends and sanctions only Natural Philosophy" whereas "Porphyry was a strange Compound of Priest, Juggler, Scholar & Philosopher".

7[7] "Diabolography", "writing about the Devil", is not in *OED*; the first instance cited of "neuropathology" is from 1857. In a signed note—most probably a draft letter—tipped into the book at this point, C. A. Tulk takes exception to C's analysis of the oracles and other forms of spiritualism as a form of animal magnetism, as degrading at the same time "all those facts of a supernatural kind which are recorded in the Holy Scripture". He concludes, "I cannot but regret, my dear Sir, this reducing of all spiritual experience to the same dead level of zoomagnetism, when, as it appears to me, they are as discretely various as the affections, reason, and intelligence of man, and the mere animal passions, and instincts of the Brute."

8[1] The "phantasmagoria" was a fashion of the early 19th century, notably in the

should I not deserve the Gallows? And would it be any palliation or not rather an aggravation of my Crime that I had suffered myself to be persuaded that the person, who had taught me these tricks, had learnt them from the accursed Spirit and enemy of God and Man, and had actually, as far as in my power lay, i.e. in my will & full belief entered into the same contract in order to obtain the same knowlege for the same devilish and murderous purposes?—Whether the making especial Laws for this particular mode of poisoning was wise or no, and whether such Laws did not & must not multiply the crime, they meant to prevent, by confirming the imaginations of the people in the previous state, requisite ~~for~~ both for Witching and being bewitched, is another Question of easy solution; but which Judge & Jury were not concerned with.

9 p 75

Whatsoever the Devil worketh, it is to bring advantage to his own Kingdom or otherwise he should act in vain. But whatsoever he worketh by a visible Covenant, is not for the advantage of his own Kingdom: and therefore it is in vain. The major is plain from the Text: *Be sober, be vigilant, because your adversary the devil, as a roaring lion, walketh about, seeking whom he may devour, whom resist stedfast in the faith.**

* It is evident that St Peter[1] alludes to the Jewish Informers and Persecutors, who, as Paul confesses of himself, went about Christian-finding just as our Bigots from James I to James IInd went a *witch-finding*—and so refers to the double name of the Devil, Satan; i.e. Circuitor, and Diabolos i.e. false Accuser, Συκοφαντης,[2] slanderous Informer, the spiritual Father of those lying Bigots.[3]

10 p 76

. . . and therefore doth St. *Paul* warn *Timothy, That a Bishop must have a good report, lest he fall into the snare of the devil,* all Sins being the snares of the Devil . . .

i.e. lest he give an advantage to our common Slanderers & Accusers who lay snares for us in the spirit of the Devil.

1802 exhibition of optical illusions created mainly by means of the magic lantern.

9[1] In 1 Pet 5.8, q in textus.

9[2] "Sycophant" or informer—a word C traced to the act of exposing someone who traded illegally in figs, in *BL* ch 10 (*CC*) I 188*.

9[3] For Satan and *diabolus* see **4** and nn.

11 p 76

If the Witches be not superlatively mad . . . they will not make a League with the Devil, knowing him to be the Devil, because they cannot but know that he was and is a Lyar and a Murtherer from the beginning, and hath deceived many before them, that were of the same way and profession. And a visible appearance can afford them no certain security, but that he may and will deceive them still, and that he continueth a lyar and a deceiver. But while the delusion is internal, and the imagination depraved, and led by the suggestions and motions of Satan, they then are so blinded, that they see not, nor understand the danger they run into . . .

An excellent argument, and one that well deserves a full explanation in detail, from the nature of Sleep and sleep-like states—as the suspension of the Volition & Comparative Power, the entire passiveness of the mind to mental Images, as the effects not the causes of morbid sensations, and instantly passing away, most often even out of the Memory, as soon as the sensation is removed, as, for instance, by turning on the other side, or discharging the oppressive air from the stomach or lower Bowels.—

12 p 78

[Quoting Bishop Hall:] ". . . Who can be afraid of a muzled and tyed up Mastive? what woman or child cannot make faces at a fierce Lyon, or a bloody *Bajazet* lockt up fast in an Iron Gate? Were it not for this strong and strait curb of divine Providence, what good man could breathe one minute upon earth? The Demoniack in the Gospel could break his iron fetters in pieces, through the help of his Legion; those Devils that possessed him could not break theirs; they are fain to sue for leave to enter into Swine, neither had obtained it (in all likelihood) but for a just punishment to those *Gaderene* owners . . ."

Surely, never was there a more unfortunate instance of the false Light, in which a plain fact may be viewed & placed by the innocent prejudices of the Beholders! Our Lord miraculously cur~~ing~~ed an Epileptic Maniac, who in the moment preceding his cure prefers a request just such as a Mad *Jew* might be expected to have hit on. Our Lord bids him go about his business—he rushes amongst a herd of swine, frightens or perhaps drives one or more down ~~a~~ the Sea Cliff, the rest, as usual, follow and are drowned—& what we should now say metaphorically was then said by the Ignorant propriè[1]—Why! the Devil must have got into the Swine.

12[1] "In the proper sense", literally. C is responding to what appears to him to be a misrepresentation, in textus, of the episode of the Gadarene swine in Luke 8.26–36.

13 pp 78–9

This pretended League [between Devil and witch] must needs be a lye and a figment, because of the effects that are feigned to follow, as to have carnal copulation with the Devil, to raise storms and tempests, to flye in the air, and to kill men and beasts. For if these things be done, they are either performed by the Witches own natural power, or by the Devils. If by the Witches natural power, or the force of her resuscitated imagination and strength of will to work *ad nutum* [at a nod] (as *Van Helmont* seems to hold) then the Devil operateth nothing, but in playing the Imposter, and deceiving the Witch, and that he may easily do by internal and mental delusion, and needs no visible League to bring it to pass.

How very close Van Helmont seems to have been to the full discovery of Mesmerism, or theletic manipulation.[1] That the Will can extend its power, by some immediate vehicle or instrument secreted, accumulated, and directed by its own *intension*, beyond the surface of the visible Body, is evident in the Torpedo, Gymnotus, and other Aquatilia Electrica/[2] that there is an appropriate electrical apparatus in these animals does not prove that there need be one in so perfect an Organismus as the human, but on the contrary the multiplication of appropriate instruments the lower we descend in the scale of animal organization & in some proportion to the descent (thus, several of the Insect Tribes and the Crustacea are a perfect *Shop* of Tools) furnishes a str/ong analogical presumption against such necessity—not to say, that our present ignorance of a galvanöid structure in the human frame is no proof of its non-existence.—This point, I meant to observe, Helmont had in full and clear view; and he had himself accidentally discovered, that the root of the Napellus, & probably other vegetable Narcotics, was capable of specifically exciting the ganglia of the pectoral Region (Plexus Solaris) so as to alter the polarity of the Nervous System.[3] All that remained therefore for him to have ascertained was whether the *Will* (say of A) could act analogously i.e. as a narcotic, on the nervous system of B, the latter being previously disposed by natural or *for-the-purpose-induced*, disease, so as to bring about

13[1] I.e. manipulation "by the will". "Theletic" is not in *OED*. For mesmerism see **7** and nn; also n 5 below.

13[2] The "electric eel, and other electric water-creatures". Cf C's reference to the electric eel in a similar context in KLUGE **7** (and n 1).

13[3] In a famous experiment, Jean Baptiste van Helmont (for whom see **2** n 1) swallowed the vegetable poison aconite—from the root of wolfsbane, not *Napellus* or monkshood, but both are plants of the genus *Aconitum*—and reported that he felt himself thinking in his stomach. See *Van Helmont's Works* (1664) 274: this ed was in RS's library, though not acquired until 1835, after C's death.

the same excited state of the pectoral Ganglia. This would have completed the discovery after made by Mesmer. Whether the Will of A act directly on B, or by means of ~~an effluence~~ material tho' imponderable effluence from the body of A; or by a peculiar ⟨narcotic⟩ secretion from ~~the~~ his Skin, as Stieglitz supposes, and applies to cases of *Fanatical* Contagion in crowded *Preachings*, or by an organ of *Temperature* in the cutaneous Nervous Net-work, a Caloric sui generis,[4] as Schelling Conjectures; or by a nervous atmosphere as Humbold, Blumenbach, Soemmering & others; are ?s that belong to the Theory not to the *Facts*.[5]

14 p 82

. . . We are sure that in these late years that are past, when so many pretended Witch-finders were set abroad in *Scotland* and *Northumberland*, they never manifested, nor could verifie any such thing, but were found and discovered to be notorious Impostors and Knaves, pretending to discover Witches by putting sharp Needles or Pins into the Warts and hollow Excrescences of divers persons . . . . By which wicked means and unchristian practices divers innocent persons, both men and women lost their lives; and these wicked Rogues wanted not greater persons . . . that did authorize and incourage them in these Diabolical courses, as though this had been some way prescribed by God or his Word to discover Witches by . . .

Q^{y}. Whether Baxter lived long enough to read this Book? And whether if he had, he had any uncomfortable Twitches of Scepticism as to his outrageous Witch-fidianism—which thro' his agents and disciples, the two Mathers and others was the occasion of the barbarous Murder of so many Hundred Christians in England and in America![1]

13[4] "Of its own kind", unique.

13[5] Drawing upon his extensive reading in monographs and periodicals dealing with animal magnetism (see **7** n 3), C summarises theories that had been brought forward to explain it. He was particularly impressed by the way that a number of eminent scientists had repudiated their original scepticism, and several of the names he cites here appear in this context also in an essay that C wrote in 1817, perhaps as part of a projected encyclopedia entry on the subject (*SW & F*—*CC*—588–95); in *CN* IV 4622; and in letters of Nov–Dec 1818 (*CL* IV 883, 886). *TT* (*CC*) I 96 n 6 summarises the history of C's interest in the subject. Here he refers to theories proposed by Stieglitz in *Ueber den thierischen Magnetismus* (Hanover 1814), which C wrote to his bookseller about in 1816 (*CL* IV 666); by Karl Eberhard Schelling, whose work C read in *Jahrbücher der Medicin als Wissenschaft* (JAHRBÜCHER); and by Alexander von Humboldt and others (Humboldt's theory of "nervous atmosphere" being mentioned particularly by Stieglitz, 74–8).

14[1] Richard Baxter lived until 1691, so he could have known about this book. C's notes for Lect 12 of the 1818 series, a lecture on magic and witches, clarify the sources and context of the remarks he makes here. One of the works he drew on for that

15 pp 84–5

And such was that of *Lots* Wife, who looking back contrary to command, was turned into a Pillar of Salt . . . and this by the divine finger was a real transubstantiation,* especially in respect of her body, the substance of which was really changed into an absolute Pillar of Salt, without regression or turning back to what it was before . . .

* That is, she loitered on her way, was surprized by the Lava Shower, and became a statue of Salt—or dissolved as Salt would in a common Rain-storm.—Thus Niobe ~~was~~ became a statue of stone—i.e. was petrified with Horror & Grief. I hope—nay, I trust, I feel, I know, thanks be to my Redeemer to whom alone we owe Light and the glorious Liberty of the Gospel,—that my Faith as a Christian would not be much hazarded even tho' I should extend a similar interpretation to the Egyptian Magi[1]—I am at least strongly inclined to believe that the account in the first documents, was written or insculpt in hieroglyphic symbols, and referred to *Predictions* chiefly—so that we may throughout render the words—& this the Priests had likewise predicted in their Almanacs, or meteoro- and astro-logical Reports to the Government.—

16 pp 101–3, pencil, P.S. in ink

The whole strength of the Christian Religion consists in the certainty of Christs Resurrection in his true and individual body. For as the Apostle argueth: *And if Christ be not risen, then is our preaching vain, and your faith is also vain: yea and we are found false witnesses of God, because we have testified of God, that he raised up Christ: whom he raised not up, if so be that the dead rise not.*

God forbid! I believe in the true death of Christ, and in his Ascension/ and on these two articles it *may* perhaps be said that the *History* of Christ as ~~d~~ to its supernatural character depends—But the strength of the Christian *Religion* is Faith and Love—Faith in our Redemption by the incarnate Word; & Love even unto Death for this stupendous Mercy. The pas-

---

lecture, Francis Hutchinson *An Historical Essay Concerning Witchcraft* (1718) 72–94 attributed the Salem witch trials in part to the fact that Cotton Mather had encouraged New Englanders to read Baxter's *The Certainty of the World of Spirits* (1691) "as a Book that was *Ungainsayable*": *Lects 1808–1819* (*CC*) II 206–7 and n 47. For C's knowledge of other works by them see BAXTER and MATHER.

15[1] The contest between the magicians of Egypt, on the one hand, and Moses and Aaron on the other (Exod 7.10–8.19) is the next example of false and legitimate transformations offered by Webster; eventually the magicians themselves gave up, saying, "This is the finger of God" (Exod 8.19).

sage in St Paul is exceedingly obscure to us from our ignorance of the particular Tenets of those, whom he here reprehends. It seems probable, that they were a species of Docetæ, who would not believe that so divine a Being as the Æon, Christ, could *die*—that he but *appeared* to die on the cross, &c/ that men might conquer *Death* by a voluntary dying to the Body, and become living Spirits. To these fancies St Paul's is a fair reply.[1] If the dead will not rise, then Christ did not rise—& vice versâ—but if this were true, if we are to expect a glorification only in this Life, we are of all men the most wretched—for such transformations and analogies to the refinement and spiritualization of Christ's Body during the interval from his Interment to his ascension, none but Fanatics and Visionaries can have faith in.—Then he proceeds to answer their objections to the resurrection of the Dead.

[a]I fear too, that in § 3. Web^r has conjured up more spirits of Doubt than seem to have been in *his* power to *lay*: or in any man's who assumes that a fact, known from a history only, is the *whole* strength (i.e. ground & key-stone) of the whole X^n Religion.[2]

17 p 105

And consequently that what strange things soever we may by sight and touch take to be the apparitions of Spirits, that to touch have the solidity of flesh and bones, we must conclude that they are not Spirits, but must be some other kind of Creatures, of whose nature and properties we are to inquire; for doubtless (as we shall manifest hereafter) there are many strange Creatures, that for their rarity or strange qualities, have been and are mistaken for the apparition of Spirits.

Webster evidently shrinks from the argument built on the tri-angelic visit to Abraham.[1] I feel, as he felt, that it is a *captious* argument—but cap-

16[a] From here the note continues in ink

16[1] C is imagining the historical context of Paul's statement in 1 Cor 15.14–15, q in textus. For the Docetae, who taught that Christ only *appeared* to suffer as a man, see FLEURY **98** and n 3.

16[2] In para 3 p 102, Webster considers the Apostles' attempts to understand in natural terms the miracles of Christ's walking on water and his resurrection. This may be the passage to which C refers, but more probably it is para 3 p 105, where Webster quotes the same passage from St Paul as has been under discussion here: "3. Therefore [to believe] that Demons do appear in the shape of Dogs, Cats, and the like . . . must suppose them to have bodies as solid and tangible as flesh and bones: and so overthrow the main proof of our Saviours Resurrection, and consequently the very foundation of the Christian Religion; *For if Christ be not risen our faith is vain, we are yet in our sins, and are of all men most miserable*, as having only hope in this life, and no further."

17[1] Webster is trying to make the case that there is a vital difference between the

tious arguments must nevertheless be answered; were it but for this cause, that their force commonly consists in some erroneous Tenet taken for granted by both parties. Hence indeed it becomes *captious*: for if it applies against A in one point, it is of equal or perhaps greater annoyance to B. in the support of his own system, in other points. But what is that to me? might a third party say, the Deists for instance. The argument in itself is good: its captiousness is an accident arising from the temper and circumstances of the Arguer, as a Christian versus Christian.—

In this case I, as a third party and yet I trust no less Christian than either of the two others, should demand of Webster, by what right he converted a [? solid] natural argumentum ad homines atque ex concessis[2] into a universal and necessary position. Our Lord argued with his Disciples from their own grounds—the only sort of argument that would have been at all to the purpose.—[3]

18 p 138 | Ch 7

There ought a due comparison be made with the judgments and sentiments of other Interpreters, according as the Apostle saith: *That no Prophecie of Scripture is of any private interpretation:* Which ought to be rendered as learned *Beza* and Dr. *Hammond* give it: "No Prophecie of Scripture is *propriae incitationis*, of a Mans own or proper incitation, motion, or loosing forth . . ."

I prefer Baxter's Sense, that the Scripture Prophecies are not to be interpreted of Individual Persons or single Events[1]—for instance, the Prophe-

---

apparition of evil spirits—which are visible but not tangible—and the truly miraculous appearances of Christ. On p 105 he addresses the potential objection about the angels that appeared to Abraham (Gen 18): "And if any do object (as we have heard some do) that three Angels did appear unto *Abraham* in the Plains of *Mamre*, as he sate in the Tent-door, and did eat and drink, and washed their feet, and therefore that they had flesh and bones; to that we return this responsion." He argues that it is not fair to bring texts in scripture to contradict one another; that the Old Dispensation was another matter; that the three angels had divine support; and that probably in fact one of them was the Son.

17[2] "Directed at particular individuals and based on premises that have already been granted".

17[3] On p 103, Webster states that Christ himself answered doubts about his resurrection by allowing Thomas to touch his body. According to him, Christ's teaching on the issue was plain: "1. He doth not at all deny the existence or beings of Spirits; neither that Spirits do not, or cannot make visible apparitions: but doth grant both. 2. But he restrains these apparitions to those inseparable properties that belong to Bodies and Spirits, that is, a body (that is to say an humane body) hath flesh and bones, but a Spirit hath neither, as Christs or humane bodies have . . .".

18[1] The text at issue is 2 Pet 1.20. C had already written about Baxter's "sound & irrefragable" interpretation—"That none of these Scriptures that are spoken of Christ the publick Person, must be interpreted as spoken of *David* or any other private Per-

cies concerning Antichrist may have been fulfilled in Paganism or as others think in Popery; but it is fanatical and by this text forbidden to apply them to any one Pope or Emperor in particular.

19 p 138

And again, *Hath not God made foolish the wisdom of this world?* σοφίαν τοῦ κόσμου τούτου [the wisdom of this world]. And the words of the Hebrew in that place of *Isaiah* do signifie all that height of wisdom or understanding, that Men either have by Nature, or acquire by Art and Industry.

O no! no! At least, not without limitation.—Had W. said all the intellect and philosophy (for this is the proper rendering of σοφια)[1] which is merely intelligential, excluding the moral postulate or *faith*—I should have agreed with him.

20 p 139, pencil

There is another rule which the learned do use, in expounding of the Scriptures, which is often either too far extended, or not rightly limited and applied, which is this: That Men in interpreting of the Scriptures should keep close to the literal sense, if it include not an absolute absurdity.

N.B. To *compare* historically the persecutions of the Lutherans & Calvinists with those of the Papists & Arminians.[1]

21 p 139

It is apparent that our Saviour Christ cured the Man that was born blind, and the means and manner is described . . . . But it were absurd so far to stick to the letter, as to believe that clay, and spittle, and washing in the poole *Siloam*, were true and real natural means to produce that effect; no, that were absurd, and therein the literal sense is not to be followed.

[a]⟨The note below reminds me of poor Woolston's fate; and that of the pers. spirit especial in the Arminians./—⟩[1]

21[a] This afterthought is written in pencil in the outer margin above the body of the note (which already filled the outer margin and foot-margin)

---

sons only, of whom they were mentioned but as Types of Christ"—in BAXTER *Reliquiae* COPY B **63**.

19[1] *Sophia* "wisdom".

20[1] C speculates about the historical consequences of the extreme positions that Webster sketches out—Protestant reliance upon the Scriptures and Romanist reliance upon the authority of the Church.

21[1] C appears to be referring to his own

But neither does the *Letter* of the Evangelist imply this. The *mode* of this miracle is so evidently intended to be emblematic, that it may at once illustrate and confirm a similar interpretation of many, nay, of most of the others. In *addition* to their miraculous character, and verity as facts and actions, our Lord's *Signs* were all *significant*: and in this divine quality *peculiar* to the Miracles of Christ do they become proper and harmonious Parts of the everlasting Gospels. As *mira* et verè *miranda*[2] they belonged principally to the unconverted Eye and Ear-witnesses, the Countrymen and Contemporaries of Jesus—both drawing their attention, mercifully agitating the~~ir~~ stagnant sediment of their prejudices, and at last leaving them without excuse of any kind; but as perfect Symbols of the Religion, Ideals of the divine Ideas, and partaking in their everlastingness, they belong to Believers.

22 p 140, pencil

. . . but Satan is bound *in chains of everlasting darkness*, and therefore cannot be said literally to appear in person before God, but by way of a Metaphor. So when the Angel telleth the Virgin *Mary*, that she should conceive in her womb, and she not understanding how that should come to pass, because she had not known Man, the Angel answered, the *Holy Ghost shall come upon thee, and the power of the highest shall overshadow thee*. Though the matter of fact be an undoubted truth, and an Article of Faith, literally so taken; yet the manner of the Holy Ghosts coming upon her, and the power of the highest overshadowing her, cannot be understood in a literal sense . . . but after a Metaphorical sense, and a most mystical meaning.

It is noticeable that no reference or allusion is made to this in all the N.T. except a suspicious gloss of one word (*supposed*) in our Copies of Luke—[1]

---

note (following), to which this insertion is a pencilled afterthought. Thomas Woolston (1670–1747), who wrote in favour of allegorical interpretations of scripture (Webster's topic in this section of his work), died in prison after being convicted of blasphemy—some thought, led on by William Whiston and others who would not run such risks themselves. C's comment may also have been influenced, however, by the account of Ahab further down on the same page, C taking Woolston's case as an example of the kind of "persecuting spirit" he detects among the Arminians: "Again concerning Ahab, thus much is literally true in matter of fact that he was perswaded to go up to *Ramoth-Gilead* by his false Prophets in whose mouths there was a lying Spirit."

21[2] "*Wonders* and truly *things to be wondered at*".

22[1] I.e. the parenthetic addition in Luke 3.23, "And Jesus himself began to be about thirty years of age, being (as was supposed) the son of Joseph".

23 Title-page, referring to p 142, pencil

Allegories may be used, and the literal sense nevertheless preserved also for the History is literally true that *Sarah* and *Hagar* were two living Women, the one *Abrahams* Wife a free Woman, the other his Servant, and a bond-woman, and yet this did not hinder but that thereby an Allegory might be used, and they might, and did signifie and express another thing than what was meerly contained in the letter.

142. Allegory & yet traditionally true.

24 p 145

Moses . . . doth purposely intitle the Devil by the name of a Serpent, because (by his effectual creeping into the interiour senses, as also by infecting Mens minds with venomous perswasions) he doth very lively represent the nature, disposition and qualities of the venemous Serpent.

Da pater, augurium, animisque *illabere* nostris. Verg. En. L. 3.[1] The Serpent coiling round the Club of Esculapius, and the little woman on one side in Tooke's Pantheon.—Q[y] taken from any antique Gem or Bas Relief?[2] If so, not improbably ⟨a⟩ Transpict from some Hieroglyphic of Eve, the Tree, the Serpent, and the Jehovah, the Healer, afterwards sent to the shades for raising from the Dead; but re-ascending & deified.

25 p 146

For neither can the going upon her belly, nor the eating of dust be any punishment at all to the natural Serpent, because (before the tentation) both those properties were peculiarly allotted unto her . . .

But *are* Serpents pulverivorous?[1]

24[1] "Grant, Father, an omen, and glide into our hearts": Virgil *Aeneid* 3.89 var, q in exactly this form in *CN* IV 4618 (Oct 1819), also in association with Webster and (n 2) with Tooke's *Pantheon*.

24[2] Andrew Tooke *The Pantheon, Representing the Fabulous Histories of the Heathen Gods, and Most Illustrious Heroes* (many editions from 1698) was a familiar textbook, and C probably recalled from his own schooldays the plate illustrating Aesculapius that he describes here. See Plate 2. What edition C used is not known; the 23rd, of 1771, has some claims (*CN* III 3683n). The image is not fully explained in the accompanying text (Tooke does not, for instance, account for the little hooded female figure), and C adapted it to his own purposes, using it in 1804 to compliment HD (*CL* II 1042) and in 1819—in a note that corresponds to this one at several points—to gloss the OT story of the Fall (*CN* IV 4618). There is no indication either in Tooke or in the Latin original by François Pomey as to whether the image was based on an "antique Gem or Bas Relief": C may have been recalling the engraving of a very similar figure from a bas-relief in Joseph Spence *Polymetis* (2nd ed 1755) 133 and Plate XX fig 3.

25[1] "Dust-eating"—a nonce-word not in *OED*.

2. Plate xxv from Andrew Tooke *The Pantheon* (1771)
See WEBSTER **24** and n 2
The British Library; reproduced by kind permission

26 p 149

The only objection worth taking notice of that *Pererius* bringeth . . . is this: That *Adam* and *Evah* being in the state of innocency could not be wrought upon by an interiour tentation, because that neither the sensitive appetite nor the phantasie were corrupted; and therefore Satan could not internally work upon them, and therefore that the whole tentation must be extrinsecal.

I should affirm now the very contrary—namely, that they could be acted on ab intra—vel internè.[1]

27 p 155, pencil

As for the changing water into blood, and the producing of Frogs, they were so easy to be done after the same manner [by trickery or sleight of hand] . . . that they need not any particular explanation . . .

What? *all* the waters of all Egypt?[1] For this is asserted, and less than this could have deceived no one, after this had been done./

28 p 155, pencil

[Glossing Exod 7.11, 22 and 8.7, 18, where "the Magicians . . . did so with their enchantments", Webster explains that the Magicians] were deeply skilled in natural and lawful Magick (as generally the *Aegyptians* and the Eastern Nations were) though they did use and apply it to an evil end, namely the resisting the power of Gods miracles wrought by *Moses* and *Aaron* . . .

Well done, Webster! Thou hadst a fine specific incredulity, a sort of Witchphobia, that yet left the throat in full possession of its swallowing faculty in all other points.[1]

29 pp 184–5, first sentence in pencil | Ch 9

[Webster outlines six arguments to show] a simple and absolute impossibility, that God should be the author of sin . . .

These Arg. form the most whimsical Logic![a1]

29[a] Last word partly overtraced in ink

26[1] "From within—or internally".

27[1] Exod 7.20: "all the waters that were in the river were turned to blood".

28[1] I.e. Webster can still swallow anything: his credulity is unimpaired.

29[1] Webster argues as follows: (1) the Scriptures explicitly deny that God is "the author of sin or evil"; (2) his perfection precludes it; (3) he is under no law, therefore cannot be said to transgress; (4) he hates sin;

[b]The absurdity implied in the obvious and apparently inevitable consequences of a controverted Position is brought to prove—what? the falsehood of the Position itself, of course.—No! but that the consequences are not the consequences of the Position. As if A should deny that $7\frac{1}{2} + 7\frac{1}{2} = 30$, because the consequence would be that half a crown would be equal to a whole Crown; & B. in reply should set forth vehemently the excessive absurdity, aye, & improbability of half being equal to the whole, and thence conclude that it could not follow from 15 being equal to 30.—

30 p 186

. . . and *Job* tells us: *If he gather unto himself his spirit and breath, all flesh shall perish together, and man shall turn again into dust.**

* Here in the most ancient work, the precious relique of patriarchal Philosophy, as elsewhere in the old Testament, the idea of creation begins with CHAOS, i.e. ⟨universal⟩ indistinction, and that of annihilation extends no further than to DUST, i.e. indistinction in relation to particulars: but yet God is every where represented as the Ground and Origin of all things, even of Chaos itself. Let Chaos represent the mere state of potentiality, the necessary result of the Apostasy or the Spiritual Fall—& so it should be. Thus ~~we~~ are solved the otherwise insurmountable difficulties of Creation e nihilo,[1] on the one hand, and the free will of the Creature, which, were there nothing not creaturely in the creature, would be impossible: and th/us do Scripture & true Philosophy reciprocally confirm each other. *S. T. C.*

31 p 202 | Ch 10

. . . we do here once for all exclude and except forth of our discourse and arguments the humane and rational Soul as not at all to be comprised in these limits . . . . Because I find *Solomon* the wisest of Men making this question: *who knoweth the spirit of man, that goeth upward: and the spirit of the beast, that goeth downward to the earth?**

* There can be little doubt, I should think that Ecclesiastes was written after the age of Alexander the Great. As to its being Solomon's—~~it~~ this

29[b] From here the note continues in ink

(5) all things that he created are good; and finally (6) "That which God is the author of, doth not make Man worse, but sin doth make Man worse, therefore God is not the author of it."

30[1] "Out of nothing".

is a supposition as rational as Garrick's *being* King Lear, or the late Mr J. Kemble Macbeth. The mono-dramatist announces his part—I am Solomon, he that *was* King at Jerusalem.[1]

32 pp 208–9

If Angels be absolutely incorporeal, then they cannot be contained or circumscribed in place, and consequently can perform no operation in Physical things. To which if they answer with *Thomas Aquinas: Quod circumscribi terminis localibus est proprium Corporum, sed circumscribi terminis essentialibus, est commune cuilibet Creaturae, tam corporali, quam spirituali* [That it is proper to bodies to be circumscribed in terms of space, but limitation in terms of essence is common to all created things whether corporeal or spiritual]; This aiery distinction might have taken place, if *Aquinas* had shewed us what essential terms and limitations are, but of this we have no proof at all, and what was never proved may justly be denied.

I deny that it is *aery*—~~the~~ mind has no relations of space; but the human mind is finite quoad the *human* mind, i.e. term. essent. Ӿ term. local.—Ӿ means in contradistinction from—

[a]But the whole of Webster's Reasoning is a tissue ~~of~~ quorum pro quibus:[1]—the confusion of Reason with Understanding, of Ideas with Conceptions, is the first Quid pro Quo, and the Source of all the rest.[2] 2nd—the antithesis of Spirit to Body, instead of Matter, tho' he himself quotes St Paul's Spiritual Body.[3] Spirit = id quod subsistit et non videtur. Materia = id quod mere videtur. Corpus = et substat et videtur, vel Spir: + Materia.[4] It would be tedious to go thro' the rest. Enough, that

32[a] Change of ink and hand—an afterthought

31[1] C makes the same point, drawing probably on Eichhorn, in BIBLE COPY B **51** (and see n 1): Eccles is to be considered a drama composed centuries after the reign of Solomon himself, the speaker adopting the role of the great king. C this time offers theatrical examples closer to home: David Garrick (1717–79) and John Philip Kemble (1757–1823), who had played the parts of Shakespeare's kings.

32[1] I.e. of quid pro quos, as C goes on to say—errors created when one thing is substituted for another.

32[2] Webster uses "reason" where C would say "understanding", and treats the imagination as a faculty of "reason" in this reduced sense, e.g. pp 206, 209. For the proper distinction between reason and understanding, see SCHELLING *Denkmal* **16** n 1; for that between ideas and conceptions, see SOUTHEY *Wesley* **13** n 2.

32[3] Webster alludes to St Paul with the phrase "spiritual bodies" p 210, but does not actually quote 1 Cor 15.44.

32[4] "Spirit = that which subsists and is not apparent; matter = that which is only apparent; body = that which both subsists and is apparent, or Spirit + Matter." For other versions of this three-way distinction see JAHRBÜCHER **25** and n 5, TENNEMANN **52** n 1.

by the very same arguments he might have proved that the *Word*, Soul, *is* the Soul; because we cannot think without words. ~~The freq~~ Add therefore, 3. the confusion of Imagination with Conception.—Imagination, i.e. Construction in Space, is the innate Language of the human Mind—of which no better proof need be given than that we express qualities & *in*tensities by visual quantities, and figured *ex*tension—a *high* note, a *low* note, a *brilliant* passage in a musical Composition.—

Nevertheless, Webster is right in his position—Whatever is finite & in communion with other finites has, ipsis terminis,[5] a *body*.[6]

33 p 209[a]

And now let us examine the objections that are usually brought against this opinion, the strongest of which is to this purpose; that if Angels be Corporeal, then of necessity they must be mortal, alterable and destructible; to which I answer. 1. Because no creaturely Nature is or can be immortal . . . Therefore the Angels whether corporeal or incorporeal, are not immortal . . .

Pity, that W. had not asked himself, whether the objective reality of Angels, as a separ⟨a⟩te *Genus* of Creatures, is any where taught in Scripture preceptively & as a revealed Fact, or only spoken of allusively, as an admitted popular Belief, in which the Writers participated? Reason decides with Augustin, that there are but three diverse kinds, ἕτερα γενῆ,[1] ~~poss~~ conceivable—God, Man, and Brute—the absolute Reason, the finite Rational, the finite Irrational.[2]

34 p 210

. . . even as he doth preserve and conserve the bodies of the Saints <u>in their Graves</u>* until the general Resurrection, and in the World to come doth keep them in immortality . . .

33[a] This note fills the space following **32** and may be a continuation of it, but the ink is different

32[5] "By its own limitations": see textus.

32[6] *CN* IV 4619, 4621 contain further comment on pp 207–11.

33[1] "Diverse kinds".

33[2] On the absence of scriptural authority for the existence of angels, especially fallen ones, see OXLEE **6** and n 4, SHERLOCK **53** and n 8. For the dictum attributed to Augustine (which has yet to be satisfactorily traced in his works) see Isaac TAYLOR *Natural History* **3** n 1. Webster himself, however, quotes (p 212) a passage from a work associated with and once attributed to Augustine (*De spiritu et anima* ch 8: Migne *PL* XL col 784) that could be construed as confirming the position C describes.

* How is it possible that Webster could have written these 3 words without remembering S[t] Paul's vehement ["]Thou *Fool*! *not* that which goeth into the Grave riseth again"—& hastily erasing them?[1]

The immortality of the Ειμι,[2] or principle of Individuality, is a deeper subject, than Webster could even distinctly propose to himself! At all events, it is an unsafe practice that of citing single Flights of Devotional Poetry from Scripture, as authorities for metaphysical dogmata. How easily might an Enthusiast ground the pernicious doctrine of Pantheism, or that of God as being the universal Soul diversely modulated in diverse bodies, in the same words!

35 p 211

. . . *Aquinas*, and the rest of the Scholastick <u>rabble</u> . . .

unworthy of a man like Webster.

36 p 211

. . . *Who maketh his Angels spirits: his ministers a flaming fire*. From whence they [the Schoolmen] would positively conclude that they are spirits, and absolutely incorporeal; but fail of their purpose for these clear reasons. 1. The Text there cannot be rationally understood of their creation, or of their creaturely nature, but of their offices and administrations . . . . And again the word רוח [*ruach*, breath] doth not alwaies or of necessity signifie an incorporeal thing but that which is a body, as the winds, and so doth *Luther* and diverse others render it . . .

There is one sense of Ruach (Spirit) and this of most frequent occurrence, in which it may be elucidated from the best if not only philosophical division of Bodies in Chemistry—viz. 1. Combinants, which we might call Spirits—Oxygen, the Magnetic; and the Electric Aura, Light, Heat. 2. Bases, including all the Metals, with Carbon and Azote. 3. Amphoterics, that are sometimes Spirits to Bases, sometimes Bases to Spirits—Hydrogen, Phosphorus—Chlorine? Iodine?/ A Spirit is not a Soul or a Life; but a Soul, a *Life*, may be the *Base* or Suppositum of a Spirit.

37 p 212

They can no more be meerly and literally said to be spirits, understanding spirit to intend an absolute incorporeal substance, than his ministers

34[1] C paraphrases 1 Cor 15.36: "Thou fool, that which thou sowest is not quickened, except it die".

34[2] *Eimi* "I am".

can be literally understood to be flaming-fire, they must either be both literally true, which is absolutely absurd, or else those words must have a metaphorical interpretation, as they may and must have, and there is no inconvenience in that exposition.

This habit of taking the rhetorical accomodations of St Paul & the Author of the Ep. to the Hebrews (probably, Apollos)[1] as the actual meaning of the texts quoted may be reckoned among the minor causes of false Doctrine. As well might we adopt Burke's application of Milton's Description of Death to the Kingly Office as framed by the ~~National Convention~~ Constituent Assembly of France for the Poet's actual meaning.[2] The far more probable Rendering of the Hebrew would be—He maketh the winds his Messengers, and the flaming fire his ministers[3]—or (still better) ~~He~~ and Fire and Flame the Executors of his Commands.—

38 p 226 | Ch 11

[Quoting from Amesius:] "They [Devils] are said to be reserved to damnation, because they are so bound up in these evils and miseries, that they never can escape; and they are hereafter *to go into that everlasting fire, that is prepared for the Devil, and his Angels*."

Poor Devils! I am sure, it makes my heart ake to read about it.

S. T. C.

39 pp 234–5, pencil

[Quoting Stillingfleet with regard to "the Message of *Jonah* to *Nineveh: yet forty days, and Nineveh shall be overthrown*":] "Comminations of judgments to come do not in themselves speak the absolute futurity of the event, but do only declare what the persons to whom they are made are to expect . . . . Comminations do speak only the *debitum poenae*, and the

37[1] C may have learnt of Luther's "happy conjecture" that Apollos was the true author of Heb from Eichhorn : see Bible copy b **134** n 1, Irving *Sermons* **5** n 4.

37[2] In Milton's description of Death in *Paradise Lost* II 672–3, "What seem'd his head, / The likeness of a kingly crown had on". Burke quotes the passage that includes these lines (II 666–73) as an admirable example of the use of obscurity, in his *Philosophical Enquiry into the Origin of our Ideas of the Sublime and Beautiful* (*Works*—1792–1827—I 122); he comments disapprovingly on the first National Assembly in France, in *Reflections on the Revolution in France* (*Works* III 68–78); but he does not appear ever to have put the two together and described the Assembly in terms of Milton's lines about Death. C however makes a similar attribution in Eichhorn *Apocalypse* copy a **10**.

37[3] C offers his own translation of the verse at issue, Ps 104.4 "Who maketh his angels spirits; his ministers a flaming fire".

necessary obligation to punishment; but therein . . . God is not bound to necessary performance of what he threatens."

Aye! but where is the evidence that the threat did come from God? And can mercy to one man or city countervail the injury done to all by weakening the conception of the ~~divine~~ immutability of the divine word? Granted, that a *Threat* confers no right—yet this was no mere threat, but a positive declaration. And after all, is not the whole Book of Jonas a manifest Apologue or Parable, in which Jonas represents the People of Israel—& so beautiful an Apologue, so concinnous and squaring in all its part[a] to the characteristics of the Nation, which it shadows out, that it would be almost miraculous if it were a mere coincidence of Chance.[1]

40 p 236, pencil

We may observe that how great soever these signs and wonders be, yet they are but lying ones, both in regard of the end for which they are done, and in respect of their substance. And therefore how great soever the signs and wonders be that evil Angels do perform, yet they are totally different from true miracles . . .

i.e. there are no true miracles but in *my* Religion, those namely of the Apostolic Age—says the low Church Protestant! None after the third Century, says the High Church Protestant! None but in the bosom of the holy Roman Catholic Church, & there they continue—says the Papist.—Thick as Hops in all religions, says the Brahmin.

41 p 236, pencil

Therefore what signs and wonders soever Satan doth work, they are no real and true miracles, for as Dr. *Stillingfleet* saith: "God alone can really alter the course of nature."

Alas! who does not know this? But teach us what does really alter the Course of Nature? How do I know, that raising bodies from what *we* now call death may not 500 years[a] cease to be a miracle just as our raising what the ancients called death, has—saving and excepting the self-complimentary metaphors of the Humane Society?—[1]

39[a] For "parts" **41**[a] Perhaps for "in 500 years"

39[1] C interprets Jonah in the same way in BÖHME **180**, LUTHER *Colloquia* **86**, *AR* (*CC*) 264*.

41[1] Founded in 1774 as the Society for the Recovery of Persons Apparently Drowned, the Humane Society renamed itself in 1776.

42 p 237, pencil

Such ["true miracles"] were the taking of *Enoch* and *Elias* into Heaven, the conserving of *Noah* and his Family in the Ark, the confusion of tongues at the building of *Babel*, the fecundity of *Sarah* being old and barren, the passage of the children of *Israel* over the red Sea and over *Jordan*, the standing still of the Sun in the Battel of *Joshuah*, its going back in the dial of *Ahaz*, its eclipse at our Saviours suffering, the preservation of *Daniel* in the Den of the Lions, and of the three companions of *Daniel* in the fiery furnace, the preserving *Jonas* in the belly of the Whale, the raising up of the dead, and the curing of the Man born blind, and all the rest of those most true and wonderful miracles wrought by our blessed Saviour and his Apostles.

What a farrago the man has brought together— 1. a Hebrew metaphor for a Cenotaph. 2. A providential act. 3. A mistranslation. 4. No miracle, mirum, haud miraculum.[1] 4. A providential series of events. 5. A quotation from a War Ode. 6. The true sense of the Passage doubtful. 7. Not necessarily an eclipse, & if it were, yet the *Date* uncertain. 8. 9. and 10. manifest fables.—11, 12, and 13 the only ones that have a fair claim to the name of miracle, according to the Author's own definition.[2]

43 p 239, pencil

1. It is <u>manifest</u> that in the times of our Saviours being here upon earth, and his Disciples, that there were many Demoniacks or Men possessed with Devils, or Men that were devillished, or over whom the Devil exercised an effective and ruling power, . . .

manifest? Say rather, contrary to clear History, & without even a hint in the N.T.—[1]

42[1] "A marvel, but hardly a miracle".

42[2] Besides quoting Stillingfleet's criterion (in **41** textus), Webster asserts (p 236) that God's miracles "are alwayes true and real, being against and above the whole power and course of nature, but those wonders wrought by Satan . . . do but all arise from natural causes . . .". C has assigned numbers to Webster's catalogue of miracles—inadvertently using "4" twice, for Sarah's late pregnancy (Gen 18.11–14) and then for the crossing of the Red Sea (Exod 14.21–31)—in order to record naturalistic explanations that had been proposed for the alleged miracles of the OT by writers such as Lessing and Eichhorn. For his lifelong interest in miracles and especially his awareness of the danger of relying on miracles as "evidences" of religion see also LIGHTFOOT **2** n 1, *Friend* (*CC*) I 431 and nn, *SW & F* (*CC*) 209–11.

43[1] C's sceptical remark is perhaps a result of the controversy about the "demoniacs" or stories of possession by devils in the NT that was carried on after Webster's time, in the mid-18th century, by such writers as Farmer and Lardner.

44 p 242 | Ch 12

[An account of an innkeeper's daughter giving a bewitched apple to a nobleman she loved, and of the generation of frogs from the apple. Webster concludes that this was not magic, but "secret poysoning".]

A good fat lie. Webster's Soli-fidianism (—for *non*) contrasted with his Omnifidence this Witch point excepted, is really *humorous*.[1]

45 p 243

[Webster tells the story of a garment, bitten by a rabid dog, that subsequently engenders "Worms altogether like little Whelps in the head".] . . . the Dog doth with his teeth catch hold of her Garment . . . and did bark a little while, and forthwith ran away.

Mad dogs never bark; but are either dumb or moan & howl.[1]

46 p 248

[Robert Boyle reports the case of a "bewitched" baby who would neither sleep nor suck until a piece of iron—"this noble mineral"—was hung "about the infants neck, so that it might touch the pit of the Stomach".] "And though I am not forward (he saith) to impute all these diseases to Witchcraft, which even learned Men father upon it; yet its considerable in our present case, that whatsoever were the cause of the disease, the distemper was very great, and almost hopeless, and the cure suddenly performed by an outward application, and that of a Mineral, in which compacted sort of bodies the finer parts are thought to be lockt up."

Q^{y}. Magnetic Iron? That the magnet has strong action on the skin & thro' it on the stomach & nervous system was put beyond rational Doubt, by the Physicians to whom Louis XVIth committed the investigation, and who denied utterly, and I fear not without personal Malignity, the *animal* Magnetism of Mesmer.[1] These reported with detail of their experiments

44[1] On the question of credulity see also **2**, **28**. "Omnifidence" (belief in everything) is not in *OED*.

45[1] C is right: dogs suffering from hydrophobia lose their characteristic bark because of constriction in the throat, and either become voiceless or develop a distinctive howl. Gillman had written on hydrophobia in a monograph that C praised (*CL* IV 776): *Dissertation on the Bite of a Rabid Animal* (1812).

46[1] A Commission led by Benjamin Franklin reported to the King of France in 1784 on the phenomena of animal magnetism, concluding that the effects were real but attributing them largely to the role of imagination; a private report by the same group cautioned the government about sexual aspects of the magnetic treatment. See KLUGE **7** n 4, *SW & F* (*CC*) 594 and n 1. The work by Stieglitz mentioned in **13** n 5 includes (658–61) comments on these reports.

to the French Government, that Mesmer's prior cures with mineral magnet were grounded in *fact*, tho' probably exaggerated. That Appendices, or Amulets, not mercurial, are in some instance medicinal, Wienholt's experience led him to believe confidently.[2]

47 pp 250–1

[A case reported by Helmont:] "So (he saith) we have in times past seen at *Lira* the children of *Orphans* to have cast up by vomit an artificial Horse and Cart, drawn forth by the hands of the by-standers; to wit a four footed board accompanied with its ropes, and wheel. And what way soever it were placed, it was easily greater than the double throat."

The *story* may be true, & the more probable from *Fits* being so common in the Foundling Hospitals of the continent: tho' the *Telling* is Self-contradictory: for how could it have been vomited if it had been too large to have been swallowed? A *most* singular instance occurred at Keswick, in my own and Robert Southey's (the Poet Laureate's) own presence—of a Pike sent us as a present from Mr Leathe's of Leathe's Water or Thirlmere, the lake between Grasmere and Keswick—& which had 3 pounds & a half of Stones in its stomach, the *smallest* of which could not be forced down the throat of the Fish without lacerating it. We made the exactest inquiries, tracing it from the persons who caught and were present at the time in the boat (two of them the young Mr Leatheses) to the moment of its delivery, and received the most solemn assurances that no trick had been played—The throat was entire & in its natural state—[1]

48 p 251

[Another report of remarkable stomach contents.] ". . . the one [woman] cast up with great strainings an head bodkin very great bended like an hook, with a great lump of Womens hair, wrapped with the pairing of nails, who died the day following. The other vomited up a Womans

46[2] C is probably remembering accounts of the success of Arnold W. Wienholt (1749–1804) with amulets in magnetic cures that he read in K. E. Schelling "Ideen und Erfahrungen über den thierischen Magnetismus" *Jahrbücher der Medicin als Wissenschaft* II i 3–46, ii 158–90, esp i 7. See JAHRBÜCHER for remarks about other points in this article.

47[1] The names Leath and Leathes are old Westmorland and Cumberland names derived originally from an Anglo-Saxon word for "barn". A. M. Armstrong et al *The Place-Names of Cumberland* pt 1 (Cambridge 1950) 35 notice Leatheswater as a name for Thirlmere in the 18th century. J. S. Leathe of Dalehead was a neighbour of RS. This incident does not appear to have been recorded elsewhere.

Quoif, pieces of glass, with three dried pieces of a Dogs tail that was hairy . . ."

These cases & the numerous similar ones on record I attribute to Epileptic Fits, during which the miserable Patient with a sort of Antagonist Action to that in Hydrophobia swallows whatever lies at hand. Hence Pins, and needles, Hair torn from their own head or as here from some domestic Animal, Rags, Glass, & the like are the stuff of most frequent occurrence.

49 p 252

[Helmont's account of the causes of such events:] . . . first the Devil, by reason of the league with the Witch, doth bring and convey the things to be injected to the place, or near the object, and makes them invisible by his spiritual power: Secondly that the Witch by the strength of her imagination and the motion of her free will, . . . doth convey or inject these strange things into the bodies of those they would hurt or torment . . .

See p. 78: and my marginal note to § 6.[1] S. T. COLERIDGE

50 p 311 | Ch 16

[Joachim Camerarius has it from Lassar Spengler that a grave man of Nuremberg was given a magic crystal "as a sign of a grateful mind".] "If he desired to be made more certain of any thing, that he should draw forth the glass, and will a male chast Boy to look in it, and should ask of him what he did see? . . . And this Man did affirm, that he was never deceived in any one thing, and that he had understood wonderful things by the boys indication, when none of all the rest did by looking into it, see it to be any thing else but a neat and pure Gemm. . . . but the Man being weary of the use of it, did give it to *Spengler*, who being a great hater of superstition, did cause it to be broken into small pieces, and so with the Silk in which it was wrapped, threw it into the sink of the House."

What![a]

This is the lamest story of all; from which we only learn, that Spengler was a *goodie*,[1] the honest grave Anonyme a Humbug—& J. Cam. his Cousin.

50[a] Written in the inner margin of p 310 against the underlined "wonderful"; the remainder on p 311

49[1] I.e. **13** above. *CN* IV 4622 offers further comment on Webster 252–3.

50[1] C was one of the first to use "goody" in the sense of weak or sentimental dogooding, and "goodiness" is his coinage: see JOHNSON **40** n 1, *EOT* (*CC*) II 91 and n 6.

51 p 311

For the most part the child tells any thing that comes into his fancy, or doth frame and invent things upon purpose, that he never seeth at all, and the inquirers do presently assimilate them to their own thoughts and suspicions.

On the propensity of Children to support, and their ingenuity in supporting, impostures see R. Southey's judicious & valuable remarks in his "Life of Wesley", Vol. II. p. 331.[1]

52 p 318

Lastly . . . it is a certain truth that two extreams cannot be joined or coupled together, but by some middle thing that participateth or cometh near to the nature of both. So the Soul which (by the unanimous consent of all men) is a spiritual and pure, immaterial and incorporeal substance cannot be united to the body, which is a most gross, thick and corporeal substance, without the intervention of some middle nature, fit to conjoin and unite those extreams together, which is this sensitive and corporeal Soul or Astral Spirit . . .

This may be ably and effectively supported on the position of the tautogeneity[1] of Substance, Mind being 1.2.3.4. &c, Body $\frac{1}{2}\,\frac{1}{3}\,\frac{1}{4}\,\frac{1}{5}$ &c; but it is clearly nugatory on Webster's scheme of an *essential diversity* (in kind & not in degree alone) of the spiritual Soul and the organic Body. Inter res diversi generis non dantur Media.[2]

53 p 319

Upon the supposition that the rational Soul be not *ex traduce* [derived from a parent stock; congenital], but be infused after the bodily organs be fitted and prepared, which is the firm Tenent of all Divines Ancient, middle and Modern, and must upon the granting of it to be simply, and absolutely immaterial and incorporeal (which is indisputable) of necessity

51[1] RS quotes Wesley's report of a girl of 15 whom he found in a trance passing from smiles to weeping and crying for pity of the damned. RS comments, "With all his knowledge of the human heart . . . Wesley had not discovered, that when occasion is offered for imposture of this kind, the propensity to it is a vice to which children and young persons are especially addicted. If there be any natural obliquity of mind, sufficient motives are found in the pride of deceiving their elders, and the pleasure which they feel in exercising the monkey-like instinct of imitation." For C's copiously annotated copy of this work see SOUTHEY *Wesley*.

52[1] I.e. being of the same kind: not in *OED*.

52[2] "Between things diverse in kind there are no intermediaries."

be infused, because no immaterial substance can be produced or generated by the motion of any agent, that is meerly material, or forth of any material substance whatsoever. And therefore I say that the Soul being infused, it must of necessity follow the organized body, that could not exist (except as a lump of flesh) without the corporeal sensitive soul . . .

This is one and not the only one instance of Problems that men have ceased attempting to solve, from indolence of mind—& not from its want of interest, nor yet from the impracticability of determining it, *subjectively* at least. The psilophists[1] of the present age in contempt "of all Divines, ancient, middle and modern["], suppose the Soul to be extraduce: tho' a few only have dared particularize the secreting Gland.

53[1] C must intend "psilosophists". A variant on his coinages "psilosophy" (slender wisdom) and "psilosopher", "psilosophist" would be even more damning than "sophist".

ADAM WEISHAUPT

1748–1830

Apologie des Misvergnügens und Uebels. 2nd ed rev. 2 pts in one vol. Frankfurt & Leipzig 1790. 8°.

British Library C 126 d 9

"S. T. C." label on title-page. James Duke Coleridge monogram "C" on p ⁻4. Unopened (Jul 1991): i 275–8; ii 35–8, 211–14, 243–6, 345–52, 355–8, 361–4. The number "2" written at the top of i 448 (the last page) and "44–2" at the top of i ⁺1 do not appear to be in C's hand.

DATE. May 1810, when C wrote in a notebook, "Interesting Thought on Education, as : Man :: transmission of Instinct to Animals. I have written it on the inward Cover of the first Volume of Weishaupt's Apologie des Misvergnügung. as a note to p. 22.—": *CN* III 3775.

COEDITOR. Raimonda Modiano.

1 i ⁻1 (inside—verso—of original paper cover)

Turn of mind into melancho[ly][a] and frequent madness & extravagance from the Turn of *Life*—the top of the Hill—at 35 to 40—different in different men—

2 i 8–9 | Dialogue 1

Ich. Wenn der Tod ein für alle Menschen so empfindliches Uebel ist, warum trinkt *Sokrates* den Giftbecher mit dieser Gelassenheit? . . . Warum sehnt sich der Krieger nach Schlachten und Gefahren? . . . Der Tod ist also wie es scheint nicht für alle Menschen ein Uebel.

[*I.* If death is such a grievous evil to all men, why did Socrates empty the cup of poison so calmly? . . . Why does the warrior long for battles and dangers? . . . Death, it seems, is not an evil to all men.]

These instances prove only that Death may be represented as a lesser evil than others—Is the extraction of a Tooth no evil, because it is deemed a lesser evil, than the Tooth-ache?—But in truth, all Reasoning on this sub-

1[a] Letters obscured in tight binding

ject must be nugatory, until the question has been satisfactorily answer[a]—what do you mean by Evil? If you mean it as synonimous with Pain and its causes, is it not idle to dispute, that Pain is Pain?

3 i 22, i $^{+}$1 (inside original paper cover)

Ich. . . . Ich denke diese Beyspiele sollen dir beweisen, dass wir Dinge suchen, oder fliehen, in so fern wir uns solche vorstellen; dass unsere Handlungen durch den Willen und dieser durch die Vorstellungskraft bestimmt werde . . .

[*I.* . . . I think these examples should prove to you that we seek or avoid things in so far as we imagine them; that our actions are determined by the will and the will in turn by the power of representation . . .]

This is all baseless. We know too well, that it is not the mere notion however clear, that restrains or impels us; but the feelings habitually connected with that notion. The Drunkard is convinced that his Drams are poison; yet takes them. [a]For once that a deep conviction is the parent of a Habit, a Habit is an 100 times the parent of the Conviction. Hence, the immense importance of Education, i.e. *training up*. Hence, the sophistry may be shewn of Rosseau's Plan of Education—in which an intellectual conviction is always to precede the appropriate action.[1]—Education is to man, what the transmission of Instincts is to animals—intwines Thought with the living Substance, the nerves of sensation, the organs of Sense, the muscles of motion, and this finally with the *Will*—the total Soul energizing, unique & unific!

4 i $^{+}$1, referring to i 27, cropped at the end

Ich. . . . Du darfst sicher glauben; dass du den wahren Gesichtspunkt entweder gar nicht hast, oder zu flüchtig darüber hinweg eilst . . . dass dir diese Vorstellungsart, noch lange nicht, zu deinem allgemeinsten und dringensten Bedürfniss geworden sey . . .

[*I.* . . . You may be certain that you either do not have the true point of view at all or are too hastily hurrying past it . . . that this way of thinking is far from having become your most general and most urgent necessity . . .]

2[a] For "answered"
3[a] The note on i $^{+}$1 begins: "p. 22. Add to the marginal note—"

3[1] For other instances of C's dissociating himself from the radical theories of education promulgated by Rousseau's novel *Emile* (1762) see ROBINSON **16** and n 2, *CL* IV 879–80.

p. 27. The Author has already abandoned his Thesis—it is no longer the mere Vorstellungsart, but the urgent & habitual Bedürfniss[1] connected with it!—How? What [. . . . .]

5 i $^{+}1$

Might we define Evil as retrogressive Imperfection, or positive Deterioration? If Progression be the end and object of the human Soul, whatever gives it a retrograde movement, is Evil—great or small as the movement is ultimately contrary or conducive to Progression. The mind may run back in order to spring forward again with greater force—may like Antæus, fall and touch the earth in order to renew its Strength.—[1]

4[1] Not merely a "way of thinking" but a "necessity": textus.

5[1] The giant Antaeus, in classical mythology, was a mighty wrestler, the son of Earth and Sea (Ge and Poseidon; Terra and Neptune). Since his mother gave him new strength every time he fell to the ground, Hercules was able to defeat him at last only by holding him up in the air and squeezing him to death.

Lost Book

Pythagoras, oder Betrachtungen über die geheime Welt und Regierungskunst. Vol I [all published]. Frankfurt 1795. 8°.

Not located; marginalia not recorded. *Green SC* (1880) 814, "with MS. notes by S. T. Coleridge on the margins, but a portion of some cut away in binding". The same lot in the sale included the title following and "other works by Weishaupt", 9 vols in all.

Lost Book

Ueber den Kantischen Anschauungen und Erscheinungen. Nürnberg 1788. 8°.

Not located; marginalia not recorded. *Green SC* (1880) 814, "with MS. notes by S. T. Coleridge on the margins, but a portion of some cut away in binding". Cf WEISHAUPT *Pythagoras*.

Ueber Wahrheit und sittliche Vollkommenheit. 3 vols. Regensburg 1793, 1794, 1797. 8º.

The title-page of Vol I (1793) has no volume number. Vol II (1794) has a fly-title before the title-page, reading *Ueber die Lehre von den Gründen und Ursachen aller Dinge*. Vol III (1797) title-page adds *Dritter Theil*, and its separately-paginated pt 2 is entitled *Ueber die Zwecke oder Finalursachen*.

Victoria College Library (Coleridge Collection)

The work is described by EHC in a pocket mounted on III +5 (p-d).

DATE. Uncertain, possibly as early as C's period in Germany, 1798–9.

1 I -1[a]

I have no recollection of any Work so verbose as this—Such a forest of *Leaves*—.—An apple brought in a whole basket of leaves—taken away, & again brought, the very same apple, another huge basket of other leaves [&][b] so forth/ It is most wearisome—

1[a] C's note, written on the original light-grey paper wrapper, has been pasted to I -1

1[b] A hole in the leaf

WILLIAM CHARLES WELLS

1757–1817

Two Essays: one upon single vision with two eyes; the other on dew. A letter to the Right Hon. Lloyd, Lord Kenyon and an account of a female of the white race of mankind, part of whose skin resembles that of a negro; with some observations on the causes of the differences in colour and form between the white and negro races of men. By the late William Charles Wells, M.D. F.R.S.L.& E. With a memoir of his life, written by himself. London 1818. 8°.

University College London: Ogden Collection A384

Bookseller's letter of 4 Jul 1866 loose inside front cover. Pasted on inside front cover a clipping from *Gillman SC* (1843) 370, describing this copy; below, in pencil, "March 31st 1843" (the date of the Gillman sale) and "C K Ogden [?P/A] 384 | £150". Loose in the volume, a single sheet of notepaper certifying the notes as C's and offering the book for sale for 10/6, and a scrap of paper that must have drifted from another book, since there are no corrections in this volume: "The MS Corrections are by Mrs H. N. Coleridge | E. H. Coleridge | May 5—1890".

CONTENTS. Pp 1–117 *On Single Vision . . . and the Experiments . . . in Optics*; 123–282 *Essay on Dew* (apparently 2nd ed); 283–6 Letter to David Hume; 287–422 Letter to Lord Kenyon; 423–39 *An Account of a Female of the White Race . . .*

DATE. Sept 1819? Cf a letter of 28 Sept 1819: "Have you seen the Memoir of Dr Wells written by himself—and prefixed to a posthumous collection of his Essays? They are very interesting . . ." (*CL* IV 950).

1 p 22, pencil, cropped | An Essay on Single Vision pt 1

Dr. Reid, however, has himself so ably shown, that we should never have acquired, by means of our eyes, any knowledge of distance, unless they had been assisted by the sense of feeling,* that I forbear to say any thing more upon this head . . .

* A sense of feeling is perhaps involved in that of Sight, at least in the organ of Sight. But this is not Dr Wells' reasoning: and in any other [i]t is a mistaken position. The Eye would of itself, tho' more slowly, acquire

the judgement of distance by the law of the relative maximum and the [. . . . .][a] There is a growth in seeing by the[b]

2 p 68, pencil | End of Essay

Before *I* could with any inward satisfaction enter on an investigation of this nature, I should find it necessary to settle what an Organ of sense is, generally. Answer: 1. To abstract *physically*. 2. To oppose or form antitheses. 3. Syntheses. 4. Judgement as to the coincidence.—Questions. What are the conditions of a physical Abstraction?—in order to the possibility of this (for primâ facie a physical Abstraction is a contradiction in terms) we must assume three terms in objective nature instead of one. viz. Matter; Material Substance; and Body. And the middle term, containing Light, Magnetic, Electric, and Galvanic Ethers, &c are the conditions of all physical abstraction & therefore the objective Correlatives of all organic Sentiency.—This is a mere Hint for the mere commencement of such an investigation.

3 p 71, pencil, cropped | Experiments and observations on several subjects in optics. I On visible position, and visible motion

"I have frequently" (says Mr. Melvill) "observed, when at sea, that, though I pressed my body and head firmly to a corner of the cabin, so as to be at rest in respect to every object about me, the different irregular motions of the ship, in rolling and pitching, were still discernible by sight. How is this fact to be reconciled to optical principles? . . ."

Just as modern Unitarians adduce against the Trinity objections that ought [to][a] have been solved in order to the possibi[lity][b] of a Godhead at all, whether uni- or tri-personal: so do the Naturalists start diffi[cul]ties[c] against particulars; which in truth apply[d]

4 p 217, pencil, slightly cropped | Essay on Dew pt 2

Air both reflects and refracts light, and all other bodies, as far as I know, acquire heat, while they act thus on the light of the sun.*

* Surely, Dr W. should have more rigorously determined the extent of the Term, Air: whether he meant to affirm these properties and qualities of Gas, generally, or of that mixture or combination of Oxygen and Ni-

1[a] Two or three words lost in cropping of the bottom of the page
1[b] Remainder of note lost in cropping **3**[a] Word lost in cropping
3[b] Letters lost in cropping **3**[c] Letters lost in cropping
3[d] Remainder of note lost in cropping

trogen supposed to constitute ⟨the⟩ Atmosphere, or lastly, the Air as it is exists in nature and in the popular use of the word

5 pp 388–9, pencil, cropped | Letter to Lord Kenyon

Perhaps too, from a well-known law of human nature, their [authors'] moral feelings may be less correct than those of many other men, in consequence of the great and frequent exercise, which is given to the powers of their understandings.*

An important Truth lurks, and a most mischievous Falsehood glares, in this position, from the ambiguity of the term "Understanding"—the former, if it be interpreted the power of adapting means to ends, no matter what the *end* may be: the latter [a][. . . . .] *Law* (το πρωθυστατον)[1] in objects of contempla[tion.][b] Men eminent in the latter from Thales to Plato and from Plato to Berkley and Kant have been eminently good men—Bacon himself is no exception, nor (his circumstances [. . . . .][c] human[d]

5[a] At least one line lost in cropping the bottom of p 388
5[b] Letters lost in cropping **5**[c] Most of a line lost in cropping
5[d] Remainder of note lost in cropping

5[1] "The last [thing] first".

BENJAMIN WHEELER

1733–1783

The Theological Lectures of the Late Rev. Benjamin Wheeler, D.D. Canon of Christ Church, and Regius Professor of Divinity in the University of Oxford. With a prefatory sketch of his life and character, by Thomas Horne, D.D., &c. Vol I [all published]. Oxford 1819. 8°.

Not located; marginalia printed from *LR* II 363–4. This vol belonged to Francis Cary: *LR* II 361.

DATE. About 1820, if Cary—whom C had known since 1817—acquired the book upon publication and lent it to C soon after.

1 I 77

A miracle, usually so termed, is the exertion of a supernatural power in some act, and contrary to the regular course of nature . . .

Where is the proof of this as drawn from Scripture, from fact recorded, or from doctrine affirmed? Where the proof of its logical possibility,—that is, that the word has any representable sense? Contrary to 2 x 2 = 4 is 2 x 2 = 5, or that the same fire acting at the same moment on the same subject should burn it and not burn it.

The course of nature is either one with, or a reverential synonyme of, the ever present divine agency; or it is a self-subsisting derivative from, and dependent on, the divine will. In either case this author's assertion would amount to a charge of self-contradiction on the Author of all things. Before the spread of Grotianism, or the Old Bailey *nolens volens* Christianity, such language was unexampled.[1] A miracle is either *super naturam*, or it is simply *præter experientiam*.[2] If nature be a collective term for the sum total of the mechanic powers,—that is, of the act first manifested to the senses in the conductor A, arriving at Z by the sensible chain of intermediate conductors, B, C, D, &c.;—then every motion of

1[1] For C's view of Grotianism as a crude attempt to defend the Christian faith by reference to such external "evidence" as that of miracles see e.g. LUTHER *Colloquia* **4** n 1, **80** n 3. This form of reasoning, C suggests, is better suited to legal process (The Old Bailey being the central criminal court in London) than to religion.

1[2] "Beyond nature" or "outside experience".

my arm is *super naturam*. If this be not the sense, then nature is but a wilful synonyme of experience, and then the first noticed aerolithes, Sulzer's first observation of the galvanic arch, &c. must have been miracles.[3]

As erroneous as the author's assertions are logically, so false are they historically, in the effect, which the miracles in and by themselves did produce on those, who, rejecting the doctrine, were eye-witnesses of the miracles;—and psychologically, in the effect which miracles, as miracles, are calculated to produce on the human mind. Is it possible that the author can have attentively studied the first two or three chapters of St. John's gospel?

There is but one possible tenable definition of a miracle,—namely, an immediate consequent from a heterogeneous antecedent. This is its essence. Add the words, *præter experientiam adhuc*, or *id temporis*,[4] and you have the full and popular or practical sense of the term miracle.[5]

1[3] Aerolithes (or aerolites), meteorites consisting almost entirely of stone as opposed to meteoric iron, had been quite recently identified: the first instance of the word in *OED* is from the 1815 supplement to the *Encyclopaedia Britannica*. Johann Georg Sulzer (1720–1779), writer on aesthetics, made observations about the effect of electricity on tasting—noting a sensation of acidity at the positive pole and of alkalinity at the negative—that anticipated by about 30 years Galvani's experiments with frogs. C appears to be referring to the electrical pattern itself rather than to the instrument known as the "metallic arc", composed of two metals, that Galvani began to use about 1786.

1[4] "So far", or "up to now, outside the realm of experience".

1[5] For C's almost life-long opposition to Hume's famous definition of a miracle as "a violation of the laws of nature" see also SKELTON **8** n 3, *SW & F* (*CC*) 209–11, *CN* III 4381.

JOHN WHITAKER
1735–1808

The Origin of Arianism Disclosed. London 1791. 8°.

British Library C 126 k 7

With the monogram of John Duke Coleridge on p $^{-}2$; "S. T. C." label and C's initials (not in C's hand) on the title-page.

DATE. Uncertain. C annotated this work on two or more occasions (**1**), at least one of them after c 1812–13 when he read EICHHORN *Apocalypse*, apparently for the first time. *LR*, without citing evidence, proposes dates of 1803 and 1810 for two readings.

1 p 30

"Therefore," as we are told, "the Jews sought the more to kill him, because he not only broke the Sabbath, but also called GOD HIS FATHER, MAKING HIMSELF EQUAL WITH GOD." In strict fidelity of translation, he "called God," not merely "*his* Father," but "HIS OWN PROPER Father," *his* in a *proper* and *peculiar* degree of filial relation; and *so* made himself *equal* with God "his Father." [Whitaker quotes John 5.18 in a footnote.]

Ευαγγ. κατα Ἰων. Cap 5. v. 16. 17. 18. 19:[1]—Whoever reads these four verses attentively, judging of the meaning of each part by the context, must needs see that the "ισον εαυτον ποιων τῳ Θεῳ", "making himself equal with God" refers—not to the αλλα και πατερα ιδιον ελεγε τον θεον, or the Ο πατηρ μου—but to the εργαζεται, καγω εργαζ~~φ~~ομαι[2]—the 19 verse which is directly called Jesus's *reply*, takes *no* notice whatever of the Ο πατ~~φ~~ηρ μου, but consists wholly of a justification of the κ' αγω εργαζω—.[3]

1[1] "The Gospel according to John" 5.16–19: "And therefore did the Jews persecute Jesus, and sought to slay him, because he had done these things on the sabbath day. But Jesus answered them, My Father worketh hitherto, and I work. Therefore the Jews sought the more to kill him, because he not only had broken the sabbath, but said also that God was his Father, making himself equal with God. Then answered Jesus and said unto them, Verily, verily, I say unto you, The Son can do nothing of himself, but what he seeth the Father do: for what things soever he doeth, these also doeth the Son likewise."

1[2] I.e. not to the "but said also that God was his Father" or the "My Father", but to the "he worketh, and I work".

1[3] I.e. takes no notice of the "My Father" but consists of a justification of the "and I work".

The above was written many years ago. I still think the remark plausible, tho' I should not now express myself so positively. I imagined the Jews to mean, "he has evidently used the words πατηρ μου[4] not in the sense in which all good men may use them, but in a literal sense, *because* (by the words that followed, εργαζεται κ' αγω εργαζομαι[5] he makes himself, or, by making himself equal to God." To justify these words is the purport of Christ's reply.

2 p 31

[In a footnote, Whitaker defends his use of the plural "devils" in opposition to a recent translator of the Gospels who pointed out that *diabolos* ("devil") is invariably singular and that a different word (*daimon* "daemon" or "power") is used for evil spirits in the plural.] And though the word *daemons* . . . might critically be more exact in a translation; yet the word *devils* better accords, with the usages of our language and the course of our ideas. Exactness therefore has been properly sacrificed to utility.

i.e. the *words* of Scripture to *my* interpretation of their sense! *Modest*! What a *useful* translation W. would have made on this plan—it would have removed all doubts from the mere English Reader of the Gospels.

3 p 34

[Whitaker quotes Eusebius *Ecclesiastical History* 2.4 on Philo Judaeus:] ". . . *what and how great advances he made*, in the knowledge of the *divine* and *Jewish* religion; is evident to all from his *writings:* and in the philosophick and liberal parts of Gentile literature, I need not say how great he was; for studying with peculiar zeal the discipline of Plato and Pythagoras, he is *reported by history* to have surpassed all his contemporaries." Philo's acquaintance with *the doctrines of the Heathens*, was known only by *historical report* to Eusebius; while the *writings* of Philo displayed his knowledge, in *the religion of the Jews*. . . . He was therefore a cotemporary with the apostles. And the *writings* of such a man as this, must be a full evidence of the opinions of the Jews, at the moment.

Strange Comment! Might I not after having spoken of Duns Scotus's works, say—he is *related* in subtlety of logic to have surpassed all his Contemporaries, yet still mean no other works than those before spoken of? Are not Philo's works full, crowded with Platonic & Pythagorean Philosophy? Eusebius knew from his works that he was a great Platonic

1[4] "My Father".

1[5] He "worketh . . . and I work".

Scholar; but that he was greater than any other man of his Age, ~~how~~ he could only learn from Report or History. That Virgil is a great Poet, I know from his Poems; but that he was the greatest of the Augustan Age, I must learn from Quintilian & others.—

4 pp 35–41, referring to p 36

. . . Philo has shown a pleasing, and yet puzzling, disquisitiveness of genius. His mind, all the while, is busily operating upon itself. And, like the silk-worm, he is spinning a multiplicity of fine threads out of his own bowels, and is continually burying himself in his own web of silk.

Philo and the Author ⟨of the W. of S.—⟩ (or rather, perhaps, Authors: for the 10 first Chapters form a complete work of themselves) were both Cabalistico-platonizing Jews of Alexandria[1]—As far as being such they *must* agree, so far they do agree—and as widely, as such men *could* differ, so widely do they differ—Not only the style of the W. of S. is generically different from Philo—so much so that I should deem it a *free* Translation from an Hebrew original—but in all the minutiæ of traditional History & Dogma it contradicts Philo.—Philo attributes the creation of Man to Angels, and they infused the Evil Principle thro' their own imperfection/ in the Book of Wisdom, God created man spotless, and the Devil tempting him occasioned the Fall—So the whole account of the Plagues of Egypt differ as widely as possible, even to absolute contradiction/ The origin of Idolatry is explained altogether differently by Philo, and by the W. of S.—In short, so unsupported is the tradition, that many have supposed an elder Philo, as the Author. That the second and third Chapters allude to Christ, is a groundless hypothesis—The just man

4[1] On a second reading (**1**), C knows where Whitaker's argument is tending and so he anticipates the later chapter that will put the case for Philo's authorship of the Wisdom of Solomon (in the Apocrypha). Whitaker points out that it had been attributed to Philo in antiquity by Basil, Jerome, and Augustine, and that the tradition of his authorship persisted through the Middle Ages (121); he further maintains, changing ground, that "The language is very similar to Philo's; flowing, lively, and happy" (132). He concludes that there is incontestable evidence "that the Wisdom of Solomon was written later than the days of our Saviour, and might be written, as historical report says it actually was, by Philo" (135). C, however, had read Eichhorn on the subject, and holds different views, notably that the work falls into two parts (chs 1–10, 11–19) and is not a coherent whole; that the traditional attribution to Philo must be rejected on the internal evidence of style and doctrine, though the author or authors of the work, like Philo, combine Jewish religion and Greek philosophy; and that its composition antedates or coincides with the lifetime of Christ, but is certainly not later. See Eichhorn *Apocrypha* **11–23** and nn. Modern scholarship generally accepts Eichhorn's views: R. H. Charles ed *The Apocrypha and Pseudepigrapha of the Old Testament in English* (2 vols Oxford 1913).

is called a child of God, hgeked Jehova, παῖς Κυριου—but Christ's specific title which was deemed blasphemous by the Jews was Ben Elohim, υιος του θεου[2]—/ and the fancy that Philo was a Christian in Heart, but dared not openly profess it, is too absurd—Why no traces in his latest works, or those of his middle age? Why not the least variation in his religious or philosophical creeds in his latter works, written long after the Resurrection of Christ, from those composed by him before, at, or a few years after Christ's Birth. Some of the earlier Works of Philo must have been written when Christ was in his Infancy or at least Boyhood—.

In short, just take all those Passages of Philo which most closely resemble others in the W. of S., and contain the same or nearly the same Thoughts, and write them in an opposite Column/ and no doubt will remain, that Philo was not the composer of the Book of Wisdom/ Philo subtle, & ƒ with long involved Periods, knit together by logical connectives/ the B. of W. sententious, full of parallelisms, assertory, & Hebraistic throughout. It was either composed by a man who tried to Hebraize the Greek, or (if a Translator) by one who tried to Greecize the Hebraisms of his original, not to disguise or hide them, but only so as to prevent them from repelling or misleading the Greek Reader—The different use of the Greek Particles in the W. of S. and the works of Philo, is sufficient to confute the hypothesis of Philo as the Author.—As little could it have been written by a Christian/ for he could not have been a Christian of Palestine—from the overflowing Alexandrine Platonism—nor a Christian at all, because he contradicts the doctrine of the Resurrection of the Body, and in no wise connects any redemptory or sacrificial virtue to the Death of his just man/ denies original Sin in the Christian sense, & explains the vice & virtue of mankind by the Actions of the Souls of men in a state of pre-existence.

No signs or Miracles referred to in the account of the just man, the hgneked Jehova/ and that it was intended as a generalization, is evidently[a] from the altering the singular into the plural Number in the third Chapter.[3]

4[a] For "evident"

4[2] "Son of God". C alludes to Matt 26.63–6, where the High Priest questions Jesus—"tell us whether thou be the Christ, the Son of God"—and charges him with blasphemy. EICHHORN *Apocrypha* **131** (not annotated) makes the same point, that the "righteous man" of Wisd of Sol is not Christ and that the Greek phrase meaning "child of the Lord" is not the same as the one meaning "Son of God"; he also gives the equivalent phrases in Hebrew, but does not transliterate them. C's "hgeked Jehova"—"hgneked Jehova" below—is not intelligible as Hebrew; it appears to be an attempt to render the Hebrew phrase given by Eichhorn, properly *ebed Jehova* "servant of the Lord".

4[3] The "righteous man" of Wisd of Sol 2.12 becomes "the righteous" (plural) in Wisd of Sol 3.1 and following.

The result is, that it was composed by an unknown Jew of Alexandria; either some time before, or at the same time with Christ.—I do not think St Paul's parallel passages amount to any proof of quotation or allusion/ they contain the common doctrine of the spiritualized Judaism, in the Cabala/[4]—And yet the work could scarcely have been written long before Christ, or it would certainly have been referred to & quoted by Philo— & most probably by Josephus. And this too is an answer to the splendid & well-supported Hypothesis of its being a Translation from a Chaldaic Original, composed by Seru~~b~~babel—The variations of Syriac Translation, which are so easily explained by translating the passage into the Chaldaic, when the cause of the mistake in the Greek or of the variation in the Syriac is seen at once, are certainly *startling*; but they are too few— & how came more of the Fathers, as Jerom, to remain ignorant of this Chaldaic Original?[5]—My own opinion is, that the W. of S. was written in Greek by an Alexandrine Jew, who had formed his style on that of the Septuagint, and led still further to an imitation of the Old Testament Manner by the nature of his fiction, and as a *dramatic* propriety—and yet deviated from it partly from the very remoteness of his platonic Conceptions from the simplicity and poverty of the Hebrew, and partly from the wordy rhetoric epidemic in Alexandria—& that it was written before the *Death* of Christ, if not the Birth, I am induced to believe—because I do not think it probable that a Book written by a Jew, who had confessed Christ, would have so soon have been received by the Christians, and so early placed in the very next Rank to Works of full Inspiration.—[6]

Taken therefore as a work ante, or at least extra, Christum,[7] it is most valuable, as ascertaining the opinions of the learned Jews on many subjects, and the general opinion concerning Immortality, and a day of Judgment. On *this* Ground Whitaker might have erected a most formidable Battery, that would have played on the very Camp & Battle Array of the Socinians—i.e. of those who consider Christ only as a Teacher of important Truths.—

In referring to the Cabala, I am not ignorant of the date of the oldest

4[4] Eichhorn 202 points out verbal parallels between Rom 1.20 etc, Eph 6.13 etc, and Wisd of Sol, and it is now generally agreed (contrary to C's conclusion) that Paul must have been familiar with Wisd of Sol.

4[5] This hypothesis that the "second Solomon"—the Jewish King Serubabel—was the author of Wisd of Sol, discussed and rejected by Eichhorn 186–92, was the work of Eichhorn's contemporary and sometime collaborator Johann Melchior Faber, in *Super libro Sapientiae* (2 pts Onoldi [Ansbach] 1776–89).

4[6] C's dating is in broad agreement with Eichhorn's: see n 1 and EICHHORN *Apocrypha* **18** and n 1.

4[7] "Before" or at least "outside Christ"—i.e. independent of him.

Rabbinical Writings which contain or refer to this Philosophy; but in coincidence with Eichhorn, and very many before Eichhorn, that the foundations of the Cabala were layed & well known long before Christ, tho' not *all* the fanciful Superstructure.[8] I am persuaded, that new Light might be thrown on the Apocalypse by a careful Study of the Book Sohar, and whatever else there may be of this kind.[9] The introduction is clearly Cabala:—the ο ων = 3, and to 7 = the 10 Sephiroth, which all together constitute the Adam Kadmon, the *second Adam* of S[t] Paul, & incarnate in the Messiah—&c &c &c.[10]

Were it not for the silence of Philo & Josephus, which I am unable to explain, if the W. of S. were written so long before Christ, I should incline to believe it composed shortly after if not during the persecution of the Jews in Egypt under Ptolemy Philopator.[11] This hypothesis would give a particular propriety to the bitter exposure of Idolatry, to the comparison between the sufferings of the Jews & those of idolatrous Nations, to the long rehearsal & rhetorical decoration of the Plagues of Egypt—to the reward of the just man after a death of Martyrdom—&c: and would besides help to explain the putting together of the 10 first Chapters, and the fragment contained in the remaining Chapters—They were works written at the same time, & by the same Author/ nay, I do not think it absurd to suppose, that the Chapters after the 10th were annexed by the Writer himself, as a long explanatory Appendix—or possibly, if ∅ they were once a separate work, these 9 latter Chapters were parts of a Book composed during the persecution in Egypt, the introduction & conclusion of which being personal, and of local application, were afterwards omitted or expunged in order not to give offence to the other Egyptians, per-

4[8] Although C's estimates about the dating of the Cabbala vary considerably, the general statement here—that the foundation was laid before the lifetime of Christ—represents a consistent position. See esp RHENFERD **4** n 1, TENNEMANN **64** and n 1.

4[9] C would have found references to the Book of Sohar (or Zohar), a storehouse of cabbalistic lore dating from the 2nd century AD, in the OT scholarship of Eichhorn and others (e.g. EICHHORN *Apocrypha* p 105 n, not annotated); an available ed was *Kabbala denudata* (2 vols St Sulzbach & Frankfurt 1677, 1684).

4[10] In Rev 1, and esp in the seven golden lampstands with one in their midst who introduces himself as "the first and the last" of 1.12–18, C recognises some features typical of the Cabbala, notably "the Being = 3" etc (for the significance of this Greek phrase to C, see BIBLE COPY B **119** n 1). In a note of 1827, C was to object to the notion that the cabbalistic system was consistent with Christian Trinitarianism because it distinguishes the first three of the ten sephiroth as "eternal subsistences of the godhead"; he maintained that "If the three first *Proprietates* are God, so are the Seven: ⟨and so are all Ten.⟩ God according to the Cabbalists is all in each and one in all": OXLEE **13**. Adam Kadmon in this system is the first emanation of the godhead, the *Urmensch* or "original man" as Eichhorn explains (103–4, not annotated); the "second Adam of St Paul" is an allusion to 1 Cor 15.45.

4[11] I.e. Ptolemy IV, who reigned 221–205 BC.

haps, to spare the shame of such Jews as had apostatized thro' fear, and in general not to revive heart-burnings.

In modern Language I should call these Chapters in their present state a NOTE on the 15–19th V. of Chap. X.[12] And indeed on a reperusal of the Book, I rather believe that these Chapters never formed part of any other work but were composed as a sort of long explanatory *Post-script*—with particular Bearing on certain existing circumstances, to which this part of the Jewish History was especially applicable.—Nay, I begin to find the silence of Philo & Josephus less inexplicable—and to imagine that I discover the Solution of this Problem in the very Title of the Book—No one expects to find any but works of *authenticity*, enumerated in these Writers—but to this a Work calling itself the Wisdom of Solomon, and both being a fiction, & never meant to pass for any thing else, could make no pretensions. To have even approximated it to the holy Books of the Nation would have injured the dignity of the Jewish Canon/ and brought suspicion on the genuine works of Solomon, while it would have exposed to a charge of Forgery a Composition, which was in itself only an innocent dramatic Monologue.

N.B. This Hypothesis possesses all the advantages, and involves none of the absurdity, of that which would attribute the ~~W. of S.~~ Ecclesiasticus to the infamous Jason, the High Priest—/[13]

More than one Commentator, I find, has suspected that the ~~W. of S.~~ & the II of Maccabees were by the same Author/ I think this nothing.[14]

5 p 36[a]

. . . Philo throws out a number of declarations, that show his own and the Jewish belief in a secondary sort of God, a God subordinate in origin to the Father of all, yet most intimately united with him, and sharing his most unquestionable honours.

5[a] **4** is written around this note, and therefore presumably later

4[12] Wisd of Sol 10.15–19: "She [Wisdom] delivered a holy people and a blameless seed from a nation of oppressors. She entered into the soul of a servant of the Lord, and withstood terrible kings in wonders and signs. She rendered unto holy men a reward of their toils; she guided them along a marvellous way, and became unto them a covering in the daytime, and a light of stars through the night. She brought them over the Red sea, and led them through much water; but their enemies she drowned, and out of the bottom of the deep she cast them up."

4[13] The theory that another book in the apocryphal canon, Ecclesiasticus or "The Wisdom of Jesus, Son of Sirach", was actually the work of Jason, the "unworthy" son of the High Priest Simon, is dismissed by Eichhorn (29–30, not annotated).

4[14] EICHHORN *Apocrypha* 271–4 surveys the scholarship proposing that the author of Wisd of Sol was also the author of 2 Macc, and considers the intellectual relationship of the two works; he concludes that they have different authors.

the belief of the Alexandrine Jews who had acquired Greek Philosophy, no doubt—but of the Palestine Jews?

6 p 48

St. John also is witnessed by a Heathen [Amelius], and by one who put him down for a Barbarian, to have represented the Logos as THE MAKER OF ALL THINGS, as WITH GOD, and as GOD . . . . And St. John is attested to have declared this, "not even as *shaded over*, but on the contrary as *placed in full view.*"

Stranger still! W. could scarcely have read the Greek.[1] Amelius says, that these Truths *if* stripped of their allegorical Dress would be plain—i.e. that John in an allegory, as of one particular man, had shadowed out the creation of all things by the Logos, and the after union of the Logos with human Nature—i.e. with all men/ That this is his meaning, consult Plotinus.[2]

7 p 107

"Seest thou not," adds Philo in the same spirit* of subtilizing being into power, and dividing the Logos in two; "that about Him Who Is are the first and greatest of Powers, the Beneficent and the Corrective? And the Beneficent is called *God*, because according to it he placed and disposed the universe; but the other is called *Lord*, to which belongs the government of the whole."

* Who that had ever rested but in the porch of the Alexandrine Philosophy, would not rather say—of substantiating Powers and Attributes into Beings? What is the whole System, from Philo to Plotinus, and thence to Proclus inclusively, but one fanciful Process of hypostasizing logical Conceptions and generic Terms? In Proclus it is Logolatry[1] run mad.

8 p 132

Such would be the evidence for that Divinity, to accompany the Book of Wisdom; if we considered it to be as old as Solomon, or only as the Son

6[1] Whitaker himself includes the Greek text in notes to p 47. His source is Eusebius Pamphilus *Evangelicae praeparationis* 540 a-d, quoting the views of Gentilianus Amelius, a pupil of Plotinus. It is not Amelius, however, who uses the phrase about being placed in full view, but Eusebius himself in his commentary on the testimony of Amelius.

6[2] This appears to be a general reference to the doctrine of Plotinus, who taught Amelius, rather than a reference to any specific passage in his work. Cf "the best parts of Plotinus" in **13** below.

7[1] "Word-worship". The *OED* quotes this note as its first example of the use of the term. For a brief survey of C's knowledge of Proclus see PROCLUS headnote.

of Sirach. But I consider it to be much later than either, and actually a work of Philo's. Tradition, that useful echo of history, has pronounced it his. Where the original voice cannot be heard, we must take the reverberation of it. This becomes decisive, when the work says nothing to the contrary. But the Wisdom of Solomon says much, in favour of the tradition. The language is very similar to Philo's; flowing, lively, and happy. !!

How is it possible to have read the short hebraistic Sentences of the Book of Wisdom and the long involved Periods that characterize the style of all Philo's known writings, and yet attribute both to one Writer?—But indeed I know no instance of assertions made so audaciously, or of passages misrepresented & even mistranslated so grossly, as in this Work of Whitaker. His System is absolute naked Tritheism.

9 p 132

The work too alludes in one place to the days of the Gospel, as evidently as the personated character of Solomon would allow it to do. The righteous man is shadowed out by the author, with a plain reference to our Saviour himself.

How then could Philo have remained a Jew?

10 p 175

In all effects that are *voluntary*, the cause must be prior to the effect, as the father is to the son, in human generation. But, in all that are *necessary*, the effect must be co-eval with the cause; as the stream is with the fountain, and light with the sun. Had the sun been eternal in its duration, light would have been co-eternal with it.

a just remark, but it cuts two ways—for these *necessary* effects are not really but only logically different or distinct from the cause—the rays of the Sun are only the Sun diffused, and the whole rests on the sensitive form of material Space. Take away the notion of material Space, and the whole distinction perishes.—

11 p 192

[Whitaker is quoting from Eusebius:] "Moses then does expressly give us the theology of two Lords; when he says, 'And the Lord rained from the Lord, fire and brimstone' upon the city of the ungodly."

Jupiter e Jove, i.e. e cælis ab æthere.[1]

12 p 266

[Whitaker uses "the dialogue of JUSTIN MARTYR with TRYPHO the JEW", dated c 155, as proof that the Jews had by then abandoned their ancient belief in the divinity of the Son of God.] "*We all,*" as Trypho rejoins, "*expect* Christ to be born *a man off men*;—answer me therefore first, how you can show that there is *any other God*, besides the Creator of all things." "Show me," he [Trypho] repeats again, "that there is *any other* confessed by the spirit of prophecy to exist, besides the Creator of all things." Justin accordingly sets himself to show, that "in the beginning, before all creatures, God GENERATED a certain Rational Power OUT OF HIMSELF, which is also called by the 'Holy Ghost' in Scripture, 'THE GLORY OF THE LORD, and sometimes SON, and sometimes WISDOM, and sometimes ANGEL, and sometimes GOD, and sometimes LORD and LOGOS' . . ."

Is it not monstrous that the Jews having fully believed a Trinity, one and all but ⟨half⟩ a century or less before Trypho, Justin should never refer to this general Faith, ~~and~~ never reproach Trypho with the present opposition to it as a Heresy from their own Forefathers, even those who rejected Christ or rather Jesus as Christ?—But no!—not a single Objection ever strikes this bigotted Priest, or appears worthy of an answer. The stupidest Forgeries become authentic—the most fantastic abstractions of the Alexandrine Dreamers substantial Realities!—!—

I confess, this Book has satisfied me how little Erudition will gain a man now a days the reputation of vast Learning, if it be only accompanied with *Dash* & Insolence—It seems to me impossible, that this Whitaker *can* have written well on the subject of Mary, Queen of Scots: his powers of Judgment appear so abject![1]—For instance—he says, that the grossest moral Improbability is swept away by positive Evidence—as if positive Evidence (i.e. the Belief I am to yield to A. or B.) were not itself grounded on moral Probabilities.—This Whitaker would have been a choice Judge for Charles the 2nd & Titus Oates!—[2] S. T. C.

11[1] "Jupiter from Jove, i.e. from the heavens from the ether"—C's point being that they are synonymous terms.

12[1] Whitaker had pub *Mary Queen of Scots Vindicated* (3 vols 1787) and announced a one-vol sequel, *The Private Life of Mary Queen of Scots*, in an advertisement at the end of this ed of *The Origin of Arianism*; but the sequel never appeared.

12[2] I.e. because of his apparent indifference to moral considerations. Titus Oates (1649–1705)—"perjurer", as the *DNB* succinctly says by way of identification—was the chief fabricator of reports of a "Popish Plot" against the life of Charles II; on the basis of his evidence several supposed conspirators were executed.

13 p 267

"Since you say," he [Trypho] subjoins, "that Christ was pre-existent AS VERY GOD, and by the will of God was made flesh, and born man off a Virgin; how can ye demonstrate his pre-existence?" Justin therefore proceeds to demonstrate it, asserting Joshua to have given only a temporary inheritance to the Jews, "as being not Christ THE GOD, or THE SON OF GOD;" and noticing the Sacrament of the Eucharist . . .

a precious Beginning of a ⟨precious⟩ Demonstration!! It is well for me that my Faith in the Trinity is already well grounded by the Scriptures, by Bishop Bull, and the best parts of Plotinus—or this man would certainly have made me either a Socinian or a Deist.—

14 p 270

That, in the first and second century, the Christians *did* discriminate themselves from the Jews, by the direct and profest adoration of our Saviour as God; is evident from a variety of testimonies . . . . St. Stephen's dying recommendation of his soul to THE LORD JESUS . . . carries the worship of our Saviour, to the highest point possible of Christian antiquity. The general mode of commencing and concluding the Epistles of St. Paul, in a prayer of supplication for the parties, to whom they were addressed; in which he says, "Grace to you and Peace from God our Father, and"—from whom besides?—"THE LORD JESUS CHRIST;" in which our Saviour is at times invoked *alone*, as "the Grace of OUR LORD JESUS CHRIST be with you all," and is even invoked the *first* at times, as "the Grace of THE LORD JESUS CHRIST, *and* the love of God, *and* the communion of the Holy Ghost, be with you all;" shows us plainly the practice of the original Christians . . .

Invoked! Surely a pious Wish is not an invocation!—May good Angels attend you! is no invocation or worship of Angels! The Essence of religious Adoration consists in the attributing by an act of prayer or praise a *necessary Presence* to an Object—which not being distinguishable if the Object be sensuously present, we may safely define Adoration as an acknowlegement of the actual & necessary presence of an intelligent Being not present to our Senses. May lucky stars shoot influence on you! would be a very foolish superstition—but to say in earnest!—O ye Stars, I pray to you, shoot influences on me—would be Idolatry. Christ was *visually* present to Stephen: his invocation therefore was not perforce an act of religious adoration, an acknowledgement of Christ's Deity.

GILBERT WHITE

1720–1793

The Works, in Natural History, of the late Rev. Gilbert White, A. M. Fellow of Oriel College, Oxford. Comprising The Natural History of Selborne; The Naturalist's Calendar; and miscellaneous observations, extracted from his papers. To which are added, a calendar and observations, by W. Markwick, Esq. F.L.S. 2 vols. London 1802. 8°.

This copy is in a "Cottonian Binding" of printed fabric patterned with blue flowers and olive-brown leaves.

British Library C 61 b 20

A note on I $^{-}$3 (p-d), "[?S. V.] June 1844 when Southey's Books were sold by Fletcher Piccadilly", indicates that this volume came from RS's library; a note pasted to I $^{-}$2, dated 1 Aug 1907, by the BM binder observes, "This book was probably bound for Southey by Mrs Wordsworth . . . in a piece of one of her old gowns". Notes in two hands other than C's appear on I 61, 107, 206, 229, 239, 289, 302, 305, 321, 353. In Vol II, a few pages of the "Naturalist's Calendar", the "Summary of the Weather", and the Index remain unopened (as of Jul 1991): 141–4, 147–50, 153–6, 275–8, 289–92.

DATE. Jul 1810: **4** is dated 7 Jul, and a series of notes based on this reading appears in *CN* III 3956–9, 3961–2.

1 I 63 | *Natural History of Selborne* Letter 12 to Thomas Pennant 4 Nov 1767

Subsist they [the swallows] cannot openly among us, and yet elude the eye of the inquisitive: and, as to their hiding, no man pretends to have found any of them in a torpid state in the winter. But with regard to their migration, what difficulties attend that supposition! that such feeble bad fliers (who the summer long never flit but from hedge to hedge) should be able to traverse vast seas and continents in order to enjoy milder seasons amidst the regions of *Africa*!

Surely from Dover to Calais—and from Gibraltar ~~Cadiz~~ (or even Toulon) to the Coast of Barbary cannot be called a traverse of *vast seas*.

2 I 168 | Letter 39 to Pennant 9 Nov 1773

Bulfinches, when fed on hempseed, often become wholly black.

* I saw a Canary Bird at Blumenbach's in Gottingen, which the Professor had changed to a bright black by the same food.[1]

3 I 194–5 | Letter 44 to Pennant 30 Nov 1780

Virgil, as a familiar occurrence, by way of simile, describes a dove haunting the cavern of a rock in such engaging numbers, that I cannot refrain from quoting the passage: and *John Dryden* has rendered it so happily in our language, that without farther excuse I shall add his translation also.

Qualis speluncâ subitò commota Columba,
Cui domus, et dulces latebroso in pumice nidi,
Fertur in arva volans, plausumque exterrita pennis
Dat tecto ingentem—mox aere lapsa quieto,
Radit iter liquidum, celeres neque commovet alas.

As when a dove her rocky hold forsakes,
Rous'd, in a fright her sounding wings she shakes;
The cavern rings with clattering:—out she flies, !
And leaves her callow care, and cleaves the skies:
At first she flutters:—but at length she springs !!
To smoother flight, and shoots upon her wings.

* *curiosa* felicitas,[1] indeed! a very *odd* way of translating a passage *happily*.[2] Except the 4 last words, and ~~there~~ it wants 5 only of having as many faults as words; & many of them gross & glaring faults.—S. T. C. (Of course, I leave the "in" "with" "and" ~~and~~ "she" "her" "a" and "the", out of the reckoning).

4 I 292–3 | Letter 18 to the Honourable Daines Barrington 29 Jan 1774

. . . what is stranger still, another bird of the same species [swallow] built its nest on the wings and body of an owl that happened by accident to hang dead and dry from the rafter of a barn. This owl, with the nest on its wings, and with eggs in the nest, was brought as a curiosity worthy the most elegant private museum in *Great-Britain*. The owner, struck with

2[1] C was at Göttingen and attending some of Blumenbach's lectures Feb–Jun 1799.

3[1] C responds to White's word "happily" with a familiar tag, "*studied* felicity", from Petronius *Satyricon* 118.

3[2] Dryden's translation of the lines from Virgil *Aeneid* 5.213–17 is very free. Cf a more literal rendering (H. Rushton Fairclough, LCL): "Even as, if startled suddenly from her cave, a dove whose home and sweet nestlings are in the rocky coverts, wings her flight to the fields and, frightened from her home, flaps loudly with her wings; soon, gliding in the peaceful air, she skims her liquid way and stirs not her sweet pinions . . .".

the oddity of the sight, furnished the bringer with a large shell, or conch, desiring him to fix it just where the owl hung . . . and the following year a pair, probably the same pair, built their nest in the conch, and laid their eggs. . . . Thus is instinct in animals, taken the least out of its way, an undistinguishing, limited faculty; and blind to every circumstance that does not immediately respect self-preservation, or lead at once to the propagation or support of their species.

This is an inadequate explanation. I would rather say, that Instinct is the wisdom of the species, not of the Individual; but that let any circumstance occur regularly thro' many generations, that then its *every-time-felt* inconvenience would by little & little act thro' the blind sensations on the organic frame of the animals, till at length they were *born* wise in that respect. And by the same process do they lose their not *in*nate but *con*nate wisdom: thus Hens hatched in an artificial oven, as in Egypt, in 3 or 4 generations (the same process having been repeated in each) lose the instinct of Brooding. I trust, that this Note will not be considered as lessening the value of this sweet delightful Book. S. T. Coleridge.
July 7, 1810 Keswick.

See p. 356.[1]

5 I 326 | Letter 23 to Barrington 8 Jun 1775

The remark that I shall make on these cobweb-like appearances called gossamer, is, that, strange and superstitious as the notions about them were formerly, nobody in these days doubts but that they are the real production of small spiders, which swarm in the fields in fine weather in autumn, and have a power of shooting out webs from their tails so as to render themselves buoyant, and lighter than air.

Permit me to observe, as a certain yet hitherto unnoticed, etymology of this word, that it is "God's Dame's Hair", and in monkish Latin (where I found it) called Fila Mariæ, *Capilla Matris Dei*—/ Thus Gossip, i.e. *God's Sib.*[1]

6 I 332 | Letter 25 to Barrington 2 Oct 1775

[Of a clan of gypsies called *Curleople*, the termination of which name "is apparently Greek":] It would be matter of some curiosity, could one meet

4[1] I.e. **8** below.

5[1] C later published a variant of this observation as a contribution to RS's *Omniana* (2 vols 1812) sec 76. The Latin means "Mary's thread", "*the hair of the Mother of God*"; C could have found a very similar etymology in Stephen Skinner *Etymologicon linguae anglicanae* (1671). Cf *SW & F* (*CC*) 1098 and n 2.

with an intelligent person among them, to inquire whether, in their jargon, they still retain any *Greek* words: the *Greek* radicals will appear in hand, foot, head, water, earth, &c. It is possible that amidst their cant and corrupted dialect many mutilated remains of their native language might still be discovered.

This has been done by a learned German, ⟨(Grellman)⟩ who has made it evident, that they are the remains of an expelled nation from between Persia & Hindostan.[1]

7 I 333

Gypsies are called in *French*, *Bohemians*; in *Italian* and modern *Greek*, *Zingani*.

The Zingani in Calabria and Apulia are not Gypsies; but Christian Greeks with a very strange religion.[1]

8 I 356 | Letter 31 to Barrington 29 Apr 1776

To a thinking mind nothing is more wonderful than that early instinct which impresses young animals with the notion of the situation of their natural weapons, and of using them properly in their own defence, even before those weapons subsist or are formed. Thus a young cock will spar at his adversary before his spurs are grown; and a calf or a lamb will push with their heads before their horns are sprouted.

See p. 292.[1]

9 I 358 | Letter 32 to Barrington, n.d.

Thus far it is plain that the deprivation of *masculine vigour* [by castration] puts a stop to the growth of those parts or appendages that are looked

6[1] Heinrich Moritz Gottlieb Grellmann *Die Zigeuner. Ein historischer Versuch über die Lebensart und Verfassung Sitten und Schicksahle dieses Volks in Europa, nebst ihrem Ursprung* (Desau & Leipzig 1783); 2nd ed 1787 tr by Matthew Raper as *Dissertation on the Gipsies* (1787). In the English text, sec 2 "On the Origin of the Gipsies" surveys theories about their origins, esp those based on linguistic evidence, and concludes that "the Gipsies come from Hindostan" (131); however, Grellmann also says that "It does not appear, that there is so much Persian, in the Gipsey language, as has been generally imagined; and even what there is of it they may have brought with them from their native country; as many Persian words are current in Hindostan" (163).

7[1] C's note may indicate direct personal experience or at least some informed discussion in Italy, perhaps about Nov–Dec 1805. The *Zingari* or *Zingani* of Italy and *Zigeuner* of Germany, though commonly considered gypsies, were a group of distinctive origin, being derived from a heretical Greek sect of Asia Minor, the Athinganoi or "Touch-Me-Nots".

8[1] I.e. **4**.

upon as its insignia. But the ingenious Mr. *Lisle*, in his book on husbandry, carries it much farther; for he says that the loss of those insignia alone has sometimes a strange effect on the ability itself: he had a boar so fierce and venereous, that, to prevent mischief, orders were given for his tusks to be broken off. No sooner had the beast suffered this injury than his powers forsook him, and he neglected those females to whom he was passionately attached, and from whom no fences could restrain him.

Blumenbach told me, that the abscission of the Horns of the Stag and Male Deer had the effect of Castration.[1]

10 II 7 | Letter 41 to Barrington 3 Jul 1778

Say, what impels, amidst surrounding snow
Congeal'd, the *crocus'* flamy bud to glow?
Say, what retards, amidst the summer's blaze,
Th' *autumnal bulb*, till pale, declining days?
The GOD of SEASONS; whose pervading power
Controls the sun, or sheds the fleecy shower:
He bids each flower his quick'ning word obey;
Or to each lingering bloom enjoins delay.

a noble Paraphrase of "*I do n't know*."

11 II 10 | Letter 42 to Barrington 7 Aug 1778

A good ornithologist should be able to distinguish birds by their air as well as by their colours and shape; on the ground as well as on the wing, and in the bush as well as in the hand. [White describes the flight of various birds.] . . . the *green-finch* in particular exhibits such languishing and faultering gestures as to appear like a wounded and dying bird; the *king-fisher* darts along like an arrow; *fern-owls*, or *goat-suckers*, glance in the dusk over the tops of trees like a meteor; *starlings* as it were swim along . . .

This Letter has disappointed me. I have myself made & collect~~ion~~ed a better table of characters of Flight and Motion.[1]

9[1] See **2** n 1.

11[1] This Table does not appear to have survived, but C did keep such notes, e.g. the catalogue of signs of different kinds of weather from the movements of birds and other wildlife in BM MS Egerton 2800 ff 151–4: *CN* II Appendix F.

12 II 101 | Letter 62 to Barrington, n.d.

On the 2d of *February* [1776] the thaw persisted; and on the 3d swarms of little insects were frisking and sporting in a court-yard at *South Lambeth*, as if they had felt no frost. Why the juices in the small bodies and smaller limbs of such minute beings are not frozen is a matter of curious enquiry.

* The more apposite question, perhaps, would be: the juices having been frozen, is it not plain from this that the vital principle subsists in the Solids? The juices in a frozen caterpillar are mere ice, and it breaks like a cylinder of thin glass of the same size: and yet thaw it with your breath & the animal crawls.

13 II 106 | Letter 63 to Barrington, n.d.

A circumstance that I must not omit, because it was new to us, is, that on *Friday*, *December* the 10th [1784], being bright sun-shine, the air was full of icy *spiculae*, floating in all directions, like atoms in a sun-beam let into a dark room.

This is not uncommon in Westmoreland & Cumberland. I have myself noticed it often in hard frosts.

14 II 111 | Letter 64 to Barrington, n.d.

In the sultry season of 1783 honey-dews were so frequent as to deface and destroy the beauties of my garden. My honeysuckles . . . being enveloped in a viscous substance, and loaded with black aphides, or smother-flies. The occasion of this *clammy appearance seems to be this, that in hot weather the effluvia of flowers in fields and meadows and gardens are drawn up in the day by a brisk evaporation, and then in the night fall down again with the dews, in which they are entangled . . .

This is now known to be the saccharine excrement of the Aphides. It is a true *sugar*; no wonder therefore, that, tho' not *directly* vegetable, the Bees are fond of it.[1]

15 II 112 | Letter 65 to Barrington, n.d.

The summer of the year 1783 was an amazing and portentous one, and full of horrible phaenomena; for, besides the alarming meteors and

14[1] C reports the current theory, but in fact the sticky substance found on the leaves of certain trees in hot weather comes from the trees themselves.

tremendous thunderstorms that affrighted and distressed the different counties of this kingdom, the peculiar *haze*, or smokey fog, that prevailed for many weeks in this island, and in every part of *Europe*, and even beyond its limits, was a most extraordinary appearance, unlike any thing known within the memory of man.

Occasioned by the ⟨eruption of⟩ four tremendous Rivers of Fire in Iceland.[1]

16 II 178 | *Observations on Various Parts of Nature* "Food of the Ring-dove"

One of my neighbours shot a ring-dove on an evening as it was returning from feed and going to roost. When his wife had picked and drawn it, she found its craw stuffed with the most nice and tender tops of turnips. These she washed and boiled, and so sat down to a choice and delicate plate of greens, culled and provided in this extraordinary manner.

a *plate* of greens found in the craw of a Ring-dove!! A *peck* of Turnip Tops would, when boiled, make little more.

17 II 181 | "Hen Harrier"

Of the great boldness and rapacity of birds of prey when urged on by hunger, I have seen several instances; particularly, when shooting in the winter in company with two friends, a woodcock flew across us closely pursued by a small hawk; we all three fired at the woodcock instead of the hawk, which, notwithstanding the report of three guns close by it, continued its pursuit of the woodcock, struck it down, and carried it off, as we afterwards discovered.

~~The~~ a most extraordinary fact of this kind I was myself witness to, in Germany, in the excessive cold vile ⟨winter⟩ of 1799. A flock of House Sparrows pounced down on a bone, as it was ⟨a⟩gnawing by a large Dog near a Dunghill—and by united force carried it off. The Dog drew back frightened: & growled.—On the day before near Zelle I saw a Crow attack another Crow, kill it, and *eat* it.[1] S. T. Coleridge—

15[1] C mentions this event of 1783 also (with "three or more vast rivers of fire", but without a date attached) in *Friend* (*CC*) I 101. His statement is confirmed by *GM* LVII (1787) 197–8, although it is unlikely that this was his own source since it does not give a figure to the number of lava-streams.

17[1] For other reminiscences of C's German period see **4** and **8**. In May 1799 C had someone copy into his notebook from the *Göttingisches Journal der Naturwissenschaften* an account of the terrain between Hanover and Zelle (Celle), but there appears to be no other record of his having been there, or near there, himself. *CN* I 439 and n.

THOMAS WHITFIELD

b c 1584

A Discourse of Liberty of Conscience, wherein the arguments on both sides are so equally laid together in the ballance, that the indifferent reader may without difficulty judge whither side weighes the heavier. London 1649. 4°.

Not located; marginalia printed from MS TRANSCRIPT (a). See CROMWELLIAN TRACTS.

MS TRANSCRIPTS. (a) VCL BT 37; (b) Humanities Research Center, University of Texas.

DATE. Perhaps 1818, along with other "CROMWELLIAN TRACTS".

1 p 16

To the first argument that it belongs to God alone to make lawes to bind Conscience &c. the answer is,

That the Magistrate doth make no lawes to bind Conscience, but only enjoynes men to doe that which the law of God requires, and restraines them from doing that which the law and word of God forbids, and this is his duty to doe, namely; to punish sinne, all sinne and breaches of Gods Law, whether it be in matters of Doctrine or Practise.

Answers unanswerable under the condition of an infallible Magistrate; but, as Magistrates are fallible, and because this is the one case in *which the being actually mistaken is the most likely to happen*, and the mistake is of most pernicious consequences, therefore the unanswerable arguments are not worth answering.

2 pp 16–17

Suppose the magistrate should enjoyne a superstitious Papist to take the Image which usually he prayes before, and breake it in pieces or cast it into the fire, this would goe against the Conscience of the Papist, but it would be no sinne in the Magistrate; because it is the command of God, that images being instruments of Idolatry should be destroyed: and this is the onely thing which the Magistrate commands, and not the doing of

it against his conscience, that is his owne fault only, who ought to have a Conscience better informed, and not to thinke good, evill.

Even this is a sophism. The Magistrate might break the image himself or by his Beadles; but to force the Papist himself to do it is gratuitous, inexcusable brutality. S. T. C.

CHRISTOPH MARTIN WIELAND

1733–1813

Comische Erzählungen. [Edition not named; possibly Reuttlingen 1785, like *Idris* following.]

Not located; marginalia printed from *Athenaeum* No. 1691 (24 Mar 1860) 409. This vol was described and C's notes published in the *Athenaeum* by Sir Matthew Digby Wyatt, who had borrowed it, as C did, from Rolandi's Circulating Library. In "Coleridge Marginalia on Wieland and Schiller" *MLR* XIX (1924) 344–6, Leonard L. Mackall points out that it was probably (but not certainly: see **1** n 5) the second of two vols, the first consisting of *Idris*, pub together in Reuttlingen in 1785 with a collective title-page identifying the series as *Sammlung der poetischen und prosaischen Schriften der schönen Geister in Deutschland*. See *Idris* headnote.

CONTENTS. 1–42 *Das Urtheil des Paris*; 43–76 *Endymion*; 77–124 *Juno und Ganymed*; 125–75 *Aurora und Cephalus*.

DATE. Between Apr 1812 and the summer of 1813, when C was living with the Morgans on Berners St and making use of Rolandi's Library.

1 front and back flyleaves

It seems almost ridiculous to make serious remarks upon a set of poems, which, as they provoke no comic, so do not suggest any serious feeling; if, indeed, we except that mixture of disgust, indignation, and sorrow at the writer, which flows like an undercurrent through the mind during the perusal. Yet I will hazard one observation—assertion I should have said—that Wieland's remark on the paramouncy and predominance of beauty on the mind of *women* in their preference of lovers, is really a calumny; of course, I mean comparatively with the influence of female beauty on the determinations of men.[1] Wilks, a man almost laughably ugly, said, and with truth, that the handsomest man in the kingdom had but half-an-hour's advantage of him.[2] The tale of Cephalus and Procris,

1[1] This is a theme repeated in the vol: *Endymion* begins with a long passage on the effects of his beauty; *Aurora und Cephalus* lines 65–77 offers authorities to show how women are attracted by beauty in young men, and lines 590–623 describe the beauty of Celadon as irresistible.

1[2] This was a well-known boast of John

or the possibility of loving the same Being in two persons, might have been worked up into a very beautiful poem;[3] but, alas! Wieland sacrificed everything *dem ewigen Einerley*[4] of concupiscence and description of nudity. The conclusion of the poem is especially unnatural and painful. If poetic justice required that Cephalus should be additionally punished for the low stratagems of his unjust jealousy; and if the monstrous up-starting of a real Celadon could be made endurable; yet Procris should have been represented as believing him to be Cephalus, and should have been rescued from the seduction. The last poem is incomparably the best, and yet in the same proportion gave me more pain than the others.[5] In the 4 preceding tales, the matter and the manner, the story and the execution, are at Par with each other—4 sister harlots—yclept—Filth, Smut, dirt, and Nastiness, flaunting in Coan robes[6] of tawdry muslin, stolen or borrowed from the rag fair of Italian Poetry. But the subject of Cephalus and Procris, as here treated, one might liken to a beautiful statue of conjugal love, the countenance of which the artist had wantonly deformed by a Faunish grin, scarcely more disgusting than inappropriate.— S. T. C.

2 pp 20–1 | *Das Urtheil des Paris*

Whatever sense or meaning there is in the original fiction; viz., the contest of Ambition (rank and power personified in Juno), of Wisdom = Pallas, and of Beauty = Venus, in the soul of a young Prince, is completely obliterated by this mode of handling it. The fable in itself is the counterpart of the choice of Hercules.[1]

Wilkes (1727–97), circulated e.g. in jest books. C makes a joke about his squint in *Omniana*: see *SW & F* (*CC*) 316.

1[3] According to myth, Aurora took revenge on Cephalus for rejecting her by promising that he would repent of his devotion to his wife Procris. She then aroused his jealousy, so that he went in disguise to court his wife as Celadon; when he revealed himself, she fled and joined the followers of Diana and was accidentally killed by Cephalus himself. In Wieland's version, Procris loves Cephalus *both* as Cephalus and as Celadon; he leaves her; but when he repents and goes back to her it is too late—there is another Celadon with her. The moral of the poem is spelled out in lines 880–2: he taught her to love him in another, and now he has to take the consequences.

1[4] "To the eternal uniformity".

1[5] If C was reading the ed of 1785, *Aurora und Cephalus* is in fact the last tale, and there are only four altogether.

1[6] Flimsy, near-transparent garments, as in *SW & F* (*CC*) 62.

2[1] I.e. the Judgment of Paris, which involves choosing the most beautiful one from three goddesses, is matched by the Choice of Hercules (Hercules, trying to decide what course of life to follow, is approached by two female figures representing Virtue and Pleasure, and chooses the former).

Idris. Ein Heroisch-comisches Gedicht. Fünf Gesänge. Reuttlingen 1785. 8°. With the general fly-title: *Sammlung der poetischen und prosaischen Schriften der schönen Geister in Deutschland: enthaltend Wielands Idris und Comische Erzählungen.* [This vol contains *Idris* only.]

The Johns Hopkins University Library (Special Collections Division)

This vol was described by its owner in 1924 as having a green label pasted to its cover to show that it came from "Rolandi's French, Italian, German & Spanish Circulating Library consisting of upwards of 300,000 Volumes in Ancient and Modern Foreign Literature . . . 20 Berners St., Oxford St., London". Inside the cover was a yellow label giving the number of vols in the library as "upwards of 25,000"—a discrepancy that suggests that the Wieland work was in the library for many years: Leonard L. Mackall "Coleridge marginalia on Wieland and Schiller" *MLR* XIX—1924—344–6. At some later date, probably after it and the following WIELAND *Neueste Gedichte* were donated to The Johns Hopkins University in 1928, the vol was rebound and the labels were removed.

Donor's inscription of Feb 1928 on $^{-}2$; pencilled check-marks on 43, 83, 100; a note in pencil not in C's hand on 146.

DATE. Presumably 1812–13, the period when C lived with the Morgans at 71 Berners Street, London.

1 p [199], facing the last page of text

I concede to the Poets of Faery Tales a full exemption from Chronology & Geography/ they have a right to live and move thro' Abstract Space, and in *mere* Time/ So is[a] with Spencer, and so with the Arab. Nights Ent:/ but I cannot allow a wanton & systematic Insult (as Rulers, Vandyk, the Druids, &c &c all higgledy-piggledy) for this destroys *all* Illusion.[1]

1[a] Presumably intending "it is"

1[1] These elements are combined in Canto 1, where stanza 73 mentions the Druids and stanza 75 Vandyck (Wieland's spelling, however, is the same as C's—Vandyk).

Wielands Neueste Gedichte. vom Jahre 1770 bis 1777. Rev ed. Reuttlingen 1780. 8°. With the general fly-title: *Sammlung der poetischen und prosaischen Schriften der schönen Geister in Deutschland. Enthaltend Wielands neueste Gedichte.*

The Johns Hopkins University Library (Special Collections Division)

Described by Leonard L. Mackall in the article referred to in WIELAND *Idris* headnote. Mackall calls it a "similar Rolandi volume", implying that it also contained the Rolandi labels; but if it did, they were removed on rebinding after 1924. Donor's inscription of Feb 1928 on p $^{-}$2; passages marked in pencil (not apparently by C) pp 88, 90, 118–19, 122, 127, 128, 129; pencilled notes in German in two different hands pp $^{+}$1, $^{+}$2; an offprint of Mackall's article bound in between pp $^{+}$2, $^{+}$3.

DATE. Presumably 1812–13, like the other Wieland vols from Rolandi's Library.

1 p $^{+}$3, referring to p 221, slightly cropped | "Das Wintermärchen" pt i "Der Fischer und der Geist"

[Wieland retells the story of the fisherman from *The Arabian Nights*, with omissions.]

221. O how vile a sacrilege [is] rash abridgement!—Not to [m]ention the terrific witness of [the] three baffled Oaths in the original Tale, the lucky Stratagem of the Fisherman, which blends such a human Interest in the Tale & lifts up Humanity from its prostration before physical Force, nor even the truly sublime moment when the Genius Spurns the Chest into the Ocean—the simple disturbance or rather subversion of the *Character* of an evil and rebellious Spirit, which is so finely sustained in the Original, and the Meanness of the reward by Wieland left [un]explained & inexplicable, but [by] the Arabian Poet formed in perfect [con]sequence & harmony—should have precluded the very Thought [of] this butcherly Excision.[1]

1[1] For C's love of the *Arabian Nights* see e.g. *CL* I 347, *TT* (*CC*) I 123 n 20. His objection to Wieland's version of the Fisherman's Tale has some validity, but Wieland's work is rather a sequel than an abridgement. The original story tells how a geni imprisoned underwater in a jar first promises (three times, in the first three centuries of his imprisonment) to reward his liberator, but then vows to kill him. The fisherman who eventually releases him manages to trick him into going back into the jar by asking how it could possibly have contained him. The geni at last swears to do him no harm and to bring him riches; when the fisherman once again opens the jar, the geni emerges,

1A p 243 | Pt ii "Der König der schwarzen Inseln"

Gott! welch ein Bild
Entblösst sich seinen erschroeckenden Blicken!—
Welch kläglich *Ecce-homo-* Bild!
Sein Leib, bis an die Hüften enthüllt,
Als wie von tausend Schlangentbissen . . . ?|δ

[God! What an image
Exposed itself to his terrified glance!
What a sorrowful *Ecce-homo* portrait! ?|δ
His body, uncovered to the hip,
[Disfigured] as though by a thousand serpent-bites . . .]

2 p 316, pencil | "Einige Erläuterungen zu bessern Verständniss des vorstehenden Gedichts"

So wie an der ganzen Geschichte des Königs Artus und der Tafelrunde, so ist auch an der Geschichte dieses Merlins unstreitig etwas wahres; aber was daran wahr ist von dem Fabelhaften scheiden zu wollen, möchte wohl vergebliche Mühe seyn.

[As with the whole story of King Arthur and the Round Table, so with the story of Merlin there is incontestably some truth to it; but wishing to separate what is true from what is fictional would probably be fruitless labour.]

Warum?[1]

---

kicks the jar far out to sea, and rewards the fisherman with exclusive fishing rights to a lake full of fabulous coloured fishes. Wieland begins with the reward of the coloured fishes, and takes the story on from there.

2[1] "Why?"

EDWARD WILLIAMS
ALIAS IOLO MORGANWG
1746–1826

Poems, Lyric and Pastoral. In two volumes. By Edward Williams, Bardd wrth Fraint a Defod Beirdd Ynys Prydain. 2 vols. London 1794. 12°.

Victoria College Library (Coleridge Collection)

Inscribed on the half-title of each vol "From the Author". "S T C" on title-page of Vol I only, not in C's hand. Typographical errors have been corrected, apparently by the author, on I xiv, II 34, 138. On II +1 in what appears to be RS's hand is a list of Welsh details: "The Harp | The Crwth | The Bow of twisted twigs | The Hirlas—a wild bull horn | Rodris shield.| Rodericus filius ceni Regis. | The Leek". RS has marked four maxims on II 256 with his characteristic "S", as indicated in the textual notes to **1**.

DATE. About 1796? C knew Williams personally by 13 May 1796: *CN* I 174 (16) n.

1 II: 256 | *Poetic Triades, or Triades of Song*

[a]6. Three things must be avoided in Poetry: the Frivolous; the Obscure; and the Superfluous.
[b]7. The three principle considerations of Poetical description: what is *obvious; what instantly engages the affections; and what is strikingly characteristic.
8. The three Dignities of Poetry: the True and the Wonderful united; Beauty and Sapience united; and the Union of Art and Nature.
[c]9. The three Utilities of Poetry: the praise of Virtue and Goodness; the Memory of Things remarkable; and to invigorate the Affections.
[d]10. The three indispensable Purities of Poetry: Pure Truth; Pure Language; and Purity of Manners.

1[a] This maxim is marked with a short line in the margin, apparently by C, and also with RS's pencilled "S"

1[b] Marked with a line in the margin

1[c] This maxim is marked with a short line in the margin, apparently by C, and also with RS's pencilled "S"

1[d] Marked with RS's pencilled "S" in the margin

[e]11. Three things thoroughly should all poetry be: thoroughly erudite; thoroughly animated; and thoroughly natural.

* I suppose, rather what ~~to~~ we ~~frequently~~ recollect to have frequently seen in nature, though not in the descriptions of it.

1[e] This maxim is marked with a short line in the margin, apparently by C, and also with RS's pencilled "S"

WALTER WILSON

1781–1847

Memoirs of the Life and Times of Daniel De Foe: containing a review of his writings, and his opinions upon a variety of important matters, civil and ecclesiastical. 3 vols. London 1830. 8°.

Not located; note printed from *N&Q* III (Feb 1851) 136.

DATE. After Nov 1829, the date of publication (*EC*).

1 II 205

[Wilson quotes an earlier biographer's comparison between Defoe and Addison and Steele:] "That Daniel De Foe wanted many of those qualities, both of mind and manner, which fitted Steele and Addison to be the inimitable *arbitri elegantiarum* [arbiters of taste] of English society, there can be no doubt . . ."

I doubt this, particularly in respect to Addison, and think I could select from Defoe's writings a volume equal in size to Addison's collected papers, little inferior in wit and humour, and greatly superior in vigor of style and thought.[1]

1[1] C writes appreciatively of Defoe's style in his annotated *Robinson Crusoe*: see DEFOE. He also discussed *Robinson Crusoe* in a lecture of 3 Mar 1818: *Lects 1808–1819* (*CC*) II 192.

JOHANN CHRISTOPH WOLF
1683–1739

Curae philologicae et criticae, in SS. apostolorum Jacobi Petri Judae et Joannis epistolas hujusque Apocal. Accedunt in calce quaedam ex Photii Amphilochiis adhuc non editis cum interpretatione Latina et notis. Hamburg 1735. 4°.

Harvard University (Houghton Library)

Autograph signature "S. T. Coleridge" on title-page; a misprint corrected p 704, possibly by C. On p $^{-}$2, the inscription "H— N— Coleridge e dono J. H. Green Nov. 1841."; also a pencilled list, largely erased, of the pages containing C's notes. A description of the vol on p $^{-}$4 by Reginald L. Hine, and his bookplate on p $^{-}$5 (p-d).

DATE. Possibly May 1810, when two notebook entries appear to be related to C's reading of this work: *CN* III 3778, 3793 and nn.

1 p 28 | James 2.1

του Κυρίου ἡμῶν Ιησοῦ Χριστοῦ τῆς δόξης][a] Vocem δόξης alii ad *fidem*, tanquam gloriae plenam & parariam, ad *Christum* alii, tanquam *gloriosum*, referunt.

[(AV) "My brethren, have not the faith of our Lord Jesus Christ, *the Lord* of glory, with respect of persons." Some refer the word δόξης to *faith*, as full of *glory* and effective, others to *Christ*, as *glorious*.]

? ? Whether it be not possible that δοξης may be ενεκα της δοξης—for opinion's sake.[1]

2 p 406 | Leonard Twells *Vindiciae Apocalypseos* pt 2 ch 1 § 1 De Justino martyre

Dissertator praeterea credulitatem ejus nimiam ex admissis *Sibyllae Cumaeae* oraculis, & Interpretum Alexandrinorum LXXII. cellis patere existimat. Sed positis his *Justinus M.* idoneus testis haberi potest *Apoca-*

1[a] Square bracket in original to separate text from gloss, in Wolf's footnote

1[1] The Greek word δόξα (*doxa*) means "opinion" and hence "good report" or "glory": C proposes an alternative translation, but he has to posit the omission of the preposition *heneka* "on account of" or "for the sake of".

lypseos sua aetate receptae. . . . Imponi porro Christianis & Justino M. poterat carminibus, *Sibyllae* alicui *antiquae* ab impostore aliquo suppositis; idem vero non aeque fieri poterat de libro, non ante annos admodum multos a Joanne sub nomine suo scripto, & a Christianis recepto.

[*The author of the dissertation* considers that his [Justin's] excessive credulity is revealed by his acceptance of the oracles of the *Cumaean Sibyl* and the tale of the 72 Alexandrian translators, shut in their cells. But when these are set aside, *Justin M*[*artyr*] can be taken as an adequate witness that the *Apocalypse* was accepted in this period. . . . Indeed, the Christians and Justin could have been imposed upon by poems attributed by some impostor to an *ancient Sibyl*, but this could not have equally been the case with a book written by John in his own name not so many years before, and accepted by the Christians.]

But surely the instance of the Sybilline Prophecies evinces gross credulity, and an eagerness to take as authentic whatever suited his purposes—Now Justin was a vehement Millenarian—and as such must have been bribed to believe the Apoc. genuine. Justin proves the antiquity of the book; but nothing more.[1]

3 p 440 | Rev 1.5

τῷ ἀγαπήσαντι ἡμας Pro ἀγαπήσαντι, *Bengelius* ex paucis aliquot codicibus exhibet ἀγαπῶντι, fortasse ideo, quod sic perpetua indicetur dilectio, quae *Grotii* ad h. l. est observatio.

[(AV) "Unto him who loved us"—From some few documents Bengel suggests *loves* for *loved*, thus perhaps that this indicates a continuing election, and this is Grotius' observation on this passage.]

The first Aorist has the force of the present, implying Habit—as *Birds fly*—would in Greek be expressed by the first Aorist.—[1]

4 p 496 | Rev 6.8

Καὶ εἶδον, καὶ ἰδου ἵππος χλωρὸς] Equum gilvum, qui alias dicitur ὠχθρὸς . . .

[(AV) "And I looked, and behold a pale horse"—A light yellow horse, which is otherwise called "pale" . . . .]

a cream-coloured Horse.

2[1] In LESSING *Sämmtliche Schriften* **50** C similarly objects to using the testimony of Justin Martyr as proof that Rev was accepted in his time as the work of St John. Indeed, he goes so far as to maintain that the words must have been an interpolation in the ms.

3[1] For a fuller discussion of C's views about this principle in Greek grammar see *SW & F* (*CC*) 1101 and n 4.

5 pp 515–17 | Rev 9.1–12

[Wolf summarises various interpretations of the horde of man-like locusts loosed from the bottomless pit to torture mankind for five months following the sounding of the Fifth Angel.]

It is strange that so many acute and learned Divines should have commented on a Prophecy professedly chronological without taking the least notice of the order of Time, stated by the Prophet himself. Mede was the first, I think, who perceived the necessity of regulating the interpretation by the Dates.[1]—Since then Whitaker and Faber have done, perhaps, almost as much as can be expected from uninspired sagacity.[2]—It is by the Dates that the Prophecy is distinguished from all but Daniel; and even from Daniel by the succession & connection of the Dates. Now, then supposing the writer not to be dreaming, these Dates are either literal—& how could so many events, be they what they may, take place in 4 or 5 years? The supposition is monstrous.—Or the day means a year—& this interpretation confutes by wholesale all the comments of the Papists.

6 pp 547–8 | Rev 13.18

[The interpretation of "the number of the beast" is in question.] Sequantur illi, qui nomina Graeca consectati sunt. Ex his primus fortasse est *Irenaeus*. Is enim . . . tria assert, nempe Ευάνθας, Λατεῖνος et Τειτάν.

[Let those who have sought Greek names follow. First among these perhaps is Irenaeus. For he . . . sets forth three: namely, Evanthos, Latinus, and Teitan.]

Λατεῖνος[1] Faber has adopted—and if I remember aright, without reference to Irenaeus, as his Original[2]—it is at once the name of a man, and

5[1] Joseph Mede *Clavis Apocalyptica ex innatis & insitis visionum characteribus eruta & demonstrata*, *In Sancti Joannis Apocalypsin commentarius*, and Παραλειπόμενα *or Remains on some Passages in the "Apocalypse"*: *Works* (1672) 419–32, 437–532, 581–605. The method of all three works, which depends upon first separating the order of the visions from the interpretation of them so that when the meaning of one is sure then the meaning of the others will fall into place, is recapitulated in the *Remains* as follows (*Works* 581–2): "For if we can once be assured of the meaning of one Vision, how evident then and ruled will be the way from it to find and discover the rest?"

5[2] For Faber see **6** and n 2. "Whitaker" is Edward William Whitaker (1752–1818), author of *A General and Connected View of the Prophecies Relating to the Times of the Gentiles* (Egham 1795)—issued in an expanded form as *Commentary on the Revelation of St John* (1802).

6[1] "*Lateinos*".

6[2] In *A Dissertation on the Prophecies* (2nd ed 2 vols 1807) II 308–16, George Stanley Faber considers the interpretation of the Number of the Beast, 666, in Rev 13.18. Like Wolf, he cites the opinion of Irenaeus, which was finally in favour of *Teitan* (*Adversus haereses* 5.30.3). He concludes, however (II 316), "*Lateinos* is at once *the name of a man, the title of an empire*, and *the distinguishing appellation of every individual in that empire*: and, when the sum of its nu-

of the beast-like Latinus and the Latin Empire/ but what becomes of the gender ~~of~~ in the latter case[3]—I think it possible, that the same may mean both the name of the Church (Λατεινος) letters Χξς[a] numerically, and the χαραγμα initially—& that the character may be Χριστος Ξυλῳ σταυρωμενος.[4] Such was the Image of Idolatry substituted for Paganism—

N.B. I had not read p. 549, when I wrote the note over-leaf.[b5] I think mine the better—for mine is the actual Χαραγμα,[6] borne in the right hand, as by the Crucifigeri, or signed in the forehead in Baptism. Observe too the τῳ θηριῳ & then the του θηριου.[7]

7 p 552

[Wolf summarises various interpretations of "the mark of the beast" that identify it—and Anti-Christ—with the Roman Church.]

And why should the Latin Church monopolize Anti-christ? Is the Greek Church one iota less gross in her Idolatry and Superstitions? Less adverse to true Knowlege & human Improvement?

8 p 578 | Rev 17.12

Καὶ τὰ δέκα κέρατα, ἅ εἶδες, δέκα βασιλεῖς εἰσιν] Per hos Reges idem designari opinatur partim Pontifices, partim Synedrii praesides. [A list follows.]

6[a] C uses the ς ligature (normally expanded in this ed but here retained to make his point about the three figures in the number)
6[b] I.e. the earlier part of this note

merical letters is taken in the Greek language, the language in which the Apocalypse is written, and in which therefore the calculation ought evidently to be made, it will amount precisely to 666. On these grounds then I do not hesitate to assert, that *Latinus*, and *nothing but Latinus* is *the name of the beast*; for, in no other word, descriptive of *the revived temporal beast*, or *the Papal Roman empire*, can such a fatal concurrence of circumstances be discovered." For other responses to the question about "the number of the beast" see BIBLE *NT Rev* **5** and n 1, *CN* III 3792–3 and nn.

6[3] C presumably expects the name for the empire to be neuter, like *imperium* "empire" itself; or feminine like the names of countries; but not the masculine *Latinus*.

6[4] I.e. both the nāme of the "Latin" Church, the letters Χξς signifying the number "666", and the "mark" initially—and that the character may be "Christ crucified on the Cross".

6[5] On 549 Wolf summarises a few of the more eccentric interpretations of 666, including the theory of C. A. Heumann, who believes that it symbolises Christ as the head of the Church.

6[6] "Mark".

6[7] C means presumably that his interpretation fits both the reference to the image made "to the beast" (Rev 13.14) and the reference of Rev 13.17 and 13.18 to the name "of the beast" and the number "of the beast".

[(AV) "And the ten horns which thou sawest are ten kings"—By these kings, it is believed, are designated partly pontiffs, partly rulers of the Synod.]

To all this Trash the collation of the Dates supplies a sufficient answer.

9 pp 646–7 | Rev 22.19

Καὶ ἐάν τις ἀφαιρῇ ἀπὸ τῶν λόγων βίβλου της προφητείας τάυτης, ἀφαιρήσει ὁ Θεὸς.

[(AV) "And if any man shall take away from the words of the book of this prophecy, God shall take away his part out of the book of life, and out of the holy city, and the things which are written in this book."]

This appears to me the most suspicious Text in the whole Apocalypse—In the works of undoubted Authority, the Gospels, Acts & Epistles, nothing like it is to be found—Besides, is it a Christian Threat? Is Hell threatened to any Vice, save in that mysterious passage concerning the Sin against the Holy Ghost,[1] with no reservation in case of after repentance—with no consideration of the motive preceding?—And this too in a Work which appears to have been sent directly to no Church, that could have been evidence of its authenticity? For if St John have actually sent Copies to all the Churches mentioned in the second Chapter & seq.,[2] could there have arisen so much uncertainty respecting its character? Could it have been among the νοθα and αντιλεγομενα[3] for 4 Centuries?

9[1] Mark 3.29: ". . . but he that shall blaspheme against the Holy Ghost hath never forgiveness, but is in danger of eternal damnation: Because they said, He hath an unclean spirit".

9[2] The seven churches of Rev 2 are those of Ephesus, Smyrna, Pergamos, Thyatira, Sardis, Philadelphia, and Laodicea (identified in Rev 1.11).

9[3] "Spurious" and "rejected" works.

KARL CHRISTIAN WOLFART
1778–1832

Jahrbücher für den Lebens-Magnetismus oder Neues Askläpieion I ii. Leipzig 1819. 8°. [C's copy not located.]

British Library C 126 g 1

It is not certain how much of this issue C read, since his note exists only as a page of ms bound—accidentally, it seems—into OKEN *Lehrbuch der Naturphilosophie*.

DATE. Probably 1819–20, but possibly later.

1 referring to I ii 50

§ 3. Nahrungsmittel und Arzneien wirken gleich Luft und Wasser durch dasselbe Grundwesen, welches vermöge ihrer Grundmischung—woraus übereinstimmende Wechselbeziehungen zum Organismus entstehen, die wir ihre Eigenschaften und Heilkräfte nennen—sich verschiedengestaltig den Wechselverhältnissen gemäss offenbart. Was diese einzeln und mehr lokal und nur mittelbar allgemein wirken, das wirkt der Magnetismus unmittelbar durch das Ganze, und dadurch vermittelt auch im Einzelnen: als der Eine Inbegriff von vielem Einzelnen.

§ 4. In so fern der Mensch mit andern Menschen lebt, empfängt und übt er, er mag wollen oder nicht, von und mit diesen den natürlichen Magnetismus. Sobald er aber dieser stillen Kraft des All-Lebens in sich bewusst wird, und indem er mit Bedacht davon Gebrauch macht, steigert sich eben der natürliche zum mesmerischen Magnetismus, der sonst auch der thierische genannt wurde.

§ 5. Das Leben selbst ist der Inbegriff eines, in Bezug auf die Allbewegung, zu einem besondern Kreis sich geschlossenen Wirkens oder Bewegens. Da das Bewegen nur in feinen und gröbern Strömungen oder Stralungen vermöge gegenseitiger Bestimmungen, d.h. im Ein- und Ausströmen besteht, so ist dadurch die allgemeine und besondere Wechselwirkung, oder der Magnetismus und die sogenannte *actio in distans* erklärlich und begreiflich, worauf denn das Wesen der magnetischen Wirkung beruht.

[§ 3. It is by means of the same basic essence that food and medicine act like air and water, their basic combination—a combination from which harmonious interrelations,

which we call properties and healing powers, result in an organism—enabling this essence to manifest itself in different forms according to the different relations. What these affect separately and more locally and only indirectly in a general way, magnetism affects directly through the whole and thus, as the one sum total of many components, also conveys in each component.

§ 4. In so far as man lives with other men, he exerts a natural magnetism on them and receives it from them, whether he wants to or not. But as soon as he becomes conscious of this still force of universal life in himself and uses it deliberately, it is elevated from strictly natural to mesmeric magnetism, which otherwise would also be called animal magnetism.

§ 5. With respect to the movement of the universe, life itself is the sum of an action or movement that is confined to a particular circle. Since the movement consists, by virtue of mutual provisions, only in its own cruder streaming or radiating, i.e. in influx and efflux, the general and particular reciprocal action (or magnetism and the so-called *actio in distans* [action at a distance]), on which the nature of magnetic action depends, is explicable and comprehensible in this way.]

P. 50 § 3.—An aboriginal *commixture* (*Grundmischung*) the source and antecedent of all Action and re-action!! Poor Wolfart is a second Nathaniel—I honor him for his believing Heart—the filial reverential affection, he bears to the memory of Mesmer is *beautiful*.[1] But his Brain-power has suffered a metastasis *ek*static:[2] and it thinks all its thinking in the Plexus Solaris of his Somnambules.—[3] A caput mortuum[4] of materialism is all that remains in his own skull.

§ 4. As soon as the Man becomes conscious of this "stillen Kraft des All-lebens"[5]—Aye! as soon as.—But who ever did attain to this consciousness? W. has grossly confounded Inference by Induction with Consciousness, i.e. immediate Presence of an Object to a Subject.

§ 5. Never surely did man ambulate in circulo[6] more like a blind Mill-Mare than Wolfart.[7]—And what then is *Motion*, of which Influx and Efflux are at best but relative Phænomena? Is it aught but a genus generalissimum[8] of all Changes under the form of Space, and per metaphoram[9] of Time? As well might he explain Corn by a Heap of Corn, generalizing the latter in the term, *Cumuleity*: as refer Action and Re-action to Motion.

1[1] Nathanael, "an Israelite indeed, in whom is no guile" (John 1.47) was one of the first of Jesus' disciples, as Wolfart was one of Mesmer's: see MESMER headnote.

1[2] I.e. a transformation "*out of* its [proper] place".

1[3] I.e. in the pit of his patients' stomachs. Typically, the patients of the mesmerists fell into trances (became "somnambulists") and were able, in the "clairvoyant" phase, to describe their bodies—obstructions, internal injuries, etc—from within. Cf SOUTHEY *Wesley* **99** and n 2.

1[4] "Dead head"—a chemical term for a residue. Cf C's use of the phrase in *BL* ch 7 (*CC*) I 117.

1[5] "Still force of universal life"—in textus.

1[6] "In a circle".

1[7] C uses the image of the blind mare turning the mill-wheel also in KANT *VS* **4** (following n 4).

1[8] "Most general kind".

1[9] "Metaphorically".

CHRISTIAN WOLFF

1679–1754

Logic, or rational thoughts on the powers of the human understanding; with their use and application in the knowledge and search of truth. Translated from the German of Baron Wolfius. To which is prefixed a life of the author. London 1770. 8°.

British Library C 43 b 2

With the initials "DC", slightly cropped, on the title-page, in an unidentified hand. C's notes, written before the vol went to the binder's, were folded in to be protected from cropping.

DATE. Possibly as early as 1800, but more likely 1819–22. C read a German edition in Jan–Feb 1801, and the editor of *CN* came to the conclusion that he must have read (and annotated) the English version first and have turned to the original when the translation proved unsatisfactory: *CN* I 891, 902 and nn. While it is true that the notebook entries and the annotations overlap, it was unusual for C to write extended notes in the margins of books (as opposed to flyleaves) as early as 1800, and an alternative hypothesis is that having read the German text, he came upon a copy in English and annotated it later, perhaps in conjunction with the philosophical lectures of 1819 or the logic class of 1822.

1 pp 18–21, slightly cropped | Ch 1 § 13

If the notion we have is clear, we can, in that case, either repeat to another the characters or marks, by which we distinguish a thing; or at least can represent them to ourselves, in particular, one after another; or we can do neither. . . . our notion of a Red colour is clear, yet undistinct or confused. We can, it is true, know a red colour, when it offers to our view, but yet are unable to express to another, by what marks we know it. . . . A notion is complete, when the characters or marks assigned, are sufficient to distinguish the thing at all times from all other things. . . . Our notion is adequate, if we have clear and distinct notions also of the characters or marks, by which we know a thing.

This is erroneous. For red is not only a clear but a distinct notion—that is, that which I can instantly distinguish from green or any other color. That I cannot distinguish its component elements, because to *us*, in our

present state of Knowlege, it is itself a simple element of visual sensation, cannot surely make it confused. But I suspect, that the error is in the Translation of *undeutlich* by *confused*: a~~s if~~nd the equivocal word, undistinct, for indistinguishable—.[1] I cannot explain the notion, Red; I can only *recall* it.—A man may never have seen the tricolored flag; but if he has seen, blue, red, and white, separately, I can give him a true notion of it. *Deutliche* Begriffe[2] are therefore always of Compounds or Conjunctions.—Indeed I doubt, whether it be not inconvenient to use the term, notion, of any mere perception or recollection of a simple sensation. Vorstellung or Representation would be preferable. For all Knowlege, *notio*, is of the combinations, relations, likenesses and differences, of Things.—Simple sensations, and their representations in the memory, being premised under the name of Elements, our Notions might be divided into 1. clear. 2. distinct. 3. contra-distinct, or essential. 4. compleat. (The distinction between compleat & adequate I do not understand, unless the latter mean *sufficient*:—which must vary ad hominem et ad usum,[3] & therefore no part of logic—or unless it be resolved into) 5. Immediate.—The contrary would be 1. Faint. 2. Confused. 3. Neither, yet not scientific. 4. Incompleat. 5. Mediate—1. I look at a Rose for the first time, as a Whole—2. I also distinguish the component parts. 3. I have discovered, which of these parts is peculiar to the Rose. 4. Neither of the Rose or of any existent thing can I have a compleat notion; tho' I may have of a~~n~~ mathematical Line, because it is only that which I define it as being. 5. It is still a controversy among philosophers, whether my notion of God is immediate, or intuitive, or whether it[a] mediate or discursive. In this sense only can I understand Spinoza's Assertion, that we have an adequate idea of God.[4]

My objection to Wolf's arrangement is its variableness, its ambulatory nature—and that it is merely Comparative, or endless and non-existent. For instance: I have distinct notions of the striking on the Bell, of the Hour, and the Indication, and W. calls this an adequate idea of a Clock[5]—

1[a] For "it be"

1[1] C's suspicion is correct: the German text makes a distinction between *klar* "clear" and *deutlich* "distinct", and says at this point that the notion of the colour red is *zwar klar; aber doch undeutlich*, i.e. "certainly clear, but yet indistinct". It is the translator who has added "or confused".

1[2] "*Distinct* notions".

1[3] "According to the man and to the use".

1[4] C is probably referring to the discussion of different kinds of knowledge in Spinoza *Ethics* pt 2 props 20–47, esp Prop 47 (tr): "The human mind has an adequate knowledge of God's eternal and infinite essence."

1[5] Wolff 21: "[Our notion] is inadequate, if we have but confused notions of the characters which distinguish a thing. For example, if one can not only say, that a Clock is a machine, which, by the strokes on a bell, indicates the hours, but has also dis-

but another man has furthermore distinct notions of gravitation, of the laws of vibrating particles, of the relation of the Clock to Time local & to Time solar—and the latter cannot be more than adequate, yet more than the former, which therefore cannot be adequate. And if by adequate he means only a knowlege sufficient to form a distinct idea, why make it different from distinct—and how ~~to~~ arbitrary to make the term, distinct, signify only a certain degree of distinctness? Now my classification corresponds to actual, different, States of Knowlege.

2 p 35 | § 31

If by the senses we are led to a notion of any thing, we are not to doubt its possibility; For, who can entertain a doubt of the possibility of a thing that really exists? And therefore, such notions afford a sure ground of solid knowledge.

This is equivocal. The senses tell me only, that I see, or hear, &c such & such sights, or sounds: it is my Judgement, that must decide on their real, i.e. extraneous, Existence/ Doubtless, whatever is real, must be possible in the sense, in which it is real. But in a fever I am led by my senses to see a Fiend with Horns & fiery Eyes at the bed-foot—but my Judgement tells me, that I am in a fever—and that this Sight does not refer to a correspondent Reality, because it is not possible. We decide almost as often that a thing is real because it is possible, as that it is possible because it is real—for instance, philosophers formerly smiled incredulously at many tales of Herodotus as Lies, which from increased Knowlege of causes they now credit.[1]

3 p 39 | § 36

If a distinct notion is complete; § 15.) that is, of such a nature, as only to agree to the individuals of the same species or genus, and consequently to be distinguishable at all times from all other things, that have any affinity with them, this I call a Definition; which consequently is a distinct complete notion of a species or genus: But if, in consequence of a notion, we can distinguish a certain thing under given circumstances only, for a given time, from other things present; this I call a Description. Thus the notion of an eclipse of the moon, namely, a privation of light at the full

---

tinct notions of the striking on a bell, of the hours, and of the indication; his notion of a clock is adequate . . .".

2[1] C makes the same point in BROWNE *Works* **11** (and see n 1): "The Veracity and Credibility of Herodotus has increased, and increases, with the increase of our Discoveries."

moon, is a definition . . . . On the other hand, if I order a person, who never saw a citron, to fetch me one from my Study, telling him, that it is a yellow, and somewhat oblong fruit, standing on a little table to the right hand, on entering the Study; this distinct notion is a description, as by it I can distinguish the citron only under certain circumstances; namely, so long as it remains on the same table in the Study.

What W. names a complete, I call a scientific, notion. My notion of the Bella Donna would be scientific, if I knew its peculiar sexual characters, joined with those marks, of leaves, color, &c which distinguish it from other sorts of Night-shade: even tho' its poisonous qualities were unknown to me; but it would not be a *compleat* notion of the Plant—So, that the Circle is a curve line, all the radii from the centre are equal—or that it is a figure formed by a line, one ~~ex~~ end of which is fixed and the other moveable—is a scientific idea; but a Circle has countless other properties equally peculiar—it can not therefore be called a compleat idea.

4 p 80 | Ch 4 § 8

. . . Three kinds of Syllogisms have been formed, which are called Figures, and in particular, Figure First, Second, and Third, some adding a fourth, wherein the Middle Term is the Predicate in the Major Proposition, and the Subject in the Minor. An example of the first Figure you have above, (§ 6.); of the second is the following;

"Every prudent Man has a regard to futurity:
Some Babblers have no regard to futurity;"
Therefore "Some Babblers are not prudent."

An example in the third Figure is this;

"No Fool has a regard to futurity:
Some Fools are rich;"
Therefore "Some that are rich have no regard to futurity."

This is not worthy the name of a logical Syllogism: or any other figure but the first. For the business of a Syllogism, and of simple Logic in general, is the Resolution of Truth: whereas these Figures are involutions.[1]

It is a wanton putting an affirmative in the major, and a negative in the minor—instead of making both negative—

4[1] For C's own lessons on the syllogism see *Logic* (*CC*) 99–103, 297–307.

Imprudent men have no regard to Futurity—
Babblers have no regard to Futurity—

Ergo, B. are imprudent men—Or if it were denied, that imprudence necessarily implies disregard of Futurity, it is but to add the word "proper," & the objection is removed—or in two syllogisms.

Prudent minds regard futurity
Some men regard futurity,
Ergo, some men have prudent minds

Those who disregard futurity, are not prudent
Babblers disregard it
Ergo, &c &c—

5 p 106 | § 29

We sometimes seem to draw a Conclusion from a single Premiss; which manner of reasoning is called *an immediate Consequence*. As if I say,

"A Triangle is a figure;"
Therefore, "Whoever describes a Triangle, describes a figure."

Here it should seem, as if I immediately drew one Proposition from another. But it is evident, that the one of these Propositions alone cannot possibly lead me to the other. . . . This appears still more evidently in other instances. For example, if I say,

"Every Animal perceives;"
Therefore, "Some Animals perceive."

This in fact is an Enthymeme, in which the Minor, viz. *Some Animals are Animals*, is omitted. And here, in passing, I observe, that the Proposition omitted is Identical (§ 13. c. 3.); and thus it appears, that the use of Identical Propositions are unavoidable in Syllogisms.

Here the major is omitted, as taken for granted; but the actual process of the mind, tho' unrememberably rapid, is still syllogistic:

Any figure described is a Figure.
A Triangle is a figure.
Therefore, Whoever describes a Triangle describes a Figure.—

In short, it is either 3 or not 2: and the latter is almost always the case. As in this instance, the Term Triangle is evidently used for the Mathematical Figure, not for a *Thing*: or the Premise would be false.—But if a math.

fig. then it is one identical prop—a Triangular Figure is a ~~triang~~ Figure. So in the next—/Some and every are here of exactly the same import—or else it would be—

All animals perceive—
But some Things are Animals—
Therefore, some Things perceive.

The true rule for syllogistic reasoning is never to divide in words, where there is no possible division in the Conception, either by ignorance or forgetfulness. Now the meaning of the word "every" in this Enthymeme is "[?~~eno~~] not *only some but all*." The second therefore instead of adding, as it should do, to our ~~view~~ distinct view, diminishes. It is not a new position; but a repetition of a part of it. When I say, Socrates is a man—I say something not self-evident—it might be the name of an Angel or a Dog.

CHRISTOPHER WORDSWORTH

1774–1846

Six Letters to Granville Sharp, Esq. respecting his remarks on the uses of the definitive article, in the Greek text of the New Testament, &c. [*Anonymous*.] London 1802. 8°.

Victoria College Library (Coleridge Collection)

Inscribed "S. T. C." on the title-page. EHC description of the vol as part of the "Green Bequest" in a pocket mounted on p $^{+}6$ (p-d). All C's notes are on a fly-leaf ($^{+}2$).

In a letter of 26 Jul 1802 (*CL* II 820–1), C explains the anti-Socinian controversy to which this work contributed. Christopher Wordsworth, WW's brother, was writing in support of Granville Sharp's proposed grammatical principle "as follows—When και connects two nouns (*not of the Plural number, and not Proper names*) if the article ὁ, or any of it's cases, precedes the first of the said Nouns or Participles, and is not repeated before the second Noun or Participle, the latter always relates to the same Person, that is expressed or described by the first Noun or Participle . . . from which rule he deduces absolute assertions of the Godhead of Christ" in a group of NT texts. In Wordsworth's further study of particular texts, however, C believes that "all the instances, but two, are to all intents & purposes *Proper Names* & consequently fall within Grenville Sharpe's own Exception—the two instances, which I have not found used as a Proper name, are Titus II. 13. & 2 Peter I. 1."

DATE. Jul–Aug 1802: *CL* II 820, 829.

1 p $^{+}2^{a}$

παρακαλω, κυριε, θεε πατερ—[1]

2 p $^{+}2$, referring to p 2 | Letter 1

The first step was, to determine to make an actual comparison of your theory with the volume of the New Testament.

But, at the same time, it occurred to me, that I should probably find some at least of those texts, the translation of which you had called in

1[a] The first of the series of brief entries and the only one not linked to any page in the text

1[1] "I call [on you], lord, god father"—C perhaps illustrating the problem: are "lord", "god", and "father" one, or two, or three?

question, cited and explained by the Greek Fathers; not indeed as instances of any [a]particular rule, but expounded by them naturally as men[b] would understand any other form of expression in their native language.

P. 2—contrasted with p. 19[1]

3 p +2, referring to p 14 | Letter 2 § 2

The text here [in Athanasius], indeed, is not Χριστου και Θεου [of Christ and God], but Κυριου και Θεου [of Lord and God]. Yet, if we consider, that Κυριου is the reading (so far as is known) of no other Father, version, or manuscript, and call to mind how easily, in any single case, the abbreviated το χ̅υ̅ might be converted into κυριου; moreover, when we observe, that this homily is edited by the Benedictines from a transcript (by Mill) of a *single* manuscript; and, most of all, that while, at *first sight*, the context might *appear* to *require* του κυριου, yet, in fact, του Χριστου is at least as suitable to the scope of the writer's argument, and the pertinency of his quotation . . . there can, I think, be little doubt but that the reading which proceeded from the hand of this writer, was του Χριστου και Θεου: and, if this be granted, of the rest there can be no dispute. He evidently understood the passage agreeably to *your* explanation.

14—exceeding strong in proof of κυριος being the proper name of Christ[1]

3A p 19, marked with an ink line in the margin | § 5

The fact may be, that like some others of the ancient Fathers, Ambrose occasionally was not strictly scrupulous about the soundness of some of the steps of his argument, provided they were specious, suitable to his purpose, and the conclusion orthodox. I mean to say (if the likelihood of his *ignorance* of the Greek text should be denied to me) that Ambrose would, upon occasion, convert a Latin passage boldly to his advantage, though he might not be ignorant that the Greek original would hardly admit of his interpretation.

4 p +2, referring to p 22, textus marked with a line in the margin | § 6

Socinianism was always a puny heresy in ancient times. A philosopher

2[a–b] There is a horizontal stroke in the margin against this line

2[1] I.e. **3A** below, which casts some doubt on the linguistic reliability of the Fathers.

3[1] I.e. *Kyrios* "Lord". C refers to this point also in **8**.

or an enthusiast now and then got puzzled, and wandered into Socinian language . . .

22 ? ? ?

5 p $^{+}$2, referring to p 24 | § 8

[Jerome is cited as an exception to "the *general* attachment of the orthodox to the interpretation of our vulgar translation", i.e. "the kingdom of Christ and of God" in Eph 5.5.] In the first place there is Jerome—himself an host. . . . "Ad haec videndum quid sentire voluerit, dicens *in regno Christi et Dei.* Utrumnam aliud regnum Christi sit, et aliud Dei: an idem regnum sit Patris et Filii. Et si quidem dixisset, in regno Filii et Patris, per Filium veniremus ad Patrem: et licet esset *diversitas personarum*, tamen esset regnantium una majestas; nunc vero quum dixerit, in regno Christi et Dei, ipsum Deum et Christum (*the God Christ*) intelligamus: quia et quum tradiderit regnum Deo et Patri, non erit Pater omnia in omnibus, sed Deus omnia in omnibus. Ubi autem Deus est, tam Pater quam Filius intelligi potest." [So we must see what he meant when he said *in the kingdom of Christ and God.* Whether the kingdom of Christ is one thing and the kingdom of God another. Whether there is one kingdom of Father and Son. And if indeed he had said "in the kingdom of Son and Father", we should come to the Father through the Son; and though there was a *diversity of persons* yet there was one majesty of rulers; now indeed, since he has said "in the kingdom of Christ and God", we are to understand very God and Christ; because even when he has handed over the kingdom to God and Father, the Father will not be all in all but God will be all in all. But where God is, both Father and Son may be equally understood.] I need hardly remark, Sir, that the following is the argument of this passage. There is no impropriety in calling the kingdom of heaven Christ's kingdom; for it is not written, that the *Father* in that kingdom, but that *God* shall be *all in all.* Now God is the name *common* to all the persons of the Trinity. Therefore this kingdom may be called, as it may suit the writer's purpose, the Kingdom of God the Father, of God the Christ, or of God the Holy Spirit.

24. Jerome's words do not necessarily bear their meaning—

6 p $^{+}$2, referring to p 27 | §§ 12, 15, 16

[Wordsworth quotes Chrysostom *De incomprehensibili Dei natura* 5.17 (tr Paul W. Harkins): "And Paul said: '. . . from whom is the Christ according to the flesh, who is over all things, God blessed forever, Amen.'

And again: 'No fornicator or covetous one has an inheritance in the kingdom of Christ and God.' And still again: '. . . through the appearance of our great God and Saviour Jesus Christ.' And John calls him by the same name of God when he says: 'In the beginning was the Word, and the Word was with God; and the Word was God.'"]

27.—Ditto. Idem de ambobus prædicatur, sunt igitur equales.[1] This is the argument—of which p. 29. is a confirmation.[2]

7 p $^{+}$2, referring to p 29 | §§ 15–16

We shall meet with better success in Cyrillus Alexandrinus. In his Thesaurus (under the title Εκλογαι ῥητων μετα συλλογισμων εκ της καινης διαθηκης, ὁτι Θεος κατα φυσιν ὁ υἱος, ει δε τουτο, ου ποιημα, ουδε κτισμα—see p. 267) after quoting the verse [Eph 5.5] he immediately continues: Ιδου παλιν Χριστον ονομασας ευθυς αυτον εισφερει και Θεον, ὡς του Θεου και Πατρος εν αυτῳ βασιλευοντος, αυτου τε αυ παλιν εν τῳ Πατρι. Κατα το παρ' αυτου λεγομενον, ὡς προς τον Πατερα, ὁτι παντα τα εμα σα εστι, και τα σα εμα. Ἑν δε των παντων ἡ βασιλεια, κοινη μεν υἱῳ προς πατερα, κοινη δε πατρι προς υἱον, συμβασιλευοντος δηλαδη του ἁγιου πνευματος. Πως ουν ποιημα, ὁ βασιλευων εν Πατρι, και μετα Πατρος Θεος Λογος; [Lo, again, having called him Christ he immediately adds God also, as though God and Father reign in him and he in the Father, in accordance with what was said to him by the Father, "All things that are mine are yours and yours are mine." There is one kingdom of them all, common to the son with the father and to the father with the son, the holy spirit of course reigning with them. How then can the God-Word reigning in the Father and with the Father be a creature?] (Thesaur. vol. v. p. 283.)

16. Again, in the sixth of the Dialogues de Trinitate (vol. v. p. 611.) A. Τι δε δη και μαθων ὁ των θειων ἡμιν μυστηριων ἱερουργος, Θεου βασιλειαν ωνομαζε την Χριστου; γραφει γαρ ᾧ δε· Τουτο γαρ ιστε γινωσκοντες, ὁτι πας πορνος, η ακαθαρτος, η πλεονεκτης, ὁς εστιν ειδωλολατρης, ουκ εχει κληρονομιαν εν τη βασιλειᾳ του Χριστου και Θεου. Ενδοιασαιμι γαρ αν ουδαμως, ὡς ὁτῳ περ αν ενυπαρχοι φυσικον αξιωμα, το χρηναι κρατειν, ἑψεται που και παντως αυτῳ, και το δειν ειναι Θεον. Η ουχ ὡδε ταυτ' εχειν νοησομεθα αν, ὡ Ερμεια; B. Πανυ μεν ουν. ειη γαρ αν ειπερ ὁλως Θεος παντως που και βασιλευς. A. Ειπερ ουν αρα καταληξει ποτε της του βασιλευειν ευκλειας,

6[1] "The same thing is predicated of both; therefore they are equal."

6[2] I.e. **7** following.

απολισθησειεν αν και του ειναι Θεος. και ζωη μεν η φως, ουκ ετι. σιωπω δε το ατοπον. Τις ουν αν ειν λοιπον ἡ του υἱου φυσις, θεοτητος τε και βασιλειας, και του ειναι φως απημφιεσμενη, και ζωοποιειν ουκ εχουσα το ζωης τητωμενον; [A. Why did the revealer of the divine mysteries call the kingdom of God the kingdom of Christ? For he writes thus: "For this ye know, that no whoremonger, nor unclean person, nor covetous man, who is an idolator, hath any inheritance in the kingdom of Christ and of God." I should have no doubt that one in whom exists the natural quality that he must reign must consequently and necessarily be God. Or are we to think that this is not the case, Hermias? B. Yes, indeed, for if he were wholly God he would be entirely king. A. If then he were ever to shed the glory of his kingship he would also cease to be God, and would no longer be life or light. But I pass over this absurdity. What would remain of the nature of the son if he were stripped of the divinity and the kingship and had not the power to give life to the lifeless?]

29—clearly mistates the reasoning of Cyrill
God first proved from the Basileia[1]—& then the elements of the Basileia from the God—a fair & rational Circle—~~th~~ not that he is *called* God here, but he is necessarily implied to be so—

8 p +2, referring to p 30 | § 17

[Wordsworth quotes from Cyril of Alexandria's *Epistles* (tr John I. McEnerney): "For we are servants, but he, by nature, is Lord and God, even if he was among us and in our nature according to the dispensation of the Incarnation. For this reason, the blessed Paul called him Christ and God, speaking as follows, 'For know this and understand that no fornicator, or unclean person, or covetous one who is an idolater, has any inheritance in the kingdom of Christ and God.' Consequently, all the others, as I said, may be anointed ones, and very reasonably, because of having been anointed, but Christ alone is true God, the Emmanuel."]

30 fair—but like p. 14. Κυριος a proper name[1]

9 p +2[a], referring to pp 30–1, yellowish crayon | § 18

18. From the two following examples, which will finish what I have to say at present upon Cyril, I will not pretend to claim more, than that it

9[a] At the end of the list, written below a line in the same crayon

7[1] "Kingdom", in textus. For the broad context of this remark see **9** n 1.

8[1] "Lord"—as in **3** above, to which C refers.

should be granted that they contain nothing *contrary* to your interpretation.

The first is in the Thesaurus, under the title Ὁτι βασιλευς εστιν ὁ του Θεου υἱος [That "King" is the son of God]. But as this is merely a transcript of the text, without any *further* comment, I shall spare myself the trouble of an extract.

18—directly against him, if it prove anything—[1]

10 p $^{+}$2, referring to pp 31–2 | §§ 20, 21

20. Theodoret's testimony to *your* interpretation is no less explicit than that of Cyril. . . . 21. Again, to the same meaning, but with a slight variation in the reading; which, however, one may affirm, did not originate in any such cause as that of a purpose of *accommodating* the passage to his service . . . . Here Χριστου του Θεου [of Christ the God] is carelessly and unsuspectingly put down as the equivalent expression to του Χριστου και Θεου [of the Christ and God].

31 & 32. Unobjectionable; but the point ought to have been proved before it can be called a *slight* variation &c—

11 p $^{+}$2, referring to p 33 | §§ 22, 23, following **10** textus

22. The following is what Theodoret writes on this verse [1 Cor 8.6], in his Commentary on St. Paul's Epistles. It determines not any thing. . . . 23. Neither is my fourth and last reference to Theodoret more determinate.

33. Fair/ but ditto.

12 p $^{+}$2, referring to p 34 | § 26

In the short Comment or Scholia of Jo. Damascenus on St. Paul, he writes thus upon the 5th and 6th verses. Μη νομιζητε, φησιν, απο του βιου τῃ

9[1] Christopher Wordsworth's Letter 2, pp 12–38, is concerned exclusively with a phrase in Eph 5.5, AV "in the kingdom of Christ and of God". Sharp had argued that the reference is to Christ and God as one, not as two Persons. After a survey of analogous and explanatory passages, Wordsworth concludes that of 21 Greek passages studied, 12 are not relevant and 9 support Sharp. Of 30 Latin passages, 14 are judged irrelevant, 3 support Sharp, 13 are against him (**13** textus). AV is derived from the Latin tradition. "I fancy, Sir, in fine, we may safely conclude, that our English translation of this verse, we have inherited, *solely* from the Latin text, and from the Latin interpreters" (38). C's reaction to Wordsworth's argument in general appears in the letter q in HEADNOTE.

πιστει μη συμπαροντος, την πιστιν ὑμας μετοχους αποφαινειν της Χριστου βασιλειας, ἡτις εστι του Θεου βασιλεια· μηδε τις απατατω κενῳ λογῳ, ὡς πιστεως αληθους ουσης εν τοις παρανομως βιουσι, και σωζειν αυτους δυναμενης, εφ᾽ οἱς οργιζεται κατα του κοσμου Θεος. [Do not imagine, he says, that when you have not lived in accordance with the faith, faith will make you partakers of the kingdom of Christ, which is the kingdom of God; nor let any be deceived by a vain word saying that true faith can exist in those who lead unrighteous lives and that it is able to save those on whose account God is angry with the world.] This passage is obscure from its extreme brevity. It might almost seem, that the interpretation was meant to be contradictory of your's.

34. !—What obscurity?—none! Manifestly against.—

13 p $^{+}$2, referring to p 36 | § 30

We have referred to *twenty-one* Greek passages in which the words εν τῃ βασιλειᾳ του Χριστου και Θεου [in the kingdom of the Christ and God] are quoted. Of these we consider *twelve* (viz. the passages in Nos. 1, 12, 13, 14, 18, 19, 22, 23, 25, 26, 27, 28) as determining nothing either way with respect to the meaning of those particular words: But then we observe, that it is not *for* the sake of those words that their quotations are made. The remaining nine (viz. Nos. 2, 11, 15, 16, 17, 20, 21, 24, 29) are with one voice, clear testimonies for your interpretation. That is, in fact, *all* the Greek authorities that do speak at all are on your side.

Of the *Latin* writers we refer to something more than *thirty* passages, *sixteen* of which we consider as *significant* testimonies (viz. Nos. 3, 4, 5, 8, 9, three in No. 7, No. 10, and in the Appendix, Nos. 6, 7, 16, 17, 21, 24, 25.) And of these *sixteen* we may perhaps claim *three* (viz. Nos. 8, 9, 10) to your side; the rest are plainly against you.

It is to be remarked, however, that such is the nature of those *three*, that were we to determine the true sense of the Greek *merely* from Latin interpreters, they ought, perhaps, to be accounted of as much value as all the rest put together.

P. 36/—No. only 2.[1] 20. /—*21. & 24*— ~~are~~ doubtful from the variation/ of the Latin no/ 10 being a mere translation can prove nothing/ those *three*, disingenuous—/ 8—not deducible—9 not proveable to be that [? Term/Text]

13[1] Tit 2.13 and 2 Pet 1.1: cf *CL* II 821.

"Who Wrote ΕΙΚΩΝ ΒΑΣΙΛΙΚΗ?" considered and answered, in two letters, addressed to His Grace the Archbishop of Canterbury. [With documentary supplement.] 2 pts. London 1824, 1825. 8°.

[Bound with] *King Charles the First, the Author of Ikôn Basilikè, further proved, in a letter to His Grace the Archbishop of Canterbury, in reply to the objections of Dr. Lingard, Mr. Todd, Mr. Broughton, The Edinburgh Review, and Mr. Hallam.* Cambridge 1828. [The latter work is unannotated, and perhaps never was in C's hands (see the description of the vol below). This pamphlet is dated at the end: Trinity College, Cambridge, May 23, 1828.]

University of Chicago

A slip of paper reading "With the Author's respects" is pasted on the title-page, and a note in pencil is written above the author's name: "Enriched with marginal notes by Sam: Taylor Coleridge." A note is written on p 53, and a word is inserted on p 69, a fist on p 61, and a "?" on p 117—none of them in C's hand. A letter from the author to T. I. Cornthwaite regarding the second title (*King Charles* . . .) is pasted in at pp ⁻5 (p-d)–⁻4; the signature "Tullis Cornthwaite. 1842" appears on ⁻5 (p-d).

DATE. c Jul 1825. For C's letter of 13 Jul 1825 to the Rev S. Mence after reading this book, see *CL* v 477–8. The debate about the authorship of *Eikon Basilike* is summarised in MACDIARMID **9** n 1: C had at one time sided with those who believed John Gauden to be the author, but his annotations here show that although he thought Christopher Wordsworth's arguments weak, he agreed with the conclusion that Charles himself had been the author.

1 p 51, pencil, cropped

In short, if there be any thing at all, assuredly, it is a very little, in the testimony, either of Walker or of Mrs. Gauden, which can be considered as of an original and independent character. By far the greatest part of what is material, is such as Gauden might easily have insinuated into them . . . . We must never forget, that Walker's book was not written till nearly five and forty years after the publication of the *Icôn Basilikè:* and that towards the close of that interval, he had been <u>gadding about</u>,* and talking, and disputing a great deal upon the subject; things very likely to make a confusion in any man's memory.

* Q^{y}? Might not the phrase have been omitted? Will it not be thought to

betray a passion of Prejudice against an old man merely because he had given credit to the solemn assurance of a friend & master?[1]

2 p 71, pencil, cropped

I am disposed to conjecture, and I please myself in cherishing the thought, that Fairfax read the book, and that feelings of respect and awe were produced by its perusal in the mind of the general, who, with all his faults, was a devout man: and that from this, as one main cause, arose a material change in his sentiments, affections and conduct towards the King.

But neve[r] the less assent[ed] to his Deat[h] when according to his own Avowal h[e] might have prevented it.[1]

3 p 155, pencil, cropped

[Wordsworth casts doubt on Walker's account of a conversation he held with Gauden before the work was finished.] No; Dr. Walker; here must be a mistake.—If any conversation ever took place of the kind here recorded . . . then, I must believe, that the date of it was *subsequent* to the publication of the *Icôn*, and not *before* it: in short, that this was one of those *after-infusions*, from which, as I shrewdly suspect, a great part, or the whole of the testimony of Walker was derived.* How could these persons hold this foolish talk of "no man drawing his own Picture," when we have consenting accounts from both sides that the title of the Book was not yet *Icôn Basilikè*, but *Suspiria Regalia*?

* Now this *is* an argument that *is* to the purpose. Pity, that Dr W. should have weakened the force of the impression, it is calculated to make, by the small or no account, he had made, of [. . . . .][1]

1[1] Anthony Walker, "tutor and inmate in Gauden's family, and his curate at Bocking" according to Wordsworth (20–1), wrote *A True Account of the Author of a Book Entituled,* Εἰκων Βασιλικη (1692).

2[1] Thomas Fairfax (1612–71), 3rd Baron Fairfax of Cameron, Parliamentary general and one of the judges in the trial of Charles I. More than one contemporary report testifies to his regret at his involvement in the trial and execution of the King, e.g. Edmund Ludlow *Memoirs* (3rd ed 3 vols Edinburgh 1751) III 8: "And the Lord Fairfax, on that subject, plainly said, That, if any person must be excepted [from a general indemnity], he knew no man that deserved it more than himself; who being General of the army at that time, and having power sufficient to prevent the proceedings against the King, had not thought fit to make use of it to that end." Walter Scott uses this passage in a footnote to his edition of Fairfax's own *Short Memorials* in the Somers Tracts, *A Collection of Scarce and Valuable Tracts* v (2nd ed 1811) 375n. Fairfax himself, in the memoirs (*Collection* v 395) says he made "earnest endeavours" to prevent the trial from taking place.

3[1] C perhaps meant, of Walker's actually having been shown the text before publication.

4 pp 174–5, pencil, cropped

But, if this account will not satisfy; if the notions which I have thrown out cannot be entertained; then I would further suggest, that Lord Clarendon, perhaps, was not so far influenced by the confident pretensions of Gauden, as we have been willing to allow. The whole meaning of his silence may be, that he felt the controversy would be every way a most inexpedient one.

Is this the way in which an impartial judge argues a disputed question? Would it be pardoned in any but an hired or official Pleader? Is not the fact, that Clarendon knew by his own case that the King did not scruple pious frauds of this sort, a sound and weighty argument for all minds, and at all periods? Not indeed decisive—nor in my opinion sufficient to counterbalance the weight of internal evidence, which assigns the Work to the King himself. I believe the authenticity of the Εικὼν βασιλικὴ *notwithstanding* D^r W's [. . .]tation in its support.

5 p 183, pencil

Then, again: if we may give credit to any thing which we receive from Walker,* we have an account from him in reference to Clarendon at this very same moment; and he favors us, (though it be thirty years after they were spoken,) with what he calls "Bishop Gauden's *own words* to him upon that occasion."

* This causeless and unjust antipathy to Dr Walker annoys & provokes me more than all the rest—

5A p 353, marked with a small pencilled cross in the margin similar to C's crosses elsewhere

You will further judge whether such writing, as the above, deserves the character which is given of Charles's acknowledged Productions by Mr. Laing and others.

5B p 353, marked with a small pencilled cross

Gauden, to be sure, as we saw before, had derived some knowledge of part of the above circumstances, from Stephen Marshall.

WILLIAM WORDSWORTH

1770–1850

“Benjamin the Waggoner” MS I.

The Wordsworth Trust, Grasmere

A notebook containing the earliest surviving complete transcription of the poem that was eventually published as *The Waggoner* in 1819, in the hand of MW. This draft has been fully described along with other versions in the Cornell Wordsworth series, and our account of the ms is much indebted to it: William Wordsworth *Benjamin the Waggoner* ed Paul F. Betz (Ithaca 1981) esp 141–2, 343–53. Line numbers here are keyed to the Reading Text of MS I in that ed. Betz prints C’s annotations (with some readings different from ours) in an Appendix, and shows that in subsequent revisions, some of them made on these same sheets, WW took C’s suggestions for improvement “very seriously” (343). The process of revision had begun before C made his comments, however (**2**). Our presentation here attempts to reconstruct the ms as C saw it in the fair copy so that textus includes previous but not subsequent layers of Wordsworthian revision.

DATE. Shortly after C’s return from the Mediterranean, perhaps as early as 26 Oct 1806 when he was reunited with the Wordsworths, but most probably between Dec 1806 and Mar 1807, while he was staying with them at Coleorton.

1 f 3v, pencil, commenting on text f 4r, partially overwritten in pencil by MW | Lines 73–7

If thou resist that tempting door
Which with such friendly voice will call
† Look at thee with so bright a lure*
For surely if no other where
Candle or lamp is burning there

* From disuse of reading poetry, and thinking like a Poet, I am probably grown dull; but this † line I did not discover the meaning or construction, for some minutes of endeavor. Might I propose the addition of

“will call,
If he resist those Casement Panes
Which o’er his Leader’s Bells & Manes

Will make th' old mossy High-way Wall
Look at him with so bright a Lure:—
For surely &c—["]

2 f 5^{v}, pencil, commenting on text f 6^{r} and WW revisions in pencil f 5^{v}; C's note overwritten by MW and WW | Lines 114–24

I'm here and with my horses yet.
He makes a mighty noise about me
And yet he cannot do without me
My jolly Team he finds that ye
Will work for nobody but me
Finds that with hills so steep and high
This monster at our heels must lie
Dead as a cheese upon a shelf
Or fairly learn to draw itself *
When I was gone he felt his lack
And was right glad to have me back

[In pencilled draft revisions on the facing leaf, WW proposes alternative lines 119–22:

That up these mountains without me
Tis vain to strive for Mastery
That neither Horse nor Wain will stir
If B—— be not the Waggoner]

* What if—

high
"This monster at the foot must lie
Or half-way up ~~on~~ the Fell-side road
~~With~~ Its wheels as lifeless as its load,
While that Hill bad, and this Hill worse is,
In spite of sober Simon's curses,
Or stinging whip of sneaking Relph,
Unless it learn to draw itself.—
When Ben was gone, he felt his Lack
And was right glad to have him back—
For neither Horse or Wain would stir, &c.?["]

The Excursion, being a portion of the Recluse, a poem. London 1814. 4°.

Private collection

Bookplate of Henry S. Northcote on p $^{-}3$ (p-d). Squiggle in ink on p 291 not by C, whose notes are all in pencil.

Most of the notes written by C on the first four books of *The Excursion* in this copy have been so effectively erased that no reconstruction is possible, though the locations of notes can be indicated, and in that case are numbered in series as though the notes were there. C's reservations about *The Excursion* were the subject of a fine letter to WW (*CL* IV 571–6). Later, the severe review of the poem in the *Ed Rev* supplied some of the impetus behind *BL*; cf *BL* ch 21 (*CC*) II 107–18. The bookplate indicates that the volume belonged to Henry Stafford Northcote (1792–1851), eldest son of Sir Stafford Henry Northcote (1762–1851), the baronet who, according to C's own account, saved his life when he was a child: *CL* I 353. C annotated this copy before it was properly bound (**5**), perhaps fairly soon after publication. Unlike the preserved notes, the erased notes did not leave traces of themselves offset on the facing pages—evidence that suggests that they were rubbed out not long after being made, perhaps by the binder, perhaps by the owner, perhaps by C himself.

DATE. Possibly Aug-early Sept 1814, while C was living in Bristol. *The Excursion* was published Aug 1814 (the Dedication being dated 29 Jul), and C had certainly read it—whether in this copy or another—and the review of Nov 1814, by Apr 1815: *CL* IV 564.

A p 9, marked with a partially erased pencil line in the margin | I 121–4

Espoused the Teacher of the Village School;
Who on her offspring zealously bestowed
Needful instruction;* not alone in arts
Which to his humble duties appertained . . .

B p 9, marked with a partially erased pencil line in the margin | I 134–8

From his sixth year, the Boy of whom I speak,
In summer, tended cattle on the Hills;
But, through the inclement and the perilous days
Of long-continuing winter, he repaired
To his Step-father's School* . . .

C p 19, pencil, marked with a partially erased line in the margin | I 328–30

> The mother strove to make her son perceive
> With what advantage he might teach a School
> In the adjoining Village;) but the Youth . . .

D pp 119–20, marked with a pencil line in the margin | III 530–61

> a sheltered Hold,
> In a soft clime encouraging the soil
> To a luxuriant bounty!—As our steps
> Approach the embowered Abode, our chosen Seat,
> See, rooted in the earth, its kindly bed,
> The unendangered Myrtle, decked with flowers,
> Before the threshold stands to welcome us!
> While, in the flowering Myrtle's neighbourhood,
> Not overlooked but courting no regard
> Those native plants, the Holly and the Yew,
> Gave modest intimation to the mind
> Of willingness with which they would unite
> With the green Myrtle, to endear the hours
> Of winter, and protect that pleasant place.
> —Wild were the walks upon those lonely Downs,
> Track leading into track, how marked, how worn
> Into bright verdure, among fern and gorse
> Winding away its never-ending line,
> On their smooth surface, evidence was none:
> But, there, lay open to our daily haunt,
> A range of unappropriated earth,
> Where youth's ambitious feet might move at large;
> Whence, unmolested Wanderers, we beheld
> The shining Giver of the Day diffuse
> His brightness, o'er a tract of sea and land
> Gay as our spirits, free as our desires,
> As our enjoyments boundless.—From these Heights
> We dropped, at pleasure, into sylvan Combs;
> Where arbours of impenetrable shade,
> And mossy seats detained us side by side,
> With hearts at ease, and knowledge in our hearts
> "That all the grove and all the day was ours."

1 p 143, pencil, erased | IV 38–42

Be mute who will, who can,
Yet I will praise thee with empassioned voice:
My lips, that may forget thee in the crowd,
Cannot forget thee here; where Thou hast built,*
For thy own glory, in the wilderness!

[a]* remembered, unconsciously I [? doubt not,] from a mss drama of mine

The Whirl[. . . .] the desert sands rise up [. . .]
themselves [. . .] from Heaven to Earth
they stand
a Temple
[. . .] by Omnipotence to its own Honor[1]

2 p 145, marked with a line in pencil, note erased | IV 99–103

those transcendent truths
Of the pure Intellect, that stand as laws,
(Submission constituting strength and power)
Even to thy Being's infinite majesty!

3 p 152, pencil, note of 4 lines erased | IV 258–61

But, methought,
That He, whose fixed despondency had given
Impulse and motive to that strong discourse,
Was less upraised in spirit than* abashed . . .

4 p 154, pencil | IV 281–92

. . . Nor unreproved by Providence, thus speaking
To the inattentive Children of the World,

1[a] This note, much erased, has been reconstructed by John Beer

1[1] C refers to an unfinished play of 1800, *The Triumph of Loyalty*, lines 338–41 (*PW*—EHC—II 1072):

The Whirl-blast comes, the desert-sands rise up
And shape themselves; from Heaven to Earth they stand,
As though they were the Pillars of a Temple,
Built by Omnipotence in its own honour!

In 1817 C was to publish the passage containing these lines as *A Night-Scene* in *Sibylline Leaves*: *PW* (EHC) I 423.

"Vain-glorious Generation! what new powers
On you have been conferred? what gifts, withheld
From your Progenitors, have Ye received,
Fit recompense of new desert? what claim
Are ye prepared to urge, that my decrees
For you should undergo a sudden change;
And the weak functions of one busy day,
Reclaiming and extirpating, perform
What all the slowly-moving Years of Time,
With their united force, have left undone? . . ."

Might not Providence have addressed the same language to Luther? To Dr Bell?[1] To every bold Benefactor of the Human Race?

5 p 155, pencil, cropped | IV 211–17

. . . the law,
By which Mankind now suffers, is most just.
For by superior energies; more strict
Affiance in each other; faith more firm
In their unhallowed principles; the Bad
Have fairly earned a victory o'er the weak,
The vacillating, inconsistent Good.

Compare this with the sa[me] Truth announced in "[The] Friend"—[1]

5A p 160, marked in pencil | IV 339–41

. . . to the Emmet gives
Her foresight; and the intelligence that makes
The tiny Creatures strong by social league . . .

6 p 168, pencil, note of 9–10 lines erased | IV 523–5

This rather would I do than see and hear
The repetitions wearisome of sense,*
Where soul is dead, and feeling hath no place . . .

4[1] Andrew Bell (1753–1832), reformer in education, whose "Madras System" in which pupils assist and tutor one another C championed in e.g. *Friend* (*CC*) I 102 (and see n 4), *Lects 1808–1819* (*CC*) I 578–89.

5[1] C must be referring to the essay on English law in which he approvingly quotes Milton's declaration, "I cannot praise a fugitive and cloistered virtue, that never sallies out and sees her adversary": *Friend* (*CC*) I 79–80.

7 p 169, pencil, marginal note of about 12 lines erased | IV 564–6

> Upon the breast of new-created Earth
> Man walked; and when and wheresoe'er he moved,
> Alone or mated, Solitude was not.

["The Prelude".] MS B.

Two notebooks, continuously paginated, containing the ms of *Prelude* I–XIII.

The Wordsworth Trust, Grasmere

The text is a fair copy of the as-yet-untitled *Prelude*, in the hand of MW, made for C between Dec 1805 and Feb 1806. The ms itself and its place in the evolution of WW's poem are described at length in *The Thirteen-Book* Prelude *by William Wordsworth* ed Mark Reed (2 vols Ithaca 1991). Line references in our headlines are keyed to the Reading Text in that ed (*Prelude 1805–6*), which provides a photograph and transcriptions (varying somewhat from ours) of the page upon which most of C's notes appear (I [148]; see Frontispiece), besides an apparatus that makes it possible to trace WW's subsequent revisions. Page references follow the original numbering in the ms, although it has also been foliated.

DATE. Between 26 Oct 1806, when C saw the Wordsworths for the first time since his return to England from the Mediterranean, and mid-Apr 1807—probably earlier rather than later in that period, but perhaps after 21 Dec 1806, when C arrived at Coleorton for an extended visit.

1 MS B i [148], referring to i 133, marked with a pencil line in the margin | Cf *Prelude 1805–6* VI 343–5

> Of College cares and study was the scheme,
> Nor entertain'd without concern for those
> To whom my worldly interests were dear . . .

p. 133 l. 14. 16. to *me* were obscure, and *now* appear rather *awkwardly* expressed. I should wish to trace the classical use of the word "Concern". These are the passages, which it is so difficult & fretsome to correct; because, if once amiss, no after genial moment can be pressed into the dull service of amending them. Yet I venture to propose, thinking dilatation better than awkwardness—

> "A disregard
> Of College objects was our scheme, say rather,
> A mere Slight of the studies and the cares
> Expected from us, we too being the~~re~~n
> Just at the close of our noviciate:
> Nor was it formed by me without some fears,
> And some uneasy forethought of the pain,

The Censures, and ill-omening of those,
To whom my worldly Interests were dear—["]

2 i [148], referring to i 135 | VI 386–7

Swift Rhone, thou wert the wings on which we cut
Between thy lofty rocks!

135. l. 5. "*we cut*". May "cut" be used neutrally in pure language? If so, tis right & the best: if not "we flew" or "we rush'd"

3 i [148], referring to i 137, marked with a small cross | VI 446–7

My heart leap'd up when first I did look down
On that which was first seen of those deep haunts . . .

137. l. 13. leap'd *up*, look'd down/ leap'd high?—or rather
O! my Heart leap'd when first &c—

4 i [148], referring to i 138 | VI 465–8

The Maiden spread the hay-cock in the sun,
While Winter like a tamed Lion walks
Descending from the mountain to make sport
Among the cottages by beds of flowers.

138. l. 7. This line I would omit; as it clearly carries on the metaphor of the Lion, & yet is contradictory to the idea of *a "tamed" Lion*/ "to make sport" &c is here at once the proof of his having been tamed, & the object of his "descending from the mountains"—which appear incompatible.

5 i [148], referring to i 141 | VI 543–6

The mind beneath such banners militant
Thinks not of spoils, trophies, nor of aught, nor
That may attest its prowess, blest in thoughts
That are their own perfection and reward . . .

141. l. 3. 4.—*aught*: *thoughts*—was a hitch to my ear—
? Seeks for no trophies, struggles for no spoils
That may attest &c.

6 i [148], referring to i 141 | VI 547–8

Strong in itself, and, in the access of joy
Which hides it like the overflowing Nile.

D? l. 7.—Was it by mere caprice or a beginning of an impulse to alter, from having looked over the latter half of this Book for the purpose of correcting, which I employed myself on for the ~~purpose~~ deadening of a too strong feeling, which the personal Passages, so exquisitely beautiful, had excited—that I wished this faultless Line to stand

"Spread o'er it, like the fertilizing Nile"—?

For fear, it should be so, I will leave off. Ὑστερον αδιον ασω.[1]

6[1] "Tomorrow I will sing another song": Theocritus 1.145, q var in the Preface to *Kubla Khan* (*PW*—EHC—I 297).

Translation of Virgil *Aeneid* bk 1

The Wordsworth Trust, Grasmere

C wrote these notes at WW's request, on the first of three notebooks containing WW's translation of *Aeneid* bks 1–3—a copy in the hand of MW. With the exception of **46** and the various marks described in the headlines, C's notes are not strictly marginalia but notes written on three leaves of paper that are now bound in as a separate booklet, with a note by DW on f 3^{v}, "Coleridge's remarks on Virgil". Other annotations on the ms appear not to be C's, neither the pencilled comment "beautiful" at lines 214–32 nor the corrections made by MW and WW in this and the other notebooks. A fourth notebook catalogued in the same group of mss (DC MS 101) contains another copy of most of the text of bks 1–3 and includes draft revisions that show WW responding to C's comments.

The numbering of lines in the ms is not quite accurate. We therefore give the line numbers as they appear (since C refers to them that way) but also include the correct numbering, in square brackets. Book and line numbers following the last vertical rule in a headline refer to the Latin original.

WW's translation is pub in full in *WPW* IV 286–357, and Graver. All English translations not otherwise attributed are by H. Rushton Fairclough (LCL).

DATE. About 8–12 Apr 1824: *CL* V 353.

1

~~First Book~~ Before I commence this revision which had it but been an original poem of yours most chearfully should I have d~~oes~~one, I must put you on your guard against the morbid hyper-critical state of my taste—to my own grievance & Damage./ I can only put a mark + to the objections, that I feel confident are worth attending to: and −, where I am myself doubtful. S. T. C.—

2 I 1–3 | *Aeneid* I 1–3

Arms, and the Man I sing, the first who bore
His course to Latium from the Trojan shore,
A Fugitive of Fate . . .

First Book.
Line.
− 3. A Fugitive *of* Fate, were it less dubious English, seems to give the

sense of fato profugus, urged by propelling fate? ~~Propelled by~~ By destiny, propelled? A fated Fugitive?—

3 I 3–4 | I 3–4

long time was He
By Powers celestial toss'd on land and sea . . .

4. By force supernal.

4 I 5, marked with pencilled + in ms | I 4

\+ Through Juno's unrelenting enmity

\+ 5. might not "through" be omitted, & the line put in Apposition? Stern Juno's unrelenting⟨forgetting⟩[a] enmity!

5 I 8–9 | I 6–7

Whence flowed the Latin People; whence have come
The Alban Sires, and Walls of lofty Rome.

\+ ∯ 8.—*came*? any thing better than flow'd—.
have come might apply to the Walls & l. R. but not to the *Alban* Sires.

6 I 10–14 | I 8–11

Say, Muse, what Powers were wrong'd, what grievance drove
To such extremity the Spouse of Jove,
Labouring to wrap in perils, to astound
With woes, a Man for piety renown'd!
In heavenly breasts is such resentment found?

10–14.—This §ph. should be retranslated—

7 I 15–17 | I 12–14

Right opposite the Italian Coast there stood
An ancient City, far from Tiber's flood,
Carthage its name

15. 16.—Dryden's seems preferable.[1] longè applies to the whole, or

4[a] The insertion is written immediately above the "relenting" of "unrelenting"

7[1] "Against the *Tiber*'s Mouth, but far away, / An ancient Town was seated on the Sea: / A *Tyrian* Colony . . . *Carthage* the Name": Dryden's translation of the same

rather the Mouth of the Tiber completes the Italiam.[2]—Distant but lying opposite to the Italian Coast, where the Tiber disembogues itself.

8 I 17–30, marked with pencilled – in ms | I 12–22

a Colony of Tyre,
Rich, strong, and bent on war with fierce desire.
– No region, not even Samos, was so graced
– By Juno's favour; here her Arms were placed,
Here lodged her Chariot; and unbounded scope,
Even then, the Goddess gave to partial hope;
Her aim (if Fate such triumph will allow)
That to this Nation all the world shall bow.
But Fame had told her that a Race, from Troy
Derived, the Tyrian ramparts would destroy;
That from this stock, a People, proud in war,
And train'd to spread dominion wide and far,
Should come, and through her favourite Lybian State
Spread utter ruin:—such the doom of Fate.

+ 18. – 21 – 26—as neither translation or poetry.—Pope; or Ha/yley, might talk giving an *unbounded* scope (i.e. no *scope* at all) to partial hope;[1] but not *W.W.*—much less in lieu of tenditque fovetque.[2] – 28—wide & far. I fear a something ludicrous in this hystero-proterizing of a familiar idiom, so bare-facedly for rhyme's sake.

9 I 47–8 [45–6], marked with pencilled + in ms | I 34–5

Sicilian headlands scarcely out of sight,
+ They spread the canvas with a fresh delight . . .

p. 3.
48. They set ~~sail~~ their sails for the open sea, and ~~keeled the~~ met the longer or bolder waves—this is the sense—by a triplet it might be expressed—

lines, from *Works* v (Berkeley 1987) 344.

7[2] The question is whether *longe* ("far" or "afar" or "far away") refers only to the mouth of the Tiber or also to Italy in lines 13–14 *Italiam contra Tiberinaque longe ostia*.

8[1] C quotes textus. He is not claiming that either Pope or William Hayley (1745–1820) committed this contradiction in terms; but Pope used the word "unbounded" frequently in translations of Homer that C considered to have been the source of a great deal of careless English verse: see e.g. *BL* ch 2 (*CC*) I 39–40*. C annotated Hayley's life of Milton: HAYLEY.

8[2] *Aeneid* I 18 "[it] was [her] aim and cherished hope", lit "she both aimed at and cherished [it]".

9A I 49–51 [47–9], pencil | I 36–7

Then Juno, brooding o'er the eternal wound,
Thus <u>inly</u>;—"Must I vanquish'd quit the ground
"Of my attempt? . . ."

9B I 56 [54], marked with pencilled + in ms | I 41

"The desperate frenzy of Oïleus' Son . . ." +

9C I 76–7 [74–5], marked with pencilled + in ms | I 58–9

+ This did he not,—sea, earth, and heaven's vast deep
Would follow them, entangled in the sweep . . .

10 I 83–9 [81–7], marked with pencilled + in ms | I 63–70

+ And give, on due command, a loosen'd rein.
As she approached, thus spake the suppliant Queen:
"Aeolus! (for the Sire of Gods and men
"On thee confers the power to tranquillise
"The troubl'd waves, or summon them to rise)
+ "A Race, my Foes, bears o'er the troubled Sea
"Troy and her conquer'd Gods to Italy.
"Throw power into the winds; the ships submerge,
"Or part,—and give their bodies to the surge. . . ."

4.[1]
83. + 88—obscure & reads uncouth—A Rāce, mȳ fo͞es, be͞ars o'er. − 91. *weak*—age diversos[2]—is more than *part*, ⟨or scatter: let the corses mount the surge?⟩ ~~&~~ at all events *their~~s~~* is unhappy—. Virgil avoids this confusion of Antecedents. The Corses?

11 I 104–11 [102–9] | I 81–6

When Aeolus had ceased, his spear he bent
Full on the quarter where the winds were pent,
And smote the mountain.—Forth, where way was made,
Rush his wild Ministers; the land pervade,
And fasten on the Deep. There Eurus, there
Notus, and Africus unused to spare

10[1] This is the page number in the ms.
10[2] *Aeneid* I 70 tr "or drive the men asunder [*age diversos*] and scatter their bodies o'er the deep".

His tempests, work with congregated power,
To upturn the abyss, and roll the unwieldy waves ashore.

108.—And bear down on the Deep. + unused to spare his tempests.—There Eurus, ~~Notus~~ here Notus, and Africus (the Seaman's Fear!)

Apt for the storm, with c. p.
Upturn &c—

12 I 135–40 [133–8] | I 104–7

Help from her shatter'd oars in vain she craves;
Then veers the prow, exposing to the waves
Her side; and lo! a surge, to mountain height
Gathering, prepares to burst with its whole weight.
Those hang aloft, as if in air; to these
Earth is disclosed between the boiling seas . . .

136 + Help from—craves. Is this a translation of Franguntur remi![1]—but the *She* render the whole description obscure—is ~~veers~~ Prow the Nom. or Accus. of *veers*—& is "veer" ever used of a *part* of a Ship. The Ship may veer; but can the Prow?—I but put the question.—*Those* & *these* occasion an ~~unnecessary~~ additional perplexity—. Item. The Voice may ~~have~~ force a metrical effect on "prepares to burst with its whole weight"—I do not like the *and lo*! it produces a pause not intended—and removes the instantaneous *in*sequence—Furit æstus arenis[2]—you imply in "*boiling*"—but surely Virgil meant to shew that the storm had driven the fleet shoreward & into shallow water.

13 I 141–8 [139–46] | I 108–12

three encounter shocks
In the main sea receiv'd from latent rocks;
Rocks stretched in dorsal ridge of rugged frame
On the Deep's surface; ALTARS is the name
By which the Italians mark them. Three the force
Of Eurus hurries from an open course
On straits and Shallows, dashes on the strand,
And girds the wreck about with heaps of sand.

142. *Encounter* a shock *received* from? ~~In brevia et syrtis urget~~[1] As to

12[1] *Aeneid* I 104 tr "The oars snap".
12[2] *Aeneid* I 107 tr "the surges seethe with sand".
13[1] *Aeneid* I 111 tr "forces . . . into shallows and sandbanks".

these Lines, however, you construe them otherwise than I should—& I doubt not, better, ~~from~~ as having studied it. I should not give all the force to Virgil's *ab Alto* that you have done. I should construe it, "from deep water"—.[2] But the "latentia" seems not a happy epithet in connection with Dorsum immane Mari summo.—[3]

14 I 164–72 [162–70] | I 124–9

> Meanwhile, what strife disturb'd the roaring sea,
> And for what outrages the storm was free,
> Troubling the Ocean to its inmost caves,
> Neptune perceiv'd incensed; and o'er the waves
> Forth-looking with a stedfast brow and eye
> Raised from the Deep in placid majesty,
> He saw the Trojan Gallies scatter'd wide,
> The men they bore oppress'd and terrified;
> Waters and ruinous Heaven against their peace allied.

16~~4~~5. &c.—And for what outrages—&c. Not *translation*—Nept. perc. incensed.—I can scarcely read, as part of a sentence. It seems to my ear as if I were repeating single words—perceived, incensed, admir'd &c—"and terrified" a rhyme to "against their *peace* ALLIED"!

15 I 173–4 [171–2] | I 130

> Nor from the Brother was conceal'd the heat
> Of Juno's anger, and each dark deceit.

+ 172, 3/—~~4~~ So simple in the original—Nor was Neptune any Stranger to his Sister's Tricks and Tempers—. *The heat of anger* is not the meaning of *Irae* (plural)—nor does *doli* mean—["]*dark* deceit".[1]

The following Speech is as good as the original—which for the life of me I could never read even at School but as a Tom Thumb Tragedy[2]—

13[2] *Aeneid* I 110 tr "from the deep", corresponding to WW's "from an open course" (he having used "the Deep" for *fluctibus* two lines earlier).

13[3] From *Aeneid* I 108, 110, tr "hidden [rocks]" and "a huge ridge topping the sea". WW chooses the more Latinate "latent" and "dorsal".

15[1] *Aeneid* I 130 *nec latuere doli fratrem Iunonis et irae* tr "nor did Juno's wiles and wrath escape her brother" (both *irae* and *doli* being plural forms).

15[2] I.e. as absurdly inflated, after the manner of Henry Fielding's burlesque *Tom Thumb, a Tragedy* (1730), enlarged as *The Tragedy of Tragedies* (1731). The "following Speech" to which C refers is *Aeneid* I 132–41, rendered thus in WW's lines 177–92 [175–90]:

> "Upon your Birth and Kind
> "Have ye presumed with confidence so blind
> "As, heedless of my Godhead, to perplex

The quos ego. Sed motos[3]—for exquisite vulgarity & boat-swain Mutter is incomparable.—Obiter dictum sit:[4] "Godhead" is far too theological & abstract a word.

16 I 191–4 [189–92] | I 142–3

> He spake; and, quicker than the word, his will
> Felt through the sea abates each tumid hill,
> Quiets the deep, and silences the shores,
> And to a cloudless heaven the Sun restores.

L. 194. Qy Unclouds the Heaven and the Sun restores

17 I 200–3 [198–201] | I 148–50

> Thus oft, when a sedition hath ensued,
> Arouzing all the ignoble multitude,
> Straight through the air do stones and torches fly,
> With every Missile frenzy can supply . . .

200. *Ensued*? coorta est?[1] This is a very remarkable instance of an inverted Simile. I imagine that Virgil's purpose was to prepare the reader's fancy for land and city imagery & interests.

18 I 211–13 [209–11] | I 155–6

> Then, when the Sire, casting his eyes abroad,
> Turns under open Heaven his docile Steeds,
> And with his flowing Chariot smoothly speeds.

213.—"Flowing" is very bold: but I think it an improvement.[1]

"The Land with uproar, and the Sea to vex,
"Which by your act, O winds! thus fiercely heaves
"Whom I—but better calm the troubled waves.
"Henceforth, atonement shall not prove so slight
"For such a trespass; to your King take flight,
"And say that not, to *Him*, but unto *Me*,
"Fate hath assignd this watry sovereignty;
"Mine is the Trident—his a rocky Hold,
"Thy mansion, Eurus!—vaunting, uncontroll'd,
"Let Aeolus there occupy his hall,
"And in that prison-house the winds enthrall!"

15[3] *Aeneid* I 135 tr by WW "Whom I—but [better to calm the] troubled [waves]" (as q in the preceding n).

15[4] "Let it be a passing remark"—or more idiomatically "by the way", "incidentally".

17[1] *Aeneid* I 148 tr "[tumult] has risen".

18[1] WW uses "flowing" to translate *volans*, lit "flying", in *Aeneid* I 156.

19 I 216–20 [214–18], marked with pencilled + in ms[a] | I 159–61

> There is a Bay whose deep retirement hides
> The place[+] where Nature's self a Port provides,
> Framed by a friendly island's jutting sides,
> Bulwark from which the billows of the Main
> Recoil upon themselves, spending their force in vain.

218. "Nature's Self", not Virgilian. I wish, the 3 first lines of this passage, There is a Place, were equal to all the rest—me judice,[1] they do not give the imagery of the original—if I understand the lines—the water splits itself into little coves or sinuses.

20 I 243–4 [241–2] | I 179

> Bruise it with stones, and by the aid of fire
> Prepare the nutriment their frames require.

244. *nutriment.*

21 I 255–6 [253–4] | I 187–8

> He stops—and, with the bow, he seiz'd the store
> Of swift-wing'd arrows which Achates bore . . .

P. 12
255. Q[y] He seized the bow; nor lack'd ~~there~~ he ample store
Of ~~swift-winged Arrows: those, Achates bore~~ feather'd Shafts, Achates' quiver bore.

22 I 276–7 [274–5] | I 203

> "Hereafter, this our present lot may be
> "A cherish'd object for pleased memory. . . ."

277. + −

23 I 280–2 [278–80] | I 205–6

> ". . . There, Fate a settled habitation shews;—
> "There, Trojan empire (this, too, Fate allows)
> "Shall be revived. . . ."

19[a] A pencilled line in the margin from line 214 to 232, interrupted by the marginal comment "beautiful", does not appear to be in C's hand

19[1] "In my opinion".

281 +. There are *unenglishisms* here & there in this translation of which I remember no instance in your own poems, one or two in the Descriptive Sketches excepted—such as the Walter Scott abrupt nudity[1] of the Article—There, *Trojan* Empire (this too Fate allows)—

24 I 288–94 [286–92] | I 210–14

> They seize the Quarry; for the feast prepare;
> Part use their skill the carcase to lay bare,
> Stripping from off the limbs the dappled hide;
> And Part the palpitating flesh divide;
> The portions some expose to naked fire,
> Some steep in cauldrons where the flames aspire.
> Not wanting utensils, they spread the board;
> And soon their wasted vigour is restored . . .

290–94. Not worth translating; but not well translated—in plain truth, Slubbered over, as by rendering the original literally & disrhyming ~~the~~ your lines, would appear—

25 I 303–6 [305–8] | I 220–2

> Apart, for Lycas mourns the pious Chief;
> For Amicus is touch'd with silent grief;
> For Gyas, for Cloanthes; and the Crew
> That with Orontes perish'd in his view.

303. Why *Apart*? secum, below, means, turned in on himself.[1]

> ? All mourn; and more than all the pious Chief—
> Him Amycus, him Lycus touch'd with Grief—
> Him Gyas & Cleanthes &c—

26 I 317–18 [313–14] | I 228–9

> Thus, sorrowing, spake: "O Sire! who rul'st the way
> "Of Men and Gods with thy eternal sway . . ."

– 315.—Is there other authority for "the way" except the disputed reading in Shakespear & Massinger?[1] We rule our *ways*.

23[1] I.e. being denuded.

25[1] By "below", C means "in the following line", i.e. *Aeneid* I 221, where *secum* (lit "with himself") occurs. His point is that Aeneas did not, as WW seems to imply, physically withdraw from his men at that moment.

26[1] C alludes to a supposed crux in

27 I 346–7 [344–5] | I 254–5

On whom the Sire of Gods and human Kind
Half-smiling, turn'd the look that stills the wind . . .

347. Why *half*-smiling.[1]

27A I 350–1 [348–9], marked with pencilled + in ms | I 257

"Thy griefs dismiss;
+ "And, Cytherea, these forebodings spare . . ."

27B I 357–8 [354–5], marked with + in ms | I 262

". . . I will raise
+ "Things from their depths, and open Fate's dark ways . . ."

28 I 368 [365] | I 271

"O'er Albalonga sternly fortified. . . ."

368. It is plain that Virgil meant to avoid the trivial name, as one of our old Poets does in "the fate of ancient Lud"—by ~~di~~ interposing three words between longum and Alba.[1] It seems likewise to require a more faithful translation—

29 I 369–70 [366–7] | I 272–3

"Here, under Chiefs of this Hectorian Race,
"Three hundred years shall empire hold her place . . ."

Philip Massinger *A Very Woman* IV ii 44 and a related one in *Macbeth* V iii 22. In the edition of Massinger by William Gifford that C annotated either the 1805 or the 1813 version of, Gifford draws attention to the line "In way of youth I did enjoy one friend" and compares it to Shakespeare's much-discussed "my way of life / Is fallen into the sere, the yellow leaf". As he points out, Johnson had proposed emending the phrase to "May of life", a suggestion that had been accepted by some commentators and challenged by others. Gifford defends the original readings in both plays by bringing forward examples to support the view that "way of life" is "a simple periphrasis for *life*; as *way of youth*, in the text, is for *youth*": Philip Massinger *Plays* (4 vols 1805) IV 304n–5n.

27[1] The word translates *subridens* in *Aeneid* I 254, lit "less than laughing".

28[1] *Aeneid* I 271 *et longam multa vi muniet Albam* tr "and, great in power, shall build the walls of Alba Longa". Alba Longa was the original of Rome, that is, the city founded on the site of Rome, the two names being sometimes used interchangeably. Similarly, "Lud" is an old name for London. The quotation is untraced.

370. Shall Empire hold *her* place = regnabitur?[1] Border on the mock-heroic?[2]—For myself, I wonder at your patience in wading thro' such a stiff mare mortuum[3] of Dullness! and that of the dullest sort, to wit, History in prosing narrative prophecy—with so ludicrously anachronical a familiarity of names and detail—old acquaintances of the last Plutonic Sexmillennium!—[4]

30 I 373–8 [370–5] | I 276–9

"... Then Romulus, the elder, proudly drest
"In tawny wolf-skin, his memorial vest,
"Mavortian Walls, his Fathers Seat, shall frame,
"And from himself, the People Romans name.
"To these I give dominion that shall climb
"Uncheck'd by space, uncircumscrib'd by time ..."

375.—*frame* walls?—If you wish to strengthen the line, why not—Offspring of Mav, Mavortian Walls shall frame.— + 377—*climb*? *by* space? *by* time—~~In~~ ⟨uncircumscrib'd in space⟩ unmeasur'd in extent and without bound in time. In Space unmeasur'd, without bound in time.—

31 I 379–80 [376–7] | I 279–80

"... Even Juno driven
"To agitate with fear earth, sea and heaven ..."

380 Even Juno, she
That ⟨Whose⟩ wild alarms ~~are~~ yet vex Heaven, Earth & Sea ⟨mad Alarum vexes Earth & Sea⟩—

32 I 383 [380] | I 282

"The Romans, lords o'er earth, The Nation of the Gown. ..."

– 383 I don't like; but can suggest nothing.—Paraphrased is ~~spoil~~ crushed/ else—[1]

29[1] WW's phrase translates *regnabitur* tr "will reign" in *Aeneid* I 272.

29[2] C describes a similar reaction in **15**. The reading here—"border" (sing) and "?" perhaps intending "!"—is odd but unambiguous.

29[3] "Dead sea".

29[4] The last "Plutonic six thousand years"—"Plutonic" having to do with a theory of geological evolution based on the working of inner fires, therefore (presumably) a long, slow cycle.

32[1] I.e. to paraphrase would be to crush the original, otherwise C would recommend the following paraphrase.

The Romans, Lords of all beneath the Sun
That in the Toga awe what clad in arms they won—

33 I 422–5 [418–21] | I 310–13

Forthwith he hides, beneath a rocky cove,
His Fleet, o'ershadow'd by the pendant grove;
And, brandishing two javelins, quits the Bay,
Achates sole companion of his way.

424. Rightly translated? Surely, they were boar-*spears* not javelins:—*lato* ferro and crispans, I imagined, means that *play* and *give* of ~~the~~ a flexile weapon.[1] Likewise, I would suggest that either concealed or some still better word should be put for *hides*, or that the whole sentence should be put in the participle absolute, as the English Reader can not quite free himself from the modern associations with the word Fleet.[2] The Fleet, concealed beneath the r. c. And overshadowed by the p. g. Two quiv'ring Spears in hand, he quits the Bay—

34 I 426–33 [422–9] | I 314–17

While they were journeying thus, before him stood
His Mother, met within a shady wood.
The habit of a virgin did she wear;
Her aspect suitable, her gait, and air;—
Arm'd like a Spartan Virgin, or of mien
Such as in Thrace Harpalyce is seen,
Urging to weariness the fiery horse,
Outstripping Hebrus in his headlong course.

428 & q. s.[1]—I am sick of finding fault, the more discomfortably because my main feeling is that of faulting you for undertaking what compared with the original is scarcely a possibility, & your name is such that comparison with Dryden, Pitt, Beresford,[2] &c &c stands you in poor stead—nulla gloria præterire claudos[3]—But I confess that I cannot read the compressed ~~dignified~~ and sustained yet simple dignity of virginis os

33[1] *Aeneid* I 313 *bina manu lato crispans hastilia ferro* tr "grasping in hand two shafts, tipped with broad steel". C's query emphasises *lato* "wide" or "broad" and *crispans* "waving" or "brandishing" (LCL "grasping").

33[2] The Fleet Prison, chiefly a debtors' prison in C's day; demolished 1848.

34[1] I.e. *quae sequuntur* "what follows".

34[2] Earlier translators of the same text, Christopher Pitt's version appearing in 1740 and James Beresford's in 1794.

34[3] "There is no glory in outstripping the lame": proverbial.

habitumque[4] (315–320) & not find the English weak—"is seen"—suitable (aspect,) gait, air—mien—"Arm'd *like* a Spartan Virgin—.["]

A *Virgin* ⟨1⟩[a] ~~might she seem in dress & charms~~ She in Habit and (in Charms)

A *Spartan* ⟨2⟩ *Virgin* ⟨3⟩, ~~she~~ seems—& such her arms—/merely, to convey my sense of the climax,123—*urge to weariness* is scarcely the dictionary meaning (me judice)[5] of *fatigat*[6]—at all events, not the poetic force—and the participles *ing*, *ing*, kill the *rapidity* of the movement—

And leaves behind swift Hebrus in her flight or course or speed (which, by the bye, with Virgil's pardon, she might have done on a Donky:)

35 I 439–42 [435–8] | I 321–4

"... Have you not seen some Huntress here astray,
"One of my Sisters, with a quiver graced;
"Clothed by the spotted lynx, and o'er the waste
"Pressing the foaming boar, with outcry chased?"

441.—Clothed *by*? 442.—This is one of the sad necessities of rhyme in translation of continuous sentences. With shrill shouts pressing on the foaming Boar, is quite in the character of an animated inquiry; but to *mortice* on a supplementary description, "with outcry chased"—.

36 I 445–9 [441–5] | I 327–9

"... O Virgin! in pure grace
"Teach me to name Thee; for no mortal face
"Is thine, nor bears thy voice a human sound;—
"A Goddess surely, worthy to be own'd
"By Phoebus as a Sister ..."

448 + worthy to be own'd. does not even answer for a rhyme-botch—and does not give Virgil's sense, worthy to be owned by Phoebus as *a* Sister. The Question is simply—Are you Diana or at least one of ~~her~~ Dian's Train?—

34[a] The figure is written under the preceding italicised word in ms, as are "2" and "3" following

34[4] *Aeneid* I 315 tr "with a maiden's face and mien".

34[5] "In my opinion".

34[6] *Aeneid* I 316 tr "out-tires"—WW's "urging to weariness".

37 I 460–1 [456–7] | I 336–7

> "... The Tyrian Maids who chase the sylvan game
> "Bear thus a quiver slung their necks behind ..."

+ 461 + Slung their necks behind—! V. T. mos~~t~~ est gestare pharetram.[1]

38 I 465–6 [461–2] | I 339

> "... But Lybian deem the soil: the natives are
> "Haughty and fierce, intractable in war...."

– 465—does not give the force of Fines[1] nor the *personality* of Libyis, which *defines* the genus intractibile bello.[2]

39 I 481–6 [475–80] | I 348–52

> He, feeling not, or scorning what was due
> To a Wife's tender love, Sichaeus slew;
> Rush'd on him unawares, and laid him low
> Before the Altar, with an impious blow.
> His arts conceal'd the crime, and gave vain scope
> In Dido's bosom to a trembling hope.

486. You have convinced me of the *necessary* injury which ~~a~~ Language must sustain by rhyme translations of narrative poems of great length.—What would you have said at Allfoxden or in Grasmere Cottage to giving vain *scope* to *trembling* hopes *in* a bosom?—Were it only for this reason, that it would interfere with your claim to a Regenerator & jealous Guardian of our Language, I should dissuade the publication. For to *you* I dare not be insincere—tho' I conjecture, from some of your original Poems (of ⟨the⟩ more recent, I mean) that our tastes & judgements differ a shade or two more than formerly—& I am unfeignedly disposed to believe, that the long habits of minute discrimination have over-subtilized my perceptions. I have ~~not~~ composed ⟨about⟩ 200 verses within the last 18 months—& from the dissatisfaction if they *could* be read ~~by~~ in the most newspaper flat reading other than strongly distinguishable verse, I found them polished almost to *sensual* effeminacy. You must therefore take my opinions for what they are—

37[1] *Aeneid* I 336 tr "Tyrian maids are wont to wear the quiver".

38[1] "Boundaries", from *Aeneid* I 339 *sed fines Libyci, genus intractibile bello* tr "but the bordering country is Libyan, a race unconquerable in war".

38[2] "A race unconquerable in war".

40 I 502–3 [496–7] | I 370–2

He answer'd, deeply sighing, "To their springs
"Should I trace back the principles of things . . ."

503. + the principles of things, the *technical* phrase ~~for~~ of the Orphic Poets—περι αρχων.[1]

41 I 511–20 [505–14], marked with pencilled + in ms | I 378–82

" . . . Aeneas I am, wheresoe'er I go
"Carrying the Gods I rescued from the Foe,
"When Troy was overthrown. A Man you see
"Fam'd above Earth for acts of piety;
\+ "Italy is my wish'd-for resting place;
"There doth my Country lie, among a Race
"Sprung from high Jove. The Phrygian Sea I tried
\+ "With thrice ten Ships which Ida's Grove supplied,
"My Goddess Mother pointing out the way,
\+ "Nor did unwilling Fates oppose their sway. . . ."

511—Æneas I, who wheresoe'er I go Carry &c—super æthera[1]—above Earth's—~~not even to the Gods unknown~~ ~~disown'd of man nor to the gods unknown~~ Not the gods confess my fame!—But the whole passage needs to be recomposed—you have so diluted* the meaning.—I *doubt* your version of genus ab Jove summo[2]—May it not be part of the Answer to ⟨Vos⟩ Qui tandem?[3] my ~~race~~ kind from highest Jove—i.e. I am Jove's Grandson.

* 515 ∤, 518

42 I 539–40 [533–4] | I 397–8

"These touch, while those look down upon, the plain,
"Hovering, and wheeling round with tuneful voice. . . ."

540. These & those strike me as uncouth, there having been no previous division made—but dedere *cantus*[1] is not with tuneful *voice*—send forth

40[1] "Concerning the principles of things". The Orphic Poems, concerned with such matters as the origin of the gods and the creation of the universe, and once ascribed to Orpheus, were known by C's day to have been written around the 2nd century AD (though based on traditional material). Cf FABER **13** n 5.

41[1] *Aeneid* I 379 *super aethera notus* tr "my fame is known in the heavens above"—lit "above earth's atmosphere".

41[2] *Aeneid* I 380 tr "[I seek] a race sprung from Jove most high".

41[3] The question put by the disguised Venus in I 369, tr "But who, pray, are ye?"

42[1] *Aeneid* I 398 tr "and uttered their songs".

the shrill strain—*chaunt*.—My main objection is that the Imagery of this ⟨(in the Original⟩ rather strongly expressed) passage is not distinctly made out in your lines.

43 I 548–9 [542–3] | I 403–4

And from the exalted region of her head
Ambrosial hair a sudden fragrance shed . . .

548. *Vertice*[1] = from the exalted region of her head?

44 I 597–8 [591–2] | I 436

while thyme-clad hills and plains
Scent the pure honey that rewards their pains.

598.—Is there *authority* for *scent*?[1]—~~no~~ Except in Perfumers & Snuff Shops?—I retract this question; but is it not obscure in this place—& with a "*while*"?

45 I 604–7 [598–601] | I 441–3

Within the Town, a central Grove display'd
Its ample texture of delightful shade.
The storm-vex'd Tyrians, newly-landed, found
A hopeful sign, while digging there the ground . . .

604.—From this line the Translation greatly & very markedly improves/ the metre has bone & muscle.

46 I 626–8 [620–2], pencil, marked with pencilled + in ms | I 454–6

nor forbears
\+ To ponder o'er the <u>lot</u> of noble cares
Which the young City for herself prepares . . .

* unfortunate, the provincial idiom of *Lot* for "a many"[1]—if instead of this line, ⟨which breaks the already too slender transition⟩ could you not improve on the original by ~~introducing~~ marking the silent labor of the Artists, or something to break the crudeness of[2]

43[1] *Aeneid* I 403 tr "from her head".

44[1] I.e. for its use as a verb signifying "give scent to". *OED* includes as its first instance Dryden's 1697 tr of Virgil's *Georgics*, and as a later one Pope's 1725 *Odyssey*—so perhaps the authority could be said to be in the translating tradition.

46[1] *OED* cites this as colloquial usage, with 1812 as its earliest recorded occurrence. WW may, however, have intended the meaning "fate" or "destiny".

46[2] Here C is finding fault with Virgil

47 I 627–33 [621–7], marked with pencilled + in ms | **46** textus and the following lines I 629–33 [623–7] | I 456–9

He meets the Wars of Ilium; every Fight,
In due succession, offer'd to his sight.
There he beholds Atrides, Priam here,
\+ And that stern Chief who was to both severe.
He stopp'd; and, not without a sigh, exclaim'd . . .

627.—To ponder &c—Destroys the already too obscure copula of *Artificum* & miratur,[1] & thus renders the He meets the wars of Ilium still cruder than Virgil's videt Iliacas[2]—OFFER'D *to his sight*: seems likewise slovenly. In my [? Morelli/Morell:] Edition as it is *Atridas*, not Atri*dem*[3]—632. Achilles' *name* is quite requisite, I think—& to both *severe*. ?And fierce to both Achilles. As the Tear ~~Swelled~~ Bedimm'd his eye, he stopped—.

48 I 670–5 [662–7], marked with a – in ms | I 484–7

– Thrice had incens'd Achilles whirl'd amain
About Troy Wall, the Corse of Hector slain,
And barters now that Corse for proffer'd gold.
What grief, the spoils and Chariot to behold!
And, suppliant, near his Friend's dead body, stands
Old Priam, stretching forth his unarm'd hands!

673.—This & the two following Lines should be altered—& the whole passage deserves it. By hurrying over what Virgil makes prominent (*Eneas*'s height of Emotion, at this particular point) "*his* friend" becomes equivocal—/—

?{ And close beside his Friend's dead body stands
Priam, still suppliant with unweapon'd hands.

---

rather than with WW. The passage shifts (too abruptly, in C's view) from a description of the building of a temple in a grove to Aeneas's reflections upon the wars.

47[1] *Aeneid* I 455–6 tr "he marvels at . . . the handicraft of the several artists".

47[2] *Aeneid* I 456 tr "he sees . . . [the battles] of Ilium".

47[3] *Aeneid* I 458 tr "the sons of Atreus". C was certainly consulting the Latin original, but he must be mistaken about the editor: Thomas Morell was at this time the editor of the standard textbook *Gradus ad Parnassum* which James Gillman Jr was currently using at school, but not of a Virgil. C might have meant Jan Minell, who did publish an edition of Virgil with elementary notes (Rotterdam 1666 and later); WW made use of it as he worked on his translation. C objects that WW's tr appears to make a plural noun into a singular one, thereby inventing a character called "Atrides".

48A I 686–8 [678–80], marked with pencilled + in ms | I 496–7

the Queen
Ascends the Temple:—lovely was her mien;
And her form beautiful+ as Earth has seen . . .

49 I 694–6 [686–8] | I 500–2

she appears
Far, far above the immortal Company:
Latona's breast is thrill'd with silent ecstasy.

696—Far far *above*/ too vague for supereminat[1]—& tho' Virgil shews great want of judgement in this outrè imitation of Homer, yet still I would give his meaning which your version submerges—

Where'er she winds her ways ⟨threads the dance⟩, the
Goddess bears
Her quiver visible—still, still appears
The ~~lucid~~ frontal Crescent far above the rest!
Mute exultation thrills Latona's breast—

seems more true to the intention.—

50 I 712–13 [704–5], marked with pencilled + in ms | I 513

+ Achates, in like sort, by what he saw
Was smitten . . .

+ 712. *by what he saw*—you would ~~not~~ scarcely write this in a prose note.

51 I 719–20 [711–12] | I 518–19

For Delegates from every Ship they were,
And sought the Temple with a clamorous prayer.

720 clamore[1]—with noise just like a parcel of *Tars*, made their way to the Temple with ~~eager~~ noisy Hail. Virgil wished to contrast the Ship Crews & inferior Officers with the *stillness* of Eneas & his *Staff.*

52 I 753–6 [745–8] | I 544–7

". . . A man to no one second in the care
"Of justice, nor in piety and war,

49[1] *Aeneid* I 501 tr "overtops".

51[1] *Aeneid* I 519 tr "with loud cries".

"Ruled over us; if yet Aeneas treads
"On earth, nor has been summon'd to the shades . . ."

753. care, war, hands, shades—*rather* too confluent?—

53 I 776 [768] | I 562

"Trojans, be griefs dismiss'd, anxieties allay'd. . . ."

776.—an *odd* line

54 I 797 [789] | I 579

For He, the Cast-away of stormy floods . . .

798—Cast-away of *Floods*—is this ever applied to the Sea—

55 I 811 [803] | I 589–90

With godlike mien and shoulders, standing in full day

811.—Here I think some substitute for humeros[1] should be ventured—

55A I 821–2 [813–14], marked with pencilled + in ms | I 597

\+ ". . . O Sole, who for the unutterable state
"Of Troy art humanly compassionate . . ."

56 I 987–94 | I 717–22

And sometimes doth unhappy Dido plant
The Fondling in her bosom, ignorant
How great a God deceives her. He, to please
His Acidalian mother, by degrees
Would sap Sichaeus, studious to remove
The dead by influx of a living love,
Through a subsided spirit dispossess'd
Of amorous passion, through a torpid breast.

The Six first lines of p. 43—tentat prævertere jam resides animos[1] &c—are obscure & run *obstructedly*. That *through* twice repeated.—Generally, however, this latter part is done with great spirit.

55[1] *Aeneid* I 589 tr "shoulders".

56[1] *Aeneid* I 721–2 var, C departing from the Latin text perhaps because he was attempting to quote from memory. Tr (based on C's wording) "she now tries to startle her settled spirits [into life]".

FRANCIS WRANGHAM

1769–1842

The Life of Dr. Richard Bentley. [*Anonymous*.] [London 1816.] 8°.

Privately printed in an edition of 25 copies. Bound in "PAMPHLETS—MISCELLANEOUS". Actually a variant version of Wrangham's article "Dr. Richard Bentley" in *The British Plutarch* ed Francis Wrangham (6 vols London 1816) v 365–414. Wrangham's own annotated copy of the latter includes holograph corrections not incorporated in the former, which therefore cannot be a later, revised version but was probably printed for the author more or less simultaneously with *The British Plutarch*. Copies of his seven lives (including Bentley's) were issued collectively as *Humble Contributions to a British Plutarch* (London 1816).

British Library C 126 h 3(9)

Inscribed in ink at the top of p [1]: "From the author".

DATE. Jan 1818? See *CL* IV 802 to Wrangham: "I was much pleased with your abridged Life of Bentley—"; the issue in **2** is then discussed in the letter.

1 pp 2–3, pencil

His son Thomas, the father of Dr. Bentley, was a respectable blacksmith at Oulton . . . . [Footnote:] The writer of his Life in the old *Biographia Britannica* says, "he was the son of a mean tradesman." This Mr. Cumberland, his grandson, in a letter to the Bishop of Oxford, stiles "a misrepresentation, debasing his condition from that of a gentleman."

* Whimsical as this protestation of Cumberland's must appear, and impossible as it is not to smile at it, there is a just feeling, a grounding Idea gleaming thro'—It is easy to *imagine* a state of Society, in which a Blacksmith would of good right rank as an Artist—at *all* times he acts, he forms—whereas a Tradesman as equidistant from the Artisan and the Merchant is merely instrumental/ We find a similar feeling in Cicero de Officiis[1]—thus too the Scottish Prejudice against Manufacturers, which does not prevail against the Cottager or Franklin who makes the whole from the fleece to the Mantle.—

1[1] Cicero distinguishes between vulgar and genteel ways of earning a living in *De officiis* 1.42: trade on a small scale is one of the meaner occupations.

2 p 5

[Footnote:] For a question upon the proportions of Nebuchadnezzar's Image of Gold in Dan. vi., which nearly lost him his mistress, "a most excellent Christian woman," and for other petty exceptions to the chronology of that prophet, of whom (though expressly quoted by our Blessed Saviour himself, Matt. xxix. 9, Mark. xiii. 14, Luke xxi. 20) "he was very desirous to get clear," as well as for his hostility to the Apocalypse, Mr. Whiston impeaches Dr. Bentley of Scepticism—"Scepticism, he says, not Infidelity: for I take the evidence for the truth of the Bible to be so prodigiously strong in all original authors, that no persons so learned as Dr. Bentley and Dr. Hare can, I believe, by any temptation proceed farther than scepticism . . ."

Not the Prophet Daniel, from whom our Saviour quotes; but the Life of Daniel, prefixed to the Prophecies by some Editor posterior to the time of Alexander the Great, as is clear by the number of Greek words, found only in these six Chapters, which are as unconnected with the VIIth, which is evidently the *Beginning* of of a Work, as their style is different. Of these six Chapters *I* too am desirous to get clear, in proportion to my sense of the importance of the Prophecies themselves.[1] S. T. C.—

[a]Causes of a moral nature excepted, few things have favored Scepticism more, than the superstition of attaching an equal importance to all the Books, and to all the parts of each, of the Old Testament. As if[b] a man's faith in the Redemption from Sin & the self-origination of the latter were dependent on the opinion, he had formed, concerning the question whether the Book of Jonah is an history or an allegory; or whether the Parenthesis in Matthew is genuine or a gloss that had slipt into the Text![2]

2[a] This paragraph is written in the outer margin above the beginning of the first paragraph

2[b] In the last space left in the margin C has written: "As if (see * above)" and continued the note in the head-margin with "* As if a man's faith . . ."

2[1] The authenticity of the Book of Daniel was a particular concern of biblical scholarship in the period. C came to hold the view that Dan fell into two parts by different authors, chs 7–12 containing the prophetic visions and chs 1–6 having been attached later as a biographical introduction to the visions. The biographical chapters he firmly rejected; the prophetic ones he was not entirely sure about. See esp EICHHORN *AT* **48**, PAULUS **43**, *TT* (*CC*) I 63, and nn. In LACUNZA **6** and LUTHER *Colloquia* **20**, C alludes to Bentley's wish to be rid of Dan—probably remembering Wrangham's evidence in this *Life*.

2[2] The reference is to a crux in Matt 12.40, "For as Jonas was three days and three nights in the whale's belly; so shall the Son of man be three days and three nights in the heart of the earth". In *LS* (*CC*) 57–9 C gives his reasons for believing, on the ground of internal evidence, that the verse is "a gloss of some unlearned, though pious, christian of the first century, which had slipt into the text". For the Book of Jonah as an "Apologue or Parable" in which "the Jewish Nation [is] collectively . . . impersonated" see *AR* (*CC*) 264* and n 64, also LUTHER *Colloquia* **86** and n 1.

Scraps, by the Rev. Francis Wrangham. 8 pts in 1 vol. London 1816. 8°.

Boston Public Library

Inscribed on title-page "From the author". Library bookplate on p ⁻3 (p-d) shows that this vol was "bought with the income of the Scholfield bequests"; inscribed in pencil on verso of title-page "Scholf, Mar. 29, 1919".

CONTENTS. All separately paginated and with separate title-pages: (i) Milton's *Second Defence of the People of England* tr by Wrangham with preface and notes; (ii) *Memoir of Caroline Symons*; (iii) *A Dissertation on the best Means of Civilising the Subjects of the British Empire in India*; (iv) *Six Hundred Threescore and Six*; (v) *Four Passages of Scripture Elucidated* (from Bryant, abridged); (vi) *Articles suggested for a Village Cow-club*; (vii) *On Village-Libraries*; (viii) Virgil's *Bucolics* tr by Wrangham, with Latin on facing pages.

DATE. Mar 1817 at the earliest. In **5** C refers to a note in his *first* Lay Sermon (*SM*, pub Dec 1816) with the implication that the second (pub Mar 1817) had also appeared.

1 i 59 | *Second Defence*

The spirit and the strength remain, still unimpaired; my eyes alone have failed: and yet they are as unblemished in appearance, as lucid and free from spot, as those which possess the sharpest vision. [Wrangham, in a footnote, cites three passages, the last of which, from *Paradise Lost*, is]

> "Blind Tamyris, and blind Maeonides,
> And Tiresias and Phineus, prophets old," &c. . . .

[and comments that the last line] would sound more harmoniously however, to a modern ear, if the two names were to change places.

rather, if the initial And were omitted. Indeed, with the and the same both arsis and emphasis ought to be given to the syllable *re-* & the first foot be a modern Anapæst

> Blind Tamyris and blind Mæonides,
> Tĭrēsĭas

or

> Ănd Tĭrē/sĭās and Phineus, Prophets old
> Milton would on no account have made it Tīrĕsiăs

2 i 71

Woe to those that mock or hurt us, protected as we are, and almost consecrated from human injuries, by the ordinances and favour of the Deity; and involved in darkness, not so much from the imperfection of our optic powers, as from the shadow of the Creator's wings*—a darkness, which he frequently irradiates with an inner and far superior light!

* I should have expected from Archdeacon Wrangham a Note on this passage, had its only purpose been to express his own admiration of, and direct the reader's attention to, ~~the~~ its pathos and sublimity ~~of this passage~~. But I almost suspect, that W. had not been much impressed by it—it is so feebly & flabbily translated.[1]

3 v 8 | *Four Passages of Scripture Elucidated*

One part of it, in particular, demands remark: "He shall smite the corners, פאחה, of Moab (where the LXX. translation, ἡγεμονας, αρχηγους, is probably the best) and destroy all the children of Seth." Now Plutarch, in his "Isis and Osiris," expressly identifies Seth with Typhon or Peor-Apis, in whose temple the Ονολατρεια was practised by the Egyptians.*

* A much more important correction might have been noted—namely, that the true version would be—he shall smite the corners of Moab and call together the children of Seth as the Hen calleth her chickens under her wings—the Hebrew verb is strictly *cluck* together. And to this sense of the Prophecy our Lord refers when he wept over Jerusalem.[1]

2[1] The Latin in C's copy of John MILTON *A Complete Collection of the ... Works* ed T. Birch (2 vols 1738) II 315–49 reads as follows (II 325): "Et sanè haud ultima Dei cura caeci sumus; qui nos, quò minus quicquam aliud praeter ipsum cernere valemus, eò clementiùs atque benigniùs respicere dignatur. Vae qui illudit nos, vae qui laedit, execratione publicâ devovendo; nos ab injuriis hominum non modò incolumes, sed penè sacros, divina lex reddidit, divinus favor; nec tam oculorum hebetudine, quàm coelestium alarum umbrâ has nobis fecisse tenebras videtur, factas illustrare rursus interiore ac longè praestabiliore lumine haud raro solet." The Columbia Milton (John Milton *Works* VIII—New York 1933—73) uses a translation based on the 1809 version of George Burnett which may provide a point of comparison for Wrangham's: "And, in truth, we who are blind, are not the last regarded by the providence of God; who, as we are the less able to discern any thing but himself, beholds us with the greater clemency and benignity. Woe be to him who makes a mock of us; woe be to him who injures us; he deserves to be devoted to the public curse. The divine law, the divine favour, has made us not merely secure, but, as it were, sacred, from the injuries of men; nor would seem to have brought this darkness upon us so much by inducing a dimness of the eyes, as by the overshadowing of heavenly wings; and not unfrequently is wont to illumine it again, when produced, by an inward and far surpassing light."

3[1] Matt 23.37 (and Luke 13.34): "O Jerusalem, Jerusalem, thou that killest the prophets, and stonest them which are sent

4 v 12–13

He [Samson], therefore, invokes God for assistance; and a miraculous discharge of water takes place from the jaw-bone, which he called En-Haccori, "the fountain of invocation."

The most natural and probable explanation of this passage is that it is a narrative Riddle, quite in the spirit of the Age & Country. Samson had taken refuge in some mountain ridge, called the Ass's Jaw—had rolled a huge stone from it on his assailants as they were climbing up the Ravine or Defile to his stronghold—this was poetically & not infelicitously called a Jaw Bone—and on returning he found a small spring or collection of water in the hollow, from which he had loosened the huge Stone or Boulder.[1] The very same thing occurred to myself on Plinlimmon, at a time when Brookes (of Jesus College, Cambridge) and myself were almost frantic with thirst.[2] S. T. Coleridge

5 v 19

The history of Jonah is attested by our Saviour, who would never have appealed for the illustration of a fact to a Galilean apologue or novel.

For the proofs, that this sentence confirming the allusion to the Whale's Belly in Matthew is a Gloss of some weak Jewish Christian that has slipt into the Text, see the first note to my first Lay-Sermon.[1]

S. T. Coleridge.

6 v 24

They [the mariners] were appalled at witnessing a real Leviathan, against which their emblematical one had no power, swallowing up a strenuous

---

unto thee, how often would I have gathered thy children together, even as a hen gathereth her chickens under her wings, and ye would not!" C links this verse with Num 24.17 (textus) again in BIBLE COPY B **96**; in BIBLE COPY B **15** n 1 the source for this speculative reading is identified as Alting, i.e. Jacobus Alting "Analysis exegetica in quatuor priores libros Mosis" *Opera omnia* (5 vols Amsterdam 1687) I 116; but Alting does not make the connection between the OT verse he is glossing and the NT texts proposed by C.

4[1] C offers the same interpretation in BIBLE COPY B **19**: "Probably, some narrow Ghyll or Rent in the mountain was named the Ass's Jaw . . . and some remarkable Rock called the Jaw-Bone".

4[2] C told this story also on 30 May 1830, a propos of *AM*, but it appears that he was himself mistaken about the name of the mountain—which should have been Penmaenwawr—and perhaps also about the name of the companion, although Brookes had indeed been a fellow-climber in 1794: *TT* (*CC*) I 149 and n 2.

5[1] Actually Note B in the Appendix to *LS* (*CC*) 57–9, which C cites again on this point in *AR* (*CC*) 264*. For the issue in general see WRANGHAM *Life of Bentley* **2** and n 2.

votary of their superstitions. This they would naturally report on their return, and it would quickly afterward be confirmed by the stranded Cetus disgorging the prophet; an event, which would brand with disgrace their boasted empress of the seas.

I should have supposed the very contrary; and that the event would have covered with glory the Empress of the Seas.[1]

7 viii 3 | *Bucolics* 1.1–2

Mel. Tityre, tu patulae recubans sub tegmine fagi
Sylvestrem tenui Musam meditaris avenâ . . .
Meliboeus. Beneath this beech you, Tityrus, thrown at ease
Pour through the reed your sylvan melodies . . .

Beneath the spreading Beech you, Tityrus! note
The Sylvan Muse upon the slender Oat.[1]

6[1] Wrangham's explanation of the story of Jonah depends upon the assumption that Jonah's shipmates were worshippers of a female deity under the form of a whale.

7[1] Virgil *Eclogues* 1.1–2 tr H. Rushton Fairclough (LCL): "You, Tityrus, lie under your spreading beech's covert, wooing the woodland Muse on slender reed . . . ."

XENOPHON

c 435–354 BC

Xenophon's Memoirs of Socrates. With the defence of Socrates, before his judges. Translated from the original Greek. By Sarah Fielding. 2nd ed rev. London 1767. 8°.

Not located; marginal note printed from *N&Q* 7 ser VII (1889) 90–1. "H. J. C.", who contributed the note, confidently identifies the edition and page references but cannot positively vouch for the handwriting.

DATE. Uncertain; perhaps about 1820 (see **1** n 1).

1 pp 338–9

[Socrates:] "The Man then, EUTHYDEMUS, who *knoweth* the Laws, that are to regulate his conduct in serving of the Gods; will serve them, according to these Laws?"

"No Doubt."

"And he, who serveth them, according to these Laws, will serve them as he *ought*?"

"He will."

"But he, who serveth them as he *ought*, is pious?"

"Assuredly."

"Then he, who *knoweth* how he ought to serve the Gods; may rightly be defined, a PIOUS Man?" [Footnote:] How sophistical is this Way of Reasoning; and how pernicious the Notion it is endeavouring to establish! But I can no way so effectively shew the ill Tendency of it, as in borrowing, for the Purpose, the Words of One who will ever be, not only a Credit to her Sex, but an Honour to her Country. "The most ignorant Persons, says Mrs. CARTER, in one of her Notes on EPICTETUS, often practice what they know to be Evil: And they who voluntarily suffer, as many do, their Inclinations to blind their Judgment, are not justified by following it. The Doctrine of EPICTETUS therefore, here, and elsewhere, on this Head, contradicts the Voice of Reason and Conscience: Nor is it less pernicious than ill-grounded. It destroys all Guilt and Merit; all Punishment and Reward; all Blame of ourselves or others; all Sense of Misbehaviour towards our Fellow-creatures, or our Creator: No Wonder that such Philosophers did not teach Repentance towards GOD."

I am convinced that the word translated "*knowlege*" and "knoweth" had nearly the same force and meaning in the mind of Socrates as *Faith* in St. Paul.[1] To the persons instanced by Mrs. Carter Socrates would have denied *knowlege*. Spinoza, in his "Ethics," adopts the same system;[2] and it is evident that the whole difference between this and Mrs. Carter's notion is merely metaphysical, perhaps merely nominal, but certainly not moral. A certain clearness of conception there is, an adducible approximation to a sense of certainty, which will preclude volition, and to these perfectly *clear* knowleges Socrates refers, involving the Practical in the Intellectual. S. T. C.

1[1] C was probably thinking esp of Heb 11.1, "Now faith is the substance of things hoped for, the evidence of things not seen." C himself wrote an "Essay on Faith" and a gloss on this verse in St Paul (commented on also in SCUDAMORE), about Jul 1820: *SW & F* (*CC*) 833–44, 845–6. His conclusion in the "Essay" is that "Faith subsists in the Synthesis of the Reason and the Individual Will."

1[2] Spinoza *Ethics* pt 2 P20–48, esp P43 (tr): "He who has a true idea at the same time knows that he has a true idea, and cannot doubt the truth of the thing."

THOMAS YOUNG

1773–1829

Lost Book

A Course of Lectures on Natural Philosophy and the Mechanical Arts. 2 vols. London 1807. 4°.

Not located; marginalia not recorded. *Green SC* (1880) 895: "with autograph Note by S. T. Coleridge, but a portion cut away by the binder".

ZEITSCHRIFT

Zeitschrift für spekulative Physik herausgegeben von Schelling. 2 vols (4 pts) in 1 vol. Jena & Leipzig 1800, 1801. 8°.

Bound with an unmarked copy of Goethe *Versuch die Metamorphose der Pflanzen zu erklären* (Gotha 1790).

British Library C 126 e 1(1)

With the "S. T. C." label on verso of title-page, monogram "C" of John Duke Coleridge on p ⁻6.

CONTENTS. I i [iii]–iv Preface; 3–48 Steffens "Recension der neuern naturphilosophischen Schriften des Herausgebers"; [51]–99 Schelling "Anhang zu dem voranstehenden Aufsatz, betreffend zwei naturphilosophische Recensionen und die Jenaische Allgemeine Literaturzeitung"; 100–36 Schelling "Allgemeine Deduction des dynamischen Processes oder der Categorien der Physik"; [139]–68 Steffens "Ueber den Oxydations- und Desoxydations-Process der Erde"; I ii 3–87 Schelling "Allgemeine Deduction des dynamischen Processes"; [88]–121 Steffens "Beschluss der Recension der neuesten naturphilosophischen Schriften des Herausgebers"; [122]–56 Schelling "Miscellen"; II i [3]–68 Eschenmayer "Spontaneität = Weltseele oder das höchste Princip der Naturphilosophie"; 69–108 Hoffmann "Ideen zur Konstrukzion der Krankheit"; 111–46 Schelling "Anhang zu dem Aufsatz der Herrn Eschenmayer betreffend den wahren Begriff der Naturphilosophie, und die richtige Art ihre Probleme aufzulösen"; 147–54 Schelling "Miscellen"; II ii iii–xiv, [1]–127 Schelling "Darstellung meines Systems der Philosophie".

DATE. Uncertain; perhaps 1821, when a notebook entry appears to echo details of Schelling's "Allgemeine Deduction" from this journal: *CN* IV 4835 and n. These notes certainly postdate C's reading of major texts of Naturphilosophie such as SCHELLING *Einleitung* and STEFFENS *Grundzüge*. See **1** n 1 below, and cf **7** n 2.

COEDITOR. Raimonda Modiano.

1 pp ⁻2–⁻1, referring to I i 21–2 | Steffens "Recension"

. . . Erstlich hat der Verf. [Schelling] als er von der Wärme als einem fluidisirenden Princip sprach, auf eine Theorie der Wärme nach diesem Grundsatze hingedeutet; die Folge wird zeigen wie wichtig es gewesen wäre diese zu liefern. . . .

Die Wärme deutet den atomistischen Weg der Natur an (vom Product zur Productivität). Durch sie kann es daher nie zur Identität, sondern nur zur Indifferenz der Gestaltung kommen (wobey die specifische Tendenz der einzelnen Actionen gesichert ist). Bey der leisesten Decombination der Actionen tritt Electricität hervor. Aber bey aller Decombination der Actionen, wo entweder Wärme frey wird . . . oder wo Wärme gebunden wird . . . kann es nur durch eine momentane freye Entgegensetzung der Actionen (das Moment der Decombination) geschehen und das Phänomen *dieser* Entgegensetzung ist die Electricität.

[. . . At first the author [Schelling], when speaking of heat as a fluidising principle, suggested a theory of heat according to this principle; the sequel will show how important it would have been to provide this. . . .

Heat indicates the atomistic path of nature (from the product to productivity). Identity of formation can therefore never be attained by it, but only indifference (in which the specific tendency of the individual actions is assured). On the slightest decombining of the actions electricity emerges. But all decombination of actions, in which heat is either liberated . . . or fixed . . . can only take place through a momentary free opposition of the actions (the moment of decombination) and the phenomenon of *this* decombination is electricity.]

P. 21, 22.

The clear-headed perspicuous Steffens, whom I love and honor with heart and head, could not but feel the obscurity and the limping of Schelling's Theory of Warmth, or the Ground-work at least of the promised Theory as given in his Enleitung:[a] and nothing, but his ~~high~~ reverential sense of Schelling's Genius, would, I am persuaded, have influenced him to adopt so implicitly his great Master's dynamico-atomistic Assumption of simple Actions. As to Warmth, far more beautiful is Steffens's own doctrine, who regards it as the Indifference between Light and Gravity.[1] And yet there must be a lower Form of Light and Warmth, in which they stand in antagonism. Why not thus? Let the highest ~~Form~~ Product of Light (n.b. not as the universal ~~opposite~~ Antithesis to Gravity, including the power of Sound &c, but) as Lux phænomenon[2] or Light commonly so called, be the outward Pole or correspondent Excitant of Organization—A lower will be a chemical or chemic-mechanical Stuff, embodying the chemical

1[a] A slip for "Einleitung"

1[1] E.g. in STEFFENS *Grundzüge* 48–9 (part of which is annotated: **12**). C also annotated the works by Schelling to which he alludes here, specifically *Einleitung zu seinem Entwurf eines Systems der Naturphilosophie* (Jena 1799). In a passage immediately following **1** textus, Steffens himself mentions approvingly Schelling's argument that a theory of warmth constructed on (tr) "dynamic-atomistic" principles is of "utmost importance" (23).

1[2] "Light as phenomenon", i.e. actual light.

powers of Contraction, as Oxygen—while the Warmth will appear as the dilation in Hydrogen, the substance or magnetic product ~~in~~ with which the one is combined & made latent being the Metal Y, the stuff representative of − Magnetism, and the other metal X, the Stuff representative of + Magnetism, not improbably Nitrogen itself. The order would be this.

Lux Phænomenon	Caloric
− Electricity	+ Electricity
Oxygen	Hydrogen.

———

Functions	Functions
1. Distinction.	1 *Diffusion*
2. Contraction	2 Dilation
3 Fixation*	3 Vis fluidifica†[4]

* i.e. when it acts on a Fluid—for a Fluid is that which has no distinguishable parts: the Oxygen acts therefore on the whole as at all and one. But for the same reason, when it acts on a Solid (= rectius,[3] Rigid) it exerts the same fixive power by ~~a~~ causing a retraction of each particle in upon itself as it were, and thus produces the phænomenon of pulverization, or multeity, and the quality of positive Hardness.—The power exerted is the same ~~to~~ in both, and differenced only by the Subjects.

† Hydrogen. Fluidum fluidissimum, æreum quidem propter levitatem ejus relativum, haud vero *Aer*[5]—*an* Air.

2 I i 44, pencil

Die höchste Desoxydation deutet sich bei ihnen [Metallen] durch Glanz (Maximum der Opacitaet) an, der Anfang der Oxydation ist der Anfang des Farbenwechsels. Die Farben erhöhen sich, wie die Oxydation zunimmt, geschieht sie schnell, so ist sie mit Lichtentwickelung verbunden, und das Maximum der Oxydation deutet sich durch Durchsichtigkeit an. . . . Indess was die Natur auf der einen Seite zu bestätigen scheint, scheint sie auf der andern zu widerlegen. Alcohol is *verbrennlich* und *durchsichtig* zugleich, Diamant ebenfalls.*

1[3] "More correctly".

1[4] "Fluidific force", or that which makes things fluid.

1[5] "The most fluid fluid, an air which indeed on account of its relative lightness is hardly really an *Air*". For the role of hydrogen as the symbol of fluidity in the Compass of Nature see OERSTED **2** and n 2.

[The highest disoxidation is indicated in them [metals] by lustre (maximum of opacity): the beginning of oxidation is the beginning of change of colour. The colours are heightened as oxidation increases; if it happens quickly, then it is combined with the production of light, and the maximum of oxidation is indicated by transparency. . . . However, what nature appears to confirm on the one hand, she seems to refute on the other. Alcohol is both *combustible* and *transparent* and so is the diamond.*]

* I have much to say on this subject, ~~of~~ the solving Idea of which neither Sch. nor Steff. appear to have caught. The Transparency of the Diamond and of Alcohol both depend on the Western or Positive Pole of the E.W. line.[1] S. T. Coleridge

3 I i 45–6, pencil

* Ferner alles was in Verbindung mit dem absolut flüssigen, zur Indifferenz der Gestaltung gebracht ist (alle Gasarten) sind, *als* solche durchsichtig, (nur eine Wärmetheorie könnte uns dieses enträthseln).

[* Furthermore, all that in combination with the absolutely fluid reach the equilibrium of form (all gaseous substances) are, *as* such, transparent. (Only a theory of heat can solve this riddle for us.)]

* It seems strange to me, that both Schelling and Steffens should so often—indeed almost always—overlook the essential difference of the Fluid and the Aeriform. Nay, more than overlook—they destroy it and refer both alike to the *absolutely* fluid. Now Repulsion (*Fliehkraft*) which[a] the Principle of the Gaseous, is opposite to Dilation or the Principle of the Fluid, as belonging to opposite Lines, and analogous only because they are both the positive Poles of the Lines to which they belong. Light and Darkness (the Mosaic,[1] I mean, or Gravity) are the two opposites, the primary Gegensätze[2] of Nature—the Gaseous is under the Pos. Pole of Darkness, the Fluid the Pos. Pole of Light—and here will be found the true solution of the difficulty.

4 I i 45, pencil | Continuing **3** textus

Der durchsichtige Wasserstoffgas, verbrennt mit dem durchsichtigen Sauerstoffgas, mit Flamme, und das Product der Verbrennung ist wiederum ein *Durchsichtiges—Wasser.

3[a] Perhaps a slip for "which is"

2[1] I.e. on hydrogen. For expositions of the basic framework of the Compass of Nature see STEFFENS *Beyträge* **16** n 1, where other cross-references are gathered.

3[1] I.e. as in Genesis, the first Book of Moses.

3[2] "Opposites".

[Transparent hydrogen burns with a flame with transparent oxygen and the product of the combustion is again something *transparent—water.]

* In this word lies the confusion/ Oxygen Gas is not *transparent* in the same sense as Water, nor is the difference in the *degree* only.

5 I i 46–7, pencil, cropped

Da nun Wärme nach der Hypothese nichts ist, als phlogistisirtes Licht, und spezifische Wärmecapacität nichts als specifische phlogistische Erregbarkeit (eine Construction der Wärmecapacität, die eben so meisterhaft, und unwiderlegbar als in der Natur gegründet ist—wovon unten ein mehreres) . . .

[Since, according to the hypothesis, heat is nothing but phlogisticated light, and specific heat capacity is nothing but specific phlogistic excitability (a construction of the heat capacity, which is established in just as masterly and irrefutable a manner as in nature—about which more below) . . .]

Was aber mag *phlogistisirtes* bezeichnen? Ist es ein zusammengesetzes Licht (Lux + Phlogiston?[)] Was denn ist Phlogiston.—Oder ein vermindertes *degradirtes* Licht? [. . .] durch Widerstehung[1] [. . .] it intelligible.

6 I i 47, pencil

[Editor's (Schelling's) note:] Ich gestehe, dass anfänglich nicht sowohl Erfahrungen, deren Mangel an Entschiedenheit ich selbst bemerkte, sondern vielmehr die gefasste Idee, *dass der Sauerstoff durchgängig sich* als *Repräsentant des negativen in der Natur* (der Attractivkraft) bewähren müsste, mich auf jene Hypothese führte, und in so fern ist auch die jetzige Theorie die vorhergehende, nur in einer höhern Abstraction ausgedrückte.

[I admit that initially it was not only practical knowledge, the lack of decisiveness of which I noticed myself, but the preconceived notion *that oxygen must universally prove* to be *the representative of the negative* (i.e. of the attractive power) *in nature* that led me to this hypothesis, and to that extent the present theory is the [same as the] previous one, only expressed by a higher abstraction.]

Here again is the Error—The Oxygen is not the Repres. of *At*tract. but of *Con*traction.

5[1] "But what can *phlogisticated* signify? Is it a compound light (light + phlogiston)? What then is phlogiston?—Or a lesser, *degraded* light? [. . .] through resistance [. . .]".

7 I i 48–[49] (at the end of the review), pencil

The greater part of Schelling's and of Steffens's mistakes or imperfections, may be traced to their oversight of the Gegensatz[1] of the Lines in their exclusive attention to the relative Identity of Poles. South and West are both indeed Positive Poles, but of opposite Lines. The great point therefore to be secured in teaching the Natùrphilosophie is to give a clear insight of the essential difference between Attraction and Contraction, and between Dilation and Repulsion. Iron is Iron by attraction, and becomes *Rust* by Contraction. Ice becomes Water by Dilation, but Water-gas (if such there be) by Repulsion, Steam being the transitional State. Hence (I suspect) that Warmth is essential to Fluidity only, not to Aerity. I have erred myself in referring Odors objectively to the W. or Dilation—which I now see to be the medium of our *sensation* of Odors—and in confounding the products of Light and Gravitation (E. and W.) with Light itself.[2] I divided Light from Grav. instead of ⟨contra-⟩distinguishing it, and made N. and S. the Poles of the latter only—in short I placed the points

	− G				G	
+ L		− L	instead of[a]	GL		LG
	G				L	

8 I i 108, pencil | Schelling "Allgemeine Deduction des dynamischen Processes" § 9b

Es wird also, wenn in der Linie ACB

A———C——————B

A den Punct vorstellt, von welchem aus beide Kräfte sich trennen, bis zu einer gewissen Entfernung von A, deren Grösse übrigens völlig zufällig ist, indem der Raum gar nicht in Betrachtung kommt,* nichts von der negativen Kraft vorkommen können, sondern allein die positive Kraft herrschend seyn . . .

[So it is, if in the line ACB [above], A represents the point from which the two forces separate, nothing of the negative force can occur up to a certain distance from A, the

7[a] C circled the second diagram in his crowded note, to isolate it from the first one

7[1] "Opposition", in the sense of oppositeness, being placed in opposite positions.

7[2] For the errors regarding odor and the confounding of "the products of Light and Gravitation (E. and W.) with Light itself", see *CL* IV 773–4 and *CL* IV 806 respectively—passages in two important letters of Sept 1817 and Jan 1818 to C. A. Tulk.

magnitude of which, by the way, is entirely contingent, since space is not in any way relevant;* the positive force alone will be in command...]

* Is this more or less than a plump Contradiction in terms? In terms only, perhaps—but than[a] an Equation should have been proved previously.

9 I i 109, pencil, rubbed at the end, referring to I i 115 | § 16

Da nun aber die beiden Kräfte, deren Entgegensetzung eine unendliche ist, auch ins Unendliche sich fliehen, so wird in der Construction der Materie irgend ein Moment vorkommen, in welchem die beyden Kräfte sich absolut trennen. Der synthetische Punkt C in der oben construirten Linie (§. 9.) fällt also hinweg, und die eine Linie ACB

\+ o − kann gedacht werden als getrennt in die beiden
A C B

Linien AC, und CB, deren jede für sich jetzt die Eine der beiden Thätigkeiten repräsentirt.

[But since the two forces, infinitely opposing each other, also flee each other to infinity, the construction of matter will contain a moment when the two forces absolutely divide. The synthetic point C on the above constructed line (§ 9) thus disappears, and the single line ACB [above] can be conceived as divided into the two lines AC and CB, each of which now represents one of the two activities.]

§ 16. Between this and § 9 there is a Link wanting. In § 9 no fleeing of each other is mentioned; but a constant overtaking of the Positive Powers by the Negative. But this can be represented by [. . . . .][a] only by an equation.

10 I i 168 (misprinted 268), pencil, cropped | End of Steffens "Ueber den Oxydations- und Desoxydations-Process der Erde"

This masterly Oration is deficient in one main point: viz. it does not explain the re-oxygenation of the Air itself. For in order to this, it is not sufficient to shew that a D~~y~~esoxydation exists proportional to the Oxydation—it must be shewn, how the Oxygen + Carbon is decarbonated. For it is found, that the injury to the air from decaying Vegetables and nightly excretions is nearly equal to the benefit derived from the *pure* oxygen supplied by them.—It seems more probable to me, that the Cycle of [. . . . .] started in each [. . . . .]

11 p $^{-}$2, referring to I ii 13–16 | Schelling "Allgemeine Deduction" §§ 34–5

Sind beide [Kräfte] sich entgegengesetzt und getrennt, so wird ebenso wie im vorhergehenden Moment jede dieser Kräfte *für sich* die Fläche

8[a] A slip for "then" **9**[a] A line and a half in ms illegible

hervorbringen (§. 18. 19.). Aber beide sollen in ihrer Trennung wieder identisch gesetzt werden für die Anschauung. Diess ist, da der Gegensatz der *Kräfte selbst*—bestehen soll, nur dadurch möglich, dass ihre *Productionen* in einer gemeinschaftlichen dritten dargestellt werden, und da, wie gesagt, jede dieser Kräfte für sich die Fläche hervorbringt, so wird das Gemeinschaftliche, (welches nicht als durch ein blosses Hinzufügen, sondern durch ein wirkliches Durchdringen oder Multipliciren der Produkte durch einander entstehend gedacht werden muss), die *zweite Potenz der Fläche* oder der *Cubus* seyn müssen.

[If the two [forces] are opposed to each other and separated, then each of these forces will produce the surface *for itself*, as in the previous moment. (§ 18, 19). But both are to be again posited in their separation as identical to perception. Since the actual opposition of *the forces* is to persist, this is only possible by representing their *productions* in a third force common to both. Since, as already mentioned, each of the forces brings forth the surface for itself, this common [factor] (which must be thought of as arising not by a mere adding of one to the other, but by a real penetration or multiplication of the products) must be the *square of the surface* or the cube.]

2nd Heft.[1] §. 34, 35. p. 13–16 Obscure and unsatisfactory—especially in the surfaces multiplying into each other & generating Cubes.

12 p $^{-}$3, probably referring to I ii 16 | § 35

Denn man setze entweder, dass beide Kräfte überhaupt gar nicht unterschieden, oder dynamisch sich entgegengesetzt seyen, so haben wir die ursprüngliche Null, oder dass beide mathematisch getrennt seyen, so haben wir entweder die Linie, in welcher ein einziger Punct ist, der die beiden Kräfte nur dadurch in sich vereinigt, dass sie von ihm aus sich nach entgegengesetzten Richtungen trennen (§. 9.), oder wenn wir auch diesen Punct wegfallen lassen, so producirt jede dieser Kräfte für sich die Fläche (§. 18. f.) und es entsteht wiederum keine Raumerfüllung. Dass eine solche entstehe, dazu gehört, dass beide Kräfte *als* entgegengesetzte gleichwohl in Ein und dasselbe Gemeinschaftliche gesetzt seyen, denn keine von beiden erfüllt für sich den Raum, also müssen auch in dem unendlich kleinsten Theil des erfüllten Raums beide Kräfte zugleich gegenwärtig seyn.

[For if it is posited either that the two forces are not different at all, or are dynamically opposed to one another—then we have the original nought: or that the two forces are mathematically separated—then we have either the line, in which there is a single point which unites the two forces in itself only by their separating in opposite directions starting from it (§ 9), or, if we drop this point also, each of these forces produces

11[1] I.e. the second Part (ii) or Number of the journal.

the surface for itself (§ 18 f) and again space-filling takes place. For this to arise it is necessary that the two forces be posited *as* opposed, yet in one and the same common ground, since neither fills the space itself; therefore in even the infinitely smallest part of the filled space both forces must be present at the same time.]

We may understand opposite directions (entgegengesetzte Richtungen) in two ways.

Either a and b~~e~~ go, a west and b east

W a__________ab__________b E

or a will go east and b west: and then they mus[t] [? start][a] at the point, where they separate.

13 I ii 16–17 | **12** textus

Depth is given *in* THE Space, but not given *by Space*. It is an Idea, or as it were a Spiritual intuition—not an Image, like Length & Surface. In all these Constructions Schelling pre-supposes the Space, and (what is worse) the Idea of *Depth* as ⟨if it were⟩ given by Space. But this potenziation of Space into *the* Space, this *substration* of the *idea*, Depth, under the *image* of relative Lengths, ⊤ or ⊥, is the very Knot to be unfolded.

14 I ii 146 | Schelling "Miscellen"

. . . Hr. *von Arnim* hat selbst zur Begründung seines Antheils an den magnetischen Phänomenen mehrere bekannte und neuaufgefundne Thatsachen zusammengestellt, wovon ich hier nur die schon . . . bemerkte Wirkung des Magnets auf ganz durchsichtige Diamanten, (Producte der Natur aus reinem Kohlenstoff nach Guyton), und die von Hrn. von Arnim bemerkte Wirkung desselben auf aus Holzkohlen der Länge nach geschnittne Nadeln anführen will.

[. . . Mr von Arnim has himself put together a number of well-known and newly-discovered facts to establish his part in magnetic phenomena, of which I shall here mention only the already . . . described effect of the magnet on absolutely transparent diamonds (natural products of pure carbon, according to Guyton) and its effect, noticed by Mr von Arnim, on needles cut lengthwise from charcoal.]

Such exceedingly small portions of Iron suffice, as has been proved, to make a body magnetic, that no experiment of this kind can be quite satisfactory.

12[a] A hole in the paper; the tops of two ascenders are visible

15 I ii 156 | § 6

Nachricht

Es ist ein grober Irrthum, wenn ich S. 93. des ersten Hefts dieser Zeitschrift Herrn Reinhold unter den Philosophen nenne, welche sich für zu gut hielten, an der Literat. Zeitung jetzt noch, Theil zu nehmen, welches ich getan habe, mehr um ihm meine Achtung zu bezeugen, als ob ich dessen völlig gewiss gewesen wäre.

[*Report*

It is gross error when, on p. 93 of the first volume of this journal, I include Mr Reinhold among those philosophers who thought it beneath their dignity to contribute to the *Literaturzeitung*. I did so more out of respect for him than out of any great certainty in the matter.]

How sorrowful to see so great a mind as Schelling's so little a man as Schelling! Vindictive and jealous as a Romish High-priest, a ferocious sullen Monk, glooming like the black Wick of a Candle, thro' ~~as~~ his own surrounding and surmounting Light and Radiance: for alas! the Monk is a Philosopher, and yet a Monk! First, Schulz—& that was only below Schelling's Dignity. Then, Reinhold: then Fichte: and last and worst, Jacobi.[1] Even to dissent from his conjectures is an unpardonable offence with this Grand Turk of Philosophy.

16 II i 32–4, pencil, cropped | Eschenmayer "Spontaneität = Weltseele"

[Eschenmayer complains of the inappropriateness of the phrase *specifische Beschaffenheit* ("specific composition"), imported from chemistry and physiology.] *Schelling* scheint diesen Begriff durch die Annahme einer *Mehrheit* von ursprünglichen Aktionen noch begünstigen zu wollen, aber ich frage, wie ist eine einfache Aktion von den andern unterschieden, wenn es nicht blos ein gradueller Unterschied seyn soll?

[Schelling still seems to want to favour this concept by assuming a *plurality* of original actions; but I wonder how a simple action is to be distinguished from others, if the difference is not simply to be a gradual one.]

15[1] C's note refers to Schelling's disputes with contemporary followers or opponents of Kant. C would have seen attacks on Johann Schulz (or Schulze or Schultz) (1739–1805) *Erläuterung über des Herrn Kant Critik der Reinen Vernunft* (Königsberg 1784) and on Karl Leonard Reinhold (1758–1823) *Briefe über die Kantische Philosophie* (Mannheim 1789) in SCHELLING *Philosophische Schriften* I 278 and 285 respectively (neither page annotated). For Schelling's increasing divergence from Fichte see SCHELLING *Darlegung* in general and SCHELLING *Philosophische Schriften* **38** and n 1 in particular. For his harsh treatment of Jacobi see SCHELLING *Denkmal* **1**, **2**, **17**, **20**, and nn. Schelling himself refers to Fichte in **22** textus below, and to Reinhold in **24** textus, **38** textus.

I was myself, I own, disappointed, mortified I might say, by this Assumption of Schelling's—It seemed like [. . . . .] Sky. Why, they come out of a closed F[. . .] (= ray of Light) as soon as it is o[?pened.] Neither can I see any reason for it [. . . . .] Omneity of the [. . . . .] [i]ts infinite Unities. S. T. C.

17 II i 35, pencil, cropped

Er geht von einem *allgemeinen Organismus* aus, welcher aber noch unentwickelt und in einer *ursprünglichen Involution* befangen ist; hier entsteht die Frage: soll in diese *Involution* schon eine Mannigfaltigkeit von künftigen Entwicklungen, eine Verschiedenheit künftiger Richtungen hineingetragen werden, oder sollen nur jene zwei ursprüngliche einfache Tendenzen: ein ursprünglich Evolvirendes und ein ursprünglich Retardirendes (Expansion und Kontraktion) darinn wohnen.

[He takes as his starting point a *universal organism*, but one still undeveloped and bound up in an *original involution*. The question thus arises whether this *involution* should be thought of as already containing a multitude of future developments, a diversity of future directions, or should only those two original, simple tendencies reside within it, the originally evolving one and the originally retarding one (expansion and contraction)?]

But d[oes] not Sc[helling's] *transce*[*ndent*] teach [that] there are *Rela*[*tions*] the [. . .] Alp[. . .] of *N*[*ature*] itself [. . .] a las[. . . . .]

18 II i 51, pencil, cropped

Der Geruch ist nur noch wenige Schritte von seinem Gegenstande entfernt, und obgleich hier genaue Beobachtungen fehlen mögen, so ist doch die Zeit der Fortpflanzung eine ohne Vergleich grössere, als nur diese bei der Fortpflanzung des Schalls.

[*Smell* is only a few steps away from its opposite, and although exact observations may be lacking, the time taken for its propagation is incomparably greater than that for the propagation of sound.]

But [. . .] not, [? is] this to [be] referr[ed in] part [? at least] to the affect[ive] differen[ce.] The m[otion] of mat[ter] on this hypothesis of Plus and Minus, co[nfining] the Odorifique, may have split in [the] divergence into a Subtlety below the minimum.

19 II i 52, pencil, cropped

Und endlich geht *das Gefühl* in eine innige Einverleibung mit dem Gegenstand über. In beiden letztern wächst die Zeit ins Unermessliche.

Welches abnehmende Verhältniss von der unermesslichen Ferne bis zur Berührung! So wie im erstern Fall die Zeit beinahe verschwindet, indem der Raum unermesslich wird, so verschwindet im letztern Fall der Raum, indem die Zeit unermesslich wird.

[And finally *feeling* passes into an intimate incorporation with the object. In the two latter the time increases until it is immeasurably great. *What a decreasing proportion from immeasurable distance to contact! Just as in the first case time nearly disappears, whereas space becomes immeasurably great, so in the latter space nearly disappears, whereas the time becomes immeasurably great.*]

[An]tithesis [. . .]—and [. . .] is it [. . .] than [. . .]de [. . .]? In [? what] [s]ense [. . .] Time [. . .] aus [. . .]—(in [. . .] sense [s]pace [. . .] instance [. . .] nebula [. . .]) in [. . .] instantaneous feeling of the prick of a Pin?

20 I i title-page, referring to II i 136, pencil | Schelling "Anhang zu dem Aufsatz"

Ich betrachte in der Naturphilosophie jenes Subject-Object, das ich Natur nenne, allerdings in seiner Selbstconstruction. Man muss sich zur intellectuellen Anschauung der Natur erhoben haben, um diess zu begreifen.—Der Empiriker erhebt sich darin nicht: und ebendesswegen ist *er* eigentlich immer das construirende, in allen seinen Erklärungen. . . . Der Naturphilosoph kann eben darum, weil er die Natur zur Selbstständigkeit erhebt, und sich selbst construiren lässt, nie in die Nothwendigkeit kommen, die construirte Natur (d.h. die Erfahrung) jener entgegen zu setzen, jene nach ihr zu corrigiren . . .

[In natural philosophy I admittedly regard that subject-object which I call nature, in its self-construction. One must have raised oneself to the intellectual intuition of nature in order to understand this.—The empiricist does not rise to this; and because of this *he* is always that which is constructing, in all his explanations. . . . The natural philosopher can never need to oppose constructed nature (i.e. experience) to independent nature, to correct independent nature in accordance with it, for the very reason that elevates nature to independence allows it to construct itself . . .]

p. 136. Distinction between the Empirist,[1] and the Philosopher, Termin. a quo ⚹ Term. ad quem.[2] Exper. equally necessary to both.

21 II i 144, pencil, cropped

[Baader, according to Schelling, considers spontaneity to be the First Principle] . . . während *mir* das, was diess alles thut, noch *in der Natur selbst*—die wirkliche *Seele* der Natur—ist da ich überhaupt nicht zwey

20[1] Not in *OED*. The term still current in C's day was "empiric"; "empiricist" was a later introduction.

20[2] "'The end from which' as opposed to 'the end towards which'".

verschiedene Welten sondern durchaus nur die *Eine* selbige zugebe, in welcher alles, und auch das begriffen ist, was im gemeinen Bewusstseyn als Natur und Geist sich entgegengesetzt wird.

[. . . whereas, in *my* view, that which performs all this is still *in nature itself*—the real *soul* of nature—for I acknowledge not two different worlds but only *one* and the same in which everything is comprehended, including that which the common understanding sets in opposition as nature and mind.]

I presume, that [. . . . .] of Schelling his intellectual Title-deed for this real property, called Nature or true yet unconscious Being.

22 II ii vii, pencil | Schelling "Darstellung meines Systems"

Nun könnte es aber sehr wohl seyn, dass der Idealismus, z.B., welchen Fichte zuerst aufgestellt . . . eine ganz andre Bedeutung hätte, als jener . . . um diese Entgegensetzung aufs verständlichste auszudrücken, so müsste der Idealismus in der subjectiven Bedeutung behaupten, das Ich seye Alles; der in der objectiven Bedeutung umgekehrt: Alles seye = Ich und es existire nichts, als was = Ich seye . . .

[Now it could well be that the idealism, for example, which Fichte originally set up . . . had quite a different significance from that idealism . . . In order to express this opposition as clearly as possible, idealism in its subjective meaning would have to maintain that the ego was everything; and idealism in its objective meaning the opposite: everything was = to the ego, and that nothing exists except that which was = to the ego . . .]

This is easily *said*; but the latter = Ich is either *ein* Ich, or Ichheiten.[1] The first is = Fichte: the second to every body.

23 II ii vii–viii, pencil

Nicht anders als mit dem Idealismus möchte es sich wohl mit dem verhalten, was man bis daher Realismus genannt hat; und fast kommt es mir vor, als seye die folgende Darstellung Beweis, dass man bis auf den heutigen Tag den Realismus in seiner erhabensten und vollkommensten Gestalt, (ich meine im Spinozismus),* in allen öffentlich bekannt gewordenen Ansichten durchaus verkannt, und misverstanden habe.

[The position with regard to what was till then called realism is probably no different from that of idealism; and it almost seems to me as if the following account is a proof that realism in its loftiest and most perfect form (I mean Spinozism)* has been absolutely misjudged and misunderstood in all those views which have become public up to the present day.]

22[1] I.e. either "*a* self, or selves".

* Curious how many twists and turns Schelling has made with regard to Spinoza, to all intents the same as his own system: for it is neither Realism, for it does ⟨not⟩ deduce cogitation from matter—nor Idealism, for it does make matter the result of cogitation but places all in the Identity of Will.[1]

24 II ii x–xi, pencil, cropped

[In a long footnote (ix–xii) Schelling makes a virulent attack on Reinhold.]

The uncandid manner, in which Schelling speaks of all who dare utter a doubt concerning the Natùr-philosophie, and still more the harsh and detracting Tone in which [. . . . .] more philosophical as well as more genial Opinions, are very unamiable Traits of Character/ Schelling could not have [. . . . .][1]

25 II ii xiv, pencil, so rubbed as to be almost illegible | End of Schelling's foreword

Kant [? did] far more. [. . .] Schelling [. . .] less [. . .] his Ladder, but its suggested & [? original road] [. . . . .] Metaphysische Anfangsgrunde [. . . . .] is puerile [. . . . .] Kant [. . .][1]

26 II ii 5, 4 | §§ 4–6

§. 4. *Das höchste Gesetz für das Seyn der Vernunft, und da ausser der Vernunft nichts ist . . . für alles Seyn* (insofern es in der Vernunft begriffen ist), ist *das Gesetz der Identität*, welches in Bezug auf alles Seyn durch A = A ausgedrückt wird. . . .

§. 6. Der Satz A = A allgemein gedacht, sagt weder, dass A überhaupt, noch dass es als Subject, *oder* als Prädicat *seye*. Sondern *das einzige Seyn, was durch diesen Satz gesetzt wird, ist das der* ***Identität selbst****, welche daher von dem A als Subject, und von dem A als Praedicat völlig unabhängig gesetzt wird.* Der *Beweis* für die erste Behauptung ist in der *Wissenschaftslehre* §. 1. geführt, der zweite Theil des Satzes folgt aus dem ersten von selbst, und ist in ihm schon enthalten. Denn da von dem Seyn des A selbst überhaupt, und inwiefern es Subject und Prädicat ist, abstrahirt ist, so bleibt als das Einzige, wovon nicht abstrahirt

23[1] For C's critical exposition of Spinoza's philosophy (with some reference to Schelling) see *SW & F* (*CC*) 607–24; for an annotated copy of his works see SPINOZA.

24[1] See **15** n 1.

25[1] For C's opinion of this work see KANT *Metaphysische Anfangsgründe*.

werden kann, was also durch jenen Satz eigentlich gesetzt ist, die absolute Identität selbst.

[§. 4. *The highest law for the being of reason, and since there is nothing except reason . . . for all being* (in as far as it is included in reason) is *the law of identity*, which is expressed as A = A in respect of all being. . . .

§. 6. The proposition A = A taken in its general significance neither means that A is at all, nor that it is as subject, *or* as object. *The only being which is posited by this proposition is* ***identity itself****, which is therefore posited completely independent of A as subject and of A as predicate.* The *proof* for the first assertion is given in the "Wissenschaftslehre" § 1, the second part of the proposition follows of itself from the first and is already contained in it. Since the being of A itself generally, and as far as it is subject and predicate, is abstracted, the only remainder which cannot be abstracted is that which is actually posited by that proposition, absolute identity itself.]

To § 6 and the preceding §§s it is enough to reply, that to identify (or confound) is not to abstract. If A = x: A − x = 0.

It is evident likewise, that Schelling has degraded Self-affirmation ~~S = Ob~~ by a retropulsion of the O⟨b⟩ + S, instead of elevating or potenziating the Objectivity by S = Ob. He turns the Self in Self-knowlege into an Object whereas the reasoning should have been—Object = Self; but Self = Knowlege; ergo, Object = Knowlege.

[a]By retropulsion I mean the forcing the second over the first, so as to make the second first and the first second.[1]

2. Ob. + S.
1. S = Ob

27 II ii 9, pencil | § 15

Die absolute Identität **ist** *nur unter der Form des Satzes A = A, oder,* diese Form ist unmittelbar durch ihr Seyn gesetzt. *

[*Absolute identity* **is** *only posited in the form of the proposition A = A or,* this form is posited directly by its being.*]

* §. 15. Here begins the Trial, whether the preceding §s *mean* any thing.

28 II ii 10–11, pencil | § 16

Zus. 1. *Was zugleich mit der Form des Satzes A = A gesetzt ist, ist auch unmittelbar mit dem Seyn der absoluten Identität selbst gesetzt, es gehört*

26[a] The first part of the note is written on II ii 5, the remainder in the foot-margin of II ii 4

26[1] This generalised meaning is not in *OED*. C has appropriated a medical term of recent introduction, the first example in *OED* being in a passage of 1794 by Erasmus Darwin.

aber nicht zu ihrem Wesen, sondern nur zu der Form oder Art ihres Seyns. Der Beweis für den ersten Theil des Satzes folgt unmittelbar aus dem vorhergehenden. Der zweite Theil des Satzes wird so bewiesen. Die Form des Satzes A = A ist bestimmt durch A als Subject und A als Prädicat. *Aber die absolute Identität selbst ist in demselben unabhängig von dem A als Subject und dem A als Prädicat gesetzt. (§. 6.) Also gehört auch, was zugleich mit der Form dieses Satzes gesetzt ist nicht zur absoluten Identität selbst, sondern nur zu der Art oder Form ihres Seyns.

[Addition 1. *Whatever is posited together with the form of the proposition A = A is also posited directly with the being of absolute identity; it does not, however, belong to its essence, but only to the form or kind of its being.* The proof for the first part of the proposition follows directly from the foregoing. The second part is proved thus: the form of the proposition A = A is determined by A as subject and A as predicate. *But absolute identity is posited in it independently of the A as subject and the A as predicate. (§ 6.) Therefore that which was posited at the same time as the form of this proposition does not belong to absolute identity itself, but only to the kind or form of its being.]

But the *sort* or *form*—why not *is* it as well as Identity? The latter is independent of A as Subject and A as Predi⟨c⟩ate[a] but are not A and A dependent on *it*? If so, either as different from I. or the same. If diff., I. [? is the] *all*—if the same, I. necessarily *is* as A and A. But I = Reason; ergo, A ⚹ A is a contemplation from the point of Reason.

⚹ = antitheticé[1]

29 p +2 (numbered "2" in ink), referring to II ii 11, pencil, badly rubbed | **28** textus

p. 11 Is not the word, independent, used sophistically in Zusatz[1] of § 16? The image of my face in a mirror is dependent on my face, but my [. . .] is independent [be]cause m[y] face is & always [. . .] without that Image. But [? could] [. . .] said that the Face was independent of its own Features?

30 pp +2–+3, referring to II ii 11–12, pencil, rubbed

§. 17. *Es giebt eine ursprüngliche Erkenntniss der absoluten Identität und diese ist unmittelbar mit dem Satze A = A gesezt.* . . . §. 18. *Alles was ist, ist dem Wesen nach, insofern dieses an sich und absolut betrachtet wird,*

28[a] Here C has written "*" and continued the note in the foot-margin with "*"

28[1] "In antithesis to", "antithetically".

29[1] "Addition": textus. Although C cites p 11, the appropriate textus is the passage given for **28**, from p 10, which contains the idea of independence.

die absolute Identität selbst, der Form des Seyns nach aber ein Erkennen der absoluten Identität.

[§17. *There is an original knowledge of the absolute identity and this is immediately posited by the proposition A = A. . . .* § 18. *With respect to its essence and insofar as this is considered in itself and absolutely, everything that exists is absolute identity itself; with respect to its form of being, however, it is knowledge of absolute identity.*]

§s 17.18. It is difficult to discriminate Schelling's Identity from the common notion of Substance, a pin-cushion of powers and qualities.

For if the knowlege knows the Identity as that of which it is itself the *Form*, it knows itself as the *Form* of the Identity—therefore it distinguishes its self from the Identity and no less the Identity from itself. But the latter thus distinguished seems = the *would-be-never-can-be* image (ειδοειδες τὶ)[1] call'd Substance.

Now what answer can be given to this which would not imply that esse and scirè, exist[er]e[a] and sciri[2] are the same—i.e. what becomes of the distinction between Schelling and the common Idealist? For egoism is not the *common* Idealism./ Besides, is it not merely arbitrary to call das Selbst-erkennen[3] the *Form* of the Identity?~~—Nay, a contradiction to Zus. I §. 16. according to [. . .]~~ welches "also gehört, auch [ni]cht[b] Zur absoluten Identität selbst, sondern *nur* zu der *Art* oder *Form* ihres Seyns![''] (p. 101. 6.)[4] What is this less than saying that Self-knowlege distinguishes itself from its own Identity, as not belonging to the latter, but only to the sort (Art) or form of its Being, which however is one and the same as the Being, ⟨to which it does not belong!!⟩—Now methinks, the more intelligible position would be that the Self-knowlege is the Identity of which the Subject and Object are the Form.—

Again, to what purpose the distinction between das Wesen = essence, and das Seyn = Being, Esse, Entity? I mean, as applied to the Absolute.[5]

31 II ii 14–15, pencil, overtraced at the end | § 23

Zwischen Subject und Object ist keine andere, als quantitative Differenz möglich. . . . Erläuterung. . . . da sie [Subjectivität und Objectivität] zur Form des Seyns der absoluten Identität, mithin zur Form alles Seyns gehören, vielleicht nicht auf gleiche Weise, sondern so beisammen sind,

30[a] Small hole in paper; letters supplied by ed
30[b] Small hole in paper; letters supplied by ed

30[1] "Something in the shape of a shape".
30[2] "To be" and "to know", "to exist" and "to be known".
30[3] "Self-knowing" or "self-knowledge"—not in textus.
30[4] Last sentence of **28** textus.
30[5] First sentence of **28** textus.

dass sie wechselseitig als überwiegend gesetzt werden können, welches alles wir aber hier noch nicht behaupten, sondern nur als einen möglichen Gedanken aufstellen.

[*Between subject and object only a quantitative difference is possible. . . . Explanation. . . .* since they [subjectivity and objectivity] belong to the form of being of absolute identity, and thereby to the form of all being, [and] are together, perhaps not in the same way, but in such a manner that they can alternately be posited as preponderant—none of which we would as yet maintain, but simply put forward as a possible thought.]

False! It is not a possible Thought except as far as the Form is taken as a Being of itself, different from the Being, or rather (for there seems no end to the contradictions) from the Being of the Being.—[a]I confess, that in this § 23. Schelling appears to me to have helped himself out with as mere a *fact* of Psychology or Reflection as ever Fichte did.[1]

32 p +3, pencil, referring to II ii 14–15 | **31** textus

§ 23. here begins the *Bridge*, which in Schelling's own opinion (see the Erläuterung)[1] requires no little courage in him who would venture to cross it. *Quantitative* difference between S. and O. when the wh[ole][a] is in each!!—S = x − 0: 0 = x − 0:—& yet S not = 0!

33 pp 16–17, pencil, rubbed | § 28

Es giebt kein einzelnes Seyn, oder einzelnes Ding an ***sich***. Denn das einzige *An sich* ist die absolute Identität (§. 8.) Diese aber ist nur als Totalität. (§. 26.)

Anm. Es *ist* auch nichts an sich ausserhalb der Totalität, und wenn etwas ausserhalb der Totalität erblickt wird, so geschieht es nur vermöge einer willkürlichen Trennung des Einzelnen vom Ganzen, welche durch die Reflexion ausgeübt wird, aber an sich gar nicht stattfindet, da alles, was ist, Eines, (§. 12, Zus. 1.) und in der Totalität die absolute Identität selbst ist. (§. 26.)

[*There is no individual being, or individual thing in* ***itself***. For the only *in-itself* is absolute identity (§ 8). This however is only as totality (§ 26).

Note: Nothing *is* in itself outside totality and if something is caught sight of outside totality it only happens by means of an arbitrary separation of the individual from the

31[a] Overtracing in ink, apparently by C, begins here
32[a] Small hole in paper; letters supplied by ed

31[1] For the rivalry between Schelling and Fichte see **15** n 1.

32[1] "Explanation"—in **31** textus.

whole which is caused by reflection, but does not in itself take place at all, since everything that is, is one (§ 12, Addition 1) and is absolute identity itself in totality (§ 26).]

Strange, that such a man should so delude himself! What after all is gained by nick-naming the whole thing *nichts*![1] *Can* any man believe pain and pleasure to be nothing or very nothing of very nothing? Does the term, ist,[2] receive any elucidation? is it not [. . . . .] [? pattern] of old [. . .] There seem to me to be but two (*essentially* different) systems, the one (Spinoza, Schelling), which assumes the Esse alone, call it reason, or matter: the other both Esse and Habere.—[3]

34 II ii 17–18, pencil | § 30

Erläuterung. Unsere Behauptung ist also auf's deutlichste ausgedrükt, *die*, dass, könnten wir alles, was ist, in der Totalität erbliken, wir im Ganzen ein vollkommenes quantitatives Gleichgewicht von Subjectivität und Objectivität, also nichts, als die reine Identität, in welcher nichts unterscheidbar ist, gewahr würden, so sehr auch in Ansehung des Einzelnen das Uebergewicht auf die Eine, oder die andere Seite fallen mag, dass also doch auch jene quantitative Differenz keineswegs *an sich*, sondern nur in der Erscheinung gesetzt ist.

[*Explanation*. Our assertion, therefore, expressed as clearly as possible, is as follows: that if we could see everything that is in totality, we would perceive in the whole a complete quantitative equilibrium of subjectivity and objectivity—that is, nothing but pure identity, in which nothing is distinguishable, however much preponderance may fall on the one side or the other, in respect of the individual; that, therefore, even that quantitative difference is in no way posited *in itself*, but only as a phenomenon.]

What, again, is this, but to assert that God sees and knows nothing because he sees and knows all—i.e. that there is no God: inasmuch as Omniscience would be nihiliscience?[1] Besides, an equal division is not indifference.—If it were answered—x is all in S. and yet all in O—then what avails it to prove the average equilibrium? *All* can have neither + or −

35 II ii 19, pencil

Wie es aber möglich sey, dass von dieser absoluten Totalität irgend etwas sich absondere oder in Gedanken abgesondert werde, diess ist eine Frage,

33[1] "Nothing"—textus.

33[2] "It is"—italicised in textus.

33[3] The "to be", or being, alone; and both "to be" and "to have". For the fundamental likeness between Spinoza's system and Schelling's, see **23**. The relationship between "to have" and "to be" is a recurrent theme in C's work; for a playful treatment of it in the 1812 *Omniana* see *SW & F* (*CC*) 315–16.

34[1] "Nihiliscience" (knowledge of nothing) is not in *OED*.

welche hier noch nicht beantwortet werden kann, da wir vielmehr beweisen, dass eine solche Absonderung nicht an sich möglich, und vom Standpunct der Vernunft aus falsch, ja, (wie sich wohl einsehen lässt) die Quelle aller Irrthümer seye.

[But how it is possible that anything separates itself from this absolute totality or is separated in the mind is a question which cannot yet be answered here, since we shall, rather, prove that such a separation is not in itself possible and that it is wrong from the point of view of reason—even that it is the source of all errors (as can well be understood).]

But are not errors somewhat, or properties of somewhat? Spite of himself, Schelling is haunted by the eye-phantom of a Substance, "a prima et unica materia".[1]

36 II ii 22, pencil | § 35

Nichts einzelnes hat den Grund seines Daseyns in sich selbst.—Denn sonst müsste das Seyn aus seinem Wesen erfolgen. Nun ist aber alles dem Wesen nach gleich (§. 12. Zus. 1.) Also kann das Wesen keines einzelnen Dings den Grund enthalten, dass es als dieses einzelne seye, es ist also als dieses nicht durch sich selbst.

[*Nothing individual has the ground of its existence in itself*—otherwise being would have to result from its essence. However everything is the same in essence (§ 12, Addition 1). Therefore the essence of no single thing can contain the ground that it *is* as this individual; it is, therefore, not through itself that it is [exists] as this individual thing.]

How can *nichts*[1] have any ground? But alles *einzelnes* ist nichts,[2] according to Schelling.

37 II ii 27, pencil | § 44

Alle Potenzen sind absolut gleichzeitig. Denn die absolute Identität ist nur unter der Form aller Potenzen. (§. 43.) Sie *ist* aber ewig, und ohne alle Beziehung auf die Zeit (§. 8. Zus. 2.) Also sind auch alle Potenzen ohne alle Beziehung auf Zeit, schlechthin ewig, also auch unter sich gleichzeitig.*

[*All powers are absolutely simultaneous*; for absolute identity is only under the form of all powers (§ 43). It *is*, however, eternally, and without any reference to time (§ 8,

35[1] A "first and unique matter". Cf *substantia unica* "unique substance", a phrase C always associated with Spinoza, e.g. *SW & F* (*CC*) 609 and n, *AR* (*CC*) 169 and n 30.

36[1] "Nothing"—in textus, and cf **33**.

36[2] "Every *individual* thing is nothing".

Addition 2). Therefore all powers are also without any reference to time, simply eternal and therefore also simultaneous with each other.*]

* Thus must Schelling go on ad infinitum/ in a legerdemain of turning something into nothing, nothing into something, & that something into another nothing, in order to arrive at *any* thing!

38 II ii 51 | § 72

Die Zu- und Abnahme der Cohäsion steht in einem bestimmten umgekehrten Verhältniss zu der Zu- und Abnahme des specifischen Gewichts. Folgt aus 58. Zus. 6.

Anm. 1. . . . Je grösser dieses Moment [der Differenz] wird, desto mehr wird die specifische Schwere überwunden, aber in desto höherem Grade tritt nun auch die Cohäsion ein bis zu einem Puncte, wo mit abnehmender Cohäsion wieder die grössere specifische Schwere siegt, und endlich beide zugleich und gemeinschaftlich sinken.

[*The increase and decrease of cohesion stands in a definite inverse proportion to the increase and decrease of specific gravity.* This follows from 58, Addition 6.

Note 1. . . . The larger this moment [of difference] is, the more the specific gravity is overcome, but the greater also is the efficacy of cohesion, up to a point at which, with decreasing cohesion, the greater specific gravity is again successful. Finally both sink together and in common.]

* But Tin. 7.299: Cobalt, 7.700, Iron. 7.788.—Can so very slight a difference in Sp. Grav. account for so vast a difference in Cohesion?[1]

38[1] Eschenmayer does not supply the figures for the specific gravities of these metals, and C must have turned to another work, perhaps a reference book, for them. A work he refers to elsewhere, William Thomas Brande *A Manual of Chemistry* (2nd ed 3 vols 1821), gives figures that are close to but not exactly the same as these.

HENRY AUGUSTUS ZWICK

fl 1823

Calmuc Tartary; or a journey from Sarepta to several Calmuc hordes of the Astracan government; from May 26 to August 21, 1823. Undertaken, on behalf of the Russian Bible Society, by Henry Augustus Zwick and John Golfried Schill, and described by the former. London 1831. 8°.

Not located. Formerly at Keats House, but had disappeared by 1959.

With the signature of William Lambe who attended Keats at Wentworth House. Presented to Keats House by H. Saxe Wyndham Esq in 1931. Pasted in the book is the library card of the Highgate Book Society to which both Lambe and Gillman were subscribers. Lambe borrowed the book from 14 to 20 June 1831 and Gillman had it from 7 to 13 July.

DATE. Summer 1831.

1 front flyleaf

A very interesting little Volume. I have read more than one "Travels &c["] in two Volumes *Quarto*, of far less substance & intrinsic value. The perfect freedom from all sectarian bigotry, Missionary enthusiasm and *bibliolatry* is as exemplary as it is remarkable. S. T. C.

ADDENDA

THOMAS AMORY

c 1691–1788

The Life of John Buncle, Esq; containing various observations and reflections, made in several parts of the world; and many extraordinary relations. London 1756. 8°.

The Rosenbach Museum and Library, Philadelphia

Inscribed on the title-page "G. T. S."—with an addition "(.trong)" to signify that "G. T. S." was the American collector G. T. Strong. Several pencilled notes in the vol are not in C's hand: on the title-page, a note in one hand, "Chas Lamb's copy with notes by Coleridge", has its own commentary in another hand, "G. T. Strong's writing"; some figures on p 23, a mark against a paragraph on p 80, a note on p 471, and a list of pages annotated on p $^{+}1$—all in pencil—are certainly not in C's hand. Typographical errors are corrected on pp 6, 118, 131, and 132, possibly by C.

Lamb recommended this work to C 24 Jun 1797: *LL* (M) I 112. C's annotations, however, appear to belong to a later period, after he went to live in the Lake District, about which he writes authoritatively in **1**.

DATE. Probably early, but not before 1800.

1 p $^{-}1$ (p-d), referring to pp 168–9

[A lake is described "above a mile in length, and more than half a mile broad" situated next to a "rocky mountain" that] stands perpendicular at one end of the lake, at the distance of a few yards, and has an opening at the bottom, that is wide enough for two coaches to enter at once, if the place was dry.

168. 169.—wholly imaginary. There is not only no such place in Cumberland, Westmoreland, Lancashire, or the borders of Yorkshire; but none which by any exaggeration could be reconciled to the description. The Yorkshire Mountains would be the most likely—but where is the Lake?—To Skeddaw, Helvellen, Scafell it is wholly inapplicable.[1]—Besides, there never was a time since the reign of William the Conqueror,

1[1] Buncle is travelling through Westmorland, but he does not give names to the particular lake and mountain that he is describing. Skiddaw, Scafell Pike, and Helvellyn, all in the Lake District, are all over 3000' high: cf other references to them in FIELDING *Tom Jones* **1** n 1, JONSON **25** n 5.

when the Traveller would not have heard the name of the vale, of the next Market-town, of the stupendous Mountain, &c &c.—It is pure fiction.—

2 p 171

The power of electricity, to be sure is vast and amazing. It may cause great tremors and undulations of the earth, and bring down all the buildings of a great city: but as to splitting the earth to great depths, and forcing up torrents of water, where there was no sign of the fluid element before, I question much if the vehemence of the elemental electric fire does this.

Why?

3 p 175

As we have two ebbs and two flows in twenty-four hours, and the moon comes but once in that time to our meridian, how can the second ebb and flow be ascribed to it?

A fine ignorant worthy fellow.

EDWIN ATHERSTONE

1788–1872

The Last Days of Herculaneum; and Abradates and Panthea; Poems by Edwin Atherstone. London 1821. 12°.

Victoria College Library (Coleridge Collection)

On title-page, bibliographical annotations by a later owner, J. P. Colby of St Louis, Missouri, indicating the locations of C's notes and giving dates for Atherstone and adding after "Panthea" "Also—*A Dramatic Sketch*". Bookseller's notations in pencil pp $^{-}$6, $^{+}$7. On p $^{-}$6 the top edge of a newspaper column, "New Notes of Coleridge", once pasted in there.

DATE. Between 1821 (date of publication) and 1827, when C refers to Atherstone as someone well-known to him—indeed, as a nuisance: *CL* VI 662.

1 p $^{-}$2, pencil

Your hunters out of the Books, from which Milton, Shakespear, & others got their fine Thoughts may be likened to those who pose themselves [? ~~from~~] with old Fuller's Question—What Load-stone touched the first Load-stone?[1]

Item—one of the 1000 exquisite instances of difficulties seriously proposed which would never have occurred at all to any Brain less felicitously fantastic than good dear Fuller's or his more magnisonant Kidney-fellow, Sir T. Brown[2]—is

How came the Load-stone to fall in love with the cold, dreary, barren, [? fishy] North instead of the spicy East, or the golden West—

2 p 4 | *The Last Days of Herculaneum*

Some in the terrible sky
Had imaged forth appalling forms;—a god
6 7 1 2 3 4 5 8
They saw, huge as an Alpine hill, who rode

1[1] I.e. what magnet magnetised the first magnet? The source of the question has not been traced. C presumably refers to Thomas Fuller (1608–61), several of whose works he annotated: Thomas FULLER.

1[2] The first instance of "magnisonant" (defined as "high sounding") in *OED* is from RS in 1843. C's jocular phrase links two favourite 17th-century authors: for annotations see Thomas FULLER, BROWNE.

Half hidden on a throne of clouds, and breathed
Red vapours from his nostrils:—and his eyes
Glared like two suns of blood through mist. One saw,
Down bending from the sky distinct, a face
[a]Horrific;—black as tenfold night;—severe,
But calm it look'd with steadfast gaze to earth,
And eyes that never closed, though all around
[b]A thousand fires unintermitting play'd.

Q^y *Unimageable? One saw*—mean as a phrase, and a spondee of two words in the last foot of an Iambic turns it into a Scazon[1] scarcely tolerable in our language.

3 p 5

And the loud roaring, smother'd and profound
Of subterranean thunders fill'd the air.

? intense[1]

4 p 5

Some shouted as in rage; and some with tears
Big rolling down their marble cheeks, stood stiff
And paralyzed.

[a]Some seem'd to shriek
And yet were silent—

4A p 6

And nostril spread, as though in manic rage
To threat the Thunderer.

4B p 7

Each where he stood remain'd:—the mother hugg'd
Her infant to her breast . . .

2[a] Short vertical stroke against this line
2[b] Short vertical stroke against this line
4[a] C's alternative wording is written between the lines of verse, beginning above "and some"

2[1] "A modification of the iambic trimeter, in which a spondee or trochee takes the place of the final iambus" (*OED*).
3[1] Written against the 1st line of textus.

4C p 8, marked with a vertical line in the margin

On that devoted group the bolt had fallen:—
And when, recovering sense, the people turn'd
To look again upon them, they beheld
No sign of man,—but on the earth there lay
A heap of whiten'd ashes.

5 p 9

Trembling/ to their ∧ homes
The citizens return'd. Darkness intense
Soon cover'd all things;—and the close, hot air,
Felt suffocating

∧ unsafe

5A p 12, pencil

His wither'd hands he tosses to and fro—
Wheezes and snorts for breath . . .

5B p 12, pencil

Soundly they
Sleep who shall wake no more. He on whom fell
The crushing ruin:—who by the red bolt
Pērish̆'d . . .

5C p 13, pencil

What is it waves
At intervals along the inky sky
Like a dark blood-red flag?

5D p 13, pencil

Whence come those distant thunder-breathings deep,
That fall with gentlest touch upon the ear,
Yet seem to fill the heavens—and reach earth's centre?

5E p 14, pencil | **5D** textus cont'd

'Tis from that mountain's vast and hollow womb,
Now first conceiving subterranean fire,
And belching earthly thunders.—

5F p 14, pencil

What is it moves with gentle heave the ground;
Like ∧ soft~~est~~ swell of ocean in a calm— ∧ the
Now rests—then comes again with tremblings soft,
~~As from the rumbling of a loaded wain~~ / δ
Felt, tho' not heard?

6 p 14, pencil

Is the great sun
Consumed too,—or darken'd?—this the time,
So oft foretold, when nature shall expire * . . .

* Turn back to Pliny's—[1]

6A p 15, pencil

. . . redder now—
And redder still the awful concave glows—
Till in its bloody, but uncertain glare,
The bolder may walk forth.

6B p 15, pencil

. . . the glistening grass,
Where, 'gainst the rich deep green, the cowslip hangs
His elegant bells of purest gold . . .

7 p 16, pencil

When the tall neighbour grass, heavy with dew,
Bows down its head beneath the fresh'ning breeze;—
Where oft in long dark lines the waving trees
Throw their soft shadows on the sunny fields . . .

gale[1]

6[1] In his Introduction, Atherstone observes that regarding the eruption of Vesuvius that buried Herculaneum and Pompeii "little is known but the two letters of Pliny the younger to Tacitus the historian" (v)—which he then reprints (vi–xvi) in Melmoth's translation. C would be recalling such passages as the following (xv): [In the darkness preceding the eruption, voices are heard,] "the greater part imagining that the last and eternal night was come, which was to destroy both the gods and the world together".

7[1] Written against textus line 2.

7A pp 16–17, pencil

The pallid statue o'er some honour'd tomb
That ever drooping hangs;—and the bronze Mars
That bares his blood-stain'd sword:—the solemn tree
That o'er the sepulchre his ⟨its⟩ dark green boughs
Hangs melancholy . . .

7B p 17, pencil

the beggar's rags,
And the cerulean blue of beauty's robe;—
All in one undistinguishable hue
Are clad, of lurid redness.

8 p 17, pencil

"Is this morn?" they ask,
"Oh! what a night ~~we've~~ ⟨has⟩ pass'd!—but is this morn?
"And what is that, high in the gory clouds,
"That orb of brighter crimson?"

ensanguined[1]

9 p +2, pencil

Spondee	Gōd spāke
Iambic	Dĕ līght
Trochee	Līghtlў̆
Anapest	Ăt thĕ clōse
Amphibrach	Dĕlīghtfŭl
Dactyl	Mērrĭlў̆[1]

8[1] Written against textus line 3.
9[1] C used some of these same examples in lessons on English prosody in 1807: *SW & F* (*CC*) 201–6.

JOHN BANIM

1798–1842

MICHAEL BANIM

1796–1874

Tales by the O'Hara Family. Second Series. Comprising "The Nowlans", and "Peter of the Castle". [Anonymous.] 3 vols. London 1826. 12°.

Victoria College Library (Coleridge Collection)

For a detailed account of these vols see BANIM in *CM* (*CC*) I. The following note was at first overlooked.

8 III 368–9 | *Peter of the Castle*

[Collum has come in great distress, at the point of death, to confess the injustice he had done.] "Collum," said Felix, "do not speak those words; your trials are over: you stand forgiven upon earth and in Heaven; the future upon earth should be happy; and it shall, if a brother's care and love can make it so; cheer up; if you have strength to walk to my house——"

"No Felix," interrupted the wretch, "that can never be; your forgiveness—your being alive to forgive me—is the greatest blessing; your fellowship I cannot, dare not court, even was there a promise of life to seek it. Oh, my soul shrinks at the thought! *How could I sit by your fire-side? *How look into your face? No, my brother, no!—give your hand again; I ask that: and now one drop of water; one drop for His sake who——." He was again silent . . .

** Suppose this tale true: & can a more frightful picture be imagined of the heart-bewildering demoralization of the Romish Doctrine of Penance—Penance—& this drawn by a Romanist?—After 20 years of Self-torture, the *Pride* still rankling, the Soul still unreconciled with itself!

RICHARD BAXTER

1615–1691

Copy A

Reliquiae Baxterianae: or, Mr. Richard Baxter's narrative of the most memorable passages of his life and times. Faithfully publish'd from his own original manuscript, by Matthew Sylvester, &c. 3 pts (in 1 vol). London 1696. F°.

Not located. The last record concerning this copy dates from 1854, when Pickering's collection was auctioned at Sotheby's: Sale Catalogue 7 Aug 1854, Lot 340. The purchaser was Richard Monckton Milnes. Annotations in *CM* (*CC*) I were printed from *NED*, but a portion of the MS TRANSCRIPT upon which the *NED* text itself had been based was subsequently identified in the Humanities Research Centre at the University of Texas, Austin. That transcript, in the hand of SC, contains three previously unknown notes and a text that is certainly closer to the original than *NED* was, for notes **44[j]–66**. Part I below records the three new notes; Part II gives the full text of the TRANSCRIPT version of all the notes (but not textus) that have even slightly different readings from those previously pub in *CM* (*CC*) I 263–77; they should be taken as superseding the earlier version. Cancelled words that are clearly the transcriber's correction of her own error are not recorded.

PART I

Following **44[k]** i 314 | **44[k]** textus

It is really idle and unmanly to defend the Church by the logical rule, *ex abusu non valet contra usum*:[1] when the experience of more than two centuries has proved, that the *abuse* is to the use at least 9.99 to 1. Thus in the rite of Confirmation. Doubtless, if the primitive instead of the Diocesan Episcopacy had been adopted,[2] it might not only have been a most

F44[k][1] I.e. a conclusion drawn "from the abuse of a thing is not valid against the [proper] use of it": cf C's use of this legal maxim in BLANCO WHITE *Preservative* **8**.

F44[k][2] It was often argued that in the early Church the *episkopos* or "overseer" had been the equivalent of a presbyter, therefore that the early Church had been presbyterian in structure and the hierarchy of ranks a later development. See Jeremy TAYLOR *Polemicall Discourses* **5** and n 2.

efficient Practice, but have supplied a satisfactory argument to all the liberal modern Baptists, who do not attach a saving and indispensable virtue to baptism. "*You* have *one* advantage, *one* occasion of Christian edification," (might the Pædo- say to the Antipædo-baptist;)[3] but *we* have *two*: and our Confirmation answers all the purposes of your adult baptism.—But as it *is*, and is *known* to be conducted, this would be little less than impudence. I myself, a boy of twelve years old, out of boyish fun, was confirmed six times over by the Bishop, I availing myself of the Crowd.

Following **49** i 373 | *Copy B* **88** textus

I have no doubt of the fact in part: and yet I believe, that the majority of Charles's judges acted from conscience. How he was brought before such judges is another case. I confess, that had I been sworn in a judge, I should have given my verdict, as Martin & Colonel Hutchinson did.[1] It is *wicked* injury to the character of our ancestors to similarize the punishment of Charles and the murder of Louis XVI.th

Following **57** i 439

[Baxter defends the position of the non-conforming clergy within the C of E after the Restoration.] And as you recount all that may aggravate their sin, so you must in justice remember all that may extenuate it: Remember therefore, I. That for the Common Prayer and Ceremonies, and Prelacy, multitudes of worthy holy Men conformed to them heretofore, from whom you would not have separated; such as Dr. *Preston*, Dr. *Sibbs*, Dr. *Taylor*, Dr. *Staughton*, Mr. *Gattaker*, and most (by far) of the late Synod at *Westminster*: and for the rest of the Conformity, remember the *Matter* and the *Temptation:* For the *Matter*, it is much about Political Things, where it is no wonder if Divines on either side are ignorant or erroneous . . . . And for the *Temptation*, remember that such horrid Miscarriages, as the Rebellious pulling down of King and Parliament, killing the one and casting out or imprisoning the Members of the other, and the attempted taking down of all the Ministry . . . are things that might easily draw Men to judge that the Covenant was but a League for the promoting of an unlawful War, and therefore is utterly null . . .

Exaggerations, which Baxter's own account confutes.—*Vide* Part I. es-

F44[k][3] Someone in favour of infant baptism (the C of E position) and someone opposed to it (the Baptists).

F49[1] The regicides Henry Martin or Marten (1602–80) and Colonel John Hutchinson (1615–64). C annotated memoirs of the latter: HUTCHINSON.

pecially the great and successful care to provide the Churches with learned and zealous ministers &c.[1]

PART II

44[j] i 314

[MS TRANSCRIPT gives only the last two lines of C's note:] of an *elect* Christian Congregation. "Cast thy bread on the waters" &c. seems the proper motto of the Established Church of England.

44[k] i 314

Poor little sinful Darlings!—This was the cant of the Age.

44[l] i 315

Me judice, a very wise omission: for the practice must inevitably lead to superstition, and to the notion of some *magical* charm infused into the elements.

44[n] i 315

This is most true; but with what tenfold force does it apply to common extemporary prayer among Dissenters!

44[o] i 317

No wonder that the Bishops and their party conquered: when the excepters gave them such advantages. Many a proselyte has *the church* gained from *the meeting-house* through the disgust occasioned by the long-winded, preaching prayers of the dissenting ministers, and the utter exclusion of the congregation from all *active* share in the public devotion.

44[p] i 321–4

Paragraphs marked thus, N., appear to me weak, those with NN., not only weak but of ill consequence.

F57[1] In bk 1 pt 1 (textus being from bk 1 pt 2), Baxter defends the Westminster Assembly against the charge that it had ejected learned ministers and replaced them with ignorant ones, for political reasons: see esp i 74, q in SOUTHEY *Wesley* **43** n 2.

44[q] i 326

If it be right and efficacious to baptize children at all, why should these poor darlings be excepted, for no other reason but that they are so unfortunate as to have wicked parents? If baptism be a good, the denial of it is a misfortune; and is it Christian Charity to add misfortune to misfortune, and that to poor worse than orphan children?

44[r] i 327

Beyond all doubt every sincere Christian is so far a priest of the Gospel, as that, in case of necessity, he may, & ought to, baptize.

44[s] i 329

This is a sound & weighty objection confirmed by constant Experience.

44[u] i 332

Sound objections. Indeed no month passes in which the common people do not make the same observation, when any one of notoriously bad character is burying.

45 i 347

I think that *this* one argument might have been fairly turned against Baxter; for by the implied allowance of genuflexion on *week*days, with the exception of the interval between Easter and Whitsuntide, it seems evident, that the standing up was intended as a symbolical remembrancing of our Lord's resurrection and of our own: *ergo* one of those mere arbitrary ceremonies which led to the final corruption and apostacy both of the Roman (or Western) and of the Greek or Oriental churches. It is, however, undeniable, that Baxter truly asserted the primitive custom to be that of receiving the sacrament sitting.

47 i 354

Most true! Alas, that the *best* of all national churches should have had an æra so disgraceful as the Restoration!

48 i369

So did the learned and saintly martyrs full of faith; yea, Luther himself. Selden too condemns the sabbatical transferred to the Dominical day, as

the basest of Judaic superstitions. The best argument for the cheerfully serious observation of Sunday in rest, meditation, sober recreation, &c. is that there *can* be no sound argument against it, or for the change of the Day or Interval. I consider it, in our present state, a *command* of Natural Religion, favoured, though not compelled, by the Gospel Revelation. Were an Angel to trumpet it from the clouds the duty of observing it could not be more manifest to my reason than it already is.

49 i 370

Bishop Jeremy Taylor. If ever book was calculated to drive men to despair, it is Bishop Jeremy Taylor's on Repentance. It first opened my eyes to Arminianism, and that Calvinism is *practically* a far, far more soothing and consoling system.

50 i 384

What Baxter suspected is now known to be true. The new acts were imposed by Sheldon's advice for the express purpose of ejecting all the old godly ministers, and to put in their places another generation, that might (as they effectively did), "wean the people from making *a fuss* about Religion"; i.e. from thinking or caring about it.

51 i 387

Baxter makes the usual mistake of writing *Fanatic* when he clearly means *Enthusiast*. The Field-Methodists are Fanatics, i.e. *circà fana densâ turbâ concalefacti*; those who catch heat by crowding together round the same *Fane*. Fanaticism is the *fever* of Superstition. Enthusiasm on the contrary implies an undue (or, when used in a good sense, an unusual) vividness of ideas, as opposed to perceptions, or of the obscure inward feelings.

52 i 411

The first instance in which have[a] found Baxter *unfair*. See the Covenant itself, p. 391, and you will find the oath not for the *preservation* of the Reformed religion in general; but to the preservation of the reformed religion in *Scotland*, and the *reformation* of the English Church—in other words for the substitution of the Knoxo-Calvinistic, Scoto-genevan form of Synodical Presbytery for the Episcopal government of the Anglican Church.

52[a] For "I have"—perhaps a transcriber's error.

53 i 412

Bo-peep with conscience. Either the Robber's oath obliges or not. I think, not. The guilt of perjury lies with the *necessitating* Imposer. But if it does, then it must be kept like any other binding oath or promise, i.e. neither in the sense of the Imposèr, nor in that of the Imposèd, but in that sense which the latter understood the former to have imposed it.

54 i 413

I never yet saw, heard of, or read any question in casuistry, which an honest man of sound logical head could not solve in an instant: not one, that ever had the least difficulty in it theoretically, though doubtless many, where it is difficult to determine the ratio of the facts in order to propound the question or problem.

55 i 414

Here Baxter seems to me wrong. Vows by compulsion, not a trifling one, but to avoid death, or perpetual jail, can never, never be in the same class with voluntary, still less with spontaneous vows or oaths. The sum is this: if tyrants and robbers know, that oaths compelled by them are void in conscience, a few lives may be lost, which might otherwise have been saved; but is this to be put in competition with the weakening of all tyranny, and the preservation of the essence of an oath, as either an act of duty (negatively, at least) or not an oath at all? Would these Casuists be mad enough to say, that you were bound to keep an oath forced upon you by a raving Madman?—But, in truth, oaths altogether are bad, foolish, unchristian things, except as mere remembrancers of the guilt of deliberate falsehood, at the same time *occasioning* the affirmer to be calm and deliberate.

56 i 432–3

With what caution ought we to take the supernatural relations even of the very best and most veracious men! Baxter says, "I and all men were convinced." How? Ex. gr. that of the woman swallowed up &c. Why not have given all the particulars of place, time, names and characters of the witnesses, &c.?—The very same story has been told and retold repeatedly by of different persons in different places and times within the last twenty five years—yet each so told as to leave no doubt, spite of all the pomp of witnesses, that they were each and all repetitions of the same old story. Besides, this whole hypothesis of preternatural judgment in this life is in direct opposition to a positive declaration of Christ concerning the wall that fell down and the blind man.

57 i 438

It is impossible to read Baxter without which[a] to admire most, the uncommon clearness (perspicuity & perspicacity) of his understanding; or the candour and charity of his spirit. Under such accursed persecutions he feels and reasons more like an angel than a man.

58 i 440

But what would come of this? Did God ever please to bring about reformation by these passive measures? Never! Did Luther act so? Did the Trinitarians restore the true faith by such measures, when the Arians were uppermost?

60 i 447

This seems unanswerable if the husband be a thorough Papist. But how *could* such a one marry such a Protestant, except for her estate, or in the full intent as well as hope of using every means to con- or rather per-vert her. Either way, it must be guilt in a woman to marry such a man. And yet if she ever hesitated, had "*half a mind to it*," I would wager a trifle, that she married him, though the Devil was grinning over the Priest's shoulder during the marriage ceremony.

61 ii 6

Oaths are 9999[a] times out of 10,000 abominations. Perhaps, I need not have made the one exception, as oaths are administered in our law. "Recollect yourself! You are in the presence of the omnipresent, omniscient God, who has declared his wrath against deliberate falsehood. Do you believe this? Are you at this moment fully aware of it?—" This would be a form of administering an oath, which the most rigid Quaker, if in his senses could not object to, and would preclude all the evil superstitions, which now transfer the essence to the ceremony.

62 ii 8–9

Much as I love the Church of England, I have no hesitation in asserting (as my belief) that nothing in the History of the Inquisition was equally *wicked*, as the conduct of Sheldon & the Court after the Restoration.

57[a] *NED*: without hesitating which

61[a] SC first wrote "9999" and then crossed out the final digit, which is required, however, for sense

63 ii 12

N.B. But here Baxter confounds the drawers up, or worders, of the oath, with the two Houses of Parliament, who with the King were the Imposers. Still, however, I could no more have taken the oath than Baxter: because it was meant to mean something beyond the former oaths, & whatever that might be, was for Diocesan Prelacy and despotism. O it was a disgraceful æra both in Church and State! How grateful ought we to be for our present truly blessed constitution in the latter, and for the mild & liberal spirit in the former. If not what a Christian Church should be, yet the Church of England injures only itself. It neither oppresses, annoys, or interferes with, those who dissent from it.

64 ii 46

O that this no less wise than amiable remark were more and more generally felt and acted upon. This is the sublime moral of Shakspeare's Shylock and Edmund.

65 iii 55

All this proves against any soul-danger in Infant-Baptism, if administered and afterwards acquiesced in, conscientiously. But it surely does not prove that it is not our duty to take the sacraments as we appear to find them in Scripture. I cannot assent to Baxter's main argument: for an ordinance of admission to Christian membership, pre-requiring on the part of the competitor knowledge, repentance and faith, is a definition that will not agree with Infant Baptism—and to deny any definition to be true which does not include the lawfulness of Infant Baptism, would be reasoning in a circle with a vengeance. The best argument is: let every man be convinced in his own mind, and agree to differ, keeping up both Love & Communion.

66 iii 57

And what is all this in opposition to the positive, oft-repeated injunctions of Christ and Scripture, demanding previous faith & repentance in the subject to be baptized. Analogies are good substitutes, but they must not master when the principals are present.

JOSEPH BEAUMONT

1616–1699

Lost Book

Some Observations upon the Apologie of Dr. Henry More for his Mystery of Godliness. Cambridge 1665. 4°.

Not located.

The vol containing this annotated work was sold by Parke Bernet Galleries, New York, 18 May 1954 (Lot 244). The Catalogue records an inscription on "an endleaf"—"S. T. Coleridge. March 23, 1803. Curry's Mitre Court, Fleet Street"—and a marginal comment in C's hand on p 11. The five tracts collected in this vol are the following:

(1) Herbert of Cherbury *De religione gentilium, errorumque apud eos causis* (Amsterdam 1663)
(2) [Benedict Spinoza] *Tractatus theologico-politicus* (4th ed Hamburg 1670)
(3) [Allesandro Sardi] *Johannis Seldeni . . . liber de nummis. In quo antiqua pecunia Romana & Graeca metitur precio ejus, quo nunc est in usu* (1675)
(4) [Philippe Labbe] *Bibliotheca nummaria* (1675)
(5) BEAUMONT

LA DANSE DES MORTS

La danse des morts, comme elle est dépeinte dans la louable et célebre ville de Basle, pour servir de miroir de la nature humaine. Dessinée et gravée sur l'original de feu Mr. Matthieu Merian. On y a ajouté une description de la ville de Basle, et des vers à chaque figure. Basle 1789. 4°.

Collection of Anthony William Poole King

Inscribed p $^{-}1$ "bought at Basle 30th August 1802 Th Poole". C's note is completed in another hand (see **1** n 2); beneath it, on p $^{+}1$, a note signed by William Poole King and dated 1850: "Written by Samuel Taylor Coleridge, in my Uncle Thomas Poole's Library at Nether Stowey where he was on a visit". Since C's last visit to Nether Stowey occurred in 1807, while all versions of the poem contained in his note belong to 1833, this statement must be discounted as sheer guess-work. Poole visited C in London at least as late as 1827, and corresponded with him to the end of his life. Other books owned by Poole and annotated by C are described in HAYLEY headnote.

DATE. 1833, probably about mid-Oct. (The poem itself refers to the author as being "threescore years" old.) For other versions of the *Epitaph* see *PW* (EHC) I 491–2.

1 p $^{+}1$

ESTESE's αυτοεπι~~φ~~ταφιον.[1]
Here lies a Poet—or what once was He.
Pray, gentle Reader, pray for S. T. C.
That he who threescore years with toilsome Breath,
Found death in Life, may now find life in death.[2]

1[1] I.e. "S. T. C.'s self-epitaph". C uses the pseudonym he had created for himself in 1799: see ANNUAL ANTHOLOGY **10** n 3.

1[2] Completed in another hand: "Mercy for Praise, *to be forgiven* for Fame / He ask'd, and hop'd thro' Christ. Do Thou the same." On these lines and other variants, see GREW **44** nn 1, 2.

DECLARATION OF PRINCIPLES

Declaration of Principles. [Anonymous.] [n.d.] 8°.

University of Texas (Humanities Research Center)

A broadsheet proposing principles for a rational religion, opposed to "ceremonial worship" and "the existing institutions of society". The opening sentence is, "I believe that to worship, by mere words or formal ceremonies, any object on the earth or in the heavens, or any thing of human device, is most opposed to the feelings of every conscientious intelligent mind, and that all such worship is necessarily destructive of the rational faculties of those trained in the practice of it."

DATE. Not known.

1 p [1]

I believe that all facts prove that there is an external or internal cause for all existence by the fact of their existence; but that man has not yet acquired a knowledge of any facts to ascertain what that cause is, or any of its essential qualities.*

* Exquisite Contradiction—to the pre-asserted discovery of its *wisdom* and *supreme goodness*—or are these *non*-essential qualities?[1]

S. T. C.

1[1] The anonymous author has already taken for granted the presence of a "supremely good principle" in human nature that merits "practical worship", and advocated a new religion or "true wisdom" founded "on facts only".

HENRY AUGUSTUS DILLON-LEE
VISCOUNT DILLON

1777–1832

The Life and Opinions of Sir Richard Maltravers, an English Gentleman of the Seventeenth Century. [Anonymous.] 2 vols. London 1822.

Previously reported as lost: *CM* (*CC*) II 212

Newberry Library, Chicago

Half-title of Vol I inscribed "From the Author—", to which note C has added "(received from his Lordship Friday, 9 Feby 1827—*S. T. C.*[)]". On the same page, C has identified the author: "By Viscount Dillon"; and someone else has identified C's hand in a pencilled note, "Samuel Taylor Coleridge". The title-page verso in I has the signature of presumably a later owner, "Thomas Dent". The title-page of Vol II again is inscribed "from the Author". Small pencilled marks against passages on I 27, 44, 45, 49, 51, 53, 55, 62, 70, 71, II 266 do not appear to have been made by C.

DATE. Shortly after 9 Feb 1827.

1 I 1–2, cropped

The accidents of my life may have been few, and, in the opinion of some, ~~considered as~~[a] even trivial; ⋀ but the period at which I have lived, and the train of thought which that epoch has left in my mind, may serve for my apology in taking up the pen, to set down such passages as I think may amuse others . . .

⋀ ⟨[? & disgusting]⟩ but the deep interest of the Period, through which I have lived, would itself be an apology for any Man, who should employ his pen in recording the events and passages which he deemed most likely to amuse others, together with the train of thought, which such an Epoch has left on his own mind. And I persuade myself, that the very attempt will secure for me a favourable Hearing with those, who &c.

1[a] C has also written a "delete" symbol in the margin

1A I 97, marked with a pencil line in the margin

We may, by cultivation, derive a greater advantage than from living under such a sun [as that of France], which, though it spontaneously produces flowers of the sweetest fragrance, yet frequently generates reptiles replete with venom.

WILLIAM GODWIN

1756–1836

MS of "Abbas King of Persia an Historical Tragedy", Acts I–III.

Collection of Lord Abinger: Bodleian Library Dep. c. 663/2

Three notebooks, one for each act, with titles on the covers: Act 1, Act 2, Act 3. Wm 1794, in each notebook. The notebooks are foliated continuously, but with the cover and title-page of the first being counted as "i" and "ii" respectively; [ii^{v}] lists "Dramatis Personae", with actors' names being pencilled in for some parts—Abbas, Mr Cooke; Sefi, Mr H. Johnston; Cartzuga, Mr Pope; Bulac, Mr Murray; Irene, Mrs Powell (cancelling Mrs Litchfield). It is assumed that since some of the underlining of questionable words and phrases accompanies notes by C, all such underlining is in his hand. A few revisions in ink have been made by Godwin himself, who has also approved some of C's suggestions with a pencilled "Yes" and rejected others with a "No" in the margins: these additions, postdating C's notes, are not recorded. Changes of scene are indicated by stage directions such as "Scene, a Forest between Bagdad and Ispahan", but the act and scene divisions indicated in headlines here are not part of the ms.

Godwin had been trying to break into London theatre, but his tragedy *Antonio*, performed at Drury Lane in Dec 1800, had been a failure. C's letters about *Abbas* which, in the event, was not accepted for production, show that he was a reluctant critic: in *CL* II 713–14 he declares himself unfit, and in *CL* II 742–3 he explains that his detailed notes on the play had been written with such "boyish freedom of censure & ridicule" that he dares not send them. The second letter explains the symbols that are used throughout the marginalia, ※ for "false or intolerable English", ⊤ for "*flat* or mean", ≢ "common-place *book* Language", # for "bad metre". Since C says that although he thought the first two acts would have to be completely rewritten, he was "much interested by the last three", it is all the more regrettable that Acts IV–V have been lost. A few brief notes outlining ideas for the development of the plot appear in Bodleian MS Dep. b. 229/6 (b).

DATE. After 25 Mar and before 8 Jul 1801: on the former date, C agreed to comment on the ms, and on the latter he returned it to Godwin (*CL* II 713–14, 742).

A f 2 | I i

1st MOB. . . . But, neighbour, what puzzles me most is that these cursed turks should chuse with their eyes open, to go thus head foremost to the

devil. Does not every body know, that whoever believes in Omar can never come to heaven?
?

B f 3

MUSTAPHA. . . . He has expell'd the Tartar and the Turk,
And crown'd his native clime with wealth and greatness:
Each province, every town has drawn in turn
Its Monarch's care; and works of public use ⊤
Rise every where around. What could he more?

C f 4

MUSTAPHA. With a small band of chosen men our sultan
into Plung'd in the desert. Calil, the Turkish visier,
With forces that three times out number'd ours,
Hung on our march, made capture of our convoys,
And tried all stratagems to cut us off. ⊤

D f 4 | Continuing **C** textus

ABDALLAH. At length through countless dangers, difficulties
That mock narration . . . ⊤

E f 4

MUSTAPHA. . . . He sought a hill, the first, had met our view,
Since we had left our Persia's fruitful confines.
He rang'd his army in three several lines
On the ascent, and gave the foremost battle
To be commanded by the prince, his son.

F f 4

MUSTAPHA. . . . while his wondring troops,
Fired at the great example, mov'd resistless.
by ?

G f 6

SEFI. My Father, all I have and am is thine:
My little merits nurs'd and shap'd by thee;
And, as a tribute, I would fain unlock, { δ
And lay them at thy feet.

H f 6 | Continuing **G** textus

ABBAS. I swear by Alla, I am much less proud
Of all my victories in war, and all
The peaceful honours of my prosperous reign, 丰
Than to be father of a son like thee.

I f 7

SEFI. I trust my ~~native~~ country does not own a man,
~~A man w~~ Who does not boast himself most true and loyal.
ABBAS. Oh Sefi, Sefi, little dost thou know
The cares, the fears, the sleepless, dire alarms,
That haunt and sting the bosom of thy father!
SEFI. How you surprise, How terrify my soul!
ABBAS. When I succeeded first to Persia's throne,
Confusion and disorder fill'd the state. 丰
I still'd the tempest, I regain'd the provinces . . .

J f 8

ABBAS. . . . Fill'd with the high conception of their valour, 丰
They tyrannis'd the nation they were hir'd,
To serve, seiz'd on all offices, frankly
Disclos'd themselves a stern, exclusive clan, ※T. 丰
And held the throne itself in basest shackles.
This corps I dar'd reduce.

1 f 8

ABBAS. . . . To rescue the dear country of our prophet
From the barbarian gripe of the profane Turk.
Persia, which, from the earliest period that records
The history of nations, still
Has been the flower of Asia, would desert
Her place among the empires of the world,
Did she not thus resolve to vindicate
And watch the land, that boasts to have been the source ※
And fountain of our pure religion. gi—on.

execrable metre.[1]

1[1] Written against line 2 of textus.

1A f 9

ABBAS. . . . Thy mother with a small, but faithful band,
Abides beleaguered in the very palace. ※
SEFI. Base, treacherous men!
ABBAS. Yes, Sefi, 'tis indeed a coward's part,
Thus to invade the moment, when their king,
Amidst a thousand forms of fear and death,
Wars, undeterr'd, to buy his country honour. — } 丰
I know these wretches; If I once return,
They'll scud to covert, fear'd by my very presence. !!
SEFI. My father let us go. Thy genius still
Shall ward all harm and misery from our Persia. δ

1B f 9

ABBAS. . . . To vulgar eyes my state, no doubt, may show
A scene of luxury and soft indulgence.

1C f 9

ABBAS. . . . Thorns plant my pillow; ease deserts my board; ※
And all is vigilance, mistrust, suspicion!

1D f 10 | I ii

IRENE. Oh, Zelica, how anxious is my state!
Where is my husband now, and where my son?
Far, far away, engaged in distant wars,
Busied in foreign and superfluous conquests!
Shall e'er these eyes be blessed once more to see them? ※

1E f 11

ZELICA. Oh, Madam, what
a thought is that!
Can you compare these rich and splendid Scenes,
With a wild solitude, was never cheer'd
With sight of son, ~~or~~ husband, or a human visage?
IRENE. That 'tis, my Zelica, ~~that~~ which makes my misery. ※
. . . thus as I am,
A hopeless prisoner, a splendid slave,
Fill'd with eternal doubts, and restless fears;
Never to know one moment's relaxation. — ⊤

2 f 11 | Stage directions

Enter a mute
(he expresses his intelligence by signs.)

Would not this be ludicrous on the stage?

2A f 11

IRENE. . . . The face of man must never meet my view, ǂ
Unless he be my husband or my son

2B f 12 | I iii

MUSTAPHA. Or all, or most,
My lord, are come, Searching on every side,
They have discover'd nought, that does not wear
The face of peace, and tranquil, rural business.

2C f 12

ABBAS. Mustapha,
Thou art right sure there was no least appearance ※
Of hostile force in any other quarter?

3 ff 12^{v}, 13

ABBAS. Why am I
Compell'd to advance with all this preparation,
Upon the bosom of my native soil!
Oh, Persia, Persia! have not I reliev'd thee, T
With cares, and watchings, and incessant toil,
From hostile ravage, anarchy and impotence: T
And this is my reward! Why do we make
Mankind our care? These labours purchase for us
A splendid name,
But no man's love, but no man's living friendship!
The time will come, I see it, faithless Persia,
When thou wilt long for such a king as Abbas, T
When barbarous Tartars, and perfidious Turks,
Mogul and Usbec chiefs; without resistance,
Shall sack thy cities, and make all a waste. T

and impotence—the equivoque latent in this word would of itself damn your play.—. This speech is the first spirited passage, I had almost said, the first tolerable passage, I have met with.

3A f 14

SEFI. 'Tis Cartzuga's self;
He waits at hand permission to salute
His master, and to lay his honours at ⚌
Your royal feet.

4 f 14

ABBAS. . . . I'll go to meet him, thus on foot, lacquey
⊙ My hero as he rides along, and be
The appendage of his triumph.

⊙ A solecism in manners.

4A f 14

ABBAS. Fair Sultana,
I have brought a gift to buy a monarchs welcome; to win
Thy son . . .

4B f 15

ABBAS. I am not angry with thee. No, I am pleas'd ⊤
To find our sentiments thus harmonise. ⚌ ⚌

4C f 16

IRENE. How is it, Sefi? Thou appear'st disturb'd:
Thy brow is stampt with gloom and perturbation. ⚌

4D f 17

SEFI. But this moment,
As I was seated reading in my chamber,
I saw it flung in through the eastern window. ⊤ ※
I rose, and hasten'd to find who had done it
But all was stillness; and no creature near.
I knew not then its devilish contents, ⊤
Or I would quick have order'd a pursuit: ⊤ ※
Ere I could read the scroll, pursuit was vain. —Why?

4E f 17

SEFI. . . . The thought alone of what this paper utters,
Hangs like a millstone, and weighs down my heart. Too bad

Henceforth I ne'er can look upon a mirror:
I ne'er shall meet the approving smiles of virtue,
But I shall smite my hand upon my brow,
And say,
This is a look, where wicked men descried
The characters and painting of a villain.

4F f 17

ABBAS. Sefi, my son, thou art the best of children.
Yes, to this secret haunt, thy mother's chamber,
Suspicion and mistrust shall never come . . .

4G f 22 | II i

SEFI. I could as soon believe the Gods were tyrants,
Malicious, cruel, deaf to mercy's plea, δ
As guilt could nestle her in his white hairs.

4H ff 22–3

IRENE. . . . My son, when Abbas was in all the ardour
Of his first love for my once lauded beauty, δ
'Twas then I ask'd my father at his hands . . . .
Ungenerous daughter! had I left my sire
In his obscureness, had I not preferr'd, ※
Thus selfishly preferr'd my own delight
To Michaels safety, he had perish'd then,
As all his fathers did, lov'd, honour'd in #
A good old age, surrounded by his kindred,
The ornament and boast of his dear country. ⊤

4I f 23

SEFI. My Mother, let us go without delay ※
Before the feet of Abbas; I will lead thee;
Thy accents, pleading for who gave thee life, ※
Must prove omnipotent.

4J f 23

IRENE. I cannot pass yon portal,
There is a circle drawn round these apartments,

Nor can I speak even with my husband, or #
My child, but when they enter here.

SEFI. These rules,
Dear mother, are not made but for occasions
Of ordinary nature. My authority
Will ope these doors, and force their dumb defenders to ∓
Fall back, and yield us egress. Come away! ※ # ∓

IRENE. No Sefi, no. This bosom's not a stranger,
I feel it is not, to heroic enterprise. ※ #

4K f 24

SEFI. Mother, I go. Trust me, I will #
Not stint my efforts in so dear a cause.

IRENE. Remember, Sefi, Michael's blood flows in #
Those veins of thine . . . .
Strike thou thy father on the heart; employ
The soft persuasion of resistless nature. ※ ?

4L ff 24–5 | II ii

ABBAS. What is this new conception of my brain?
My son my rival! Sefi my cause of fear!
Whence came this monstrous notion? I must strangle it,
Or else farewel for ever the peace of Abbas! #
. . . unnatural sons, urg'd by #
The hey day of the blood, that fret, and cry,
Our fathers live too long! But, no; Sefi #
Is not like them! When ever was a youth
So dutiful, so childlike?—Cursed malcontents! . . .
Have you no bowels? ⊤

5 f 25

ABBAS. . . . There are conceptions so accurs'd and black
That but to have them, but that they should cross
Our brain, though like a thin, unresting vapour,
Leaves a reproach never to be remov'd.

well written[1]

5[1] Written against line 3 of textus.

5A f 25

CARTZUGA. Great Sultan, what is't that disquiets thee?
ABBAS. Nothing, my soldier: nothing, dearest friend.—
Tell me the business that brought thee hither! #
What paper's that?
CARTZUGA (*with hesitation*). My Lord,—it is—the catalogue
Of the ringleaders in the late sedition. ⊤

5B f 26

CARTZUGA. Were it not better, oh, most mighty prince,
<u>To stay the torrent of this bloody vengeance</u>, ǂ
Till it <u>were seen the fruit of</u> temperate rigour? ※ ǂ
I know, your Persian maxims place the power
Of life and death without reserve
In the sole voice of him who <u>sways the sceptre</u> . . . ǂ

5C f 26

ABBAS. . . . I had one friend I priz'd above the world,
One bosom where I treasur'd all my confidence,
My love—Sefi, my son—him they endeavour'd to #
Corrupt, to make my son my foe—this is
A crime no torture, and no death can expiate. #

5D f 26

ABBAS. . . . Look to thyself. An Eastern monarch does #
Not easily endure to have his passions
Thus thwarted . . .

5E f 27

GUARDS (*without*). My lord, you cannot enter.
SEFI (*without*). Insolent!
Dost thou not know me? <u>I say</u>, I will. # ⊤

5F f 27

SEFI. I have delay'd his speed, till I had time
<u>To move a question</u> to thee. ⊤

5G f 28

SEFI. . . . Thus, in ignorance,
Had I not done this, thou'dst have caus'd #
A guileless, honourable, old old man,
To die a traitor's death.

5H f 28

SEFI. . . . Michael, in whose mild aspect first I read
The festive reverence, due to silver age? ※ T. ∓.

5I f 28

SEFI. Poor Michael, sweet old man! what venom'd tongue
Has slander'd his mild innocence? Drawn from #
His lonely, rustic home . . .

5J f 28

ABBAS (*aside*). . . . Who knows
That this poor boy, with all this native eloquence,
Feels not that he is pleading for an accomplice?— #
I will dissemble.

5K f 31 | II iii

AMBASSADOR. . . . wherefore hast thou presum'd
With force and arms to tread the holy ground,
Made sacred by the dwelling of our prophet?
Why hast thou, heretic, polluted with
Fantastic novelties his sainted tomb? #

5L f 31

AMBASSADOR. Your upstart sect pays hollow service to #
Our prophet, while with contumelious scorn
You trample on the sequence of our caliphs . . . ※

5M f 32

SEFI. . . . Has he so soon forgot
Derbend and Erivan, Orumi and
The field of Trebisond? Bear not all these
The blooming memory of Persian valour? ※ ∓

6 f 32

ABBAS. I'll not be jealous! no, I'll not be made
An instrument for fools to palm their jests on!—
Who's there?—Is this mean lacquey of the court
Noting my starts?—What is thy office, fellow?

BULAC. I come, dread king, commission'd by your son.

very well[1]

7 f 33

ABBAS (*aside*). My son!—still of my son, and nothing but
(*to him*) My son!—Well, sir, utter your commission! δ

vary

7A f 33

ABBAS. This is the Mirza's prayer?—It likes me well.— ※

7B f 34

ABBAS. Go forth, my son; unfold the Persian standard!
Thou art thy father's pupil; I have train'd
Thee in the rudiments of glorious war;
Thy earliest laurels were atchiev'd beneath ǂ
My guardian eye; and now 'tis time thou shouldst
Begin thyself the quest of great adventures, ǂ
And show thee worthy of the unusual grace,
Which from thy birth I have awarded thee.

8 f 37ᵛ (facing ms on f 38) | III i

BULAC. . . . The shadows, that the glorious light of heaven
† Makes nothing of, seem to my slumbering sense
Evils unconquerable, mountain mischiefs,
Loftier than Taurus. Why do I call them shadows?

† This is a natural & affecting thought; & the first clause is well expressed.—loftier than Taurus is ridiculous. We never speak of an evil as *lofty*—it is a blunder for ~~an~~ *Irishm~~a~~en*, who, I presume, derive their pe-

6[1] Written against last line of textus.

culiar Talent from the Muses that reside on Mount Taurus rather than those on the Mount Parnassus.—[1]

8A f 39

ABBAS. What, no disorder? Have you not o'erheard
Strange shrieks & groans, and whisperings, like the murmur
Of dark assassins hastening to their quarry?
BULAC. My liege, I still have been observant, but
Have heard no smallest sound. ※

8B f 39

ABBAS. . . . What has poor Sefi done,
That he should be the business of my terrors?
He play'd a shining part in our late combat:
Did he not with most exemplary duty,
Lay all his well earn'd honours at my feet? ⊤ ǂ
The malcontents, the pests of me and Persia,
Sought to seduce him by a proffer'd crown:
Was he allur'd? did he not place their offer
In my own hands? did it not vex and grieve him? ⊤

8C f 41

ABBAS. Is not this Persia? Am not I the Sultan? ⊤ δ
I'll not be trifled with; thy life shall answer it! δ
BULAC. Menace not thus the ever-loyal slave!

8D f 41

ABBAS. . . . This seems a story worth a monarch's treasure.— δ

8E f 42

ABBAS. I see it all!—What, while I struggled with
My doubts, sternly suppress'd, and drove them from me,
Stands treason off thus plain to all my Court? ※

8[1] For the self-contradicting statement known as an Irish Bull see SKELTON **5** n 4. Mount Parnassus is sacred to poetry; the name of the Taurus range in Asia Minor, which was chosen by Godwin presumably for local colour, means "bull".

9 f 42

ABBAS. Tis done! My doubts, and struggles have an end.—
Horrors and darkness! who would be a king!
Cut off from nature and her sweet content;
Thrust out a gloomy, uncompanion'd monster!

These 3 lines would be enough to *damn* your Play.

9A ff 42–3

ABBAS. . . . Henceforth my heart be steel, my breast remorseless!
I will not be insulted thus for nought; ⊤
I will not patient wait their ripening plots; ※ ※
I will prevent them, and "confound their malice."—
Bulac, I thank thee! Well thou hast approv'd
Thy truth. Be watchful still; and whatsoe'er
Thou find'st, haste me to know it. ※

9B f 44

ABBAS. My dearest Sefi! my most gallant son!
Art thou at bay? humbled almost to death,
Driven to the toils by this ferocious Turk?
Nature, I feel thee here! Sefi is still ‡
My son!—Unnatural father! Yes, 'twas I
That drove him forth, just in the opening bloom
Of manhood, to contend alone with war,
With every hideous guise and shape of death! ‡

9C f 44

ABBAS. . . . While Sefi sweat in blood, and laugh'd at danger, ※
So he might serve his father and his country . . .

9D f 45

BULAC. In death, great king, I honour you; and love
That virtue ∧ leads you blindfold to destruction. ※

9E f 47

BULAC. . . . Great is your struggle, sir; 'tis in these struggles
We see the man himself, no more set off
With pomp, and thrones, and state, the trash of monarchs ⊤

9F f 49 | III ii

CARTZUGA. δ { . . . In these blest climates loyalty is still
Mix'd and confounded with religion's dictates.

9G f 50

CARTZUGA. Spoke like my sovereign, like the genuine blood
Of our great imams, who in this excell'd
All mortal men, forbearance, charity,
And melting kindness. ⊤

9H f 51

ABBAS. What means this woman? whence this vast emotion? δ

10 f 51

IRENE. Forgiven my son! forgiven Sefi! what
Has he e'er done that might demand forgiveness? . . .
ABBAS. He came to ask reprieval for thy father;
'Twas an ungrateful suit, but he succeeded.
IRENE. Abbas, I fear this answer's an evasion.—

—WHOO!![1]

11 f 52

IRENE. Oh, tyrant! nature can endure no longer!
I knew thee for the assassin of my race,
And curs'd my womb, when it grew great by thee.

a *foul* line.

11A f 53

IRENE. . . . and thy own flesh and blood, ⊤
Sefi, must die, because Irene is his mother!

11B f 53

ABBAS. . . . It is too plain she hates me!
Has she not had the forming of the mind
Of Sefi? Has he not imbib'd her views,
Her thoughts, her aims? 'Twere idiotism to doubt it! ⊤

10[1] C's exclamation is written against the last line of textus.

IRENE. What have I done?—Oh, Abbas, mighty Abbas,
Heed not the ravings of a frantic mother!
Give me my Sefi, shield his guiltless head,
And I will swear, thou art a God in mercy . . . ‡

JOHN HASLAM
1764–1844

Medical Jurisprudence, as it relates to Insanity, according to the Law of England. London 1817. 8°.

British Library 7510 cc 1 (1)

Bound as first with Charles Thomas Haden *Practical Observations on the Colchicum Autumnale, as a general remedy of great power, in the treatment of inflammatory diseases, both acute and chronic; and therefore as a substitute for bleeding, in disorders which are connected with increased action of the heart and arteries* (1820); and with SCUDAMORE. This collection of pamphlets was bound after C's notes had been made: the annotated pages in HASLAM have been folded in to protect them from cropping, but the notes in SCUDAMORE were overlooked.

Bookplate of James Gillman on p $^{-}3$; booksellers' marks and prices in pencil on p $^{-}3$, together with the words "Coleridge" and "With MS. Notes by Samuel Taylor Coleridge" in an unidentified hand, in pencil; and in a smaller hand, also in pencil, "Patterson". A typographical error is corrected on p 9 in ink, not in C's hand. A leaf with the signature "W. S. Jackson", now loose in the vol, was perhaps once a flyleaf.

DATE. Probably 1817–18, not long after the date of publication.

1 p 16

Respecting the quantum of reason which the lunatic possesses, the physician may safely conclude where he bewrays no derangement, that on such topics he is of sound mind; and the fact is firmly established, that those who are insane on particular subjects, will reason correctly on ordinary and trivial points; *provided they do not become associated with the prevailing notions which constitute their insanity.* Ordinary persons have been much deceived by this temporary display of rational discourse, and it generally occurs that we are disposed to form a hasty conclusion, in proportion to the paucity of our knowledge on any given subject:—most minds feel more invited to indulge in the convenience *of a syllogism, than to undergo the toil of *induction.

* This general partiality for syllogism, i.e. reduction of Rhetoric to the forms of Logic, is new to me; but still more so, that the major of a Syllo-

gism does not imply a previous Induction, self-evident truths excepted, the known universal assent to which is indeed a species of Induction. What D[r] Haslam meant to say, however, is: that men are more disposed to receive a general opinion on the strength of its being the general opinion, than to cross-examine it by recorded, well attested, facts. N.B. A writer's *mea⟨n⟩ing* is not so often erroneous, as his choice of words, (*knowing*, *clever*, *well-turned*, *antithetic words*) whereby to convey his meaning. ~~The~~ With exception of this sentence the § is judiciously conceived and well-expressed. *S. T. C.*

2 p 17

This occasional display of rationality, although admitted by all who have had experience of the insane, excites a doubt in the minds even of learned and intelligent persons who have merely speculated on this disease. They have conceived, from the existing philosophy of the intellect, that reason is the directress of human actions,—that this high arbiter of thought is an undivided principle,—that where the rudder is attached the ship may be steered—and that he who reasons must be rational: and so he is, *as long* as he *does* reason.

a Sophism which has deceived the writer himself. *Reasoning* is taken as identical with *Reason*: the Idiom of a particular Language with an Objective Idea, of universal validity.

3 pp 22–3

As the word BELIEF is important, it will not be considered unnecessarily digressive to attempt an investigation of its legitimate meaning. . . . Without descending to the minutiae of verbal examination, and tracing back its derivation to its Gothic or Saxon radical, it may be safely asserted, that to BELIEVE, originally implied to belove: to be attached or partial to, independantly of any evidence which would lead to demonstration.

I doubt this. Glauben is = lauben + ge; and "ge" = the assemblage, ~~or~~ collectivity or contraction. Thus in the Gothic, Rasna is a House, Gerasna a village.—Now "Laube" is = our "Leave", or Permission, as Erlauben, to permit, to grant leave; and thus by the usual nami⟨ng⟩ of effect from Cause, is of the same meaning as Lien or Lief, in Lieftenant. The meaning of the word, Belief, is therefore = a vicarious Conviction, a holding on the authority of another.[1] Belief and Facts are as different in meaning

3[1] This speculative etymology, like others in C's letters and notebooks, is partly founded on entries in Johann Christoph Adelung *Grammatisch-kritisches Wörter-*

as in origination/ Dr H. might have spared p. 23, if he had seen that a man is mad because he does not *believe*, but in the depths of self-sufficiency appears to himself to *know*, and will not allow to the authority of others any share in the formation of his convictions.

4 p 52

In those cases where insane persons have deliberately destroyed others there has been some existing and prominent delusion which has been fully believed to be TRUE and GOOD and RIGHT, which has constituted the motive, and urged on the miserable victim of this delusion to the accomplishment of his purpose.

? Is not this too broad an assertion? Does it not perilously confound two diverse sorts of Madness, say rather *three* sorts? ⟨1⟩[a] Loss of Reason, ⟨2⟩ Derangement of the Understanding, and ⟨3⟩ pure Frenzy? And this confusion is the more strange, from the Author having him self given a̸ clear instances of the latter in the pages immediately following: so that the whole is a specimen of the art of saying and unsaying, only too common in medical writers of the present Day.

5 p 62

The members of the medical profession have long and anxiously endeavoured to frame a definition of insanity, which is an attempt in a few words to exhibit the essential character of this disorder; so that it may be recognized when it exists;—these efforts have been hitherto fruitless, nor is there any rational expectation that this desideratum will be speedily accomplished.

The attainment seems to be more useless than difficult. Like most definitions of a Genus, that comprizes many and diverse species, it would rather subserve the purposes of artificial arrangement, than of practical

4[a] C's arabic numerals, superscript in ms, have been brought down to the line to avoid confusion with editorial matter

buch der Hochdeutschen Mundart (2nd ed 4 vols Leipzig 1796). Of *ge-* Adelung notes that it may have a collective function, and one of the instances that he cites is *Gehäuse* ("housing" in the general sense of a container or casing, *Haus* itself meaning "house"); *glauben* he connects with *lauben*, *Erlauben*, and *Liefern*, as C does. His analysis is confirmed by contemporaries, e.g. *Praktische Anweisung zur Kenntniss der Hauptveränderungen und Mundarten der teutschen Sprache* (Leipzig 1789) 56, where *Holz* and *Gehölz* "wood" are given as an example. (For C's education in Gothic, see VAUGHAN **9** n 1.) G. H. Balg *A Comparative Glossary of the Gothic Language* (Mayville WI 1887) lists *razn* as "house" and *garazna* as "neighbour".

determination. Thus I would define Madness, "The Absence of the necessary conditions of Free Agency by the privation or perversion of the Judgement, the Volition remaining." But this is evidently the same as "Such a privation or perversion of the Judgement, as precludes Free Agency by the absence of its indispensable Conditions".—Consequently, the whole practical worth of the Definition depends on the filling up of the *Blank* in our knowlege designated by the word, "Such".

6 pp 81–2

This appears however to militate against the dictum of law, which states, "Whatever may be the degree of weakness or imbecility of the party—whatever may be the degree of incapacity of the party to manage his own affairs, if the finding of the jury is only that he was of an extreme imbecility of mind, that he has an inability to manage his affairs: if they will not proceed to infer from that, in their finding upon oath, that he is of *unsound mind*, they have not established, by the result of their enquiry, a case, upon which the Chancellor can make a grant constituting a committee either of the person or estate."

To be sure, the Chancellor's Dictum is too much like Bardolph's account of "accomodate".[1] But the meaning seems evident—on a case so important to the Individual the Jury are required to use positive terms, and not comparative ones. They must have made up their minds, that the Individual was not merely a very weak man, to whom they would not entrust any affairs of their own, and such as would lead them to *expect* mismanagement; but that he was positively incapable, by the existence of a morbid state, different in kind, in the same sense as a man in a fever would be very imperfectly described by saying that he was *extremely hot*.—But this is the great defect, ὡς ἔμοιγε δοκεῖ,[2] in Dr Haslam's mind, that he is predisposed to detect the nonsense ⟨of the words⟩ rather than to seek out the sense of the man who used them.

7 pp 83–4

If the word unsoundness be particularly examined, and for that purpose we consult Dr. Johnson's Dictionary . . . the adjective unsound has a dozen different meanings, but none in the sense of vitiated intellect. From

6[1] "Bardolph's account" in *2 H IV* III ii 77–80 represents meaningless or tautological definitions: ". . . Accommodated: that is, when a man is, as they say accommodated, or when a man is being whereby 'a may be thought to be accommodated—which is an excellent thing."

6[2] "As it seems to me, at least".

authority therefore we obtain no information. If we proceed to its derivation, we shall find that our Anglosaxon ancestors by the word SUND (whence our SOUND) meant precisely the Latin SANUS. USUND Anglosaxon, or unsound English, would therefore be of equivalent meaning with the Latin INSANUS.

I speak diffidently; but feel inclined to conjecture, that our English, sound, is equivalent to the Latin sincerus, i.e. sine cerâ, without any *crack* that has been luted or cemented by wax.—Sonat sincerum—it *rings.*[1] This seems to receive confirmation from the common phrase for the opposite state—The man is *cracked.*—It is not unusual in Etymology for an adjective to be derived from a compound substantive—thus, A sound, thence a sounding or soundness, i.e. power of giving out a sound—hence the adjective, sound. So, Glum = Gloom, Glumness = the form or habit of Gloom, and then glum = gloomy. So in the idiom, a home stroke, a home question.

8 p 150 (end of text)

The reader must be aware that this is general reasoning, as no particular case has been the subject of discussion. The search has been directed to a broad and general principle, without prying into subtil distinctions;—it is reasoning as far as a knowledge of the human intellect, in its sane and disordered state, may be expected from medical opinion; but it presumes not to dictate to that constituted authority denominated law, which in all civilized nations, has been wisely established for thc protection and happiness of the community.

I have seldom read a book, which has left me so incapable of conjecturing the Author's Object in writing it.

7[1] C offers this old but incorrect etymology for "sincere"—as derived from the Latin meaning "without wax"—also in *C&S* (*CC*) 92*. *Sincerum sonere* "it rings true" appears (in the negative) in Lucretius 3.873.

JOHANN GOTTFRIED HERDER

1744–1803

Verstand und Erfahrung. Eine Metakritik zur Kritik der reinen Vernunft. Leipzig 1799. 8°.

Not located; marginalia published from *Westmorland Gazette* 28 Aug 1819.

This note, submitted by De Q as an anonymous contribution to the *Westmorland Gazette*, is the first recorded publication of any of C's marginalia, as D. S. Roberts has pointed out: *N&Q* n.s. XLI (Sept 1994) 331. It is of a piece with C's marginalia in other works by Herder, and with his opinion of this work as it is expressed elsewhere: see esp HERDER *Kalligone* **1**, *Briefe* **11** and nn.

DATE. Winter 1809–10, when C and De Q were both staying with the Wordsworths at Allan Bank, Grasmere. In the article that includes this note, De Q refers to the book as one "which about ten years ago we lent to Mr. Coleridge by way of affording him winter evening's diversion". C appears to have been already familiar with this work: see HERDER General Note.

1 Title-page

What Hume said of Beattie's Work may be more truly applied to these volumes: *it is one big lie in octavo*.[1] Like a Surinam Toad, it begins with a mother lie; and, every step it crawls, young lies sprout out on its back.[2]

1[1] Of James Beattie's *Essay on the Nature and Immutability of Truth*, which attacked him, Hume is reported to have remarked, "Truth! there is no truth in it; it is a horrible large lie in octavo": *GM* XLVII (1777) 159n. C's attitude towards the work was consistently dismissive: cf *Friend* (*CC*) I 28, *BL* ch 12 (*CC*) I 270, *Logic* (*CC*) 193*.

1[2] For the image of the Surinam Toad that gestates its young in its back see DONNE *Sermons* COPY B **60** n 5. It appears also in a letter of 28 Apr 1808, relatively close to the probable date of this note: *CL* III 95.

IMMANUEL KANT

1724–1804

Copy D

Immanuel Kants vermischte Schriften. 4 vols. Halle & Königsberg 1799–1807. 8°.

Not located: marginalia pub from De Q's anonymous account in *Blackwood's Magazine* XXVIII (Aug 1830) 244–68. It seems most likely that in this set C read and annotated only one essay, "Der Streit der Facultäten" in III 457–576. The page references given in the headlines are the pages on which the textus appears, the exact location of C's notes not being known. (They may have been on fly-leaves: De Q describes **2** as having been written "in a blank leaf of that volume which contains the Essay in question" [251].) The German has been taken from *Vermischte Schriften* directly rather than from *Blackwood's*.

TEXTUS TRANSLATION. Immanuel Kant *The Conflict of the Faculties* tr Mary Gregor (New York 1979).

DATE. Possibly 1809–10, when C and De Q were both staying with the Wordsworths at Allan Bank, Grasmere. De Q left for London Feb 1810 and did not return until Nov, by which time C had gone; but De Q must have left books behind. See HERDER *Verstand* preceding.

1 III 550n

Im römisch-catholischen System des Kirchenglaubens ist, diesen Punkt, (das Bibellesen) betreffend, mehr Consequenz als im protestantischen.—Der reformirte Prediger, *La Coste*, sagt zu seinen Glaubensgenossen: "schöpft das göttliche Wort aus der Quelle (der Bibel) selbst, wo ihr es dann lauter und unverfälscht einnehmen könnt; aber ihr müsst ja nichts anders in der Bibel finden, als was wir darin finden.—Nun, liebe Freunde, sagt uns lieber, was ihr in der Bibel findet, damit wir nicht unnöthiger Weise darin selbst suchen, und am Ende, was wir darin gefunden zu haben vermeinten, von euch für unrichtige Auslegung derselben erklärt werde."—Auch spricht die catholische Kirche in dem Satze: "Ausser der Kirche (der catholischen) ist kein Heil," consequenter als die protestantische, wenn diese sagt: dass man auch als Catholik selig werden könne. Denn wenn das ist (sagt *Bossuet*), so wählt man ja am sichersten,

sich zu ersteren zu schlagen. Denn noch seliger als selig kann doch kein Mensch zu werden verlangen.

[On this point (the reading of the Bible), the Roman Catholic system of dogma is more consistent than the Protestant. The reformed preacher La Coste says to his co-religionists: "Draw the divine word from the spring itself (the Bible), where you can take it purer and unadulterated; but you must find in the Bible nothing other than what we find there. Now, dear friends, please tell us what you find in the Bible so that we won't waste our time searching for it ourselves, only to have you explain, in the end, that what we supposed we had found in it is a false interpretation." Again, when the Catholic Church says: Outside the (Catholic) Church there is no salvation, it speaks more consistently than the Protestant Church when it says: Catholics too can be saved. For if that is so (says Bossuet), then the safer choice is to join the Catholic Church; for no one can ask for *more* salvation.]

It may well surprise one to find in Kant a confirmation of so ridiculous a sophism as that of Bossuet and the Romanists. The Protestant does not say that a man can be saved who chooses the Catholic religion, not as true, but as the safest; for this is no religion at all, but only a pretence to it. A faith sincere, from honest intentions, will save Catholic or Protestant. So St. Paul on meats and holy days.[1]

2 III 551n–3n

70 apokalyptische Monate (deren es in diesem Cyclus 4 giebt), jeden zu 29½ Jahren, geben 2065 Jahr. Davon jedes 49ste Jahr, als das grosse Ruhejahr, (deren in diesem Zeitlaufe 42 sind) abgezogen: bleiben gerade 2023, als das Jahr, da Abraham aus dem Lande Canaan, das ihm Gott geschenkt hatte, nach Egypten gieng.—Von da an bis zur Einnahme jenes Landes durch die Kinder Israel, 70 apokalyptische Wochen (= 490 Jahr)—und so 4mal solcher Jarhwochen zusammengezählt (= 1960) und mit 2023 addiert, geben, nach *P. Petau* Rechnung, das Jahr der Geburt Christi (= 3983) so genau, dass auch nicht ein Jahr daran fehlt.—Siebzig Jahr hernach die Zerstörung Jerusalems (auch eine mystische Epoche.)—Aber *Bengel, in ordine temporum pag. 9 it. p. 218. seqq*, bringt 3939, als die Zahl der Geburt Christi, heraus? Aber das ändert nichts an der Heiligkeit des Numerus septenarius. Denn die Zahl der Jahre vom Rufe Gottes an Abraham, bis zur Geburt Christi, ist 1960, welches 4 apokalyptische Perioden austrägt, jeden zu 490, oder auch 40 apok. Perioden, jeden zu 7mal 7 = 49 Jahr. Zieht man nun von jedem neun und vierzigsten das *grosse* Ruhejahr und von jedem *grössten* Ruhejahr, welches das

1[1] E.g. Col 2.16–17: "Let no man therefore judge you in meat, or in drink, or in respect of an holyday, or of the new moon, or of the sabbath days, which are a shadow of things to come; but the body is of Christ." And cf Rom 14.1–12.

490ste ist, eines ab (zusammen 44), so bleibt gerade 3939—Also sind die Jahrzahlen 3983 und 3939, als das verschieden angegebene Jahr der Geburt Christi, nur darin unterschieden: dass die letztere entspringt, wenn in der Zeit der ersteren das, was zur Zeit der 4 grossen Epochen gehört, um die Zahl der Ruhejahre vermindert wird. Nach *Bengeln* würde die Tafel der heil. Geschichte so aussehen:

2023: Verheissung an Abraham, das Land Canaan zu besitzen:
2502: Besitzerlangung desselben:
2981: Einweihung des ersten Tempels:
3460: Gegebener Befehl zur Erbauung des zweiten Tempels:
3939: Geburt Christi.

Auch das Jahr der Sündfluth lässt sich so *a priori* ausrechnen. Nämlich 4 Epochen zu 490 (= 70 × 7) Jahr machen 1960. Davon jedes 7te (= 280) abgezogen, bleiben 1680. Von diesen 1680 jedes darin enthaltene 70ste Jahr abgezogen (= 24), bleiben 1656, als das Jahr der Sündfluth.—Auch von dieser bis zum R. G. an Abraham, sind 366 volle Jahre, davon eines ein Schaltjahr ist.

Was soll man nun hiezu sagen? Haben die heiligen Zahlen etwa den Weltlauf bestimmt?—*Frank*'s *Cyclus iobilaeus* dreht sich ebenfalls um diesen Mittelpunkt der mystischen Chronologie herum.

[70 Apocalyptic months (of which there are 4 in this cycle), each 29½ years long, equal 2065 years. Subtract every 49th year of this, as the great year of rest (there are 42 of them in this period) and we get exactly 2023 as the year Abraham left the land of Canaan, which God had given him, for Egypt. From then to the occupation of that land by the children of Israel 70 Apocalyptic weeks (= 490 years)—multiply these week-years by 4 (= 1960) and add 2023, and this gives, according to P. Petau's reckoning, the year of Christ's birth (3983) so exactly that it is not even a year off. 70 years after this, the destruction of Jerusalem (also a mystical epoch). But Bengel (*in ordine temporum*, page 9 and pages 218 ff) gets 3939 as the date of Christ's birth? That changes nothing in the sacred character of the *numerus septenarius*; for the number of years between God's call to Abraham and the birth of Christ is 1960, which comprises 4 Apocalyptic periods each of 490 years, or also 40 Apocalyptic periods each of 7 × 7 or 49 years. Now if we subtract 1 from every 49th year for the great year of rest, and 1 for every greatest year of rest, which is the 490th (44 altogether), there remains exactly 3939. Hence the dates 3983 and 3939, as different years assigned to the birth of Christ, differ only in this: that 3939 is obtained from 3983 by subtracting the number of years of rest from what is included in the time of the 4 great epochs. According to Bengel, the table of sacred history is as follows:

2023 Promise to Abraham that he would possess the land of Canaan
2502 He takes possession of it
2981 Consecration of the first temple
3460 Command given to build the second temple
3939 Birth of Christ.

The year of the Flood, too, can be calculated a priori in the same way: 4 epochs of 490

(70 × 7) years makes 1960. Subtract from this every 7th (280) and this leaves 1680. From this 1680 subtract every 70th year contained in it (= 24), and this leaves 1656 as the year of the Flood. Also, from this to God's call to Abraham are 366 full years, of which 1 is a leap year.

What are we to say to this? Have the sacred numbers perhaps determined the course of events in the world? Frank's *Cyclus iobilaeus* also revolves around the center of this mystical chronology.]

In this attack on the New and Old Testament from Cabala of Numbers, how came it that Kant did not perceive that Jews could not join with Christians? And one of the events, at least, is downright history, the destruction of Jerusalem. A single perusal of Eichhorn (no believer himself in the supernatural) dashes to earth all these objections.[1] Besides, how unfair to subtract every 49th year in the first 2065 (= 2023), and not to subtract them in the 70 times 4 Apocalyptic weeks that follow; to make the Apocalyptic month 295 years, and then four Apocalyptic weeks = 28! What coincidences may not be produced by these means? I doubt not you might fix on some one number in the Greek or Roman history, and play the same marvels off with it. Petavius may omit, and Bengel introduce, the subtraction of the 49th year, and all is fair;[2] but Petavius must not now omit and now introduce *ad libitum*. In short, the whole range is included in 10; and what wonder if, with such license allowed, half a dozen remarkable events, in the course of 6000 years, should be brought all to some one number? Every man's own experience would furnish equal coincidences in every year, if he examined minutely.

2[1] C had heard Eichhorn lecture at Göttingen in 1799–1800, and later annotated at least five of his works—some in more than one copy. It appears that he is referring not to a particular work but to the general tendency and method of Eichhorn's work, i.e. to his treatment of the Bible as an historical document.

2[2] Petavius and Bengel—Denis Petau or Petavius (1583–1652) and Johann Albrecht Bengel (1687–1752)—are both cited as authorities in textus.

ROBERT LEIGHTON

1611–1684

Copy B

The Genuine Works of R. Leighton, D.D. Archbishop of Glasgow: with a preface by Philip Doddridge, D.D. A new edition, with corrections and additional letters. To which is now prefixed, the life of the author, by the Rev. Erasmus Middleton. 4 vols. London 1819. 8°.

Victoria College Library (Coleridge Collection)

James Gillman's copy, listed in *Gillman SC* (1843) 454; C mentions its not belonging to him in *CL* v 205. Bookplate of Robert, Marquess of Crewe, in each vol. Some notes were published in *CM* (*CC*) III from MS TRANSCRIPTS, before the originals were located. Rather than send the reader back and forth between vols, all the notes—new and old—have been retranscribed and footnotes reprinted in this version, which supersedes the earlier one. Entry **28** in the original version now becomes an ANNEX.

In accord with his complaints about the printing of Greek and Latin in this ed (e.g. **11**, **23**, **26**), C has corrected typographical errors on III 11, IV 19n, IV 464. There is also a typographical correction, not by C, on II 145. Passages are marked with a line in pencil at several points, but these markings appear to be by another reader, most likely Gillman: I 7, 10, 74 (with "Sp" for "Spiritual Aphorisms"—a reference to *AR*), 92, 99; II 120–1; IV 18. A correction and comment in pencil on III 115, and a pencilled correction on III 119, are also in another hand, possibly Gillman's.

CONTENTS. I v–vi Advertisement; ix–x Preface by the Rev. Henry Foster; xi–xviii "Preface by Dr. Doddridge"; xix–xxxvi "Life of Robert Leighton, D.D., Archbishop of Glasgow" by Erasmus Middleton; I 1–507, II i–354 *A Practical Commentary upon the First Epistle General of St. Peter*; 355–429 *Expository Lectures on Psalm XXIX; on Isaiah VI; and on Romans XII*; 431–51 *Charges, &c. to the Clergy of the Diocesan Synod of Dunblane*; 452–64 *Seven Letters*; 465–80 *Rules and Instructions for a Holy Life*; III 1–226 *Eighteen Sermons*; 227–63 *An Exposition of the Creed*; 264–333 *An Exposition of the Lord's Prayer*; 334–400 *An Exposition of the Ten Commandments*; 401–14 *A Discourse on Matthew XXII.37, 38, 39*; 415–18 *A Short Catechism*; 419–533 *Ten Sermons, from the Author's Manuscripts*; IV [vii]–xv "Preface by the Publisher of the Latin Edition [of *Praelectiones theologicae*] (1693)", James Fall; 17–257 *Theological*

Lectures; 259–327 *Exhortations to the Candidates for the Degree of Master of Arts in the University of Edinburgh*; 329–426 *Meditations Critical and Practical, Psalms IV. XXXII. and CXXX.*; 427–55 *A Sermon, preached to the Clergy*; 457–84 *Letters*.

DATE. From about summer 1819 to at least Sept 1823 (**27**), and probably with some additions from early Nov 1823 to the publication of *AR* in May 1825. Two notebook entries referring to this edition in c Jan 1822 are *CN* IV 4853–4; it was also in Jan 1822 that C broached with Murray the possibility of a collection of "The Beauties of Archbishop Leighton": *CL* v 200.

1 I 2–3, pencil, partly overtraced in ink | *A Practical Commentary*: 1 Pet 1.1

. . . this first chapter is much on that [subject, i.e. *faith*], persuading them of the truth of that mystery they had received and did believe, *viz.* their redemption and salvation by Christ Jesus; that inheritance of immortality bought by his blood* for them, and the evidence and stability of their right and title to it.

* Blood. line 24. ~~Of~~ By the Blood of Christ I mean this. I contemplate the Christ, 1. as [a]Christus Agens,[1] the Jehovah Christ, God the Word: 2. as Christus patiens,[2] the God incarnate.[b]—In the former (Christus Agens) he is—relativè ad Intellectum humanum Lux lucifica, Sol Intellectualis; relativè ad Existentiam Humanam, Anima Animans, Calor fovens.[3] In the latter (Christus patiens) he is Vita vivificans, Principium Spiritualis, id est, veræ Reproductionis in vitam veram.[4] Now this Principle, or Vis Vitæ vitam communicans, considered in formâ passivâ, assimilationem patiens,[5] at the same time that it excites the Soul to the vital Act of assimilating—*this* is *the Blood* of Christ, really present thro' Faith and actually partaken by the Faithful. Of this the body is the continual Product, i.e. a good Life—the Merits of Christ acting on the Soul redemptively.

1[a-b] Overtraced in ink

1[1] "Christ acting".

1[2] "Christ suffering", i.e. "being acted upon".

1[3] As "Christ Acting" he is, "relative to the human intellect, light-making Light, intelligible Sun; relative to human existence, he is the animating Soul, the cherishing Heat".

1[4] As "Christ Suffering" he is "life-giving Life, the Principle of Spiritual (that is, of true, or really existing) Rebirth into true life".

1[5] This "Life-Force communicating life", considered "in its passive form, undergoing assimilation".

2 I 7

Scattered in the countries, and yet gathered in God's election, chosen or picked out; strangers to men amongst whom they dwelt, but *known* and *foreknown* to God; removed from their own country, to which men have naturally an unalterable affection, but made *heirs* of a better, as follows, ver. 3, 4. and having within them the evidence both of eternal election, and that expected salvation, the *Spirit of Holiness*, ver. 2.*

* Leighton avoids all metaphysical views of Election relatively to God—and confines himself to the practical—in relation to man, and in that sense in which every man can judge of it.

3 I 13–23 | 1 Pet 1.2

[Commenting esp on the phrase "elect unto obedience", Leighton observes that 1 Pet 1.2 describes both the state and the causes of election, in which all three persons of the Trinity are active, since "eternal election" is attributed to God the Father and election in a second sense, "effectual calling", to the Holy Spirit, while justification of the elect is achieved by the purifying blood of Christ. Leighton insists that no mortal is without "the natural pollution" of sin, and that no mortal effort can purge it: "There is nothing in religion further out of nature's reach, and out of its liking and believing, than the doctrine of redemption by a Saviour, and a crucified Saviour, by Christ, and by his blood, first shed on the cross in his suffering, and then sprinkled on the soul by his Spirit" (11)]

That the Doctrines asserted in this and the two or three following pages[1] cannot be denied or explained away without removing (as the modern Unitarians) or (as the Arminians) unsettling and undermining the foundations of the Faith,[2] I am fully convinced; and equally so that nothing is gained by the change, the very same logical Consequences being deducible from the tenets of the Church Arminians, scarcely more so from

3[1] On pp 13–14 Leighton concentrates on the term "obedience", which he takes to consist "in the receiving Christ as our Redeemer" and in the "entire rendering up of the whole man to this obedience". He asserts that such obedience can be made possible only by "grace renewing the hearts of believers" and changing "their natures".

3[2] For C at this time, the "foundation" involved belief in the Trinity (rejected by Unitarians) as well as in the doctrines referred to at the end of this note, original sin with redemption and "change of Heart" as its consequences. Cf *AR* (*CC*) 197–8. For C's frequent attacks on "modern Unitarians" see *LS* (*CC*) 111–12, *BL* ch 24 (*CC*) II 245–6, *AR* (*CC*) 208*–12*. He uses the term "Arminian" interchangeably with "Grotian" (Grotius having been a follower of Arminius) to refer loosely to an episcopal high-church party associated with Laud or with Laudian principles: see n 4 below, and cf *C&S* (*CC*) 135 and n.

those which they still hold in common with Luther, Zuinglius, Calvin, Knox, Cranmer and the other Fathers of the Reformation in England, and which are therefore most unfairly entitled Calvinism—than from those which they have substituted.[3] See this proved in my Mss Notes to Taylor's Letter on Original Sin.[4] Nay, the Shock given to the Moral Sense by these Consequences is, (to *my* feelings) aggravated in the Arminian Doctrine by the thin yet dishonest Disguise.

Meantime the Consequences appear to me, in point of Logic, legitimately concluded from the Terms of the Premises. What shall we say then? Where lies the Fault? In the original Doctrines expressed in the Premises? God forbid! In the particular Deductions, logically considered? But these we have found legitimate. Where then? I answer: in deducing *any* Consequences by such a process, and according to such rules! The Rules are alien and inapplicable: the Process presumptuous, yea, preposterous. The error, τὸ πρῶτον ψεῦδος,[5] lies in the false assumption of ~~the~~ a *logical* deducibility, at all, in this instance. First, because the Terms, from which the Conclusion must be drawn [a](termini in Majore præmissi, a quibus scientialiter et scientifice demonstrandum erat),[6] are Accomodations, and not scientific—i.e. proper and adequate: not per *idem*, but per ~~max~~ quam maxime *simile*, or rather quam minime *dissimile*.[7] Secondly, because the Truths in question are *transcendent*, and *have* their *ev-*

3[a] Square brackets in the original are given as parentheses to avoid confusion with editorial matter

3[3] In the history of the Church, Arminianism arose as a reaction against Calvinism, and the two names are commonly used to denote contrasting beliefs. C here emphasises, however, the common ground that Arminian doctrine shares with the "Fathers of the Reformation"—Luther, Zwingli, Calvin, Knox, and Cranmer. In *AR* (*CC*) 162 he says, ". . . the Doctrines of Calvin on Redemption and the natural state of fallen Man, are in all essential points the same as those of Luther, Zuinglius, and the first Reformers collectively." Modern Calvinism C believed to have less in common with original Calvinism than had Arminianism: see n 11 below and COPY C 13.

3[4] C records in several places his horror at Jeremy Taylor's "Arminian" minimising of the significance of original sin, and his emphasis on the sinner's responsibility for repentance, e.g. *Friend* (*CC*) I 434, BAXTER *Reliquiae* COPY A **49**. The notes he refers to here are probably the eight annotations on *An Answer to a Letter from the Bishop of Rochester Concerning the Chapter of Original Sin, in the "Unum Necessarium"*, in J. TAYLOR *Polemicall Discourses* **173–180**, particularly **179**: ". . . Deny original Sin, & you will soon deny free will—Then virtue & vice—and God becomes Abracadabra—a sound!!" C quotes Taylor on original sin in *AR* (*CC*) 265–6, and quotes one of his own notes on Taylor 282.

3[5] "The fundamental error": see BAXTER *Reliquiae* COPY B **92** n 1.

3[6] "The terms in the major premise, from which philosophically and scientifically the demonstration was to be made".

3[7] Not "through [being] *the same*", but "through [being] in the greatest degree *similar*" or rather "in the least degree *dissimilar*".

idence, if any, *in* the *Ideas* themselves, and for the *Reason*; and do not and cannot *derive* it *from* the *Conceptions* of the *Understanding*, which cannot comprehend the Truths but is to be comprehended in and by them. Vide I John: v. 5.[8] Lastly, and chiefly, because these Truths, as they do not originate in the intellective Faculty of Man, so neither ⟨are they⟩ addressed primarily to our Intellect; but ~~in~~ ⟨are substantiated *for us* by their⟩ correspondence to the Wants, Cravings, and interests of the Moral Being, for which they were given, and without which they would be devoid of all meaning—vox et præterea nihil.[9] The only Conclusions, therefore, ⟨that dare be drawn from them,⟩ must be such as are implied in the origin and purpose of their revelation; and the~~ir~~ legitimacy ⟨of all Conclusions⟩ must be tried by their Consistency with those Moral interests, those Spiritual necessities, which are the proper *final cause* of the Truths & of our Faith therein. For *some* of the Faithful these Truths have, I doubt not, an *evidence* of Reason; but for the whole Household of Faith their *Certainty* is in their *Working*.[10] Now it is *this*, by which ⟨in all cases⟩ we know and determine *Existence* in the first instance. That which *works* in us or on us, *exists* for us. The Shapes and Forms that follow the Working as its results or products, whether the Shapes cognizable by sense or the Forms distinguished by the Intellect, are after ⟨all⟩ but the *particularizations* of this Working; as it were its proper names, as John, James, Peter, in respect of Human Nature⟨. They are⟩ all derived from the relations, in which finite Beings stand to each other; and are therefore heterogeneous and except by *accomodation* devoid of meaning and purpose when applied to the working in and by which *God* makes his Existence known to us, and (we may presume to say) specially exists for the Soul in whom he thus works. On these grounds, therefore, I hold the doctrines of Original Sin, the Redemption therefrom by the Cross of Christ, and Change of Heart as the *Consequent*: [? ~~nor~~] without adopting the additions to the doctrines ~~made~~ *inferred* by one Set of Divines, the Modern Calvinists,[11] or acknowleging the Consequences burthened on the doctrines by their Antagonists. Nor is this, my faith, fairly liable to any inconvenience—if only it be re-

3[8] John 1.5, "And the light shineth in darkness; and the darkness comprehendeth it not."

3[9] "A voice and nothing more", a Spartan's comment upon eating a nightingale: Plutarch *Moralia* 233A.

3[10] The emphasis on the "working" of the spirit here may be derived from the textus, e.g. p 16: ". . . and so [sanctification] comprehends justification, as here, and the first working of faith, by which the soul is justified. . . . The spirit or soul of a man is the chief and first subject of this work, and it is but slight false work that begins not there . . .".

3[11] For C at this time the phrase "modern Calvinists" had specific reference to Edward Williams: see COPY C **13** n 2, and *AR* (*CC*) 158, where his objection is that Williams and his party conceived of the human will as "absolutely passive, clay in the hands of a Potter".

membered, that it is a spiritual Working, of which I speak, and a spiritual Knowlege—not thro' the medium of *Image*, the seeking after which is *Superstition*; nor yet by any *Sensation*, the Watching for which is *Enthusiasm*, and the Conceit of its presence Fanatical Distemperature.[12] "Do the will of the Father: & ye shall *know* it.["]—[13]

4 I 25–7, perhaps referring to 23, where **3** was already written

Find thou but within thee sanctification by the Spirit, and this argues necessarily, both justification by the Son, and the election of God the Father, 1 John iv. 13. *Hereby know we that we dwell in him, and he in us, because he has given us of his Spirit.*

* We must distinguish the Life and the Soul:[1] tho' there is a certain sense in which the Life may be called the Soul—i.e. The Life is the Soul of the *Body*. But the Soul is the life of *the Man*, and Christ is the Life of the Soul. Now the Spirit of Man, the Spirit *sub*sistent, is deeper than both, not only deeper than the Body & its life, but deeper than the Soul; and the Spirit descendent and *super*sistent[2] is higher than both—In the regenerated Man the Height and the Depth become one—the Spirit communeth with the Spirit—and the Soul is the Inter-ens, or Ens intermedium[3] between the Life and the Spirit—the Participium, not as a Compound, however, but as a Medium indifferens[4]—in the same sense, in which Heat may be designated as the Indifference between Light and Gravity.[5] And what is the Reason? The Spirit in its presence to the Understanding abstractedly from its presence in the Will—nay, in many, during the negation of the latter.—The Spirit present to Man but not appropriated by him is the Reason of Man—the Reason in the process of its identification with the Will is the Spirit.—

5 I 158 | 1 Pet 1.22

* The chief point of obedience is believing; the proper obedience to truth is, to give credit to it; and this divine belief doth necessarily bring the

3[12] C's distinction between enthusiasm and fanaticism is fully worked out in BIRCH **1**; these two are further related to superstition in BAXTER *Reliquiae* COPY A **51**.

3[13] John 7.17 (var).

4[1] Cf **7** below; and for further development of this theme see COPY C **7**.

4[2] "Standing *over*". C's coinage by analogy with "subsistent" above, and perhaps contrasted with "superstition" in **3**.

4[3] The "Inter-being" (or being *between*) or "intermediary Being".

4[4] The "Partaker" as an "indifferent Midpoint".

4[5] In the method of analysis of the natural world that C learnt chiefly from German *Naturphilosophen* such as Heinrich Steffens (*Grundzüge der philosophischen Naturwissenschaft*—Berlin 1806—64), light and gravity are polar powers, with heat the product of their meeting in equilibrium. The same statement appears in e.g. BÖHME **79**.

whole soul into obedience and conformity to that pure truth, which is in the word . . .

* This is not quite so perspicuous and single-sensed as Archb. Leight. is in general. This effect is occasioned by the omission of the word "this" or "divine" or the truth "in Christ." For Truth in the ordinary and scientific sense is received by a spontaneous, rather than chosen by a voluntary, Act:—and the apprehension of the same (Belief) supposes a position of Congruity rather than an Act of Obedience. Far otherwise is it with the Truth that is the object of Christian Faith: and it is this Truth of which Leighton is speaking. Belief indeed is a living *part* of this Faith; but only as long as it is a *living* part. In other words, Belief is implied in Faith; but Faith is not necessarily implied in Belief.[1] "*The Devils believe*."[2]

S. T. C.

6 I 166 | Pet 1.23

Hence learn, 1. That true conversion is not so slight a work, as we commonly account it. It is not the outward change of some bad customs, which gains the name of a reformed man in the ordinary dialect; it is a new birth and being, and elsewhere called *a new creation*. Though it be but a change in qualities,* yet it is such a one, and the qualities so far distant from what they before were, that it bears the name of the most substantial productions . . .

* I dare not affirm that this is erroneously said; but it is one of the comparatively few passages that are of service as reminding me that it is not the Scripture, that I am reading. Not the qualities merely but the Root of the Qualities is trans-created.[1] How else could it be a Birth? A Creation?

7 I 170–5 | 1 Pet 1.24

This natural life is compared, even by natural men, to the vainest things, and scarce find they things light enough to express it *vain*; and as it is here called *grass*, so they compare the generations of men to the leaves of trees. But the light of Scripture doth most discover this, and it is a lesson that requires the Spirit of God to teach it aright. *Teach us*, says Moses, Psal. xc. 12. *so to number our days that we may apply our hearts unto*

5[1] There is a longer exposition of the distinction between faith and belief in BLANCO WHITE *Letters* **1**.

5[2] Jas 2.19 (var), alluded to also in COPY A **7** at n 2.

6[1] Apparently C's coinage, given as a nonce-word in *OED*. For other compounds with the prefix "trans-" see DONNE *Sermons* COPY A **4** and n 6.

wisdom; and David, Psal. xxxix. 4. *Make me to know my life, how frail I am*. So Ja. iv. 14.; and here it is called *grass*. So Job xiv. 1, 2. *Man that is born of a woman is of few days, and full of trouble. He cometh forth like a flower, and is cut down*.

It is the fashion to decry scholastic distinctions as useless subtleties, or mere phantoms—entia logica vel etiam verbalia solum.[1] And yet in order to secure a safe and christian interpretation to these and numerous other passages of like phrase and import, in the Old Testament, it is of highest concernment that we should distinguish the Personëity, ⟨or Spirit,⟩ as the Source and principle of Personality, from the person itself as the particular product at any one period, and as that which cannot ~~subsist~~ be evolved or sustained but by the Co-agency of the system and circumstances, in which the Individuals are placed.[2] In this latter sense it is that *Man* is used in the Psalms, in Job, and elsewhere—and the term ⟨made⟩ synonimous with Flesh. [a]That which constitutes the Spirit *a man*, both for others and for itself, *is* the Man: and to this the elements and elementary powers contribute its *bulk* (τὸ videri et tangi)[3] wholly, and its phænomenal *form* in part, both as co-efficient, and as Conditions. Now as these are under a Law of vanity and incessant change, τα μη οντα αλλ᾽ αει γινομενα[4]—so must all ⟨be⟩ to the production and continuance of which the~~y~~se are indispensable. On this hangs the doctrine of the Resurrection of the Body, as an essential part of the doctrine of Immortality—on this the scripture (and only true and philosophical) sense of the Soul, Psyche or Life, as resulting from the continual Assurgency of the Spirit thro' the Body; and ⟨on this⟩ the Begetting of a new Life, a regenerate Soul, by the descent of the divine Spirit on the Spirit of Man.[5] When the spirit by sanctification is fitted for an incorruptible Body, then shall it be raised into a world of Incorruption, and a celestial Body shall ~~be born to it~~urgeon forth thereto, the Germ of which had been

7[a] Note continues on I 172 with "*from over-leaf*" at top of page

7[1] "Things that exist in logic or rather only in words". C often had occasion to defend "Scholastic distinctions", e.g. the use of "subjective" and "objective" in *BL* ch 10 (*CC*) I 172, and of "aureity" in *SW & F* (*CC*) 496.

7[2] An important distinction that appears elsewhere in C's writings, e.g. IRVING **11**, "that divine Humanity which is the *Ground* of the humanity or spiritual Personëity in every Person".

7[3] "The [capacity] to be seen and touched".

7[4] "Things that do not exist but are always becoming": cf C's observation that *natura* is a future participle, as implied in his definition of "nature" as "Natura, that which is *about to be* born, that which is always *becoming*" in *AR* (*CC*) 251, also *CL* VI 897.

7[5] Cf the distinction between life and soul in **4**.

implanted by the redeeming and creative Word in this World.[6] Truly has it been said of the Elect—They ~~sink to~~ fall asleep in Earth; but awake in Heaven. So St Paul expressly teaches: and as the passage (Cor. I. xv.) was written for the express purpose of rectifying the notions of the Converts concerning the Resurrection, all other passages in the N. T. must be interpreted in harmony with this.[7] But John, likewise, describing the same great event, as subsequent to and contra-distinguished from the partial or Millenniary Resurrection which (whether we are to understand the Apostle symbolically or literally) is to take place in the present World—~~he describes~~ beheld a new Earth and a new Heaven as antecedent to, or co-incident with the Appearance of the New Jerusalem—i.e. the state of Glory, and the resurrection to Life Everlasting.[8] The Old Earth and its Heaven had passed away from the face of Him on the throne, at the moment that it gave up the Dead.[9]

8 I 175 | 1 Pet 1.25

Ver. 25. *But the word of the Lord endureth for ever.* . . . with respect to those learned men that apply them [the Prophet's words] to God, I remember not that this *abiding for ever* is used to express God's eternity in himself.

No! nor is it here used for that purpose; but yet I cannot doubt but that either the Word, Ο Λογος εν αρχη,[1] or the divine Promises in and thro' the incarnate Word, with the gracious influences proceeding from him are here meant—and not the written ῥηματα, or Scriptures.[2]

9 II 242–3, pencil | 1 Pet 4.14–16

And thus are reproaches mentioned amongst the sufferings of Christ in the gospel, and not as the least; the railings and mockings that were darted at him, and fixed to the cross, are mentioned more than the very nails that

7[6] The issue of the nature of "body" and the doctrine of a "twofold" body (based on 1 Cor 15.40–4) are prominent in marginalia to LUTHER *Colloquia*, e.g. **40**, and IRVING *Sermons*, esp **27**, **29**.

7[7] 1 Cor 15, esp 40–4 and 51, "Behold, I shew you a mystery; We shall not all sleep, but we shall all be changed".

7[8] See Rev 21, esp 1–4: "And I saw a new heaven and a new earth. . . . And I John saw the holy city, new Jerusalem, coming down from God. . . . and there shall be no more death . . .".

7[9] From Rev 20.11–13 (var).

8[1] "The Word [who was] in the beginning"—from John 1.1 (var).

8[2] The distinction between the Word and spoken or written words appears also in a notebook entry of c 14 Mar 1826 (*CN* IV 5338): see BÖHME **145** n 1. The same Greek words are used with different meanings, however, in *AR* (1825) 25n (omitted from 1831 on): *AR* (*CC*) 534.

fixed him. And, Heb. xii. 2. the *shame* of the cross, though he was above it, and despised it, yet that shame added much to the *burden of it; so ver. 3. *He endured the contradiction of sinners.*

* I understand Archb. L.[n] thus: that tho' our Lord felt it not as *shame*, nor was wounded by the revilings of the people in the way of any correspondent resentment or sting, which yet we may be without blame; yet he suffered from the same as *Sin*, and as an addition to the guilt of his persecutors which could not but aggravate the burthen which he had taken on himself, as being Sin in its most devilish form.

10 II 293, pencil | 1 Pet. 5.5

This therefore is mainly to be studied, that the seat of humility be *the heart*. Although it will be seen in the carriage, yet as little as it can; as few words as may be concerning itself; and those it doth speak must be the real thoughts of the mind, and not an affected voice of it differing from the inward sense; otherwise humble speech and carriage only put on without, and not fastened in the inside, is the most refined and subtile, and indeed the most dangerous kind of pride. And this I would recommend as a safe way: ever let thy thoughts concerning thyself be below what thou utterest: and what thou seest needful or fitting to say to thy own abasement, be not only content (which most are not) to be taken at thy word, and believed to be such by them that hear thee, but be desirous of it; and let that be the end of thy speech, to persuade them, and gain it of them, that they really take thee for as worthless and mean as thou dost express thyself.

Alas! this is a most delicate and difficult subject: and the safest way, and the only safe *General Rule*, is the Silence, that accompanies the inward act of looking at the *contrast* in all that is of our own doing and impulse! So may Praises be made their own Antidote.

11 III 9 | Sermon 1, on Jas 3.17

Nor rests it in an affecting sympathy, its *mercy* is helpful, full of mercy, *and good fruits:* and it both *forgives* and *pities*, and *gives: without* partiality, and without hypocrisy, [a][αδιακωεοσκ ανυποκωτος] the word αδια<u>κωτος</u> may as well bear another sense . . .

αδιακριτος και ανυποκριτος.[1] N.b. the Greek words are more often mis-

11[a] Square brackets in original

11[1] C corrects the obvious misprinting of Greek words quoted from Jas 3.17 (var) "without partiality, and without hypocrisy" (AV).

printed than otherwise throughout this edition: the dissenting Clergy not addicting themselves ordinarily to such acquirements—

12 III 20–1

They shall see God. What this is we cannot tell you, nor can you conceive it: but walk heavenwards in purity, and long to be there, where you shall know what it means; *for you shall see him as he is.*

We say: Now I *see* the full meaning, force and beauty of a passage—we see them *thro'* the words. Is not Christ THE WORD? the substantial, consubstantial Word, ὁ ων εν κολπω πατρος,[1] not as *our* words, arbitrary: nor even as the words of Nature, phænomenal merely? If even thro' the words[a] a powerful and perspicuous Author (as in the next to inspired Comment^{y} of Archb. Leighton—for whom God be praised!) I identify myself with the excellent Writer and his thoughts become my thoughts: what must not the Bliss be, to be thus identified first, with the filial WORD, and then with the Father in and thro' him?

13 III blank leaf following III 68, referring to III 63 | Sermon 5, on Isa 60.1

In this elementary world, light being (as we hear) the first visible, all things are seen by it, and it by itself. Thus is Christ, among spiritual things, in the elect world of his church; *all things are made manifest by the light*, says the apostle, Eph. v. 13. speaking of Christ, as the following verse doth evidently testify. It is in his word that he shines, and makes it a directing and convincing light, to discover all things that concern his church and himself, to be known by its own brightness. How impertinent then is that question so much tossed by the Romish church, how know you the scriptures (say they) to be the word of God, without the testimony of the church? I would ask one of them again, how they can know that it is day-light, except some light a candle to let them see it? They are little versed in holy scripture, that know not that it is frequently called light; and they are senseless that know not that light is seen and known by itself. If our gospel be hid, says the apostle, it is hid to them that perish; the god of this world having blinded their minds against the light of the glorious gospel, &c. no wonder if such stand in need of a testimony. A blind man knows not that it is light at noon-day, but by report: but to those that have eyes, light is seen by itself.

12[a] For "words of"?

12[1] John 1.18, "Which [i.e. who] is in the bosom of the Father". For the special significance of this verse to C see BIBLE COPY B **119** n 1, and *AR* (*CC*) 313* and n 30.

P. 63 On the true test of the Scriptures. Oh! were it not for my manifold infirmities, whereby I am so all unlike the white-robed Leighton, I could almost conceit that my Soul had been an emanation from his! So many and so remarkable are the co-incidences, and these in parts of his Works that I could not have seen—and so uniform the congruity of the whole. As I read, I seem to myself to be only thinking my own thoughts over again, now in the same and now in a different order.

14 III 68–71, P.S. on blank leaf following III 68

The author of the epistle to the Hebrews calls him [Christ] ἀπαυγασμα, "the brightness of his Father's glory, and the character of his person", Heb. i. 3. And under these expressions lies that remarkable mystery of the Son's eternal relation to the Father, which is rather humbly to be adored than boldly to be explained, either by God's perfect understanding of his own essence, or by any other notion.*

Certainly not by a transfer of a *notion*: ~~of an~~ and this too a notion of a faculty itself but notional and limitary to the Supreme Reality.[1] But there are *Ideas* which are of higher origin than the notions of the Understanding, and by the irradiation of which the understanding itself becomes a human Understanding. Of such veritates verificæ[2] L. himself in other words speaks often. Surely, there must have been an *intelligible* propriety in the terms, Logos, Word, Begotten before all creation,[3] Adequate Idea or Icon, &c:[4] or the Evangelists and Apostolic Penmen would not have *adopted* them. *They* did not *invent* the terms; but took them and used them as they were taken and ~~im~~applied by Philo and both the Greek and oriental Sages.[5] Nay, the precise and orthodox, yet frequent use of these Terms by Philo and by the ⟨Jewish⟩ Authors of that traditional Wisdom degraded in after times, but which in its purest parts, existed long before the Xtn Æra, is the strongest extrinsic argument against the Arians, Socinians, and Unitarians, in proof that St John must have meant to deceive his Readers, if he did not use them in the known and received sense.—To be a Materialist indeed, or to those who deny all knowleges

14[1] C objects both to the attribution to God of mere *understanding* and to the assumption that the transcendent could be apprehended by that limited faculty.

14[2] "Truth-making truths".

14[3] As in e.g. John 1.14, or in the words of the Nicene Creed, "begotten of his Father before all worlds".

14[4] In COPY C **7**. C expands upon the connection between "Word" and "Icon" (εἴκων): "The Logos is the substantial-Idea ⟨= Εικων⟩ in whom all Ideas are contained and have Being: it is the Idea of God."

14[5] C's knowledge of the significance of "logos" etc to Philo Judaeus (c 30 BC–c AD 40) and the "Greek and Oriental Sages" may come from his reading of Eichhorn: see EICHHORN *NT* COPY A **32**, *Apocrypha* **23**.

not resolvible into notices from the 5 senses, these terms as applied to Spiritual Beings must appear inexplicable or senseless—But so must *Spirit* itself. To *me* (why do I say, to *me*?) to Bull, Waterland, to Gregory Nazianzen, Basil, Athanasius, St Augustin, the terms, Word & Generation ⟨have⟩ appeared admirably yea, most awefully pregnant & appropriate[6]—but as the Language of those who know that their Minds are placed with their backs to Substances—and which therefore they can name only from the correspondent *Shadows*—Yet not (God forbid!) as if the Substances were the same with the *Shadows*[7]—which yet Leighton supposes in this his censure—for if he did not, he then censures himself & a number of his most beautiful passages.—These and 2 or 3 other sentences (slips of human infirmity) are useful in reminding me that Leighton's Works are not inspired Scriptures.

P. 68. On a second consideration of this passage, and a renewal of my marginal animadversion—yet how dare I apply such a word to a passage written by a Minister of Christ so clearly under the especial Light of the divine Grace as was Archbishop Leighton?—I am inclined to think that Leighton confined his censure to the attempts to *explain* the Trinity—and this by *notions*—and not to the assertion of the adorable Acts implied in the terms both of the Evangelists & Apostles, and of the Church before as well as after Christ's Ascension; ~~and~~ nor to the Assent of the pure *Reason* to the *Truths* and more than Assent to, the affirmation of the *Ideas*.—

S. T. C.

15 III 73, end of Sermon 5

The preceding Sermon, excellent in parts, is yet on the whole the least excellent of Leighton's Works—and breathes less ⟨of either⟩ his own character as a Man, ~~and~~ or the character of his religious philosophy. The Style too is in many places below Leighton's ordinary style—in some places even turbid, operose, and *catachrestic*—ex gr. to trampl~~ing~~e on smilings with one foot, and on frownings with the other.[1]

14[6] C invokes great defenders of Trinitarianism capable of using such terms as "word" and "generation" symbolically to describe the spiritual relationship between the first two persons of the Trinity. Cf his strong objection in 1805 to Samuel Horsley's definition of "generation" (in a theological context) as "The inducement of a Form on a pre-existing material": *CN* II 2444.

14[7] Using the allegory of the cave from Plato *Republic* 7, C defends the Trinitarians' use of the language of this world to describe a transcendent realm.

15[1] The example comes from III 69, where Leighton says that the true Christian "can generously trample upon the smilings of the world with the one foot, and her frownings with the other".

16 III 77 | Sermon 6, on Ps 42.8

Though the multitude and weight of Job's afflictions did force out of him some bitter words, and made him look back upon the day of his birth, and curse it; yet faith recovers him from his distemper, and makes him look forward with joy, even as far as to the blessed day of his resurrection, Job xix. 25. *"I know that my Redeemer liveth, and that he shall stand at the latter day upon the earth: and though after my skin, worms destroy this body, yet in my flesh shall I see God."

* Leighton, I presume, was acquainted with the Hebrew Language; but he does ⟨not⟩ appear to have studied it much. His observation on the Heart, as used in the Old Test., shews that he did not know that the ancient Hebrews supposed the Heart to be the seat of Intellect & therefore used it exactly as *we* use *the Head*—[1]

17 III 104 | End of Sermon 7, on Ps 119, 136

The preceding (VIIth) Discourse admirable throughout, Leighton throughout! O what a contrast might be presented by publishing *this* and some Discourse of some ~~pre~~ Court Prelate or Divine (South for instance)[1] preached under the same State of Affairs—and printing the two in columns!—

18 III 106 referring to III 107 (**19**) | Sermon 8, on Song of Sol 1.3

The lines on p. 107, noted by me,[1] are one of a myriad instances to prove, how rash it is to quote single sentences or assertions from the correctest Writers, without collating them with the known system or express convictions of the Author. It would be easy to cite 50 passages from Archbishop Leighton's Works in direct contradiction to the sentence in ques-

16[1] C makes this point frequently. Cf HEINROTH **40** and n 1. His reference to Leighton's "observation on the Heart, as used in the Old Test." may mean a passage earlier in this sermon, III 75, where Leighton quotes passages from the Psalms to suggest that God comforts troubled mankind by cheering his heart: "The believing soul hath but one comfort whereon he relies, but it is a great one, which alone weighs down all the rest. *Bread strengthens, and wine makes glad the heart of man*, Psal. civ. 15. *But God is the strength of my heart* (says the Psalmist) Psal. lxxiii. 26. *and the gladness of it too. Thou has put gladness in my heart, more than they have when their corn and wine increaseth*, Psal. iv. 7."

17[1] Robert South (1634–1716), chaplain for a time to Clarendon (1660) and to the Duke of York (1667). There are records of C's reading—on the whole, approvingly—his *Sermons* (1737) in 1797 and 1810: *CN* I 319–28, III 4003–4, 4008. C quoted South in an epigraph for *Friend* (*CC*) I 176.

18[1] I.e. **19** following.

tion—which he had learnt in the Schools when a Lad, and afterwards had heard and met with so often that he was not aware that he had never sifted its real purport— S. T. C.

19 III 107

In all love, three things are necessary. (1.) Some goodness in the object, either true and real, or apparent and seeming to be so; for the soul be it ever so evil, can affect nothing but what it takes some way to be good.*

* This assertion in these words has been so often made, from Plato's times to ours,[1] that even wise men repeat it without perhaps much examination whether it be not equivocal—or rather (I suspect) [a]true only in that sense in which it would amount to nothing—nothing to the purpose at least. This is to be regretted—for it is a mischievous equivoque, to make good a synonime of pleasant, or even the Genus of which Pleasure is a Species. It is a grievous mistake to say, that bad men seek pleasure because it is *good*—no! like children they call it good because it is pleasant.—Even the useful must derive its meaning from the good, not vice versâ.[2]

20 III 120, pencil | End of Sermon 8

Yet another most admirable Discourse.

21 III 121, pencil | Sermon 9, on Rom 8.7

The reasonable creature, it is true, hath more liberty in its actions, freely choosing one thing and rejecting another; yet it cannot be denied, that in acting of that liberty, their choice and refusal ∧ I follow the sway of their nature and condition.

VI.[1] l. 6 I would fain insert "are most often *determined*, and always *affected*, by the sway &c["]: I do not deny that the Will follows the Nature; but then the Nature itself is a Will.

19[a] Having begun his note at the foot of the page, C continues at the top of the page with a note, "(*continued from below*)"

19[1] E.g. in *Symposium* 205A–206A.

19[2] For C's attempt to discriminate the "useful" from the "pleasant", the "good", the "agreeable", etc, in 1811 see "Hints Respecting Beauty" in *SW & F* (*CC*) 277–80.

21[1] Not a volume-number, nor the number of the sermon. C's marginal marks are actually a caret and a roman "I"; he may have meant to repeat them here but have turned the caret over.

22 III 121, pencil | Continuing **21** textus

As the angels and glorified souls, (their nature being perfectly holy, and unalterably such) they cannot sin, they can delight in nothing but in obeying and praising that God, in the enjoyment of whom their happiness consisteth . . .

So the next sentence. If Angels be other than Spirits made perfect or as L. writes glorified Souls—the "unalterable by Nature" seems to me rashly asserted.

23 III 121, continued on blank leaf following III 68; pencil

The *mind* φνημα φρονημα Some render it the prudence or wisdom of the flesh. Here you have it, the carnal mind, but the word signifies, indeed, an act of the mind, rather than either the faculty itself, or the habit of prudence in it, so as it discovers what is the frame of both those. ?

I doubt.[a] Φρονημα signifies an *act*: and so far I agree with Leighton. But φρονημα σαρκος is "the Flesh" (i.e. the natural man) in the act or habit of minding—but those Acts taken collectively is the *Faculty*—the Understanding.[1]

How often have I found reason to regret, that L. had not clearly made out to himself the diversity of the Reason and the understanding.[2]

24 III 196, pencil | Sermon 15, on Ps 119.32

A narrow enthralled heart, fettered with love of lower things, and cleaving to some particular sins, or but some one, and that secret,* may keep foot a while in the way of God's commandments, in some steps of them; but it must give up quickly, is not able to run on to the end of the goal.

* One of the blessed privileges of the Spiritual Man (& such Leighton was) is a piercing insight into the diseases of which he himself is clear. Ελεεινε!—[1]

23[a] For want of space on the page, C here writes "See blank Leaf at the beginning" and starts over on the original flyleaf, now bound in facing III 68, with "P. 121."

23[1] The Greek phrase is from the text for this sermon, Rom 8.7—lit "the mind of the flesh" as C has it in *AR* (*CC*) 259* glossing "the understanding"; AV "the carnal mind", with marginal alternative "the minding of the flesh"; Art 9 of the Articles of Religion in BCP renders it as "the lust of the flesh". There is an extended discussion of the phrase as C found it in John WEBSTER *Displaying of Supposed Witchcraft* (1677) in *CN* IV 4618 (c Oct 1819); cf HOOKER **28**, LACUNZA **11**, LUTHER *Colloquia* **46**.

23[2] C published several explanations of this distinction, e.g. *SM* (*CC*) 59–62, *Friend* (*CC*) I 154–61, *AR* (*CC*) 216–32.

24[1] C uses the vocative of *eleeinos*,

25 III 204–5 | Sermon 16, on Rom 8.33–4

The great evidence of thy election is love. Thy love to him gives certain testimony of his preceding eternal love to thee, so are they here designed, they that love God; thy choosing him is the effect and evidence of his choosing thee. Now this is not labourious, that needs to be disputed, amidst all thy frailties; feel the pulse of thine affection, which way beats it, and ask thy heart whether thou love him or not, in this thou hast the character of thy election.

Know you not, that the redeemed of Christ and he are one, they live one life, Christ lives in them, and if *any man hath not the Spirit of Christ, he is none of his*, as the apostle declares in this chapter? So then, this we are plainly to tell you, and consider it, you that will not let go your sins to lay hold on Christ, have as yet no share in him.

*But on the other side: the truth is, that when souls are once set upon this search, they commonly wind the notion too high, and subtilize too much in the dispute, and so entangle and perplex themselves, and drive themselves further off from that comfort that they are seeking after; such measures and marks of grace, they set to themselves for their rule and standard; and unless they find those without all controversy in themselves, they will not believe that they have an interest in Christ, and this blessed and safe estate in him.

To such I would only say, are you in a willing league with any known sin?

* an admirable Antidote for such as too sober and sincere to pass off feverous sensations for Spiritual Realities have been perplexed by Wesley's Assertions—that a certainty of having been elected is an indispensable Mark of Election.[1] Whitfield's Ultra-Calvinism is Gospel Gentleness and Pauline Sobriety compared with Wesley's Arminianism in the outset of his Career.[2] [a]But the main and most noticeable Difference be-

25[a] Having begun at the foot of III 204 and continued at the foot of III 205, the note takes up again at the top of III 204 and ends at the top of III 205

which may be used either of one who *shows* pity, or of one who is *deserving* of pity. In this case, referring to Leighton, "[O] he who shows pity" implies also a plea for pity.

25[1] E.g. John Wesley *Sermons on Several Occasions* (1825) I 108 (Sermon 10): "It all resolves into this: Those who have these marks are children of God: But we have these marks: Therefore we are children of God." But cf SOUTHEY *Life of Wesley* (1820) I 295, II 181–2, where Wesley's retreat from this position is given in his own words.

25[2] C's views on the conventional contrast between Calvinism and Arminianism are expressed in **3** at n 3 above. For C's opinion of the differences between Wesley and Whitefield, the best source is his notes in SOUTHEY *Life of Wesley*, a book he reread (apparently several times) in the 1820s.

tween Leighton and the modern Methodists is to be found in the uniform *Self*ishness of the latter—Not do you wish to love God? Do you love your neighbour?—Do you think O how dear and lovely must Christ be—or—but are you certain, that Christ has saved *you*, that he died for *you*—*you*—you—you yourself—on to the end of the Chapter—this is *Wesley's* Doctrine.

26 IV ⁻5

Memorandum
In respect of the Latin and Greek Citations, the latter particularly, this (E. Middleton's) Edition is inferior to the rival Edition by Dr Jerment.[1] It is both more frequently and more grossly incorrect: so grossly indeed as to render it difficult even to conjecture the original words, and so frequently that speaking of the *Greek* Quotations I had almost said *always*. On the other hand, Dr Jerment's can boast only a *comparative* accuracy, the "*clauda gloria prœterire claudos*" (the lame glory of outrunning the Lame)[2] and the Paper, Type, Printing, and Frontispiece of this Edition are so strikingly superior, than[a] on the whole I give it the decided Preference.[3] Above all, in respect of the Portrait, which in this Edition may be supposed a resemblance, a *somewhat of a Likeness*, of the Arch-bishop; but which in Dr *Jerment's is a Libel, and in Mr Wilson's Selections[5] little less than Petty Blasphemy. S. T. Coleridge

* I speak of that in *four* Volumes. The Edition in Six Volumes and containing the original Latin of the Lectures &c[4] I have not yet seen.
16 Septr 1823.

27 IV 96–7 | Lecture 9 "Of the Pleasure and Utility of Religion"

For that this was his fixed purpose, Lucretius not only owns, but also boasts of it, and loads him [Epicurus] with ill-advised praises, for en-

26[a] For "that"

26[1] George Jerment's edition, *The Whole Works of Robert Leighton, D.D.* (4 vols 1820), was the one C used for *AR*: see LEIGHTON COPY C.

26[2] Proverbial. C uses the phrase also in W. WORDSWORTH "Translation of *Aeneid*" **34**.

26[3] See Plate 3 for the preferred frontispiece.

26[4] The Jerment ed that C used (see n 1) replaced an earlier version in 6 vols (1805–8), the final vol of which (1808) contained the Latin text of Leighton's theological lectures.

26[5] *Selections from the Works of Archbishop Leighton* ed W. Wilson (Oxford 1822). C made similarly disparaging remarks in a letter of 9 Sept 1823: *CL* v 203; cf *AR* (*CC*) xcvii n 163.

Freeman sc.
Robert Leighton, D.D.
late Arch Bishop of
Glasgow.
Ætat. 40-1654.
Pub. Nov. 1-1804 by W. Baynes, 54 Paternoster row.

3. Frontispiece portrait of the author from Robert Leighton
The Genuine Works I (1819). See ADDENDA LEIGHTON **26** and n 3
Victoria University Library, Toronto; reproduced by kind permission

deavouring, through the whole course of his philosophy, to free the minds of men from all the bonds and ties of religion* . . .

* But surely in *this* passage Religio must be rendered Superstition, the most effectual means for the removal of which Epicurus supposed himself to have found in the exclusion of the "Gods many and Lords many"[1] from their imagined agency in all the phænomena of Nature and the events of History, ~~con~~substituting for these the belief in fixed Laws, having in themselves their evidence and necessity. On *this* account, in *this* passage, Lucretius praises his Master.

28 IV 105 | Lecture 10 "Of the Decrees of God"

They always seemed to me to act a very ridiculous part, who contend, that the effect of the divine decree is absolutely irreconcilable with human liberty; because the natural and necessary liberty of a rational creature is to act or choose from a rational motive, or spontaneously, and of purpose; but who sees not, that, on the supposition of the most absolute decree, this liberty is not taken away, but rather established and confirmed? *For the decree is, that such an one shall make choice of, or do some particular thing freely. And, whoever pretends to deny, that whatever is done or chosen, whether good or indifferent, is so done or chosen, or, at least, may be so, espouses an absurdity.

* I fear, I fear, that this is a Sophism not worthy of Archb. Leighton! It seems to me tantamount to saying—I force that man to do so or so without my forcing him.—But however this may be, the following sentences[1] are more precious than Diamonds. They are *divine*.

29 IV 114, referring to IV 113–14

For, that this world, compounded of so many, and such heterogeneous parts, should proceed, by way of natural and necessary emanation, from that one first, purest, and most simple nature, nobody, I imagine, could believe, or in the least suspect: can it possibly be thought, that mortality should proceed from the immortal, corruption from the incorruptible,

27[1] C uses this phrase from 1 Cor 8.5 to characterise pagan polytheism, a form of "superstition" and not "religion" proper as he defines it, e.g. in COPY A **5**.

28[1] Continuing textus, pp 105–6: "But, in a word, the great difficulty in all this dispute is, that with regard to the *origin of evil*. Some distinguish, and justly, the substance of the action, as you call it, or that which is physicial in the action, from the morality of it. This is of some weight, but whether it takes away the whole difficulty, I will not pretend to say. Believe me, young gentleman, it is an abyss, it is an abyss never to be perfectly sounded by any plummet of human understanding."

and, what ought never to be so much as mentioned, even worms, the vilest animalcules, and most abject insects, from the best, most exalted, and most blessed Majesty? But, if he produced all these things freely, merely out of his good pleasure, and with the facility that constantly attends almighty power; how much more consistent is it to believe, that this was done in time, than to imagine it was from eternity?

It is a very difficult matter to argue at all about that, the nature whereof our most enlarged thoughts can never comprehend. And though, among philosophers and divines, it is disputed, whether such a production from eternity is possible or not; there is probably something concealed in the thing, though unknown to us, that might suggest a demonstration of the impossibility of this conceit . . .

It is inconceivable how any thing can be created in Time; and *production* is incompatible with interspace.[1]

30 IV 152–3 | Lecture 15 "Of Regeneration"

The Platonists divide the world into two, the sensible and intellectual world; they imagine the one to be the type of the other, and that sensible and spiritual things are stamped, as it were, with the same stamp or seal. These sentiments are not unlike the notions, which the masters of the cabalistical doctrine among the Jews, concerning God's *sephiroth* and seal, wherewith, according to them, all the worlds, and every thing in them, are stamped or sealed; and these are probably near akin to what Lord Bacon of Verulam calls his *parallela signacula* [corresponding marks], and *symbolizantes schematismi* [symbolic figures]. According to this hypothesis, these parables and metaphors, which are often taken from natural things to illustrate such as are divine, will not be similitudes taken entirely at pleasure; but are often, in a great measure, founded in nature, and the things themselves.*

* I have asserted the same thing, and more fully shewn wherein the difference consists of Symbolic and metaphorical, in my first Lay-sermon;[1] and the substantial correspondence of the genuine Platonic Doctrine and Logic with those of Lord Bacon, in my Essays on Method, FRIEND Vol. III.[2]
S. T. Coleridge

29[1] C makes the same point about the unthinkability of a creation in time in JACOBI *Ueber die Lehre* **19**.

30[1] *SM* (*CC*) 59–93 (App C), esp 79. The distinction between symbol and metaphor plays an important part in *AR* (*CC*) 205–6, 318–34.

30[2] *Friend* (*CC*) I 482–95.

31 IV 201 | Lecture 19 "That Holiness Is the Only Happiness on This Earth"

* Even the philosophers give their testimony to this truth, and their sentiments on the subject are not altogether to be rejected: for they, almost unanimously, are agreed, that felicity, so far as it can be enjoyed in this life, consists solely, or at least principally, in virtue: but as to their assertion, that this virtue is perfect in a perfect life, it is rather expressing what were to be wished, than describing things as they are.

* And why are the Philosophers to be judged according to a different rule? On what ground can it be asserted that the Stoics believed in the actual existence of their God-like Perfection in any Individual? Or that they meant more than this—~~No~~ To no man can the name of the Wise be given in its absolute sense who is not perfect even as his Father in Heaven is perfect?[1]

32 IV 225 | Lecture 21 "Of the Divine Attributes"

In like manner, if we suppose God to be the first of all beings, we must, unavoidably, therefrom, conclude his unity: as to the ineffable Trinity subsisting in this Unity, a mystery discovered only by the sacred scriptures, especially in the New Testament, where it is more clearly revealed than in the Old, let others boldly pry into it, if they please, while we receive it with an humble faith, and think it sufficient for us to admire and adore.

But surely, it having been revealed to us, we may venture to say—that a positive Unity, so far from excluding, implies plurality: and that the Godhead is a fulness = πληρωμα.[1]

33 IV 245 | Lecture 24 "Before the Communion"

Ask yourselves, therefore, <u>what you would be at</u>, and with what dispositions you come to this most sacred table?

In an age of colloquial Idioms, when to write in a loose Slang had become a mark of Loyalty (see Barrow's Works, as often as the dignity of his thoughts and the precise accuracy of his language, rendered it possible) this is the only *Sir R. L'estrange* vulgarism, I have met in Leighton.[1]

31[1] The last clause echoes Matt 5.48.

32[1] "Pleroma", "fulness", occurring 12 times in AV; cf C's use in LEIGHTON COPY C **50**, IRVING *Sermons* **55** at n 4.

33[1] C associated slangy prose with Sir Roger l'Estrange (1616–1704), who he believed had introduced slang into English literature: AURELIUS **62**.

34 IV 252 | "An Exhortation to the Students, upon their return to the University after the Vacation"

Study to acquire such a philosophy as is not barren and babbling, but solid and true; not such an one as floats upon the surface of endless verbal controversies, but one that enters into the nature of things; for he spoke good sense, that said, "The philosophy of the Greeks was a mere jargon, and noise of words."

If so, then so is all Philosophy: for what System is there, the elements and Outlines of which are not to be found in the Greek Schools? Here L. followed too incautiously the Fathers.

35 IV 442 | "A Sermon, Preached to the Clergy"

For these incongruous honours, to speak it in a word, raising some from contempt, teach them to contemn and insult over their brethren; to say nothing of their affronting of higher quality, yea, of princes and kings themselves, while they pretend to be the only supporters of their crowns. And if this their insolency in advancement devolve them back again into contempt, and their honour become their shame, they may thank themselves for it.

I fancy that ⟨(had he been present at the preaching of this Sermon)⟩ Archbishop Laud would have glared on Archbishop Leighton with much the same sweet expression as Archangel Satan did on Archangel Michael over the Body of Moses.[1]

36 IV 463 | Letter 3

. . . and though . . . this base clod of earth I carry still depresses me, I am glad that even because it does so, I loathe and despise it; and would say, major sum et ad majora genitus, quam ut mancipium sum <u>reles corpusculis</u> [I am greater and born to greater things than being the slave <u>reles corpusculis</u>].

? vilis corpusculi.[1]

35[1] A playful allusion to Jude 1.9: "Yet Michael the archangel, when contending with the devil he disputed about the body of Moses, durst not bring against him a railing accusation, but said, The Lord rebuke thee."

36[1] C suspects a typographical error, since the last two words of Leighton's text make no sense. Leighton's Latin means, "I am greater and born to greater things than being the slave . . ."—but the final phrase *reles corpusculis* is nonsense. C suggests "of a worthless little body".

37 IV 463

The one is of a good pen, and an acquaintance and friend of yours, *Paulus Nolone~~d~~us*, and his Life of Martin of Towers I think you will relish . . .

Tours[1]

38 IV 465 | Letter 4

I thank you for the notice of your capuchin; but I almost knew that he was not here before I looked.* It is true the variety of his book refreshes us, and by the happy wording, the same things not only please, but sometimes profit us; but they tell us no new thing, except it may be some such thing as, I confess, I understand not, of essential unions and sleeps of the soul; which because I understand them not, would rather disorder and hinder than advance me; and therefore I begin to be unwilling to look over these and such like, unless I could pick out here and there such things as I am capable of, and not meet with those steep ascents which I dare not venture on: But dear *a-Kempis* is a way to it, and oh! that I could daily study more and attain more sublime humble devotion there drawn to the life . . .

* It would be interesting to know, which work of the mystic writers Leighton speaks of.

Annex

C appended the following note (without textus) in his own hand, to Watson's MS TRANSCRIPT of some of the notes in COPY B: VCL S MS F 2.2. Although no specific page is indicated in C's note, he might have had in mind such a passage as the following.

A IV 214 | Lecture 20 "Of Our Happiness . . ."

It would be quite silly to ascribe to the church a decisive power, as if, when a book were first presented to it, or brought out of any place, where it had been long concealed, it could immediately pronounce whether that book was a divine authority or not. The church is only a witness with regard to these books we acknowledge, and its testimony extends no farther than that they were received, in the first ages of Christianity, as sacred and divinely inspired, and as such handed down from age to age, to the church that now is; and he that would venture to discredit this testimony, must have a heart of lead, and a face of brass.

There is no occasion to dispute so fiercely about the inward testimony of the

37[1] The text is corrupt and C has made an attempt to correct it, but the reference is probably to St Paulinus, bp of Nola (Paulus Nolanus, c 353–431), who knew St Martin of Tours and corresponded with his biographer, Sulpicius Severus. In that case, Leighton's phrase "acquaintance and friend" would not be meant to be taken literally.

Holy Ghost: for I am persuaded that those who talk about it, understand nothing more by it, than that the Holy Spirit produces, in the hearts of men, that faith whereby they cheerfully and sincerely receive these books, and the doctrine contained in them, as divine; because such a faith either includes, in the very notion of it, or at least is necessarily connected with, a religious frame of the mind, and a sincere disposition to universal obedience.

It is certain that the Fathers of the Latin Church to the time of Jerom gave the name of canonical and ~~extended~~ the attribute of inspiration to all the Books, "which the use of God's Church approved as profitable, and containing matter of good instruction["]—for instance, the Book of Wisdom—.[1] On the other hand the Greek Fathers did not unanimously receive all those found in the Hebrew—ex. gr. the Book of Esther. And tho' Origen, as might be expected from his great Learning, and ~~the~~ other Greek Fathers following his authority, paid greater attention to the difference between the Books existing in Hebrew, and those either written in Greek, or now extant only in Greek Translations from the Hebrew, yet I do not find that they confined the notion of inspiration to the Hebrew Canon exclusively/ And even if they had attributed a higher grade of inspiration to this than to the Wisdom and Ecclesiasticus, yet let it not be forgotten that different degrees, nay *sorts*, of Inspiration were affirmed of different parts of the Hebrew Scriptures—: Inspiration κατ' εξοχην[2] to the Pentateuch—a somewhat inferior to the Prophets—and a lower to the Hagiographa—: indeed so much lower, that Philo assigns little more to the Historians and Sententiaries than he claims for parts of his own Writings[3]—⟨In what sense the Scriptures are the Rule of our Faith, see Field p. 365, whose authority, I see, bears me out in my assertion of the necessity of a right Idea of God as an antecedent Criterion/ "the infinite excellency of God as that whereby the truth of the heavenly doctrine is proved".⟩[4]

ANNEX A[1] Richard Field *Of the Church* (1635) 381. C's account of the biblical canon here is taken from Field bk 4 chs 22–4; cf C's annotated FIELD in *CM* (*CC*) II.

ANNEX A[2] "Eminently".

ANNEX A[3] The chapters of Field that C drew upon for this note do not contain the reference to Philo Judaeus. C had extensive knowledge of scholarly debates about the canon: see e.g. BIBLE *Apocrypha* **4** n 4, KANT *Religion* **3** at nn 14–17.

ANNEX A[4] Field begins with the phrase quoted by C but goes on to other "rules": "Thus then we see, how many things, in severall degrees and sorts, are said to be rules of our faith. The infinite excellency of God, as that whereby the truth of the heavenly doctrine is proved. The articles of faith, and other verities even knowne in the Church, as the first principles, are the canon, by which wee judge of conclusions from thence inferred. The Scripture, as containing in it all that doctrine of faith, which *Christ* the Sonne of God delivered. The uniform practice, and consenting judgement of them that went before us, as a certaine and undoubted explication, of the things contayned in the Scripture."

PIETRO METASTASIO
1698–1782

Opere di Pietro Metastasio. 12 vols. London 1782–3. 12°.

Victoria College Library (Coleridge Collection)

Inscribed "Ellen Coleridge 1861" on I $^{-}$2, "S. T. Coleridge" (not in C's hand) on V title-page. The vols were rebound at some point after C made his notes, and several of the notes were cropped in the process. The binding itself is tight, with some loss of legibility where the notes run into the gutter.

Someone—surely not C—at some point went through the footnotes to these vols carefully crossing through "v." (for Italian *verso*—"verse") in references to the Bible. These cancellations have not been recorded.

A large group of notes in pencil, all apparently in the same neat hand but most of them so brief that it is not possible to be absolutely certain, simply provide English translations for isolated words in the Italian text: these occur on I 7, 14, 33, 60, 90, 93, 99, 111, 113, 122, 123, 195, 291; II 19; VI 13; VII [101], 102, 103; IX 88, 142, 187. Several of these are certainly not in C's hand, and since the practice of such glossing also is not customary for him, the group as a whole is not presented here.

Passages are marked with pencilled crosses, short horizontal lines, curved lines or braces on I 22, 60, 165, 291, 297, 298; II 12, 49, 103, 210, 212; IX 144, 168, 169. The curved line and the brace in this form (a figure "3" or a backwards "3") are not usual in C's books, and this group is therefore also assumed to be the work of another reader.

What seems to be the offset and illegible trace of a pencilled note appears at the top of XII 121, but there is no corresponding note (or impression in the paper) on XII 120.

CONTENTS. I 1–108 *Artaserse*, 109–204 *Adriano in Siria*, 205–320 *Demetrio*, 321–44 *Il Sogno di Scipione*, 345–70 *Il Natal di Giove*, 371–8 *La Danza*; II 1–108 *Olimpiade*, 109–202 *Issipile*, 203–314 *Ezio*, 315–50 *L'Isola Disabitata*, 351–76 *Le Cinesi*, 377–88 *Il Vero Omaggio*, 389–400 *L'Amor Prigioniero*, 401–6 *Il Ciclope*; III 1–100 *Didone Abbandonata*, 101–208 *La Clemenza di Tito*, 209–316 *Siroe*, 317–48 *L'Asilo d'Amore*, 349–72 *La Pace fra la Virtù, e la Bellezza*, 373–86 *Le Grazie Vendicate*; IV 1–142 *Catone in Utica*, 143–250 *Demofoonte*, 251–342 *Alessandro nell'Indie*, 343–80 *Il Tempio dell'Eternità*, 381–404 *La Contesa de' Numi*, 405–18 *Il Sogno*; V 1–102 *Achille in Sciro*, 103–224 *Ciro Riconosciuto*, 225–328 *Temistocle*, 329–46 *Il Palladio Conservato*, 347–68 *Il Parnaso Accusato, e Difeso*, 369–92 *Astrea Placata*, 393–439

Sonetti, e Canzonette; VI 1–92 *Zenobia*, 93–172 *Ipermestra*, 173–264 *Antigono*, 265–310 *Gioas Re di Giuda*, 311–52 *Betulia Liberata*, 353–81 *Sant'Elena al Calvario*; VII 1–98 *Semiramide*, 99–169 *Il Re Pastore*, 169–244 *L'Eroe Cinese*, 245–84 *Giuseppe Riconosciuto*, 285–326 *La Morte d'Abel*, 327–46 *La Passione di Gesù Cristo*, 347–66 *Per la Festività del Santo Natale*, 367–406 *Isacco, Figura del Redentore*; VIII 1–92 *Attilio Regolo*, 93–188 *Nitteti*, 189–230 *Alcide al Bivio*, 231–94 *Epitalami*, 295–304 *La Strada della Gloria*, 305–26 *Egeria*, 327–50 *Il Parnaso Confuso*, 351–92 *Cantate*; IX 1–84 *Il Trionfo di Clelia*, 85–160 *Romolo, ed Ersilia*, 161–244 *Il Ruggiero*, 245–70 *Il Trionfo d'Amore*, 271–90 *I Voti Pubblici*, 291–308 *La Pubblica Felicità*, 309–66 *Partenope*, 367–75 *La deliziosa Imperial Residenza di Schönbrunn*; X [1–2] Avvertimento, [3–4] Avviso del Bettinelli, 5–40 *La Galatea*, 41–80 *Gli Orti Esperidi*, 81–104 *Il Convito degli Dei*, 105–48 *L'Endimione*, 149–58 *La Morte di Catone*, 159–66 *L'Origine delle Leggi*, 167–82 *Il Ratto d'Europa*, 183–8 *Pe'l Santo Natale*, 189–236 *L'Angelica*, 237–336 *Giustino*, 337–72 *Lettere sopra la Musica*, 373–82 *Lettera sul Tasso, e l'Ariosto*; XI [1] Avviso, 3–50 *L'Atenaide*, 51–82 *Traduzione della Satira III. di Giovenale*, 83–98 *Teti, e Pelèo*, 99–112 *La Ritrosia Disarmata*, 113–40 *La Corona*, 141–54 *L'Ape*, 155–70 *Satira VI. del Libro secondo di Q. Orazio Flacco*, 171–80 *La Gara*, 181–8 *Tributo di Rispetto, e d'Amore*, 189–96 *La Rispettosa Tenerezza*, 197–202 *Augurio di Felicità*, 203–24 *La Pace fra le tre Dee*, 225–30 *Invito a Cena d'Orazio a Torquato*, 231–3 *L'Inverno*, 234 *Madrigale*, 235–6 *Riposta ad Orazio*, 238 *Versetti*, 239–44 *Il Quadro Animato*, 245–8 *Complimento*, 249–52 *Canzonetta*, 253–7 *Complimento*, 258 *Complimento*, 259–60 *Primo Omaggio di Canto*, 261–2 *Complimento*, 263–4 *La Virtuosa Emulazione*, 265 *La Scommessa*, 266 *Complimento*, 267 *Complimento*, 268 *Complimento*, 269–70 *L'Aurora*, 271–2 *L'Estate*, 273–4 *Complimento*, 275–7 *L'Armonica*, 278–80 *Strofette*, 281–7 *Sonetti*, 288–9 *Traduzione del di contro Epigramma*, 290–8 *Strofe per Musica da Cantarsi a Canone*, 299–344 *Indice delle Arie, Cori, e Duetti*; XII 1–322 *Estratto dell'Arte Poetica di Aristotile*, 323–70 *Dell'Arte Poetica, Epistola di Q. Orazio Flacco a Pisoni*, 371–427 *Annotazioni alla Poetica di Q. Orazio Flacco*, 433–40 Tavola generale, 441–4 Ordine cronologico con cui furono scritte le seguenti Opere.

TEXTUS TRANSLATION. Konrad Eisenbichler.

DATE. After 1806, when C returned from Italy; perhaps c 1810–12. Though he had read some Metastasio before, it was not in this London ed: *CN* II 2184, 2224, 3190 and nn. On the other hand, later public references are quite independent of these notes: *BL* ch 22 (*CC*) II 122, *Lects 1808–1819* (*CC*) II 118.

1 VII 22–3, cropped | *Semiramide* I v

IRCANO. E il Re qual dritto
Ha di frapporre a' miei cortesi affetti
O limiti, o dimore?

TAMIRI. Che! Tu conosci amore? Il tuo piacere
E' domar combattendo uomini, e fere.
IRCANO. E' ver; ma il tuo sembiante
Non mi spiace però: godo in mirarti;
E curioso il guardo
Più dell'usato intorno a te s'arresta.

[IRCANO. And what right does the King
have to place either limits or stays
to my courteous affections?
TAMIRI. What! You know love? Your pleasure
lies in conquering in battle men and beasts.
IRCANO. It is true; but your face,
however, does not displease me: I enjoy admiring you;
and, curious, my gaze
stops more than it is accustomed upon you.]

The Italian Critics themselves admit this *Ircano* to be a very insufferable sort of Gentleman because, forsooth, he is not dignified enough—not (for the true reason) because it is a stupid Abortion of Dullness from Timidity. Metastasio had not courage, if he had power, to present a rude, half-wise Savage

2 VII 50–2, cropped | End of II ii

I could not have believed, that M. could have written, or even an an[a] Austrian Court-Audience have [. . . . .][b] the whole Play is the worst in [the] collection—a continued untrag[ic] improbability (but that is a trifle[)] [. . . . .][c] sacred human [. . .]veed[d] up her own Child to effeminacy [and] loathsomeness, in order to usurp his Throne & gratify her own passions![1]

3 VII 66–7, slightly cropped | End of II ix

There is something absolutely shocking to my moral feelings (& has been so from [e]arliest youth) in a man's continuing to woo a woman, after proofs of her contempt. What does ~~s~~he wish? her body?—Love without Love ~~can n~~ is a contradiction—it is an hypocrite Lust. Yet Novels & Plays swarm with these situations.

2[a] Word repeated at turn of line
2[b] At least one line lost through cropping at the bottom of VII 50
2[c] Two or three words lost through cropping
2[d] It is possible that a line has been completely lost through cropping before this word, the first on VII 52

2[1] The opening scenes of the play show Semiramis masquerading as her son Ninus (who remains hidden in the palace) in order to reign in Assyria.

4 VII 71 | End of Act II

O de~~s~~testable/ verily it is αμαρτημα κατα φυσιν[1] in an evil kind!

5 VII 77, slightly cropped | III i

SIBARI *solo*. Quell'ira, ch'io destai,
Molto giovar mi può. Scitalce estinto
Dal timor mi difende
Ch'ei palesi il mio foglio;
E di lei, che m'accende,
Un'inciampo mi toglie al letto, al foglio.
Questa dolce lusinga
Di delitto in delitto, oh Dio! mi guida.
Ma il rimorso or che giova?
Quando il primo è commesso,
Necessario diventa ogni altro eccesso.
Or che sciolta è già la prora,
Sol si pensi a navigar.
Quando fu nel porto ancora,
Era bello il dubitar.

[SIBARI *alone*. That wrath, which I awoke,
can help me greatly. Scitalce, dead,
keeps me from fearing
that he may disclose what is on my page;
and he removes a stumbling block from the bed and door
of her for whom I burn.
This sweet enticement
leads me, oh God! from crime to crime.
But of what benefit is remorse now?
Once the first [crime] is committed
every subsequent excessive act becomes inevitable.
Now that the bow is already set loose,
let us think only of sailing forth.
While it still lay in port,
it was a pleasure to think [about this].]

Sibari—Iago—I feel the blasphemy of joining the nam[es] yet the Italians—phoo!—Mr Fox dare—*prefer* Metastasio to—no [. . .] that name I dare not [? write][1]

4[1] "Crime against nature".

5[1] The name must be Shakespeare, *Othello*'s Iago being likened to Metastasio's villainous Sibari. Charles James Fox (1749–1806) was a colourful and cultivated politician, and anecdotes about his tastes and interests circulated during and after his lifetime. C gives a version of a story told also

6 VII 98–9, cropped | End of *Semiramide*

It would be unjust and cruel to Judge of Metastasio by this Drama/ Surely, the Subject must have been forced upon him by royal command—and yet he cannot wholly be acquitted. Such hateful outrages has he committed on the [. . . . .][a] gross violations of historic probability & Asiatic[b] Customs I leave out of the Question. These are mino[r] faults—yet one would suppose th[at] instead of a [? crowd] of ~~of~~ Babylonic Courts she were before an Atheni[an] Agora—or parliament of Democr[ats][c]

7 VII 244–6, cropped | End of *L'Eroe Cinese*

L'Eroe Cinese

The superfluity of surprizes, & reverses make this up and down, down and up Drama somewhat ridiculous, which with greater temperance would have been, and but for this defect is, an interesting Plot interestingly devel[. . . . .][a] narrated in elegant Dialogues—this is the Italian Ideal of the Drama, and after this Ideal Metastasio's Works are Master-pie[ces.] Doubtless, they approach nearer to t[he] Idea than those of any other athe[. . .] but the Idea is poor, hungry, meagre. A Poet must have lived among the poor human sacrifices, [th]e Voces et præterea nihil,[1] in [or]der to have a mind sufficiently [e]ffeminated to have been enabled [to] realize[b] this so excellently well, & [y]et have been content to aim at [n]othing higher.— S. T. C.

8 VII 293–6, cropped | *La Morte d'Abel*

ABEL. Più gradito comando
Eseguir non potrei. Quanto m'è cara
La mia greggia fedel, madre, tu sai.
Sai tu quanto tormento,

6[a] The bottom of the page is cropped, with the loss of at least one line

6[b] After this word another word has been completely crossed out—possibly not by C or not at the time of writing

6[c] This appears to be the last word of the note: it is followed by a horizontal line, in ink, across the bottom of the page

7[a] End of word and remainder of line lost in cropping of VII 244

7[b] "realize" replaces another word completely crossed out

by Samuel Rogers (whom C knew) and pub in *Recollections of the Table-Talk of Samuel Rogers* (1856) 90–1, following Fox's dismissal of Milton: "He thought so highly of the *Isacco* of Metastasio, that he considered it as one of the four most beautiful compositions produced during the century; the other three being Pope's *Eloisa to Abelard*, Voltaire's *Zaire*, and Gray's *Elegy*."

7[1] "Voices and nothing more". C adapts a tag from Plutarch *Moralia* 233A, as in KLUGE **28** at n 2.

Quanto sudor mi costa, ed io no'l sento.
Quel buon pastor son'io,
Che tanto il gregge apprezza;
Che per la sua salvezza
Offre se stesso ancor.
Conosco ad una ad una
Le mie dilette agnelle;
E riconoscon quelle
Il tenero pastor.

[ABEL. A more welcome order
I could not carry out. You know, Mother,
how dear my faithful herd is to me.
You know how much torment,
how much sweat it costs me, and I feel it not.
I am that good shepherd,
that the herd greatly appreciates;
who, for its salvation
offers even himself.
I know one by one
my dear little lambs;
and they recognise
the tender shepherd.]

Never to be sure was a worse *Example*[a] chosen. That Abel, the Emblem of Pastoral Life—a state, in which the fetters of Property are light and golden, should be the Innocent[—]and that Cain—emblem of Agriculture[—]which introduces & supposes Cities, Lan[d] boundaries, avarice & inequality,—sho[uld] be the first Murderer—is a fine [. . . . .][b] *men* [ar]e presented [in]dividually, to bring in an innocent Abel, [w]ho has just been butchering his Lambs, [? no]t no purpose (for they did eat Flesh, it [s]eems)—and a bloody Cain offering [. . .]acts & grains on his grassy altar—is [. . . . .][c] the poetic Vision—the dichterische *Anschauung*.[1]

S. T. C.

N.B. It would be no bad theological Conceit to suppose, that Cain was conceived in the Interval of the Fall and the Penitence, in the first love-

8[a] "*Example*" replaces another word completely crossed out

8[b] The bottom of the page is cropped, with the loss of at least one line

8[c] Two or three words lost in cropping

8[1] C translates the phrase himself—"the poetic Vision"—but is perhaps using it in a negative form and arguing that the Abel who presents himself as a loving shepherd should not be shown (as he is) coming proudly from the sacrifice of his best lamb. For a set of cross-references to the significance of the term *Anschauung* in C's work generally, see FICHTE *Bestimmung* **9** n 3.

less Lust—Abel, after Peniten[ce,] when Love consented to dwell with [h]is negro *Lettersake*,[2] and with the [?s/n]ame gave origin to us poor Mulattoes.

9 VII 298–9, cropped

ANGELO. So che vuoi dirmi.
No, non è vero. Il tuo peccato è sempre
Soggetto a te: tu dominar lo puoi
Con libero poter. L'arbitro sei
Tu di te stesso; e questo arbitrio avesti,
Perchè una scusa al tuo fallir non resti.
Con gli astri innocenti,
Col fato ti scusi;
Ma senti che abusi
Di tua libertà.
E copri con questa
Sognata catena
Un dono, che pena
Per l'empio fi fa.

[ANGELO. I know what you wish to tell me.
No, it is not true. Your sin is always
subject to you: you can be its master
with [your] free will. You are your own
arbiter over yourself; and this power was given to you
so that there be no excuse for your failing.
With the innocent stars,
with Fate you excuse yourself;
but you know that you abuse
your own freedom.
And you cover with this
imagined chain
a gift, which becomes
an affliction for the wicked.]

OH! it is too bad!—Unlaughable absurdity is a torment. Whatever is lawless, & unnatural, must be either ridiculous, or painful. [. . . . .][a] refuge of Nature, followed by a Satyr, & escaping by a Metamorphosis.

9[a] The bottom of the page is cropped, with the loss of at least one line

8[2] I.e. Lust, which begins with the same letter as Love. C conceives of the two as opposites, white and black (hence "negro") mythologically speaking, but as united in actuality ("us poor Mulattoes").

10 XII 24, pencil, cropped | *Estratto dell'Arte Poetica d'Aristotile* ch 1

Convien quì stabilire (e si proverà poi più prolissamente) che la circostanza essenziale, che distingue l'imitazione del Poeta da tutte le altre imitazioni, *è la misurata, armoniosa favella, con la quale i primi uomini inventori della poesia, inclinati per natura al canto, ed alla imitazione, hanno imitato, cantando, il semplice parlar naturale. E che questa lingua canora divenne il materiale necessario e distinto, con cui l'imitator Poeta fa poi le altre sue imitazioni, come lo statuario col marmo, ed il pittor co' colori. E che senza la favella canora non avrebbe la poesia alcun proprio distintivo: poichè le invenzioni, e l'espressione de' caratterì, degli affetti, e de' costumi non sono sue qualità private, ma comuni alla pittura, alla scoltura, e ad altre arti imitatrici.*

[It is necessary to establish here (and this will be proven at greater length later on) that the essential characteristic that distinguishes a Poet's imitation from all other imitation *is the measured, harmonious speech with which the first people who invented poetry, inclined by nature to song and imitation, imitated, with song, simple natural speech. And that this musical language became the necessary and specific material with which the imitating Poet then creates his other imitations, just as a sculptor [does] with marble or a painter with colours. And that without musical speech poetry would have nothing distinctive of its own: since inventions and the description of characters, feelings, and habits are not its own particular qualities, but common to painting, sculpture, and to other imitative arts.*]

This whole dispute origina[?tes] in the rage of *distinguishing*[.] Poetry belongs [to] all the arts, [. . . ?ulp] only [? to] [? g]raphic, and [m]etrical [P]oetry.

11 XII 25–6, pencil, cropped

Nulla di comune v' è fra Omero, ed Empedocle, a riserva del Metro; onde Poeta dee quello giustamente chiamarsi, e questo piuttosto Fisico, che Poeta (1). [*Footnote:*] (1) Οὐδὲν δὲ κοινόν εστιν Ὁμήρῳ καὶ Εμπεδοκλεῖ, πλὴν τὸ μέτρον· διὸ τὸν ποιητὴν δίκαιον καλεῖν. τὸν δὲ φυσιολόγον μᾶλλον ἢ ποιήτην. Aristot. Poet. Cap. I, Tom. IV, p. 2.

[(Metastasio gives an Italian translation and the Greek original from Aristotle *Poetics* 1447b:) Homer and Empedocles, however, have really nothing in common apart from their metre; so that if the one is to be called a poet, the other should be termed a physicist rather than a poet (Greek tr I. Bywater).]

If the first *senten*[*ce*] be true, [the] last is inevita[ble.] In Homer there is [? pa . . .] and images and thought and expressions of Feeling produce[?d] following each other according to the nature of passion tempered by pleasu[re.] If Empedocles have not this, he ~~is~~ was no [. . . . .] Aristotle

falsely [. . . . .][a] [be]tween him and Homer [. . .] [es]sential to Poetry is ⟨possessed⟩ in common

12 XII 30, pencil, cropped

Onde, se poi, per correr dietro al maggior verisimile, ad onta dell'impegno già preso, egli avvilisce lo stile; cade nell'error puerile d'uno sconsigliato Scultore, che, per dare alle sue statue maggior somiglianza col vero, s'avvisasse di colorirne il marmo, o le fornisse d'occhi di vetro.

[As a result, if then, in order to chase after greater similitude, in spite of the commitment already undertaken, he weakens the style; he falls into the childish error of the heedless sculptor who, in order to give his statues greater similitude with reality, takes it upon himself to paint the marble or to furnish them with glass eyes.]

An utterly misapplied Simile—He who is to keep up a mock dignity, [? burlesques] mean things by pompous language, he[?ars] not the true Voice of nature, [? singes] the Statue, & puts glass eyes in its head.

13 XII 31, pencil, cropped | End of ch 1

La favella sempre grande, sempre ornata, e sempre sonora di Virgilio, di Torquato, han riportata fin'ora, e riporteranno eternamente la maggior parte de' voti, mercè quel difficile, e perciò mirabile uso, che hanno essi saputo farne nell'imitar la natura. E che che dicano, o abbian saputo dire molti de' nostri per altro eruditissimi Critici, per farci venerare come esquisiti tratti di maestra imitazione le frequenti bassezze, le negligenze, le ineguaglianze, le mancanze d'eleganza e d'armonia, e la fastidiosa copia delle licenze, che s'incontrano in alcuni, eccellenti nel resto, così moderni, come antichi Poeti; non giungerà mai a costringere il buon senso universale a compiacersi degli errori, nè a contar fra i pregi i difetti.

[The always grand, always adorned, and always sonorous speech of Virgil, of Torquato [Tasso], have till now received, and will forever receive, the greater number of votes thanks to that difficult, and therefore admirable, use that they have been able to make of it in imitating nature. And whatever many of our otherwise most learned critics have said, or have been able to say, in order to make us venerate as exquisite strokes of masterful imitation the frequent base elements, negligences, inequalities, lack of elegance and harmony, and the bothersome surplus of licence, that are found in some otherwise most excellent poets, both modern and ancient, will never be enough to compel universal good sense to be satisfied with errors, nor to count the defects among the merits.]

11[a] The bottom of the page is cropped, with the loss of at least one line

This i[s] bully[?ing] not rea[son.] Big assert[ions] & appea[ls] to the Mob[a] are they negligences, vulgarities[,] inequalities in rebus equalibus,[1] &[c] &c—Besides, it is false t[hat] the greater number of Readers have voted thus in reality?[b] [. . .], they do not like Poetry because they have been taught to consider a [. . . . .], i.e., [. . . . .] its diction as poetry—but (they [? would reply] [. . .][c]

13[a] This word may have been followed by a full stop or a linking word, but the margin is cropped

13[b] C often forms a question mark where one would expect an exclamation mark

13[c] The bottom of the page is cropped, with the loss of at least one line

13[1] "Among equal things".

APPENDIX

SOME MISTAKEN ATTRIBUTIONS

SOME MISTAKEN ATTRIBUTIONS

The following is a list of works that have been erroneously described as containing annotations by Coleridge. It aims to settle notorious disputed claims, not to present an exhaustive catalogue. The works on this list have been examined personally by one or other of the editors. Neither "lost books" (books plausibly reported as containing C's notes, but lost to sight) nor "ms facsimiles" (books containing transcriptions from attested originals in C's hand) are included in the list, since they can be found in their places in the alphabetical series of the *Marginalia*. "Marked books" (containing only an inscription, a signature or an ownership label) are omitted as not actually containing marginalia.

[Bentham, Jeremy.] *Not Paul, but Jesus. By Gamaliel Smith, Esquire.* London 1823. University College, London: Ogden 578. The notes are not in C's hand nor in his style; there is no evidence that he ever read the work.

Bowles, William Lisle. *The Spirit of Discovery; or, The Conquest of Ocean.* Bath 1804. Duke University Library: Tr.R. 821.69 B787S. The notes are not in C's hand and there is no good reason to associate them with him.

Browne, Sir Thomas. *Religio Medici.* London 1831. McGill University Library: Osler Collection. The notes are not in C's hand and do not appear to have been of his composition; some are dated as late as 1840.

Bruno, Giordano. *De monade, numero et figura* [*etc*]. Frankfurt 1591. Oxford: Bodleian Library 8° B 143 Art. This copy belonged to Robert Burton. It contains a few marked passages but no notes.

Coleridge, Hartley. *The Worthies of Yorkshire and Lancashire.* Pt 1. London & Leeds 1832. Interleaved copy of Pt 1 "The Life of Andrew Marvell", with copious notes and addenda. Harvard University Library: 19478.135. The notes alleged to be C's are not in his hand and appear to be editorial revisions.

Cunningham, Allan. *The Lives of the Most Eminent British Painters, Sculptors, and Architects.* Vol I (of 6). London 1829. BM: C 61 d 3. The marginalia are not by C but by HC.

Euclid. *The Elements of Euclid.* Ed Robert Simson, M.D. 5th ed. Edinburgh 1775. Whereabouts unknown. This book was withdrawn from a Sotheby's sale of 25–7 June 1956 (Lot 327) in spite of documented testimonials to its having been C's copy from his Cambridge days, when the hand was declared to be certainly not C's and the notes proved to be written on paper watermarked 1812.

Francis, Sir Philip. *A Letter Missive . . . to Lord Holland.* London 1816. BM: C 126 i 3 (3). Although it is now bound with several other tracts some of which are annotated by C, these notes are not in his hand and there is no evidence to suggest that the pamphlet belonged to him.

Helvétius, Claude Adrien. *De l'esprit.* Paris [Liège] 1759. Oxford: Bodleian Library Walpole e 1035. Bookplate of JHG; ex libris Arthur Symons. Brief note not in C's hand.

Horace. *Opera.* Glasgow & London 1796. University of Birmingham Library (Heslop Room): PA 6393 A2. None of the notes—most of them typical student glosses—is in C's hand.

Milton, John. [*Poems.*] Two odd vols, the first *Paradise Lost* (London 1751), the second lacking a title-page but containing *Paradise Regained, Samson Agonistes, Poems upon Several Occasions, Sonnets,* and *Psalms.* BM: C 61 a 5, 5*. CL's copy, with his and his sister Mary's notes in ink and pencil; some rubbed-out pencil notes apparently also theirs; and a series of notes glossing the text. The last have been thought to be in C's hand, but are not, nor are they the sort of note he habitually wrote.

Paracelsus. *Opera omnia.* Geneva 1658. Library of the Royal College of Surgeons. The notes are not in C's hand.

Priestley, Joseph. *Hartley's Theory of the Human Mind, on the Principle of the Association of Ideas.* 2nd ed. London 1790. Johns Hopkins University, Milton S. Eisenhower Library. The one substantive note and the markings in this copy are not in C's hand and there is nothing in the provenance of the book to link it to him.

Sachs, Hans. *Sehr herrliche schöne und wahrhafte Gedicht Fabeln und gute Schwenk.* Nuremberg 1781. BM: C 43 b 3. Although they are in C's hand, the notes in this copy are not marginalia but a transcription of Sachs's poems from another edition, together with a couplet from Shakespeare's *Troilus and Cressida,* the whole written originally on a separate sheet of paper and later tipped in.

Scholz, Johann Martin Augustin. *Solemnia natalitia regis augustissimi ac potentissimi Friderici Guilelmi III.* Bonn 1825. BM: C 44 g 4 (4). Al-

though this pamphlet is bound with others annotated by C, the single note is not in his hand.

Scriptores de re rustica. 5 pts in 2 vols. Paris 1543. Cornell University Library: Wordsworth Collection. This book belonged to WW. The notes are not in C's hand.

Selden, John. *Seldeniana.* London 1721. NYPL: Berg Collection. The notes are transcriptions, probably from *LR*, of C's notes on Selden—i.e., a posthumous ms facsimile.

Smedley, Edward. *Religio Clerici: A Churchman's First Epistle.* 3rd ed rev. London 1819. Duke University Library (Rare Books Dept.). The notes are not in C's hand and there is no reason to associate the work with him.

Swedenborg, Emanuel. *Divine Providence. Angelic Wisdom Concerning the Divine Providence.* London 1833. Swedenborg Society, London: L/287. The notes are not in C's hand nor of his composition.

Webster, Daniel. *An Address Delivered at the Laying of the Corner Stone of the Bunker Hill Monument.* 5th ed. Boston 1825. BM: C 126 h 3 (8). A presentation copy inscribed "S. T. Coleridge Esqe with the respects of [? J./I.] Wheeler". The work is annotated, but not by C.

Willich, A. F. M. *Elements of the Critical Philosophy.* London 1798. BM: C 43 b 6. Bookplate of JHG. The notes are not C's but JHG's.

Wrangham, Francis. *Thirteen Practical Sermons.* London 1800. Victoria College Library: Coleridge Collection 132. Presentation copy from the author to C, with an inscription. The notes are not in C's hand.

INDEX

B&F	= Beaumont and Fletcher	pref	= preface
ed	= edited	q	= quoted
MT	= marginalia text	tr	= translated
n	= editorial footnote	†	= lost book

A note number in italic (for example, "Trent, Council of [3]*232n*") indicates an especially comprehensive note.

I BRIEF GUIDE

All works appear under the author's name when it is known; anonymous works, periodicals, etc are listed by title; institutions are listed under the name of the place in which they are or were located. Entries are arranged alphabetically, sometimes in three parts, the first containing general references, the second particular references, and the third specific works.

When a word is referred to rather than used (as, for example, when its use or etymology is discussed), it is placed within quotation marks and indexed separately. Every effort has been made to give in the index entries the actual words that appear on the page. Spellings on the page that depart significantly from the norm (for example, "ouran outang" for "orang-utan") and circumlocutions ("conjugal state", for instance, for "marriage") are placed in quotation marks and given in parentheses after the page number or, if they occur frequently, after the conventional spelling in the heading of the entry. Words whose meaning would otherwise be ambiguous may be accompanied by a parenthetical explanation: for example, "foot/feet (metrical)". In order to facilitate rational grouping, some paraphrasing has been admitted in the subentries. Greek and Hebrew words and phrases have been transliterated.

Birth and death dates are provided where they are known, but birth dates of persons now living are not given. Pseudonyms and nicknames (e.g. "J. W. T." for James Webbe Tobin and "Asahara" for Sarah Hutchinson) are explained in parentheses, or cross-referenced to the real name when a work is involved (e.g. "Lyndsay, David" *see* Dodds, Mary Diana). For figures known by two names, such as scholars publishing under Greek or Latin versions of their birth names, the more familiar name (e.g. Melanchthon) becomes the main entry, but if there is no clear favourite we use the name that occurs more commonly in our text. Names of literary characters to whom Coleridge refers in his notes are accompanied by the title of the work in which they appear or by the name of the author in whose writings they are found, for example "Satan (*Paradise Lost*)" or "Pantagruel (in Rabelais)". Names invented by Coleridge for purposes of play or illustration are identified as "(fiction)".

Abbreviations of the names of persons frequently referred to (e.g. DC, JHG, RS) are alphabetised under their surnames (Coleridge, Green, Southey). Standard abbreviations for the books of the Bible found in footnotes and those for C's works listed among the Abbreviations continue to be used here in sub-entries. The page numbers for C's marginalia text are designated MT and are set off from surrounding numbers by semicolons.

The section devoted to Coleridge has been modified slightly from series practice. Al-

though the standard editions are indexed when they are themselves the subject in the text, routine cross-reference to other volumes of the *Collected Works* and to the *Notebooks* and *Collected Letters* has otherwise been avoided, the names, titles, and subjects being already indexed in their own right. For further minor departures see the list of categories at the beginning of the entry for "Coleridge, Samuel Taylor".

II EXTENDED GUIDE

The index to the volumes of *Marginalia* conforms to the general guidelines of the series. This extended introduction explains those guidelines and accounts for some special variations.

We index proper names of people, places, and compositions, but places of publication are excluded, as are place-names in titles of honour. Works are listed under the names of their authors, anonymous works by their titles alone; buildings and institutions are listed by location, e.g. "Bristol, Broadmead Meeting House". We also index subjects, and—this is an important point—by a key-word system, which is to say that the word that appears in the index can be expected to appear on the page(s) listed. There are several advantages to this policy, which produces what one reviewer referred to as a "concordance-like" index. The reader is spared the annoyance of hunting for something that appears not to be where it was said to be (when another sort of index might give "Puritans", for example, but the text reads "Cromwell and his party"). The element of subjectivity in the indexing process is reduced, as is the influence of passing intellectual fashions, since the indexer is prevented from translating the words on the page into such general categories as might seem convenient at the time of indexing. Furthermore, for an author as eccentric as Coleridge, a literalist policy has the effect of revealing certain kinds of connections, as when a significant term such as "multeity" is carried over from theological subjects into science or literary criticism. We emphasise, however, that, comprehensive as it seems, this index is not a concordance and that words have to meet the requirement of a certain level of significance. Hence common phrases such as *a priori* are indexed when Coleridge treats them as subjects but not necessarily when he simply uses them. Even "God" is not indexed in every passing reference, e.g. "as God wills", or we would have had to say "God, *passim*". "Rat-catchers in England" are indexed under "rat-catchers" and not under "England".

The key-word policy has, however, a number of practical disadvantages. It is better calculated for those readers who already know the text and are trying to recover something from it than for those who, coming to Coleridge perhaps from other fields of study and with specific interests to pursue, are encountering the material for the first time and want an index that will lead them into the text. To recur to the previous example, historians who wanted to know what Coleridge had to say about the Puritans would not find "Cromwell and his party" listed under that convenient umbrella term unless it happened to appear in the editorial footnotes; and they might not have the ingenuity or the patience to check for listings under "Roundheads", "Cavaliers", "Charles I", "Presbyterians", etc.

Being tied to the Coleridgean vocabulary also raises some distinctively Coleridgean problems. The terms Coleridge uses are often unconventional, especially in writings like the marginalia that were not prepared for publication. Then too he behaves, linguistically, as both a lumper and a splitter: he took pride in (and indeed has been celebrated for) a scrupulous "desynonymisation" of words which common usage tended to confuse (famous examples are "fancy" and "imagination", "talent" and "genius", "reason" and "understanding"); but he also on occasion used synonyms interchangeably ("Son", "Word", "Logos", "Lord", "Redeemer", "Saviour", etc). Sometimes these synonyms are the consequence of a conscious stylist's wish to avoid the obvious or repetitive; sometimes (as with

"flint broth" where "stone soup" might be the commoner phrase) they appear to be idiosyncratic. Finally, an indexer quickly becomes aware of the extent to which Coleridge's theory about nouns as relative late-comers in language is embodied in his own work, in which key concepts are often to be discerned in verbs and adjectives—especially in verbs—rather than in the nouns that are usually the basis of an index.

Although the volumes of the Bollingen Edition are uniform in format and superficially so in their indexing policies, no two titles made quite the same demands on the indexers and no two indexes follow exactly the same practices. We have therefore assumed a licence to depart from the examples before us so long as we adhered to the basic policies of indexing proper names and of indexing subjects according to key words. Where consistency seemed to us to be at odds with convenience to the reader, we have given up consistency.

The marginalia present some special problems. The sheer length of the text produced enormous entries and although the practice of analytical breakdown (still by key words) is well established in the edition, further measures had to be devised to subdivide exceptionally long entries such as that for the Bible (see the statement at the beginning of that entry). The miscellaneous character of our volumes meant that we could not, like the editors of shorter and more focussed works, expect to work within the lexicon of a relatively narrow subject, say logic or religion or statesmanship. On the other hand, it was agreed early on that we would be indexing Coleridge, and not the authors whose works prompted his marginal reflections; so the textus—the passage that elicited Coleridge's comment—is only lightly covered in the lists that follow, at a considerable saving of space. ("We" refers now not to the editors of the Bollingen Coleridge all together, but to those of us responsible for the index to the *Marginalia*—Heather Jackson, Marion Filipiuk, and a small but dedicated group of undergraduate and post-graduate students, especially Joseph Black, Shalender Jolly, Dylan Reid, and Helen Smith.) Fictional characters (dramatis personae, for example) in the books Coleridge annotated are named in the index only if Coleridge himself mentions them in his notes.

Finally, because the individual volumes of the marginalia have emerged one by one without indexes, the editors found it necessary to repeat material in their footnotes (the reader having no way of tracing the definitive—or even the *first*—note on a given subject, say the Duke of Buckingham or the theory of caloric) and to supply more than once sets of references to other passages in Coleridge's works—whence the common feature of editorial notes that end with "cf" and a paper trail of references to the *Collected Works*, the *Collected Letters*, and the *Notebooks*. This practice led us to a radical rethinking of the especially complex "S. T. Coleridge" entry—of which more later.

The remainder of this introduction will describe some of the problems peculiar to the *Marginalia*, together with the practical solutions adopted here.

(i) The Key-word Policy

Two of the difficulties inseparable from this system have been described already. The first is the use of a form of circumlocution, as in "Cromwell and his party". If, in an involved account of the relationship of God the Father, God the Son, and God the Holy Spirit Coleridge does not make use of the word "Trinity", then that account cannot appear in the index under "Trinity". The presence of the subject is not necessarily reflected in the key terms of the discussion. A second is the use of virtual synonyms, as in "Son", "Saviour", "Word", "Redeemer", etc, or "tolerance" and "toleration". A third arises with homonyms, that is, when the same word is used with different meanings and the word appears so frequently as to produce a daunting number of page-references, as in the case of "spirit", which may mean "spirit" as opposed to "body", or "spirit" in the sense of "immaterial being"—ghost or angel

or demon—or "spirit" in the sense of "Holy Spirit", the third Person in the Trinity. We have tried to respond to these problems and to minimise the inconvenience to readers by breaking down long entries and giving some of the context for each use of the key term, and by attaching to the end of important entries like "Trinity" a list of closely related terms for further exploration, even when the list cannot be absolutely exhaustive. The full list of cross-references generally appears only at the central entry; all other entries on the list are cross-referenced to the central entry. (We have not, however, attempted to propose related terms as cross-references in all cases. To find out what Coleridge thought about snakes, for example, readers will have to exercise ingenuity and check "snake", "serpent", "adder", "viper", "reptile", etc.) From Volume Three onward an effort was made to get the standard term into the editorial footnote, so that footnote references may signal the presence of the subject (though not the word) in the text above.

(ii) Capitalisation

This heading refers not to Coleridge's practice in capitalisation, which is erratic but typical of his period, but to the effect that regular capitalisation has on a proper noun, namely that of denoting a narrowly specific instance within the general range of the meaning of the word. In the marginalia, these cases nearly always separate the lexicon of religion from the common lexicon, for example in "flood" and "Flood" or "father" and "Father". This phenomenon, like the homonyms mentioned previously, becomes a problem only when the index-entry becomes too long to encourage a complete survey. Capitalisation in the index therefore reflects this distinction and serves as a way of subdividing long entries; the lower-case general use precedes the upper-case specific use, as in "god(s)" and "God".

(iii) Verbs and Adjectives

Indexes implicitly give priority to nouns—as Coleridge did not, either in theory or in practice. Where a verb or adjective is of special significance, a conventional index might absorb it silently under the nearest available noun, but a key-word index requires that the word on the page appear in the index. We offer a compromise solution, sometimes listing adjectival uses under the noun ("historical evidence" appears under both "evidence" and "history") and sometimes listing adjectives and verbs on their own account ("intuitive", "be").

(iv) Paired Terms

Paired terms are a recurrent feature of Coleridge's writing, one almost invariably accompanying the other like horse and carriage. We have gathered such habitual pairings according to the following principles. We use the conjunction "and" to cover all forms of relationship between terms, whether correlation (north and south, negative and positive), discrimination (fancy and imagination, genius and talent), or opposition (matter and spirit, ecclesia and enclesia). For every such pair the main entry will be found under the word that comes first in the alphabet (head and heart, object and subject), with a cross-reference at the later one ("subject and object *see* object and subject").

(v) Internal Cross-Reference

It has been a regular feature of the indexes to the *Collected Works* that internal cross-references should not be included. In a work that contained three references to Agnes Ibbetson therefore, with three editorial notes—the first identifying Ibbetson and the next two referring readers back to the first—the three references in the text would be indexed along with the first explanatory note, but the two following notes (of the "cf p 49 above" sort) would be ignored. On the other hand, if the cross-reference was not a purely internal one referring

to the same work, but one that directed readers to further references to Ibbetson in other works by Coleridge, such as the letters or notebooks (in the form "cf *CL* III 100"), the rule was that these further references would be listed both under "Ibbetson" and in the "S. T. Coleridge" entry under the relevant work *with a further subdivision* for the key-word topic ("S. T. Coleridge—*Letters*—Ibbetson"). The marginalia being produced volume by volume without indexes, the editors have found it necessary, as mentioned earlier, to include in their footnotes an unusual number of these cross-references both to the marginalia and to other works by Coleridge, and to include them repeatedly. Virtually every page therefore includes, among the editorial footnotes, at least one reference to parallel passages in Coleridge's works, especially to the marginalia themselves, the letters, and the notebooks. Given the scale of the marginalia, a list of undiscriminated page numbers under "Letters" in the Coleridge entry would not be much use to anyone. The parallel passages are seldom, however, identical with the text in the marginalia and consequently every such cross-reference would have to be checked and tagged with a key word (which might or might not be "Ibbetson") in order to provide an analytical entry under *The Friend* or *Letters*.

We have taken the view that the subject as identified by a key word in the text of the marginalia is the main thing, that the other *Collected Works* have their own indexes, and that it is not for us to index the letters and notebooks. The page number that takes readers to Coleridge's mention of Ibbetson will lead them also to the editorial footnote if there is one, and so to comparable references in the Coleridgean corpus. Therefore we have treated all cross-references to Coleridge's works as other titles in the series treated "internal" cross-references, and we index Coleridge's works (*Friend*, *Letters*, *Notebooks*, etc) only if they are themselves subjects in his notes or in the editorial apparatus.

(vi) Errata

The process of making the index has uncovered occasional errors (for instance in dates) and discrepancies which we now take the opportunity of correcting: for example, where a footnote incorrectly refers to Charles Maitland when it should have been to John Maitland, the index reads (a) "Maitland, Charles *see* Maitland, John" and (b) "Maitland, John [3]593 ('Charles')".

"A" [5]833, 833n
a posteriori [4]175
a priori [2]1058–9, [3]259, 957, 957n, 958, 958n, 965, 965n, 966n, [4]112, 112n, 217–18, 217n–18n, 280, 355, 355n, 378–9
Aaron (Bible) [1]419, [2]387, 396, 396n, 489, [4]683, [5]52–3, 52n, 64n, [6]105n, 112
Aarsleff, Hans *The Study of Language in England 1780–1860* [5]732n–3n
Abaddon (Bible) [2]308, 512
Abbadie, Jacques/James (1654–1727) [3]673
Abbot, Charles, 1st Baron Colchester (1757–1829) [2]696
Abbot, George, Archbishop of Canterbury (1562–1633) [2]1100
Abbott, Charles, 1st Baron Tenterden (1762–1832) [3]500
Abbott, Mr (fl 1735–50) [5]187
Abbott, Thomas Kingsmill (1829–1913) *see* Kant *Critique of Practical Reason*, *Fundamental Principles*, *Introduction to Logic* tr Abbott
Abbt, Thomas (1738–66) [1]lxix q, 6 ("T. Abbot")
Vermischte Werke MT [1]3–6
Abednego (Bible) [2]570, 570n, [4]50n
Abel (Bible) [2]177, 177n, 450, 574n, 780, 898, [3]43n, [5]591, 593, [6]324–6, 325n
Abelard, Peter (1079–1142) [3]135n, [4]291, [5]778
Theologia Christiana [5]778 q
Aberdeen [2]979, 979n, [5]651
Abergavenny see *Earl of Abergavenny*
Abernethy, John (1764–1831) [1]550n, 624n, 843, 843n, [4]5
Enquiry into . . . Mr. Hunter's Theory of Life [3]844n; *Reflections on Gall and Spurzheim's System* [2]1012n, [4]5

"abeternal" [1]696, 696n
abhorrence of guilt [5]420
Abhorson (*Measure for Measure*) [4]695, 695n
Abiah (Bible) [1]423
abiding, the [5]95
abiding-place [4]743
Abinger, Lord *see* Scarlett, James Richard
ablative (case) [3]19, 19n, 835
ablution(s) [4]625
abnegation [5]795
abolitionist(s) [6]35
aborigines [5]309
abortion [1]772, [3]809, [5]468
  wretched [5]476
abracadabra [3]317, 516n, [4]626, 626n, [5]615, 615n, 679 ("Abra is Cadabra") 679n, [6]298n
Abraham (Bible) [1]463n, 686, 787, 788n, [2]151, 280, 329, 378, 384–5, 385n, 395, 414, 497, 674, 702, 743, 895n, 897, 916, 1165, [3]19n, 21n, 106, 109, 427, 429, 456, 462, 464, 469, 604, 728, 757, [4]47, 246n, 249–50, 251, 252, 663, [5]416, 417, 535, 649, 830, [6]110, 292–4
  angels' visit to [6]106; descendants of [5]623, 624; God of [6]92; sham [4]97
Abrahamidae [2]916
Abraxas [4]626, 626n
abridgment [6]159
abrogation [1]877
Absalom (Bible) [3]768
Abscheu [4]430–1
Absehen [3]90
absence [4]299
absolute, the [6]241
absolute(s) [1]679, [2]854n, [3]15, 66, 849n, [4]364n, 381, 381n, 439, [5]18, 32, 201, 356n, 483, 744, 749, [6]241
  as Almight [2]995; atheistic [3]1050; forms of [3]15; God the a. [2]1186, [3]24, 460, 720; idea of [1]602, [5]455, 484; impersonal [6]5; and nature [1]138; plenitude in [2]553; priority of [2]1019n; prothesis [2]995n; and relative [2]554n, [5]356; schemes of [5]806; terms for [2]278; unity of [5]357
absolution(s) [1]309, 470, [2]26, 722, 1096, [4]86, [5]163, 587, [6]13
absorption [1]641, [2]1167, [5]244
abspection [2]612n
abstract(s) [5]10, 117n, 306, 446, 792, 806
  and concrete [3]272, [5]697; logical [1]550; realism of [2]433n; visual [5]94
abstraction(s) [1]432n, 602, 620, 627, 631, 632, 641, 673, [2]482, 611, 637, 638n, 798, [3]76, 261–2, 276, 947n, 957, [4]116, 228–9, 450, [5]173, 185, 274, 751, [6]145
  arbitrary [5]730; Aristotelian [3]913; barren [4]364; comedy as [2]82; fictions of [3]301; and generalisation [3]126–7, 127n, [5]481n; God as [3]79; historic [4]808; and idea [3]261–2, [5]364, 364n; images are all a. [3]792; infirmity of [3]85; logical [3]348; mere [5]460; a.-mongers [2]426; physical [6]132; power of [2]961; in Proclus [4]426; pure [5]744; substantiated [3]86, 919; use of [2]612; verbal [3]101
absurd, the [3]332n, [5]842
absurdity/absurdities [1]304, 562, 634, 782, [2]205, 278, 539, 1055, 1144, [3]77, 89, 333, 644, 1023, [4]409, 597, 818, [5]7, 354, 457, 467, 524, 530, 551, 597, 752, 780, 811, [6]78, 83, 85, 326
  laughable [4]827; likeness to truth [2]177; metaphysical [2]560; of RC dogma [2]282; of transubstantiation [5]543
Absyrtus (myth) [1]537, 537n
abuse
  abusive terms [1]876; and use [1]517, 517n
abysm [3]30
abyss [1]693, 694
  of being [1]659; see also *abyssos*
Abyssinia [5]102n
abyssos [1]618, 618n, 636
Academus/Academy (Plato's) *see* Athens
Acatius (legend) [2]752
accent [1]377, [2]230, [3]903
  rustic [2]230
accent (in verse) and quantity [5]690
"accersive" [1]569, 569n
accerso [1]569n
accident(s) [1]4, 602, 611, [2]854, [3]23, 24, 182, 1062, [4]157, 582, 857, [5]4, 83, 156, 167, 443
  in drama [4]718–19; interpretation of [1]350; sensible [2]282; and substance [1]524–5, [2]625, [5]548, 551–2, 580
accidental, the [4]718
acclamatus [5]38
"accommodate" [6]288, 288n
accommodation [1]788, 788n, [3]177, 177n
"according to" [4]472, 472n
"accrescence" [4]845, 845n
accumulation [3]382
accuracy [2]637
accusative (case) [3]15, 831, 834
accuser [2]799, [3]436, [6]98
  false [5]422, [6]101

Acer (in Homer) [1]374
"acerb" [1]591, 591n
Achaean(s) [1]461, 461n
Achamoth (myth) [4]257
Achates (in Virgil) [6]204, 208, 214
"ache(s)" [4]721, 721n, 768, 768n
Achilles (myth) [1]790, 799, [2]346n, [3]407, 408, 413, [5]712, 712n, [6]213
heel of [2]633, [5]522, 522n
Achilles (*Troilus and Cressida*) [4]810, 811, 812
Achitophel (in Dryden) [2]308, [3]141, 141n
achronos [2]728, [5]186
acid(s) [1]613, [2]246, 572, [3]1005, 1031, [4]89, 320n, [5]438
and alkali(s) [3]1003, 1004, 1005, [4]168; carbonic [3]1032–3; hydatic [3]1032; hydrochloric [5]343n; muriatic [3]1027, 1028, 1028n, 1031, 1032–3, [5]343, 343n; oxymuriatic [5]343, 343n, 346n; prussic [5]137; vegetable [5]257
acidity [1]611
d'Acier *see* Dacier
Ackermann, Jacob Fidelis (1765–1815) [1]654, 654n ("Ackerman")
Ackermann, Johann Christian Gottlieb (1756–1801) [1]654, 654n ("Ackerman")
Ackers, Charles (?1702–59) [1]701
Ackworth School [2]76, 76n
aconite [6]103n
aconitum [6]103n
acorn(s) [2]1200, [3]11, 102, 697, 1020
Acosta, José de (c 1539–1600) *Geschichte von Westindien* [4]489–90
acoustics [4]503, 503n, [5]294n, 295n
acquiescence [2]645
Acragas [2]570n, [4]246n
acre(s) [3]808
square [3]807, 808n
act(s) [1]627, [2]198, [3]13, 15, 1004, [4]442, [5]66
absolute [1]827; adorable [6]307; antonym for [3]913, 913n; baffled [1]646; and being [1]460, [3]15, [4]166; of Christ [5]535; circling [3]460; constructive [5]600, [6]8; creative [2]419, 640; and deed [3]753; discursive [2]656; divine [1]719; *esse* as [5]410; eternal [1]564, [3]12, [5]210; extroitive and retroitive [1]680; first [5]650; free [5]784; God as [2]287, [4]200, 200n; ground of existence [3]1065; ground of reality in [5]443; image abstracted from [3]947; immediate [5]15, 410; immoral [4]277; individual [5]578; initiative [1]601; intellectual [1]702, [5]469; intervening [5]348; lawless [1]336; manual [3]846; mental [5]654, 734; moral [4]429–30, 661–2, [5]561; organic [1]634; outward [3]233; particular [5]494; and pass [3]910, 910n; and passion [5]680; in play(s) [1]72, [4]864; polar [5]348; poor in [3]909; positive [1]685; as power [1]70; of power [5]654; primary [4]445; pure [2]193, 1106, [3]79, [5]25, 25n, 26, 66; reciprocal [1]694; redeeming [5]66; reflex [5]27; religious [1]781; of self-consciousness [3]357, [4]453; of self-constitution [1]659; self-ponent [5]725; separate [1]401; sinful [1]342; spiritual [3]927; and substance [1]667; supernatural [3]708; and thing [3]273; and thought [5]93; total [5]500; transcendent [3]29; of trust [2]1166; visible [5]650; will as [2]251; of will [4]460
Act(s) of Parliament *see* Parliament: Acts/Bills
Acta martyrum see Ruinart
Acta Seminarii Regii . . . Lipsiensis ed C. D. Beck [1]clxx; MT [1]7–8
actio
a. in distans [3]384, [5]131; *a.* and *passio* [5]25, 25n
action(s) [3]83, [4]127, 421, [5]776
and agency [3]959; and agent [3]305; antagonist [6]122; bodily [1]754; cant of [5]90; consciousness of [5]614; consequences of [4]465; continuous [4]520; for damages [5]67; defect of [1]692; at a distance [3]284, 286–7, 289, 384, 384n, see also *actio in distans*; ground of [6]56; inceptive [5]256; indivisible [1]868; outward [1]496; and passion [3]266, 266n, 274, *see also* active and passive, agent(s) and patient, *agere* and/*et pati*; polar [5]733; positive [1]649; power of [5]207; pure [5]594; and reaction [3]23, [6]170; simple [6]226; source of [5]497; and thought [3]84; unity of [4]826, 863–4; universal condition of [3]1007
active and passive [1]662, [2]1025, [3]836, [4]450n, 451n, [5]706–7, 784n; *see also* action(s), and passion
activity [2]624, 624n, 630, 631, 632, 633n
inward [1]516; of mind [2]639; springs of [5]363; unlimited [1]647
Acton, W. H. *see* Swedenborg *Concerning the White Horse* rev Acton
actor(s) [1]384, 395, [2]776, [3]406–7, 407, 814, 917, [4]42, 42n, 726, 743, 780, 781, 844
alter texts [4]717; interpolates [4]735; want of [4]734; *see also* player(s)
actual, the [1]138, [2]279, [3]345
and ideal [2]140, 853–4, 853n, [4]418; and

actual, the—*continued*
potential [1]138, 694, [2]326, 431, 566, 1185, 1185n, [3]545, 545n, 876, [5]424–5, 460, 649, 784; and real [1]231–2, [2]1186, [4]223, 350, [5]615
actuality/actualities [1]691, [2]542, [3]67, 331, 705, [4]403n, 404, [5]424, 580
eternal [1]669; overflow of [1]565
actus purissimus [1]232, 232n, [2]287, 1186, 1186n, [3]79, 643n, 710, [4]200
acuteness [5]528, 541, 558
acyanoblepsia [3]986
ad [1]434n
adage [5]99
"adagy" [2]819, 819n
Adam (Bible) [1]124, 176, 606, 645, 654, 657, 692, 707, 733, 786, 787, [2]177n, 247, 378, 384–5, 387, 576, 723, 780, 789, 915, 916, 1052–3, 1053, 1055, [3]39, 41, 47, 48, 64, 65, 65n, 475, 493, 494, 613, 735, 757, 876, 925, [4]246n, 615, 644, [5]133, 139n, 162n, 202, 248, 368, 394, 426, 487, 590, 590n, 591, 591n, 592, 593, 595, 597, 600, 602, 608, 609, 611, 613, 615, 629, 648, [6]5n, 16, 112
and the Adam [2]87; birth of [5]465; bisexual [5]248n; curse of [5]594; death of [2]388; and Eve [3]105, [5]251, 594, 594n, [6]5n; example of [4]655–6; before Fall [2]1185; Fall of [1]676n, [3]729, [5]598; fertility of [1]784; history of [5]603; Kadmon [6]141, 141n; old [3]770; "red earth" [2]334; ruinous [2]495; second (Christ) [3]720, [6]141; sentence of death [5]609; sons of [5]611; threat to [3]66; two [5]600
Adam (*Paradise Lost*) [3]402, 560, 1093n, [4]799n, [5]477
Adam, Charles (b 1857) *see* Descartes *Oeuvres* ed Adam and Tannery
Adam, Mrs [2]87
Adam, Thomas (1701–84) *Private Thoughts on Religion* [1]lxxxiv, lxxxv; MT 9–19; [2]967
adamah [2]334n
Adamites [3]494n
Adams, G. (probably George Adams M.A., ?1698–?1768) *see* Fleury *Ecclesiastical History* tr Herbert and Adams
Adams, Joseph (1756–1818) [1]550n, [2]363
An Illustration of Mr. Hunter's Doctrine [1]550n, [4]5
Adams, Mr (fl mid 17th century) [2]1174n
adaptivity [4]542
adder(s) [2]771, [4]309, [5]506, 506n
Addington, Henry, 1st Viscount Sidmouth (1757–1844) [2]847n
Addison, Joseph (1672–1719) [1]38, 60, 157, 157n, [2]815, 1173n, [3]154n, 992n, [4]292, 632, 840–1
and Defoe [6]163; on ghosts [2]700; prose style [1]157, 157n, 182n
Cato [4]838, 838n q, 841n. See also *Spectator*; *Guardian*
addition [5]487
Address to the Commons [2]532
addressees [1]468
Adelantado [5]106, 107
Adelung, Johann Christoph (1732–1806)
Deutsche Sprachlehre für Schulen MT [1]20–3; *Grammatisch-kritisches Wörterbuch* [6]286n–7n; and others *Mithridates* [3]24n–5n, [4]170, 186–7; *Versuch eines . . . Wörterbuches der hochdeutschen Mundart* [4]35, 35n, 36n
adept [1]685
"adequate" [4]413, 413n, [6]172–3
Aders, Carl/Charles (1780–1846) [1]xcvii, xcviii, cvi, clxi, [2]*179–81*, 194n, [4]270, 278n, 469, 811n, [5]268
Aders, Eliza (née Smith) (d 1857) [2]180, 194n, [4]469
letter to [2]904n, 905n
adherence [2]1164
adhesion [1]645
and centrality [1]549; and cohesion [1]549
adiaphora [1]253
adiaphorites [2]22
adiaphoron [4]145, 145n
adit [5]81, 81n
adjective(s) [2]960, [4]166, 167n, [6]289
semi-adjective [4]661; substantive [5]740; and substantive powers [1]611, 611n
"admensate" [2]200, 200n
Admetus (myth) [2]1083–4
"Administration of the Lord's Supper" see *BCP*
administrators [1]339
Admiralty, Court of *see* London: Admiralty, Court of
admiration [1]61, [2]808, [4]35, 718, 817
admission
promiscuous [1]355; a.-ticket [6]62
admixtures [2]346
admonition(s) [5]578
public [6]56
adnoun [3]450, [4]166, 167n
Adonijah (Bible) [2]836
Adonis (myth) [2]573

adorability [4]670, [5]656
adoration [1]435, [2]652, [3]494
of Cross [2]1158; defined [6]146; inward [1]576; lazy [4]280; religious [2]1159, [5]417
Adrian *see also* Hadrian
Adrian VI (Adrian Dedel), Pope (1459–1523) [5]636 ("Adrianus")
"adsedent" [4]682, 682n
adulation [2]970, 1132, 1132n
adult [5]169
adultery [1]877, [3]496, [4]240, 718, [5]575, 575n, [6]98, 98n–9n
adunare [3]46n
advancement [5]67
Advent [4]665, [5]662
Adventure Bay [2]74
adverb [4]166
adversity [1]262
advice [3]896
advocate [5]560
of a bad cause [1]807
Adwitamists [2]340, 340n
Ady, Thomas (fl 1656) *A Candle in the Dark* [6]98 q
Aecius (in B&F) [1]393, 393n, 396
Aeetes (myth) [1]537n
aeiparthenia [1]504n
"aei-partheny" [1]504, 504n
Aelfric, St (c 955–c 1020) [2]983, 983n, [6]21
Aelius Donatus (fl 4th century) [3]1072n
Aeneas/Eneas (in Virgil) [1]xci, 109n, [2]930n, [6]205n, 211, 213, 214, 215
Aenesidemus of Cnossos (c 2nd half of 1st century BC) [1]781, 781n
Aeolian harp *see* harp, Eolian
Aeolus/Eolus (myth) [1]609, [6]200
nature of [5]227
aeon(s) [2]32, 33n, 487, 714–15, [3]60, 60n, [6]64, 106; see also *aion*
Aeon (myth) [2]575, 576, [3]913
"Aepio" (Amelia Opie) [1]90
ae-position [5]231
aer [1]479, 479n; *see also* air
aeriform [5]451, [6]228
aerity [5]358n, [6]230
and fluidity [3]997, 997n
aerolithes [6]135, 135n
"aeroseptic" [4]149
Aeschines (c 397–322 BC) [5]581, 581n
Aeschylus/Eschylus (525–456 BC) [2]458n, 1090, 1090n, [3]886, 894, [4]631
ed Brunck [2]1090n; ed Porson [2]1090n; ed Schütz [1]27n, [2]1090n; ed T. Stanley [2]1090n
Agamemnon [1]26, 565n, [3]57n, [4]864, 864n, ed C. J. Blomfield [1]24n, ed Denniston and Page [1]24n, ed Fraenkel [1]25n, ed James Kennedy MT [1]24–5; 100; *Choephoroe* ed C. J. Blomfield [1]26; *Oresteia* [4]864n; *Persae* ed C. J. Blomfield [1]26, 526; *Prometheus Bound* [1]cxli, 25, 377n, 432, [2]892, 1089, [4]845–6, 845n–6n, *see also* Coleridge, S. T. VI "On the *Prometheus* of Aeschylus"; *Prometheus vinctus* ed C. J. Blomfield MT [1]26–7; 26n q, 526, [2]1090n, tr H. W. Smith [1]26 q; *Septem contra Thebas* ed C. J. Blomfield [1]26; *Suppliants* [6]8n; *Tragoediae* ed Dindorf [2]1090n
Aesculapius/Esculapius (myth) [2]343, 344n, 346n, [3]177, [5]384, [6]110, 110n
Aesop (c 620–560 BC) [2]1051, [3]656, 680, [4]561
Fables [4]504n
aesthetic(s) [1]6n, [3]259, 259n
transcendental [4]157, 158n, [5]81
Aethelred II (968–1016) [3]784 ("Ethelred")
aether *see* ether
Aetius (pseudo-Plutarch) (1st or 2nd century) [1]584n, 778, [2]741
De placitis philosophorum [5]227
aeviternity [3]91
aevum [3]60, 60n
affect [5]216, 217
affectation [4]283
affection(s) [1]169, 752, [2]682, 689, 1113, [3]242, 265, 741, [4]278, 335, 598, 702, 777, 819, [5]292, 795
and appetite [2]402; carnal [1]12; disinterested [2]347; domestic [2]636, [4]729; filial [1]398; inmost [1]426; parental [5]476; profound [4]810; purifying of [5]480; seat of [5]136; selfish [4]814; of space [5]720; spiritual [4]275
afficients [3]741
affinity/affinities
chemical [3]324; elective [3]59n; finer [1]537
affirmant, absolute [2]745
affirmation [5]459
affirmative and negative [5]413
Africa [1]245, 528, 539, 746, 771n, [2]6, 384, 717n, [3]129, 159, 233, 883, 1080–2, [4]87n, 88, 299, [5]262, 337, 352
East A. [5]262; map of [4]601; travels in [4]29–31
African(s) [1]540, [2]200, 1207, [3]1082, [5]336, 337
African Association *see* London
African Institution *see* London
Africus [6]200–1

Afrites (in Aeschylus) [4]845
after-birth(s) [1]663, [3]866
after-life [1]283, [3]553n
after-pains [1]663
after-thought [3]920
after-wit [2]846
Agadoth see *Haggadoth*
Agamemnon (myth) [1]799, [2]833
Agamemnon (*Troilus and Cressida*) [4]810
agate(s) [3]636, 898
agathon [1]115, [2]205, 425, [3]151, 460, [5]740
age(s)
  above the a. [2]934; of anxiety [4]610; apostolic [1]317, 345, 447, 533, [2]35, 495, [3]17, 20, 28, 446, 448, 454, 595, 613, [4]49, 260, [5]51, 512, 529, 659, [6]63, 118; Augustan [4]336, 336n, [6]138; barbarous [5]811; character revealed in sermons [2]328; characterisation of [4]28n; disease of the [1]495; distant [3]20; doctrine of [5]571; Elizabetho-Jacobaean [1]389; enlightened [4]670–1, [5]866; fashion of [1]378, [5]442; Father of [5]800; former [5]319; genius outruns [2]781; golden [4]336, [5]301n; heroic [1]423; idols of [3]877; influence of [2]1138; iron [3]286; old [2]1185; philosophy of [3]235; present [1]164, [3]754, [5]390; Shakespearean [3]172; spirit of [3]831, [5]421, 659; vices of [2]813; weakness of [4]21; witty [2]824; writing for, not with [5]89. *See also* dark ages; middle ages; time(s)
The Age MT [1]28–30
agency [2]248, [5]172
  and action [3]959; collective [5]73; continuous [1]401; denial of [2]802; divine [6]134; God's [5]644; instrumental [4]496; material [1]178; mechanical or magical [6]97; spiritual [2]402, [6]28
Agenor (in B&F) [1]371
agent(s) [3]428, [4]815, [5]267, 548
  and action [3]305; actualising [2]1185; all-wise [4]113; free [1]124, [4]465, [5]614; human [1]719; individual [5]599; informing [3]46; living [4]540; moral [1]342, [5]385; patible [5]26, 26n; and patient [1]54, [3]275, [5]443–4, 444n, *see also* action(s), and passion; personal [5]765; prime [2]255; responsible [5]516, 791; sole [4]408; spiritual [3]33, [5]172; and works [2]1162–3
agere and/*et pati* [4]450, 451, 815n, [5]784; *see also* action(s), and passion
aggregate [1]740, [3]44, 79, 157, 678, 741, 856, [4]117, 228–9, 386, [5]133, 267, 406, 456, 568, 715, 716, [6]7–8
aggregation [2]206
agility [2]633, [5]169
agitators [2]510
Agnes, Princess of Meran (widowed 1293) [3]196
agnition [4]477
agnomen [2]898, 898n, [5]31
agnos [2]339, [3]61, 61n
agnus [3]61, 61n
  a. Dei [1]522–3
agony/agonies [5]613
  convention of [4]824; epileptic [5]584
agora [6]324
agreeable, the [4]653
  and beautiful [4]677
agreeable(s) [3]259
Agreus (myth) [2]576
Agricola, Johann (1492–1566) [3]756, 759 ("Grickle")
agricultor [5]271
agriculturalists [2]1192
agriculture [2]64, [5]380, [6]22, 44, 325
Agriculture, Board of [1]279, 360, 360n
  Agricultural State of the Kingdom [1]360n
agriculturist [3]807
Agrigentum [5]226
agrios [2]576n
Agrippa von Nettesheim, Heinrich Cornelius (c 1486–1535) [3]308, 308n, [5]810n
  De vanitate scientiarum [5]810, 810n
Agruerus (myth) [2]577
ague(s) [4]149
Aguecheek, Sir Andrew (*Twelfth Night*) [1]404, [4]756, 756n
Ahab (Bible) [2]830, [5]565, [6]109n
Ahad [3]913
Ahaz (Bible) [2]270, 270n, [6]119
Ahnung-drivel [2]203
Ahnungsvermögen [5]723
aidance, supernatural [5]678
Aikin, Arthur (1773–1854) [3]937, [4]283, 283n; see also *Annual Review and History of Literature* ed Aikin
Aikin, John (1747–1822) [3]1064
aim(s) [5]168
  spiritual [5]622
ainigmatode [1]450
Ainsworth, Robert (1660–1743) *Thesaurus linguae latinae compendarius* [4]420n q
aion [2]576n, [5]57, 57n; *see also* aeon(s)
"air" [6]132–3
air [1]569–70, 639, [2]853, [3]12, 43, 90, 150, 324, 998, 1027, 1028, 1029, 1063, 1086, 1087, [4]169, 317, 387, [5]357–8, 450, 451, 687, [6]227, 227n
  a.-blight [2]364; deadly [1]48; a.-fire [1]662;

fixed [2]246, 246n; infected [2]362–3; in motion [1]479n; musical [4]500; primal [5]719; principle of [1]642; pulses of [2]604; re-oxygenation of [6]231; a.-vessels [2]859; see also *aer*
aisthesis [5]174, 174n
aistheta [5]4–5, 592, 592n
aites [1]42n
Aix [1]111–12
Ajax (myth) [3]365, 365n
Ajax (*Troilus and Cressida*) [4]810, 811
Ajora [5]837
Akenside, Mark (1721–70) [1]38
Akiba ben Joseph (c 40–c 135) [5]806–7
ala [3]652, 652n
Aladdin (*Arabian Nights*) [5]167n
Alakaluf [5]252
Alanus de Insulis (c 1114–1203) [4]661–2 q, 662n q
Alanus Magnus *see* Alanus de Insulis
Alathe [4]693, 693n
Alba
  Alban sires [6]198
Alba/Alva, Ferdinand Alvarez de Toledo, Duke of (1508–82) [2]163n
Alba Longa [6]206, 206n
Albani of Merate, Ignazio (fl 1602) [2]7n, 8
Albany (*King Lear*) [4]815, 820, 821
Albaris (2nd half of 6th century BC) [5]226
Albemarle, Duchess of *see* Monck, Anne
Albemarle, Duke of *see* Monck, George
Alber, Erasmus (c 1500–53) *Der Barfüsser Münche Eulenspiegel und Alcoran* [2]765n
Albertus (in B&F) [1]405
Albertus Magnus, St (c 1200–80) [1]538 q, 538n, [2]11–12
Albigenses [1]857n, [4]43, 43n, [6]14
  Albigensian heresy [1]349n, [2]69n
"Albinus" *see* White, Gilbert
Albion [2]845
Albion (myth) [2]577
album [4]602, 602n
albumen [2]546, 546n
Alcaeus (fl c 590 BC) [4]339, 339n, [5]144, 144n
alcaic [3]814 ("alchaic")
alchemist(s) [1]547n, 629n, 631, 656n, [2]621, 727n, 788, *825n*, [3]635, 1024, 1088, [4]635
alchemy [1]215–16, [2]42, [3]935, [4]513n
  childishness of [2]824–5; corporeal [1]817; definition [2]824–5; metaphors [1]668; nonsense [3]1029, 1029n; symbolic [5]700
Alcides (myth) [1]71
Alcmaon/Alcmaeon (5th century BC) [5]701, 701n, 702
Alcmena (myth) [3]234n
alcohol [1]551, [2]1186, [4]169, [6]227–8
alcoholics [5]252n
Aldhelm, Bishop of Sherborne (c 640–709) [6]17
Aldrovandi, Ulissi (1522–1605) [3]1088, 1089n
ale, Goslar [3]1072
Aleppo [4]29
aletheia [2]205, [3]23, 23n, 163, 460
alethes [3]151, [5]740
Aleutian Islands [2]178
Alexander, St, Bishop of Alexandria (d 328) [2]728, 731n, [3]825
Alexander VI (Rodrigo Borgia), Pope (1431–1503) [3]794, [5]103
Alexander I, of Russia (1777–1825) [3]250n
Alexander of Aphrodisias (fl late 2nd century) [1]188, [5]227
Alexander of Hales (c 1170–1245) [3]1085, 1085n
Alexander Polyhistor (Lucius Cornelius Alexander Polyhistor) (c 105–35 BC) [2]893, 1082n, [5]230, 231
Alexander the Great, King of Macedon (356–323 BC) [1]50, 440, 799, 850n, [2]416, 416n, 434, [3]110, 111, 447, 466, 542, 573n, 722, 786n, 925n, [6]113, 217
  rules of [2]1058; successors of [3]419
Alexander, William, 1st Earl of Stirling (c 1567–1640) [2]14
Alexandria [1]447, 468n, [2]381n, 416n, 417n, 451, 586, 713n, 740, 843, 919n, 1106, [3]6, 467, 595, 728, [4]473, 473n, 474, 650n, [5]27n, 841, 842, 843, [6]3, 4, 138
  bishops of [3]440n; Church of [2]502, [5]660n; dialect of [3]19; Jew of [6]140
Alexandrian(s)/Alexandrine(s) [2]472, 472n, 725, [4]421n, [5]667, 740n, 746
  philosophy of [2]203, 426, 433, 478, [4]158, 158n; *see also* school, Alexandrian
alexandrine (verse) [1]57n, [2]1035, [5]688
Alexis (c 375–c 275 BC) [4]147
Alfieri, Vittorio, Count (1749–1803) [3]712, [5]165
Alford, Henry (1810–71) [2]244; *see also* Donne *Works* ed Alford
Alfoxden [1]89, [6]210
Alfred the Great, King of Wessex (849–99) [2]1139, [3]1083, [5]79
algarroba [5]104
Algazel *see* Ghazali
algebra [1]616, 633, [2]962, 1133, 1160, 1160n, [3]130, [5]434
algebraist(s) [3]322, [5]244, 789
Algerus (d 1131) [2]672

Algiers [1]322
Dey of [1]32
Algripe (in B&F) [4]693, 693n
Ali Baba (*Arabian Nights*) [3]877n
Ali ben Abu Talib (c 600–61) [2]1025, [4]357, 357n
alien(s) [1]692, 877, [3]142, 148; *see also* Parliament: Acts/Bills: alien bills
alienation [1]356, [4]145
from communion [6]56
Alihu (Bible) [2]489
Alinda (in B&F) [1]400
Alisio, Cammillio (Cammillo Cateni) (fl 1792–1817) [1]206
Alistra (myth) [2]580
aliud [2]33, 33n
alkali(s) [1]569, [2]572, [3]951, 1001, 1005, 1030–1, 1031n, 1033n, [4]320n, 531n, [5]438
and acid(s) *see* acid(s)
alkaline [1]667
all [3]12, 741, [4]492
a.-being [5]716; a.-common [3]258, 258n; a.-commonness [1]123; in each [5]360; A.-father [4]61; and God [5]354; A.-good [2]279; A.-perfect [5]20; a.-to [3]897
All Saints' Day [3]310n
Allah [6]272 ("Alla")
Allan Bank *see* Grasmere
allegiance [3]160
oath of *see* oath(s)
allegorising [4]427
allegorist [2]433
"allegory" [4]427n
allegory/allegories [1]54, 801, [2]88, 336, 715, 879n, 898, 986, 1080, 1152, [3]19, 154, 230n, 417n, 564n, 570, 759n, 767, 778, 835, 927, 992n, 1075, [4]41, 194, 195, [5]415, 676–7, [6]110, 143, 217
arbitrary [5]698; beautiful [3]510; Böhme's [1]559; of cave [3]525n; defective [1]813; degenerates into pun [1]821; of devil [2]164; of fall [2]1052–3; faulty in *Pilgrim's Progress* [1]811–12, 812–13; in gnosticism [2]482; allegorical and literal [5]594, 629; and mythology [1]794, 812n; Persian [3]92; personification [1]432, 432n; picture [3]676; in Rabelais [4]196; religious [4]191n; and symbol [2]1053n, [3]472, [5]698n; allegorical visions [5]413
alleity [3]1024
Allen, Helen Mary (fl 1906–34) *see* Erasmus *Opus epistolarum* ed Allen and Allen
Allen, Percy Stafford (1869–1933) *see* Erasmus *Opus epistolarum* ed Allen and Allen
Allen, Robert (1772–1805) [2]574n
Allen, William (1770–1843) [2]857, 857n–8n, [3]937, 1002n, 1033n, [4]385n, 390n
Allerdale [5]389n
Allestree, Richard (1619–81) [2]409n
alleys [5]321
allgemein [3]258, 258n
Allgemeine Bibliothek der biblischen Litteratur ed Eichhorn *see* Eichhorn
Allgemeine Encyclopädie der Wissenschaften und Künste [2]1026n
Allgemeine Literaturzeitung [6]225, 234
Allgemeine Zeitschrift von Deutschen für Deutsche [2]188n
Allgemeinheit [1]123n
Allheit [5]369
alliteration [2]241
Allmacht [5]718, 718n
Allmight [1]636, 653, 659, 693, [2]995, [3]100
allness [2]206
allogeneity [5]70
"allogeneous" [5]484, 484n
allon [2]825, [3]1024–5, [4]315, 315n
allos [2]932n
Allsop, Thomas (1795–1880) [1]clxix, [2]529n q, [5]392n
letter(s) to [1]xcix, cxvii q, cxviii, [4]577 q
Letters, Conversations [1]lxixn q, xcviiin, cxxxvii, cxliiin, 48n q, 63n q, 120n q, 230 q, [2]1070n
Allston, Washington (1779–1843) [1]58n, [2]20, 792, 1066, 1066n, [3]899, 899n
letter to [2]20–1 q, 22n q
Diana and Her Nymphs in the Chase [3]899n
allusion(s) [2]1079, [3]29, [4]121, 746, [5]524, 861
almah [4]255
almanacs [2]387, 1107, 1108n, [6]105
metallic [1]419
Almight *see* Allmight
Almighty, accusation of [5]75
alms [3]608
a.-basket [5]598; a.-giving [5]587; a.-houses [1]755; a.-offerings [2]670
Alogi [3]441n, [5]513, 513n
Aloidae [3]413
alpha and omega [1]678, 678n, [3]5, 5n, [5]702, 702n
alphabet(s) [1]787, [2]574n, [4]37n, 165, [6]27
of dynamics [5]434–9; of sufferings [5]236
Alphabet of Ben-Sira see Talmud
Alphabeta linguarum [4]5

Alphonso (in B&F) [1]375, 399
Alpinus, Prospero (1553–1617) [3]104, 104n
altar [1]322, 333, [3]21, [5]661
alter [2]33, 33n
a. ego [3]660; *a.* and/*et idem* [1]601n, 690, 694, [4]440, 444, [6]32, 32n; *a. et ipse* [5]121
alterity [1]601, 601n, 652, 680, [2]33, 745, 881, [3]13, 17, 18, 18n, 24, 24n, 107n, 428, 720, [4]258, 400, 454, [5]24, 789, 799
divine [3]106; filiation of [1]640; and ipseity [1]646, 646n
Altick, Richard Daniel *The Shows of London* [4]13n, 169n, 488n, [5]832n
Alting, Jacobus (1618–79) *Opera omnia* [6]220n
Alting, Johann Heinrich (1583–1644) [1]421n
Altseidenberg [1]566n
alum [3]1023
aluminium [3]481n
alumium [3]481, 481n
Alva *see* Alba
Alypius (4th century) [2]746
Amalek (Bible) [1]475, 475n, [4]683
Amalekites [4]682
Amant, Friar [3]235
Amantius (legend) [2]718
amanuensis/amanuenses [3]435, 446, [4]536, [5]473
Amarus *see* Ananas/Ananus
amathia [2]871–2, 871n–2n
amativeness [5]422n
amaurosis [2]492n–3n, [5]184n
Amazon(s) [4]192
Amazon (river) [1]226, [2]827n
ambassador(s) [1]523, [3]450
ambiguity [1]618, [2]799, 1150, [3]19, 351, 352, 915, [5]494, [6]133; *see also* equivocation
"ambition" [2]972
ambition [2]846, 971, [3]222, [4]341, 798, [5]161, [6]59, 157
of appearances [2]159; human [5]745; worldly [2]1100
Ambleside [1]cx, cxn, clxviii, [3]977
Ambrose, St (c 339–97) [2]284, 306, 683, [3]486, 765, [5]559 q, [6]178
ambrosia [2]167
ambush [4]287
Amelias, triad of [4]489–90
Amelius Gentilianus (fl 246–70) [6]143, 143n
amendment(s) [3]544–5
conjectural [3]192
America [1]528, 539, 764–5, 765n, 782, 797n, 799, [2]176, 178, [3]884, [5]337
climate in [1]359; fictional heroes in [1]212; history of [3]816–26; Methodism in [5]186; persecution of witches in [6]104; Spaniards in [2]163, 163n; transportation to [4]15; vulgarisms in [3]110; Wesley in [5]122; woodmen [3]586; *see also* United States
American(s) [1]540, [3]356n, [5]253n
hatred of England [3]133; rebellion of [1]13
Ames, William (Giulielmus Amesius) (1576–1633) [3]795n, [6]117 q
"amiable" [2]591, 591n
Amiens, Peace of [2]845, 847n, [5]195n, [6]45
Aminta (in B&F) [1]394
"ammaximation" [1]579, 579n
Ammianus Marcellinus (b c 330) [2]746
Ammon (myth) [3]419
ammonia [1]569, 569n, 570n, [3]951, 998, 1001, 1027n, [4]526n
Ammonites [1]442n, 873
ammonium [3]44, 45
Ammonius Hermaeus (6th century) [5]748
amoeba [1]736 ("amoebean")
"amorphosing" [5]265, 265n
Amory, Thomas (c 1691–1788) *The Life of John Buncle* [1]lxxxviii, xc–xci, clxiii, 30; MT [6]249–50
amphibia [4]501, 502
amphibion/amphibii [2]346
amphibrach [1]377, 671, [6]255
Amphictyonic Council [3]108 ("Amphyctyonic"), 108n
Amphilochius, St, Bishop of Iconium (c 340–95) [5]683
amphimacer [1]379, 858, [2]1039, [3]903, [5]118
Amphis (4th century BC) [4]147
"amphoteric" [4]243n, 320n, [5]689n
amphoteric(s) [3]6, 6n, 379, [4]315, 315n, 320, [6]116
"amphoteros" [4]243
amphoterosis [5]663
amplification [2]513
amplitude [5]406
Amsterdam [1]218n, 687, [3]926, [4]176
amulet(s) [2]592, [3]373, 373n, [4]189, [6]97, 121, 121n
Amulet [1]154, [2]616n
"amusement" [4]610n
Amyntas (in Tasso) [2]10
Amynus (Bible) [2]577
"an" [3]367–8
ana [1]464, 464n, [4]471
Anabaptist(s) [1]247, 256, 270, 310, [2]327n, 496, 1143, [3]724, 761n, 926n, [4]28, 28n, [5]501, 501n, 502, 562, 563, 647, 648, 648n, 649, 651

"anachoresis" [5]579
anachronism(s) [1]417, [3]834, [4]608, 804n, [5]119
 in Jonson [3]178; in Shakespeare [3]174
Anacreon (c 570–c 475/485 BC) [2]354, 984, [4]291, 691, 691n
Anahita (myth) [3]92 ("Anahid"), 92n
anaktodouleia [1]257, 257n
analogon [1]583, [3]16, 259, 1010, [4]168
 transcendent [5]751
analogous, the [3]1000
analogy/analogies [1]114, 201, 236, 345, 620, 685, 719, [2]143, 250, 545, 545n, 564, 657n, 799, 949, 1028, [3]102, 280, 312, 433, 611, 663, 671, 689, 739, 776, 841, 850, 920, 997, 1035, [4]114, 323, 453, 496, 520, 669, 768, [5]26, 32, 32n, 70, 156, 231, 413, 622, 654, 771, 796, 798, 825, [6]8, 52, 264
 abuse of [2]860; of circumstances [1]492; deceptive [5]780; distant [5]39; Donne's taste for [2]273; evil of [4]225; of faith [3]452, [4]473, [5]563, 563n, 575; good substitutes [1]277; intimate [4]267; of life [3]62; logic of [6]70; and metaphor(s) [1]123, [3]311n, 551, 551n; mock [3]866; to prayer [4]682; of spirit [5]579; true [1]610; wilfulness of [2]232
analysis [3]344, 834–5, [4]111, [5]242
 differential *see* calculus; transcendental [2]673
Analysis of the Report on the Extinction of Slavery MT [1]31–6; [4]8
anamnesis [1]510n
anamorphoses [3]393n
Ananas/Ananus (Bible) [2]509 ("Amarus"), 509n, 517, 707, [3]476, 477n, [5]402n
Ananias (Bible) [1]294, [2]492, 509n, [3]987, 987n, [5]645, 645n, [6]55, 55n
anapaest/anapest [1]403, [2]129, 221, 762 ("anapestic"), [3]814, [6]255
anarchists [2]510, 512
anarchos [6]78, 78n
anarchy [1]423
anarthrous [1]574, 574n
anastasis [3]436, 436n, 663–4
anathema(s) [1]339, [2]1152, [3]780, 819, [5]8, 683
 a. maranatha [3]216, 562, 562n, [5]643
anatomist(s) [1]626, [2]343, [5]175, 180, 481
anatomy
 comparative [2]268, 1026n, [3]841–2, 1043; phytological [4]82
anav [4]254
Anaxagoras (c 500–428 BC) [1]557, 557n, [5]719n
 system of [5]721
Anaxandrides (4th century BC) [4]147
Anaxarchus (fl c 340 BC) [5]728
Anaximander of Miletus (c 611–546 BC) [1]669n, 691n
Anaximenes (fl 380–320 BC) [5]694, 719
"ancestry" [1]392
Anchises (in Virgil) [1]xci, 109n
"ancient" [2]260
ancient(s) [4]604, [5]689, 690
 phraseology of [4]136; Swedenborgianism of [5]710; veneration of [4]105
Ancillon, Johann Peter Friedrich (1767–1837) [5]305
 Über die Staatswissenschaft [5]305
Ancrum, Earl of *see* Carr/Ker, Robert
"and" [4]36, [5]402n, 487, 516, 516n
Andala, Ruardus/Ruardo (1665–1772) [4]242
Anderson, Adam (d 1846) [3]942
Anderson, Alexander (d 1811) [3]937, 940
Anderson, John Parker (b 1841) [1]cli, clii
Anderson, Robert (1750–1830) [1]50, 55, 55n
 Works of the British Poets [1]lxxi, lxxxi, lxxxiii, civ, cixn, cx, cxxvi, cliii, 413n, 766, 766n, [2]102, 213, 760n, 769n, 1033, 1170n, [3]882, 882n; *Copy A* MT [1]37–51; *Copy B* [1]cxxxixn; MT 52–75; *Copy C* [1]cxxxixn; MT 76–87
Anderson, William (probably the marine painter, 1757–1837) [3]937
Anderton, Lawrence ("John Brerely") (1575/6–1643) [2]670, 673, 673n
 Protestants Apologie for the Roman Church [2]673n
Andes [3]859, 920, [5]387
Andover [3]107
 Theological Seminary [3]107n
Andreini, Giovanni Battista (b 1578)
 Adamo [2]973, 974
Andrew, St, the Apostle (1st century) [2]252, 256, 257
Andrewes, Lancelot (1555–1626) [1]73, *73n–4n*, [2]260, 260n, 294n, 338, 1100–1, 1101n
 XCVI. Sermons [2]1101n
Andrews, Dr [5]78
Andrews, Dr (fl 1612) [2]232
androgyne/androgyny [3]906n, [4]611n
andronicon [1]551
Andry, Charles Louis François (1741–1829) [3]1067n
anebe [1]464, 464n
"anecdote" [2]149n
anecdote(s) [1]50n, 699, 818, [3]204, 222, 307, 308n, 726, 964, [5]49
 of Christ [4]471; hearsay [6]63; traditional [2]439

anecdoton/anecdota [2]149, 149n, [3]41, 41n
aner [1]551, 551n
aneurism [4]164
Anfang [1]608n
angebohrnes [3]266, 266n
"angel" [2]267
angel(s) [1]269, 273, 297, 375, 457, 573, 575, 576, 618, 644, 681, 706, 773, 783, [2]267, 269, 306, 360, 429, 429n, 433, 510, 514, 662, 723, 723n, 743, 901, 901n, 993, 1077, 1105–6, 1146, 1147, 1186, 1186n, [3]200, 214, 474, 477, 526, 564, 595, 768, 769, 884, 985, 1086–7, 1086n, 1088, 1089, 1089n, 1090, [4]53, 302, 303, 445, 548, 678, [5]33, 33n–4n, 54, 54n, 56, 404n, 406n, 407, 407n, 411, 415, 417, 474n, 493, 494n, 505n, 607, 612, 656, 670, [6]114, 138, 176, 261, 310
 and Abraham [6]106, 107n; accusing [5]85, [6]97; apostate [1]656; black [4]538; angelic body [3]46; brethren of the [1]687n; Christ an [2]743; evil [6]118; existence of [6]115, 115n; fall of [1]708, [2]510, 652, 652n, 653, 973, 1146, [3]14, 14n, 417n, 436n, 473, 473n; fallen [2]571, 1105–6, [3]25, 48, 48n; fifth [6]166; guardian [3]436–7; deliver/give law [1]468, 468n; [2]472, 472n; meaning [2]919–20, 919n; in *Paradise Lost* [3]411–13; pitying [1]149; of the Presence [3]102, 594; rebel [5]424n; repeating [3]436; "seen of" [3]30; single [2]429, 429n; sociable [1]485; at Sodom [1]418, 418n; worship of [6]146
Angelina (in B&F) [1]385
Angelo (*Measure for Measure*) [4]693, 693n
angelos/angeloi [3]1086n, [5]33, 33n
anger [1]165, 165n, [2]255, 637, 1158, [3]867
 holy [1]730–1
Angerstein, John Julius (1735–1823) [2]1195n
angle(s) [1]463, 463n, [5]202
anglers [4]802
Anglesey, Earl of *see* Annesley, Arthur
Anglo-Americans [3]133
Anglo-Saxon (language) [3]633, [6]17, 289
anguish(es) [4]809
 chaotic [5]425; child of [1]638
anhippos [5]47n
anility/anilities [4]146, 514
anima [4]420, 420n, 542n
 a. animans [6]296; *a. humana* [5]448; *a. mundi* [1]180n, [2]788, 788n, [3]854, [5]715, 715n, 733, 830; *a.* physical [5]453; *see also* world-soul
animadversions [5]500
animal(s) [1]538, [2]689, 856, 860, 1008n, 1026, [3]841, 998, 1002, [4]420, 494, [5]286, 286n, 287n, 290, 292, 310, [6]80
 blessing of [5]652n; chemistry [3]1002n; cruelty to [4]96n; Descartes on [4]389, 389n–90n; domestic [5]380; elemental [3]1037; genera of [5]388; generic immortality [3]317; graminivorous [5]246; human [4]196; inferior [5]731; instinct in [6]126; kingdom [5]442, 446, 447; language in [1]111; life of [5]715; machines [4]211–12, 212n; and man [1]126, [2]1000, 1000n, [4]420, [5]728, [4]530–1, 531n; most hateful [5]476; microscopic [3]1043; no noblest [2]1000; prehistoric [2]862; realm [5]259; reason in [1]111, 111n; respiring [4]492; sinless [2]1109; souls of [3]424, [4]91–8; species of [5]387; spirit-world [3]197, 198; torpid class of [5]445; *a. triplex* [1]166; and vegetable [4]493; visible [4]142
animal magnetism [1]535, 581, *581n–2n*, 582, [2]452n, 492n–3n, 533, 549, 1011n, 1016, [3]94, 94n, 364–5, 364n, 371–99, 598n, 715–17, 867–8, 872, 1067, 1067n, [4]270–8, 496, 496n, 497, 497n, 498–9, 514, 592, 592n, 681, 682n, [5]141n, 191, 404n, 467n, 517, 517n, 723n, 726n, [6]99, 99n, 104n, 169–70
 1784 report on [6]120, 120n. *See also* clairvoyance; grade, magnetic; mesmerism; zoomagnetism
animal magnetists [2]458n
animalcule [4]394, [5]409
animalia [5]287
animalisation [5]348
animality [1]589, 596n, [4]420
animation [2]999–1000
 spirit of [1]675; suspended [2]69, 1087, 1099, [3]613, 733, [4]137, [5]191, 622
animity [4]420, 420n
animus [3]1087, 1087n, [4]420, 420n, 542, 542n
Anlagen [5]738
anlehnen [4]284, 284n
Anmuth [4]254, 254n, 358
annal(s), abridged [2]377
Annalen der Philosophie [5]768
Annales du Muséum national d'histoire naturelle [4]532n
Anne, Queen of England (1665–1714) [1]182, [3]141n, 483, [4]336, 336n
 accession of [1]182; reign of [1]122, [4]79, 180n, [6]81; Test Acts of [4]20, 20n
Anne of Bohemia, Queen of England (1366–94) [2]823, 823n

Annesley, Arthur, 1st Earl of Anglesey (1614–86) [1]255
Annianus, Bishop of Alexandria (1st century) [4]473n
annihilation [1]184, [2]669n, [3]317, 433, [6]113
  of the wicked [5]584
anniversary [5]550
annotation(s) [1]440, [2]394, [5]500
Annual Anthology [2]351
  II ed RS [1]lxxx, cxiii; MT [1]88–99; [4]283n
Annual Register [1]356n
Annual Review and History of Literature ed A. Aikin [2]849n, [3]805, [4]283n
annunciation [4]477
anodynes [5]163, 419
anomaly [4]730
anonymity
  anonymous reviews [3]418–19, 419
"anordinated" [4]500, 500n
anothen [2]485, 485n
anous [5]391, 391n
Anschauen [4]131–2, 132n, 460, [5]265
anschaulich [4]185
Anschauung [1]568, [2]607, 607n, 610, [3]80, 80n, 90, 90n, 241, 242, 283, 333, 393, 641n, [4]131, 223, 223n, 351n, 393, 393n, 394, 394n, [5]369, 751, [6]325, 325n; *see also* intuition(s)
Anselm, St, Archbishop of Canterbury (c 1033–1109) [2]664, [3]785, [4]108, 108n, 347n, [5]769–77
  error of [5]789
Anson, George, Baron Anson (1697–1762) *Voyage round the World* [2]754n
anstatt [1]20–1
Anster, John (1793–1867) [1]24, 100, [2]140, 1116, [4]6
  Poems [1]clxiv–clxv; MT 100–3; *Solitude* MT [1]103; *The Times* MT [1]100–3
Anstey, Christopher (1724–1805) *New Bath Guide* [5]690, 690n
ant(s) [2]689, 861n, [3]558, 581, 581n, [4]87–8, 531, [5]731
  a.-hills [4]88
Antaeus (myth) [1]71, [6]127, 127n, [4]198 ("Antheus")
antagonism [5]78
antagonist [5]70
ante [1]*562n*
antecedent [5]65, 788
  and consequent [5]6; universal [2]543, [5]443
ante-columbianism [1]528
ante-diluvian(s) [1]782 ("anti-"), 783n
antelope [4]535
Ante-Nati [4]105
antennae [3]671
antepasts [5]796
anteriority [2]1162
anthelmintic [3]377
Antheus *see* Antaeus
Anthony, St *see* Antony, St
"anthropogony" [3]355, 355n
anthropoid(s) [3]811, [4]15
anthropology [2]51–2, 998–1031, [3]715
anthropomorph [5]406, 731
"anthropomorphic" [2]1175, 1175n
anthropomorphism [1]201, 566, 566n, [2]152, 255, 901, 1174, [3]357, 1091, [4]308, [5]129, 456, 730, 730n, 741
anthropomorphitism [4]547
"anthropophagous" [2]73n, 73n
anthropos [5]21
  a. misoumenos [5]475
anti-bases [4]320
"Antichrist" [4]20n
Antichrist [1]473, 473n, [2]592, [3]442, 449n, 471, 697, [4]20, 20n, 548, [5]178, [6]14, 167
  church of [4]21n, [6]16n; prophecies of [6]108
antichristianism [3]698
antichthon [2]557, 557n, [5]228, 229n, 700–1, 700n, 701n, 703, 703n
anti-churchman [1]808
anticipation [4]379, 799, 800, [5]192
anticlimax [5]841
Anticyra [1]768 ("Anticera"), 768n, [4]191, 191n
Anticyre, herb of [5]529, 529n
antidote(s) [3]112, 522, 1083, [5]131, 189, 552
  moral [1]812
anti-episcopalians [2]61
anti-episcopists [4]591
anti-figure [3]1011
anti-friction [1]527, 527n
anti-frictionist [1]527
Antigonus (c 80–35 BC) [2]157n
Antigua [1]32, [3]990
anti-Jacobin [3]148
Anti-Jacobin [2]755n, 794, 850, [5]145n
anti-light [1]685n
anti-liturgists [5]510
antimony [1]215, 215n–16n, [5]261
Antinomian(s) [1]804, [2]788, 788n, 1178, [3]735, 743, 743n, [4]596, 596n, [5]471
antinomianism [1]814, *814n*, [2]496, 496n, 655, [4]596n, [5]189, 189n, 496, 588n
antinomies of reason [5]750
Antioch [2]450, 451, 506n, 670, [3]49n, [5]525, 832
  Church of [5]660n; Council of [2]736, [5]632
Antiochus IV (Antiochus Epiphanes), King

of Syria (c 215–163 BC) [2]36n, 155, 155n, 156, 157, 157n, 377, 411, 411n, 416, *416n–17n*, 420, 1074, 1075, [3]34n, 111–12, 111n, 112n, 420n, 923, [4]65
reign of [1]441n
Antiochus Epiphanes *see* Antiochus IV
anti-paedobaptism [1]810
anti-paedobaptist(s) [1]247, 263, 355, [2]1143, [3]470, [5]563, 650, [6]41
English [5]501
Antipater (398–319 BC) [2]416
antipathy/antipathies [2]163, 812, [5]150
of English and French [4]239–40, 240n; national [5]195
Antiphanes (c 408–c 334 BC) [4]147
anti-philtre [4]620, 620n
antiphos [1]785, 785n
antipode of faith [3]764
Antipodes [1]764–5, 797
antipole [1]653
anti-pope [2]507n
anti-prelatism [1]319
anti-prelatists [1]805, [2]61, [4]591
antiquarian [3]174, [2]815–16
antiquarianism [4]586
antiquity/antiquities
accident of [2]260; Christian [5]526, 561; ecclesiastical [2]1041; pagan [6]99
"Anti-Reformer" [4]14
"antiscriptural" [1]736, 736n
anti-Sinai [1]846
Anti-Slavery Society *see* London
Antisthenes (c 455–c 360 BC) [2]872, 872n, [3]650
antithesis/antitheses [1]348, 563, 597, [2]249, 683, 989n, 990, 991, 993, 1186, 1193, [3]6, 12, 18, 130, 137, 223, 223n, 416, 449, 450, 451, 453, [4]399, [5]185, 283, 680, 776, [6]132
of creature to God [2]676; false [3]224; language of [5]131; philosophical [2]170; primary [5]273; and thesis [2]316, [4]722, [5]49, 444, 460, 661; *see also* polarity
antithet(s) [3]913, [5]264
antitheton/antitheta [4]319, [5]446
anti-trinitarian(s) [6]87, 91
antitype(s) [2]749, [3]78, 78n, [5]59, 413
of water [3]594, 594n
"antizote" [1]594, 594n
antlos [1]769n
Anton, Paul (1661–1730) [1]492n
Antonines/Antonini [1]315, [2]299n, 692, 692n, [4]627, 627n, [5]829, 829n
Antoninus, Marcus *see* Aurelius Antoninus, Marcus
Antoninus Pius (86–161) [5]829, 829n
Antonio (in Godwin) [4]95n
Antonius, Marcus (Mark Antony) (c 83–30 BC) [2]157n, 878, 919n, [3]447
Antony of Egypt, St, (c 251–356) [2]568, 727–8, 728n, 733–4, 737–8, 742, 1041, [4]93, 95, 95n, 96n, [5]121n ("the Great")
Antony of Padua, St (1195–1231) [1]725, [4]96, 96n, [5]652, 652n
Antony *see* Antonius, Marcus
Antony (*Antony and Cleopatra*), [4]737
Antony (*Julius Caesar*) [2]522, [4]733, 735 ("Ant.")
Antwerp [2]65n, 938n, [3]993, [4]48
Museum voor Schone Kunsten [3]993n
anvaan [4]254
anvnuth [4]254, 254n
anxiety [4]774, [5]122
age of [4]610
anything [2]887–8
aoratos [2]419, 419n, 422, 425n
aorist [2]711, 711n
first [6]165
aorta [3]717
"apagogic" [5]803
"apagogical" [5]792
"apagogically" [5]780
ape(s) [2]346, 346n, 800, 869–70, 870n, [4]431, 530
apeiron [1]107n, 114n, 548n, 585, *585n*, 653, 653n, 669n, 691n, [2]563n
Apel, Johann Gottfried Jakob (1771–1816) [2]579
Apella (in Horace) [5]651
aphesis [1]466, 466n
aphids [6]152
aphorism(s) [2]118, 123, [3]21, 220, 223, 225, [4]475, 783
"aphorisming" [1]141, 141n
aphorisming [1]55
aphorist [1]137
aphrodisiac [2]693n, [4]694, 694n, [5]254n
Aphrodite (myth) [3]92n, 391n; *see also* Venus
apiary [5]831
Apocalypse [5]349n, 494, 578, 607 ("apocalyptic")
interpretations of [5]630n; of Jesus Christ [3]421, 448, 477; *see also* Bible: NT: Rev
Apocalypt [1]486, [5]85
apocope [5]566
"apocrypha" [1]493n
Apocrypha *see* Bible: Apocrypha
apodictic [3]966, 966n
Apollinarius, the Younger, Bishop of Laodicea (c 310–c 390) [2]749

Apollo (myth) [1]147, 219, 399, 403, [2]134–5, 135n, 214, 217, 505, 575, 578–9, 583, 583n, 869n, 1127, [3]177, 616, 616n, [4]189n, 648, 835, 835n, [5]117n, 227, 522n, 657, 745n
oracle of [2]727, 733. *See also* Helios; Phoebus; Sol
Apollo Belvedere [5]117, 117n
Apollo Daphneus [3]921
Apollodorus (fl c 300–260 BC) [4]147
Apollodorus (fl c 140 BC) [3]234n
Apollonius of Tyana (c 4 BC–c AD 98) [1]162, 188, 454, 454n, [2]704, 705, 706, 708, 708n, [3]922, 922n, 923, 923n, [5]741, 741n
Apollonius Rhodius (3rd century BC)
tr F. Fawkes [1]38
Argonautica [2]583n
Apollos/Apollo (fl c 54) [1]467, 468n, [2]563, 563n, 706, 706n, [3]20, 20n, 310, 310n, [5]395, 395n, 536, 667, [6]117, 117n
Apollyon (Bible) [2]308, 512
apologising for Christianity [5]513, 513n
apologist [1]523
apologue(s) [1]695, [3]154, 595, 767, [6]118
admonitory [5]415
"apology" [3]539
apomnemoneumata [4]470, 470n–1n, 473, [5]526, 526n
Apomti (myth) [4]489–90
apoplexy [4]183, 183n
"apostasis" [1]675, *675n–6n*
apostasis [1]609, 609n, 649, 649n, 678, [2]*675n*, [3]436, 436n, [5]761
consequence of [2]326; creature as [2]676; defined [2]326; of spirits [2]562; in stasis [1]678, 678n; *see also* Fall
apostasy/apostacy [1]601, [2]147, 601, [3]27, [5]85, 127, [6]113
apostate angels [1]656; from Christ [2]592; first [1]708; fundamental [5]662; original [1]460; papal [2]707; primal [2]658; Romish [4]20; *see also* Fall
apostate(s) [1]874, [2]710
hierarchy [3]14, 14n
apostle(s) [1]316, 543, 719–20, 832, 833, 847, [2]254, 256, 439, 442, 447, 453–4, 455, 468, 475, 483, 492, 673, 681, 710, 712, 744, 811, 921, 1059, 1078, 1081, 1111, 1159, [3]74, 309, 310, 431, 446, 448, 669–70, 685, 696, 725, 766, 1069, [4]55, 248n, 251, 260, 471, 477, 484, 627, 627n, 638, [5]122, 129n, 140, 505, 512, 513, 522, 522n, 524, 526, 529, 535, 539, 553, 561, 570, 583, 608, 621, 623, 635, 641, 645n, 659, 666, 667, 680, 682, 823, 859n, [6]119, 307
age of *see* age(s), apostolic; authority of [5]683–4; baptism by [2]736; beloved [5]554; books of [5]10; chief of [2]502; of the Circumcision [3]467, 467n; competent recorders [4]479–80; constitution of [6]19; discourses of [4]471, 475; epistles [3]697; fallibility of [2]495; foundation [2]670; gifts of [1]309; infallibility of [5]622; inspiration of [3]20; instruction of [3]27; linguipotence of [1]317; lives of [4]474, 474n; marriage of [2]703; miracles of [3]8; as missionaries [4]473–4; missions of [3]6, 6n–7n; oral and written instructions [2]701; philosophic [4]348; preaching of [2]452; records of [5]526, 526n; spirit [2]811; strong-minded [4]254, 255n; succession from [3]720, 720n–1n, [4]550, [5]634n; system of faith [3]685; testimonies of [2]436–7
Apostles' Creed *see* Creed, Apostles'
"apostolichrony" [4]67, 67n
apostolicity [6]64
apostrophe(s) [2]662, [3]404
apothecary [4]785
apparatus of experiment [5]562
apparition(s) [2]1077, 1081, [3]197, 214, 824, 920, [4]781, 839, 845, 849, [5]175, 598, 605
Irish [5]599; luminous [3]128
appearance(s) [1]774, [3]23, 273, [4]129n, 210, 271–2, 448, [5]175, 405
categories of [5]615; and illusion [3]249, 249n; language of thoughts [5]416
appetence [1]685, [3]18n
and will [3]18
appetible [1]773
appetite(s) [1]171, 819, [2]689, [3]63, [4]268, 445, 731, [5]168, 784
animal [3]401; inherent [5]600; sinful [3]402
apple
bewitched [6]120; a.-dumpling [4]115; of knowledge [5]598; in leaves [6]130; pie [2]641, [4]162; tree(s) [3]167, 373
Appleyard, Joseph Albert *Coleridge's Philosophy of Literature* [2]1055n
appointments, extraordinary [5]537
Appollinarius *see* Apollinarius
"apponible" [4]384, 384n
"apprehend" [6]82, 82n
apprehend and comprehend [4]302
apprehension and comprehension [1]567, [2]1192, 1192n, [5]792
apprentice(s) [1]873, [2]521, 909
apprenticeship [5]378
appropriation [5]653

approximations [5]156
apriority [3]966, 967
Apsley, Sir Allen (?1569–1630) [2]1191
Apuleius, Lucius (b c 125) [2]87
Apulia [6]150
aqua [3]193n
a. cristallina [5]557, 557n; *a. intima* [1]622
aqua vitae [3]1070
Aquaster (myth) [1]654
aquiform [5]451
Aquila Ponticus/of Pontus (fl early 2nd century) [2]270, 270n, 379, 714, [4]255
Aquinas, Thomas, St (1225–74) [1]xci–xcii, civ, 286, 301, 479n, 538n, 862n, [2]11–12, 12n, 183, 255, 272, 653 q, 913, [3]142n, 972, 973, 1078, 1078n, [4]643, [6]114 q, 116
not annotated by C [1]lxiii; C's reading of [1]50, 50n; commentary on Aristotle [5]802, 802n; pun on [3]193, 193n
Quaestiones disputatae de malo [2]299n; *Summa theologia* [1]232n q, 802, [2]29n, [5]804
Arab(s)/Arabian(s) [1]540, [2]727, 739n, 1017, [3]355, [4]354n, [5]352, 844
Arabia [1]764n, 797, [2]384n, 414, 455, 455n, 493, 830, 1113, [3]21, 673, 1080, [5]308, 309
Arabian Nights [2]159n, 196n, 1119, 1119n, [3]405 ("Arabian Tale"), 877n, [4]28, 846n, [5]167n, [6]158, 159, 159n
Arabic (language) [2]12n, 375, 574n, 683, 836, [4]243, 243n, 846n, [5]237, 337
Aragon [3]104n
Aral [2]528
Aramaic (language) [2]400n, 485, 561, [3]466n, [4]248, 248n, 473–4, [5]237n, 396n
Arber, Agnes (née Robertson) (1879–1960) [1]lxviii
arbiter [1]331
arbitrary, the [4]169
arbitrator [2]813
infallible [2]36
arbitrement [3]311, [4]141
and volition [2]247; *see also* will(s)
arbitrium [2]247, 1099, [3]359, 709
Arbouin, James (1742–1822) [5]464 ("Arboyin"), 464n
Arbuthnot, John (1667–1735) [1]156n
arc, metallic [6]135n
Arcadians [4]201
arcanum/arcana [2]1107n, 1152, [3]682
grand [5]433
d'Arcet *see* Darcet
arch [1]683, 683n, [2]182
of bridge [1]682; galvanic [6]135; geometry of [5]300; mathematical [3]989, 989n
archaism(s) [5]49, 861n
archangel [2]920
highest [5]202
Archas (in B&F) [1]366
archaspistae [6]66
"*archaspistes*" [6]93n
archaspistes [2]26, 26n, [3]45, 45n, 562, 562n, [5]274n
of Trinitarianism [6]93
archbishop(s) [1]308, 310, 352, [2]1043, 1043n, 1198, [5]503, 508, 537
arche [1]340n, 466n, 539n, 681, [2]466, *466n*, [6]5
Archelaus of Miletus (5th century BC) [5]719n
archers, English [3]165
archetype [3]304
archeus [1]569, 569n, 577, 589, 634n, [3]722
"archic" [1]570
archiereis [2]510
Archilochus of Paros (fl 714–676 BC) [2]759
archimage [2]409
archimager [3]420, 420n
archimandrites [5]509, 509n
Archimedes (c 287–212 BC) [1]121, 127n, [3]624
archipelago, Indian [5]262
architect(s) [2]429, [3]741
architecture [4]160
Archiv für den thierischen Magnetismus ed Eschenmayer, Kieser, and Nasse [2]533, [3]376n, 389, 389n, [4]497n, [5]136n, 141n
Archiv für Magnetismus und Somnambulismus ed Boeckmann [3]376n
Archiv für Physiologie ed Reil [3]376n, [5]141n
archives [2]399
arch-Jesuit [2]1079
Archontici [4]257
arch-philosopher [2]1147
arch-presbyter [1]339
Archytas (c 428–347 BC) [5]694, 695, 701n, 702
Arcona [4]489–90
Arctic [1]204n, [2]1112, [3]989n, [4]507
Arcudius, Petrus (1562/3–1633) [5]527
area [1]563
aredphogu [1]121
Ares (myth) [4]607n
Argand, Aimé (1755–1803) [1]303, 303n
Argens, Jean Baptiste de Boyer, Marquis d' (1704–71) [1]699n
Kabbalistische Briefe MT [1]104–15
Argentina [3]1077
Argonaut(s) (legend) [2]1031n
Argonautica [4]631

argument(s) [2]405, [4]409, [5]63, 396, 560
ad affectum caritatis [1]314; *ad hominem* [2]31, 563, 798, 798n, [4]95, 673; captious [6]106–7; in a circle [2]253; circular [5]31, 31n, 33, 33n, 287, 287n; conveyance of [2]31; cosmological [4]347, 347n; as edge-tools [5]75; appealing to hatred [2]1141; Kantian [5]790; of materialists [4]266–7; mode of [5]70; negative [5]677; ontological [4]347, 347n; road of [5]50; two-edged [1]313, 317; from universality of being [5]82; weak [3]983
argumentation [3]222
agility of [5]541; copiousness of [5]558
Argus (myth) [2]385–6
Ariadne (in B&F) [1]375
Ariadne (myth) [1]374, [5]836
Arian(s) [2]306, 740, 742n, 743, 744, 992, 992n–3n, [3]145n, 230, 524, 692–3, 692n, 762, 825, [4]302, 302n, 672, [5]7n, 8, 11, 11n, 19, 20, 24, 26n, 33, 51, 56, 58, 69, 569, 633, [6]80, 81, 87, 263, 306
Arianism [1]145, 145n, 274, 358, 587, [2]32–4, 296n, 728–36, *731n*, 732n, 740, 740n–1n, 741, 743n, 748n, [3]232, 232n, 673, [5]16n, 633n, [6]63, 71, 78, 81, 91, 136
anti-A. [5]25; in C of E [1]343; high [5]563; hypothesis of [3]673n; inconsistency of [6]80; relation to Socinianism and Unitarianism [2]265
Ariel (*Tempest*) [4]611, 611n, 786, [5]130n
Ariminum (Rimini), Council of *see* Rimini
Arion (legend) [2]239, [4]533n
Ariosto, Ludovico (1474–1533) [1]lxiii, 117n, 543, 543n, [2]131, [4]605, [5]110
Orlando Furioso MT [1]116–17; 217n
Aristaenetus (fl c 450) *Epistolae graecae*† [1]118
Aristeas [2]380, 381n, 831, *831n–2n*, 895, 895n
Aristides the Just (c 520–c 468 BC) [2]936, 936n–7n
Aristion (1st century) [3]4n
Aristippus of Cyrene (c 435–c 366 BC) [2]872, 872n, [5]226, 227, 227n
Aristobulus I (fl 103 BC) [3]112, 112n
Aristocles (2nd century) [5]728–9
aristocracy [1]727, [2]101, [3]799, [4]16, [5]124, 272–3
in England [2]68–9; of wealth [4]79
aristocrat [5]396
Shakespeare as [1]380
Aristogeiton (d 514 BC) and Harmodius [1]337, 337n
Aristophanes (c 450–c 386 BC) [2]631, 757n, 774, 775, [3]765n, 894, 1075n
Aristophanic sheep [3]828; discussed with J. H. Frere [1]xcviii; tr Frere [2]794–5; metres [1]387, 387n
The Birds [1]669n, [2]864, tr H. F. Cary [1]clxvi; MT 119–20; *The Clouds* [2]632n, 871n; *The Frogs* [1]872n, [2]794, [3]189, 189n, [4]864, 864n, tr Frere [1]119; *The Knights* [4]595n; *Plutus* [2]632n
Aristotelian(s)/Aristotelean(s) [1]73, 73n, [2]788, 1147, 1185n, [3]94n, [4]174n, [5]698n
born [5]771; exaltation [4]110; formula [3]158n; and Platonists [4]135, 135n, [5]732, 732n, 770, 772–3
Aristotelism [5]802
Aristotle (384–322 BC) [1]cxxiii, cxxxi, 368n, 525, 557, 566, 567n, 578n, 622n, 791, [2]11–12, 68, 135n, 318, 355, 466, 657n, 665n, 867n, 869, 968, 999n, 1110, 1136n, [3]84, 211n, 257n, 347n, 366n, 478n, 619, 622, 792n, 877n, 901n, 915n, 968, 973, 1085, [4]94, 105–6, 109, 113, 135 ("Stagyrite"), 235, [5]42, 43, 228, 446, 447, 554, 691, 695, 702, 713–14, 726n, 732 ("Stagyrite"), 734, 735–9, 736n, 737n, 761, 801–2, 801n, 804–5
not annotated by C [1]lxiii; and Archytas [5]694–5, 695n; attribution(s) [2]869n; authority of [5]805n; categories [3]901, [4]108, 108n; on creation [1]119; days of [6]51; disciples of [5]826n; ethics [4]654; faith of [4]200; on the good [1]185, 185n; infallibility of [5]800–1; Kant a modern A. [3]322n; on light [3]1018, 1018n; and Locke [4]105, [5]732, 732n; logic [3]411; logical works [5]803; and Plato [2]1146, 1146n, 1147, *1147n*, [3]913, [4]382, 382n, [5]698, 698n, 732, 732n, 735–6, 736n; and Pythagoras [5]702; race of [2]1146; remark by Fielding [1]50, 50n; and Schoolmen [2]12, 12n; on soul [2]542, 542n–3n, 552; spiritual children of [5]770; substantial forms of [5]470, 470n; successors of [5]743n; on tragedy [1]72, 72n
Categories [4]108n, 450n; *De anima* [1]354n, [3]1018n, [4]108n, [5]233n q, 554n, tr Hett [5]233n; *Ethics* [1]773, [5]39; *Eudemian Ethics* [4]654n; *Magna moralia* [4]654n; *Metaphysics* [2]869n, [5]701, 731, tr Tredennick [1]557n; *Nicomachean Ethics* [4]654n; *Organon* [4]291, 291n; *Physics* [2]869n, [3]916n, [5]733, tr Hardie and Gaye [5]699 q; *Poetics* [1]368n, [2]141n, [3]173n q,

[4]797n, [5]689n, [6]327–9, tr Bywater [6]327; *Politics* [5]39; *Posterior Analytics* [1]253n, [2]543n, [4]674n; *Prior Analytics* [1]340n; *Rhetoric* [5]689n; *Topics* [4]108n
arithmetic [3]201, 807, [4]105, 156, 218–19, 505, 505n, [5]227, 487, 656
infinitesimal [1]4; synthetic character of [3]966
arithmeticians [5]228
arithmoi [5]229n, 703, 703n
Arius (c 250–c 336) [2]32–3, 32n, 728, 728n, 730, *731n*, 732n, 734, 735, 736, 743, [3]692, 693, 761, 728 ("Arrius")
Ark (of Covenant) [1]424, [2]893, [3]108, 109
ark (Noah's) [2]391, 574n, 576, 580, 581, 584, [3]480, 593, 594, [5]387, 387n, [6]119
Arlington, Earl of *see* Bennet, Henry
arm [5]65
Armado, Don (*Love's Labour's Lost*) [4]783, 783n
Armageddon [2]47, [3]470, 470n
Armenians [2]660, [3]820
Arminian(s) [1]199n, 302, 524, 560, 674, 819, 821, [2]57, 651, 913, 913n, 916, 1157, 1157n, 1177n, 1193, [3]515–16, 515n, 738, 738n, 747n, 761, 823, [4]634, 672, [5]5, 81n, 596, 596n, 661, [6]109n, 297
ascetic [5]498; and Calvinists [1]351, 817–18, *818n*; clergy of C of E [1]327; persecutions of [6]108; *see also* clergy, Arminian
Arminianism [1]230, 269, 269n, 346, 346n, 358, 476, [2]31, 651n, 810, 810n, 914n, [3]307n, 515, 515n, 528n, [5]81n, 163n, 597, 678n, 683, [6]261, 298n, 311n
and Calvinism [1]476, [3]515, 515n, [5]584–5, 586, [6]311n; hollowness of [1]674–5; peccant part of [5]585; Wesley's [3]528, [6]311
Arminiensis, Henricus (Henry of Rimini) (d c 1314) [1]301
Arminius, Jacobus (Jacob Harmensen) (1560–1609) [1]269n, 351, [2]810, 810n, 913, [3]515n, 764, [4]644, [6]297n
armour [2]914, [3]444, [4]838
chain [5]528
Armour, George A. (fl 1884) [1]800
Armour, Richard Willard (b 1906) *see* Coleridge, S. T. IX *Coleridge the Talker* ed Armour and Howes
arm-pit(s) [1]179
Armstrong, Aileen M., and others *The Place-Names of Cumberland* [4]692n, [5]389n, [6]121n
Armstrong, Arthur Hilary *see* Plotinus *Plotinus*; Porphyry *Life of Plotinus* tr Armstrong
Armstrong, John (1709–79) [1]38
army/armies [1]850, [2]970, [3]157, 165, [4]735, [5]377n, 378, 379, 396
Austrian [5]379, 379n; British [5]379; mixed [3]419; Prussian [5]379n; reform of [5]377–81; standing [3]168
Army List [4]575n
Arnaud, Antoine (1612–94) *see* Lancelot and Arnaud
Arndt, Ernst Moritz (1769–1860) *Geist der Zeit* [1]lxivn
Arnim, Ludwig Joachim von (1781–1831) [3]127, [6]233
Arnobius, Afer (d c 330) [2]706, [5]602, 602n
Adversus gentes [5]602n
Arnold (in Solger) [5]88
Arnold, Lorna [1]clxin
coeditor [4]117, 243
Arnold, Matthew (1822–88) [1]160n
Arnold, Thomas (1795–1842) [2]44
Arnold, Weld [2]214
Arnold, William Harris (fl 1903) [2]213, 1117, 1169, [4]203
Arnot, Captain (fl c 1660) [2]1171n
"aroint" [3]188, 188n
Arran [2]578
arrangement [1]537, [2]1016, [3]331, [4]221
artificial [6]287; of particles [5]827
Arrian (Flavius Arrianus) (2nd century) [1]cv, 161n
arrogance [2]1024, 1024n, [3]957
arrow [2]993
Arrowsmith, Aaron (1750–1833) [4]601, 601n
Arrowsmith, R. (fl 1830) "Abstract of the Prize Essay of Dr William Horn" MT [2]366–7
arse, singing [2]772
arsenic [1]551, [2]615, 856, [3]1063, [5]264
arsis [1]403
arson [5]103
art(s) [1]515, [2]1065, [4]196, 451
antedate Flood [2]414; dishonest [6]59; fine [2]1018n, [3]993; history of [1]143; and nature [2]1052, [4]417–20, [5]737, 737n; work of [4]421n
Artaxerxes Longimanus (465–425 BC) [1]771, [2]149n, 374, 374n, 375, 377, 378, 416
artefact(s) [2]788, [5]552
Artemis, temple of [6]5n
Artemisia absinthium [1]851
arteriality [3]123, [4]149
artery/arteries [3]123, 123n, [4]164, [5]289–90, 789
arterio-muscular system [1]624

Arthur (*King John*) ^{4}711, 711n

Arthur, King of Britain (legend) ^{2}779n, 794, ^{6}160

Arthurian legend ^{2}410n

article(s) (of belief)

essential ^{5}432; fundamental ^{5}57, 617, ^{6}93; new ^{4}630–1; of revealed truth ^{5}61

article(s) (in grammar)

definite ^{1}455, *455n*, 465n, 471n, ^{2}880n, ^{3}11, 11n, nudity of ^{6}205, Greek ^{1}467n, ^{1}489–90, 490n, ^{2}423, ^{6}177

Articles . . . for the Establishing of Consent ^{4}681

Articles of Religion (C of E) ^{1}358, 359, 836–8, ^{2}35, ^{3}456n, 698, ^{4}642, 658, ^{5}5n, 53n, 467n, 471, 513, 566n, ^{6}79–80, 79n, 310n

Luthero-Calvinistic sections ^{5}498, 498n; Six Articles ^{1}809n; Thirty-nine Articles ^{1}316 q, 330, 360, 712n, 809, *809n*, ^{2}298n, 531n, 651, 651n, 1098, 1098n, 1104, ^{3}139n, 698, ^{4}298n, 307n, 659n, 664, ^{5}138, 156; specific Articles: 2 ^{6}79n; 6 ^{1}316n q, ^{5}567n q; 9 ^{3}526n q, ^{5}185n, 591, 591n q, 668n q; 10 ^{5}394n; 11 ^{5}597n, 670n q; 13 ^{5}138n q; 17 ^{5}156n q; 19 ^{5}660, 660n q, 661; 20 ^{1}316n q; MT ^{1}711; ^{2}1098; 25 ^{5}398n q; 28 ^{1}509; 29 ^{5}673n q; 30 ^{5}683n q, ^{6}21n; 37 MT ^{1}711

articulation ^{3}24, 61

of nature ^{1}537

artificers ^{3}109

artillery ^{2}125–6

artisan(s) ^{1}423, ^{5}378, 481, ^{6}216

Scotch ^{4}657

artist(s) ^{1}423, ^{3}20, 21, 109, 447, ^{4}450, ^{6}216

historian as ^{1}448; Italian ^{6}6

Artugon (myth) ^{4}489–90

Arundel, Earl of *see* Howard, Thomas

Arundel, William (fl 1691) ^{2}1095

"as" and "so" ^{5}502, 502n

as in praesenti ^{3}154n

Asa (Bible) ^{2}894

"Asahara" (SH) ^{1}lxxxvii

Asaph (Bible) ^{5}178, 178n

ascension ^{2}327, 940

re-a. ^{4}266; of Steffens ^{5}295

Ascension Day ^{3}666, 667

Ascension of Christ ^{2}1086, 1088, ^{3}45, 925, 926, ^{5}397–8, 529, 535, ^{6}105–6, 307

ascent ^{3}12, 564, ^{4}500

and descent ^{5}445n, method of ^{1}598; of individuation ^{1}597; in nature ^{3}580–1 ("ascend"); of soul ^{5}771

ascetic ^{2}728n

asceticism ^{2}872n, ^{3}625, 625n, 626

Ascham, Roger (1515–68) ^{2}64–9, 68n

aseity ^{1}585n, ^{3}944, 944n

Asgill, John (1659–1730) ^{1}cvi, cviii, cxlin, ^{2}158, ^{3}159, 159n, 425, 425n, 743, 743n

A Collection of Tracts ^{1}lxv, xcviii, cxlin; MT 121–9

ash(es) ^{1}750, 784, 790, ^{4}531, 531n, ^{5}257

of vegetables ^{5}262

Ash, Charles Bowker (b 1781) *Adbaston*† ^{1}130

Ash, Samuel (fl 1809) ^{1}130

Ashburn ^{1}272

Ashby, Anna Lou ^{5}866

Ashby de la Zouch ^{2}245

Ashe, Thomas (1770–1835)

Memoirs of Mammoth, and Various Other . . . Bones ^{4}532n; *Travels in America* ^{4}532n

Ashe, Thomas (1836–89) *see* Coleridge, S. T. IX *Miscellanies* ed Ashe

Ashley ^{2}649, 686

Ashley, A. J. (fl 1930) ^{2}840

Ashley, Baron *see* Cooper, Anthony Ashley

Ashley Cottage ^{1}cxin, ^{2}668

Asia ^{2}6, 178, 418, 474, 1017, ^{3}159, 419, ^{4}299, 507, ^{5}386, 494n, 634, 634n, ^{6}272

Asiatic courts ^{4}165; churches of ^{3}466; science in ^{2}702; travels in ^{4}29–31

Asia Minor ^{2}919n, 1017, ^{6}150n, 281n

Asiatic Researches ^{2}585n, ^{6}8n q

"ask at" ^{4}601, 601n, 613

askesis ^{5}86

Asklepieion ^{3}864

Asmodeus (Apocrypha) ^{4}514

asparagus ^{3}1075

Aspasia (5th century BC) ^{2}1069, 1069n

Aspatia (in B&F) ^{1}374, 375 ("Aspasia")

aspect, total ^{2}631

aspections ^{4}156

asphyxia ^{4}164

"aspicience" ^{2}607n

aspirate ^{3}828, 1068

aspiration(s) ^{1}356, 781

aspist ^{5}578

aspistes ^{5}578n

ass(es) ^{1}375, ^{2}662, ^{3}47, 97, 744, 873, ^{4}759, ^{5}652

brayless ^{2}240; a.-flings ^{1}6; jawbone of ^{1}422–3, *423n*; shadow of ^{3}234

assassin(s) ^{2}614, ^{3}220, 801, ^{4}774, 775, 792, 792n

assassination [1]337n, 422, [3]757n, 787n, 819, [4]74, [5]143
assent [2]644
  royal [4]20; supposed [5]638
assentation [2]76
assertion(s) [2]893, 1005, 1014, [3]65, 120, 213, 296, 395, 397, 456, 586, 598, 916, 1032, 1062, [4]272, [5]349, 372, 382, 396, 525
  arbitrary [4]482; blind [3]216; confidence of [3]420; groundless [5]3; mere [2]641; paradoxical [5]767; rash [1]850, [4]379; undocumented [5]707; unqualified [5]72; unsupported [4]480
assimilability [3]177
assimilation [4]320, [5]287, 650, 715, [6]296, 296n
  laws of [5]410; spiritual [5]674
association(s) (of ideas) [1]516, 561, [2]960, 961, [3]791–2, 792n, [4]218, 543
  accidental [1]60; accidents of [3]265; creatures of [2]971; of disease [3]913; doctrine of [1]580n; Hebrew [2]514; influence(s) of [3]914, [4]701; law of [1]693, [3]117, 117n, 213, 790, 792, [4]92, 106–7, 106n, 222, [5]789; link of [4]735; local [4]145; passive [4]221, [5]726; peculiar acts of [1]602; play of [4]856; swarm of [5]173; train of [2]635; vicious [1]394; visual [2]639
association(s) (social) [4]796
  visiting [1]530
associationism [3]242n–3n, [4]108n, 222n
assonance [3]891
assumption(s) [1]691, [2]609
  arbitrary [5]244
Assur (Bible) [1]444; *see also* Assyria/Assyrian(s)
"assurance" [5]126, 137–8
assurance(s) [2]828, 1166, [3]566, 662, 735, [5]125, 155, 172, 173
  false [5]188
Assyria/Assyrian(s) [1]443, 444, 444n, 707, 832n, [2]417, 832, [3]419, 478, [6]322n
  empire [3]923
Astarte (myth) [1]864, 864n, [2]580
astartolators [1]864
Astbury, John (?1688–1743) [3]634
asterisk [2]36, 36n
asterisms [2]932
Asterius, Bishop of Amasia (fl c 400) [5]587, 587n
asteroids [2]557n
"astheny" [6]26, 26n
Astraea (myth) [1]385, [4]339
astriction [3]1022, 1027
astrictive [3]1000
astringency/astringent, the [1]589, 595, 596, 598, 600, 604, 612, 613, 614, 631, 632, 633, 638, 665, 667, [3]1004; *see also* harshness
astrognosy [2]557
astrologers [5]234
astrology [1]642, [2]42, 825, [3]645, 653, 654, 779, 933, [4]144, 582, 614, [5]560
astronomer(s) [1]213, [2]276, 338, 648, [3]1080
  court [2]387; modern [5]225, 232; telescopic [2]1164
astronomy [2]825, 903, [3]426, 426n, [4]505–11, 513, 515–23, [5]560–1, [6]52
  Pythagorean [5]700; true [5]232. *See also* comets; planets; solar system; stars; sun
Astruc, Jean (1684–1766) [1]417n, 616, 616n
  Conjectures sur les mémoires originaux [1]616n
Asturius (legend) [2]725
Ate (myth) [4]629, 629n
Athanasian(s) [3]25, 692n, 825, [5]632–3, 657
Athanasius, St, Bishop of Alexandria (c 296–373) [1]587n, [2]306, 665n q, 733n, 736, *740n–1n*, 742, 742n, 744–5 q, 745n, 748, 748n, 750, 843, 938, [3]369, 442n, 524, 692, 762n, 1038n, 1038n, [4]95, 300n, 513, 514, 643, 650, 650n, [5]8n, 96–7, 558n, 573, 632, [6]72n, 91 q, 178, 307
  Creed of *see* Creed, Athanasian; death of [5]578; pseudo-Athanasian Creed *see* Creed, pseudo-Athanasian
  De symbolis [2]334n; *De synodis* [5]633n; *Oratio in Arium* [2]730n; *Vita Antonii* [2]728, 728n, [4]95n
atheism [1]114, 302, 514, 516, 645n, 679, 679n, [2]194, 346, 883, 935, 1205, [3]137, 205, 342, 493, 671, 1050, 1091, [4]27–8, 94, 548, 719, [5]71n, 76n, 145, 203, 208, 383n, 592, 614, 716
  akin to idolatry [3]77; decorous [5]456; Epicurean [1]120, 120n, 646; Epicurean veil [2]251; forms of [2]344; God makes the ground [1]585; in gown and surplice [2]1010; modest [3]358; moral [1]120, 120n; moral arguments [2]664–5; negative [2]345; Oken's [3]1042; painted [3]1083; Schellingian [2]554, [3]123; speculative [6]75–6; of Spinoza [1]239n; Spinozistic [3]296; supersensual [1]659
atheist(s) [1]173, 223, 239, 256, 281, 566, 804, [2]48, 497, 564, 1155, 1175, [3]1038n,

atheist(s)—*continued*
1038n, [4]834, [5]10, 118n, 615, 655n, 703, 729
Bruno not [2]976; Epicurus [5]386
Atheista Fulminato [1]390n
Atheling [3]786
Athena/Athene (myth) [1]617, 617n, [2]135n, 583n, [3]92, 92n. *See also* Minerva; Pallas
Athenaeum ed A. W. Schlegel, K. W. F. Schlegel, and Schleiermacher MT [1]131–53
Athenaeum (London) [1]cli, clxvn, 28, 760, [2]873, 874, [3]1064, [6]156
Athenaeus (fl c 200) *Deipnosophists* [1]299n
Athenagoras (2nd century) [1]105, [6]88
Athenians [1]178, [3]555, [4]201, 296
Athens [1]877n, [2]154, 558n, 919n, 981n, [3]143n, [4]296, [5]224, 642n, 733
Academus/Academy [1]174n, 616n, [2]154, 872, 872n, [5]642, 642n, 736, 752; Lyceum [5]736, 736n; other [2]918; Stoa [5]739
Atherstone, Edwin (1788–1872)
Fall of Nineveh [1]154; *The Last Days of Herculaneum* [1]154; MT [6]251–5
Atherton Moor [2]62
Athinganoi [6]150n
Athos, Mount [5]387n
Atkins, Mr *see* Atkyns
Atkins, Will (in Defoe) [2]165, 165n, 168
Atkyn, John Tracy (d 1773) *Reports of Cases* [3]500, 500n
Atkyns, Richard (1615–77) [1]334–5 ("Mr Atkins")
Atlantic Ocean [3]586, [4]533n
Atlas (myth) [2]577, [3]649
Atlas, Mount [4]81
atmosphere [3]205, 372, 1061, [4]397, 487, 539, [6]133
boundary line [5]734; density of [5]349
atom(s) [1]51, 108n, 307n, 596, [2]788, 890, [3]283n, 335, 344, 916, [5]460
in Epicurus [4]435; of the human frame [5]548; life-a. [3]1041–2; Mesmer's system atomic [3]865; organic [3]1037–8, 1038n; solid [1]108; *see also* corpuscles
atomism [1]107–8, 108n, [3]916n, [4]271n
Epicurean [5]552n
atomist(s) [1]596, [2]889, [4]160n, [5]714, 714n
atomology [3]1043
atonement [2]489, 659, [3]46, 47, 47n, [4]64, 64n, 630, [5]166, 766
at-one-ment [3]18
Atreus (myth) [6]213n
atrichismos [3]25n, 25n
Atrides (myth) [6]213, 213n
atrocity/atrocities [4]95, 178, [5]106, 415, 416n
atrophy [1]524
attainments, personal [5]529
attention [1]633, [2]539, [3]91, 399, 563, [5]581
power of [4]159
Attic (dialect) [3]830, 830n; *see also* Greek (language)
Atticus (109–32 BC) [4]80, 80n
Attila (c 406–53) [2]525
attönen [3]46, 46n
attorney general [3]436, [6]97
attraction [1]82n, 177, 578, 589, 599, 604, 623, 641, 643, 660, 665, 666, 667, 776, [2]788, 789n, 853, 853n, 854–5, 855n, 886, 996–7, 997n, 1186, [3]63, 129, 139, 280n, 286–7, 287–8, 288–9, 292, 293, 1003, 1004, 1006n, 1008, 1021, 1021n, 1022, 1060, [4]396, 417, [5]131, 264n, 266, 342
appropriative [5]435; and centrality [1]549; and contraction [1]549, [3]996, 996n, 998, [6]229, 230; elective [5]294; and gravity [3]286, 286n; and repulsion [1]563, 571, 573, 633, [2]311, [3]282, 297, 302, 343, 851, 851n, 1006, [5]231, 442, 451, 460; specific [1]862; *see also* polarity
attractive, the [1]595, 611, 638
attribute(s) [3]17, 24, [4]108, [5]6, 7, 203, 614, [6]32, 143
of Deity [5]406, 780; divine [3]617, [5]61, 75, 556, 635; God's [5]590; incompatible [1]601, [5]729; physical [5]481; substance(s) and [5]448; windy [2]38
attribution, act of [1]460
attrition [2]26, 27, 28, [5]585, 585n, 682
Atwood, George (1746–1807) [2]182n
Atys *see* Catullus *Attis*
Aubrey (in B&F) [1]398
Aubrey, John (1626–97) [1]55, 55n, 56, [2]111, [3]985 ("Audley"), 985n, [4]724, 724n
Brief Lives [4]724n, ed Dick [1]870 q; *Letters Written by Eminent Persons* [4]724n; *Miscellanies* [1]55n, 282n, [3]985n, [4]724n
audience(s) [4]742, 820, 839, [5]658
court [6]322; interest of [3]307; prejudiced [5]60; private [5]642; quest for [2]999; Shakespeare's [4]861
auditor(s) [4]604, 800, 845, [5]658
of Christ [1]513; inattentive [4]860
Audley *see* Aubrey
Aufidius (*Coriolanus*) [4]767, 804
Aufklärungsstolz [2]480
Auge [1]688n
augrim [4]814

Augsburg [3]756 ("Auspurg"), 762 ("Augspurg")
Confession [5]76, *76n*
augur [3]110
August II of Poland (1670–1733) [3]217, 217n
August/Augustus, Prince of Gotha (1747–1806) [4]187
Augustan age *see* age, Augustan
Augustine, St, Archbishop of Canterbury (d c 604) [5]138, 138n, 532
Augustine/Austin, St, Bishop of Hippo (354–430) [1]467n, 478, 490, 565, 565n q, 605 q, 605n q, 624n, [2]52, 53n, 247 q, 266 q, 283, 288, 294, 299 q, 301, 305, 317, 317n, 327 q, 335, 335n, 655n, 664, 667, 675, 680 q, 699, 743, 810, 823, 913, 923, 1137 q, 1138, 1192n, [3]28n, 452, 459, 459n, 470 q, 486, 509n, 524, 668, 687, 744, 744n, 748, 765, 765n, 771 q, 818n, 907, 985, 985n, 1078n, 1089, [4]231, 238n, 266, 266n, 644, [5]20, 25, 76n, 543 q, 545, 573, 573n, 574, 574n, 586–7 q, 593, 603, 603n, 613, 619, 629, 630, 641 q, 643, 662n, 663, 666 q, 671 q, 671n q, [6]23, 23n, 67n, 70–1 q, 93, 115, 115n, 138n, 307
not annotated by C [1]lxiii; on belief [2]29, 29n; *durus pater infantium* [5]586, 586n; on fortune [2]325; on heresies [2]272; Luther's admiration [2]272, 304; on marriage of cousins [2]91; on three genera/kinds of being [2]1147, 1147n, [5]483
City of God [2]199n, [5]402n; *Confessions* [1]645, 645n q, 709n, [3]618 q, 619, 619n q, [5]176, 176n; *Contra Manichaeos* [1]756 q; *De civitate dei* [2]575n, 792, 923n; *De fide et symbolo* [2]882n; Letter 164 [2]334 q, 334n
Augustus Caesar (Gaius Julius Caesar Octavianus) (63 BC–AD 14) [1]109n, 176, 486n, [2]108n, 755–6, 878 ("Octavius"), 919n, 949, 1018n, [3]240, 240n, 447, 722, [5]371, 487, 681 ("Octavius"), 829, 829n
age of [2]157, [4]336, 336n; time of [1]8
Augustus Frederick, Duke of Sussex (1773–1843) [2]955n, [6]48, 48n
Aulus Gellius *see* Gellius
aura electrica [5]445, 445n, 508, [6]116
aura ignea [1]618, 618n
aureity [3]520n, [6]302n
Aurelian (Lucius Domitius Aurelianus) (215–75) [1]8n
age of [1]8
Aurelius Antoninus, Marcus (121–80) [1]lxxxvi, cxxviii, 176, 799, [2]427 ("Marc Antonine"), 427n, 692, 727, [4]627n, [5]658, 658n, 829, 829n, [5]40, 40n, [6]27
"Life" by Dacier MT [1]156–9
His Conversation with Himself, together with Cebes *The Mythological Picture* tr Jeremy Collier MT [1]155–96; *Communings with Himself* tr Haines [1]164n; *Meditations* [1]lxxxii; MT [1]159–81, 192–6, tr Farquharson [1]164n q, 168n q, 169n q, 174n q
Aurifaber (Johannes Goldschmidt) (1519–75) [2]774n, [3]749, 779n
aurora(s) [5]814, 814n
a. borealis [5]814n
Aurora (myth) [6]157n
Aurora (ship) [2]586
Auschwitz [1]35n
Ausdehnung [4]209
auseinandersetzen [1]560, [3]262, 262n, [5]242
Ausonius, Decimus Magnus (c 310–95) [1]109, 109n
Mosella [1]109n
austerity [1]649
Austerlitz [5]379n
Austin, St *see* Augustine, St, Bishop of Hippo
Austin TX
University of Texas, Humanities Research Center [1]cxli, clxviiin, clxxiv, [2]966, [4]656n, marginalia in [2]3, 49, [3]838, [5]475, [6]154, 267, transcript(s) of marginalia in [2]42, 44, 357, 558, 828, 837, 967, 1110, [3]507, 1064, [4]11, 170, 294, 341, 469, 675, [6]257
Australasia [6]35–7
Australia [2]74n, 861n,
New Holland [2]176; *see also* Australasia
"Australis" (R. Southey) [2]74n
Austria [1]698, [5]312n, 379n, 507, [6]322
RC Church in [1]846
Austrian(s) [5]276n, 280
Austrian Succession, war of [1]698
Autenrieth, Johann Heinrich Friedrich von (1772–1835) [3]378–9
authenticity [2]477, 522, 888, [3]111, [4]260
of Bible [4]669; works of [6]142
author(s) [5]89
of all ages [5]811; bi-partite [5]134; gives authority [2]893; Jewish [3]524, [6]306; modern [2]77; perspicuous [3]522, [6]305; sensible [2]438
authority/authorities [1]430, [2]601, 644, 810, 893, 1098, 1111, [3]150, 204, 450, 558,

authority/authorities—*continued*
603, 899, [4]93, 260n, 646, [5]10, 425, 598, 683–4, [6]23
apostolic(al) [2]471, [6]13; appertinent [5]707; binding [3]20, 487; in Church [1]353, [3]686; of Church [2]195, [3]48, [5]574; of church or scripture [2]40; civil [5]501n; co-ordinate of [5]568; credible [5]63; of creed [5]620; dispensing [3]157; of early Church [5]578; of gospels [2]439; joint [1]834; of Kant [5]809; lawful [1]321, 352; learned [3]179; legitimate [2]510; Milton's reverence for [1]72; own [5]572; patristic [2]925, [5]526, 670n; and power [1]333, [3]157, 157n; revered [5]658; scriptural [1]824, [4]260; of Scriptures [4]260, [5]570; spiritual [5]68; spirit of [5]173
auto to pragma [5]4
autobiography [2]840, [3]773
autobiographical vein [5]810
Autochthon (myth) [2]577, 578n
autographs [4]473
autohuios [1]690, 690n
autokatakritos [6]56, 56n
automatism [3]790
automaton(s) [1]114, [3]429, [4]629
passive [5]530
autonomy [3]296
autopator [1]689, 690n, [3]30
autos [1]466, 466n
autotheism [2]883, 883n
autothetes [1]690, 690n
autumn [3]889, [5]349
Auxenius *see* Auxentius
Auxentius, Bishop of Milan (d 373/4) [2]747 ("Auxenius")
avarice [3]502, 650, [6]325
Ave Maria [5]819
Avenel (in Scott) [4]595, 598, 598n, 600, 600n
Averroes (1126–98) [3]243, 243n, [5]784–5, 786–7
aviary [3]976n
Avignon [6]22
Avila, Juan de (1500–69) [5]818
awe [4]653
ax [2]734, [5]729
Axen, von *see* Pappen
Axieros (myth) [1]665, 692n, [2]583, 583n, [3]399, 473
Axiokersa (myth) [1]665, 692n, [2]583, 583n, [3]399
Axiokersos (myth) [1]692n, [2]583, 583n, [3]399, 473
axiolatroi [1]257n
axiom(s) [3]354, 809, 1050, 1091
of ethics [5]37; moral [4]57; priest's [5]641; universal [5]459
axis, magnetic [1]663, [5]265, 344, 347
axle-tree [3]1004
Axon, William Edward Armitage (1846–1913) [1]761
ayin [2]54n
Aylmer, John, Bishop of London (1521–94) [2]68 ("Aelmer"), 68n, 69
Aynard, Joseph S. (fl 1909–34) [1]clin, cliin, clxvii
Ayr (ship) [5]862n
Ayscough, Samuel (1745–1804) [4]808, 808n; *see also* Shakespeare *Dramatic Works* ed Ayscough
Azara, Felix de (1746–1811) [5]254
Azores [2]213
"azote" [5]247, 247n
azote (nitrogen) [1]571n, 572 ("azoote"), 573, 589, 590, 594, 595, 596, 598, 599, 611, 617, 635, 641, 643, 660, 775, [2]546, [3]998, 998n, 1004, 1007, 1026, 1031, 1057, 1057n, 1058, 1063, [4]324, [5]258, 335n, 342, 344, 356, [6]116
and hydrogen [1]648; *see also* nitrogen

"B." [2]11
B., Hon Mr [3]893, 893n
B., Miss [1]153n
Baader, Franz Xaver von (1765–1841) [2]1002n, [3]115, 129, 292, 292n, 294n, [4]427, 444n, [5]325, [6]236
followers of [2]1002
Baal (myth) [1]845, [2]383, 399
Baalzebub (Bible) [3]57n; *see also* Beelzebub
Babbitt, Frank Cole (1867–1935) *see* Plutarch *De Pythiae oraculis* ed Babbitt
babble [1]313
babbling [5]640
babe(s) [5]466, 495, 648, 649
innocent [5]613; soul of [5]653
Babel [1]843n, [2]527, [3]722, [4]176, 257n, [6]119
baby/babies [4]650
heathen [1]246
Babylas, Bishop of Antioch (d c 250) [3]921
"Babylon" [5]635, 635n
Babylon [1]439, 708, 844n, 846, [2]148, 416, 417, 451, 473, 474, 513, 514, 832, [3]6, 422, 461, 462, 465, 467, 467n, 468, 542, 694, 721, [4]176, 474n, 513n, [5]226, 396n
captivity of Jews in *see* Captivity; Rome as [1]471

Babylonia [2]418
Babylonians [2]893, [3]480, [5]226n, 234
bacallao [4]692, 692n, 755 ("Baccalà")
baccalaureus [3]821
Bacchation [5]227
Bacchic rites [1]237n
bacchius [1]671
Bacchus (myth) [1]8n, [2]573, 576, 579n, 582, 584, 584n, [3]189, [5]227, 836; *see also* Dionysus
"bachelor" [3]821n
bachelor(s) [1]754, [2]919, [3]907
Bacon, Francis, 1st Baron Verulam and Viscount St Albans (1561–1626) [1]lxix, cxxiii, 156n, [2]648, 648n, 673, 679n, 825n, 882n, 933, 933n, 1131, 1143n, [3]133, 221, 251n, 531, 539, 540n, 558, 622, 877n, 882, 882n, 950, [4]632, [5]174, 200, 201, 201n, 208, 208n, 448, 695, 695n, 812, 826n, [6]133
 not annotated by C [1]lxiii; British Plato [3]919n, 950n; *confessio fidei* [4]664; ingenuity [2]88; and Kant [3]919n; and Plato [6]315; Platonist [4]159–60, 160n, [6]50n; tribute to [4]403n; view of reason [2]333n; Baconian work [2]954, 954n; on Xenophon [4]310n
 The Advancement of Learning [2]648n, [3]573n, [5]124n; *Apophthegms* [5]360n q; "A Confession of Faith" [4]664n q; *De augmentis scientiarum* [3]557n, 558n, 950n; *History of King Henry VII* [5]532, 532n q; *Novum Organum* [2]277, 1024 q, 1024n, [3]557, 557n, 919, [4]403, 403n, tr *New Organon* [3]919n, 950n; "Of Heresies" [4]632n; "Of Unity in Religion" [4]632n q; *Works*: ed Mallet (1740) [1]75n, 766, 766n, [3]558n, 724n, 882, 882n, [3]950n, [4]632n q, 664n q, [5]75n, 124n, 360n q, 532n q; (1765) [1]766, 766n; (1803) [1]766, 766n, [3]882n; (1807) [3]882n; ed B. Montagu (1825–37) [1]527, 527n; ed Spedding, Ellis, and Heath (1857–68) [3]950n, [4]664n, [5]360n, 532n, [5]124n, 360n q
Bacon, Roger (c 1214–c 1294) [2]12n, [3]645, 645n, [5]695, 695n
bacteria [2]362n
baculus [1]419
Badams, John (d 1833) [3]191, 191n
Baddeley, St Clair (fl 1893) [2]116
Baden, Duke of *see* Karl Friedrich
Baer, E. (fl 1945) [2]830
Baevius (1st century) [5]831
Bage, Isaac (fl 1817–24) [1]xcviii, [2]689
Baghdad [4]29, [6]270
baguette [4]497, 497n
Bahrdt, Karl Friedrich (1741–92) [1]197
 Glaubens-Bekänntniss ed J. F. Jacobi MT [1]197–202
Bailey, Nathan (d c 1742) *Universal Etymological Dictionary* [2]38n, [4]181n
Baillie, William (fl 1638–48) [2]1171n
Bailly, Jean Sylvain (1736–93) [3]1067n, [4]508
Baines, Peter Augustine (1786–1843) *Faith, Hope, and Charity* MT [1]203–4; [4]3
Baird, Dr (fl 1810) [3]940
Bajazet [5]832, [6]102
baker [1]878
Baker, Rachel (b 1794) [1]205
 Devotional Somnium [1]205; *Remarkable Sermons . . . Delivered During Sleep*† [1]205
Balaam (Bible) [2]143–4, 144n
 children of [6]59
Balaamites [2]506, [5]624, [6]59
balance [4]358–9, 603–4, [5]98
 of trade [1]123, 123n; verbal [3]224
"bald" [3]25n
Baldovini, Francesco (1634–1716) *Lamento di Cecco da Varlungo* MT [1]206–10
Baldwin (in B&F) [1]397
Baldwin, T. W. [3]719
Bale, John (1495–1563) [2]819, 819n
 Illustrium Majoris Britanniae scriptorum [2]819 q, 819n
Balfour (in Scott) [4]588
Balg, Gerhard Hubert (1852–1933) *A Comparative Glossary of the Gothic Language* [6]287n
Bali (myth) [2]342
ball(s) [3]362, 362n, 1034, [5]32
 in electric machine [5]349
Ball, Alexander John, 1st Baronet (1757–1809) [1]738, [2]158, 889n, 1204n, [3]149n, [5]831, 831n
ballad(s) [2]387, [4]90
 metre of [5]689; popular [4]815
ballets [2]191
balloon [2]321, 321n, [5]346
ballot [2]90
Balthasar (legend) [4]55n
Baltic [1]537, [5]196
Baltimore MD
 The Johns Hopkins University Library, marginalia in [1]488, [6]158, 159
Bamberg [2]1086n
banana [4]89, 89n
Bancroft, Richard (1544–1610) [2]813, 813n, 1100

band [5]285
indissoluble [1]646; Pythagorean [5]541, 541n; Theban [1]42, 42n
bandbox [2]1066
bang/bhang [1]777, 777n, [4]84–5, 85n
Banim, John (1798–1842)
The Boyne Water [1]211; *The Nowlans* [1]211; and Michael Banim *Tales by the O'Hara Family* MT [1]211–14, [6]256
Banim, Michael (1796–1874) *see* John Banim and Michael Banim
bank, Church as [6]19
banknote(s) [6]19
forged [5]298
Banks, Sir Joseph (1743–1820) [1]ciii, 528n, 535, 536, *536n*, [2]861n, [3]937, 942, [4]85, 85n
banner [6]55
banquet(s) [2]655
vampire [5]102
Banquo (*Macbeth*) [4]774, 775, 787, 788
"Baptism" [6]86
baptism/Baptism [1]235, 236, 236n, 245–7, 265–6, 349, 355, 846, [2]449, 734, [3]41–2, 427–8, 477, 593, 594n, 597, 597n, 599, 607, 691, 693, 758, [4]258, 635, [5]12, 192–3, 274, 398, 398n, 490, 490n–1n, 546, 566, 566n, 608, 609, 615, 619, 620, 646–55, 658, 664, 674, [6]167, 258, 260
adult [6]258; Apostles' practice [2]736; of Christ *see* Jesus Christ, baptism of; in C of E [2]1158; and Confirmation [5]662; Creed of [1]311, 312, [3]689; cross in [1]322, 329; doctrine of [2]40–1; etymology [2]495–6; form of [5]636–7; history of [4]306, 306n; infant [1]42n, 263, 263n, 276–7, 532, 810, [2]41, 724, 724n, 1143, 1199–1200, [3]470, 725, 725n, 761, 761n, [4]306, [5]495, 501n, 647, 653, 655, 659, 664, [6]41–3, 258n, 264; of Jesus *see* Jesus Christ, baptism of; as light [5]650; and Quakers [1]323, 821; sacrament of [3]440, 440n; significance of [2]1157–9; and sin [1]470; *sine qua non* [5]593
Baptist *see* John the Baptist, St
Baptist(s) [2]801n, [3]761, [4]306, 588, [5]501n, 654
missions of [4]651n, [5]105n–6n; modern [6]258
Baptist Missionary Society *see* London
baptizein [3]15
bapto [2]495–6
baquet [4]497n, 682, 682n
bara [2]580, 580n
Barabbas (Bible) [2]1040
Barachias (Bible) [2]450
Barak (Bible) [1]823n
Barbados [2]93
barbara [1]770, 770n
Barbara Allen [4]90
barbarism(s) [3]109, [4]509
exotic [5]866; symptom of [4]42
Barbary [2]418, [4]84, 85, 861, [5]831, [6]147
Barbauld, Anna Laetitia (1743–1825) [2]1119n, [4]283n
Works [1]clxviiin
barber [4]612, [5]669
Barbeyrac, Jean (1674–1744) [6]71, 72, 72n
Barbieri, Carlo (1717–93) *see* Francis of Sales *Il teotima* tr Barbieri
Barchusen, Johann Conrad (1666–1723)
Elementa chemiae MT [1]215–16
Barclay (probably Robert Barclay, 1648–90) [1]275
Barclay, John (1582–1621)
Argenis Copy A (Latin) MT [1]217–21; *Copy B* tr Le Grys and T. May [1]219n q; MT 222–5; tr K. Long [1]220n; *Satyricon* [1]217, 218, 218n–19n; *The Phoenix* tr C. Reeve [1]220n
Barco Centenera, Martin del (b 1535) [3]1077
bard(s) [2]1170n, [5]306
cyclical [2]386; divine [2]947; scholarly [2]867
Bardili, Christoph Gottfried (1761–1808) *Grundriss der ersten Logik* [3]258
Bardolph (*1 Henry IV*) [3]182; (*2 Henry IV*) [6]288, 288n
Barfield, Owen (1898–1997) *What Coleridge Thought* [2]859n
bargain [5]66
Baring family [1]723, 723n
barites *see* barytes
barium [5]261
barley [2]648
Barlow, Peter (1776–1862) [3]936, 940
Barlow, Thomas, Bishop of Lincoln (1607–91) [1]352
barmaids [4]719
barn, Methodist [1]30
Barnabas, St (1st century) [1]491n, [2]706, 710, 710n, [3]1084, [4]254–5, [6]68
Barnabus, Epistle of *see* Bible: Apocrypha: NT
Barnard, St *see* Bernard of Clairvaux, St
Barnard, Fulke Tovey (b 1797) [2]5, 586
Barnard, John (d 1683) [2]1133
Barnardine (*Measure for Measure*) [1]393
Barnes, Joshua (1654–1712) [1]833, [2]354, 354n
Barnet [1]cxxxviii

Barnet-Heath [2]127
barons [3]693, 799, 800, [4]15
barrel-organ [3]248, 248n
Barrington, Daines (1727–1800) [6]148, 149, 150, 151, 152
barrister(s) [2]476, [5]98, 581
Old Bailey [4]646; theological [5]575
Barrow, Isaac (1630–77) [1]182, 182n, [2]294n, 558, [6]316
Sermons [1]182n; *Works* [1]182n
Barrow, John (1764–1848)
Account of Travels into the Interior of Southern Africa [3]1074n; *Travels in China* [5]407n q
Barrow, Samuel (b c 1625) [3]165, 165n
In Paradisum Amissum [2]77, 77n
barter [2]98
Barth, J. Robert, S.J., coeditor [3]707, 816, 874, 1083
Coleridge and Christian Doctrine [3]742n q, 1078n, [4]133n, 589n, 596n, 682n, [5]5n, 85n, 394n q
Bartholomew Fair see Jonson
Bartlett and Welford *see* New York
Barton, Bernard (1784–1849) [1]240, [2]140
Bartram, Harry (in Scott) [4]582
Bartram, William (1739–1823) *Travels through North & South Carolina* [1]lxiii, lxxx, lxxxvii; MT 226–7
Baruch (Bible) [1]439, 439n, [2]450; *see also* Bible: Apocrypha: OT: Baruch
Barwell, Mr [1]350
barytes [1]570, [4]526n, [5]261
bas relief [3]68, [6]110, 110n
basaltes [3]630
base(s) [1]579, 597, 663, [2]546, [3]951, [4]320, 526, [5]255, 255n, 344, [6]116
common [1]614, [3]918; congruous [2]402; metallic [3]1030–1
Basel/Basle [4]537, [6]266
Council of [2]506–7, *507n*, [5]633
baseness [1]212, [4]819
Basil, St (c 330–79) [2]296n, 750, 751, 751n, 752, 1081 q, [3]524, 582, [5]683, [6]138n, 307
Basilides (fl c 125) [2]713, 713n, 923
basin [2]333
basis [5]721
basket-work [2]165
Basques [3]104n
Bassarius (myth) [5]227
Bassenthwaite [3]974
Bassolis, Joannes de (d c 1347) [5]549
bastard(s) [4]701, 701n, 756, 759, 785, 822, [5]760
bastardy [4]817
basting [3]45
Bastwick, John (1593–1654) [4]176, [5]616, 616n
bat(s) [3]453, 716
Bateman, Thomas (1778–1821) [1]228, 505n, [2]361, [3]126, 126n
A Practical Synopsis of Cutaneous Diseases MT [1]228–9
Bates, Joshua (1788–1864) [2]952
Bates, William (1625–99) [1]259, [4]76
bath(s) [2]981–2, [5]834
blood *see* blood-bath; king's [1]546
Bath [1]xciv, civ, 130, [2]169, 649, 668, 686, [3]636, [4]183n
bathos [3]783
battering-ram [4]739
Battersby, Mr (? Nicholas) (fl 1662) [4]72
battery [3]948n
battledore(s) [3]167, [5]134
battlements [5]321
Battus (legend) [5]831–2, 832n
Bauddhists *see* Buddhist(s)
Bauer [3]779
Bauer, Mr [5]771, 771n
Bauer, Walter (1877–1960) *Greek-English Lexicon of the New Testament* [1]462n, 490n, [2]315n q, 745n, [3]328n
Baumgarten, Alexander Gottlieb (1714–62) [1]6, 6n, [3]326, 326n, 853, 853n
Baumgarten-Crusius, Ludwig (1788–1842) [1]7
Bavaria, Church in [1]846
Bavarian [5]280
Baxter, Andrew (?1686–1750) [1]civ
Baxter, Richard (1615–91) [1]lvii, lxiv, lxv, cxxxi, cxxxviiin, 280, 297n, 565, 803 q, 807n, [2]61, 294n, 651, 651n, 1043n, 1198n, [3]142n, 166n, 363n, 920n, 921, 921n, [4]73, 175 q, 632, [5]67, 146, 146n, 509, 520, 521n, 646, 646n, [6]104n
on early Church [5]128–9, 128n–9n; "Life" by M. Sylvester [4]591; on prophecy [6]107, 107n–8n; on toleration [4]175, 175n; on witches [6]104
Catholick Theologie MT [1]231–9; 351, [3]877 ("Catholic Faith") 878n; *The Certainty of the World of Spirits* [6]105n; *A Holy Commonwealth* [1]230, 341, 341n, [2]935n, [4]632, 632n q; *A Key for Catholicks* [1]350; *Paraphrase of the New Testament* [1]230; *Practical Works* [1]288n; *Reasons of the Christian Religion* [1]244; *Reliquiae Baxterianae* ed M. Sylvester

Baxter, Richard—*continued*
[1]ci, cxx, cxxvi, 230, 803, 803n, [2]650, 650n, 1198, 1198n, [3]795, 795n, [4]73n, [5]67n q, 120, 120n, 129n q, 145, 145n, 146n q, 509n q, 598, 598n q; *Copy A* [1]lvii, xcii, 230; MT 240–78; [2]650, 650n; MT 970n–1n, [6]257–64; *Copy B* [1]lix, lixn, clviii, 230; MT 279–361; [2]736, 736n, 1191, [3]438n, 667, 667n; *The Saint's Everlasting Rest* [1]230, 244, 244n, 288, 288n; *Universal Concord* [5]129n; *The Unreasonableness of Infidelity* [1]244
Bayards [1]212
Bayle, Pierre (1647–1706) [2]771n, [3]506 q, [4]230, [5]313
Dictionnaire historique et critique [4]230n, tr *Dictionary Historical and Critical* [2]765–6 q, [5]719, 719n–20n
Baynes, Paul (d c 1617) [3]795n
bazaar [5]832
"be" [4]36n
be [1]*461n*, [2]992, [3]279, 279n, 836n, [4]457, 531, [6]9n; *see also* being
and have [1]149, 149n, [2]403, [3]87, [4]757, [5]95n, [6]155
Beacon, Joseph (fl 1667) [3]824, 824n
beadle(s) [3]587, [4]757, [6]155
Beadsmoore, John (fl 1799) [2]245
beam (ceiling) [3]203–4, [4]739
bean(s) [1]767, 767n, [3]68, 539n
abstain from [3]539, 539n; blue [2]354; and hops [3]269–70, 270n
bear(s) [1]399
b.-garden [4]77; white [2]1112; constellation(s) [1]399, 399n
beards, women's [3]1072–3
beast(s) [2]920, [3]558, [4]97, 266, [5]271, 360
in chains [2]140; epics [2]772n; number of [6]166, 166n–7n, *see also* six hundred and sixty-six; in Rev [1]483, 483n–4n, [3]923–4, 924n; scarlet [1]471; seven heads [3]929n; within [3]620–1
"beastify" [3]325
beatifications [5]662
beatitude [3]29, 60
Beatrice (in Dante) [1]485
Beatrice (*Much Ado about Nothing*) [4]783
Beattie, James (1735–1803) *Essay on the Nature and Immutability of Truth* [3]101n–2n, [6]290n
Beauclerk, William Aubrey de Vere, 9th Duke of St Albans (1801–49) [2]808
Beaufort, Margaret, Countess of Richmond and Derby (1443–1509) [2]70 ("Margaret of Lancaster")
Beaumont family [1]xcvii, clxi, [2]794, 1118n, [3]400
suppliers of books to C [2]131, 132
Beaumont, Francis (c 1584–1616) and John Fletcher (1579–1625) [1]lxvii, lxxxix, xci, xcii, xciv, cvi, cviii, cxxi, cxli, cxlviii, clii, 43, 43n, [3]171n, 702, [4]717–19, 717n, 718n, 798
in C's lectures [1]cxxxix; compared with Shakespeare [2]778; imitators [3]187; imitators of Shakespeare [4]715, 715n, 719; in *LR* [1]cxli; royalist(s) [1]380, 389
The Beggar's Bush [1]362, 373, 376n; MT 388; [2]76, 76n; *The Bloody Brother* MT [1]368–9; *Bonduca* [1]366, 400; *The Chances* [1]376n; *The Coronation* MT [1]402–3; *The Custom of the Country* MT [1]383–4; 402n; *Dramatic Works*: ed Bowers [1]363, 375, 379n, 383n; *Copy B* ed Colman MT [1]373–408; ed A. Glover and A. R. Waller [1]363, 375, 379n, 384n, 388n, 390n, 399n, 406n, ed P. Whalley [3]170; *The Elder Brother* [1]373; MT 384–6; 402n; *The Fair Maid of the Inn* MT [1]405; *Fifty Comedies and Tragedies Copy A* [1]cviii, cxxi; MT 365–72; *The Honest Man's Fortune* MT [1]408; *The Humorous Lieutenant* MT [1]388–9; *A King and No King* MT [1]380–1; *The Knight of the Burning Pestle* [4]714–15, 715n; *The Laws of Candy* MT [1]366, 392–4; *The Little French Lawyer* [1]362; MT 394–5; *Love's Pilgrimage* [1]362; *The Loyal Subject* [1]366; MT 389–90; *The Mad Lover* [1]366; MT 389; [4]718, 718n; *The Maid in the Mill* [1]393, 394n, 397; *The Maid's Tragedy* [1]374–5; MT 378–80; 394n; *Monsieur Thomas* [1]362, 376n; *The Noble Gentleman* MT [1]401–2; *Philaster* [1]385; *The Pilgrim* [1]362, 373, 376n; MT 399–400; [2]76, 76n; *The Prophetess* MT [1]369–70; *The Queen of Corinth* [1]397; MT [1]370–2, 400–1; *Rule a Wife and Have a Wife* MT [1]391; *The Scornful Lady* MT [1]381–3; [4]817, 817n; *The Spanish Curate* [1]373; *Thierry and Theodoret* [1]362; *The Tragedy of Rollo* [1]362; MT 397–8; 620n; *The Two Noble Kinsmen* MT [1]406–7; *Valentinian* MT [1]366–7; 375; MT 395–7; *A Wife for a Month* [1]375; MT 399; *The Wild-Goose Chase* MT [1]398–9; *Wit at Several Weapons* [1]402n; MT 403–4; *Wit*

without Money [1]373; MT 386–7; *The Woman-Hater* MT [1]407–8; *The Woman's Prize* MT [1]401; *Works: Variorum Ed* ed R. W. Bond and Greg [1]363, 375n, 379n, 383n, 384n, 385n, 386n, 388n, 389n, 390n, 391n, 396n
Beaumont, George (fl 1826) [3]983n, 984, 990
The Anti-Swedenborg [3]983
Beaumont, Sir George, 7th Baronet (1753–1827) [1]xciv, 58n, 160, 160n–1n, [2]245, 879n, 947n, 1195n, [4]821, 821n, 836, 836n
letter to [1]172n; supplier of books to C [1]xcviii
Beaumont, Joseph (1616–99)
Some Observations upon the Apologie of Dr Henry More† [6]265
Beaumont, Lady Margaret (née Willes) (1758–1829) [1]182n, [2]117, 1191, [4]836n
letter(s) to [1]554, 630n q, [4]156n q, [5]490n
Beausobre, Isaac de (1659–1738) [1]305, 305n–6n
Histoire critique de Manichée et du manichéisme [1]306n; *Remarques historiques* [1]306n
"beautiful" [5]212
beautiful, the [1]483, [3]460, [4]604, [5]138, 740
and agreeable *see* agreeable; defined [2]1069, 1069n; love of the [2]186; sense of [2]403, [5]681; and sublime [4]408
beauty/beauties [1]483, [3]60, [4]268, 292, 418, 421n, 835, [5]369–70, [6]157
accidental [1]367; defined [2]792; and faults [4]161, 807; must be felt [2]551; female [4]865n; feminine [5]821; insolence of [1]392; and love [6]156, 156n; masculine [5]117n; moral [3]677; in nature [5]363; personal [1]159; ought to please [2]355; principles of [3]259; prostituted [4]816; b.-spots [2]1159; synonym of Holy Spirit [2]305; and truth [5]859; of universe [4]141; as Venus [6]157; of virtue [2]1178; world of [2]583–4
Beauty and the Beast [2]1135
beaver [1]653n, 773, 773n, 777–8, [6]80
bebaisteron [5]59, 59n
"became" [3]919, [5]470, 470n
"because" [2]21
Becher, Johann Joachim (1635–82) [1]63n, 546, [5]331–2
beck(s) [4]721–2, 722n
Beck, Christian Daniel (1757–1832) see *Acta Seminarii* ed Beck
Beck, Jacob Sigismund (1761–1840) [3]319, 319n
Grundriss der critischen Philosophie [3]319n
Beck, Lewis White (1913–97) *see* Kant *Kant's Latin Writings* ed Beck
Becket, Thomas à, St, Archbishop of Canterbury (c 1118–70) [1]cvi, 528, 528n, 870, 872, 872n
Béclard, Pierre Augustin (1785–1825) [4]164
becoming [2]988, 989–90, 990n, 991
and being [1]579, 696, 696n, [3]1020n, [4]139–40, 379, 444n; surface sphere [1]579
bed [3]615, 615n
Procrustean [4]669, [5]744; of Ware [2]888, 888n
bedclothes [5]726
Bedad (Bible) [1]418
Beddoes, Thomas (1760–1808) [1]63n, 163, 163n, 282n, 535, 780n, [2]85, 787n
Chemical Experiments and Opinions [3]1011n; *see also* John Brown *The Elements of Medicine* pref Beddoes
Bede, the Venerable, St (673–735) [1]213, 878, 878n, [2]984, 984n, [5]79n, [6]17
Ecclesiastical History [1]clxx
Bedell, William, Bishop of Kilmore and Ardagh (1571–1642) [3]803n, [5]508, 508n–9n; *see also* G. Burnet *Life of William Bedell*
Bedford, Countess of *see* Russell, Lucy
Bedford, Duke(s) of *see* Russell, Francis and John
Bedford, Grosvenor Charles (1773–1839)
An Elegy Written in a London Church-Yard. A Parody MT [1]97; *97n*
Bedlam *see* London
Bedlamites [1]393
Bedouin [2]727
bedside [5]512
bee(s) [2]689, 861n, 983, [3]479, 581, 581n, [4]493–4, 496, 530, 531, [5]39, 39n, 198n, 731, 831, 831n, [6]152
b.-hive [5]306, glass [3]479, 479n; queen [1]203, *203n*, [2]28, 953, [3]829, [5]469, 484; in winter [2]829
beech [3]230–1, [4]814, 827
Beecroft, John (fl 1740–79) [1]701
beef [2]1113, [5]249
beefsteak [5]363, 370
Beelzebub (Bible) [1]451, [3]57, 57n, [4]514
Beelzebub (*Paradise Lost*) [4]841, 841n
beer [3]45, 1072, 164, [5]548
Beer, Georg Joseph (1763–1821) [4]164
Beer, John, coeditor [3]508, 538
Coleridge the Visionary [2]1070n; *Coleridge's Poetic Intelligence* [3]868n; "William Ellery Channing Visits the Lake Poets" [4]76n

Beersheba [1]424
Beethoven, Ludwig van (1770–1827) [2]65 q, 65n q
beetle(s) [1]421, [3]1036, [5]225, 226
"began" [2]1036
begetting [3]12, 139, 139n, 329
 horrible [1]646
beggar(s) [5]40n, 484
 b.-girl [2]840
beggary [5]645
beginning [1]618, 636, 678, [2]989, [3]91, 91n, 434, [5]304, 594, [6]78, 79
 miraculous [3]721
"begotten" [2]33, 722n, 732, 732n, [3]16, 524, [5]26, 26n, 57, 465, [6]306
begotten [1]466
 and created [5]620, 626, 627; the eternally [5]470; thrice [2]584, 584n
Begriff/Begriffe [2]626, [3]120, 857, [5]279, 299, 701, 751, 760, 778
beheading [5]65
behemoth [1]426, 427, 427n, [3]770–1, 771n
Behmen, Jacob *see* Böhme, Jakob
Behmenists [1]270, 296, 297, 297n, [4]676, [5]509n
Behn, Aphra (1640–89) *Abdelazer, or The Moor's Revenge* [1]50, 50n
beholder(s) [5]175, 406
 gifted [5]415
beholding [1]609, [3]209
 immediate [1]632, 632n, [3]641, 641n, [5]137n, 751
being (state of) [2]249, 250, 629, 734n, 988, 990n, 991–2, 993, 996, 996–7, 1028, [3]83n, 128n, [4]403n, 404, 451, 548, [5]182, 201, 409, 776, [6]241
 and act *see* act; act of [1]665, [4]457; actual [4]141; antecedent of [2]287, 423; and becoming *see* becoming; of the being [6]242; birth of [4]459; cessation of [5]609; change of [1]184; conception of [4]131; corporeal [5]496; of Deity [5]406; depth(s) of [2]1167, [4]403, [5]161; and doing [2]693, [5]725; essential [3]50; and existence [1]595, 636, [2]989, 989n–90n, [3]86, [4]131, 227, [6]26, 241, 241n; and existing [1]573, 579; first act of [1]665; form(s) of [3]46, [5]460; God ground of [2]324; ground of [3]876, [5]75; and having [1]682; idea of [3]861; immutable [5]370; interior [1]537; and knowing [3]849, 849n, [4]447, 447n, 460, [5]273; manifested [5]360; modes of [3]76; moral [2]191, 1148, [3]516, [4]220, 625, [5]176, 562, [6]299; moral and intellectual [4]399; necessity of [5]424; objective [4]543, [5]714; original [5]443; to be perceived [3]440, 440n; positive [1]115; potential and actual [2]1019, 1185–6; really b. [2]671, 671n; related to mind and spirit [2]248; sacramental [2]672; scale of [3]1093n, [4]429; spiritual [4]616; as subject [3]85; substantive [6]87; total [4]200; true [5]453, 459; unconscious [6]237; vital [2]250, [5]673. *See also* be; *ousia*
being(s)/Being [2]249, 250, 629, 734, 884, 988, 990n, 991–2, 993, 996, 996–7, 1028, 1185, 1186, [3]15, 82–3, 128, [4]137, 269, [6]143
 absolute [1]824, [2]324, 423, [3]90, [5]203, 410, 790, [6]8, 241; absolutely good [2]162; all created [2]732; all-perfect [5]729; of being(s) [3]24, [5]756n, [6]242; bond of [4]269; co-eternal [2]293; divine [1]105, 573, [5]68; eternal [4]365; ever-present [4]729; evil [2]164; finite [1]681, [4]445, [6]299; God as [2]305; imperfect [4]440; incorporeal [3]1087; infinite [1]618, [5]155; intelligent [6]146; living [5]431; moral [5]724; necessary [3]333, 345–6, 346–7, 859, 860, [5]208, 730; and notions [5]764; omniscient [5]656; progressive [5]591; rational [5]37; self-conscious [5]7; self-grounded [5]730; spiritual [2]198, [3]524, [5]613, [6]307; supersensual [4]409; supreme [1]435, [3]332n, [4]258, 300, [5]483, 657, 793, [6]76; three genera/kinds [2]920, 920n, 1147, 1147n, [3]985, 1089, [5]483; universe of [2]884
Des bekannten Diebes, Mörders und Raübers . . . Leben [1]829n
Bela (Bible) [1]418
Belch, Sir Toby (*Twelfth Night*) [4]756, 756n
Belfast [4]199
Belgium, Inquisition in [1]281n
Belgrade [1]698
Belial (Bible) [1]518, [2]269
 son of [6]32
Belial (*Paradise Lost*) [2]125n, [3]1065n, [4]842n
"belief" [6]286–7
belief(s) [2]828, 1005, 1192, [3]508, 509, 615, [5]759
 another man's [5]408; apostolic [5]607; articles of [1]123, 471; avowals of [5]664; blind infatuated [3]825; and certainty [2]645, 645n; conscious [5]540; dramatic [3]405; expansion of the [1]232; explicit [2]682; and facts [6]286–7; and faith [1]123–4, 503–4, 744, 783–4, [2]31, 267, 299, 299n, 300, 689, 695, 695n, 1006, 1061n, 1162, [3]519, 519n, 752, 764, [4]216, 398, 669n, 672, [5]11, 272, 272n, [6]301, 301n; habit of

[2]1175; and idea [3]859; individual's [5]516; inward [5]639; and knowledge [1]128, [3]662; meaning of [3]860; points of [5]562; Popish [5]163; popular [6]115; proportional [2]699; rabbinical [5]606; reward of [2]29; right [5]798; scheme of [5]513; and science [1]128; strange [1]296; and unbelief and disbelief [5]771; universality of [5]82
"believe" [1]281
believer(s) [5]50, 654, 659, [6]109
arguments for [2]148, 149; Catholic [3]686; experiences of [5]516; individual [5]568; loose-living [2]1178; sincerest [1]823; true [1]815, [5]66, 529
bell(s) [5]641
b.-ringing [5]254
Bell, Andrew (1753–1832) [2]857n, 980n, [4]438, 438n, [6]192, 192n
Bell, Sir Charles (1774–1842) *The Hand* [2]883n
Bell, George (fl 1745–90) [5]184, 184n
Bell, Henry (fl 1650) *see* Luther *Colloquia* tr Bell
Bell, John (1745–1831) *Poets of Great Britain* [2]213
Bell, Robert (1800–67) [5]194
Bell, Thomas (1792–1880) *The Anatomy, Physiology, and Diseases of the Teeth* [2]368
belladonna [6]174
Bellarmine/Bellarmin, Roberto Francesco Romolo (1542–1621) [2]664, 672, 672n, [3]153, 153n, 459, 459n, 1064, [4]269, 551, 551n, [5]525, 525n, 545, 546, 546n, 574, 640
Bellarminisms [5]525
Bellaston, Lady (in Fielding) [2]672, 694
Bellona (myth) [2]8
bellows [1]868–9
Bellula (in Cowley) [2]105, 105–6, 106n
belly [3]1036
Belsham, Thomas (1750–1829) [1]316, 316n, [3]692, 738, 738n, [5]7n, 162, 162n, 657, 657n
ed *The New Testament* [2]482n
Belshamites [5]7
Belur Mountains [2]178
Bemerton [2]1046, 1046n
Bemis, Frank Brewer (1861–1935) [5]854
Ben Nevis [2]691, 691n
ben trovato [5]225
benchers [1]124, 124n
Bendyshe, Thomas (1827–86) *see* Blumenbach *Anthropological Treatises* tr Bendyshe
Benedick (*Much Ado about Nothing*) [4]783 ("Benedict")
Benedict, St (c 480–c 550) [2]969n, 984, 984n
Benedicta (in Aurelius) [1]162
Benedictine(s) [5]662, [6]178
benefactor [5]642
beneficence [1]814, [4]626
benefits, public [1]356
benevolence [1]4, [3]645, [4]655
"Ben-Ezra, Juan Josafat" *see* Lacunza y Diaz, Manuel
Bengel, Johann Albrecht (1687–1752) [3]1081, [6]165, 293, 294, 294n
Benjamin (Bible) [1]798
tribes of [3]461, 462
Ben-Kiber [1]110, 112
Benneke, Mr (fl 1817) [5]142n
Bennet, Henry, 1st Earl of Arlington (1618–85) [1]353n, [4]74
Bennet, Henry Grey (1777–1836) [3]893n
Bennett, James (1774–1862) *see* Bogue and Bennett
Bennett, Jonathan *see* Leibniz *New Essays* tr and ed Remnant and Bennett
Beno/Benno, Cardinal (11th century) [5]577
Bentham, Jeremy (1748–1832) [1]579n, 740n, [2]616n, 954n, 955n, [4]280n
Defence of Usury [2]310n; *Not Paul, but Jesus* [6]333
Bentham, Joseph (fl 1740–78) [1]701
Bentinck, William Henry Cavendish, 3rd Duke of Portland (1738–1809) [4]13, 13n
Bentley, Richard (1662–1742) [1]90n, 376, *376n–7n*, 387n, [2]52–3, 54n, [3]421, 589, 589n, 731, [4]6, [6]216–17
Proposals for a New Edition of the Greek Testament [3]421n. *See also* Horace; Milton *Paradise Lost* ed Bentley
Bentley, Thomas (d 1675) [6]216
Bentley, Thomas (1736–80) [3]628, 628n, 630, 639
Benvolio (*Romeo and Juliet*) [4]832
Beor (Bible) [1]418
Beotia *see* Boeotia
bequests [5]587
Bérard, E. (possibly Etienne Bérard, 1764–1839) [3]938
Bérard, Jacques Etienne (1789–1869) [3]938, 940
Berea [3]147
Berengarius (Berengar of Tours) (999–1088) [2]283, [3]439, 439n, 657n, 706, 706n, 1068, 1068n, [5]393, 393n, [6]20, 21, 21n
Berenice (legend) [1]403

Beresford, James (1764–1840) *see* Virgil *Aeneid* tr Beresford
bergamot [1]736
Bergenaars [4]152
Berina (in Reynolds) [4]237, 237n
Bering Strait [2]178
Berith [2]579
Berjew, John Paine (fl 1808) *see* A. Parsons *Travels* ed Berjew
Berkeleianism [1]525, [3]916, [4]448
Berkeley CA
  University of California, transcript(s) of marginalia in [1]555
Berkeley, George, Bishop of Cloyne (1685–1753) [1]cxxiii, 198n, 409, 410n, 638n, 774n, [2]623n, 1203, [3]957, [4]222n, 353, 354n, 415n, 447–8, 447n–8n, [5]382, 382n, [6]133
  C's acquaintance with works [1]409; Berkeleian formula [3]128n; idealism [2]547n, 613n, [4]132; and Platner [4]126n; scepticism of [3]966; and Jeremy Taylor [5]533
  Alciphron [2]36n, [4]114, 114n q; *De motu* [2]628, 628n; *Essay towards a New Theory of Vision* [4]126 q, 126n; *Principles of Human Knowledge* [2]631n; *Siris* [1]lxxxvi; MT 409–10; [2]69n, [5]533n; *A Treatise concerning the Principles of Human Knowledge* [2]631n, [3]916, 916n, [4]126n, 354n q; *Works* ed Luce and Jessop [3]916n, [4]115n, 126n q, 354n q, [5]4n
Berlin [3]217n, 955, 955n, 969, [5]87
Berlinische Monatsschrift [2]754, [4]225
Bernard of Clairvaux, St (1090–1153) [2]260n, 273, 274n, 292, 303 q, [2]716n ("Barnard"), 982–3, 983n, [3]605 q, 610, 625 q, [4]642, [5]662, 662n
Bernard, Sir Thomas (1750–1818) [2]1195n, [4]821, 821n
Bernardo (*Hamlet*) [4]839, 840, 845
Berners, Baron *see* Bourchier, John
Berni/Bernia, Francesco (c 1497–1535) [2]795n
Bernouilli/Bernoulli, Jacques (1654–1705) [4]376, 376n
Bernouilli/Bernoulli, Jean (1667–1748) [4]376, 376n
Beroaldo, Filippo (1472–1518) [2]7
Berowne (*Love's Labour's Lost*) *see* Biron
Berridge, John (1716–93) [5]182
berries [3]889
Bertha von Lichtenstein [3]196
Berthollet, Claude Louis, Comte (1748–1822) [3]942, 1020n, [4]539n
  Eléments de l'art de la teinture tr William Hamilton [2]496n
Bertram (Ratramnus of Corbie) (d c 868) [5]547, 548
Bertram, Harry (in Scott) [4]584 ("Bartram"), 585, 594n, [5]547, 548
Beruth (myth) [2]577, 578n, 579, 580
Berwick, Lord, [2]822
Berwick-upon-Tweed [2]1055
Berzelius, Jöns Jacob, Baron (1779–1848) [1]548n, 779, 780n, [3]942, [5]256, 256n, 331–2
Bessus (in B&F) [1]374
beta [6]26–7
Betham, Sir William (1779–1853) [4]7, 9
Bethany [2]747
Bethel(s) [3]602, [4]662n
Bethlehem/Bethlem [1]442, 443, 444n, [2]258, 276, 301, 917, [3]729, [4]476
  star of [3]653, 653n
Bethsaida [2]256, 747
Betrachtungen über das Universum see Dalberg
better, the [4]435
better
  and other [1]513, [4]174, 174n, [5]229; and wiser [5]229n, 791, 791n
Betterton, Thomas (c 1635–1710) [4]42, 42n
Betty Martin *see* Martin
Betylus (myth) [2]577
Betz, Paul F. [4]574; *see also* WW *Benjamin the Waggoner* ed Betz
Bewick, Thomas (1753–1828) *A General History of Quadrupeds* [3]1066n
bewitching of soul [2]592
Bewusstsein [2]1030
Beza (Théodore de Bèze) (1519–1605) [1]878n q, [2]1135, [3]795n, [5]548, 549n, [6]107
Béziers [6]14
bhang/bang see *bang*
Biancafiore (in Boccaccio) [1]543–4, 544n

BIBLE

Arrangement in this section is alphabetical, and from the general or comprehensive to the particular, references to the Bible as a whole preceding those to the Apocrypha and the New and Old Testaments and, within particular books, general references and those to whole

chapters coming before those to specific verses. All standard references are taken from the "Authorised Version"—or "King James Version" in modern orthography (AV). Standard abbreviations of the names of particular books are used.

The Bible [1]lxiv, cxxxi, 148, 148n, [2]828, [4]667 ("Book"), 667n, [5]96, 152n, 253, 473 ("canonical writings"), 651

Copy A [1]lxxvii; MT 411–13; *Copy B* MT [1]414–74; *Die Bibel nach . . . Luthers* [2]474n; *Die Heilige Schrift* ed Cohen *see under* OT; *Holy Bible, with Notes* ed Mant and D'Oyly [1]416, [3]594n, 595n, 605, 605n, [5]189n; *New English Bible* [1]137n q, 175n q, 415, 418n q, 421n q, 425n q, 426n q, 427n q, 429n q, 430n q, 431n q, 432n q, 433n q, 434n q, 435n q, 436n q, 437n q, 441n q, 444n q, 449n q, 450n q, 451n q, 455n q, 459n q, 462n q, 463n q, 464n q, 466n q, 467n q, 469n q, 471n q, 490n q, 510n, 519n q, 703n q, 709n q, 710n q, [2]34n q, 144n q, 270n q, 302n q, 372n q, 384n q, 400n q, 469n q, 473n q, 567n q, 1029n q, 1179n q; The [American] Revised Standard Version of the Bible [1]427n q; The Revised Version of the Bible [1]427n q

above comparison [1]802; allegory in [2]1052–3; Apocalypse *see* NT: Rev; the Book for the Man [2]338; canon [2]374, 441, 446, [3]14, 20, 310, 310n, 443, 533, 533n, 763, 771, 1086, [6]319, 319n; canonical books [2]500; Celtic translation [6]17; chronology [2]387, 387n, [6]292–4; C and textual criticism [1]416; C's reading of [3]466; C's systematic study of [2]369; and HC [1]42; corrupted texts [5]629; criticism of [2]561, [3]3, 3n, modern [5]72; divinity of [6]20; division into verses [2]314; Donne on [2]336; easy to understand [5]480n; English [1]804, [2]920; and English law [1]807, 807n; erring fancies in [6]19; Geneva B. [2]415n, [3]452n–3n; Hebrew [2]314, 314n, 377; Hebrew books of [6]319; interpretation of [1]416, 521, 673, 675, 758n, [2]37–8, 286, 571, 1050–1, 1079–80, [3]14, 33, 44–5, 49, 55, 72, 419, 435–9, 443, 444, 449, 463, 463n, 465, 468–9, 472, 520, 602–3, 616, 686, 731–2, 734, 875, 876, 904, 922, 923, 928–9, 1086–7, 1088, [4]304–5, 643n, 668n, [5]413n; Jewish commentators [3]1088; language of [5]66; as law-book [3]72; literal truth [2]807n; mirror of faith [2]423; misinterpretation [4]305–6; no notes [2]261, 261n; not a plain, easy book [4]304–5; notes in [2]278; oath [3]183n; only book [2]320; only code of Christians [3]487; parts of [5]507; perplexing [3]19–20; plan of study [5]167–8; poetry and history [1]446n; power of [2]1123; printed [5]433; prophecy/prophecies [2]544, [3]468–9; prophetic [3]425n; reading(s) of [5]317, 507, [6]291–2, promiscuous [1]804; and reason [5]664–5; revisal of [6]77; rule of faith [5]572; sacred drama [3]436–7; and science [3]948n; B. society *see* London: British and Foreign Bible Society; spirit of whole [3]418; spiritual unity of [2]1036, 1037n; and reason [5]318; system of revelations [3]365; testimony of [5]662; textual corruption in [2]36–7; Tischendorf text [1]416; translations [1]444, 455, 462, 463, 466, [3]1065n, [6]77, 77n; Tyndale [1]416; Vulgate [1]469, 472, 491n, 493n, 710n q, [2]52n, 375n, 415n, 439n, 454n, 683n, [3]33n, [5]634n, 682, [6]77n, 97n; Welsh [6]17n; word of God [3]722; B. worship [5]805n. *See also* bibliolatry; Gospel(s); Scripture(s)

APOCRYPHA [1]468n, [2]261, 261n, 316, 316n, 374, 375, 375n, [3]17n, 40n, 310, 310n, 466n, 469, [4]476n, [5]272

NEW TESTAMENT APOCRYPHA

The Apocryphal New Testament ed Hone [1]528n; MT 488–93; [2]482n, [3]17n, [4]255n; *The Apocryphal New Testament* ed M. R. James [1]489; Acts of Paul and Thecla [3]772n; Acts of St Paul [3]7n; Acts of St Thomas [3]21n; 1 Clement [1]492, 493n, [2]441, 441n, 442; 2 Clement [2]441, 441n, 442; General Epistle of Barnabas MT [1]491–3; 817, [2]482, 482n, [4]254–5, 254n–5n; Gospel according to the Hebrews/Nazareans *see* NT: Matt *below*; Gospel of the Birth of Mary MT [1]490–1; [2]437n; Shepherd of Hermas [1]492, 493n, 817, [2]707, [3]452, 452n, 688

OLD TESTAMENT APOCRYPHA

Baruch [2]375n, 377, 377n, [3]462; Bel and Dragon [1]320, [3]466n; Ecclus (Wisd of Jesus, son of Sirach) [2]421–2, 423, [3]533, [4]475, [5]272n, [6]142, 143–4, 319, Eichhorn on [2]421–2; 10.28 [1]137 q, 137n; 44.7 [2]933 q, 933n; 49.16 [2]1072 q; Enoch [1]320n, 468, 468n, [2]712n, 1074n, [3]41, 41n, 310, 310n; ch 37–71 [3]668n; 1 Esdras 4.37–8 [3]767, 767n; 1–2 Esdras

The Bible—*continued*
[1]433n, [2]415, *415n*, 417n, 426, 426n, [3]41, 41n, 452 q, 453n, 476, 476n; 2 Esdras [2]375n, 417, 712n; Judith [1]320, [3]767, 767n; 1 Macc [2]434, Eichhorn on [2]434; 1–2 Macc [2]157n, 375n, 376n, 1075n, [3]595n, 607n; 2 Macc [2]376, 1075 [6]142, 142n, omitted from canon [3]595, ch 7 [2]718, 718n; Prayer of Manasses [2]415n, [5]520; Song of the Three Holy Children [3]466n; Susannah [3]466n; Tobit [1]320, [2]1105, 1106, 1106n; Wisd of Jesus, son of Sirach *see* Ecclus; Wisd of Sol [2]369, 421, 422–33, 426, 1074, [3]74, 533, [5]667, [6]138–42, 138n, 143–4, 319, Eichhorn on [2]422–33; 1.8 [2]427n q; 1.16–2.24 [2]1075, 1075n; 2.12 [6]139n q; 2.23 [3]875 q, 875n; 3.1 [6]139n q; 4.12 [2]415 q; 5.10 [2]427n q; 7.22 [2]427n q; 7.22–3 [2]425n q; 10.15–19 [6]142n q; 11.20 [2]1137n q. *See also* R. H. Charles ed *The Apocrypha . . . of the Old Testament*; Eichhorn *Einleitung in die apokryphischen Schriften des Alten Testaments*

NEW TESTAMENT [1]175, 232, 253, 317, 334; MT 446–73; 521, 607, 846, [2]207, 435–502, 480n, 737, 743, 786n, 1016, [3]73, 102n, 106n, 200, 212, 424n, 446, 597, 763, 925, 1086n, [4]227, 247, 300, 308, 637, 649, 656, 669, 864, 864n, [5]13, 14, 19, 63, 65, 77, 126, 127, 298, 330, 465 ("Evangelic or Apostolic Writings"), 473, 519, 523n, 527, 527n, 535, 537, 567, 568, 572, 583, 623, 658, 672, 798, [6]7, 28n, 41, 91, 119, 119n, 294

New Testament (1622) [1]cvi; *The New Testament . . . with a Commentary* ed Clarke [4]256n q, 486n q; *Nieuwe Testament* [2]474n; *Novum Testamentum* ed Koppe [1]480; annotations by Grotius [1]199n; canon [1]491, 492, *492n–3n*; common editions [2]473; definite article in [6]177–83; divinity of [1]816–17; doctrine of [6]74

EPISTLE(S) [4]646, 667, [5]152, 570; Catholic E. [3]445–6, 446n; of St John [4]174, [5]667, *see also* 1–3 John *below*; Pastoral E. [1]492, 492n, [2]568, 568n, [5]629, 629n, *see also* 1 and 2 Tim, Titus *below*; of St Paul/Pauline [2]436, 503, [5]140, 391, 434, 434n, 665, 667, 766, Eichhorn on [2]466–76, *see also* NT: Col, 1 and 2 Cor, Eph, Gal, Heb, Phil, Philem, Rom, 1 and 2 Thess, 1 and 2 Tim, Titus *below*; of St Peter [4]174, *see also* 1 and 2 Pet *below*

GOSPEL(S) [1]452, 710, [2]38, 435, 436, 436n, 452, 493, 902, 902n, 1057, 1081–2, [3]3, 4n, 7n, 697, 726, [4]646, 649, 659, 664, 666, 667, 668, 673, [5]72, 152, 606, 607, 667; *A Harmonie upon the Three Evangelists . . . with the Commentarie of M. John Calvine* tr Paget MT [1]476–9; according to the flesh [1]512, 512n; aim of [5]674; authenticity of [5]62; authority of [2]436–7, 439–45; begin with baptism of John [3]36; canon [2]439n; composition of [4]469–84, [5]513; credibility of [5]51; facts of [5]63; first three [5]535; four [5]434; harmony of [2]34–5, 36–7, [3]666–7; how to read [1]446–7; of the infancy see *evangelium/evangelia infantiae*; interpretation [4]40–68; interprets Ps [1]710; Latin [5]637; oral [4]55; order of composition [1]235n; original [2]270, 270n, 453, [4]41; rejection of [6]69; revision of [3]458, 458n; synoptic [2]270n; three [4]479, [5]630. *See also* NT: John, Luke, Mark, Matthew *below*; gospel(s); *Urevangelium*

NT Greek [2]683, editions: Bowyer [1]416, Erasmus [2]52n, Griesbach [1]416, 490n, E. Harwood [1]416, Lachmann [1]416, 490n, Mace [1]416, Tasker (*NEB Gk*), [1]466n, 490n, Whittaker [1]416, *see also* Bauer *Greek-English Lexicon of the NT*; as guide [2]813; inspiration of [5]575; interpretation of [4]244, 253, [6]303; language of [2]1084; letters on [1]cxviii; miracles [3]708; neat copy [2]1118; need for new translation [1]471, 471n; sense of Devil [3]876; silence of [4]56, 56n; truths of [6]19; works of undoubted authority [6]168; writers of [1]127; *see also* Eichhorn *Einleitung in das Neue Testament*

Acts [1]474, 491n, 511, [2]435, 455, 470, 495, 709–10, 1159, [3]3, 4n, 7n, 9, [4]474; 1.1–6 [3]666; 1.14 [2]272n; ch 2 [2]703n, [3]732, 1069, 1069n, [4]248n, [5]741; 2.1–4 [1]236n; 2.3 [5]651n; 2.4 [2]701n q, 751n, 1045n, [4]250n–1n q, [5]741n q; 2.6–11 [2]1045n, [4]248n; 2.14–18 [2]1045n; 2.14–36 [4]476, 476n; 2.16–18 [3]668, 668n–9n q, 1069n; 2.16–21 [2]653n; 2.24 [2]334n, 923, 924n, [3]663 q, 663n–4n q; 2.27 [2]334n; 2.30 MT [1]458; 2.31 [3]663 q, 664n q; 2.36 [2]328 q, 328n q, 329–35; 2.36–8 [5]628; 2.38 [1]235, 235n q, [2]736n q, [5]628, 628n q, 653n; 2.39 [2]653n q; 2.46 [6]41; 3.10 [1]656q, 656n; 3.12 [1]490n q; 3.14 [2]293 q; 3.22 [2]799n; 4.32 [6]41; 5.1 [6]55n; 5.1–10 [5]645n; 5.1–11

[1]294n; 5.15 [5]859n q; 5.31 [2]1187n; 5.34 [1]463n; 6.5 [2]506n; 6.30 [2]901n; 6.38 [2]901n; 7.22 [2]144n; 7.53 [1]468n, [2]472n; 7.55–6 [4]297n q; 7.59 [1]829; 7.60 [1]829n q; 8.4 MT [1]458–9; 8.9–24 [3]922n; 8.14–25 [5]666n; 8.16 [2]736n q, [5]666n q; 8.17 [5]665 q, 666n; 8.20 [5]666n q; ch 9 [3]745; 9.3 [2]252n q; 9.4 [2]252, 336–7; 9.7 [1]459, 459n q; 9.10–16 [3]987n; 9.10–18 [2]492, 492n; 10.9–20 [2]470n; 10.33 [2]704n; 10.34–5 [2]498 q; 10.38 [2]751n, [5]60 q; 10.40–1 [1]863n; 10.46 [2]701n; 10.48 [2]736n q; 10.9–20 [2]470n; ch 11 [5]567; 11.19 [3]7n q; 11.30 [2]1042n; 13.8–11 [5]645n; 13.18–20 [3]108n q; 13.33 [2]584 q, 584n, [3]49 q, 49n; 13.43–8 [3]6n q; 14.23 [2]1042n; 15.1–29 [5]623, 623n; 15.9 [3]609 q; 15.22 [2]1042n; 15.39 [4]254 q; 16.3 [2]661n; 16.30 [5]514n q; 17.28 [3]87n q, [4]226n q; 17.37 [2]799n; 18.18 [4]252; 19.1–9 [2]701n; 19.6 [2]701 q, 701n q; 19.12–16 [3]39n; 20.17 [2]1042n q; 20.28 [2]1042n q, 1161 q, 1161n, [3]544, [5]503n; 20.35 [1]252n; 21.20–4 [2]470; 21.20–5 [4]250, 251; 21.39 [2]919n q; 22.1–21 [2]455n, 564, 564n; 22.3 [1]463n; 22.9 MT [1]459; 23.12–35 [2]456n; 24.15 [2]184n q; 24.21 [2]184n q; 26.7 [2]832n; 26.18 [2]1187n; 27.43 [2]665n q; 28.16 [5]635n; 28.24 [1]468n

Colossians MT [1]465; [2]436, [3]7n, 31; Eichhorn on [2]498–9; 1.3 [1]702n; 1.11 [4]560 q; 1.12–23 MT [1]465–7; [2]498; 1.13–20 [3]107n q; 1.14 [2]497n; 1.15 [2]419n q, 722 q, 722n q, [3]545n q, [4]62–3 q, [5]29n q, 577, 577n q, 620 q, 620n q; 1.15–16 [4]63n q; 1.15–18 [2]498, 498n q; 1.15–23 [1]465n–6n; 1.16 [1]236n; 1.18 [3]40n q; 1.19 [2]716n; 1.19–20 [2]263–9, [3]31 q; 2.2–3 [3]24 q, 24n q, [5]59n q, 628n; 2.3 [1]478n; 2.9 [2]716n; 2.16–17 [6]292n q; 2.18 [4]298n, [5]505n; 2.23 [5]142n, 505n; 3.1 [4]562 q; 3.2 [4]556 q; 3.3 [3]582 q; 3.5 [3]585n q, [4]557; 3.11 [2]291n; 3.12–25 [1]252n; 3.17 [2]668n q; 3.23 [2]668n; 4.14 [4]480n q

1 Corinthians [1]415, [2]436, 564; Eichhorn on [2]468–9; ch 1 [5]20; 1.2 [2]468–9 q; 1.10–11 [6]42n q; 1.10–12 [6]42; 1.12 [2]705n; 1.22 [3]988n; 1.22–5 [3]6n; 1.24 [1]478n; 1.26 [1]512n; 1.27 [1]252n; ch 2–4 [6]42; 2.2 [2]208n; 2.4 [2]789n q; 2.4–16 [1]824n; 2.9–11 [1]588n; 2.10 [5]14 q, [6]54 q, 54n q; 2.11 [1]10n, [5]15 q, 15n; 2.12 [3]548 q; 2.13–14 [1]819, 819n, [5]169n; 3.6 [5]395 q, 395n; 3.10 [2]705n; 3.16 [1]179n; 4.15 [2]732n q; 4.17 [2]471; 4.21 [3]550n q; 6.1 [3]12n; 6.1–7 [1]253n; 6.3 [1]474; 6.4 [1]252n; ch 7 [2]984n; 7.1 [2]705n; 7.6 [2]467; 7.8–9 [2]984n; 7.10 [2]468; 7.12 [2]467; 7.17 [4]251; 7.19 [4]251; 7.25 [2]467; 7.32 [2]984n; 7.40 [2]467; 8.1 [2]285 q, 285n q, 483n, [3]19n q; 8.1–2 [4]255n q; 8.5 [3]529 q, 529n, [6]314 q, 314n; 8.5–6 [2]344 q, 344n; 8.6 [5]58, 58n q, [6]182; 9.5 [2]703n q; 9.14 [2]468; 9.16 [3]748 q; 9.22 [3]69q, 69n; 10.4 [2]486n; 10.16–21 [4]484n; 10.31 [2]668n q, [3]558 q, 558n q; ch 11 [5]683n; 11.10 [2]919; 11.13 [4]256n; 11.13–14 MT [1]461; 11.23–5 [5]673n–4n q; 11.23–6 [2]267n; 11.23–9 [4]484n; 11.24 [1]510n q, 714 q, 714n, [3]28n; 11.25 [1]510n q; 11.26 [1]510n q; 11.28 [3]624 q; 11.29 [5]683n q; ch 12 [6]42; 12.3 MT [1]462; [2]247–8; 12.4–6 [5]654n; 12.4–11 [6]57n q; 12.8 [5]514 q, 514n; 12.8–11 [2]751n; 12.12–27 [1]510n; 12.13–18 [2]670n; 12.16–17 [3]87n; 12.27 [3]545 q, 545n q; 12.28 [3]6n; 13.12 [1]237n q, [4]126n q; ch 14 [5]390, 517–18, 517n, 518n; 14.1–3 [5]391n q; 14.1–6 [2]701n q; 14.3 [1]294n; 14.20 [4]560 q; 14.20–5 [5]518n; 14.26 [5]391n, 517n; 14.29 [5]391; 14.40 [4]256n q; ch 15 [1]166n, 863n, [2]924n, 1029n, [3]39n, 424n, 433 q, 433n, 444, 594n, [6]303; 15.1 [1]702n, see also *BCP*: Bible: NT: 1 Cor 15.1; 15.1–2 [1]232n; 15.1–4 [1]235, see also *BCP*: Bible: NT: 1 Cor 15.3; 15.1–13 [2]469; 15.3 [1]702n–3n q; 15.6 [4]248n; 15.12 [2]184n q; 15.12–44 [2]184n; 15.13–14 [3]691, 691n q; 15.14–15 [6]105 q, 106n; 15.19 [1]128 q, 128n, [3]444n; 15.20 [3]40n; 15.20–58 [1]127, 127n; 15.21–3 [2]564, 564n; 15.22–8 [4]62; 15.23 [3]444n; 15.24 [5]59 q; 15.25–8 [3]461 q, 461n q; 15.26 [2]308–14; 15.35–54 [2]309n; 15.36 [1]470n, [2]565 q, 565n, 918 q, 918n q, [6]116 q, 116n q; 15.36–7 [1]737 q, 737n; 15.36–8 [2]184n; 15.39–40 [2]309n q; 15.40 [3]39 q, 39n, 46 q, 46n q, 732, 732n q; 15.40–4 [3]520–1, 520n, 521n, [6]303n q; 15.41 [1]438n; 15.44 [1]175n q, [4]69 q, 69n q, [5]703n, [6]114n; 15.45 [1]124n q, [2]273n q, 302n q, [3]39n q, 444n, 876 q, 876n, [5]600 q, [6]141n q; 15.47 [2]683 q, 683n q, [3]39 q, 39n, 444n; 15.50 [2]184n, 313 q, 313n; 15.51 [3]444n, 521n q, [6]303n q; 15.51–2 [2]685, 685n; 15.52 [3]444n; 15.52–7 [2]497n; 15.53–4 [2]1185n; 15.57 [3]444n; 15.59 [3]444n; 16.1–2 [2]1153n; 16.22 [3]562n q, [5]642–3 q, 643n

2 Corinthians [1]415, [2]564; 1.12 [1]684, 684n

The Bible—*continued*
q; 1.20 [3]609; 1.22 [3]17n; 3.5–6 [1]200n q; 3.6 [3]441 q, 464 q, 464n; 3.18 [1]237n q, [3]711 q, [4]562 q; 4.11 [2]717n; 4.18 [3]617 q, 617n; 4.19 [3]610 q; 5.1 [1]474; 5.10 [5]563n, 578n; 5.15 [1]703n; 5.16 [1]512n, [2]271n, 1082 q, 1082n, [4]473n q, 477n, 479 q, 479n; 5.17 [2]343n; 5.19 [1]490n, [5]165–6 q, 166n; 5.20 [3]543; 7.1 [3]518, [5]582; 7.10–11 [5]582; 7.11 MT [1]462; 8.2 [1]564n q; 10.8 [1]294n; MT 462; 10.10 [2]705; 11.2 [1]752n; ch 12 [3]772n; 12.2 [4]477 q, 477n; 12.2–4 [2]360n q; 12.7 [2]705, 706n q, [3]772n q; 12.9–10 [1]252n; 13.10 [1]294n

Ephesians [1]415, 459, 459n, 465, [2]493, [3]7n; ch 1 [5]548n; 1.4 MT [1]463–4; 1.6 [1]438n; 1.7 [2]497n, 1187n; 1.12 [1]438n; 1.13 [2]1162n, [3]17n; 1.14 [2]1161 q, 1161n, 1162n; 1.17 [3]710 q; 1.19 [1]675 q, 675n; 1.19–23 [2]670n; 2.1–8 [2]1061n; 2.2 [3]496 q, 496n; 2.2–10 [1]232n; 2.10 [2]732n q; 2.14–16 MT [1]464; 2.18 [6]42; 3.6 [6]42; 3.7–9 [3]7n q; 3.8–11 [3]22 q; 3.9 [2]732n; 3.18 [2]709; 4.1–13 [6]42; 4.1–17 [1]504n; 4.7–8 [5]513n q; 4.8 [2]564 q, 564n; 4.9 MT [1]464; 4.11 [3]6n; 4.11–13 [5]513 q, 513n; 4.13 [2]662 q, 662n; 4.16 [1]529; 4.17 [1]529n q; 4.21 [2]742 q, 742n; 4.23 [4]45–6; 4.24 [3]876 q, 876n, 878 q; 4.30 [3]17n; 4.31 [4]560 q; 5.5 [2]742n, [6]179 q, 180, 182n q; 5.13 [3]523 q, [6]305 q; 5.23 [3]678, 678n q; 5.23–32 [1]752n; 5.29–32 [3]678, 678n q; 5.32 [1]472n; 6.13 [6]140n

Galatians [1]415, [2]436; Eichhorn on [2]495–7; Luther on [4]631, 631n; 1.2 [1]822; 1.6 MT [1]463; 1.6–9 [2]1085n; 1.8 [5]519 q, 519n, 657n q; 1.10 [1]463n q; 1.12 [2]468, [3]421n; 1.17 [2]455, 455n q; 1.18–19 [2]455n–6n q; 1.20 [2]299, 1162; ch 2 [2]700; 2.7–21 [2]705n; 2.14–17 [1]512n; 2.16 [1]822n, [5]492n q; 2.16–17 [2]592n; 2.20 [1]821n, 822n, [2]592 q, 592n, 1162, 1162n q; 2.20–1 [2]299n; 2.21 [2]592 q, 592n; 3.1–12 [2]592n; 3.6–29 [5]623n; 3.7–9 [5]778n; 3.11 [3]332n, [4]348n q; 3.16 [1]705n q; 3.19 [1]468n, [2]472n; 3.19–20 MT [1]463; 4.1 [1]245n; 4.4 [2]271n q, 273n q, 275n; 4.4–5 [2]273–9; 5.2 [4]252; 5.2–4 [4]251, 252n q; 5.19 [6]56n; 5.20–1 [6]42; 5.22 [4]560 q; 6.1 [3]550n q; 6.7 [5]561n q; 6.12–15 [5]623n q; 6.14–15 [2]343 q, 343n; 6.15 [4]251

Hebrews [1]415; MT 467; 493n, [2]436, [3]310, 310n, 421, 595, [5]54, 76n, 590–1, 667, 668, [6]77; by Apollos [3]20, 20n; attributed to St Paul [2]400, 400n, 502; [3]19, authorship of [2]563–4, 563n, 706, 706n, [6]117, 117n; canonicity of [3]19–20, 20n; Eichhorn on [2]472, 499–500; ch 1–3 [1]438n; 1.3 [1]466n q, [3]523 q, [6]306 q; 1.4–5 [5]54n q; 1.5 [2]584 q, 584n; 1.6 [2]722n q, 732n q; 2.1–4 [1]468n; 2.2 MT [1]468–9; [2]472n q; 2.4 [2]751n; 2.7 [5]33n q; 2.16 [3]14 q, 14n q, 19–20, 19n q, 21 q, 21n q; 3.2 [2]500n q; 3.12 [5]516n q; 3.14 [1]466n; MT 469; 4.12 [3]546 q, 546n; 5.5 [2]584 q, 584n; 5.12–14 [1]312n, [5]620n; 6.2 [5]578n; 6.4–6 [1]821n; ch 8–9 [3]28n; 9.11 [3]28n q; 9.22 [2]563 q, [3]544; 10.22 [3]517–18; 10.25 [5]578n; 10.26–7 [5]583, 583n q; 10.29 [5]583; 10.38 [3]332n, [4]348n q; 11.1 [2]689 q, 689n, [4]298n, 616, 616n, [6]223n q; 11.17 [2]732n q; 11.21 [3]616n q; 11.26 [2]807 q; 11.33–4 [3]595n q; 11.33–8 [3]595; 11.35 [3]595, 595n q; 11.40 [1]853; 12.2 [3]521 q, [6]304; 12.5 [3]556 q; 12.9 [1]239n q, [5]482n; 12.14 [5]491 q, 491n; 12.22–3 [5]728n q; 12.22–4 [4]552 q; 12.23 [1]729n; 12.29 [2]567 q, 567n; 13.8 [3]562 q; 13.17 [1]474

James [1]474, 493n, [2]436, 469, 832, [3]446n, 724, 724n–5n, [4]252; Eichhorn on [2]472, 500–1; an epistle of straw [3]725n; 1.1 [2]832n; 1.17 [1]556 q, 556n, 729 q, 729n, [2]884 q, 884n, [2]1166n q; 1.21 [1]675 q, 675n q, [3]568 q; 1.22 [3]498, 498n q; 1.23 [1]237n q; 1.25 [3]429 q, 429n q, 498, 498n q; 1.26 [2]655 q, 655n; 1.27 [2]655 q, 655n, [3]721 q, 722, 724, 725n, [4]625 q, 625n q; 2.1 [6]164 q; 2.5 [2]1185n; 2.8–10 [2]19, 19n q; 2.10 [5]612, 612n q; 2.19 [1]504 q, 504n q, [2]1083 q, 1083n, [3]510 q, 510n, 519 q, 519n, [6]301 q, 301n; 2.23 [1]470n; 3.17 [3]522–3, [6]304, 304n q; 4.1 [5]277 q, 277n q; 4.14 [3]519 q, [6]302; 5.14–15 [4]259 q

John [1]178, 415, 452, 474, [2]36, 203–4, 342, 435, 436n, 470, 493, 503, 1055–6, 1084, 1159, 1162n, 1187n, [3]4n, 441n, 664–5, 673, 673n, 683, 727, 730, 732, 922, [4]57, 67, 226, 304, 348, 407n, 473, 646, [5]58, 77, 140, 363, 434, 434n, 516, 554, 676, 766, 778, [6]17, 23; allegorised [2]715; authorship of [3]442n; catholicity [6]65; C's projected commentary on [1]624; collated with St Paul [2]267; divine oracle [3]24; Eichhorn on [2]456–65, 478–87; St Paul in harmony with [1]463; purpose [1]447; rejection of [6]69; ch 1 [1]624, 624n, 676, 706, [2]270, 479n, 582, 582n, 798, [4]200n, [5]567; ch 1–3 [6]135; ch 1–6 [2]565–6; 1.1 [1]477–

8, 574n, 675 q, 675n, 681, 681n q, 690n q, [2]466n, 598 q, 598n, 741 q, 741n q, 798n, 970 q, 970n, [3]11 q, 11n q, 24 q, 24n q, 73n, 77n q, 521 q, 521n q, [4]394n q, [5]35 q, 35n q, 160 q, 385, 385n q, [6]5 q, 5n q, 83n, 180 q, 303 q, 303n q; 1.1–3 [1]236n; 1.1–4 [2]208n, [3]60n q, [5]630n, 663; 1.1–16 [2]462n; 1.1–18 [2]798, 798n; 1.3 [3]12n q, [4]492n q, [5]484 q; 1.3–4 [1]658, 658n q; 1.4 [1]123 q, 123n, 624 q, 624n, 630n, 675 q, 675n, 712 q, 712n q, 824n, [2]583n, 750n q, [3]61n, [5]628, 628n q, [6]64 q, 64n; 1.4–5 [2]1000 q, 1000n q; 1.4–9 [1]465n; 1.5 [1]465, 465n, 824n, [2]298 q, 298n, [3]516, 516n q, [6]299, 299n q; 1.6–9 [2]479n; 1.7 [1]465, 465n; 1.8 [2]484n q, 726 q, 726n; 1.9 [1]465, 465n, 675 q, 675n, 712 q, 712n, 824 q, 824n, [2]297 q, 297n, 1175 q, 1175n, [3]23 q, 23n, 61n, 558 q, 558n, 696 q, 696n, 723 q, 723n, [5]8 q, 8n, 155 q, 155n, 189 q, 189n, 400 q, 400n; 1.9–12 [1]713n; 1.9–13 [1]713; 1.10 [2]584 q, 584n, [3]763; 1.11 [2]183n, 479n, [3]876 q, 876n; 1.11–12 [3]150–1 q, 151n q; 1.12 [1]462n, 484n, 676 q, 676n q; 1.13 [2]279n; 1.14 [1]438n q, 446n q, 687n, [2]33n, 271 q, 271n q, 273n q, 315 q, 315n q, 457 q, 486n, 732n q, 750n q, 798n, [3]14 q, 14n q, 16 q, 16n q, 17, 17n, 41n, 524n, 545 q, 545n q, 610 q, 610n q, 876 q, 876n q, [6]65n q, 306n; 1.15 [2]479n; 1.16 [3]876n q; 1.18 [1]420n q, 460, 461n q, 575 q, 575n q, 681, 681n q, 785 q, 785n q, [2]33n, 457 q, 458 q, 458n, 489, 489n q, 570 q, 570n q, 723 q, 723n q, 732n q, [3]11 q, 11n q, 16 q, 16n q, 17 q, 53, 57 q, 57n, 66–7 q, 67n q, 106, 106n q, 431 q, 431n q, 522 q, 522n q, [4]57n, [5]33 q, 33n, 56n q, [6]61, 61n q, 78, 78n q, 83n, 85 q, 85n q, 305n q; 1.20 [2]150n; 1.21 [3]41n; 1.25–6 [4]49; 1.27 [2]479n; 1.29 [2]489, 489n q, 497 q, 497n; 1.29–34 [2]481n; 1.31 [2]798n; 1.31–3 [2]463n; 1.32 [3]730n; 1.32–4 [4]64–5; 1.36 [2]489, 489n q; 1.42 [3]458n q, [4]49; 1.43–51 [4]682n; 1.47 [6]170n q; 1.49–51 [3]432, 432n q; ch 2 [2]37, 37n q; 2.1–11 [2]262n, 1015n; 2.1–12 [4]65; 2.4 [1]519 q, 519n q; 2.11 [4]66n q; 2.13–22 [4]66; 2.18 [3]6n; 2.19 [1]466, [2]1088n; 3.1–7 [4]659n; 3.1–13 [5]193n; 3.3 [1]202n q, 574n, [4]621n; 3.5 [3]605n; 3.7 [1]574n, [4]621n; 3.8 [1]14, [4]635 q, 635n q, [5]157 q, 157n q; 3.10 [5]583n; 3.12 [3]427n; 3.13 [2]457 q; 3.15 [2]559n q; 3.16 [1]198–9 q, 200n q, 202n q, 826 q, 826n, [2]457 q, 732n q, [3]720, 720n q; 3.16–17 [3]545n; 3.18 [2]457 q, 732n q; 3.31 [2]485 q; 4.7–26 [3]659n; 4.21–3 MT [1]457; 4.21–4 [3]1079n; 4.23–4 [4]46; 4.24 [1]179n; 5.3–14 [2]1109, 1109n; 5.4 MT [1]457; 5.16–19 [6]136 q, 136n q; 5.18 [2]798n, [6]136; 5.19 [1]466n–7n q; 5.21 [2]184n q; 5.23 [2]39n; 5.25 [2]566 q, 566n; 5.28–9 [2]184n; 5.29 [2]564–5 q; 5.30 [2]644n, [5]54 q; ch 6 [1]624, 669n, 673, 673n, [4]668, [5]151, 548, 549, 551; 6.1–15 [2]1159, 1159n; 6.5 [1]815n; 6.5–14 [4]67; 6.10 [2]1086, 1086n; 6.30 [3]6n; 6.30–58 [1]510n; 6.31–58 [1]469, 469n, [2]1084, 1084n q; 6.32–65 [3]439n q; 6.35 [2]670, 670n; 6.39 [2]644n, 652n; 6.40 [2]652n; 6.44 [2]332 q, 332n, 652n; 6.47–51 [2]670, 670n; 6.47–58 [1]863, 863n; 6.51 [1]469n q, [6]21, 21n q; 6.52–60 [5]396–7, 397n q; 6.53 [2]670n q, [4]668n q, 6.53–8 [2]670, 670n; 6.54 [1]469n, [2]267n; 6.56 [2]267n, [5]673n q; 6.60 [1]673 q, 673n q, [5]151n q; 6.63 [1]179n, [3]163n, 439n q, 1086n q, [5]778n q; 6.65 [2]332n; 6.69 [3]76n q; 7.17 [2]644 q, 644n, [3]517 q, 517n, [6]300n; 7.22 [4]251; 7.24 [2]566 q, 566n; 7.39 [5]666n q; 7.46 [1]448 q, 448n q; ch 8 [5]575n; 8.42 [2]732n q, [3]16n q; 8.44 [3]120 q, 121n, 446n, 769n, [4]14, q, 14n, [5]424n q; 8.58 [3]429 q, 429n; 9.2 [3]707–8; 9.39–41 [1]273n; 10.7–8 [3]752, 752n q; 10.9 [5]580n q; 10.10 [1]564n q, [2]291–6; 10.16 [6]41; 10.25–6 [2]564, 564n; 10.30 [2]798n q, [3]588 q, 588n; 10.34 [1]438n, [2]183n, 799n, [3]904n; 10.34–6 [1]708n, [2]798, 798n q; 11.1–44 [2]1159, 1159n, [3]613n; 11.17–44 [2]262n; 11.24 [2]652n; 11.25 [2]184n; 11.27 [5]618n; 11.33–44 [4]256, 256n; 11.35 [1]13n, [2]314–17; 11.38–44 [2]1086, 1086n; 11.52 [3]876 q, 876n; 12.24 [1]470n; 12.25 [2]559n q; 12.28 [1]428n, [5]11n; 12.38 [2]287–90, 1076n q; 12.48 [2]652n; 13.7 MT [1]457; 13.13 [4]57 q, 57n q; 13.15 [4]566 q; 13.23 [2]262n, [5]540n; 13.31–2 [3]14n; ch 14 [4]646n; 14.3 [2]484n q; 14.6 [3]23n q, [5]580n q; 14.9 [5]56, 56n q; 14.10 MT [1]457–8; [3]689n q; 14.11 [4]673n q; 14.15 [2]193 q, 193n; 14.16 [3]584n; 14.16–17 [3]689n q; 14.17 [1]179n; 14.19–20 [6]67, 67n q; 14.20 [1]574q, 574n q, [5]551 q, 551n; 14.23 [1]713n, [2]462n, 463 q, 463n q, 598 q, 598n, [4]145n q, 300n q, [5]55 q, 55n; 14.26 [2]752n, [3]584n, [4]646n q; 14.28 [3]588q, 588n, [4]394 q, 394n, [5]9–10 q, 10n, 55 q; 15.1 [5]580n q; 15.1–5 [5]396 q, 396n q; 15.2 [1]179n; 15.5 [3]678, 678n q; 15.12 [5]132n q; 15.15

The Bible—*continued*
[5]563 q, 564 q; 15.26 [1]179n, [2]732n q, [3]16n q; 16.13 [1]179n; 16.23–4 [4]299n; 16.26–7 [4]299n; 16.33 [3]582 q; 17.1–5 [3]14n; 17.3 [2]427 q, 427n; 17.5 [3]50 q, 50n q; 17.6 [1]428n; 17.11 [6]41; 17.26 [1]428n; 18.19–23 [4]51n; 18.33–9 [2]1173n; 18.36 [1]252n q, 675 q, 675n q, [3]72 q, 72n, [4]51n, [6]55 q, 55n q; 18.36–37 [4]50; 19.10 [1]462n; 19.11 MT [1]458; [2]485 q, 485n; 19.14 [2]902n; 19.14–15 [2]1173n; 19.14–22 [3]6n; 19.21 MT [1]458; 19.26 [2]262n; 19.26–7 [5]524 q, 524n q; 19.29–30 [4]745n; 19.30 [2]1107n q; 19.34 [2]362n, [3]612n q; 19.35 [4]61; 20.15 [2]1078n; 20.19 [2]1077n; 20.22 [5]536 q, 536n; 20.22–3 [2]722n, 751n, [3]734n; 20.23 [1]847 q, 847n; 20.24–31 [2]37n q; 20.26 [2]1077n; 20.29 [1]283 q, 283n; 20.31 [4]61, [5]618n, 622n; ch 21 [1]493n, 514–15, 515n, [2]463, 484, 484n, [3]542, 667, [4]61n, [5]629, 629n; 21.15 [1]514 q; 21.15–17 [5]634n; 21.22 [3]608; 21.22–3 [2]38n–9n q; 21.23 [2]484n q; 21.24 [2]463 q, 463n–4n q
1 John [1]415, [2]436, [3]446n, 477, 732, 922, [4]174; catholicity [6]65; Eichhorn on [2]487; 1.1–3 [5]553–4, 553n; 1.5–6 [6]66n; 1.1–8 [4]645 q, 645n; 2.4 [3]549 q; 2.6 [1]473n; 2.15 [2]568 q, [4]556 q; 2.17 [2]568; 2.20 [3]541n q; 3.2 [3]569; 3.4–10 MT [1]469–70; 3.6 MT [1]470; 3.10 [1]656 q, 656n; 3.23 [5]628, 628n q; 3.23–4 [1]470n; 4.1 [3]986 q; 4.1–3 [2]750n; 4.2 [1]470n, [2]487, 487n, [5]618n, 628, 628n q; 4.8 [2]249 q, 249n, 527 q, 527n, [3]76 q, 76n; 4.9 [1]703n, [2]732n q; 4.9–10 [1]470n; 4.12 [1]179n; 4.13 [6]300 q; 4.15 [1]179n, [5]540n q, 618n; 4.15–17 [1]470n; 4.16 [2]249 q, 249n, [3]76 q, 76n; 4.18 [3]64 q, 64n; 4.20 [1]729 q, 729n q, [2]449 q, 449n q, [4]298n; ch 5 [3]516; 5.1 [2]732n q; 5.7 [1]489, 562n q, [2]52 q, 52n q, 752n, [3]477n q; 5.7–8 [6]67, 67n q; 5.8 [2]52n q; 5.18 [2]732n q; 5.20–1 [1]820 q, 820n q
2 John [3]732; catholicity [6]65; 7 [2]487, 487n, 750n; 10–11 [6]58 q, 58n q
3 John [1]474, [3]732; 5 [2]668n
Jude [1]493n, [2]436, [3]446n; Eichhorn on [2]476–7; 6 [2]571, 571n q, [3]14n; 9 [3]535n q, 594, 594n q, 595, [6]317n q; 14–15 [1]320, 320n, 468, 468n, [3]310, 310n; 25 [1]576n q
Luke [1]415, 444, 448, [2]37n, 270, 270n, 316, 362, 435, 436, 442–3, 445–50, 448n, 493, 661, 918n, 999n, 1078, [3]3, 4n, 36, 606, 683, 726, 730, 926n, [4]55, 56, 56n, 67, 250, 251n, 469–84, 640, [5]77, 434, 434n, 607; date of [4]56, 56n; Eichhorn on [2]451–2; purpose [1]447; relation to Marcionite Gospel [2]438–9, 438n, 439n; ch 1–2 [2]34–5, 35n, 487, [3]730n, [4]41n, 52, 251n, 478, 479, [5]515, 515n, 629, 629n, [6]64, 64n, 69; 1.1–2 472n q; 1.1–4 [2]444, 444n q, 902, 902n, [4]55n; 1.2 [2]436n q; 1.3 [1]476–7; 1.5 [1]446 q, 446n; 1.5–2.52 [1]506, 506n, [2]266, 266n; 1.17 [5]402n; 1.26–38 [3]17n; 1.35 [4]57; 1.74 [1]445n q; ch 2 [2]446n; 2.1–20 [4]476; 2.7 [2]915; 2.8 [2]918; 2.9 [2]918; 2.22–39 [4]54; 2.22–40 [4]477; 2.29–30 [2]279–84; 2.33 [4]55n q; 2.41–52 [4]478; ch 3 [1]493n; 3.2 [4]481n q; 3.8 [3]464 q, 464n; 3.16 [1]471n q, [5]650 q; 3.21–3 [3]730n; 3.22 [4]481n q; 3.23 [6]109, 109n q; 3.23–38 [4]55; ch 4 [3]107n; 4.1–13 [2]921, 921n; 4.2 [2]443; 4.16–30 [4]480; 4.35 [3]475n; 4.38–9 [2]703n; 4.39 [3]475n; 5.32 MT [1]455; [4]644n q; 5.36 [2]566n q; 5.37–8 [2]566n; 6.20–49 [3]7, 7n; 6.26 [4]746 q 746n q; 6.31 [2]118n; 6.39 [1]273n; 6.41–2 [3]71n; 6.47–9 [1]273n; 7.19–23 [4]298n; 7.23 [2]798 q; 7.29 [4]59n; 8.6 [3]67 q; 8.19 [3]440n q; 8.19–21 [2]272n; 8.26–36 [6]102n; 8.30 [4]782 q, 782n q; 8.33 [4]782 q, 782n q; 8.41–8 [1]450, 450n; 8.43–8 [4]637n; 8.46 MT [1]455; 8.52 [2]404 q, 404n; 9.10–17 [4]67; 9.12 [1]815n, [2]461; 9.14 [2]1086n; 9.18–22 [4]646n; 9.20 [5]622n, 635 q, 635n; 9.28–36 [3]40n; 9.32–3 [3]40n q; 9.33 [2]922; 9.51–6 [2]447, 447n; 9.51–ch 18 [2]444; 9.54–6 [3]820n; 9.56 [3]820n q, [5]645 q, 645n q; ch 10 [5]129n; 10.1 [1]309n, [4]474n q; 10.1–16 [3]696n; 10.1–20 [2]722n q; 10.21 [1]586 q, 586n; 10.25–8 [4]659n; 10.27 [2]193 q, 193n, [5]161 q, 161n; 10.27–8 [4]626n; ch 11 [3]35; 11.2 [3]453 q, 453n; 11.4 [2]1179 q, 1179n; 11.9 [1]709n; 11.13 [2]1166n; 11.20 [1]457 q, 457n q; 11.24 [3]39n; 11.24–6 [5]411n q; 11.29–30 [4]735n; 11.32 [3]7n q; 12.8 [5]540n; 12.45–51 [3]422n; 13.34 [6]219n–20n q; ch 14–23 [2]36–7; 14.22 [2]1107n q; 15.1–17.10 [4]481; 15.7 [2]787n q; 15.11–22 [1]202n; 16.17 [1]437n, [2]470n; 16.19–31 [2]1029n; 17.10 [3]456n; 17.13 [1]512n; 17.20–37 [3]421, 421n, 477, 477n; 17.21 [1]675 q, 675n, [3]453 q, 453n; 17.24–37 [3]449, 449n; 17.29–30 [3]477n q; 18.1 [1]702n q; 18.8 [1]247n, [3]452 q, 452n, 454n; 18.9 see *BCP*: Bible: NT: Luke; 18.15–34 [4]482; 18.16 [1]289n; 18.34 [4]482 q, 482n; 19.12 [3]454 q; 19.41 [1]13n; ch 20 [4]482; 20.19–

23 [4]482; 20.35–8 [2]184n; ch 21 [4]482; 21.9–19 [1]453n; 21.20 [6]217; 21.27 [3]454n q; 21.27–8 [3]447 q; 21.33 [3]53n q; 21.36 [1]702n q; 22.1–23.49 [4]483–4; 22.8 [2]902n; 22.11 [2]902n; 22.13 [2]902n; 22.19 [1]510n, 714 q, 714n, [2]267n, 672 q, 672n, [3]156n q, [5]396 q, 396n q, 673n; 22.19–21 [3]28n; 22.24–7 [2]972n; 22.26 [5]539n; 22.31 [3]474; 22.32 [3]458 q; 22.36 [3]696n q; 22.62 [3]988n q; 23.36 [4]745n; 23.56 [1]334n, [3]664n q; ch 24 MT [1]456; 24.2 MT [1]456; 456n; 24.13–25 [1]456n; 24.25–7 MT [1]456; 24.29 [3]666; 24.33–53 [3]666; 24.36 [1]456n q; 24.39 [5]555 q, 555n q; 24.41–3 [1]456n

Mark [1]415, 448, [2]37, 319, 320, 435, 442–3, 445, 448, 918n, 1159, [3]4n, 666, 926, 926n, [4]470, 472, 473, 473n, 474, 474n, [5]396, 434, 434n, 567, 629, 629n; Eichhorn on [2]450–1; end of [1]455; purpose of [1]447; ch 1 [3]107n; 1.6 [5]105n; 1.7 [2]121n; 1.12–13 [2]921, 921n; 2.17 [4]644n q; 3.17 [2]496n, [5]402n; 3.19 [1]450n; 3.29 [6]168n q; 3.31–4 [2]272n; 4.27 [1]14; 5.9 [3]138n q; 5.25–34 [4]637n; 5.39 [2]404 q, 404n; 6.3 [2]476–7; 6.7–13 [2]722n; 6.15 [2]150n; 6.30–45 [4]67; 6.35 [1]815n, [2]461; 6.44 [2]1086n; 7.7–9 [5]567n q; 7.29 MT [1]454–5; 7.36 [4]646n; 8.9 [2]1086n; 8.12 [3]988 q, 988n; 8.25 [2]835; 8.29 [5]635 q, 635n; 8.30 [2]1173n; 8.34–8 [4]659n; 9.2–13 [3]40n; 9.4–13 [2]150n; 9.24 [2]1061 q, 1061n, [3]509 q, 509n, [4]683 q, 683n q; 9.30 [4]646n; 9.31 [2]1088n; 9.44 [2]569 q; 9.46 [2]569 q; 9.48 [2]569 q; 10.14 [1]289n; 10.15 [5]650n q; 10.17–22 [3]650n; 10.30 [2]559n q, [5]630, 630n q; 10.41–4 [1]250n; 10.43 [5]539n; 12.17 [1]838n q, [5]363n q; 12.30–1 [2]193 q, 193n, [4]626n; 13.9–13 [1]453n; 13.10 [1]528n; 13.14 [3]111n, [4]58n, [6]217; 13.15 [2]482n; 13.26–32 [2]34n q; 13.31 [3]53n q; 13.32 [2]32n, 992 q, 992n q, [3]709 q, [4]302 q, 302n q, [5]33 q, 56 q, 56n, 57 q, 57n q, 58, [6]90n q; 14.12 [2]902n; 14.16 [2]902n; 14.22 [1]839n q, [2]267n, [3]156n q; 14.22–4 [3]28n; 14.28 [2]1088n; 15.34 [1]427n q, [3]34n, 55 q, 611n, [5]523 q, 523n; 15.36 [4]745n; 15.40 [2]272n; ch 16 [1]493n; 16.1 [2]272n; 16.7 [3]666; 16.8 MT [1]455; 16.9–20 [1]455n, [2]441n, [3]3, 3n–4n, [4]474n, [5]629, 629n; 16.15 [3]659n, [4]474 q, 474n q; 16.17 [5]565, 565n; 16.18 [3]137 q, 137n

Matthew [1]415, 448, 451, 452, 474, 879, [2]29, 37, 400, 400n, 435, 442–3, 487, 661, 918n, 1056, 1078n, [3]3, 4n, 36, 606, 607, 683, 730, 731, 926n, [4]56, 56n, 58, 67, 68, 68n, 251n, 470, 471, 472, 478, 478n–9n, [5]72, 72n, 140, 396, 434, 434n, 516, 526, 567, 635 ("first Gospel"), 637 ("first Gospel"), [6]23, 64, 64n, 67, 69; authenticity of [5]77; date of [1]235, 235n, [4]56, 56n, [5]637n; distinctive character [3]7; Eichhorn on [2]445–50; first gospel [2]270, 270n; Gospel according to the Hebrews [1]490, 491, 491n, [2]467, 493, Eichhorn on [2]436–7; Gospel according to the Nazareans [1]490, 491, 491n; in Hebrew [4]248; last written [1]447; non-apostolic [2]736; purpose [1]446–7; and Talmud [1]513; versions of [5]607, 607n; ch 1 [1]493n, [3]421; ch 1–2 [2]34–5, 35n, [4]41n; 1.1 [3]606–7; 1.1–17 [4]55; 1.1–18 [4]53; 1.18–25 [3]17n; 1.18–2.23 [1]506, 506n, [2]266n; 1.22 [2]1076n q; 1.23 [2]270n q; ch 2 [2]446n, [4]55n; 2.1 [1]446 q, 446n; 2.1–2 [3]607; 2.2 [3]653, 653n; 2.4 [4]470n; 2.12–23 [4]54; 3.1 [3]607; 3.2 [4]56; 3.4 [5]105n; 3.9 [3]464 q, 464n; 3.11 [1]471n q, [3]598n q, [5]650 q; 3.13–17 [4]298n; 3.14 [5]635n; 3.14–15 [4]481n; 3.16 [2]463 q, 463n q; ch 4 [3]107n; 4.1–11 [2]921, 921n; 4.2–3 [2]443; 4.4 [3]16 q, 16n q; 4.8 [2]921; 4.14 [2]461; 4.17 [4]56 q, 56–7; 4.18–20 [2]252–3, 254; 4.24 [2]1109 q, 1109n q; ch 5–7 ("Sermon on the Mount") [1]456, [3]7, 7n; 5.1–12 [3]607; 5.2 [2]303–6; 5.3 [4]254 q; 5.16 [2]296–302; 5.17 [2]615 q, 615n; 5.17–18 [1]832n, [4]251n q, 481n q, [6]60n q; 5.17–19 [5]522n; 5.18 [1]437n, [2]470 q, 470n q; 5.19 [1]833n, [6]59 q; 5.22 MT [1]448–9; 512, 512n; 5.26 [1]512, 512n; 5.29 [1]512, 512n; 5.44 [2]564 q; 5.48 [3]306 q, 306n, 532 q, 532n, [5]170 q, 170n, 725 q, 725n, 820 q, 820n; ch 6 [5]523n; 6.1–4 [4]622n; 6.3 [3]608; 6.9 [5]522n–3n q; 6.9–13 [3]432n, [5]95n, 520n; 6.10 [3]417 q, 417n, 453 q, 453n; 6.11 [3]765n; 6.13 [1]561–2 q, 562n q, [2]1179 q, 1179n; 6.25 [3]765n; 6.30 [5]785 q, 785n; 6.34 [2]800 q , 800n; 7.1 [5]180 q, 180n, 646 q, 646n; 7.3–4 [3]71n; 7.7 [1]709n; 7.9 [3]408, 408n; 7.11 [2]1166n; 7.12 [4]639 q, 639n q; 7.17–18 [2]1109n; 7.20 [2]644 q, 644n, [5]744 q, 744n; 7.21–3 [4]622n; 7.26–7 [1]273n; 8.17 MT [1]449; 8.21 [2]448–9; 8.25 [3]512 q, 512n; 9.13 MT [1]449; [4]644n q; 9.14 MT [1]449–50; 9.15 [1]450 q; 9.15–17 [1]449n q, 450n q; 9.17 MT [1]450; 9.20 [2]716n; 9.20–2 [4]637n; 9.22 MT [1]450; 9.24 [2]404 q, 404n; 9.29 [5]587 q, 587n q; 9.30 [4]646n; 10.5–42 [3]8n; 10.8 [3]8n; 10.28 [3]37n q;

The Bible—*continued*
10.32 [5]540n; 10.34–9 [4]659n; 10.38 [1]821n; ch 11 [1]649; 11.2–6 [4]298n; 11.4–6 [1]450n q; 11.5–6 [3]775n q; 11.7 [2]483; 11.11–12 MT [1]450; 11.14 [2]150n, [3]457n, [5]402n; 11.25 [1]586 q, 586n; 11.27 [5]563 q, 563n q; 11.28 [5]683 q, 683n; 11.29 [4]566 q; ch 12 [2]722n; 12.18 [5]59; 12.24 [3]57n q; 12.25–7 MT [1]451; 12.31 [2]251, [4]300n q; 12.32 [4]244n q; 12.38 [3]6n q; 12.39 [4]735n q; 12.40 [2]1088n, [4]735n q, [6]217, 217n q; 12.41 [3]7n q; 12.43 [3]39n; 12.43–5 [5]411n q; 12.46 [2]272n q; 12.48 [1]520 q, 520n q; 12.49 [1]520, 520n q; 12.50 [2]644n; 13.19 [4]234n, [5]85n q; 13.55 [2]272n, 476–7; 14.13–22 [4]67; 14.17 [1]815n; 14.21 [2]1086n; 14.26 MT [1]451; 15.15 MT [1]451; 15.18 [3]518; 15.22 [3]527n; 15.32 [1]815n; 15.38 [2]1086n; 16.4 [4]735n; 16.7 MT [1]451; 16.14 [2]150n; 16.15–17 [4]641n q, 646n; 16.16 [3]76n q, 458n, [5]618n, 622n; 16.18 [2]670n q, [3]458 q, 458n, [6]15n; 16.18–19 [1]511 q, [3]234, 234n q, [5]634n; 16.19 [1]309n, [2]722n, 1096n, [5]535n q; 16.20 [3]687n, 733n, [4]646n; 16.20–1 [2]1173n; 16.21 [2]1088n; 16.24 [1]821n; 17.1–13 [3]40n; 17.9 [2]1173n; 17.10–12 [1]446, 446n, 452, 452n q; 17.10–13 [3]41n q, 457n; 17.12 [2]150n; 17.15 [3]527n; 17.20 [4]668n q; 17.23 [2]1088n; 17.24–7 [6]60n; 17.25–6 MT [1]451–2; 17.26 [1]451n; 17.37 [2]834; 18.1–4 [2]972n; 18.18 [2]722n, [5]535n; 19.6 [1]185n; 19.8 [2]1160n; 19.12 MT [1]452; [2]984n; 19.14 [1]289 q, 289n, [5]648n, 650n; 19.16–22 [3]650n; 19.16–24 [2]322n; 19.17 [2]317–28, [4]113 q, 113n; 19.21 [3]650n q; 19.24 [5]417n q; 19.28–9 [1]232n; 19.35 [1]512n; ch 20 [2]716n; 20.1–16 [1]202n, [5]582n; 20.16 [2]1166 q, 1166n; 20.20–2 [2]972n; 20.25–7 [1]250 q, 250n q; 20.26 [5]539n; 21.18–22 [2]47; 21.20–2 MT [1]452–3; 21.25 [4]59n; 21.42 [1]649n q; 22.11 [1]714 q; 22.14 [2]1166 q, 1166n; 22.21 [1]838n q, [5]363n q; 22.23 [4]663n q; 22.23–32 [3]478n; 22.30 [3]478n q; 22.36–7 [5]457 q, 457n q; 22.37–9 [2]193 q, 193n; 22.37–40 [4]626n; 23.9–10 [4]57 q, 57n q; 23.37 MT [1]453; [3]894n q, [6]219n–20n q; ch 24 [3]416n, 447n, 448; 24–5 [3]731n; 24.9 [1]453; 24.9–13 MT [1]453n; 24.14 [1]528n, [2]448, 448n q; 24.15 [3]111n–12n q, 421n, [4]58n q; 24.16 [2]833, [6]217 ("xxix, 9"); 24.24 MT [1]454; 24.36 [4]302n q, [5]33 q, 56 q, 56n, 58, 58n q [6]90n q; 24.39 [3]480 q; ch 25 [1]852; 25.14–30 [4]596n; 25.20–1 [4]622n q; 25.31–46 [4]662n–3n q; 26.17 [2]902n; 26.19 [2]902n; 26.26 [1]839n q, [2]267n, [3]156n q; 26.26–8 [3]28n; 26.53 [2]1077n, [4]782n q; 26.63 [4]50 q; 26.63–4 [4]51n; 26.63–6 [6]139n q; 26.64 [2]494, 494n q; 26.75 [3]988n q; 27.19 [1]447n; 27.24 [1]447n; 27.43 [1]484n q; 27.46 [1]427n q, [3]34n, 55 q, 611n, [5]523 q, 523n; 27.47–9 [2]150n; 27.48 [4]745n; 27.52–3 [2]446n q; 27.56 [2]272n; 27.62–6 MT [1]454; 27.64–6 [1]447, 447n; 28.3 [2]631, 632n; 28.7 [3]666; 28.11–15 MT [1]454; 28.12–15 [1]447, 447n; 28.16–20 [3]667; 28.19 [1]235n q, 528 q, 528n q, [2]154 q, 154n, 736 q, 736n, 752n, [3]309 q, 309n, 659 q, 659n, 691 q, 691n, [4]474n q, [5]637n q, 653n q; 28.20 [1]468n, [2]1163 q, 1163n q, [3]458 q; 28.45 [2]902n; 28.51–4 [2]902n

1 Peter [1]474, [2]436, 469–70, 502n, 1084, [3]445–6, 445n–6n, 669n, [4]174, [6]296–304; authenticity of [5]668, 668n; Eichhorn on [2]473–5, 501–2; Leighton on [3]508–22, 541–603; ch 1 [3]669; 1.1 [3]541–3; 1.2 [3]514–17, 544–52; 1.3 [2]732n q; 1.3–4 [3]552–4; 1.5 [3]554–5; 1.6 [3]508, 555–6; 1.7 [3]508, 556; 1.8–9 [3]509, 556–61, [5]599n; 1.10–12 [3]561–4; 1.12 [5]575, 575n q; 1.13 [3]509–10, 564–5; 1.14 [3]510–11; 1.14–16 [3]565; 1.17 [3]565–7; 1.18–19 [2]139n q, [3]511; 1.20 [3]511, 567; 1.21 [3]568; 1.22 [3]517–19, 568; 1.23 [1]574n, [2]1185 q, 1185n, [3]519; 1.24 [3]519–21; 1.25 [3]521; 2.1 [4]560 q; 2.1–2 [3]511–12, 568–7, [5]613 q, 613n q; 2.3 [3]512, 571; 2.4–5 [3]512–13, 572; 2.5–8 [1]649n q; 2.6 [3]513, 572; 2.8 [2]486n; 2.9 [3]572; 2.13–24 [3]573; 2.17 [3]573–4; 2.24 [1]449n; 3.3–4 [3]574; 3.8 [3]574; 3.10 [3]574; 3.11 [3]578; 3.12 [3]578–81; 3.13 [3]581–2; 3.14 [3]582; 3.15 [3]583–8, [4]562 q; 3.16 [3]588–90; 3.18 [2]1187n, [3]28 q, 590–3; 3.19–21 [3]593–5, 594n q; 3.21 [3]595–600, 595n, 597n q; 3.22 [3]600–1; ch 4 [5]578, 578n; 4.2–3 [3]601; 4.4–5 [3]601–2; 4.6 [3]602–3; 4.14–16 [3]521–2; 4.19 [2]33n; 5.5 [3]522; 5.8 [6]97n, 101 q, 101n; 5.13 [2]473, 474, 473n–4n q, 703n, [3]467n, [4]474n, [5]635, 635n q; 18.19 [1]452n

2 Peter [1]490n q, [2]436, 469–70, 502n, 1084, [3]445–6, 445n–6n, 478, 478n, 669n, [4]174, [5]59 q, 59n q; authenticity of [5]668, 668n; Eichhorn on [2]475–6; 1.1 [6]177, 183n; 1.13–14 [2]486n q; 1.19 [2]288 q, 288n q, [3]422n, 668, 668n, 691 q, 691n, [5]59, 59n q; 1.20 [1]316n q, [3]603n q, [6]107,

107n; 1.20–1 [3]421–2, 422n; 2.4 [2]571n q, [3]14n; 3.2 [2]475 q, 475n; 3.6 [3]480 q; 3.8 [2]712n, [3]603n q; 3.8–10 [3]445n q, [4]244n; 3.10 [3]445 q, 478n q, 925; 3.16 [4]304n; 3.18 [3]697, 697n q

Philemon [3]7n; 10 [2]732n q

Philippians [1]415; MT 464; [3]7n; 1.6 [4]244n; 1.10 [4]244n; 1.23 [4]552 q; 1.29 [3]561 q; 2.1–2 [6]42; 2.6 [5]30n; 2.7 [2]273n q, 315 q, 315n q; 2.8–9 [5]30; 2.9–10 [5]59; 2.10 [2]1083 q, 1083n, [5]31 q, 31n; 2.13 [4]408 q, 408n q, [5]207 q, 207n q; 2.24 [2]500, 500n q; ch 3 [1]235; 3.15–16 [6]42; 4.5 [5]578n; 4.7 [2]296 q, 296n, [5]822 q, 822n; 4.8 [1]29n, [2]291n, [4]256n

Revelation/Apocalypse [1]415, 474, 492, 493n, [2]55n, 336, 436, 458–9, *459n*, 484, 502n, 900n, 1048–9, [3]309, 417, 417n, 418, 421, 430, 441n, 442n, 449, 452, 464, 467, 472, 474, 476, 477, 481, 725, 928–9, [4]300, 304, [5]84–5, 85n, 166 ("St John"), 166n, 167, 349n, 434, 494, 515, 607, 667, 807, 807n, [6]164–8; *Apocalypsis graece* ed Heinrichs [1]cxliv; MT [1]480–7; [2]707n; authenticity of [3]922; authorship of [2]465–6, 488, 489–90, [3]477n, 684, 684n, 732, 732n; Bentley's hostility [6]217; canonicity of [3]442, 442n, 443–4; date of composition [2]459; drama of [3]929; Eichhorn on [2]465–6, 487–94, 503–20, *see also* Eichhorn *Commentarius in Apocalypsin Joannis*; interpretation(s) of [3]922n, [5]494n, 630n; prophecies of [3]694; as prophetic drama [2]505; symbolic [3]443–4; wilderness in [1]817, 817n; ch 1–3 [5]494n; 1.1 [3]421n; 1.1–8 [2]505n; 1.5 [2]466, 489, 490, 490n q, 505, 722n q, 732n q, [6]165 q; 1.7 [2]144 q; 1.8 [1]678n q, [3]5 q, 5n q, [5]702n q; 1.9 [2]488; 1.9–3.22 [2]505n; 1.11 [3]422n, [6]168n; 1.12–18 [6]141n; 1.20 [2]920n q; ch 2 [6]168n; 2.1 [2]920n q; 2.6 [2]506; 2.11 [2]559n; 2.12 [2]920n q; 2.14 [2]506; 2.17 [3]571 q; 2.22 [4]190 q; 2.25 [2]38n q; 2.28 [1]575n; 3.14 [2]466 q; 4.1–11 [2]488n; 4.1–22.21 [2]505n; 5.9 [2]489; 5.13 [4]298 q, 299n; 6.8 [6]165 q; 7.14 [2]489, 490n; ch 8–11 [2]512n; 8.3–4 [2]920n; 8.6–12 [2]509; 8.10–11 [2]508; 8.11 [2]509n q; 8.13 [2]509, 510; ch 9–10 [2]509; 9.1 [2]510; 9.1–12 [6]166; 9.7 [2]511 q, 515n; 9.8 [2]512 q, 512n q; 9.10 [2]515n; 9.11 [2]512 q; 9.13–15 [2]505n, 513; 9.14 [2]513; 9.15 [2]514 q, 515 q, 515n; 9.19 [2]515 q, [3]924n; 10.5–6 [3]334 q; 11.1 [2]516 q, 516n; 11.1–14 [2]518; 11.2 [2]516 q, 516n; 11.3 [3]476n q; 11.3ff [5]402n q; 11.3–4 [1]445n q, *see also* witnesses, two; 11.3–13 [1]445n; 11.3–14 [2]517; 11.6 [2]517 q; 11.7–14 [3]476; 11.15–19 [2]518; 11.16 [4]298n; 12.1 [3]469 q, 471 q; 12.2 [3]470 q; 12.4 [5]85n; 12.5 [3]472 q; 12.6 [1]817n q; 12.7 [3]200n; 12.7–9 [3]14n, 417n, 449n, 472–3 q; 12.10 [3]31 q; 12.11 [2]489, 490n; 12.14 [1]471 q, 817n q, [3]471n; 13.1–2 [1]483n–4n q; 13.2 [1]484n q; 13.3 [1]481–3; 13.8 [1]484n, 707n q, [2]279n; 13.11 [1]481–3; 13.11–12 [1]484n q; 13.14 [6]167n; 13.16–18 [1]484n; 13.17 [6]167n; 13.18 [3]929n q, [6]166 q, 166n, 167n; 14.1–4 [1]575n; 14.11 [3]623 q; 14.13 [2]717n; 15.3 [1]10n; 16.16 [3]470n; 16.17 [2]1107n q; ch 17 [3]448, [5]396n; 17.3 MT [1]471, 817n q; 17.5 MT [1]471–3, [3]467n q; 17.11 MT [1]483–4; 17.14 [1]707n; ch 19 [2]505n, [5]432–9; 19.9 MT [1]484; 19.10 MT [1]484–5; 19.16 [1]707n; ch 20 [1]863n q, [2]712, 712n, [3]9, [5]629–30, 20.1–7 [3]442 q; 20.4 [3]443, 443n q; 20.4–6 [4]247n; 20.6 [2]335–6; 20.7 [3]442 q; 20.7–8 [3]481n q; 20.10 [2]569, 569n; 20.11 [3]61n q; 20.11–13 [3]521 q, 521n, [6]303n; 20.14 [2]559n; 20.14–15 [3]61n q; ch 21 [3]983; 21.1–2 [5]463; 21.1–4 [3]521, 521n q, [6]303n q; 21.3 [2]486n; 21.8 [2]559n q; 22.8 [2]488, 488n q, [3]477; 22.9 [3]477, 477n q; 22.16 [1]575n; 22.19 [6]168 q; ch 23 [1]316 q

Romans [1]415, 474, 825n, [2]184n, 436, 670, 670n, 706, [3]744n, [6]15, 15n; collated with John [2]267; Eichhorn on [2]469–71, 498; ch 1 MT [1]459–60; 1.3 [2]273n q; 1.4 [4]653n; 1.17 [3]332 q, 332n, [4]348n q; 1.20 [2]343 q, 343n, [6]140n; 2.4 [3]592; 2.12 [2]1160, 1160n; 2.14 [3]735n q; 2.16 [2]451; ch 3 [5]572; 3.2 [4]251; 3.4 [2]677 q, 677n; 3.15 [1]14; 3.25 [2]497n; 3.28 [2]298n q, [3]307 q, 307n; 4.1–13 [5]778n; 4.5 [4]236 q; 4.11 [1]470n, [4]249–50; 4.22–4 [1]470n; 5.7 [3]12n; 5.12–21 [3]54n; 5.13 [1]824n q, [3]53 q; 5.14 [3]65n; 5.21 [1]703n q; ch 6–8 [2]278, 278n; 6.3–10 [2]267n; 6.5 [2]315 q, 315n q; 6.6 [1]821n, [5]582; 6.9–11 [3]605n; 6.11–13 [5]582; 6.14–15 [2]677n; 6.15–23 [1]832n; 6.18–19 [5]582; 6.20 [2]326n; 6.21 MT [1]460; 6.23 [2]326n; ch 7 [3]497, 498, 498n, 738; 7.1 [3]738n q; 7.1–6 [1]832n; 7.4–6 [5]582; 7.6 [3]498n q; 7.7 [2]677n; 7.13 [2]26n; 7.24 [1]470 q, 470n q, [2]690 q, 690n, 1177n q, [3]747 q, 747n, 963 q, 963n, [5]545 q, 545n, 796 q, 796n; 8.2 [3]709 q; 8.3 [2]315 q, 315n q; 8.4 [2]1076n q; 8.5 [5]583n q; 8.6 [3]424n;

The Bible—*continued*
8.6–7 [1]358 q, 358n q, [2]1151 q, 1151n q; 8.7 [1]504 q, 504n, [3]525–6, 526 q, 526n, 563n, 746 q, 746n, [4]168n q, [5]185 q, 185n, [6]309, 310n; 8.9 [1]302 q, [3]550 q; 8.9–11 [1]179n; 8.16 [2]248–9; 8.21 [5]603n q; 8.26 [2]752n; 8.29 [2]722n q; 8.33–4 [3]527–8, [6]311; ch 9 [1]lxxviii, [3]745; 9.3 [2]922 q; 9.3–5 MT [1]460–1; 9.5 [1]461n q, [2]33n, 1084 q, 1084n q, [5]34 q, 34n q; 9.7–10 [5]212; 9.19 [2]665n q; 9.19–21 [1]412, 412n q; 9.20–1 [2]162, 162n q; 9.33 [2]486n; 9.34–9 [2]913, 913n; 10.1 [5]618 q, 618n; 10.9 [5]540n q, 618n q; 10.9–10 [1]232 q; 10.19 [3]457 q; 11.1–8 [3]457 q; 11.13 [4]474n; 11.16 [3]455 q, 455n; 11.17–24 [3]455, 455n q; 11.17–25 [3]456, 456n; 11.25 [3]457 q, 457n; 11.26 [3]62 q, 62n; 12.5 [2]670n; 12.6 [5]563n; ch 13 [3]153; 13.1–2 [3]150 q; 13.6–7 [3]152, 152n q; 13.7 [2]302–3; 13.11–13 [5]582; ch 14 [1]268, [6]42; 14.1–12 [6]292n; 14.23 [2]566 q; ch 15 [1]268; 15.1 [1]252n; 15.1–7 [6]42; 15.4 [3]711 q; 15.15–16 [3]7n q; 15.17 [6]42; 16.25 [3]7n q; 16.27 [1]576 q, 576n
1 Thessalonians [1]474, [2]436; Eichhorn on [2]494–5; 1.5 [2]751n; 3.15–17 [3]732n; 4.13–18 [2]313n; 4.14 [2]313 q, 313n q; 4.16–17 [2]494n q; 4.17 [4]552 q; 5.10 [1]703n; 5.17 [1]702n q, [3]615 q, 878 q, 878n; 5.21 [1]lxii q, lxiin q; 5.23 [1]166n q
2 Thessalonians [1]415, 474, [3]732; 1.6–12 [2]567–8; 1.11 [1]702n q, [3]878n q; 1.12 [1]438n; MT 467; [2]742n; 2.1–10 [1]473n, [3]448 q; 2.2 [4]244n; 2.2–3 [3]732n q; 2.3 [1]474, 675n–6n q
1 Timothy [1]415, 459, 459n; MT 467; 490n q, 492, 492n, [2]436, 502, 502n, 999n, [4]485n, [5]128, 128n; authorship of [1]490n; doubtful status [3]30, 30n; Eichhorn on [2]471–2; not by Paul [2]568; 1.9 [3]735n; 1.17 [1]576 q, 576n q, [2]419n q, 786n q; 2.5 [4]299n; 2.7 [3]7n q; 2.10 [4]256n; 3.2 [2]684n q; 3.4 [4]256n; 3.8 [4]256n; 3.11 [4]256n; 3.15–16 [2]471; 3.16 [1]468 q, 468n, 489–90, 490n, 713n, [2]204n, [3]30 q, 30n; 5.9 [4]485, 485n, 486n q; 5.11 [2]568 q; 5.11–12 [4]486n; 5.12 [2]568 q; 5.22 [1]532, 532n q; 6.10 [1]474, [3]5n q; 6.15 [1]707n q; 6.17 [3]556 q
2 Timothy [1]459, 459n, 490n q, 492, 492n, [4]485n, [5]128, 128n; 1.11 [3]7n q; 3.16 [1]492n; 3.16–17 [2]1061n; 4.11 [4]480n; 4.11–13 [3]726n; 4.13 [3]7n
Titus [1]459, 459n, 467n, 492, 492n, [4]485n, [5]128, 128n; attribution of [6]55; 1.5 [2]1042n q; 1.7 [2]1042n, [5]503n; 1.10–14 [2]35n; 1.15 [1]657 q, 657n, [3]589, 589n q; 2.1 [4]256n; 2.7 [4]256n; 2.13 [2]742n, [6]177, 183n; 3.5 [1]262n q; 3.5–7 [1]232n; 3.10–11 [6]55 q; 3.11 [6]56n
OLD TESTAMENT [1]316; MT 417–46; 607, 675, 785, [2]208, 343, 467, 743, 796, [3]73–4, 102n, 107n, 658, 763, 775, [4]57, 253, 471, 475n, 649, 649n, 669, [5]65, 74, 127, 298, 330, 337n, 338n, 473, 495, 497, 519, 523n, 527, 527n, 567n, 572, 583, 676, [6]7, 76, 91, 113, 294, 302, 308; *Die Heilige Schrift* ed Cohen [1]415–16, 418n, 425, 425n, 426n, 427n, 432n, 441n, 708n; annotations by Grotius [1]199n; books not of equal importance [6]217; Books of Moses [5]434, [6]5; Hagiographia of [3]533; on immortality of man [1]675; inspired [3]553; interpretation by Fathers [6]72; letters on [1]cxviii; literal meaning [3]19; manner of [6]140; miracles of [6]119n; Pentateuch [2]382, 387n, 394, 395, 416, 416n, 832n, 894, 894n, [3]54, 489, 533, [4]250, 304, 634, [5]635, [6]319, later than Moses [2]390; prophecies [3]418n, 462; prophetic books [2]403; prophets [2]151, 1075, [4]304, [5]575, [6]319, chapter-titles of [5]512; quoted in NT [4]58; Samaritan text [1]418, 418n; Scottish martyrs' predilection for [2]1175; Septuagint [1]415, 427 q, 427n q, 439, 444n q, 669n, 681n q, [2]208n, 270n, 375n, 377, 379–81, 381n, 415n, 416, 416n, 451, 578n, 714, 714n, 722n, 737, 786n, 831–2, 831n–2n, 895n, 901, 1107n q, [3]32n, 466n, [4]255, [5]567n, [6]77, 140; *see also* Eichhorn *Einleitung ins Alte Testament*
Amos 3.6 [2]164 q, 164n
1 Chronicles [2]379, 409, 409n; 1.8 [2]577n; 1.11 [2]577n; 1.13 [2]831; 15.17 [5]178n; 16.29 [2]305 q, 305n q, [5]130n q, 510n q; 17.18 [2]1029n; 22.5 [2]147 q; 29.20 [4]298n q
2 Chronicles [2]379, 409, 409n, 415n; 2.3 [3]109n q; 7.1–3 [2]465n; 17.14–18 [3]461n; 18.18 [3]1087; ch 20 [1]442; 20.21 [2]305 q, 305n q; ch 21 [3]699n; 26.20 [2]838; 34.8–35.19 [2]894n; 35.22 [3]470n q
Daniel [1]707n, [2]14, 155, 155n, 156, 294, 377, 377n, 408, 409, 409n, 420, 420n, 503, 570, 570n, 712n, [3]9, 417, 417n, 419–21, 430, 449, 464, 466n, 472, 474, 481, 573, 573n, 594n, 731, 765n, 922, 923, 923n, [4]58; authenticity of [3]420–1, 420n, [6]217n; dream-book [3]34; Eichhorn

on [2]410–12; non-canonical [3]111–12, 111n; spurious [3]*34n*, 731n; ch 1–6 [1]433, 433n, 734n, [2]36, 36n, 376, 376n, [6]217, authenticity of [3]465–6, 466n; ch 1–12 [2]376n; 1.17 [5]653n q; 2.31–45 [3]419n; 2.33 [3]419n q; 2.36–40 [2]155n; 2.40–3 [1]440n–1n q; 2.44 MT [1]440; 3.8–30 [2]570n q; 3.16 [3]583 q; 3.25 [4]50n; 4.19 [3]103n; 4.27 [5]587n; ch 6 [6]217; ch 7 [2]516n, [3]419, 573n, 923; ch 7–12 [2]409, [5]434n; 7.13 MT [1]441; 441n q, [4]65; 7.13–14 [1]733 q, 734, 734n, [3]421n, [4]58, 58n, 62n q, [5]463; 7.25 [3]420n q; 8.18 [3]614n q; ch 9 [2]516n, Jahn on [3]103; 9.1–3 [3]103n; 9.3 [3]563; 9.1–23 [3]103n; 9.9 [2]1187n; 9.24–7 [3]103, 103n; 9.26 [3]479 q, 479n; 10.2–3 [2]517n; 10.9 [3]614n q; 10.11 [3]563; 10.13 [3]417n, 594n; 10.20 [2]578n; 11.2 [2]578n; 11.31 [3]112n q; 12.10 [3]593 q

Deuteronomy [3]471; Eichhorn on [2]395–8; 1.14–18 [2]1109n; 4.24 [2]567 q, 567n; 4.29 [1]709n; 4.40 [2]654–5 q, 655n; 5.5 [1]463n; 5.6–7 [2]901n; 7.1–3 [4]257n; 7.2–3 [2]384n; ch 8 [3]471n; 10.5 [2]893; 12.25 [2]654–5 q, 655n; ch 14 [1]417n; 15.10 [4]625n q; 17.14–15 [4]48n q; 17.14–20 MT [1]421–2; 423; 17.18–19 [1]423n q; 18.10–14 [2]1108n; 18.15 [2]144, 144n q, 799 q, 799n; 18.15–19 [3]738; 18.15–22 [5]656n q; 18.16 [2]145n; 25.1–8 [3]417; 25.5 [5]393n q; 26.18–19 [3]417n–18n q; 32.2 [1]815n q; 32.4 [5]635n; 32.7–8 [2]397n q; 32.15 [5]635n; 33.2 [1]463n; 33.27 [1]239n q; 34.9 [2]145n q; 34.10 [2]145n q

Ecclesiastes [1]433, 433n, [2]377, 379, 409n, [4]304, [5]811 ("Solomon"), [6]113–14, 114n; 1.12 MT [1]433; [2]460, 460n q; 1.18 [3]619 q; 8.12 [2]654–5 q, 655n; 9.5 [4]200 q; 10.15 [3]617–18 q; 11.1 [1]263 q, 263n q; 12.7 [1]675 q, 675n

Esther [1]433, 433n, [2]354, 369, 377, 409n, 411, [3]533, 767, 767n, [6]319; Eichhorn on [2]401; 3.9 [2]401n; 3.13 [2]401n; 8.9–11 [2]401n; 9.1–19 [2]401n

Exodus [1]415, [2]136n; Eichhorn on [2]395–8; ch 1–14 [2]383, 383n; ch 3–14 [2]387n; 3.8 [2]831; 3.14 [1]239n q, 435n q, 458n q, 460 q, 460n, 461n q, [2]379n, 392, 392n q, [3]12n, 30 q, 30n q, 659 q, 659n, 1065n, [4]407n, [6]76n q; 3.17 [2]831; 4.9–11 [3]987, 987n q; 4.13 [2]284–7; 4.20 [2]387n; 6.3–8 [2]392; 7.10–8.19 [6]105n; 7.11 [2]1107n, [6]112; 7.15–8.11 MT [1]419; 7.17–20 [2]1015n; 7.19–25 [5]64n; 7.20 [6]112n q; 7.22 [2]1107n, [6]112; 8.7 [2]1107n, [6]112; 8.18 [2]1107n, [6]112; 8.19 [1]457n q, [6]105n q; ch 13 [1]417n; 13.5 [2]831; 13.21–2 [3]108n, 540n; 14.20 [3]248n q; 14.21–31 [6]119n; 15.23 [2]508, 509, 509n q; 16.23 MT [1]419; 17.8–14 [1]475n q; 17.11 [4]682; 18.26 [4]48; ch 19–31 [1]463n; 19.3–5 [4]47; 20.3–5 [5]406n q; 20.4 [3]1087n q, [5]554, 554n q; 20.4–5 [3]108n; 20.7 [3]1087n q; 20.8 MT [1]419; 20.8–11 [1]269n; 20.10–11 [1]334n; 20.17 [2]146n q; 21.4–6 [2]898; 21.21 [2]899; 22.3 [2]899; 22.4 [2]899; 22.18 MT [1]420; 22.20 [6]81 q; 23.28 [2]831; ch 24–31 [2]489n; 24.9–18 [2]489n; 24.10–11 MT [1]420; 24.12–15 MT [1]420–1; ch 25–7 [2]901; 25.18–20 [2]488, 488n; 25.20 [3]924n q; 25.40 [2]488, 488n q, 489n; 33.18–20 [1]785n; 33.19 [3]102n q; 33.20 [1]794, 794n–5n q; 34.11–16 [4]257n; 34.14–16 [2]384n; 34.30–5 [2]138n; 35.7 [3]109n; 40.34–8 [2]465n

Ezekiel [1]707n, [3]462, 739, [4]252, 304, [5]434; Eichhorn on [2]408–10; ch 1 [5]775n; 1.4–28 [2]403, 403n, 488, 488n; 1.26 [1]441, 441n q, [4]65, 65n q; ch 4 [1]437; 4.6 [2]516n; 10.1–22 [2]403, 403n; 14.14 [2]409n; 14.20 [2]409n; 18.20 [5]61 q; 18.30–2 [5]674n q; 27.13 [2]578n; 28.3 [2]409n; 29.18 [3]478–9 q, 479n; 33.32 [3]570 q; 36.26 [3]711 q; ch 37 [1]708, 708n, [2]1074 q; 37.3 [2]829 q, 829n; 37.12 [2]1074n q; 37.12–14 [1]708n; 38.2–6 [3]70; 39.15 [2]449; ch 41 [4]252n

Ezra [2]409, 409n, 415n, 426, 426n, [3]453n; 1.1–2 [2]148, 148n–9n q; ch 2 [3]461; 2.64–5 [2]378n; 6.14 [2]149, 149n q; 9.6–15 [2]832, 832n

Genesis [1]415, *417n*, 473, 612 ("Mosaic"), [2]136n, 383, 414, 1052–3, [3]39, 950n, 998n, [4]47, 300, 583, [5]430n, 603, [6]228n; author of [1]616, 616n; commentary on [5]139, 139n; Eichhorn on [2]384–95; ch 1 [1]708n, 783, [2]137n q, 138, 324n, 562, [3]60n, 139n, 1016n, [4]513, [5]348n; ch 1–2 [1]783, [5]248; ch 1–3 [1]719; 1.1 [1]608n, 681n q, [2]419, 419n q, 466n q, [3]348, 348n q; 1.1–2 [1]418n, [5]385, 385n q; 1.1–2.4 [1]684n, [2]389n; 1.2 [1]604 q, 604n q, [2]208n q, 246, 246n q, 391n, [3]876; 1.2–3 [5]452 q, 452n q; 1.3 [5]470 q, 470n q; 1.4 [1]418n; 1.7 [2]391n; 1.9–10 [2]391n, 1038n; 1.9–25 [1]664, 664n; 1.15 [2]915n q; 1.16 [4]513n q; 1.22 [3]808 q, 808n q; 1.26 [5]60 q; 1.26–7 [1]29n; 1.27 [5]248 q, 248n q; ch 2 [1]684, 783;

The Bible—*continued*
2.1–17 [2]390n; 2.3 [1]419n q; 2.4 [3]581 q, 581n, [5]430n q; 2.4–3.24 [2]389n; 2.7 [1]332n q, 636 q, 636n, [2]334n q, [4]531 q, 531n q; 2.19–23 [1]684, 684n; 2.21–2 [3]614n q; ch 3 [3]105; 3.1 [2]915, 915n q; 3.5 [1]438n; 3.15 [1]457, 457n, 707n; 3.19 [2]1072 q; 3.22–4 [2]571n; 4.1 [2]302n q; 4.4–16 [2]177n; 5.1–28 [1]418n; 5.3–8 [5]594n; 5.21–4 [3]39, 39n q; 5.22 [2]1074n q, [3]39n q; 5.27 [4]201n q; 5.30–2 [1]418n; 6.4 [1]328 q, 328n, [2]1113 q, 1113n; 6.9–22 [1]418n; 6.9–8.22 [2]390n; 7.8–9 MT [1]417; 7.17–20 MT [1]417–18; ch 9–10 [4]583n; 9.4 [1]624n; 9.8 [2]579 q; 9.11 [2]579 q; 9.18 [4]257 q; 9.18–27 [2]177n; 9.20–5 [1]112n q; 9.25ff [4]257; ch 10 [2]177n, 397, 397n; ch 10–11 [2]397n; 10.1–32 [5]337n; 10.2–5 [2]578n, [5]337n q; 10.6 [2]577n; 10.7 [2]390n; 10.13 [2]577n; 10.15 [2]831; 12.6 [2]394 q; 13.7 [2]831; 15.18 [2]390n; 15.19 [2]831; ch 16 [2]395; ch 17 [4]249–50; 17.10 [4]251; 17.16 [2]395; ch 18 [6]107n; 18.11–14 [6]119n; 19.1 MT [1]418; 21.33 [1]434n q; 22.1–18 [3]604n; 22.12 [3]555 q; 24.3 [4]257n; 25.23 [2]928n; 25.29–34 [2]928n; ch 27 [2]928n; 28.1 [4]257n; 28.12 [3]348n; ch 32 [3]906n; 32.24–31 [2]489; 32.30 [2]489n q; 35.11 [2]395; 36.31 [2]394–5; 36.31–6 MT [1]418; 38.9 [1]640 q, 640n q; 47.31 [3]615n–16n q; 48.13 [1]687n; 49.4–5 MT [1]418; 49.10 [4]44n q
Habakkuk [5]434
Haggai [5]434; ch 1 [5]574; 2.7 [3]33n q, 738 q, 738n
Hosea [1]415, 442n, [5]434; ch 1–2 [1]437; 1.10 [1]452n; 2.1 [1]452n; 2.2–17 [1]441n; 2.14 MT [1]441; 2.18 [1]18; 6.1–2 [2]1074 q; 12.10 [1]817n q; ch 13–14 MT [1]442; 13.3 [1]815n; 13.10 [2]1074 q, 1074n; 13.14 [2]1074 q, 1074n
Isaiah [1]415, 474, [2]148, 405–6, 406n, [3]110, 110n, 441, 462, 465, 468, [4]255, [5]434, [6]108 q; Eichhorn on [2]404–8, *408n*; 1.10 [1]823 q; 1.10–20 [4]638, 638n; 2.2–4 [2]153 q, [6]16n; 2.22 [1]332n; 7.9 [1]605n q, [2]29n q; 7.14 [2]269–73; 8.20 [3]986 q; 9.6 MT [1]433–4; 434n, [2]786n q; ch 11 MT [1]434; [4]49; 13.2 [6]56n q; 14.12 [2]553 q, 553n; 19.18 [4]257n; 22.5 [3]564 q; 25.6–8 [2]1074n; 28.19–20 [3]671, 671n q; 29.14 [3]775n q; 29.18–19 [5]75 q, 775n; 30.15–19 [3]528; 30.33 [2]559n; 31.3 [3]1086 q, 1086n; ch 38 [2]829n, [3]110n; ch 40–55 [2]148n ("Deutero-Isaiah"), [3]110n, 462, 462n; 40.28 [1]434n q, [2]786n q; ch 41 MT [1]434; ch 42 [1]434; 42.1 MT [1]434–5; 435n q, [5]59; 42.1–4 [1]435n; 42.5 [1]435n q; 42.7 [3]593 q; 42.8 MT [1]434–5; [5]514 q, 514n q; 42.15 MT [1]435; 44.8 [6]76 q; 44.28 [2]148n; ch 45 [3]461–2; 45.1 [2]148n; 45.5 [6]76 q; 45.7 [2]164 q, 164n; 45.9–10 [2]162n; 45.16 [3]585; 46.9 [6]76 q; 49.1–6 [1]435n; 49.15 [2]1176 q; ch 50–1 MT [1]435; 50.3 [3]465; 50.4–9 [1]435n; 52.3 [1]452n; 52.13–53.12 [1]435n; ch 53 [2]279n; 53.1–9 [1]734, 734n; 53.3 [1]736n; 53.4 [1]449n; 53.4–6 [1]449n; 55.8 [3]558 q, 558n, [5]730 q, 730n, [6]80 q, 80n q; 57.15 [2]1029n, [3]32n, 584n q; 57.21 [3]552 q; 58.13 [1]876; 59.5 MT [1]436; 60.1 [3]523–5, [6]305; 61.1 [3]593 q; 61.1–2 [2]798; 61.1–6 [2]1061n; 61.10 [2]544n q; 63.1–6 MT [1]436; 63.9 [3]102n q, 594 q, 594n q; 65.17–18 MT [1]436–7; ch 66 MT [1]437; [4]252; 66.17 [2]569; 66.19 [2]578n; 66.24 [1]437 q, 437n q, [2]569 q, [3]25n q, 62, 62n
Jeremiah [1]415, 707n, [2]409n, [3]34n, 462, 467, 481, [5]434; 1.1–3 MT [1]437; 2.22 [3]544; 4.23 [1]604 q, 604n q; 6.16 [2]655n; 7.31 [2]559n; 10.16 [5]482n q; ch 13 MT [1]437; 13.11 MT [1]438; 14.7–9 [3]528; 17.9 [1]10n; 17.13 [3]592 q; 31.30–2 [5]61; 32.26–44 MT [1]438; ch 33 MT [1]438–9; 38.23 MT [1]439; 38.28 [1]439n q; ch 50–1 [3]465; 50.8–9 MT [1]439–40; 51.6–9 [3]468n; ch 52 MT [1]440; 52.4–14 [3]480, 480n
Job [1]415, [2]55n, 313, 409n, 433, 895–6, *895n*, 968n, 969n, 1051–2, 1053, [3]75, 520, [5]85, 86n; Eichhorn on [2]413–14; model for Milton [2]968; most precious poem [1]426; ch 1 [6]97–8, 98n; ch 1–2 [2]896n, [3]436–7, 437n; 1.7 [6]97n q; ch 2 [3]474; 2.1 [2]896n; 3.13–19 [1]431, 431n q; 3.25–6 MT [1]424–5; 5.6 [1]425n; 5.7 MT [1]425; 5.23 [1]425n; 7.7–10 [2]313n; 7.9 [2]565 q, 565n; 7.12 MT [1]425; 7.20 MT [1]425; 8.17–18 MT [1]425–6; 9.7 [2]895, 895n q; 9.30–1 [3]544; 13.7 [1]823 q, 823n q, [3]573n; 13.15 [1]823 q, 823n q; 14.1–2 [3]519 q, [6]302 q; 15.20–30 [2]313n; 15.25 [3]585; 16.17–19 [2]306–8; ch 19 [2]924, 924n; 19.25 [6]308 q; 19.25–6 [1]426n, [2]313 q, 313n q; 19.25–8 MT [1]426; 19.26 [2]923–4 q; ch 21 MT [1]426; 27.3–4 [1]332n; 32.8 [1]675, 675n q; 32.19 [2]1108n; 34.14–15 [6]113 q; ch 40–1 [3]770–1; 40.15 MT [1]426–7; 41.1 MT [1]426–7
Joel [1]415, [5]434; 2.28–32 [2]653, 653n, [4]476n; 3.2 MT [1]442

Jonah [1]695, [3]767, 767n, [5]434, [6]117–18, 118n, 217, 217n, 220, 221n; 1.6 [3]614n

Joshua [1]422n, [2]258, [5]434; Eichhorn on [2]398–9; 3.10 [2]831; 6.20 [4]503n q, [5]294n–5n q; 10.12 [2]897; 10.12–14 [2]895, 895n; 10.13 [2]897, 897n

Judges [1]415, [2]379, [3]108n, 109, [5]307n, 434; ch 1 MT [1]422; 2.12 [1]864n q; 3.5–7 [4]257n; 3.15 [2]771n q; 3.15–30 MT [1]422; [2]771n; ch 4 [1]823n; ch 5 [1]823n q; 5.3 [2]379 q; 5.19 [3]470n q; 5.23 [2]835; 10.6 [1]864n; 11.29–40 [2]833, 833n q; 11.31 [2]833n; 11.37–9 [2]834 q, 834n; 11.39–40 [2]834n q; ch 14 [1]423n; 14.8–18 [3]508n; 15.15–20 MT [1]422–3; 16.15 [2]1029n

1 Kings [1]440, [2]379, [3]39, 476n, [5]434; 9.7–8 [2]147n; 15.13 [3]585; 19.4–8 [4]472n; 19.11–12 [5]187 q, 187n; 22.19–21 [3]474; ch 28 [1]110n

2 Kings [1]440, [2]379, [3]39, 476n, [5]167, 434; 1.2 [3]57n q; 2.11 [3]39–40, 40n q, 476n; 5.1–19 [1]832n q; ch 18–19 [2]408n; ch 20 [3]110n; 20.1–11 [2]829n; 23.10 [2]559n; 23.29 [3]470n; 24.18 25.30 [1]440n

Lamentations [2]409n, [5]434

Leviticus [1]415, [2]395; 9.23–4 [2]465n; ch 11 [1]417n; MT 421; 11.29–32 MT [1]421; 14.12 [3]657–8; 17.11 [1]624n; ch 18 [3]778n, [5]393

Malachi [1]415, [2]375, [5]434; 2.17–3.6 [3]101; 3.13–14 [3]101; 3.14–18 MT [1]445–6; 4.2 [1]815 q, 815n q, [2]150, 150n q; 4.5 [1]446n q, [2]150n, [3]41n, 457, 457n

Micah [1]415, [5]434; Eichhorn on [2]371–2; 1.4 [1]442n–3n, [2]372, 372n q; 5.2–6 MT [1]442–4; 5.5 MT [1]444; 5.6 [1]444n–5n q; 6.6–8 [4]638, 638n; 6.8 [1]601n, [2]343 q, 343n, 560 q, 560n, 744 q, 744n, [3]62 q, 62n; 6.9 [3]556; 7.1 [1]453, 453n q, [2]47

Nahum [5]434; 3.8–19 [2]515n

Nehemiah [2]409n, 415n, [3]453n; 2.12–15 [2]1118n; 7.66–7 [2]378n; ch 9–10 [2]832, 832n; 13.15 [1]876; 13.21 [1]876; 13.23–31 [1]418n

Numbers [1]415, [2]395; 12.1 [2]384n q; 12.15 [2]838; 14.34 [2]516n; 15.32–6 [4]287; 17.1–10 [5]52n q; ch 22–4 [2]144n; 24.17 MT [1]421; 421n q, 453 q, [2]144n q, [6]220n; 31.5 [1]443, 443n q

Obadiah [5]434

Proverbs [1]415, [2]409n, 422, 423, 433, [4]475; ch 1–2 [6]84, 84n; 2.6 [6]84n q; 3.17 [3]623 q; 7.26 [3]576 q; ch 8 MT [1]432; 8.16 [2]208n q; 8.30 [5]35; 9.10 [3]583 q, 583n; 10.5 [3]614n; 11.7 [3]553 q; 12.20 [1]321 q; 14.32 [3]553 q; 24.17–18 MT [1]432–3; 24.18 [1]433 q, 433n q; 25.20 [3]553 q; 25.22 [1]433 q, 433n q; 26.10 MT [1]433; 26.16 [3]573 q; 27.22 [4]811n q; 28.1 [3]567 q; 30.33 [2]932 q

Psalms [1]415, 473–4, 707n, 710, 712n, [2]377, 406, 409n, 1052, 1052n, [3]520, 739, 775, 904, 904n, [5]178–9, 178n–9n, 434, 497, 635, [6]17; Brady and Tate *A New Version of the Psalms of David* MT [1]475; [5]179n; Eichhorn on [2]412–13; new translation needed [1]429; 1.20 [3]576 q; 2 [3]727 q; 2.7 [2]584 q, 584n, [3]49n; 2.12 MT [1]427; 4 [2]1052n; 4.5 [3]604; 4.7 [3]553 q, [6]308n q; 5 [2]1052n; 6 [2]1052n; 6.3 [3]527n; 6.8–10 [2]337–8; 12.2 [3]576 q; 14.1 [2]345 q, 345n q, 1029 q, 1029n, [6]66 q, 66n; 15.2 [3]577 q; 16 [3]732; 16.2 [3]603 q; 17 MT [1]427; 18.2 [5]635n; 19.1 [5]95 q, 95n; 19.4–5 [1]815n; 22 MT [1]427–8; 428n, [3]34, 55, 611, [6]91; 22.1 [5]523, 523n; 22.27–31 [1]428n q; 23.3 MT [1]428; [5]11n; 27.4 MT [1]428; 29.2 [2]305 q, 305n q, [5]130n q, 510n q; 33.6 [2]208n q; 38 MT [1]428–9; 39.4 [3]519 q, [6]302 q; 41.10–11 MT [1]429; 42 [1]429n; 42.8 [6]308; 43 [1]429n; 45.1 [4]475 q, 475n; 45.6 [4]49 q; 46 [3]912, 913n q; 46.4 [3]479 q; 47.5 [5]690 q, 690n; 48.5 [1]431n; 49 MT [1]429–30; 49.9 [2]1030 q, 1030n; 50 MT [1]430; 51.10 [4]174, 174n q; 52.2 [3]575 q; 53.1 [2]345 q, 345n q, 1029 q, 1029n, [6]66 q, 66n; 54 [2]1052n; 54.2–3 MT [1]430; 55 [2]1052n; 62.10 [3]556 q; 67 [2]1052n; 68.18 [2]564 q, 564n; 68.29 MT [1]430; 71.16 [3]723, 723n q; 72 [1]706n; 72.1 [1]707n q; 72.17 [1]706n q; 73 MT [1]431; 73.26 [6]308n q; 73.27 [3]592 q; 74.6 [3]491 q; 74.14 MT [1]431; 76 [2]1052n; 76.6 [3]614n q; 82 [3]904, 904n; 82.6 [1]438n, [2]183, 183n, 798n q, 799 q, 799n; 84.3 [1]24, 24n; 88.5 MT [1]431; 90.2 [5]456n q; 90.4 [2]712n; 90.12 [3]519 q, [6]301–2 q; 91.5–6 [3]575 q; 94.9 [3]87 q, 87n; 95.1 [5]635n; 96.9 [2]305 q, 305n q, [5]510n q; 104 [1]708, 708n–9n; 104.2 [2]544n q; 104.3–6 MT [1]432; 104.4 [3]1086–7, 1086n q, [6]117n q; 104.15 [6]308n q; 110.3 [2]305 q, 305n; 111.10 [3]583 q, 583n; 119 [3]767–8, [6]308; 119.32 [3]526–7, [6]310; 130.3 [3]604–6; 130.4 [2]1187n; 136 [6]308; 139.8 [5]187 q, 187n; 143.1 [1]829, 829n q; 145.17 [1]10n; see also *BCP*: Bible: OT: Ps

Ruth [2]379, 409n

1 Samuel [1]415, [2]379, 399–400, [5]434; Eichhorn on [2]399–400; 1.4 [3]49n q; 1.11 [2]833, 833n–4n q; 1.20 [3]49n q; 1.28 [2]833,

The Bible—*continued*
833n–4n q; 6.14 [2]830; 7.3–4 [1]864n q; 7.15 [2]400n q; 8.19–20 MT [1]423–4; 10.25 [1]424, 424n q; 11.14 [2]830; ch 28 [3]771n; 28.7 [2]1108n; 28.7–25 [1]420n
2 Samuel [1]415, [2]379, 399–400, [5]434; Eichhorn on [2]399–400; 24.1–15 MT [1]424
Song of Solomon [2]55, 55n, 409n, 505n, 1051–2, [4]304, 642, 656, 656n, [5]81, 81n; 1.2–3 [1]629 q, 629n q; 1.3 [6]308
Zechariah [1]415, 707n, [2]409, 503, 894 ("Zachary"), [5]434; 4.12–14 MT [1]445; 5.11 [2]513; 6.9–15 [3]112; 6.12–13 [3]112 q, 112n; 10.12 [3]103, 104
Zephaniah [5]434

Bible, political [2]118
biblical criticism *see* Bible, criticism of
bibliography [3]372
bibliolatria [5]805
"bibliolatry" [5]805n
bibliolatry [1]257n, 804n, [2]37, 1155, 1155n, [3]310, [5]568n, 656, [6]246
Protestant [2]35, 35n, 37–8
bibliophiles [2]702
"Bibliotheca Britannica" *see* R. Southey
Bibliotheca Sacra [2]377
Bibliotheca Theologica [4]667
bicentrality [4]327, 327n
Bichat, Marie François Xavier (1771–1802) [2]1008n
Bicheno, James (d 1831) [3]922
The Destiny of the German Empire [3]923n; *The Signs of the Times* [3]923n
Bickerstaff, Isaac (in *Tatler*) [3]586, 587n
Bickerstaffe, Isaac (c 1735–c 1812) *The Padlock* [2]428n q
Biddle, John (1615–62) [1]297, 297n
Biel, Gabriel (c 1420–95) [2]11–12, [5]549, 549n
Collectorium . . . sententiarum [5]804, 804n
Biester, Johann Erich (1749–1816) [1]3
Bigham, Charles Clive, Viscount Mersey (1872–1956) *The Roxburghe Club* [2]702n
bigot(s) [3]663, 663n, 787, 826, [4]160, 189, 639, [6]101
ignorant [1]357; infallible [1]872; lying [4]180; b.-slime [4]647
bigotry [1]204, 695, 728, [2]951, [3]144, 147, 483, 600, 622, 670, 698, 802, 819, [4]81, [5]529, 632
acts of [5]651; calumnious [1]257; high-church [1]331; narrow [2]969; patristic [3]143
Bildungstrieb [4]432, 432n, [5]473, 473n
poetic [5]858
bile [5]98
black [5]151
bill(s)
of imagination [4]662; parliamentary *see* Parliament: Acts/Bills
billiard ball [2]198
Billingsgate *see* London
Billingsley, John (fl 1794–1809) [3]937
Bilson, Thomas, Bishop of Winchester (1546/7–1616) [1]275, 337, [3]149 q, 150, 795n
The True Difference between Christian Subjection and Unchristian Rebellion [3]148 q, 149n
binding [5]46, 284
cottonian [1]cxxii, [4]29, [6]147
bindweed [3]813
Bingley, F. E. (fl 1833) [2]49
biographee [2]56
biographer(s) [1]849, [5]149, 154
character of [2]56; Johnson as [2]76, 76n; minute [3]665
Biographia Britannica [5]669n, [6]216
biography/biographies [3]142, 307, 636, [4]183, 473, 478, [5]167
biographical anecdotes of Jesus [4]473; HC's [2]71; most delightful [5]154; esoteric [2]601; and history [2]51; of Jesus [2]452; Puritan [2]1173; spirit of [3]629; traditions [2]411
biology [3]243n
Bion (fl c 100 BC) [2]55, 55n, [4]147
tr F. Fawkes [1]38
bios [1]822, [5]176, 176n
Biot, Jean Baptiste (1774–1862) [3]942
bipolarity [1]70n, [3]327n, [4]326, 327, 327n
birch [4]827
Birch, Thomas (1705–66) [2]972n, [3]881, 883, 883n; *see also* Milton *A Complete Collection, Works* (1783); Thurloe *A Collection*; J. Tillotson *Works* ed Birch
Birch, Walter (c 1774–1829) *A Sermon on . . . Infidelity and Enthusiasm* [1]cxlin; MT 494–7
bird(s) [1]642n, [2]165, 580, 634, 860–1, [3]129, 325, 579, 581, [4]164, 273, 303, 494–5, 500–1, [5]69, 292, 360, 476, [6]151
birdifies [3]325; bush b. [3]1074; C's identification with [1]482, 482n; as colons [1]133; b.-fanciers [4]702; b.-lime [1]515, 515n, [5]251; mocking-b. [4]76; of prey [1]425; song of [2]862n; on a string [3]833

Bird, W. (fl 1854) [4]294
Birdcage Walk *see* London
Birkbeck, George (1776–1841) [2]979, 979n, 981n
Birmingham [3]191n, 637, [6]20n, 49
  Keele University, marginalia in [3]627
Birnam Wood [4]864, 864n
Biron/Berowne (*Love's Labour's Lost*) [4]696, 696n, 783 ("Byron")
birth(s) [1]618, 619, 620, 640, [2]658, 659, 1185–6, [3]519, 866–7, [4]816, [6]301
  creaturely [1]601; eternal [1]602; form of time [1]605; of ideas [5]372; new *see* new birth; b.-place [5]644; recommencement of [1]643; in soul [4]653; b.-throe(s) [1]609, [5]172, 181; twin [1]580
Biscay [3]104
bishop(s) [1]250, 265, 329, 333, 339, [2]72, 439, 476, 531, 711, 711n, 827, 920, 931, 941, 948, 1042, *1042n–3n*, 1095–7, 1138, [3]48, 459, 685, 686, 688, 693, 720, 766, 801, 803n, 825, [4]173, 659, 665, 666, [5]50, 129n, 503, 508, 508n, 537, 538, 539, 659, 662, 684, [6]14, 259
  of Alexandria [3]440n; Asiatic [6]63; and Baxter [1]331; Christian [1]526; dead [1]353; discourses of [5]571; in early Church [4]473; exauctoration of [5]531; governing right of [1]309; Irish Catholic [5]660; of Jerusalem [2]471, [3]440n; of London [4]548–9, 549n; making of [5]399; no b. no king [1]310n, [3]803–3; parochial [1]308; rights of [3]490; of Rome [3]440n; Romish [5]395, 396; triple-crowned [1]473; two species of [1]338; Whig [1]836; *see also* episcopacy
Bishop, Cortlandt Field (1870–1935) [5]490
Bishop, William, Bishop of Chalcedon (1554–1624) [2]936
bishoprics [2]937
Bither [3]1084
Bithynia [5]525n, 634, 634n
"bitter" [1]611, 613, 613n, 637
bitter, the [1]589–91, 595, 598, 600, 604, 611, 612, 613, 614, 637, 641–2, 641n, 667, [2]509n, [4]323
  and sweet [1]613
bitterness [1]631, 641, 643, 651, [2]508, 509
blabs [2]93
black (colour) [1]641–2, [3]1059, [4]98, 167
black(s) (people) [5]271
Black, David (d 1603) [2]1171
Black, John (1783–1855) *see* A. W. Schlegel *A Course of Lectures* tr Black
Black, Joseph (1728–99) [2]246n
Black, Matthew see *Peake's Commentary on the Bible* ed Black and Rowley
black pudding *see* pudding
Black Sea [5]832
Black, William (fl 1875) [1]162n
Blackadder, John (1615–86) [2]1181n
blackamoor(s) [2]384, [4]861, 861n, [5]377
blackberry/blackberries [1]246, [2]919
blackguard(s) [1]805, 817, [3]682
"blackies" [5]613, 613n
blacking [3]441, 441n
Blacklock, Thomas (1721–91) [1]38
Blackmore, Sir Richard Dodderidge (1723–80) [1]38
blacksmith [6]216
Blackstone, Sir William (1723–80) [2]68, [4]12, 15, 16, 646
  Commentaries on the Laws of England [2]68n, [4]12n, 646n
Blackwood, William (1776–1834) [1]cxviii
Blackwood's Edinburgh Magazine [1]cxv q, cxvn, cxviii, cxx, cli, clxvn, 765n, [2]1064, 1115, 1169, [3]882n, 891n, 946n, [4]595n, [6]291
  publishes Browne marginalia [1]795–9
bladder [2]56, 1108, 1108n, [3]771n, [4]634, [5]365 ("bladdery"), 560
  b.-woman [1]420
blade [4]131, 761
  two-edged [5]75
Blainville, Henri Marie Ducrotay de (1777–1850) [4]164
Blair, Hugh (1718–1800) [3]402, 403, [4]624
Blair, Robert (1699–1746) [1]38
"blaired" [4]16, 16n
Blake, William (d 1694)
  founder of charity school [1]xcix
  The Ladies Charity School-house Roll MT [1]498–9; *Silver Drops* [1]clxi, 498, 499n
Blake, William (1757–1827) [2]180
  ed by Yeats [1]553
  An Island in the Moon [4]501n; *Songs of Innocence and of Experience* [1]cviii, 371n, 687n, 779n, [5]403
Blakeney, Edward Henry (1869–1955) *see* Horace *Ars poetica* tr Blakeney
Blanco White, Joseph ("Leucadio Doblado") (1775–1841) [1]500, 814, 861, [2]142, 1189, [3]459n, [6]13
  letter(s) to [1]856 q, [5]51n, 68n q; owner of annotated books [1]c; and RS [1]500; supplier of books to C [1]xcviii
  A Letter to Charles Butler MT [1]501–2; 855, 856, 857n, 859, 859n, 861; *Letters from Spain* [1]clxi, 500, 508; MT 503–7;

Blanco White, Joseph—*continued*
Life . . . Written by Himself ed Thom [1]500; *The Poor Man's Preservative against Popery* [1]500, 503; MT 508–10; 855; *Practical and Internal Evidence against Catholicism* MT [1]511–25; 855, [6]13n
Bland, Robert (?1779–1825) and others *Collections from the Greek Anthology* [4]170
Blandford, Marquis of *see* Spencer, George
Blane, Sir Gilbert (1749–1834)
Elements of Medical Logick [2]1182, 1182n–3n q; *Observations on the Diseases of Seamen* [2]1183n
blank verse [1]217–18, 218n, 383, 407, [2]216–17, 761, 761n, 1120n, [3]192, 403, 814, [4]162–3, 759, [5]688–9, 689n
in B&F [1]382; Italian [4]290; printed as prose [1]408
blanket [4]727n
Blashfield, Edwin Howland (1848–1936) ("Blushfield") *see* Vasari *Lives of the Painters* ed Blashfield, Blashfield, and Hopkins
Blashfield, Evangeline Wilbour (d 1918) ("Blushfield") *see* Vasari *Lives of the Painters* ed Blashfield, Blashfield, and Hopkins
blasphemy/blasphemies [1]6, [2]233, 485, 883, 929, 977, 978, 1054, 1160, 1173, [3]401, 485, 696, 972, [4]182, 638, [5]354, 585, 590
against the conscience [5]616; ingenious [2]970; of lust [1]6; ribald [4]256; supralapsarian [5]613
blatt [2]1042, 1042n
Blaustoff [5]260, 260n
Blavier, Jean (fl 1810) [3]936
blaze [2]571
bleat [2]67
bleeding [6]38, 39
"bless" [1]54, 54n
blessedness [3]617
blessing, cup of [5]551
Blifil (in Fielding) [2]693
blind, the [4]824
b.-born [3]389; case of b. girl [1]112; b. man/men [1]273, 397, [2]491, 610, 835, [3]388, [5]184, 415, [6]119, 262; pictures to [2]98; b.-worm [3]970
blindman's buff [6]25
blindness [2]492, 491n–2n, 631, [3]26, [5]184n, 613
human [5]759
bliss [5]582, 723–4
exclusion from [1]847
blisters [6]39
blituri [3]504, 505n
blockhead [1]399
Blomfield, Charles James, Bishop of London (1786–1856) [1]lxx, cxxiin, 24, 26, 26n, 27n, 377n, 526, [2]1090n
A Charge Delivered to the Clergy [1]lxiii, cxxii; MT 526–34; *see also* Aeschylus *Agamemnon*, *Choephoroe*, *Persae*, *Prometheus Vinctus*, *Septem contra Thebas*; *Poetae minores graeci* ed Blomfield
Blomfield, Edward Valentine (1788–1816) *see* A. H. Matthiae *A Copious Greek Grammar* tr Blomfield
Blondel/Blondell, David (1590–1655) [3]795n
"blood" [5]478, 478n
blood [1]548, 550, 623, 624n, [2]857, 1177, [3]42, 43n, 44, 60n, 324, 375, 612, 708n, 717, 1002n, [4]83, 94, 493–4, 739, 744, 762, [5]64, 98, 233, 411, 444n, 462
arterial and venous [4]521; b.-bath [1]457, 457n; carbonised [2]367–8; of Christ *see* Jesus Christ, blood of; circulation of [4]618, [5]789; curdled [3]377; and flesh [1]313, 673, 863, [2]167, 670, 670n, [3]431, 439–40, [5]4, 542, 545, 546, 547–8, 553, 672–3, 679, 680, [6]66; iron in [1]577, [4]274, 274n; issue of [4]637, 637n; kept by Jews [2]274; and life [1]466; life of [4]5; oxygen in [4]390; poles in [2]859; pride of [4]583; red [5]445, 445n; royal [2]1196; rush to head [2]981–2; sacrificial [5]31; shedding of [3]21; sinful [4]234; b.-thirstiness [5]640; treason in [5]596; b.-vessel(s) [1]671, [2]859; and water [6]65–6; water changed to [6]112
bloodhound [5]293
"bloods" [4]739, 761, 762, 812
Bloody Assizes [1]230
Bloomfield, Robert (1766–1823) [2]755, 755n
Farmer's Boy [2]755n
Bloomington IN
University of Indiana, Lilly Library, marginalia in [1]clxi, 498, [2]102, 815, 967, 1169, [5]36
blossom [3]580
blotch, black [5]153
Blount, Thomas (1618–79) *Glossographia* [2]279n
blow [5]552
blue [3]1017, 1018, 1034, [4]167
Bluebeard [3]797, 797n

blue-stockings [2]1016
Blumenbach, Johann Friedrich (1752–1840) [1]535, 550, 550n, [2]369, [3]948, 948n, 1040, 1040n, [4]432n, [5]141, 141n, 473n, 858n, [6]104, 148, 148n, 151
C's acquaintance with [1]535; on race [3]356, [5]253, 253n
Anthropological Treatises tr Bendyshe [5]338n; *De generis humani varietate nativa* tr Gruber [1]535, [5]337n; *Handbuch der Naturgeschichte* [1]535, [3]1041n, 1045n, [4]502n, 533n; *Institutiones physiologicae* [1]535, 550n, tr Elliotson as *Institutions of Physiology* [1]548n, [4]432n; *Über die natürlichen Verschiedenheiten im Menschengeschlechte* tr Gruber MT [1]535–41; [5]253n
Blumenbach, Jr (fl 1799) [1]204n, 535
Blunden, Edmund Charles (1896–1974) see *Coleridge: Studies* ed Blunden
Blunden, Humphrey (fl c 1650) [1]554
blunder [1]608
blunderbuss [3]144
blunderer [2]355, [4]672
blundering [4]726
blunts [1]739
blush [3]494
Blushfield *see* Blashfield
Blyenbergh, Willem van (d 1696) [5]201, 201n, 202
boa constrictor(s) [1]327, [3]701 ("boa contractors")
boar [2]983, [6]151
Antinomian [5]588
boast [3]681
boasting [4]759
Fichte's [2]611
Bobadil (in Jonson) [3]1019, 1019n
bocage [3]976 ("boccage")
Boccaccio, Giovanni (1313–75) [1]542, [2]702n
Il Filocopo [1]542; *Genealogia degli Dei* [1]542; *Opere* [1]clxx, ed Ciccarelli MT [1]542–4; *Vita di Dante* [1]542
Bocchio (fiction) [2]8–9
Bochart, Samuel (1599–1667) *Geographia sacra* [2]577n, 578n
Bocking [2]524n
Bode, Johann Elert (1747–1826) [3]944, [4]506
Bodrou [5]838, 840
Bodryddan [4]101
"body" [1]735, [3]43–5, *43n*, 742–3, 742n, 768–9, [4]247n, 492n, [5]175, 308
body/bodies [1]178, 597, 614, [2]852, 891, [3]28n, 67, 276, 559, 742n, [4]275, 275n, 420, 420n, 461, 491–2, [5]94, 171, 460, [6]132
acting on [4]273; celestial [2]309, [3]520, [6]302; celestial and terrestrial [3]46, 46n, 443n; in chemistry [6]116; of Christ *see* Jesus Christ, body of; Christ's meaning [2]924; in communion service [3]156, 156n; component particles [2]1205; composite [3]344, [5]452; construction of [3]1006; corporate [1]724; as *corpus phaenomenon* [1]283; death of [5]591; of the/this death [1]430, 470, 470n, [2]565, 566, 690, 1177n, 1178, [3]747, 963; defecated of [5]606; defined [1]737, [2]166, 1003, [3]278, 293, 911; derived from death [2]542; dying to the b. [6]106; dynamic [2]566; effigy of spirit [2]976, 976n; Fichte's view [2]630–1; four functions of [5]451; generic term [3]366; grave of soul [2]284; health of [5]98; human [5]260, 553; individual [4]228; laws of [5]423; bodily life [2]1167; life in [5]496; life the soul of [3]518; living [4]317, 317n; living harp [2]1003; Lord's [5]397, *see also* Jesus Christ, body of; manifest powers [3]1022; material [5]600; and matter [1]125, [3]130, 130n, 277–8, 293n, 294n, 303n, 324, 1087n, [5]357, 357n, 734, 764, 764n; matter of [4]159; means personality [2]924; and mind [1]159, 172, 180, 186, [4]171n, 775, 851, [5]4, 86, 181, 215, 217, 219, 822, [6]123; in motion [5]711–12; natural [5]452; natural and spiritual [4]69; none simple [5]264; noumenal and phenomenal [1]839, [2]431; as organ [1]132; organic [1]125, [6]8; organised [1]550, [3]600, 841, [5]430, [6]20; partibility of [5]713; phantom [2]598; phenomenal [1]863; physical or spiritual [3]431n; politic [1]356, [2]1142, [3]53, [4]251n, [6]51; ponderable [1]785; ponderable substances [1]780; and power [2]853, 853n; powers manifest in [1]780; primary [1]780; properties of [5]4; reaction of [5]181; redemption from [2]1177–8, [3]747; represents powers [3]1021; represents progenitors [3]596; resurrection of *see* resurrection; shaken [5]72; shape of the [5]475; sign of [3]14; simple [3]1001, [5]445; and soul [1]166, 171, 582, 620, 676–7, 677n, 713, [2]170–1, 171n, 219, 263, 264, 306, 310, 311, 316, 335, 431, 547, 566, 572, 1003, 1010, 1029–30, 1185–6, 1185n, [3]37, 432, 554, 559, 596, 612, 790n, 910, 935, [4]247n, 262, 268, 391–2, 545–6, [5]82, 227, 362–3, 421, 591, 601, 609, 672, 679,

body/bodies—*continued*
726, 751–2, 783, 826, 828–9, [6]88, 123–4; soul of [6]300; source of consciousness [1]676–7; specific gravity of [2]189, 189n–90n; Spinoza's definition of [2]631; and spirit [1]126, 178, [2]166, 1193, [3]130, 393, 1087, [5]172, 334, 394, 418, 423, 544, 545–6, [6]8, 114–15, 114n, 302; spiritual [1]246, [3]28, 732, [5]568, [6]114; spiritual and natural [2]924n; subfacial [5]431; synthesis of matter and spirit [3]130; very thin [5]565; twofold [3]38, 38n, 520n; union of [1]754; visible [1]445, 673, [5]672; visible and invisible [2]565; vital [6]66; as weight [2]855

Boeckmann, Johann Lorenz (1741–1802) see *Archiv für Magnetismus und Somnambulismus* ed Boeckmann

Boehler, Peter (1712–75) [5]156, 156n

Boehm, Andreas (1720–90) [3]203–4 ("Böhm")

Boeotia/Beotia [2]567n, 580, 584

Boerhaave, Hermann (1668–1738) [1]clin, 545, [3]314, [5]811, 811n
a Socinian [1]197
Aphorismi de cognoscendis et curandis morbis [1]545; *Elementa chemiae* [1]545; *Institutiones et experimenta chemiae* [1]545; *Institutiones medicae* [1]545; *A New Method of Chemistry* tr P. Shaw and Chambers MT [1]545–52; [6]96n

Boerner, Christian Frédéric (1683–1753) *see* Luther *Des theuren Mannes Gottes* ed Boerner

Boethius, Anicius Manlius Severinus (c 480–c 524) [1]232n, [2]12n, [4]608, [5]24
Consolations of Philosophy [1]219n, 220, 221n

bog(s) [4]149n
b.-ground [1]527; b.-land [4]22; Serbonian [2]615n

Bogue, David (1750–1825), and James Bennett *History of Dissenters* [4]170, 171

Bohemia [1]858n, [3]174, 174n, [5]127, 128

Bohemian (in Scott) [4]612–13

Bohemians [6]150

Böhm *see* Boehm

Böhme/Behmen, Jakob (1575–1624) [1]lxiii–lxiv, lxx, ci, cxxiii, cxxxviii, cxlin, clin, 296, 296n, 297, 297n, 347n, 410n, 553–4, 719n, [2]13n, 615n, 755, 755n, 885n, [3]84, 142n, 705, 705n, 855, 991, [4]259, 259n, 424, 424n, 425, 425n, 432n, 676, 676n, [5]123n, 153n, 165, 166, 166n, 203, 203n, 809, 813–14, 814n, [6]99
birthplace [1]558; Brooke a Behmenist [1]730, 731, 732; and Buffon [1]625, 625n; C's revised view of [1]660n; derivation of body [2]542; and Eichhorn [1]616; error of [1]601–2, 617, 618, 679, 694; fault [1]557–8; follower of [3]47; on Gen [2]137–8, 138n; genius of [1]621–2; German text [1]667n q, 688; on God [2]665–6; how to read his works [1]560–1; language of nature [5]467; and W. Law [5]123, 123n; "Life" MT [1]558–60; lunatic [4]501, 501n, 502; metaphors in [4]635, 635n; original thinker [1]645; oscillates between truth and error [1]619; overcame pantheism [1]677; pantheistic [1]562n; and Plato [1]575; and Plotinus and Proclus [1]656; ridiculed [3]381–2; and Schelling [1]619, 620, [3]330, 330n, [4]425, 427, 427n, 432, 432n–3n, 434; a seer [1]628; spelling of name [1]565, 565n; strength of [1]633–4; and Swedenborg [5]433, 433n; visionary [1]558; wholly intuitive [1]632; *see also* Behmenists
Aurora [1]553, 555; MT 560–628; 607, 607n, 625n, 634, 637n, [2]138n, 542n q, [3]382n, [5]433n q, 814n; *The Clavis* MT [1]672; *Forty Questions concerning the Soul* MT [1]670–2; 672n; *Mysterium magnum* MT [1]672–88; 679n q; *Of the Election of Grace* MT [1]693–5; *Sämmtliche Werke* ed Schreiber [1]688n; *Signatura rerum* MT [1]689–93; *The Three Principles of the Divine Essence* [1]555; MT 628–61; [2]138n; *The Threefold Life of Man* MT [1]661–70; 672n; *The Way to Christ* [1]553; *The Works* ed Law, Langcake, and Ward, tr Sparrow [1]lxxxvi; MT 553–696

Bohn, Gottfried Christian (fl 1726) *Der wohlerfahrner Kaufmann* MT [1]697

Bohn, Henry George (1796–1884) [1]clxi

Bohn, James Stuart Burges (1803–80) [2]830

Bohte, J. H. (fl 1818–23) [1]cv ("Bothe")

Boileau-Despréaux, Nicolas (1636–1711) [2]75

Bolingbroke (*Richard II*) [4]796, 798, 799

Bolingbroke, Viscount *see* St John, Henry

Bologna [3]945n

Bolognian Stone *see* Bononian Stone

Bolton [1]243

Bolton, Geoffrey Curgenven *The Passing of the Irish Act of Union* [5]659n

Bolton, Mr *see* Boulton

bombast [1]706, [2]498, [3]701

Bombay [4]29, 30, 30n
Bonaparte *see* Napoleon
Bonario (in Jonson) [3]180
Bonaventura/Bonaventure, St (1221–74) [2]11–12
Opera [1]xc
Bond, Donald Frederic (1895–1970) see *Spectator* ed Bond
Bond, Richard Warwick (1857–1943) *see* B&F *Works: Variorum Ed* ed Bond and Greg
bondage [5]123
bone(s) [1]183, 638, 671, [5]295, 296, 411
human [1]783, [5]296; *see also* marrow-bones
"boned" [5]295, 295n
bonelessness [1]778, 778n–9n
Bones, James (d 1809) [1]92n
Lines to Sarah [1]92
bonhommie [4]156
boni socii [4]595, 595n
"bonice" [5]133, 133n
Boniface, St (c 680–c 754) [2]63, [5]636
Boniface VIII, Pope (c 1235 or 1240–1303) [5]194
Bonn [5]142n
Bonner, Edmund, Bishop of London (c 1500–69) [1]318, 318n, [2]71, 813, 813n, [3]803, 803n
bonnet [4]747
Bonnet, Charles Etienne (1720–93) [2]527n, [3]128, [5]824–5, 826–7
Betrachtungen über die organisirter Körper [5]826n
Bonneval, Claude Alexandre, Comte de (1675–1747) *Memoirs of the Bashaw Count Bonneval* [1]xcii; MT 698–9
Bononian Stone [3]944, 945n
book(s) [4]99–100, 99n, 194, 258, [5]373–4
age of [2]409; burnt [2]702; for children [4]658, 658n; child's [1]728; of chivalry [5]821; b.-club, German [2]179; C's *see* Coleridge, S. T. I (1) book(s), library; common [5]812; darling [5]134; deifications of [2]39; devotional [2]409; easy [4]304; evil fortune of [5]502; falling [1]299; forged [5]229; for girls [2]190; holy [6]142; how to read [2]561; impatience to [2]636; influence of [1]150; inspired [5]803; b.-knowledge [1]668; and lecture [3]307; of life [3]60, [5]638; b.-maker [3]955, 960; b.-making [3]809, [5]812; medical [3]843; modern [4]99; b.-monger [3]955; moral or religious [1]783; of nature and of revelation [3]919; old [6]96; one [2]338; b.-pirates [3]256; of poor men [2]300, 301n; price of [4]343; prophetic [5]515; sacred [2]411; society/societies [5]866; for the soul [5]362; spoiled [1]372; as treasure [1]285; unintelligible [4]305; of the Word [5]434
Book Collector [1]xcvn, clxiin
Book of Common Prayer [1]cxxxi, 250n, 259–67, 287n, 323, 324–8, 330, 360, 429, 429n, 472n, 562n, 587n, 712n, 805, [2]264n, 522n, 651n, 751n, 970n, 1098n, 1166n q, 1198n, [3]28n, 526n, 723, 723n q, 778n, 798n, 1078n, 1086n, [4]74n, 630n, 665n, [5]144n, 185n, 208n, 393n, 505, 506, 508, 512, 530, 530n, 546n, 591n q, 668n, 670n q, [6]42, 43, 310n
fallible origin [1]838; Knee-Book [2]574n
Copy A MT [1]700; *Copy B* with *A Companion to the Altar* [1]414; MT [1]701–14; "Administration of the Lord's Supper" MT [1]703–4, *see also* Eucharist; Bible: NT: 1 Cor 15.1 in MT [1]702; 15.3 MT [1]702; Luke 18.9 MT [1]703; OT: Ps 8.2 MT [1]705; 8.5 MT [1]706; 68.34 MT [1]706; 72 MT [1]706; 72.1 MT [1]707; 74.2 MT [1]707; 74.15 MT [1]707; 82.6–7 MT [1]707–8; 87 MT [1]708; 88.10–12 MT [1]708; 104 MT [1]708; 104.6 MT [1]709; 105.3 MT [1]709; 110 MT [1]709–10; 118 MT [1]710; 126.5 MT [1]710; "The Catechism" [4]642, [5]393, 393n q, 546n, [6]21n; "Collect for the 25th Sunday after Trinity" MT [1]703; "Communion of the Sick" MT [1]704–5; *A Companion to the Altar* [1]701; MT 711–14, 712n, [2]651n; "Solemnisation of Matrimony" MT [1]704; "Table of Kindred and Affinity" [5]393n
The Book of Discipline [1]531n
Booker, John (1603–67) *Almanack* [4]72
bookish(ness) [1]150, [3]813
bookseller(s) [2]519, [3]882, 955, 955n, 960, 969, 970, [4]270
order of [5]812
Bookworm [2]964, 1032
boor [3]779
Boosey, Thomas (1767–1840) [1]cv, 870–1, [3]114
letter(s) to [1]131, 718 q, 871, [3]75 q, [4]463, [5]307 q
boot [5]91n
booty [1]394, [3]187
Bo-peep [1]271, [6]262
Borchling, Conrad (fl 1931), and Bruno Claussen *Niederdeutsche Bibliographie* [2]773n

Bordeaux, Archbishop of [4]272, 272n
border [3]567
Borders [5]857n
bore [2]820, 820n, [5]168
Borgia, a [4]267
Borgia, Cesare (1476–1507) [3]851, 851n
"boring" [3]29
Borkowski *see* Dunin-Borkowski
"born again" [4]635
Borrowdale [1]cx, [5]389
borrowers [3]187
borrowing(s) (literary) [2]973–4, [3]175, 893–4; *see also* plagiarism
Bosanquet, Miss [3]990
Boscovich, Ruggiero Giuseppe (1711–87) [1]569, [3]645, 645n, 646n
  De solis ac lunae defectibus [3]283, 283n; *Theoria philosophiae naturalis* [1]569, 569n
Bosphorus [5]833
Bossuet, Jacques Bénigne, Bishop of Meaux (1627–1704) [1]478n, 503, [2]283, *283n–4n*, [6]291–2 q
  Discours sur l'histoire universelle [2]284n; *Exposition de la doctrine de l'église catholique* [2]284n; *Histoire des variations des églises protestantes* [2]284n
Bostock, Bridget [5]191
Bostock, John (1773–1846) [3]938, 939
Boston [3]822, 824
  Public Library, marginalia in [6]218; Bunker Hill Monument [4]6; Harvard University, Houghton Library, marginalia in [1]217
Boston Daily Advertiser [2]952n
Boswell, James (1740–95) [2]774 ("Bozzy"), [3]142
  Life of Johnson [1]221, 221n, ed G. B. Hill [5]124n, 867n, ed Hill, rev L. F. Powell [2]980n
Boswell-Stone, Walter George (1845–1904) [3]811
botanist(s) [4]531n, [5]142, 481
botany [3]1035n, [4]326, [5]167, 175
  few ideas in [2]527
Botany Bay [1]536n, [2]861, 861n
Bothe *see* Bohte
"bothness" [2]1186, 1186n
Bottari, Giovanni Gaetano (1689–1775) [2]7
Böttiger, Karl August (1760–1835) [1]7
bottle(s) [2]566, 608
bottom [1]379, 379n
  b.-winds [2]220, 220n
bouches, bonnes [5]102, 102n
Boudet, Michel, Bishop of Langres (1469–1529) [5]549n
boughs [3]697
Bouillon-Lagrange, Edme Jean Baptiste (1764–c 1840) [3]940
boule [5]75
boulema [5]21–2
Boulger, James Denis (1931–79), coeditor [1]9, 203, 494, 501, 503, 508, 511, [2]784, [3]3, 10, 416
Boulton, Matthew (1728–1809) [1]243, [3]637 ("Bolton")
bound [4]458
  boundless [3]730; infinite [3]48
boundary [5]104
  natural [4]341
Bounty (ship) [1]536n
Bourchier, John, Baron Berners (1467–1533) [1]368n
"bourd" [3]184–5
Bourne, Hugh (1772–1852) [5]135n
Bourrienne, Louis Antoine Fauvelet de (1769–1834) *Private Memoirs of Napoleon Bonaparte* MT [1]715
Bovillus, Carolus (Charles de Bovelles/Bouillé) (1475–c 1553) [1]793, 793n
bow [3]5, 340
  and arrow [2]620; b. making [5]650
Bowditch, Nathaniel (1773–1838) [3]941
bowel(s) [3]381, [6]102
  b.-movements [5]711n
Bowers, Fredson Thayer *see* B&F *Dramatic Works* ed Bowers
Bowle, John (1725–88) [3]893, 893n
Bowles, Caroline Anne *see* Southey, Caroline Anne
Bowles, William Lisle (1762–1850) [1]lxxvii, [2]15n, 94, 650
  Elegiac Stanzas [1]717; *On Mr Howard's Account of Lazarettos* [1]700n; *On the Death of Mr. Headley* [1]700n; *Poetical Works* [1]717; *Sonnets, and Other Poems* [1]lxxviii, 700n; MT 716–17; *The Spirit of Discovery* [1]717, [6]333; *Two Letters to the Right Honorable Lord Byron* [1]716, [4]5
Bowyer, James *see* Boyer, James
Bowyer, William (1699–1777) *see* Bible: NT: Greek: ed Bowyer
Box [2]649, 668, 686
boxer, statue of [2]789
boxing [4]702
"boy" [4]697
boy(s) [3]329, 350
  American [4]505, 505n; in brook [2]554;

favourites [1]161; b.-friends [1]525; in Jonson [3]185, 185n; love of [1]42n; at school [5]174
Boyce, Samuel (1709–49) [1]38
Boyd, Henry (d 1832) *see* Dante *Inferno* tr Boyd
Boydell, John (1719–1804) [2]1195n
Boyer, James (1736–1814) [1]354, *354n*, 513n, [2]76, 76n, 406n, [3]154, 154n, [4]174n, 175 ("Bowyer"), 679n, [5]860n
Boyer, P. J. (fl 1908) "An Eighteenth Century Pedagogue" [1]354n
Boyle, Charles, 4th Earl of Orrery and 1st Baron Marston (1676–1731) [3]589n
Boyle, Charles, Lord Clifford of Lanesborough (d 1694) [2]78
Boyle, Richard, 1st Earl of Burlington (1612–97) [2]78
Boyle, Robert (1627–91) [1]114n, 549, 552, [2]788, [3]128, [6]96, 96n, 120
a Socinian [1]197
Boys, Johannes [2]1117
Bozrah [1]436
Bozzy *see* Boswell, James
Brabant, Robert Herbert (1781–1866) [2]649
letter to [2]677n
Brabantio (*Othello*) [4]861
"brachyology" [4]463–4, 464n
Braconnot, Henri (1780–1855) [3]940, 941
Bracton, Henry de (d 1268) [3]150, 150n–1n
De corona [3]166
Bradbury, T. (fl 1753) [6]34
Bradford [1]203, [4]3, [5]394
siege of [2]61
Bradley, James (1693–1762) [3]824, 824n
Bradshaw, John (1602–59) [2]950n, 970, *970n*, [3]795n
Bradshawe, Henry (1831–86) [3]909
Bradwall [3]633
Bradwardine, Thomas, Archbishop of Canterbury (?1290–1349) [6]15
Brady, Nicholas (1659–1726) [1]475, [5]178, 178n
and Nahum Tate *A New Version of the Psalms of David* [1]701
Brahe, Tycho (1546–1601) [3]540n
Brahma [3]59n, [5]519, 822
Brahman(s)/Brahmin(s) [2]200, 340, 347, 348, [3]21, 21n, 59, 659, [4]508, 644, [6]118
Brahmanism [2]344, 345
Braidwood, James (fl 1866) [3]503
brain(s) [1]762, 796, 868, [2]538, 539, 860, 1012n, [3]125–6, 716, 716n, [4]160, 389, 448, 461, 544, [5]136, 260, 291–2, 444, 444n, 517, 824–5, 827
b.-cracker [5]173; disease of [1]112; living [5]247; organised [4]639; principle of [1]590
Bramah, Joseph (1748–1814) [2]227n
hydraulic press [2]227, 227n
bramble(s) [1]246
b.-bush [1]873
bran [3]877
branch(es) [3]697, 1025, [4]43, [5]455, 471
Brande, William Thomas (1788–1866) [1]642n, [3]936, 938, 941, [4]503n
Brande's Dictionary of Science, Literature and Art [1]641n q; *A Manual of Chemistry* [1]595n–6n, [3]68n, 600n, 945n, 950n, 1002n, 1033n, [4]319n–20n, 539n q, [5]557n, [6]245n
Brandeis University *see* Waltham MA
Brandenburg [2]936n
Brandes, Ernest (1758–1810) [1]535
Brandl, Alois Leonhard (1855–1940) [1]clxxi
brandy [3]1071, [5]252, 418
b.-sop [2]310
brass [2]322, 914, 914, [3]649, 1067n, [5]172
front of [2]585
Brathwait, Richard [1]155
Braunstein [5]261–2, 262n
bravado(es) [2]883, [6]75
Braybrooke, Baron *see* Neville, Richard Griffin
Brazil(s) [2]167, [5]101–7
bread [3]408, 741
consecrated [3]579–80; form of [5]657, of life [2]298, 919; shew-b. [5]374; and wine [1]264, 313, 525, [2]301, [3]757, [5]4, 5n, 542, 546, 553, 555, 665, 673–4, 680, *see also* Eucharist
breadth [1]579, [3]123, 123n, 139, 949, 1011, [5]825
poles of [1]660; power of [1]662
break-water [5]738
breast-plate [5]522
breath [1]332, [3]23n, 150
of God [3]13, 24; sovereign [1]332
breathing(s) [1]868, [3]54, 372, 831, [4]323, 390, [5]462
rough and smooth [3]827–8, 1068 ("harsh")
Brechin [2]1099 ("Brechen")
Breda [1]332, [4]75
Declaration of [1]333n
breeches [5]306
blue [5]296, 296n
Breerwood *see* Brerewood

breeze [3]248, 312, 466, 697, [4]124, 124n, [5]25, 861
Bremhill [1]716
Brenkmann, Hendrik (1680–1736) *Historia Pandectarum*† [1]717
Brennstoff and *Brinnstoff* [3]1020, 1020n, 1026, 1027, 1028, 1029
Brennus (fl 389 BC) [2]416
Brent, Charlotte (b 1783) [1]53, 684n, [2]242n, 525, 1120n, 1121, 1121n, [3]682n, [4]403, 403n, 686
 letter(s) to [1]xcvi, [5]101
Brentius *see* Brenz, Johann
Brenz, Johann (Brentius) (1499–1570) [3]724, 750
"Brerely, John" *see* Anderton, Lawrence
Brerewood, Edward, ("Breerwood"/"Bryerwood") (c 1565–1613) [1]lxxv, cvi, cviii, 872, 873, 874 q, 876
 A Learned Treatise of the Sabaoth [1]871, 873 q; *A Second Treatise of the Sabbath* MT [1]718–21; 870, 871
Brerewood, John (fl 1611) [1]871
Breschet, Gilbert (1784–1849) [4]164
Breslau [2]1016n, [5]142n
brethren [2]1156
Brethren of the Separation [2]512n
Breton, Nicholas (1545–1626) [1]382, 382n, [2]119n
Brett, Raymond Lawrence ed *S. T. Coleridge* [1]cxxxiiin
breves [3]904
brevity/brevities [3]965, [4]239
brewer(s) [5]317n
breweries [5]250, 250n
Brewerton, T. le Gay (fl 1810–18) [3]939
Brewster, Sir David (1781–1868) [3]943
 Letters on Natural Magic [5]252n
Briareus (myth) [2]311, 311n
bride
 and bridegroom [3]753; kindled [1]600
bridge [1]682, [5]601, [6]242
Bridgenorth, Major (in Scott) [4]609
Bridges, Mr (fl 1880) [1]clxvi
Bridgwater [2]820n
Bridgwater, Earl of *see* Egerton, Francis Henry
"Bridgwater Treatises" [2]883, 883n
Brief Notes on the Creed of St. Athanasius [5]10 q, 13 q, 14
Briefe, die neueste Litteratur betreffend see Nicolai
Bright, George (d 1696) [3]707
brilliance [1]765
brimstone [1]351, 370, 551, 629, [2]611, [3]760, [5]188
Brinckley, John (1763–1835) [3]941
Brindley, James (1716–72) [3]628
Brinkley, Roberta Florence (1892–1967) [1]cxlvin q, cliv, [4]105
 "Coleridge Transcribed" [1]cxxxviiin, cxlvin, 555; *see also* Coleridge, S. T. IX *Coleridge on the Seventeenth Century* ed Brinkley
Brisbane, D. O'Donovan [3]827
Brissot, Jacques Pierre (1754–93) [4]634
Bristol [1]lxxxv, xciv, xcvii, civ, cx, cxi, 32, 88, 89n, 130, 158n, 198n, 228, 334, 358n, 710n, 806n, [2]5, 6n, 169, 586, 587n, 753, 801, 820n, 889, 1184, 1196, 1196n, [3]672n, 899n, 1011n, [4]182, 294, 295, 772, [5]81n, 830, 844, [6]189
 Bristol Central Library [1]354n; Bristol Library [1]lxxviii, 120n, 409, [2]131, 985, [5]108, 486; Bristol Library Society [1]ciii, cv, cxiii, 89n, 830, [2]172n, 413n, 804, 1203, [3]646n; Broadmead Meeting House [4]3; Pneumatic Institute/Institution [1]90n, [4]183n; St Mary Redcliffe Church [1]411; RS lectures in [1]806n; Wesley at [5]137
Bristol Channel [2]820n
Britain [2]163n, 577, [3]420, [5]195n, 397n
 Church of [6]17; and Denmark [5]312–13; provinces of [6]16
Britannia [2]51
British and Foreign Bible Society *see* London
British Catholic Association *see* England
British Critic [2]850
British Journal [3]163n
British Library *see* London
British Library Journal [4]334
British Magazine [2]11
British Museum *see* London
The British Plutarch ed Wrangham [6]216
British Poets see Anderson, Robert
Briton(s) [4]657, [5]253
brittleness [5]306
Broad, James (fl 1810) [3]937
Broade/Broad, Mr (fl 1756) [3]627
Broadwater [3]974, 980, [5]390n
Brobdingnag (in Swift) [2]202, [5]476 ("Brogdignag")
Brock, John (1620–88) [3]821
Brockbank, Philip *see* Shakespeare *Coriolanus* ed Brockbank
Brodie, Benjamin Collins (1783–1862) [3]943 ("D. C.")

Broicher, Charlotte (b 1848) "Fries und Coleridge" [2]186n q
bronchitis [1]822
bronze [3]135
brooding [5]326, [6]149
brook [2]554, [3]898
Brooke, Baron(s) *see* Greville, Fulke and Robert
Brooke, Henry (c 1703–83) *The Fool of Quality* [1]cxl; MT 722–37
Brookes (fl 1794; possibly John Brooke, c 1772–1821) [6]220, 220n
Brooks, Harold Fletcher *see* Shakespeare *Midsummer Night's Dream* ed Brooks
Brooks, Phillips (1835–93) [1]206
Broome, William (1689–1745) [1]38
broth, flint [4]645
brothel(s) [3]193n, 397, [5]476
brotheller [3]802
brother(s) [4]335, 466
by gore [3]708; b.-hate [1]560; spiritual [5]280; Theban band of [1]42, 42n; younger [5]367
brotherhood, symbols of [1]418
Brougham, Henry Peter, 1st Baron Brougham and Vaux (1778–1868) [1]356, 356n, *738–9*, [2]909, 909n, 954n, 955n, 979n, 980n, 981n
An Inquiry into the Colonial Policy of the European Powers [1]356n, 738, [2]949n, [3]149n, [5]102n–3n; *A Speech on the Present State of the Law of the Country* [1]356n; MT 738–40; [5]851
Broughamers [2]979
Broughton [2]111
Broughton, Baron *see* Hobhouse, John Cam
Broughton, Hugh (1549–1612) [2]69
Works ed Lightfoot [3]723n
Broughton, Leslie Nathan (1877–1952)
Sara Coleridge and Henry Reed [2]864, 867n q; *Some Letters* [2]1189
Broughton, Nicholas *see* Breton
Broughton, Thomas Duer (1778–1835) *Letters Written in a Mahratta Camp* [4]170
Broughton, William Grant (1788–1853) [6]184
Brown, Arthur W. *Always Young for Liberty: a Biography of William Ellery Channing* [2]20
Brown, Christopher *Van Dyck* [3]993n
Brown, John (1722–87) *Dictionary of the Holy Bible* [4]656, 656n
Brown, John (1735–88) [3]lxxixn, 871, [4]385n
Brunonian medicine [3]398n; Brunonianism [4]385
Elementa medicinae [3]871n, tr as *Elements of Medicine* pref Beddoes [2]85, [3]871n; *Works* [2]85, [3]871n
Brown, John (fl 1806–21) [1]550n
Brown, John, of Ambleside (fl 1859) [1]clxviii
Brown, John Russell *see* Shakespeare *Merchant of Venice* ed Brown
Brown, John Taylor (1811–1901) [2]794
"Bibliomania" [5]108; *Odds and Ends* [5]108
Brown, Thomas (1663–1704) [1]38, 182, 182n, 803, [3]680, 680n
Brown, Tom
Tom Brownism [2]72, 72n
Browne, Robert (c 1550–1644) [1]283n
Browne, Sir Thomas (1605–82) [1]lxiv, lxxxiin, lxxxvi, 55, 653n, 741, 845, [2]348n, [3]780, 780n, 882, 882n, [5]810n, [6]251
on Copernicus [2]668, 668n; and Johnson [1]845
The Garden of Cyrus [1]764, 775; MT 791–5; *Hydriotaphia* [1]741, 763; MT 790–1; 797; *Pseudodoxia Epidemica* [1]741, 742; MT 766–80; [2]170n, 668n, [3]780n; *Religio Medici* [1]lxi, lxxxi, lxxxvii, 741; MT 742–59, 781–90; 788n q, [2]668n, [3]266n q, [4]804, 804n, 849–50 q, 850n q, [6]333; *Urne Buriall* [1]xc; *"Works"* [1]lxxxii, lxxxvii, cxv–cxvi, cxlin, 282n, 741, 742; MT 760–99; [2]1191, [3]266n, 780n, [4]804n
Browne, William (c 1590–1645) [1]37, 59, 59n
"Life" by Anderson MT [1]59
Britannia's Pastorals MT [1]47; [2]128n
Brownists [1]283n
Brownrigg, Elizabeth (d 1767) [5]145n, 371, 371n
Bruce, James (1730–94) *Travels to Discover the Source of the Nile* [4]87n
Bruce, Michael (1746–67) [1]38
Bruce, Robert (1554–1631) [2]1174
Brucker, Johann Jakob (1696–1770) [2]172, [3]642, 649n
Historia critica philosophiae [2]172n, [4]354n
Brun, Sophie Christiane Friederika (1765–1835) *Lebensansicht* [1]132
Brunck, Richard Franz Philipp (1729–1803) *see* Aeschylus ed Brunck
Brunetti, Cosimo (c 1620–c 1680) *see* Pascal *Les provinciales* tr Wendrock, Cordero, and Brunetti

Bruno, Giordano (1548–1600) [1]lxx, cvii, 117n, 177n, 559, *559n–60n*, 568, 568n, 602, 603n, 622n, 770n, [2]13n, 131, 702n, [3]84, 142n, 991, [4]424, 424n, [5]444n, 810, 812n, 830, 830n

not annotated by C [1]lxiii; philosophy of [5]812–13

De la causa, principio et uno [3]75; *De l'infinito* [2]976, 976n; *De monade* [2]976n, [6]333; *De progressu et lampade venatoria logicorum* [1]347n, 560n; *De umbris idearum* [1]568n; *The Expulsion of the Triumphant Beast* [2]976, 976n; *Ode* in *De monade* [1]183n q; *Von der Ursache, dem Prinzip und dem Einem* [3]84

Brunonian medicine/Brunonianism *see* Brown, John (1735–88)

Brunswick Clubs [2]474, *474n*

Brussels [2]938n

brute(s) [4]91, 97, [5]177, 471, 483

and man [4]394, [5]842

Brutus (*Julius Caesar*) [4]733, 733n, 735, 806–7

Brutus (legend) [2]577

Brutus, Lucius Junius (fl 509 BC) [1]392, 610n, [3]787, [4]189, 189n

buffoon [1]610; honoured [1]361

Brutus, Marcus Junius (c 85–42 BC) [1]174, [3]787n, [4]79, 79n, 807, 807n, [5]40, 41, 128n, 681, 747, 747n

and Cassius [1]337, 337n

Bryant, Jacob (1715–1804) [6]218

The Sentiments of Philo Judaeus [2]434n

Brydone, Patrick (1743–1818) *A Tour through Sicily and Malta* [5]846n

Bryerwood *see* Brerewood

Bryskett, Lodowick (fl 1571–1611) [1]74n

bubble(s) [1]675, [2]195, 1010, [3]644, [5]495

bubble and squeak [4]667, 667n

Buccleuch, Duke of [3]152

Bucer, Martin (1491–1551) [1]477n, 509, 509n, 835, 839, [2]668, [3]795n, 877, 877n, 881, [5]392, 399, 399n–400n, 661, [6]18, 18n, 21, 21n

Buchanan, Francis Hamilton (1762–1829) [5]416

An Account of the Kingdom of Nepal [5]416n; *Genealogies of the Hindus* [5]416n; *A Journey from Madras through the Countries of Mysore, Canara, and Malabar* [5]416n

Buchanan, George (1506–82) [2]129, 129n

De jure regni apud Scotos [3]178n; *Rerum Scoticarum historia* [3]178

Buchanan, Thomas Ryburn (1846–1911) [3]934

Bucholz, Christian Friedrich (1770–1818) [3]940, 943

Buckingham, Duke of *see* Villiers, George

Buckland, William (1784–1856)

On Geology and Mineralogy [2]883n; *Reliquiae diluvianae* [2]164, 164n

buckler [5]83

bud(s) [4]82n

Buddha [2]340, 1023n, [3]587n, 1054

Buddhism [2]1023n, [3]1053 ("Buddhaism")

Buddhist(s) [2]340, 341 ("Bauddhists"), [5]71, 71n

Buenos Aires [4]532n, [5]316n

buffalo(es) [2]862, [4]86, 88

Buffon, George Louis Leclerc, Comte de (1707–88) [1]623, 623n, [2]885, 885n, [3]1037, [4]201n, [5]271n, 430, 430n

and Böhme [1]623, 625, 625n; theory of solar system [5]339

Histoire naturelle [1]623n, 625n, tr Smellie as *Natural History* [3]1037n, [5]339n q

buffoon [1]610, [4]820

buffoonery [4]189, 626

bug-bear [4]366

Bugenhagen, Johann (1485–1558) [3]718

builder [3]779

bull(s) (cattle) [2]580, 581, 637, [4]86, 95, 96, 96n, 534

brazen [2]570n, [4]246, 246n, [5]634, 634n; calf [6]51; b.-fights [4]95

bull(s) (Irish) [2]17, 570, 835, 835n, [3]1029, 1068, [4]96n, 246, 246n, [5]51n, 842, [6]281n

bull(s) (papal) [3]760, 760n, [4]96, 96n, [5]143n, 634

Bull, George, Bishop of St David's (1634–1710) [1]478n, [2]264, 294n, [3]369, 524, 877, 877n, [5]7, 7n, 8n, 12n, 16n–17n, 20, 54, 64, 64n, 97, 174, 174n, 542–3, 543n, 576n, 626, 627, [6]66, 66n, 67, 68, 68n, 72, 73, 73n, 77, 79, 84 q, 90, 93, 146, 307

Corruptions of the Church of Rome [1]478n; *Defensio Fidei Nicaenae*† ed Grabe [1]478, 478n, 800, [2]265, [3]369n, 877n, [5]7n, 54n, 576, 576n–7n, 601n, 626n, 730n; *Opera omnia* [1]800; *Some Important Points of Primitive Christianity* [1]800

bullet(s) [1]868, [5]202

pewter [3]1080; steel [3]1081

Bulletin of the New York Public Library [2]16n

bullfinch(es) [2]581, [6]147

bull-frog [3]1061, [4]352

bull-froggery [2]498, 499n
Bullinger, Johann Heinrich (1504–75) [3]724, 762–3, 763n
bullion [1]123, 123n, [5]276n, 686n, 687, [6]19
nature is b. [3]984; of Scripture [6]20
bullocks [3]383
bully [2]712, [3]158, [4]584, [5]51, 51n
bullying [4]771, 772, 772n, [5]251
bum [2]1005, 1005n
b.-brusher [3]154
Bum-Bay [4]30
Bunyan, John (1628–88) [3]1076n, [4]608 q, 608n, 619, 650, 652–3, 657n
genius not fanatic [1]818; not Calvinist but Lutheran [1]810; style [1]802
Grace Abounding [1]801, [4]631n, 651n, 653n; *The History of the Town of Man-Soul* [1]801; *Holy War* [4]653n; *The Pilgrim's Progress* [1]lxxxix, cxiii, cxlivn, 811n, [3]1076, [4]588, 650–2, 651n, 653n, 654, 514 q; *Copy A* ed R. Southey [1]488; MT 802–15; 817; [4]588n, 651n; *Copy B* ed W. Mason MT [1]816–27; [4]588n, 651n, [5]514n; ed Sharrock [4]651n q; ed Wharey [1]811n
Bunyon, Frances Sarah (1816–93) [4]334
Buonaparte *see* Napoleon
Burckhardt, Johann Gottlieb (1756–1800) [3]719
burden [1]813
Burdett, Sir Francis, 5th Baronet Burdett (1770–1844) [3]146n
Burdy, Samuel (?1760–1820) *see* P. Skelton "Life" by Burdy
Bürger, Gottfried August (1747–94), [4]466n
Gedichte [1]lxxviii; MT 828–9; *The Lass of Fair Wone* [1]828; *Lenore* [1]91n; *Sämmtliche Schriften* ed Reinhard [1]828; see also *Musenalmanach* ed Bürger
Burges, Caroline Eliza Ann (fl 1832) [4]337n
Burges, Cornelius (?1589–1665) [3]795n
Burgh, Albert (fl 1668–75) [5]213
Burghley, Baron *see* Cecil, William
burglary [5]103
Burgundy [3]961–2
Burgundy, Duke of (in Commines) [2]100
burial [1]266–7
Burke, Edmund (1729–97) [3]209, 209n, [5]274n, 689, 689n, [6]117
A Letter . . . to His Grace the Duke of Portland on the Conduct of the Minority in Parliament [4]13, 13n; *Letter to a Noble Lord* [4]634; *Observations on a Late State of the Nation* [2]1173n; *Philosophical Inquiry into the Sublime and the Beautiful* [2]1069n, [3]404–5, 404n, [6]117n; *Reflections on the Revolution in France* [2]511, 511n, [6]117n; *Works* [1]cviin, [2]511n, [6]117n
Burke, William (1792–1829) [3]742n
Burkitt, Mr (fl 1806) [4]402
burlesque [1]182, 749, [4]638, 848
Burlington, Earl of *see* Boyle, Richard
Burlington VT
University of Vermont Library, marginalia in [2]169
Burma [3]1054
Burmese Gymnosoph [5]71
Burmese (language) [5]71n
Burn, Richard (1720–85) *see* J. Nicolson and Burn
Burnet, Gilbert (1643–1715) [1]850, [2]294n, 970n, [3]665n, 704, 704n, [5]145, 146, 146n
rash and credulous [1]843; a whig [1]836, [3]166, 166n
History of His Own Time† [1]clxii, 830, [3]166n, 167n q, 704n, [5]145n; *The History of the Reformation of the Church of England* [1]803, 803n; MT 831–9; [3]166n, 704n; *The Life of William Bedell* [1]xciii, clin, clxvii; MT 840–9; [3]166n; *The Memoires of the Lives and Actions of James and William Dukes of Hamilton and Castle-herald* MT [1]850; [2]60n, 1169, [3]166n; *see also* T. More *Utopia* tr Burnet
Burnet, Thomas (c 1635 1715) [1]183n, [3]644, 704, 704n
Latin and English styles [1]182–3
Archaeologiae philosophicae [1]183n, 851, [3]704n; *De statu mortuorum* [1]lxxviii; MT 851–3; *Telluris theoria sacra* [1]lxxviii, 851, [4]82n, tr as *Sacred Theory of the Earth* [1]182–3, [3]707n, [4]82
Burnett, George (1776–1811) [6]219n q
Burney, Charles (1726–1814) *A General History of Music* [2]413n q
Burney, Frances (1752–1840) [2]139
Burney, James (1750–1821) [1]365
Burney, Martin Charles (c 1788–1852) [1]365
Burnham-on-Sea [2]820n
burning [5]276
Burns, Robert (1759–96) [1]158, 158n, [2]94, 999n
and Scots [1]75n
Tam o'Shanter [1]158n
Burrard, Sir Harry (1755–1813) [2]940n
Burre, Walter (d 1622) [4]199
Burrow, Edward John (1785–1861) [3]936
Burrow, Sir James (1701–82) *Reports of Cases* [3]500, 501n

Burslem [3]632, 633, 636, 638, 639
Burton [1]cx
Burton, Henry (1578–1648) [2]932, 932n, [4]176
Burton, John, of Preston [1]clxviii
Burton, Mr [4]337, 337n
Burton, Robert (1577–1640) [1]cxvi, [6]333
The Anatomy of Melancholy† [1]xc, xci, 299n q, 768n, 854, [2]739
Bury, Robert Gregg (b 1869) *see* Plato *Epistles, Protagoras*; Sextus Empiricus *Outlines* tr Bury
Bury St Edmunds [1]156
Busby, Richard (1606–95) [2]76
bush [5]720
flame in [5]398; flaming [2]402; b.-rangers [6]37
business [4]831
religion as [1]319
Bussora [4]29
bustard [1]482n
"but" [4]166, 166n, 167
"but what" [4]579, 611
butcher(s) [4]612, [5]295n, 363, 531
Bute [2]578
Buthia [2]578
Buthoè [2]578
Butler, Alban (1710–73) *The Lives of the Fathers, Martyrs, and Other Principal Saints* [2]1058n
Butler, Charles (1750–1832) [1]500, 522, 857n, 858, 858n, 859, 864, [3]459, 459n, [6]13, 13n
The Book of the Roman-Catholic Church [1]511, 522 q, *855*; MT 856–60; [3]459n; *Life of Fenelon* [4]170; *Some Account of . . . Bossuet* [4]170; *Vindication of "The Book of the Roman Catholic Church"* [1]855, 856, 857n; MT 861–6
Butler, James, 12th Earl and 1st Duke of Ormond (1610–88) [1]255, [5]659
Butler, Joseph (1692–1752) [1]409, [4]132, 132n
The Analogy of Religion MT [1]867–9; [4]132n–3n q; *Sermons* [1]867
Butler, Samuel (1613–80) [1]37, 488, [2]17n, 351, 763, [4]466n
wit of [2]17
Genuine Remains in Prose and Verse ed Thyer [3]86n; *Hudibras* [1]182n, [2]17n, 707n, 762n, 763n, 971, 1144, 1144n q, [4]72, 77, 77n, [5]690 q, 690n; *Miscellaneous Thoughts* MT [1]49; [3]86 q, 86n
Buto [2]578
Butt, John Everett (1906–65) *see* Pope *Poems* ed Butt
butterfly/butterflies [1]525, 525n, [2]565, [3]505, [4]93, 267n, 647n, [5]289, 591, 592n
Buttmann, Philipp Carl (1764–1829) *Lexilogus* [2]825n; see also *Museum* ed Wolf and Buttmann
button [3]964, 964n, [5]675
Buxton [4]617–18
Buxton, Thomas Fowell (1786–1845) [6]29, 29n
by-laws [1]340
Byblus [2]577
Byerley, Thomas (d 1826) [3]627
Byfield, Nicholas (1579–1622) [1]871, 872, 873n
Byfield, Richard (c 1592–1664) [1]lxxv, cvi, cviii
The Doctrine of the Sabbath Vindicated [1]cxxvi; MT 870–9; 718
"Byondo" (R. Southey) [1]90
Byrom, John (1692–1763) [2]35n
Byron, George Gordon, 6th Baron (1788–1824) [1]379n, 742, [3]485, [4]5
letter to [1]376n q; overrated [6]74, 74n; on Pope [4]76, 76n; a wicked Lord [4]76; WW's opinion [4]76
Beppo [2]795n; *The Bride of Abydos* [4]170; *Childe Harold's Pilgrimage* [4]76n; *Don Juan* [1]217n, [2]795n, [4]76n q, ed EHC [1]clxxiin; *English Bards and Scotch Reviewers* [4]76n, [5]866; *The Giaour* [4]170; *Letter on the Rev. W. L. Bowles's Strictures on Pope* [4]76n; *Letters and Journals* ed T. Moore [5]866; *Poetical Works* [5]866, ed EHC [1]clxxiin
byssos abyssos [3]12, 12n, 30n
Bythinia [2]474
Bywater, Ingram (1840–1914) *see* Aristotle *Poetics* tr Bywater
Byzantium [2]729n

"C" see *The Rape of Helen* tr "C"
C., D. [6]171
C., H. J. [6]222
"C. H. S." (Christopher Hardy Sherive) [1]90
C., S. T. *see* Coleridge, S. T. I (1) initials
cabal/cabbal [1]353, 353n, [3]156
popish [3]156
Cabasilas, Nicholas (b c 1322) [5]662, 662n
cabbage(s) [1]201, [3]68, [4]318, [5]175
Cabbala/Cabala/cabbalistic(al) [1]119, 438n, 645n, 719, *719n*, [2]397, 427n, 430, 430n,

712, [3]81, 308n, 925, 1090, 1090n, 1090–1, [4]245–6, 246n, 258, 259n, [5]630n, 740, 806–7, [6]140–1, 141n
dating of [5]740n; doctrine [3]531, 622, [6]315; fancies [3]41; logodaedaly [3]476; mss [3]594; of numbers [6]294; of Paul [5]667; process in Böhme [1]670
Cabbalist(s)/Cabalist(s) [1]438, [3]1091, [4]257, [5]483
Cabeza de Vaca, Alvar Nuñez (16th century) [5]106
cabinet [1]763
c.-work [4]610
Cabiri [1]660, 660n, 665, 678, 692, [2]574, 575, 583, 583n, [4]594–5, 594n–5n, [6]5n
Cabiric metaphysician [5]153, 153n; Cabiric mysteries [1]616, [3]682; Cabiric rites [1]237n; *see also* mysteries, Samothracian
cable [5]420
cacata carta [1]lxxii, [3]887, 887n
cachexy [5]127, 127n
cacodaemony [1]88
cacophony [1]158, [3]194, [4]509
Cacus (myth) [4]198
Cadamust, Gerald (fl 1518) [2]7
Cadet/Cadet de Gassicourt, Charles Louis (1769–1821) [3]937
cadetships [5]378
Cadiz [1]223n, 500
Cadmaean (language) [4]37
Cadmilus (myth) [1]692, 692n, [2]576n, 583, 583n
Cadmus (myth) [1]799, [2]578, 580, [4]37n
Caesar(s) [2]61, [3]153, [5]537
despotism of [5]643; and God [5]363, 363n
Caesar, Gaius Julius (c 100–44 BC) [1]218n, 233, 337n, 838, 949, [3]345, 405, 447, [4]79, 79n, 311n, 336n, 735, 807, 807n, [5]69, 70, 536
death of [2]950, [3]787n; heavenly [1]339
Caesarea [2]37n
Caesario (*Twelfth Night*) [4]706
Caesarius of Nazianzus, St (d 369) [2]748
Caeso/Kaeso, Fabius Vibulanus (d 479 BC) [1]176
Caffraria [3]1074, 1074n
Caiaphas (Bible) [2]485, [4]51n, [6]33
Caille (fl 1784) [3]1067n
Cain (Bible) [2]177, 301, 302n, 574n, 576, 717, 780, 788, 1185, [3]285, [4]640n, [5]593, [6]325–6
generations of [2]576
Caine, Sir Thomas Henry Hall (1853–1931) *Life of Coleridge* [1]cli
Cainists [2]717
Cainites [6]5
Cairo [4]29, 30
Caistor [5]853
Caius (fiction) [5]5, 9
Cajetan (Thomas de Vio), Cardinal (1469–1534) [3]235
cake [5]579
c. paperlets [2]599
Calabria [4]86, 86n, [6]150
Calais [2]981n, [5]196, [6]147
calamity/calamities [2]160, 508, [4]434, 785, [5]167
Calamy, Edmund, the Elder (1600–66) [1]254, 259, 332, 332n, 352, 352n, 357n, [2]651, 651n, [4]183, [5]520, 520n
Calamy, Edmund, the Younger (1642–86) [1]353n, 357n
Calamy, Edmund, the Youngest (1671–1732) *An Historical Account of My Own Life* [1]357, 357n
Calas, Jean (1698–1762) [6]32
Calbeck [3]975
Calchaquina [3]1077
calcination [3]945
calcium [3]481, [5]257, 258, 261, 397
calculation [1]812
calculus [5]96
Calcutta [3]673, 1081
Calderón de la Barca, Pedro (1600–81) [1]390n, 506n, [3]1066
influence on B&F [1]398
Autos sacramentales, allegoricos y historiales [1]398n; *La Devoción de la Cruz* tr A. W. Schlegel [1]398n
calendar of saints [6]82
calf, golden [1]785, [3]924n
Caliban (*Tempest*) [3]186–7, [4]786, 811, 820
Caligula (Gaius Julius Caesar Germanicus) (12–41) [1]486n, [2]622, 622n, [3]505, [5]43, 829, 829n
Calixtus (Georg Calixt) (1586–1656) [1]307n
Callidora (in Cowley) [2]105–6, 106, 106n
Callimachus (fl 250 BC) [1]299n, [4]147
Bath of Pallas [1]145
calling, effectual [3]547
Callistratus (2nd/3rd century) [4]289
callus [4]164
calm(ness), philosophic [2]928, [5]145
Calne [1]xciv, cvi, 374, 392n, 716, 871, [2]526, 668n, [3]170, 321, 810
calomel [5]137, 181

caloric/calorique [2]426, 426n, [3]46, 46n, 278, 278n, 323, 858, [5]244, 244n, 438, 450, 451, 557, 557n, [6]104, 227
Calprenède, Gauthier des Costes de la (1610–63) *Cassandre* [5]821n
calumny/calumnies [3]649, [4]671, [5]151, 154, 624, [6]14
  posthumous [5]102
Calvary [3]51, [5]775n
Calvin, John (1509–64) [1]198n, 224, 225n, 346n, 358, 477, 477n q, 805, 805n, 835n, [2]183, 300, 304, 313, 496n, 668, 679 q, 680 q, 680n, 801, 1097n, 1192n, [3]31, 77n, 309, 515, 515n, 562, 727, 922, [4]640, 643, 644, 652–3, 655, 669, 670, 670n, 747, [5]75, 75n, 76n, 156n, 158n, 160, 202, 395, 505, 506n, 595, 603, 603n, 609, 614, 643, 661, [6]15n, 298, 298n
  C's reading of [1]476–9; on free will [2]676, 677; on prayer [1]674; predestination [1]835; and Servetus [1]478n, [2]666–7, 667n
  Institutio religionis christianae [5]75n, tr *Institutes of the Christian Religion* [4]640n, [5]160n, tr Norton as *Institution of the Christian Religion* [4]640n; *see also* Bible: NT: GOSPEL(S): *A Harmonie . . . with the Commentarie of M. John Calvine*
Calvinism [1]230, 269, 269n, 358, 801, 803n, [2]20, 31, 677, 677n, 1099, [3]25n, 26n, 47, 307n, 528n, [4]429n, 588, 651–2, 658, [5]81n, 158, 159, 159n, 162n, 182, 678n, [6]261, 298, 298n
  and Arminianism *see* Arminianism; Calvinist Methodists [3]495; charge against Leighton [3]567; compared to Socinianism [2]797–803; denial of free will [3]737; fashionable definition [1]810; high [5]163n; highest [5]162; in Irving [3]26–7; modern [3]26, 26n, 435, 515n, 562, [4]429n, [5]202n; perverted [3]59; radical error of [3]26; spread of [1]224; ultra-C. [3]528, 879–80, [6]311
Calvinist(s) [1]199n, 257n, 284, 302n, 307n, 810, 820, [2]260, 496n, 839, 913, 916, 1157n, [3]31n, 69, 71n, 232n, 747n, [4]43, 429, 647–8, 659, 669, 672, [5]15n, 137, 408, 433, 433n, 469, 593, 596, 613
  and Arminians *see* Arminian(s); doctrine of redemption [2]263; errors of [1]820, 824; French [1]225, 225n; minatory [5]163; modern [3]308–9, 517, 517n, 876, [6]299, 299n; persecutions of [6]108
Cambrai [4]193
Cambridge [1]809n, [3]283n, 318, 905, [4]294, [5]16n, 118n, 390, 400n, 478, 540n, 553n, 669, 853
  Cambridge University [1]72n, [2]352, 794, 956n–7n, 978, [3]821n; Catherine Hall [3]707; C's days at [3]927n; Jesus College [1]99n, 615, 615n, 700, [2]819n, [3]349, [6]220; King's College [1]cxxxiv; Pembroke Hall [1]74n; Pepys Library [4]71; Platonists *see* Platonists, Cambridge; St John's College [1]cxiv, 98n, [2]56, 71, 650, 937, 954n; St Peter's College [5]78; Trinity College [1]99n, [2]71, 914n
Cambridge Bibliography of English Literature [1]clin
Cambridge MA
  Harvard College [3]821; Harvard Divinity School [2]20; Harvard University, marginalia in [1]clxiii, clxvi, clxvii, clxix, clxxiv, 119, 279, [2]50, 116, 245, 698, 753, 952, 985, 1112, [3]886, 934, [4]90, 101, 237, 754, [5]80, 426, [6]38, 164, transcript(s) of marginalia in [2]214, 215
Cambyses (fiction) [2]570
Camden, William (1551–1623) [1]213
  Institutio graecae grammatices compendaria MT [2]3–4
camel(s) [3]21, [4]534
camera
  lucida [4]337, 337n; obscura [3]716, 716n, [4]82n, 337n
Camerarius, Joachim (1500–74) [1]233 ("Camero"), [2]1097n, [6]122
Camilla (legend) [4]192
Camillus, Marcus Furius (447–365 BC) [1]176, 315
Camisards [5]166
Camoëns, Luis de (1524–80) [1]543, 543n
Campanella, Tommaso (Giovanni Domenico) (1568–1639) [5]807–9
Campbell, Hugh John Vaughan, Viscount Emlyn [3]492
Campbell, James Dykes (1838–95) [1]clii, clxxi, clxxii, [5]108
  owner of annotated books [1]100; and Scots [1]75n
  ed "Coleridgeana" [1]cli; "Narrative of the Life of S. T. Coleridge" [1]cli; *Samuel Taylor Coleridge* [1]100; *see also* Coleridge, S. T. II *Poetical Works* (1893) ed Campbell
Campbell, John Frederick, 1st Earl Cawdor of Castlemartin (1790–1860) [3]492 ("S. F.")

Campbell, Thomas (1777–1844) [2]180, 954n
Campe, Joachim Heinrich (1746–1818) [3]656
camphor [1]777 ("camphire"), [5]251, 252
Campion, Thomas (1567–1620) [2]116
"can" and "may" [3]678–9
Cana [2]204, 262, 1015, [3]35, [4]65
Canaan (person) (Bible) [1]540, [4]257, [6]5
Canaan (place) [2]151, 342, 392, 831 ("Canaanitish") [3]108n, [5]504n, [6]292–3
Canaanites [1]864, [2]394, [4]257, 257n
Canada [2]977
 Canadian savage [4]303
canal(s) [3]627–8, 629
 c.-like [2]1024
canary [6]148
Canberra
 National Library of Australia, marginalia in [6]35
Cancer [1]399n
candidate(s) [4]24
 gown of [4]731
candle(s) [2]568, 568n, 631, 884, [3]373, 386, 783, 1015, [4]375, 375n, 461n, 538, [5]264, [6]234
 c.-flame [4]864; c.-light [1]763, 797
Candolle, Augustin Pyramus de (1778–1841) [3]942 ("Decandolle")
candour [4]425
Candy [4]84
cannabis [4]84–5
Cannia [4]89
cannibal(s) [5]102
cannibalism [2]73, 73n, [5]101–2 ("banquets")
Canning, George (1770–1827) [2]511n, [4]20, 20n, [5]145n, [6]45
cannon [2]620, [5]101, 101n
 c. ball [3]301, 302, 362n, [4]634
Cannon, John *see* Junius *Letters* ed Cannon
Cannus, Melchior (Melchior Cano) (1525–60) [5]549
"canon" [5]13, 13n
canon [3]595, 726, [5]667
 biblical *see* Bible: canon; Christian [1]467; compilers of [2]405–6; of credibility [3]661, 700; of faith [5]571; formation of [3]763; Hebrew [2]481, [3]376, 377, 409, 466, [6]319; heretical [5]570; intermediate [1]492; of interpretation [2]561, [3]438; Jewish [2]374, 374n, 375, 376, 377–81, 409, [3]310, [4]253, [6]142; of logic [4]426; lower [1]492; of philosophy [3]328; prophetic [2]409; of Scripture [5]464, 527; secondary [1]493n; superior [1]492; Trent or Lateran [2]283; of truth [3]689, 689n
canon fidei [1]345, 345n
"canonical", misuse of [1]491
canonicity [3]20, [6]65; *see also* Bible: canon
canonisations [5]662
canonists [5]661
cant [1]264, [2]999, [4]505, 645, 653, 667, [6]259
 mystifying [5]296; sentimental [2]1199; wearisome [5]90
Cantabs [3]902
Canterbury [2]819n, 1198, [5]138n
 Cathedral [1]cvi, 872; Convocation at [2]1150n; Court of [1]clvin
Canterbury, Archbishop of (*Henry V*) [4]717
Canterbury Tale [2]1135
cantharides [1]777, 777n, [2]693n, [5]254, 254n
cap [4]747
capacity
 of Christ [3]747; minimum of [2]39
Cape of Good Hope [2]586, 1112n, [4]534, 534n
Cape Town
 South African Library, marginalia in [4]151
Cape Verde/de Verds [5]102
Capell, Edward (1713–81) [1]373, [4]696n
caper [2]1006n
Capernaeum [2]256, 258
Capilupi, Lelio (1498–1560) [2]764
capital (financial) [1]724, [2]619, [4]622
 defined [2]311; negative [5]146
capital punishment [4]241n
capital(s), small [5]117, 117n
capitalists [5]686
Cappadocia [2]474, 981n, [5]634, 634n
Cappe, Newcome (1735–1800) [1]316, 316n
 Critical Remarks on Many Important Passages of Scripture [1]316n
Capper, Benjamin Pitts (b 1761) [1]clxn
 A Topographical Dictionary of the United Kingdom MT [2]5–6
capriccio [3]1035, 1035n
"caprified" [4]663, 663n
"captious" [6]107
captiver [5]451
captivity [1]438, 710
 to evil [2]1166
Captivity/Captivities (of Jews) [1]422, 431, 438, 674, 707, [2]147, 376, 377, 378, 419, 421, 514, 785, 894, [3]437, 461n, 462, 473, 658, 1086, 1089

capuchin [3]535, [6]318
caput mortuum [1]618, 618n, [4]412n, [6]170
Caracalla, Marcus Aurelius Antoninus (188–217) [5]829, 829n
Caractacus (d 54) [3]419, 419n
Caratach (in B&F) [1]366
carbon [1]551, 570, 571, 572, 589, 596, 597, 598, 611, 614, 633, 635, 643, 663, 667, 737, 780, [2]546, 546n, 852n, 853n, 854–5, 854n, 855–6, 855n, 857, 1186, [3]44, 45, 129, 443, 951, 998, 998n, 999, 1004, 1007, 1021n, 1022, 1027, 1029, 1029n, 1031, 1061, [4]16, 169, 315, 315n, 316, 324, 385, 388n, 396n, 492, 521, [5]247, 247n, 257, 259, 260, 260n, 264, 264n, 342, 344, 344n, 347–8, 356, 397, 435, [6]116, 231
  acid gas [4]492; in blood [2]367–8; Böhme's view of [1]611; dioxide [2]246n, 857, 858n, [3]68n, [4]492n; oxide of [1]633; and plants [5]347; principle of fixity [1]573; role in animal life [3]68; role in vegetation [3]68
carbon-azote/carbonazot(e) [1]573, 573n, 579, 597, 641n, 663
carbonic acid *see* acid(s)
  c. a. gas *see* gas(es)
carbuncle [3]779
"carcass" [1]177, 177n
carcass(es)/carcase(s) [1]735, 735n, [2]316, 335, 1185, [3]44, [4]317, 322, [6]88
  human [5]431
card(s) [3]389
  house of [4]637, [5]668
Cardan, Girolamo (Jeronimus Cardanus) (1501–76) [1]634n, 772, [2]804, 824n, [3]656
cardo [5]73
care(s) [4]162
carelessness, seeming [1]268
caret [3]818
Carew, Thomas (1594/5–1640) [1]37, [2]14
Carey, William (1761–1834) [2]339
caricature(s) [1]393, 346, [2]824, [3]182, [4]190, 505
Carios [5]104
Carisbrooke Castle [2]522n
Carlestad *see* Carlstadt
Carlisle [4]584
  Cathedral Library [1]ciii, 758n, [3]979, 979n
Carlist [2]260
Carlstadt, Dr (Andreas Rudolf Bodenstein) (c 1480–1541) [2]1097 ("Carolostadius"), [3]753
Carlyle, Jane Welsh (1801–66) *see* Carlyle, Thomas
Carlyle, Thomas (1795–1881) [2]1115, [3]501n, 627, 630n, [4]610n, [5]365n
  and J. W. Carlyle *The Collected Letters* ed C. R. Sanders [3]191n
Carlyon, Clement (1777–1864) [1]149n–50n, 150n q, 204n, 535
  Early Years and Late Reflections [2]369 q, [3]1071n
Carmel, Mount [3]470, 470n
Carmelites [5]818
Carmina illustrium poetarum italorum MT [2]7–10
Carmina quadragesimalia [2]95n
carnal, psychical equivalent to [3]44
Carnarvon, Earl(s) of *see* Dormer, Robert; Herbert, Henry George and Henry John George
Carneades of Cyrene (c 215–130 BC) [5]747, 747n
Carnero, Dr [1]504–5
carnifex [5]396
carob [5]104
Carolina USA [2]499n
Caroline, Queen of England (1768–1821) [1]738
Carololatria [1]257, 257n
Carondelet [2]941
Carpalim (in Rabelais) [4]193, 196
carpenter [5]714, 756
carpentering [2]165
Carpocrates (2nd century) [2]713 ("Carpocras")
Carr/Ker, Robert, 1st Earl of Ancrum (1578–1654) [1]167n, [2]18n
Carr/Ker, Robert, 6th Earl of Somerset (c 1587–1645) [2]942n
carrack [2]230 ("carack")
carrier [1]590
carrion [4]762–3, 846, 847, [6]88
carrot [4]318
Carter, Elizabeth (1717–1806) [6]222, 223
Carter, George Goldsmith *The Goodwin Sands* [2]520n
Carter, James (1792–1853)
  Lectures on Taste [2]754n; *A Lecture on the Primitive State of Man* [2]754n
Carter, John (d 1856) [1]cxii
Carteret, Sir George (d 1680) [4]72
Carthage [5]831, 832n, [6]198
cart-wheels [5]159
Cartwright, Christopher (1602–58) [1]232

Cartwright, Thomas (1535–1603) [1]351, 351n, [2]812, [3]795n, [4]643
Cartwright, William (1611–43) *The Siedge* [1]751n–2n
carvings [1]684
Cary, Henry (1804–70)
Commentary [3]500; *Memoir of the Rev. Henry Francis Cary* [1]237n, 494 q, [2]133, [4]677
Cary, Henry Francis (1772–1844) [1]lxxiiin, lxxxvn, cvii, cxlin, clxvi, 231, [2]94, 131, *133–4*, 140, 805, [4]677
and Asgill project [1]lxv; and Dante [4]101, 101n; death [1]clxi; letter(s) to [1]121 q, 836n–7n q, [2]213–14 q, [3]425n, [5]120; owner of annotated books [1]26, 494, [6]134; supplier of books to C [1]xcviii, [4]101 ("Carey"), 101n
Memoir of see Henry Cary *Memoir*; *Sonnets and Odes* [2]133; *see also* Aristophanes *The Birds*; Dante *The Vision* tr Cary
Cary, Jane Sophia (d 1815) [4]101n
Cary, Lucius, 2nd Viscount Falkland (1610–43), [2]358, 358n, 523, 945, 945n, [3]803
Discourse of Infallibility [3]803n
Caryl, Joseph (1602–73) [4]182
Casaubon, Isaac (1559–1614) [3]650, [4]99, [5]223; *see also* Persius ed Casaubon and Casaubon
Casaubon, Meric (1599–1671) *see* Persius ed Casaubon and Casaubon
Casca (*Julius Caesar*) [4]734
case(s) (in grammar) [3]830, 831, 832, 832–5
confusion of [5]775
cases, extreme [1]337, 361
Casimir (Maciej Kazimierz Sarbiewski) (1595–1640) [1]civ
casket [3]37
Caspar (legend) [4]55n
Cassandra (myth) [2]155n
cassava [2]298n
Cassilane (in B&F) [1]366
Cassio (*Othello*) [4]746, 865
Cassiopeia [2]396n, [3]540, 540n
Cassius (Gaius Cassius Longinus) (d 42 BC) [1]191, 337, 337n
Cassius (*Julius Caesar*) [4]733, 733n, 806
Cassius (myth) [2]576
Castabala [1]859n
caste(s) [5]234 ("casts"), 234n
in India [2]342, 342n, 347, 348
Casti, Giambattista (c 1721–1803) [2]795n
Castile
Castilian dialect [3]830
castle [3]301, 362n, [5]212
Castle of Turpitude [5]845
Castlereagh, Viscount *see* Stewart, Robert
Castor and Pollux (myth) [2]810, [5]197, 197n
castration [6]150, 151
castus [3]61n
casuist(s) [1]272, [6]262
Polish [5]496; Roman [5]562; Romish [5]497
casuistry [1]271, [2]522, 926, 941, [3]360, [5]561, [6]262
books of [5]562; C's hatred of [1]342; Jesuitical [5]525n
cat(s) [4]711n, [5]387, 388, [6]75
black [1]519, [2]285, 285n, [5]274; Katterfelto's [3]9; c.'s paw [2]263; sparks from [5]577
catachresis [1]862, [2]496n, [3]525, [6]307
catacomb(s) [2]314, [4]810
catalepsy/catalepsies [3]374n, [4]514, 592, [5]122
cataleptic state [5]517
cataleptic, the [6]99
catalogue [3]629
of books [5]167; of names [5]638
Catalonia [3]104
Catanea, Giovanni Maria (d 1529) [3]235
cataphysical [3]376, 376n
cataract (eye) [1]810, 810n, [4]164, 647, 647n
cataract (waterfall) [4]408, 817
catch-pennies [4]270
catechism(s) [1]266, 311, 509, 705, [2]193, [3]1078n, [4]306n, [5]192, 515, 629, [6]19
C of E see *BCP*: Catechism; Westminster [5]540, 540n
catechist [3]563
catechumen(s) [1]236, 311, 312, 312n, 324, 345, 685, [3]445, 445n, 689, [5]619, 620, [6]62
categorical imperative *see* Kant
category/categories [3]80, 243n, [4]108, [5]592
of appearance [5]615; Aristotle's [3]901, [5]701; defined [1]655; Kant's [3]249, 381; Pythagorean [5]701; table of [3]95, 95n–6n, 248n
catenation [3]105
Cateni, Cammillo *see* Alisio
caterpillar(s) [2]545, 1004, [4]267, 267n, 647, [5]591, [6]152
cathedrals, Gothic [3]994
Catherine I, of Russia (1684–1727) [1]213n
Catherine of Aragon, Queen of England (1485–1536) [1]318n, 422, 422n

Cathery, Richard (fl 1810) [3]942
"catholic" [1]848n, [2]674, 724, [3]446n, [5]539
Catholic(s) [1]198n, 307n, [2]195, 972, 1106, 1201, [3]231, 669, 686, 883, [4]22, 33, 68, 260, 672, [5]552, 567, 569, [6]87, 88, 292
anxious for reform [6]15; bigotted [5]379; conscientious [1]520; French [1]258; German [1]223n, 607; Irish [4]25; C. League [5]104n; pseudo-C. [4]20; reasonable [1]314; Spanish [1]258; universal [6]19; Vico as [6]18; *see also* church(es): Roman Catholic
Catholic Apostolic Church *see* church(es): Holy Catholic Apostolic
Catholic Association *see* Dublin
Catholic Bill *see* Parliament: Acts/Bills: Catholic Emancipation Bill
Catholic Church *see* church(es): Roman Catholic
Catholic Emancipation [1]733n, 855, 866n, [2]474n, [3]489n ("Relief"), [4]18–24, [6]13n, 48n; *see also* Parliament: Acts/Bills
Catholicism [3]785, [5]143, 507
and Charles I [1]222; dialogues on [2]208; Roman [5]274n; *see also* church(es): Roman Catholic
catholicity [2]674, 918, [3]444, 445, [5]569, [6]65
"catholism" [2]141, 141n
Cato, Marcus Porcius, the Elder (234–149 BC) [1]176, 315, [4]804
Cato, Marcus Porcius, the Younger (95–46 BC) [1]315
Cato's Letters see Trenchard
Catos [1]315
Cattermole, Richard (?1795–1858) [1]795n
A Sermon [4]3
cattle [1]877
Catullus, Gaius Valerius (c 84–54 BC) [1]lxxii q, cvn, 188, [2]240, 520n, [3]887n q, [4]336n
Attis [2]354 ("Atys"), 354n; *Carmina* [1]487n, [2]519n, tr Cornish [1]7 q; *Opera* [1]lxxviii
Caucasian(s) [3]356n, [5]253n
Caucasus [2]783, [5]387, 387n
cauliflower [4]318
causa causans [5]826n
causa causarum [3]309; *see also* cause(s) of a cause
causa sui [3]13, 30, 151, [5]210, 779
causality [3]30, [5]615
causation [2]1145, [3]206, [4]92, 106, 543, [5]201, 552
cause(s) [1]780, [2]1028, [3]90–1, 270, 346, 855, [4]211, 221, 702, [5]204
absolute [5]372; acting at a distance [4]417, 417n; bad [1]807; best [2]42; as category [1]238; of a cause [2]299, 299n, [5]564, 564n, [6]28, 28n, see also *causa causarum*; continual [5]418; desiderata of [4]386; and effect [1]201, [2]802, 1185, 1193, 1205, 1205n, [3]705, 791, 850, 950, 950n, [4]47, 174, 292, 375, 386, 405, 416–17, 787, [5]32, 65–6, 84, 125, 162, 206, 209, 211, 267, 356–7, 559, 595, 598, 649, 670, 730, [6]144; for effect [3]734; effective [1]683, [5]643; efficient [3]559, [5]159, 213, 562, 605, 644, 701, 702; exciting [5]738; for existence [6]267; final [1]536, [3]516, 853, [4]137, [5]37, 159, 211, 214, 788, [6]299; finite [5]207; first [3]332, [5]788–9; and ground [5]206; imaginary [5]252; infinite [3]78, 89; instrumental [5]653; intrinsic [1]787; knowledge of [3]546, 578; material [5]559; meaning of [4]354; not to be multiplied [3]345; natural [3]205; necessary [4]408; occasional [4]354; in philosophy [5]7, 7n; of pleasure [4]766; potentiative [2]1185; secondary [3]77; of self [3]1065, 1065n; sufficient [2]1010n, 1145, [3]676, [5]159, 175, 175n, 457, 721, 721n; superessential [1]565; supernatural [2]249; transcendent [5]798
"causeless" [4]702
caustic(s) [5]163
lunar [3]129
Cavalier(s) [2]60, 512, 835, [3]489, 802, [4]594, 657n
cavalry [3]774, [4]193, [5]377
Cavanagh, John (d 1819) [1]223n
cave(s) [2]164
allegory of [3]525n, [6]307n; Pope's [1]814
Cave, William (1637–1713) [1]492, [5]401, 401n
Antiquitates Apostolicae [4]474, 474n; *Antiquitates Christianae* [2]11; *Scriptorum ecclesiasticorum historia literaria* [1]lxxx; MT [2]11–13; [5]401, 401n
Cavell [3]795n
Cavendish, Christiana, Countess of Devonshire (d 1675) [3]879n
Cavendish, Henry (1731–1810) [1]779, 780n, [3]938
Cavendish, William, 1st Duke of Newcastle (1592–1676) [2]1197, 1199, [3]172
cavern [2]958
Cawdor (*Macbeth*) [4]789
Cawdor, Earl *see* Campbell, John Frederick
Cawthorne, James (1721–61) [1]38
Caxton, William (c 1422–c 1491) [2]699n
Cayley, Sir George (1771–1857) [3]937

Cazotte, Jacques (1720–92) [3]207, 207n, 208, 209
Cebes [3]992. See also *Picture of Cebes*; *Tablet of Cebes* [3]2
cechin *see* chequin
Cecil, William, 1st Baron Burghley ("Burleigh") (1520–98) [3]794–5, [5]143, 143n
cedar [1]442n
 c.-wood [2]372
Celadon (myth) [6]156n, 157, 157n
"celebrious" [2]527, 527n
celebrity [2]571
céleste mécanique [2]825
celestial and terrestrial [1]138
Celestial City (in Bunyan) [4]653n
Celia (in Jonson) [3]180
celibacy [1]518, [2]742n, 937n, 938n, 984, [3]808, [6]14
 of clergy [3]310, 785, 785n, [6]13; soul-poisoning [1]530
celibates [3]907
Cellarius, Christopher (1638–1707) [2]980, 981n, [5]693n
Celle [6]153 ("Zelle"), 153n
Celsus (fl c 178) [2]722, [4]627, 627n
 The True Word [2]317, 317n
Celt(s) [4]15, 78, 583, 583n, [5]195n, 337
 anthropoid [4]15; as mixed race [1]540
Celtic (language) [4]282n
cement [4]739
cenocranion [4]188
cenotaph [6]119
censors [4]647
censure [2]103
centaur(s), [2]346, [4]198, 418
Centenera *see* Barco
cento [3]220
centrality [1]604, [3]139, [4]323, 529, [5]265, 266, 438
 and adhesion *see* adhesion; and attraction *see* attraction; and cohesion [1]549; and contraction [1]549; and dilation [1]549; and repulsion [1]549; and surface powers [1]641
centre [1]629, 646, 775, [4]396, 443, [5]131
 Christ as [3]72–3; eccentric [1]691; false [1]560; necessity of [4]43; origination of [3]325; and periphery [1]562
centrifugal
 and centripetal [1]569, 594, 643, 651, [3]876, [5]438; c. force *see* force
centripetal and centrifugal *see* centrifugal
Centuries of Magdeburg [5]298, 298n
Cephalus (myth) [6]156, 157, 157n
Cephas (Bible) [3]458n, [5]536
Cephites [3]458
Cerberus (myth) [4]670
"cercoceronychous" [1]351n, [5]82, 82n, 83, 83n
cerebellum [5]422, 422n
ceremonials [1]358
ceremoniousness [2]1034
ceremony/ceremonies [1]253, 275, 318–19, 339, 809, 847, [2]26, 300–1, 655, 1139, [4]625–6, [5]192, 397, 562n, 639, 651
 arbitrary [1]267, [6]260; of Church [1]329; and essence [6]263; indifferent [1]253; of the law [3]722; outward [1]323
Ceres (myth) [1]639, 639n, 653, 653n, 665, 665n, 678, [2]573, 575, 583n; *see also* Demeter
Cerinthians [2]272
Cerinthus (fl c 100) [2]487, [3]441, 441n, 1068, 1068n, [4]249, [5]625, [6]58, 63
cerium [3]1033, 1033n
"certain" and "positive" [1]*520n–1n*, [3]733, 733n
certainty [1]106, 283, [2]1061, 1133, [3]17, 326, 517, 682, 959n, [4]109, 123, 219, [5]16, 96, 771
 of adherence [2]1164–5; and belief *see* belief; no degrees of [1]520; of election [3]528; and evidence [2]1160, 1164, 1164n; of geometry [4]156; and positiveness [3]849, 849n, 850, 968n, [5]664; sense of [6]223; subjective [1]303; Jeremy Taylor's [5]557; in working [6]299
Cervantes Saavedra, Miguel de (1547–1616) [1]367n, 390n, [2]689, [3]207n, [4]192, 192n, 779
 capable of tragedy [1]367
 Don Quixote [1]cxxxix, 392, [3]207, 207n
Cesario (in B&F) [1]405
Cévennes [5]166
Ceylon [2]342, [4]84–9
ch [2]1092, 1092n
Chablais [1]516n
Chactaws [1]226
chaff [5]306
chain(s) [2]291, [3]26, 26n, 424, [4]408, [5]155, 242, 243n, 754n
 dances to [2]140, 140n; dependent [5]754; of facts [1]536; great [3]675–6; invisible [3]823; iron [5]279; links [2]510, [3]853; of motives [3]423; of truths [5]568
chair [2]613
 easy [5]135; majestic [1]725
Chaldaic (language) [3]466, [5]237, 237n, [6]140
Chaldea [1]440, [2]390, 419, [3]462, 465, 467

Chaldean(s) [1]439, 540, [5]233, 234
C. fables [3]1090
chalk [4]148n, [5]257, 654
Chalmers, Alexander (1759–1834) [1]cxxxviiin
silly remarks [2]15
ed *The Works of the English Poets* [1]cxln, cxlin; MT [2]14–18; 586, 1033, 1170n, [4]809
Chalmers, George (1742–1825) *Caledonia* [6]94n
Chalmers, Thomas (1780–1847) [3]747, 747n
On the Adaptation of External Nature to the Moral and Intellectual Constitution of Man [2]883n; *Select Works* ed Hanna [3]747n q
Cham, Great [3]779
chamber-pot [1]768
Chambers, Ephraim (c 1680–1740) *see* Boerhaave *New Method of Chemistry* tr Shaw and Chambers
Chambre, Robert (fl 1659) *Some Animadversions upon the Declaration of . . . the Army* MT [2]19; 111
chameleon [3]552 ("camelion")
Chamfort, Nicolas Sébastian Roch (1741–94) [3]207
chamois-hunter(s) [1]331n, [2]1158n
champagne [3]217n
Champel [1]478n
Champion ed J. Thelwall [4]837n
chance [1]706, [2]694, [3]206, [5]141
belief in [6]75
chancellor(s) [2]72, 375, 941
Chancery, Court of *see* London: Court of Chancery
change(s) [3]261, 520, 676–7, [5]591
causes of [5]232
changeling [3]161, [5]274
changing [5]342
Chanina *see* Hanina ben Dusa
channel [5]168
exclusive [5]157
Channing, William Ellery (1780–1842) [2]20–1, 181, [4]5, 76n
A Discourse Delivered at the Installation of the Rev. Mellish Irving Motte MT [2]20–2; [4]3; *Memoir of the Life of William Ellery Channing* [2]21; *Remarks on the Character and Writings of John Milton* [4]5
chaos [1]119–20, 562, 601, 604, 609, 609n, 610, 663, 669, 669n, 767, 791, [2]562, 578, 583, 615n, 665, 769, 852, 891, 973n, [3]22, 22n, 66, 325, 325n, 333, 417, 493, 493n, 834, 1024, [4]217, 491, 491n, [5]439, [6]5, 5n, 113
coagulation of [1]679; and cosmos [2]583, [4]162, 162n; dove of [2]580, 581n; of fancy [5]726; far from God [4]524, 524n; and God [1]677–8; gods of [2]575; indistinction [1]600; of wills [5]165
chapel(s) [1]30, 349, 522
Chapman, George (?1559–?1634) [1]lxxxvii; *see also* Homer *Chapman's Homer* ed Nicoll, *Whole Works* tr Chapman
chapters, headings of [2]998
character(s) [2]778, [3]182, 886, [4]241, 718, 742, 784, [5]73, 99
bad [6]260; common [5]599; decent [5]189; in drama [3]180; female [4]851; French [5]379; generic [5]771; germ of [4]855; historical [4]797; imaginative [4]598; Jonson's [3]173; loss of [4]689; national [5]195n, [6]16; secret [5]228; shades in [4]844; Shakespeare's [4]783; Spanish [5]104; strength of [4]817; unnatural [1]366; violation of [3]190; want of [4]860
Characteristick der alten Mysterien [5]602n
characteristics, personal [5]407
charcoal [2]69, 1057
animal [5]257
charewoman [2]815
charge, circular [1]465
chariot [3]898, [4]543, 624
fiery [3]40; of sun [5]745
charity/charities [1]123, 203, 204, 330, 504, 751, 755, 878, [2]286, 702, 1051, 1151, 1161, [3]787, [4]180, 238, [5]11, 50, 169, 193, 521, 641, 642, 646, 667
argument addressed to [1]314, 314n–15n; breach of [1]329, 350; Christian [1]13, 266, [4]660, [5]135, 145, [6]260; and faith [5]468, 471–2; and religion [5]562; trial for [1]395
Charke, Ezekiel ("Chark") (fl 1600) [2]1134, 1135
charlatan(s) [3]315, [4]41n
Charlemagne (742–814) [2]779n, [3]134, [5]309, 309n
Charles I, King of England (1600–49) [1]73, 223n, 224n, 249n, 250, 257n, 282, 323n, 334, 359, 374, 401, 728n, [2]62–3, 114, 114n, 260n, 521–4, 796n, 797–8, 798n, 818n, 827, 925, 927n, 928, 929, 933, 940, 941, 942, 946, 949n, 970–1, 1095, 1102n, 1194–5, 1195n, [3]141n, 157, 171, 178, 227, 228, 801, 801n, 803n, 878, [4]74,

74n, 590n, 594, [5]80, 146n, 518n, 526, 661, 670n ("martyred")
age of [4]723; arbitrary monarch [2]358; *BCP* service [2]970–1, 970n; and Buckingham [2]943n; capture of [1]318; and Catholicism [1]222–3; character [2]59, 59n, 60; conflict with parliament [2]947; correspondence [2]1199; cruelties under [1]807; death of [1]278, 289–90, 335, 336, 395, [2]43, 43n; demure Jesuit [5]670; and *Eikon Basilike* [1]336, 336n, [2]948, 948n, [3]798, 798n, [6]184–6, see also *Eikon Basilike*; epitaph on [1]257; execution of [1]292, 1100n; history of [4]675; judges of [6]258; liar [2]947, 948, 1103, 1194n; lie-martyr [5]616; marriage [2]931n; as martyr [1]398, [5]540, 540n, 670n; narrow-minded [2]1104; reign of [1]250, 282, 374, 398, [2]827, 925, 946, [3]632, [4]657, [5]531; and Prince Rupert [2]1196–7, 1196n; Scottish supporters [1]301n; Spanish match [2]931n, 936, *936n*; time of [5]124n; trial [2]969–71; uxorious [2]948, 948n
Charles I, King of Sicily, Count of Anjou (1220–85) [1]502
Charles II, King of England (1630–85) [1]73n, 250, 250n, 257n, 259, 280, 328, 332, 333, 711n, 762, [2]238, 522n, 651, 651n, 818n, 823n, 827, 827n, 835, 1131, 1132, 1201n, [3]141n, 143, 144n, 156, 156n, 539n, 540n, 802, 802n, 803n, 918, 976n, 1079, 1079n, [4]20n, 74, 75, 80, 833, 833n, [5]41, 146, 660, 660n, [6]145, 145n
brotheller [2]1133, [3]802n; cruelties under [1]807; despotic [1]249; in exile [1]333n; promise to Baxter [1]291; reign of [1]245, 762, 796, 803, [3]153, [4]71, 75, 657, [5]80, 531, 553n; Restoration of [1]182, [3]801n; time of [5]659; tyrant [2]818, [3]420, 420n
His Majesties Reasons [1]257n
Charles V, Holy Roman Emperor (1500–58) [3]232n, 756
Charles IX, King of France (1550–74) [2]411n
Charles X, King of Sweden (1622–60) [2]62, 62n
Charles Edward *see* Stuart
Charles Emanuel I, Duke of Savoy (1562–1630) [2]8
Charles, Robert Henry (1855–1931) ed *The Apocrypha and Pseudepigrapha of the Old Testament* [6]138n
Charles-Town Advertiser [4]96
Charlotte, Princess (1796–1817) [2]1188
charm(s) [1]702, [2]1158, [4]626
for cramp [4]11–12, 12n; for foot [1]129; magical [1]264, [6]259
charnel-houses [4]546
Charon (myth) [4]645, 645n
Charron, Pierre (1541–1603) [5]810–11, 810n
charter(s) [2]933, [5]308
of the Church [6]19
Charterhouse *see* London
chasm(s) [2]607, 1000, [3]217, 661, [4]763, [5]354
of causation [1]599; between creator and creature [1]573–4; between finite and infinite [3]855; manifest [5]350
chastity [1]397, 519, [2]694, 926
of elephants [4]489; obligation of [6]13
Chat, Dame (*Gammer Gurton's Needle*) [2]777
Chateaubriand, François René, Vicomte de (1768–1848) [4]185, 185n
Chatham, Earl of *see* Pitt, William, the Elder
Chatterton, Thomas (1752–70) [1]38, [2]126, 351
Chaucer, Geoffrey (c 1343–1400) [1]37, 40, [2]121, 375, 755n, [4]808
and Greek [1]73n; and S. C. Hall [1]52, 53; marginalia by WW [1]76; modernised by Dryden [4]291, 291n; satire [2]759
Canterbury Tales [2]1135; *The House of Fame* [4]809n; *Troilus and Criseyde* [3]1070 q, [4]808n–9n
cheat [1]699
"cheated" [4]185
cheese, moon made of [4]16
cheiromancy [3]645, 779
Cheke/Cheek, Sir John (1514–57) [2]66, 68n, 938, 938n–9n
Chelsea *see* London
chemism [3]125
chemismus [3]948, 949, [4]319–20
chemist(s) [1]779–80, 779n–80n, 817, [2]338, 621, [3]817, 1088, [4]160, 317, 531n, 673, [5]346, 481, 811
Davy as [4]128; experimental [5]346; French [3]127n, 278, 278n, 1032; German [3]1043; modern [1]63, 590, [5]450; present [1]596; prince of [1]650; speculative [3]1001
chemistry [1]410n, 545–52, 779–80, [2]1012, 1015, [3]325, 325n, 790, 843, [4]28, 317, 320, [5]557, 811n
analysis [2]546; animal [3]1002n; bodies in [6]116; Davy's discoveries [4]836; dynamic [2]546; echo of spiritual truths [1]648; ele-

chemistry—*continued*
ments [2]852n, 854–5, 854n; empirical [3]1001; history of [1]545; ideal [5]344; metaphor from [3]709; modern [1]410; nomenclature [1]570n; chemical phenomena [3]1010; present state of [1]650; problems of [2]825; spiritual [1]602; vocabulary of [3]1005; *see also* power(s), chemical
chemy [3]935
Chenevix, Richard (1774–1830) [3]939
chequin [5]846 ("cechin"), 846n
cheres(h) [1]665, 665n
Cherokee country [1]226
Cheronaea [2]416
cherub(s) [2]488, 900
aim of [2]42; carrier [1]590
cherubim [2]488, 920, [3]924, 924n, 1089
Cheshire [3]628, 629, 631, [5]191
Chester [1]871
Chester, John (fl 1798–1801) [1]204n
chestnut [5]838
Chetwode, A. L. (fl 1903) [2]1032
Chevreul, Michel Eugène (1786–1889) [3]943
Chiabrera, Gabriello (1552–1638) [4]290, 290n
Delle opere† [1]clxvi, [2]23, [4]290n
Chiause [3]183
Chicago IL
Newberry Library, marginalia in [6]268; University of Chicago Library, marginalia in [3]881, [6]184
Chichester [2]1103, [5]551n
chicken(s) [1]453, [4]30–1, [5]326
skin [4]705
chiefs, patriarchal [6]94
child/children [2]1201, [3]239, 472, [4]115, 305, 453, 597, 817, [5]74, 278, 281, 323, 366, 598, 634, 651
abstraction in [2]638; begetting of [5]636; of believers [5]654; books for [4]658, 658n; concept of self [3]236–7, 239; defective [4]23; dying [2]922; education of [4]27–8, 28n; fables for [2]1051; in the first form [1]224; of God [1]484, 484n, [3]151, 569, [6]139; handkerchief gardens [2]918; Holy [1]507; and impostures [6]123, 123n; language of [2]535–6; of light [1]605; c.-like [2]1051n; love of [5]223; orphan [1]266, [6]260; quarrels of [5]681; reading [5]174; shown prints [2]508; sick [5]675; between sleep and wake [5]790; teaching [4]306; tossed into air [4]430; unbaptised [1]247; watching them [2]601, 601n; wishes of [2]42; in womb [2]535
childbirth [2]6
childhood [1]285, [2]536, 601, 1175
evil in [4]438; faith of [4]287; reading of [5]821
childishness of alchemy [2]824–5
Chile [3]1077
chiliagon [1]326
Chillingworth, William (1602–44) [1]xcii, [2]24, 290, [3]803n, [4]301n, [5]568, 568n, [6]61
inferior to Stillingfleet [2]31; as a Socinian [2]34
Religion of Protestants [2]24, [3]487, 487n; *The Works Copy A* MT [2]25–31; *Copy B* MT [2]32–41
chimera(s)/chimaera(s) [2]38, 38n, 394, [3]493, [5]575n, 638
chimney(s) [3]952, [4]530
c.-cleaning [3]952n; c.-sweep [3]971
china [3]480
China [2]73, 76, 528, 849, 1023n, [3]631, [4]169, 483, [5]262, 366n, 407n, 651
John Wordsworth's voyage to [1]76; missions to [3]309–10; natives of [5]415; schools in [5]366; trade with [1]724n
Chinese (language) [3]429, [4]243, 243n
Chinese (people) [2]527, 585, [5]130, 353, 406, 407n, 416
music of [4]511; Tao of [4]490; vices of [4]656
Chiny *see* Chunee
Chio [5]837, 838
Chios [2]779n
Chipewyans [2]986n
chirocosmetic [4]705
Chiron (myth) [2]346n
chirurgery, thelematic [5]137; *see also* surgery
Chisholm, Mrs (fl 1823) [5]306, 306n
Chiswell, Richard (1639–1711) [3]486
"chit chat" [1]763, 796
chit chat [1]763n, [2]15
literary [5]527
chivalry [4]811, [5]821n
books of [5]821
Chladni, Ernst Florens Friedrich (1756–1827) [5]294, 294n, 339, 340
Ueber Feuer-Meteore [5]339n
Chloe (Bible), house of [6]42n
chloride [5]438
chlorine [1]589, 590, 613, 822, [2]546n, [3]127, 127n, 1001, 1001n, 1004, 1017, 1020, 1020n, 1021, 1021n, 1022, 1028, 1028n, 1032, [4]315, 315n, 387, 387n, 539n, [5]335, 335n, 343, 344, 346, 346n, 438, [6]116
"Chloroesteesian" [3]1021n
chloros [4]327n

chlorosis [4]785, 785n
choice [3]79, 359n, [4]98, 194, 444, 641, 810
 free [1]4, [5]367; and freedom [2]603, 603n, 641; and will [5]358, 410n; is will [2]678
chole [5]98
choler [4]762
cholera [4]149n
Chorazim [2]256
chorea [2]739, 739n
choriambic(s) [1]377, [3]904
choriambus [1]384
chorography [3]41
chorus [4]731, 731n, 864, 864n
 Greek [4]797
chosen, the [2]1166; *see also* elect
"Christ" [1]281, [5]621, 622
Christ, a [5]603; *see also* Jesus Christ
Christ Church *see* Oxford
Christendom [4]669, [5]51, 196, 282, 407, [6]14
 commonwealth of [4]240; establishment of [5]644; European [5]195; Gotho-celtic [4]43; rights of [5]312; spiritual [3]454; witchcraft in [4]145–6
christening [1]266n
 unchristian foolery [1]42
Christensen, Merton A. (d 1985), coeditor [1]481, [2]373, 415, 435, 478, 505, 519
Christian(s) [1]106, 420, 435, 675, 699, [2]314, 381n, 1153, [4]249, 258, [5]11, 133, 529, 622, 639, [6]68, 294
 abominations attributed to [3]695; against Christians [5]678, 678n; all agree [4]672; assurance of [2]828; atheists [5]716; may baptise [1]266; C of E [5]97; code of [3]487; C as [5]96–7; after Constantine [3]142; of all denominations [5]123; differences between [1]674; duty of [3]688, [6]29; duty to [5]304; early [4]660, [5]85n; of early Church [2]738, 749n, [3]146, 448, 925; and Elpistics [3]642; error of [5]53; faith of [2]558–9, [4]479; first [5]57, 607; French [3]754; full-grown [5]132; generality of [5]182; Gentile [2]811, [4]244, 253, 260, [6]67; gnostic [2]713, 714; assured hope of [2]655; immoral [4]624; imperfect [5]682; inconsistency of [4]623; individual [5]561; and Jews [6]146; Jewish [1]833, [2]437n, 470–1, 710, [3]1084, [4]244, 252, 260, [5]522n, 624, 645, [6]220; Judaising [6]69; life of [2]998, 998n–9n, [5]650; lowest rank [4]251; marks of [4]238, [5]491; mass of [2]741, 1080; in name only [2]1162; needs of [1]877; new-made [5]644; of 19th century [5]51; nominal [3]776, [5]385; NT determination of [5]189; *omne et nihil* [2]199; opposition [2]1156; orthodox [2]1034; Palestinian [4]250, 251, 252, 253, [6]67; persecution of [2]739–40, [3]694, 695; philosophic [2]695; and prayer [5]520; primitive [2]39, [3]603, [4]514, 627, [5]51; privilege of [6]54; problem of [2]1143; progression of [5]10; Protestant [2]666, 1156, [5]308; regenerate [3]478; religion of [4]479; in Rhodes [5]841; Roman [3]458; in Roman Empire [3]143; rule of [5]562; rules for [5]578; Scriptural [5]179; self-ignorant [1]302; serious [2]273; must feel sin within [1]819; sincere [5]665, [6]260; slave-owners [6]35; soul of [5]516; state consisting of [2]58; as subjects [1]833; superstition of [4]299–300; true [3]669, [5]15, 133; unlearned [5]513; vital [1]621; warmest [2]1062; world of [5]651; young [2]343
Christian (in Bunyan) [1]812, 813, 814, 820, 821, 821n, 822n
Christian Examiner [2]952n, [4]5
Christian Observer [2]651n, 1177n
Christian Remembrancer [6]12
Christianising of slaves [3]1082
Christianism
 Pagan [5]670; Roman [5]670
Christianity [1]51, 297n, 307n, 438, 813, [2]931, [3]443, [4]668, 669, [5]169, 329, 583, 621, [6]23, 134
 not *a* Church [4]20; adversaries of [3]698, 698n; affairs of [1]447; apologising for [5]513, 513n; arguments against [4]651; attribute of [5]480; beliers of [3]586; ceremonial part [2]655; characteristic doctrine [5]497; Christian dispensation [3]743; C's faith in [2]36; common philosophy of [2]36; corruption(s) of [1]529, [5]669n, [6]13n; criteria of [2]319; defence of [2]1080; defended against its defenders [3]562; and deism [2]434; divine philosophy [5]385; divinity of [5]822; doctrine of [1]303, [2]454; doctrine of redemption [5]524; effects of [2]1081, [6]14; essential [3]669; establishment of [2]712; evidence(s) of *see* evidence(s); faith its object [1]503; first principles [2]716; foundations of [5]529; founders of [2]1080; fundamental article [5]57, 617; genuine [1]807, [3]625; glory of [2]278; importance of gospels in [5]516; Grotian defence [1]244; historic [5]644; historical [2]247, 454, [3]729, 926, [5]642; fact of history [1]446, [2]204; history of [5]127; idea of [6]57; and idolatry [2]1125; institution of [5]560; and Jewish history [1]710; Johannine [1]299n; and Judaism [2]504, [3]470; Kant's system friendly

Christianity—*continued*
to [2]185–6; light and energy [3]72; mean conception of [3]622; means of establishing [2]1061; moral effect [2]321; mysteries in [1]201, [2]671, [5]82; orthodox [3]662; paganised [2]304; pantheistic [2]199; paralysis of [5]515; Pauline [2]469–70; pentad of [2]290; and philosophy [5]384–5, 766–7; as philosophy [4]663; popular [2]1007; powers glorified by [5]518; practical [4]626; presuppositum of [2]1106; no pretext for sedition [4]481; primitive [5]532; principles of [2]697; a process [3]697; professors of [1]675; progression of [5]560–1; purposes of [1]473; real and nominal [3]454; offers regeneration [2]495; accords with reason [1]576; revealed [5]677; rule of [5]43; satire on [5]416; scheme against [4]145; scheme of Christian faith [3]919–20; and slavery [6]28–9; sophism on behalf of [2]253; and Spinozism [3]23; spirit of [6]28–9; spiritual proof of [1]302; spread of [4]651n, [5]643; and Stoicism [1]172–3; subversive of [5]557; success of [5]142–3; supernatural in [5]746; sure signs [4]625; teaching of [4]306–7; triads in [5]235; tri-unity *is* C. [3]369; true practical [1]305; true skin of [1]815n; truth of [5]72; Unitarians as demi-semi-quaver of [1]346; victory of [4]146; vital truths [2]343; whole scheme of [6]19
Christmas [1]327, [2]921
Christoduly [2]662, [4]299n
Christolatry [2]662, [4]299n
"Christopaedia" [4]41, 41n
Christopaedia [2]35n, 266, 266n, 270, 487, 661n, [3]49n, 730n, [4]55, [6]64, 64n, 68, 68n, 69n; see also *evangelium/evangelia infantiae*
Christopher, St (?3rd century) [3]779
Christophilus (in Lacunza) [3]463
Christ's Hospital *see* Hertford; London
chromium [5]261
"chronical" [1]497, 497n
chronical and temporal [1]497
chronicle(s) [2]123, 1053
chroniclers [5]561
"chronochorhistorical" [3]926, 926n
chronology [1]446, [2]387, 902
of Bible [2]387, 387n, [6]292–4
Chronos [2]578n
chrysalis [4]647n
Chrysippus (c 280–206 BC) [1]174, [5]225
Chrysler, Walter Percy (1875–1940) [1]clxxiii, [2]1169
chrysopoets [2]824n
chryso-poietic [1]546, 546n
chrysor [2]576, 576n
Chrysor (myth) [2]576
Chrysostom, John, St (c 347–407) [1]853, [2]674, 924, 924n, [4]643, 650, 650n, [5]395 q, 518, 575, 575n, 601, 684–5, 684n
prayer [1]327n
De incomprehensibili Dei natura tr Harkins [6]179–80 q; *Homilies* [5]518n
Chrystsostom *see* Chrysostom
Chunee [4]488 ("Chiny"), 488n
"church" [1]837, [2]39, 680, 680n, [3]50, [5]638
church(es)/Church(es) [2]655, 1202, [3]416, 450, [4]190, [5]52, 192, 507, 569, 631, 632, 663, [6]79
abusive sense of [1]529; admission into [5]622; after 145 AD [5]677; ages of [5]516; Alexandrine [5]54; the alone saving [1]232; ancient [5]578; Anglican [1]271, [6]261, *see also* C. of England *below*; of Antichrist [4]21n; anti-Christian [5]178; Apostolic [2]471, [6]43, 55, of England and Ireland [5]75; of Asia [3]422; C.-Aspist [5]578; attendance at [2]1156; authority of [1]711, [3]48, [5]568; body of Christ [3]545; Brahman [5]177; and canon [2]446; Catholic [1]307, 339, [2]30, 205, 707n, 724, 1138, [3]20, 36, 70, 369, 686, 1069, [4]33, [5]78, 123, 166, 210, 418, 491, 639, [6]14, 15–16, *see also* c., Roman Catholic *below*; central [1]349; centre is Christ [3]72–3; ceremonies of [1]329; child of [2]1034; Christ in [1]434; in Christ [2]1139, [3]21; of Christ [1]315, 355, 452, 527, 531, 806, 806n, [2]21, 295, 682, 747, 747n, 1136, 1136n, [3]34, 453–4, 756, [4]20n, [5]144, 164, 467, 529, 561, 608, [6]14, 14n; under Christ [1]528, 531
Christian [1]275, 446, 530, 531, [2]288, 448, 560, 796, 937, [3]147, 424, 474, [4]43, 244, [5]10, 127n, 128, 644, [6]23, 28, 60, 264, charter of [6]19; Christ's [1]710; Christ's sayings about [5]535; of the Circumcision [5]645; collective wisdom [5]530; of common sense [5]795; communion with [6]56; comprehensive [1]307; confused with clerisy [3]156; Constitutional [1]809; Corinthian [2]656, [3]691; corruption(s) of [2]707, 724, 740, [5]463; councils of *see* Council(s); Cyprian's definition [1]846; damage to [2]24; definition of [2]195, 195n; dignitaries of [2]57; diocesan [1]245, 250, 253, 254, 257, 308, 338; discipline [1]309, 339–40, 341, [6]22; doctrine of [5]162; early

[1]543, [2]375, [3]146, 766, 1084–5, [4]646, [5]7n, 667n, 669n, [6]307; in the East [2]657; Eastern [1]267, 311, 345, [3]689, [5]551, 577n, [6]260 ("Oriental"), *see also* c., Greek *below*; edification of [2]286; effects on [5]579

C. of England [1]263, 295, 308, 309, 316n, 317, 322n, 355–60, 805–6, 805n, 809, 837, [2]20, 40, 274n, 290, 297, 496n, 650, 980n, 1038, 1101, 1150n, 1198, [3]144n, 157n, 163, 167, 308, 440n, 823, 1089, 1090, [4]172n, 177, 298n, 336, 366n, 551, 568, 621n, 630n, 631, 641, 659n, 746n, [5]5n, 8n, 31n, 81n, 97, 129n, 146, 152, 155n, 173, 384, 389, 467n, 471, 491, 495, 503n, 507, 508n, 540, 544n, 558, 566n, 574, 591, 640, 646n, 683n, [6]29n, 93, 258n, the most apostolic [6]43, apostolic succession [3]720, Articles of *see* Articles of Religion, authority of [2]1098, on baptism [6]42, 42n, beauty of [2]651, best period of [3]459n, bestirring herself [1]514, biography of [1]844, bishops of [5]503, brand-mark on [5]616, bulwark of toleration [2]651, burial service [1]127n, Catechism [1]10n, 509n q, [5]393n q, ceremonies [1]253, under Charles I [1]250, [2]925, under Charles II [1]245, 250, C's attachment to [4]172, constitution of [5]568, Convocation of [5]532n, credulity in [3]921, 921n, creeds of [5]568, defended [5]499, derived from RC Church [2]1097n, discipline of [5]568, Donne worthy of [2]333, edging towards Roman Catholicism [2]675, enemy of freedom [2]951, 951n, epochs of [1]358, error of [6]12, establishment [5]508, 508n, fault of early divines [2]684, founders of [5]505, glories of [3]918, high church [1]352, 357, [3]146, high-church tendencies [3]153n, honour of [5]521, injures only itself [1]275, lay readers [2]1156n, liberal spirit [6]264, liturgy [3]368–9, martyrs of [3]561, misfortune of [4]549–50, and Moravians [3]493n, neglect of hymns [5]512n, objects of [6]14, obligations of member [2]352, overthrow of [5]531, and Presbyterians [2]1043n, present and former [4]179, present condition [5]49, proper motto [6]259, reconciles tradition and scripture [3]686, reformed [1]356, after Restoration [6]263, sacramental ritual of [5]568, sacraments [5]398n, saints of [6]82, schisms in [1]321–2, a sect [1]527, 531, separation from [2]912–13, sign of cross in [2]1158, stars of [5]661, under Stuarts [2]1041, no occasion for subscription [2]531, tolerance of [5]509n, toleration in [3]368, 368n, two eras [2]264–5. *See also* Articles of Religion; *BCP*; c., Anglican *above*; c., established *below*

English [1]271, 478, [4]306, 643, [5]548, Fathers of *see* Fathers; of Ephesus [1]485; episcopal [1]321n, [5]616; errors of [2]919; established [1]254, 281, 353, 865, [2]48, 838, [3]107, 156, 369, [4]642, 658, [5]67, 521–2, 532, *see also* C. of England *above*; establishment [1]322, [3]70, [5]67, 662n; fabric [5]510n; faith of [4]200, [5]665; fallibility of [2]813; fallible [6]42–3; Fathers of *see* Fathers; first Christian [5]517; forms of [2]1034; Founder of [1]448; French [4]192 ("Gallican"); general [1]307; of Geneva [5]505; government [1]294, 339, [2]1136, 1175, [5]537; governors [1]309; Greek [1]267, [2]423, 705, 1162, [5]527, 576, 835, [6]167, *see also* c., Eastern; guardian angel of [5]588; Head of [1]456; Hebrew [2]400, [3]36, [4]62; heretical [6]71; history [1]512, [2]649–86, 698–752, 808–14, 1097, [3]231n, [5]812; Holy Catholic Apostolic [3]71n; an idea [5]638; idea of [1]355, [5]662, 662n; ideal [3]472, [5]638; independent [1]307, 320; infallible [1]313–14, [2]30; infant baptism in [5]659; interpretation of [5]662; interprets Scripture [5]572; invisible [3]72–3; in Ireland [4]21; as Israel [2]51–2; of Jerusalem [2]705, [6]61

Jewish [1]282, 706, [2]156, 495, 560, 567, [3]424, 446, 455, 470, 471, 472, 595, [4]62, 244, 471, [5]11, 177, 504n, 523n, 607; Jewish-Christian [1]486; Latin [2]21, 703, 917, [3]533, 994, [5]505, 576, 578, 627, 639, [6]12, 167, *see also* c., Roman Catholic *below*; low [2]26; Lutheran [4]670, [5]81n, 540, 548; Lutheran Episcopal [5]152; machinery of [4]173; Manicheanism in [2]721; marriage of [3]684; mediaeval [5]143n; members of [2]1142; membership [1]324, [5]129; militant [1]427, [5]607; misfortune of [2]749; mixed [6]69; Moravian [5]130, 149, 149n, 151, 152; Mother [5]510, 510n, [6]68; national [1]233, 233n, 263, 264, 268, 321, 339, 531, 534, 806, 806n, 809, [2]20, 69, 72, 295, 333, 747, 747n, 943, 943n, 1136, 1136n, 1139, 1142, [3]231, 759, 874, 874n, [4]20n, [5]67, 78n, 179, [6]22, 260, and universal [1]531; necessary for [5]568; New *see* Swedenborg: New Church; no C., no Christ [1]310, 310n; overseer of [5]537; of Pales-

church(es)/Church(es)—*continued*
tine [2]709; parish [1]349; parochial [5]129; parties in [5]521; Pauline [1]486; peace of [1]330; pentad [1]806, [2]290; persecution of [5]596; policy [5]433; power of [1]308, 318–19, 329, [6]55; prelatic [1]347; prerogatives of [1]330; Presbyterian [4]591; primitive [1]339, [2]41, 304, [4]473, [5]575, 578, 582, 650, 677, 683; as profession [2]321; proper power of [1]805; property of [1]359, [2]943; Protestant [1]258, 345, [2]260, 1162, [4]24n, 172, [6]291–2; on Purgatory [5]605; Reformation [3]561; Reformed [1]314, [2]916, 1143, [4]669, 670, [5]128, 504; regenerated [1]310; reunion of [5]548; revenues of [1]356
Roman [1]258, 267, [2]40, 669–70, 1162, [3]212, 234, [5]177–8, 548, 561, 835, *see also* c., Roman Catholic; Roman Catholic [1]247, 305, 344, 846, 848, 855–6, [2]480n, 663, 1043, 1097n, 1139, 1140n, 1149, [3]595n, 645n, 772n, 775, 1069, [4]68n, 632n, [5]143n, 396n, 495, [6]16n, 118, 291–2, councils of [3]234, errors of [1]203 ("Romish"), [2]707, 707n, fundamental assumption [1]313–14, hay and straw of [3]310, idolatry [2]1043, influence on fine arts [3]993–4, and James I [2]936n, Latin in [2]653, and Laud [4]177, Protestant revolt against [3]232n, power of [4]20n, regime [3]757n, and F. Schlegel [1]145, in Spain, Italy, Sicily, Germany [1]845, transubstantiation [1]861, doctrine of works [2]298n. *See also* Catholic(s); Catholicism; c., Catholic, Latin, Roman *above*, of Rome, Romish, Western *below*; doctrine(s), RC; papist(s); Roman Catholic(s); Roman Catholicism; Romanism; Romanist(s)
of Rome [1]478, [2]269, 274n, 681, [3]189, 720, [4]550–1, 568, 664, [5]8n, 504, 543, 565, 574, 577, 580, 611, 632, 636, 660n, [6]69, religious forms of [5]644, tyranny of [5]509n, *see also* c., Roman Catholic *above*; Romish [1]203, 311, 514, 530, 805, 844, [2]26, 673–4, 1140, 1162, [3]42, 70, 85, 523, 993–4, [4]195, [5]105, 128, 568, 636, 656, 665, *see also* c., Roman Catholic *above*; ruin of [5]135; Scotch [3]425, 425n, [5]540; of Scotland [1]531, 866n, [2]1136, [3]59, 540, 540n, [4]657n, [5]67, 68n, history [1]850; Scoto-anglican [3]540; Scottish [5]660, [6]47; and scripture [2]40, 289, 290, 295, 680–1, [3]451; seven [5]494n, [6]168, 168n; Spanish [4]43; spirit of Socinianism in [5]516; spiritual [2]1142; and state [1]249, 275, 318–19, 360, 807, [3]72, [5]527, 532, 661, 733; superstition in [2]725; Swedenborgian *see* Swedenborg; three forms of [1]527; tradition of [4]256, [5]630; true [1]421, 521, 846, [5]570; true and orthodox [5]568; Turkish [5]177; two-foldness of [3]1084; unity of [5]147, [6]15; universal [1]294, 339, 447, 492, 531, [2]663, 701, [5]78n, 503, 659, [6]71; vices destroy [3]775; visible [2]30, 1175, [3]72, 73, [5]642, 644; voice of [1]339; Western [1]267, 311, 345, [2]657, 674, 1199, [3]689, [5]10, 127, 551, 627, [6]260, *see also* c., Roman Catholic *above*; earliest writings of [1]817
Church, Frederic C. *The Italian Reformers 1534–1564* [2]292n q
Church, Thomas (1707–56) [5]148
Churchill, Charles (1731–64) [1]38, [2]768, 768n–9n
The Duellist [2]768n–9n; *The Ghost* [2]768n
Churchill, John, 1st Duke of Marlborough (1650–1722) [4]180
Churchill, Sarah (née Jennings), Duchess of Marlborough (1660–1744) [2]84
churchman/churchmen [1]358, 359, 509, [2]835, 1041, [3]70, 883, [5]433, 521, 532
ambitious [6]19; exemplar of [5]510; high [3]156, [4]24, [5]636; moral corruption [2]740; Oxford [1]531; Parliamentary [1]313; of Restoration [3]163; Roman [5]495; of 17th century [2]1100; unamiable [2]1097
Churchman, John (fl 1582) [2]914n
Churunti (myth) [4]489–90
chyle [3]1002n
ciarlatan [4]41, 41n
Cibber, Colley (1671–1757) [1]402, *402n*, [2]769n, 779
An Apology for the Life of Mr. Colley Cibber [1]402n; *Love Makes the Man* [1]402n; *The Non-Juror* [1]402n; *The Rival Fools* [1]402n
Ciccarelli, Lorenzo (fl 1712–30) *see* Boccaccio *Opere* ed Ciccarelli
Cicero, Marcus Tullius (106–43 BC) [1]cvii, 174n, 315 ("Tully"), [2]68, 276, 318, 693–4, 695, 763n, 923, 950, 969n, [3]509n, 618, 767, [4]80n, 82n, 99, 336n, 508, [5]128n, 581, 581n, 689, 689n, 726n, 747, 747n, [6]4, 4n
age of [1]150; letters of [1]512, [2]476, 476n; manuscripts [2]36; spirit of [5]414; spurious work [2]36n; style [2]763; texts of [2]36
Academicae quaestiones [2]800n; *Ad Brutum* [5]128n; *De divinatione* [2]1173n; *De finibus* [5]612n, [6]3 q, tr Rackham [6]3 q; *De natura deorum* [2]36n, [5]12n; *De officiis* [4]720n, [6]216, 216n; *De republica* [2]923n;

Divinatio in Caecilium [6]99n; *Letters to Atticus* [2]476n; *Tusculanae disputationes* (*Tusculan Disputations*) [2]792
Ciceronianism [2]36
Cilicia [2]733
cima [1]421, 421n
Cimarosa, Domenico (1749–1801) [4]168, 169n
Gli Orazi ed i Curazi [4]168n–9n
cinnamon [5]105
Cintra [5]316n
Convention of [2]100n, 101n, 794, 940, 940n
cipher *see* cypher
Circe (myth) [6]99 ("Circëia")
circle(s) [1]679, [2]671, 671n, 1110, [3]79, 80, 85, 118, 341, 349, 357, 460, [4]46, 108–9, 112–13, 115, [5]427, 431, 750, 815n, [6]174
argument in *see* argument; concentric [2]747, [4]527, [5]548; of contract [5]299; defined [2]1183, 1183n; demonstrable [5]656; equal radii [2]252; of fire [4]223; as God [4]224, 224n; God as [1]562n, 564, [2]271, [3]729, [5]407; idea of [5]209, 209n; infinite [2]638; intuition of [4]109; living [5]815; mathematical [2]793, 793n; never open [2]1018–19; perfect [4]224; point in [1]507; pure [2]425, [3]967; and radii [5]412, 412n; radii of [4]108–9; of sciences [5]655–6; and square [5]617; square [2]75, 853, [5]202n; squaring of [4]444, [5]811n; squared [3]680; three-cornered [5]450
circle-animal [3]357
Circuitor [3]436, [5]85, 422, 422n, [6]97, 101
circulation [2]1167, [3]46
circumcision [2]660–1, [4]249–50, 251–2, [5]623–4, 623n, 647, 649, 830–1, 830n
Apostle of the *see* Peter, St; Christians of the [2]474
circumference [1]646, [3]357, [4]443, [5]131, 548
"circumincession" [5]704n
circumincession [4]400n, 682, 682n
circumscribing [2]626
circumscription [5]815
circumstance(s) [3]520
accidents of [1]541; influence of [5]66
circumstantials [1]254
Cistercian [5]121n
citadel [6]60
citizen(s) [1]833, [2]1148, [3]142, 148, 367, 818, [4]251, 313
duties of [4]735, [6]60; fellow [5]280, 304; non-c. [5]315; unhired [5]381; useful [5]103, [6]6
city/cities [1]164, 783, [3]63, 468, 480, 806, [6]325
central [3]108; destruction of [5]624; at a distance [5]321; free [2]1017; of God [3]62; symbolical [3]468; vast [2]514
civil war(s) [1]833, [2]124–5, 129, [4]145
Civil War(s) (in England) [1]230, 833, [2]512, 926, 1195, 1196n, 1200, [3]801n, [4]307n, [5]146n, 503n, 539n, 596
"Civil War Tracts" MT [2]42–3; 357
civilians [1]686
civilisation [2]530, 943, 1114, [3]984
and cultivation [1]132, 132n, 356, [5]253, 253n–4n; general [5]301; history of [1]148; progress of [5]834; traces of [1]783
civility [2]300, [5]103, [6]58
Clairvaux [2]983n
clairvoyance [2]402, 551n, [3]377n, [4]496, 536n, 592, [5]183n, 404n, 726. *See also* clear-seeing; animal magnetism
clairvoyant(s) [2]551, [3]376–7, 377n, 389n, 717n, [4]271, 496, 497n, 536, 592, [5]391, 391n, 404; *see also* inside-seers(s)
Clapham Sect [1]322n, 736n, [3]602n
Clare Market *see* London
Clarence, Duke of *see* William Albert Victor
Clarendon Code [3]157n, 801n
Clarendon, Earl(s) of *see* Hyde, Edward and Henry
claret [1]379, 379n
Clarges, Sir Thomas (fl 1810) [3]936
Clark, William Andrews, Jr (d 1934) [4]69
Clarke, Adam (?1762–1823) *see* Bible: NT: *The New Testament . . . with a Commentary* ed Clarke
Clarke, Charles Cowden (1787–1877) [2]65n
Clarke, James Freeman (1810–88) *see* De Wette *Theodor* tr Clarke
Clarke, James Stanier (?1765–1834) *see* Dicconson *Life of James the Second* ed Clarke
Clarke, Mary Anne (1776–1852) [2]100n
Clarke, Samuel (1599–1683) [1]259
Clarke, Samuel ("Clark") (1675–1729) [1]458n, 492, [3]165, 165n, 814n, [4]111, [6]71, 71n, 73, 74, 74n
The Scripture Doctrine of the Trinity [3]165n, [6]71n
Clarkson, Thomas (1760–1846) [1]31, [2]587n, [4]241, 241n
letter to [1]lxxxvn, [3]643n q; supplier of books to C [1]xcvii
History of the Abolition of the Slave Trade [2]983n; *Memoirs of . . . William Penn*

Clarkson, Thomas—*continued*
[3]928n; *A Portraiture of Quakerism* [2]811n q, [3]928n
"Clasio, Luigi" *see* Fiacchi, Luigi
class(es) [1]220, [3]63–4, 1025, [4]23, 196
governing [1]359; higher [4]580, 594; influencive [5]362; labouring [2]847; learned [1]355, [3]109; lower [4]633; lower and middle [2]1062; manufacturing [2]1192; middle [2]159, 159n; privileged [2]562, [3]358; representatives of [5]362; specific [2]159
class-fellow [5]642
classic(s) [4]723
English [5]581; favourite [3]891. *See also* Greek; Latin
Classic Fairy Tales ed I. A. and P. Opie [4]630n
classification [2]146, [3]1032, 1035
clumsy [3]629; scheme of [4]500; scientific [2]146; systems of [1]537; terms of [3]1025; words of [2]12
Claude, Jean (1619–87) [4]294 ("John")
Claude Lorraine (Claude Gelée) (c 1600–82) [4]337, 337n
C. L. Glass [4]337, 337n
Claudia (in B&F) [1]396
Claudianus, Claudius (Claudian) (c 365–c 408) [3]413, [5]386 q
Quae exstant ed Heinsius MT [2]44–5; *In Eutropium* [2]44
Claudio (*Measure for Measure*) [4]694
Claudius (fiction) [5]420
Claudius I (Tiberius Claudius Nero Germanicus) (10 BC–AD 54) [1]486n, [3]928, 929n
Claudius, Matthias (1740–1815) [3]97
Claussen, Bruno (fl 1931) *see* Borchling and Claussen
Clavigero, Francisco Xavier, Abbé (1731–87) *History of Mexico* tr C. Cullen [5]337n q
clay(s) [1]548, [2]1193, [3]419, 600, 600n, 633, 850, [5]202n
Clayton, John (1780–1865) [4]631
"clean" and "unclean" [1]417, 417n
cleansing [5]650
Cleanthes (c 331–232 BC) [1]174n, [3]934, 935n, [5]225
Clearchus (c 450–401 BC) [4]147
clear-seeing [5]726; *see also* clairvoyance
cleavers [5]295
clemency [2]934
Clemens Alexandrinus *see* Clement of Alexandria
Clemens, James B. (fl 1944) [1]clxxiii, [2]963
Clement VII (Giulio de' Medici), Pope (1478–1534) [1]831
Clement XIV (Lorenzo Ganganelli), Pope (1705–74) [1]213
Clément, Nicolas (c 1778–1841) [3]941
Clement of Alexandria (Titus Flavius Clemens), St (c 150–c 215) [1]491, 491n, [2]33n, 665n q, 706, 713n, [3]446n, [5]228, 547, 548, 548n, 563n, 571 q, 572, 572n, 637
Adumbrationes in Epistolam Judae [2]477n; *Opera* [2]477n; *Paedagogus* [3]687–8 q, 688n, 689; *Stromateis* [3]504, [5]225–6; *Writings* tr William Wilson [3]688 q, 690 q
Clement of Rome (Clemens Romanus), St (d ?101) [1]312, 312n, 852, [2]441, 442
Epistles [1]491n; *see also* Bible: Apocrypha: NT: 1 and 2 Clement
Cleopatra (69–30 BC) [1]799, [2]878, 919n, [3]897
Cleopatra (*Antony and Cleopatra*) [4]737, 761
Cleremont (in B&F) [1]395
clergy [1]340, 341, 352, 353, 355, 526, [2]321, 935, 948, [3]70, 155, 774, 874–80, 1089, 1090, [4]665, [5]79, 175, 507, 662, 684, [6]23, 47
Arminian [1]327, [5]495; Calvinistic [5]469; celibacy of [3]310, 785, 785n, [6]13; C of E [5]144n, 527; court [5]531; dignified [1]250; dissenting [6]304; efficacy [2]1156; emancipation of [6]14; Episcopalian [5]146; established [2]294–5, [4]657; high church [1]290; libraries of [3]877; of the Lord [5]538; Lutheran [4]269, [5]634; married [1]356; monastic [6]17; on Mosaic law [2]184; nonconforming [6]258; papistical [5]144; pastoral [2]937n; power of [1]833; prelatic [2]1156; read sermons [3]732; regular [5]162; responsibility of [1]234; role of [1]529–30; Romish [1]865; not salaried dependents [1]359; Scotch [4]657; sequestered [5]146, 146n; since 1688 [2]1167 ("1668"); taxes [5]532; Tory [1]808n. *See also* divine(s); minister(s); priest(s)
clergyman/clergymen [1]529–30, [2]475, [3]107, [4]272n, [5]67, 538, [6]23
greedy [4]630n; idle [5]66
"clerisy" [1]355n
clerisy [1]322n, 531, [2]57–8, 72, 295, 338, 943, 943n, 1138, [3]50, 51n, 156, 156n, 874, [6]14n
national [1]528, 529, [5]78, [6]14, 23; Roman [6]13
clerk(s) [2]294, [3]666
articled [6]79

Cleve, C. (fl 1700) [2]102
clew of argument [1]426
Cliffbank [3]635
Clifford, Anne, Countess of Dorset, Pembroke, and Montgomery (1590–1676) [1]lxvii, [2]49, 63–4, 119n, [5]834n
Clifford, George, 3rd Earl of Cumberland (1558–1605) [2]119n
Clifford, John de, 7th Baron Clifford (?1435–61) [2]64
Clifford, Margaret, Countess of Cumberland (?1560–1616) [2]117
Clifford of Lanesborough, Lord *see* Boyle, Charles
Clifford, Thomas, 1st Baron Clifford (1630–73) [1]353n
Clifton Pneumatic Institute [1]163n
climate(s) [1]539, 541, 878, [2]74, 417–18, 700, 700n, 1113, [3]679, 976, [4]164, 258, [5]252, 271, 271n, 309, 349n
  cold [4]788
climax [2]241
clinamen [1]307, 307n, [4]168, [6]75, 75n
Clinton, Harry (in Brooke) [1]723, 732, 736
Clissold, Augustus (?1797–1882) *see* Swedenborg *The Economy of the Animal Kingdom* tr Clissold
"Clito" [3]786
clitoris [1]779, 779n
Clitus Mela (d 328 BC) [3]786n
Cloanthes (in Virgil) [6]205 ("Cleanthes")
clock(s) [2]555, [3]589
  idea of [6]172–3, 172n–3n
clog [1]658, 658n
Clonard [1]213n
closet [4]712, [5]157, 296, 512
cloth, outward [1]815
clothes [2]617
  best [1]758
cloud(s) [1]706, [2]489, 887, [3]35, 454, 454n, 616–17, [5]157, 176, 296, 383, 615, 670–1, 677
  coming in [3]447; of darkness [3]248; gorgeous [5]371; of metaphysics [5]74; c.-specks [5]491
Cloud, Joseph (c 1770–1845) [3]942
cloudage [4]400
Clowes, John (1743–1831) [5]463
Clowes, William (1780–1851) [5]135n
clown(s) [4]185, [5]175
  and Hamlet [4]858
"club" [4]331
club [1]141, [2]474
  c.-regulation [1]340
club, iron [2]1155
"cluck" [1]421, 421n
clump [2]431
clutch [5]664
Clutterbuck, Henry (1767–1856) [6]38
  Inquiry into the Seat and Nature of Fever [6]38n
co-acervation [1]496, 496n
coach [3]946, [4]450
coacruation [1]740, 740n
coadunation [1]175, *175n*, [2]267, [3]266, 266n, [5]15 ("coadinatively")
co-agency [6]302
co-agent(s) [5]195, 548
coagulation of chaos [1]679
coagulum [5]445, 545–6, 545n
coal [3]157, 1000, [4]528, 538
  c.-blasts [2]746; glowing [5]244
coarseness [3]171
coasters, piratical [2]88
"coasting" [4]812, 812n
coat [5]680
  powdered [2]817
Coat, Mrs [3]1013
cobalt [3]817, 817n, [5]261, [6]245
Cobbett, William (1762–1835) [1]860, 860n, [2]211n, 900, 900n, [3]146, 146n, [6]46, 46n
cobbler [4]650, [5]366, 814n
Cobbler (*Julius Caesar*) [4]805
cobbleries [1]683
Cobham [1]90n
Coblenz [3]160n
Cobolt(s) (myth) [4]594
Coburn, Kathleen Hazel (1905–91) [1]cliv, [2]526
  owner of annotated books [1]206, [6]32; *see also* Coleridge, S. T. VI *Philosophical Lectures* (1949), IX *Inquiring Spirit*, XII *Notebooks*; Sara Hutchinson *Letters* ed Coburn
cobweb(s) [1]764, 797, [3]1088, [4]57, 197
Cocceius, Johannes (Johann Koch) (1603–69) [1]lxxiii, cxxii, clxi, 416, 443n, 458n, [2]503, 504, 505n, 506, [3]438, 438n, [5]139, 139n, 167, 167n, [6]59n
  Commentarius in Epistolas Pauli [2]46; *Opera omnia*† [1]443n, 451, 451n, [2]46–7, 504n, 506n, [5]139n, 624n
Cochläus (Johann Dobneck) (1479–1552) [3]656
Cochrane, Nathaniel Day (fl 1806–16) [4]534, 534n
Cochrane, Spencer (fl 1810) [3]938
cock [2]344, [3]587n, 975
  c.-crow [4]841; c.-fighting [5]97; shy [1]259, [5]35, 35n; c.-sure [3]197, 213n; c.-surety [3]213

Cock Robin [3]438 q, 438n q
cockade [5]675
cockatrice [1]436
Cocker, Edward (1631–75) *Cocker's Arithmetic* [3]808, 808n
Cockermouth [2]529n
Cockney College [2]955n
coconut [4]30n
cod [4]96, 692, 692n, 755, 782
code(s)
  esoteric [5]228n; moral [3]455; national [3]112; religious [2]146; sacred [1]539
Coelho, Gonzalo (fl 1504) [5]102n
Coelites [2]974n
Coenobite [2]982
co-factor [5]784
coffee-house [3]222
coffin(s) [1]764, 797, [3]373
Coffman, Ralph J. *Coleridge's Library* [4]545
cogitability [5]790
cogitanda [1]575
cogitatio [4]112, 227, [5]210
  c. infinita [1]566; *c. sine centro* [5]710
cogitation and matter [6]238
cogito [4]122–3
  c. ergo sum [2]629, 629n, [3]95
cognition [1]634, [2]192
  distinct [5]409
co-heirs [1]339
cohen see *kohen*
Cohen, Salomon Jacob (1772–1845) *see* Bible: OT: *Die Heilige Schrift* ed Cohen
coherence [1]573, 589, [4]314n, [5]263–4
  power of [1]596
"coherentific" [1]780n
coherismus [4]314, 314n
cohesion [1]589, 776, 862, [2]249, 855, [3]129, 325, 325n, 1004, 1061, [4]314n, 395, 395n, [6]245. *See also* adhesion and cohesion; centrality and cohesion
coin(s) [1]123, [3]67
coinages [1]634n, [3]926n
coincidence(s) [1]350, 834, [3]216, [4]537, 788, [5]141, 372, [6]294
Coindet, Jean François (1774–1836) [4]164
co-inherence(s) [1]635, 643, [2]865, [3]424, 449, 558, [4]676, [5]458
co-instantaneity [4]416
coir [4]30, 30n
coition [1]768
coitus [2]857
Coke, Sir Edward (1552–1634) [2]931n, [3]981
Col [2]584
Colborne, Henry *see* Colburn
Colburn, Henry (d 1855) *A New System of Practical Domestic Economy* [2]616n
Colburn, Zerah (1804–39) [4]505n
Colby, J. P. [6]251
Colchester [2]211n
Colchester, Baron *see* Abbot, Charles
Colchester Gazette [3]986
cold [1]775, [2]1112
  and warm [5]706–7
cole [3]68
Colebrooke, Sir George (1729–1808) *Six Letters on Intolerance* MT [2]48
Colenso, John William (1814–83) [4]334
Coleorton [1]lxxxvi, 218n, [2]4, 222n, 245, 947n, 1191, [3]400, [6]187, 194
Colepeper, John, 1st Baron (1600–60) [2]358 ("Culpepper"), 358n, [3]798
Coleridge, Alwyne Hartley Buchanan (b 1914) [1]clxxiii, [4]99
  coeditor [2]50, 92; owner of annotated books [1]411, [3]993
Coleridge, Anthony Derwent (1916–68) [1]clxxiii, [2]650, 967, [5]853
  owner of annotated books [2]649–50
Coleridge, Arthur Duke (1830–1913), owner of annotated books [3]838
Coleridge, Berkeley (1798–99) [1]409
  birth [1]412n, 413; death [1]671, 671n
Coleridge, Bernard John Seymour, 2nd Baron Coleridge (1851–1927) [1]clvin, clxxiii, 816, [5]463
  owner of annotated books [5]48, 403
  The Story of a Devonshire House [2]91
Coleridge, Derwent (1800–83) [1]lxvii, cli, 39, 413, 480, 801, [2]49, 794, 875n, 1129, 1190n, [3]16, 16n, [4]737n
  as annotator [2]80n, [4]100n; birth [1]412, 412n; christening [1]42, 42n; C's books and [1]xcii, cxii, clvi, clxiv; coxcomb [2]92, 92n–3n; death [1]clxix; in *DNB* [1]clxxii; as editor [1]cxxv, cxxxiii, cxxxvin, cxlix–cl, *see also* HC *Essays and Marginalia* (1851), *Lives of the Northern Worthies* (1852), *Poems* (2nd ed 1851); Coleridge, S. T. II *Dramatic Works*, *Poems* (1852), *Poetical Works* (1863), IV *LS* (1852), *C&S* (1852), *SM* (1852), IX *NED*, *NTP* ed DC; Greek grammar for [2]3, 4; illness of [1]671, 671n; letter from [3]101; C's letter to [5]601n; library [1]clxix–clxx, clxxn, 855, 867, [2]824n; marginalia addressed to [1]c, cxx, 615, [2]369, 675; ordination [2]651n; owner

of annotated books [1]cxlin, clviii, clxiii, 542, [2]10, 350, 649–50, [4]117, 147, 469, 574, 578; on *TT* [1]cxliiin; taught Greek by C [1]7; transcriber of marginalia [2]558, [3]101

The Philological Library of . . . Derwent Coleridge [4]468; *A Portion of the Library of . . . Derwent Coleridge* [2]350, 910

Coleridge, Derwent Moultrie (1828–80) [2]1190, [3]16n

birth [1]413

Coleridge, Edith (1832–1911) [1]cxxxv, clxiii, 411, 413, [2]90, 977

owner of annotated books [1]542, [2]49, 50, 132, [3]838, [4]102, [6]30; *see also* SC *Memoir* ed Edith Coleridge

Coleridge, Edward (1800–83) [1]cxxvi, 88, [2]*142*, 573, 599n, [3]175n, [5]51n, 68n

letter(s) to [1]508, [2]91, 93n, 142 q, [3]577n q, [5]167n; marginalia written for [1]c; owner of annotated books [1]cxlin, [2]142, 1154, [3]827, [5]48; supplier of books to C [1]xcviii

Coleridge, Ellen (née Philipps) (1829–1909) [6]320

Coleridge, Ernest Hartley (1846–1919), [1]clii, 760, [2]91, 339, 852, 874, 966, 1169, 1203, [3]10, 656, 863, 1083, [4]5, 99, 213, 242, 332, 578, [5]463, [6]25, 30, 73, 94, 130, 131, 177

as editor [1]clxix–clxxii, *see also* Coleridge, S. T. II *Complete Poetical Works*, *Poems* (1905), IX *Anima Poetae*, X *Letters* ed EHC; letter to [1]800 q, [2]44 q; owner of annotated books [1]clxix–clxx, 88, 116, 121, 542, [2]649–50, [3]537, 655, 838, 934, 993, [4]578, [5]3, 373; transcriber of marginalia [1]cxxviiin, 26, 131, 197, 555, [2]4, 245, 361, 503, 504, 519, 526, 647, 796, 1129, [3]75, 837, [4]143, 294, 402, [5]403, 454

Letters . . . to Daniel Stuart [1]clxxiin; "Life of Coleridge" [1]clxxi, clxxin; *Life of . . . Lord Coleridge* [1]clxxiin; *The Life of Thomas Coutts, Banker* [1]clxxiin

Coleridge, Geoffrey Duke (1877–1955) [1]clxxiii

Coleridge, George (1764–1828) [2]94

donor of books [1]lxxviii; letter(s) to [1]lxxxi, 88 q, [2]95n q

Coleridge, Gerard Hartley Buchanan (1872–1945) [1]clxvii, clxx, clxxin, clxxii–clxxiii

owner of annotated books [2]91, 649–50

Coleridge, Gerard P. D., owner of annotated books [2]91

Coleridge, Hartley (1796–1849) [1]lxxixn, lxxxix, cxxvii q, 671n, 808n, [2]505n, 875n, [3]165n, 400, 934, [4]384n, 737n

as annotator [1]39–40, 49n, 65n, [4]574, 656n; baleful influence of RS on [1]c; birth [1]411; books associated with [1]cv; burnt [1]412, 412n; christening [1]42, 42n; and C's books [1]cxii; death [1]cxlix; in *DNB* [1]clxxii; fellowship withdrawn [4]107n; flight from London [1]671n; German grammar for [1]20; Greek grammar for [2]3, 4, 66n; letter to [2]369; letter to JHG [1]clixn q; library [1]clviii, clixn; marginalia addressed to [1]lxxxi q, 41, 615, [2]926; marginalia by [6]333; owner of annotated books [1]cxlin, clixn, 7, 39–41, [4]574, [5]488, [6]34; Prometheus project [3]92n; prose style [2]54, 54n, 63, 77; provision for [1]cxlixn; reaction to *LR* [1]cxliin; reaction to *TT* project [1]cxliin; taught Greek by C [1]7

Essays and Marginalia ed DC [1]cxlix, 39, 40, 46; *Letters* ed Griggs and Griggs [1]lxxxvn q, cixn q, cxliin q, cxliiin q, clxn q, [2]49 q, 54n q, 93n q, 1190n q; *Lives of the Northern Worthies* (1852) ed DC [1]cl, [2]49, 63n q, 82n q, marginalia added [1]lxvii; *Poems* [2]49; *Poems* (2nd ed 1851) ed DC [1]cxlix, 39, [2]4 q; *The Worthies of Yorkshire and Lancashire* [1]lxvii, lxviin, c, cl; MT [2]49–85, 119n, [6]333

Coleridge, Henry Nelson (1798–1843) [1]cii q, cxii, clxviiin, 52, 93n, 413, 481, 722, 801, [2]142, 904n, 905n, 911, 967, [3]140, 507, [4]11, 102, 161, 337n, 804n, [5]120, 667

as annotator [2]50; and Asgill project [1]lxv; assists C as editor [1]cxxiv; biography [1]cxxxiv–cxxxv; C's executor [1]cxlixn; death [1]cxxv, cxlviii, clxi; in *DNB* [1]clxxii; as editor [1]lxviiin, cxxvi, cxxvii, cxxxiii–cxlviii, clxxi, *see also* Coleridge, S. T. III *AR* (1843), *BL* (1847) with SC, *C&S* (1839), *Friend* (1837), *LS* (1839), *SM* (1839), IX *CIS* (1840), *LR*, *TT* ed HNC; engagement to SC [3]778n; essays on C [1]cxxxvii, cxxxviiin, cxliii q, cxliiin; letter from Barnard [2]586 q; letter(s) from C [1]122, 122n, 723n, [2]90 q; letter from RS [1]clixn q; letter to Gillman [1]cxxxviiin q, [2]259 q, 590 q; letter to Head [2]977 q; letter(s) to Poole [1]cxxiv–cxxv q, cxxivn, cxxxviin q; letter(s) to RS [1]lixn–lxn q, clxviiin; marginalia addressed to [1]cxxii, 526, 527, [2]978, [4]11, 13, 14n, 334, 336n, 337n; ed marginalia [1]cxxiv–cxxxvi, cxxxviii–

Coleridge, Henry Nelson—*continued*
cxlix; marginalia written for [1]c; marriage [6]31; naming of [1]177n; owner of annotated books [1]lxvii, cxxii, clviii, clxix, 526, 802, [2]49, 50, 86, 910, [4]11, [5]194; presentation copy of *TT* [1]clxixn; relations with Pickering [1]clxii, clxiin; supplier of books to C [1]xcviii; as textual editor [1]cxliv–cxlvii; transcriber of marginalia [1]lxxiii, cxxviiin, cxli–cxlii, [5]499; use of C's marginalia [1]cxxxiv

Prefaces to *LR* [1]lxvi–lxvii q, cxxxiii–cxxxiv q, cxxxvi–cxxxvii q, cxxxix q, cxlii q, cxliv–cxlv q, cxlvii q, clx q; *Introductions to the Study of the Greek Classic Poets* [2]892n; "Life and Writings of Hesiod" MT [2]86–9; *Notes on the Reform Bill* MT [2]90; 210, [4]7; *Remarks on the Present State of the Roman Catholic Question* [5]851; *Six Months in the West Indies in 1825* [1]cxxxiv; MT [2]91–3

Coleridge, Herbert (1830–61) [1]cxxxv, 413, [2]7, 905n, [5]108
in *DNB* [1]clxxii; library sale [1]cli, clxiii, [2]7; owner of annotated books [1]802, [2]7, [3]838

Coleridge, James (1759–1836) [1]cxxxivn, clxxii, [2]142, [5]152n

Coleridge, Jane (née Hart) (d 1834) [2]91 ("Hunt")

Coleridge, John (1719–81), prophetic dream [1]cii–ciii, 163, 163n

Coleridge, John Duke, 1st Baron Coleridge (1820–94), owner of annotated books [1]clxxii–clxxiii, 24, 476, 501, 508, 553, [2]32, 373, 415, 435, 558, 647, 959, 1203, [3]10, 134, 140, 196, 367, 371, 415, 537, 782, 839, 954 ("James"), 974, 1078, 1083, [4]3, 5, 7, 154, 341, 465, 469, 578, [5]3, 36, 46, 334 ("James"), 392, 401, 403, 669, 830, [6]73, 95, 125 ("James"), 136, 225

Coleridge, John Taylor (1790–1876) [2]90, 94, 755n, 830, [4]40, 792n
editorship of *QR* [1]148n; letter to [2]840n q, 1189 q

Coleridge, Luke Herman (1765–90) [1]282n

Coleridge, Mary Simpson (née Pridham) (1808–87) [1]413, [2]1190
as annotator [1]411; transcriber of marginalia [3]101, [4]148

Coleridge, Nicholas F. D. (b 1926) [1]clixn, clxxiii, [5]488
owner of annotated books [1]542, [2]132, 1182, [4]143

COLERIDGE, SAMUEL TAYLOR (1772–1834)

I BIOGRAPHICAL AND GENERAL: (1) Biographical (2) Character and opinions (3) Marginalia (4) Word-coinages
II POETICAL WORKS III PROSE WORKS IV CONTRIBUTIONS TO PERIODICALS AND NEWSPAPERS V ESSAYS VI LECTURES VII MSS VIII PROJECTED WORKS IX COLLECTIONS AND SELECTIONS X LETTERS XI MARGINALIA XII NOTEBOOKS

I BIOGRAPHICAL AND GENERAL

(1) *Biographical*
struggle against addiction [5]844n; at Allan Bank [1]xcii–xciii, [6]290, 291; staying with Allsop [5]392n; annuity [4]151n; in Antwerp [3]993; at Ashley Cottage [2]668n; Attic nights with CL [5]531
lot resembles Baxter's [1]285–6, 299; at Berners St [3]930n; reading of Bible [3]466; family Bible [1]411; birthday [1]340, *340n*, 411, 411n, [2]106, 106n, 269n, 29th b. [3]837, 837n; and *Blackwood's* [1]cxviii; and Blumenbach's wheel-animal [3]1040, 1040n–1n; read Böhme at school [1]637n; wants German Böhme [1]688, 688n; book-buying in Germany [2]1048; his books [4]99–100, [5]120; selling or pawning books [1]xcvi, cxxiii, [2]753; spending on books [2]519–20; and Boyer [4]174n, 175 ("Bowyer"); at Bristol [1]ciii, 130, [2]586, 587n, [6]189; and BM Library [2]1169, [6]54, 57, 57n; burial [2]905n
at Calne [1]xcvi, cvi, 130; at Cambridge [2]794; meets H. F. Cary [1]494, [2]133; childhood reading [4]658; his Christian name [3]165, 165n; at Christ's Hospital [1]42n, 710n, [3]163, [4]11–12, 12n; longs to read

Church Fathers [5]601, 601n; at Coleorton [1]cx, [3]400; and HC [1]671n, [2]49; collection on flight [6]151, 151n; collection on zoomagnetism [5]141–2; colour theory [5]452n; confirmed six times [6]258; meets Fenimore Cooper [1]212n; "Cordomi" (C) [1]90, 99n; at Corsham House [4]183, 183n; countless intentional works [3]142; *Courier* period [5]377; cowardice of pain [4]10; seeks Craven scholarship [1]377n; crawls through a book [4]336–7; on cuckoo in Germany [2]67, 67n

and Davy [1]99n, 220, 220n, [5]343; his death [1]cii; and death of Berkeley Coleridge [1]671, 671n; and death of John Wordsworth [5]824, 825n; near despair [5]163, 678n; expects to die 1811 [2]243; distress in 1810 [1]197; disuse of reading poetry [6]187; domestication with Wordsworths [4]289; dreams [1]755, [2]403, [5]496, 726, 726n; Durham Cathedral library [1]50n, 255, 255n, [5]597n

education [4]100; and Eichhorn [2]369, 396, 396n, [6]294n; electrical experiments [5]577, 577n; ends proposed in his work [3]606; and SC engagement [3]778n; "Esteesi"/"Ess Teesi"/"Estese" [1]93n, [3]68, 68n, [4]488; in Essex 1818 [3]1049n; ascent of Etna [5]387n

read Fichte in Germany [2]594; fish on board ship [3]1044, 1044n; flogged as schoolboy [1]566n; frantic with thirst [6]220; and J. H. Frere [2]794–5; frost experience [4]275

German lessons [2]188n; departure for Germany [4]837, 837n; in Germany [1]cvn, 535, [5]46, 97n, [6]153; and W. Gilbert [3]990, 990n; and H. Gillman [2]599n; and Godwin [1]173n, 745n, [2]847, 847n–8n; wins Gold Medal [5]118n; at Göttingen [1]149n–50n, [5]141n, [6]17n; offered grant of £200 [2]907; discusses his gravestone [2]180; Greek grammars for his sons [2]3, 4, 66n; and JHG [1]131, [4]313, 327n, 345, 373, 391, [5]784n, [6]32; move to The Grove [1]xcix

habit of opiates [5]419; Harz walking tour [1]204n ("*Harzreise*"), [3]1071, 1071n; and Hazlitt [1]cxviii, [4]837, 837n; health [1]184n, 228, 286, 372n, 838n–9n, [2]120; health of mind [1]286; knowledge of Hebrew [1]415, 513n, [2]1188; at Highgate [1]cxi, cxiv–cxv; and Hurwitz [2]955n, 1188–9; and SH [1]227, 227n, 761, [2]695n

an Iapetides [4]583; initials [1]cxxviiin, *93n*, [2]904, 904n, 905n, [3]512, 512n; insulated position of [3]71–2; inscription for his tombstone [2]993; Irving's use of his conversation [3]64–5, 67, 68; and Italian [1]lxxxi, 542, [2]976, [4]290n; in Italy [3]932, [5]277n, [6]150n

at Jesus College [1]615; journalist [3]882n; read Kant in Germany [2]594; meets Keats [4]606n; at Keswick [1]lxxix, cviii–cix

at Lamb's fireside [2]119; as leader-writer [5]104n–5n; at Leghorn [4]168, 168n; and letters [2]1122, 1122n; library [1]cxxiii, clvi; life saved [6]189; logic class [6]171

and Mackintosh [5]533, 533n; in Malta [1]lxxxiii, 697, [2]1204n, [3]500, [4]35, [5]831, 831n; Malta reading [2]1064; voyage to Malta [1]155–6, 769n; marriage [1]528n; neglect of mathematics [1]615, [3]349, [4]503; Mediterranean experience [1]167n, [2]417–18; his memory [1]cxxix, cxxxi, [5]402; Messina inscription [2]647; and Hannah More [1]736, 736n; and Morgans [1]53, [2]242n, 243n, 526, [4]403, 403n, [6]156, 158

at Nether Stowey 1807 [6]266; and nitrous oxide [4]183n; in Noto (Sicily) [4]235, 235n; obscurity [5]173–6; old and suffering [5]860; omitted words [2]*124n*; and opium [1]xciv, xcvii, 4, 714n, [2]859n, 1122n, [3]237n, 510n, 747n, [4]10n, 503n; Oxford trip 1820 [4]107, 107n

and Paulus [4]40; and Poole [1]lxxxiv–lxxxv, [4]312; portraits of [2]235n, 1066n; hears *Prelude* [1]218n; prescribes for infertility [2]365; prescription for [5]307; productions of *Remorse* [2]776n; pronunciation of name [2]686n; as prosodist [2]216n; and Quakers [6]60n

reading with Mrs C [5]488; reading in sickness [5]120–1; reading speed [4]336–7; return to England 1806 [1]lxxxiii–lxxxiv, [6]187, 194; rheumatism [2]1190, 1190n; Rhine tour [2]180; HCR's first visit [3]321; in Rome [5]652n, 835, 835n; and Royal Society of Literature [1]31, 738–9, 795n; knowledge of Russians [3]884

and A. W. Schlegel [4]836–7, 836n–7n; school experience [1]726, 726n; reading of Scott [4]577; seal [1]93n; sees letters all blood [4]83; in Sicily [4]86, 86n, 235, 235n, [5]80, 277n, 846n; "Siesti" [2]1120n; his signs or logical symbols [2]600n, [3]1005n, [5]48–9, 131, 357, 357n, 432, 434–9, 461, 500, 541; smokes *bang* [4]84; in Somerset [4]236; and RS [1]cxiii–cxiv, 173n, [5]119,

Coleridge, Samuel Taylor—*continued*
119n; assists RS with review [4]619; examined by Spurzheim [5]422n; and Steffens [5]241, 347, 359; and John Sterling [5]373; study of Apocalypse (Rev) [2]1048, of Bible 1827 [2]369, of Plato and Aristotle 1824 [5]691; in Syracuse [1]cv
with L. Tieck in London [3]378n; with Tiecks in Rome [4]427, 427n; with James Tobin in London [1]762n, [3]974; trip in 1828 [4]40; and C. A. Tulk [5]403; and Unitarianism [4]429n, [6]25; verse polished to effeminacy [6]210
wedding-day [1]411; assists in biography of Wedgwood [3]627; will of [1]cxxiii–cxxiv q, cxxivn, clvin; and WW [1]xciii, cxi, 173n, 372n, [2]245, 535n, [3]210, 210n; holiday with Wordsworths [4]48n; working hours [1]392, 392n–3n

(2) *Character and opinions*
makes abstracts from books [1]lxxviiin; "alone" [1]754, [3]476, 476n, 863; assent to Articles of Religion [1]836–8; a zealous Athanasian [3]369
on baptism [5]490, 490n–1n, 647, 647n; reverence for Bible [4]304; and birds [1]47n, 482, 482n; birthday remorse [1]661; does not consider body as self [4]461; Browne "paints" him [1]744; opposed to bullionists [5]686–7, 686n
hates casuistry [1]342; on Catholic Emancipation [4]18; on Charles I [6]258; as Christian [5]96–7; and C of E [1]317, 357, 360, [3]163, 878, [6]43; conceals doubts [3]466; conscience does not err [5]298; constitutional softness [2]1176; contempt for *plebs* [2]511n; content not to know [2]271; conviction of weakness [2]1176; cypher [1]173n
no fear of death [5]862; could not be Deist [1]531; delay in opening letters [1]755n; desynonymises [5]3n; dislike of his name [1]93n; drug experiments [1]777n
Episcopalian [1]309; errors about odour [6]230, 230n; and etymology [1]61, 61n; "Extremes meet" [1]518n, [2]1178n; faith in Trinity [6]146; favourite books [5]134; favourite comedies [2]778n; first scruple [2]1060; fondness for old books [6]96; against French [1]6n, 162n, [2]176n, [4]78, 78n, [5]373, 373n, 835n, 840
golden rule [1]lxi q, [3]71n q, 120n, 1088n–9n q, [5]360, 360n; habit of digression [3]138n; handwriting [1]lxxiv–lxxvi, lxxivn; homoousian [6]90; hopes of a pension [2]511n; humble poet [1]482; hyper-critical [6]197
identifies with Leighton [3]523, [6]306; identifies with writer [6]305; incurious [2]978; inscription in books [1]cxxviiin; abhors intolerance [4]178; regrets Irving connection [3]67
distaste for Johnson [1]55n; love of old writers [2]121; love-creed [2]225; master passion [3]222; interest in medical science [1]*282n*; metrical sensibility [2]1040n; misuse of genius [1]164n; preference for Moravian Church [5]152, 152n; mottophilist [1]lxvi
neglect of talents [1]769; never mutilates a book [2]875; never played at school [3]632; obstinate hoper [5]534; ocean of papers [3]987; opposed to Emancipation and Reform Bills [3]159
philo-parenthesist [1]lxvin; his philosophy [4]15, ground of [2]423; charges of plagiarism [1]cxlviii; as pointer [1]lix; political religion [3]801; prayer for enlightenment [1]453; presentiment of death [1]372n; his puns [3]175, 175n, 1065, 1066n, [5]111n, 478n, 801n, for CL [5]525, 525n; a Puritan on issue of holy days [1]327; purpose of his life [5]485
as reader [1]cii–cxv, 758n, [2]220; experience of reading [1]lx, lxix, [3]523; reading of history [1]*795n*; rebuilding the doctrine of realism [5]800; religious doubts [1]288; experience of rose [2]625; and round-abouts [2]1158
sabbatarianism [1]871; theory of sacrament [5]398; scepticism about Chinese and Hindu myths [2]585; his scheme [2]1007, [3]1020, 1020n–1n, [4]400–1; school charm [1]129; against Scots [1]57n, 75n, [3]795n, [4]577; self-portraiture [2]455n; and character of RS [1]330–1, 331n, 808; spelling [1]lxxv; respect for Steffens [5]280, [6]226; on Stuarts [1]808; contemplates suicide [1]167n, [2]236n; views near to Swedenborg's [3]732, 732n; his system [2]554, 554n, of divinity [3]436, tetradic [3]1006; systematising mind [1]cxxvi
love of Jeremy Taylor [5]617; theism of [4]28; thinks freely [3]436; tormented culprit [3]512; touchstones of faith [3]1085n; trinitarianism [2]24
and Unitarianism [1]198n, 566, [3]137n, 305n; a visionary [1]758; wild notions [4]520; interest in witchcraft [4]145n; emphasis on words [1]533n; differs from WW [6]210; on greatest works of Christian era [4]403

(3) *Marginalia see also* Coleridge, S. T. XI

for specific references to authors and works

abbreviations in ^{3}59; on additional blank leaves ^{3}31; additions after ten years ^{2}644; addressed to himself ^{2}441; at Allan Bank ^{1}xcii–xciii; apologies for ^{1}cxxi–cxxii, ^{2}118, 118n, 787, ^{5}284n; archaisms in ^{5}49

docked by binder ^{4}431; on a blank leaf ^{5}867; at Bristol ^{1}lxxviii–lxxix; cancellations in texts ^{1}768n; HNC's use of ^{1}cxxxiv; complaints about paper ^{2}519–20, 519n, 520n; do not compromise book ^{2}395; correction fifteen years later ^{2}405; corrects a note ^{2}103

dating of ^{1}cxxviii–cxxx; dispersal of ^{1}clvi–clxxiv; earliest ^{1}lxxvii; in early eds of C's works ^{1}cxxxv–cxxxvi; editorial tradition ^{1}cxlvi–cxlvii; of 1810–16 ^{1}xciv–xcvii; error in early Böhme marginalia ^{1}660; favourites not annotated ^{2}804; at Greta Hall ^{1}xciii

C's habit ^{3}373, ^{5}480; handwriting in ^{1}lxxiv–lxxvi, cxxviii; at Highgate ^{1}xcvii–cii; history of writing ^{1}lxxvi–cii; notes usually in ink ^{1}lxx–lxxii, cxxviii–cxxix, ^{5}829; in Lamb's books ^{2}118, 118n, 217, 217n, 243; in library books ^{2}698; limited space ^{3}875, 887, 989; listening and talking ^{5}121; in *LR* ^{1}cxxxix–cxlviii

C made for writing notes ^{1}331; in Malta ^{1}lxxxiii; marginal illustrations ^{4}283; marked books ^{6}333; mistaken attributions ^{6}333–5; in Morgan's book ^{4}721; notes improve book ^{2}221; notes record present knowledge ^{1}774–5; on outward leaf ^{5}74

pencil or ink ^{1}lxxii, ^{2}520, 520n; pencil too perishable ^{1}lxxi, 632; plans to publish ^{1}121–2; posthumous editions ^{1}cxxxiii–clv; practice in writing ^{1}lvii–lxxvi; not always on first reading ^{2}1050; propensity for ^{1}526; publication of ^{1}cxv–cxxvii, 53, ^{2}214; published in *Blackwood's* ^{1}796–7; punctuation ^{1}lxxv; qualities of ^{1}lvii–lxxvi

to "any after reader" ^{4}332; reasoning with books ^{4}453; turn book to relic ^{1}372; during residence with Poole 1807 ^{1}lxxxiv–lxxxv; scandalised owner ^{2}46; scanty space ^{2}17, 1163, ^{5}644; signs in ^{1}765, ^{2}118, 416, ^{3}130, 130n, 137–8, *137n*, ^{5}500; bequeathed to RS ^{5}120; spelling ^{1}lxxv; style of conversation ^{1}lxxxv; under other eyes ^{5}408; value of ^{6}149

(4) *Word-coinages*

abeternal ^{1}696, 696n; accrescence ^{4}845, 845n; adagy ^{2}819, 819n; admensate ^{2}200, 200n; adsedent ^{4}682, 682n; Adwitamists ^{2}340, 340n; aei-partheny ^{1}504, 504n; aero-septic ^{4}149; all-commonness ^{1}123; allogeneous ^{5}484, 484n; ammaximation ^{1}579, 579n; amorphosing ^{5}265, 265n; animity ^{4}420, 420n; anordinated ^{4}500, 500n; antizote ^{1}594, 594n; aphorisming ^{1}141, 141n; apostolichrony ^{4}67, 67n; apponible ^{4}384, 384n; astheny ^{6}26, 26n; bothness ^{2}1186, 1186n; bull-froggery ^{2}498, 499n

cacodaemony ^{1}88; caprified ^{4}663, 663n; Catholism ^{2}141, 141n; cenocranion ^{4}188; cercoceronychous ^{1}351n, ^{5}82, 82n, 83, 83n; Christopaedia ^{4}41, 41n; chronochorhistorical ^{3}926, 926n; chryso-poietic ^{1}546, 546n; clerisy ^{1}355n; coacruation ^{1}740, 740n; coherentific ^{1}780n; colluvion ^{2}387, 387n–8n; cometarian ^{3}323, 323n; communify ^{4}331; concircularly ^{3}341, 341n; concomparable ^{4}194, 194n; confabrication ^{2}1173, 1173n; *confacciamento* ^{2}377, 377n; contraversy ^{2}569, 569n; convolition ^{5}418, 418n; co-persons ^{2}321, 321n; corporific ^{3}949, 949n; cosmolater ^{4}581, 581n; cosmotheism ^{1}643n, ^{5}251, 251n; counterpay ^{5}198, 198n; crambist ^{1}528, 528n; creability ^{2}578, 578n; credentialise ^{2}39, 39n

definient ^{4}380, 380n; deuteroptis ^{4}83, 83n; diabolography ^{6}100, 100n; diabolosophy ^{4}145, 145n; digenerations ^{3}356, 356n; *disfacciamento* ^{4}808, 808n; disimaged ^{2}1028, 1028n; displanations ^{2}798, 798n; distinctity ^{2}300, 300n, ^{3}52, 52n, 102, 102n; dormitate ^{2}516, 516n; ecdotes ^{3}307, 307n–8n; egometical ^{1}346, 346n; elanguescing ^{4}238, 238n; empirist ^{6}236, 236n; enclesia ^{5}67, 67n–8n; entelechism ^{5}827, 827n; epopsy ^{1}652, 652n; esemplastic ^{1}113n, 595, 595n, ^{2}396n, 397, ^{3}790, 790n; esenoplastic ^{1}113n, ^{3}790, 790n; ethometer ^{2}6, 6n; evenomate ^{2}298, 298n; evoer ^{2}582, 582n; existential/existentially ^{1}288, 288n; exition ^{1}667n; extroitive ^{1}667n, 680, 680n

facciamenti ^{3}926, 926n; facticity ^{3}310n; factity ^{3}310, 310n; factuality ^{3}310n; faith-mate ^{3}418, 418n, 476; ferruminator ^{4}291, 291n; filiety ^{3}16, 16n; fixive ^{1}596, 596n; fluidising ^{1}638, 639n; fore-tact ^{2}1136, 1136n–7n; friendism ^{4}801, 801n;

Coleridge, Samuel Taylor—*continued*
gallocristan [2]92, *92n–3n*; glycydor [1]614, 614n; gnathonism [2]931, 931n; goodiness [6]122n; grelly [5]301, 301n; heautophany [5]589, 589n; hierolatry [1]297, 297n–8n; hitty [2]56; hodiernity [1]410, 410n; holomery [4]466, 466n; *Homereumenoi* [2]779n, 1130n; hominifact [2]980, 980n; homoiogeneous [4]218, 218n; hurraer [2]582, 582n; hydroseptic [4]149; hypertheological [3]66, 66n; hypo-criticism [3]955, 955n; hypopoesis [1]108, 108n; hystero-proterise [5]159, 159n; hystery [1]536, 536n

iamböid [4]603, 603n; Ideatae [5]770, 770n; idiosymbolic [3]138, 138n; idoloplastic [4]234, 234n; ignivomist [1]872, 872n; illucence [3]560, 560n; imparticipability [1]60, 60n; impetite(s) [1]819, 819n, [3]910n; incendent [4]396, 396n; incitivity [4]389, 389n; incoherentic [1]780, 780n; indifferentism [5]365, 365n; infrasocinian [3]434, 434n, [4]269, 269n; intellecturition [1]lix, lixn, 653, 653n; interinanimate(s) [2]223, 223n; intermundium [4]263, 263n; interpocular [2]63, 63n; intertrusion(s) [2]52, 52n, [5]530, 530n; introition [1]667n; introitive [1]667n; Laudites [4]20, 20n; linguipotence [1]317, 317n; lininess [5]133; logolatry [6]143, 143n

magnetopathia [3]374, 374n; merder [3]894, 894n; metallology [1]639, 639n; micranthrope [1]671, 671n; minimifidian(ism) [1]512, 512n–13n, [3]557, 557n; misepiscopy [2]1173, 1173n; miso-fanatic [5]124, 124n; misosophy [2]1147, 1147n; mononomian [5]588, 588n; moonery [5]296, 296n; multeity [1]152, 152n, 304n; multisciolous [2]999, 999n; multivocal [2]1150, 1150n; murthero-maniacal [4]238, 238n; *mythosophisch* [4]504, 504n; nationalty [6]22, 22n; neologist(s) [1]305, 306n; neuropathology [6]100, 100n; nihiliscience [6]243, 243n; notionalise [3]429, 430n; omnifidience [6]120, 120n; omnify [5]508, 508n; *Oneirosoph/Oneirosophen* [4]504, 504n; one-side-mindedness [1]808, 808n–9n; ourishness [4]827, 827n; outerance [1]637, *637n–8n*

papoduly [2]38, 38n; papophobists [2]935, 935n; papyrologiophagous [1]88; parthenolatry/parthenolatries [1]519, 519n; particularism [1]639, 639n, [2]674, 674n; pasch [3]913, 913n; pass [3]913, 913n; *Pauloeides* [1]459, 459n; pedoeuvre(s) [1]862, 862; personëity [1]304, 304n; phantastery [2]1026, 1026n; phenomenically [5]734, 734n; philagathocaletheists [5]470, 470n; philochristianism [4]269, 269n; philo-despot [2]927, 927n; philogynic [2]73, 73n; philoparenthesist(s) [3]138, 138n; philopoesy [5]271, 271n; philopsophy [2]1147, 1147n; philosopherists [3]383, 383n; phosopyr [5]335, 335n; physiogonist [1]537, 537n; physiogony [1]537n, [5]445, 445n; physiographer [1]537, 537n; *Physiosoph/Physiosophen* [4]504, 504n; physiosophy [2]539n, [5]427n–8n; phytomet [1]572; piafraudish [2]1173, 1173n; picturative [3]289, 289n; ploutonomist [6]19–20, 20n; polarly [2]859n; potenziate [1]344, 344n, [3]386n; praenunciations [3]209, 209n; praeterscriptural [3]66, 66n; pregenite [2]723, 723n; preposterise [1]602, 602n; propiority [4]168, 168n; prozoote [1]594, 594n; pseudosophy [2]614, 614n; psilanthropism [4]253, 253n, [5]563, 563n, [6]71, 71n; psilanthropist(s) [2]22, 22n, [3]692, 692n, [4]46, 46n; psilanthropy [4]46n; psilology [2]1147, 1147n; psilo-phaenomenonism [2]547, 547n; psilosopher(s) [4]627, 627n, [6]124n; psilosophists [5]201, 201n–2n, [6]124n; psilosophy [2]265, 265n, [3]199, 199n, 339n, 511, 511n, [4]627n, [5]202n, 309, 309n, [6]124n; psychologist [4]181, 181n–2n; psychooid [3]935, 935n; pulmonists [5]147, 147n; pulverivorous [6]110, 110n; pyrophose [5]335, 335n

quasific [5]155, 155n; *Realitabilität* [4]406, 406n; re-fundence [1]694, 694n; reintroitive [1]667, 667n; retroition [1]667n; retroitive [1]667n; sapientise [5]506, 506n; sarcomorphic [2]1175, 1175n; sciolism [5]110, 110n; sciously [4]542 542n; sebanthropism [2]344, 344n; self-ponence [3]852, 852n; semperfuity [3]91, 91n; simultenise [4]314, 314n; somniloquist [1]808, 808n; spatiuncles [5]712, 712n; sterilifidianism [1]814, 814n; subemphatic [2]124, 124n; sub-existence [4]301, 301n; subposed [4]234, 234n; successry [1]392; suffiction(s) [2]886, 886n, [4]13, 13n, [5]825, 825n; superbiloquies [5]372, 372n; supersistent [3]518, 518n; sussorption [3]1073, 1073n; synenergema [5]654, 654n

tautogeneity [6]123, 123n; tetraxy [4]400, 400n; theletic [6]103, 103n; theophysy [1]660, 660n, [6]5, 5n; too-muchness [1]725, 725n; totalism [1]638, 639n; trans-con-

ceive [2]882, 882n; transcreated [3]519, 519n, [6]301, 301n; transcriptural [1]736, 736n; transdate [5]297, 297n–8n; transimaginate [3]90, 90n; transimagine [2]882, 882n; transinfusion [2]250, 250n; transsensual [2]802, 802n; transteverine [3]7, 7n; trocheised [1]403, 403n; ultrafidianism [1]513n, [3]557n; undivulsed [1]653, 653n; unicism [3]77, 77n; unicist [2]799, 799n; unintroitive [1]667n, [4]787, 787n–8n; uni-personalists [2]22, 22n; unpossessedness [4]787, 787n; up-swing [2]1181, 1181n; uppropment [1]507, 507n; valdisonant [2]582, 582n; zoics [3]278, 278n; zooseptic [4]149; zote [5]247, 247n

II POETICAL WORKS

Complete Poetical Works ed EHC [1]cxlixn q, clxxi, clxxiin, 8, 39, 67n, 90n, 91n, 92n, 93n, 94n, 95n, 96n, 97n, 98n, 99n, 165n, 185n, 218n, 222n, 280n, 385n, 427n, 544n, 594n, 654n, 672n, 723n, 734n, 758n, 765n, 857n, [2]14, 23, 70n, 133, 180, 197n, 214, 217n, 233n, 353n, 403n, 498n, 513n, 515n, 535n, 551n, 560n, 561n, 586, 587n, 615n, 646n, 686n, 760n, 847n, 859n, 861n, 865n, 869n, 873, 874n, 875n, 877n, 904n, 905n, 964, 985, 1003n, 1033, 1048, 1116, 1120n, 1121n, 1175n, 1188, [3]61n, 230n, 445n, 459n, 510n, 564n, 712n, 740n, 769n, 863n, 869n, 1068n, 1071n, 1073n, [4]30n, 241n, 267n, 313n, 335n, 544n, 583n, 602n, 603n, 605n, 614n, 665n, 787n q, 792n, [5]84n, 149n, 242n, 282n, 501n, 521n, 592n, 817n, 819n, 821n, 855n, 861n, [6]40n, 191n, 196n, 266

Dramatic Works ed DC [1]cxxxvi, cl, cln

Poems (1796) [2]95n, 96n

Poems (1797) [1]lxxin, 716, [2]95n, 353n, 865n

Poems (1803) [2]95n

Poems (1844) ed SC [1]cxxxvi, cxlviii

Poems (1852) ed SC and DC [1]cxxxvi, cxlix, cl, cln

Poems (1905) ed EHC [1]clxxiin

Poetical and Dramatic Works [1]cxxivn

Poetical Works [1]cxviii

Poetical Works (1828) [1]95n

Poetical Works (1834) [1]cxxiv, cxxivn, cxxxvii, 857n [2]86, 904n, 905n, 964

Poetical Works (1852) [1]857n, [2]95n

Poetical Works (1863) ed DC [1]cxxxvin, cln

Poetical Works (1893) ed JDC [1]cli, clii, 857n, [2]586, 587n, 904n

Lyrical Ballads (1800) [1]cxxxiv, 89; *see also* WW *Lyrical Ballads*

Sibylline Leaves [1]xcvi, cxviin, 95n, 392n, 851, [2]16n, 586, 587n, 794, 985, [5]501n, [6]191n

British Stripling's War-Song MT [1]96; *Brockley Coomb* [1]26n; *Christabel* [1]lxxxiii, lxxxiv, cxviin, clxxi, clxxiin, 48n, 62n, 88, [2]947n, 983n, 1204n, [4]162n, 577, 583n, 603n, 611n, 665 q, 665n, [5]817 q, 817n; *A Christmas Carol* [1]88; MT 93; 93n, [2]70 q, 70n; *Constancy to an Ideal Object* [6]40n q; "conversation poems" [1]120n, 218n; *Cupid Turn'd Chymist* [1]lxxvii, [2]94–5; *Dejection: an Ode* [1]409, 760, 762n, 765 q, 765n, [2]498n q, 551n; *Delinquent Travellers* [2]834n, 861n, 1108n; *Egoenkaipan* [2]615n; *Eolian Harp* [2]535n, 560n, 1003n, [3]248n, [4]313n q; epigram on Donne [2]16 q, *16n* q; *Epigrams* MT [1]97–8; 97n–8n; *Epitaph* [1]594n q, [2]880, 903–4 q, 903n, 904n q, 905–6 q, 905n, 906n q, [6]266 q; *Faded Flower* [2]55n; *Fall of Robespierre* [5]282n q; *Fancy in Nubibus* [1]cxix; *Farewell to Love* [2]874, 877 q, 877n; *Fire, Famine, and Slaughter* MT [1]97; 97n, [5]501n; *Fragment 64* [2]1116; *France: An Ode* [5]241, 242, 242n; *Frost at Midnight* [2]49, 233 q, 233n, [3]445 q, 445n, [4]605 q, 605n, [5]821n q; *Garden of Boccaccio* [1]544n; Greek "Ode on the Slave Trade" MT [5]118; *Hendecasyllabi* [1]90n; *Home-Sick* [1]90n; *Human Life* [2]16n; tr Hurwitz [2]1188; *Improvisatore* [1]385n, [2]197n; *Knight's Tomb* [4]593n; *Kubla Khan* [1]clxixn, [2]134n, 859n, [4]544n q, [6]196n; *Lewti* [1]88; MT 91; 91n; *Limbo* [1]672n, 685n, 776n, [2]217n, 218n, 561n, 685n; *Lines on a Friend Who Died of a Frenzy Fever* [2]1175n; *Lines on a King* [2]873; *Lines Suggested by . . . Berengarius* [3]439n; *Lines Written . . . at Elbingerode* MT [1]93; 93n; *Love* [2]1066n, 1121, *1121n*; *Love and Friendship Opposite* [2]197n; *Metrical Experiments* [2]875n; *Metrical Feet* [2]874n; *Moles* [2]217n; *My Baptismal Birth-day* [2]964; *My Godmother's Beard* [3]1073 q; *Nightingale* [1]9, 91n; *A Night-Scene* [6]191n; *O! Christmas Day* [1]227; *Ode on the Depart-*

Coleridge, Samuel Taylor—*continued*
ing Year [2]514, 515 q, 515n, [5]855 q, 855n; *Ode to Georgiana* MT [1]96–7; 96n; *On Donne's First Poem* [2]217 q, 217n; *On Presenting a Moss Rose* [1]lxxvii; *On Revisiting the Sea-Shore* [5]819 q, 819n; *Osorio* [1]xciv, 716, [2]513 q, 513n, [3]564n, [6]49n; *Pains of Sleep* [1]228, [3]510n q; *Pang More Sharp Than All* [1]758n q; *Plot Discovered* [2]126n; *Psyche* [4]267n, [5]592n; *Raven* MT [1]97; 97n; *Recantation* MT [1]92; *Reflections on Having Left a Place of Retirement* [2]353n, [4]241n; *Religious Musings* [1]165n q, 427n, [2]122n, [3]740 q, 740n; *Remorse* [1]xciv, 130, 373, [2]753, [3]712 q, 712n, [4]770, 770n, [6]49, 49n; *Rime of the Ancient Mariner* [1]lxxvii, lxxviii, cxxv, 594n q, 615, 615n, 764n, 828, 851, [2]165n, 213, 586, 668n, 1119n, [3]466 q, 466n q, [4]162n, 335n q, 581n, 614, 614n q, [5]861, 861n, and Bartram's *Travels* [1]226, epigraph of [1]183n, genesis of [1]clxixn, "moon" gloss [1]180n, origins of [1]clxxi, sources of [1]clxix, 9; *Rose* [2]94, 95n; *Sancti Dominici Pallium* [1]436n, 501, 855, 856, 857–60, 857n, [3]459 q, 459n; *Sheet of Sonnets* [1]lxxviii, lxxxvii, [2]133, [3]712; *Something Childish, but Very Natural* [1]90n; *Sonnet XII* MT [1]95; *This Lime-Tree Bower* [1]88, 89; MT 94–5; 94n–5n; *Three Graves* [2]985; *To a Critic* [5]149 q, 149n; *To a Friend* MT [1]94; 94n; *To a Young Lady* MT [1]92; *To an Unfortunate Woman* MT [1]99; 99n; *To Mary Pridham* [1]758n q, [5]821n q; *To Two Sisters* [1]100, [2]1120n; *To William Wordsworth* [1]218n q; *Tombless Epitaph* [2]23; *Triumph of Loyalty* [6]191n q; *Two Founts* [2]180, [3]869 q, 869n; *Two Round Spaces on the Tombstone* [2]759n–60n; tr *Wallenstein* [4]787n q; *Work without Hope* [2]1033; *Written in a Blank Leaf of Faulkner's "Shipwreck"* [2]586; *Youth and Age* [1]185n; *Zapolya* [1]cxviiin, "Glycine's Song" [1]91n

III PROSE WORKS

Aids to Reflection [1]cxxxiiin, 231, 237, 237n, 351n, 644n, 713n, [2]289n, 722n, 809n, 814n, 1033, [3]486, 509n, 537, [4]469, [5]61, 61n q, 75, 75n q, 131, 173–6, 175n q, 186, 186n, 480, 480n q, 599, 691, [6]54, 55, 55n
on baptism [1]532, 532n; a brain-cracker [1]488, [5]173; and Charles Butler [1]501; cited by C [1]509; Hooker in [2]1131, 1163n; and marginalia [1]lxiv, cxvi, cxix–cxx; praises Hurwitz [2]1189; proofs of [1]c; (1825) [1]ci, cxxx q, 197, 200n, 283, 283n, 669, 669n q, 813, 813n–14n q, 831, [2]87, 87n q, 277, 277n q, 582, 582n, 657n q, 658n, 922n, 1177, 1177n, [3]5, 5n q, 42 q, 42n q, 64, 64n, 423, 423n, 431, 431n q, 433, 433n, 514, 564n, 606n, 618n, 725n, 875, 875n q, 1082, 1082n, [4]233, [5]495n, 501n, 510n, 669, [6]41; (1831) [1]cxxiv, cxxxvii; (1843) ed HNC [1]cxxxvi, cxlvi, cxlviii; (1854) [1]cln
"Allegoric Vision" [1]653n–4n
Biographia Literaria [1]xcvi, cxviin, cxxvi, 393n, [2]20, 794, 983n, 1033 q, 1050, [3]75, 433, 789, [4]27, 122, 143, 259, 259n q, 264, 344, 402, 447, [5]468, 468n q, [6]189
critique of WW in [1]cxlviii; final paragraph of [1]576n; Kant q in [3]87n; proofs of [1]373–4; (1847) ed HNC and SC [1]cxxivn, cxxxvi, cxlvi, cxlvii, cxlviii, 82n, [3]781, and German marginalia [1]cl; (1907) ed Shawcross [1]lx q, lxn, cxxxi–cxxxii q, cxxxiin, [2]356n q
"Formula Fidei" [1]cxliii
Friend [1]xciii, xcv, cxi, cxviin, cxxxii q, cxxxiin, cxliin, 160n q, [2]20, 359, 985, [3]503, 531, 531n, 557n, [4]310, 654, 654n, [5]170 q, 174, 297–8, 298n q, 301, 301n q, 309, 309n q, 602, [6]192, 192n q, 315, 315n
Aristophanes in [1]119; Aurelius in [1]155; Bacon in [1]766n; Chiabrera in [4]290n; circumstances of [1]xcii–xciii; "Essays on the Principles of Method" in [2]954n, 1204n, [6]315; Hooker in [2]1131, 1143, 1143n, 1147n; inception of [1]lxxxvi; "Specimens of Rabbinical Wisdom" in [1]513n, [2]1189; subscriber to [1]130; on wit [1]144n; (1809–10) [1]cxxi, clxviiin, 157n, 230, 393n, 840n, [2]935n, 1033 q, [3]189n, [4]93, 93n, 282, 289; (1818) [1]279, 840, [2]23, 133, 1184, [3]75, 93, [4]472, 472n q, 675, [5]286, 286n q, 302, 302n q; (1837) ed HNC [1]cxxxv, cxlvi, [2]872, 872n
Lay Sermons [1]cxviin, 100, 644n, [2]1116, [4]328n, [6]218
(1839) ed HNC [1]cxxxvi, cxlviii; (1852) ed DC [1]cxxxvi, cl; see also *Statesman's Manual*

Logic [1]cxix, [2]596, 1115, 1147n, [3]75, 91, 91n, 618n, [5]269n
"My Nightly Prayer" [1]cxliii
On the Constitution of the Church and State [1]cxx, 28, 155, 170n, 711n, [2]655n, 808, 809n, 935n, 1190, 1190n, [4]11, 17, 17n, 341, [5]68n, 78, 78n, 480 q, [6]16, 16n
1st ed (1829–30) [1]lxxvi q, cxvi q, cxvii q, [2]58, 58n, 111, 505n, [3]72, 72n, 106; 2nd ed (1830) [1]cxxiv, cxxxvii, [2]505n, [3]106; (1839) ed HNC [1]cxxxvi, cxlviii; (1852) ed DC [1]cxxxvi, cxlix
Statesman's Manual [1]cxviin, 100, 279, 801, [2]320, 320n, 722n, 983n, [3]47n, 75, 115, 531, 723n, [6]218, 220, 220n, 315, 315n
(1839) ed HNC [1]cxxxvi, cxlviii; (1852) ed DC [1]cxxxvi
Theory of Life [1]cxxxiiin
(1816) [3]842n, 844n, [5]241; (1848) [1]175n q, [2]268n, [3]123n

IV CONTRIBUTIONS TO NEWSPAPERS AND PERIODICALS

"Character of Sir Thomas Browne as a Writer" [1]cxv–cxvi, cxix
Courier [1]840
Essays on His Own Times ed SC [1]cxxxiiin, cxxxvi, cxlix
"Historic and Gestes of Maxilian" [1]37, [2]533, 1115, [3]882n q
"Letters on the Spaniards" [5]105n, 195n
"Letters to C. J. Fox" [6]45, 45n
"Letters to Mr Justice Fletcher" [2]696
Morning Post [4]18, [6]45, 45n
review of Clarkson's *History* [2]983n
The Watchman [1]lxxviii
"What Is an English Sonnet?" [3]891n

V ESSAYS

"Apologetic Preface to *Fire, Famine, and Slaughter*" [1]280n
"Essay on Establishment and Dissent" [5]67, 68n
"Essay on Faith" [1]lxxiii, cxliii, clixn, [2]990n, [3]558n, [4]615, [5]469, 469n, [6]223n q
"Essay on Scrofula" [2]363n
"Essay on the Supernatural" [4]581n
Introduction to *Encyclopaedia Metropolitana* [1]cxviin
"Notes on Atheism" *see* "Remarks on Atheism"
"On Animal Magnetism" [6]104n
"On Poesy and Art" [4]402
"On the Passions" [2]172n, [3]910n
"On the Principles of Genial Criticism" [1]152n, 632n q, [2]1066n, [3]259n, 883n, 899n, [4]143, 677n
"Remarks on Atheism" [1]lxxviii

VI LECTURES

lectures on Shakespeare [1]212n, 362, [4]684
lectures 1808 [1]lxxxv–lxxxvi, 53, 158n, 180n, [2]117, [3]400, [4]677n
lectures 1811–14 [1]xciv, xcv, 53, [2]753, 1147n, [3]888, 888n, [4]764
literary lectures 1818–19 [1]cxvii, 763n, 801, [2]131, 133, 213, [3]146n, 170, [4]463, 778–9
and B&F marginalia [1]374, Hooker in [2]1131, reconstructed by HNC [1]cxxxiv, cxxxix–cxl
Lectures 1808–1819 ed Foakes [4]677n, 684; *see also* IX *Coleridge on Shakespeare* ed Foakes, *Coleridge's Miscellaneous Criticism* and *Coleridge's Shakespearean Criticism* ed Raysor
lectures on the history of philosophy 1818–19 [1]lxix, cxvii, 119, 756n, [2]554n, 794, [3]75, 146n, 304, 307–8, 307n, [4]463, [5]691; see also *Philosophical Lectures* below
"On the *Prometheus* of Aeschylus" [1]cxxxix, cxli, cxlin, 432n, 473n, 624n–5n q, [2]345n, 665n, [3]92n, [4]463, [5]70n
Philosophical Lectures (1949) ed Coburn [1]cliv, 119
Seven Lectures ed J. P. Collier [1]cxlviin, 67n

VII MSS

BM Add Ch 66314 [1]cxxivn, cxlixn
BM Add MS 27902 [5]853; 32566 [1]277n; 34225 [1]clxxiin, 655n q, [2]858n; 34225 ff 81–3 [3]1073n; 34225 ff 146–7 [3]598n; 36532 [2]533; 36532 ff 5, 7–12 [3]374n, 598n
BM Ashley 3506 "Liber Aureus" [1]354n
BM MS Egerton 2800 [1]lxxviiin, [4]779n; ff 26–7 [4]779n; f 49[v] [1]801; f 53 [2]525; f 54 [2]102; f 59 [1]378n; f 71 [2]1069n; f 105 [2]165n, 981n; f 106 [3]149n q; ff 106–8 [1]738; f 155[v] [3]68n; f 169 [2]936n q; f 170 [2]929n; f 170[v] [2]927n; f 188[v] [3]468n

Coleridge, Samuel Taylor—*continued*
BM MS Egerton 2801 [1]clxxiin, [2]11; f 84 [3]742; f 140 [3]394n; f 171[v] [3]543n; f 188 [3]535; f 194 [2]1095; ff 212[v]–215 [1]lxxviiin; f 232 [2]370; f 234[r] [3]509n; f 237 [3]486; f 252 [3]588n–9n
BM MS Egerton 2825–6 [1]230, [3]262n
Huntington Library
MS HM 8195 "On the Divine Ideas" [1]70n
Leatherhead MS [1]800, [2]5, 44, 586
Logic MS *see* BM MS Egerton 2825–6 *above*
"Opus Maximum" *see* VCL S MS 29 *below*
Pierpont Morgan Library MS [2]166n–7n q
University of Waterloo MS [2]615n
Victoria College Library
Leatherhead Collection [1]clxvii, clxxii–clxxiii
MS 8 [1]clvin
MS F 14.3b [1]738
MS LT 8 [2]4
S MS 11.6 [2]252n
S MS 29 ("Opus Maximum") [1]cxviii, [3]295n, [4]327n, 381n q, 391, [5]777n, *see also* VIII *Opus Maximum*
S MS F 2.2 [6]318
S MS F 2.6 [2]3
S MS F 11.2 [2]573

VIII PROJECTED WORKS

analyses of Ariosto, Calderón, Cervantes, Chaucer, Dante, Donne, Milton, Rabelais, Spenser [1]cxvii; "Apology for Conceits" [2]238; "Apology for Puns" [2]238, 238n; second volume of *AR* [1]cxix–cxx; "Assertio Fidei Christianae" [1]cxix; "Assertion of Religion" [3]365, 365n, 764n, [5]777n; "Beauties of Archbishop Leighton" [2]1177n, 1178n, [3]514, 537, [6]54; Bible: commentary on [2]481, on John chs 1 and 6 [1]624, 624n, on Rev [1]480–1, [3]467, 467n–8n, letters on OT and NT [1]cxviii; "Bibliotheca Britannica" [1]156n, 297n; "Biographical Memorials of Revolutionary Minds" [3]142, 142n, [5]143n, 208n
"Characteristics of Shakespeare's Dramatic Works" [1]cxvii; "Christianity Defended against Its Defenders" [3]562; "The Church as a Profession" [2]321; "Concerning Poetry" [2]755n; "Constructive Philosophy" [2]958, 958n; "Consolations and Comforts" [2]15n, 116; "Defence of Christianity" [4]627n; "Diadestè" [1]373, 376, *376n*; "Dictionary and Grammar Writers" [3]930
edition(s) of Asgill [1]lxiv–lxvi, 121–2, 230, 526, of J. Butler *Analogy* [1]867, of W. Collins [2]94, 864, of Gray [2]94, 864, of J. Taylor *Liberty of Prophesying* [5]501; "Elements of Discourse" [3]557, 557n, 618, 618n; "Encyclopaedia Biblica" [1]416, 440n; encyclopedia entry on animal magnetism [6]104; essay(s) on faith [3]558n, on Luther and Calvin [1]476, on prayer [3]754n–5n, [4]336n, [5]510n, on punning [5]111n, on taste in religion [5]130, on words of Christ [5]578; "Examination of the Style of our English Prose Writers under Charles I and the Commonwealth" [2]1131; "Excursions abroad and at home" [1]cxix
Gentleman's Magazine, record of pilgrims for [1]cvi; German grammar [1]7; "great Work" [2]1055; Greek grammar [1]7; Greek lexicon [1]7; "Heraclitus redivivus" [1]780n; history of German poetry [1]131, of philosophy [1]cxvii, of Whiggery [3]141, 141n, 799n; "Hymns on the Elements" [1]120n, 400n, [2]173n
"Life": of Böhme [1]559n–60n, of Bruno [1]559n, [2]976n, [5]812n, of Hölty [2]1116, of Leighton [1]831, [2]911, 926, 1095, 1169, [3]483, 486, 539, 539n, 626, [5]221, [6]54, of Lessing [1]xcvii, [3]640; "Locke book" [1]756, *756n*; "Logosophia" [1]559n, 693n, 756n, [2]170, 722n, 1055n, [3]142n, 295, 295n, 935, 935n, [4]381n; "Mysteries of Christianity" [1]197; "Noetic" [3]742; "Observations on Egypt" [1]738; *Opus Maximum* [1]481, [2]289n, 481n, [3]742n, *see also* VII "Opus Maximum"; "Organum verè Organum" [2]648n
poem(s) on death of Homer [1]757, *757n*, on Mahomet [3]230 q, 230n, on Thor [2]131; "Pioneers of the Reformation" [2]1178n; "Practical Logic" [1]552, 552n; "A Review of old Books" [2]804, 824n; selections on style [1]845n; Swedenborgian projects [5]403; theological novel [2]724n; "Tithes and Church Establishment" [2]899n; translation(s) of Arndt [1]lxivn, of Bacon [4]403n, of Blumenbach [1]535, of Boccaccio [1]542, of T. Burnet [1]851, of *Faust* [1]cvii, from OT [2]369, of Rev [1]480–1, [2]459n, 504, *505n*; treatises on the Logos

[4]407n; "Vindiciae Heterodoxae" [1]347n, [2]717n, 755n, [3]142n, 990–1, 991n; "Weatherbound Travellers" [2]958n; "The Will" [1]693

IX COLLECTIONS AND SELECTIONS

Anima Poetae ed EHC [1]clii, clxxi, clxxiin
Coleridge on Logic and Learning ed Snyder [1]552n, 624n, [2]289n
Coleridge on Shakespeare ed Foakes [1]cxlviin
Coleridge on the Seventeenth Century ed Brinkley [1]cliv–clv, 70n, 183n, 230, 280n, 378n, 801, 854, [2]214, 259
Coleridge the Talker ed Armour and Howes [2]21 q, 252n, 964, [3]18n, [6]73
Coleridge's Miscellaneous Criticism ed Raysor [1]clii, cliii q, cliv, 49n, 62n, 155, 801, [2]214, 864
Coleridge's Shakespearean Criticism ed Raysor [1]clii–cliv
Complete Works ed Shedd [1]cxxxiii, cxxxiiin, 37, 121, 566n, [2]21, 169, 214
Confessions of an Inquiring Spirit [1]713n, 804n, [2]35n, 917n, [3]908n, [4]470n, [5]33n, 516n, 805n
(1840) ed HNC [1]cxxxiiin, cxxxvi, cxlvii, cxlviii, [2]*289n*, 290n, [3]655, [4]260n; (1849) ed HNC and SC [3]655; (1956) ed Hart [1]cxlvn q
Inquiring Spirit ed Coburn [1]cliv, 117n, 738; [2]102, 525
The Literary Remains of Samuel Taylor Coleridge ed HNC [1]cxxiv–cxxvi, cxxxiii, cxxxiiin, cxxxiv, cxxxv, cxxxviii–cxlvii, cxlviin, cliii, clixn, 3, 52, 217, 558n, 617n, 629n, 700 q, 736, 742, 743, 761, 796, [2]14, 142, 214, 244, 573, 590, 797, 921n q, 966, 1105, 1117–18, 1147n, [3]170, 175n, 220, 415, 416, 514, 718, 918, 1064, 1083, [4]99, 102, 161, 189, [5]3, 48, 499, [6]73, 136, 335; *see also* HNC Prefaces
Miscellanies, Aesthetic and Literary ed Ashe [2]533, [3]911n
Notes and Lectures on Shakespeare ed SC [1]cxxxiiin, cxxxvi, cxlviii, clii, cliii, 403n, [2]691, 864, 1038n q, [3]813, [4]279
Notes on English Divines ed SC [1]cxxxvi, cl, 240, 816, [2]244, [3]1083, [6]257
Notes, Theological, Political, and Miscellaneous ed DC [1]cxxv, cxxxiiin, cxxxvi, cl, clii, cliii, clxi, clxiii, 480, 831, [2]42, 110, 214, 815, 954, 966, [3]101, 500, 952n, 1069n, [4]11, 71
Omniana with RS *see* Southey, Robert
Specimens of the Table Talk of the Late Samuel Taylor Coleridge ed HNC [1]cxxiv, cxxxiiin, cxxxiv, cxxxv, cxxxvii, cxlii, cxliin, cxliiin q, cxlixn q, clxviiin–clxixn, 121, 132, 500 q, 800 q, 801 q, 802 q, 830 q, [2]977, 978n, 979n, 1105, 1131, [3]140

X LETTERS

"Catalogue of copies" [1]clvin
"Letter to a Godchild" [1]cxliii
Letters ed EHC [1]clii, clxxi, clxxiin
Unpublished Letters ed E. L. Griggs [1]clxxi

XI MARGINALIA

The references below are exclusively to mentions of, or commentary on, C's marginal notes on an author and his work(s), or on specific works where no author is given. Full references to the texts of the marginalia will be found under the individual author(s) or titles. *See also* Coleridge, S. T. I (3) for more general references to the marginalia and to C's habit of writing notes.

Abbt, T. [1]lxix q
Acta Seminarii Regii . . . Lipsiensis [1]clxx
Adam, T. [2]967; *Private Thoughts on Religion* [1]lxxxiv, lxxxv
Aeschylus *Agamemnon* [1]100; *Prometheus vinctus* [2]1090n
Amory, T. *The Life of John Buncle* [1]xc–xci, clxiii
Anderson, R. *The Works of the British Poets* [1]lxxi, lxxxi, lxxxiii, cx, cxxvi, cliii; *Copy B* [1]cxxxixn; *Copy C* [1]cxxxixn
The Annual Anthology II [1]lxxx
Anster, J. *Poems* [1]clxiv–clxv
Ariosto [1]lxiii
Aristophanes *The Birds* [1]clxvi
Asgill, J. [1]cvi, cviii; *A Collection of Tracts* [1]lxv q, xcviii, cxlin
Aurelius, M. [1]lxxxvi, cxxviii; *Meditations* [1]lxxxii
Bartram, W. *Travels through North & South Carolina* [1]lxiii, lxxx, lxxxvii
Baxter, R. [1]lxiv, lxv, cxxxviiin, 122;

Coleridge, Samuel Taylor—*continued*
Reliquiae Baxterianae [1]ci, cxx, cxxvi; *Copy A* [1]lvii q, xcii, [2]650, 650n; *Copy B* [1]lix q, lixn, clviii, [2]1191
Beaumont and Fletcher [1]lxvii, lxxxix, xci, xcii, xciv, cvi, cxli, cxlviii, clii; *Fifty Comedies and Tragedies Copy A* [1]cxxi q
Berkeley, G. *Siris* [1]lxxxvi
Bible [1]lxiv; *Copy A* [1]lxxvii; *Copy B* [1]817n; *Apocalypsis Graece* ed Heinrichs [1]lxxiii q, cxliv; Apocrypha: NT [3]17n; NT: Rev [1]817n
Birch, W. [1]cxlin
Blake, W., of Highgate [1]xcix, *Silver Drops* [1]clxi
Blanco White, J. *Letters from Spain* [1]clxi
Blomfield, C. J. [1]lxx q; *A Charge Delivered to the Clergy* [1]lxiii, cxxii q
Boerhaave, H. [1]clin
Böhme, J. [1]lxiii–lxiv, ci, cxxviii, cxlin, clin; *The Works* [1]lxxxvi
Bonneval, C. A. *Memoirs of the Bashaw Count Bonneval* [1]xcii
Bowles, W. L. *Sonnets, and Other Poems* [1]lxxviii
Brerewood, E. [1]lxxv, cvi, cviii
Brooke, H. *The Fool of Quality* [1]cxl
Brougham, H. P. *A Speech on the Present State of the Law of the Country* [1]356n
Browne, T. [1]lxiv, lxxxvi; *Religio Medici* [1]lxi q, lxxxi, lxxxvii; *"Works"* [1]lxxxii, lxxxiin, lxxxvii, cxv–cxvi, cxlin, 741 q, [2]1191
Bunyan, J. *The Pilgrim's Progress* [1]cxiii, cxlivn
Bürger, G. A. *Gedichte* [1]lxxviii
Burnet, G. *History of His Own Time*† [1]clxii; *The Life of William Bedell* [1]xciii, clin, clxvii
Burnet, Gilbert *Memoires* [5]221
Burnet, T. *De statu mortuorum* [1]lxxviii
Burton, R. [1]cxvi; *The Anatomy of Melancholy*† [1]xci
Byfield, R. [1]lxxv, cvi, cviii; *The Doctrine of the Sabbath Vindicated* [1]cxxvi
Capper, B. P. [1]clxn
Cave, W. *Scriptorum ecclesiasticorum historia literaria* [1]lxxx
Chalmers, A. [1]cxxxviiin; *The Works of the English Poets* [1]cxln, cxlin
Chiabrera, G. *Delle opere*† [1]clxvi
Chillingworth, W. [1]xcii
Cocceius [1]lxxiii, cxxii, clxi
Coleridge, H. *The Worthies of Yorkshire and Lancashire* [1]lxvii q. lxviin, c, cl
Collier, J. P. *History of English Dramatic Poetry*† [1]clxx
Collins, W. *The Poetical Works* [1]lxxvii
Colquhoun, P. [2]967; *A Treatise on Indigence* [1]lvii q, lxxxiv
Commines, P. de *The History* [1]lxxxix, clxiii
Cornwall, B. *see* Procter, Bryan Waller
Cowley, A. *The Works* [1]lviii q, lxxx
Crashaw, R. [1]53
"Cromwellian Tracts"† [1]lxxixn, cvi, [2]954
Daniel, S. [1]lxvii, cxvi; *The Poetical Works* [1]lxxxvi, lxxxviii, cxxi q, cxxin
Dante *Divina Comedia* [1]lxiii
La danse des morts [2]903n, 967
Defoe, D. *Robinson Crusoe* [1]cxxxix–cxl
Descartes, R. *Opera philosophica* [1]clxv–clxvi
De Wette, W. M. L. *Theodor* [1]xcviin
Donne, J. [1]xcii, cxxxviiin; *Poems* [1]lxxxix, xcn, xci, cxxi q, cxln, clxiii; *Sermons* [1]lxiii, lxvii, lxxi, cxxvi, cxlivn, clxix; *Copy A* [1]xcii
Drayton, M. [1]53
Dunbar, W. *Poems*† [1]clxx
Dyer, G. *Poems* [1]lxxx
Eichhorn, J. G. [1]ci, cxviii, cxx, [2]651, 651n; *Commentarius Copy B* [1]lxxii q; *Einleitung ins Alte Testament* [1]417n, [2]1129
Eschenmayer, A. C. A. [3]114
Eternal Punishment [1]lxi q
Fénelon, F. [1]cxxxviiin, cxlin, [3]750
Fichte, J. G. *Die Anweisung zum seeligen Leben* [1]clin, [2]594; *Die Bestimmung des Menschen* [2]594; *Der geschlossne Handelsstaat* [2]594; *Grundlage der gesammten Wissenschaftslehre* [2]594; *Grundriss des Eigenthümlichen der Wissenschaftslehre* [2]594; *Das System der Sittenlehre* [2]594; *Ueber den Begriff der Wissenschaftslehre* [1]lxxx; *Versuch einer Kritik aller Offenbarung* [2]594
Erigena *see* Joannes Scotus Erigena *below*
Field, R. *Of the Church* [1]cxx
Fielding, H. *Jonathan Wild* [1]cxlin; *Joseph Andrews* [1]xcviii; *Tom Jones* [1]cxlin, [1]215
Fitzgibbon, J. *Speech* [1]lxxx
Fletcher, P. [1]53
Fleury, C. [1]clin
Flögel, C. F. *Geschichte der komischen Litteratur* [1]xciii, clxvii
Forbes, D. *The Whole Works* [1]cxxii q, 279

Friedländer, D. *Sendschreiben* [1]clxvii
Fuller, A. [1]lviii q, [2]967; *The Calvinistic and Socinian Systems . . . Compared* [1]lxxxiv
Fuller, T. [2]804–5; *The Appeal of Iniured Innocence* [1]cxlin; *The Church-History of Britain* [1]cxlin; *The Holy State* [1]cxlin; *A Pisgah-Sight of Palestine* [1]clxi
Godwin, W. *Spital Sermon* [1]lxxx, [2]696
Gray, T. *The Works* [1]cxxxviii
Greville, F. [1]lxxxiv, cviii q, cxvi; *Certaine Learned and Elegant Workes* [1]xci, clxiii
Grotius, H. *De jure belli et pacis*† [1]clxx
Hacket, J. [2]259; *Scrinia Reserata* [1]cxlvin
Hartley, D. *Observations on Man* [1]lxiii, lxxviii
Hayley, W. *The Life of Milton* [1]lxxxiv, [2]1191
Hegel, G. W. F. [1]clii; *Wissenschaft der Logik* [1]lxiii, lxviii
Heinrichs, J. H. [1]cxliv; *see also* Bible *above*
Herbert, G. *The Temple* [1]xcii
Herder, J. G. *Kalligone* [1]lxviii q; *On the Resurrection/Von der Aufstehung* [1]lxix q
Hermann, J. G. J. *De emendenda ratione graece grammaticae* [1]lxxxvi, clxx
Heylyn, P. [2]259
Hillhouse, J. A. *Hadad* [1]cxl, clxix
Hobbes, T. *Leviathan* [2]966
Hölty, L. H. C. *Gedichte*† [1]clxv
Homer [1]lxxxvi, lxxxvii–lxxxviii, clviii, clviiin, clx, clxix
Homeric Hymns (*Homeri hymni*) [1]lxxxvi
Hooker, R. [1]cxxxviiin, 280n, [2]259
Howie, J. *Biographia Scoticana* [1]cxxii q
Hugh of St Victor [1]cviii; *De sacramentis* [1]cvi
Hutchinson, L. [1]lviii q
Hutton, J. *An Investigation of the Principles of Knowledge* [1]lviii q
Irving, E. *Sermons, Lectures* [1]cxxxi q, cxxxin
Jacobi, F. H. *Werke* [3]846
Jahn, J. *Appendix hermeneuticae* [1]480
Joannes Scotus Erigena [1]lxvin q
Jonson, B. [1]lxvii, xciv, cvi, cxli, cxlviii, clii
"Junius" [1]lxxxv
Kant, I. [1]lxiii, lxiv, lxxiv, ci, cxxviii, clii, cliv, [2]594; *Critik der Urtheilskraft* [1]653n; *Grundlegung zur Metaphysik der Sitten* [1]lxxxi; *Logik* [1]lxviii; *Metaphysische Anfangsgründe der Naturwissenschaft* [1]xcv; *Vermischte Schriften* [1]lxxi q; *Copy C* [1]lxii q
Klopstock, F. G. *Messias*† [1]lxxxi
Kluge, C. A. F. *Versuch einer Darstellung des animalischen Magnetismus* [1]lxxvi q
Knight, R. P. *An Analytical Inquiry into . . . Taste* [1]lxxxvi
La Cépède, B. G. E. *Les âges de la nature*† [1]clxvi
Laud, W. *The History of the Troubles and Tryal* [2]1095; *The Second Volume of the Remains* [2]1095
Law, W. *A Serious Call to a Devout and Holy Life* [1]clin
Leibniz, G. W. *Theodicee* [1]xcii
Leighton, R. [1]cxvi, cxxvi; *The Expository Works and Other Remains Copy A* [1]ci, cxx, cxlivn; *The Genuine Works Copy B* [1]ci, cxx, cxlivn; *The Whole Works Copy C* [1]ci, cxx, cxlivn
Lessing, G. E. *Sämmtliche Schriften* [3]640
Lightfoot, J. [1]clixn
Luther, M. [1]cxxviii, cxliv; *Colloquia Mensalia/Table Talk* [1]lxxxix–xc ("Luster's Tables"), ci, cxxxviiin, [2]1038n
Macdiarmid, J. [1]cxxxviiin
Malthus, T. R. *An Essay on the Principle of Population* [1]lxxxi
Mandeville, B. *The Fable of the Bees* [1]clxv
Mather, C. *Magnalia Christi Americana* [1]lxxi, lxxin–lxxiin, xciii, clxvii
Matthisson, F. *Gedichte Copy A* [1]lxxx
Meckel, J. F. *System der vergleichenden Anatomie* [2]1026n
Mendelssohn, M. *Jerusalem* [1]lxxx; *Philosophische Schriften*† [1]clxvi
Milton, J. *A Complete Collection* [1]lxiii, lxxxvi, 280n; *Paradise Lost*† [1]clxii
More, H. [1]cxliv; *Observations* [3]915; *Philosophical Poems* [1]xcii, clin
Nicolson, J. and R. Burn *The History . . . of Westmorland and Cumberland Copy A* [1]lxxxiii
Odes and Addresses to Great People [1]clxi, clxin
Oersted, H. C. [1]clii
Oken, L. [3]114; *Lehrbuch der Naturgeschichte* [1]642n q
"Pamphlets—Divinity" [1]203
Parnell, T. *An Historical Apology for the Irish Catholics* [1]lxxxiv, [2]48, 966
Pascal, B. *Les provinciales* [1]lxiiin, lxxxi
Paullini, C. F. *Disquisitio* [1]lxix q, lxxxi
Pepys, S. *Memoirs* [2]1191
Percy, T. *Reliques of Ancient English Poetry* [1]lxxx

Coleridge, Samuel Taylor—*continued*
Pereira, G. *Antoniana Margarita* [1]lxxi, xciii, clxvii
Persius [1]cvii q
Petrarch [3]265n
Petvin, J. *Letters concerning Mind* [1]lxxxix, clxiii
Plato [1]lxiii, xcii
Plotinus [1]lxxxiii
Poetae minores graeci [1]cxxxn q
Procter, B. W. ("Barry Cornwall") *Dramatic Scenes and Other Poems* [1]cxlin
Ralegh, W. *The History of the World* [1]lxxxv, clin
Rehberg, A. W. *Ueber das Verhältniss der Metaphysik zu der Religion* [1]lxxxiii, clxvi
Reynolds, J. *The Triumphes of Gods Revenge agaynst... Murther* [1]lxxxix, clxiii
Rhenferd, J. [1]cxxxi q, cxxxin, [2]830
Richter, J. P. F. *Museum* [2]180
Rimius, H. *A Candid Narrative of the ... Moravians*† [1]clxvii
Ritson, J. [1]lxxi; *Ancient Songs* [1]xcii; *A Select Collection of English Songs* [1]xcii
Robinson, R. *Miscellaneous Works* [1]lxxxv, clxi
Royal Society *Philosophical Transactions*† [1]lxxvii, lxxxv, [2]967, [4]88n
Sandford, D. *Remains* [1]cii
Sannazaro, J. *Opera omnia* [1]37 q, 60n
Scapula, J. *Lexicon graeco-latinum* [1]lxxxvi
Schelling, F. W. J. [1]lxxiv, ci, cxxviii, clii, cliv, [2]594; *Denkmal* [1]lxix q; *Einleitung zu ... Naturphilosophie* [2]180; *Philosophische Schriften* [1]lxxiv q; *System des transcendentalen Idealismus* [1]lxix q
Schlegel, A. W. [1]lxiii; *Vorlesungen*† [1]xcvi, clxvi
Schleiermacher, F. D. E. *A Critical Essay on the Gospel of St. Luke* [1]clxx
Schubert, G. H. [1]clii; *Allgemeine Naturgeschichte* [1]cliin, clxvii
Scott, Sir W. *Novels and Tales Copy A* [1]801 q
Sedgwick, J. *Hints ... on ... Evangelical Preaching* [1]xciii, clxvii, [2]874
Selden, J. *Table Talk* [1]lxxxvn, cxlin
Sermons or Homilies [1]712n
Shakespeare [1]lxvii, xcii, xciv, cxxvi, cxxxviiin, cxl, cxln–cxlin, clv, clxiv; *Works Copy A* [1]cxxii q, clii, [1]53; *Stockdale's Edition Copy B* [1]clii; *Dramatic Works Copy C* [1]clin, clii, cliii, cliiin; *Dramatic Works Copy D* [1]lxx, clii; *Tempest* [1]cxln
Sidney, A. *Works* [1]clin, [2]966
Sidney, P. *Arcadia* [1]lxxxviii–lxxxix, cviii q
Skelton, P. *Complete Works* [2]1154
Smith, J. *Select Discourses* [1]cxl
Solger, K. W. F. *Erwin*† [1]clxvi, [2]1069n q
Southey, R. *Annual Anthology* II [1]cxiii; *The Doctor* [1]cxiv; *History of Brazil* [1]clxvii; *Joan of Arc* [1]cxiii, clin; "Life of Bunyan" [1]cxiii; *Life of Wesley* [1]lxiii, lxiv, lxv, lxvii, xciii, ci–cii, cxiii, clxviii, 122, [2]496n q; *Lives of the British Admirals* I [1]cxiv; *Omniana* [1]cxiii, clxi, clxin; *Poems* [1]clxi
Spenser, E. [1]cxxxviiin, cxxxixn
Spinoza, B. [1]clixn, [3]75; *Opera* [1]lxviii, 104n–5n, 283n
Stanley, T. [1]cxviii; *The History of Philosophy* [1]clxi
Starke, M. *Travels on the Continent*† [1]clxvi
Steffens, H. [1]ci, clii, [2]594, [3]114; *Caricaturen des Heiligsten* [2]180; *Grundzüge der philosophischen Naturwissenschaft* [2]546n
Stillingfleet, E. *Origines Sacrae* [1]lxxxiv, lxxxv, [2]967
Swedenborg, E. [1]lxiii; *True Christian Religion* [1]606n q; *The Wisdom of Angels* [1]clxvii
Taylor, I. [1]lxxvi; *Natural History of Enthusiasm* [1]cxvi
Taylor, Jeremy [1]cxxviii, 280n; *An Answer to a Letter* [3]515, 515n–16n, [6]298, 298n q; *Eniautos. A Course of Sermons* [1]lxxx; *Symbolon Theologikon: Polemicall Discourses* [1]lxvn, lxxxviii, lxxxix, xc, xci, ci, cxlvii, clv, [2]507n q, 1177n q, [3]515, 515n–16n q, [6]298, 298n q
Tennemann, W. G. [1]lviii q, cxviii, cxxviii, [3]347n; *Geschichte der Philosophie* [1]ci, cliv
Teresa, St [1]cxliv; *Works* [1]xciii
Tetens, J. N. [1]lxxxiii; *Philosophische Versuche* [1]lx q
Tindal, W. *The History and Antiquities of ... Evesham*† [1]cxli
Todtentanz see *La danse des morts*
Tooke, J. H. *Epea Pteroenta or, The Diversions of Purley*† [1]lxxx
Valckenaer, L. K. *Diatribe de Aristobulo Judaeo* [2]339

Vaughan, R. *The Life and Opinions of John de Wycliffe* [3]142n
Vincent, W. *The Greek Verb Analysed* [1]lxxx
Virgil *Georgical/Georgics* [1]cvi, clxiii
Voss, G. J. *Poeticarum institutionum libri tres* [1]lxxxi
Wall, W. *Conference between Two Men* [1]cxvi, cxvin
Waterland, D. *The Importance of the Doctrine of the Holy Trinity* [1]800; *A Vindication of Christ's Divinity* [1]clxvii, 358n
Weishaupt, A. *Ueber Wahrheit und sittliche Vollkommenheit* [1]lxviii q
Wheeler, B. *Theological Lectures* [1]cxlin
White, G. *Natural History of Selborne* [1]xciii, civ, cxxii q, clxviii
Wolff, C. *Logic* [2]1016n
Wordsworth, C. *Six Letters to Granville Sharp* [1]lxxxi
Wordsworth, W. *Prelude* [1]lxiii, lxxxiv

XII NOTEBOOKS

notebook(s)
as confidants [1]cxix; "Day-Books" [3]428, 428n; early list of [1]clvin; "Fly-Catchers" [3]428n; Hooker in [2]1149n; on Kant *Grundlegung* [1]lxxixn; "Mem: Book" [3]668; in Ottery Collection [1]clxxii; "Prognostics of the Weather" in [1]lxxviiin; to be read dramatically [1]cxxvi; transcription of marginalia in [1]cxxvi; use by HNC [1]cxxxiv
Gutch Memorandum Book [1]lxxviii, cliv, 226, [2]1203
N 27 [2]1007n
N 28 [2]1007n
N 29 [1]3, [2]1129
N 30 [1]850
N 35 [2]46, 698
N 36 [2]574n q
N 38 [1]808n q
N 39 [2]505n q
N 45 [1]808n–9n q
N F° [1]414, 489, 669n q, [2]482n q, 503, 504 q, 511n q, 1072
N Q [1]34n, 480 q, [2]837
N R [1]lxxiii q
N Y [4]264n
Notebooks ed Coburn [1]cliv, clv, [4]327n

Coleridge, Sara (née Fricker; Mrs C) (1770–1845) [1]xcvin, cxii, clixn, 116, 329n, 697, [2]7, 132, 242n, 753, 905n, [3]863, 1049, [5]488
age of [1]340, 340n; as annotator [1]411; and C's books [1]clxvii, clxix, 41; letter(s) to [1]cvii q, 329n q; teaches SC Italian [4]102; wedding [1]411; as wife [2]166n
Minnow among Tritons ed S. Potter [2]49 q
Coleridge, Sara (SC) (1802–52) [1]lviii–lix q, lxvii, lxxiv q, cvi, cxii, 52, 413, [2]7, 49, 132, 242n, 905n, 998n, 1038n, [3]781, 930n, [4]391
as annotator [1]411; baptism [1]42, 42n; biography [1]cxxxiv–cxxxvii; birth [1]413; character [6]30; C's bequest to [1]cvin; death [1]cxxv, clxi; in *DNB* [1]clxxii; tr Dobrizhoffer [1]cxxxv; dying [1]839n; as editor [1]lxviiin, cxxvi, cxxvii, cxxxiii–cxlix, clxxi, *see also* Coleridge, S. T. II *Poems* (1844 and 1852), III *BL* (1847), IV *EOT*, IX *NLS*, *NED* ed SC; engagement to HNC [2]91, [3]778n; inscription by [1]116; learns Italian [4]102; letters [2]259 q, [3]101; marriage [6]31; owner of annotated books [1]clviii, clxix, [2]977, [3]400, 838, [6]34; on Henry Reed [2]864; relations with Pickering [1]clxii, clxiin; "Sariola" [3]930; as transcriber of marginalia [1]cxxviiin, cxli–cxlii, 545, 701, 831, 867, [2]19, 110, 112, 113, 357, 815, 828, 954, [3]132, 508, 514, 784, 843, 844n, 943, 952n, 1080, [4]11, 164, 170, 341, 402, 447, [5]120, [6]131, 257; Virgil bequeathed to [6]30
tr *History of the Chevalier Bayard* [1]cxxxv; *Memoir* ed Edith Coleridge [1]lxxiv q, clxviiin q, 413n, [4]283n q; *Phantasmion* [1]cxxxv; *Pretty Verses for Children* [1]cxxxv
Coleridge, Sarah (née Hart) (d 1830) [2]91 ("Hunt")
Coleridge, Stephen William Buchanan (1854–1936), owner of annotated books [2]526, 815
Coleridge: Studies by Several Hands ed Blunden [1]clxxxin
Coleridge, Walter Henry Praed (1886–1967) [1]clxvii, clxxiii, 802

Coleridge, William Hart, Bishop of Barbados (1789–1849) [1]cxxxiv, [2]91
Coleridgeism [3]25n
colic [5]236, 360, 795
collapse [5]372
collation [1]688
collect(s) [4]665
"Collect . . . 25th Sunday after Trinity" see *BCP*
collectaneum/collectanea [2]780, [4]304
Collection of Old Plays see Dodsley
collector [5]552
college for missionaries [3]8
Collier, Jeremy (1650–1726) [1]lxxxii, 155, 183n, [3]992n
  prose style [1]155–61, 166–8, 177, 181n, 182–4
  Ecclesiastical History [2]83; *see also* Aurelius *His Conversation* tr Collier
Collier, John Payne (1789–1883) [2]632n, [3]171n, [4]693n, 723n
  History of English Dramatic Poetry [1]clxx; *An Old Man's Diary* [3]795n; *see also* Coleridge, S. T. VI *Seven Lectures* ed Collier
colligation(s) [1]452, [3]833
Collingwood, Dr (fl 1818) [2]363
Collins, Anthony (1676–1729) [1]248n
Collins, William (1721–59) [1]38, [2]864, [4]605
  Ode on the Poetical Character [2]94; *Poetical Works* [1]lxxvii; MT [2]94–6; *Popular Superstitions of the Highlands of Scotland* [4]605n q
Collinson, Peter (1694–1768) [2]85 q
colloquy, ease of [2]58
"colluvion" [2]387, 387n–8n
Colman, George, the Elder (1732–94) [1]373, 379, 379n, 381, 384, 387, 388, 390, 391, 392, 396, 398, 399, 402, 406, 407n
Colman, George, the Younger (1762–1836) [1]183n, [2]75; *see also* B&F *Dramatic Works* ed Colman
Colombo [4]86–7
colon(s) [1]133, [3]890, 891
colonel [5]378
colonisation [2]311, [5]102n, [6]35, 44
  national [5]283
colonisers [5]106
colonists [2]908, [5]103
  Dutch [5]106
colony/colonies [3]1082, [5]102, 323
  role of Church in [6]29n; Roman [3]309
Colossae [1]465
colour(s) [1]589, 642, [2]403, 608, 1115, [3]384, 389, 944–5, 1017–18, 1025, 1033–4, 1059, 1060, [4]98, 167, 187, 208–9, 209n, 313n, 460, [5]599, 704, [6]171–2, 227–8
  blind man and [2]491; c.-blindness [3]986n; glittering [2]545; intentional [3]919; law of [4]167; origin of [1]637–8; in silk [1]762, 796; c.-theory [3]1014, 1018n, [4]164, 167n, [5]452, 452n; *see also* light
Colquhoun, Patrick (1745–1820) [2]967
  A Treatise on Indigence [1]lvii, lxxxiv; MT [2]97–8; 967; *Treatise on the Police of the Metropolis* [2]97
Colson, Francis Henry (1857–1943) *see* Philo Judaeus *De confusione, De legum allegoria, De migratione* tr Colson and Whitaker
Columbia University *see* New York City
Columbus, Christopher (1451–1506) [1]528n–9n
Colver, A. Wayne *see* D. Hume *Natural History of Religion* ed Colver
Combe, George (1788–1858) *Essays on Phrenology* [3]716n
Comber, William Turner (fl 1807) *An Inquiry into the State of National Subsistence* [4]170
combinant(s) [1]676, [6]116
combination [3]129, [4]128
comburent [4]396, 396n
  and combustible [4]428, 428n
combustibility [1]662, [3]995–6, 996, 999
combustible [1]612, 780
  and comburent *see* comburent; and combustive [1]570, [3]1026
combustion [1]590, [3]1000, 1003, 1009, 1011, [4]428n, 539, [6]228–9
  spontaneous [5]252n
Come, Landlord, Fill a Flowing Bowl [1]369n
"come-at-able" [1]399, 399n
comedy/comedies [3]192, 405, [3]702, [5]98, 595
  of B&F [1]393; and Christianity [2]82; comic literature [2]753–83; demands characters [3]182; elder [4]817; English [2]74–5; fused with tragedy [1]366, 367; Greek [2]74, 775n; higher [4]842; modern [3]172; Roman [2]775; and wickedness [2]83, 84
Comenius, Johann Amos (Jan Amos Komensky) (1592–1670) [5]128
Comestor, Petrus (d 1179) [2]11–12
comet(s) [1]623n, [2]144n, 276, [3]285, 323, 944, 945–6, 946n, [4]201, 515–16, 517–22, [5]231, 232, 249, 249n, 263, 385, 701

Comet (steamboat) [5]862n
cometarian [3]323, 323n
comfits [2]919
comfort(s) [2]617, [3]611
  spiritual [5]636
comforter(s) [5]134
  Job's [5]75
Comforter (God) [1]602, [3]584, [5]535
comic, the [4]838
  and tragic [4]693
Coming, Second *see* Jesus Christ: Second Coming
comma(s)
  as insects [1]133; Johannine [2]52n
command(s)
  categorical [4]409–10; divine [2]26; explicit [1]334; of God [1]877; universal [5]123
commandment(s) [5]457
  divine [5]604; God's [5]123, 656; Ten *see* Ten Commandments; universal [6]59
commemoration [2]662
"commend" [3]4
comment, running [1]633
commentary, revealed [3]448
commentator(s) [1]591, [3]465, [4]195, 357
  prognosticating [2]516
commerce [1]515, 724, [2]619n, 1192n, [5]262, [6]20
  domination of [5]428; extended [2]1192; with Heaven [1]123; intellectual [6]14
commination(s) [6]117
Commines/Comines, Philippe de La Clyte, Sire de (c 1447–1511) [1]368, 368n
  The History [1]lxxxix, clxiii, 368n; MT [2]99–101
commission [5]634
Commission under Charles II [1]328
committees, secret [1]332
commixtion [5]352
commixture [1]562, [6]170
Commodus, Lucius Aurelius (161–92) [1]298, 298n, [2]692, 692n, [5]40, 40n
common, the [5]269
common law [1]124
common sense [1]6, 212, 313, 318, 329, 520, 675, 734, [2]78, 206, 547, 559, 604, 648, 788, 803, 930, 930n, 1058, [3]328, 737, 817, 1006, 1043, [4]40, 52, 262, 297, 304, 425, 478, 604, 645, 665, 668, 863, [5]74, 156, 276, 319, 541, 552, 564, 664, 743
  Church of [5]795; dictate of [1]495; divines [5]553; English [2]204; limitations of [5]543n; profound [5]589; and science [5]480; true [1]675
Commonalty, Jewish [1]451
commonplace(s) [1]773, 673, [2]12, 1071, [3]221, 1054
  erroneous [2]68
commonwealth(s) [1]789, [2]827, 827n, 1201, [3]801, [4]78, 715, [5]146n, 508
  of ants [3]581; of Christendom [4]240; Hebrew [3]106–13, 426; of nations [1]733; Parliamentary [1]313; *see* also England: Commonwealth
Commonwealthmen [4]594
communicant(s) [3]13, [5]555
  presumptuous [5]685
communication(s) [5]481
  draw-bridge of [1]140; of ideas [2]636; intercourse of [1]350; miraculous [5]622; organs of [5]796; premature [5]325–6
"communify" [4]331
communion [5]678, [6]56
  with God [1]621; of saints [2]673
Communion [1]340, 704, 713, 838, [2]787n, [3]340, 512n, 527n–8n
  in both kinds [6]21n; exclude from [5]634; Romish [1]514, 810; *see also* Eucharist
"Communion of the Sick" see *BCP*
community/communities [1]601n, [2]745, 881, [3]13, 17, 18, 157, 428, 460, [4]258, [5]93, 175, 638, 799
  Christian [1]324, [2]1162, [5]512, 665; old [2]311; representative of [5]530
compact [3]154, 159n
  social [3]233
compactness [5]455
compages [2]26, 26n
companion [3]786, 786n
A Companion to the Altar see under *BCP*
company, loose [4]662
Comparative Literature [2]1115
comparatives [2]278
comparison [2]345, 1069, [3]94, [4]173, 498, 595–6, [5]820
  faculty of [5]720
compass [3]868, 868n
  in Donne [2]223; dynamic [5]263; needle *see* needle, magnetic; of powers [3]1020, 1020n, 1022; reversed [3]478
compass of nature [1]578–9, 775, [2]546, 854n, [3]61n, 139n, 325n, 951, 996n, 1006n, 1017n, *1020n*, 1021n, 1063n, [4]314n, 315n, 323n, 387n, 395n–6n, [5]228n, 241, 247n, 263n, *265n*, 334n, 335, 342, 342n, 346n, 352, 352n, 355n, 358n, 435n, 451n, [6]227n, 228n; *see also* polarity

compatibility, negative [5]302
"compatible" [6]28
compensations [5]587
competence [4]162
compilation [4]270, 272, [5]802, 812
compiler(s) [1]456, [2]377, 405, 411, 448, [4]478
of liturgy [5]519
complacency [4]817
parental [2]37
complaints [5]464
compliance [5]642
components [4]383–4
"componible" [4]384, 384n
componible and decomponible [4]383–4, 384n
composition(s) [3]897, 915–16, 948, [4]358, [5]324, 672
chemical [5]260; fragmentary [4]162; historical [1]448; musical [6]115
compositor(s) [1]766, [2]216, [3]882–3, [4]762, 813
compositum [2]311, [3]44, [5]548
compost, hybrid [1]811
compound(s) [2]621, 1119n–20n, [4]383, 387, [6]172, 300
Greek [4]326
"comprehend" [5]6, 595, [6]64, 82, 82n, 86, 86n
comprehend and apprehend *see* apprehend
"comprehension" [2]250
comprehension [1]358, 567, [2]626, [4]95, [5]6
and apprehension *see* apprehension; forms of [1]201
compression of thought [2]238
compromise [3]162, 166, 166n, 799, [4]14, 17, [5]484
of principles [3]141, 141n; spirit of [1]331
Compton, Henry, Bishop of London (1676–1714) [4]549n
compulsion [2]802, [3]720, [5]208
and necessity [2]641; and obligation [1]495–6, [2]641; of senses [1]282
compunction [4]770
concave and convex [5]268–9
"conceit" [2]1145
conceit(s) [2]238, [4]735
equipoise [5]424; theological [6]325
conceivability [3]755
conceivable [4]430, 430n
"conceive" [5]6
conceiving, mode of [5]443
Concentus et gratulatio musarum Cantabrigiensium [1]68n
concept(s) [3]242, 242n, 244–5, 791
of Hebrews [3]108; and ideas [2]729n
"conception" [2]250, 1148
conception(s) (mental) [1]496, 645, [2]673, 729, 1160, [3]45, 49, 248, 248n, 853, 857, 860, 901, 957, 968, [4]122, 401, [5]299, 408, 449, 615, 744–5, 799
abstract [5]481; alien [2]153, [5]131; anthropomorphic [5]156; clearness of [6]223; distinct [2]674, [3]101, [5]612, 803; of God [3]643; and idea(s) [1]236–7, [2]295–6, 295n, 332, 478, 500, 729, 884, 1134, 1145, 1147, 1148, [3]744, 744n, 755, 848–9, [4]17n, 234, [5]126, 126n–7n, 131, 135, 135n, 156, 481, 481n, 599–600, 638, 751, 751n, 752, 756, 756n, 760–1, 761n, 770, 771, 772–3, 773n, 776, 776n, 793, 797, 797n, 828, 828n, [6]80, 86, 86n, 87, 114, 114n, 299; and image [4]217, 217n, 234–5; and imagination [6]115; impossible [3]671; indistinct [3]788, [5]317; internal words [2]1148; logical [6]143; most general [5]806; necessary [5]809; and notions [4]131, [5]828, 828n; Platonic [6]140; precise [5]481; products of understanding [3]991; purification of [5]751; of understanding [5]795
conception(s) (physical) [3]329, 350
immaculate [1]44, 504, 506; of Jesus *see* Jesus Christ, conception of; miraculous [4]256, [5]465;
conceptionist(s) [2]1146, [5]692, 770
conceptualist [2]1147, [5]657
sensible [2]478
"concern" [6]194
public [5]642
concerningness [2]662
concert [4]610
concessions [2]210, [3]54
conch [6]148–9
conciliare [2]271, 271n
concircularly [3]341, 341n
conclave, papal [3]232
conclusion(s) [3]94, 163
legitimacy of [6]299; practical [1]468
"concomparable" [4]194, 194n
concord [1]347, [2]1021
concordance(s) [2]314, 314n
Concordantia discordantiarum [5]573, 573n
Concordia discordantium canonum see Gratian
concordia discors [4]238n
concrescents [1]595
concrete(s) [4]166, [5]599, 702
and abstract *see* abstract; chaotic [1]595
concubine [5]633
concubinism [3]699
concupiscence [1]30, [5]615, [6]157

concursion [2]206
condemnation [2]495
abiding [5]497
condescension [2]327, [5]817, 439
ineffable [5]466
"condescensive" [1]161
Condillac, Etienne Bonnot de (1714–80) [2]648, 648n, [3]877 ("Condilliac"), 877n, [5]703n, 827, 828n
error of [3]354n; theory of knowledge [2]341
Logic [1]39
conditio sine qua non [2]943
condition(s)
generic [5]383; material [5]825; moral [3]453; negative [4]301
Condorcet, Marie Jean Antoine Nicolas Caritat, Marquis de (1743–94) [2]849n, [3]207, 806n, [5]703n
conduct
law of [5]37; outward [5]562; reform of [5]650; root of [1]821
conductor(s) [3]382, [5]358
of power [4]389
"confabrication" [2]1173, 1173n
"confacciamento" [2]377, 377n
confederacies, literary [5]812
confessio ignorantiae [3]340–1
confession(s)/Confession [1]324, [2]1096, [3]145, [4]176, 549, 662, [5]496
Augsburg [6]60; of ignorance [3]340–1; Peter's [5]634; seal of [5]577n; of witches [6]99
confessor(s) [2]717, [3]442
gullible [5]823; Scottish [2]1175
confidant [4]466
confidence(s)
improper [5]585; reckless [3]750
confirmation, outer [1]496
Confirmation [1]263, 266, 349, 532, [3]440n, [4]306, [5]398n, 535–6, 537, 566n, 636, 658–67, [6]257–8
relation to Baptism [1]247
conflagration(s) [5]252, 578, 610
self-kindled [5]373
conflict [2]564
Confortator [5]134
confusion [1]137, 496, 631, 634, [2]300, [3]22, 22n, [5]269, 290, 304, 342, 470, 588, 789
advantages [1]143; Jeremy Taylor's [5]614; verbal [4]458; visionary [5]611; of words [2]1164
confutations [5]347
"congenerous" [5]418
congregation(s) [1]234, 265, 307, 308, 321n, 339, 359, [2]319, 323, 654, 655, [3]756, 758, 759, 875, [5]144, 530, [6]259
Christian [6]259; crowded [2]328; elect [1]263; and priest [1]246; promiscuous [1]264, [2]1082; sober [1]328
Congregationalist(s) [1]311; *see also* Independents
Congress
American [4]96; of Munster [3]993; of Vienna [3]250n, 852n
Congreve, William (1670–1729) [1]38, [2]17n, 74–85, 779
error of [2]83; wit of [2]17
Love for Love [3]985n; *The Mourning Bride* [2]83; *The Old Bachelor* [2]77, 78, 81; *The Way of the World* [2]84
Conistonmere [3]974
conjecture(s) [2]445, 451, [3]649, [5]525
bold [1]396
conjunction(s) [4]166, 166n, [6]172
disjunctive [1]246, [4]466, 466n, [5]653
conjuration [5]271
conjurer(s)/conjuror(s) [2]257, 1108, [4]146, [5]306, 390
conjuring [2]611, [4]143
connate and innate [6]149
connection(s) [5]37, 487
cause [4]107; continuing [3]833; forms of [3]172, 222, 223
connexus [1]527
Connor *see* O'Connor
conquaintances [1]688
conquassare [1]710n
conqueror(s) [4]807, [5]273
conquest [2]564, 784, 1017, [3]161, [6]10
Conquest, Norman [4]15
Conradus [2]301
consanguinity, prohibited degrees of [5]393; see also *BCP*: "Table of Kindred and Affinity"
conscience(s) [1]178, 223, 271, 283, 334, 504, 685, 807, 875, [2]143, 183, 186, 297, 332, 591, 613, 618, 663, 663n, 768, 927, 1140, 1141, 1179, [3]25, 94, 105, 265, 266, 266n, 267n, 306, 317, 393, 579, 588–9, 590, 599, 605, 677, [4]74, 77, 216, 239, 241, 262–3, 367, 409–10, 650–2, 674, 702, 728, 771, 784, 789, 791, 792, 793, 841, 854, [5]68, 155, 302, 311, 425, 475, 592, 612, 677, 820, 822, [6]91
bad [5]564; binding of [1]342; Bo-peep with [6]262; Christian [3]735; complacent [3]488; and consciousness [4]239n; counterfeit peace of [3]750; court of [3]328, 496, [4]96; deification of [3]928; egotism of [5]496; does not err [5]298; erring [3]787; of fact [3]879; false [2]1178; india-rubber [2]940; individ-

conscience(s)—*continued*
ual [1]352; influence of [5]728; law(s) of [1]201, [2]614, [3]267, 956, 958, [5]168, 656; liberty of [6]154–5; mask of [1]319; purifying of [3]597; quasi [4]799; related to reason [2]189; remonstrating [2]160; restless [5]122; seared [3]879; struggle of [4]770; stupefied [3]751; stupor of [4]137; uncorrupted [5]618; wounded [5]419
"conscious" [3]177, 177n
"consciousness" [5]175
consciousness(es) [1]561, 679, 868, [2]547, 604, 630, 999–1000, 1008, 1030, [3]75–6, 77, 86, 95, 297, 379, 382, 550, 670, 716, 850, [4]115, 124n, 225, 261–2, 314, 411, 653
of actions [5]614; antecedent of [4]216; below [2]1167; central [5]474; clear [5]612; collective [3]312; common [4]448; condition of [5]814; and conscience *see* conscience; dawn of [1]647; after death [1]125; defined [6]170; degree of [2]635; depends on body [1]676–7; dim [2]1148; direct path [2]605; distinct [1]818, [3]91; divine [1]564, [5]16, 18; empirical [3]243, 243n; energies of [1]566; equivocal use [2]629; everlasting [2]559; of fact [3]879; facts of [5]756; human [1]566, [2]615, [3]588, [5]159; of imperfection [5]93; inherited [6]16; intermutual [5]12; inward [5]514; meaning of [5]94, 94n; moral [5]298–9; multiplied [3]975; mutual [5]14; original unity [3]243, 243n; predicate [3]85; primary and secondary [2]610n, [4]374, 374n, 451, 451n; primary law of [2]631; recollective [4]374; reflective [4]542; reflex [2]160; resistance to [2]632; of the Revelation [2]189; of self [2]552; self-c. *see* self-consciousness; spontaneous [4]448n; survival of individual [1]283; twofold [2]606–7; underneath [3]265; unthought-of [4]845
consecration [3]597, 597n
consent [3]154
fullness of [1]310
consequence(s) [1]342, 812, [2]806, 807n, [4]465, [5]10, 37, [6]298
captious [5]9; chain of [5]626; Christian [1]827; false [5]803; moral calculation of [1]223, 223n; practical [2]107–8
consequent [1]679, [4]267, [5]788
and antecedent [5]6
consequentiality [1]201
conservatio [5]680n
Conservative [4]151, [6]47
consideration [4]9
consistency [2]893, [3]353, [4]787
consistory [1]341
consolation [4]52
consonance [3]891
consonants [5]434, 435
conspiracy [5]226
conspirator [4]806
constable [2]357
Constance, Council of [2]505–7, *507n*, [5]143n, 633; *see also* Costnitz
Constantine VI, Emperor of Eastern Roman Empire (771–?797) [2]272
Constantine the Great (c 274–337) [1]721, [2]72, 287n, 721, 729, 729n, 730, 731n, 734, 734–5, 735, 735n, 741n, [3]142, 142n, 143, 144, 235, 235n, 417, 417n, 481, 761, [4]184, 307, [5]538, 538n
Constantinople [1]698, [2]12n, 670, 1139, [3]145n, [5]69, 70, 832, 833
Council of [2]296n, 731n, 732n, 740n; Santa Sophia [2]305, 305n
Constantinopolitan(s) [2]68
C. Creed [2]732n
Constantius II (317–61) [2]732n, 738, [3]143, 143n, 144, 145, 145n, 692–3, [5]663n
constellation(s) [1]399, 399n, [2]235, [3]540, [4]762
constipation [3]399
constituent(s) [3]21, [5]300
constitution (personal) [2]210, [3]787
bodily [2]521; of the human mind [1]508; of mind [4]130; moral [3]803; necessity of [3]720
constitution (political) [1]224, 275, 809, [2]1150, [3]149, 154, 157, 163–4, 228, 678, 755, 787, [4]11–17, 19, 24n
Baxter on [1]294; best [5]301; blessed [6]264; British [1]224, 864, [3]680, [4]23; Church and [1]809; of Church [2]1139, [5]128; of C of E [5]568; is the country [6]48; danger to [1]724; ecclesiastical [5]67; English [1]331, [2]68–9, [3]799, [5]539; free [5]405; Hebrew [3]107–8, 112; as idea [4]12; maxims of the [1]290; Mosaic [2]146; political [5]301–2; of realm [2]933, [3]143; spirit of [1]332; theory of [4]12; uterine life of [4]79; wicked [5]277; wounds to [1]356
construction(s) [1]776, [3]62, 138, 289, 1011, [4]401
constructive act [3]949; of matter [3]295, 295–6; mental [5]600; polar [1]639; of relations [5]410; of Schelling [6]233; of the sense [5]828; successive [5]750
construing, false [5]775
"consubstantial" [2]725, *725n–6n*, 732, 733, 734, [3]233, [5]627, 633n, [6]85–6, 86n

consubstantial [2]743, 744, 749, [3]757
consubstantialis [6]86n
consubstantialists [2]745
consubstantiality [2]725, *725n–6n*, 751, [3]233, 233n, [5]573
consubstantiation [2]280, 304n, 1038, 1038n, [3]761n, [5]5, 5n, 398n, 554, 554n, 835, [6]21n
 Luther on [1]297, 297n, 862, 862n, [2]671, 671n; *see also* Eucharist
consubstantiationist [5]11
consul [1]610
consummation of this world [5]607
consumption [6]55
contact [1]794, [3]865
 plane of [3]293; spiritual [5]796
contagion [1]356, 496, [3]46, 62
 fanatical [6]104; of infidelity [5]512; salutiferous [5]404
"contagious" [2]362, 362n
contemplatio [4]12
contemplation [1]659, [2]1025, [3]561, [4]421, [5]781, 795, 797
 form of [5]631; objects of [6]133; silent [5]627; of truth [5]776
contemporaneity [3]792n, [4]221, 222n
contemporary/contemporaries [4]723
 of Shakespeare [3]179, 187; testimony of a [2]444
contemporeity [3]791–2
contempt [2]942, 1055, [3]625, 1065, 1068, [4]842, [5]753
 dread of [4]860; philosophic [4]805
Contender, grand [3]817
context [2]286, [5]571, [6]20
 and text [5]15
Conti *see* Quinziano Stoa, Gianfrancesco
Continent, the [4]817, [6]14, 45n, 121
contingency [2]152, 153, [3]746, [4]109, 543, 548, [5]465
continuity [1]537, [2]855, [3]119n, 129, 319, [4]604
 breach of [1]457; distinction in [5]360
continuous, the [1]625
continuum [4]211
 streamy [5]726
contraband [1]252
contract(s) [5]379, [6]101
 breach of [1]360; marriage [5]550; original [5]299; robberies by [1]343; social [2]1148, 1148n, [3]154n
contraction(s) [1]589, 599, 604, 612, 641, 660, 665, 666, 667, 776, [2]853, 853n, 854–5, 855n, [3]61n, 62, 123, 123n, 996, 999, 1003, 1008, 1021, 1021n, 1022, 1060, [4]387–8, 388n, 396, [5]266, 342, 344, 346, 430, 431, 438, [6]227
 and attraction *see* attraction; and centrality *see* centrality; contractive power [3]997; and dilation [1]633, [5]451
contractive [1]595, 611, 624, 625, 638, 639, [3]61, 1004
contradiction(s) [1]304, 601, [2]152, 191, 200, 247, 446, 601, 729, 844, [3]346, 363, 588, 667, [4]362, 436, 450, 451, 669, 864, [5]3, 269, 285, 298, 349, 459, 470, 680, 754, 771, 842, [6]51, 78, 267
 apparent [4]743, [5]340; childish [2]950; in essence [5]425; French [2]347; gross [5]656; idea and [5]600 ("contradictory"); invisible [3]916; to law of nature [2]202; palpable [2]270; seeming [1]175; tangle of [5]622; in terms [1]201, 252, [3]428, 743, 1050, 1054, [4]381, [5]450, 542, 710, 794, [6]132, 231; unsurmountable [5]708; verbal [1]107
contradistinctions [3]372
contrariety [3]130, [4]351
contrary/contraries [2]855n, [3]1003n, 1026n, [5]231, 400, 459
 counteracting [5]292; not negation [2]559; and opposite(s) [1]331, 678, 678n, [2]1030, [3]327, 361, 361n, 1026, [4]450, 450n, 603, 603n; philosophy of [5]452n; potential [5]784
contrast(s) [1]647, [3]791, [4]221
"contraversy" [2]569, 569n
contrition [1]324, [2]27, 28, [5]585, 585n, 682
contrivances, mechanic [5]297
controversialists, Protestant [2]38
controversy/controversies [1]316, 456, [2]569, [3]589, [4]305, [5]547
 endless [5]571; fair conduct of [2]1156n; Protestant [1]317; quinqu'articular [5]15; religious [5]589; sacramentary [2]280; Trinitarian [6]61
conundrum(s) [1]486, 673, [3]1047, [5]712, 719, 747
convalescence [2]1166, [5]125, 181
convalescent [5]583
convent *see* nunnery
conventicle [1]30, 872, [4]190
convention
 of agonies [4]824; legitimate [2]506
conversation(s) [1]150, [2]190, [3]589, [4]723, 786, [5]416, 527
 feeling of [2]123; of ladies [3]171; of a poet [1]91; rhythm of [1]390; in Scott's novels [4]612; serious [5]484; of souls [1]754

conversion(s) [1]304–5, [2]204, [3]209, 519, 542, 605, 991, [4]621n, 633, 637, 657, [5]65, 125, 125n, 156, 156n, 163, 171, 172n, 582, 586, [6]42, 301
of Christians [5]644; individual [5]642; of Jews [2]916, 916n; mark of [5]650; of St Paul [2]492, [5]172; religious [5]229n; by the sword [3]699; to truth [1]645
convert(s) [3]20, 520, 602, 673, 1069, [4]474, 475, [5]85, 172, 628, [6]303
admission of [5]608; Corinthian [5]518; Gentile [1]832, [5]623, 623n, [6]69; Italian [1]447; Jewish [1]832, [3]9, [4]471, [5]623, 635; new [2]653; pagan [1]315, [2]471; from paganism [5]522; of Palestine [5]645; to RC Church [1]844; Saxon [5]138
convertendi [5]635
convex and concave *see* concave
conviction(s) [1]496, 675, [2]1154, 1160, [3]661, [5]424
and habit [6]126; heat of [4]181; inward [5]318; positive [5]204; spiritual [2]143
convict-ship [2]460
Convocation [1]341, [2]115
at Canterbury [2]1150n; of C of E [1]359, 359n, [2]1149–50, 1150n; loss of [5]532; at York [2]1150n
"convolition" [5]418, 418n
convulsion [3]375n
Conyngham, Elizabeth (née Denison), Marchioness Conyngham (c 1766–1861) [4]608, 608n
Conyngham, Henry, 1st Marquis Conyngham (1766–1832) [4]608 ("Cunningham"), 608n
cook [1]873
Cook, B. (fl 1810) [3]936, 937
Cook, James (1728–79) [1]536n, 615, 615n, [2]73–4, 74n, 861n, 980, 981n, [3]1074
First Voyage [3]1073
Cooke, George Frederick (1756–1811) [6]270
Cooke, Thomas (1703–56) *see* Hesiod tr Cooke
cookery [3]44
Cookson, H. E. (fl 1926) [4]139
coolness [4]860, [5]372
coomb [1]26, 26n
Cooper, Anthony Ashley, 1st Baron Ashley and 1st Earl of Shaftesbury (1621–83) [1]353n, [3]141, 141n, 144n
Cooper, James Fenimore (1789–1851) [1]211–12, 212n
Gleanings in Europe ed Spiller [1]212n; *The Red Rover* [1]212n
Cooper, John Gilbert (1723–69) [1]38
Cooper, Sir William (fl 1653) [2]1132
co-operation [5]652
moral [5]654; negative [1]820
co-ordination [1]805
Copeland [5]389, 389n, 390n
Copenhagen [5]312n
battle of [1]177n
Copernicus, Nicolas (1473–1543) [1]559, [2]668n, [3]201
Copernican system [3]780, 780n, [4]508, 522, [5]232
De revolutionibus orbium celestium [1]559n
co-persons [2]321, 321n
The Copie of Three Petitions [2]42
copiousness of argumentation [5]558
Coplestone, Edward (1776–1849) [2]164n, [4]107, 107n
Copley, John Singleton, Baron Lyndhurst (1772–1863) [2]1190, 1190n
copper [1]546, [2]985
green venom of [1]786
Copper Indians [2]985
Coppermine (river) [2]987n
Coptic (language) [1]483, 574n, [2]380–1, [4]257
copula [1]616, 646, 690, [3]43–4, 443, 830, [4]113, 830, [5]171, 177, 285, 409, 680
of electricities [4]359; logical [5]174; vital [2]611
copulation [1]768
copy/copies
and imitation [3]172, 172n, 892, 892n, [4]168, 168n, 765, 765n, 780; and original [5]10; prompter's [4]723; of verses [2]1120, [3]901
copyist(s) [1]439, [2]135, [3]819, 892, [5]402, 515
inspired [5]473
copy-right [1]69
copy-soul [2]553
coral(s) [2]74, [3]1037, [5]360
Corbet, Richard, Bishop of Oxford and Norwich (1582–1635) [2]14
"Life" by Chalmers MT [2]15
Certain Elegant Poems [2]15n; *The Fairies' Farewell* [2]15n
Corcoran, Thomas H. *see* Seneca *Seneca* tr Corcoran
Cordatus, Conrad (1480–1546) [2]774n
Cordelia (*King Lear*) [1]394, [4]818
Cordero, Gratien (fl 1634) *see* Pascal *Les provinciales* tr Wendrock, Cordero, and Brunetti
Cordilleras [5]105
Cordoba/Cordova [3]927, 927n

"Cordomi" (i.e. C) [1]90, 99n
cordon [4]419
Core (Bible) [2]717
Coriat *see* Coryat
Corinth [1]400, [2]655–6, 701, 749, [5]391n, 517–18, 517n, [6]56, 56n
 Church at [5]390; Temple of Venus [2]701, [5]517n
Corinthian(s) [2]703, [5]391, 515n, 518n, 522, 683n
Cork [5]179
cormorant, library [1]cii–cxv
corn [3]308, [5]304
 c.-grinding [5]730; heap of [5]568, [6]170; c.-laws [3]800; *see also* Parliament: Act(s)/Bill(s): Corn Bill
Cornbury, Lady Theodosia (née Capel) (d 1662) [4]83
Corneille, Pierre (1606–84) [4]736
Cornelius Agrippa *see* Agrippa von Nettesheim, Heinrich Cornelius
Cornell University *see* Ithaca NY
corner-stones [3]436
Cornford, Francis MacDonald (1874–1943) *see* Plato *Theaetetus* tr Cornford
corning [3]44
Cornish, Francis Ware (1839–1916) *see* Catullus *Carmina* tr Cornish
Cornthwaite, Tullis I. (fl 1832–42) [2]521, [6]184
Cornwall [1]47, 99n, 293, [2]512n
"Cornwall, Barry" *see* Procter, Bryan Waller
Cornwall, Duke of (*King Lear*) [4]815, 820, 822
corolla [2]61 ("corona")
corona *see* corolla
Coronation Oath *see* oath(s)
corporations, literary [5]812
"corporeity" [4]492n
corporeity [1]614, 682, 682n, [4]492, [5]546
"corporific" [3]949, 949n
corpse [5]834; *see also* corse
corpus [3]139, 156, 156n, 431
 c. intelligibile [1]863; *c. mortuum* [1]618, 618n, [2]1029, 1029n, [4]412, see also *caput mortuum*; *c. noumenon* [2]566, [3]443; *c. phaenomenon* [1]283, of Christ [1]863; *c. politicum* [3]678, [4]251, [6]60; *see also* body
Corpus juris civilis [4]666n
corpuscles [3]202, 286, 296
 corpuscular atom(s) [3]46; *see also* atom(s)
correction, letch of [1]399
corrector [2]216
correlate [1]517
correlative(s) [3]12, [5]231
 objective [6]132
correspondence(s) [5]459
 dictionary of [5]403; relation of [5]370; two-fold [5]766
correspondents [2]455, [5]159, 413
 and opposites [1]678
corrosiveness [1]546
corruptible, the [6]65
"corruption" [1]164
corruption(s) [3]41, 444, [5]545
 in Church [5]578, 677; in early Church [2]740, [5]683; of gospel faith [5]662; of Latin Church [6]12; popish [1]473
corse [2]446
 Hebrew word [2]446; maggoty [1]719
Corse, John (fl 1792–9) [2]527
Corsham [1]494, [4]183
 C. House [4]183n
Corsican, paltry [1]715
Corston, William (fl 1810) [3]943
Cortes, Hernando (1485–1547) [2]163n
Corvino (in Jonson) [3]180
Cory, Mr [3]893, 893n
Coryat, Thomas (c 1577–1617) [2]820 ("Coriat")
Cosin, John (1594–1672) [1]254, 255, 255n, 328
cosmogony [2]1144, [3]325, [5]430
 of Indians [2]986, 986n–7n; Mosaic [2]346, 393
"cosmolater" [4]581, 581n
cosmology [3]296
cosmoplasm [4]386
cosmoplasts [5]430
Cosmopolis [2]753
cosmopolitism [3]250
cosmos [1]602n, [2]583, 684, [3]313
 and chaos *see* chaos; see also *kosmos*
"cosmotheism" [1]643n, [5]251, 251n
cosmotheism [5]769, 769n
 Böhme's [1]643
Cossacks [6]60
Costnitz (Constance) [3]765n
costume [3]21, 492, [4]717n
 of Judaism [3]40; of truth [3]69
co-symbolists [5]619
Cotelier, Jean (Cotelerius) (1627–86) [1]491
 SS Patrum qui temporibus apostolicis floruerunt [2]711n
Coton, Pierre (1564–1626) [5]543
cottage(s), comfortable [1]755
cottager [3]478, [6]216

Cotterel/Cottrell, James (fl 1649–68) [1]742
Cottle, Amos (d 1800) [1]89, 97n
Icelandic Poetry [1]97n
Cottle, Joseph (1770–1853) [1]cxiii, clxix, 97n, [2]1184
death [1]clxi; letter(s) to [1]lxxxiv q, 736n q, [2]559n, [3]508n q, 509n; as printer [1]cviii; supplier of books to C [1]lxxxvii, xcvii, cv, 411
Early Recollections [1]cxxxvii; *Reminiscences* [4]294
Cotton, Charles (1630–87) [1]763n
Cotton, John (1585–1652) [3]818
Cotton, Nathaniel (1705–88) [1]38, [2]864
cotton-factors [4]342, 342n
cottonian binding *see* binding
couching-needle [1]810, 810n
Couchman, G. W. [2]586
Council, Amphictyonic *see* Amphictyonic Council
Council(s) (of Christian Church) [2]*732n*, 1140, 1149, [3]73, 234, 825, [5]661
general [2]1149–50, [3]231–3, 760–1, [5]632–4, 639, 665; Lateran [5]633; orthodox [5]627; of 72 [3]113, 113n. *For particular Councils see the place-names*: Antioch, Ariminum (Rimini), Basel, Constance, Constantinople, Ephesus, Florence, Jerusalem, Laodicea, Milan, Nicaea, Pisa, Sardica, Seleucia, Sirmium, Toledo, Trent, Tyre
Council, Privy [5]13
counsel [5]578
counsellors [2]58
"count" [3]786, 786n
countenance(s) [4]762, 813, [5]65
beautiful [5]416; flushed [1]173
counter(s) [5]789
counter-action [4]604
counterbalance [1]508
counterfeit(s) [3]132, 755
"counterpay" [5]198, 198n
counterplay [5]198n
counterpoise [3]679
counter-power [1]563
Counter-Reformation [5]104n
counter-sleep [5]726
counting house [2]999
country/countries
free [5]280, 300, 378, 381; liberty of [1]332; love of [5]115; polar [5]263; popish [1]352; sacred idea of [1]740
county [5]174
couplet(s) [3]404, [4]828, [5]768
courage [4]775, 811, 817, 830, [5]29, 829
Courier [1]lxxxv, xciv, 197, 654n, 738, 857n, [2]117, 685, 696, 873, 877n, 1120n, [3]882n, 884n, [5]104n, 686n
courses, academic [3]626
court(s) [1]314, [4]80
Babylonic [6]324; Catholic [5]507; Christian [2]826; criminal [1]29; c.-dress [2]64; of Exchequer [3]166n; French [1]359; high [2]375; of High Commission [2]937, 937n
courtesans [5]323
courtesy [2]236, 329 ("curtesy")
phrase of [2]322
courtiers [2]827, [4]739, [5]484
Court-preachers [5]662
cousin(s)
german [2]1051, [5]287; marriage of [2]91, [3]778, 778n; second [5]287
cove(s) [6]204
covenant(s) [1]445, [2]579, 1179–80, [3]465, [4]663, [5]598, 649
divine [3]455; of faith [5]623, new [5]674; of grace [5]623; new [4]256; oath *see* oath(s); of works [5]623; *see also* Solemn League and Covenant
Covenanter (God) [4]531
Covenanters [1]351, [2]1171n, [3]141n, [4]587, 591, 594
Coventry [1]230
Coventry, Sir William (?1628–86) [4]79
Coverdale, Miles (1488–1568) [1]429n
"covet" [2]146
cow [2]200
c.-broth [1]397; c.-club [6]218; c.-dung [5]225
coward [3]280
cowardice [2]126, 1201, [4]771, 789
of pain [4]10
Cowley, Abraham (1618–67) [1]37, 184n, 223, 223n, 428n, [2]17n, 224n, [4]583n
C's opinion [4]76, 76n; and Crashaw [1]63n, 67, 67n; and Donne [2]219; and Greek [1]73n; and Milton [2]254, 654, 654n; prose style [1]157, 157n, 182, 182n
De plantis [2]102; *Hymn to Light* [3]888 q; *Loves Riddle* MT [2]105–6; *The Mistress* MT [2]104–5; *Ode upon His Majesty's Restoration* MT [1]73; *Piramus and Thisbe* MT [2]105; *A Vision* [1]219n; *The Works* [1]lviii, lxxx; MT [2]102–6
Cowper, William (1731–1800) [1]*218n*, 220, 220n, [2]761, 873, 1156n, [5]830
tr Andreini [2]974–5, 974n; blank verse of [1]218; superior to Thomson [1]74n
The Flatting Mill [3]783n, [4]60n; *Poems* ed

John Johnson [4]60n; *The Progress of Error* [2]1068n; *The Task* [1]218n, 254n q, 519n; *Yardley Oak* [2]879 q, 879n, [3]250–1 q, 251n; *see also* Homer tr Cowper
Cox, Charles F. [1]215
Cox, Richard, Bishop of Ely (c 1500–81) [5]505n
coxcomb(s) [1]105, [2]92n–3n, 1012, [3]672, 754, [4]97n, 188
coxcombry [4]721
coy [3]890
cozening [5]287
crab [2]565, [3]444
Crabb (fl 1820; possibly J. Crabb, fl 1811–34) [1]816
Crabb Robinson, Henry *see* Robinson
crab-sticks [2]1155
Crackanthorpe family [3]980
"cracked" [6]289
crackers [4]13
crackpates [3]698
craft, Devil's [5]105
Craik, Thomas Wallace *see* Shakespeare *Twelfth Night* ed Lothian and Craik
cram, lobby [3]157
crambe [5]809, 809n
crambe bis cocta [4]647, 647n, [5]809, 809n
"crambist" [1]528, 528n
cramp
  charm for [1]129, [4]11–12, 12n; of strength [2]228
Cranae [3]402
craniology [2]1012n
cranioscopy [2]1012n
Cranmer, George (1563–1600) [2]1131
Cranmer, Thomas (1489–1556) [1]329n, 422n, 809, 809n, 834, 835, 839, 1097n, [3]515, 515n, 1079, [5]392–400, [6]298, 298n; *see also* Strype *Memorials of . . . Cranmer*
cranny [5]514
Cranz, David (1723–77) *The History of Greenland* [1]431n
Crashaw, Richard (1612/13–49) [1]37, 53, [2]17n, 103
  and Cowley [1]63n, 67, 67n; "Life" by Anderson MT [1]47–8; 62
  The Flaming Heart [1]48n; MT 62; *A Hymn to . . . Saint Teresa* MT [1]65–7; *In the Glorious Epiphany of Our Lord God* MT [1]68; *Music's Duel* [1]63n; *Natalis Principis Mariae* [1]68n; *On a Prayer-Book* MT [1]63–5; *On Hope* MT [1]49, 67–8; *On the Birth of a Princess* MT [1]68; *Out of the Italian* MT [1]68; *To the Name Above Every Name* MT [1]68; *To the Queen* MT [1]49, 68; *Upon the Death of . . . Mr. Herrys* [1]63n; *Verses to St. Teresa* MT [1]48; *The Weeper* MT [1]62–3
crassament [3]612
crassness [5]423
"cratemen" [3]633, 633n
Crates (fl c 470 BC) [4]147
Cratilinth, King of Scotland (legend) [2]1171
Cratinus (c 519–423 BC) [2]757n, [3]828n
craving(s) [4]814, [6]299
  instinctive [5]822; of soul [4]647
crazy [2]82, 82n
"creability" [2]578, 578n
cream [2]1056, 1057
  Devonshire [2]365; skimmed [1]731
"create(d)" [2]732, 732n, [5]465
creation(s)/Creation [1]114, 767, 784, 787, 873, 877, [2]340, 393–4, 419, 584, 723, 1144, [3]29, 59n, 519, 609, 755n, 915, 919, 944 ("Creative Week"), [4]135, 295, 354, 383n, 444, [5]626, 680, 766, [6]301
  absolute [3]348; account of [5]603; an act [3]643; atheistic scheme [1]120; Böhme's account [1]600–1; continuous [3]949, 949n, [5]207; entails redemption [2]293; eternal [2]748; *ex nihilo* [3]138–9, 138n, [6]113; external [5]743n; first act of redemption [3]22, 66; c.-form [3]64; not generation [6]78–9; of man [3]60; new [1]574, 582, [3]594, 611, 876, [5]607; outward [1]674; perpetual [5]385, polar scheme of [1]663–4; positive [3]1091; possibility of [1]690; redemptive [2]293; related to fall of spirits [1]645, 649; scale of [3]580–1; before time [2]34; in time [3]89, 531n, [6]315n; three moments of [1]652; unsubstantial [2]425; whole [5]523; to will causatively [3]139; the Word in [1]600
creativity [2]580
creator/Creator [1]173, 527, [2]1085, [3]109, [4]299, [5]26, 83, 369, 482
  all-wise [5]809; emanations from [5]652; intelligent [5]618; invisible [1]729; self-conscious [2]665; will of [4]414
creature(s) [1]564, 602, [2]1186, [3]101, [5]10, 626, 810
  as apostasis [2]676; born c. [3]913; fallen [5]135; free will of [6]113; rational [5]407, 476, 483; responsible [2]328; spiritual [5]15; time innate in [5]814; c.-worship [5]626; worship of [2]743, [4]298–9
creatureship [2]1102

"credentialise" [2]39, 39n
credibilising [4]839
credibility [4]641, [6]96
canon(s) of [3]661, 700
credit
bills of [2]621; in the world [3]585
creditor [2]659, [3]26, 47, [5]66
credulity [2]454, 710, [3]780, 919, [5]516, [6]96, 112n, 120n
of G. Burnet [1]843; in C of E [3]921, 921n; malignant [4]249
Creech, Thomas (1659–1700)
tr Lucretius [1]38; MT 51, 82
creed(s)/Creed [1]324, [2]657, [3]668, 690, 766, [4]80, 260, 479, 669, [5]619, [6]19, 85
Apostles' [1]236, 236n, 311, 311n, *312n*, 345, 464, 836, [2]69, 69n, 184n, 334, 335n, 657, 681, 1099, [3]56, 56n, 445, 445n, 608–14, 610n, 689, 689n, 691–2, 691n, 732, 732n–3n, 766, 766n, 768, 768n, [4]175, 175n, [5]129, 556, 570, 570n, 619–22, 619n, 627–8, 637, 642, 646, 646n, [6]62–3, 92, 92n; Athanasian [1]586–7, *587n*, 836, [2]751n, [3]369, 369n, 762n, [5]558n, 643, [4]300, 300n, [5]3, 8–9, 8n, 9n, 10, 13–14, 49–50, 50n, [6]72, 72n, *see also* C., pseudo-Athanasian; baptismal [1]311, [3]692, [5]571, 572, 642; Baptist [5]501; blundering [6]72; of Cerinthus [6]63; cheerless [4]158; in Christian Church [1]344–5; C of E [4]641, [5]129, 568; common [4]663, [5]13; Constantinopolitan [5]576; copies of [5]637; defined [5]10; federal [3]691; of a freeman [5]829; Gentile [3]474; of Gregory [6]61 q; history of [5]619n, [6]62n; humourist's [1]126; and individuals [3]367n; initiatory [5]620; of Jerusalem [6]61; John's [5]628; of Melanchthon [6]60; Nicene [1]236n, 312, 312n, 345, 478, 478n, 707n, 712n, 836, [2]35, 69n, 184n, 661, 735n, 740n, 751, 751n, 788n, [3]16n, 77n q, 145n, 232n, 524n, [4]300, 673, [5]7n, 9, 10, 13, 14n, 50, 50n, 576n, 618, 633n, [6]306n q, *see also* faith, Nicene; oscillatory [2]265; papist's [2]30; Paul's [5]628; Peter's [5]628; of Pius IV [5]14n; Pope Paul's [5]14, 14n; popular [5]578, 655; pseudo-Athanasian [1]836–7, 836n–7n, [2]732n, 737, 737n, [3]52, 52n, 762, [4]300n, [5]8n, 9n, 558; purpose of [3]368; of Quakers [3]928; Roman [6]62; secular [2]940; Sedgwick's [4]669; simple [5]540; of Sirmium [2]744n; sufficient [5]628–9; of Theophronius [2]736–7; true [5]620; truth of [6]62; Wesley's [5]155
Creek Confederacy [1]226
crepitus [3]721, [5]287
crescent [1]705, 705n
Cressida (*Troilus and Cressida*) [4]810
Crete [2]573, [5]44
cretic [3]652n
Creuzer, Georg Friedrich (1771–1858) [2]389n, 1089
Symbolik und Mythologie [2]86; *see also* Hermann and Creuzer
crew [5]862
Crewe-Milnes, Robert Offley Ashburton, 2nd Baron Houghton, Marquess of Crewe (1858–1945) [4]189, [6]295
crick in neck [5]295
cricket [1]222, 222n–3n
Cricklade [2]821
crime(s) [1]47, 369, 812, 874, [2]107, 980n, [3]787, [4]241, 662, 774, 809, 815, 854, [5]316, 521, 641, 728, [6]101
aggravation of [1]834; all equal [5]612; three classes [5]103
criminals [4]241n, [5]102–3, 315, [6]36
crimson [5]813
cripple, sturdy [2]16
crisis/crises [5]517, 591
ecstatic [5]759; highest [5]404
Crisp, Thomas Steffe (1788–1868) [2]1184, [4]3
Crispin, Moll (fiction) [4]650
Cristogalli [3]754
criterion/criteria [1]825, [3]726, [5]9
double [5]579; of heretic [5]570; moral [2]328
critic(s) [1]402, [3]886, 901, [4]863, [5]768
of art [1]143; biblical [1]433, 455, [2]1106; candid [1]50, [5]149; favourable [4]466; genial [2]406; German [4]836, 836n, [5]325; historical [2]452; Hurdite [3]894; Italian [6]322; Johnson as [2]76, 76n; judicious [4]470; modern [1]50, [2]296; moral [4]866; philosophical [4]596; Scotch [1]60; sensible [4]250; sorry [2]969; sturdy [1]407; as toad [1]216, 216n
Critical Review [4]654n
Critici sacri ed J. Pearson and others [1]416, [5]167, 167n
criticism(s) [2]14–15, 864, 999, 1156n, [3]418, 451, 702 ("criticise"), 889, [4]408, [5]149n
of Bible *see* Bible: criticism; cold [1]730; court of [1]378; definition [2]710; easy [1]527–8; French [4]779, 780; genial [4]779; higher *see* Higher Criticism; historical [2]895, [3]309, [5]694; interpret a poem [1]482; Johnson's [3]651–2; Kantian [5]405n;

matter-of-fact [1]388; minute [2]440; particular [4]849; philosophical [4]836; poets above c. [3]886; verbal [3]589, 647, [4]297; as vivisection [5]102n; wholesome [2]1058; *see also* Bible: interpretation of

criticismus [5]405, 405n

critique [5]753

of intellect [3]919; Kant's [5]714

Crito (5th century BC) [2]343

croaking [5]319

crockery [5]395

crocodile [1]427, 427n, [3]771n, 935n

crocus [6]151

Croesus (6th century BC) [1]723

Croget's Isle [2]74

Croker, John Wilson (1780–1857) [2]90, [5]124, 124n

and Asgill project [1]lxv

Cromwell, Oliver (1599–1658) [1]73, 223n, 224n, 245, 247, 248, 300, 333n, 335, 336, 336n, 728, 728n, 803, [2]19, 363, 522, 818n, 823n, 838, 838n, 949, 949n, 954, 970, 970n, 973, 1196n, 1200–1, 1200n–1n, [3]141, 141n, 169, 801, 801n, 802, [4]181, 182, 591, 657n, [5]124n, 145, 146, 146n

baseness of [2]109; despair over commonwealth [1]313; and Independents [1]283n; "Old Noll" [3]188, 188n; "Sultan" [2]950, 950n

Speech to the Parliament . . . 4th of September, 1654 [2]111; *Speech to the Parliament . . . 12th of September, 1654* [2]111; *Speeches to the Parliament in the Painted Chamber* MT [2]107–9

Cromwell, Thomas, 16th Earl of Essex (?1485–1540) [5]393 ("Crumwel")

"Cromwellian Tracts"† [1]lxxixn, cvi, [2]110–12, 357, 954

Cronus (myth) [2]575, 577, 578n; *see also* Saturn

Crook/Crooke, Andrew (d 1674) [1]742

crop(s) [5]256

increase of [2]785

cross/Cross [1]343, [2]267, 923, 1080, 1177, [3]42, 43n, 465, 517, 606, 613, 663, [4]656, 665, 745, [5]30, 524, 548, 680

adoration of [2]1158; in baptising [1]322; of Christ [5]492, 496, 497, 670; images of [2]1158; mental idol [1]820; miraculous [2]734; in polar scheme [1]636; redemption by [5]152; shame of [6]304; virtue of [4]633

"cross-catching" [4]182, 182n

Cross, Frank Leslie (1900–68) see *Oxford Dictionary of the Christian Church* ed Cross

Crossfell [4]29

crossing in baptism [1]329

crotchet [2]36, 36n

crow(s) [3]1045, [4]669, [5]69, 296, [6]153

crowd(s) [1]496, [5]487

crown(s)/Crown [2]511, [5]796

dispensing power of [1]323; flower as [2]933; and king [2]1043n; patronage of [1]724; prerogatives of [2]60; represents nation [3]801; as seed and flower [2]61; of thorns [5]608; Triple [1]872

Crown and Anchor *see* London

Croye, Isabelle, Countess of (in Scott) [4]613

Crucifigeri [6]167

crucifixes [1]821

Crucifixion [1]284, 713, 714, 821, [2]279, 343, 497, 671, 902n, 1173, [3]42, 55–6, 611, [4]41, [5]535, 465

scene of the [5]523

Cruciger, Casparus (1504–48) [3]718

crudity/crudities [2]63

cruelty/cruelties [4]693, 823

foul [1]807; unmanly [1]353

Cruikshank, Ellen (b 1775) [1]9

Cruikshank, John (b 1773) [1]9

Cruikshank, William (d 1802) [1]9, [2]15

Crummock [3]980

Crumwel, Lord *see* Cromwell, Thomas

crusaders [2]739

Crusoe, Robinson (in Defoe) [5]106, 688, 688n

crust, opaque [2]922

crustacea [6]103

crutches [1]169

crypto-papist [1]842

crypto-Romanism [5]308, 497n

crystal(s)/chrystal(s) [1]299, 685–6, 775, 775n, [3]325, 1023, 1042, [4]332n, 529, [5]265, 491

magic [6]122; polished [5]529

crystallisation/chrystallisation [1]589, 594, [5]294

mineral [5]350

Ctesias (fl 398 BC) [1]771–2

cube(s) [3]1007, [6]232

of nature [1]663; cubo-c. [1]581

cubit(s) [4]166, [5]387

cuckold [4]785

cuckoldism [4]700

cuckoo [2]67, 67n, 806, [4]539

cucumber(s) [5]751, 767

Cuddy (in Scott) [4]594

Cudworth, Ralph (1617–88) [1]lvii, 113n, 119–20, 119n–20n, 358, 358n, 557n, 582n, [2]340n, 348n, 788n, 1173n, [4]581n, [5]80, 81n
  not annotated by C [1]lxiii
  True Intellectual System [1]119n, 358n
cui bono [2]251, [5]62
Cul [2]584
Cullen, Charles (fl 1804) *see* Clavigero *History of Mexico* tr Cullen
Cullen, William (1710–90)
  First Lines of the Practice of Physic [4]149n; *Synopsis nosologiae methodicae* [1]505n
Cullender, Rose (fl 1662) [3]190n
"culminant" [3]565n
Culpepper *see* Colepeper
cult(s) [3]492, [4]625–6
cultivation [3]1087, [5]301, 770
  and civilisation *see* civilisation
culture, Jewish [4]40n
cum hoc ergo propter hoc [1]298, 298n, 953
Cumae [1]449n
Cumberland [1]cxxxv, 75, 777n, [2]529n, [3]795, 974–82, [4]737, 737n, [5]234, 389, 389n, [6]95, 121n, 152, 249
Cumberland, Countess of *see* Clifford, Margaret
Cumberland, Earl of *see* Clifford, George
Cumberland, George (1752–1848) [3]940, 941
Cumberland, Richard (1632–1718) [2]75
Cumberland, Richard (1732–1811) [6]216
Cumpstone, George (fl 1723) [3]977
"cumuleity" [6]170
cumulus [5]719
cunning [2]928, 945, [4]196, 846, 860
  of instinct [4]809; malignant [5]476
Cunningham, Allan (1784–1842) [1]38, 365, [2]140, 1095, *1169*, 1173–4, 1174n
  marginalia addressed to [2]1173–4; owner of annotated books [1]cxxii
  The Lives of the Most Eminent British Painters, Sculptors, and Architects [6]333
Cunningham, Francis (1820–75) [1]365
cup [4]517
  reclaiming of [6]20; exclusion of laity [5]683, 683n
Cupid (myth) [2]94–5, 875, 876, 876n, [3]1066n, [5]100
  and Psyche [2]87, 87n, [3]*1066*
cupidity [2]80
Cuquilla [4]489–90
Cuquisako [4]489–90
curate [4]783
curds and cream [2]859
cure(s) [3]398, [4]657
  magnetic [3]397; miraculous [1]872, [2]41, 722
Curiatii [4]168
curiosity/curiosities [1]168, 280, 370, 763, [3]45, [4]788
  active [1]763, 796; interest of [5]474
"curious" [2]130, 130n
curious, the [1]763, 796
Curleople [6]149
Curley, Edwin *see* Spinoza *Collected Works, Ethics* tr Curley
currency [2]620, [3]132, [3]565
  British [2]621; metallic [6]20; reform of [5]686n
current(s) [2]640, 820n, [4]543
Curry, Kenneth [1]90n
  "The Contributors to *The Annual Anthology*" [1]89n; *see also* RS *New Letters* ed Curry
curse(s) of the law [2]147
  mythic [1]539
"cursed" [2]660
cursing [5]146
curtain [5]395
Curteys, Richard, Bishop of Chichester (?1532–82) [5]395
Curtius Rufus, Quintus (1st century) *De rebus gestis Alexandri Magni* [2]1058, 1058n
curve [2]889
Cusanus (Nicholas of Cusa) (1401–64) [5]806
Cushites [2]384, [5]337
custard [2]641
custom(s) [1]161, 383, [2]601, [3]469, [4]239, [5]159, 167
  ancient [5]298; arbitrary [1]159; Asiatic [6]324; Jewish [5]551, 651; of parliament [4]12; primitive [1]267; universal [4]23
custom house [3]152
customer [4]612
"cut" [6]195
Cuthbertson, John (fl 1810) [3]938, 940
Cuthell and Martin *see* London
Cuthlac (8th century) [6]17
Cuvier, Georges (1769–1832) [1]62n, 460n, [2]177, 177n, 862n, [3]842, 842n, [4]491, 532, 532n, [5]141, 141n
cyanic acid [5]260
cyanogen [4]315, 315n, [5]260n
Cybele (myth) [1]7, 8n, [2]354n, [3]448n
Cyclades [2]820, 820n
cycle(s) [3]160, 160n, 1008, [5]267
cycloids [1]601

Cyclops (myth) [3]410, 468n, 817, 817n
Cydnus (river) [2]919n
cylinder [3]1004
optic [3]716, 716n
cymbal [1]7, 7n
cymbalum [1]7–8, 7n–8n
cynicism [2]872n
cypher(s)/cipher(s) [1]689, [3]102, 1071, [5]585
Arabian [5]228; C's [1]173n
cypherers [5]457
cyphering [5]160, 226, 324
Cyprian, St (c 200–58) [1]233, 245, 470, 470n, [2]53n, 272n q, 669, 699, 722, 723, 916, [3]764, 764n, 818 q, [4]513, [5]605 q, 619, 643, 684 q, [6]84–5 q
definition of Church [1]846
Cyprus [2]95n, [4]254, 863
Cyrano de Bergerac, Savinien de (1619–55) *Histoire comique des états et empires de la lune* [4]501n
Cyrenaics [2]872n, [5]227n
Cyrene [5]832n
Cyril, St (827–69) [2]298, 337
Cyril/Cyrillus, St, Archbishop of Alexandria (d 444) [5]24, 591n, [6]61, 182
De trinitate [6]180–1 q; *Epistles* tr McEnery [6]181 q; *Thesaurus* [6]180–1 q, 182 q
Cyrillus, Glossator [1]26n
"Cyrus" [2]897–8, 898n
Cyrus (d 529 BC) [1]844n, [2]148, 148n, 149, 149n, 378, 416, [3]461–2, 465, 479, 479n, 569
Cyrus (in Xenophon) [5]725–6
czar [3]756–7

D., S., transcriber of marginalia [2]966, [4]11
Dacier, André (1651–1722) [1]155
dactyl [1]384, 671, 858, [2]1039, 1040, [5]118, [6]255
dactylo-spondaic hexameter [5]689
daemon(s)
in the distance [1]223; giant [2]514; of sea [1]425; of Socrates [5]722–3; *see also* demon(s)
dagger [2]614, [3]220
Dagon (myth) [2]575, 577
daher [2]856, 856n
Dahomey [3]883, 883n
daimon [1]179n, [5]170, [6]137; *see also* demon(s)
daisy [5]278
Daja (in Lessing) [3]217
Dalai Lama [2]1023, 1023n
Dalberg, Karl Theodor Anton Maria von (1744–1817) *Betrachtungen über das Universum,* tr as *Observations on the Universe* [4]276
Dalehead [6]121n
Dalgetty, Dugald (in Scott) [4]591–2, 591n
Dalilah *see* Delilah
Dallison, Charles (fl 1648), [2]113
The Royalist's Defence [2]42; MT 113–15
Dalrymple, Sir Hew (1750–1830) [2]940n
Dalton, John (1766–1844) [1]596n, [2]889, 889n, [3]941, [4]377n
Dalyell, Sir John Graham (1775–1851) *see* F. Huber *New Observations* tr Dalyell
Dalyell/Dalzell, Thomas (c 1615–85) [2]1171n ("Dalziel")
Dalzell, Alexander *see* Erasmus *Letters 1535 to 1657* tr Dalzell
damages, action for [5]67
Damascene *see* John of Damascus
Damascus [2]455, 492
Damis (1st century) [5]741
"damnation" [2]568
damnation [2]565, [3]62, [5]10–11, 188n, 613
damnatory clauses [3]368
"damned" [2]567
damned, state of the [1]449
Dampier, William (1652–1715) [2]165, *165n*, 861n, 980
Collection of Voyages [2]165n; *The Voyages and Adventures* [1]lxxviiin, [2]165n, 981n
damsels, hapless [5]236
Dan [1]424
dance(s) [3]62, 172, 221
motley [4]827; tragic [4]168
dancing [2]190–1, [2]739n
d.-master [1]160, 160n
Danes [5]196
danger [5]588
Daniel (Bible) [1]843n, 844n, [2]155, 343n, 375, 409n–10n, 412n, 894, [3]731, [4]58, 645, [5]652, 653, [6]119
life of [6]217
Daniel, Henry (fl 1814) [1]xcvii, 228, 505n
Daniel, Peter Augustin (1874–1913) [1]379n–80n
Daniel, Samuel (1562–1619) [1]lxvii, cxvi, 37, [3]165n, 581 q, 581n
laureate [1]56n; "Life" by Chalmers MT [2]14–15; marked passages [1]53; sober-minded [2]119; well-languaged [2]127–8
Civil Wars see *The History of the Civil War*; *Cleopatra* [2]119n; *A Defence of Rhime* [2]119n; *Delia and Rosamond Aug-*

Daniel, Samuel—*continued*
mented[2]116; *A Description of Beauty* MT [1]59; *The History of the Civil War* MT [1]58, [2]116, 118–30, 119n–20n q, 120n; *History of England*[2]117; *Hymen's Triumph* [2]116, 117, 120n, [5]99; *The Passion of a Distressed Man* MT [1]46–7; *Poems of Daniel and Defence of Rhyme* ed Sprague [1]45n; *The Poetical Works* [1]lxxxvi, lxxxviii, cxxi, cxxin; MT [2]116–30; *To the Angel Spirit . . . Sidney*[2]116; *To the Lady Lucy* MT [1]46; *To the Lady Margaret* MT [1]4–5; 44n, [3]426 q, 426n, 546 q, 546n; *To the Lord Henry Howard* MT [1]44; 44n

Danish (language) [5]197

Danish (people) [1]540

La danse des morts (*Todentanz*) [2]903n, 967; MT [6]266

Dante Alighieri (1265–1321) [1]lxiii, 117n, [2]213–14, [3]886, 900, 903n, [4]509n, 796, 824, 824n, 114

and Byron [3]485; his gallant bark [2]579; Hebrew [1]485; and H. F. Cary [4]101, 101n

Canzoni [2]131, [5]114n; *Convivio* tr W. W. Jackson [5]114n q; *De vulgari eloquentia* [4]796n, tr Howell [5]109n q, 114n, tr (Italian) *De la volgare eloquenza* [4]796, 796n, [5]109 q, 114n; *Divina Commedia* [2]131; *Copy A* ed Placidi MT [2]132, tr J. D. Sinclair *Divine Comedy* [2]137n q; *Inferno* tr Boyd [2]131; *Opere* [2]131, [5]109n; *The Vision . . . of Dante Alighieri Copy B* tr H. F. Cary [2]131; MT 133–8

Danton, Georges Jacques (1759–94) [2]510n

Danube [1]191

Danvers, Charles (c 1580–1627) [2]1046n

Danvers, Charles (d 1814) [1]xcivn, cx, clxi, 89, 851

Danzig [2]755

dao [4]36, 36n, 166, 166n

Daphnis (myth) [1]23

Darbishire, Helen (1881–1961) *Some Variants in Wordsworth's Text* [1]clxxiiin; *see also* WW *Poetical Works* ed de Selincourt and Darbishire

d'Arblay, Alexander Charles Louis (1794–1837) *The Vanity of All Earthly Greatness* MT [2]139; [4]3

Darcet, Jean Pierre Joseph ("d'Arcet") (1777–1844) [3]939, 942

Darcy, John (fl 1799–1820) [1]688n

daring [5]745

Darius I, King of Persia (548–486 BC) [2]149n, 434, [3]465, 466, 466n

dark, the [5]264–5

dark ages [2]786

darkness [1]576, 605, 631, 663, 678, 685, [2]298, [3]17, 61, 62, 139, 139n, 1060, [4]443, 443n, [5]27, 615

Böhme on [1]665; cloud of [3]248; kingdom of [3]305; and light [1]585, 686, 824–5, [2]298, 325, 568, 1000, [3]997n, 1018, [4]427, 441, 537, [6]64, 228; Mosaic [3]1024; mystery/mysteries of [1]518, [2]891; of negation [5]595; papal [1]515; spiritual [1]13; state of [4]492; world of [1]170

Darley, George (1795–1846) *Sylvia* MT [2]140–1

darling(s)

poor [1]266; sinful [1]264, [6]259

Darnelly, Daniel (c 1604–59) *In obitum . . . Donne* MT [2]238–40

Darnley, Lord *see* Stewart, Henry

Darnton, Robert *Mesmerism and the End of the Enlightenment in France* [4]325n

dart [4]292

Darwin, Charles Robert (1809–82) [5]388n

Darwin, Erasmus (1731–1802) [1]120n, [2]27n, 102, 353, 794, [4]91, 91n, 97n, 638, [5]388n, [6]239n

The Botanic Garden [2]507n–8n q, [3]630 q, 817n, [4]202n; *The Economy of Vegetation* [4]202n; *The Loves of the Plants* [4]263n, 313n; *The Temple of Nature* [3]1073n, [4]202n q; *Zoonomia* [1]589n (*Phytologia*), [4]91n, 638n q, [5]388n

Darwinian [4]97, 97n

darwinising [5]388

Dasein [4]403n, 404

dash [6]145

Dashwood, Anna Maria (fl 1835) [4]101

date(s) (in time) [3]628, 629

collation of [6]168; distinguish prophecy [6]166; omission of [3]636, 638

dative [3]831, 833–5, 833n

datum [4]359

datur, non intelligitur [1]567

daughter(s) [2]273, [4]334–5, 718

Davenant, John, Bishop of Salisbury (1576–1641) [2]913, [5]155, 155n

Davenant, Sir William (1606–68) [1]lxxviii, 37, [4]77n, 724n

The Death of Astragon [1]413, 413n, [2]162n; *Gondibert* MT [1]49

David (Bible) [1]110, 316, 423, 424, 427, 458, 798, [2]65, 144, 144n, 147, 149, 257, 286, 301, 308, 329, 399, 406, 483, 674, 785, 829, 836, 894, 917, 1153, [3]109, 519,

542, 606, 697–8, 711, 754, 758, 767, 768, 775, [4]48, 49, 50, 55, 58, 298, 298n, 299, 304, 483, [5]178, 178n, 416, 417, 590, 590n, 681, [6]107n, 302
descendant of [5]635; magnificent [3]34; psalms of [1]428, 428n; sceptre of [2]483; son of [5]652; throne of [1]458, [4]52–3, [5]606; time of [2]395
David, Christian (1690–1751) [5]128, 131
David Evangelizans [5]179
Dávid/Davidis, Francis (1509–79) [4]670, 670n
David, Richard (b 1912) *see* Shakespeare *Love's Labour's Lost* ed David
Davies, John (?1627–93) [2]954n
Davies, Sir John (1569–1626) [1]37, [2]14
On the Immortality of the Soul [1]52
Davies, Julian *The Caroline Captivity of the Church* [5]492n
Davis, Bertram Roland (1897–1972) [2]615n
Davis, K. [2]214
Davison, John (1777–1834) *Discourses on Prophecy* [1]441n; MT [2]142–57
Davy (*2 Henry IV*) [4]589, 589n
Davy, Sir Humphry (1778–1829) [1]lxxii, 63n, 89, 90n, *99n*, 220n, 282n, 546n, 626n, 648n, 650, 779, 779n, [2]520, 520n, 746n, 787n, 848n, 857n, 883, 889n, [3]104, 104n, 127n, 481n, 936, 939, 940, 951n, 1000–1, 1017n, 1020, [4]122, 160, 160n, 315n, 319n–20n, 358, 359n, 392, 392n, 526n, 531, 531n, 837n, [5]169n, 255n, 346, 346n, 564n, 811, 811n, [6]110n
not annotated by C [1]lxiii; an atomist [1]572; and BM [6]57n; on chlorine [5]343, 343n; C would give his life for [1]571; discoveries [1]177n, [5]564; great man [1]220, 220n; isolation of elements [5]261, 261n; knighthood [1]572, 572n; lectures of [1]569n, 570n, [2]246; letter(s) to [1]lxxxiv q, 535, [2]1169 q; merit of [4]128, 128n; and nitrous oxide [3]375, [4]836; and phlogiston [1]639n, 662n; and plagiarism [5]261n; Pneumatic Institute [1]163n; and science of mind [1]566; vetch experiment [5]256, 256n
"The Bakerian Lecture for 1809" MT [3]950–2; *Collected Works* [1]650n q, [2]546n, [3]1020n, 1021n, 1027n q; *Elements of Agricultural Chemistry* [4]531n q, [5]256n q; *Elements of Chemical Philosophy* [2]546, 825n q, [3]375n, 1001n q, 1020n, 1028n q, 1032n, 1033n q, [4]526n, [5]261n; *Fragmentary Remains* ed J. Davy [1]99n; *Lines Descriptive of Feelings* MT [1]99; "Of Potassium" [4]526n; "On Some Chemical Agencies" [3]948, 948n, 950; "On Some New Electro-chemical Researches" [3]950; *Researches . . . concerning Nitrous Oxide* [3]376n, [4]183n; "Some Experiments on . . . Carbonaceous Substances" [2]69n q, [3]1027n; *A Syllabus of a Course of Lectures on Chemistry* [3]323n q
Davy, John (1790–1868) [3]941; *see also* H. Davy *Fragmentary Remains* ed J. Davy
Dawe, George (1781–1829) [2]1066, *1066n*
dawn [1]515
day(s) [1]576
Gospel [1]515; d.-hirelings [5]283; holy [1]327, 878; of Judgment *see* judgment(s); last [2]652, [3]446, [5]578; of the Lord/the Messiah see *Dies Messiae*; and night [1]631; symbolic [2]516–17, 516n; ten [3]923; thousand years [3]603; of week *see* week; words for [1]608; as years [5]349
daydream [1]370, 722, [4]431, 587
daydreamer [4]776n, 789, 789n
dazzle [1]558
de [4]36, 36n, 166, 166n
De anima (attributed to Hugh of St Victor) [5]780
De ecclesiasticis dogmatibus see Driedo
de facto and *de jure* [2]129, 129n, 949
De haeretico comburendo [1]248, 248n, 255n, [4]670, 670n
de jure and *de facto* see *de facto*
De spiritu et anima [6]115n
De Xenophane, Zenone et Gorgia [2]869n
deacon(s) [2]321, 1199, [3]688
deaconesses [4]486n
"dead" [4]322, [5]622
burial service [1]127n; prayer for [1]781; raising of [6]110, 119; restored to life [4]514; resurrection of *see* resurrection
deaf/deafness [3]238, 389, [4]638n
and dumb [4]164, 165
dean [2]72
Deans, Effie (in Scott) [4]589n
Deans, Jeanie (in Scott) [4]597
"death" [6]118
death [1]577, 589, [2]247, 284, 312, 1008, [3]14, 54, 62, 317, 612–13, 645, 739, 739–40, [4]241, 435, 480, 733, 776, [5]117, 186, 276, 559, 591–2, 591n, 609, 821, [6]125
d.-bed [2]970, [3]145, [4]800; body as [5]545; body derived from [2]542; body of *see* body of the/this death; call by [3]422; car of [1]483; chamber of [3]740; of Christ *see* Jesus Christ, death of; concept of [1]125;

death—*continued*
consolation of [4]825; beyond d. of body [2]565; an eclipse [2]524; end of life [2]309; eternal [2]559, 559n, 669, 1109, [3]25, [5]618; eternal sleep [2]344–5; exemption from [3]476; fear of [5]862; in God [1]609; goddess [2]924, 924n; judgment after [2]565, 567; of just man [6]139; and life [1]597, 648, [2]566, 788, 1088, [3]61, [5]127n, 251, 425, 529; in life [1]594, [2]236n; lot after [1]283; d.-men [2]562; and more vital life [2]615; mystery of [5]589; out of life [2]788; passion of [1]646; penalty [4]241n; premature [3]39; preparation for [5]488–98; presumptuous to pretend to know it [1]47; prothesis of life [1]597; quaternion of [1]579; realm of [2]1073–4; reduction to potential state [2]566; region of [3]581; rescue from [3]741; second [3]433; sentence [5]103; and sin [2]802, [5]618; of sin [3]743; and sleep [2]1008–9; spiritual [2]1074, [3]739n; stimulus of [3]612; sudden [1]163, 163n; truly such [4]260; d.-tubes [5]101; two forms of [3]61; universality [2]1185; white [4]785, 785n
Death (*Paradise Lost*) [6]117, 117n
debauchee [1]699, [4]801
debauchery [1]383
Deborah (Bible) [1]823, 823n, [2]835
debt(s) [1]739, [2]659, [5]66, 146
liquidation of [1]200; national [2]311, 311n, 979; payment of [2]657–8
debtor [3]26, 47, [4]661
and creditor [2]263
debutants, theological [3]462
decad [1]643, [5]701, 701n
Decalogue [1]324, 419n, 877; *see also* Ten Commandments
Decandolle *see* Candolle
decantatus [1]253n
decarbonisation [4]385
decay [5]514
deceit [5]168
decency [4]732n
decisiveness [5]686
declamation [5]370
rational [2]217
Declaration of Principles MT [6]267
Declaration of Rights [1]866n
Declaration of the Rights of Man and of the Citizen [3]960n, [4]342n
decline [1]356
decomposition [3]948, 1011, [4]148n, [5]252, 260, 445, 790
decorum [2]945, [4]777
poetic [3]1086; theological [2]422
decree(s)
absolute [5]597; irreversible [5]154, 155
dedication(s) [2]78, [5]533
Latin [2]812
deducibilia [2]450, 450n
deduction(s) [3]328, [5]126, 383
intellectual [1]774
deed(s) [3]741, [5]594, 604
and act [3]753; faith in [1]821–2; outward [5]561; value of [5]562
deed-poll [1]124
deer [1]327, [2]862, [4]535, [6]151
d.-stealing [4]724
default of man [5]598
defect(s) [1]234, [3]135
inherited [2]249; signs of [3]64; supposed [4]697; symptomatic [2]1193
deficiency, inherent [2]43
"definient" [4]380, 380n
definite(s) [1]595, [3]670–1
and indefinite [4]647; sensuous [2]456
definiteness [1]158
false [1]157, 186
definition(s) [2]994, [3]1090, [4]371, [5]448, 768, [6]79, 287
choice of [5]471; contra-d. [1]352; and description [2]1183, 1183n, [6]173–4; forced [5]547; general [5]63; generic [1]550; Kant's [3]294; negative [5]604; real [1]231, [4]405; strict [2]608; verbal [3]261, [5]176; of words [4]320
Defoe, Daniel (1660–1731) [1]366n, [2]816, [3]141, 141n, 146, 146n, [6]163
career [2]767–8; prose style [2]167; and Swift [1]126n
Colonel Jack [4]658, 658n; *The Life and Adventures of Robinson Crusoe* [1]cxxxix–cxl; MT [2]158–68, 573, 767n, 980, [3]484, 484n, [5]106n, [6]163n; *Royal Religion* [3]163, 163n; *The Shortest Way with the Dissenters* [2]767 ("*Nonconformists*")
deformities, moral [1]516
Degen [4]761, 761n
degeneracy [1]356, 540, [2]1016
degenerous race *see* race(s), degenerous
degma [1]444n
degradation [3]676
degree(s) [2]808, [3]326, 343, 363
difference of [5]405, [6]229; genera of [1]590; and kind [1]817, [2]338, [3]115, 158, 206, 259, 259n, 380, 380n, 682, [4]107, 390, 443,

781, [5]189, 270, 286, 428, 564, 565, 581, 612, 729, [6]123; susceptible of [5]582
Deianira (myth) [2]90, 90n
deification [4]429
deinon [1]397n, [4]797
deisidaimonia [3]76
deisitheotes [3]77
deism [1]288, 514, [3]205, 670, 684, 698, [4]297, [5]614
in Eichhorn [2]454; Kantian [5]746; sceptical [2]434; sword and buckler of [5]83; vulnerable [5]71
deist(s) [1]248, 248n, 341, [2]786–7, [3]49n, 658, 683, 698, 764, [4]41, [5]63, 71, 71n, 76, [6]80, 107, 146
cunning [5]75; pious [5]677; rejection of gospel [2]263
deitas [3]151
deity/deities/Deity [1]175, 573, [2]198, 247, [3]13, [5]32, 557
absolute [3]233; attributes of [1]114, [5]780; conceptions of [2]421; diffused [3]755; energies in [1]602; equal [3]588; exclusive [5]656; ground of [1]694; as identity [3]17; incarnate [4]655; inspiring [2]405; intuitions of [1]657; life of [5]704; and matter [4]141; metaphysical [3]683; moral attributes of [3]478; mystery of [2]247; national [2]149; nature and [5]446; objective and subjective [6]89, 89n; omnipresence of [1]524; physiological [2]575; presence of [5]777; proof of [4]231; pure [1]620; as spherical [5]407; subjective [6]76, 76n; substance of [5]718; synthesis of opposites [1]568; time in [4]421; tripersonal [3]661; union with humanity [3]27; Unitarian view [4]429; unity of [3]660. *See also* god(s); God
deka [4]38
Dekker, Thomas (c 1570–c 1641)
The Honest Whore [2]217n; *The Seven Deadlie Sinns of London* [2]870n, [3]193n; *see also* Ford and Dekker
Delagoa [3]1082
Delametherie *see* Lamétherie
Delamotte, Charles (1714–96) [5]133, 133n, 134
Delaroche, François (1743–1812) [3]942
delators [3]471
delegation [3]450
Delia (fiction) [6]27
Delia (in Ritson) [4]293
deliberation [3]79, [5]529
delicacy [4]162, 192
"delicious" [1]227, 227n, [2]1039n
Delilah/Dalila(h) (Bible) [2]941, [3]47
Delille, Jacques (1738–1813) *see* Virgil *Georgica . . . hexaglotta* tr Delille
deliquium/deliquia [3]461, 461n, [5]821, 821n, 822
delirium/deliria [1]172, 608
and mania [4]822n
deliverance(s) [2]1177, [5]171
Deliverer [2]302
De Lolme, Jean Louis (c 1740–1807) [2]68
Delos [2]578–9, [5]836
Delphi [2]255n, [3]108n, [4]189n, [5]391n, [6]5n
oracle at [1]420n
delta [3]950, 950n
Deluge [1]709, 782–3, [2]385, [3]356n, 480, 644, [4]491, [5]386, 645, [6]5
Burnetian [4]82; Mosaic [4]83; Noachic [5]253; *see also* Flood
delusion(s) [1]621, [2]63, [3]214, 404–4, 405–6, 550, 879, [4]51, 168, 437, 780–1, [5]141, 168, 171, 183, 344, 406, 424, 465, [6]8, 8n
enthusiastic [5]515; pagan [5]471; Popish [5]471; Romish [3]467; serviceable [5]819
Demades (fl 350–319 BC) [2]416
demagogues [4]811
French [2]511
dementato [5]427
Demeter (myth) [2]583n, 1091n; *see also* Ceres
Demetrius (Grigoriy Otrepieff) (d 1606) [3]757n
Demetrius of Phalerum (c 345–283 BC) [6]3, 4, 4n
demi-semi-quaver [1]346, [2]1053n
demi-semi-quavering [2]1053, 1083, 1083n
demission of Comforter [5]535
demiurge [1]692n, [3]692, 692n, [5]84
democracy/democracies [2]68, [4]16, 145
relique of [3]240
democrat(s) [1]341 ("democratical"), [6]324
Democritus (c 460–c 370 BC) [1]168, 168n, 176 q, 773, [3]790n, [4]827, [5]644n, 728, 729
system of [5]721
demon(s) [2]720, [5]236. *See also* daemon(s); *daimon*; devil(s)
demoniac(s)/daemoniac(s) [4]668, [6]102, 119, 119n; *see also* possession
demonology/daemonology [2]533, [6]100
"demonstrate" [5]744, 744n
demonstration(s) [3]328, 332, 619, 619n, 829n, [4]114, 364, 409, [5]201, 561
geometrical [4]273; mathematical [2]642; oc-

demonstration(s)—*continued*
ular [3]817; scientific [2]143; strict sense of [4]265
"demonstrative" [4]114
demonstro [5]793, 793n
demoralisation [6]256
Demosthenes (384–322 BC) [2]416, 696, [3]227, 227n, 767, [5]223, 581, 581n
Demours, Antoine Pierre (1762–1836) [4]164
den(s) [5]544
Denbigh [3]188n
dendrite [2]1185
Denham, Sir John (1615–69) [1]37
On Mr. Abraham Cowley's Death MT [1]73; *The Progress of Learning* MT [1]74
denial [2]644
Denmark [2]62n, [3]133, 166, [4]170, [5]141, 312–13
denominations, different [4]672
density [3]294–5, 325, 325n, 344
increase of [5]431; of planets [5]263
Dent [5]390n
Dent, Thomas [6]268
"denude" [4]723, 723n
deo [4]166, 166n
Deodati *see* Diodati
dependence/dependency [1]201, [3]832, 835, [4]23, 140, [5]93, 729
relation of [5]370
"dependent" [3]859, 859n
dependent(s) [5]283, 455n, 759
depopulation [3]462
depravation [2]1163–4
heretical [1]834
depravity [1]30, [2]687
depth(s) [1]579, 597, 605, 637, 670, 694, [3]24, 30n, 139, 949
of being [2]1167; deeper [3]17; depthless [3]12n; gravity the power of [3]139; and height [3]518, [6]300; idea of [6]233; positive [4]385; power of [1]571
"depurated" [1]620, 620n
De Quincey, Thomas (1785–1859) [1]153n, 340n, 550n, 761, [2]940n, 1116, [3]376n, [4]280n
attacks on C [1]cxxxvii; book inscribed to [2]1032; death [1]clxi; describes "German Coleridge" [2]1048; on Herder [2]1048; letter to [2]1089 q; owner of annotated books [1]xcii, [3]503, [6]290, 291; supplier of books to C [1]lxxxvi, cvi, 553, [2]1089, 1129
"The Lake Poets" [1]cxvin q; tr *Laocoon* [1]72n; "William Wordsworth and Robert Southey" [1]cviin; *Works* [1]cviin, 9 q, 553 q, [3]539n, [4]283n
Derbend [6]279
Derby [1]clxviii, [4]91n
Derby, Countess of *see* Stanley, Charlotte Margaret
Derby, Earl of *see* Stanley, Edward George Geoffrey Smith
Derbyshire [1]272
Derosne, Louis Charles (1780–1846) [3]938
Derwent (river) [1]272
Derwentwater [3]974, 980
Descartes, René (1596–1650) [1]clxvi, 82, 82n, 409, 524, [2]629n, 788, 886 ("Cartesian"), 956, [3]43n, 155, 330n, 790n, 793, 793n, 1087, [4]78, 93, 106, 108, 108n, 130, 209n, 227, 354n, 376n, 377, [5]199, 200, 812
animal machines [4]389, 389n–90n; on animals [4]93n, 211–12, 212n; Cartesian mechanics [3]920; Cartesian system [3]1087n; *cogito* [3]95n; dualism of [2]310, 310n, [3]432–3, 433n; error of [2]171, 171n, [5]789; on existence of God [5]800; Leibniz attacks [3]343, 343n; letter by [4]93, 93n; and Locke [1]756n, [4]25, 25n, [5]732, 732n; misunderstood [3]972–3, 973n; proof of existence of God [3]329–30, 331, 858–9; semi-Cartesian notions [3]926; and Voetius [4]106n; vortices of [4]13, 13n
De methodo [2]170; MT 173–5; [4]442 q, 442n, tr as *Discourse on Method* [4]212n q; *Discours du Monde* [1]744n q; *De passionibus animae* MT [2]170–3; *Epistola . . . ad D. Gisbertum* [4]106n; *Epistolae* [4]106n; *Meditations* [1]82, 82n q; *Oeuvres* ed C. Adam and Tannery [4]93n; *Opera philosophica* [1]clxv; MT [2]169–75; [4]106n; *Philosophical Works* tr Haldane and Ross [2]170, [4]212n q; *Principia philosophiae* [1]82n, [2]170
descendants [5]651
descent [3]564, [5]152, 439
and ascent [5]445n; discontinuity in [5]97; method of [1]598
description [1]138
Daniel's [2]120; and definition *see* definition; poetical [6]161; verbal [2]173
Desdemona (*Othello*) [3]407, [4]865, 866, 867
de Selincourt, Ernest (1870–1943) [4]139; *see also* WW *Letters* ed de Selincourt and others, *Poetical Works* ed de Selincourt and Darbishire

desert [1]471, [2]899–900, 900n, [5]383, 608
true [1]4
desiderium/desideria [1]146, 600, [3]34n, [5]453, 467
d. gentium [3]33
design, argument from [3]848, [5]730n
desinence [2]1021
desire(s) [2]201, [3]585, [4]342, 463, 810, [5]216
arose from negation [1]574; in desire [1]326; fond [2]824; sexual [3]265; of willing [5]784
Desmoulins, Antoine (1796–1828) *Histoire naturelle des races humaines* MT [2]176–8
desolating [5]276
Desormes, Charles Bernard (1777–1862) [3]941
desoxydation [6]231
despair [2]560, [3]735, [4]9, 595, [5]163
toys of [5]588; of truth [5]642
despondence/despondency [2]313, [4]794
weakens memory [1]109
despot(s) [5]124, 484
philo-d. [2]927, 927n; virtuous [5]40
despotism(s) [2]418, 692, 846, 951, 1017, 1139, [3]429, 467, [4]81, 145, [5]270, 311, 745, 829, [6]264
Austrian [5]281, 312; of the Caesars [5]643; defined [2]1206–7; military [5]279; oriental [2]826; papal [1]514; priestly [3]819; Russian [5]281, 312, 315; tributary [1]740
despotist [1]224
destiny
over-ruling [4]601; of the world [4]51
"destroy" and "kill" [3]38
destruction [2]672, [3]59, 59n, 60, 62
personification of [2]515; principles of [1]643
desynonymisation [1]152n, 258n, 495–7, 533n, [2]*654n*, 822, [3]18n, 889n, [5]724n
desynonymising [1]496–7, 497n
detail, difficulties in [5]351
detection [5]424
deterioration, positive [6]127
determination(s) [1]827, [2]995–6
determinism [4]435, 436, [5]792
detestants [2]806
detraction [2]999, [3]575
deus
d. alter [1]785n; *d. alter et idem* [1]694, 694n, [2]423, [6]32; *d. ex machina* [1]557, 557n; *D. Patiens* [2]279, 279n; *D.*, subauditur of [4]629
"deutero-canonical" [1]493n
Deutero-Isaiah *see* Bible: OT: Isa ch 40–55
"deuteroptis" [4]83, 83n
deutlich [6]172, 172n
deutoxide [3]127
Deutsche Monatsschrift [3]960
Deva (myth) [2]200
development [4]266
intellectual [5]271
de Vere *see* Beauclerk
deviate [3]18
"devil(s)" [2]692, [6]137
devil(s) [1]780, [2]661, 706, 727, [3]305n, 769, 985, [4]644, 712, 782, 849, [5]140, 160, 164, 170, 471, 612, 613n, [6]117
Assyrian as [1]444; believe [1]504, [3]510, 519; d.'s-bit [2]168, 168n; blue [3]384, [5]165; d.-combats [2]1175; defeat of [3]9n; distinct genus of beings [3]742, 742n; doctrine of [5]150; English [3]884; evil will [2]279; false translation [1]455; inconstant [5]236; Milton's [4]842; not quite [4]862; prince of [3]57n; she- devil [1]370; and spirits [2]1109; *see also* demon(s)
Devil [1]618–19, 640, 643–4, 810, [2]41, 168, 286, 292, 512, 559n, 705, 725, 727, 739, 802n, 1022, 1106n, 1109n, [3]121n, 446n, 471, 471n, 594, 594n, 770, 771, 771n, 876, 926n, 984, [4]234n, 235, 235n, 341, 428–9, 429n, 549n, 668, [5]83n, 84, 85–6, 85n, 86n, 383, 383n, 421, 422n, 614, [6]97, 97n, 98n, 100, 101, 102, 103, 110, 119, 122, 263
before time [2]748; not in Bible [2]164; children of [1]656; converse with [6]98; craft of [5]105; and devils [3]774; existence of [3]742, 742n; has no one body [3]769; and hell [1]811; imaged with horns [1]626; a liar [4]14, [5]424; Luther's vision of [3]198n, 212n, 305n; and miracles [5]823n; mystery of [2]1109; objective existence [3]436, 436n; possessed by [5]819; reality of [3]305; in strait-waistcoat [5]453; tempting [6]138; winds of [4]288. See also *diabolos*; evil; Lucifer; Satan
Devon [1]47, [2]512n
Devonshire [1]59
Devonshire, Countess of *see* Cavendish, Christiana
Devonshire, Duke of [3]152
devotees [2]728
pagan [5]517
devotion(s) [4]140, [5]642, 667
private [1]324; public [5]512, [6]259; pulley of [1]325; Scripture model of [5]484; three species [5]510

dew [6]132
d.-drops [1]709, [3]460, 741, [5]444, images of sun in [1]815, 815n
De Wette, Wilhelm Martin Leberecht (1780–1849)
Lehrbuch [2]181; *Theodor* [1]xcviin; MT [2]179–209, tr J. F. Clarke [2]181, 186n q; *Vorlesungen über die Sittenlehre* [2]181
dia [1]466
diabolism [5]158
"diabolography" [6]100, 100n
diabolos/*Diabolos* [2]692, 692n, 896n, [4]234, 234n, [5]421–2 ("*Diabolus*"), 422n, [6]98n, 101, 137; *see also* Devil
"diabolosophy" [4]145, 145n
diagnostic [5]515
of ideas [5]599
diagram, intellectual [5]32
dial [1]674, [2]561, [5]569
dialect(s) [2]653, [3]830, 830n, [5]651
provincial [3]633
dialectic [2]989–90, 990n, [3]364, [4]156, [5]767–8, 803
Kant's transcendental d. [3]242n; logic of ideas [5]796; Platonic [4]157
dialogue(s) [3]813, [4]797, 848
dramatic [4]718; mock [1]402; Scott's [4]586, 613
A Dialogue on Parliamentary Reform MT [2]210–11; [4]7
Der Diamant und der Bergcrystall [4]332n
diamond(s) [1]570, 572, 663, 666, [3]529, 635, 1022, 1027, 1027n, 1033, 1033n, [4]332n, 466, 691, [5]153, 257, 257n, 263, 344, 344n, 834, [6]227–8, 314
becomes charcoal [2]69; factitious [1]446; specks in [2]155
Diamond, William (fl 1800–30) [2]75
Diana (myth) [2]7–8, 581, [6]157n, 209
diarrhexis [5]181
diarrhoea [3]870n
Dibdin, Charles (1745–1814) [2]75, 83
Dibdin Club *see* New York City
Dibdin, Thomas Frognall (1776–1847) [2]702n
Dicconson, William (1633–1701) [1]357n
The Life of James the Second ed J. S. Clarke [1]357, 357n, 359
dice [1]782
dichotomy [1]231, 347, [2]1193n
logic of [2]1193, [3]363, [5]459
Dick (fiction) [1]484
Dick, Oliver Lawson *see* Aubrey *Brief Lives* ed Dick
Dickens, Charles (1812–70) *Bleak House* [5]252n
Dickon (fiction) [5]858, 858n
Dickson, Dorothy [3]980, [4]282, 289
dictation/dictate [1]439, [2]561, [3]439, 663, 663n
Lord's [5]520; miraculous [5]515; oral [5]473
dictator(s) [1]439, [4]145
diction [1]366
Browne's [1]774; classical [5]861; dramatic [4]848; felicity of [5]448; Gray's [2]866; pedantry of [3]882; poetic [1]401, [3]403, [4]840–1, 841n, [6]329; real-life [4]787; *see also* word(s), choice of
dictionary/dictionaries
of human nature [4]629; ideal of [4]35; medical [4]745; morals of d. writers [3]930
A Dictionary of Buckish Slang [3]164n
Dictionary of National Biography [1]clxxii, 723n, [2]858n, 939n q, [3]178n, 631, [4]96n, 283n, 721n, [5]17n, 162n, 811n, [6]145n
Diderot, Denis (1713–84) [3]698, 698n, [4]170, [5]703n
Dido, Queen of Carthage (legend) [2]930n, [3]365, 365n, [5]831–2, 832n
Didoclavius (David Calderwood) (1575–1650) [3]795n
"die" [1]157n
"die game" [4]636, 636n
Diels, Hermann (1848–1922) *Die Fragmente der Vorsokratiker* ed Krantz [2]425n
Dierbach, Johann Heinrich (1788–1845)
Die Arzneimittel des Hippocrates, review of MT [2]365
dies [1]608n
Dies Messiae [1]863, [3]445, 445n, 446, 461, 470, 478, [4]244, 244n, 246n, [5]606–7. *See also* Lord, Day of; Messiah, day(s) of
diesparmenoi [1]458, 459n
diet [5]137
Dietrich, Veit (Vitus Dietericus) (1506–49) [2]774n, [3]718
difference(s) [1]563, 752, [2]825, [4]780, [5]481
and diversity [1]331, 331n; essential [5]408; and indifference [1]550–1; in kind [2]1133, [4]107; and likeness [4]169, 222; and sameness [4]603
"difficult" [5]420
difficulty/difficulties [3]283, [5]61
not objections [1]421
diffusion [5]287, [6]227
diffusive, the [3]325
digamma [1]377n, 604n, [2]53, *53n–4n*, 577n,

789, [3]59, 828, 828n, 829, [4]37, 37n, [6]27, 27n
Digby, Sir Kenelm (1603–65) [1]742, 758, [2]824, [3]817n
Two Treatises [1]758n
"digenerations" [3]356, 356n
digestion [1]657, [5]86
affects memory [1]109
digitus [4]38
dignitaries, Church [2]827
dignity/dignities
ascent in [5]406; dignifying [2]945; spiritual [3]603
digression(s) [2]81, [3]613, [4]831, [5]528
in C [1]lxvi
dilatability [3]996
dilatation [5]344
dilation [1]589, 590, 604, 631, 641, 660, 666, 776, [2]853, 853n, 854–5, 855n, [3]61n, 997n, 999, 1003, 1009, 1017n, 1021, 1021n, 1022, 1060, [4]387–8, 395, 396, [5]266, 287, 342, 438, [6]227, 228
and centrality *see* centrality; dilative power [3]997; and repulsion [1]549, [3]996, 996n, 998, [6]230
dilative, the [1]595, 611, 612, 625, 638, [3]61, 1000, 1004
dilativity [4]314
dilemma, assertion of [5]697
Dillon, John (fl 1857) [5]866
Dillon, Wentworth, 4th Earl of Roscommon (c 1633–85) [1]37
Dillon-Lee, Henry Augustus, Viscount Dillon (1777–1832) *The Life and Opinions of Sir Richard Maltravers* [2]212; MT [6]268–9
dimension(s) [3]123, 123n, 139, 321–2, 333
equilibrium of all [1]548
dimness, sensuous [4]409
Dinant (in B&F) [1]394, 395
Dindorf, Karl Wilhelm (1802–83) *see* Aeschylus *Tragoediae* ed Dindorf
Ding/Dinge an sich [3]326, [4]125, 125n, 126, 346, 346n, [5]580, 701, 718; *see also* thing-in-itself
dining [5]370
Dinmont, Dandie (in Scott) [3]716, 716n, [4]594, 594n
dinner [3]360
diocesan(s) [1]319, [5]503; *see also* church(es), diocesan
diocese, moral [4]653
Diocletian (Gaius Aurelius Valerius Diocletianus) (245–313) [2]336, 336n
Diodati/Deodati, Charles (?1609–38) [3]902, 905
Diodorus of Sinope (fl 284 BC) [4]147
Diodorus Siculus (fl 60–21 BC) [4]631, [5]234
Diogenes (413–317 BC) [6]56, 56n
Diogenes Laertius (fl 1st half of 3rd century) [1]174n, 584n, [3]650, [5]223–4, 225n, 386n q, 604n, 693, 703
"Life of Pythagoras" [5]703n–4n; *Lives of Eminent Philosophers* tr Hicks [5]709n q, 714n q, 728–9 q, [6]5n q, 56n q
Diogenes of Apollonia (fl 460 BC) [5]718–19, 719n, 721
Diomedes (late 4th century) [2]758, [4]289
Dionysius, St, Bishop of Alexandria (c 200–64) [1]485n, [2]724 q, 725 q, 725n, 748, 748n, [3]441–2, 442n, 477n, [5]683, 685, 685n
Dionysius, St, Bishop of Rome (fl 259–68) [2]725n
Dionysius of Halicarnassus (d c 8 BC) [2]53n–4n, 831
Roman Antiquities [4]189n
Dionysius Periegetes (fl c 300) [2]981n
Dionysius the Areopagite (1st century) [5]149, 483; *see also* Pseudo-Dionysius
Dionysus (myth) [1]592n, 617, 617n, [2]579n, 581, 582, 583, 584n; *see also* Bacchus
Dioscorides, Pedanius (fl 1st century) [1]770
Dioscorus/Dioscuri (myth) [5]197n, 227
Diphilus of Sinope (b c 360 BC) [2]775n, [4]147
diphthongs [2]68, 1092, 1092n
"diphysis" [5]579
diplomatists [1]331
direction(s) [5]244, 451
ideal [5]343; opposite [5]424, [6]233; potenziating [1]614
Directory for the Public Worship of God [5]508, 509, 530, 530n
disanimation [2]170, 170n
disappointment [2]637
disbelief [2]1079, [5]620
dogmatical [5]771; presumptuous [1]682
disbeliever [4]592
discernment of reason [1]820
discerpibility [2]547, 547n
discerption [5]438n
disciple(s)/Disciples(s) [1]453, 847, [2]297, [3]696, [4]57, [5]56, 128, 151n, 535, 553, 607, 677, [6]107, 119
beloved [5]540; of Christ [3]659, 668; crass apprehensions of [1]451; dupes [4]63; elder [5]642; first [5]608; interpretation of [5]607; Palestine [2]918; prohibition to [2]1173; of

disciple(s)/Disciples(s)—*continued*
Pythagoras [5]541; seventy [5]128; uncomprehending [4]482; uneducated [3]731–2
disciplinarians [5]67
discipline [1]339, [2]515, 656, [3]497, [5]304, 639
Christian [1]254, [5]67–8, 67n; church [1]340, 341; of C of E [5]568; and law [3]759; moral [1]803
discontinuity [1]597–8, [5]169
in descent [5]97
discord(s) [4]313
resolution of [2]1021
"discourse" [5]492–3, 493n
discourse(s) [2]656, [4]648
free [3]732; inward [1]146; mental [4]92, 93n; in NT [1]448; philosophy as [1]108n; of reason [3]150, 150n, [4]543; *see also* faculty, discursive
discoursing, method of [3]91
discovery/discoveries [1]774, [3]871, [5]811
history of [6]50; law of [2]161, 161n
discretion [1]813
age of [4]306
discrimination
minute [6]210; power of [4]159; rules of [2]1058
"discursive" [2]656
discursive and intuitive [1]587n
discursus [5]493
disease(s) [1]172, 429, 449, 868, [2]362n, 363, 364, 604, 705, 739, 1185, [3]64, 67, 312, 373, 396–7, 398, 772, 913, [5]137, 148, 168, 180, 190, 425, 678, [6]103
Baxter's [1]344; contagious [5]165; insight into [6]310; mistaken for witchcraft [3]822; mode of life [2]564; nervous [3]213, [4]83n, [5]122; new [6]46; organic [5]184; and sins [3]734; in the will [1]201
"disembodied" [3]742
disensoul [1]517
"disfacciamento" [4]808, 808n
disguise(s) [3]516, 1083, [4]466–7, [5]161, [6]298
disgust [3]913, [4]273, 818
dishonesty [2]453, [5]646
dishonour [4]810
"disimaged" [2]1028, 1028n
"disingenuous" [5]154
disinterestedness [4]814, 830–1
disjunction [2]241, [4]604
dislike [4]842
disobedience [5]611
disorder [5]168
disorganisation [3]61
disornaments [2]85
disparate(s) [2]854–5, 855n, [3]670, 1003n, 1026n, [5]231
dispensation(s) [3]696, [5]61
Christian [5]54, 63, 514; gospel [4]251; Jewish [1]719n; Mosaic [5]63; Patriarchal [5]63; three [3]427
dispersion [1]776
"displanations" [2]798, 798n
display, ostentatious [6]59
dispondoeuses [1]377
dispositions, moral [2]29
dispute(s)
daemon of [5]159; between good men [1]280; religious [5]528
disputing [5]460
disquiet, storm of [1]425
D'Israeli, Isaac (1776–1848)
Calamities of Authors [3]991n; *Vaurien* [2]1029n
disse [1]608, 608n
dissectors [1]626
dissembler [1]54
dissent [4]619, [6]42
dissenter(s) [1]325, 348, 353, 357, 711n, 738, [2]48, 1136, [3]70, 156, 877, 883, [4]178, 179, [5]123, 129n, 145, 510
grand error [1]324; orthodox [6]14; and prayer [1]264, [6]259; present [1]339–40; rise of [1]531; *see also* minister(s), dissenting
dissentients [1]323
dissolution [5]37
distance [3]322
acting at a [4]417, 417n; power of [3]1015; relative [5]430
distant, the [5]415
distemperament [5]99
distillations [4]494
"distinct" [6]172–3
distinct(s) [1]562
distinction(s) [1]286, 355, 562, [2]995, [3]12, 13, 59, 748, [4]326, 604, [5]77, 265, 789, [6]227
arbitrary [2]605; conceptual [5]803; in continuity [5]360; without difference [3]674; and division [1]175, 175n, 331n, 528 ("distinguishing"), [2]250, 1154–5, 1193, [5]19n; easy to make [2]618; in grammar [3]834; organ of [1]655; philosophical [2]1030; profound [1]603–4; real [2]198; reverential [4]426; rule of [3]696; in Schelling [4]424; scholastic [6]302, 302n; of Schools [5]673; and separation [1]233, [4]366, 366n, [5]19; of terms [1]632; true [5]771; in unity [5]408; unphilosophic [4]322; verbal [4]456

"distinctity"/"distinctities" [2]300, 300n, [3]52, 52n, 102, 102n
distinctity/distinctities [3]17, 66, 74, 102, 102n, [5]443
eternal [3]13; and unity [2]300, [3]52
distinctive, the [1]625
distinctness [1]565, [3]313, [5]291, 372, 449
distribution, distinctive [1]348
district, petty [5]644
ditheism [2]797
diverse [3]1003n
diversions, sinful [1]825
diversity/diversities [4]107, [6]64
and difference [1]331, 331n
divertisement [5]289
Dives (legend) [2]979
divestment [1]466
divi [2]344, 344n
"divide" [4]166
dividuity [2]279, 279n
dividuous, the [1]625
divine, the [1]675–6, [5]710n
and human [3]311–12
divine(s) [2]844, 926, [3]844, [4]669, [5]533
anti-prelatic [1]327, [5]577–8; Arminian [5]5, 578; Catholic [3]369; Christian [1]113, [2]254, [3]136, [5]202; church [1]316, [5]510; C of E [2]265, 650, 684; clerks of a guild [6]79; contemporary [1]686; dissenting [2]360; early [5]393; elder [3]918, [5]495; eminent [3]561; English [2]260, *273n–4n*, 294, 318, 322, 323; Evangelical [5]471; favourite [3]435; of 15th to 17th centuries [2]926; German [2]205; Grotian [3]308, [5]561; high-church [3]143; Italian [5]519; Jesuit [5]519; Latitudinarian [5]82, 553, 561; learned [1]345, 521, [3]606, [5]500, [6]166; Lutheran [3]1078, [5]394; modern [1]171, [2]342, 882–3, [5]27; neologic [2]999n; orthodox [3]33; Paleyan [3]308; party of [5]661; pious [3]36; polemic [5]662; Pontifical [5]399; pontificial [2]38; practical [2]186; prelatic [5]521; Presbyterian [1]339, 674, [2]651; professional [5]664; Protestant [1]256, 345, 516, [5]554, 568, [6]12, 23, 60; Puritan [2]651, 1156, [4]182; rational [5]384; of Reformation [2]1167; RC [6]93; Romish [1]256, 472, [2]295, [5]568, 572, 578, 632, 660, 665; Saxon [5]394; School [3]1088; Socinian [4]642, [5]561; sound [5]803; Spanish [1]524; supra-lapsarian [5]162; systematic [2]659, [5]81, 596; textual [2]923; ultra-Calvinistic [3]69; Venetian [1]846; wire-drew their texts [2]338; Westminster [5]508, 520; young [5]50; *see also* clergy
divining power in man [1]163
divinity/Divinity, the [2]40, [5]54, 524
absolute [5]633; of Christ *see* Jesus Christ, divinity of; out of us [5]822; representations of [2]255; of Scriptures [5]53; union with [6]88
divinity (i.e. theology)
Christian [3]743; C's system [3]436; marrow of [1]819; misty [2]334; School [5]803; slippery [2]300
divisibility [3]118
division(s) [1]331, 348, [2]995, [3]748, [4]316, 604, [5]27
arbitrary [5]487; and distinction *see* distinction
divolution, polar [2]992
divorce [3]497, 883, [5]38
of Catherine of Aragon [1]422
divorcement [1]824
Dixon, Robert (fl 1827) [5]478
"Doblado, Leucadio" *see* Blanco White, Joseph
Dobrizhoffer, Martin (1717–91) *An Account of the Abipones* [1]cxxxv
Docetae [3]45, [4]61, 61n, [5]397, 398n, [6]106, 106n
error of [2]750, 750n,
doctor(s) [2]1141, [3]21, [5]278, 661
of abstractions [1]673; high-church [5]659; individual [1]314; Jewish [3]1090, 1091, [5]606; pontifical [5]5; primitive [1]263; Roman [1]315; Romish [5]51, 492, 578, [6]21; sainted [2]748
doctrine(s) [1]318, 358, 834, [4]473, [5]53, 135, 560, 639
accursed [5]559; Apostolic [5]568; Catholic [5]568; Christian [3]743, [5]208; contradictory [3]69–70; distinct [5]393; distinguishing [2]26; essential [1]302, 469–70; general [3]697; immoral [5]519; inefficacious [3]63; intelligibility of [3]31; Lutheran [5]561; Luther's [5]466; Methodist [5]586; Moravian [5]171; natural [1]352; passive [2]601; peculiar to Christianity [5]535; pernicious [5]172; philosophy of [5]582; proves miracle [5]384; agreeable to reason [3]606; religious [4]513; RC [5]5n, 587, *see also* church(es): RC; Romish [5]678; subversive [5]656
document(s) [2]453, [4]473, [5]308
historic(al) [5]10, 635; test of [5]145
"Documentary Hypothesis" [1]417n
Dod/Dodd, Benjamin (fl 1745–64) [1]701
Doddridge, Philip (1702–51) [3]537; *see also* R. Leighton *Expository Works* rev and

Doddridge, Philip—*continued*
pref Doddridge, *Genuine Works* pref Doddridge
Dodds, Eric Robertson (1893–1979) *see* Proclus *Elements of Theology* tr Dodds
Dodds, Mary Diana ("David Lyndsay") (fl 1822) *Dramas of the Ancient World* MT [3]782–3
dodo [1]487
Dodsley, Robert (1704–64) [1]38
A Select Collection of Old Plays [1]xc, cxxi, [2]117, 217n, 759n, 777n
dog(s) [2]704, 1110, 1132, 1150n, [3]558, 586, 1048, [4]93, 272, 273, 385, 498, 498n, 535, 535n, 597, 598, 600, 762–3, [5]177, 293, [6]75, 80, 153, 176
acute sense of smell [1]657; barking [1]477; catch fear [5]122; dead [4]763, 846–7; ghosts of [3]197; mad [2]771; Newfoundland [4]73; rabid [5]260, [6]120, 120n; without spleen [5]567–8; taught to speak [1]111
doggerel [5]178
dogma(s)/dogmata [1]504, [2]1062, 1062n, 1081, 1081n, [3]7n, 436, [5]597, 766
Calvinistic [3]70; Christian [4]643–4; Jewish [5]85; mysterious [5]541; Romish [2]282; truth of [4]265
dogmatism [1]105, [3]249, 249n, [4]408, [5]208, 771
rational [5]750
dogmatist [4]130
doing and being [2]693, [5]725
Dolce, Lodovico (1508–68) [1]116
Dolet, Etienne (1509–46) [2]769–70
De Cucullatis [2]770 q
Döllinger, Johann Joseph Ignaz von (1799–1890) [3]114
Dollond, John (1706–61) [4]187, 187n ("Dolland")
dolphin [4]532–3, 533n
domes [5]321
domestics [4]827
domination
lust of [5]167; papal [5]661; spiritual [5]151
Dominic, St (c 1170–1221) [1]323n, [5]121, 121n
Dominican(s) [1]281n, 349n–50n, [3]99, 99n, 667n, 794, [4]33–4, [5]167
Dominicanism(s) [5]149, 149n
dominion [5]59, 614
domino [5]309
Domitian (Titus Flavius Domitianus) (51–96) [1]790, [2]459, 1111, [3]57, 57n, 608
Domville, Mrs (fl 1830) [5]389
Domville, Sir James Graham [3]483
Domville, Sir William, 1st Baronet (1742–1833) [5]389
Domville, Sir William, 2nd Baronet (1774–1860) [5]389
Don (river) [3]1047
Don Quixote (*Don Quixote*) [1]392, [3]207, 207n
Doncaster [5]97n
donkey [6]209
Donkin, Bryan (1768–1855) [3]942
Donne, John (1573–1631) [1]xcii, cii q, cxxx q, cxxxviiin, 37, 377, [2]14, 131, 294n, 759, 1041n, 1101n, 1177n, [3]309n, 511
on interpretation of Bible [2]336; in Chalmers MT [2]16–18; Christian [2]220; C's lectures [1]cxln; and Cowley [2]103, 219–20; marked passages [1]53; metre [2]221; opulence of [2]219, 220; Pope's opinion [3]174; satires [2]216; and Shakespeare [2]218; spirit of [3]900; uncritical age of [2]274; versification [1]377; wit of [2]17; worthy of C of E [2]333
Air and Angels [2]215; MT 222; *The Anatomie of the World* [2]234n; *Anniversaries* [2]231n; MT 234–5; *Biathanatos* [1]166n; MT 167; *167n*, [2]235; *235n–6n*, 766n; *The Blossom* [2]225, 225n; *Breake of Day* [2]214; *The Calme* [2]213; *Canonization* [2]215; MT [2]220; *The Dissolution* [2]215; MT [2]225; *LXXX Sermons* [1]lxiii, lxvii, lxxi, cxxvi, cxlivn, clxix, [2]244; *Copy A* [1]xcii; MT [2]245–58; [4]742, 742n; *Copy B* MT [2]259–338; [4]742, 742n; *Elegie IV* [2]216; MT 225; *Elegie XVI* [1]lxxxixn; *Elegies* [2]213; *The Elegies and the Songs and Sonnets* ed Gardner [2]215, 218n, 221n, 222n, 223n, 225n; *The Extasie* [2]215; MT 223–4; *A Feaver* [2]215; MT 221–2; *The Flea* [1]166n, [2]215; MT 217–18; *The Good-morrow* MT [2]17; 215; MT 218; *Holy Sonnet XVIII* [1]709n; *Human Life* [2]16n; *Ignatius His Conclave* [2]766, 766n; *The Indifferent* [2]215; MT 219; *Letters* [2]213; MT 232–6; *Letters to Severall Persons of Honour* [1]167n; *Loves Deity* [2]215; MT 224–5; *Loves Exchange* [2]214; *Loves Growth* [2]214; *Metempsychosis* see *The Progress of the Soul*; *A Nocturnal upon S. Lucies Day* [2]215; MT 223; *On the Blessed Virgin Mary* [1]43; MT 43–4; [2]213, 216; *Poems* (1669) [1]lxxxix, xcn, xci, cxxi, cxln, clxiii; MT [2]213–43; "Elegies

upon the Author" MT ²237–43; *Poems* ed Grierson ¹44n, 776n, ²18n, 213, 215, 218n, 221n, 223n, 225n, 226n, 227n, 228n q, 229n, 230n, 231n, 238n, 239n, 240n, 241n; *The Primrose* ²215; MT 225; 225n; *The Progress of the Soul* (*Metempsychosis*) ¹776, 776n; MT ²18; 234n; *Pseudo-martyr* ¹166n, ²766n; *The Relique* ¹cxxin, 372n, ²225, 225n; *Satires, Epigrams and Verse Letters* ed Milgate ²215, 226n, 227n, 228n, 229n, 230n, 231n; *Satyre III* ²216; MT 225–8; *Satyre IV* ²216; MT 228; *Satyre V* MT 228–30; MT 228; *Satyre VI* ²216; MT 231; *Satyres* ²16n, 760n; *Sermons* ed G. R. Potter and E. M. Simpson ²244, 245, 271n; *Song: Goe, and catch a falling starre* ¹776n, ²215; MT 218; 221n; *Song: Sweetest Love, I doe not goe* ²215; MT 221; *Songs and Sonets* ¹754n, ²16n; *The Storme* ²213; *The Sun Rising* MT ²18; 215, MT 219; *To M. T. W.* ²218n; *To Sʳ Nicholas Smyth* ²231n; *To the Praise of the Dead* ²216, 231, 231n; *The Triple Fool* ²215; MT 220–1; 221n; *Twicknam Garden* ²215; MT 223; *The Undertaking* ²215; MT 219; *A Valediction: Forbidding Mourning* ²214, 215; MT 223; *A Valediction: of the Booke* ²214; *The Will* ²225, 225n; *Womans Constancy* MT ²18; 215; MT 218; *Works* ed Alford ²244 ("*Sermons*")
Donne, John (1604–62) ¹167n
Donne, Mrs ²353
Doomsday ⁵487; *see also* Judgment, Day of
door ⁵177, ⁶9
Doradoes ¹789
Dorchester House *see* Highgate
Doric (dialect) ⁵695; *see also* Greek (language)
Dörien (in Jung) ³216
Dormer, Anna Sophia (née Herbert) (d 1643) ²78n
Dormer, Robert, 1st Earl of Carnarvon (d 1643) ²78n
"dormitate" ²516, 516n
Dornedden, Carl Friedrich (1768–1840) ²371
"Erläuterung der aegyptischen Götterlehre" ²144n
Dorset, Earl(s) of *see* Sackville, Charles, Richard, and Thomas
Dorset(shire) ²827n, ³638, ⁶44
Dort, Synod of ²913n, ⁵15, 15n, 81, 81n, 509n, 596n
dotage ⁵242
dotards ⁴55
Douai ²24
double entendre ¹390
double-land ²577
double(ness) ³46
double touch *see* touch, double
doubt(s) ¹508, ²313, 1165, ³283, ⁴208, ⁵75–6
concealed ³466; impossible ⁵742; natural ²1088; Simonidean ⁵12; uneasy ⁵598
doubting, appetite for ²464
Douglas, John, Bishop of Salisbury (1721–1807) ¹317, 317n, ⁵140, 140n
The Criterion; or, Miracles Examined ⁵140n
Douglass, Mr (fl 1815) ¹205
douleia ¹257n
Dousterswivel (in Scott) ⁴578
Dovaston, John Freeman Milward (1782–1854) ⁴292n
dove(s) ²574n, 1086n, ⁴65, 65n, ⁵229, 363, ⁶148, 148n
of Chaos ²580, 581n; d.-cote ⁴802; Holy Ghost as ²330
Dove Cottage *see* Grasmere
Dover ¹333n, ²122, 190n, 520n, 981n, ⁶147
Treaty of ¹353n
dove-tailing ⁵309
Dowden, Edward (1843–1913) ¹clxvi, ²102, 615n
Dowling, Mr ³1081–2
Downham, George, Bishop of Derry (d 1634) ³795n
doxa ²1081, 1081n, 1082n, ⁴254n, 256, ⁶164, 164n
doxology ¹576n
doxy ³144
Doyle, James Warren (1786–1834) ³459, 459n
Doyle, Martin (fl 1817–42) ¹688n
Doyle, R. (fl 1820) ¹688n
D'Oyly, George (1778–1846) ⁵495n; *see also* Bible: *Holy Bible, with Notes* ed Mant and D'Oyly
doze, temporary ⁵483
drag-net ⁵811
dragon ²515, 717, ³470, 471, 474, 922n, ⁵84, 85n, 841
in Rev ¹483–4, 483n–4n
dragonfly ²646, 646n, ³26
drake ³1072; *see also* duck(s) and drake(s)
drakestone ⁴10n
"drallery" ¹396

drama(s) [2]757, [3]94, 894, [4]765, [5]121
comic [1]367; didactic [4]638, 638n; dramatic poetry [4]162; Dryden's vulgar idea of [3]182, 182n; earnest [4]797; Eccles as [1]433; epic [2]896; examples in [2]206; fictitious [4]798; genus [3]182; Greek [4]864n, [5]688; historic [4]794, 798; imitates reality [4]780; Italian ideal of [6]324; juvenile [4]783; legendary [4]809; mixed [4]712; object of [4]780–1; as poetry [1]376; present [3]172; prophetic [2]505; of Rev [3]929; Roman [2]776; romantic [4]779, 811; satirical [4]809; Sophoclean [4]168, 796; symbolic [3]417n, 452; tragic [1]367
dramatic, the, and epic [4]737, 848, 848n
dramatis personae [3]182
dramatist(s)
Elizabethan to Caroline [1]401; English [3]171; Greek [1]376; Italian [1]384; rule of [3]173; sacred [3]436–7; sentimental [4]598; Spanish [1]384, 398; vulgar [4]726
drapery [1]543, [3]21, 511
Paracelsian [1]668; poetic [4]47; verbal [4]246
draw-bridge [3]550
drawing, schoolboy's [5]296
draxasthe [1]427n
dray-horses [5]250
Drayton, Michael (1563–1631) [1]37, 53, [2]127
epitaph [1]56; "Life" by Anderson MT [1]55–7; marked passages [1]53; pastoral [3]890; sonnets MT [1]57
England's Heroical Epistles [1]382, 382n; *Ideas* [1]40; *The Muses Elysium* MT [1]81; *Nimphidia* MT [1]57; 57n; *The Owle* MT [1]382; 382n; *Polyolbion* [1]55, 57n, [2]114n, [3]898, [5]389–90, 390n q; *To Proverbs* [1]57n
dreadnoughts [3]420
dream(s) [1]163, 554, 558, 669, 755, [2]410, 607, 607n, 883, [3]207n, 212, 216, 317, 377, 479, [4]51, 60, 210, 223, 268, 477, 503, 505, 581, 781, 861, [5]164, 169, 174, 181, 300, 306, 379, 496, 552, 605, 775, 795
aweful [5]559–60; of the blind [3]389; Böhme's [1]631; d.-book [3]34; C's [1]755, [5]559n; in common [3]249; croaking in [5]319; distinctive characters of [3]717; Eve's [3]105; with eyes open [5]569–70; are ghosts [3]198; d.-images [4]781; incoherent [1]286; interpretation of [4]541–4, [5]726; language of [3]376; Nebuchadnezzar's [3]419n; novel as [1]730; objection from [2]644; of Paulus [4]50; philosophising [4]431n; Pilate's wife's [1]447; and prophecy [2]403; prophetic [1]163n; remarkable [1]163; silly [2]622; systematic [1]808; theory of [2]624, [3]217; d.-waking [4]776; wilful [4]360; winged [3]895
dreamer(s) [2]1076, [5]474
Alexandrine [6]145
dreamery [5]251
dreaminess [5]372
dreaming [4]143, 781, [5]181n
dreamland [3]869
drengage [3]977, 977n, 981
Dresden [4]171
dress(es) [4]525, 717
allegorical [6]143; biblical [3]1091; mannish [1]389
Driedo, Johannes (1480–1535) *De ecclesiasticis dogmatibus* [5]586
Drillman, Corporal (fiction) [1]50, 50n
drink, meat and [5]362, 372
drinkers, dram [5]252
drinking [3]360
Drinkwater, John (1882–1937) [1]816, [3]886
dromedary [2]16, 81
dromois [1]24, 24n
drop(s) [1]562
paste [1]448
dropsy/dropsies [1]173, [5]252
drosois [1]24, 24n
dross [3]984
drowned, the [5]168
drowning [4]275
drudge(s) [2]279, 512, [3]734, [5]622
drug(s) [3]398, [4]320
Thessalian [5]528
druggists [5]361
Druids [6]158, 158n
drum [3]953
Drummond, Henry (1786–1860) [3]10, 70, 70n–1n
Drummond, Henry (1851–97) [2]46
Drummond, William (1585–1649) [1]37, [2]14, 231n
Conversations [3]174
drunkard [5]190, 584, [6]126
drunkenness [1]172, [2]570, [5]146, 559
Drury, Amy (fl 1662) [3]190n
Drury, Elizabeth (1595–1610) [2]234, 234n–5n
Drury, Mrs [2]353
Drury, Sir Robert (d 1536) [2]235n
"dry" [5]113
dry rot [1]250, [3]901, [5]516
Dryden, John (1631–1700) [1]37, 377, [2]79,

83, 216, 955n, 973, [4]779, 779n–80n, 808, 833
C's attitude towards [4]76, 76n, 291n; moderniser of Chaucer [4]291, 291n; plays of [3]182, 182n; prefaces [4]779; prose style [1]157, 157n, 182, 182n
Absalom and Achitophel [3]141, 141n; *Alexander's Feast* [2]484n; "Dedication" [2]757n q; *The Hind and the Panther* [2]78, q 78n; Preface to Fresnoy [4]779n; *Works* [6]198n–9n q. *See also* Juvenal; Lucretius; Persius; Virgil *Aeneid*, *Georgics* tr Dryden
drying [5]266
duad [5]230–1
dual [5]201
dualism [2]310, 725n, [4]128n, 171n, 262, [5]714n
Cartesian [6]88; Descartes' [3]432–3, 433n; Kant's [3]291; Schellingian [2]1007n; *see also* Descartes
dualist [5]752
duality [2]87, [3]1052
Dubawnt Lake [2]987n
Dublin [2]413n, 558, [6]38, 38n
Catholic Association [1]859n; Trinity College [1]100
Dublin Magazine [1]100
Dublin University Review [4]6
Dubois, Jean Antoine (1765–1848) *Description of . . . the People of India* MT [2]339–49
Du Chat, M. *see* Le Duchat
Duchesne, Joseph ("Quercetanus") (c 1544–1609) [3]816, 817
duchess [4]599
duck(s) [2]190, [3]952, [4]92–3
and goose [2]192
duck(s) and drake(s) [4]9, 10n
ducklings [5]594
ductility [4]314, 314n
Dudley, Joseph (1647–1720) [3]817
Dudley, Robert, 1st Earl of Leicester (?1532–88) [2]837, [5]390
duel(s) [4]238, 238n, 241
duelling [4]580, 584
Du Fresnoy, Charles Alphonse (1611–65) *Art of Painting* pref Dryden [4]779n
Duhamel, Jean Baptiste (1623–1706) [3]128
duke(s) [2]219, [5]278, 280
Duke, Richard (c 1659–1711) [1]37
Duke University *see* Durham NC
dulia [2]663n
dullness [4]289, [6]207, 322
-duly [1]257n, 663n
Dumain (*Love's Labour's Lost*) [4]696
Duméril, André Marie Constant (1774–1860) [3]941
Dumfriesshire [4]574
Dümmler, Ferdinand [1]131
Dunbalrase [5]390n
Dunbar, Earl of *see* Home, George
Dunbar, John (fl 1810) [3]937
Dunbar, William (c 1460–c 1520) *The Poems*† [1]clxx, [2]350
Duncan (*Macbeth*) [4]789
Duncan, P. (fl 1833) [1]34
Dundas, Henry, Viscount Melville (1742–1811) [3]1080, 1080n
dung [1]657, [2]1065, [3]728
d.-hill [2]345, [3]587, [4]665; d.-yard [2]764
dungeon [1]308
dungeonings [5]544
Dunin-Borkowski, C. S., Count (fl 1809–10) [3]939
Dunmow [1]160n, [2]1118n
Dunn, S. G. [2]259
Duns Scotus, Johannes (c 1265–1308) [1]153n, 254n, 255n, 286, 301, 479n, 524, 524n–5n, [2]11, 11–12, 183, 183n, 1136, [3]135n, 136n, 142n, 365, 366n, [5]478n, 597, 597n, 603n, 768–9, 787–92, 792–3 q, [6]137
De Sententiis [1]255, 255n, [2]1136n, [5]597n; *Sententia* [5]787 q; *see also* Scotist
Dunsinane [4]864, 864n
Dunstan, St (c 909–88) [1]858
dupe(s) [1]402, [2]194, [3]659, [4]55, 63, [5]396, 641
duplication [3]660
duplicity [3]357n
of human nature [4]412
duplique [3]660
Dupuis, Charles François (1742–1809) [1]492
Durandus of Saint-Pouçain (c 1275–1334) [1]286, 301, [5]5n
Durchbruch [4]227, [5]181, 181n
Dürer, Albrecht (1471–1528) [4]810, 811, 811n
Durham [2]945, [3]975, [4]132n
Cathedral Library [1]ciii, civ, 50n, 255, 255n, [2]1136n, [5]597n
Durham NC
Duke University Library [1]717, marginalia in [1]clxvii, [4]619, [5]377, microfilm at [2]117, transcript of marginalia in [5]854
duri per durius [5]74

Durling, Robert M. *see* Petrarch *Petrarch's Lyric Poems* tr and ed Durling
Durward, Quentin (in Scott) [4]612, 612n
Dusch, Johann Jakob (1725–87) *see* Pope *Collected Works* ed Dusch
dust [3]12, [6]113
Dutch (language) [3]978, [4]289
Dutch (people) [2]756, [5]106, 106n
Dutchman [5]296, 296n
Dutens, Louis (1730–1812) *see* Leibniz *Opera omnia* ed Dutens
duty/duties [1]4, 326, 751n, [2]614, 614n, 618, [3]263–4, 312, 644, 958, 959, 969, 970, [4]162, 214, 335, 410, 776, 777, 810, [5]37, 38, 104, 169, 493, 529, 677, 829
act of [6]262; aweful [5]181; Christian [3]72; of conscience [5]494; in duty [1]326; in Fletcher [1]395; of friend [4]9–10; to mankind [1]13; moral [4]638; negative [2]496; notion of [2]129; pastoral [1]813; preventive [5]102; of public life [4]145; religious [4]549, 855; of reverence for rank [1]499; and right(s) [2]210n, [3]178n, 875, 960, 960n–1n, [4]341–2, 342n, [5]37, 302–4, [6]24; rules of [3]688; sense of [4]341; spiritual [3]1089
Dutrochet, René Joachim Henri (1776–1847) [2]1026n
dwarf [2]346, 346n, 1112, [3]869, [4]594, 595n
dyad [1]582, 643, [2]751n, 1186, [3]1054–5, [5]733, 733n
of manifestation [1]653
Dyce, Alexander (1798–1869) [1]89n, 386n, 389n, [2]7, [4]727n
dye, main [1]762, 796
dyer(s) [2]496
Dyer, George (1755–1841) [1]clx, [2]*351*, 848n, [4]294
Academic Unity MT [2]352; *Four Letters* [5]851; *Poems* [1]lxxx; MT [2]353–6; 696, 845; *Poetic Sympathies* MT [2]354–5; *The Poet's Fate* MT [2]354; *Privileges of the University of Cambridge* [2]351; *The Redress* MT [2]355–6
Dyer, John (1699–1757) [1]38
Grongar Hill MT [1]75
Dyer, Mrs [1]295
dying [3]62–3
Dymock, Thomas W. (fl 1648) *Englands Dust and Ashes Raked Up* [2]42; MT [2]357–8
dynamic(s) [2]727, [4]421
abstract [2]1015; material [3]997; d. philosophy *see* philosophy, dynamic; physical [5]434
dynamis/*dynameis* [2]452, 751, [3]73, 135, 135n, 202, 1029, [4]328, [5]550, 665–6, 666n, 763; *see also* power(s)
dynamodynamis [1]581, 592
dynasty, Austrian and Spanish [5]275
dyspepsy [5]559

E Os [5]502, 502n
each, all in [5]360
eagle [1]482–3, 482n, 487, [3]76, 453, 471, [4]525, [5]651, 862
ear(s) [1]638, 683, [3]87, 217, 1087, [4]273, 509, 674, 759, [5]296, 544, 583
Böhme's "counsellors" [1]577; boring of [3]29; box of the [4]766; decorous [4]637; educated [3]904; hard bones in [1]577; Milton's [3]905; subtlety of [3]827; e.-witnesses [1]306, [3]207
Earl of Abergavenny (ship) [1]76, [5]824n, 825n
"earth" [1]663
earth(s) [1]126, 625n, 685, [2]557, [3]39, 1015, 1030–1, 1057, [4]526, 526n, [5]232, 256, 257, 263, 266, 340, 357, 438, 451, 610
absorbs blood [3]42, 43n; core of [5]245, 247; duration of [5]606; e.-element(s) [3]1019–20, 1019n–20n, 1022; fire-matter in [4]202; formation of [4]516–17, 517n; fuller's [2]816, 816n; and heaven [1]138, 436, 437, 832, 877, [2]470, [4]251, 481, [5]433, 624, [6]60, 303; Heraclitus on [5]714; history of [4]526; major magnet [5]267; metallic [5]247; new [2]1022; origin of [5]430, 430n; e.-rind [4]491; subfacial body [5]431; water as mother of [1]661–3
"earthly" [3]427
earthquake(s) [1]370, [2]388, 446, [3]481, [4]490–1, 809, [5]187, 514
earthworm [4]431
"earthy" [1]785n
earthy [1]764, 797
ease, graceful [1]763, 796
East [2]1017, [5]156, 256, 266
allegory [2]1053; ideal [5]438; poor gold in [5]262; punctual [1]611; Roman [4]483; spicy [6]251; superstitions of [5]226; *see also* compass of nature
East Anglia [2]327n
East India Company [1]724, 724n, [2]979n, [3]1081, [4]30, 170; *see also* London: East India House
East Indies [2]230n, [4]534, 534n, [5]387n, 830
Eastbourne [2]179

Easter [1]327, [3]666, 667, [6]260
Eastlake, Sir Charles Lock (1793–1865) *see* Goethe *Zur Farbenlehre* tr Eastlake
Easton, James (fl 1799–1825) *Human Longevity* [4]201n
ebb and flow [6]250
Ebeling, Christian Daniel (1741–1815) [1]697
"Ebenezarites" [4]662, 662n
Ebenezer(s) [3]602
Eber (Bible) [4]257
Eberbach [2]982
Eberhard, Johann August (1739–1809) [3]672
Ebert, Johann Arnold (1723–95) [3]656
Eberus, Paulus (1511–69) [3]718
Ebionites/Ebionim [1]491, [2]437, 437n, 700, 709–10, 710n, [3]730, 730n, 1084, [4]253, 254, 255–6, [5]623, 625n, [6]54, 67, 68, 68n, 69, 645
ebullience [2]922
eccalumeni [1]529, *529n*
ecclesia [2]654, 654n, 1139, 1142, [3]1084n, [5]503
 and enclesia [2]69, 943, 943n, 1140, 1141n, [5]67, 67n–8n, 78, 78n
Ecdicius (fl 362–3) [4]99n
ecdotes [3]307n–8n
echo(es) [2]632, [3]48, 121, 539n, [5]82, 790
 confused [2]1000; mental [4]477; worship the e. [3]539
Eck, Johann Maier von (Eckius) (1486–1543) [3]696
eclat [3]175
Eclectic(s) [4]125, 421n, [5]743n
 philosophers [2]1002
Eclectic Review [1]306n; MT [2]359–60; [3]1076–7
eclecticism [2]1015
eclipse(s) [1]609, [4]129, [5]264, [6]119
 of documents [5]635; lunar [3]426; of the truth [2]882
eclogue(s) [2]54, 55n
 amoebean [1]736
economics [2]64n, 616–22
 Keynesian [2]953n
economy [4]649
 severest [1]394
ecstasy/extasies [2]402, [3]868 ("extatic")
 religious [2]701, 701n; temple [5]517
Edda [4]489–90
eddy [5]186
Eden [1]779, [2]1074n, [3]41, 105
Eden, John (d 1840), letter to [1]xcvi q, xcvin
Edgar (*King Lear*) [4]818
Edgar Aetheling (c 1050–c 1125) [3]784, 785n
edge-tools [5]75, 75n
Edgeworth, Maria (1767–1849)
 Patronage [4]170; and R. L. Edgeworth *Practical Education* [4]658
Edgeworth, Richard Lovell (1744–1817) [3]938, 942; *see also* M. Edgeworth and R. L. Edgeworth
edification [5]155
edifice [4]652
 foundationless [5]668; old [5]89
Edinburgh [2]1204n, [3]141n, 627
 Edinburgh University [2]979, 979n, 981n; *see also* Medico-Chirurgical Society
Edinburgh Encyclopaedia [1]123n
Edinburgh Medical and Surgical Journal MT [2]361–8; [3]126n
Edinburgh Monthly Magazine [1]cxviii; see also *Blackwood's Edinburgh Magazine*
Edinburgh Review [1]147, 216n, 725, 860, [2]914n, 980n, 983n, [3]60n, [4]5, 26n, 201n, 627, 627n, 630n, [5]102, 102n, [6]184, 189
Edinburgh Weekly Journal [4]76n
Edith (in B&F) [1]398
edition(s) [4]768
 comparison of [6]312; expensive [3]705; incorrectness of [3]882–3; instructive [1]389; modern [4]99; pirated [3]887
editor(s) [1]387, 399, [4]723
 entitled to correct [1]384
Edmund (*King Lear*) [1]212, 212n, 276, 276n, [4]732n, 815–18, 822, [6]264
Edom [1]418, 436, [2]390, 394–5
Edomite [2]414
educated, the [4]775
education [1]531, [2]530, 954n, [3]312, 621, [4]27–8, 100, [5]37, 102, 273–4, 320, 321, 322, 366n, [6]125
 bad [2]636; blunders in [4]438; Christian [4]306n; C's lecture on [1]158n; C's principles of [2]722n; C's scheme of [5]324, 324n; foreign [4]818; German [5]326; importance of [6]126; irreligious [3]513; learned [4]258; liberal [3]91, 91n; noble scheme of [2]722; persons of [5]651; of poor [3]700; prejudice of [4]239; religious [4]597; of soul [5]496; technical [1]632
"educe" [3]91, 91n
Edward I, King of England (1239–1307) [2]155n, [4]291
 reign of [2]929
Edward III, King of England (1312–77) [2]826n, [5]195, 196

Edward IV, King of England (1442–83) [2]938n
Edward VI, King of England (1537–53) [1]129, 280, 286n, 318n, 329, 329n, 835, 866, [2]264, 264n–5n, 277, 663, 819n, [5]41, 393, 519, 661
 "First Prayer Book of Edward VI" [2]89n
Edward the Black Prince (1330–76) [2]826
Edward the Confessor, King of England (c 1003–66) [3]784, [5]38
Edwards, Bryan (1743–1800) *History . . . of the British Colonies* [2]985
Edwards, Jonathan (1703–58) *A Careful and Strict Enquiry into . . . Freedom of the Will* [2]802n, [5]202n
Edwards, R. (fl 1820) [1]816
Edwards, Thomas (1599–1647) *Gangraena* [4]176 q
Edwards, William Frederic (1777–1842) [4]164
eel [3]635, [4]431
 electric [3]868n, [6]103n
"effect" [5]649
effect(s) [2]1145, [4]221, [5]65
 cause and *see* cause; moral [5]585; purely relative [1]791; transitory [2]1185
effeminacy [4]162, 838, [6]210, 322
efficacy
 magical [5]675; saving [2]496; spiritual [1]832, [3]597, 597n, [5]835
effluence [1]525, [5]714
effluents [5]604
effluvia [6]38
effluviation [5]340
efflux [2]479, [6]179
efforts, mental [5]181
effrontery [4]195
effusion, harmless [5]866
"efreet" [4]846n
Egede, Hans (1686–1758) [1]431n
egeneto [2]273, 273n, 750, *750n*, [3]876n, [5]470, [6]88
 e. sarx see *sarx*
Egerton, Francis Henry, 8th Earl of Bridgewater (1756–1829) [2]883n
egg(s) [1]119, 792n, [4]92, 273, 273n, [5]110, 504n–5n, 811, *811n*
 broad end [1]318; containing snake [1]436; everything from [2]367, 367n; of universe [5]429–30, 431
Eglon (Bible) [1]422
Egmont, Lord *see* Perceval, John James
ego [4]347–8, 364n, [5]204
 e. agens [5]594; *e. contemplans* [2]602; *see also* I
egoism [2]636, [6]241
egoismus [2]595, [4]41, [5]94n
egoity [4]454
"egometical" [1]346, 346n
egotism [1]763, 796, [2]622, 622n, [3]955, 963, 1068, [5]111
 anxious [5]496; becoming [1]763, 796; Wesley's [5]133n, 161n
Egremound [5]390n
Egypt [1]419, 457n, 540, 684, 771n, [2]284, 383–4, 385, 396, 416, 417n, 418, 573, 577n, 579n, 584, 728n, 737, 737n, 809, 831, 1012, 1015, 1041, [3]419, 422, 473, 474, 722, 1086, [4]29, 99n, 176, 201, 513, 513n, [5]64n, 142, 226, 352, 465, 811n ("Egyptian"), 846, [6]149, 292–3
 connection with Jews [3]111; double-land [2]577; Egyptian pebble [3]630; Exodus from [2]378; flight into [2]661, [4]54; Hebrews settle in [2]395; Jews in [3]658, [6]141; magicians [2]1105, 1107, 1107n, [6]105n; mythology [3]92n; plague(s) of [2]363, [6]138, 141; serpent symbol [1]684; waters of [6]112
Egyptian (language) [2]380–1
Egyptian(s) [1]778, 783, 785, [2]578, [5]62, 225, 226n, [6]112, 219
Ehre [4]287, 287n
Ehud (Bible) [1]422, [2]771n, [4]304
ei [5]711, 711n
Eibinger [2]982
Eichhorn, Johann Gottfried (1752–1827) [1]ci, cxviii, cxx, 305, 306n, 416, 458n, 481, 719n, [2]37n, 38, 144, 149n, 270n, *369–70*, 568, 651, 651n, 707, 707n, 736n, 902n, [3]3n, 20n, 30n, 421n, 524n, 669, 732n, 922, [4]40, 58, 59n, 60n, 468, 469, [5]85n, 128n, 402n, 526n, 540n, 624n, 667n, [6]59n, 114n, 117n, 119n, 138n, 140n, 141, 141n, 294, 294n
 effrontery of [2]497; Eichhornian reading [3]929n; on four kingdoms [2]155; great error of [2]512; hypothesis of *Urevangelium* [4]452n, 469–70, 475; on Jeremiah [1]439; learning praised [2]491; lectures of [2]445n; on Pastoral Epistles [4]485; no philosopher [2]478, 500; his theory [4]471
 ed *Allgemeine Bibliothek der biblischen Litteratur* [2]144n; MT 371–2; [3]612n, [4]56, 56n; *Commentarius in Apocalypsin Joannis* [1]cvi, 471n, [2]369, 651, [3]922n; [5]494n, [6]136 ("*Apocalypse*"); *Copy A* MT [2]503–18; *Copy B* [1]lxxii; MT [2]519–20; *Einleitung in das Neue Testament* [1]414, 452n, 468n, [2]38n, 651, [3]669n, [4]56n, 485n; *Copy A* [2]415; MT 435–77; *Copy B*

MT [2]478–502; *Einleitung in die apokryphischen Schriften des Alten Testaments* MT [2]415–34; 435, 651, [6]142n ("*Apocrypha*"); *Einleitung ins Alte Testament* [1]417n, 418n, 439n, 616, 616n, [2]148, 148n, 155n, 369; MT 373–414; 415, 435, 481, 481n, 651, 895n, 896n, 1129, [4]253n
Eichner, Hans, coeditor [1]3, 132, [2]181, 753, 852, 1112, [4]465
-*eides* [1]459n
Eidgenoss [3]250n
eidolon/*eidola* ("idola") [2]679, 679n, 685, 685n, 882n, [3]90, 90n, 431, 431n, [4]42, 42n, 124n, [5]17, 17n, 409, 729n
eidos [3]194, [4]42, 42n, 313–14, 313n–14n
eidouranion [4]13, 13n
eight [4]37, 37n
VIII Problems Propounded to the Cavaliers [2]42
"eighth" [1]483
eikon [1]345n, 431n, 466n, [3]107n, 524n, 545, 545n, [4]653n; *see also* icon(s)
Eikon Basilike [1]336, 336n; MT [2]521–4; *522n*, 948, 948n, 971, 971n, 1132n, [3]798, 798n, [5]146n, [6]184–6. *See also* Charles I; Gauden
eimarmenon [5]717, 717n
"*eimi*" [5]175
eimi [1]*461n*, [2]379n, [3]279n, 830, 834n, 836n, [5]189, 711n, [6]85, 116, 116n; *see also* I am
eimids [2]891
einai [3]279, [4]36n
Einbildungskraft [3]790
Einhof, H. E. (1778–1808) [3]938
eirgastai [2]1107, *1107n*
eis [1]575n, [3]834
e. and *en* [5]653, 653n; *e. allo genos* [1]253, 253n
"eisel" [4]745
Eisenbichler, Konrad [6]321
-eity (-*eitas*) [1]*152n*
ejaculation [2]541
ejection [5]146
ekdikesis [1]462n
Ekins, Nathaniel (fl 1630–60) [1]760
ekkaloumenoi see *eccalumeni*
Ekkehart I, Dean of St Gall (c 910–73) *De prima expeditione Attilae regis Hunnorum in Gallias*† ed Fischer [2]525
Ekkehart, Meister (c 1260–1327) [2]525
ekklesia [1]529n
Ekron [3]57n
El Dorado [5]106
El Jah [3]24, 24n
Elagabalus *see* Heliogabalus
"elanguescing" [4]238, 238n
elasticity [1]653, [3]276–7, [4]395, 395n
Elba [3]160n
elbow-room [3]671
elder(s) [2]489, 920, 1097, 1199
lay [6]47; Moravian [3]493–4
elderly, the [3]360
Eldon, Lord *see* Scott, John
Eleanor (*King John*) [4]711n
Eleatic(s) [2]869, 869n, 872n
philosophy [2]340, *340n*
Eleazar (Bible) [2]895n
Eleazer (fl 64) [2]509, 509n
elect, the [1]284, 454, 464, 729, [2]562, 1164, [3]50, 62, 520, 527, 528, 547n, 548, 550, 589n, 602, 818, [5]137n, 606, 607, 665, [6]303; *see also* chosen, the
election (in religion) [1]222, 824, 827, [2]802, [3]51–2, 62, 514–15, [4]640, [5]75n, 154, 155, 156, 156n, 162n, 185, [6]297
Calvinist doctrine [1]284; mark of [3]543, [6]311; of ministers in church [1]308, 339
election(s) (in politics) [2]90, [3]799–800, [4]19, 96, [5]39n, 300 ("electing"), 644
interference in [4]13, 13n
elective affinity *see* affinity
elective attraction [3]984
elector(s) [4]22, 23, 24, [6]49
divine [5]156
electricity/electricities [1]177, 579, 582, 650, 660, 662, 663, 775–6, 780, [2]853, 853n, 854n, 855n, 863, 890, 1007, 1008n, [3]61, 61n, 94, 123, 123n, 205, 210, 211, 256, 325, 325n, 364, 399, 947, 949, 997, 997n, 999, 1002, 1011, 1017n, 1032, 1060, [4]149n, 353, 358–9, 392, 392n, 393, 492, 494n, [5]265, 266, 347, 348, 435, 438, 451, 764, [6]226, 227, 250
belief in [3]373; forces of [3]1006; opposite [5]714; positive [1]590; static [5]577n; and taste [6]135n; *see also* fluid, electric
electrisation [3]872
electromagnetism [3]104n
elegance [5]455
"elegant" [3]318
elegeia [1]146n
elegy/elegies [2]237
defined [1]146, 146n
element(s) [1]119, 120, [3]43, 790, 1019, 1021n, 1022–4, 1026, [4]809, [5]344
actual [5]346n; centrifugal [1]569; confusion of [2]246; four [5]231; love as [3]265; primal [5]721; simple [5]816

elements (of Eucharist) [1]264, [2]281–2, [3]598, [5]393, 542, 552, 555
elenchi, Zeno's [5]712
elenchus ab ignorantia [3]934
elephant(s) [1]111, 427, 427n, [2]527, 862, 933, [3]558, 1046, 1047, 1082, [4]488–9, 488n, 489n, 530, 534, [5]250, 385, [6]80
Elers/Ellers, David and John Philip (fl 1695) [3]633, 634
Eleusa [2]739
Eleusinian mysteries *see* mysteries, Eleusinian
Eleusis [1]665n
elevation [4]723
  moral [1]430
Elfric *see* Aelfric
"Elia" *see* Lamb, Charles
Elias *see* Elijah
Eliezer (Bible) [2]823
eligibility [4]22, 23–4
Elihu *see* Elijah/Elias
Elijah/Elias (Bible) [1]452, 845, [2]150, 1072–3, 1082, 1085, [3]39–41, 40n, 41n, 457, 457n, 475–6, 476n, [4]296 ("Elihu"), 472, 472n, [5]402 ("Helias"), 402n, 535, 564, [6]119
  and John the Baptist [2]150; type of Messiah [2]150n
elimination [4]321
Eliogabalus *see* Heliogabalus
Eliot, John (1604–90) [3]820
Elisha (Bible) [1]832n, [6]72
elision [3]903
Eliun (myth) [2]577, 578n, 579
Elizabeth (Bible) [2]323, [4]51, 297
Elizabeth I, Queen of England (1533–1603) [1]287n, 321n, 395n, 401, 501, 531, 559, 762, 831, 865, 866, [2]64, 127, 260, 294, 327n, 675, 818–19, 819n, 837, 940, 943, 943, 1136, 1139n, 1194, 1199, [3]171, [4]173, 336, 336n, 681, 766, [5]143, 143n, 519
  age of [4]767; rebellion against [3]144; reign of [1]357, 389, 762, 796, 813, 831, [2]235, 813, 1120, [3]918, [4]75, 657, [5]144, 389; statesmen of [3]251; statute of [3]144; writers of [2]240
Elizabethans [3]221n
elk [2]1185
Ellers *see* Elers
Ellington, James *see* Kant *Metaphysical Foundations* tr Ellington
Elliotson, John (1791–1868) [1]822n; *see also* Blumenbach *Institutions* tr Elliotson
ellipsis/ellipses [3]370, [4]326, 723, [5]431
Ellis, Daniel (fl 1807–11) [4]531, [5]256
  Farther Inquiries [4]531n q, [5]256n; *Inquiry into the Changes Induced in Atmospheric Air* [4]531n, [5]256n
Ellistone, John (d 1652) [1]554
elm [4]318, 318n
elocution [3]37
Elohim [1]417n, 660n, 679, [2]385–6, 389–90, 389n, 419n, 578n, [4]49, 49n
"eloigne" [3]188
eloquence [3]431, 452, 767, [4]25
  impetuous [4]845; of inferiors and superiors [2]319; manly [3]8; poetic [5]528; and poetry [5]689; spirit of [5]651; of Jeremy Taylor [5]597
Elphiston (possibly John Elphinstone, d 1649) [2]1104
Elpistics [3]642
Elwes, Robert Harvey Monro (b 1853), *see* Spinoza *Chief Works*, *Ethics*, *Tractatus politicus*, *Tractatus theologico-politicus* tr Elwes
Elwyn, Alfred (1804–84) [1]cxlin
Elwyn, William Brame (1774–1841) [1]xcvii, [3]507–8, 508n
Elxai (Bible) [2]709, 710
Elymas (Bible) [5]645, 645n
Elysium [2]167, 1074
Elzevir, Abraham (1622–52) [1]218n
Elzevir, Bonaventura (1583–1652) [1]218n
Elzevir, Daniel (1626–80) [1]218, 218n, 219n
Elzevir family [2]219n, 526
Elzevir, Jean (1622–71) [1]218, 218n
Elzevir, Louis (1540–1617) [1]219n
Elzevir, Louis (1604–70) [1]218n
Elzevir Press [1]218, *218n–19n*
emanation(s) [1]563n, 568n, 652, [2]478–9, 562, 748, [3]122, 122n, 755, 755n, 949n, 1091n, 1092, 1092n, 1093, 1093n, [4]383, 383n, 525, [5]652, [6]314
  ancient heresy [1]645, *645n*
emanationists [2]479
emancipation [1]33, 34–5, 36, [4]24n
  mental [1]515; of slaves [3]1082. *See also* Catholic Emancipation; Parliament: Acts/Bills: Catholic Emancipation Bill
emasculation [1]356
embers, walking on [3]308
emblem [1]345n, [4]502
embryo [2]1025–6, 1026n
emendation [1]381
emeralds [3]898

Emerson, Ralph Waldo (1803–82) [2]21, 181, 964
Essays [1]clxixn
emetics [6]39
emigration [2]311, 849, [5]283
of Jews [2]401
emigré [5]143n
Emili, Paulo (Paulus Emilius Veronensis) (d 1529) [1]522, 523
eminenter [1]567, 567n, [2]1110, [3]29, 79
eminently and formally [1]567, 567n
Emlyn, Thomas (1663–1741) [6]90
Dr Bennet's New Theory of the Trinity Examined [6]89
Emlyn, Viscount *see* Campbell, Hugh John Vaughan
Emma of Normandy (d 1052) [3]784
Emmaus [1]456
emotion(s) [4]781
noblest [1]393; of sublimity [2]1069
emou [5]58, 58n
Empedocles (fl c 450 BC) [1]767, [2]349, 425n, 1123, [6]327–8
emperor(s) [2]949, [3]149
dying [3]146; poet as [5]749; Roman [1]486, [3]471, [5]829n
Empfindung [1]692, 692n, [3]264, 662, 663n; *see also* self-finding
emphasis [1]377, [2]217, [3]815, [4]743
empire(s) [4]81, 145
Babylonian [2]409; in Dan [3]923; French [2]847; of Great Britain [1]732–3; Greek [3]447; heterogeneous [5]644; Latin [6]167; Roman [1]436, 441n, 472, 472n, [2]155, 513, 663, 674, 712, [3]143, 309, 442, 447, 470, 573, 1069, [4]474, [5]674, [6]28n; succession of [2]157, 157n
"empiric" [6]236n
empiric(s) [1]631, 631n, [4]657
empiricism [3]920
empirical medicine [3]365; prejudice of [5]828
"empiricist" [6]236, 236n
empirickqutique [4]804n
Empirie [4]379–80, 380n
empirism [2]538n
"empirist" [6]236, 236n
employment [1]878
empress of the seas [6]221
empyrean [5]656
of ideas [2]1146
emulation [1]525, 726
and envy [1]726
en [5]31
"Enchanter, Northern" (Walter Scott) [3]484–5, 484n
enchantments [1]419, [2]1107
enchantress, fratricidal [1]537
"enclesia" [5]67, 67n–8n
enclesia [2]1139, 1142, [3]1084n
and ecclesia *see* ecclesia
encyclopaedia [2]781
French [4]272; of prayer [5]520
Encyclopaedia Britannica [1]cviii, [4]518n, [5]376, [6]135n
Encyclopaedia Judaica [1]416
Encyclopaedia Londinensis ed John Wilkes [1]218n; MT [2]526–31
Encyclopaedia Metropolitana [2]1204n
Encyclopaedia of Religion and Ethics ed J. Hastings [2]901n, [5]105n
encyclopaedists [1]143
Encyclopédie [3]698n, [4]272n
end(s) [2]1161, [3]29, [5]788
faculty of [3]424; fallible judgments of [1]4; and means [1]185, 367, 446, 827, [2]322–3, 356, 1018, 1066, [3]5, 263–4, 317, 423, 424, 459, [4]23–4, 113, 426, 780–1, 789, 863, [5]185, 399, [6]29, 53, 133; medial [5]425; ultimate [5]177, 425
Endeavour (ship) [1]536n, [2]861n
ending [2]1021n
Endor, Witch of [1]110, 110n, 420, 420n, [2]1105, 1108n, [3]771n
enduring, reverence of [2]186
enemy/enemies [1]442, [5]132
common [6]98; inveterate [5]625
energeia [1]479, 479n
energema [5]654, 654n
"energic" [2]1175, 1175n
energy/energies [2]261, 580, [4]165, [5]176
articulative [3]24; of consciousness [1]566; conservation of [3]323n; creative [2]723; focal [4]398; immanent [1]564; moral [4]810; negative and positive [4]167; nervous [5]136, 141; of non-resistance [1]820; opposing [4]128, 128n, 359; pleasurable [1]692; polar [1]663; qualitative [3]1004; single [4]827; source of [5]438; total [4]399, 399n; in Trinity [1]564; vital [2]1182, [5]137; of will [3]26, 307
Enfield, William (1741–97) [2]172n, [3]191n
Engels, Johann Jakob (1741–1802) [1]513n, [2]429n
"Stück VI" in *Der Philosoph für die Welt* [1]756n
engine(s) [5]207
fire-e. [5]351

enginery [1]325

England [1]244, 254, 788, 840, [2]210, 233, 236n, 321n, 348, 964, 1055, [3]149, 153n, [4]24n, 185, 200, 227, 227n, 421n, 483, 534n, [5]38, 43, 44, 68, 97, 196, 295n, 315, 319, 508, 644, 650, 686, 689n, 834, [6]15, 52

Americans' hatred of [3]133; British Catholic Association [1]203, 857n; Church of *see* Church of England; Civil War [3]801n, [4]307n, [5]124n, 596; Commonwealth [4]78, 176, [5]124n, 146n, 508; compromise characteristic [4]17; constitution of [3]799; extinction of [2]1179; and Germany [5]372, 372n; gold in [5]276; history of [3]784; Independent churches in [1]346; infidelity in [5]630; Jews in [3]700; king of [3]1082; law(s) of [3]164, [4]633–4, 646; English medicine [3]372–4; English metaphysicians [3]877–8; mind of [2]1150; English nationalist [3]165; negotiations with Denmark [5]312; persecution of witches in [6]104; philosophy in fashion in [4]125; English prose [3]887, classics of [3]882; Protectorate [1]807, [2]827, [4]675; Reformation in [2]1158, [3]515, [4]184, [5]144n; religion in [5]142; Restoration [4]336, 336n, 723n; Revolution (1688) [3]168, 757n, [4]282, 594, 817; Revolutionary War [1]92n; and Rome [6]14; and Scotland [4]591

English (language) [4]326n, 595n, [5]111, 113, 114, 283, 428, 566, [6]4, 77

composite language [1]496; and French [3]1074; harmonious [3]1076; imperishable [2]15; Middle E. [4]284n; mother-E. [4]717, 780; Old E. [5]389; pure [5]651; RS's use of [4]172n; *see also* style

English (people) [5]280

advantages of [4]235; character of [1]733, [5]195n; common sense of [2]204; and French [4]239–40, 240n; as generous/Iapetic race [1]540; intolerant of charlatans [3]315; lack metaphysical genius [2]1136; lose in cabinet [2]101; rival to Greek [3]403; and Scots [4]765–6; as soldiers [2]100

English Catalogue of Books [2]5, 840n, [3]810, [4]151, 578, [5]78, 817, 848, [6]163

English Channel [2]190n

English Place-Name Society [4]692n

"English Tracts"† [2]532

Englishman/Englishmen [5]83, 327, [6]16

better [2]120; illiterate [4]301; invent English fools [1]212; Jacobinised [4]795; Kant as [3]314; loyal [2]932; murder of [3]1081; privileges [1]360; style worthy of [5]533

engraving(s) [4]82

in Homer [2]1126; mezzotint [2]1196, 1196n

enigma(s) [1]472, 776, 789n, [2]343, 714, 785, [3]467

"enigmatise" [5]85

enjoyment, sensuous [1]655

"enkindle" [4]788, 788n

enlegeia [1]46

Enlightenment

pride of [2]480n; Scottish [4]657n

enmity, national [5]195

Enmore [1]9

ennea [4]37

ennead [1]643, 691, 691n, [3]910, [5]22, 701n

Ennerdale [3]980

Ennius, Quintus (c 239–169 BC) [2]59n, 757, 757n

ennui [2]1022, [3]57, [5]122

Enobarbus (*Antony and Cleopatra*) [3]897n

Enoch (Bible) [2]576, 1072–3, 1074, 1074n, 1082, 1085, [3]39, 39n, 40, 40n, 475–6, [5]402, 402n, [6]119; *see also* Bible: Apocrypha: OT: Enoch

enochos [1]448n

enough and more than e. [1]183, 183n

ens

e. entium [3]332, [5]756; *e. imaginarium* [3]43; *e. logicum* [2]1028, [3]43, 77, 135, [4]235, 460, [5]4, 446, 550; *e. non e.* [1]574, [2]889; *e. non vere e.* [4]14; *e. rationalis* [3]919, 919n; *e. rationis* [3]83; *e. reale* [1]114, 114n, [2]685, [3]43, 80; *e. realissimum* [3]345; *e. spirituale* [3]754, 755n; *e. super e.* [2]324, 676, 889; *e. supremum* [5]372; *e. vere e.* [2]889, [4]235

entangler [5]451

entelechia [3]82

"entelechism" [5]827, 827n

"entelechy" [5]827n

entelechy [3]1055, 1063

enthousiastoi [1]496, 496n

enthusiasm [3]338n, 408, 517, 560, [5]189, 510, [6]300, 300n

defined [1]494–5, [6]261; and fanaticism [1]270, 270n, 495–6, [2]198n, [3]517n, 1079n, [6]261; and genius [1]818; rank [5]652; religious [5]480–5; and superstition [2]198, 198n; wise [2]254

"enthusiast" [1]270, 270n

enthusiast(s) [2]754, [3]331, 494, [4]55, 63, 183, 623, 626, [5]134, 568, 568n, 569, [6]116, 261

generous [4]633; high-flying [5]229; sublime [1]762, 796

enthymeme [3]94, 94n–5n, 362, [4]235, [6]175–6

Entick, John (c 1703–73) [1]560, 560n
 New Spelling Dictionary [1]560, 560n
entireness [1]763, 764, 797
entity/entities
 absolute [2]611; fictitious [5]244; logical [5]756; metaphysical [1]632; and non-entity [2]604; potential [5]424; spiritual [5]452
entomology [2]527
entozoa [1]460, 460n
entrails [1]657
"enucleate" [1]620n
envelopes, ceremonial [1]878
envenomer [2]945
"envy" [4]358
envy [2]637, [4]141, 141n, 816, 860
 and emulation *see* emulation; plebeian [2]76
eo [6]25n, 26–7
Eolian harp *see* harp, Eolian
Eolus *see* Aeolus
Eon *see* Aeon
Epaphras (Bible) [1]465
epaulette [5]675
epecho [1]229, 229n, 836
Epeus/Epeius (myth) [3]648, 649
Ephesians [2]704, 710, 711
Ephesus [2]459, 471, 490, 702, [3]6, 477, [4]61, 474, [5]551, 558, 629, [6]168n
 Church at [1]485, 485n, [3]422n, 684n, [5]807n; Council of [5]576; proconsul of [1]481, 482, 482n
ephorim [3]426
Ephraim (Bible) [1]442
epic(s) [2]413, 413n, 968, [3]484, [4]604, 604n, 787, 794, 853, 864, [5]110
 blank verse in [5]689; and dramatic *see* dramatic; Homeric [4]811; *see also* poem, heroic
Epicharmus (c 540–450 BC) [2]775, 775n, 1123
"epician" [5]111, 111n
Epictetus (c 55–c 135) [1]cv, 161, 161n, 174n, 175, 175n, 177n, [2]427, 427n, [3]570–1, 622, [5]385, 658, 658n, [6]222
 Apophthegmata [1]161n; *Enchiridion* [1]161n
Epicurean(s) [1]174, 433, 631, 631n, [3]498, [4]663, [5]81n, 135, 272
 atheism [1]646, [2]251; onion [1]652, 652n; philosophy [4]663; principles [1]305; reasoners [2]291
Epicuri, Christian [5]552
Epicurism [2]1080, [4]548
 of genius [4]162
Epicurus (341–271 BC) [1]307, 307n, 646n, 773, [2]867n, [3]242, 243n, 529, 532, 623 q, 968, [4]435, [5]382, 382n, 386 q, 386n, 811, 811n, [6]75n, 312, 314
 an atheist [5]386; physiology of [5]811n; species of [5]604, 604n
 On Nature [6]75n
epicycles [3]1008
epidemic [2]363, [5]308
epidermis [1]814
epigenesists [3]243n
Epigeus (myth) [2]577, 578n
epigram(s) [2]770, 917, [3]222, [4]864
 pointed [3]701; A. Pope's [2]1120
epigrammatisers [1]845
epilepsy [2]454, 705, 720, 739, 739n, [3]375, 375n, 772, 772n, [4]497n, [6]122 ("fits")
epileptics [5]819
Epimetheus (myth) [2]86
Epiphanius, St, Bishop of Constantia (c 315–403) [1]490, [2]316, 709, 833, 833n, 923, [3]441, 495, 928, 929n, [4]250n, 251, 258, [5]181, 623, 623n, [6]63
 Adversus haereses (*Panarion*) [2]437, 437n, 441 q, 713, 713n, 717; *Heresies* [4]249 q, 252–3 q, 257, [5]181n
"Epiphany" [6]86
epiphany [1]434, [2]279, [3]454, 732, [4]480, 481n
 of the will [2]1193
epiphonemas [1]876, 876n
episcopacy [1]233, 294, 308–10, [2]523, 838, 1099, 1138, [3]801n, 803, [5]129n, 147n, 503, 503n, 508, 531–40, 660
 in Church of Scotland [3]540n; diocesan [6]257; episcopal spirit [2]811; misepiscopy [2]1173; moderate [4]172; and prelacy [2]61, 61n
Episcopalian(s) [1]311, 327, 332, [2]1042n, 1136, 1149, 1198, [4]591n, [5]508
episcopus/episcopi [2]1138, 1138n, [5]503
episkopos/episkopoi [5]503n, [6]257n
 e. koinoi [1]308
episteme [4]113
Epistemon (in Rabelais) [4]196
epistles, heroic [1]382
Epistles of NT *see* Bible: NT: EPISTLES
epistolikon [2]704
Epistolists [5]473
episynagein [1]453n
epitaph [1]56, [2]1180, [3]160, 1071
 for C [2]993
epithet(s) [1]25, 25n, [2]559, [4]186
 compound [2]865, 1119, 1119n; deceptive [2]662; double [2]1119n; reverential [5]643
epitrite(s) [1]377, [2]1040
epitritus primus [2]1039

epoch(s) [3]60–1, 60n, 461n, 478, 1021, [4]244, [5]57, 57n, 341, 800
five [3]60; principal [5]607; of reproduction [3]60; second [3]1024; third [3]461, *461n*
epopsy [1]652, 652n
epopt [1]598, 598n
epoptae [1]616, 616n, 628, [3]99n
epos [4]794n
Epstein, Isidore (b 1894) *see* Talmud: *Babylonian Talmud* tr Epstein
Epworth [5]164
"equal" [5]410–11, 435
equal [3]137, 137n
equality/equalities [4]768, [5]278
different sorts of [5]410; with God [5]30; of possessions [5]304
equation [6]231
mark of [5]435; of supreme reason [2]182–3; theory of [3]947
equator [1]775, [3]327, 327n, [4]491, [5]248, 262, 386
equilibrium [1]549, 775, [3]1007, [4]488, [5]421, 423, 424, 614, [6]243
of forces [5]442
equipoise [4]733, [5]424
equivocal [2]1160
equivocation(s) [2]990n, [3]33, 853, 1003, [4]379, 800, 842, [5]6, 9, 803
Augustine's [5]176; defined [3]277; latent [5]409. *See also* ambiguity; equivoque; meaning, double
equivoque [1]148, 184, 238, 287, [2]615, [3]345, 347, 532, 858, 1054, [4]155, 276, 540, 746, 864, [5]83, 223, 792, [6]274, 309; *see also* equivocation
era [5]308 ("aera")
eradiation(s) [1]601, [2]479, [5]244
Erasmians [4]192
Erasmus, Desiderius (c 1466–1536) [1]144n, 458n, 833, [2]52n, 304n, 528–9, 703, 969n, [3]736, 764n, 774, 774n, 774–5, 775n, [4]243, 614, 644, [5]391, 391n, 544 q, 649, 649n
on 1 Cor 14 [5]517, 517n; epigraph from [5]302n; letters of [2]763 q; and Luther [3]774–5; ridicule of pedants [2]763
Adagia [3]234n; *Collected Works* [3]234n; *Collected Works* XXVIII ed A. H. T. Levi [4]614n q; *Dialogus Ciceronianus* [2]763n, [4]614n; *Diatribe de libero arbitrio* [3]736n; *Hyperaspistes* [3]736n; *Letters 1535 to 1657* tr Dalzell [5]549 q, 549n q; *Opera omnia* [2]704n, [5]391n; *Opus epistolarum* ed H. M. and P. S. Allen [2]763n; *Paraphrasis in Acta Apostolorum* [2]703n; *Praise of Folly* [2]528–9, 529n; *see also* Bible: NT: Greek: ed Erasmus
Erastians [1]308
Erastus, Thomas (1424–83) [2]1135
Eratosthenes (c 285–194 BC) [4]147
Erdkugel [3]1020n
Erdman, David Vorse, coeditor [3]220, 500, 784, 794, 932
Erdmann, Johann Eduard (1805–92) *see* Leibniz *Opera philosophica* ed Erdmann
eregertai [1]450n
Erennius (fl 240) [5]748
Erfurt [4]187
"ergo" [4]194, [5]577
Erhard, Johann Benjamin (1766–1827) [3]954
Erigena, Joannes Scotus *see* Joannes
Erinnius (myth) [5]227
Eriphus (4th century BC) [4]147
eristic [5]460
Erivan [6]279
erkennen [3]366
Ernest, Duke [4]187
ero [4]98
Eros (myth) [1]119, 661, 661n, [4]464
e. and *heros* [1]392, 392n
Erota (in B&F) [1]392
erratum/errata [3]882, 887, [4]761
error(s) [1]142, [3]65, 260, 368, [4]9, [5]121, 150, 308, 384, 521
begets error [5]390; in Church [2]1140; dangerous [5]483; epidemic [1]283; four enormous [1]645–6; fundamental [2]26, 990, 990n, 996, 996n; generates error [2]745, [3]233; of great men [3]755; guilt reduced to [3]851; of half truth [2]266, 328, 1139, [3]33; of history [2]1198; hive of [2]953, [5]469, 484; of Irving [3]66; neutralised [5]452; perilous [1]566; personal [5]562; positive [1]234; quenching [5]188; in religion [4]260; of RC Church [3]42, [4]589, [5]469; of sects [5]157; shifting of [5]738; source of [5]571; speculative [2]685, 685n; supposed [5]470; of Swedenborgians [3]989; and truth [1]495, 556–7, 619, [2]735, [5]552, 561–2; typographical [1]766; of the understanding [1]823, [4]181; vulgar [1]774, 774n, [2]1198; of the will [5]624
Erscheinung/Erscheinungen [3]249n, [4]129, 129n, 210, 413
Erse (language) [2]574n
Erse (people), as mixed race [1]540
Erskine, Thomas, 1st Baron Erskine (1750–1823) [4]14, 96n

Erskine, Sir Thomas, 1st Earl of Kellie (1566–1639) [5]834n
"Erthusyo" (R. Southey) [1]89
erudition [2]274, [5]541, [6]145
antiquarian [6]64; Jonson's [3]179; Jeremy Taylor's [5]524; trammels of [5]591
eruption [5]766
Erxleben, Johann Christian Polycarp (d 1777) [4]187
erysipelas [2]1190
Esaias *see* Isaiah
Esau (Bible) [2]928n
escapes [2]160
Eschenbacher [5]762, 762n
Eschenburg, Johann Joachim (1743–1820) [3]656
Eschenmayer, Adolph Carl August (1768–1852) [1]556, [2]186, 188, 188n, [3]114, [4]398–9, [5]141, 141n, 183, 183n, 427, 428n, 762n, [6]225, 234, 245n
Psychologie MT [2]533–57; [5]183n; see also *Archiv für den thierischen Magnetismus* ed Eschenmayer, Kieser, and Nasse
Esculapius *see* Aesculapius
Esdras *see* Bible: Apocrypha: OT: 1 and 2 Esdras; OT: Ezra
"esemplastic" [1]113n, 595, 595n, [2]396n, 397, [3]790, 790n
"esenoplastic" [1]113n, [3]790, 790n
eskimo(s)/esquimaux [2]834, 1108, [5]252, 337, 337n, 353
esoptron [1]237, 237n
esoteric, the [5]573, 732
Español [1]500
Espencaeus, Claudius (Claude Togniel d'Espence) (c 1511–71) [5]548, 549n
Esquirol, Jean Etienne Dominique (1772–1840) [4]164
essay(s)
Montaigne's [5]810; philosophical [5]468
"An Essay on Electrical Attractions and Repulsions" MT [3]947
esse [3]128, 326, 440, [6]87n
e. absolute [5]410; *e.* and *habere* [5]95, 95n, [6]243; *e.* and *percipi* [3]916, [5]4; *e. est percipi* [5]4n; *e.* and *posse* [4]233; *e.* and *scire* [6]241; *see also* be
essence(s) [2]135, 611, [3]75, 85, [5]216
common [1]648; essential being [3]50; and existence [1]288, 288n, 579, [3]851, [5]360; free [2]554; of God [3]79, [5]205; identical with existence [1]596; infinite [5]213; intelligent [2]249; line of [1]579, 636; potenziated [3]46; primary [3]1024; of soul [4]292; substantial [1]573
essentia [6]87, 87n
essential(s) [1]254
essentialiter [1]653, 653n
essentiality [2]41
Essex [2]211n, [4]149, 681, 848n
C's 1818 trip to [3]1049n
Essex Street Chapel *see* London
"est" [6]87
Establishment [1]309
of C of E [1]360
estate(s) (land) [1]739, [2]295, [5]193, 273, 283, 614
estate(s) (social) [1]833, 865, [2]1139, [3]50, 800–1, [4]11
Estcourt, Mr (fl 1809) [1]697
esteem [4]612
"Este(e)se"/"Esteesi" (STC) [1]89, 91, 93, *93n*, 97, 98, 285, 288, [3]68, 68n
Esteesian [3]1021n
estesismos/*estesmos* [3]25, 25n, 59, 59n
esti [5]396
Estienne, Henri (Henricus Stephanus/Henry Stephens) (1528–98) [1]472n, 496n, [2]1130n
Thesaurus graecae linguae [1]26n, [2]386n, [4]343, 343n, [6]26
Estifania (in B&F) [1]391
Estlin, John Prior (1747–1817) [1]198n, 867, [3]657, 672, 672n, [4]133n
letter to [4]171n
Evidences [1]719n q
esto [5]711, 711n
esurience [3]1024
et cetera oath *see* oath(s): Etcetera
"etemporal" [5]95
Eteocles (myth) [2]584
"eternal" [2]560, [5]157, 157n
eternal, the [4]266, [5]32, 95, 203, 470, 482
act of [6]5; infinite [1]564
Eternal Punishment Proved to Be Not Suffering, but Privation [1]lxi; MT [2]558–72
eternity [2]559, 728, [3]32, 60n, 306, 710, 989, [4]126, 200, 303, 413, [5]68, 155, 385, 557, 615, 699, 761, 780
divine [2]1145; idea of [2]152, 1069; image of [3]875; production from [6]315; and time [1]825, 825n, [2]559, 560, 560n, 1161–2, [3]66; time the life of [3]89; timeless [1]825
eth [2]714, 714n
Ethelred *see* Aethelred II
Ethelwulf (d 858) [5]79 ("Ethelwolf"/"Etherwolf"), 79n
"ether" [4]494n
ether(s)/aether [1]597, 622, 622n, 675, [3]285,

ether(s)/aether—*continued*
323, 729, 1016, 1018, 1024, 1057, 1058, 1059, [4]273, 275, 395, 395n, 519, [5]132, 159, 231, 438, [6]132
black [1]170; organic [2]550; tension of [3]1015n; true [6]8; vitreous [3]867, 867n
etherist [5]714
ethics [3]201, [4]109, 280 ("*Ethice*"), 280n, 654, [5]208
ascetic [2]707; axiom of [5]37; *cui bono* system [2]250, 251; Epicurean [5]135; Platonic [5]135; and politics [5]535, 535n; science of [2]181; Stoic [5]135; system of [2]250; Jeremy Taylor's [5]604
Ethiopia [1]721 ("Aethiopia"), [2]383–4, [3]70, 233
Ethiopian(s) [3]356n, [5]253n
ethometer [2]6, 6n
Etna [1]421, 421n, [3]1038, [5]387, 387n
Eton College [1]cxxxiv, [2]4, 66, 88, 142, 599n, 979, 980, 1034n, [3]827, [5]48
Etonian [2]88, 979, 980
Etruria [3]631
Etruscan [1]237n, [2]776n
Etymologicum Magnum [1]26n
etymologists [5]732
etymology/etymologies [1]61n, 392, [2]528, 574n, 1071, [3]981, 1079n, [5]22, 104, 284n, [6]286n, 289
joke on [4]741; of numbers [4]36–8; of "quality" [1]656; best service [2]653–4; *see also* Coleridge, S. T. I (2): and etymology
etymon [4]98
eu [1]27, 27n
Euanthas [3]929n
Euboea [2]820, 820n
Eubulus (4th century BC) [4]147
"Eucharist" [6]86
Eucharist [1]673, 705, 713, 846, 861–3, 862n, [2]670, 672n, 749, 998, [3]43n, 439–40, 439n, 477, 598, 761, 761n, 763n, 1078n, [5]5n, 393n–4n, 397n, 398n, 524, 652, [6]146
in Böhme [1]668–9; Bucer on [1]839, [5]392; C receives "in Bucer's sense" [1]509, *509n–10n*; C of E doctrine [5]554; controversy about [6]21n; errors about [1]524; extension of incarnation [3]757–8, 758n; institution of [5]548; as life [5]650; turned into magic [5]684; in RC Church [2]26; sacrament of [3]440n; symbol [1]469; symbolic [1]524, 862. See also *BCP*: "Administration of the Lord's Supper"; bread, and wine; Communion; consubstantiation; Lord's Supper; real presence; Sacrament; transubstantiation
Euclid (fl 300 BC) [2]491, 1183, [3]726, [4]113, 641, [5]656, 709
Elements [4]113n, 114–115, 114n, commentary by Proclus [4]154–60, ed Simson [6]334
"eudaemonism" [4]280, 280n
eudaimonism [4]548
Eugene of Savoy, Prince (1663–1736) [1]698
Eugenius III, Pope (Bernardo Pignatelli) (fl 1145–53) [1]383
Eugenius IV, Pope (Gabriele Condulmaro) (1383–1447) [2]507n
Euler, Leonhard (1707–83) [3]944
eulogies [4]736
Eumenius (3rd–4th century) [3]143
eunuch(s) [1]5, 452, [4]704, [5]618n, 840n
euoriazein [1]26, 27, 27n
euphemism [2]834
Euphrates [1]779, [2]513, 514, [3]467
euphuisms [2]929
Eupolis (fl 429 BC) [2]757n
eupraxy [3]617, [5]724
eureka [3]399
Euripides (480/5–406 BC) [1]377n, [2]1090, 1090n, [3]894, [4]631, [5]867n
Cyclops [2]757n; *Medea* [2]1107n; *Orestes* [2]1107n
Euripus [2]820, 820n
Europa (myth) [2]580
Europe [2]74, [3]159, 250n, 419, 493n, [4]165, 196, 670, 672, 817, [5]101n, 281n, 372, 651, 659
abuse of [2]342; armies in [5]379; cat of [5]387; commonwealth [1]733; duped [3]659; fog over [6]153; hot climates [2]417; characterised by impatience [2]648; insularity of [5]337; Jews in [5]234; modern [5]328–9; Protestant churches of [4]172; unified [2]618–19, 619n; *see also* nation(s), European
Eurus [6]200–1, 201
eusebeia [1]490, 490n
Eusebians [2]741–2
Eusebius, Bishop of Caesarea (c 260–c 340) [1]472n, 485, 485n, 491, [2]287n q, 400n, 488, 501, 502, 576, 713n, 731n, 733, 735, 832n, 893, 918, [3]7n, 441, 442n, 688, 689, 692, 692n, [4]242, 513, 643, [5]575n, 620, 620n, [6]7 q, 8, 144 q
on Philo Judaeus [6]137–8
Evangelicae praeparationis [6]143n, tr E. H. Gifford as *Preparation for the Gospel*

[5]728; *Historia ecclesiastica* [4]253n, 473n, tr as *Ecclesiastical History* [1]485n, [2]490, 490n, 918n, [3]145n, 440, 440n, 477n, 691n, [5]748–9, [6]137 q, tr as *History of the Church* [3]232n, 762n
Eusebius of Nicomedia (d 342) [2]729n, 730, 731n, 741n, 745, [5]626
error of [2]729
Eustace, John Chetwode (?1762–1815) *A Tour through Italy* [4]170, 185–6
Eustathius (fl 1160–74) [2]67, 386n, 1130n, [3]828n
Eustathius of Antioch, St (fl c 325) [2]728
Euthydemus of Chios (5th century BC) [6]222
Euthymius, St (377–473) [5]575n
Eutyches (c 384–c 456) [2]660, 660n, [3]369, 369n
Euxine Sea [2]981n
"Evangelical" [4]621n
Evangelical(s) [1]322, 322n, [2]562n, 913n, 1174n, [3]309, 309n, [4]549n, 619–74, 746n
missions of [5]105n–6n
Evangelical Magazine [3]309n, [4]633
Evangelical Revival [3]309n
Evangelicalism [1]734, 736, [2]1015, [5]162n
evangelist(s)/Evangelist(s) [1]171, [2]164, 275, 494, 570, 681, 902, 918, 1057, [3]74, 310, 482, 524, 663, 683, 696, 927, [4]304, 621, 646, 646n, [5]27, 52, 473, 522, 570, [6]306, 307
books of [5]10, *see also* Bible: NT: GOSPEL(S); infallibility of [5]622; object of [4]61; pseudo-e. [4]621, 621n; veracity of [5]62
Evangelist (in Bunyan) [1]814, [4]651n
Evangelist, John the *see* John, St
evangelium/evangelia [3]685, 686, 726, [6]68
e. infantiae [1]506, 506n, [2]35, 35n, 266n, 446n, 448, 487n, 661n, [3]17, 17n, 36, 49, 730n, [4]41, 41n, 55, 55n, 67, 67n, 251, 251n, 253, 478, 478n, [5]629, [6]64n. *See also* Christopaedia; infancy, Gospel(s) of the
evangely/evangelies [2]441, 441n
Evans, Elizabeth (née Strutt) (fl 1776–1802) [1]511n
Evans, Ernest (b 1889) *see* Tertullian *Adversus Praxean, Tertullian's Treatise on the Incarnation* ed and tr Evans
Evans, Sir Hugh (*Merry Wives of Windsor*) [4]692, 692n, 755
Evans, Roger [5]853, 854
Evanthos [6]166
evaporation [1]793, [4]491, [5]715
Heraclitus on [5]713–14
evaporators [3]41
evasion [5]157, 503
Eve (Bible) [1]788, [2]301, 302, 576, 780, 789, 915, 916, 1052–3, [3]105, 614n, [5]133, [6]110, 112
Adam and *see* Adam; creation of [5]248n; manufacture of [1]684
Eve (*Paradise Lost*) [3]402, [4]731, 731n, 799n
Evelyn, John (1620–1706) [3]501n, [4]73, 74, 81, 82
Sculptura [2]1196n
Evening Standard [1]856
"evenomate" [2]298, 298n
events [5]70
external [5]598
"everlasting" [1]434, [2]786, 786n
Everyman [2]776–7
"evidence" [5]65
evidence(s) [1]520–1, [2]651, 1062, 1133, 1166, [3]163, 326, 516, 561, 763n, [4]52, 640, [5]51, *51n*, 64–5, 77, 140, 141, 516, 618, 656, 672, [6]66
a priori [2]1059; affirmative [2]31; balancing of [4]180; and certainty *see* certainty; circumstantial [5]668; choice of [2]149; of Christianity [2]493, [3]308, 308n, 708, 722, 763, [4]40n, 642, [5]598, 644; degrees of [1]520; external [2]247, [4]643, [5]72; external and internal [2]36; false [3]183; gap in [4]301; of the Gospel [2]651; historic(al) [2]785, [3]661, 662, [5]519, 598; internal [1]430, 448, [2]445, 522, [3]110, [5]516, 630, 634, 668; judicial [5]822; of miracles [4]40n, moral [2]454; negative [2]567, [5]146; objective [1]303; outward [4]641; passion for [1]317; positive [6]145; of reason [6]299; scheme of [5]514; semblance of [5]369; of the senses [4]110; sensuous [3]641
evil(s) [1]238, 685, 731, 732, [2]559n, 664, 1109n, 1163n, [3]447, 505–6, 579, 675, [4]134, 233, 233n, 689, 776, 827, [5]85–6, 231, [6]126
absolute [2]326; actual [3]875; birth of [2]1106; bodily consequences of [5]420; in Böhme's scheme [1]563; captive to [2]1166; cause of [4]428–9; in childhood [4]438; choice of [3]265, 312; connate [3]266; contingent [1]875; defined [6]127; direst [2]559; disindividualised [3]433; essential [5]424; generates evil [5]684; and good [2]162, 164, 278–80, 1022, 1153, [3]62, 136, 880, [4]262, 423, 424–5, 430, 434, 441–2, 443–5, 496, 596, 629n, 854, [5]162, 189, 218, 298, 424, 470, 592, 616; out of good

evil(s)—*continued*
[3]728; of guilt [2]800; inevitable [2]529; inflicted by God [5]611; moral [3]879, [5]74, 752; mystery of [5]424; nature of [2]199; necessity [5]381; E. one [3]73; origin of [1]574, 645, 685, [2]251, 748n, [3]473, 529n, 742n, [4]431, 444, 444n, [5]424n, 752n; outward [1]261; and pain [2]251, 251n; positive [5]373; potential [3]876, 880; principle [3]305; problem of [4]433; public [1]356; pure [2]559n; of Puritanism [5]123, 124; radical [4]439; removal of [6]28; spirit of [3]708; transforming [5]423; of universe [5]592. *See also* Devil; vice(s); wickedness; will(s), evil
Evites [3]496n
evocation [3]59
evoe [2]581, 582
"evoer" [2]582, 582n
evolution(s) [1]151, 401, [2]884, 933, 1026, [3]286, [4]531n, [5]756, 824–5
arcana of [2]1152; of chaos [1]120; mutual [1]635; of planet [5]430; of spiritual life [5]562
evulsion [1]778
evyon [4]254
ex abusu [6]257
exaggeration, sportive [2]236
exaltation(s) [5]169
Aristotelian [4]110
Examiner [2]861n
example(s) [3]312, [5]341
Christ as [4]655–6; good and bad [4]656; illustrious [4]655; and model [2]206
"exantlation" [1]768–9, 769n
excellence [4]865
absence of [4]24; characteristic [5]520; essential [1]367; female [4]335
exceptions, rule for [5]567
excerpta [5]571
excess [1]565, [3]135, [5]99
of light [2]974; neutralise [5]363
"excitability" [4]385, 385n
excitability [2]700, [3]398, 399, 741, 871, 871n, [4]389
excitancy [3]741
excitants [3]94, 398
excitement [3]871, 871n, [4]507, [5]141, 172
craving for [2]999; language of [2]1067
exclamation [4]167
excommunication(s) [1]309, 339, [2]683, 697, 750, 751n, [3]758, [5]67, 395, [6]55, 58
execution [2]978n
exegesis [1]681, [6]83n
eternal [6]83; historic [3]666
exeis [2]542, 542n–3n
exelthousan [1]455n
exemplar [3]55, [4]324
exercise [3]397
devotional [5]512
exertion [1]516
Exeter [1]cv, [2]95n
Exeter, Duke of (*Henry V*) [4]717
Exeter, Duke of *see* Holland, Henry
exile(s) [1]439, [2]405, [3]110, 462, [6]3–4, 4n
exinanition [2]135
existence [1]595, 596, [2]562, 989–90, 990n, 991–2, 993, 996–7, 1003, 1145, 1185, [3]43, 82, 331, 345, 346, 349, 517, 858, 859, 876, [4]108, 131, 224, 403n, 404, 411, [5]75, 213, 410, [6]299
and being *see* being; concept of [3]860, 860n; after death [2]432; divine [1]693; and essence *see* essence; etymologised [1]573, 573n; external [5]713; future [2]1186; of God *see* God, existence of; ground of [4]425; grounded in act [3]1065; kinds of [4]266; knowledge of [3]660; logical and real [5]772; and non-e. [5]37; proof of [3]956; real [5]455; sense of [2]1167; subjective [5]459; and subsistence [5]429, 429n
"existential"/"existentially" [1]283n, 288, 288n, 663, 663n
existentialism [1]288n
existents [5]203
"exition" [1]667n
"exlex" [2]771, 771n
Exodus, the [1]431
exorcism(s) [2]41, 739, [4]514, 514n, [5]274
exorcists [2]256, [3]212, 822
exossation [1]778n
exosseous [1]778
exoteric [5]573
exousia [1]462n, [3]150
expansion [1]563, [3]123, 123n, 277, 292, [4]395n, [5]264, 346, 487
expansive, the [5]356
expectancy, docile [5]413
expectation, time of [5]606
expedience [1]527, [3]166, [4]799, [5]302, 741
expediency [3]4–5
experience(s) [2]679, 1133, [3]41, 63, 166, 204, 248, 248n, 285, 848, 989, [4]109, 212, 223–4, 224, 379, 648, [5]70, 172, 463, 820, [6]135
Christian [5]512; facts of [3]312, [5]592; familiar [5]251; generalised [3]163; horizon of [5]755; inductions of [5]457; inward [2]639, [3]764; nature of [5]425; outward [5]803; progressive [1]724; sensible [2]824, [5]771; sen-

suous [1]683; spiritual [5]168, 171, 180, 181, 181n; subjective [5]465; Swedenborg's [5]407; unconscious [5]723; of world [3]328
experiment(s) [2]608, 825n, [3]364, 396, 850, 950, 1006, [4]28, [5]41, 201
counter-e. [3]1014; Davy's [5]256; de Luc's [3]948; electrical [5]562; modern [1]817; recent [2]1015; scientific [6]96
experimentalism [3]920
experimentalist [3]211
experimenter [4]860
experimentum crucis [5]247
expiation [2]489, [3]544, [4]651, 855
"explain" [1]560
explanation [3]76, 312, 715, 753
expletive(s) [2]59, [5]755
explication [3]834, [4]405, [5]595
explicit and implicit [1]836
explosion(s) [5]266, 338, 339
nervous [5]181; of solar system [5]430 ("explosive part"), 430n
exponent(s) [1]688, [5]672
exposure of children [3]809
expounder [2]38
expounding [1]349
expression(s) [5]37
figurative [2]829; literal [5]66; rapturous [5]371
exquisiteness [4]162
extensio [4]227, [5]210
extension [1]105, [2]563, 639, [3]344, [4]209n, 227, 227n, 229–30, 392, [5]210n, 214, 215, 442, 734, 753, 786, [6]115
extensity [2]646
extensive and intensive [3]272, 454
exterior, smiling [5]683
"extraduce" [6]123–4
"extreme" [1]549
extreme(s) [2]483, 1178, [3]372, 434, 1091, [5]124, 420
cases [1]337, 361; Germans in [5]692; Germans' motto [2]512; law of [3]280; meet [1]lxvi, 518, 518n, [3]454, 454n, [4]98, 98n, 448, [5]23, 99, 162, 487
Extreme Unction [3]440n, [5]398n, 566n
extremity [1]337
extroition [3]1024
"extroitive" [1]667n, 680, 680n
eye(s) [1]674, 683, 684, [2]402, 604, 1046, [3]87, 217, 357, 390, 552, 559n, [4]273, 375, 422, 674, [5]17, 165, 175n, 296, 358, [6]131
analogy for soul [3]121; "(all) my e. and Betty Martin" [3]438, 438n, 842, 842n, [5]296n; black [2]1121; bodily [2]679; bodily or mental [5]406; Böhme's "counsellors" [1]576; buxom [1]638; convulsion of [3]213; despotism of [3]373n; disease(s) of [1]810n, [3]653, [4]164; dissection of [5]175; enslaves mind [3]138, 138n; extracted [6]20; e.-falsehood [2]1158; e.-glass [3]973, [4]375, [6]328; hexameters on [1]672; inward [5]15, 191; mastering [6]58; material [5]418; mental [5]175; of mind [3]437; mind's [1]822, [3]248, 437, 991, [5]650; my e. [5]296, 296n; naked [3]9; organist of light [3]559; ox's [1]397; e.-phantom [6]244; pinched out [5]149; power of [4]98; public [5]41; pulled out [3]26; e.-reading [4]404; scratched out [5]609; and sight [5]297; of spirit [4]616; spiritual [1]517, [3]561; most superficial of the senses [3]1036; telescope of soul [1]671; unarmed [2]508
eye-witness(es) [1]282, 402, 447, 450, [2]453, 468, 494, 1056, 1086, [3]211, 661, 667, 868, [4]55, 471, 479, 838, [5]50–1, 63, 72, 142, [6]109, 135
Eynsham [2]983n
Eytzinger, Michael (d 1598) *De Leone Belgico* [1]281n, [2]163n
Ezekiel (Bible) [1]785, [2]313, 403, 409n–10n, 410, 412n, 894, 1074n, [3]70, 478, 1090, [5]775
Ezra (Bible) [1]844n, [2]149, 149n, 377, 420, 894, [3]437, 437n

"F. R. S." (Francis Wrangham) [1]90
fabas, Venetian [1]506
Faber, George Stanley (1773–1854) [2]47, 516n, [3]922, 923n, [6]166
A Dissertation on the Mysteries of the Cabiri MT [2]573–85; [3]683n, 923n, [4]594n–5n; *A Dissertation on the Prophecies* [2]518, 518n, 573, [3]923n, [6]166n
Faber, Johann Melchior (1743–1809) [2]429, 429n
Super libro sapientiae [6]140n
fable(s) [1]772, 772n, [2]234, 895, 928, 1051, 1052–3, 1084, [3]207, 309, 445, 473, 594, 691, 919, 922, [6]119
absurd [5]621, 646; of Apostles' Creed [6]63; Indian [2]772n; Judaic [3]1090; rabbinical [2]915, [3]437
fablers [2]194
fabling [2]275, [3]437
Fabricius, Johann Albert (1668–1736) [2]417n, [3]833n
Fabricius, Lucinus Caius (fl 282 BC) [1]315
fabulists [2]1106

face(s) [3]231, [6]240
bi-frons [3]735; female [2]1121; handsome [3]417; image of [1]753
facility [5]419
facimento/facimenti [3]926 ("Facciamenti"), 926n, [4]808n
facsimile(s) [2]1028, [3]790, [4]765
manuscript [1]clviii
"fact" [3]248, 248n
fact(s) [1]303, [2]605, 658, 674, 803, 953, 1061, 1062, 1148, [3]23, 41, 43, 60, 63, 94, 182, 204–5, 205n, 248n, 307, 389, 395, 470, 691, 805, 842, 879, [4]95, 437, 473, [5]62, 63, 70, 77, 92, 125, 141, 289, 299, 425, 473, 481, 782, 795
actual [5]201; of animal magnetism [3]373, [4]499; anomalous [5]252; anti-f. [5]152; awe-striking [2]328; and belief [6]286–7; in Bible [1]446–7; of Christianity [2]204; combinations of [2]460; of consciousness [5]465; criminal [5]642; deductions from [5]153; not subject of demonstration [2]143; different aspect [5]496; discrimination of [1]410; evident [5]60; of experience [3]312; and fancy [5]415; and fiction(s) [2]1139, [3]989, [4]478, 479, [5]65; fundamental [5]595; heart-withering [5]242; historic(al) [1]783, [2]1082, 1148, [3]49, 927, [4]52, [5]71, 308, 309, 467, 707; and hypothesis [2]605; and ideas [3]36; imagined [2]886; inference from [3]997, 998; insulated [3]364; knowledge of [1]446; known [5]413; matter(s) of [3]848, [5]415, 751; meagre [4]272; of mind [4]647; in minds [5]594; new-naming of [5]350; novel founded on [5]226; of original sin [2]247; palpable [2]480; physiological [5]411; potential [5]203; psychological [5]411, [6]242; quasi-f. [3]822; ratio of [1]271; reference to [5]366; in religion [2]482; of Roman Church [5]561; rule of [4]458; of sense [2]1160; single [1]368; startling [3]222; statement of [3]374; store-house of [5]743; and theory [2]552, [6]104; of time and space [5]615; translated into general terms [3]871; and truth [3]967, 967n, 968; unaccountable [3]352, [5]592
"facticity" [3]310, 310n
faction [2]1104, [3]222, [5]146
mark of [5]632; trick of [1]212
factionary [2]1097, [6]59
factionists [1]353
"factity" [3]310, 310n
factors [5]264
dynamic [4]488
factory [2]999
f.-owners [4]342n; of the understanding [2]295
"factuality" [3]310n
faculty/faculties [4]93, [5]640, 666
of being [4]219–20; conceptive [5]803; corrupted [1]429; culture of [5]493; demonstrative [5]743; discursive [4]353; human [5]37; imperfection of [3]260; intellective [5]15; intellectual [5]743; intuitive [4]353, [5]599, 600; judicial [5]156; Kant's critique [3]354; locomotive [5]603; logical [3]746; of means [3]423, 424; mediate [5]599; mental [3]1091; of mind [2]640–1, [3]893; natural [5]529; percipient [5]410; of presentiment [5]723; progressive [3]317; somniative [3]991; of thinking [5]770
faeces [3]374n
fair play [2]492
Fairclough, Henry Rushton (1862–1936) *see* Horace *Epistles*, *Satires*; Virgil *Aeneid, Eclogues* tr Fairclough
Fairfax, Thomas, 3rd Baron Fairfax of Cameron (1612–71) [2]54–63, 1196n, 1197n, 1199, [6]185, 185n
fairy/fairies [1]763, [2]920, [4]594–5, 595n
fairy tale(s) [3]634, [4]658n, [6]158 ("Faery")
"faith" [4]399, 399n
in St Paul [6]223
faith [1]123, 283, 685, 847, [2]702, 807, 828, 998, 1150, 1151, 1161, [3]4, 307, 307n, 332, 454, 466, 493, 558–61, 558n, 566, 604, 606, 606n, 609, 640–1, 750–3, 868, [4]181, 262, 306, 346, 348, 629, 633, 810, [5]32, 466, 523, 608, 639, 652, 653–4, 654, 667, 670, 678, 803, [6]264
accompaniment of [5]467; act of [2]300; analogy of [4]473, [5]563, 563n, 575; article(s) of [1]281, 315, [2]39, 276, 531, 681, [3]436, 446, 474, 690, 771, 774, [4]177, 258, 475, 477, [5]14, 151, 152, 182, 235, 407, 524, 540, 597, 649, [6]19; Asgill on [1]128; assimilative [1]704; babes in [5]13; and belief *see* belief; binding on all [5]564; Calvinistic articles of [5]76; canon of [2]1081, 1081n, [5]571, 572; catholic [2]462, 674, 785, 882, [3]417, [5]11, 572, 665, [6]66, 74, 75, 85; and charity [5]468; in Christ [1]435, [2]291, [3]722, [5]50; of Christ [3]743, 750; Christian [1]29, 513, [2]663, 1161, [3]200 ("Xtn"), 328, 519, 1083, [4]482, [5]9, 25, 61, 82, 176, 190, 266n, 535, 564, 592, 596, 618, 626, 644, [6]89, 93; of Christians

[4]479; C of E doctrine [2]34–5; C's [3]517; commanded [2]497; and common sense [1]313; f.-compact [3]691; confessions of [5]408; conflict of [5]172; consistency in [5]66; continuation of reason [1]576; with contrition [5]585; corrupters of [3]487; covenant of [5]623; defined [1]460, 503–4, [2]267, 277, 297, [3]560, [5]500, 500n; departing [6]71; dimness of [4]409; disposition of [5]620; distortion of [1]58; doctrine of [1]826; dogmas of [2]1062; eating by [5]558; effectual [5]72; efficient [5]125; elevates the soul [3]556; energy of soul [3]558; essential doctrine [1]470; essentials of [1]846; evangelical [1]865; exists in sphere of noumena [1]201; fealty of will [2]1151; f.-fellows [5]395; Fichte's use of [2]610; foundation(s) of [3]515, 686, [5]383, 617, [6]297; four points [2]1166; in free will [1]172; fullness of [5]622, fundamental article of [5]626; gift of [3]690, 693; gospel [2]270, [5]662; Grotio-Paleyan [1]288; ground of [3]662; growth in the [1]232; harmony of [5]798; in the heart [1]823; Herder's [2]1080; heroic [2]272; highest sense of [3]104; and history [2]1079–80, 1082; hooded falcon [5]656; household of [6]299; humble [3]554; ideas the objects of [5]640; implicit [1]824, [2]654, [5]540, 548; injured [2]660; intellectual [5]621; intelligible [5]805; intense [4]514; Jewish [2]419; judgment of Church in [1]711; justification by *see* justification; justifying [1]11; keystone [1]29; laugh out of [3]786; lax [4]269; life of [1]464, [2]37, [6]57; is love [1]814; man of [2]561; meaning of [4]640–1, 640n, 641, 668, 668n, [5]12; measure of [1]492; and metaphysics [1]819–20; mirror of [2]423; mongrel [2]314; moral [5]789; as moral postulate [6]108; moral state [2]29, 31; mysteries of [2]1151, [5]32; of nature [2]547; necessity of [4]672, [5]61, 677; negative [4]587; Nicene [2]34, [5]57; nursery [2]419; object of [3]312; not mere opinion [2]28–9; orthodox [3]744, [5]657; patriarchal [5]535; St Paul's definition [4]616, 616n; perfect [1]781, [2]1165; pillar(s) of [3]686, [5]570, 570n; poetic [4]479; point of [1]308; popular [4]717; positive [1]304, [2]644; practical reason [1]685; and prayer [1]702; preservative of [1]343; product of spirit [2]496; profession(s) of [1]345, [3]689–90, [5]432, 548; proper objects of [3]989; and prophecy [2]150, 405; rational [5]770; rays of [1]782, [2]1178; and reading [5]514; reality of [5]132; and reason [1]170, 170n, 203, 576, 789, [2]267, 331–3, 1046, [5]97n, 484; of reason [4]446, [5]701n, 766; rectitude of heart [5]624; and redemption [5]535, 587, [6]105; religion is [2]186; rents in [1]515; restorative [2]591; rise of [5]156; robe of [1]316; rooted in will [1]287; rule of [1]312, 312n, [2]38, 1081, 1081n, [3]533, 766, 766n, [4]175n, [5]571, 572, 619, [6]79, 319; salvation by [1]847, [2]1162; sap of [1]823; saves us [1]821–2, [5]126; saving [2]682, 1166, [4]643, [5]561; and scepticism [3]56; scheme of [5]123, 568; and science [1]128, [3]682; Scriptural [2]790; self-reflected [3]749; Semitic [4]257; sincere [6]292; sinking of [1]320; soul of [3]17; species of [3]641; speculative [5]618–19; Swedenborg's definition [5]469, 469n; symbol of [5]13, 13n, 620, 620n; system of [3]685; test of [1]249; theory of [5]661; Tridentine [3]232n, [5]14n; underminings of [3]722; universal [4]484; wilful [5]664; will prime agent of [2]678; withholds belief [3]62; and works [1]460, [2]297, 298, 299–300, [4]623, [5]176, 469, 471n; without works [3]495

faithful, the [4]647, [6]296

Faithful (in Bunyan) [1]803, [4]653n

faithlessness [2]591

"faith-mate" [3]418, 418n, 476

falcon [1]483, [5]656

Falconbridge (*Merchant of Venice*) [4]780

Falconer, William (1732–69)
The Shipwreck MT [2]586–8; *Universal Marine Dictionary* [2]586, 587

Falkland, Viscount *see* Cary, Lucius

fall/Fall [1]460, 609, 609n, [2]86, 87n, 716, 1106, 1185, [3]65, 381, 729, 767, 875, 878–9 [4]502n, 580, 615, 656, [5]162n, 248n, 394, 439, 593, 594n, 597n, [6]110n, 138, 325
of Adam [5]598, 602, 610n; as allegory [1]183n, [2]1052–3, 1053–5; of angels [3]25, 436n, 904; antecedent to creation [3]66; consequent of [1]602; equivalent to descent [1]598; hour of [3]767, 767n; of man [1]124, 670, 675, 685, [2]137, [3]19, 22, 27, [5]583; as myth [5]603n; mythos of [3]473–4, 473n; original [3]876; possibility of [3]67; and present state [3]46; of spirits [1]645, [2]326, [3]436; spiritual [6]113; *see also* apostasy

Fall, James (c 1646–1711) [3]514, 537, [6]295

fallacy [3]935
fall-outs [5]49
falsehood(s) [1]675, [2]236, 1051, [3]54, 54n, 367, 586, [4]480, 668, 672, 743, [5]168, 308, 348, 616, 776
abhorrence of [3]9; antinomian [3]743; deliberate [6]262; effect of [3]749; expediency of [2]1194; negative [3]466; by omission [5]575; and paradox [5]612; in partial truth [2]969; and truth [1]224, 530–1, [2]328, [5]99, 617, [6]133; virtual [5]554
falseness [5]469
"falsetto" [4]594n
falsetto [2]866, 1068, [4]589, 594
falsity [3]948, [5]215, 244, 409, 452
Falstaff (in Shakespeare) [1]212n, 374, [2]17n, [3]174, 174n, 187, [4]55, 55n, 239n, 589n
fame [3]222
and reputation [1]165, 165n, [3]173, 173n
familiarity [4]841
Familists [2]327, *327n–8n*, 1137, [3]926n, [5]568, 569
family/families [3]1025, [5]38
ancient [2]1196; enduring [1]739; f.-feuds [4]827; Jewish [3]606; large [4]719
famine [2]1109n, [5]274
"fanatic" [1]270, 270n, [3]1079n, [6]261
fanatic(s) [1]272, 353, [2]515, 714, 725, 754, 771, 984, 1057, [3]705, 735, 764, [4]665, [5]134, 395, 569, [6]106
dangerous [5]229; high-church [2]1097; judaising [1]875
fanatici [1]496, 496n
fanaticism [1]30, 560n, 818, [2]286, [3]147, 317–18, 318n, 483, 517n, 557, 694, 1079n, [5]171, 510, 743n, [6]300n
and enthusiasm *see* enthusiasm; religious [5]125
fancy/fancies [1]178, 321, 638, 647, 682, 763, 797, [2]250, 344, 447, 627, 768, 824, [3]12, 42, 42n, 58, 194, 202, 395, 565, [4]13n, 51, 145, 233, 702, 787, 830, [5]83, 126, 588, 598, 615, 638, 795
active [1]610; assent of [2]300; cabbalistic [3]41; chaos of [5]726; craving of [5]442; danger of [4]789; f.-dress [3]1083; f.-drolleries [1]394; drunk with minutiae [1]397; English [4]691; and fact [5]415; fancyette [2]646; of females [3]872; figures of [4]41; general [2]452; harmless [5]173; idoloplastic [4]234; image of [1]753; and imagination [1]497, [2]418, 654, 673, [3]117, 117n, 224, [4]583, 583n, 596–7, 610n, 611, 822n, [5]541, 545, 782, 798; as imagination [3]138, 138n, 790; influence of [3]117; insubordination of [1]685; insufficient to poet [2]219–20; inventions of [5]759; inventive [4]78; Jewish [3]9, 34; Judaic [3]1090; materialising [3]1087; f.-medal [5]658; and memory [3]38; mischievous [5]561; particular [5]570; picture-word of [3]949; power of [4]248; seething [1]558; sensuous [1]238, 774, [2]1144, [4]196, 542; strong [5]406; superstitious [3]774; theory framed in [1]58; things of [5]755; and truth [5]406; unhallowed [3]55; *vis flammea* [5]783; and wit [1]67n; witty [1]67; wooden-jointed [4]360; f.-work [5]732; youthful [4]810
fancying [4]355
"fane" [3]1079n
Faneromeni [5]835
fangen [4]38
Fanshawe, Sir Henry (1569–1616) [2]1125n
fantasts [1]762, 796, [2]725, 725n, [3]653
faquirs [3]1054
far niente [1]873
Faraday, Michael (1791–1867) [2]905n, [3]104, 104n, [4]503, 503n
farce [3]182, [4]600
fardle [1]813
Farey, John (1766–1826) [3]936, 937, 943
farina [4]318
Farington, Joseph (1747–1821) *Diary* ed Greig [2]1195n
farm(s) [5]283
farmer(s) [1]527, 876, [5]283
hard-hearted [6]44; soul of [5]271–2
Farmer, Hugh (1714–87) [1]317, 317n, [6]119n
A Dissertation on Miracles† [1]317n, [2]589; *An Essay on the Demoniacs of the New Testament* [1]317n, [2]589
Farmer, Priscilla (d 1795/6) [3]714
Farmer, Richard (1735–97) [4]741n, 813, 842, 869
Farnese, Alessandro, Duke of Parma (d 1592) [4]199
Farquhar, George (1678–1707) [2]779, 779n, [4]779, 780n
The Beaux' Stratagem [2]779n; *A Discourse upon Comedy* [4]780n; *The Recruiting Officer* [2]779n
Farquharson, Arthur Spenser Loat (1871–1942) *see* Aurelius *Meditations* tr Farquharson
farrago [3]809, [5]677, [6]119
Farrand, Mrs Max (fl 1935) [4]105
Farren, Margaret (d 1804) [2]169
far-sightedness [5]268

fart [2]1005, 1005n, [3]721n, [4]193, [5]287n
fascinati [1]622, 622n
fascination [2]522, [3]449
fashion(s) [1]256, 280, 398, 810, [2]545, [3]565, 813
accidental [1]186; of age [5]442; among Protestants [1]317; universal [5]416
fast(s)/fasting [1]178, 826, [2]202, 716, [3]486, 608, [5]147
fatalism [3]205, [4]410, 436, [5]792, 842
fatalists [5]842
fate [3]346, [4]408, 794, [5]614, 730
Fates [2]88, [4]786, 809
father(s) [2]915, 1148, [4]718, [5]466
Augustine a hard f. [3]765; of Church *see* Fathers; and daughters [4]334–5; of a family [1]201; God as *see* Father (God); maculate [1]506; and mother [1]620, 647, [5]634, 751; and son [5]626, 789
"Father" [2]264, [5]34, [6]66
Father (God) [1]466n–7n, 561, 659, 992, 993n, [3]11–14, 16, 18, 53, 66, 77, 106, 151, 428, [4]258, 277, 300, 400, 492, 548, 647, 672, [5]11n, 15, 58, 66, 653
of ages [1]434; alone [4]302; from all eternity [4]441; everlasting [1]434, [2]786n; gospel of [3]427; of (all) lights [2]1166, [5]484; Persons of [5]19; revealed [6]83; and Son [1]458, [2]33, 39, 741, [5]16, 18, 32, 56, 71, 626, 633, [6]67, 82, 86, 178; of spirits [5]482; in Trinity [5]9–10; unbegotten [2]735; will of [5]58. *See also* God; Trinity
Fathers (in Church) [1]lxix, 805, 817, [2]11, 31, 38, 260n, 292, 423, 438, 584, 665, 665n, 680, 683, 684n, 916, 917, 1081, 1152, [3]441, 459, 465, 486, 534, 561, 669–70, 684, 728, 758, 763, 764, 766, 1078n, [4]64, 253, 253–4, 643n, 669, [5]11, 21, 23, 181, 202, 564, 570n, 572, 573, 581, 601, 638, 646, 646n, 669, 669n–70n, 680, [6]140, 317
on absolution [2]722; African [5]643; Alexandrian [2]502; ante-Nicene [2]32–4, 41, [5]13 ("anti-"), 13n, 571, [6]82, 91; Apostolic [2]711n; ascetic ethics [2]707; Asian [5]643; assertions of [5]619; austerity of [5]683; authority of [5]658, 661; best [1]263; Catholic [5]625; Christian [2]584, [6]92; of Church [4]64; C's reading of [5]601n; credulity of [4]249; early [2]274n, [5]547, 573, 582, 637, [6]71; of early Church [5]662n; of English Church [4]300, 301n, [5]8, 466–7; of English Reformation [6]298; evil as negative [2]199; gentile [2]437, 710, [3]1084; enemies of gnosticism [2]464; gossip of [6]63; Greek [1]478, [2]723, 1022, [3]77n, 533, [5]75n, [6]178, 319; Greek and Latin [1]245; on heresy [5]570; ignorance of [6]91; immortality of [5]567; instances in [5]666; Latin [1]345, [2]882, [3]533; of Latin Church [6]319; before the law [5]398; their logic of analogy [6]70; Luther's low estimation of [2]272, 304; lying [2]707, 710n; Nicene [2]749, [5]625, 626, 627; partiality for [2]273; patristic leaven [2]1041, in Donne [2]301; polygamy of [2]1160; post-Nicene [2]743, 749; precepts of [3]686; primitive [2]710; of Protestant Reformation [5]662n; of the Reformation [3]515, [5]582; reliability of [6]178n; inestimable service of [6]93; spiritual [4]474, [5]530; stultifying effect [2]925; taste for [2]260; as tritheists [2]748; wanton fancy of [2]335; Waterland's defence of [6]71–2; writings of [5]298, 663
fathom-line [1]601
fatigue [2]624
Fatima (d c 632) [4]357n
fault(s)
and beauties *see* beauties; characteristic [5]520; of Constantine [2]735; f.-finders [5]121; f.-finding [5]281
Faustus of Milevis (fl 383) [5]545
favere linguae [3]577, [5]158, 158n
favouritism [1]147
Fawkes, Francis (1720–77) *see* Apollonius Rhodius, Bion, Moschus, Musaeus, Sappho, Theocritus tr Fawkes
Fawkes, Guy (1570–1606) [4]97n, 757, 757n
fealty [2]297, 1151, [5]642
fear(s) [2]507, 927, 1163–4, [3]64, 408, 409, 410, 509, 583, [4]265, 489, 676, [5]83
boastfulness of [2]712; godly [3]566; law of [2]143; prudential [4]728; spirit of [5]123; thraldom of [3]466
fearful, the and hateful [1]371n
feast, triumphal [1]714
feather(s) [2]471, 683, [4]669
feculae [1]630, 630n
Feder, Johann Georg Heinrich (1740–1821) *Institutiones logicae et metaphysicae* [4]133
Federkraft [5]277
Fee! Fa! Fum! [4]630
feeling(s) [1]331, 674, 751, [2]198, 607, 624, 624n, 1004, [3]264, 409, 1036, [5]25n, 86, 290, 467, 475, 795, [6]235–6
beaten road of [4]855; blind [3]963; not in brain [2]538; change of [4]241; deep [5]110;

feeling(s)—*continued*
enthusiastic [4]513; excess of [3]173; faculty of [2]552; fluttering [5]857; French [4]184; gentlemanly [4]22; habit of [3]720, [4]814; hardened [5]562; and ideas [2]959; and imagination [4]773; impel us [6]126; and intellect [1]751; intense [4]238; and intuition [3]393; inward [1]270, [6]261; language of [2]300; moral [2]254, [4]770, [5]385, [6]322; natural [1]372, [4]599; new [4]728; organised [1]579; of people at large [5]512; poetic [2]637; religion of [2]200–1, 200n; religious [1]602, 825; reptile [1]395; rudiment of other senses [1]579; sense of [6]131; serious [6]156; strong [1]743; suppressed [4]704; tender [4]662; and thought [1]848; and touch [3]1036n; transient [2]221; unconquerable [4]437

Felicitas, St (d 203) [2]719

feliciter audax [4]736

"felicitously" [4]15

felicity [4]625

Felix (Bible) [2]456n, [3]614

Felix Farley's Bristol Journal [2]586, 587n, 1066n

Felix, Orlando (fl 1813) *see* Ruiz de Padron *Speech*; Jovellanos *Bread and Bulls* ed Felix and others

fell(s) [3]975–6, 981, 981n

Fell, John, Bishop of Oxford (1625–86) [1]182n, 492, 492n, [2]409n, [3]764n

Fellowes, Robert (1771–1847) *Religion without Cant* [4]660

fellowships [2]937

Felltham, Owen (1602–68) *An Answer to the Ode* [3]194, 194n

felon(s) [5]315
f.-trappists [2]980

felspar [5]246

Felton, John (?1595–1628) [2]1103

female(s) [1]654, [2]1017, [4]865, [5]517n
community of [2]938; and male [1]654, [2]276n, 541–2, 541n, 857, 1017, [3]906, [4]432, 432n, 600, [5]248, 291; and mesmerism [2]700, 700n; nervous [3]872; nothingising of [5]97; seminal fluid [2]1001, 1001n; true beauties [2]1121

feminine, the [1]662, [6]30
and masculine [1]662, [4]649, [5]782; negative correlative [2]580; *see also* woman/women

Fénelon, François de Salignac de La Mothe (1651–1715) [1]cxxxviiin, cxlin, 213, 503, [2]848, [3]750, 970 q, [5]178, 178n
Les Aventures de Télémaque [2]590, tr as *Telemachus* [1]220, 220n; "Extracts" MT [2]590–2; *Maxims of the Saints Explored* [2]590

Fenelons [5]178

Fenton [3]636

Fenton, Elijah (1683–1730) [1]38

Fenton, Mr (in Brooke) [1]723, 727

Fenwick, John (1739–1823) [2]845

Ferdinand (*Tempest*) [4]688, 831

Ferdinand III, Holy Roman Emperor (1608–57) [1]546, 546n

ferment [5]256, 814

fermentation [4]529

fern(s) [1]772, [4]827
f.-owls [6]151

Ferrara [2]507n

"ferruminator" [4]291, 291n

fervour [5]169

Fescennine [2]756

Fest, Johann Samuel (1754–c 1797) *Versuch über die Vortheile der Leiden und Widerwärtigkeiten des menschlichen Lebens*† [2]593

festival(s) [3]704
Christian [1]874

Festus, Sextus Pompeius (late 2nd century) ed *De verborum significatu* [3]505n

Fetherstone, Christopher (fl 1584) [1]476

fetish ("fetisch") [1]863, [2]200, 220

fetlocks [5]476

fetters of mechanic philosophy [1]410

fever(s) [3]125, 475, [4]148–50, 222, 263, 415, [5]641, 821, [6]173, 288
hectic [3]1047; f.-marsh [5]277; of Methodism [5]180; f.-spots [3]37

few and many [5]770

Fiacchi, Luigi ("Luigi Clasio") (1754–1825) [1]206

fiat [3]326, [4]14

"fib" [5]13, 13n

fibre(s) [3]325, [5]452, 826

fibril(s) [5]452
primordial [5]444

Fichte, Johann Gottlieb (1762–1814) [1]cxxiii, 556, [2]193, 539n, *594–5*, 863n, [3]97n, 954, 973, [4]132, 158, 361, 364n, 369, 393n, 412, 421n, 439, 453, 458, 458n, [5]89, 90n, 95, 203n, 320 q, 347n, 753, [6]237
followers of [2]1002; injuries to [3]971, 971n; and Kant [2]615, [4]354, 357; and Schelling [4]421, 425, 425n, [6]234, 234n, 242, 242n; Schelling on [4]344–59; silly dreams [2]622; system of [3]249; tail of [5]95; vanity [2]599, 617; his *Wissenschaftslehre* [4]357, 442, 442n

Die Anweisung zum seeligen Leben [1]clin, [2]594; MT 596–9; [4]351n; *Appellation an das Publikum* [2]594; *Die Bestimmung des Menschen* [2]594; MT 600–15; [4]352, 352n; *Einige Vorlesungen über das Wesen des Gelehrten* [4]346n, 347n; *Einige Vorlesungen über die Bestimmung des Gelehrten* [2]594; *Der geschlossne Handelsstaat* [2]594, 600; MT 616–22; *Grundlage der gesammten Wissenschaftslehre* [2]594; MT 623–5; 626, 627, 638; [4]132n, 348n; *Grundriss des Eigenthümlichen der Wissenschaftslehre* [2]594, 623; MT 626; 638; [4]412n; "Philosophie und Religion" [4]347–8 q; *Philosophisches Journal* [4]155n; *Das System der Sittenlehre* [2]594, 623, 624, 624n; MT 627–37; *Ueber den Begriff der Wissenschaftslehre* [1]lxxx, [2]594, 623, 626; MT 638; [3]266n, [4]158n; *Versuch einer Kritik aller Offenbarung* [2]594, 596n q; MT 639–46

Fichtean(s) [2]628, [4]155

Ficino, Marsilio (Ficinus) (1433–99) [3]308n, [5]237, 237n
Platonica theologia de imortalitate animorum MT [2]647–8; *see also* Plotinus . . . *operum . . . libri LIV* tr Ficino

"fictile" [3]501, 501n

fiction(s) [1]58, [2]886, 1076, [3]57, 154, 172, 328, 405, 408, 865, 948, [4]48, 712, [6]140, 142
of abstraction [3]301; arbitrary [4]597; clumsy [1]397; of devil [2]164; and fact(s) *see* fact(s); and history [4]798, 809; infidel [5]667; of law [2]1139, [3]159, 159n; legal [2]59; of logic [2]1002; Newtonian [5]452; poetic [4]479; of purgatory [1]512

fiddle [3]870

fiddlers [6]99

fideles [5]197n

fidelity [2]297, 347, [4]819, 820
unhired [4]827; in marriage [3]496

Fidus (fl 258) [2]723

Field, Barron (1786–1846) [2]214, 215
Botany-Bay Flowers [2]861n; *First Fruits of Australian Poetry* [2]861n

Field, Edwin Wilkins (1804–71), [2]179, [3]321, 719, [4]261, 270, 373, [5]199, 241

Field, Miss (fl 1916) [4]270, [5]241

Field, Richard (1561–1616) [1]312n, [2]264, 265n, 273n, 294n, 309, 309n
Of the Church [1]cxx; MT [2]649–86; [3]533, 533n q, 561, 561n–2n, [6]319 q, 319n

Fielding, Henry (1707–54) [2]727n, 764n, 779
on Aristotle [1]50, 50n; and Garrick [2]779, 779n; Hogarth's portrait of [2]779n; and Richardson [2]692–3
Amelia [1]50n, [2]693; *The History of the Adventures of Joseph Andrews* [1]xcviii; MT [2]689–90; 693, [3]370n; *The History of Tom Jones, a Foundling* [1]cxlin, 3; MT [2]691–5; [3]94, 94n q; *The Life of Mr Jonathan Wild the Great* [1]cxlin; MT [2]687–8; *Tom Thumb* [6]202, 202n; *Works* [2]779n

Fielding, Sarah (1710–68) *see* Xenophon *Memoirs of Socrates* tr Fielding

fiend(s) [4]735, 867, [6]173
f.-hag [2]515

fiendishness [4]817, 855

Fiennes, William, Lord Say and Sele ("Seal") (1582–1662) [3]486, 488

Fifth Monarchy men [1]270, 272, 382

fig(s) [2]1141n
f.-leaves [5]396; f. tree [1]401, 452, [3]896

fighters [1]379

figure(s) [1]551, [3]293, 294, [4]127–8, [5]457, 580, 599
anti-f. [3]1011; Chladni [5]294, 294n; destruction of [3]433; distinction of [5]443; figuration [3]79; and fluid [1]550; geometric(al) [1]601, [4]224; of individual [3]917; mathematical [3]670; principal [1]375; in sand [1]735; sculptured [1]684; of speech *see* speech; of sphere [5]406; and symbol [5]550; symbolic [1]472

filiation [1]564, 626, 640, [2]249, 249n, 992, [3]77, 730, 857, 857n, [4]548, 646, [5]799

"filiety" [3]16, 16n

filings [2]1110, [3]1004

filioque [5]576, 576n–7n

filius [2]271, 271n

film, carnal [5]650

Filmer, Sir Robert (d 1653) [5]38, 42
Patriarcha [5]38n

filter [2]214, [3]231, [5]737, 737n

filth [1]393, [4]190
f.-harvest [2]764

final cause *see* cause, final

finality [5]296

Finch, Jermiah Stanton (b 1910) [1]clxiiin
"Charles Lamb's Copy of *The History of Philip de Commines*" [2]99

finding [4]131

fine arts [2]1018n, [3]993, [4]168, 169, 604, 766n, 864

fineness [3]753

fineries [2]1071

finger(s) [3]129, 211, [4]38, 266
f.-active [2]648; counting on [4]36n; of God [1]457, 457n; of spirit [3]563

finis coronat opus [4]613n
finite(s) [2]996, 1106, 1186, [3]15, [5]355, 406, 455, 708, [6]114–15
  forms of [3]16; and infinite [2]278, 992, 996, 1186, [3]79, [4]414, 449, 647, [5]458, 459–60; irrational [5]483; rational [5]483; symbol of [5]457
finiteness [1]574, [2]425, [4]444, [5]19, 729, 752
finition [1]562
Finland [5]103
  Fish of (Henry Gillman) [5]103n
Finnian, St (d 550) [1]213n
fire(s) [1]172, 238, 339, 448, 552, 632, 633, 635, 638, 639, 641, 643, 662, 692, [2]425, 489, 591, 611, 1021, 1022, [3]38, 60, 61–2, 61n, 351, 352, 383, 433, 481, 694, 925, 950n, 999, 1003, 1016, 1023–4, 1087, [4]417, 418, 428, 443, 443n, [5]350–1, 351, 451, 471, [6]117
  active and passive [1]780; *agnos* and *ignis* [2]339; balls of [2]746; Böhme on [1]638–9, 642, 649–50, 654, 664; calling down [5]645; central [1]629, [3]869; circle of [4]223; coffins from [3]373; f.-eater *see* ignivomist; elements [3]1023–4; eternal [5]717; f.-flash [1]611, 612, 617; form of [5]719; funereal [2]569–70; f.-god [2]419; God as [2]567–8; from Heaven [5]634; Heraclitus on [5]713, 714, 721, 722; images of [5]60; f.-lake [5]158; f. of London [2]1179, 1179n; f.-maker [4]538; f.-matter [4]201, 202n; moist [5]714, 714n; office [4]658, 658n; f.-place [3]212; plastic [1]177; primal [5]707; rivers of [6]153; sacred [3]108; shower of [2]836; spirit [1]654; f.-squibs [3]721; as symbol [3]1024; tongues of [5]650–1; in water [1]649–50
fire-arms [2]126, [5]101, 101n
firedamp [2]746n
firefly/fireflies [1]210n, [2]440, [5]130
firmament [2]296
Firmilian, St, Bishop of Caesarea (d 268) [5]643
firmness, moral [4]649
first, the [5]721
  absolute [1]602; f.-fruits [1]602; mover [3]347n; self-originated [5]626
firstborn [5]57, [2]722, 722n
Fischart, Johann (c 1545–90) [2]771n
Fischer [1]3
Fischer, Friedrich Christoph Jonathan (1750–97) *see* Ekkehart *De prima expeditione* ed Fischer
fish(es) [1]778, [2]346, 545, 672, 834, 860–1, [3]1043, 1044, 1073, 1073n, [4]112, 164–5, 500, 802n, 846, [5]177, 360, 681, [6]60
  arm of [5]103; coloured [6]160n; dead [5]467; fishifies [3]325; flat [3]132, 132n; flying [3]761, [5]681; and government [2]87–8; odd [5]837; as semi-colons [1]133; full of stones [6]121
Fisher, John, St, Bishop of Rochester (1469–1535) [2]70, 72
"Fisher, John" *see* Percy, John
Fisher, Timothy (fl 1810) [3]939
fisherman/fishermen [2]256, [5]181, [6]159
  riddle of [1]757
fishing [5]100
  f. smacks [2]88
fister [5]70, 70n
fit(s) [1]680
  apoplectic [1]163; epileptic [6]122
fit et facit [5]444n, 473
fitness, moral [5]608
Fitzclarence, George Augustus Frederick, 1st Earl of Munster (1794–1842) [4]74, 74n
Fitzgibbon, John, 1st Earl of Clare (1749–1802) [2]353
  Speech . . . on . . . the Bill for the Relief of His Majesty's Roman Catholic Subjects [1]lxxx, [2]845; MT 696–7
Fitzroy, Augustus Henry, 3rd Duke of Grafton (1735–1811) [3]224, 224n
five(s) [1]222, 222n–3n, 798–9, [3]1053, [4]37, 37n
  little [3]837. *See also* pentad; quincunx
fixation [3]998, [5]545, [6]227
fixity [1]573, 579, 588, 637, [5]344, 435
"fixive" [1]596, 596n
fizzle [3]867n
Flacius, Matthias, Illyricus (1520–75) [2]765–6
flag, tricoloured [6]172
flagellation [1]487
flame(s) [3]125, [5]719
  in bush [5]398; pillar of [3]539; sacred [1]328; world in [5]528
Flanders [1]334, [2]100n
flash [1]619, 647, [4]418
flashlets [1]808
flat(ness) [1]371, [4]289
flattening [2]449, 449n
flatterer [2]1141n, [5]682
flattery [1]51, 160, 523, 560, 736, [2]353, 827, [3]809, [4]762, [5]858, 858n
  Donne's [2]233; rancid [2]818; white [2]236
flatting-machine [3]783, 783n

flatting-mill [4]60n, 67
flatus vocis [5]777
Flaugergues, Honoré (1755–1835) [3]939
Flavel, John (?1627–91) [4]182, 183
Flavius (*Julius Caesar*) [4]732, 732n, 733, 805
Flaxman, John (1755–1826) [2]180, [4]787, 787n
flea(s) [1]25, [2]217, 1004, [3]307, [4]802, 802n, [5]229, 442, 442n, [6]75
  f.-skip [2]1012
Fléchère, Jean Guillaume de la ("John William Fletcher") (1745–85) [5]185, 185n
fleece [6]216
"fleet" [6]208, 208n
fleet(s) [2]620
  Danish [5]312, 312n
Fleming, Robert (1630–94) [2]1181
Flemish (people) [2]163n
"flesh" [3]27–8
flesh [2]313, [3]41, 42, 324, 520, 526, [4]420, [5]310, 411, 466
  address of [2]1036; and blood *see* blood; to come in the [2]487; dead [1]517; death in [4]435; eyes of [5]418; fleshly corruptions [3]12; or life [1]166; man as [6]302; mind of the [1]430, 504, [2]332, 1151, [3]424, 424n, [6]310n, see also *phronema sarkos*; noumenal [5]573, 573n; pound of [4]718, 815; and spirit [2]659, [3]602, 1086, [4]473, 473n; two senses [3]14, 14n; will of [2]279; wisdom of [1]684; Word become [3]17; Word made [6]65
Fletcher, Frank [5]426
Fletcher, Giles, the Younger (c 1585–1623) [1]37
Fletcher, John (1579–1625) [1]362, [3]703n, [4]736
  good scholar [1]385; and Greek [1]73n; imitator of Shakespeare [1]397–8; plays of [3]172
  and Shakespeare *Two Noble Kinsmen* [5]178 q, 178n; *see also* B&F
Fletcher, Joseph (1784–1843) *The Constitution of the Bible Society Defended* [4]3
Fletcher, Phineas (1582–1650) [1]37, 53
  "Life" by Anderson MT [1]59–61
  Piscatory Eclogues [1]60; *The Purple Island* [1]59 q, 60n, 61 q
Fletcher, Richard, Bishop of Worcester (d 1596) [1]395n
Fleury, Claude (1640–1725) [1]clin
  The Ecclesiastical History tr H. Herbert and G. Adams MT [2]698–752
Flexner, Bernard (b 1865) [1]clxvi, [4]207
flight [6]151
fling [2]73
flint(s) [1]775, [3]634, 1023, [4]418, 645, [5]257, 257n
"flocci-nauci-nihili-pilificating" [1]329n
flock(s) [1]575, [3]21, [5]538, 589
Flögel, Carl Friedrich (1729–88) *Geschichte der komischen Litteratur* [1]xciii, clxvii; MT [2]753–83
flogging [1]354
"flood(s)" [6]215
flood [4]273
Flood [2]164n, 390, 390n, 391, 574n, 579, 973n, [3]14, 61, 61n, 417n, 644, [5]337n, 368, [6]292–4; *see also* Deluge
Florence [3]251n, [4]144, 701, [5]275 ("Fiorenza"), 275n, 279
  Council of [5]633; Uffizi Gallery [3]899n
Florence, Duke of [5]39n
Florentine [4]746
Florizel (*Winter's Tale*) [4]709
Florus (fl 122) *De qualitate vitae* [2]601n
flounder(s) [1]371, [3]132, [4]706
  flat as a [1]98
flow, rhythmical [1]803
flower(s) [1]367, 602, [2]689, [3]342, 580, 813, [5]287–9, 780
  bed of [1]401; brimstone [3]760; of cobalt [3]817, 817n; f.-names [2]168n; and sun [2]302–3
Flower, Benjamin (1755–1829) [4]294
flowing, the [5]95
Fludd, Robert (1574–1637) [1]630n
  Philosophia Moysaica [1]clxx
Flüe, Niklaus von (1417–87) [2]202, 202n
"fluid" [5]442, 450, 453
fluid(s) [1]177, 548n, 550, [2]854n, 1013, [3]61, 129–30, 293, 294, 325, 382, 383, 383n, 387–8, [4]386, 395, 395n, 448, 523, [5]386, 442–3, 444, 444n, 448–9, 449, 449n, [6]228
  defined [1]548, [6]227; elastic [2]853, [5]410, 450; electric [3]945–6, 947–9, 950, 950n; and figure [1]550; hypothetical [3]211; of life [3]383–4, 386, 395; life-infusing [3]374; magnetic [2]550n; nervous [3]372, 372n; plastic [5]445; positive [5]347; qualities of [3]383; and solid [5]344; spirituous [5]442, 444n, 446, 453; subtle [3]952, [5]450–1; universal [3]865n, 867n
fluidific, the [3]61
"fluidising" [1]638, 639n
fluidity [1]550, [5]263, 266, 357, 358n, 451, [6]230
  aboriginal [5]347; and aerity [3]997, 997n; of quicksilver [1]548

fluidum [4]519
flumen [2]496, 496n
fluoric gas *see* gas(es)
fluorine [3]1032n
flush, genial [5]242
flux [2]750, 802n, [3]39, [5]273
bloody [2]615; continual [1]737
"fluxion" [1]*153n*
fluxion(s) [1]153, [2]526
fly/flies [1]25, [3]57, 57n, 438, [4]267, 336, 497, [5]177
flesh-f. [2]1068, 1068n; Reading [5]619n
fly-catcher(s) [2]545, 545n, [3]428n
defined [1]lxvin
flying in sleep [5]771
fly-wheel [2]545
Fo/Foh [2]1023, 1023n, [3]587, 587n
Foakes, Reginald Anthony *see* Coleridge, S. T. VI *Lectures 1808–1819,* IX *Coleridge on Shakespeare* ed Foakes
foal [4]636
foam, rabid [2]496
focus/foci [1]560, 599, 687, 687n–8n, 782, 1019, [3]116, 381, 393, [4]326, 527, 531, [5]243–4, 484
of percipient [4]269
foetus [2]857, 1025–6, 1026n, [3]1046
fog [6]153
Foh *see* Fo
foibles [2]735
folktales [3]103n
folly/follies [2]1054, [3]173, [4]827, [5]121, 279, 541
dangerous [1]254; impudence of [2]1180; negative [4]366
fomes [3]66, [5]277
fondness [4]810, 814
Fontanini, Giusto, Archbishop of Ancyra (1666–1736) [2]976
Fontenelle, Bernard Le Bovier de (1657–1757) [3]503
food [1]10, [3]64, 695, [5]552, 673
abstinence from [1]826; defined [4]320, [5]137; divine [3]42; general [5]674; as metaphor [5]672–3; and wine [3]360
fool(s) [1]433, [3]698, [4]584, 707, 737
honour to [5]682
Fool (*King Lear*) [4]820
fooleries [6]15n
tolerable [5]505, 506, 506n
foot/feet [4]38, 166
charm for [1]129; elephantine [2]429; washing of [1]457
foot/feet (metrical) [4]686–7
composite [4]604, 604n, 687; *see also* metre
football [4]634
Foote, Maria (?1797–1867) [4]607, 607n
Foote, Samuel (1720–77) [5]534
Dramatic Works [5]534n
fop [3]985, 985n
fopperies, Romish [2]1041
"for" [2]906n
"for 't" [1]158
Forberg, Friedrich Karl (1770–1848) [3]971n
Forbes, Duncan (1685–1747) [1]74
A Letter to a Bishop [2]787n; *The Whole Works* [1]cxxii; MT [2]784–90
force(s) [1]625, [2]891, 1009, [3]1029, [4]131n, 416, [5]176, 244, 279
in actu [1]688; antagonist [3]139, [5]442, 460; balance of [4]603; centrifugal [5]714, c. and centripetal [1]lx; coherentific [1]780; defined [4]389; degree of [5]719; dilative [5]266; electric [5]247; equal [5]424; fundamental [3]283–4; moral [5]822; of one power [1]70; opposite [3]289, [5]714; opposition of [6]232–3; physical [6]159; and power(s) [1]623, 632–3, 648, [3]286, 288, 289, 378, 378n, 1006, 1006n, 1022, [4]131, [5]460, 714; primary two not four [1]660; substantiative and modifying [3]1005; two [5]78; *see also* power(s)
Ford, John (c 1586–c 1640) [4]168
and T. Dekker *The Sun's Darling* [3]175n q
Foreign Slave Trade [4]8
foreigners [5]143n
foreknowledge [3]139, [4]481, [5]57, 68
foresight [4]421
gifts of [2]1156; logical [5]70
forests [4]170
"fore-tact" [2]1136, 1136n–7n
foretastes [5]796
forethought [2]453
forge [1]838n–9n, [2]16
forgery/forgeries [1]699, [2]107, 155, 443, [4]241n, 250, [5]561, 693n, 695, 695n, [6]142, 145
"forgiveness" [1]466, 466n
forgiveness [4]655, [5]130, 559, 681
God of [5]420
"form" [4]42, 42n
form(s) [1]151n–2n, 152, 625, 670, 683, 683n, 689, [2]135, 489, 641, 655, 1090, [3]13, 16n, 17, 95, 741, 755, [4]93, 316, 460, 579, 601, [5]123, 208, 407, 409, 410, 592, 704, [6]240, 242, 299

aboriginal [1]561; absolute [3]16; from absolute [3]15; antecedent and consequent [5]409; categoric [3]249; change of [4]322; common [3]127; of comprehension [1]201; confused [5]581; constitutive [1]655; of contemplation [5]631; continuance of [3]600; correlative [5]460; correspondent [5]459; development of [5]287; element of [1]638; elementary [3]1024; essential [2]423, [5]451, [5]172; eternal [5]796; existing [5]405; of faith [3]691; finite [3]16; first [3]1052; of forms [3]24; four primary [5]451; and ground [3]60; human [5]173, 406; and idea [5]470; of all ideas [5]627; identical with matter [1]596; of the identity [6]241; incorporeal [5]230; innate [5]297; of intellect [3]45, 332; intelligible [5]408; of law [1]125, [3]54; of logic [3]18; logical [4]461; mathematical [3]248; and matter [3]354, 354n, 789–90, [4]234–5, 415, [5]719; from mind [4]217; necessary [5]542; particular [5]343; of perception [3]85; permitted [5]657; phenomenal [3]520, [6]302; power of [3]278; preceding [5]659; principle of [5]715, [6]8; of reality [3]331, [5]788; reason manifest in [2]713; of representation [3]301; of sense [1]569, [2]729, [3]201, 848, 968, [5]599; and shape [1]792, 792n, [5]405; solid [1]569; source of [5]457n; of space and time [3]966; Stoic view [1]175; subjective [3]270; and substance [1]448, 563, [3]746, [4]235; substance of [1]353; substantial [1]524, [5]826, 826n, 470; supreme [5]799, 799n; in Swedenborg [5]427; of thinking [5]708; transitive of [5]451; of truth [6]78; of understanding [1]683, [3]357; unity of stuff [3]129; universal [3]80; vegetable [1]589; visible [4]316

forma/formae

f. apparens [3]44; *f. fidei* [3]691; *f. formans* [3]129, [5]405, 470, and *f. formata* [5]826; *f. formantes* [3]741; *f. informans* [3]44; *f. substans* [3]44

formalis and *formosum* [3]259, 259n

formalism [2]553

formalist(s) [3]268

Formalist (in Bunyan) [1]821, 821n, 822

formaliter [2]1110, [3]79

formality [2]1034, [3]483

formally *see* eminently, and formally

Forman, Harry Buxton (1842–1917) [2]50, 753

formation(s) [3]138, 916

of mountains [1]664; selfless [1]679

formula/formulae [2]146, [5]456

Trinitarian [5]653n; universal [6]73

fornication [6]59

Forster, Sir Humphry (fl 1543) [2]817

Forster, Johann Reinhold (1729–98) *see* Kalm *En resa til Norra America* tr Forster

Forster, John (1812–76) [1]52, [4]161

Forster, Thomas Ignatius Maria (1789–1860) [3]939, 940, 941, 942

Sketch of the New Anatomy and Physiology of the Brain and Nervous System [3]716n ("Foster")

Forsterus, Joannes (1495–1556) [3]718

fort esprit [2]987, [4]97

Fortescue, Sir John (?1394–?1476) [3]152, 169

fortification [5]196

fortune [1]183–4, [3]180

caprice of [2]818; competent [2]325; independent [5]366; f.-tellers [5]234; f.-telling [3]645, 920, [4]788

fossils [3]1047, [5]310n, 338

Fossombrone, Ludovico di (fl 1530) [1]4, 4n

Foster, Benjamin Oliver (fl 1899–1919) see *Livy* tr Foster

Foster, Henry (fl 1818) [3]514, 537, [6]295

Foster, James (1697–1753) *The Usefulness . . . of the Christian Revelation Defended*† [2]791

Foster, John Leslie (c 1781–1842) [4]18, 18n

Foster, Sir Michael (1689–1763) *A Report of Some Proceedings* [2]129, 129n

Foster, Mr [3]820

Foston-le-Clay [4]630n

Fothergill, John (1712–80) [2]85, 85n

foundation [5]72

of faith [5]617; of religion [5]596

founder(s) [4]357

divine [5]560; of C of E [4]643, [5]466–7

fountain(s) [1]649, 656, [2]247, 333, 702, 1069, [3]1051, [5]133, 351, 385

of lovers [5]845

fountain-head [3]1090

four [4]37, 37n

fourfold [1]633, 635

Fourcroy, Antoine François, Comte de (1755–1809) [1]641, 641n, [3]938, 942

Fowler, Harold North (1859–1955) *see* Plato *Phaedo* tr Fowler

fox [1]399n

black [1]399; f.-hounds [3]716

Fox, Charles James (1749–1806) [3]146n, 148, 148n, 884, 884n, [4]13, 13n, [6]323, 323n–4n

Fox, George (1624–91) [1]lxx, 297n, [2]717n, 755, 755n, [3]77n, 142n, 826, 927, 928, 928n, [4]182, 643, [5]123n
Journal ed W. Penn [4]181 q, 181n, [5]569n q
Fox, Henry Richard Vassall, 3rd Baron Holland (1773–1840) [1]500
Foxe, John (1516–87) *Book of Martyrs* [2]1173n
Foxley, Barbara (fl 1911) *see* Rousseau *Emile* tr Foxley
Foxon, David Fairweather (b 1923) "The Printing of *Lyrical Ballads*" [1]91n
Fracastoro, Girolamo (Frascatorius) (1483–1553), not annotated by C [1]lxiii
fraction(s) [2]699, 1142, 1154, [3]127, 233, [5]734
Fraenkel, Eduard (1888–1970) [1]25n
fragment(s) [3]743
deficiency of [1]234; fragmentary composition [4]162; Parmenides's [5]705; Pythagorean [5]695; of truth [4]259
fragrance, vernal [1]602
frailty/frailties [4]137
earthly [1]280
frame [5]284
France [1]698, [2]60, 177n, 321n, 770, 779, 809, 931n, 936n, 1118n, [3]638, 852n, 864, 883–4, 883n, [4]43n, 290, 299, 341–2, 505, 628n, 701, [5]44, 45, 103, 141, 143, 195n, 196, 222n, 507, 833, 835n, [6]14, 269
Calvinists in [1]225; conflict with [5]638; Constituent Assembly of [6]117; history of [2]99, [5]373; infidelity in [5]630; Jacobins in [3]495; King of [5]639, 639n, [4]73; Minister of Police [3]436; National Assembly [6]117n; population of [5]270; reformed clergy [3]785; RC country [1]733; St Bartholomew's Day Massacre [3]803n; school for deaf and dumb [4]165
franchise [2]90, [3]800
Franciosini, Lorenzo (fl 1622) *Grammatica spagnuola ed italiana* [1]clxvi
Francis (fiction) [2]683
Francis of Assisi, St (1181–1226) [2]765, 765n, [3]73, 427
Francis of Sales, St, Bishop of Geneva (1567–1622) [1]516, 714n, [2]765, 765n, [3]60n
Il Teotima o sia il trattato dell' amor di Dio tr Barbieri [1]516n; MT [2]792–3; *Lettres à des gens du monde* [1]516n
Francis I, Grand-Duke of Tuscany, Holy Roman Emperor (1708–65) [5]275, 275n
Francis I, King of France (1494–1547) [2]7n
Francis, Sir Philip (1740–1818) [3]220n
A Letter Missive . . . to Lord Holland [5]851, [6]334
Franciscan(s) [1]506, [3]73, 73n, 645n, [5]662
F. cowl [3]786; Irish [2]309
Frank(s) [4]290, [5]834, 842
Frank, Johann Georg (1705–84) *Cyclus jobilaeus* [6]293–4
Frankfurt [5]46n, 505, 505n, 506
Frankfurt-am-Main [1]723n
Frankfurt-on-Oder [1]6n
franklin [6]216
Franklin, Benjamin (1709–90) [1]244n, 581n, [3]43n, 104, 104n, 376n, 1067n, [6]120n
Franklin, Sir John (1786–1847) [1]549n
Narrative of a Journey to the Shores of the Polar Sea [1]lxxviiin
frankness [5]527
Fraser, Alexander Campbell (1819–1914) *see* Locke *Essay* ed Fraser
fratres fideles [5]197
fraud [1]517, [5]279
pious [2]1173n
Frauenfeld [3]864
Frederick II, the Great, King of Prussia (1712–86) [2]1016n
Frederick III, Duke of Schleswig-Holstein-Gottorp (1597–1659) [2]62n
Frederick Augustus, Duke of York (1763–1827) [2]100, *100n*, 586
"free" [1]431
free will [1]303, 824–5, [2]152, 153, 160, 554, 642, 675, 676–7, 801, 1109, [3]75–6, 76n, 81, 102n, 137, 206, 312, 379, 736n, 737n, 956, [4]125, 409, 436, 439, 543, 629–30, 629n, 639n, 643–4, 662, [5]68–9 ("free being"), 305, 394, 394n, 466, 470, 476, 583, 592, 594, 596, 603, 603n, 615, 783, [6]113
abdication of [1]172; arose from negation [1]574; denial of [3]737; of the Devil [2]292; Luther's error [3]736–7, 737n; Luther's opinion [2]1099; and original sin [2]247; proof of [4]652; suspension of [5]726
free-agency [3]110, 464, [4]175, 787
free-agent [1]827, [2]1109
"freedom" [6]52
freedom [1]201, 656, 825, [2]152, 692, 802, 899, [3]466, 478, 677, [4]225, 421, 436, 438–9, [5]165, 182, 277, 284, 421, 769
absolute [2]641, [3]30, [4]412; argument against [4]435–6; and choice *see* choice; essence of [4]433; fitness for [2]909; friends of [5]282; in God [5]207; idea of [4]434; inward [5]302;

light of [2]846; moral [3]464, [5]752; and necessity [2]641, 802, 1193, [4]445, [5]208; outward [5]305; perfect [3]670, [5]208; religious [2]973; securities of [5]378; sphere of [5]302; spirit of [2]929; and spontaneity [2]604–5, 611; theory of [3]80–1, [4]443–5; true [5]829; of will [3]311–12
freeman [2]899
creed of a [5]829
Freeman, William Henry (fl 1863) [1]clxiv
Freemasons [1]340, 340n; *see also* Masons
free-thinker(s) [2]832, 987n, [4]637
freezing [1]596
Freiheit [5]305
Freke, William (1662–1744) *Select Essays* [3]654
French (language) [3]394, [4]101n, 289, 291, 326n, 612, 780, [5]142, 827, 866, [6]150
C's ignorance of [1]162n; defect of [1]161; and English [3]1074; pun in [1]76; in Shakespeare [4]717
French (people) [2]163n, [3]160, 1003, [4]341–2, 655n, [5]97, 373n
anthropoids [4]15; braggards [4]717; chemists *see* chemist(s), French; Christians [3]754; as colonists [5]103; contradictions [2]347, and Danish [5]312; Dubois as example [2]341; and English [4]239–40, 240n; feeling [4]184; fops [1]148, 148n; Gallo-jacobinical heart [2]345; on love [2]527, 527n, [3]1003; lust of blasphemy [1]6; metaphysicians [3]877–8; as mixed race [1]540; national character of [1]699n, [5]195n; pride of [1]477; Protestants *see* Protestant(s), French; psilosophists [4]97, 97n; quintessential [2]176; *sciences d'observation* of [4]15; steal from their neighbours [4]185; wicked race [5]373; wit [2]1022
French Revolution [2]108n, 400, 510, 511, 845–51, 846n, [3]160n, 208, 250, 785n, 884n, 923n, 984, [4]213–14, 279–80, 342n, [5]89, 270, 282, 297, 630n, [6]33n, 45, 81n
atheism in [4]28; leaders of [4]68; Revolutionists [3]250; Sheridan's support for [1]92n
Frenchery [5]292
Frenchman/Frenchmen [2]100, 348, [3]216, 577, 577n, 883, [4]78, 655, [5]840
intense [2]176
Frend, William (1757–1841) [1]99n, 615n, [2]848n, 913n
Evening Amusements [1]clxix
Freneau, Philip (1752–1832) [3]133
frenzy/frenzies [5]189, [6]287
Frere, George (1774–1854) [1]xcviii, cxxii, clviii, 279, [2]784
Frere, James Hatley (1779–1866) [2]516n, [3]70, 70n–1n, 378n
A Combined View of the Prophecies of Daniel, Esdras, and S. John [3]70n
Frere, John Hookham ("William and Robert Whistlecraft") (1769–1846) [1]xcvii, xcviii, 279, [2]351, 794–5, 979, 979n, [3]765, 765n, 1075, 1075n, [5]854
Prospectus and Specimen of an Intended National Work [1]217n; MT [2]794–5; *see also* Aristophanes *The Frogs* tr Frere
Freud, Sigmund (1856–1939) [1]582n
Frey, Andreas (fl 1749) [3]495–6
A True and Authentic Account [3]494n q, 495, 495n q, 496n q
Freya (myth) [4]489–90
friar(s) [3]754, 774, [4]195, 731, [5]542
Friar John (in Rabelais) [4]191, 192
Friar Lawrence (*Romeo and Juliet*) [4]831
Fricker, George (1774–1854) [1]lxxxi, [4]32, 32n
friction(s) [4]418, 536, [5]184, 252
Friedländer, David (1750–1834) *Sendschreiben . . . von einigen Hausvätern jüdischer Religion* [1]clxvii; MT [2]796
Friedman, Arthur *see* Goldsmith, Oliver *Collected Works* ed Friedman
Friedrich Wilhelm, Duke of Nassau-Weilburg (1768–1816) [2]983
friend(s) [2]693, [3]750, [4]597, [5]74
duties of [4]9–10; of freedom [5]282; old [5]121; precious [1]405
"friendism" [4]801, 801n
Friends, Society of *see* Quakers
friendship [3]265, 670, [4]9–10, [5]476
and love [1]751–2, [2]197, 262, 262n
Friendship's Offering ed T. Pringle [1]31, [2]964, [4]151n
Fries, Jakob Friedrich (1773–1843) [2]186n
frigidity [5]38
frippery [2]544
The Frisky Songster [1]369n
Frith, John (1503–33) [1]833, [3]1068
frivolity [2]636
frog(s) [1]778, 872, [2]1126, [4]352, [6]75, 112, 120
f.-critic [1]148n; f.-man [1]148; paradoxical [3]1073, 1073n; plague of [1]419; swimming [1]148
Froissart, Jean (c 1333–c 1404) [1]368, 368n
"fromme" [3]192, 192n
front [5]105
Fronto, Marcus Cornelius (c 100–c 176) [1]160

frost(s) [1]238, [2]190, [3]44, 158, [4]275, 358, 543, [5]266, [6]152
froth [3]877
frowning(s) [3]525, 525n, [6]307, 307n
fruit(s) [2]689, 1037, [3]776, [4]529, 780
 forbidden [5]593
fruition [5]169, 309, 449, 796
Fry, Elizabeth (1780–1845) [4]241n
Fryssbe, Thomas [1]155
fuel [1]328
Fuge, John Hele (fl 1818) "Case of Gunshot Wound of the Heart" MT [2]361–2
fulfilment [3]23
"fulgent" [5]112, 112n
Fulgentius (468–533) [3]765, 765n
Fülleborn, Georg Gustav (1769–1803) [3]640
Fuller, Andrew (1754–1815) [1]lviii, [2]801n, 967
 The Calvinistic and Socinian Systems Examined and Compared [1]lxxxiv; MT [2]797–803
Fuller, Thomas (1608–61) [1]xci, 366n, [2]72, 158, 294n, *804–5*, 816, [3]824, [4]179 q, [5]97, 138, 139, [6]251, 251n
 The Appeal of Iniured Innocence [1]cxlin; MT [2]806–7; 808, 1102n; *The Church-History of Britain* [1]cxlin; [2]806; MT 808–14; 1102n; [5]147n; *Davids Hainous Sinne* [1]576n, [2]805; *The History of the University of Cambridge* [2]808; *The History of the Worthies of England* [2]116, 804; MT 815–21; 1023n q; *The History of Waltham Abbey* [2]808; *The Holy State* and *The Profane State* [1]cxlin, [2]804; MT 822–7; 830; *Life Out of Death* [2]804; MT 828–9; 837; *A Pisgah-Sight of Palestine* [1]clxi; MT [2]830–6; *A Triple Reconciler* [2]804, 809n, 828; MT 837–9
fullness [5]455, 520, [6]316
function(s) [1]623, [2]891, 1008, 1067, [3]242
 cycle of [5]462; deranged [5]678; reciprocal [5]578
functionaries [5]536
fund(s) [2]311, 311n
 f.-owners [2]295
"fundamental" [2]25–6
fundamentals [1]249
Fund-ort [5]263
funeral [1]764, 797
"funest" [5]566, 566n
fünf [4]36n
fungi [4]528
fur [1]399
furnace [1]868, [2]570
furniture [2]617
 of soul [2]98
Furse, W. [5]401
Fury/Furies [4]786, 809, [5]584
Fuscus Salinator, Gnaeus Pedanius (fl 106–36) [1]757
Fuseli, Henry (1741–1825) [2]235, 235n, [3]899, *899n–900n*
 "Milton Gallery" [3]900n
fusibility [4]314
fusion(s) [3]858, [5]265
 of spirit [5]821
future, the [3]163, 836n, [4]356, [5]415
 anxiety about [3]645; and past [1]280, 361; scene set in [1]150; f. state *see* state
future (in grammar) [3]830
futurition [4]110
futurity [6]175
 continuous [2]569; distant [1]446
Fyfe, Sir William Hamilton (1878–1965) *see* Longinus *On the Sublime* tr Fyfe

Gabii [5]533n
Gabriel (*Paradise Lost*) [3]413n
Gadshill [4]55, 55n
gag [5]396
gait of manhood [2]126
Galatia [2]474, [5]634, 634n
Galatians [5]623
galaxy [4]162, 516
 of learning [5]661
Galba, Servius Sulpicius (3 BC–AD 69) [1]486, 486n, [3]929, 929n
Gale, Thomas (c 1635–1702) *see* Joannes Scotus Erigena *De divisione naturae*; *Opuscula mythologia* ed Gale
Galen (Claudius Galenus) (c 130–c 201) [1]748, [2]65 q, 66, [4]804, 804n
Galenist [4]622, 622n
Galilean(s) [5]651
Galilean (Jesus) [2]798
Galilee [2]515n, 1015, [3]51, 667, [5]651
 Sea of [2]255
Galileo (Galileo Galilei) (1564–1642) [3]645n–6n
 Mathematical Collections and Translations [2]1164n
gall [5]98, 151
 g. apples [5]838; g.-sickness [4]148, 149n
Gall, Franz Joseph (1759–1828) [2]1011, 1012, 1012n, 1016, [3]716n, [4]5, 360, 422
 and J. C. Spurzheim *Physiognomical System* [3]716, [5]422n

Gallasius (Nicolas Des Gallars) (c 1520–c 1580) [5]549n
Galli [5]840n
gallicanus [3]177n
gallicinate [2]177n
Gallienus, Publius Licinius (d 268) [5]748–9
gallina [4]97n
Gallio, Junius Annaeus (1st century) [3]574
Gallo-barbarism [4]172
"gallocristan" [2]92, *92n–3n*
galloi [5]840n
Galloway [2]1099
gallows [3]665, [4]51, 241
Galt, John (1779–1839)
The Entail [2]840; *The Provost* MT [2]840; *Sir Andrew Wylie*† [2]841
Galvani, Luigi (1737–98) [6]135n
galvanism [1]579, 582, 597, [2]1008n, [3]94, 125, 210, 211, 399, 868, 949, 1011, [4]494n, [5]266
Gamaliel (d c 50), school of [1]463, 463n
Gambold, John (1711–71) *see* Zinzendorf *Maxims* ed Gambold
game(s) [2]492, [5]134, 161, 789
of guess [4]158
gaming [6]28
Gammer Gurton's Needle [2]777, [3]702
gamut [4]313n
gander [3]973
Ganganelli, Lorenzo *see* Clement XIV
Ganges [2]178, [4]507
ganglia [2]860
ganglions [3]84
garden(s) [5]283, 593, 831, 832, 843
father's [4]236; handkerchief [2]918; of lovers [5]845; pleasure [5]642
gardener, will of [1]401
Gardiner, Helen (fl 1601) [2]1172–3
Gardiner, Stephen ("Gardner"), Bishop of Winchester (c 1483–1555) [1]255, 255n, 318, [2]66, 71, 813, 813n, [3]803, 803n
Gardner, Dame Helen Louise (1908–86) *see* Donne *The Elegies* ed Gardner
Gargantua (in Rabelais) [4]78n, 191, 630, 630n
garland [5]660
garment(s)
of righteousness [1]815; seemly [5]530
garnet [5]843, 844
Garnett, Richard (1789–1850) [1]502, [4]778
Garnett, Richard (1835–1906) [1]116
Garnock, Robert (d 1681) [2]1181n
Garrick, David (1717–79) [2]779, 779n, [4]42, 42n, 632, [6]114, 114n
Miss in Her Teens [4]38n
garrulity [3]713
garter [2]826
Garter, Order of the [2]826n
Garth, Sir Samuel (1661–1719) [1]38
Garve, Christian (1742–98) [1]clxvi, [2]429, 429n
Fragmente zur Schilderung des Geistes . . . und der Regierung Friedrichs des zweyten† [2]842; *Uebersicht der vornehmsten Principien der Sittenlehre*† [2]842; *Vermischte Aufsätze*† [2]842; *Versuche über verschiedene Gegenstände aus der Moral*† [2]842
gas(es) [1]177, [3]325, [5]837, [6]228
carbonic acid [1]613, [2]69n, [3]68; fluoric [5]438; indecomponible [5]347; mastering [2]69; muriatic acid [3]127, 127n; nitric [3]1027; nitrous [3]1027; oxymuriatic [5]346; ponderable [5]258; qualities of [6]132; theory of [3]1006
gaseous, the [6]228
Gass, Joachim Christian (1766–1831) [4]485 ("C. H. Gass")
Gassendi, Pierre (1592–1655) [1]107 q, [5]81n, 552, 552n
Syntagma philosophicum [3]95n
Gassendist [5]80–1, 81n, 615
Gataker, Thomas (1574–1654) [1]155, 196, [6]258
gate(s) [4]461, [5]121, 580
five-bar [2]447
Gathorne-Hardy, Robert and W. P. Williams *A Bibliography of the Writings of Jeremy Taylor to 1700* [5]501n, 510n
Gauden, Elizabeth (née Russell) (d 1671) [6]184
Gauden, John, Bishop of Worcester (1605–62) [2]1132n, 1173n, [5]146, 146n, 510n
and *Eikon Basilike* [1]336n, [2]522, 522n, 523, 523n, 524n, 948, [3]798, [5]146n, see also *Eikon Basilike*
The Tears, Sighs, Complaints, and Prayers of the Church of England [5]510n; *see also* R. Hooker *Works* ed Gauden
Gauls [3]769, [4]807
Gaunilo (11th century) [5]772–3 ("Gunillo")
Gay, John (1685–1732) [1]38, 156n, [2]779
Gay, Robert (fl 1695) [1]222
Gaye, Russell Kerr (b 1877) *see* Aristotle *Physics* tr Hardie and Gaye
Gay-Lussac, Joseph Louis (1778–1850) [2]520, 520n, [3]942, 943, [4]315n, [5]260n
gaze [5]112, 113
gazette [3]104

ge/Ge [2]577, 578n, 579, [5]347n
ge- [6]286, 287n
gecko [4]502, 502n
Geddes, Alexander (1737–1802) [2]246, *246n*
Gedicke, Friedrich (1755–1803) [2]754
geese [3]769
Gefühl [2]200–1, [5]795
Gehenna [1]448, [2]559, *559n–60n*, 1074n, [3]37, 38; *see also* hell
Geist [1]137, 598, 654, [5]801
Gelée *see* Claude Lorraine
Gellert, Christian Fürchtegott (1715–69) [2]842
Gellius, Aulus (c 126–c 180) [1]767, [2]250n, 272, [5]531n
gem(s) [5]528
  antique [6]110, 110n
Gemara [1]513n
genders [3]830, 831n[3]
Genea (myth) [2]576
genealogist [3]109
genealogy [5]760
Génébrard, Gilbert, Archbishop of Aix (c 1537–97) [2]272
"geneic" [2]431n
genera *see* genus
general(s) [3]545, [5]99, 99n
  observations [2]972; words [2]482
General(s) (military) [1]379, [3]978, [6]98
generalisation(s) [1]620, [2]637, 639n, 729, 953n, [3]83, 163, 166, 395, 834–5, 947n, [5]185, 336n, 365n, [6]50, 139
  and abstraction *see* abstraction; disguised [1]620; vague [4]106
"generalise" [2]844, [3]423, 425
generalising, use of [2]639
generality/generalities [2]1156n, [5]321
  vague [2]1071
generalship [5]783
"generation" [1]164, [3]524, 524n, [6]78, 307, 307n
generation [1]792, [2]748, [5]626
  Adam and Eveless [5]251; circulating [5]579; and creation [6]78–9; eternal [1]677, [2]584, [5]799; rising [5]534, 866
generous race *see* race, generous
genesis/*geneseis* [1]401, [4]114, [5]347, 347n
genesis/geneses [2]88
  of the dilative [1]612; dynamic [4]324; of Hell [1]647; historic [2]60; ideal [3]11; order of [3]24; perpetual [5]714; of planet [5]430
genetics [5]410
genetrix [1]652
Geneva [1]303n, 478n, [2]226, 666, 667, [4]670, [5]145, 505
  Church of [5]504; G. malcontents [5]510
Gengulphus, St (legend) [2]772
genial [2]1174, [3]11, 886. *See also* critic, genial; law, genial
geniality [5]809
  moral [1]722
Genie [3]231; *see also* Genius/Genii
Genie Prince of Persia (St Michael) [3]417
genitive (case) [3]19, 57, 832–5, 833n, [4]283–4, 284n
  absolute [3]833, 833n; personal [1]723, 725, [3]831, 887
geniture(s) [1]618, 619, 620
  divine [1]610
genius(es) [1]136, 152, [2]254, 754, [3]632, 893, [4]270, 471, 604, 783, [5]110n, 755
  architectural [1]328; Barry Cornwall's [4]161; of B&F [4]719; better [4]868; of Böhme [5]813; borrowings of [2]973–4, [3]175; cannot be superseded [2]781; caprice of [2]234; combines extremes [1]143–4; a creative power [3]176; defects of [1]367, 367n; definition of [1]cxxxi, 747; degeneracy of [1]223; of Duns Scotus [5]789; English [5]152, 152n–3n; and enthusiasm [1]818; epicurism of [4]162; evident [5]367; and fanaticism [1]818; Flaxman's [4]787; forms taste [2]781; German [5]152, 152n–3n; of Junius [3]225; man/men of [2]411, 422, 716, [3]703, [4]96, 162, 427; metaphysical [2]1136; might of [5]503; minutial [4]244; of the moment [4]772; original [4]538; philosophic(al) [2]824, [3]918, [4]221, [5]427, 444, 452, 744; poetic [1]216n, [3]472, 889, 918, [4]104; presiding [2]788; pseudo-genius [3]701; resembling [3]888; rich [5]527; ruling [5]127; Schelling's [6]226; of Scott [4]586; and sensibility [1]cxxxi; Shakespeare's [4]818, 820, 836; sleeping [1]684; some [2]876; superhuman [4]735; tact of [2]167; and talent [1]144n, 149, 153, 367, 367n, 401, 401n, [2]1066, *1066n*, 1147, [3]176n, 1019, [4]610, 610n, 826, [5]127, 127n; Jeremy Taylor's [5]528; Tieck's [5]848; of times [2]972; turns of [5]477; two classes [2]804, 816n; of Swedenborg [5]421; Welsh [6]17; work(s) of [5]520, 783
Genius/Genii [5]167n, 422, [6]159, 159n; *see also* Genie
Gennadius I (d 471) [5]684 q, 685, 685n

gennema [1]640, 640n
Gennesaret, Sea of [2]461
Genoa [5]279
genomenon [2]273, 273n, [6]88
genos [2]576n
gentile(s) [1]434, 437, [2]437, 451, 578n, 700, 706, 709, [3]22, 54, 309, 427, 456, 457, 464, 474, [5]337n, 415, 641
Apostle of (St Paul) [4]474; conversion of [1]236; missions to [3]6, 6n–7n; prejudices [2]709
Gentilly [5]576
gentleman/gentlemen [1]212, 874, [2]159, 684, [4]830, [5]533
country [2]118; gentlemanly feelings [4]22; no time for reading [2]1016; refined [2]969
Gentleman's Magazine [1]62n, 240, 870, 871, [2]211n q, [4]603, 607, 607n, 619, 811n, [6]153n, 290n q
gentry [1]290, [2]948, 1142, 1192, [4]138, [5]175, [6]24
Gentz, Friedrich von (1764–1832) [5]274, 274n, 308n
genuflexion [1]267, [6]260
genus/genera [2]816, 844, [3]127, 182, 423
of being [3]985; determinate [1]146; generalissimum/generalissima [2]198, [5]698, [6]170; gradation of [5]388; philanthropic [5]293; and species [1]551, [2]778, [3]318, 641, 746, [4]97, 165, 314, 314n, 461, 864, [5]94, 233, 592, 599, 790, [6]287, 309, mathematical [4]157
Genus (myth) [2]576
Geoffroy, Etienne François (1672–1731) [1]547
Geoffroy Saint-Hilaire, Etienne (1772–1844) [4]164–5
geologists [3]60, 61n
geology [3]481n
geometer [3]644
geometrician(s) [2]930, 930n, [4]376, [6]8
geometry [1]615–16, [2]491, 890, 1133, 1160, 1160n, [3]118n, 201, 273, 302, 333, 357, 726, 966n, 1051, [4]145, 156, 863, [5]96, 600, 656
certainty of [4]156; confuted [5]299; geometrical construction [3]289; elements of [5]811; geometrical figures [3]276; in India [2]341; Kant's predilection for [3]362; pure [3]275; synthetic character of [3]966; wholly ideal [1]107–8, 108n
"George" [3]779, 779n
George I, King of England (1660–1727) [4]336, 336n
reign of [6]32, 74, 81
George II, King of England (1683–1760) [3]163, 661, [4]640
reign of [6]81
George III, King of England (1738–1820) [2]1055, 1188, [3]149, 149n, 661, [4]19, [5]41
reign of [1]374, [6]74
George IV, King of England (1762–1830) [2]511n, 955n, [3]72, 154n, 250, 250n, 657, 661, 661n, [4]3, 74, 74n, 608n, [5]368
funeral sermon on [2]139; perjuries of [3]154
Geraldus (fl c 900) [2]525
Gerard, John (1545–1612) *Herball* [3]896–7
Geree, John (?1601–49) *The Character of an Old English Puritane* [2]111
Gerizim, Mount [2]416
germ(s) [2]201, [5]90, [4]106
of character [4]855; divine [1]430; of growth [4]106; organic [5]430; spiritual [3]50
German (language) [1]123, 503, 607, 608, [2]271, 380, 739, [3]633, [4]90n, 254n, 284, 285, 291n, 326n, 346n, 595n, 613, [5]142, 197, 198, 245, 283, 325, 325n, 866
genius of [5]688–9; genuine [3]1011; grammar for HC [1]20; and Greek [3]646–7, [5]688; high [5]651; high and low [3]978; idioms [2]994; low [3]46, [4]282; Luther's [5]395n; philosophy in [2]999; richest [4]290
German(s) (people) [1]146, 146n, [3]46, 1003, [4]185, 358, 836n, [5]45, 97, 104, 253, 294, 565
always in extremes [2]512, [5]692; ancient [4]666, 666n; character [1]146n, [3]372; generalisation [1]148n; as generous/Iapetic race [1]540; later [4]350; G. mind [4]325; modern [4]187; neologists *see* neologist(s), German; philosophers *see* philosopher(s), German; undervalue Protestantism [4]269; uprightness of [2]204
Germany [1]166n, 177n, 191, 559, 697, [2]67, 594, 780, 1048, [3]133, 142, 333n, 754n, [4]35, 227, 227n, 299, 837, 837n, [5]45, 141, 208, 280, 295, 319, 539, 634n, 636, [6]14, 150n, 153
C in [5]97n; Counter-Reformation in [5]104n; and England [5]372, 372n; in Europe [5]372; ideaists in [2]1066; influence of Voltaire in [2]480; Jews in [3]700; lacks common sense [4]52; national character of [5]195n; nature-philosophers of [3]909; North [4]269; opposition to *Naturphilosophie* in [5]327; phi-

Germany—*continued*
losophy in fashion in [4]125; Protestant [2]480, [5]512; Reformed States [5]145; Roman Catholicism in [1]845; universities of [3]318; wars in [2]101; youthful genius of [2]863
Gernutus the Jew of Venice [4]815n
Gerson, Jean le Charlier de (1363–1429) [2]655, [5]794–8, 795n ("Gersome")
Gesenius, Heinrich Friedrich Wilhelm (1786–1842) [2]384n
gesticulation [1]580
gestures [3]382
Getulius (legend) [2]718
Ghazali, Abu Hamid Mohammed al- (1058–1111) [5]785–6 ("Algazel")
Ghent [3]160n
Gherano-Esteesian [3]1021n
Ghert/Gheert, Pieter Gabriel van (1782–1852) [3]389, 389n
ghosis [2]285, 285n
ghost(s) [1]764, 797, [2]184, [3]197, 365, 395, 824, [4]87, 581, 771, 775, 838–40, 845, 849, [5]164, 565, 598
Addison's "Ghost-faith" [2]700; appearing [2]166; belief in [1]281; holy *see* Holy Ghost; g.-monger [3]197; story/stories [2]446, [4]605; theories of [3]196–217
ghyll *see* "gil"
Giambullari, Bernardo (fl 1500) [4]290
giant(s) [2]1113, [3]307, [4]630n, [5]406, 483n, 841
double-jointed [2]228; rebellion against Zeus [3]473, 473n; war of [5]347, 347n
gibbon [1]538
Gibbon, Edward (1737–94) [1]462n, 845n, [2]698, [4]660n
distaste for Johnson [1]221n; prose style [1]156n, 157, 157n, 182n, [5]533; "Unfriend" of Christian Church [3]147
The History of the Decline and Fall of the Roman Empire [1]157n, [2]746, 746n q; MT 843–4; [3]147n–8n q, [4]514n, 627n, 651n, 666n q, [5]85n, 643, 643n
Gibbons, Brian *see* Shakespeare *Romeo and Juliet* ed Gibbons
Gibraltar [6]147
Gichtel, Johann Georg (1638–1710) [1]687n
Gichtelians [1]687
Giddy, Davies *see* Gilbert, Davies
Gieseler, Johann Karl Ludwig (1792–1854) *Historisch-kritischer Versuch* [4]471, 473, 475, 475n
Gifford, Edwin Hamilton (1820–1905) *see* Eusebius *Preparation* tr Gifford
Gifford, George (d 1686) [4]78
Gifford, William (1756–1826) [2]755, 755n
Baviad [2]755n; *Maeviad* [2]755n; *see also* P. Massinger *Plays* ed Gifford
gift(s) [2]751, [4]260
and giver [1]432; giver of [2]1166, 1166n; and giving [5]536; of God [3]453; miraculous [1]353, [5]529, 665, [6]57; sacrificial [2]318; of the spirit [3]550; spiritual [1]687; of tongues [5]518n
Gihon (river) [1]779
"gil" [1]423, 423n
Gilbert of Poitiers (Gilbert de la Porrée) (1070–1154) [5]779
Gilbert/Giddy, Davies (1767–1839) [2]883n
Gilbert, William (c 1760–c 1825) [3]990, 990n
The Hurricane [3]990n
Gilchrist, Octavius Graham (1779–1823) [2]15n
Giles/Gillis, Peter (c 1486–1533) *Hexastichon Anemolii Poetae Laureati* [2]766n
Gillet de Laumont, François Pierre Nicolas (1747–1834) [3]940
Gillman, Alexander William (1843–1903) [1]488, [3]719
Gillman, Anne (née Harding) (c 1779–1860) [1]xci, clx, clxn, clxi, [2]830
accident [1]xcix–xcx; as amanuensis [1]227; as annotator [2]339; as ideal wife [2]167n; marginalia written for [1]c; owner of annotated books [1]231, 414, 488, 503, [2]590, 822, 1191, [3]750, 886, [4]615, 754, [5]490; possible transcriber [1]555; transcriber of marginalia [2]1105, [4]616; *see also* Gillmans
Gillman, Henry Anthony (1814–58) [2]142, 599, 599n, 1191, [3]484, 827, [4]593, [5]103n
marginalia addressed to [1]701; owner of annotated books [2]158
Gillman, James (1782–1839) [1]clx, clxix, 282n, 854, [2]474, 533, 590, 794, [3]485n, 844n, [6]246
C's bequest to [2]795; C's executor [1]cxxiv; and C's study [1]cxv; death of [1]clxi; fond of puns [3]1066n; on hydrophobia [1]590; introduced to C [1]xcvii; Lamb's letters to [1]xci q; letter from HNC to [1]cxxxviiin q; letter of [1]cxliin q; library of [1]854, [3]504n, 794, 943; library sale [1]cli, clxi–clxii, [2]830; marginalia addressed to [3]801,

1064; note on literary lectures [1]cxxxix; owner of annotated books [1]cxlin, 488, 498, 545, [2]14, 133, 361, 687, 808, 840, [3]514, 544, 813, 918, 1064, [4]189, 617, 778, [5]499, [6]285, 295; in Paris [2]808; publication of marginalia [1]cxvi; reaction to *LR* [1]cxlii; transcriber of notes [1]279; and J. H. B. Williams [1]215
Catalogue of . . . the Library of James Gillman [1]488, 506n, 543n, 545, 761, 830, 831, [2]14, 42, 99, 110, 361, 532, 589, 794, 954, [3]374n, 514, 654n, 845, 885, [4]206, 333, [5]240, 847, 850, [6]131, 295; *A Dissertation on the Bite of a Rabid Animal* [5]260n, [6]120n; *Life of Coleridge* [1]ciin, clxiin; *see also* Gillmans
Gillman, James, Jr (1808–77) [1]215, 232n, [2]259, 650, 673n, 911, 1107n, [4]167n, [6]213n
letter(s) to [1]694n, [2]1183n q, [3]158n, [4]167, 167n, 350n; marginalia addressed to [2]844; owner of annotated books [1]414, 816, [2]691, 843, 911, 926, 1131, [4]778
Gillman, Lucy Eleanor *see* Watson, Lucy Eleanor
Gillman, Sophia (née Riley) (fl 1854) [1]816
Gillmans [1]xciv, xcvii, cxvii, cxxxv, 231, 469, 761, [3]309n, [4]69, 403n, 538n, 826n
affectionate friends [1]557; HC and DC visit [1]671n; the G. boys [3]831n; owners of annotated books [1]clvi, clviii, clxix, 701, [2]259; suppliers of books to C [1]lxx, xcviii; transcribe marginalia [1]clviii, clx
gills [3]1036
gin [5]252
ginomenon [2]135, 135n
Giotto di Bondone (d 1337) [4]824n
Giovio, Paolo (Paulum Jovium), Bishop of Nocera (1483–1552) [4]338
giraffe [4]534
girdle [2]557
girl(s) [3]329, 350, [4]788
charity school for [1]498; deaf and dumb [3]383; ignorance of [2]432; lovely [5]133; as readers [4]610; reading of [2]190
Giulio Romano (Giulio Pippi de' Giannuzzi) (c 1492–1546) [3]174n
glaciers [2]1140
glades [3]564
gladiators [2]775
gland [1]671, [2]548, [6]124
Glanvill, Joseph (1636–80) [3]920, [6]98
Saducismus triumphatus [3]920n, [5]598, 598n
glare, animal [5]795
Glasgow [1]cxxxiv, [2]1099
Andersonian College [2]981n; Mechanics' Institution [2]981n
"glass" [1]237
glass(es) [1]149, [3]609, 947, [4]271, 375, [5]306, 344, 418
beehive of [3]479, 479n; burning-g. [3]479, [5]311; coloured [1]822; concave and convex [5]269; crown [2]325; cylindrical [3]393; doubling [4]375; foci of [4]527; magnifying [1]25, [2]508; and mirror [1]237; musical [3]43, 43n; of telescope [5]297; windows [3]759, 760; *see also* mirror
glassblower [3]479n
Glaube [1]503, [3]752, [4]215–16, 346, 346n, [5]271–2
glauben [6]286
gleanings of the past [2]1053
glebe [5]79
glee, episcopal [4]307
gleichsam [2]1004, 1004n
Gleim, Friedrich Wilhelm (1719–1803) [3]656
Glendinning, Sir Halbert (in Scott) [4]596, 599, 599n, 600, 600n
Glendower, Owen (*1 Henry IV*) [4]758
glitter [2]604
"gloaming" [5]857, 857n
globe(s) [3]479, 1020n, [5]406, 431, 704
celestial [5]157; hollow [5]338; perfect [5]245; solid [5]430
globoseness [1]548, 548n
globosity [1]579, 594
globules [3]1041, [5]444
glocitando [1]421n
gloom [4]145
"glooming" [5]857, 857n
"gloomy" [6]289
glorification [3]720, [6]106
"glorious" [2]529, 529n
glory [1]385, 435, 438, 438n, 575, 657, [2]489, 998, 1142, [3]14, 35, 40, 50, 62, 106, 548, 616n, [4]252, 646, [5]66, 189
divine [3]29; face of [5]523; faery [1]763, 797; of the Father [5]56; of God [1]561, [3]616–17, [5]95; King of [3]50; state of [3]521, [6]303; of the world [4]795n
gloss(es) [2]246, 915, [4]735, 785, [6]217, 217n, 220
in Bible [2]394, 395; Calvinist [2]263; intruded [6]66; marginal [1]457, [2]52–3, [6]67n; Socinian [5]651; suspicious [6]109; and text [2]393n

glossers [2]917
Glossin, Gilbert (in Scott) [4]584–5
glossolalists [5]391n
Gloucester [1]297 ("Glocester")
Gloucester/Gloster (*King Lear*) [4]816–17, 822, 825
Glover, Arnold (1865–1905) *see* B&F *Dramatic Works* ed Glover and Waller
Glover, Richard (1712–85) [1]38
Leonidas [3]484, 484n; *see also* Hearne *A Journey* ed Glover
Glover, Terrot Reaveley (1869–1943) *see* Tertullian *Apology* tr Glover
gloves [4]705
glow-beast [3]1077
glow-worm [1]169, 210n, [3]1015
Glückseligkeit [2]491, 491n, [4]135–6, 136n, [5]724, 725
"glum" [6]289
gluten [1]595, [3]68n
gluttony [4]193
"glycydor" [1]614, 614n
Gmelin, Eberhard (1751–1808) [4]270
Über den thierischen Magnetismus [4]270n
Gmelin, Johann Friedrich (1748–1804) [3]872, 872n, [5]183, 183n
gnain/gnang see *ayin*
gnat(s) [4]802
"gnathonism" [2]931, 931n
gnomonics, Solomon's [3]698
gnosis [2]482–3, 483n, [2]502, [3]19–20, *19n*, [4]255, 255n
and knowledge [2]285, [3]19, 19n
Gnostic(s) [2]32, 32n, 33, 482, 712n, 713, 713n, 715n, 716, 725n, 726n, 738n, [3]16n, 495n, 612n, 690, 1068n, [4]257, [5]624–5
charges against [2]714; Christian [4]258–9, 259n; doctrine of [5]553; error of [6]64; heresy of [3]21, 612–13, [4]735
Gnosticism [1]493n, [2]285n, 464, 464n, 481–3, [4]735n–6n, [5]624n
Goa [3]1081
goad, compelling [2]319
goat(s) [4]663, 663n, [5]836
ghosts of [3]197; he-g. [2]1053; g.-imp [3]1035; songs of the [3]894; g.-suckers [6]151
gobe-mouche [2]545
goblin [5]122
god(s) [3]715, [5]728, 732
anthropomorphic [5]386; baby [4]364–5; of chaos [2]575; and Christianity [1]543; finite [5]7; and God [3]328; Greek [2]665; heathen [4]514; many [5]34; Melissus on [5]708–9, 710; pagan [1]543, [2]810–11, 811n; Pliny on [4]648, 648n–9n; three [5]18, 21, 27, 28; tri-une [5]16; and world [6]7–8
"God" [1]281, 750–1, [3]699, [6]74–5, 85, 143
God [1]12, 179, 185, 256, 281, 423, 617, 750, 823, [2]29, 145, 152, 176, 246, 278, 281, 327, 660, 829, 882, 891, 920, 1084, 1085, [3]50, 332, 985, 989, [4]266, 341, 492, 644, 646, 652, [5]6, 7, 15, 93, 139, 159–60, 162, 213, 383, 405, 406, 435, 476, 483, 602, 656, 708, 752, 790, 792, 806, 814, 819, [6]7, 16, 23
abracadabra [5]615; absolute [2]880n, 1186; absolute being [3]90; absolute Fullness [2]1109n; absolute good [2]326; absolute I [2]623, 623n; absolute identity [3]11, 1055; act without potentiality [4]127, 127n; all as [3]136–7, [5]354; for all [1]148–9; all in all [5]201, 777; all Being [5]29; all eye [5]704, 704n; all *have* the same [3]699; Allmight [3]100, 100n; all-might of [1]636, 693–4; *alter et idem* [4]444, 444n; amanuenses of [5]473; antagonist of [2]164; and anthropomorphism [4]308; appeared as Jesus [2]598; assertions of [5]58; attribute(s) of [1]731, [2]203, 568, [3]670, [5]66, 585, 596; bargain with [4]628n; beginning in [2]553; beholdeth the end [2]1161; being of [1]287, [5]182; and Belial [2]269; below [3]1086; blasphemed [2]32; bodiless [2]309; and body [2]283; without body [3]768–9; and Caesar [5]363, 363n; Calvinist representation of [3]70; Calvinist view [4]429; Cartesian proof of [3]858–9; causative ideas of [3]326; as cause [4]354, [5]206; chaos far from [4]524, 524n; character of [3]24, 24n; child of [6]139; children of [3]151; Christ as [5]620, [6]296; in Christ [2]1162; a circle [1]562n, [3]729, [4]224, 224n; City of [3]62; coexistent [4]443; as Comforter [3]584; command of [1]329; commandment of [1]819; communion with [5]169; concealment from [1]767; concept(s) of [2]417–19; conception of [3]643; conscience his voice [2]614; contrivance of [5]597; covenant [2]1179–80; and creation [5]207; before Creation [6]26; creator [3]944, [4]413–14; decrees of [5]155; defined [4]127n; definition(s) of [1]564n, [2]249; domestic [5]723; duty of princes to [5]538; his own End [3]30; *ens realissimum* [3]345; epithets of [5]482n; equal to [6]137; equality with [5]30; equivoque on [5]83; essence of [1]106; eternal act [4]200; and evil [4]433, [5]231, 592; exasperated [5]590; exclusion from [2]800; existence of [2]1175,

[3]97, 329–30, 331, 332–3, 348, 504, 658, 848, 848n, 956, 970, [4]109, 114n, 347, 347n, 409–10, 411, 443, [5]82–3, 207–8, 455n, 728, 729, 772, 773–5, 792–3, [6]299; exists in soul [3]517; extended [5]214; eye of [5]185; face of [1]794, 794n; familiarity with [2]1174; and Fate [5]614; applied to Father [5]59; as Father [1]696, [2]992–3; the Father [1]564, 694; fear of [3]583; fiat of [4]14; filial [1]507; filiation of [1]626; finger of [1]457, 457n; as fire [2]567–8, [5]716–17; first-born presented to [2]280; foreknowledge of [5]791; of forgiveness [5]420; form of [5]651; free gifts of [2]1193; and free will [4]465; free will of [5]424, 424n; freedom in [5]207; fruition of [5]796; as generic being [4]422; gift(s) of [1]825, [3]453; glorification of [3]29; glory of [1]629, [3]616; and god(s) [2]149, [3]328; of G. [1]707; and "the G." [2]735, 741, *741n–2n*; and Godhead [5]779; goodness of [2]251–2; grace of [2]592, 1176, 1178, [4]643; as great mind [2]665n; ground of good works [1]460; ground of things [6]113; hand of [3]416, 416n; happiness of [4]112; hating [2]664; from Heaven [5]12; hidden [5]75; human form [5]409; as I AM [4]460, 460n; as Idea [1]237; idea in [2]995; idea(s) of [1]787, [2]183, 249, 884, 1145n, [3]151, 206, 326, 357, 545, 600, 857, 859–60, 877, 1091, [4]114, 132, 350–1, 410, 615, [5]61, 203, 450, 481, 483, 741, 756, 766, 780, 799–800, 830, [6]172, 306n, 319; identity of will and power [3]206; identity of will and reason [3]547; image of [1]731, [2]333; and impossibilities [4]423; incarnate [5]524, 589, 621; includes all true entity [3]826; increase given by [5]395; ineffable self-cause [2]676; not to be called infinite [2]996; infinitely modified [2]803; in instrument of grace [5]675; intellect of [3]78, 79, [5]210; Jewish concept of [1]674–5; as judge [1]10, [2]108, [5]74; justice in [3]677; justice of *see* justice, of God; Kant's concept of [3]357–8, 358–9; Kant's doctrine [2]181–2, 183, 185–6; keystone of philosophy [1]585; and King [5]543; kingdom of *see* kingdom, of God; knowledge of [2]330, [3]554, [4]351, [5]780, 781, 795; lawgiver [2]596n, 677; living [3]76, 76n, 77, 729, [4]226, [5]718; the Lord [1]435, 435n; and love [2]193; as love [2]527, [3]76, [5]122–3; love and mercy [5]819; love of [1]729, 790, [2]27, [4]597–8, 652–3, [5]161, 471, 682; G.-man [1]429, 707, [2]87; and man [1]11, 29, 114, 124, 288n, [2]249, 265, 390, 404, 566, 663, 671, 803, 919, [3]447–8, 591–2, 621, [4]589, 634, 682, [5]16, 25–6, 25n, 471, 551, 597–8, 613, 618, 796, 799, [6]80, 101, 297; and man and nature [5]445; in man [1]434; manifest [1]679, 713; manifested [1]434, 468, [5]635; materiality of [5]493; meaning of [1]239; as measure [4]367n–8n; merciless [5]496; mercy and judgment [2]295; mercy of [3]63, 307; mere [5]96; metaphors of time [4]123; mind of [3]151, [5]202; and miracles [5]823, 823n; not mocked [5]561–2; moral governor [3]166; moral laws of [3]696; most real being [3]1051, 1051n; "Mother of" [2]661–2; multiplication of [3]120; name(s) of [1]239n, 264, 628, 706, 729, [2]287, 325, 392–3, 901, 903, [3]33, 1087, [4]366–7; and nature [1]180, 410, [3]46, [5]83n, 446, 453, 468, 830; in nature [5]272; nature of [1]410, 573, [2]665, [5]12n, 385; and neighbour [1]171–2; "no *Thing*" [3]1054; no man hath seen [2]570; the not-G. [3]22, 22n; and nothing [3]1091; notions of [1]587; and oaths [6]263; obedience to [5]176; Oken's "Nothing" [3]1056; omnipotent [2]652; omnipresence of [5]706; omnipresent [1]862, [5]810; omniscience [6]243; one [2]790, 901, [4]300, [5]19, 27, 34; ontological proof [4]108n; G.-orators [1]319; ordinary Providence of [5]536–7; originating impulse [1]525; originator of moral law [4]410; partibility of [3]1093; peace with [3]551–2; perfect [6]70; perfect understanding [6]306, 306n; perfection of [3]201, [5]798, [6]316; person of [2]571; personal [1]242, [3]88; personality of [4]44; personeity of [3]720; Philo's concept [2]433; plan of Redemption [5]167; as point [5]733; power of [5]383; prayer to [3]437; prescience [1]827; presence of [5]493, 644; prime mover [5]457, 457n; principle separate from [4]425; promises of [2]560, 674; prothesis [2]554n; providence of [1]304; punishes sinners [3]25–6; pure act [1]232; and reason [2]1010, 1011, [5]97; Redeemer [4]596; Redeeming [5]171; and redemption [2]263; our relation to [5]481; revealed [5]75; right idea of [3]533; of riot [3]896; and salvation [5]562; scriptures and [2]679; seat of [3]431; seen in human form [2]489; self-existing [1]561; self-grounded [3]84; self-sufficiency of [1]585; service of [1]877; and sin [6]112, 112n–13n; slandered by Irving [3]65–6; Son of *see* Son; and soul [1]395, [5]84;

God—*continued*
source of doubt [5]186; a sphere [5]131; a spirit [5]394; and spirit [5]421; Spinoza's [1]566n, [3]78, 79–80, 854, 855, [4]228–9, [5]83n, 205; spirit of [2]208n, [3]546, [5]177, 653, 654; is spirit discerned [1]824; of Stoics [1]175; substitute [5]740; successive manifestations [1]355; as sun [5]703; supermundane [2]1106; Supreme [5]386; symbol of [3]108; synonymous with good [4]113; tetrad as [5]227; thoughts of [1]815, [3]88, [5]130; threats of [2]560; three in one [4]258; three knowledges of [1]793; threefold [1]681; total [1]618, 618n, [5]22; transcends intellect [2]334; and trifles [2]480; tri-une [1]574, 687, 688n, [2]270, [5]771; true [4]371, 371n; true Unity [2]1186; is truth [3]849; of truth [3]661, [5]484; truths of [5]417; as tyrant [4]662; and universe [1]179, [3]82, [4]141, 142; in universe [5]451; union with [3]417, 591–2, 919, [4]524n, [5]582; unity of [3]660, [5]54, 54n, 769; universal soul [6]116; unjust [5]154; unseen [3]431, 431n; in us [2]676; within us [1]178, 178n–9n; veracity of [5]617–18; very [5]626, 627; watchmaker [2]324, 342n; ways of [5]596; what he is not [2]745; not will [1]694; will not do impossibilities [4]423; will of [1]293, 311, 659, 820, 825, [2]666, [3]723, [4]341, 629, 656, [5]211, 385, 394, 410, 466, 606, 784; as wisdom [3]87, [4]366; wisdom of [3]674–5; word of *see* Word, of God; work(s) of [4]524, [5]616; and world [1]242n, 601, 621, 645–6, 649, 679, [2]629, 665, 788, 885, 1107, [3]296, 326, 416, 545, 649, 1091, [4]362, 407–9, 585, 585n, [5]368–9, 456, 461, 715, 730, [6]75–6; worship of [1]204, [3]1079, [4]681–2, [5]657; wrath of [1]605, [2]661, [3]747; Zinzendorf's theory [2]422–3. *See also* Deity; Father (God); Jehovah; mind, supreme; *theos*; Trinity; Tri-unity; Word

goddess(es) [1]654, [3]448, [5]227, 228, 732

"goddify" [6]75

Goderich, Viscount *see* Robinson, Frederick John

Godesberg [2]180

"godhead" [6]203

godhead [1]601, [3]534, [5]9n, 29, 59, 394, 717, 779, [6]132, 316
divinity of [2]21; filial [2]270, 1175, [5]717; living [1]602; tri-une [2]264; unity of [2]744, 790; Zinzendorf on [3]493

godlike, the [2]343, [5]93, 725

godlikeness [3]600

godliness [1]233, [3]250, 601

The Godly and Pious Institution of a Christian Man [5]393

godmother [3]1073, 1073n

Godolphin, Sidney, 1st Earl of Godolphin (1645–1712) *Elegie on D. D.* MT [2]242

Godwin, William (1756–1836) [1]511n, 745, *745n*, [2]117, 353, 847, *847n–8n*, [3]737, 806n
death of [1]clx; letter(s) to [1]cviii q, cix, [2]64n q, 845 q, [4]291n; quarrel with C [1]173n; supplier of books to C [1]741
"Abbas" MT [6]270–84; *Antonio, or the Soldier's Return* [4]95, 95n, [6]270; *Enquiry concerning Political Justice* [1]745n, [2]847, 847n, 850, [4]342n; *St Leon* [1]lxxix, lxxixn; *Thoughts Occasioned by the Perusal of Dr. Parr's Spital Sermon* [1]lxxx, [2]696; MT 845–51; [4]27

Goede, Henning (d 1521) [3]733 ("Hennage")

Goedecke, Karl (1814–87) *Grundriss zur Geschichte der deutschen Dichtung* [2]780n–1n

Goerwitz, E. F. (fl 1900) *see* Kant *Dreams of a Spirit-Seer* tr Goerwitz, ed Sewall

Goethe, Johann Wolfgang von (1749–1832) [1]100, 139, [2]179, 190, 863n, 1025, [3]395 q, 1014, 1018n q
on colour [3]1018; his descriptive style [1]138; Scott's imitation of [4]610, 610n, 611
Dichtung und Wahrheit [4]478n; *Faust* [1]cvii, [2]190n–1n; *Versuch die Metamorphose der Pflanzen zu erklären* [6]225; *Wilhelm Meisters Lehrjahre* [4]610n, 611; *Zur Farbenlehre* [1]131, 637n, [4]170, 187–8, [5]452n, 698n, tr Eastlake [3]1014n q, 1018n

Goeze, Johann Melchior (1717–86) [1]350, 350n, [3]667n, 670, 670n

Gog (Bible) [3]70
and Magog [3]481, 481n

goggles [2]199

Golconda [5]263

gold [1]215, 351, 545–6, 546n, 547n, 594, 603, 663, 775, 785, [2]311n, 619, 683, 855, [3]43, 286, 325, 916, 921, 1006, 1006n, 1007, [4]359, [5]260, 262, 264, 265, 275–6, 341, 540
image of [6]217; ingot of [5]451; leaf [2]238, [3]1059, [5]451; noble [5]283; rod of [4]189, 189n

Goldfuss, Georg August (1782–1848) [4]448n
Handbuch der Zoologie MT [2]852–63

Goldingham, John (fl 1808–29) [3]936

Goldschmidt, Joannes *see* Aurifaber

Goldsmith, Oliver (c 1730–74) [1]38
Collected Works ed Friedman [3]200n; *History of England* [3]184, 184n; *A Reverie at . . . Eastcheap* [3]200, 200n; *The Vicar of Wakefield* [3]184, 184n
Goldthwait, John T. *see* Kant *Observations on . . . the Sublime* tr Goldthwait
Golgotha [1]41n
Goliath ("Goliah") (Bible) [2]914, 1179
Gomer (Bible) [3]70, [5]337
Goneril (*King Lear*) [1]393, [4]732, 732n, 772, 817, 818, 819, 820, 821
"good" [2]562, [6]309, 309n
good, the [2]930, [3]13, 18, 460, 532, 558, 989, [4]421n, [5]410, 740
absolute [1]435, 460, 620, 824, [2]326, [3]30, [6]83; abysmal [3]30, 428; adequate [1]875; built on error [5]308; and evil *see* evil; fruition of [5]796; in Gen [2]137; greatest [2]559; hate of [1]731; idea of [3]12; love of [2]186, [3]9; manifested [2]305; as means or end [1]185, 185n; nature [4]429; one absolute [5]482; personal [3]151; public [4]733; radical [5]373; relative and absolute [2]322–3; supreme [5]796; temper [5]652; true [5]37; and true [3]459; ultimate [1]185
Good Friday [1]327
Gooden, James (fl 1815–22), letter to [1]409
"goodiness" [6]122n
goodness [1]397, 573, [4]111, 113, 744, 817
divine [3]456; equivocal [1]803; free [1]573; of God [4]444, [5]613, 653; infinite [2]562; overflowing of [1]564; perfect [4]819; process to [2]27
goods [2]325–6
community of [5]645; worldly [2]569
Goodwin, Albert *The Friends of Liberty* [5]282n
Goodwin, George (fl 1798) [1]92n
"Goodwin, J." (fl 1800) *Lines to Sarah* MT [1]92; 92n
Goodwin, John (b c 1680) [3]822
Goodwin Sands [1]lxxii, [2]520, 520n
"goody" [6]122, 122n
goody/goodies [3]161, [5]103, 103n
Googe, Barnabe (1540–94) *see* Palingenius *Zodiacus vitae* tr Googe
goose [2]192, 809n, [3]587, 765n, 769, 952
gooseberry [4]267
gooseturd [5]835, 835n
Gordon, Sir Cosmo (1777–1867) *The Life and Genius of Lord Byron* [4]76n
Gordon, John, Viscount Kenmure (?1599–1634) [2]1169 ("Kinmuir"), 1176 ("Kenmuir")
Gordon, Thomas (d 1750) *see* Trenchard and Gordon
gore, brother by [3]708
gorge [2]136
Gorgias of Leontium (c 485–c 375 BC) [2]869, *869n*, [5]719n, 720–2
On Nature [2]869n
Gorgonia, St (4th century) [2]748–9
Görlitz [1]553, 558, 565, 566n, 597
Gorman, T. H. *see* Swedenborg *Concerning the White Horse* tr Gorman
Goslar [1]672n, [3]1072
"gospel" [1]702n
gospel(s) [4]623, 628, 638, 640, 641, 643, 645, [5]81n, 272, 417, 505
Christian [2]708; dispensation of [3]496; doctrine of [5]162; everlasting [2]452, [5]535; every Church has [6]68; of Father [3]427; of Holy Ghost [3]427; hope in [5]483; of infancy see *evangelium infantiae*; institute [5]661; according to Irving [3]56; knowledge of [1]446; and law [3]744–6; liberty of [2]37, 676, [3]776, [5]603, [6]105; light of [5]85; mean between extremes [5]420 ("Gospeal"); meaning of [3]726; a mockery [5]154; plain [5]151–2; preached in fragments [3]743; precepts of [3]696; process of [3]741; purpose of [5]394; as remedy [6]28; saving truths of [2]1156; of Son [3]427; spirit of [1]329, [2]266; spurious [1]492; Syro-chaldaic [4]68, 68n; tenets [1]845; true idea of immortality [2]1186; truth of [5]188; veracity of [5]65; verity/verities of [3]42, [5]52; *see also* Bible: NT: GOSPEL(S)
"gossamer" [6]149
gossamer [3]1067
Gosse, Sir Edmund (1849–1928) [2]926
"gossip" [6]149
gossip(s) [1]763, 796, [2]667, 917, [3]1067, [4]55, 121, 272, 724, [6]58, 63
gossiping [2]667, [5]319
Goth(s) [1]540, [4]308, [5]337
Gothenburg [3]203, 351, 351n, 352
Gothic (language) [2]271, 380, 898, [3]400, [4]37, 37n, 282, 282n, 290n, [6]17, 17n, 286; *see also* Teutonic
Gothic, the (race) [4]37n, 78, 583
Gottesthal [2]982
Göttingen [2]146n, 188n, 369, 396n, 796, [3]794n, 1040n, [4]164, 282n, 432n, 466n, [5]91n, [6]148, 294n
C in [1]149n–50n; University [2]146n, 373, Library [1]ciii
Göttingisches Journal der Naturwissenschaften [6]153n

Gottsched, Johann Christoph (1700–66) *see* Leibniz *Theodicee* ed Gottsched
Gouge, Robert (1630–1705) [1]353n
Gouge, Thomas (1609–81) [1]352, 352n
Gouger, Robert (1802–66) *see* E. G. Wakefield *A Letter from Sydney* ed Gouger
Gough, John (1757–1825) [3]937, 952n
  "On the Place of a Sound, Produced by a Musical String" 943; MT 952–3
gourmandise [4]193
gout [1]786n, [2]159
governing [1]164, 341–2
government(s) [2]1206, [3]142, 150, [4]21, [5]36–43, 102, 278, 301, 321, 361–2, 362, [6]36, 51
  American [6]37; of Church [5]537; Danish [5]312; despotic [1]305; duties of [6]44; existing [5]146; free [6]46; French [6]121; good [5]40; highest act of [1]339; Indian [5]416; jealous [5]596; kingly [5]307; law of [4]12; Locke's theory of [4]12n; mixed [4]79; papistic [2]1104; prelatical [1]809; principles of [6]51; prudent [4]483; Roman [2]1153; a science [6]52; and state [3]787–8; theory of [4]12
governor(s) [1]309
  moral [5]519; Roman [2]485; of world [2]404
Gowa, Juliette (fl 1853) *see* J. P. F. Richter *The Campaner Thal* tr Gowa
Gowan, J. R. (fl 1810) [3]937
Gowar, F. R. (fl 1810) [3]941
Gower (*Pericles*) [3]893
Gower, Barry [2]853n, 863n q
Gower, John (?1330–1408) [3]1070 q, [4]809, 809n
gown [4]731, [5]504
Gozzi, Carlo (1722–1806) [1]506, *506n*
  Opere [1]506n
Grabe, Johannes Ernst (1666–1711) [1]800, [2]417n, [6]69; *see also* Bull *Defensio* ed Grabe
Gracchi, the [3]797, 797n
Gracchus, Caius Sempronius (153–121 BC) [3]797n
Gracchus, Tiberius Sempronius (163–133 BC) [3]797n
"grace" [4]663
grace(s) [1]483, 574, 757n, [2]265, 281, 496, 592, 642, 998, 1062, 1162, [3]50, 54, 55, 310, 434, 552, 564, 740, 741, 744, 747, 752, 776, [4]260, 629, 635–6, 644, 648, 672, 691, 738, [5]72, 159, 182, 593, 596
  Attic [2]774; auxiliary [1]358, [2]332; babes of [5]544; of Christ [5]610; covenant of [5]623; divine [1]283, 344, 820, [5]470; enlightening [5]569; estate of [5]598; free [1]149, 601, [4]634; gift of [5]602–3, 820; of God [2]592, 1176, 1178, [4]643, [5]463, 516, 516n, 584; infused [2]331; instrument of [5]675; irrefragable [3]818; meaning of [1]826; means of [2]326, [5]670; before meat [5]546; prevenient [2]327; reasonless [1]824; restraining [3]771; spiritual [1]582, 813; superadded [5]529
Graceless (in Bunyan) [4]653n
gradation(s) [1]752, [3]755
  of species [5]388
gradative [1]550, 550n
grade(s)
  in animal magnetism [3]377, 377n, 386, 387, 868; Böhme's [1]610, 611n; ecstatic [5]183; magnetic [3]375, *see also* animal magnetism
gradual, the [1]619, [5]360
Gradus ad Parnassum ed Morell [6]213n
Graeme, James (1749–83) [1]38
Graeme, Roland (in Scott) [4]598, 598n, 599, 600
Graf, Karl Heinrich (1815–69) [1]417n
Grafton, Duke of *see* Fitzroy, Augustus Henry
Graham, James, Marquis of Montrose (1612–50) [1]301n
grain [1]468, [3]68
Grainger, James (c 1721–66) *see* Tibullus tr Grainger
grammar [2]881n, [3]15, [4]164, 167n, 292, 322
  common error of [3]829; English [3]897; false [2]992; German [1]7, *see also* Coleridge, S. T. VIII German grammar; Greek [1]7, [3]827–36, *see also* Coleridge, S. T. VIII Greek grammar; Italian [3]930–1; Latin [3]154n, 513, 897, [5]174; morals of g. writers [3]930; pentad of [3]1012n, [4]166n; philosophic(al) [3]647n, 832, [4]156; of philosophy [5]95; universal [4]166n; use of [3]834–5
grammarians [1]756
grammatici [2]36, [3]447, [5]225, 225n
grampuses [1]431, [4]533
Granada [3]927 ("Grenada"), 927n
Granby, Marquis of *see* Manners, John
grand, the [2]1070
Grand Monarque (Louis XIV) [4]75
grandchildren [5]278
grandfather [5]730
Granger, Mrs (fl 1721–4) [5]49
granite [1]572, [3]302, 630, [5]245–6, 338
grannams [3]373, 373n
Grant, Colonel [4]489–90
grantee [4]381

granulation [2]365
Granville, George, Baron Lansdowne (1667–1735) [1]38
grape(s) [1]246, [3]879, [5]496
g.-vine [4]278
Grasby [5]853
Grasmere [1]xciii, cx, cxn, 227n, [2]1118n, 1122, [3]499, 503, 974, [6]121, 210
Allan Bank [1]lxxxvi, lxxxviii, xcii, cxi, cxii, clviii, clixn, clxvii, 41, 52, 217, 393n, 698, 743, 761, 854, [2]117, 132, 245, 474n, 647, 787, 874, 973n, 1119n, 1203, [3]178n, 980, [6]290, 291; Dove Cottage, Wordsworth Library/Trust [1]lxxx, cix, cx, clxviiin, clxxiv, 39, 76, 227n, 698, 760, [2]116, [3]837n, [4]282, marginalia in [1]76, 226, [3]980, [4]139, 282, 289, [6]187, 194, 197, transcript(s) of marginalia in [1]761, [5]108, WW mss in [2]132n
grasp [2]960
grasshopper(s) [1]421, [2]646n, [5]105
Gratian (Augustus Gratianus) (359–83) [1]109, 109n, [2]930
Gratian (Franciscus Gratianus) (12th century) [4]238n, [5]573n, 633, 634
Concordia discordantium canonum [4]238n, [5]573n
gratifications [5]379
Grattan, Henry (1746–1820) [4]22, 24n
Gratz, Peter Alois (1769–1849) [3]421n, [4]469–70, 474n
grave(s) [1]764, 797, [2]569
gravel, deluvial [2]164
Graver, Bruce Edward *see* WW *Translations of Chaucer and Virgil* ed Graver
Graves, Robert Percival (1812–99) [1]clxviii
Gravina, Giovanni Vincenzo (1664–1718) [2]949, 949n
De romano imperio [2]949, 949n, [3]149, 149n; *Opera* [2]949n, [3]149n
gravitation [1]547, 572, 593, 597, 599, 604, 623, 624, 643, 651, 660, 793n, [2]201, 787n, 788, 789n, 853n, 855n, [3]729, 1008, 1025n, [4]20, 94, 396, 506, 516, [5]159, 438, [6]173
and gravity [1]665; law of [5]351, 351n; and light [6]230; power of depth [1]571
gravity [1]590, 637, 663, 665, 785, 862, [2]854n, 1019–20, [3]139n, 286, 286n, 518, 518n, 546, 851, 946, 1056, [4]522–3, [5]438, [6]226, 228, 300
and attraction *see* attraction; body of [3]1057n; centre of [2]147, [3]379, 379n; and gravitation *see* gravitation; humorous [1]763, 796; as hypothesis [1]108; law of [5]351n, 425; mousing [5]767; peculiar [5]338; poles of [1]663; power of depth [3]139; power stronger than [4]535–6; specific [2]189, [3]1031n, 1033, 1033n, 1068, [5]351, 438, [6]245, 245n
Gray, Robert, Bishop of Bristol (1762–1834) [2]1105
Gray, Thomas (1716–71) [1]cix, 38, 240, [3]412, 893n, [4]105, 107, 291n, [5]117n
on Plato [5]749, 749n–50n
The Bard [2]155, 155n, 224n, 864, [3]411 q, [4]291; *De principiis cogitandi* [2]867n; *Elegy* [2]864, [6]324n; *Ode for Music* [2]140n q; *Ode on a Distant Prospect* [2]864; MT 865–6; *Ode to Adversity* MT [2]866; *Odes* [1]566n, [2]94; *Poems* [1]566n, ed R. Lonsdale [2]867n; *The Progress of Poesy* [2]140n q; *Some Account of . . . Plato* MT [2]866–72; *The Works* ed T. J. Mathias [1]cxxxviii; MT [2]864–72; [4]105n, [5]750n
grazier [2]210
"great" [6]39
great, the [5]99n
Great Britain [2]474, 951, 979, [3]478, 680, [4]672, [5]41, 144, 196, 866
empire of [1]732–3; limited king of [2]1101; medicine in [3]843; richest country [2]621; ruin of [6]44; and Spain [3]696, 696n
greatness [1]715, [3]168
Greatrakes/Gretrakes, Valentine (1629–83) [2]452, 452n
Greece [1]430, 771n, [2]416, 480, 570, 573, 578n, 820n, 1123, [3]419, 474, [4]191n, 507, [5]39n, 127, 337n, 645, 693n, 747, [6]5n
ancient [3]649; conquest of [2]156n; history [3]110; literature [4]100, 691, 723; lyrics [2]413, 413n; mythology [3]92n, 473; numbers [4]36–8; pantheism [3]901; philosophers *see* philosophers, Greek; philosophy *see* philosophy, Greek; polytheism [2]664–5, [3]135–6, 135n; satires [2]757; states [3]108n; tragedy *see* tragedy, Greek
greed [2]1113
Greek (language) [1]73, 377, 415, 461, 470, 607, 670, [2]380–1, 427, 485, 514, 561, 653, 706, 734, 739, 1119n, [3]442, 466, 550, 1086, 1087n, [4]37, 37n, 38, 90n, 168, 185, 248, 248n, 251n, 290, 473–4, 509, 509n, 595n, 687, [5]9, 10, 238n, 396, 688, [6]4, 25–7, 59, 140, 149–50, 295, 304–5, 304n, 312
ambiguity in [3]19; antediluvian language [2]576; aorist tense [2]711, 711n; Apocrypha mostly G. [2]374; Attic [4]37; blest [2]1119; dialects of [2]89; elegant [6]27; and English

Greek (language)—*continued*
[3]403; English pronunciation of [2]1092; Faber's knowledge of [2]581–2; and German [3]646–7; grammar *see* grammar, Greek; grammars for DC and HC [2]3; hebraised [6]139; Hellenistic [2]469; influence on Hebrews [2]419; Jonson's [3]194; in middle ages [2]12n; modern [3]831, 831n, [4]171, [6]150; neuter plural [2]226, 226n; pronunciation of [2]66–7, 66n, 68, [3]828; in Septuagint [2]379–81; tongue-twister [2]354, 354n

Greek(s) (people) [1]431, 485, [2]410, 421, 758, 759, 1016, 1022, 1052n, 1071n, [3]206, 429, 820, [4]454, 513, 780, 810, [5]10, 234, 307, 328–9, 337, 551, 702, 786–7, 830, 830n, 843
anthropomorphism of [2]901; borrowed Hindu fable [2]584; Christian [4]672, [6]150; cosmogony of [1]120; dispersed [3]447; eulogised [2]1071; games of [5]323; Iapetic race [1]540; mathematician [3]726; modern [4]184; monarch [3]722; sages [3]649; had slaves [5]323

Greek Anthology [2]377

Greeking [2]446

Greeklade [2]821

green [3]1018, [4]167, 358

Green, Ann Eliza (née Hammond) (d 1879) [1]clvi, clxiv, clxivn, clxix, [2]180, 650, 905n

Green, Frances (née Cline) (c 1763–c 1853) [4]681, [6]32

Green, Joseph Henry (1791–1863) [1]481, 553, 761, [2]35n, 794, 825n, 966, 967, [3]295n, 378n, 900n, 1019n, 1060n, [4]327, 327n, 402, 681, [5]175n, 771n, [6]32, 334
annotations by [2]896n, [3]239, [6]335; bequest [1]clxx, 211, [2]852, [3]863, 993, [4]32, 213, 332, [5]373, [6]25, 177; book annotated for [6]73; burial of [2]905n; Calvinist [1]476; C's amanuensis [5]777n; C's executor [1]cxiv, cxviii, cxxiii, cxxiv, cxxvii, cxxxiii, cxxxiv, cxln, cxliii, cxlixn, cl, cli, clvi, clviii–clx, clxix; collaboration with C [5]784n; death of [1]clxi, clxiv; first meeting with C [2]958; Green List [1]clvi, clvin, clxiv, [2]650, 1169, [3]178n; introduction to C [4]538n; "Ja-aitchgee" [4]488; lectures at Royal College of Surgeons [5]252n; letter(s) from C to [1]414 q, 556, 602n, 660n q, 822n q, [2]361 q, 435 q, 595 q, 904n, 958 q, [3]1050n, [4]10, 11, 375n, 381n, [5]762n q; letter from J. Gillman to [1]cxliin; letter from SH to [2]1117 q; letter to Wade [2]5; library [1]55n, 288n, 390n, 425n, 655n, 854, [2]91, 181, 824n, 1033, 1101n, 1112, 1189, [3]184n, 504n; library sale [1]cli, cliin, clxiv–clxv, clxvi, 6n, [2]180; *LR* dedicated to [1]cxxv; marginalia addressed to [2]1002, 1002n, 1007, 1007n, 1015, 1015n, 1026, 1026n, [3]348, 348n, 1019, [4]487, 538n, [5]268, 287n, 296, 691, 744n, 772, 776, 777n; medical career [1]cxxxviiin; and *Opus Maximum* [3]295n; "our Scheme" [3]1020, 1020n–1n; owner of annotated books [1]lxxiv, cxlin, clviii, clxx, 131, 535, [2]478, 503, 519, 623, 880, 988, 998, 1050, [3]256, 316, 336, 655, 811, 906, 1019, [4]487, [5]96, 101, 691; his reaction to *LR* [1]cxlii; retirement of [1]cxxxviii, clx; studies with C [4]327, 327n, 345, 373, 391, 488n, 504; supplier of books to C [1]xcviii, cvi, 131, 513n, [2]373, [3]257, [4]156n, [5]87, 748n, [6]164; transcriber of marginalia [2]558, 689; use of "Green" wm [4]10n
Catalogue of the Library of Joseph Henry Green (1880) [1]154, 205, 296n, 425n, 513n, 627n, 688n, 719n, 761, 800, [2]14, 23, 44, 131, 181, 212, 474n, 525, 577n, 593, 791, 796, 804, 814n, 841, 842, 958, 1033, 1050, 1064, 1072, 1115, 1116, [3]184n, 239, 252, 263, 314, 414, 811, 862, [4]39, 232, 468, 680, [5]46n, 87, 91n, 221, 239, 376, 440, 849, [6]128, 129, 224; *Catalogue of Scarce and Valuable Books* (1884) [2]593, 791; *Dissector's Manual* [5]175n; *Distinction without Separation* [4]366n; *Mental Dynamics* [1]clxn; *Spiritual Philosophy* ed J. Simon [1]cxxxviiin, clxn, [2]859n; *Vital Dynamics* [1]clxn, 344n, 550n

Green, Matthew (1697–1737) [1]38

Green, Thomas Hill (1836–82) *see* Hume *Essays* ed Green and Grose

Green, T. M. *see* Kant *Religion within the Limits of Reason Alone* tr Green and Hudson

Greene, Richard (fl 1810) [3]936

Greene, Richard Wilson (1792–1861) *Report of the Trial of James Forbes* [3]500

Greene, Robert (1558–92) *Tu Quoque* [2]217n

green-finch [6]151

Greenlander(s) [1]431, [2]1113, [4]303

Greenough, George Bellas (1778–1855) [1]lxxxii, 204n ("Charles")

Greg, Sir Walter Wilson (1875–1959) *see* B&F *Works* ed Bond and Greg

Gregor, Mary J. *see* Kant *Anthropology, Conflict of the Faculties, Doctrine of Virtue* tr Gregor
Gregor, William (1761–1817) [3]941
Gregories [4]643
Gregory, St (c 240–332) [2]317
Gregory I, the Great, St, Pope (c 540–604) [2]969, 969n, [3]763, 765, [5]138n
Letters [2]969n; *Moralia* [2]423n, 969n
Gregory III, St, Pope (d 741) [5]636
Gregory VII, St (Hildebrand), Pope (c 1020–85) [5]577
Gregory of Nazianzus, St ("Nazianzen") (c 329–c 390) [1]245, [2]295 q, 296 q, 296n q, 746, 746n, 747, [3]143, 143n, 145 q, 147, 489, 490n, 524, [6]92 q, 307
Gregory of Nyssa, St ("Nyssen") (331–95) [2]296n, [3]620, [5]20, 21, 22, 22n, 24, 25, 26, 28, 524, 636
De pauperibus amandis ed von Heck [2]364 q, 364n q
Gregory Thaumaturgus, St, Bishop of Neocaesarea (c 210–70) [6]61
Gregory XIII (Ugo Buoncompagni) Pope (1502–85) [2]1153
Greig, James (1861–1941) *see* Farington *Diary* ed Greig
Grellmann, Heinrich Moritz Gottlieb (1756–1804) [6]150
Dissertation on the Gipsies tr Raper [6]150n; *Die Zigeuner* [6]150n
"grelly" [5]301, 301n
Gren, Friedrich Albert Karl (1760–98) [4]396
Grenville, Sir Richard (1600–58) [1]293 ("Greenvile")
Greta (river) [1]43n, [4]520n
Greta Bridge [4]520
Greta Hall *see* Keswick
Greville, Fulke, 1st Baron Brooke (1554–1628) [1]lxxxiv, cviii, cxvi, clxiii, [2]976, 976n, [3]250, 251n, [4]620
Alaham [2]873, 874, 874n; *Caelica* [2]873; MT 875–7; *Certaine Learned and Elegant Workes* [1]xci, clxiii; MT [2]873–9; [4]620n; *An Inquisition upon Fame and Honour* [2]874, 874n; *The Nature of Truth* [2]873; *A Treatie of Warres* [2]873; *A Treatise of Humane Learning* [2]873, 874, [4]620 q, 620n
Greville, Robert, 2nd Baron Brooke (1608–43) [2]1200 ("Brook"), 1200n
Nature of Episcopacy [2]1200n
Grew, Nehemiah (1641–1712) [1]114, 114n
Cosmologia Sacra MT [2]880–906
Grey, Charles, 2nd Earl Grey (1764–1845) [1]724n, [2]907, 909n, [3]141, 153, 164, [6]46, 46n, 47, 47n, 49
Grey, Henry George, Viscount Howick (1802–94) *Corrected Report of the Speech ... on Colonial Slavery* [1]33n, 35n; MT [2]907–9; [4]8
Grey, Lady Jane (1537–54) [2]938n
Grey, Richard (1694–1771) *Memoria Technica* [1]771n
Grey, Zachary (1688–1766) [3]183
greyhound [1]lix, [2]1158n, [5]293
RS as [1]331, 331n
Gribbel, John [5]486
Grickle *see* Agricola, John
grief [1]54, 483, [2]173, [3]553, [4]267, 480, 709
Grierson, Sir Herbert John Clifford (1866–1960) *see* Donne *Poems* ed Grierson
Griesbach, Johann Jakob (1745–1812) [1]466, 490n, [2]473n, 518n; *see also* Bible: NT: Greek: ed Griesbach
Griffith/Griffiths, George (fl 1657) [4]182
Griffith, Thomas (d 1883) *Life a Pilgrimage* [4]3
Griggs, Earl Leslie (1899–1974) [1]clxxi, [2]1118n
Coleridge Fille [1]lviii–lix q, cxlixn q; *see also* HC *Letters* ed Griggs and Griggs; Coleridge, S. T. x *Unpublished Letters* ed Griggs
Griggs, Grace Evelyn (née Riley) (b 1900) *see* HC *Letters* ed Griggs and Griggs
Grille, E. A. [2]1032
Grille, R. H. [2]1032
Grimm, Friedrich Melchior von, Baron (1723–1807) *Correspondance littéraire ... par le Baron de Grimm et par Diderot* ed Suard [4]170
Grimm, Jacob Ludwig Carl (1785–1863) [3]870n
and W. C. Grimm *Deutsches Wörterbuch* [1]829n, [5]181n, 497n
Grimm, Wilhelm Carl (1786–1859) *see* Grimm, Jacob Ludwig Carl
grin(s) [3]382, [4]627
Grindal, Edmund, Archbishop of Canterbury (c 1519–83) [1]531, 531n, [2]1139n–40n, 1142, 1157, [5]389–91
grindstone [2]734, [3]660, 661
Grisdale Hawes [1]cx
Groningen [6]71
Gronovius, Johann Friedrich (1611–71) [3]505n

groom [5]366
Grose, Thomas Hodge (1845–1906) *see* Hume *Essays* ed Green and Grose
Grosschopf, Arnold Heinrich (1772–1844) see *Die Orakel des Propheten Mica* ed Grosschopf
grossness [3]171
of language [3]171, 171n
Grotian(s) [2]450, [3]612, 613n
G. mode of defending Christianity [1]244, 244n
Grotianism [6]134, 134n
Grotius, Hugo (Hugo de Groot) (1583–1645) [1]199n–200n, 244n, 258, 258n, 269n, 275, 317, 346n, [2]528, 528n, 897, 913n, [3]308, 515n, 562, 664, 666, 722, 722n, 763n, 923, 924, 924n, 926, 929n, [4]256n, [5]34, 35, 81, 81n, 513, 513n, 522, 523, 598, 649, 649n, 667 ("Grotian"), [6]18, 71, 165, 297n
anti-Grotian [3]666; "Grotio-Paleyan"/"Paleyo-Grotian" [1]200n, 244n, 288, [2]450n, 651, [5]598; over-rated [3]928; between popery and Socinianism [2]652
Annotata ad Vetus Testamentum [2]897n; *Annotationes in libros evangeliorum* [5]523n q; *De jure belli et pacis*† [1]clxx, 199n, 292 q, 292n, [2]910, [6]18n, tr as *The Rights of War and Peace* [1]292n; *De veritate religionis Christianae* [1]199n, [5]598n; *Discussio Apologetici Rivetiani* [1]257
Grotta del Cane [2]69 ("Grotto"), 69n
Grotthuss, Theodor (Christian Johann Dietrich) von (1785–1822) [3]941
grotto [2]164
"ground" [1]238
ground(s) [2]666, [3]86, 87, 855, [4]443
absolute [3]359, [5]210; abysmal [3]66; alien [6]65; antecedent [5]738; of being [2]324, [3]876, [5]75; and cause [5]206; and existence [1]584–5; of existence [4]425; of existents [5]203; and form [3]60; formal [1]647; in God [1]561; of God [1]636–7, [3]84; of humanity [3]27; idea of [3]90–1; immanifestable [3]12; insight into [5]269; intelligent [2]665; of life [1]646; material [5]397; of necessary things [3]347; objective [5]291; g.-power [5]784; triune [5]742; g.-work [2]687
grounding, eternal [3]90
grove(s) [1]764, 797, [5]99n
Grove, Sir George (1820–1900) [2]361, [3]1064
Grove, The *see* Highgate
growth [1]401, 468, 692, 792, [2]367, [4]428, [5]583
bodily [5]825; eternal [1]574; in the faith [5]623; form of [1]612; full [5]169; germs of [4]106; mental [1]508; spiritual [5]578; of truth [5]561
Grub Street *see* London
Grübelgeiste [5]767
Gruber, Johann Gottfried (1744–1851) [1]535; *see also* Blumenbach *De generis humani varietate, Über die natürlichen Verschiedenheiten* tr Gruber
grudge [1]347
Grumbkow, Friedrich Wilhelm von (1678–1739) [3]217 ("Grum Cow"), 217n
Grundkraft/*Grundkräfte* [2]1009, [3]284, 296
Gruter *see* Gruytere
Gruytere, Jan (1560–1627) [2]102 ("Gruter")
Gryphius (Andreas Greif) (1616–64) [2]781–2
Peter Squenz [2]782
Guarani (language) [5]104
guardian(s) [1]395, [4]466, [5]193
Guardian [1]60n q
Guarini, Giovanni Batista (1538–1612) [1]lxxxiv
guerilla(s) [2]163
guess(es) [5]561
game of [4]158; Kantean [5]707
guessers [5]597
guessing [5]640, 705
guest [1]587
guild [6]79
Guilford, Earl of *see* North, Frederick
guillotine [3]42
guilt [1]691, 812, [2]602, 802, [3]18, 63, 120, 306–7, [4]234–5, 503, 503n, 590, 652, 718, 729, 788, 792, [5]425, 559, 588, 592, 613, 614, 656, [6]304
abolition of [2]657; consequences of [2]559; degree of [2]108; of drunkard [5]584; essence of [4]662; evil of [2]800; extenuation of [1]342; of falsehood [6]262; of habit [4]854; hereditary [5]594, 596; original [5]592, 650, 655; originating [5]420; reduced to error [3]851; and sin [3]18, [5]616
guilty, the [4]238
guinea(s) [5]16, 341
Parnassian [2]238
"Gulielmus" [3]986
Gulielmus Antistodorensis (? Altissiodorensis, d 1237) [2]685
gulls [5]396
gums [3]44
gun [1]868
gunner [3]301
gunpowder [3]301, 302, [4]757

Gunville [3]627
Gustavus Adolphus, King of Sweden (1594–1632) [1]850, 850n, [3]754, 754n
Gutch, John Matthew (1776–1861) [4]27
letter to [1]870 q
Guthkelch, Adolph Charles Louis (d 1916) *see* Swift *Tale of a Tub* ed Guthkelch and D. N. Smith
Guthrie, William (1708–70) *A New Geographical, Historical, and Commercial Grammar* [5]309, 309n, 846n
guts [1]655, 657
gutta serena [1]810, 810n, [2]492n
gutter [2]1064
Guy of Dampierre, Count of Flanders (1225–1305) [5]194
Guyon du Chesnoy, Jeanne Marie Bouvier de La Motte, Mme (1648–1717) [1]557n
Guyton de Morveau, Louis Bernard, Baron (1737–1816) [3]937, 938, 940, 943, [6]233
Guzman, Juan de (16th century) *see* Virgil *Georgica . . . hexaglotta* tr Guzman
Gyas (in Virgil) [6]205
"gymnosoph" [5]71, 71n
"gymnosophist" [5]71n
gymnotus electricus [3]868, 868n
gypsy/gypsies [4]583–4, 584–5, 788, [5]106, 861, [6]149, 150, 150n
king of [2]824; learned [3]646; g. questions [3]644

Habakkuk (Bible) [1]453n
Habassines [2]660
"habit" [5]175
habit(s) [1]4, [2]29, 636, [3]63, 237, 237n, 501, 579, 963, [4]461, 662, 796, [5]99
acquired [1]657; aorist implies [6]165; of certainty [3]682; condemned by [5]419; cultivation of [3]312; evil [1]12n; guilt of [4]854; involuntary [3]265; of memory [3]265; moral [5]592; parent of conviction [6]126; of presentiment [5]723; sinful [5]463n; tyranny of [3]510, 512, [4]465, 465n; unchristian [5]562; of virtue [2]603
Hacket, Colonel (fl 1665) [2]1171n
Hacket, John (1592–1670) [1]850, [2]260, 260n, 1041n, 1101n
A Century of Sermons MT [2]911–25; [5]662, 662n; *Scrinia Reserata: a Memorial . . . to . . . John Williams* [1]cxlvin, [2]259, 911, 917, 917n, 925; MT 926–51; 1102n
Hackforth, Reginald (1887–1957) *see* Plato *Phaedrus* tr Hackforth
Hackney *see* London
Hadad (Bible) [1]418
Haddesley, C. R. [5]854
Haden, Charles Thomas (1786–1824) *Practical Observations on the Colchicum Autumnale* [4]617, 285
Hades [1]431, 464, [2]69, 239, 278, 327, 334, 564, 583, 583n, 584, 891, 891n, [3]28, 28n, 37, 46n, 56, 57, 62, 215, 433, 612–13, 1024, [4]491, 491n, [6]63; *see also* hell
Hadley [1]cxxxviii, cxxxviiin, clx
Hadrian/Adrian (Publius Aelius Hadrianus) (76–138) [1]176, 191, [2]692, 718, [3]106, 448, 448n, [4]251, 251n, [6]60
haecceitas/haecceitates [5]789, 790
haemony [2]974n
Haemus, Mount [1]464
Hagar (Bible) [2]1137 ("Agar"), [6]110
Haggadoth [3]103, 103n
Haggai (Bible) [2]149n, 894
hagiographa [2]156, 376n, 377, 408, 409n, 467, 894, [6]319
hagiographist [3]310
hagiolatry [1]257n, [2]35, 35n, 37
hagiopneumatists [3]73
hagios [3]151
Hague, The [1]699
hail [2]897, [5]340
Haime *see* Hayme
Haines, Charles Reginald (1859–1935) *see* Aurelius *Communings with Himself* tr Haines
hair(s) [2]178, 611, [3]488, [4]283, 283n, 461, [5]834
of Cavaliers [2]512; of horse [2]800, 800n, [4]737; h.-lines [4]758; long [1]461; sparks from [5]577
haireo [5]11n
hairesis [4]98
Hakluyt, Richard (c 1552–1616) [2]165n
halb [1]20–1
Haldane, Elizabeth Sanderson (1862–1937) *see* Descartes *Philosophical Works* tr Haldane and Ross
Haldat du Lys, Charles Nicolas Alexandre de (1770–1852) [3]938, 947
"hale" [1]169, 169n
Hale, Sir Matthew ("Hales") (1609–76) [1]807, *807n*, [3]190, 190n, 920, 920n
Pleas of the Crown [2]129, 129n
Hale, Nathan (1755–76) [2]952n
Hale, Nathan (1784–1863) [2]*952n*
The American System MT [2]952–3; *Epitome of Universal Geography* [2]952n
half
better [2]87; and whole [1]725, 848n; h.-

half—*continued*
truth(s) [1]331, [2]266, 328, 940, 1139, [3]33, [5]81, 136, 349, 617, *see also* truth(s)
halieus [2]576n
Halieus (myth) [2]576
Halifax, Earl of *see* Montagu, Charles
Halifax/Hallifax, Samuel, Bishop of Gloucester (1733–90) [1]867
Hall, John (1627–56) [2]954, 954n
Hierocles [2]954n; *An Humble Motion to the Parliament . . . Concerning the Advancement of Learning* [2]110, 111; MT 954–7
Hall, Joseph, Bishop of Exeter and Norwich (1574–1656) [1]37, 156n, 332n, 845n, 849, [2]14, 759–60, 1131, [5]384, 646, 646n, [6]102 q
blot of the C of E [1]844–5
To the Praise of the Dead, and the Anatomy [2]231n; *Virgidemiarum* [2]760n; *Works* [5]384n q
Hall, Marshall (1790–1857) [3]940, 941, 942
Hall, Robert (1764–1831) [2]850, 1184, [4]3
Hall, Samuel Carter (1800–89) [1]55n, 74n, 75n, 154
annotator [1]52–3, 54n
ed *Amulet* [1]154; *The Book of Gems* [1]52–3
Hallam, Arthur Henry (1811–33) *Letters* ed Kolb [5]817n
Hallam, Henry (1777–1859) [4]16, [6]184
The Constitutional History of England [4]16
Halle [3]319n, [5]540n
Halle University [2]981n, 999n, 1016n, [3]764n
hallelujahs [4]53, 409
Haller, Albrecht von (1708–77) [1]100, [2]1026n
a Socinian [1]197
Halley, Edmund (1656–1742) [4]395–6, 396n, 518n
Halloy, J. J. Omalius d' *see* Omalius d'Halloy
halo [3]454
halogen [3]1027, 1031, 1032
Halyburton, Thomas (1674–1712) [5]172 ("Haliburton"), 172n
Memoirs of the Life [1]714n, [5]172n
Ham (Bible) [1]539, 541n, 684, 685, [2]177, 177n, 577, 577n, [4]257, 583n, [5]336–7, 337n, 352, [6]5n
land of [1]540; race of [6]5
Haman (Bible) [2]401
Hamann, Johann Georg (1730–88) [2]188n, [4]372, [5]325
hamartia [2]490
Hamburg [1]lxxviii, lxxix, cv, 350, 671, 697, 828, [2]1048, [4]90
Hamilton, James (1749–1835) [6]39
Observations on the Utility and Administration of Purgative Medicines [3]843, 843n–4n, [6]39n
Hamilton, James, 1st Duke of Hamilton and Castleherald (1606–49) *see* G. Burnet *Memoires*
Hamilton, Robert (fl 1818) "On the Early History and Symptoms of Lues" MT [2]362–4
Hamilton, William (1704–54) [1]38
Hamilton, William (fl 1791) *see* Berthollet *Eléments* tr Hamilton
Hamilton, William, 2nd Duke of Hamilton and Castleherald (1616–51) [2]60; *see also* G. Burnet *Memoires*
Hamilton, Sir William (1730–1803) *Campi Phlegraei* [1]449n
Hamilton, Sir William Rowan (1805–65) *On a General Method of Expressing the Paths of Light, and of the Planets* [4]6
Hamlet (*Hamlet*) [1]394, [4]42, 743, 744, 745, 763, 763n, 805, 836–7, 841, 844–5, 846, 849, 850, 851, 852, 853, 853n, 854, 856, 857, 858, 859
hammer [1]822, [3]815
Hammersmith *see* London
Hammond, Henry (1605–60) [1]280, 280n, 338, [2]409n, [3]149–50 q, 438, 438n, 795n, [4]173, 173n, [6]107
Paraphrase and Annotations [1]280n; *Works* [1]280n
Hammond, James (1710–42) [1]38
Hammond, Nicholas Geoffrey Lempriere (b 1907) see *Oxford Classical Dictionary* ed Hammond and Scullard
Hammond, William (fl 1818) [1]cxxxix
Hammonic (language) [4]257
Hampden, Richard (1631–95) [1]336, [3]140
Hampshire [2]767
Hampstead *see* London
Hampton Court [1]336n, [2]812, 812n
hand(s) [1]671, [2]933, [3]404, [4]38, [5]65
back of [5]449; dead [5]386, 386n; God's [3]416, 416n, [5]266n; human [5]476; imposition of [1]353, 354, [5]535–6, 536, 667; joined [4]658, 658n; laying-on of [1]532n; of Nature [5]266; trick of [2]1005
handcuffs [3]754
Handel, Georg Friedrich (1685–1759) [1]62n
Messiah [2]413, 413n
handelnde [2]613–14

handgun [5]101n
handicraft [2]1065
handicraftsmen [3]633, [5]234
handkerchief [2]599, 1092, 1092n, [5]680
h. gardens [2]918
Handlung/Handlungen [1]3–4, [2]1066
Handlungsweise [3]80, 80n, 86, 118, [4]126
"handsome" [1]159
Haney, John Louis (1877–1960) [1]clxv, clxvi, clxvii, [3]811
Bibliography of Samuel Taylor Coleridge [1]clii, [5]440
hanging [3]1082, [5]862
hangman [5]281n, 396
Hanina ben Dusa (1st century) [3]1090 ("R. Chanina")
Hankey, William Alers (fl 1830) [1]33
Hanmer, Sir Thomas (1677–1746) [4]698n, 701n, 710n, 711n, 716n, 763n
Hanna, William (1808–82) *see* T. Chalmers *Select Works* ed Hanna
Hannah (Bible) [2]833n–4n
Hannibal (247–182 BC) [1]4n, 177n, [3]470n, 652
Hanover [3]228, 229, [6]153n
House of [1]122, [3]226
Hanoverians [3]226
Hansard [3]489n, [4]79n
Hansard, Thomas Curson (1776–1833) [4]18
Hanuman (myth) [2]346, 346n
"hap" [4]136
hapax legomenon [1]27, 27n, [5]565
Happer, Mysie (in Scott) [4]597, 597n
"happiness" [3]617, 617n, [5]724, *724n*
happiness [1]169, [2]642, [3]120, 264, 582, 617–18, 808, [4]112, 134, 135, 214, 444, [5]724, 822, [6]316
definition of [4]135–6; final [3]644; of others [1]4; spiritual [4]663
"happy" [4]112, 112n
Har (myth) [4]489–90
harangues [5]147
"harberous" [2]649, 684, 684n
harbinger [2]393
harbours [5]831
Hardenberg, Friedrich Ludwig von ("Novalis") (1772–1801) [1]145n, 148n, [3]127n, 383
Blüthenstaub [1]132; *Heinrich von Ofterdingen* [1]131, [2]958; *Hymnen an die Nacht* [1]132; *Novalis Schriften* ed J. L. Tieck and K. W. F. Schlegel [3]384n; MT [2]958
hard-heartedness [4]823
Hardicanute, King of Denmark and of England (1018–42) [3]784
Hardie, Robert Purves (b 1864) *see* Aristotle *Physics* tr Hardie and Gaye
Harding, James [4]754
hardness [1]589, 649, 653, [2]1205, [3]1009, [4]131, [6]227
Hardouin, Jean (1646–1729) [5]692, 692n–3n
Chronologiae ex nummis antiquis restitutae [5]693n
Hardwicke, Earl of *see* Yorke, Philip
hare(s) [1]331n, 421, 779, [5]712n
March [3]990
Hare, Francis, Bishop of Chichester (1671–1740) [6]217
Hare, Julius Charles (1795–1855) [1]cxxiv, cl, 211, [2]332, *332n–3n*, [3]781, [5]143n
supplier of books to C [1]xcviii
The Children of Light [2]332n–3n q; *see also* J. L. Tieck *The Old Man of the Mountain* tr Hare
Hare, Mr (fl 1812) [1]cvii, [2]702n
Hare, William (fl 1829) [3]742n
Harecastle [3]627
harelip [3]130
harem [3]906
Harfleur [5]114
Harington, Lucy, Countess of Bedford *see* Russell, Lucy
Harkins, Paul William *see* Chrysostom *De incomprehensibili Dei natura* tr Harkins
Harley, Doris H. *see* Swedenborg *Heaven . . . and Hell* tr Harley
Harley, Robert, 1st Earl of Oxford (1661–1724) [1]156n
harlot(s) [1]473, 473n, [6]157
Babylonian [5]396
Harmer, James (1777–1853) [1]807, 807n
Harmodius (d 514 BC) [1]337, 337n, [4]289
harmonica, glass [3]43n
Harmonics [2]548n, [3]396, 396n
harmonists [3]666
harmony [1]201, [3]953, [4]313, 313n, 498, 603, [5]227, 749
of consequences [2]182; *harmonia* [3]854; imitative [3]651–2; in landscapes [4]827; manly [1]377; in multeity [1]679; predetermined [4]452; pre-established [2]172, 172n, 555–6, 556n, [3]243, 243n, 644, 790, 790n, [5]4 ("harmoniam"), 4n, 278; of Scripture [5]398; sobs of [1]110; universal [4]511n; of universe [4]511; of world [2]629
Harold II, of Wessex (c 1022–66) [2]808, [3]784, 785n

harp [2]968, 968n, [4]124n, [5]728
  Eolian [1]609, [2]1003, [3]248, *248n*, [4]124, 124n, [5]25; *see also* lute
Harpalyce (myth) [6]208
harpasmon [5]30, 30n
harpers [6]99
Harpocration, Valerius (2nd century) [2]386n
harrier [5]293, [6]153
Harrington, Sir James (1611–77) [1]223, 224n, 341, [3]877n, 882, 882n, 884
  Commonwealth of Oceana [1]224n, 341n, [3]802, 802n
Harris, Errol Eustace *see* Schelling *Ideas* tr Harris and Heath
Harris, James (1709–80) *Hermes* [3]15n, [4]168n
Harris, John (1820–84) [1]376
Harris, Otis [5]854
Harris, William (1720–70) [1]cxxxn
Harrison, John (d 1798) [3]635
harrow [2]648
Harrowby, Earl of *see* Ryder, Dudley
Harry (in Brooke) [1]723
Harry IV of France *see* Henri IV
harshness [1]407, 643
  in Böhme [1]650; *see also* astringency
Hart, E. H. [5]462
Hart, Henry St John *see* Coleridge, S. T. IX *CIS* ed Hart
Hart, John (d 1574) *Orthography* [3]828n
Harte, Walter (1709–74) [1]38
  Life of Gustavus Adolphus [1]850n
Hartley, David (1705–57) [1]198n, 409, 566, 580n, [2]1203, [3]86n, 242, 737, 792, 792n, 877n, [4]27n, 124n ("Hartleian"), 494n, 645n, [5]825n, 827, 827n
  on association [3]242n–3n, [4]221–2, 222n; moral character of [2]961; piety of [4]27; theory of knowledge [2]341
  Observations on Man lxiii, lxxviii; MT [2]959–62; [4]27n, 209n, [5]827n–8n
Hartley, David (1732–1813) [2]959
Hartley, Thomas (?1709–84) [5]463, 464, 464n
Hartlib, Samuel (c 1600–70) [2]954
Hartman, Robert S. (1910–72) *see* Kant *Logic* tr Hartman and Schwarz
Harut (myth) [3]92, 92n
Harvard *see* Cambridge MA
Harvard Studies in Classical Philology [4]809n
harvest(s) [1]cxviii, [3]807, [4]809
harvesting [4]149
Harvey, Christopher (1597–1663) [5]192
  The Bishop MT [2]1042–3; *Church Festivals* MT [2]1043; *The Communion-Table* MT [2]1042; *The Font* [5]192n; *The Nativity* MT [2]1044–5; *The Sabbath* MT [2]1043–4; *The Synagogue* [2]1034n; MT [2]1042–6; [5]192n; *Trinity Sunday* MT [2]1046; *Whitsunday* MT [2]1045
Harvey, Daniel Whittle (1786–1863) [2]211, *211n*
Harvey, Gabriel (c 1550–1630) [3]251n
Harvey, Henry Auber (b 1824) [2]259
Harvey, William (1578–1657) [1]802, [2]367n, [5]811
  Exercitatio anatomica de motu cordis et sanguinis [1]792, 792n; *Exercitationes de generatione animalium* [1]792n, [5]811n
Harwood, Edward (1729–94) *see* Bible: NT: Greek: ed Harwood
Harwood, Thomas (1767–1842) *Annotations Ecclesiastical and Devotional*† [2]963
Harz Mountains [3]1071
Harzreise [1]204n
Hase, Theodor (1682–1731), and C. Iken *Thesaurus novus theologico-philologicus* [2]506n
hashish [4]85n
Haslam, John (1764–1844) *Medical Jurisprudence* [4]617; MT [6]285–9
Hassell, John (d 1825) [3]942
Hassenfratz, Jean Henri (1755–1827) [3]938, 941
hässliche [4]187, 187n
Hastings, James (1852–1922) see *Encyclopedia of Religion and Ethics* ed Hastings
Hastings, Selina, Countess of Huntingdon (1707–91) [5]162, 162n
  A Select Collection of Hymns† [2]964–5
Hastings, Warren (1732–1818) [2]784n
hat(s) [2]687, 687n, [3]394, [5]651
hatchets [3]223
hate [1]560, 731, [5]471
hateful, the [1]371n, 397, [3]913; see also *miseton*
hatred [4]816
  argument appealing to [2]1141; divine [1]315; fiendish [3]133; of sin [4]133
Hatteraick, Dirk (in Scott) [4]585
Hatton, Christopher, 1st Baron Hattonhaven (?1605–70) [5]616
haughtiness [5]396
hauntings [5]349
haut ton philosophique [4]105
Haüy, René Just (1743–1822) [3]940, 942
have and be *see* be
Haven, Richard (b 1924), coeditor [1]556

having and being *see* being
Haweswater [3]974
hawk [5]226, [6]153
Hawker, Robert (1753–1827) [4]636, 636n, 639, 641, 650, 661, 662
Letter to a Barrister [4]633, 634, 636n
Hawkshead [2]4
Haxey [5]165n
hay [1]876
Hay, James, 1st Baron Hay (d 1636) [1]167n
haycocks [3]759
Haydon, Benjamin Robert (1786–1846) [2]235n
Hayley, William (1745–1820) [6]199, 199n
The Life and Posthumous Works of William Cowper [1]clxx, 220n, [2]879n; *The Life of Milton* [1]lxxxiv; MT [2]966–75; 1191
Haym, Nicola Francesco (1679–1729) *Notizia de' libri rari nella lingua italiana* MT [2]976
Hayman, Francis (1708–76) [2]196n
Hayme/Haime, John (1708–84) [5]170, 171, 171n, 174, 174n–5n
Hayter, Charles (1761–1835) [3]937
Hayward, Abraham (1801–84) [4]11; *see also* Savigny *Of the Vocation of Our Age* tr Hayward
haze, vibrating [5]372
Hazlitt, Sarah (née Stoddart) (d c 1842) [1]lviii, [2]1203, 1204, *1204n*
Hazlitt, William (1778–1830) [1]clxn, 58n, [2]180, 1195n, 1203, 1204n
abusive reviews of C [1]cxviii; on C's plagiarism [4]837, 837n; death [1]clx
Abridgment of the Light of Nature Pursued [2]787n; *Complete Works* ed P. P. Howe [1]218n q, 223n, 295n, [5]108
Hazlitt, William (1811–93) [2]116
Hazlitt, William Carew (1834–1913) [2]964, 1032
head(s)
Christ as our h. [3]678; of executive [5]536–7; and heart [1]817, [2]342, 384, 847, [3]122, 225, 401, 493n, 512, 527, 876, 972, [4]723, 817–18, [5]49, 124, 564, [6]66, 66n, 308; heresies of [3]137; human [5]751; organs of [2]546; of state [3]50
Head, Francis Bond (1793–1875) [2]977, 979n
Bubbles from the Brunnens of Nassau MT [2]977–84; [4]337, 337n
Headley, Henry (1765–88) [2]14–15, 15n
Select Beauties of Ancient English Poetry [2]15n
head-master [2]999
head-work [1]394, [4]589, 598
Healey, George Harris (b 1908) *The Cornell Wordsworth Collection* [1]701, [2]1105, 1169, 1170, [3]415
healing [1]533n
gift of [1]532; miraculous [3]734; spirit of [4]682
health [2]325, 1185, [3]64, [4]119, 846, [5]86, 98, 652
healths, drinking [5]396
healthy, the [4]644
heap [5]304
hearing [1]578, [2]1115, [3]389, [5]236, 265, 294, [5]554
Hearne, Samuel (1745–92) [1]549n
A Journey from the Prince of Wales's Fort . . . to the Northern Sea ed R. Glover MT [2]985–7
hearsays [4]480
"heart" [6]66, 66n, 308, 308n
HC's use of word [2]79
heart(s) [2]535n, 682, [3]717, 853, [4]521, [5]291–2
absence of [4]594; all deep affections [2]402; of all mankind [4]850; amendment of [3]268, [4]623; antidote to head [3]137; h.-armour [4]794; badness of [1]621; believing [5]821, [6]170; betrays judgment [3]451; h.-burnings [6]142; change of [1]438, [3]517, [6]299; cheerful [4]625; contradicts reason [2]614; crushed [4]640; cultivated [3]317; deceitful [1]722; errors from [4]181; faith in [1]823; feeling [1]763, 796; female [4]689; fleshly [4]98; flow of [1]327; good [1]5, [3]670, [4]594, [5]782, 813; guilelessness of [2]37; hardened [1]165; and head *see* head; in Hebrew [2]1029, 1029n, [3]526–7; ignorant [4]407; insulated [6]20; law written in [5]61; lifted to God [1]325; as living will [5]156; h.-lore [4]730; mended [5]73; and mind [1]763, 796; music of [1]325; narrow [4]589; and nerves [1]577; new [4]174; praying [1]712; pure [5]618; pure in [5]796; purified [1]560; rectitude of [5]624; religion of [1]754, 754n; secret movements of [5]562; singleness of [3]360; tablets of [3]54; unbelieving [2]288; understanding [2]680; want of [1]326; warts on [3]377; wise man's [4]678
hearth [1]587, 687n, 688n, 692
heat [1]177, 238, 590, [2]890, 1113, [3]158, 325, 518, 518n, 546, 850, 984, [4]358, 417, 429, [5]244, 267, 349, 358, 383, 471, [6]225–6, 229, 300
abstraction of [4]149; conducted or radiant [6]97; defined [1]597; generated by nerves [1]623; indifference of light and gravita-

heat—*continued*
tion [1]624; latent [3]323, 323–4, 323n; rays of [3]29n; vital [4]704; white and red [1]496; *see also* warmth
heath [4]827
Heath, Peter *see* F. Schelling *Ideas* tr E. E. Harris and Heath, *System* tr Heath
heathen(s) [1]304, 315, [2]255, 343, [3]474, [5]34, 609, 611
baptised [5]586; pious [5]658
heathenism [1]288, [3]473
"heautophany" [5]589, 589n
heaven(s)/Heaven [1]863, [2]135, 901, 1074n, [3]39, 471, [4]246, 549, 552–61, 644, [5]12, 56, 611
admission to [5]608; cope of [5]157; and earth *see* earth; as emancipation from wishes [2]774; h.-gate [4]628; generations of [5]430; and hell [1]138, [3]985, [5]403–25, 582, 593, 601, 612; host of [3]617; kingdom of [1]452, [2]313, [3]445, [6]60; material [5]561; meaning of [5]397–8; mock [3]581; new [2]1022; starry [1]576, [2]1024, [4]115; Swedenborg's [5]301; third [2]360; translation to [5]402; war in [3]472–3
Hebdomadal Council *see* Oxford
Heber, Reginald (1783–1826) "Life of Jeremy Taylor" [1]532, 532n; *see also* Jeremy Taylor *Whole Works* ed Heber
Heber, Richard (1773–1833) [1]240, [3]893, 893n
Hebraicae grammatices rudimenta [2]54n
Hebraism(s) [1]471, [2]426–7, [3]467, 550, [5]545, [6]139
Hebrew (language) [1]434, 470, 607, 708, 738, [2]69, 116, 302, 334, 334n, 374, 380, 380–1, 413n, 437, 449, 488, 574, 577n, 580, 582, 653, 704n, 709, 714, 769, 789, 1108, 1188–9, [3]466, 526, 584, 585, 828, 1088, [4]49, 243, 243n, 248, 248n, 251n, 253, 254, 254n, 257, 257n, [5]9, 237n, 337, 421, 607, 845, [6]77, 138, 219, 308
biblical canon [3]466, 533; C's ability in [1]513n; C's knowledge of [1]415; "darkness" in [3]139, 139n; Faber's knowledge of [2]582; and Greek hymns [2]1091; John thought in H. [3]1086; in OT [2]379–81; oracles [3]452; poesy [3]32; poetry [2]1052, [3]472; translation from [2]426–7; word for "corse" [2]446; word for "person" [2]446; word for "soul" [2]446; word for "virgin" [2]270, 270n
Hebrew(s) (people) [2]145, 147, [3]21, [4]254, 257n, [5]352
ancient [3]1087, [6]308; before Christ [2]261; commonwealth [3]426; converted [2]436; defects of H. constitution [3]112; Exodus of [2]385; Gospel of *see* Bible: NT: Matt: Gospel according to the H.; learning [3]1084; religion [3]108; sacred books of [1]447; settle in Egypt [2]395; *see also* Jew(s)
Hebrides [4]83n
Hebron [3]109
Hebrus (river) [2]980, 981n, [3]892–3, [6]208–9
Hecate (myth) [2]573
hecatombs [2]220, [3]399
Heck, Arie von *see* Gregory of Nyssa *De pauperibus amandis* ed von Heck
Hector (in Homer and Virgil) [3]1019, [4]168, [6]213
hedge [1]873, [2]1060, [4]236, [5]609
hedonism [2]872n
Hedwig Leonora of Sweden (1636–1715) [2]62, 62n
heel [1]457
Heeren, H. M. (fl 1691) [2]474n
Hegel, Georg Wilhelm Friedrich (1770–1831) [1]clii, [3]97n, [5]95, 95n
Wissenschaft der Logik [1]lxiii, lxviii; MT [2]988–97; [5]95n
hegemonikon [1]164n
Heidelberg [2]186n, 195n, [4]45, 52, 55
heifer [2]580
height [1]670, [3]17, 30n, 32
and depth *see* depth
Die Heilige Schrift ed Cohen *see* Bible: OT
Heinecken/Heineken, Johann (1761–1851) [3]376
Heinrichs, Johann Heinrich (1765–1850) *see* Bible: NT: Rev ed Heinrichs
Heinroth, Johann Christian (1773–1843)
his scheme atheistical [2]1010
Lehrbuch der Anthropologie MT [2]998–1031
Heinsius, Nicholas (1620–81) [2]44; *see also* Claudianus *Quae exstant* ed Heinsius
heir(s) [2]295
h.-loom [1]337
heis [4]36, 36n
Helen of Troy (myth) [2]1124
Helena (*Midsummer Night's Dream*) [4]689
Helias *see* Elijah/Elias
Helicon, Mount [5]109, 109n, 528n
Heliogabalus/Eliogabalus (c 204–22) [1]307n, [2]622, 622n ("Elagabalus"), [3]797, 797n
helios [2]271, 271n
Helios (myth) [2]583, 583n; *see also* Apollo
hell(s)/Hell [1]119, 352, 448, [2]69, 135, 560n,

661, [3]28n, 38n, 57, 62, 215, 250n, 433, 501, 612–13, 1064
descent into [2]1099, [3]56, 56n, 57, 732; and Devil [1]811; fear of [1]786; h.-fire [4]653, 663, [5]610; flames of [1]315; foretaste of [3]510; genesis of [1]647. *See also* Gehenna; Hades
hellebore [1]768, [4]191, 191n, [5]529n
Hellespont [3]907, [5]833
helluo librorum [1]cii
helm wind [4]29
Helme, Mathew [1]476
helmet(s) [1]345, [2]1155, [5]651
Helmholtz, Hermann Ludwig Ferdinand von (1821–94) [4]209n
Helmont, Jean Baptiste van (1577–1644) [2]824, 824n, [3]128, 817n, [6]96, 96n, 99, 103, 121 q, 122
Works [6]103n
Helmonts, the [5]809
helps, spiritual [5]636
Helston [1]clviii, clxix, 413
Grammar School [2]1129
Helvellyn [1]cx, cxn, [3]183n, 975, [5]371, 390n, [6]249 ("Helvellen"), 249n
Helvétius, Claude Adrien (1715–71) [1]545, [2]635, [3]602n, 877
De l'esprit [6]334
Helvidius (4th century) [2]272, 272n, [3]730
Helvig, Amalie von (née Imhoff) (1766–1831) *see* Tegnér *Die Frithiofs-Sage* tr Helvig
hemera [1]608, 608n
hemlock [1]713, [2]481, [5]5n, [6]21
hemp [1]777, [5]420
Indian [4]84–5, 85n
Hemsterhuis, Franciscus (1720–90) [4]207, 207n
Aristée; ou De la divinité [3]82, [4]207n; *Lettre sur l'homme et ses rapports* [4]207n
hen(s) [1]421, 436, 453, [3]1072, [4]31, 92, [6]149, 219, 220n
hen kai pan [1]175n, 242, 242n, [2]631, 666, 666n, [4]548, [5]251, 251n, 830
henad(s)/*henad* [1]586, 586n, 689, 691n
heneka [6]164, 164n
Hennage, Dr *see* Goede, Henning
Hennecke, Edgar (1865–1951) [1]489, 493n q
Henri IV, King of France (1553–1610) [1]727, [4]78, 181n, [5]543
Henrietta Maria, Queen of England (1609–69) [1]223n, [2]59, 59n, 62–3, 931, 931n, 936n, 948n
Henry (fiction) [2]658
Henry I, King of England (1068–1135) [3]786–7
Henry II, King of England (1133–89) [1]213, [3]784
Henry III, King of England (1207–72) [2]817, 826, [4]282
Henry IV, King of England (1367–1413) [2]124
Henry V, King of England (1387–1422) [2]124
Henry VI, King of England (1421–71) [2]118
Henry VII, King of England (1457–1509) [1]356, 834, [2]70, [3]169, [4]75, [5]532
Henry VIII, King of England (1491–1547) [1]cxxx q, 318n, 357, 422n, 809, 831, 833, 866, [2]238, 407, 926, 928, [3]760, 760n, 795–6, 1072, 1078
Convocations under [2]1150n; destruction of monasteries [2]733, 733n; martyrs under [1]809; overbearing character [1]833; reign of [1]831; tyranny of [4]180
Henry of Avranches (13th century) [3]1072 ("Auranches")
Henry, Prince of Wales (1594–1612) [2]936n
Henry, William (1774–1836) [3]936, 938, 939
hensbane [2]168, 168n, [4]325
Henschel, Edward [5]688
Hephaestos (in Aeschylus) [4]846n
Hephaestus (myth) [1]692n, [2]16n, 576n, 583n, [3]648, [5]522n; *see also* Vulcan
hepta [2]1092, [4]37
heptad(s) [1]563n, 643, [4]167, 167n
of colours [4]167
he-queen [2]63
Heracleon (2nd century) [2]464, 464n
Heracleonites [4]258
Heraclitus (fl 500 BC) [1]lxix, cxxxi, 166n, 168, 168n, 177 q, 177n, 347n, 410n, 584, *584n*, 622, 622n, 639, 639n, 678n, 719n, 774, 774n, [2]143, 343n, 425, 430, 869 q, 1123, [3]724n, 949, 950n, 1088n, [4]128, 128n, 383n, 827, [5]84, 360n, 713–18, 722, [6]5, 5n q
philosophy of [1]410; system of [5]721
Heraclitus (of *Peri Apiston*) [3]649, 649n
herald(s) [3]450, 450n, 594
evangelising [2]436
Heraud, John Abraham (1799–1887) [3]18n
Legend of St Loy [1]clxv
herb(s) [1]662, [4]87
Herbert, Anna Sophia *see* Dormer, Anna Sophia
Herbert, Edward (in *London Magazine*) [1]xcixn

Herbert, Edward, 1st Baron Herbert of Cherbury (1583–1648) [5]81
De religione gentilium [6]265; *De veritate* [5]81n
Herbert, George (1593–1633) [2]*1033, 1046n*, [5]192, 510, 510n
imitates Petrarch [4]102n
Affliction MT [2]1036; *Antiphon* [2]1038n; *The Bosom Sin* [3]312, 312n; *The Church Militant* MT [2]1041; *Divinity* MT [2]1038; *Faith* MT [2]1036; *The Flower* [1]xcvi q; MT [2]1038; *Holy Baptism* [5]192n; *The Holy Scriptures* MT [2]1036; *Judgment* MT [2]1041; *Love Unknown* [2]1038n, [4]102n; *Man* MT [2]1037; *Perirrhanterium* MT [2]1034–5, 1046–7; *Remains* [2]1032; *Repentance* [2]1033n; *The Reprisal* MT [2]1035; *Self-condemnation* MT [2]1040; *Sin* MT [2]1035; *The Temple* [1]xcii; MT [2]1032–41; [3]312, 773, 773n q, [5]192n; *The 23. Psalm* MT [2]1040; *Virtue* MT [2]1037
Herbert, H. (fl 1727) *see* Fleury *Ecclesiastical History* tr Herbert and Adams
Herbert, Henry, 2nd Earl of Pembroke (c 1534–1601) [2]119n
Herbert, Henry George, 2nd Earl of Carnarvon (1772–1833) [4]79, 79n
Herbert, Henry John George, Viscount Porchester, 3rd Earl of Carnarvon (1800–1849) [4]79n
Herbert, Mary, Countess of Pembroke (1561–1621) [2]116, 119, *119n*, [3]888
Herbert, Philip, 4th Earl of Pembroke (1584–1650) [2]78n, 119n
Herbert, William, 3rd Earl of Pembroke (1580–1630) [2]78n, 119n
Herculaneum [6]251–5
Hercules (myth) [1]799, [2]90n, [3]234, 234n, 701, [4]197, [5]227, 607 ("Herculean"), [6]127n
choice of [6]157, 157n; H. *furens* [1]354; Kant as [3]99, 99n; Pillar of [1]566
herd
bestial [1]803; unthinking [5]277
Herder, Johann Gottfried (1744–1803) [1]481–2, 481n, [2]188, 518n, 707, 707n, 999n, 1022, *1048–9*, [3]3, 476, [4]207n, [5]402n
German Coleridge [2]1048; no ideas [2]1068; Jacobi's letters to [3]99–100; and Kant [2]1071, [3]99n, 365n; psilanthropic Christianity [2]1079n; school of [2]205
Briefe, das Studium der Theologie betreffend [2]1048; MT 1050–63; 1064, 1065n, 1072; *Fragmente über die neuere deutsche Litteratur* [1]297n; *Ideen zur Philosophie* [2]429n, 1048, 1065, 1065n, [3]365; *Kalligone* [1]lxviii, [2]1048, 1050; MT 1064–71; 1072, [3]365n; *Die Metakritik der Urtheilskraft* [2]1048, 1059, 1059n, 1064, 1064n, [3]97n, 365n; *Sämmtliche Werke* [2]518, 518n; *Verstand und Erfahrung* [3]365n; MT [6]290; *Von der Auferstehung* [2]1048, 1050, 1060, 1064; MT 1072–88, tr as *On the Resurrection* [1]lxix; *Zerstreute Blätter* [2]1048, 1064, 1065n
Herderists [2]1085
hereafter [2]1010
heredity [3]596
hereditary right [4]19
Herefordshire [1]777n
"heresy" [2]660, [5]11, 11n, [6]55n–6n
heresy/heresies [1]516, 477, 644, [2]21, 439, 660–8, 682, 702, 710, 833, [3]230, 285, 308, 689, 755n, 766, [4]98, 181, 235, 235n, 249n, 251, [5]210, 524, 553, 570, 617, 623, 624, 625, [6]59, 74, 145
anti-trinitarian [2]657; Arian [2]736; ascetic [1]465; of Athanasian Creed [3]369; buttress of [1]507; Cerinthian [6]63; charges of [5]620; defined [5]166; and Fathers [5]638; Franciscan [3]427; freedom from [1]345; gnostic [3]612–13, [4]735; of head [3]137; of manner [4]632; meaning of [2]660; minimifidian [1]512, [3]557; origin of [3]86; Pelagian [2]809; puny [6]178; rising [2]69; statute [4]630; Wesley's [5]173
heretic(s) [1]256, 248, 248n, 256n, 305, 315, [2]317, 735, 923, [3]495n, 686, 826n, 1068, 1084, [4]185, 249, 258, 670n, [5]11, 70, 181n, 553, 570, 570n, 579, 645, [6]55–6, 57, 58, 59, 62, 65, 68, 74
catalogue of [2]765; non-existent [5]624; pretended [5]623
Herford, Charles Harold (1853–1931) *see* Jonson *Ben Jonson* ed Herford and Simpson
Heringa, Jocodus (1765–1840) [1]480
"heriot" [3]977
herkos odonton [1]327
Hermann, Johann Gottfried Jakob (1772–1848) [1]7, [2]88–9, 88n
De emendenda ratione graecae grammaticae [1]lxxxvi, clxx; MT [2]1089–93; *Elementa doctrinae metricae* [2]579, 579n; *Epistola* [2]86; and G. F. Creuzer *Briefe über Homer und Hesiodus* [2]86; *see also* Homeric Hymns: *Homeri hymni; Hymn to Ceres* ed Hermann
hermaphrodite [4]611, 611n

Hermas (2nd century) [2]699; *see also* Bible: Apocrypha: NT: Shepherd of Hermas
Hermes (myth) [1]692, 692n, [2]575, 576n, 583n, [4]170–1; *see also* Mercury
Hermesianax of Colophon (b c 300 BC) [1]145, 146
Hermione (*Winter's Tale*) [4]706–7
hermit [2]958
Hermolaus Barbarus (1454–93) [1]756
hernia [4]164
"hero" [2]1123
hero(es) [1]656, [2]1123, [3]15, 142, 280, 449, 449n, [4]718–19, 734, 811, [5]124
children of the Devil [1]656; of paganism [4]146; Scott's [4]600; Luther as [3]770
Hero (myth) [5]833, 833n
Herod (74–4 BC) [1]446, [2]615n, 711, 776, 917, [4]55n, 470, 470n, 476, 483, 748
Herodians [1]253
Herodotus (c 485–425 BC) [1]770, 771, 771n, 772n, [2]394, 394n, 831, 897, 898, 898n, 1053, [4]311n, 533n, 631, [5]832n, [6]173, 173n
pseudo-H. [2]386, 386n
heroic age *see* age, heroic
heroic poems *see* poems, heroic
heroine(s) [4]811, 718–19
heron [3]1048, 1048n
herring [3]128
Herrnhut [5]126
Herrnhuter [2]999n, [3]493n, [5]181n
Hersart, Charles (fl 1806–14) [3]940
Herschel, Sir William (1738–1822) [2]885n q, [3]29n, 73n, 379, 379n, 869, 936, [4]326n, 516, [5]232, 232n q, 291
"Observations . . . [on] the Nature of the Sun" [3]869; "On the Power of Penetrating into Space" [5]291n
Hertford
Christ's Hospital [2]888n
Hervey, James (1714–58) [2]103
Herzen, Mr (fl 1793) [4]126
Herzknirschen [4]640, 640n
Herzlehre [4]730
Hesiod (8th century BC) [1]38, [2]344, 973n, [3]493, [4]147, 631
HNC essay on annotated [2]86–9; tr Cooke [1]38
Theogony [1]645, 645n, [2]88–9, 88n, 89n, 311n, [3]493n; *Works* [1]725n; *Works and Days* [1]725, 725n q, 848 q, 848n q, [2]88, [5]530 q, 530n q, [6]5n
Hessey, James Augustus (1785–1870) [2]1169
letter to [1]831 q, 850, [3]626n q
Hessians [1]xcv, xcvn
Hester (Bible) [1]844n
hestia [1]587n
Hesychius of Miletus (early 6th century) [1]27n, [2]1130n
heterogeneity [2]547, [5]418
"heterogeneous" [6]86
heterogeneous, the [5]418
heterogenes [3]262
heteros [4]37, 37n
heterozetesis [4]106
Heth (Bible) [2]813, 814n
Hetherington, William Maxwell (1803–65) *Twelve Dramatic Sketches* [1]clxv
Hett, Walter Stanley *see* Aristotle *De anima* tr Hett
Heumann, Christoph August (1681–1764) [2]506, [3]642, [6]167n
Acta eruditorum [2]506n
Heuss, Eduard (fl 1833) [1]417n
Hew, R. H. [3]811
Hewitt, John (1614–58) *Sermons*† [2]1094
hex [2]1092, [4]37
hexameter(s) [1]671–2, [2]8, 259, 579, 757, 757n, 761, 762, [3]479, 652, 814, [5]689; *see also* metre
Heylyn, Peter (1600–62) [1]850, [2]259, 260, 260n, 269, 806, 814, 850, 914, 914n, *1102n*, [3]486
high-church fanatic [2]1097; worldly [2]1102
Aerius redivivus [2]1102n; *Cyprianus Anglicus; or, the History of . . . William [Laud]* [2]260n, 814n q; MT 1095–1104; *Ecclesia restaurata* [2]1102n; *Examen historicum* [2]807, 1102n; *History of the Sabbath* [2]1095
Heyne, Christian Gottlob (1729–1812) [3]656 ("Gottlieb"); *see also* Pindar ed Heyne
Heywood, John (c 1497–c 1580)
A Merry Play [2]777, 777n; *The Playe called Foure P.P.* [2]759, 759n, 777
Heywood, Thomas (c 1574–1641)
prose Shakespeare [2]75, 75n
A Woman Killed with Kindness [4]168
Hezekiah (Bible) [2]674, 828–9, 828n, 829n, 894, [3]110, [4]296, [5]59
Hibernian [3]680; *see also* Irishman/Irishmen
hic jacet [1]764, 797
hiccaeity [1]152, 152n
Hickes, George (1642–1715) [1]843n
Hicks, Robert Drew (1850–1929) *see* Diogenes Laertius *Lives* tr Hicks
hiding-hole [2]280
hiera phalanx [1]42n

hierarch(s) [5]669
Church [3]686; Romish [2]260
hierarchy [2]57, 1139, [3]53, 212, [4]251, [5]124, 508, 661, 662
apostate [3]14, 14n; Church [5]503n; of intelligences [5]482–3; Jewish [4]481; papal [6]22, 23; of RC Church [1]517, 865, 866, [4]21, [5]569; secular [5]541
hiereus [1]529, 529n
Hierocles of Alexandria (fl 430) [3]539n
hierocracy [1]242
Irish [4]18; Romish [4]20, 20n
hieroduly [2]663
hieroglyph(ic)s [1]419, 419n, 684, 747, 778, [2]271, 956, [3]949, [5]225, 226n, 244, 248, 845, [6]105, 110
hierokeryx [1]665, 665n
"hierolatry" [1]297, 297n–8n
hierolatry [1]257n, [2]663, 663n, 673
Hierome *see* Jerome
Hierosalamites [2]471
Higgins *see* Higgons
Higginson, Francis (1586–1630) [3]818, 819
higgler [4]639
Higgons, Bevil (1670–1735) [2]77 ("Higgins")
High Church *see* Church of England: high church
higher and lower [1]719
Higher Criticism [2]369, 370, 373, 391, 398n, 435, 482, 923, [5]434n
highest
in the highest [1]601; and lowest [5]445
Highet, Gilbert (1906–78) *The Classical Tradition* [4]809n
high-fliers [2]1174
high-flying [5]67
Highgate [1]xc, xci, xciv, xcvii, cxii, cxvii, cxxxviii, 230, 393n, 494, 500, 513n, 710n, 716, 761, [2]10, 132, 180, 558n, 590, 650, 794, 904n, 1188, [3]765n, 813, [4]101n, 237, 310, 403n, 826n, 107, 151n, 684, [5]80, 306n
Book Society [6]12, 246; C's study [1]cxiv–cxv; Dorchester House [1]498; Grammar School [2]905n; The Grove [1]clixn, 498, 838n, 871; Hebrew Academy [4]41n; "H. List" [2]1032; Moreton House [1]xcvii, 838n, 871; oaths [3]164, 164n; Old Cemetery [2]905n; St Michael's Church [2]905n
Highlanders [2]1171n
Highlands [2]311
highnesses [5]278
high-priest, Romish [6]234
highway [3]601
highwayman [5]476
"higre" [2]819–20
Hilario, St *see* Hilary of Poitiers
Hilary of Arles, St (403–49) [3]369n, [5]8n, [6]72n
Hilary of Poitiers, St (c 315–c 368) [2]666, 666n, 738–9 ("Hilario"), 747, 748, 748n, [3]487, 693 ("Hilarius")
De trinitate [3]587 q, 587n–8n
Hildebrand, Pope *see* Gregory VII
Hildenbrand, Johann Valentin von (1763–1818) [4]164
Hilkiah (Bible) [2]894n
hill [1]420–1
Hill, Aaron (1685–1750) [1]38, 74
Hill, Alan G. *see* WW *Letters; . . . The Later Years* ed de Selincourt, rev Hill
Hill, George Birkbeck Norman (1835–1903) *see* S. Johnson *Lives of the Poets*; Boswell *Life of Johnson* ed Hill
Hill, Robert (1699–1777) *Christianity the True Religion* [2]754n
Hill, Rowland (1744–1833) *Village Dialogues* [4]622–3, 649–50
Hillhouse, James Abraham (1789–1841) *Hadad* [1]cxl, clxix; MT [2]1105–9
Himeros [4]463
Hinchman, Dr (fl mid-17th century) [1]254
Hindu(s)/Hindoo(s) [1]397, [2]340, 341, 342, 344, 347, 584–5, 1123, [3]59n, [5]769, 769n
Hindustan/Indostan [1]400, [2]784, 784n, [3]646, [4]651, [5]105, 262, 415, [6]150
Hindustani (language) [4]243, 243n
Hine, Reginald Leslie (b 1883) [6]164
Charles Lamb and His Hertfordshire [1]clxiiin
hinge [3]66
Hinnom, Vale of [1]448, [2]559, 559n, [3]38, 38n
"hint" [6]6
hints [5]252
Hiph [2]584
Hipparchus (4th century BC) [4]147
Hipparchus (in Plato) [2]870
Hipparis (river) [4]119
Hippias (6th century BC) [1]337n
Hippias of Elis (5th century BC) [2]868–9, 868n
hippocampus [5]411
Hippocrates (b c 460 BC) [1]798, 799, [3]175, 868–9, [5]319
Hippocrene (myth) [5]528, 528n
hippogryph [2]646, 646n
Hippolytus (myth) [3]186

hippopotamus/hippopotami [1]427, 427n, [3]771, 771n, 1080, 1081, [4]533, [5]841
hireling(s) [1]260, [5]381
Hirschberg, Valentinus Theocritus (1597–1639) *see* P. Sidney *Arcadia* tr Hirschberg
Historia Britonnum [2]1170n
historian(s) [1]850, [2]470, 480, [3]533, 665, [4]161, 310, 646, 669, [6]319
ancient [1]448, [4]310–11, 311n; as artist [1]448; church [5]298; critical [5]755; ecclesiastical [5]646, 666; first [1]446; great [5]643; inspired [5]666; Italian [3]251; modern [3]802; old [5]39; parliamentary [2]1196; royalist [2]1196; Southey as [2]929; worth of [4]180
historiography [5]318
history/histories [1]368, [2]421, 1053, [3]405, 425n, 484, [4]260, 478 ("historical literature"), [5]60, 167, 324, 560–1, 594, 710, [6]52, 138, 207
aberration from [5]562; allegoric [5]248; ancient [4]804; authentic [3]606, [4]479; in Bible [1]446–8; and biography [2]51; canon of historic credibility [3]700; of Christ [4]479; Christian [3]720; of Church *see* church(es): history, h., ecclesiastic(al) *below*; corporate effort proposed [5]812–13; credibility of [2]459, [5]513; credulity in [3]780; ecclesiastic(al) [1]849, [2]439, 831, [5]127, 835, [6]17; of England [3]784; English [3]1078–9; errors of [2]1198; eternal [4]269; events of [6]314; evidence in [4]52; fact(s) of [1]446, [2]274, [3]49, [5]51, 782, 795; and faith [2]1079–80, 1082; faith of [5]145; and fiction *see* fiction, and history; fictitious [4]809; genuine [1]368; getting rid of [3]694; Greek and Roman [3]110, [6]294; of Greeks [2]1071; h.-hash [3]484; higher sources than [5]514; historic(al) evidence [3]661, 662; historic pole [3]21; human [5]644; imitation of [5]226; Jewish [1]817, [3]21, 470, [5]307, [6]142; man an historic being [3]729; of man [3]919; march of [3]417; mausoleum of [4]810; medical [1]282; minute [3]634; modern [4]60, 75; Mosaic [5]54; mythic [3]105; national [3]801; natural *see* natural history; of New England [3]816–26; and novel [2]448; philosophical [2]1012; of philosophy [3]318; h.-piece [4]811; in plays [4]712; and poetry [4]679; prosaic [1]58; and religion [3]36; revealed [3]436; Roman [5]576; Scottish [6]94, 94n; in Shakespeare [4]807–8; spirit of [3]483; study of [2]1197; truth of [5]124; use of [1]795; writing of [4]59
hit, sly [2]56
"hitty" [2]56
hive(s) [3]308, [5]469, 484
Hoar, George Frisbie (1826–1904) [3]881
Hobbes, Thomas (1588–1679) [1]cxxiii, 49, 255n, 495, [2]636, 636n, 954, [3]503, 793, 793n, [5]812
ignorance of mathematics [5]811
De corpore [5]811n; *Leviathan* [2]966; MT 1110–11; [3]793n, [5]615n q
Hobbesian [2]1013, 1013n
Hobbists [2]636
hobbitihoy [2]126, 126n
hobby horse [4]387
"hobby-horsical" [2]121, 121n
Hobhouse, John Cam, Baron Broughton de Gyfford (1786–1869)
A Journey through Albania [4]170, 184–5; *Recollections of a Long Life* [1]807n
Hobson, Thomas (c 1544–1631), Milton's poems on [3]413n, 901–2, 902n
hodge podge [5]296
Hodgson, Robert (c 1773–1844) [5]79n
"hodiernity" [1]410, 410n
Hody, Humphrey (1659–1707) [6]3
Hoel *see* Hywel Dda
Hoffbauer, Johann Heinrich (b 1796) *Der Mensch in allen Zonen der Erde* MT [2]1112–14
Hoffer, William [2]1203
Hoffmann, Christoph Ludwig (1721–1807) [6]225
Hoffmann, Ernst Theodor Amadeus (1776–1822)
Fantasiestücke in Callot's Manier MT [2]1115; *Die Serapions-Brüder* [2]1115
Hoffmann, Friedrich (1660–1742) [5]517
Opera omnia physico-medica [3]374, 374n, [5]517n
Hoffmann von Fallersleben, August Heinrich (1798–1874) *Williram's Uebersetzung des Hohenliedes* [1]629n
hog [2]764, [4]86
Hogan, Charles Beecher (1906–83) see *The London Stage* ed Hogan
Hogarth, William (1697–1764) [1]366, 366n, [2]158, 196n, 816
Election series [3]189, 189n; ed J. Nichols and G. Steevens *Genuine Works* [2]779n; *The Rake's Progress* [1]160n
Hogg, Edward [5]688
Hogg, James (1770–1835) [1]75n
Hohenlohe-Waldenburg-Schillingsfürst, Alexander Leopold Franz, Prince of (1794–1849) [2]1086, *1086n*

hoi polloi [1]477, 477n
Holborn *see* London
Holcroft, Louisa (b 1806) [3]191n
Holcroft, Thomas (1745–1809) [1]90n
Hölderlin, Johann Christian Friedrich (1770–1843) [4]207n
Holderness [4]80n
Holdsworth, Dr (presumably Richard Holdsworth, 1590–1649) [2]912
holidays [1]253
holiness [1]470, [2]800, [3]25, 26, 29, 264, 564, 597, 677, 709, [4]410, 429, 625, 629, 656, [5]132–3, 179, 491, 605
  beauty of [2]305, [5]130, 510, 510n; divine [3]464; essential [5]135; meaning of [2]1177; meditation on [5]589; offended [5]618; of spirit [4]653; Jeremy Taylor's [5]584
Holinshed, Raphael (d c 1580) *Chronicles* [2]396n
Holland [2]60, 327n, [3]141n, 633, 638, 639, 639n, 978, [5]279, 596, 596n
  Inquisition in [1]281n
Holland, Baron *see* Fox, Henry Richard Vassall
Holland, Henry, 4th Duke of Exeter and Earl of Huntingdon (1430–75) [2]122
Hollar, Wenceslaus (1607–77) [5]46n
Holles, Denzell, Baron Holles of Ifield (1599–1679/80) [1]255, [3]797
Hollis, Lord *see* Holles, Denzell
hollowness [5]822
Holm, Ellen [4]754
Holmes, Edward (1797–1859)
  Life of Mozart [2]65n; *A Ramble among the Musicians of Germany* [2]65, 65n q
Holofernes (Bible) [2]76
Holofernes (*Love's Labour's Lost*) [4]609, 609n
"holomery" [4]466, 466n
Holstein [5]312
Hölty, Ludwig Heinrich Christoph (1748–76)
  Adelstan und Röschen [2]1116; *Gedichte*† [1]clxv, [2]1116
holy, the [5]482
Holy Alliance [3]250, 250n
"Holy Ghost" [5]665–6
Holy Ghost [1]432, 478, 478n, 561, 568, [2]305, 423, 882, 1085, [3]11–14, 27, 36, 44, 310, 460, 674, 685, [4]53, 258, 300, 641, 646, [5]11, 20, 58, 512, 514, 515n, 536, 639, 651, 652, 798–9
  blasphemy against [5]585; descent of [2]653, 659, 1045, [5]650; distinct power [3]73–4; divinity of [2]751–2; female [2]709; gospel of [3]427; Irving on [3]42, 67; personeity of [2]751, 751n; procession of [5]576–7; sin against [1]872, [6]168. *See also* God; Holy Spirit; Trinity
Holy Spirit [1]479n, 507, [2]286, 704, [3]50, 77n, 434, 438, [4]645, 672, [5]15, 473, 514, 530, 653
  distinct hypostasis [6]67; gifts of the [1]339; guidance of [5]519; implicit doctrine of [3]428; in pentad [2]290; personality of [2]751; procession of [1]564; synonyma of [2]305; workings of [1]820; *see also* Holy Ghost
home [4]335, 743
  h. question [6]289; h. stroke [6]289
Home, Sir Everard (1756–1832) [3]936, 937, 938, 940, 942; *see also* J. Hunter *A Treatise on the Blood* ed Home
Home, George, Earl of Dunbar (d 1611) [2]1100
Home, Henry, Lord Kames (1696–1782) [3]259, [4]96 ("Kaim"), 96n
  Sketches of the History of Man [4]96n
Homer (8th century BC) [1]lxxxvi, lxxxvii–lxxxviii, cxxxi, clviii, clviiin, clx, clxix, 38, 374, 606n, 675n, 799, [2]54, 727n, 779n, 865, 894n, 928n, 968, 973n, 1071, [3]407, 413, 886, [5]690, 728, [6]327–8
  authorship of [2]397, *397n–8n*, 891–2, *892n*, 1124, 1125–6, 1126n; Bible of Greek faith [2]1123; tr Chapman [3]177n; tr Cowper [2]1120, 1120n; death of [1]757; "Life" by pseudo-Herodotus [2]386, 386n; name [2]386, 386n, 1130, *1130n*; nods [1]684, 684n, [2]516n; parodied [2]759n; personality of [2]1129; tr Pope [1]38, [6]199n; text of [2]89n; Virgil's imitation of [6]214
  Batrachomyomachia [2]1117, 1126; *Chapman's Homer* ed Nicoll [2]1125n; *Homer* tr Pope [2]1120 ("*Epigrams*"), 1120n; *Iliad* [1]327n, 461n q, [2]53, 397, 397n, 535n, 779n, 892–3, 1090, [3]612, 612n, 814 q, 814n q, 829, [4]114–15, 114n, 301 q, 301n q, 607 q, 607n q, [5]307n, 614 q, 614n q, 743n, *Odyssey* superior to [2]1119, tr Pope [3]177n, 402 q; *Margites* [2]758–9; *Odyssey* [2]87, 397, 397n, 779n, 892, 1090, [3]468n, 647–8 q, 648n, 817n q, [4]835n, [5]307n, heart in [2]535n, tr Pope [6]212n; *The Whole Works* tr Chapman [1]lxxxviii; MT [2]1117–28; [3]703
Homereumenoi [2]779n, 1130n
Homeric Hymns [2]1091

Homeri hymni ed Ilgen [2]1130n; *Homeri hymni et epigrammata* ed Hermann [1]lxxxvi, [2]88n, 1091n; MT [2]1129–30; see also *Hymn to Ceres* ed Hermann, ed Ilgen, and others
Homeridae [2]89n, 779, 779n, 1130n
Homerton [4]3
homilies [2]338, [4]631, 643, 658, [6]19
of C of E [1]359, [2]651, 651n, [5]471, [6]42
homines [5]287
"hominifact" [2]980, 980n
"hominify" [2]980n
homo
h. archetypus [1]73, 73n; *h. maximus* [5]405; *h. noumenon* [3]265, 312; *h.-ousiotes* [5]24; *h. phaenomenon* [3]265, 312, 313; *h. representativus* [1]783, 783n; *see also* man
homogeneity [4]773, 826
"homogeneous" [6]86
"homoiogeneous" [4]218, 218n
homoioma [2]315, 315n
"homoiomery" [5]406
homoiousian and homoousian [2]219, [3]145
homoiousios and *homoousios* [2]219n, [3]145n
homoousian(s) [2]734, [6]79, 79n, 90
and homoiousian *see* homoiousian
homoousios [1]478n, [2]*725n–6n*, 730–1, *731n*, 732, 733n, 734, [3]232–3, 233n, [5]21, 626–7, 627n, 633n, [6]79n, 85–6, 86n
and *homoiousios* see *homoiousios*
homos pusfacti [1]388, 388n
homosexuality [1]147n, [3]796n
homousian [6]90
Hone, William (1780–1842) [1]488 q, [2]437n, 532, [5]173, 173n
ed *The Every-Day Book* [1]488, [2]214; *The Table Book* [1]488; *see also* Bible: Apocrypha: NT: *Apocryphal NT* ed Hone
honestum [4]720
honesty [1]51, 178, [2]347, [4]73, 624, [5]783
meaning of [4]720
honey [1]596, [2]822, 829, [5]105, 831
in lion [3]508, 508n
honey-bird [4]87, 87n
honeycomb [4]494
honey-dews [6]152
Honigmann, E. A. J. *see* Shakespeare *King John* ed Honigmann
honorificabilitudinitatibus [4]509
honour(s) [1]51, [2]530, [4]73, 580, 584, 733, 733n, 816, 860, [5]314
God's [5]617; throne of [5]421
hood [3]357
Hood, Thomas (1799–1845), and J. H. Reynolds *Odes and Addresses* [1]clxi, clxin
Hood, William [5]108
Hood, William (fl 1808–17) [1]228
Hood, Mrs William (fl 1814) [2]587n
Hood's *see* London
hoof, Devil's [1]351
Hooker, Joan (née Churchman) (d 1603) [2]1134–5, 1135n
Hooker, Richard (c 1554–1600) [1]cxxxi, cxxxviiin, 156n, 259, 280, 280n, 292, 297n, 632n, [2]273n, 277, 290n, 294n, 338, 558, [3]169 q, 309n, 641n, 795n, 882, 882n, [4]179, 336, 336n
giant among Aristotelians [2]1146; "Life" by Walton [2]1131; marriage [2]914, 914n; rule of [2]1141; sermon of [1]826, 826n; "Thomas" [1]243, 292–3; wife of *see* Joan Hooker
Ecclesiastical Polity [1]303, 453, 826, lost books of [2]1134–5, 1135n; *Works* ed Gauden [2]1135n, ed J. Spenser [2]1135n; *The Works* [1]453, 453n; MT [2]1131–67
Hoole, Joseph (fl 1730) [5]165n
hoop [3]340, 341
hope(s) [1]575, [2]186, 507, 1075n, 1151, 1161, 1162, 1166, [3]64, 509, 566, 642, [4]9–10, 52, 265, 359, 788, 810, [5]644
assured [2]655; awful [5]483; beckoning [2]319; Christian [1]782, [3]553; false [5]585; religious [5]181; steadfast [5]523; trembling [5]678
hoper, obstinate [5]534
Hopkins, Albert Allis (1869–1939) *see* Vasari *Lives of the Painters* ed Blashfield, Blashfield, and Hopkins
Hopkins, John (d 1570) [3]904n, [5]178, 178n
Hopkins, Mrs Timothy [1]840
hops [2]165, [3]269–70, 270n, [6]118
Hopton, Ralph, 1st Baron Hopton (1596–1652) [2]512, 512n
Horace (Quintus Horatius Flaccus) (65–8 BC) [1]71, 756, [2]240, 582, 678, 756n, 757, 758n, 759, 760, 761, [3]175, 656, 765, [4]289–90, 336n, 736n, [6]32
ed R. Bentley [1]civ; a gentleman [2]353
Ars poetica [1]72n q, 684 q, 684n, [2]355 q, 355n q, 498n q, 514 q, 514n, 516n q, 688n q, 1092n, [3]334n q, 403 q, 403n, [4]191n q, 596–7 q, 597n q, tr Blakeney [1]72n q; *Epistles* [3]498, 498n, [4]238n q, 736n q, 809n, tr Fairclough [2]775n q; *Epodes* [2]760n, 761, 761n; *Odes* [1]692 q,

Horace (Quintus Horatius Flaccus)—*continued*
692n, [2]583n, [3]577n; *Opera* [6]334; *Satires* [1]763 q, 763n, [2]231n, 353n, 363 q, 363n, 756 q, 757n, 760n, 761n, 762 q, 776n q, [4]238 q, 238n, [5]226n, 271 q, 271n q, 651 q, 651n q, tr Fairclough [2]756 q; *Sermones* [1]388n q
Horatii [4]168
Horatio (*Hamlet*) [4]839, 840, 844–5, 859, [5]588n
Horeb (Bible) [2]150
horizon [1]576, [5]487
of experience [5]755; of knowledge [4]601
Hormby, Mr *see* Hornby
horn(s) [1]626, [3]324, [4]700, 827, [6]51, 151
of Devil [1]626; little [3]923; man of [4]429
Horn, Wilhelm von (1803–71) [2]366
Hornby, Edward Thomas Stanley (c 1782–1825) *Childhood*† [2]1168
Horne, George, Bishop of Norwich (1730–92) *A Commentary on the Book of Psalms* [1]429n
Horne, Thomas Hartwell (1780–1862) *see* Wheeler *Theological Lectures* pref Horne
Horner, Leonard (1785–1864) [3]371
hornet [3]26
Hornsey [2]558, 558n, 904–5, *904n–5n*
horologe [2]517
horologium [1]686
horology [5]814
horrible, the [1]397
Horrogan, Mike (in Banim) [1]212–13
horror(s) [2]160, [4]816, 820, [5]419, 597
h. vacui [5]644
horse(s) [2]194, 346–7, 581, 662, 862, [3]383, 1086, [4]96, 97n, 534, 535, 650n, 802, [5]159, 250, 476, 477
Barbary [4]861, 861n; h.-hair [4]737, 737n; master's [5]732; pale [6]165; Przewalski's [2]528n; in Rev [2]515, [3]924; as symbol [2]347; tail of [2]611, 800, 800n, [3]158, 158n; wild [2]528; wooden [3]649n
horsewhip [4]494
horsewhipping [3]63
Horsley, Samuel, Bishop of St Asaph (1733–1806) [1]478n, [2]404n, [3]45, 524n, 594n, [4]301n, 303, 665, 665n, [5]397, 398, [6]307n
on resurrection [1]863
Letters . . . in Reply to Dr Priestley [4]303n; *Nine Sermons* [1]863n q, [2]750, 750n q, [3]45n, [5]398, 398n; *see also* Newton *Works* ed Horsley
Hortensius, Quintus (114–50 BC) [2]276
Horton, Thomas (d 1673) [1]259
hortus siccus [5]642
Hosius, Bishop of Cordova (c 256–357) [2]730, 731n
hospital(s) [3]116, [4]96, [5]190
h. fever [6]38; foundling [6]121; lunatic [4]501, 502
host of heaven [3]617
hot, the [1]604
Hotham, Charles (1615–?72) [1]554
Hotham, Durand/Durant (?1617–91) [1]554
hoti/hoties [1]772, 772n
Hotspur (*1 Henry IV*) [1]374, [2]922, 922n
Hottentot(s) [3]355, 356, [5]83
Houghton [1]162n
Houghton, Arthur Amory, Jr (b 1906) [2]16n
Houghton Library *see* Cambridge MA
"house" [1]443
house(s) [1]443, 774, [3]341, 741, 855, 1025
h.-breakers [3]167; consecrated [1]530; enormous [2]204; h.-loom [2]98
House of Commons/Lords *see* Parliament
Houses of Parliament *see* Parliament
Houyhnhnms (in Swift) [2]347n, [5]475–7
hovellers [2]953
Howard, Bernard Edward, 12th Duke of Norfolk (1765–1842) [4]583, [6]48, 48n
Howard, Henry, Earl of Surrey (c 1517–47) [1]37
Songes and Sonnettes [1]53
Howard, John (?1726–90) [4]241n, [5]65n, 371, 371n
Howard, Luke (1772–1864) [3]938, 942
Howard, Sophia Raby (née Gillman) (b 1851) [4]778
Howard, Theophilus, 2nd Baron Howard de Walden and 2nd Earl Suffolk (1584–1640) [2]1125, 1127–8
Howard, Thomas, 4th Duke of Norfolk (1536–72) [2]508n–9n
Howard, Thomas, 2nd Earl of Arundel (1585–1642) [5]836, 836n
Howe, H. W. *Greta Hall* [1]cixn
Howe, John (1630–1705) [1]352, 352n, [2]558
Howe, John (fl 1775–85) [5]147
Howe, Percival Pressland (1886–1944) *see* W. Hazlitt *Complete Works* ed Howe
Howe, Will (fl 1683) [4]81
Howell, Alan George Ferrers (b 1855) *see* Dante *De vulgari eloquentia* tr Howell
Howes, Raymond Floyd (b 1903) *see* Coleridge, S. T. IX *Coleridge the Talker* ed Armour and Howes
Howick, Viscount *see* Grey, Henry George

Howie, John (1735–93) *Biographia Scoticana* [1]cxxii, [2]1095; MT 1169–81
Howison, James (fl 1798–1808) [3]937
hoy [4]645, 645n
Hoy, Cyrus Henry [1]407n
hrachidzalalagos [2]126
Hubbard, J. P. (fl 1810) [3]938
hubbub [4]648
Huber, François (1750–1831)
  History of Bees [1]lxxxviii; *New Observations . . . on Bees* tr J. G. Dalyell [2]1119, 1119n, [5]731, 731n
Huber, Pierre (1777–1840) *The Natural History of Ants* tr J. R. Johnson [5]731, 731n
Hucks, Joseph (c 1772–1800) [1]99n
huddle [1]158, [5]50
hudibrastic, the [2]762
Hudson, Hoyt Hopewell (1893–1944) *see* Kant *Religion within the Limits of Reason Alone* tr T. M. Green and Hudson
Hudson's Bay [2]985
Hudson's Bay Company [2]985, 987n
Huet, Pierre Daniel (1630–1721) *Demonstratio evangelica* [2]1082, 1083n
Hufeland, Christoph Wilhelm (1762–1836) [5]141, 141n
Hug, Johann Leonhard (1765–1846) *Einleitung in die Schriften des neuen Testaments* [2]181
Huggard, Eveleen M. *see* Leibniz *Theodicy* tr Huggard
Hugh of St Victor (Hugo de Sancto Victore) (1096–1141) [1]cviii, [2]679, 679n, 1182, [3]682, 682n, [4]259, 259n, [5]779–83, 795, 795n
  De sacramentis [1]cvi; MT [2]1182–3; [5]781n
Hughes, John (1677–1720) [1]38
Hughes, Joseph (1769–1833) [2]*1184*
  The Believer's Prospect and Preparation MT [2]1184–7; [4]3; *A Tribute of Friendship* [4]6
Hughson, David ("Edward Pugh") (d 1813) *Walks Through London* [2]196n
Hugo of St Cher (d 1263) [2]314n
Huguenot(s) [1]225, 740n, [2]1198n, [5]166
Hull [1]336, 337n, [2]60, 947, [5]162, 162n
hullo-bulloo [2]847
Hülsen, August Ludwig (1765–1810)
  Natur-Betrachtungen [1]132; *Ueber die natürliche Gleichheit der Menschen* [1]132
"human" [2]1051
human, the [1]675–6
human being [3]641; *see also* man/men
human nature [1]169, [2]98, 616, 671, [3]95, 266, 401, 494, 517, [4]308, 412, 629, 647, 651, 796, [5]20–1, 27–8, 475, 543, 595, 822
  essence of [4]653; laws of [3]331; limitations of [3]260; mystery of [2]247; perceptions of [4]366; politics of [1]389
human race [1]283, [2]404, 1076, [3]545, 594, 663, [5]252n, 336, 336n, 599, 724
  childhood of [1]718; origin of [2]414
Humane Society [2]388, 388n, [6]118, 118n
humanisation [1]704, [3]324–5 ("humanises"), [5]372
humanists [3]308n
humanities [5]54, 169
Humanities Research Center, University of Texas *see* Austin TX
humanity [1]169, [2]261, [3]23, 42, 434, 581, 720, 846, [4]653, 653n, [5]21, 233, 277, 377, 524, 647, 673, 822
  character of [5]483; of Christ [1]704, [3]51, [5]394, 546, 547–8, 580, [6]65; conscious [4]824; constituents of [5]425; dictates of [1]877; distinctive character of [1]878; distinguishing features of [1]29; divine [1]429, 863, [2]281, [3]27, 545, [5]466, 472, 650, 678; ideal of [2]191; imperfect [3]306, [6]20; intellection a part of [1]233; and language [1]538; mere [1]358; moral nature of [2]938; natural [4]588; perpetual [1]575; powers of [5]784; proper [2]186, [5]465; spiritual [1]202, 303; tap-root [2]987n; united to divine [3]311–12; victories of [2]846; *see also* man/men
humankind [5]730
Humber (river) [3]628
Humboldt, Alexander, Baron von (1769–1859) [1]244n, [3]384n, 938, 939, [4]427n, 491, [6]104, 104n
Humboldt, Karl Wilhelm, Baron von (1767–1835) [4]427n
humbug [1]835, [4]325, [5]93n, [6]122
humdrumming [2]960, 961
Hume, David (1711–76) [3]708n, 877, 877n, 950n, [4]260n, 646, 839, 839n, [5]65n, 124, 124n, 140n, 640, 640n, 802n, 812, [6]131
  on Beattie [6]290, 290n; definition of miracle [5]53n, [6]135n; "idea" in [2]627; Kant on [4]348, 348n; on miracles [1]317n, [5]63, 63n q, 65n; over-rated [4]75; scepticism of [3]966; and Scots [1]75n; sneer of [5]729
  Dialogues Concerning Natural Religion [3]848, 848n q, [5]729n–30n; *Enquiries Concerning the Human Understanding and the Principles of Morals* ed Selby-Bigge [5]63n q; *Essays Moral, Political and Literary* ed T. H. Green and Grose [4]839n q; *History of England* [4]75, 75n,

Hume, David—*continued*
[4]646n, [5]124n; *The Natural History of Religion* [3]848n, ed Colver [3]848
Hume, Joseph (1777–1855) [1]255n, [2]27n, 979, 979n, [3]96n, 153, 153n
Hume, Mr (fl 1811) [3]941
Humfrey, John (1621–1719) [1]348–9
humility [2]1179, [3]522, 582, [4]254, [5]148, 539, [6]304
breach of [1]350; and pride [5]820
humming [5]767
"humour" [5]98n
humour [2]917, 1126, [3]173–4, 702, [4]194, 195, 243, 360, [5]98n, 99n
confused with "character" [2]778; defined [1]139; inimitable [2]15; low [2]777; and wit [2]17n, 144n, [3]174, 174n, [6]163
humourist [1]126, 762, [5]98–9, 99n
humours, four [3]565n, [4]762, [5]98–9, 285
Humphrey, John *see* Humfrey
Humphreys, Arthur Raleigh (b 1911) *see* Shakespeare *1 Henry IV*, *2 Henry IV* ed Humphreys
Humphreys, James (d 1830) [5]478, 478n
Observations on the . . . Laws of Real Property [5]478n
hums and has [2]59
humus [1]663, [4]322
Hungary [2]1086n, [3]1062
hunger [1]665, 665n, 678, [2]1055, 1109n, [3]399, 401, 806, 808, [5]249, 370
Hunmanby [1]90n
hunt, analytic [5]789
Hunt, Henry (1773–1835) [2]211, 211n, [3]441, 441n
Hunt, Leigh (1784–1859) [1]615n, 738, [2]351 q, 964
owner of annotated book [4]101, [5]99; see also *Reflector* ed Hunt
Hunt, W. A. (fl 1827) [2]698
Hunter, George Kirkpatrick *see* Shakespeare *All's Well* ed Hunter
Hunter, John (1728–93) [1]550, 550n, 624, 624n, [3]842, 842n, 844n, 868n, [4]5, [5]504n
A Treatise on the Blood ed E. Home [1]624n q, [3]612n
Hunter, William (1755–1812) [3]937
Hunting [5]38 q
Huntingdon, Countess of *see* Hastings, Selina
Huntington Library *see* San Marino CA
Huntington Library Quarterly [3]400, [4]105
huntsman/huntsmen [1]764–5, 797, [4]96
Huon (in *Huon of Bordeaux*) [4]827, 827n
Hur (Bible) [4]683
Hurd, Richard, Bishop of Worcester (1720–1808) [3]894, 894n, 896
An Introduction to . . . the Prophecies Concerning the Christian Church [3]894n
"hurraer" [2]582, 582n
Hurst, Chance & Co *see* London
Hurwitz, Hyman (1770–1844) [1]415, 427n, 513n, 708n, 710, 710n, 719n, 738, [2]153n, 334n, 955n, *1188–9*, [3]463n, 606n, 715, [4]41, 41n
letter(s) to [2]371 q, [3]835n, [4]49n q, 166n; supplier of books to C [1]xcviii
The Elements of the Hebrew Language [2]54n; MT 1188–90; *The Etymology and Syntax of the Hebrew Language* [2]1188; *A Hebrew Dirge* [2]1188; *Hebrew Tales* [2]1189; *The Tears of a Grateful People* [2]1188; *Vindiciae Hebraicae* [2]1189
husband [1]699
jealous [4]598; reluctant [1]369; and wife [2]167n, [3]670, [4]790, [5]550, [6]263
Husenbeth, Frederick Charles (1796–1872) *A Defence of the Creed and Discipline of the Catholic Church* [1]855
Husham (Bible) [1]418
husk [1]468
of spirit [2]1003
Huskisson, William (1770–1830) [6]45
Huss/Hus, John (c 1369–1415) [1]858, 858n, [2]507n, [3]765n, [4]710n
Husseian (i.e. Southeian) *see* R. Southey
Hussein Pasha, Dey of Algiers (fl 1818–30) [1]32, 32n
"Hussey" (R. Southey) [2]932n, [5]151, 151n
Hutchinson, Francis (1660–1739) [6]105n
An Historical Essay Concerning Witchcraft [6]105n
Hutchinson, George (b 1618) [1]767n
Hutchinson, Joanna (1780–1841) [1]clxixn
Hutchinson, John (1615–64) [1]223, 223n, 278, 335, 335n, 336n, [2]43n, 971n, 1191, [4]73, 73n, [6]258, 258n; *see also* L. Hutchinson *Memoirs*
Hutchinson, John (1674–1737) *Moses's Principia* [2]787, 787n, 788, 789
Hutchinson, Julius (c 1751–1811) [2]1191, 1194, 1194n, 1198
Hutchinson, Lucy (née Apsley) (1620–c 1676) [1]lviii, 335n, [2]1191–2, [4]73n
Memoirs of the Life of Colonel Hutchinson [1]335, 335n, 766, 766n, 767n q, [2]970, 970n q; MT 1191–1202; [3]657, 705, 705n, [4]73n

Hutchinson, Mary *see* Wordsworth, Mary
Hutchinson, Sara (1775–1835) [1]lxxix, xcii, xciii, 76, 259n, 601n, 762n, 768n, 796, [2]45n, 695n, 877n, 1120n, 1121n, 1203, [3]837, 837n, [4]35, 207, 282, 292n, 804n, [5]486, 824, 824n
anagrams [1]571, 571n, [2]242n; books associated with [1]cv; C's awe of [1]9, 9n; and C's notebooks [1]533n; death [1]clx; DW letter to [1]cx; in 1835 [1]clixn; hair [4]283, 283n; images associated with [1]ciii; "Isulia" [2]117; her letter to JHG [1]clviii–clix q; letter(s) to [5]810n q, 824, 824n; marginalia addressed to [1]lxxxii, c, 762–5, 795; marginalia associated with [1]lxxxi, lxxxiii, lxxxvi–lxxxviii, cxv, cxlin, clviii, clxvi, clxix, 226, 227, 227n; owner of annotated books [1]clixn, clxxiv, 90n, 741, 742, 760–1, [2]1117–18; separation from [1]cxi, [3]863n; transcriber of marginalia [2]168n, [4]91
Letters ed Coburn [1]clviii–clix q, clviiin, clixn q, 761, [2]93n q, 1117
Hutchinson, Thomas (1773–1849) [3]837
Hutchinson, Winnifred Margaret Lambert (b 1868) *see* Pliny *Letters* tr Melmoth, rev Hutchinson
Hutchinsons, the [2]845
Hutton, Charles (1737–1823) [4]312
Hutton, James (1715–95) [5]126
Hutton, James (1726–97) [3]60n
A Dissertation upon Light, Heat, and Fire [3]59n; *An Investigation of the Principles of Knowledge* [1]lviii, lxxxiv, 409; MT [2]1203–7
Huygens, Christiaan (1629–95) [4]271n
Huysum, Jan van (1682–1749) [4]780 ("Vanhuysen") 780n
hvima [1]124n
Hyacinth (myth) [1]147
Hyades [1]764, 797
"hyberno-fumiflammant" [3]1029, 1029n
hybrid [4]169
hydatic acid *see* acid(s)
hydatid(s) [2]367, [3]444, [4]431, 432n, [5]468, 468n
Hyde, Edward, 1st Earl of Clarendon (1609–74) [1]290, 808n, [2]114, 114n, 358, 358n, 522, 523n, 945, 945n, [3]798, 801, 801n, 802, 803, 803n, [4]74, 74n, 79–80, [6]186, 308n
History of the Rebellion [1]290n q, [2]114n, 358n, 818, 818n, [5]147n
Hyde, Henry, 2nd Earl of Clarendon (1638–1709) [4]83
hydor en hydati [1]579, 579n, 594, 622
Hydra (myth) [1]788n, [2]900n, [3]234n, [4]198
hydra-head [3]797
hydrarch [1]570
hydrate(s) [1]579, 663, [4]319, [5]438
hydraulis [3]248n
hydrazotocarbons [3]1005
hydrocarbonazotes [3]1005
hydrocephalus [4]164
hydrochloric acid *see* acid(s)
"hydrogen" [5]346
hydrogen [1]551, 590, 594, 596, 597, 598, 611, 614, 628, 635, 636, 639n, 641, 643, 660, 662, 663, 666, 737, 780, [2]546, 546n, 852n, 853n, 854–5, 854n, 855, 1186, [3]43, 44, 45, 61, 61n, 67, 127, 129, 443, 950, 951, 951n, 952, 997, 997n, 999, 1000, 1002, 1004, 1007, 1017, 1020, 1021n, 1022, 1027, 1027n, 1031, 1032, 1060, 1061, [4]13, 16, 169, 315n, 316, 324, 387, 388n, 428, 492, [5]246, 246n, 247, 259, 266, 335n, 342, 343, 344, 346, 397, 438, [6]116, 227, 228–9
associated with female [1]654; and azote [1]648; chloride [1]569n; dynamic [5]265; magnetic [1]775; and nitrogen [1]650; peroxide [3]1032n; renamed [1]570; role in animal life [3]68; role in vegetation [3]68; in water [2]1144, 1144n
hydrographer [4]534n
hydrophobia [1]590, 590n, [2]739n, [5]260, 260n, 679, 679n, [6]120n, 122; *see also* rabies
hydroseptic, the [4]149
hydrosulphurate [4]168
hydroxides [3]1005
hydryl [1]570
hyena(s) [1]778, [5]387
hylarchs [2]788, 788n
hyle [1]570, 582, 609, [2]425, 431, 431n, [3]130, 247, 248n, [4]328, [5]165; *see also* matter
hylotheist [1]619, 620n
hylozoism [2]340n, 554n, [3]99n, [4]523, 523n, [5]296, [6]75, 75n
hylozoists [2]340, [5]716
Hyman, Leonard [2]1189
Hyman, Robin [2]1189
hymn(s) [2]785, 964, [3]21, 455, [5]162n, 512, 525, 526–7, 835
h.-book [3]211, [5]651; Christian [5]179; congregational [5]510; Gen 1 as morning h. [2]393; Homeric *see* Homeric Hymns; mystic [4]472; Orphic [1]592, 776n, [2]581 q, 582, 582n, [6]7; prophetic [3]55

Hymn to Ceres
ed Hermann [2]1091n, ed Ilgen [2]1091n, ed A. H. Matthiae [2]1091n, ed Mitscherlich [2]1091n, ed Ruhnken [2]1090, 1091n
hyperbola [2]557
hyperbole(s) [1]706, 755, [2]498, [3]508, 673
hyperbolism [1]725
hyperbolist [4]668
hyperdulia [2]662, 662n
hyperduly/hyperdulies [1]257n, 519, 519n
hyperlatinistic [1]762, 796
hyperorthodoxy [1]477
hyperousion [1]665, 665n
hyperstoicism [4]352
"hypertheological" [3]66, 66n
"hypertrophied" [4]77, 77n
"hypertrophy" [4]77n
hypistos [3]32n
hypnosis [3]364n
hypo [1]570
hypochondriac [3]210
hypochondriasis [2]720, 728, [5]414, 414n
hypochondriasts [5]819
hypocrisy [1]308, [2]19, [3]317, 483, 550, 879, [4]599, 645, 652, 818, [5]150, 616
Hypocrisy (in Bunyan) [1]821, 821n, 822
Hypocrisy Unveiled [2]947n
hypocrite(s) [1]426, [2]984, 1076, 1076n, [3]268, 797, [4]689
"hypo-criticism" [3]955, 955n, 963
hyponeirosis [2]886, 886n
"hypopoesis" [1]108, 108n
hypopoesis/hypopoiesis [2]445, 445n, 605, 605n, 886, 886n, [3]328, 328n, 1026, 1026n, [4]13
and hypothesis [1]108, *108n*, [2]388n, [3]328n, [4]13, 13n, 433, 433n
"hyposode" [1]570
"hypostasis" [5]579, [6]86, 87, 87n
hypostasis/hypostases [1]434, 466n, 469, 469n, [2]641, 726, 726n, 731, 731n, 798, [3]11, 17, 17n, 23n, 24, 93, 233, 233n, 428, 606n, [5]626, 627, 680, 799, 799n, [6]76
of the Holy Spirit [6]67; mistranslated "person" [2]21, 21n
"hypostatic" [6]86
hypostatikos [5]633, 633n, 799, 799n
"hypothesis" [4]13, 13n
hypothesis/hypotheses [2]445, 445n, 460, 609, 610, 886, 886n, [3]210–11, 242, 328, 328n, 395, 397, 436, 465, 1022, 1026n, [4]13, 234n
arbitrary [2]1029, [4]451; Arian [5]657; cold-blooded [2]410; Eichhorn's *see* Eichhorn; and fact *see* fact; and hypopoesis *see* hypopoesis; and hypopoiesis *see* hypopoiesis; improbable [2]414; objection to [4]458; and theory [4]12n
Hypsistus [2]578n
Hyrcanus (d 78 BC) [2]157n
Hyssus (river) [2]981n
hysteria [1]582n, [2]720, [5]136n
hysterics [3]823
hysteron proteron [1]647, 647n, [3]462, [5]159n
"hystero-proterise" [5]159, 159n
hysteroproterising [6]199
"hystery" [1]536, 536n
Hywel Dda (Hywel the Good) (d 950) [2]1170 ("Hoel"), 1170n

"I" [2]1177, [4]456, [5]94, 203, 723, [6]82
I [1]153, [2]297, 690, 1109, [3]120, 121n, 122, 236–7, 239, 297, 387, 444, 909, 909n, [4]159, 375, 459
absolute [1]648, [2]623, 623n; and consciousness [2]625; double [3]46; easily contented [2]610; equivocal [2]611, 615, 615n; Fichte's [2]596; inseparable [2]630; by itself I [2]622; in Jacobi [3]95, 96; limits itself [2]633; logical [4]454; meaning [2]535, 535n, 602, 602n; and not-I [3]266, 266n; real and empirical [3]96; I-ship [1]304n, see also *Ichheit*; simple element [5]816; spiritual [5]172; as verb [3]852; vice-I [5]296. See also *ego*; *Ich*; self
I am/I AM [1]239, 435, 458, 460, 618, 694, 824, [2]24, 203, 287, 292–3, 293n, 321, 324, 379, 379n, 392, 392n, 596, 726, 726n, 882, 891, 901, [3]12, 12n, 18, 66, 151, 429, 659, 1012, 1054, [4]122n–3n, 123, 166, 258, 348n, 406, 407n, 459, 460, 460n, 542, [5]177, 481, 790, [6]76, 82, 83, 85n, 89, 91
in absolute [1]138; equals will [2]930; meaning [3]1065; mystery of [5]616; see also *eimi*
Iago (*Othello*) [1]212, 212n, 393, [4]818, 822, 850, 850n, 860–1, 862, 865, 866, 867, [6]323, 323n
I.-ism [4]862
iambic(s) [1]377, 384, 403, [2]874, [3]712n, 839, 903, [4]290, [6]252, 255
hexameter [5]688, 689; pentameter [1]377, [2]1039, [5]688
Iamblichus (c 250–c 325) [1]690n, [3]539n q, [5]224, 226, 226n, 758
unreliability of [5]224n, 229, 229n
De mysteriis Aegyptorum [1]civn

"iamböid" [4]603, 603n
Iaones [2]578n
Ibbetson, Agnes (née Thomson) (1757–1823) [3]939, 940, 941, 942, [4]82, 82n, [5]344, 346n, 771, 771n
Ibn Ezra, Abraham ben Meir (c 1092–1167) [3]1088 ("Aben Ezra"), 1088n
Ibrahim Pasha (1789–1848) [1]32, 32n
Icarus (myth) [2]706
ice [1]505, 650, [2]1058, [3]323n, 1022, [4]491, [5]105, 244, 248, 265, 267, 557, [6]152, 230
icebergs [2]1140
Iceland [4]528, [5]263, [6]153
Ich [4]131, 346, 413, 456, 459, 460, [6]237; *see also* I
Ichheit/*Ichheiten* [2]631, 1109, [4]347–8, 443, 460, [5]816, [6]237
ichneumon [4]86–7
ichor [3]612, [6]66
icon(s) [3]106, 107n, 135, 524, 524n, 545n, [4]653, 653n, [6]306, 306n
  more than image [1]466; see also *eikon*
Ida, Mount [2]354n, 901, [6]211
Idalaea [2]95n; *see also* Venus
Idalus [2]95n
Iddo (Bible) [2]149n
"idea" [1]530, [2]631–2, 632n, [3]859–60, [5]230, 230n, 409, 565n, 581, 729, 729n, 751n, 793, 828, 828n, [6]6, 6n, 32, 80–1
  abuse of [3]177; adequate [3]524; degeneration of term [4]115n; misused by Herder [2]1068
idea(s) [1]670, [2]478, 552, 553, 716, 882, 961, 1066–7, 1113, 1155, 1186, [3]21, 90n, 177n, 516, 643n, 904, 904n, 957, [4]224, 258, 259, 314, 400, 401, 411, 731, [5]29, 79, 90, 118, 161, 173, 269, 279, 425, 444, 615, 721, 800
  absence of [3]948; absolute [1]347, [2]198; of absolute [5]455; and abstraction [3]261–2; adequate [1]573, [2]1084, [4]413, 413n, [6]306; affirmation of [5]131, [6]307; antecedent to thing [2]1134; of beautiful [3]460; birth of [5]372; of birth of evil [2]1106; causative [3]705; causes of [2]960; of Church [5]662, 662n; clear [3]859; complete [6]174; and concept(s) [2]729n; and conception(s) *see* conception(s); confused with historic genesis [2]60–1; constitutive or regulative [5]813; containing [2]429; of contract [5]299; converted to assertion [3]65; of creation [3]139; creative [2]1144; criterion of [5]131; debasement of [5]31; defined [2]152, 1134, [3]762, [5]789; degenerates [4]124; of depth [6]233; diagnostic of [5]599; discriminate [1]495; distinct [4]230; distinctive character [5]450; divine [1]464, 574, [3]28, 545, [4]349, [6]109; doctrine of [2]151, [5]738, 776; dynamic [3]999; Empyrean of [2]1146; energic [3]136, 136n; eternal [3]617, 617n; of eternity [2]1069, [4]126; ethical [5]578; and facts [3]36, 989; of fallen spirits [2]1106; and feelings [2]628; few in botany [2]527; as flash in mirror [1]619; fleshly [3]12; and form [5]470; of free will [4]439; of freedom [4]434; general [4]113, 787; and general or abstract words [2]482; and generalisations [3]163; in/of God *see* God; of gospel institute [5]661; grand [5]350, 467; great [6]71; ground of C's philosophy [2]423; grounding [6]216; harmony of [4]115; hauntings of [5]349; Heraclitus on [5]714; huddle in [1]158; of the I AM [6]82; without i. [2]153; of i. [6]77, 77n; ideal grounds [3]997, 998; identified with object [3]857; and idol(s) [2]679n, [3]42, 42n, 162, 431; and idolon [4]42; and image [1]574, [3]967, 967n, [5]17n, 409, 564–5, 565n, 581–2, 638, 729n, 793, [6]233; immoral [4]275; and impression [2]627; inconceivable [2]1145, [5]600, 771; indivisible [2]250; inexpressible [5]627; infinite [1]574; influence of [5]315; innate [2]543, [3]965n, 967; intelligible [3]31; involution of [1]599; inworking [3]755; Jung's usage [3]206, 206n; just [5]413; Kant on [5]714; of king [2]70; and law [5]372; law as [5]305; of life [2]1026, [3]60; living [1]463; of Locke [4]115; contained in Logos [1]573; *Logos protogenes* [3]92; of all mankind [5]487; material [5]825n; meagre [6]324; of a miracle [5]63; mirror of [3]20; misuse as plan [1]530; modifying power [1]822; Mosaic [5]364; of a mystery [3]878; in myth [2]177; of nation [3]158n; nature of [5]640; necessarily universal [1]368; negative definition [5]776; noetic [1]794; and notion(s) [2]295–6, 295n, 359, [3]430n, 524, [4]17, 17n, [5]699n, [6]306–7; and number(s) [5]230, 703, 703n; and object(s) [1]565, [5]208–9; objective [6]286; of one [4]364; of 1 = 3 [6]83; order of [5]214; organ of insight [5]755; and organisation [4]375; Paley on [4]638–9; perfection of [5]687; of personeity [2]456; phenomenon and [4]379; philosophy of [2]673; philosophy the science of [2]500; plant-making [3]1023, 1023n; Plato on [4]127, 156, [5]229n, 735; Platonic [1]73, 73n, [2]424, 449, [3]913, [5]748–9, 750–2; of Platonists [4]115; in Plotinus

idea(s)—*continued*
[5]758; of a poker [3]860; possession by [2]159, 160; and power [1]706; of power [5]719; power of [2]1148, [4]93; prayer is [3]754; primitive material sense [2]631–2; privilege of [5]744; in Proclus [4]426; of pure reason [4]157; of Pythagoras [4]115, [5]230; and reason [1]682; regulative [5]698, 698n, 732, 732n; in religion [2]482; religion of [2]295; of Schelling [2]187; self as [5]177; self-contradiction in [3]428; seminal [1]527–8, [3]835; shadowy [3]435–6; source of [4]78; of space [3]916, [4]115; spiritual [3]49; spiritual intuition [1]122; spiritual truths [3]743; like stars [5]795; stuffed with [5]91; sublime [2]263; subsistent [3]18; substantial [1]694, [3]545, [5]577; supernatural [2]298; in Swedenborg [5]409–10; and symbol [4]42; symbol of [2]1069; synthetic [1]571; and theory [4]13; theory of [5]750–2; and thing [2]1134, [3]158; transcendent analogon [5]751; transcendental [3]247; of Trinity [3]761–2, [5]25, [6]74; true in [1]347; truth as [3]23; of truth [6]71; truth-powers [2]297, 881n, 1151, [3]163, 163n; ultimate end [3]423, 424; unique [3]12, [5]131; unity of [1]180, [5]782; universal [3]23–4; verb substantive in [6]9; of virtue [3]317; in visual symbols [2]410; vivid [2]959; vividness of [1]270, [6]261; want of [6]83; of will [2]324, [3]12; wise only possess i. [2]159; of Word [3]101; and words [2]209, 732, 744; words in place of [2]482; of the world [5]730
ide(a)ist(s) [2]1066, 1147, [5]699, 770, 770n
ideal(s) [2]793, [3]127, [4]689, [5]170
and actual *see* actual; divine [3]545; of divine ideas [6]109; perfect [5]820; of proportion [5]98; and real [1]108, [4]168, 401, 452, 457, [5]201; in reason [5]52
"idealism" [1]145n
idealism [2]547n, 607n, [3]249, 857, 957, [4]262, 351, [5]203, 743n
all systems of i. fall [2]631; Berkeley's [1]409, [4]132; dogmatic [1]105; Fichte's [6]237; foundation-stone of [2]603; German [4]460n; ground(s) of [2]628, [4]453; in Hamlet [4]844; insufficing [5]201; lifeless [4]116; objective [4]421n; psilo-phaenomenism [2]547; pure [5]718; and realism [1]145n, [6]237–8; self-shaping [2]610; subjective [4]447n, [5]410; transcendental [3]966n, [4]447–62
idealist(s) [2]607, [5]692, 698n, 720n, 770n
common [6]241; German [3]909n; post-Kantian [5]90n; sane [3]850
ideality [5]687
Ideatae [5]770n
idem see *alter*
identity/identities [2]249, 745, 750, 881, 1186, [3]13, 17, 18, 138, 266, 449, 865, [4]258, 454, 542, 603, [5]159, 458, 460, 799, 799n, [6]92
absolute [2]1019, [3]11, [6]237–44; contemplation of [1]348; in difference [1]665; hidden [4]427; law of [1]662; love of [1]562; not sameness but union [2]598; personal [3]1071n, [4]69, [5]547; of real and actual [2]554n; of reason and will [5]176; of subject and object [5]203; will principle of i. [2]250
Ideotae [5]770
ideotis [3]686
idiom(s) [1]156–7, 157n, [2]141, 141n, [3]331
colloquial [3]534, [6]316; English [6]9; familiar [6]199
idiosymbolic [3]138
idiosyncrasy [5]577
idiot(s) [3]324, [4]23
idiotes [2]404, 404n
idleness [2]98, 168 ("idle")
"idol" [4]42n
idol(s) [2]882, 882n, [3]42, 42n, 136, 431, 431n, 584–5, [4]124n, 280, 429, [5]730, [6]21
of age [3]877; of cross [1]820–1; domination of [5]738; heathen [4]58; and idea *see* idea(s); mechanism as [2]788; mental [1]820; Protestant [2]1155; Quakers idolise words [3]809; of rabbinical fabling [3]437; unhappy [5]596; visual image [5]409
idolators [1]864, [4]109, [5]657
Jews as [2]785, 785n
idolatry [1]225, 523, [2]662, 1125, [3]5n, 77, 108, 434, 448, 467, 468, 473, 495n, 585, 924n, [4]145, 226, 296–7, 298–9, [5]31n, 158, 406n, 580, 626, 641, 657–8, 835, [6]146, 154–5, 167
essence of [4]299; exposure of [6]141; horror of [3]692; image of [6]167; kinds of [2]25; origin of [6]138; popish [1]297; of present [1]280; RC [1]845–6, [2]1043; Romanist [2]344; sensational [5]189
idolism [3]135, [5]716
idololatria [5]406, 406n
idolon [4]42
"idoloplastic" [4]234
idolum [4]124
Idumaea/Idumea [2]414, 739
Temple of Venus [2]739
Idumaeans [2]707, [3]476
idylls [2]738
"if" [5]711, 711n

Igloolik [2]1108n
Ignatius of Antioch, St (c 35–c 107) [1]233, 308, 492, [2]710n, [3]486, [4]473, 473n
Epistle to the Romans [2]717, 717n; *Epistles* [2]710–12, *710n–11n*
ignis [2]339, [3]61, 61n
i. fatuus [4]218, [5]96n
ignition [5]351
"ignivomist" [1]872, 872n
ignominy [5]68, 103
ignoramuses [2]868
"ignorance" [1]13, [2]871, 871n–2n
ignorance [1]423, 558, 874, [4]647, 662, 670, [5]83, 146, 476, 613
age of [5]561; happy [1]162; human [5]592; meritorious [2]712; mutual [5]469; popish [5]163
ignoranza [1]491
ignoratio elenchi [3]934n
Iken, Conrad (1689–1753) *see* Hase and Iken *Thesaurus*
Ilgen, Karl David (1763–1846) [2]88n; *see also* Homeric Hymns: *Homeri Hymni* ed Ilgen
Ilissus (river) [2]980, 981n
"illaqueate" [5]597, 597n
illation [1]770
Illinois, University of, marginalia at [2]521
illness [5]298
imagery of [5]125n
illucence [3]560, 560n
illusion(s) [2]643, [4]61, 129n, 781, 781n, [5]141, 772, [6]158
dialectic [5]742; dramatic [4]863n; mere [5]371; optical [6]101n
illustration(s) [1]685, [3]222, [5]341, 780
glimmer of [1]689; modes of [1]763, 797; poetic [4]418; want of [5]372
Illyricum [2]578
Illyricus *see* Flacius
Ilus (myth) [2]577
"image" [5]442, 442n
image(s) [1]431, 431n, 466, 563, 565, 573, 651, 774, [2]542, 632, [3]24, 135, 318, 377, 460, 517, 545n, 741, 865, 900, [4]144, 394, 647, 648, 653, 653n, 735, 737, 738, 781, [5]29, 125, 168, 406, 453, 614, 615, 734, 792, 813, [6]87
abstract [3]261; are abstractions [3]792; act and [3]947; allegoric [1]821; from brain [3]212, 217; called substance [6]241; in churches [2]1097; coloured [3]389; commonplace [1]59; and conception *see* conception; connate [2]543; defined [5]442; disgusting [1]157; distinct [1]110, 394, [4]278; divine [1]29; doubled [2]646; in dreams [5]559, 726; express [6]61; eye-i. [4]739; of fancy [1]753; form of [1]864; general [5]173; of God [1]815; God's [3]875; humorous [4]706; and icon [1]466, 466n; of ideas [1]573–4, 574; imageless [5]117; of loved ones [1]789; man in God's i. [4]531; material [2]250, 425; as medium [6]300; mental [6]102; in mirror [6]240; noble [5]856; obscure [1]822; optical [3]284; original [1]442; power of [5]588; primary [3]832; primitive [3]834; projected [2]1028; reflected [3]581, [5]405; repetition of [3]341, 362; retrojected [2]1028; of sense [5]795; sensible [1]516; sensuous [3]197, [5]442, 738; sensuous imaging [3]89; or shape [5]409; during sleep [5]122; soliciting [5]588; spirit not imageable [3]301; substantive [3]106; of sun [1]815; symbolic(al) [3]991, 1089, [5]494; taken literally [3]44; unimageable [3]363; unimaginable [2]539, [4]263; unreal [5]552, unstable [5]581; usual [1]811; visible [1]523; visual [1]354, [2]200, 1142, [3]431, 565, 720, [4]166, [5]409, 657; vivid [2]933; wavering [4]278; of wheel [4]450; wooden [5]753; i.-worship [2]1152, [5]497
imagery [3]468, 898, [6]204, 212
city [6]203; sublime [1]430; of visions [2]1146
imaginability [2]890
imagination(s) [1]70n, 135, 157, 375, 609n, 610, 632n, 640, 674, 686, [2]359, 622, 670, 713, 1014, 1168, [3]11, 44, 63, 197, 203, 206, 213, 224, 247, 273, 342, 376n, 400, 409, 789–93, 832, 910n, [4]92, 109, 193, 212, 229, 229n, 292, 369n, 384n, 398, 479, 727, 727n, 786, 820, 830, [5]110, 130, 136n, 210, 210n, 217, 361, 475, 756, 780–1, 785–6, [6]120n
act of [4]217; bars to [3]406; bills of [4]662; combined with sensibility [2]173; in conception [2]857n; constructive [3]275, 343; contradiction for [5]269; in critic [2]969; defined [1]175n, [6]115; delusions of [1]823; diagram in [6]8; disciplined [3]401; distemperature of [1]813; disturbed [3]223; endurable by [4]582; esemplastic power [1]113n; evil [2]160; excited [2]167; extinction of [1]327; and fancy *see* fancy; fantastic self [1]620; and feeling [4]773; finer [5]476; fixed on Christ [1]434; function of [5]796; gastric [5]101; grandeur of [1]327; habit of [3]499; in hot countries [2]418; idea of [3]118; idealising power [4]78; imperfection of [5]794; indefinite [2]160; inflated [5]154; influence of [3]117; innocent [2]273; intelligential [3]16n;

imagination(s)—*continued*
Isaiah's [5]59; Knight lacks [3]410; as laboratory [1]lxi; law(s) of [2]609, [3]118; Locke on [4]25–6; loose [1]826, [5]494; man of [3]929; may supersede perception [4]864; as medium [6]100; mere [3]9; Milton wrote from [3]403; modifying power of [3]402; of mother [3]392; necrosis of [4]77; oscillations of [5]750; other [4]503; of the people [6]101; in perception [4]217; poisoned [2]693; polluted [5]562; pollution of [1]714; power of [3]215–16; power of living in past ages [1]280; power over [2]741; primary and secondary [4]374n; pure [4]856; purity of [3]171; rare gift [3]20; of readers [2]514; reasoning with [2]864; representatives in [3]301; role in animal magnetism [3]376; role in conception [3]329; role in perception [3]377; Scott's failures of [4]598n; sensuous [5]406, 822; sensuous fancy [2]1144; shadows of [4]790; sin acts through [1]819; Skelton's [5]70; spiritual intuition [5]751; stimulants of [5]184; subjective [5]460; sympathy of [1]397; transimaginate [3]90; unity essential [4]382; unpreoccupied [3]444; visual [3]138, 138n
imaginative, the [4]833
imago [5]442n
imitation [2]206, [3]306, [4]715, [5]117n, 820
of Christ [4]656; and copy *see* copy; an improvement [1]369; of Shakespeare [1]367, 407; *see also* plagiarism
imitator(s) [3]187
free [3]892
Immaculate Conception *see* conception(s), immaculate
immanence [4]155, [5]207
Immanuel *see* Manuel I
"immediate" [6]97
immediatecy [5]599
immersion [5]664
immorality [1]544, [2]6, [4]303
"immortal" [5]177
immortal(s) [2]562
immortality [1]125, 824, [2]269, 695, 695n, 828, 1010, 1061, 1075n, 1140, 1185–6, [3]88, 305, 317, 425n, 520, 732, 743n, 875, 956, [4]246, 265, 652, 676, 676n, 695, [5]177, 374, 598, 618, [6]140
happy [5]600–1; idea of [2]1186; in OT [1]675; personal [2]261; of the soul [3]670; terror of [1]284
impanation [5]5
impartiality [4]23, 182, 804
"imparticipability" [1]60, 60n
impatience [1]605, [2]636–7, 648
impenetrability [1]82, 82n, [2]1205
imperative, categorical [5]755, 756, 791
imperator [2]949, [3]143
imperfection(s) [2]247, 671, [3]64, 776, [4]212, 434, [5]19, 93, 729, 820, [6]127
imperium/imperia [3]149
i. in imperio [1]308, [2]697n, [4]18n, [5]37
impermanence [5]360
impersators [4]42, 42n
impersonation [2]344, 345, [3]406
impery [3]149
"impetite" [1]819, 819n
impetite(s) [1]819, [3]910n
imp-flies [3]884
impieties, idolatrous [2]147
impletion [6]79
implicit and explicit [1]836
imposer(s) [1]271, 275
of oath [6]262, 264
imposition(s) [1]320, 352, [5]141, 157, 287
impossibility/impossibilities [1]448, [4]268, 423
impostor(s) [4]26, 614, [5]656
imposture(s) [1]730, [2]194, [3]708, [4]145, 662, [5]141, 287, 517, 656, [6]100, 123
impotence [1]777, [2]676, [6]274
impotency [1]777
imprecation [3]770
impregnation [2]541, 542
impress, passive [5]409
impression(s) [2]608, 959, [3]262, 790, 791, 829, [4]93, 216, 401, 416, [5]443
and idea [2]627; maternal [3]392n; from objects [5]382; through the senses [5]828; sensible [2]1133; sensual [2]632; total [3]20, 792, 914, [5]750; unity of [2]865, [4]773; visual [4]217; worldly [4]409
imprisonment [2]980, [4]667
improbability/improbabilities [1]213, [4]586, 600, 612, 717–18, 815, [5]339, 415, [6]145
"improve" [2]681, 681n
improvement(s) [3]634
human [6]167; progressive [1]356
imprudence [5]632
impudence [2]914, 1180, [4]646
impulse(s) [1]525, [2]160, 640–1, 922, [4]268
collective [2]261; vegetative [5]350; see also *Trieb*
impurity [4]654
imputation [4]620, [5]182
inaction [5]421
inactivity [2]624
inanimates [4]420
incantations [3]576
incarnation/Incarnation [1]284, 507, 644,

704, ^{2}40, 454, 671, 749–50, 916, 920–1, 923, 1175, ^{3}13n, 14, 19, 27–8, 29, 30, 43n, 72–3, 369, 606, 662, 1083–93, ^{4}407, ^{5}9, 12, 25, 152, 210, 372, 524, 553, 597, 597n, 598, 606, 617, 651, 842
continuation of ^{5}650; of elements ^{5}393; extension of ^{3}758, 758n, ^{5}675; first ^{5}680; of Logos ^{1}574; miracle of ^{1}507; primal ^{3}763; temporary ^{5}418; visual ^{4}313
"incendent" ^{4}396, 396n
incendiaries ^{3}694, ^{6}46
incense ^{3}572
incentives ^{4}728
incidents, improbable ^{1}366, ^{4}794
incitivity ^{4}389, 389n
incivism ^{2}108, 108n
inclination ^{5}588
inclusion ^{3}94
"incoherentic" ^{1}780, 780n
income ^{4}23
"incompatible" ^{6}28
incompatibles ^{1}372
"incompossibility" ^{1}254, 254n
"incompossible" ^{2}671, *671n*
incomprehensibility ^{1}304
"incomprehensible" ^{5}409, ^{6}54
incomprehensible(s) ^{2}626, 628, 671, 882n, ^{5}842
incongruity ^{4}590, ^{5}61
inconsistency/inconsistencies ^{1}823, ^{2}421, ^{3}47, ^{4}112, ^{5}121, 415, 476
inconstancy ^{2}18, ^{4}810
inconvenience and sin ^{1}352
incorporation ^{3}28
incorrupt, the ^{6}65
incorruption ^{3}39, ^{6}301
incredulity, specific ^{6}112
incredulus odi ^{4}611
indecency ^{2}273, ^{5}510, 530
indecision ^{2}604–5
"indecomponible" ^{4}384, 384n
indecomponible(s) ^{4}387, ^{5}335n
indefinite and definite ^{4}647
indefiniteness ^{1}157, 158
indemonstrability ^{4}265
independence ^{1}322, ^{4}23
"independent" ^{6}240
Independent(s) ^{1}248, 248n, 256, 283n, 309, 321n, 336, 345, 346, ^{4}308, 609, 609n, 676, ^{5}146, 508
indeterminacy ^{2}39
indeterminateness ^{3}412
indeterminism ^{5}792
index
chronological ^{5}401; double ^{5}402
India ^{1}76, 771, ^{2}46, 259, 339–40, 586, 784n, 865, 1012, ^{3}473, 474, 500, 1047, 1073, ^{4}29, 508, 525, 651n, ^{5}105, 119n, 248, 262, 337, 415, 416n, 811n ("Indian")
British subjects in ^{6}218; castes in ^{2}342, 342n, 347, 348; geometry in ^{2}341; gold in ^{5}262; missions to ^{3}309–10; ownce of ^{5}387; pantheism in ^{1}646
India-men ^{2}579
Indian(s) (of the Americas) ^{1}226, ^{2}985–7, ^{4}28, 748, ^{5}105, 122, 337, 337n, 353
Indian(s) (of India) ^{4}489–90, ^{5}353, 416, 741, 741n, ^{6}4, 4n
indictment *see* indightment
indifference ^{1}352, 563, ^{2}559, 854n, 858, 859, 935, ^{3}6, 15–16, 82, 138, 449, 450, 451, 453, 518, 546, ^{4}183, 439, ^{5}11, 49, 265, 444, 451, 460, 661, ^{6}243, 300
absolute ^{2}666, 666n; and difference ^{1}550–1; point of ^{1}594, 643, ^{2}659, ^{3}379; polarised ^{2}419; religious ^{1}256, 257; and synthesis ^{1}641
"indifferentism" ^{5}365, 365n
indigena/indigenae ^{3}883, ^{5}262, 813
indigence and poverty ^{2}97–8
indigestion ^{3}770, ^{4}268
indightment, bill of ^{2}64
indignatio fecit ^{1}856
indigo ^{4}167
indiscernibles ^{3}853, 853n
"indispensable" ^{5}567
indistinction(s) ^{1}152, 600, 663, ^{2}892, ^{3}60, 1024, ^{4}491, ^{5}452, ^{6}113
indistinctness ^{4}579
individual(s) ^{1}339, 496, ^{2}813, 816, 1075, 1142, 1166, ^{3}545, ^{4}23–4, 362, 798, ^{5}37, 182, 304, 355, 409, 418, 487, 556, 587, 599, 730, 745, ^{6}28, 243, 244, 302
actions of ^{1}834; and age ^{6}96; anonymous ^{5}50; character of ^{5}73, 99; Charles I as ^{1}336; in childhood ^{4}829; choice of ^{5}10; conscious ^{4}268; and creeds ^{3}367n; damnation of ^{5}11; figure of ^{3}917; first ^{5}248; perjured ^{5}280; rights of ^{2}129; and species ^{6}149; and state ^{2}51–2, ^{6}51; suffering ^{5}585; will of ^{1}4, ^{4}233, ^{5}282
individualisation ^{5}431
individuality/individualities ^{1}153, 175, ^{2}197, 614, 660, 781, 863, ^{3}38, 50, 278, 433, 545, 715, 731, ^{4}443, 454, 819, ^{5}93, 207, 357, 769
principle of ^{1}137, 137n, ^{6}116
individuation ^{1}153, 664, ^{2}431, ^{3}94n, 266, 286n, 317, 317n, ^{5}581

individuity [3]127 ("individity"), 720, [5]285
individuum/*individua* [2]547, [5]306
indivisa [5]790
indivisibility [5]408
indolence [5]135, 174, [6]124
induction(s) [2]605, [3]328, 850, [4]109, 110, 111, 160, [6]170, 285–6
of experience [5]457; physical [2]604; of senses [3]957
indulgence [2]1152, 1176
industry [1]515, [2]617
constant [2]98; independent [1]755; springs of [5]363
indwelling [1]331
ineptia/*ineptiae* [5]505, 506, 506n, [6]15
Ineptus religiosus [3]656
inequality/inequalities [5]304, [6]36, 325
inertia [1]661, [3]44, 1010, 1010n, [4]429, 821
infallibility [1]327, 513, 514, 515, 805, [2]30, 39, 40, 495, 679, 1140, 1140n, 1155, 1172, [3]233, 234, 803, 818, [5]617
of Apostles [5]622; God's [5]622; papal [2]744, 744n, 806, 807n
infancy [4]819, 829, [5]414, 647
gospel(s) of [1]492, [3]17, 17n, [4]41n, 251, 253n–4n, [6]64n, see also *evangelium/evangelia infantiae*; poem of the [3]730; spiritual [5]650
infans [1]245, 245n
"infant(s)" [1]245, 245n
infant(s) [1]246, [2]601, [3]94, 350, [4]489, [5]648, 652
Baptism *see* baptism/Baptism, infant; cruel/harsh father to [3]765, [5]586, 586n; droll looks of [2]191; lovely [5]834; massacre of [4]476; as a riddle [2]1145; sin in [1]289; unbaptised [5]612
infantry [5]378
"infectious" [2]362, 362n
inference(s) [1]468
by induction [6]170; fine-drawn [5]658
inferenda [1]477
inferiority, natural [5]476
inferiors and superiors [2]319
infidel(s) [1]304, 699, [2]30, 148, 150, 220, 398, 704, [4]672, [5]10, 70, 180, 379, 399
acute [5]384; arguments of [5]63; error of [5]53; honest [6]60; learned [1]317, [2]155, [3]462; sensual [5]75; shallowest [5]514; sturdy [2]1057
infidelism [6]81
infidelity [1]349, [2]31, 419, 1088, [4]287, [5]512, 630, [6]81
in disrepute [5]484; obtrusive [1]748; reign of [3]452
"infinite" [2]563, 638, [5]712
infinite, the [1]562, [3]117–18, [4]224, [5]99n, 210, 454–7, 458, 693–4, 694n
absolute [3]850; difficulty about [1]585n; finite [5]233; and finite *see* finite; God and [2]996; idea of [5]455, 484
infinitive [3]450, [4]166, 167
Greek [3]15, 15n, 279, 279n, 449; *see also* verb(s), substantive
infinity/infinities [3]409, [4]302–3, [5]287, 315, 406, 481
co-existing [2]205; definition of [1]107, 107n; measure of [5]482; proof of [3]118, 118n; unity in [1]667
infinitude [3]319
infirmities [4]137, [5]678
inflammation [3]124, 125
influence(s) [3]501, 697, 872, [5]135
divine [5]452; foreign [4]18; outward [5]304; spiritual [4]663, [5]653
influx [5]474n, [6]170
physical [3]790, 790n, [5]404
information [5]866
of people at large [5]512; undoubted [5]415
informer(s) [3]471, [6]98, 101
Jewish [6]101
informis [4]187
infra-protestant [1]863
"infrasocinian" [4]269, 269n
infrasocinian [3]434, 434n
infula [3]110
infusion(s) [5]514, 515
infusoria [2]545, 545n, [3]1037, 1039, [5]445
ing [3]730
"ingenious" and "ingenuous" [1]258, 258n, [2]822, 822n, 823, 829
ingenuity [1]765
"ingenuous" *see* "ingenious"
"ingenuousness" [2]822
Ingersoll, Charles Jared (1782–1862) *Inchiquin the Jesuit's Letters* [4]171
Inghirami, Francesco (1772–1846) *Monumenti Etruschi* [1]237n
Ingleby, Clement Mansfield (1823–86) [1]cli, [3]909
owner of annotated books [4]199, [6]32
"On Some Points Connected with the Philosophy of Coleridge" [3]499; "On the Unpublished Manuscripts of Samuel Taylor Coleridge" [1]clin
Inglis, Sir Robert Harry (1786–1855) [3]492
ingot [1]351
ingrate [2]818, 942
ingratitude [4]718, 820, [6]28
Ingulph/Ingulphus (?1030–1109) [5]38 q

inhabitation [4]155
inheritance, law of [5]478, 478n
inhibitor [3]139
inhospitality [5]394, 395
inhumanity [4]95
iniquity [3]60, [4]718
initials, C known by [2]904, 904n, 905n
initiation [1]598, [5]650
initium [5]650
injuries, organic [5]678
injustice [4]171
ink [1]487, [2]165, [3]129n, [5]397
i.-hum [2]520
innate and connate [6]149
in-ness, absolute [4]385
innocence [3]137, 494, 566, 596, [4]868, [5]336
of a nature [2]840; overzeal of [4]867
Innocent VIII (Giovanni Battista Cibo), Pope (1432–92) [3]794
innocent(s) [4]238, [5]416, 819
innovation [2]1158
Innys, William (fl 1734–56) [6]72
inoculation [4]149 ("inoculated"), [5]766
inorganic, the
and organic [4]385, 526; and organised [1]662
inquietudes [5]467
inquilinus [3]185, 185n
inquirer, learned [5]513
inquiry, dispassionate [5]413
inquisition/Inquisition [4]134, 178, [5]121n, 396, 678, [6]263
British [3]418; Italian [1]559n; I.-jails [1]522; Romish [6]55; Spanish [1]204, 258, 275, 281, *281n*, 308, 349n, 844n, [2]163, 530, 697n, [4]28, 28n
inquisitor(s)/Inquisitor(s) [3]787, [4]28, [5]617
I. General [5]422; logic of [1]252; of Star Chamber [5]616
"insane" [5]99, 99n
insanity [3]986, [6]285–9
insect(s) [2]527–8, 689, 861, 861n, 995, 1008n, 1026, [3]581, 1036n, [4]333, 493, 495–6, 496n, 498, 500, 520, 830, [5]250, 287–9, 290–1, 360, [6]103, 152
brainless [5]260; church compared to [1]246; as commas [1]133; divided [5]260n; eggs of [4]530; eyes of [3]1036; i. spirits [3]671; water-i. [3]352, 352n
insectivity [2]689, 861n
"insectology" [2]527, 527n
insecurity [4]793
dread of [2]507; public [4]776
insensilis [1]851n
inside-seer(s) [4]497n, 592n; *see also* clairvoyant(s)
insight [1]287, 824, [2]332, 679, [3]23, 79, 558, 663n, 849, 850, [5]84, 93, 627
direct [5]803; miraculous [5]608; previous [4]259; psychological [3]662; purpose of philosopher [3]715; quiet [5]664; and sights [5]474; in the Spirit [1]695; subjective [3]989; superior [5]297
insipidity [4]187
insolence [6]145
inspector [6]98
"inspiration" [5]473
inspiration [1]140, 327, 492, 560, 687, [2]402, 421, 561, [3]305, 451, 508, 561, 603, 663, 663n, 698, 763, 766, [4]260, 260n, [5]33, 33n, 77, 231, 391n, 515, [6]88
Apostolic [3]20; of Bible [3]310; continuous [5]657; of Creed [5]621; degrees of [3]533; different sorts of [6]319; direct [1]345; episcopal and apostolic [2]811; lowest grade of [2]409; miraculous [5]516; negative [3]771; of NT [5]575; plenary [2]500, [4]646, [5]622, prophetic [3]40; of scripture [6]42; supernatural [2]147; works of [6]140
"inspired" [5]519, 571, 571n
instances [5]325, 415
want of [5]372
instinct(s) [2]332, 642, 689, [3]424, 581, 867, 1048, 1072, [4]91, 93, 94, 221n, 496, 497–8, 498n, 647, [5]291, 822, [6]150
arithmetical [4]505; C's hypothesis [4]31, 31n; cunning of [4]809; fortunate [5]614; holy [1]283; natural [3]99; sexual [4]488–9; transmission of [6]126; wisdom of the species [6]149
instinctivity [4]389, 498n, 500
institutes
Hebrew [2]147; of Jewish state [6]59–60; positive [1]874; Mosaic [3]112
institution(s) [1]539, [5]304, [6]28
British [6]47; divine [5]507; national [2]486; peculiar [5]644; positive [5]103, 659; sacrificial [4]481; symbolic [5]398
instruction [3]622, [5]362
instrument(s) [2]612, [3]428, [4]251, [5]17, 185
material [5]825; for perception [5]418; servile [5]643
insubordination [5]510
insufficiency [4]24
insularity [5]337
insulators [3]382
insult [5]651
intaglio [5]83
integer(s) [2]634, [3]127, [5]406, 409, 730
integral(s) [5]304
integrality, relative [5]304

integrity, moral [5]465
integuments [1]468
"intellect" [5]200, 202, 202n
intellect(s) [2]345, [3]516, 641, 860, [4]142, 154, 154n–5n, 217, 217n, 375, 548, 811, 817, [5]203n, 210, 457, 702, 780–1, [6]299
active [1]743; antithetic [2]249; banished from Spinoza's system [1]566–7; canal-like [2]1024; childhood of [2]824; creative [3]705; critique of [3]919; discontinuous [3]883; discursive [1]685, [4]458, 653, [5]615, 800; distinctive [1]655; ever-active [5]122; fertility of [5]524; fervent [1]459; finite [3]12; form of [3]45; free [3]670; freedom of [2]824; gallant [4]93; grades of [4]583; impassioned [4]786; language of [3]261; law of [3]332; limited [2]203; march of [1]129; marrow of [2]783; masculine [2]1201, [4]82; mere [5]457; mode of [5]206; narrow [4]589; Paley on [4]638; persistency of [2]952; powerful [4]816; profound [1]393; puniness of [4]134; pure [2]729; scientific [2]695; seat of [6]308; and sense [4]156, 174–5; speculative [3]95, 97; striving of [4]838; substratum of [4]220; two powers of [2]135; vice of [5]767; waking [5]726; and will [1]702, [4]862, [5]216
intellection [1]233
intellective, the [5]461
intellectuals [2]1080
"intellecturition" [1]lixn, 653, 653n
intellecturition [1]600n, 601n
intellectus [5]202
intellegere [4]154n
intelligence(s) [1]lx, 653, 653n, 693, [2]249, 633n, [3]86, [4]127, 137, 375, 448–9, 457, 460, [5]234, 730, 738, 776, 792
attributed to God [3]358–9; distinctive [4]492; essence of [4]224; of the Father [5]56; finite [3]90; heavenly [5]57; human [5]208; life and [2]624; and nature [4]451; pure [2]198, 419, [3]1087; supreme [3]317; unconscious [4]374, 374n; wicked [3]851
Intelligencer [2]118
intelligentia carnis [1]359n
intelligibile [5]175
intelligibility [2]204, 1145, [5]642
intelligible, the [5]234, 721
intemperance [2]1185, [4]465, [5]584, 682
intense [2]1070
intensio [3]832
intension [6]103
intensity/intensities [2]541, 639, 646, 1181, [3]755, [4]413, [6]115
scale of [5]370
intention(s) [1]361, [3]38
inferred [6]62; primary [6]64; pure [5]562; right [2]41
"intentional" [3]919n
intents [1]331
interagent [6]97
interbreathings, lyrical [1]407
intercession [2]207, 673
of Christ [5]678
Intercessor [5]606
interchange [3]46
"intercirculation" [5]704n
intercommunion [1]676, [3]559
intercommunity [1]395
intercourse, promiscuous [2]321, 938
interdependence [1]152
interdependents, unity of [4]12
inter-ens [3]518, 546, [6]300
"interest" [1]140, 140n, [4]644, 644n–5n
interest(s) [1]370, 865, [4]864, [5]194, 563
common [2]328; compound [3]807; deep [1]747; human [6]159; living [5]644; man's [5]135; moral [1]468, [2]183, [5]413; temporal [1]866; totality of [4]826; of truth [3]347; unity of [4]852, 863–4
interfusion [1]401, [4]141
interinanimate [2]223, 223n
interiority [5]404n
interjection [4]167
interlinks [1]811
intermarriage(s) [4]257, [5]336
intermediaries [6]123n
intermediate [6]97
necessity of [3]999n
intermedium/intermedia [1]574, 597, [2]281, [3]518, 546, [5]410, 418, 423, [6]300
intermittents [4]148–9
"intermundium" [4]263, 263n
intermundium [2]891, [5]298
International Critical Commentary [1]416
interpenetration [1]579, 594, [4]167, 604, [5]18, 361, 500
interpocular [2]63, 63n
interpolation(s) [1]384, 404, 492, 772, [2]443, 454, 585, [3]56, [4]784, [5]455, 575, [6]55, 68
interpolator [3]105
interpretation(s) [1]467, 674, 783, [2]489, 495, 518, 659, 921, [3]26, 235, 306, 437, 602–3, [4]62, 193, 304, 814, [5]10, 118 ("interpretable"), 571–2 ("interpreted"), 619n, 680, 701, [6]64, 71, 109
allegorical [3]472; of Apocalypse [3]449; of Bible [3]686; of Böhme [1]606; canons of

[2]561, [3]420, 438–9; Catholic [5]72; Christian [3]520, [6]302; common [5]741; conditions of [1]560; conjectural [3]40, 726; crass [5]715; depends on writer's meaning [2]569; Donne on [2]336; of dreams [5]726; edifying [1]834; of facts by ideas [5]795; false [2]472, [3]1086; historical [3]105; interpreting-away [1]358; Jesuitical [3]444; kinds of [2]682–3; law of [5]755; of law [2]43; laxity of [3]103; legitimate [3]482; licences of [2]1152; literal [2]571, 685, [3]105, 443, 465, 987, [6]74; literal and symbolic [3]731–2; mistaken [3]5; natural [2]320; necessity of [2]38; NT sense of [3]876; obvious [2]442, [5]524; of OT prophets [2]150; ordinary [2]394; orthodox [2]575; partial [5]691; by Paulus [4]60; of phenomena [4]271; principles of [3]33, 452; private [1]315–16, 495; of prophecies [1]434; of Rev [6]166; rule of [6]62; of Scripture [1]339, 805, [2]722, 1106, [5]28, 28n, [6]137; Spinoza's scheme of [2]412; spiritual [1]787, [2]267, [3]463; spiritual and literal [2]267; symbolic [3]929; of texts [1]521, [5]57; true [2]798, [3]55; unnecessary [5]5; verbal [3]859; wilful [5]545; *see also* misinterpretation

interpreter(s) [1]316, [2]1179, [3]14, 928, [5]515
  Apocalyptic [3]420; authorised [2]38

Interpreter (in Bunyan) [1]812, 814

Interpreter's Bible [2]383n, 384n, 387n

Interpreter's Dictionary of the Bible [1]416

interspace [3]531, [5]16, [6]315

"intertexed" [1]246, 246n

"intertrusion(s)" [2]52, 52n, [5]530, 530n

interval [5]16

intestines [1]460, 460n

Intiaquacqui [4]489–90

intolerance [1]247, [2]743, [3]98, 98n, 216, [4]178, 307–8, 308n, 587, [5]11, 31, 469, 521

intolerancy [2]1199

intrigues [1]398

Introduction to Latin Grammar for the Use of Christ's Hospital [1]329n

"introition" [1]667n

"introitive" [1]667n, [4]412, 412n

introitive [1]680

introsusception [5]466, 616

intruders [5]520

intueri [1]632n, [4]132n

"intuition" [1]632n, [5]755–6

intuition(s) [1]527, 587n, 632, 729, [2]604, 607, 607n, 626, 639n, 991, 1154n, [3]23, 49, 77, 79, 80, 80n, 201, 241, 242, 282–3, 332, 333, 641, 641n, 791, 1000, 1091, [4]131–2, 132n, 217, 292, 393–4, 393n, 394, 394n, 414–15, 416, 441, [5]32, 32n, 368, 409
  a priori [2]1002n; Böhme's [1]620; empirical and pure [3]242n; forms of [1]655; genetic [1]607; geometry as [1]108n; great man's [5]714; ideal [5]755; intellectual [2]644, [4]155, 351–2, 351n, 399–400, [5]751, 757–8; intellectual and sensuous [5]49; mathematical [5]750; metaphysical [5]137; moral [5]76, 813; not sensuous [5]771; pure [4]156, 158n; pure and mixed [5]599; purest form of [1]568; sensuous [3]270; single or complex [4]462; of space [2]563; of space and time [2]729, [4]125, [5]297; spiritual [5]408, 450, 751, [6]233; of Swedenborg [5]433; see also *Anschauung*

"intuitive" [2]656

intuitive
  and discursive [1]587n; and sensuous [5]49; sensuous [5]461

intuitus [4]156

inturbidate [2]332, 332n

inundation(s) [1]431, [2]388

invalids [3]360

invasion [4]720

invention [1]684, [4]502
  figures of [1]375; opulence of [1]63

inversion [3]403

investigation, laws of [4]160

invisibility [5]563

"invisible" [6]61–2

invisible, the [1]320

invocation(s) [2]1152, [6]146
  of saints [3]444; of the dead [3]310

involution [1]561, [3]102, 357, [5]438, 754, 756, [6]235

"involve" [2]486, 486n

"involvent" [6]78, 78n

involvent of truth [6]78

inward and outward [1]813

inwardness [1]670
  relative [4]385

Io Paean [4]633

Iodama (myth) [2]580

iodide [5]438

iodine [1]590, 613, [3]1001, 1001n, 1004, 1017, 1021, 1021n, 1022, [4]387, 387n, [5]335n, 346, 438, [6]116

Iolaus (myth) [3]234n

"Iolo Morganwg" *see* Williams, Edward

Ion [1]757

Iona [2]578

Ionia [2]578n, [5]337n

Ionians [5]703, [5]337 ("Ionionians")

ionics [1]377
iota [3]833, 833n
iotacism [5]198
Iphigenia (myth) [2]833, 834
ipse dico [4]480
ipse dixit [1]72, 808, [3]122, 122n, 1014, [4]216, 480n, [5]111, 275, 698
ipseity [1]152n, 601n, 646, [2]734, 734n, 745, 881n, [3]13, 17, 18, 18n, 428, [4]258, [5]799, [6]92
 and alterity *see* alterity
Irad (myth) [2]576
Ircano (in Metastasio) [6]322
Iredale, Mr (fl 1887) [1]542
Ireland [1]844, [2]474, 523, 696, 751, 751n, 900n, 953, [3]72, [4]18n, 20, 24n, [5]195n, 866, [6]22, 47, 49
 Catholic schools in [1]214n; Church Establishment in [5]659; Church of [1]837; double priesthood in [2]936; Established Church in [4]21; in fiction [1]211–14; Irish Emancipation [3]159; hierocracy in [4]18; learning in [1]213, 213n, 214; pacation prevented [1]359; Union with [4]591
Irenaeus, St, Bishop of Lyons (c 130–c 200) [1]312n, 485, 486, 486n, [2]33n, 270n, 273, 274n, 439n, 442–3, 501, 502, 505, 506, 506n, 699, 709, 833, [3]446n, 684–5 q, 686, 686n q, 687, 929, 929n, 1084, [4]258, [5]570 q, 570n, 571, 571n q, 619, 629, 643, [6]58, 63, 63n, 69, 70 q, 70n, 72, 89 q, 166
 Adversus haereses [4]255 q, [6]166n, tr Keble [1]485, [2]713, 713n
Irene, Empress of Eastern Roman Empire (c 752–803) [2]272
Ireton, Henry (1611–51) [1]336, 336n
iridium [2]825, 825n, [5]261
iris [4]323, 325
Irish, the [3]148, 1029, [5]195, 280, 281n
 bull *see* bull, Irish; bullies [5]51; I. Franciscan [2]309; perjury of [3]183
Irishman/Irishmen [2]536, [6]280–1; *see also* Hibernian
iritis [4]164
iron [1]546, 546n, 547, 548, 737, 775, 785, [2]572, 825, [3]43, 44, 45, 126, 129, 286, 419, 850, 858, 1062, 1067, 1067n, [4]359, 418, [5]172, 255, 259, 262, 263, [6]230, 233, 245
 in blood [1]577, [4]274, 274n; club of [2]1155; frames of [2]428; magnetic [6]120; i.-mongers [3]988; moulding i. [2]119
irony [1]139, [2]687, 763, 774, 866, [3]223, 225, 226, [4]72, [5]161
 bitter [3]56; of Christ [1]451; dignified [5]565, 581; self-tormenting [4]851
irradiation [3]524, 746
irrational, the [1]617, 653, 653n
irreligion [4]21, [5]521
irreverence [3]77, [5]530
irritability [1]577, 626, 813, [2]689, 861n, 1008, 1008n, 1026n, [3]81, 81n, 123, 123n, 126, 581, [4]149n, 273, 388–9, 389n, 390, 498n, 500, [5]258, 259, 260, 784
 fever of [4]149; life of [3]1036
Irving, Edward (1792–1834) [1]cvi, 307, *307n–8n*, [2]46, 47, 142, 180, 287, *287n*, 504n, 505n, 712n, [3]111n, 747n, 772, *772n*
 beliefs of [3]449; Irvingite Church [3]71n; on C [3]423n q; and C's books [1]cxii; C's disagreement with [3]22n; C's respect for [3]26; donor of book [2]1182; echoes C [3]47, 48; errors of [2]572n, 822, [3]66; extent of C's agreement with [3]416; extravagances [3]731, 731n; fellow combatant [3]430; Gospel according to [3]56; vehement intellect [3]11; led C to study Rev [2]503; letter to [2]516n–17n q ("Henry"); love of the good [3]9; Luther-hearted [3]431; Luther-like [3]3, 426n, 434; misrepresents C's opinions [3]64–5, 67, 68; owner of annotated books [1]c; popularity of [3]57; presentation copy from [3]3, 10, 415; saner days of [3]58; style [3]36–7; supplier of books to C [1]xcviii; system of [3]418; transcriber of marginalia [4]294; uncritical [3]451; weakness of [3]469
 Babylon and Infidelity Foredoomed [3]71n; *Christ's Holiness in the Flesh* [3]14n; *For Missionaries after the Apostolical School* MT [3]3–9; *Sermons, Lectures, and Occasional Discourses* [1]cxxxi, cxxxin, [2]339; MT [3]10–74; *see also* Lacunza *The Coming of Messiah* tr Irving
Irvingism [3]59n
Irvingismos [3]59, 59n
"is" [4]380, [5]680, 680n, 790, [6]9, 76
Isaac (Bible) [2]385–6, 897, 1103, [3]109, 604, 728, [5]506, 624
 God of [6]92
Isaac (in Scott) [4]593
Isaacson, Stephen (1798–1849) [1]861
Isabella (in Scott) *see* Wardour
Isabella (*Measure for Measure*) [3]171, 171n, [4]693n
Isabella, Queen of France (1389–1409) [2]823n

Isabelle (in Scott) *see* Croye
Isaiah ("Esay") [1]449 ("Esaias"), 705, 734, 807, [2]148, 149, 285, 291, 405–6, 409n, 412, 440, 674, 828, 896, 897, [3]105, 110, 767, [5]583
his imagination [5]59; as Israel [1]435n; shaving rag of [2]917
Iselin, Isaak (1728–82) [3]846
Ishmael (Bible) [2]390, [3]728
Ishmaelites [5]786–7
Isis (myth) [2]144, 573
Islam [3]927n
island(s) [2]459, 1037, 1038n, [5]36, 337
happy [5]773n, 777; spirit as [1]70; uninhabited [2]161; wild [1]375
isle
Elysian [4]489; floating [4]858
Isle of Wight [1]336n, [2]522n, [4]18
Islington *see* London
"isms" [3]367
"isochrony" [4]603, 603n
Isocrates (436–338 BC) [2]870, 870n, [3]227, 227n, 622
Isola, Emma *See* Moxon, Emma
Ispahan [6]270
Israel [1]421, 421n, 422, 424, 433, 434, 438, 441n, 442, 443, 443n, 444n, [2]150, 278, 284, 398–9, 785, 832, 1153, [3]34, 62, 477, [4]245n, 474, [5]565, 583, [6]77
children of [1]418, 420, 747, [3]108n, [6]119; as Church [2]51–2; dispersion of children of [3]463; God of [1]420; history of [2]373; house of [2]328, 329; inferior to Judea [2]383; Isaiah as [1]435n; Israelitish nation [3]767; maps [2]830; people of [3]658, [6]118; saviour of [4]477
Israelite(s) [1]463n, 874, [2]144, 508, 830, [5]54, 64n, 142, 465
idea of Word [3]101; illiterateness of [2]399; *see also* Jew(s)
Issachar (Bible) [2]836
Issus [2]980
"ist" [3]367–8
isteity [2]881
isthmus [5]189
Isulia (in S. Daniel) [2]117
"it" [5]551, 833, 833n
Itagybe [5]103
Itala [2]454, 454n
Italian (language) [1]lxxxi, 206–10, [2]431, 1092, [3]831, 831n, 930–1, [4]101n, 102, 168, 329–31, 780, [5]142, [6]150
C learns [1]542
Italian (literature)
lyric metres of [4]290, 290n; Milton's I. verse [3]902–3; poets [3]909–10, marginalia on [2]7–10
Italian(s) (people) [2]100
as generous/Iapetic race [1]540
italic(s) [2]577, [4]379
Italus [2]577
Italy [1]244, 831, [2]53, 131, 140, 235n, 296, 573, 577, 964, 1118n, [3]133, 142, 693, 974, [4]189n, 290, 299, 338, 628n, 808, [5]141, 222n, 277, 277n, 832, [6]13, 14, 15, 160n, 199n, 200, 211, 321
C's I. of writers [1]117n; Florence [1]206; higher [4]701, 755, 784–5; oppressors of [5]281; RC Church in [1]845, 846; sciences in [5]311
itch [2]362, 363, 364n, [3]1061, [6]58
to dogmatise [2]84, 84n; holy [2]982, 983
Ithaca NY
Cornell University Library (Wordsworth Collection) [1]clxxiv, [3]483, 484, marginalia in [2]1129, [4]545, marked book(s) in [1]174n, transcript(s) of marginalia in [1]701, [2]1105, 1169, [5]848
"ities" [3]367
itinerants [1]308
Iupiter *see* Jupiter
"-ive" (suffix) [1]161
ivitates [1]153n
ivory [3]324
ivy [3]889
"izzes" [2]992, 992n

J., G. E. (fl 1898) [4]84
"J. W. T." (James Webbe Tobin) [1]89
Jack
a/o' Lanthorn [4]53, [6]25; of all trades [2]859; of all work [2]1015; Tar [3]394
Jack and the Bean Stalk [5]174
Jack the Giant Killer [4]28, 630n, 658n
jacket [5]309
Jackson, Andrew (1767–1845) [1]32, 32n
Jackson, Charles [3]906
Jackson, Heather Joanna [2]1115
Jackson, James Robert de Jager ed *Coleridge: The Critical Heritage* [1]cxxxviin, [2]86
Jackson, Thomas (1579–1640) [1]287, [5]80, 80n–1n
Treatise of the Divine Essence and Attributes [5]81n

Jackson, W. S. [4]617, [6]285
Jackson, William (d 1809) [1]lxxixn, xcvii
Jackson, William Walrond (1838–1931) *see* Dante *Convivio* tr Jackson
Jacob (Bible) [1]421, 421n, 687, [2]384–5, 395, 489n, 743, 899, 928, 928n, [3]34, 109, 455, 580, 906n
  descendants of [2]395–6; God of [6]92; J.'s ladder [2]609, [3]348, 348n
Jacobatius, Dominicus (Domenico Jacobazzi), Cardinal (c 1444–1521) [5]509n
Jacobi, Friedrich Heinrich (1743–1819) [1]198n, 585n, [2]186, 186n, 609, [3]649n, 698n, 790n, [4]108n, 207n, 224–5 q, 363, 369, 370n–1n q, 416, [5]320 q
  captious spirit of [3]96; golden mists of [4]360; misrepresented Kant [3]97; Reimarus on [4]215–16; and Schelling [6]234, 234n; Schelling on [4]360–72; on Spinoza [4]224–6, 227, [5]208; on tolerance [3]846n
  David Hume über den Glauben [3]640–1, 640n–1n; *Ueber die Lehre des Spinoza* [2]172n; MT [3]75–92; 789, [4]207n, [5]208n; *Von den göttlichen Dingen und ihrer Offenbarung* [4]360–72; *Werke* [2]996n; MT [3]93–100; 846
Jacobi, Johann Friedrich (1712–91) [1]198n; *see also* Bahrdt *Glaubens-Bekänntniss* ed Jacobi
Jacobin(s) [1]291, *291n–2n*, [2]1195, 1195n, [4]79, 195, 342n, [5]152, 501
  in France [3]495; "Gallo-jacobinical" [2]345; nonsense [2]195
Jacobinism [2]432n, 847, 847n, [3]788, [4]20, [5]143, 521
  arguments of [2]529; definition of [2]529n
Jacobite(s) [1]295, 359 ("Jacobitical"), [2]1150n, [4]20, 79, 594
  Rebellion [5]316n
Jacobitism [2]118
Jacomb, Thomas (1622–87) [1]259
Jael (Bible) [1]822, 822n, [2]917, [4]304
Jafhnar (myth) [4]489–90
Jago, Richard (1715–81) [1]38
Jahn, Johannes (1750–1816)
  Appendix hermeneuticae seu exercitationes exegeticae [1]480; MT [3]101–5; *The History of the Hebrew Commonwealth* tr Stowe MT [3]106–13
Jahrbücher der Medicin als Wissenschaft ed Marcus and F. W. J. Schelling [2]533, 1002n; MT [3]114–31; 292n, [4]344, 345, 368, 368n, 369, 369n, 428 q, [5]360n q, [6]104n, 121n
Jahrbücher der preussischen Monarchie [3]964n
jail, perpetual [1]272
Jainas [2]340
Jaki, Stanley L. *see* Kant *Universal Natural History* tr Jaki
jalap [5]137, 711, 711n
Jamaica [1]32, 33, [2]907
James (fiction) [2]658, [4]167, [5]21, 23, 28, 177, [6]299
James, St (d 44) [2]470, 476, 477, 477n, 655, 717n, 833n, [4]250, 402n, 526, 667
James, St, Bishop of Nisibis (early 4th century) [2]742
James, St, brother of Jesus (1st century) [2]477, 477n
James I, King of England (James VI of Scotland) (1566–1625) [1]55, 56n, 166n, 310n, 359, 401, 834, 842, [2]75, 127, 264, 265n, 269, 304, 359, 522, 813n, 815, 826, 827, 927n, 928, 929, 930, 933n, 936n, 942n, 945, 1099–1100, 1196n, [3]171, 178, 483, 561, 796n, 1067, [4]608n, 609, 766, 766n, [5]553n, 834, 834n, [6]94, 101
  age of [4]767; and Buckingham [2]942; character of [2]944; error of [2]60–1, 933; reign of [1]217, 357, 389, 398, 870, [2]235, [4]657, [5]80, 221; rise of dissenters under [1]531; Scotch Solomon [2]1134; source of errors [2]936; time of [2]650; toleration under [2]934–5; writers of [2]240
James II, King of England (1633–1701) [1]295, [2]277, 767, 827n, 951n, [3]140, 141n, 144, 144n, 161, 161n, 162, 167n, 539n, 756, 921, [4]19, [5]144, 145, 660, 660n, [6]32, 101, 308n ("Duke of York")
  abdication [1]866n; bigotry [4]81; benefactor [2]950–1; Declaration of [3]166; as Duke of York [1]353n, [3]141n; reign of [3]153, [4]71, [5]531, 661; *see also* Dicconson *Life of James the Second*
James VI of Scotland *see* James I of England
James, Montague Rhodes (1862–1936) *see* Bible: Aprocrypha: NT: *The Apocryphal NT* ed James
James, Thomas (fl 1711) [1]850
Jameson, Mrs [3]507
Jan, Johann Wilhelm (1681–1725) *De Nicolaitis* [2]506n
Janus (myth) [2]506, 575n, [3]735, 735n, [4]861, 861n, [5]611n
  statue of [5]611

Japan [2]1111, [4]169
missions to [3]309–10; Nagoya University, marginalia in [3]236, 811
Japetic (languages) [4]37n
Japhet (Bible) [1]539, 541n, 686, [2]177, 177n, 578n, [4]583n, [5]337, 337n, 352, [6]5n
descendant of [4]583; posterity of [5]337; *see also* race(s), Japetic/Iapetic
Jaques ("Jacques") (*As You Like It*) [3]406, [4]850, 850n
jargon [1]807, [3]398, 1055, [4]290, 290n, [5]481n
of astrology [4]614; gypsy [5]861; of modern prose [1]156
Jariges, Carl Friedrich von (1773–1826) [4]227
Jäsche, Gottlob Benjamin (1762–1842) *see* Kant *Logik* ed Jäsche
jasmin [5]831
Jason (myth) [1]73, 537n, [2]346n, [6]142, 142n
jaundice of party [1]291
Javan (Bible) [2]578, *578n*, [5]337, 337n
javelin [4]673
jaw
ass's [6]220, 220n; j.-bone [6]220, 220n
jealousy [4]814, 868, [5]104, 135, 150, [6]157
Jean Paul *see* Richter, Johann Paul Friedrich
Jeckle *see* Schenk, Jakob
Jefferies, Mr (fl 1791) [3]881
Jeffery (poltergeist) [5]122, 140n, 165n
Jefferson, Thomas (1743–1826) *Memoirs, Correspondence, and Private Papers* ed T. J. Randolph MT [3]132–3
Jeffrey, Francis, Lord Jeffrey (1773–1850) [1]230, 860, 860n, [2]979n, 983, 983n, [5]534n
Jehoiakim (Bible) [1]437
Jehoram (Bible) [3]699, 699n
Jehoshaphat (Bible) [1]442, 442n, [2]894, [3]461, 461n, 699n
"Jehovah" [5]658, 658n
Jehova(h) [1]417n, 420, 458, [2]325, 392, 404, 420, 423, 798, 901, 903, 1146, [3]13, 102n, 106, 107n, 151, 545, [4]296, [5]25, 97, 97n, 514, 830, [6]77, 85, 110, 139
Christ as [2]728, [5]497, 497n, 635, [6]296; and Elohim [2]389–90, 389n; Hebrew [1]675, [3]108–9; incarnate [1]706; king [2]146; J.-man [2]302, 302n, [4]44, 62; manifested [6]68; Mendelssohn's [3]699; on mount [2]489; omnipresent [4]299; priests of [2]399; pronunciation of [3]903; temple of [2]486; voice of [3]105; J.-Word [1]435, 458n, 461n, [2]24, 486, 486n, 728n, 743n, 880n, [3]13n, 24n, 77, 101–2, 102, 545n, 775, [5]497n; *see also* God
Jehovaism of the Son [6]82, 82n
Jehovaship [3]103
Jena [2]194, 195n, 1016n, [3]319n, 971n
Jena Recensent [1]lxxixn
Jenkins, Harold (b 1909) *see* Shakespeare *Hamlet* ed Jenkins
Jenkinson, Robert Banks, Earl of Liverpool (1770–1828) [1]724n, [2]511n
letter(s) to [3]877n, [4]28n
jenny-ass [5]812, 812n
Jenyns, Soame (1704–87) [1]38
Jephtha(h) (Bible) [2]833n, [4]847
daughter of [2]833–4, 833n, 834n
Jer [1]433
jeremiad [5]89n, 318
Jeremiah (Bible) [1]439, 705, [2]149, 149n, 286, 409n, 412n, 893, [3]105, 468, 480, [5]89
Jericho [4]503, 503n, [5]294
jerkin, leather [5]609
jerkiness [2]54
Jerment, George (fl 1805) [3]537, [6]312; *see also* R. Leighton *Whole Works* ed Jerment
Jeroboam I (10th century BC) [2]383n
Jerome/Hierome, St (c 342–420) [1]416, 443n, 467n, 490, 491, 491n, 493n, [2]46, 52n, 301, 306, 317n, 335 q, 335n, 415n, 454n, 568, 662, 666, 666n, 667, 668, 683, 742n, 747n, 836, [3]20n, 111 q, 441, 533, 763, 765, 1072n, 1078n, [4]242, 252, 643, [5]524, 536 q, 547, 548n, 573n–4n, 574 q, 575n, 629–30, 630, 660 q, [6]63, 138n, 140, 179, 319
Commentary on Daniel [3]573n; *De perpetua virginitate B. Mariae* [2]272n; *De viris illustribus* [1]491n; *Dialogus adversus Luciferianos* [5]11n q, 633n; *Omnia opera* [1]444n
Jerome of Prague (c 1365–1416) [1]858n
Jeronymo see Kyd *Spanish Tragedy*
Jerry the Author [5]89
Jersey [2]767n
Jerusalem [1]430, 433, 437, 439n, 442n, 449, 453, 457, 481–2, [2]37n, 157n, 276, 416, 416n, 417n, 455, 455n, 468, 470, 471, 509, 509n, 513, 515, 559, 559n, 670, 674 ("Hierusalem"), 705, 707, 833, 833n, 836, [3]38, 51, 417, 422, 441, 454, 461, 461n, 467, 468, 480, 550, 666, 667, 707, 730, 1069, 1079, 1084, [4]54, 248, 248n, 251n, 473, 474, 476, 655, [5]56, 565, [6]18, 114, 219, 219n, 292–3
bishops of [3]440n, [4]473; captivity of [1]707; Christ wept over [1]13; Church of [5]660n, [6]61; Council(s) of [2]734, [5]623, 623n; de-

Jerusalem—*continued*
struction of [1]832n, [2]459, [5]57, [6]294; fall of [2]504, 512, 515, 515n, 516; New *see* New Jerusalem; sack of [3]924; siege of [1]832–3, [5]522, 667

Jerusalem, Carl Wilhelm (1747–72) [3]677

Jesse (Bible) [1]434

Jessop, Thomas Edmund (1896–1980) *see* Berkeley *Works* ed Luce and Jessop

jest [3]175

Jesuism [1]198n

Jesuit(s) [1]359, 699n, [3]153, 232n, 439, 445, 448, 449, 451, 457, 459, 465, 468, 645n, [4]32–4, 671, [5]121n, 167, 254, 274, 308n, 525n, 633
apostate [1]699; demure [5]670; Jesuitical dishonesty [4]360; Donne plays [2]304; Herder an arch-J. [2]1079; Jesuitical interpretation [3]444; untricking [3]440

Jesuitism(s) [5]149, 149n

Jesuitry [1]522, [2]942, 948

Jesus Christ/Jesus/Christ (c 7 BC–c AD 29) [1]29, 48n, 200, 273, 277, 281, 309, 420, 434, 435n, 436, 574, 692, 729, 800, 806, 815, 820, [2]33, 194, 267, 278, 285, 315, 489, 829, 903, 1175, 1187, 1201, [3]14, 23n, 48, 101, 368, 430, 443, 453, 478, 646, 711, 726, 734, 1069, [4]245, 245n, 253, 300, 407n, 483, 629, 638, 641, 643, 645, 646, 649, 652, 660, 665, [5]31, 31n, 32, 58, 63, 66, 76n, 118, 122, 123, 128, 139, 179, 192, 272, 465, 466, 512, 513n, 514, 514n, 534, 539, 540, 561, 597, 600, 621, 622, 628, 634, 637, 648, 650, 657, 659, 682, 739, 767, 863, [6]16, 23, 28n, 32, 109n, 136, 136n, 137
act of [2]454; actions of [4]479; and Adam [3]65; adorability of [4]670; aeon [2]32, 33n; *agens* and *patiens* [3]536, [6]296; aliens from [5]132; alone saves us [2]1162; angel [2]743; the anointed [4]244n; Apollonius and [2]708n; apostasy from [5]538; army of [3]759; ascension of *see* Ascension; assertions of [1]673; baptism of [3]730n, [4]58–9, 59n, 260, 297–8, 298n, 480, *480n–1n*, [5]535, 635, [6]32, 36, 49, 83; in the beginning [3]919; begotten [3]49; belief in [5]620; biography of [2]452; birth of [1]421, 442, 915, 917, [6]292–3; blood of [2]139, 267, 268, 497, 707, 858n, [3]42, 536, 544, 545, [5]5n, 55, [6]296; on "body" [2]924; body of [1]297, 863, [2]263, 283, 559, 670, 672, 674, 750, [3]42, 47, 545, 612, 613, 664–5, [4]61, 61n, [5]5n, 132, 394, 544, 545, 546, 547–8, 550, 553–4, 555, 558, 672, 680, [6]106; body and blood of [5]5n; born again in [1]574; born of [5]600; brother(s) of [2]477, 477n, [3]440, 440n; as bud or blossom [2]285; character of [4]41; charge against [2]485; childhood of [3]49n, [6]64n; Ch. and J. [5]371–2, 535, 535n; and Christianity [3]491; and Church [1]310, 310n, [3]72–3, 73, 745, [4]233–6; Church of *see* Church, of Christ; cling to [3]747; co-heirs of [5]608; coming of [3]53; command(s) of [1]294, 833, [3]8, 489; conception of [1]506–7, [3]17, 36, 610; contemporaries of [4]44, [6]109; as cosmos [3]313; as criminal [2]497; on cross [2]671, [4]745; cross of [5]492, 496, 497, 596, [6]299; crucified [2]208, [5]74; crucifixion of *see* Crucifixion; cures blind man [6]108; dead flesh of [3]44; dear and lovely [6]312; death of [2]69, 267, 362, 563–4, 918, 1099, [3]56, 56n, 612–13, [5]535, 585, 859n, [6]63, 105–6, 140; declaration(s) of [4]482, [6]262; deity of [2]652, 744, [3]683, [6]146; descent [3]925, into Hell [1]464, [2]334–5, 1099, [3]56, 56n, 57, 612–13, 732; died through our sins [1]702; and Dionysus [1]592n; disciples of [3]668; divinity of [1]462, 734, [2]35, 269–71, 454, 657, 722, 730, 730n, 742n, 749, 797–9, 1155, [3]611, 673n, 692, 692–3, 709–10, 762n, 1089, [4]269n, 295–8, 301–2, 580, 641, 670n, 672, [5]9, 58, 59, 618, [6]68, 69, 74; doctrine(s) of [3]697, [5]85, [6]19; as dupe [4]55; enthusiast [4]63; example of [3]305–6, [4]655–6; exclusive identity with Father [2]597; express words of [5]396; faith in [1]123, 504, [2]497, [3]722, [5]50, 559, 665; false [1]454; first-born from the dead [3]40, 40n; flesh and blood of [5]542; food of soul [5]671–2; fulfilment of Jewish law [1]877; functions of [5]626; garment of righteousness [1]815; genealogies of [4]55–6; of Gnostics [3]21; and God [5]71; good shepherd [2]322; and grace [5]593; grace by [5]609; graces bequeathed [5]529; growth in [1]202; as head [1]427, [3]678; as healer [5]654; as high priest [1]529, [3]874, [5]606; history of [2]1060, 1061, [3]58, [4]479, [6]105; human character [2]205; human soul of [3]720; humanity of [3]51, [5]394; ideal of [3]97–8; imitation of [4]145; incarnation of *see* Incarnation; infancy of [4]41n, see also *evangelium infantiae*; injunctions of [6]264; invitation of [5]683; as Jehovah [1]458, 706, [2]743, [5]497, 497n; Jehovah-Word [2]728, 728n, 743, [3]13n; J. the Ch. [1]435, [2]264, 462, [3]49, [4]475, [5]371–2,

535, 535n, [6]145; of John's gospel [2]597, 598; kingdom of [1]252, [3]72, 741, [5]537; kingdom on earth [4]244; as Lamb of God [1]522–3; language of [4]635, 635n; and law [4]251, 481; as life [2]293; life as symbol [2]279–80; life of [1]513n, [4]40–68, 471; life of the soul [3]518, [6]300; as light [1]630, 824, [3]523, [5]189, [6]305; as Logos *see* Logos; love and goodness [2]207; the man [2]264, 1175; as Mediator *see* Mediator; as medium [3]568; meek and holy [1]822, [3]34; memoirs of [4]471–3; memorabilia of [2]902, [4]68; mere man [6]63; merit in [5]182; as Messiah *see* Messiah; messiahship of [4]470; millenary reign of [5]629–30; mind of [3]744, [5]589; miracles of [2]262, 288, 453–4, 835, 988, 1005, 1059, 1159, [3]709, [5]383, [6]109; model [3]306; and Mohammed [3]673; moral of [5]766; and Moses [2]145; mystic conception of [2]711; name of [1]233, [6]178; nature of [3]305, [5]563; new law of [5]582–3; and Nicodemus [2]322; omnipresence of [1]297; one with [5]673; Order of [5]103; parables [1]201–2; in *Paradise Regained* [2]969; passes through closed doors [2]1077, 1078; differs from Paul [4]45; peccability of [3]49; in pentad [2]290; perfect man [6]70; perfect righteousness [2]591; perfection of life [2]206–7; personal divinity [1]490; as pleroma [2]291; power of [4]633; precepts of [3]696; predictions of [2]1087; pre-existence of [3]57; presence of [2]492; prohibition to disciples [2]1173; promise of [5]662; prophecies of [3]691; prophesied [3]738; and Pythagoras [5]226; raising of dead [2]566; really died [2]1080, 1088; reasoning of [4]673; redeemed of [6]311; as Redeemer *see* Redeemer; redemptive power of [2]657; refers to practical reason [2]644; reign on earth [3]452; religion of [4]548, 625, 667; representative of [1]523; Resurrection of *see* Resurrection; return of [2]484n; revelation in [5]57; revelation of [3]421; and rich man [3]650; righteousness of [1]470, [2]1166, 1177, [5]171; salvation by [1]786–7; the Saviour *see* Saviour; sayings of [1]448, [3]7; scale of [2]683; Second Coming [1]436, 452, 863n, [2]39n, 144n, [3]9, 415–82, 602, 731, 732n, [4]247n, [5]606–7, 630; as Second Person [5]57; seed of [1]430, 470, [2]689–90; Sermon on the Mount [2]297, [3]7, *see also* Bible: NT: Matt ch 5–7; servants of [3]773; service of [2]253; simplicity of [5]133; and Socrates [2]872n, [5]12, 724–5; as Son *see* Son; soul of [1]456; speeches of [4]476 ("Lord"); spirit of [2]1176, [3]511, 726; spoke propaideutically [1]513; substitute of [5]651; sufferings of [3]26–7, [6]303; suprahumanity [5]621; symbol [1]821; synopsis of faith in [3]20; system of [4]626; taught nothing new [3]662; teaching of [4]663; in the Temple [2]280, [4]477; temptation of [2]443–4, 447, 921–2, [3]30, 49; thoughtfulness of [3]34; threefold generation [2]584, 584n; title of [6]139; on traditions [5]567; train of souls [3]443; Transfiguration of [2]922, [3]30, 39, 40, 40n, 542, [5]651; true man [4]61; as Truth [3]23; truth in [1]235, [2]296, [5]140; two natures [1]435, 575; twofold being [2]672n, [3]73; types of [1]316, [6]108n; ultra-scriptural speculations [2]316; union of soul with [5]559; universal idea [2]183; under the veil [1]468; and St Veronica [1]41n; vision of [3]422; wept [1]13, [2]316; whole truth in [5]135; in wilderness [3]106–7, 107n; will of [4]233; wisdom [2]207–8; within us [1]675; in the womb [2]487; as Word *see* Word; his words are spirit [3]439; words of [1]339, 340, [4]399, 399n, 642, 644, 668, [5]580, 650, 677; work of [3]876; works in Elect [3]50; worship of [4]299; worshipped as serpent [2]717; Zinzendorf's theory [2]422–3

Jesus, son of Sirach (Apocrypha) [2]421–2, 517, 707, [3]476, 477n, [5]272, 272n, 402n, 520 ("Sirach"), [6]142n; *see also* Bible: Apocrypha: OT: Ecclus

Jew(s) [1]144, 420, 438, 441, 446, 807, 807n, [2]150, 314, 381, 485, 653, 785, 796, 919, 1076, 1081, 1103, 1103n, [3]55, 110, 165, 309, 463, 474, 531, 573, 622, 657–8, 668, 816, 817, [4]249, 258, 471, 638, [5]10, 61, 74, 128, 352, 364, 416–17, 523, 567, 591, 606, 611, 835, [6]18n, 66, 69, 294

Academy in Highgate [2]1188–9; on afterlife [2]828n, [3]553n; of Alexandria [1]463, 467, [2]427, [5]668, [6]138, 140, 143; annual conflux of [4]474; apostatised [6]142; author of 1 Pet [3]28; belief in resurrection [2]832; belief in Trinity [6]145; beliefs of [4]663; biblical [4]41; J.-blackguards [2]1080; borrowings from Greek philosophy [3]446; burial customs of [3]664; cabbalistical doctrine of [6]315; and Christ [6]139; Christian [2]470–1, 490, 833n, [6]68; and Christians [6]146; Jewish Church *see* Church, Jewish; circumcised [5]624; and circumcision [5]647, 831; common tongue of [5]651, 651n; contemporaries of Jesus [4]44; con-

Jew(s)—*continued*
version of [2]916, 916n; converts to Christianity [1]832, [2]740n, 916, 917n, [3]456; Jewish culture [4]40n; cup of blessing [5]551; custom of [1]448; degeneration of [2]421; degradation of [3]34; dignity of [4]481 ("Jewish People"); doctrines resembling Christian [3]684; duties of [6]60; educated [4]57; and Egypt [3]111; in Egypt [1]447; emigration of [2]401; fancy/fancies of [3]9, 34; as generous/Iapetic race [1]540; German and English [3]700; German prejudice against [2]480; concept of God [2]417–20; notion of God [1]674–5; God unknown to [2]422; Heb addressed to [3]21; history of [1]817, [2]830–6; ignorant [2]570; interpretation of scripture [2]153; "Jew-Ethic" [3]700; Jewdom [3]467; King of [1]458, [6]33; lame [5]845; later [2]314; and law [2]471; law(s) of [1]877, [2]495–6, [6]4, 4n; laws binding on [5]535; learned [2]153, 270, 467, [3]38, 462, 606, 1085, [4]244, [6]140; legendary custom of [2]274; Lessing on [3]700n; literality of [3]731; looks of [2]830–1; mad [6]102; and marriage law [5]393; and Messiah [3]738, 925n, 988n, [4]246; in the middle ages [5]234; and miracles [2]1060; missions to [3]6, 6n–7n; orthodox [2]567; of Palestine [1]447, [2]475, 478, [6]143; Palestinian and extra-Palestinian [2]451; St Paul on [5]76; persecution of [3]112n, [6]141; persecution of Jesus [6]136n; Persian [2]401; pious [5]582, 677; Platonising [2]429; Portuguese [1]113n, [2]54n; promises made to [3]464–5; realm of shadows [2]1073–4; religion of [2]421; require a sign [3]988; restoration of [3]417, 457; Rhenferd on [2]700; in Rhodes [5]841; and Roman yoke [2]372; sabbath of [1]873; sacred books of [2]377, 453; sensuality of [4]673; Spanish [1]113n, [2]54n; on "spirit" [2]246; spiritualising of [2]499; state of [3]53–4, 448, 646; symbolical language of [2]712, [6]630n; and Trinity [2]797–8; unconverted [3]477; Jewish university [3]467; unjudaic [3]699; Wandering J. [2]755, [3]646, [5]775. *See also* Hebrew(s); Israelite(s); Judaism

jewel(s) [1]446, [3]37, 566, [4]658, [5]276

jeweller(s) [1]448, [3]636

Jewish Historical Society *see* London

Jewish War [1]832, 832n, [2]512n, 517, [3]475, 696

Jezira/*Yetsira* [4]246n, [5]807

jingle(s) [1]406, [4]742, [5]111

Joab (Bible) [1]424

Joachim, King of Naples (1767–1815) [5]276n

Joachim of Fiore (d 1202) [3]73n

Joachimites [3]73n, 427n

Joannebrot [5]105

Joannes Scotus Erigena (c 810–c 860) [1]lxvin, 624n, [3]136n, 326n, 1083, [5]444, 444n, 473n
De divisione naturae ed Gale MT [3]134–9; 1083n, [4]235n q

Job (Bible) [1]425n, 823, [2]313, 923, 924, [3]921, [6]308

job, bookseller's [5]500

Jobab (Bible) [1]418

Jocasta (myth) [2]584–5

jockey [5]250

Joel (Bible) [1]423, [2]653, [3]668n, 1069

Johanan/Juchanan, Rabbi (c 200–c 280) [3]1090

Johannes, Prince Elector of Saxony (1467–1532) [3]756

John (fiction) [2]658, [5]21, 23, 28, 177, [6]299

John, St, the Baptist (Bible) [1]323, 450, 452, [2]252, 462, 479n, 481, 483, 489, 489n, 497, [3]41, 41n, 456, 760, 987, [4]49–50, 51, 56, 58, 61, 63, 64, 297–8, 298n, 480, 480n–1n, 637, [5]99, 105, 105n, 402, 402n, 621, 635, 648, 651, 832, [6]63, 83
baptism of [3]36, 49, 926, [4]59, 59n; disciples of [1]449, 450, [2]798; as Elijah [2]150

John, St, the Evangelist (1st century) [1]200, 236, 340, 437, 482n, 485, 485n, 687, 712, 807, 843n, [2]35, 37, 58, 64, 184, 256, 273, 276, 280, 307, 440, 442, 489, 494, 496, 569, 582, 582n, 592, 707, 708, 712, 720, 735, 1078, 1080, 1085, 1162, 1177, [3]14, 24, 34, 36, 55, 467, 477, 481, 521, 524, 611, 678, 684, 684n, 738, 743, 922, 926, 928, 1085, 1085n, 1090, [4]41, 60–1, 296, 303, 473, 474, 474n, 638, [5]58, 96, 372, 385, 402, 402n, 516, 523–4, 554, 582, 591, 628, 651, 667, 674, 677, 807n, [6]58, 63, 70, 77, 85, 91, 143, 165n, 168, 303, 306
Epistles of [5]667; and 4th Gospel [2]484, 484n, 489–90; identity of [1]486; and boiling oil [2]459–60; Palestinian Jew [2]478; privilege of [2]262; on redemption [2]658; and Rev [2]460, 465–6, 488, 488n, 489–90, [3]684, 684n, [5]807n, *see also* John the Theologian; scheme of [2]726; successor [2]484; thought in Hebrew [3]1086; words of [4]40, 399, 399n; writings of [1]734, 816, [3]74, [6]66–7. *See also* Bible: NT: EPISTLE(S); GOSPEL(S); John; Rev

John Chrysostom, St *see* Chrysostom
John II, of Aragon (1397–1479) [3]104n
John, Johann Friedrich (1782–1847) [3]940
John of Cyzius (6th–7th century) [3]134
John of Damascus/Damascenus (c 676–c 754) [2]324 q, [5]24, [6]182–3 q
De orthodoxa fide [2]683
John of Gaunt, Duke of Lancaster (1340–99) [3]155
John of Gischala (fl 66–70) [1]481–2, 481n
John of Salisbury (c 1115–80) *Metalogicon* tr Mcgarry [3]682
John, "phrsphrr" [4]864, 864n
John the Theologian (John the Elder) (1st century), supposed author of Rev [1]486, [2]488, [3]421, 467–8, 477, 477n, 684, 684n
Johnes, Thomas (1748–1816) [3]188, 188n
Johns Hopkins University Library *see* Baltimore MD
Johnson, Anthony [2]245
Johnson, Esther (1681–1728) [4]466n
Johnson, J. R. (fl 1820) *see* P. Huber *Natural History of Ants* tr Johnson
Johnson, John (1769–1833) *see* Cowper *Poems* ed Johnson
Johnson, Joseph (1738–1809) [1]828, [3]882n
Johnson, Mary Lynn "How Rare is a . . . Copy of Coleridge's *Sibylline Leaves*" [2]16n
Johnson, Samuel (1649–1703) [3]166n
no Whig [3]162, 165
Works [2]512n; MT [3]140–69
Johnson, Samuel (1709–84) [1]cviii, 38, 727n, 742, 845n, [2]14, 27n, 75–6, 613n, 768n, 815, 969, 972, [3]165, 165n, 223n, [4]632, 698n, 701n, 705n, 709n, 716n, 722n, 731n, 740n, 741n, 760n, 762, 763n, 767n, 806n, 848, 869, [5]123n, [6]206n
Anderson's imitation of [1]55, 55n; antitheses [3]223; and Boswell [3]142, 142n; C's distaste for [1]55n, 221n; on Congreve [2]83; criticism of [3]651–2; on dramatic illusion [4]781, 781n; frog-critic [1]148n; overrated [6]74, 74n; pension [3]146n; poetry of [2]240; prose style [1]156n, 183n, 845, [5]533; on prosody [2]579, 579n; on Shakespeare [4]757, 761, 762, 785n, 812, 813, 825n, 847, 852, 855, 855n, 863; and sycophancy [2]75–6, 76n; on Thomson [1]74n, 75n
Adventurer [5]360n; "Cowley" [2]224n q; *Dictionary of the English Language* [3]141n q, 161n, 634n, [6]288; *History of Rasselas, Prince of Abyssinia* [5]102n; *Johnson on Shakespeare* ed Sherbo [4]781n q; *A Journey to the Western Islands of Scotland* [3]654n, [4]83n; *Lives of the Poets* ed G. B. Hill [3]178n, [4]14n, 76n q, 246n; "Milton" [4]246n q; "On Milton's Versification" [2]579n; *Rambler* [1]60n q, 156 q, 156n, [2]795, [3]651n–2n q, [4]727n; "Watts" [2]1170n; *Works* ed Sherbo [4]781n q
Johnston, Henry Erskine (1770–?1830) [6]270
joke(s) [1]144, [2]832, [3]175, 496, 902, [4]741
j.-bully [4]626–7, 627n; flat [2]1126; spoilt [3]1068
"jokesmith" [4]627n
jokesmith(s) [4]627, 630
Jonah/Jonas (Bible) [3]55, 767, 767n, [4]735, 735n, [5]434n, [6]72, 117, 119
symbol of Jewish nation [1]695
Jonas, father of Simon Peter (Bible) [1]514
Jonas, Justus (1493–1555) [3]718, 727, 756
Jonas *see also* Jonah
Jonathan (Bible) [5]590n
Jones, David *Epoch and Artist* [1]580n
Jones, Herschel Vespasian (1861–1928) [5]120
Jones, Jeremiah (1693–1724) *New and Full Method* [1]488, 491n
Jones, Maurice (fl 1801–16) [3]882n
Jones, Thomas (1765–1811) [3]188n
Jones, Tom *see* Fielding *Tom Jones*
Jones, Sir William (1746–94) [4]489, 489n, 509
Asiatic Researches [2]339; *Institutes of Hindu Law* [2]339, [6]4, 4n; "On the Gods of Greece, Italy, and India" [6]8n q; *Works* [4]489n, 509, 509n q, [5]119n; *see also* Kālidasā *Sacontalá* tr Jones
Jones, William Henry Samuel (1876–1963) *see* Pausanias *Description* tr Jones
Jonson, Ben (1572–1637) [1]lxvii, xciv, cvi, cxli, cxlviii, clii, 37, 43, 43n, 362, 365, 390, 407, [2]16, 75, 119n, 121, 231, 231n, 760n, [4]291–2, [5]98
and *Two Noble Kinsmen* [1]407; and Chapman [2]1122; characters of [3]173; C's admiration for [3]171–2; in C's lectures [1]cxxxix; Drayton epitaph [1]56, 56n; and Greek [1]73n; and Juvenal [1]62; as laureate [1]56, 56n; "Life" by Anderson MT [1]61–2; in *LR* [1]cxli; marked passages in [1]53; no humour [2]778; not a genius [3]176; and Shakespeare [2]778n, [3]176n, 182–3, 186–7, 187n

Jonson, Ben—*continued*
The Alchemist [2]691; MT [3]183–4; *Bartholomew Fair* MT [3]186–9; [4]78, 724; *Ben Jonson* ed Herford, P. Simpson, and E. M. Simpson [3]170; *Catiline* MT [3]184–6; *Cynthia's Revels* [3]194n; *The Devil Is an Ass* MT [3]189–91; *Dramatic Works* ed P. Whalley [1]61n, 373; MT [3]170–95; *Epicoene* MT [3]180–3; *Every Man in His Humour* [3]1019n; *Every Man Out of His Humour* MT [3]175; [5]98n; *The New Inn* MT [3]192–5; *Philaster* [1]lxxxixn; *Poetaster* [3]181n; MT [3]175–7; *The Sad Shepherd* [3]171; *Sejanus* MT [3]177–80; *The Staple of News* MT [3]191–2; *To the Memory of . . . Shakespeare* [3]187n; *Underwoods* [1]246n; *Volpone* [3]171; MT 180

Jordan [2]830, 833, [3]51, 108n, [5]105, [6]119

Jordan, Dorothea (née Bland) (1761–1816) [4]704n–5n

Jordanus de Quedlinburg (d 1380) [2]1182

Jortin, John (1698–1770) [3]1084, 1084n, [4]243, 243n
Life of Erasmus [4]243n

Joseph, husband of Mary (Bible) [1]48n, [2]271, 275, 329, 477, 711, 915, 921, [3]14n, 440, 606, 730n, [4]53, 55n, 58, 253, 255
son of [5]118, 118n, 513, 513n, [6]70

Joseph of Arimathea (Bible) [2]256, [3]664–5

Joseph, son of Jacob (Bible) [1]798, [2]383, 414, 895n, [3]606, [5]138

Josephedites [5]118

Josephus, Flavius (c 37–c 100) [1]468n, [2]156, 157n, 375, 376, 376n, 381, 381n, 382n, 831, [3]110, 111, 468, 468n, 607n, [6]68, 140, 141, 142
Antiquitates Judaicae [2]149, 149n, 832n, tr as *Jewish Antiquities* [2]381n, [6]68n; *Contra Apionem* tr Thackeray [2]374 q, 374n q; *Genuine Works* [5]693n; *Jewish War* [2]509, 509n, [3]476, 476n, tr Whiston [5]693n; *Works* ed Whiston [6]68n

Joshua (Bible) [1]420, 423, [2]145, 145n, 342, 785, 895, [3]108n, 738, 780, [4]257, 682, [6]119, 146

Josiah (Bible) [1]437, [2]894, 894n, [3]461, 461n, 470n

jour [1]608n

Journal of Natural Philosophy, Chemistry, and the Arts [3]1033n q, [4]82n

journals, London [4]578

journeyman [2]447

"Jove" [5]658, 658n

Jove (myth) [1]71, [2]345, 583, 1000, 1000n, 1125, [3]888, [5]658, [6]145, 145n, 211, 211n
bird of [1]482; mind of [6]8; *see also* Jupiter

Jovellanos y Ramirez, Gaspar Melchior de (1744–1811) *Bread and Bulls* ed Felix and others [4]170

Jovinian (d c 405) [2]272, 667

Jovius, Paulus (Paulo Giovio) (1483–1552) [4]338

Jowett, Benjamin (1817–93) [2]569n

joy(s) [3]553, 620, 741, [4]278, 444, 480, 489, [5]168, 171, 424
and boiled mutton [2]1006; intellectual [3]670; in light [5]814; spiritual [3]566

jubilee [2]785, [3]460

Juchanan *see* Johanan

Judaea/Judea [1]481–2, [2]383, 398–9, 470, 509, 512, 515, 515n, 830, 832, 1153, [3]34, [4]53, 248, 248n, 253, [5]539

Judah/Iuda(h) (Bible) [1]424, 443, 444n, [2]256, 832, [3]480, [4]44n, [5]565
tribes of [3]461, 462

Judaism(s) [1]288, 307n, 832n, [2]495, 811, [3]470, 874, 1083, [5]577
converts from [4]256; popular [3]40; spiritualised [6]140; triumph of Christianity over [2]504; *see also* Jew(s)

Judas Iscariot (Bible) [1]365, 491n, [2]63, 671, 711, 717, 728, [3]917, 1059–60, 1060n, [4]640n

Jude (Bible) [2]476, 477, 477n

judex [1]852n

judge(s) [2]38, 72, 115, 476, 618, [4]238, 634, [5]321
abusive language [1]727; competent [2]108; final [5]626; in Jewish history [5]307; millions of men as [2]30; omniscient [1]342; philosophical [2]255; rightful [1]422

judgment(s)/Judgment [1]327, 367, 808, [2]1136, 1160, 1168, [3]20, 451, 790, [5]415, 820, 821, [6]173
acts of [4]863; aesthetic [4]408; analytical [3]344; committed to Son [5]31–2; Day of [1]10, [3]60, [4]549n, 662n, [5]57n, 487n, 563, [6]140; after death [2]564, 565, 567; determined [5]420; divine [5]167; erroneous [3]260; error of [4]744; exquisite [4]758; future [4]637; genial [3]886; of God [1]350; last [3]925–6, [5]276; matchless [4]717; measure of [2]831; popular [2]140; reason to doubt [5]61; right of [5]614; rule of [5]714; j.-seat [4]662, [5]592; Shakespeare's [4]815, 827, 836n–7n, 838; sound [4]604; superlative

[1]393; suspended [5]726; temperance of [2]809–10
"Judian" [4]747–8, 748n
Judicia de scriptis antiquis [1]7
judicious [2]1146
Judith (Bible) [2]323, [5]520; *see also* Bible: Apocrypha: OT: Judith
juegos [1]506
Juggernaut [3]587, 587n
juggle(s) [1]522, [2]1005
juggler(s) [2]614, 727, [4]673, [5]554, [6]99
jugglery [2]942, [3]708
Julia (d 46 BC) [1]790
Julian, St (legend) [2]752
Julian the Apostate (Flavius Claudius Julianus) (331–63) [2]256, 746, 746n, 747, 758n, [3]143, 143n, 144, 145, 146, 147, 490n, 722, 921, [4]627n, [5]533
letter to Ecdicius [4]99 q
Opera quae extant omnia [4]100n; *Works* tr W. C. Wright [4]99n q
Juliet (*Romeo and Juliet*) [4]742, 828, 829, 834
Julius (in Solger) [5]93
Julius II (Giuliano della Rovere), Pope (1443–1513) [1]831
Julius III (Giovanni Maria Ciocchi del Monte), Pope (1487–1555) [3]232n
Julius Caesar *see* Caesar, Gaius Julius
Julius, Duke of Brunswick and Lüneberg (1528–89) [2]781, 780n–1n
Jung, Johann Heinrich ("Jung-Stilling") (1740–1817) [3]394, [5]291n
Theorie der Geister-Kunde MT [3]196–217; 985, 985n, [5]414n
jungle [3]466
"Junius" (fl 1768–73) [1]lxxxv, [2]815
character of [3]222–3; prose style [1]156n, [5]533
Letters MT [3]220–9, ed Cannon [3]220n
Juno (myth) [1]639, 799, [3]234n, 255, [6]157, 198, 199, 200, 202, 207
Junot, Andoche (1771–1813) [2]940n
Jupiter/Iupiter (myth) [1]178, 543, 639, 793, 799, [2]901, [3]234n, 410, 413, 448n, [4]201, [5]7, 386, 562, 562n, 681, 730, [6]8, 145, 145n. *See also* Jove; Zeus
Jupiter (planet) [1]625n, [2]920n, 1164, [3]859, [4]511, 517–18, 518n, [5]249, 249n, 339
jure divino [1]380, [3]490
jurgium [4]254
Juridical Letters [3]500
Jurieu, Pierre (1637–1713) *History of the Council of Trent* MT [3]230–5
jurists, private [2]375
juror [3]158
jus [2]1098
j. divinum [1]295, *295n*, [4]173
Jussieu, Antoine Laurent de (1748–1836) [3]1067n
justice [1]731, [2]618, [3]677, 699, [4]238, 429, 663, 693, [5]179, 227
divine [2]263, [3]671, 737, [4]234, 629, 816, 836, [5]159, 682; of God [1]323, [3]26, 307, [5]75, 609, 610, 611, 670; poetic [1]543; public [3]797; punitive [5]103, 497; true and false [2]9
Justices, Chief [2]375
justification [1]11, 11n, 703, [2]207, 1161, [3]232n, 515, 517n, 544, 548, 748, 749, 752, 755, [4]634, [5]129, 131, 138, 138n, 498n, 597n
by faith [1]358, [2]298n, [3]748, 749, 752–3, 760, 776, [4]647–8, [5]408n, 467, 467n, 604n; by works [5]497n
Justin the Martyr, St (c 100–c 165) [2]440, 446, [3]683–4, 1084, [4]471n, 473, 473n, [5]513, 514, 526, 526n, 559 q, 579 q, 629, 635, 635n–6n, 643, 766, 766n, [6]67, 68, 69–70, 85n, 92, 145, 146, 164–5, 165n
Dialogue with Trypho [2]440n, 442n q, 443, 443n q, [5]526n, 636n, [6]68n q; *First Apology* [2]718q; *Works* tr Pusey [2]718n q
Justinian (Flavius Petrus Sabbatius Justinianus) (482–565) [1]298, 298n, 299n, [2]305n, 1139, [4]666, 666n
Juvenal (Decimus Junius Juvenalis) (c 55–c 140) [1]38, 777 q, [2]84n q, 693–4, 748n, 757n, 758, 760, 760n, 1198n, [3]41, 41n, 175, 420n, 919n q
tr Dryden [1]38, [2]757n; and Jonson [1]62; style [2]761
Satires [1]857n q, [2]928n q, [3]681 q, [4]78 q, 78n q, 508 q, 508n q, 784 q, 784n q, [5]784n q, [6]73 q, 73n q
Juxon, William, Bishop of London (1582–1663) [2]521
juxtaposition [1]525, [4]384, 384n

K, Miss [2]586, 587, 587n
Kabbala denudata [6]141n
tr Rosenroth [1]719n
Kaeso *see* Caeso
Kaffirs [3]355
kai [5]402, 402n, 516, 516n
kaio [3]61n

kairos akairos [3]751
kaleidophone [4]313–14, 313n
kaleidoscope [4]82, 82n, 313n, [5]737, 737n
mental [1]822
kalesantos [1]463n
Kālidasā (?5th century) *Sacontalá* tr Sir W. Jones [5]119, 119n q
Kalk [5]258
Kalm, Pehr/Peter (1716–79) *En resa til Norra America* tr J. R. Forster [3]586, 586n
Kalmyk [5]253
kalon [2]425, [3]460, 460n
Kalzi (myth) [4]489–90
Kamchatka (river) [3]1047
kangaroo [2]861n
kanon [1]493n
k. tes pisteos [1]312
Kant, Immanuel (1724–1804) [1]lxiii, lxiv, lxxiv, ci, cxxiii, cxxviii, cxxxi, clii, cliv, 340n, 409, 539n, 622n, 632n, 751n, [2]188, 193, 481n, 557n, 594, 595, 611n, 641n, 990n, 995, 995n, 1016, 1016n, 1051, 1203–4, [3]43n, 137n, 381, 954–73, [4]36n, 107n, 130, 158, 158n, 225, 265, 351n, 361, 369, 421n, 440, [5]82, 88n, 89–90, 320 q, 405n, 581, 719n, 724n, 744, 755, 756, 788, 812, [6]133
and *a priori* [4]217–18, 217n–18n, 355, 355n; aim of [4]280, 423; and *Anschauen* [4]131–2, 132n; as astronomer [5]225, 225n; authority of [5]809; back-sliding from [2]994, 994n; and Bacon [3]919n; Baxter anticipates [1]230; beauty of method [2]607n; on Berkeley [4]132; British [4]403n; cant im manuale [4]505; categorical imperative [3]96, 357, 958, [5]791; categories [3]95, 95n–6n, 381n; and Christianity [2]186; C departs from Kantian usage [3]80n; C's admiration for [5]90n; critical philosophy of [4]157–8, 279–80, 280n; and Descartes [3]329–30, 330n; and *Ding an sich* [4]125, 125n, 126; distinction between art and handicraft [2]1065–6, 1065n; distinction between existence and attributes [4]108; distinction between genius and talent [2]1065–6, 1066n; doctrines of [3]641; error of [3]277, 286, 286n, [4]143, [5]750, 750n; on *Erscheinung* [4]129n; on existence [4]130–1; and Fichte [2]615, [4]354, 357; followers of [4]280; on free will [3]737, *737n*, [4]435–6, 445; on God [2]181–2, 183, 185–6; good sense of [4]372; great man [3]275; on happiness [4]136; and Heinroth [2]1013n; a Hercules among thinkers [3]99, 99n; on Hume [4]348, 348n; on ideas [5]714; importance of [5]206; improvement on [3]130n; indebtedness of *Naturphilosophen* to [5]297; ingratitude towards [2]192, 192n; intellectual mechanique [1]793, 793n; on intuition [4]393–4, 393n, 394n, [5]32n; Jacobi's objection to [3]95n; and Laplace [1]74n; Latin essays [3]318n; on Leibniz [3]966n; and Mendelssohn [3]297, 297n, 298; modern Aristotle [3]257n, 322n; more talked of than read [2]207; philosophy of [3]242, 954–73, [4]124–5, 217; polarity in [1]660; post-Kantian philosophy [3]12n; post-Kantian school [3]598; pun on [4]505n; quoted in *BL* [3]87n; on race [3]355–6, 356n, [5]338n; on reason and conscience [2]189; on reason and understanding [1]655n, [4]214n; review of Herder [2]429n, 1059, 1059n, 1065n; and Schelling [2]187, 187n, [3]97, 99n, 286n, 289n, 291n, 292, 330–1, [4]354, 357, 386, 386n, 439, 445–6, [5]698, 698n; Kantian scholastic [4]354; on science [4]363, 363n–4n; and shallow morality [2]429; silly remarks [2]535; slights on [4]357; on space [4]217, [5]706; on space and time [2]1002, 1002n, [4]124–6; spectacles of [5]728; and Steffens [5]242, 243; subjectivity of [5]357, 357n; sublime mystery of [3]96; superiority of [5]211; system of [2]185, 187, [5]243n, 714; theology of [3]956; trichotomies in [1]347; understanding defined [3]423, 425, 557, [5]599
Allgemeine Naturgeschichte und Theorie des Himmels [4]376, 376n, 386, 417n, tr Jaki as *Universal Natural History and Theory of the Heavens* [3]321, 338; "An Fräulein Charlotte v. Knobloch" [3]351–2, 351n, tr as *Letter to a Noble Lady* [3]985, 985n–6n; *Anthropologie in pragmatischer Hinsicht abgefasst* [2]535, [4]456, [5]241–2; *Copy A* [2]535n; MT [3]236–8; [4]456n; *Copy B* [2]535n; MT [3]239–40; [4]456n, reviewed [1]151, tr Gregor as *Anthropology from a Practical Point of View* [3]236; *Critik der praktischen Vernunft* [2]182n q, 185n, 189n, [3]737, 958, 968–9 q, 969–70 q, [4]422, C's reading of [1]676, 676n, tr as *Critique of Practical Reason* [3]97, 97n, tr T. K. Abbot [3]959n–60n q, [4]136n q; *Critik der reinen Vernunft* [2]183n, 185n, [3]205n q, 318–19, 318n, 319n, 324, 330n, 331n q, 619n, 737, 919,

956, 956n, 965, 966n, [4]218n, 223–4, 223n q, 230, 265n, 403n, 409n, 436n, 446n, [5]581n, 707, 756, [6]290, C's reading of [1]676, 676n, purpose of [4]219–20, (2nd ed 1787) [4]112n, 157n, 346 q, 348n, [5]297n, 435n, 581n, 750n, (5th ed 1799) MT [3]241–9, tr as *Critique of Pure Reason* [1]347, [2]429n, 1059n, 1152n, 1204n, [3]80n, 201n, 619, 641n, 901n, 919n, [4]112n, 124, 403, critic of [3]283n, tr N. Kemp Smith [3]97n q, 241, 557n q, 957n q, [4]157n q, 346n q, 348n q, 363n q, [5]297n q, 750n q; *Critik der Urtheilskraft* [1]348n, 653, 653n, [2]186n, 187, 187n; MT [3]250–1; 919, [4]376, 376n, [5]211, C's reading of [1]676, 676n, tr Meredith as *Critique of Judgment* [1]348n q, [2]1064, 1065n q, 1066n q, 1067–8 q, 1068n, 1069n, 1070 q, 1070n q, 1071, 1071n; *De mundi sensibilis atque intelligibilis forma et principiis* [2]612n, 623n, 1204n, [3]285n, 318–19, 318n, 966n, [4]124–5, 125n, 156, 156n, [5]409, 409n, 706n; *Dreams of a Spirit-Seer* tr Goerwitz, ed Sewall [3]316, 321, 338; *Der einzig mögliche Beweisgrund zu einer Demonstration des Daseyns Gottes* [3]87, 330, 956n, [4]108n, [5]211, 211n; *Gedanken von der wahren Schätzung der lebendigen Kräfte* [3]343n, [4]376, 376n, [5]706n, tr Gregor as *Conflict of the Faculties* [6]291; *Grundlegung zur Metaphysik der Sitten* [1]lxxixn, [2]183n, 192n, 960n; MT [3]252–5; [4]280n q, tr T. K. Abbott as *Fundamental Principles of the Metaphysics of Ethics* [3]252; *Himmelssystem* [2]997n; *Kant's Latin Writings* ed L. W. Beck [3]316; *Logik* ed Jäsche, [1]632n; MT [3]256–62, tr T. K. Abbot as *Introduction to Logic* [1]lxvii–lxviii, tr Hartman and Schwarz as *Kant's Logic* [3]256; *Die Metaphysik der Sitten* MT [3]263–8, 679n, 956, [4]153n, tr as *Metaphysic of Morals* [4]136n, tr Gregor as *The Doctrine of Virtue* [3]263; *Metaphysische Anfangsgründe der Naturwissenschaft* [1]xcv, [2]853n, 997n; MT [3]269–303; 362, 919, [4]376, 376n, 417, [6]238, 238n, tr Ellington as *Metaphysical Foundations of Natural Science* [3]269; *Observations on the Feeling of the Beautiful and Sublime* tr Goldthwait [3]316; *Principiorum primorum cognitionis metaphysicae* [2]1204n; *Die Religion innerhalb der Grenzen der blossen Vernunft* [2]181n, 183n, 185n q, 186, 186n, 207n, 985, [3]267, 267n; MT 304–13; [5]701n, C's reading of [1]676, 676n, tr T. M. Green and Hudson as *Religion within the Limits of Reason Alone* [3]304; *Sammlung einiger bisher unbekannt gebliebener kleiner Schriften* ed Rink MT [3]314–15, tr Kerferd and Walford as *Selected Pre-Critical Writings and Correspondence* [3]314; *Theorie des Himmels* [1]793n, [2]1204n; "Ueber die Buchmacherei" [3]955n; *Untersuchungen über die Deutlichkeit der Grundsätze der natürlichen Theologie und der Moral* [3]959n; *Vermischte Schriften* [1]lxxi, [2]623n, 1204n, [3]87n, 203, 261n, [4]376n, 417, [5]409n, 701n; *Copy A* MT [3]316–20; *Copy B* MT [3]321–35; *Copy C* ed Tieftrunk [1]lxii, lxiin; MT [3]336–66; [5]88n; *Copy D* MT [6]291–4; *Versuch den Begriff der negativen Grössen in die Weltweisheit einzuführen* [4]376, 376n; *Von den verschiedenen Racen der Menschen* [4]376–7, 377n; "Was heisst sich im Denken orientiren?" [5]701n

Kantian(s) ("Kantean[s]") [2]594, 628, [4]155, 158n, 653, [5]701, 704, 743, 759, 766, 789 sturdy [5]735

Kantianism [5]691–2, 692n, 697

Kantism, literal [5]753

karakar [1]421n

Karl August, Grand-Duke of Saxe-Weimar (1757–1828) [4]187

Karl Friedrich, Grand-Duke of Baden (1728–1811) [3]985

Karlson (in Richter) [4]265, 268, 268n

Karroo [4]152

Käsebier (in Bürger) [1]829, 829n

Kastner, Karl Wilhelm Gottlob (1783–1857) [3]127

kata [2]436, 436n, [3]834, [4]472n, [5]72

k. sarka [1]512, [2]918, 918n, [3]3, 7, 7n, 14n

kat'exochen [1]126, 126n

katholon [1]368, 368n, 524n, [4]718

kathos [4]472, 472n

Katterfelto, Gustavus (d 1799) [1]519, *519n*, [2]285, 285n, [3]9, 9n, 27, 27n

kayak [4]303 ("kajak")

Kaye, Frederick Benjamin (1892–1930) *see* Mandeville *Fable of the Bees* ed Kaye

Kean, Edmund (1787–1833) [4]42, 42n

Keats, John (1795–1821), [1]lxvi, 223n, [6]246 *Letters* ed Rollins [1]lxvin q, [2]1112n q, [4]606n

Keble, John (1792–1866) *see* Irenaeus *Adversus haereses* tr Keble
Keck, Thomas (fl 1656) [1]742
"keeping" [1]58, *58n*, [3]914
Keese, John (1805–56) [1]clxiiin
Kehama (in RS) [5]121, 121n
Keilah [2]917
Keiling, Caspar [5]3
Kelliher, Hilton "A Stray Notebook" [4]334, 337n
Kelly, John Norman Davidson *Early Christian Creeds* [3]692n
Kelsick, John (fl 1723) [3]977
Kemble, John Philip (1757–1823) [4]42, 42n, 721, 721n, [6]95, 114, 114n
Kemp, Grover (fl 1811) [3]942
Kemp Smith, Norman (1872–1958) *see* Kant *Critique of Pure Reason* tr Kemp Smith
Kempis, Thomas à (1379–1471) [2]1178, 1178n, [3]535, 622 q, [4]643, [6]318
  The Imitation of Christ [2]1178n, [3]209n q, 588, 588n
Kendal [1]519n, [4]675
  Sandes Library [1]255n
Kenmure/Kenmuir/Kinmuir, Viscount *see* Gordon, John
Kennedy, James (1793–1864) *see* Aeschylus *Agamemnon* ed Kennedy
Kennedy, Jane (1833–1912) [1]760
Kenney, James (1780–1849) [1]xci
Kenocranioni [4]188
kenon [5]698–700
Kent [2]977, [6]46
Kent (*King Lear*) [4]818, 819
Kentmere [3]974
Kentucky, University of *see* Lexington KY
Kenyon, John (1784–1856) [1]lix, 330, 330n, [2]1118n, [3]368n, 810
  Rhymed Plea for Tolerance [1]331n; MT [3]367–70, presentation copy to C [3]367
Kenyon, Lloyd, Baron (1732–1802) [6]131, 133
Kepler, Johannes (1571–1630) [2]668n, 1024, 1024n, [3]426, 426n, [4]505, 505–6, 522–3, [6]52
Ker, John, 3rd Duke of Roxburghe (1740–1804) [2]702
Ker, Robert *see* Carr/Ker, Robert
Kerby, F. (fl 1810) [3]940
Kerby-Miller, Charles *see* Pope *Memoirs of . . . Scriblerus* ed Kerby-Miller
Kerferd, G. *see* Kant *Selected . . . Writings* ed Kerferd and Walford
Kerguelen's Land [2]74
Kermode, Frank *see* Shakespeare *Tempest* ed Kermode
kern [1]580
Kern, Jerome David (1885–1945) [5]108, 854
kernel [1]603
Kero (8th century) [1]151, 151n
Kerslake, Mr (fl 1859) [1]clxviii
Kerslake, Thomas (1812–91) [4]294
kerugma/*kerugmata* [1]452, 452n, [2]436, 439, 1081, 1081n, 1082n, [3]7, 7n, 421, 435, 435n, [4]253–4, 256
keryx [3]450, 450n–1n, 594
Keswick [1]ciii, cv, cxn, cxi, 227n, [2]111, 170, 359, 753, 874, 1048, 1072, [3]492, [4]91, 520n, 676n, [5]81, 145, 818, [6]31, 121
  Greta Hall [1]lxxxiv, xciii, cviii, cix, cixn, cx, cxi, cxii, cxiii, cxxxiv, clviii, clxvii, clxix, 39, 40, 41, 52, 89, 116, 226, 699, 742, 743, 840, [2]4, 7, 691, 753, 874, [3]183n, 816, 930n, [4]29, 39, 620, 656n, books annotated at [1]lxxix–lxxxi, C's study in [1]lxxix–lxxxi; Vale of [5]389; *see also* Coleridge, S. T. I (1) at Keswick
Ketch, Jack (d 1686) [2]537, [5]281, 281n
Ketcham, C. H. *see* John Wordsworth *Letters* ed Ketcham
kettle [4]38
Kew, Royal Botanic Gardens [1]536n
key(s) [2]1096n, [4]103, 259
  listless [5]857; power of [1]309, [5]507–8, 534
Keynes, Sir Geoffrey (1887–1982)
  A Bibliography of Sir Thomas Browne [1]760, 774n; *William Pickering* [1]clxiin
Keynes, John Maynard, 1st Baron (1883–1946) [2]953n
keystone [1]29, 585, [5]621
  of philosophy [1]585
Kidd, John (1775–1851) *On the Adaptation of External Nature* [2]883n
Kiddell, Caroline (fl 1809–15) [2]587n
Kiddell, George (fl 1809–15) [2]587n
Kiddell, H. Grove (fl 1781) [2]1032
Kidder, Richard (1633–1703) [4]637, 637n
Kidderminster [1]264
kidney [5]560
  k.-fellow [6]251
Kierkegaard, Sören Aabye (1813–55) [1]288n
Kieser, Dietrich Georg (1779–1862) [4]326, 497 ("Keiser"), 497n; see also *Archiv für den thierischen Magnetismus* ed Eschenmayer, Kieser, and Nasse

Kilham, Alexander (1762–98) [5]135n
kill and destroy [3]38
"killcrop" [4]658, 658n
Kimchi, David (c 1160–1235) [3]1089
kin and kind [4]842
kind(s) [2]844, [3]1025
and degree *see* degree; difference in [2]1133; essential [3]1089; of living existence [4]266; in poetry [2]968
"kinde" [2]127
kindisch [2]1051, 1051n
"kindle" [4]788, 788n
kindliness [5]138
kindlings [2]553
kindness [1]748, [4]212, [5]642
"Kindred and Affinity, Table of" see *BCP*
kinesis [1]479, 479n
"king" [1]243, 537, [2]1111
king(s) [1]423, [2]39, 57, 621, 826–7, 929, 941, 1172, 1201, [3]72, 152, 153, 162, 168, 228, 677, 734, 786, 800, 1082, [4]20, 42, 240, 483, 739, 807, [5]38, 38n, 280, 311, 362, 396, 399, 537, 626, 640
of anarchists [2]512; arbitrary [3]149; authority of [2]1110–11; bound by coronation oath [1]864; congress of [3]603; and crown [2]1043n; Davidic [4]50; dethronement of [3]144; divine right of [5]544; duty of, in OT [1]421, 422n; executive power of [1]294; extinct [3]154; fool-k. [5]281; and God *see* God; of gods [5]386; as head of Church [1]806; head of clerisy [3]50; Homeric [5]307, 307n; invisible [5]607; of kings [5]658; and law [2]939, [3]164; limited [2]1101; limited power of [3]149; meaning of [2]357; necessity of [2]200; Norman [4]15; oath of [3]158; and parliament [1]291–2, 331–2, [3]796; and people [2]58; poet as [5]749; power of [1]243; prayer for [1]325; prerogatives of [3]150; provision for [4]48; rapscallion as [2]511; reforming [1]832; represents nation [1]865, [2]115; rights of [2]43; role of [1]294, 395; Saxon [5]79; she-k. [2]63; taxes and [3]152; k.-worship [2]219
King, Anthony William Poole [6]266
King, Edward (1612–37) [3]413n
King, Henry, Bishop of Chichester (1592–1669) [2]1135n
To . . . Doctor Donne MT [2]237–8
King, Robert Wylie (fl 1925) *"Parson Primrose"* [2]94
King, Sarah (fl 1796–1818) [2]587n
King, William (1663–1712) [1]37
King, William, Archbishop of Dublin (1650–1729) [3]505, 505n
piety of [4]27, 27n
Origin of Evil [3]505n–6n, [4]27n
kingdom(s) [2]950
celestial [5]607; of Christ [3]72, 741, [5]537, 630, [6]55; of Christ on earth [5]607; in Dan [1]440, 440n–1n, [3]419, 419n, 573, 923n; of darkness [3]305; on earth [3]478; four [2]155–7; of God [1]561, [3]264, 453–4, [4]482–3, 641; of heaven [1]452, [3]445, [5]648, 650, 664; of the Lord [5]606; republican [2]1201; two [2]1153
kingfisher [6]151
King's Bench, Court of *see* London: Court of King's Bench
King's College *see* London
king's evil [2]1174
kingship [2]101, 946, [5]539
kingsman/kingsmen [2]948, [3]165
"Kingston Mercantile Advertiser" [4]97n
Kingston ON
Queen's University Library, marked book in [1]clxvi
kinship, prohibited degrees of [3]778n; see also *BCP*: "Table of Kindred and Affinity"
Kippis, Andrew (1725–95) *Biographia Britannica* [5]531, 531n
Kirby, William (1759–1850)
On the Power, Wisdom, and Goodness of God [2]883n; and W. Spence *Introduction to Entomology* [2]1068n
Kircher, Athanasius (1601–80) [2]824, [3]817, 817n
Mundus subterraneus [2]824n; *Prodromus Coptus sive Aegyptiacus* [2]824n
Kirkcudbright [2]1180
Kirke, C. H. [1]365
Kirkpatrick, James Achilles (fl 1797) [1]121
Kirkpatrick, William (1754–1812) [1]lxv, xcviii, cvi, 121
Kirkpatrick, William George (c 1801–28) [1]121
Kirkton, James (?1620–99) [2]1169
Kishon (river) [3]470n
kissaros [5]836
kisses [4]706
kitten [5]355
Kittredge, George Lyman (1860–1941) "Chaucer's Lollius" [4]809n
Klangfiguren [5]294
Klaproth, Martin Heinrich (1743–1817) [3]938, 940, 942, [5]261, 262n

kleitos [3]786, 786n
Klingender, Francis Donald (1907–55) [2]158
Klopstock, Friedrich Gottlieb (1724–1803) [1]100, 697, 828, [2]1062–3, 1063n
Messias [1]lxxxi, [4]479, 479n
Kluge, Carl Alexander Ferdinand (1782–1844) [3]372, 872, [5]142 ("Klug"), 142n
Versuch einer Darstellung des animalischen Magnetismus [1]lxxvi; MT [3]371–99; 872n, [4]270n, [5]142n, 183n
knaves [2]927
knee [3]396
k.-breeches [4]190n
kneeling [1]323–4, 328
KNF [4]264, 264n
knife/knives [3]394, [5]75, 75n, 730
knight(s)
whimsical [1]765, 797; without horse [5]47, 47n; of St John [5]841
Knight, Richard Payne (1750–1824) [4]677, 677n–8n
Account of the Remains [3]401, 401n; *An Analytical Inquiry into the Principles of Taste* MT [3]400–13, WW notes in [3]401–13
Knight, Thomas (d 1820) [2]169
Knight, Thomas Andrew (1759–1838) [3]936, 940, 941, 942, 943
Knighton, Henry (fl 1363) [3]166 ("Knyghton"), [6]18 q
Knobloch, Charlotte Amalie von (1740–?94) [3]351n
knot (speed) [2]889, 889n
knot(s) [1]557, [2]612, [3]26, 130, 242, 756, 1042, [4]386, [5]491, 680, 726, [6]233
cut [3]1037, [5]404; Gordian [4]269; of Ulysses [3]468, 468n–9n
"Knott, Edward" *see* Wilson, Matthew
Knott, Tomas (fl 1723) [3]977
"know" [5]84
know thyself [3]919n
"knowing" [2]330
knowing
and being *see* being; direct [4]131; faculty of [4]155; and knowing of [2]612; and perceiving [5]15; and thinking [5]772
"knowledge" [6]223
knowledge(s) [1]878, [2]611, 628–9, [3]643, [4]404–5, [5]17, 18, 81, 201, 756
a priori [4]355; and belief [1]128; definitions of [4]115; degrees of [5]564; discursive and intuitive [1]632; distinct [2]1028, [4]348; divine [3]202; empirical or speculative [3]1001; exact [5]481; exactest [3]546; and faith [3]332; of the Father [5]56; fundamental [4]122–4, 122n; knowledge and *gnosis* see *gnosis*; hard [2]228; by ideas [5]755–6; immediate [3]550; imperfect [2]153; by insight [3]23; kinds of [6]172n; limitations of [3]967; means of [3]641; Mendelssohn on [3]366; momentous [5]175; negation of [5]271; not limited to senses [3]524; not to know [3]62; objectivity of [5]755; objects of [4]114; overloaded with [5]318; passive [4]157; popular [1]515; ports of [1]764, 797; and power [5]274; progression in [3]697; saving [5]418, 672; and sensation [2]341; spiritual [3]517, [6]300; states of [6]173; of supersensuous truths [5]752; three kinds of [3]366n; of things [6]172; treasures of [3]24, [5]59, 628; tree of [1]684, [2]1052–3; true [1]615; wisest [3]578; withholding of [5]37
Knowler, William (1699–1773) *see* Wentworth *Earl of Strafford's Letters* ed Knowler
Knox, John (c 1513–72) [1]531, 531n, 805, 805n, [2]129, 129n, 254, [3]178n, 515, 515n, [4]643, [5]505, 505n–6n, 506, [6]298, 298n
First Book of Discipline [2]254n, 1138, 1138n; *History of the Reformation* [3]819, 819n
Knox, Ronald Arbuthnott (1888–1957) [2]1029n
Knut (Canute the Great) (d 1035) [3]165
Knyghton *see* Knighton
koax koax [1]872
Koblenzer-Hill, Mrs [2]179
Kobold [4]595n
Koch, Johann *see* Cocceius
Koen, Gisbertus (fl 1766–1815) [3]833n
kohen [1]529, 529n
Kolb, Jack *see* A. H. Hallam, *Letters* ed Kolb
Koppe, Johann Benjamin (1750–91) *see* Bible: NT: *Novum Testamentum* ed Koppe
Koran [2]375, 1123, [3]92n, 673, 674
Körner, Karl Theodor (1791–1813) [1]100
kosmios [2]684, 684n
kosmon [4]158, 158n
kosmos [4]162, 162n, [5]228, 228n
k. noeros [1]201; *see also* cosmos
Kotzebue, August Friedrich Ferdinand von (1761–1819) [4]598, 718–19, 718n, [5]307n
Lovers' Vows [4]598n; *The Spaniards in Peru* [4]598n; *The Stranger* [4]598n
Kraft [1]21–2

kraken [2]1112, *1112n*, [4]534, 534n, 605–6, 606n
Krämerin [5]183, 183n
Kranz, Walther (b 1884) *see* Diels *Die Fragmente der Vorsocratiker* ed Kranz
Krenides [1]464
krinozometer [6]25n
kriozometer [6]25, 25n
Krishna [2]346n, [3]587n
Krüdener, Barbara Juliane, Baroness von (1764–1824) [5]291, 291n
ktistes [2]33
kushi [2]384n
kyamos [1]768n
Kyd, Thomas (c 1558–94) [1]62
  Spanish Tragedy [4]724 ("*Jeronymo*"), 724n
Kyrie eleison [3]527n
Kyrios [1]467n, [2]469, [6]77, 139, 178, 178n, 181

L., Mr *see* Lambe, Thomas
Labbe, Philippe (1607–67) *Bibliotheca nummaria* [6]265
labels, temporary [5]789
"Laberius" (STC) [1]92
labour(s) [2]627, 1065, [5]103, 380
  bodily [2]98; confederacies of [6]36; delight in [2]1066; ministerial [5]521; pains of [5]468; stimulus to [2]953
labourer(s) [4]236, [5]582
  parable of [1]201
labyrinth [1]516–17, 632, [4]479, [5]37, 125, 836
La Calprenède, Gauthier de Costes de (c 1610–63) *Cassandre* [5]821n
lace [3]693
La Cépède, Bernard Germain Etienne de la Ville sur Ilion, Comte de (1756–1825) *Les âges de la nature*† [1]clxvi, [3]414
Lachmann, Karl Konrad Friedrich Wilhelm (1793–1851) *see* Bible: NT: Greek: ed Lachmann
lackey(s)/lacquey(s) [5]520, 866
Lackington, James (1746–1815) *see* London
La Coste, Pierre (fl 1790) [6]291–2 q
Lactantius, Lucius Caecilius Firminianus (c 250–c 317) [2]665, 666, 666n, 923n, [5]384, 402, 629, 643
  Divine Institutions [5]402n; *Opera* [1]clxvi
Lacunza y Diaz, Manuel ("Juan Josafat Ben-Ezra") (1731–1801) [3]9, 451, 731, [5]402n
  garrulous [3]451
  The Coming of Messiah in Glory and Majesty tr Irving [2]504, 511n; MT [3]415–82
ladder [1]525, [3]146, 741, [5]444
  Jacob's [2]609, [3]348
lady/ladies
  blue [2]1016; chaste [1]397; coarseness of [3]171; Spanish [5]821; white [3]196; young [4]529; *see also* woman/women
Laelius, Caius (b c 186 BC) [5]747, 747n
Laertes (*Hamlet*) [4]841, 857, 858
Lafeu (*All's Well*) [4]700
Lagado (in Swift) [5]751n
La Grand *see* Lagrange
Lagrange, Joseph Louis (1736–1813) [6]75 ("La Grand"), 75n
  Leçons sur le calcul des fonctions [6]75n
La Harpe, Jean François de (1739–1803) [3]208, 209, 216–17
  Oeuvres choisies et posthumes [3]207n, 209n
La Hode *see* La Mothe
Laing, David (1793–1878) [2]350
Laing, Malcolm (1762–1818) [6]186
  The History of Scotland [1]301, 301n, [2]1170; MT [3]483
laity [1]517, [2]935, 1158, [3]50, 774, [5]574, [6]23
  and communion cup [5]683, 683n, [6]20; ignorance of [6]14
lake(s) [2]220, [3]974, 980, [6]249
Lake District [2]691n, [4]737n, [6]249, 249n
Lake, Kirksopp (1872–1946) [2]711n
Lalande, Joseph Jérôme Le Français de (1732–1807) [6]75n
Lama *see* Dalai Lama
La Mancha [3]207n
lamantines [4]533
lamb(s)/Lamb [1]161, [3]61, [4]92, 94, [5]385, 586
  of God [1]523
Lamb, Charles ("Elia") (1775–1834) [1]lxxxiii, xciv, xcvii, xcviii, civ, cxvi, cxvii, 161n, 240, 329n, 331n, 488, 489 q, 615n, 724n, 762n, [2]4, 16n, 94 q, 142, 180, 806, 815, 848n, 1195n, [3]191n, 321, 484, 768n, 881, [4]837, [5]99
  death [1]clx; dramatic writings [1]150n; final illness [1]cxln; gentle-hearted [1]95, 95n; and Hazlitt [4]837, 837n; dislikes Herbert [2]1033; library of [1]clxii, [2]66n, [4]105; marginalia addressed to [1]183n, 372, 372n, [2]118, 119, 243, [3]140, 146, 719, 754, 754n, [5]500, 525n, 531, 597n, 667–8; marginalia associated with [1]lxxxii, lxxxvi, cxlvii, [2]121n; and Newgate mar-

Lamb, Charles ("Elia")—*continued*
ket [1]183n; owner of annotated books [1]lxxi, lxxx, lxxxiv, lxxxvi, lxxxviii–xcii, xcv, cxxi, 30, 365, 368n, 760, 854, [2]99, 116, 213, 217, 260n, 353, 696, 845, 873, 874, [3]766n, [4]237, [5]486, 499, [6]249; poet [4]161, 161n; pun by [2]760n; recommends books to C [1]lxxxviii; *Spectator* project [1]158n; stammer [2]123n; supplier of books to C [1]cv, cvi, 230, 741, [2]117, 935n, [3]719, [5]608n; treatment of books [1]cviii; writer of marginalia [2]116, 213, [6]334
Adventures of Ulysses [2]1118; *Books from the Library of Charles Lamb, Offered for Sale by Bartlett and Welford, New York City* [1]30, [2]873; "Christ's Hospital Five and Thirty Years Ago" [1]ciin; "A Dissertation upon Roast Pig" [2]126n q; *The Letters of Charles Lamb to Which Are Added Those of His Sister Mary Lamb* ed Lucas [1]lxxivn q, lxxxix–xc q, xcn, xci–xcii q, xcin, cviiin q, cix q, cixn q, cxxi q, cxxin, 30, 39, 53, 56n, 89, 91n, 97n, 218n, 329n, 362 q, 365 q, 372n q, 488, 763n, 802 q, 828 q, [2]76n q, 117, 118n q, 121n, 140 q, 179 q, 217n q, 351, 353, 804, 808q, 861n q, 1119n q, 1169 q, 1204n, [3]719 q; *The Letters of Charles and Mary Anne Lamb* ed Marrs [2]1118 q, 1120n q, 1121n, 1204n, [4]837n q, [5]531n q, 597n q, [6]249; "Mrs. Battle's Opinion on Whist" [4]240n q; "Old China" [1]365; "On the Genius and Character of Hogarth" [1]366, 366n, [3]189n; "Specimens from the Writings of Fuller" [2]804, 809n; *Specimens of English Dramatic Poets* [1]lxxxviii, lxxxviiin, lxxxixn, 365, [2]75n q, 117, 120n, 1119n q, 1120n q, [4]162n; "Two Races of Men" [1]lxxiv q, lxxivn, lxxxix–xc q, xc q, xci, cxvi q, 741, 854, [2]217n, 873 q, [3]719; *Works* (1818) [1]xcviii, [4]161n; *Works of Charles and Mary Lamb* ed Lucas [1]lxxivn, [3]189n q, [4]162n q, 240n q
Lamb, Mary Ann (1764–1847) [1]lxxx, clxii, [2]116, 119, 214, 1204n, [3]191n, [4]105
death [1]clxi, clxii; writer of marginalia [6]334
Mrs Leicester's School MT [3]484–5; *see also* Lamb, Charles: Charles and Mary Lamb *Letters* ed Lucas and ed Marrs, *Works* ed Lucas
lambda [3]950, 950n
Lambe, Thomas (fl 1658) [1]277 ("Mr L.")
Lambe, William (1765–1847) [6]246
Lambert, Johann Heinrich (1728–77) [3]261n, 280, 280n, 282
letter to Kant [3]353–4, 354n
Lambeth *see* London
Lambethism [1]358
lame, outrunning the [6]312
Lamech (Bible) [2]384–5, 385n, 387, 576
lamed [5]845, 845n
Lamétherie, Jean Claude de (1743–1817) [3]936, 939
lamina [2]387
Lamont, Corliss (b 1902) [2]245
La Mothe, called Père La Hode (c 1680–c 1740) [1]699, 699n
La Motte-Fouqué, Friedrich Heinrich Karl, Baron de (1777–1843) [4]595
Undine [4]595, 595n
lamp(s) [3]324
Argand's [1]303; of heaven [1]200; of light [2]296; of reflection [5]130; slaves of [5]167, 167n
Lampadius, Wilhelm August (1772–1842) [5]255–6
lampoons [2]758, 759, 760n
Lancashire [6]249
Lancaster, Duke of *see* John of Gaunt
Lancaster, Joseph (1778–1838) [2]857n, 980n, [4]438n
Lancelot, Claude (c 1615–95), and Antoine Arnaud *Grammaire générale et raisonnée* (*A General and Rational Grammar*) [4]322, 322n q
land(s) [3]800, [4]23, [5]263
lineage-l. [5]79; price of [2]311
Landen, John (1719–90) [6]75n
landing-places [2]609, 609n
landmarks, ancient [1]833
Landor, Walter Savage (1775–1864) [2]180, [4]627n
Gebir [1]clxv
landowners [1]527, [3]799
neglectful [6]44
landscape(s) [4]271, 375
natural [4]827
lanes [5]321
Langcake, Thomas (fl 1764–81) *see* Böhme *Works* ed Law, Langcake, and Ward
Langdon, David (d 1848/9) [5]866
Langen-Schwalbach [2]981–2
Langhorne, John (1735–79) [1]38, [2]94
Langland, William (c 1332–c 1400) *Piers Plowman* [2]759, 759n
Langton, Stephen (c 1150–1228) [2]314n

"language" [1]538
language(s) [3]450, 861n, [4]162, 700, [5]95, 118, 425
abuse of [2]491; *Alphabeta linguarum* [4]5; analogous to algebra [2]962; antediluvian [2]576; of antithesis [5]131; beautiful [5]744; beauty of [2]1120; of Bible [2]1050, [5]66n; broad [2]730; browbeating [1]727; of Canaanites [4]257; catachrestic [5]81; chaste [3]1076; child's [2]535–6; common [2]250, 1145, [4]640, [5]651, [6]14; common ancestor [4]290n; of common life [4]837; common origin of [3]646–7; of common sense [5]552; composite [1]496; confusion of [5]290; contemptuous [4]379, [5]665; conventional [2]300; correct [5]755; corrupted [1]629; corruption of [4]292; dead [3]318; defect of [3]423, 424; defined [1]538; dignity in [5]240; direct [5]317; dramatic [4]812; of dreams [3]376; education in [5]324; error of [2]1152; European [5]9; evolution of [1]606, [3]565n; of excitement [2]1067; familiar [2]1084, [4]837–8; figurative [4]47, [5]66; of the finite [1]696; first [4]38; fixed [3]1043; foreign [5]666; God's gift [4]652; grossness of [3]171; growth of [3]834, [4]489; guardian of [6]210; heated [3]492; of high birth [4]599; human [5]814; human attribute [4]489, 489n; ideal of [1]629; idiomatic [1]156; idioms of [6]286; imperfection of [1]326, 358, 565, [2]741, [5]794; incautious [3]732; innate [6]115; of intellect [3]261; Japetic [4]37n; of the law [5]539; learned [2]381; man alone has [1]538; Massinger's [3]813; metrical [4]507; minatory [3]438; misused [4]668; modern [1]667, [4]687, [5]714, [6]142; of Moravians [5]130n; most perfect [4]509; multiply words [3]889; mysterious [4]484; names shadows [3]524–5, 525n; nature as [3]279; of nature *see* nature; new words in [3]177; original [4]257n, [5]433; parts of speech in [4]166; of St Paul [5]76; at Pentecost [4]248n; perversion of [5]774; philosophical [1]667; philosophy of [3]827, 829n; picture-l. [1]647, [2]346; plain [1]803n; poetic(al) [5]309n, 528; pompous [6]328; popular [3]474; primitive [1]61; puns in [3]976; pure [6]195; resemblances in [4]186; safe [5]131; of Scripture [3]312; Semitic [2]582, [4]243, 243n, 257, [5]170, 337, *see also* Arabic, Aramaic, Chaldaic, Hebrew, Phoenician, Syriac, Syro-Chaldaic; of sensation [4]838; A. Sidney's [5]37; sophisticated [5]480n; spiritual [1]629, [5]467; of statutes [2]210–11; Steffens on [5]325n; structure of [6]25; symbolic(al) [1]706, [5]702, 814n; technical [3]565; testimony of [3]61; of thoughts [5]416; too strong [3]468; of types [5]59; unconscious [5]148; universal [1]608, [2]141; vernacular [3]1069; visible [5]650; visual [2]173, [3]597, [4]114; of Western Church [5]627; of Zinzendorf [3]493. *See also* Anglo-Saxon; Arabic; Aramaic; Burmese; Cadmaean; Chaldaic; Chinese; Coptic; Danish; Dutch; Egyptian; English; Erse; French; German; Gothic; Greek; Guarani; Hammonic; Hebrew; Hindustani; Italian; Latin; Phoenician; Provençal; Romaic; Sanscrit; Saxon; Scottish; Slavonic; Spanish; Syriac; Syro-Chaldaic; Tartar; Teutonic; Theotiscan; Tudesque; Tupi; Welsh
languescence [4]525
Languet, Hubert (1518–81) *Stephani Junii Bruti vindiciae contra tyrannos* [2]770–1, 770n–1n
Lansdowne, Baron *see* Granville, George
Lansdowne, Marquis of *see* Petty-Fitzmaurice, Henry
lantern, magic [6]101n
lanthorn-fly [3]1077
Laocoön [4]419n
Laodicea [1]721, [3]422n, [6]168n
Council of [1]721
lapidaries [1]779
lapis infernalis [5]163, 163n
Laplace, Pierre Simon, Marquis de (1749–1827) [3]940, [5]225, 225n, 351, [6]75
and Kant [1]74n
Exposition du système du monde [1]793n, [6]75n, tr Pond as *System of the World* [4]202n q; *Traité de mécanique céleste* [1]642n, 793n, [3]325n, [4]376, 376n, [5]351n, 743n, [6]75n
Laputa (in Swift) [5]476
larch [4]829
larder [5]789
Lardner, Dionysius (1793–1859) [5]194
Lardner, Nathaniel (1684–1768) [1]305, 306n, [2]746, 746n, [3]766, 766n, [6]119n
The Credibility of the Gospel History [1]306n, [3]766n, 925n, [4]472n; *Works* [3]766n q, [4]472n, 481n
lark [1]515, [2]768n
La Rochelle [1]223, 223n
La Rovière, Pierre de (fl 1614) [2]632n
larva [2]565
larynx [1]608
Lascaris, Constantine (d 1493 or 1500) [5]832

Lateinos [1]485, 486, [3]929, 929n, [6]166n
latency [5]777
Latham, Agnes Mary Christabel *see* Shakespeare *As You Like It* ed Latham
lathe [3]639
Latimer, Hugh (c 1485–1555) [1]809, 809n, [2]357, [3]368, 368n
Latin [1]50, 55, 113n, 206–10, 503, 607, [2]380, 653, 731, 739, 898, [3]318, 428, 1087n, [4]37, 37n, 38, 290, 291, 509, 509n, 595n, 687, 780, [5]9, 283, [6]289, 295, 312
of Barclay's *Argenis* [1]220–1; as common language of Europe [2]528; derivatives of [1]845; grammar [3]19; Milton's L. verse [3]904–5; modern L. verse [2]240; monkish [1]870, [6]149; pronouns in [3]890n; of Schoolmen [2]12; universality of [6]14
Latin(s) [2]734
Latinists [5]142
Latinity
barbaro-African [2]33; Tertullian's [6]89
Latinlade [2]821
Latinus [1]482n, [6]166, 167, 167n
Latinus, King (legend) [2]577
latitude(s) [1]539, [5]814
Latitudinarian(s) [5]80, 163, 661
Latitudinarianism [1]358, [5]553n, 583
destructive of principle [2]31
Latium [2]577, [6]197
Latona (myth) [6]214
latreia [1]257n
latria [2]663n
-latry (suffix) [1]257n, [2]663n
"latten" [4]692, 692n
Lattrig [3]183, 183n
Laud, William, Archbishop of Canterbury (1573–1645) [1]lvii, 323, 323n, 349, 352, 359, 359n, 492, 803, 803n, 805, 805n, 808, 808n, [2]24, 260, 260n, 269, 274n, 651, 651n, 873, 911, 916, 932, 933, 957n, 1095–1104, 1157n, 1169, [3]148n, 515n, 535, 738n, 796, 878, 922n, [4]20n, 74, 74n, 173, 173n, 176, 177, 308n, [5]81n, 491, 491n, 492n, 497n, 510n, 521, 521n, 525n, 537n, 540, 544, 544n, 574, 578, 596, 616, 616n, 636, 636n, 638, 640, 662, 669n, 670, [6]12–13, 297n
autopapist [3]153, 153n; death of [4]178; and Herbert [2]1046n; inhumanity of [2]932n; and R. Leighton [6]317; philo-despot [2]927
The History of the Troubles and Tryal ed Wharton [1]850, [2]1095; MT [3]486–7; *The Second Volume of the Remains* ed Wharton [1]850, [2]512n q, 932n, 1095; MT [3]488–91
laudanum [3]410, [5]836; *see also* opium
Laudensians [3]148
Lauderdale, Earl of *see* Maitland, John
Laudism [1]358
"Laudites" [4]20, 20n
laughing [2]1121
l.-gas *see* nitrous oxide; l.-stocks [1]528
laughter [2]191, 191n
Laugier, André (1770–1832) [3]940, 941, 942
Laumont *see* Gillet de Laumont
Laureate [5]194
laurel [2]134, [3]821n, 889
Laurentius, Jacobus (1585–1644) *Hugo Grotius Papizans* [1]258
Lausanne [2]507n
laut [1]21–2
Lauterbach, Anton (1502–69) [2]774n, [3]718
lava [6]105
l.-streams [6]153n
Lavington, George (1684–1762) *The Moravians Compared and Detected* [2]717n; MT [3]492–8
Lavoisier, Antoine Laurent (1743–94) [1]63n, 545, 641n, [2]852n, 854–5, 854n, 857n, 858n, [3]1011, 1011n, 1020n, 1033n, [4]390, 390n, 396n, 428n, [5]331–2, 548n
"law" [3]49–50
law(s) [1]250, 252, 303, 384, 398, 602, 873, [2]147, 953n, 1028, [3]500–2, [4]258, 324, 603, 662, [5]37, 155, 159, 278, 299, 315, 594
a priori [3]259; adherence to [5]677; administration of [4]80; given by angels [1]463, 463n, 468, [2]472, 472n; antedating of [1]417; assigns prerogatives [3]150; of assimilation [5]410; of association [3]213, [4]92; authority of [1]318; autonomy of [3]735; Bible as "Law-book" [3]72; of bicentrality [4]326–7; binding [1]833; of body [5]423; book of [1]423, [3]109; canon [2]1150n; l.-cats [4]196, 197, 198; ceremonial [2]470, 655, [3]49, 53, [4]250, 252; ceremonies of [3]722; code of [2]1139, [5]73; cold [2]322; of colours [4]167; compels [2]654; compulsory [1]254; and conscience [3]267, 956, 958, [4]650–2, [5]656; confused with principle [4]496; constitutive [2]1144, [3]23, [5]425; corn-laws [3]800; courts of [1]253; cruellest [5]596; dead [1]832; defined [1]360, [2]529; denial of [6]75; dictated by Supreme Reason [1]421; and

discipline [1]254, [3]759; divine origin of [2]146; doctrine of [3]54; of duelling [4]584; and education [5]274; of eligibility in elections [4]23; of England [1]807, 807n, [2]1139, 1139n, [3]164, [4]633–4, 646; equal [5]829, [6]52–3; especial [6]101; eternal [4]487; of experimenting [5]201; fiction(s) of [2]1139, [3]159, 159n; fixed [5]578, [6]314; general [3]675, 679; genial [4]798; German [4]666; l.-giver [1]875, [3]740, [4]548; from God [5]453; of God [1]877, [2]677; God's [2]899, [5]537; God's will [1]293; and gospel [3]744–6; of government [4]12; of gravitation [4]506, [5]351, 351n; gypsy [2]784; of historic drama [4]798; historical origination of [4]666; Hooker's definition [2]1143–5; human [1]124, [2]747; of human nature [3]331; human need [5]728; and idea [5]372; of identity [1]662; inconsistency of [1]740; of inheritance [5]478, 478n; initiated [2]144; international [6]14; interpretation of [2]43; of investigation [4]160; Jewish [1]877, [2]1153, [4]251, 481, [5]393, 522n; juridical and moral [3]267; Kant's [3]302; of the land [1]331–2, [5]189, 537, 577; language of [2]210, [5]539; against l. [1]343; and life [4]168; is light [1]825; light and life of [5]613; of marriage [5]647; masters of the [3]466; in matter [3]944; of mind [4]123, [5]372; moral [1]874, 877, [2]182–3, 183n, 297, 544, 596n, [3]50, 53, 470, 489, [4]214, 410, 647; moral and material [3]696; and morality [2]529–30; Mosaic/of Moses *see* Moses; above nature [5]590; in nature [5]734; of nature [2]202, [4]379, [5]383; new [5]583; no l. after Reform Bill [3]154; no salvation by [2]592; obedience due to [1]875; objects of [2]530; observation of [2]471; outward [3]497, 735n; passion for evidence [1]317; of patronage [1]309; St Paul on [2]184, 184n, [3]751–2, 753; Pauline sense [2]278; peculiar [5]327; penal [1]320, [4]145, 241, [6]58; of perception [2]608; physical [1]620, [2]1144; plastic [4]12; of pleasure [4]183; of polarity *see* polarity; poor-l. [3]810, 810n; under popery [3]166; a power from without [3]150; practical [2]529; of psychology [3]204; public [6]36; public justice [3]797; punitive [2]1138; quick [3]896; of realm [3]143; of reason [1]819, [5]425; and religion [1]281, [5]622; repeal of [2]939; reverence for [3]317; of right reason [1]878; Roman [2]459, [3]144, [4]666n; and rule [1]377; rule of [5]269n; after sanction [5]632; of science [3]104; of sense [3]201; shallow [4]16; of similitude [5]410; and sin [1]824, 824n; of Solon [1]877; Spartan [2]899; of spirit [3]311, 454; of the state [5]304, [6]58; statute [2]146; strictness of [1]874; subordinate [3]1062; subversion of [2]107; super-parliamentary [1]865; suspending [2]771; l.-syllogism [4]633; of tenure [4]284; and theory [4]12n, 13; time and space as [4]436; twofold use of [3]737–8; uncertainty of [2]529; universal [3]254, [5]201; of universe [3]860; unwritten [3]847; of variety [3]520; of vision [5]269; of the whole [5]305; works of the [3]740, [5]492; world of [2]583; world's [2]1175, [5]99; l.-writers [3]152; written in the heart [5]61

The Law Magazine; or, Quarterly Review of Jurisprudence MT [3]500–2

Law, William (1686–1761) [1]553, 669n, [5]123, 123n, 165, 166, 166n

A Serious Call to a Devout and Holy Life [1]clin; MT [3]499; [5]123n; *The Spirit of Love* [5]123n; *The Spirit of Prayer* [5]123n; *see also* Böhme *Works* ed Law, Langcake, and Ward

Lawes, Henry (1596–1662) [3]902

Lawrance, Matthew [1]121

Lawrence, Sir Thomas (1769–1830) [2]180

Lawson, George (d 1678) *Theopolitica* [1]347

Lawson, Sir Gilfrid, 9th Baronet (c 1710–94) [2]111, [4]675n

his library [4]675n–6n

Lawson, Sir Wilfrid (c 1764–1806) [1]lxxix, ciii, cviii–cix, [4]675

lawyer(s) [3]21, 166, [4]90, 90n, [5]97

sorry moralists [3]501; Tory [2]113

Lax, William (1761–1836) [3]939

laxity [5]683

layman/laymen [1]531, [2]1199, [3]21, [5]578, 658

Lazarillo (in B&F) [1]407, 408

lazarone [5]40, 40n

Lazarus (Bible) [1]13, [2]262, 314, 342, 1086, 1159, [3]35, 613, 613n, [4]256, 256n, 645

Leach, William Elford (1790–1836) [4]333

lead [1]546, 782, [3]883, 1062

sugar of [1]596, 596n

Lead/Leade, Jane (1623–1704) [1]297n

leader [5]536

leaf/leaves [2]993, 995, [4]93, 211, [5]186, 455, 815

dry [1]325; forest of [6]130; mellowing [3]889

"lean" [4]284, 284n

Leander (myth) [5]832–3, 833n

leap
Rhodian [5]84, 456, 456n; ultra-rhodian [5]580; l.-frog [3]759
leaper, Rhodian [4]504, 504n
Lear (*King Lear*) [1]394, [4]42, [6]114
learned, the [1]631, 845, [2]1141, [5]675
and half-learned [6]97; office of [2]1141
learning [1]327, [2]1041, [3]20, 690, 918, 1085, [4]243, 267, 471, [5]9, 463, 558, 615, 661
decay of [5]145; Hebrew [3]1084, [6]91; Leighton and [3]625; men of [1]634, [2]933, [5]812; notional [1]561; omnifarious [5]528; patristic [2]917, [5]526; profane [1]873; in Rabelais [4]194; republic of [3]232; reputation of [6]145; Scholastic [5]803n; unnecessary [2]734
leasing [1]499, 499n
Leathe, J. S. [6]121, 121n
leather [4]705
Leatherhead Collection/Leatherhead MS *see* Coleridge, S. T. VII
The Leathern Bottel [2]566n
Leatheswater [6]121, 121n
leaven
Galatian [5]492; patristic [2]260, 260n, 301, 1041, [5]510n
leb [2]1029n
Le Bas, Charles Webb (1779–1861) [6]12
Lebenskraft [3]398, [4]385
Le Caan, Charles (fl 1805–10) [3]937
lech/lecher/lechery *see* letch
Lechlade [2]821
Leckie, Gould Francis (fl 1805) [1]cv, 161n
Le Clerc, Jean (Johannes Clericus) (1657–1736) [6]69, 69n
lecture(s) [1]176, [5]180
l.-courses [3]462; oratorical [2]1016; Steffens's [5]365
lecturer [3]307, [5]89, 175, 789
Lectures on Scripture Facts [4]661
ledger [3]60
Le Duchat, Jacob (1658–1735) *see* Rabelais *Works* tr and ed Le Duchat and others
ledum [5]836
leech(es) [4]802
escape of [6]42
Leeds [2]49, 76, 76n, [6]49
Leem, Knud (1697–1774) *De Lapponibus Finmarchiae* [1]431n ("Leemius")
Leeuwenhoek, Anton van (1632–1723) [1]792, 792n
legalism [5]492n, 496n
legalist(s) [2]926
national [2]72
legality [1]821, [2]530, [4]653
Judaic [5]605; principles of [3]72
Legality, Mr (in Bunyan) [1]812, [4]651n, 653n
legend(s) [2]831, [3]310, 689, 772, [4]472, 476, [5]96, 821
absurd [2]274; of Josephus [2]149; ridiculous [2]301
legerdemain [1]868
verbal [3]589
Leghorn [2]964, [4]168
legion(s) [2]1077, [3]138, 138n
race of [1]872
legislation [1]293
maxim of [1]299
legislator(s) [2]480
for Church [5]659; Hebrew [4]48; temporal [1]339
legislature [1]332, [4]666–7
determines elegibility [4]22, 23–4; mind of [5]300; power of [5]67; supreme [5]280; votes of [6]52
legitimacy [3]250
Le Grice, Charles Valentine (1773–1858) [1]222n
Le Grys, Sir Robert (d 1635) *see* J. Barclay *Argenis* tr Le Grys and May
Le Hardy, C. (fl 1810) [3]940
Lehmann, Christoph (1570–1638) *Florilegium* [3]647 q
Lehmann, Helmut T. *see* Luther *Works* ed Pelikan and Lehmann
lehnen [4]284n
Lehrjahre [2]493
Leibniz, Gottfried Wilhelm von, Baron ("Leibnitz") (1646–1716) [1]lxxvi, cxxiii, 153n, 184, 184n, 198n, 340n, 793n, [2]665n, 995, 995n, 1000n, 1004, 1016n, 1051, [3]75, 79, 81, 89, 243n, 314, 644n, 672, 790, 790n, 853, 966–7 q, 968, [4]174, 174n, 185n, 376n, 422, 444, 444n, [5]4n, 6n, 150, 150n
and calculus [1]4, 5n; conciliatory mind [5]469, 469n; on creation [3]674–5, 675–6; and Descartes [3]343, 343n; his distinction [2]665; and Kant [3]290, 290n, 965, 965n, 966n; last years of [3]324; monad(s) of [3]282–3, 282n, [5]410; and Newton [1]74n; philosophy of [2]628; plan to reunite Church [4]185, 185n; pre-established harmony [2]555–6, 556n; Rosicrucian [3]315,

315n; a Socinian [1]197; and Spinoza [2]172, 172n, [3]649, 649n; system of [3]80
Essais [3]965–6 q; *Lettre à Clarke* [3]853n; *Monadologie* [2]556n, 628n, [3]853n; *Nouveaux essais* [1]82n, 198n, 354n, [3]649n, 853n, tr and ed P. Remnant and J. Bennett *New Essays on Human Understanding* [5]410n; *Opera omnia* ed Dutens [1]354n, [3]504n; *Opera philosophica* ed Erdmann [2]556n, [3]853n; *Protogaeis* [3]644; *Reply to the Questions of a Provincial* [3]506; *Theodicee* [1]xcii, [2]556n; MT [3]503–6, ed Gottsched [3]503, tr Huggard *Theodicy* [3]503
Leibnizians [4]208–9
Leicester, 1st Earl of *see* Dudley, Robert
Leicestershire [2]942
Leighton, Alexander (1568–1649) [5]521n, 616, 616n
An Appeal to the Parliament [2]813–14, 814n q; *Sion's Plea* see *An Appeal to the Parliament*
Leighton, Robert, Archbishop of Glasgow (1611–84) [1]cxvi, cxxvi, 351, 351n, [2]265n, 294n, 814n, 1167, [3]423, 511n, [5]495, 495n, 521n, [6]94n
and C's *AR* [1]cxx; C's identification with [3]523; defect in [3]626; definition of understanding [3]425, 557, [5]599; letter to a lady [1]813, 813n q; next to inspired [3]523; portrait [6]312; projected biography of [3]483, 486; on repentance [2]1176–7; and Taylor [5]586; theological lectures [6]312, 312n; white-robed [6]306
The Expository Works and Other Remains rev and pref Doddridge *Copy A* [1]ci, cxx, cxlivn, [2]1177n q; MT [3]507–13; *The Genuine Works* pref Doddridge *Copy B* [1]ci, cxx, cxlivn; MT [3]514–36, [6]295–319; *Selections from the Works of Archbishop Leighton* ed W. Wilson [6]312, 312n; *The Whole Works* ed Jerment *Copy C* [1]ci, cxx, cxlivn; MT [3]537–626; [6]312, 312n; *Works* (1820) [1]813n q; *see also* Coleridge, S. T. VIII "Beauties of Archbishop Leighton", "Life" of Leighton
Leipzig [2]373, 1016n, [3]777, 978
Leisegang, Hans (1890–1951) *Index verborum* [2]429n, 430n
leisure [2]432, [5]90
Leith [3]819
Leland, John (1506–52) [2]558, 819 q, 821
Lelius (fiction) [5]420
Lelivec/Le Livec, H. (fl 1810) [3]936
lemming [5]686
Lemnius, Simon (c 1505–50) [3]656
lemon tree(s) *see* tree(s), lemon
lemonade [5]231
Lemprière, John (c 1765–1824) [2]887n q, 919n q
A Classical Dictionary [5]224, 224n
lemur [4]489n
length(s) [1]579, 667, [3]123, 123n, 139, 949, 1011, [4]314, [5]825, [6]233
abstraction of [4]166; manifestation of [5]245; relative [6]233
Leningrad
Hermitage Museum [1]162n; *see also* St Petersburg
lenis [3]827
Lennep, Johannes Daniel van (1724–71) [4]37n, [5]733n
Etymologicum linguae graecae rev ed Scheid [2]380n, [4]36n, 37n, [5]711n
Lennox, Duke of *see* Stuart, Ludovick
lens [2]1020
Leo X (Giovanni de' Medici), Pope (1475–1521) [1]221, 627n, 831
Leo (astrology) [1]399n
Leonardo Da Vinci (1452–1519) [1]627n
Leonardus, Bishop of Sidonia [2]660n
Leopold II, Emperor of Austria (1747–92) [5]275, 275n
Lepanto, battle of [1]789
leprosy [1]250, [2]454, 838n
episcopal [5]617
Le Sage, Georges Louis (1724–1803) [4]376, 377, 377n, 386
Lesbos
Lesbian shore [3]892
Leslie, Charles (1650–1722) [5]140 ("Lesly"), 140n
A Short and Easie Method with the Deists [5]140n
Leslie, Charles Robert (1794–1859) [4]578
Leslie, John (1766–1832) "Some Account of the Life of Josiah Wedgwood" MT [3]627–39
Lesly, Ludovic (in Scott) [4]612, 612n
Less, Gottfried (1736–97) *Auferstehungsgeschichte Jesu* [3]612 ("Lessius"), 612n ("K. R. Less"), 688
Lessing, Gotthold Ephraim (1729–81) [1]xcivn, cxxxi, 297, 297n, 350, 828, [2]38, [3]3, 75, 78, 79, 81, 82, 99–100, 790n,

Lessing, Gotthold Ephraim—*continued* 856–7, 955, 955n, [4]221n, 337n, 412–13, 419, [5]582n, [6]119n
on Berengar [6]21n; compares Sophocles and Shakespeare [1]72n; honest infidel [6]60; on language [4]290n; letters [3]672; on Wissowatius [3]657n
Anti-Goeze [1]350n; *Die Erziehung des Menschengeschlechts* [3]683, 683n; *Freundschaftlicher Briefwechsel* [3]655; *Der Juden* [3]646n; *Laokoon: oder Über die Grenzen der Mahlerey und Poesie* [4]419, 419n, tr De Quincey as *Laocoon* [1]72n; *Leben* ed K. G. Lessing MT [3]640–54; 655; *Nathan der Weise* [1]148 q, 350n, [3]217 q, 217n, [5]688, 689n; *Neue Hypothese über die Evangelisten* [1]452n; *Sämmtliche Schriften* [1]297n, [3]640, 647; MT 655–706; [4]419n, [5]570n; *Sogenannte Briefe an verschiedene Gottesgelehrte* [2]38n; *Theologischer Nachlass* [2]35n; *Von Adam Neusern* [3]683, 683n; *Wolfenbüttel Fragments* [1]350n, [5]570, 570n q; *see also* Coleridge, S. T. VIII "Life" of Lessing
Lessing, Karl Gotthelf (1740–1812) [3]656; *see also* G. E. Lessing *Leben* ed K. G. Lessing
Lessius *see also* Less, Gottfried
Lessius, Leonard (Léonard Leys) (1554–1623) [3]1064
lessons, old [2]472
Lester, William (fl 1810) [3]943
L'Estrange, Sir Roger (1616–1704) [1]181n, 182, 182n, 803n, [3]534, 534n, 680, 680n, [6]316, 316n
Fables [1]182n
letch [3]1061
letcher [1]394
letchery [1]397
lethargy [5]188
moral [1]786
letter(s) (correspondence) [2]455, [3]389, [5]680
book of [2]704n; of Cicero and others [2]476, 476n; circular [2]474; dead [1]673, [5]744, 757; intercepted [1]336; model for [3]224; next to best style [2]232; painful [1]755; unopened [2]1122
letter(s) (written character[s])
of alphabet [2]1152; awe for [2]267; black [5]284; l.-fancying [4]246; in John [1]200, 200n; and life [1]684; literal sense [2]335–6; man of [3]673; plain [3]19; Samian [3]230, 230n; significance in Böhme [1]591; and spirit [1]431, 866, [3]330, 439, 441, 464, 597, 724; superstition of [1]779; tampering with [3]444; world of [3]232
A Letter from an Irish Beneficed Clergyman, Concerning Tithes [5]851
"A Letter on Comets" MT [3]944–6
lettersake [6]326
letter-writers [2]449
lev [4]254
Levellers [2]512
lever [4]273, [5]421
Lever, Julius Walter *see* Shakespeare *Measure for Measure* ed Lever
Levere, Trevor Harvey *Poetry Realized in Nature: Samuel Taylor Coleridge and Early Nineteenth-Century Science* [4]359n, 376n, [5]265n, 452n
Levi (Bible) [1]418, 418n, [2]256
house of [5]52n; tribe of [2]396
Levi, Anthony Herbert Tigar *see* Erasmus *Collected Works* ed Levi
Levi, Primo (1919–88) *Se questa e un huomo* tr Woolf [1]35n
leviathan [1]426, 431, 707, [3]771n
levigation [3]294
Levites [1]423n, [2]899
levity [1]63, [3]29, [4]816
Lewgar, John (1602–65) [2]25
Lewis, Matthew Gregory (1775–1818) [4]654
The Monk [4]654n
lex merchetae [1]383
Lexel(l), Anders Johann (1740–84) [4]517–18
lexicon, ideal of [4]35
Lexington KY
University of Kentucky, marginalia in [4]343
Leyden [1]218n, 219n, 545
liar(s) [3]780, [4]14, 671–2, [5]553, 635
Devil as [5]424; family of [5]165
Libanius (314–c 395) [2]746n
Libanus (myth) [2]576
libel(s) [1]360, 808, [3]143, 173, [4]665
libellula [2]646, 646n
liber conciliorum [3]761
liber conformitatum [3]821, 821n
liberal(s)
defined [1]151, 151n; ultra-l. [5]106
liberalism [5]616
liberality [4]22
Liberius, Bishop of Rome (d 366) [2]744, 938
libertine(s) [4]621, 621n, 763, [5]569
libertinism [1]165

liberty [1]254, 300, [2]127, 529, 846, [3]169, 250, 529, 755, [4]184, 587, [5]208, 828
of conscience [2]530–1; English [3]166; glorious [3]776, [5]603; of gospel *see* gospel; love of [3]222, [5]195n; magnanimous [1]73; and necessity [1]827; personal [2]929; political [1]515, [2]692, [5]124; religious [2]48; of subject [4]80
"libidinise" [3]884
libido [1]518, 518n
library/libraries [5]373
Carlisle cathedral l. [3]979, 979n; of clergy [3]877; clergyman's [2]155; Lawson's [4]675n–6n; public [5]167; Rolandi's *see* London; temple [2]377; village [6]218
library-cormorant [1]cii
Library of Congress *see* Washington DC
"librating" [4]168
Libya/Libyan [2]750, [3]70, [6]210, 210n
licence [1]384, [4]734
poetic [1]47; to teach [4]666–7
licentiousness [2]496
lichens [4]827
Lichtathmung [4]323
Lichtenberg, Georg Christoph (1742–99) [4]187
Liddell, Henry George (1811–98), and Robert Scott *Greek-English Lexicon* [1]462n, 466n, [2]355n, 745n, [3]328n
"lie" [1]61
lie(s) [1]61, 395, 560, 691, [3]159, 342, 401, 769, 809, 923, [4]97, 171, 479, 702, 789, [5]124, 424, 759, [6]49
blasphemous [5]656; double [2]978; for God [1]823, [3]573; to God [2]531 ("Maker"); father of [1]646, [3]120, 121n, 446; of Fathers [5]638; good fat [6]120; life of [5]425; l.-martyr [5]616; mother-l. [3]1052; one big [6]290; stupid [1]58; swearing a [5]392; thousand [2]1154; and truth [5]564; for truth's sake [3]459; and veracity [5]820; wicked [2]814
Liège [2]101
"life" [4]527, 527n, 528–9, [5]175
life/lives [1]171, 178, 551, 605, 679, 735, [2]863, 882, 891, 999–1000, 1000n, 1009, 1009n, 1155, 1192, [3]13, 18, 42, 44, 76, 520, 715, 850, 1087, [4]93, 98, 539–40, [5]6, 73, 93, 171, 176, 208, 210, 321, 453, 457, 460, 618, [6]302
absolute [6]8; act of [1]646; active and passive [3]741; analogies of [3]62; analogon of [3]1010; animal [1]175, [2]1182, [5]171, 795; of animals [5]715; not answerable for [1]47; l.-atoms [3]1041–2; audital [1]578; beginning of [1]590; beginning and end [3]417, [4]524n; in body [5]496; of body [5]172; bodily [2]1167; Böhme's view of [1]661; book of [3]60; of Christ *see* Jesus Christ, life of; Christian [2]591, [3]743; of Christian [5]650; classification of [5]784; to come [4]52; commercial [5]480; common [5]372; consists in water, heat, light [1]597; consolation in [4]52; controversies over [1]550–1, 550n; after death [2]565; and death *see* death; in death [1]594, [2]236n; death out of [2]788; defined [3]278, [4]445; deity diffused [3]755, 755n; dependent [1]609; dialectic of [2]624n; disease a mode of [2]564; diversity of [5]286; divine [3]434, [4]258; Donne on [2]293–4; double [3]46; essential [6]70; eternal [1]124, [2]559, 559n, 1074n, 1109, [4]70, [5]189; everlasting [2]333, [3]88, [5]424, 629, 673, [6]303; excrescences of [4]432; exemplary [4]267; false [1]637, [5]425, 452; fluid of [3]383–4, 395; l.-force [3]94, 398, 398n; force of [2]1009; forms of [4]500–1; future [4]246; generic [5]189; genial [5]512; in God [1]609; godlike [5]87; a good [6]296; ground of [1]646; higher [4]493–4; history of [1]537, [3]919; idea of [2]1026, [3]60; ideal of [4]201; imperishable [5]177; impure [4]620; infinite [2]563; intelligence reciprocal [2]624; intention of [4]465; of irritability [3]1036; and law [4]168; of law [5]613; of lies [5]425; and light [1]123, 624, 630, 638, 675, 705, 786, 824, [3]60, [4]316, [5]484, 628, 630, 650, 796, [6]19, 64; light of [3]61; light of men [1]123; long [4]844; lore of [5]347; loss of [1]165, 184–5; magnetic power [2]1008; magnetism in [3]125; in man and animals [1]126; l.-men [2]562; military [5]380; and mind [2]1000, 1000n, [5]443; moral [1]818; of muscles [4]542; natural [6]301–2; of nature [5]336; nature of [4]322n; negative and positive [4]385; new [3]520, [5]181, [6]302; organic [2]431, [3]842; outward [1]822; of oyster [5]176; particular [5]369; passive [2]173; philosophy of [2]268; plastic [3]841, [5]190; pleasures of [4]729; portrait of [1]736; potential [6]75; powers of [4]165, 389; principle of [4]384–5, [5]728; private [6]94; of probation [4]465; proceeding [2]726; product of [4]274; prothesis of [3]399; public [4]145; l.-rays [4]494; retarded [1]661; seat of [3]21; self-balancing [6]75; shaped by resistance [1]692; shortening of [2]385; solar [2]1142; and soul [1]166, 166n, 171, 175, [3]518, 545–6, [5]233, [6]302n; of soul [2]1004–5; soul of body

life/lives—*continued*
[6]300; and spirit [6]116; spirit of [5]545; spiritual [1]634, 636, [2]348, [3]29, 46, [5]172, 562; Steffens's concept of [5]285–6; sum of pleasurable feeling [3]253; Supreme [2]882; symbolic [1]684; synonym of Holy Spirit [2]305; tendency to individualisation [5]431; three forms of [2]1026; tree of [2]1053; true [4]260; truly human [1]280; turn of [6]125; Unitive [2]198; unity of [2]1036; universal [4]526; uterine [2]535; vegetative [2]1008; vegetive [3]68; vegetive, insectile, animal [2]689; vital principle [2]1026, [4]149–50; whole [5]99; will as nucleus of [1]580; woman's [4]727. *See also* principle, vital; vitality

Life of a Lawyer [3]500

Life-guardsman [5]184

lifeless, the [5]421

ligament [1]671

ligature [4]164

light(s) [1]177, 605, 623, 624, 637, 663, 665, 693, 785, [2]297, 403, 489, 852, 853, 853n, 854n, 855, 855n, 860, 1000, 1019–20, [3]13, 24, 28n, 29, 72, 128, 139, 150, 202, 323, 390, 390n, 518, 518n, 546, 559, 617, 696, 723, 919, 1000, 1024, 1025, 1025n, 1028, 1029, 1059, 1087, [4]315, 315n, 358, 388, 395–6, 396–7, 426–7, 443, 443n, 448, 487, 492, 531, 539–40, [5]8, 15, 96, 189, 191, 383, 400, 410, 438, 470, 472, 640, 642, 714, 764, [6]116, 132, 226, 226n, 229, 300
a priori [5]514; from above [3]564; becomes fire [2]1020–1; Berkeley on [2]623n; in Bible [1]465; body of [3]1057n; chemical effects of [3]29; Christ as [3]523; of Christ [1]630; Christian [1]817; created and begotten [1]603, 603n; cross l. [1]600; and darkness *see* darkness; in darkness [2]825; defined [1]597; direct and reflected [3]472; divine [1]824–5, [2]206; divinity as [2]417–19, 424–6, *425n*; dry [3]724n; excess of [1]547, [2]974, [4]98; of faith [1]820; Father of [2]884, 1166, [5]484; of the Father [5]56; at fingertips [2]301; flash of [3]373; form of [1]593; formal [3]746; in fountain [1]649; garment of spirits [3]211; genesis of [1]599; green [3]1059; heart of nature [1]623; of idea(s) [5]131, 600, 782; images of [5]60; indwelling [6]19; infusion(s) of [5]529, 536; intellectual [1]818; intelligential [3]16; joy in [5]814; of law [5]613; laws of [5]159; and life *see* life; of life [3]61; life-giving [1]712; from light [1]712; of light [1]707, [5]26; lighteth every man [2]1175; of love [5]466; *lux lucifica* [1]624, *624n*; material [5]410; mere [5]467; mixes with l. [1]10; and music [4]313–14, 313n; of nature [1]296; new [1]296, [2]695, 695n; no l. of nature [2]298; not its own [5]491; of one's own [1]763, 797; only a [2]484; origin of [2]419; outward [2]297; polarised [3]999; poles of [1]663; power of [1]624; properties of [3]59–60; rays of [2]604; of reason [1]123, [5]68, 155, 797n; reflected [2]423, [3]212; of reflection [5]130; related to matter [2]1007n; revealed [6]78; from robe [2]544; scanty [5]374; second degree of [1]590; seeth l. [5]758; and shade [4]167; and shadow [5]452, 452n; smoke from [2]788, 788n; solar [5]452; from soul [1]558; in soul [1]824–5; sphere of [3]386; spiritual [1]515, [2]663, 1151, [3]72, 746, 746n; subjective [3]128; successive action [4]271; supernatural [3]439; symbol of Trinity [1]687–8, *687n–8n*; theory of [2]424–5, 425n, [3]944–5, 945n, 1013–18, [4]271n, [5]264; of vision [5]15; visual is immaterial [2]425

Lightfoot, John (1602–75) [1]clixn, 259, [3]438, 438n, 803n, [4]637, 637n, [5]508, 508n–9n, 522
Horae Hebraicae [5]523n; *The Works* MT [3]707–11; *see also* H. Broughton *Works* ed Lightfoot

light-headedness [4]822

lightning(s) [2]1022, [3]104, 204, 205, 478, 721, 945, 1087, [4]286, [5]562

Ligne, Charles Joseph, Prince de (1735–1814) [1]699n
Mémoire sur le Comte de Bonneval [1]699n; *Mémoires et mélanges historiques* [1]699n

lignum vitae [4]622

"like" [2]145

like(s) act(s) on like(s) [5]15

likeness [3]791, [4]221, 603
ridiculous [1]610; substantial [1]466

liking [2]319, [4]810

Lillibullero [4]97, 98n

Lilliput (in Swift) [2]202, 687, [3]1043, [4]188, [5]476

Lillo, George (1693–1739) [2]75

Lilly Library *see* Bloomington IN

lily [3]460, 790

Lily, William (c 1466–1522) [2]881n

Lima [4]28n

limb(s) [5]11, 476

limbo [1]786, [2]559n, 654

Limbus (myth) [1]654

lime [1]570, 613, 737, [2]246, 246n, 546, [3]44, 45, 129, 998, 1001, 1062, [4]274, 526, 526n, [5]255, 256, 257, 261, 397, 840, phosphate of [3]443, [5]296
limit(s) [1]563, [3]85, [4]115, [5]442, 719
limitation(s) [2]346, 671, [3]860, [4]459–60
Limousin [4]193
Linasu (myth) [2]584
Lincoln [2]926, 1196, [3]1065, [4]287
Minster [2]1022, 1022n–3n; Tennyson Research Centre, Central Library, marginalia in [5]853
Lincolnshire [2]210, [5]164, 853
Lindsay, Lady Anne (1750–1825) [1]313 ("Lindsey"), 315
Lindsay, Julian Ira (b 1886) [2]169–70, [3]40
Lindsey [4]287
Lindsey, Theophilus (1723–1808) [4]296, 298 q, 299, 299n
Apology [4]298n, 302 q
line(s) [2]607, [3]653, 653n, 832–3, 1004, [5]734, 750
bipolar [5]542, 714; equatorial [5]813; hemispheric(al) [3]1008, [5]265; horizontal [4]314; mathematical [6]172; and poles [5]715; of verse [5]689
linea [3]139, 653
Lingard, John (1771–1851) [1]861, [6]184
lingua arcana [2]1107, 1107n
lingua communis [5]651
"linguipotence" [1]317, 317n
linguist [2]140, [5]9
lininess [5]133
lining [1]815
link(s) [1]537, [2]291, 348, 466, 510, [4]86, 408, 459, [5]155
of association [4]735; associative [4]860; follows link [1]576; missing [3]347, 348; triple [5]569
Linley, Thomas, the Younger (1756–78) [3]248, 248n
Linley, William (1771–1835) [1]95
Linnaeus, Carolus (Carl von Linné) (1707–78) [2]865, 1068n, [3]104n, 1088, 1089n, [4]606, 606n
Linnaean method [2]85; Linnaean system [3]1035n
Systema Naturae [4]606n, tr Turton as *A General System of Nature* [4]606n
Linnell, John (1792–1882) [2]180
linnet [1]483
linseed oil [1]548
Linton [4]574
Lintot/Lintott, Bernard (1675–1736) [2]1106
Linus (myth) [4]147
lion(s) [1]399, [2]1109n, [3]97, 1066, [4]390, 551, [5]293, 387, 388, 594, 811
alchemical symbol [1]215–16, 216n; honey in [3]508, 508n; tamed [6]195; teeth of [2]512
lip(s) [1]607, [4]407
l.-brother [2]123; l.-work [1]702
Lips (in Bürger) [1]829, 829n
liquefy [3]60, 60n, 61
liquid [3]61
liquor [5]190
suffused [5]445
Lira [6]121
Lisbon [3]1081
Lisle, Edward (?1666–1722) [6]151
lisping [5]622
litany [1]261, 264, [4]665
Litchfield, Harriett (1777–1854) [6]270
literal, the
and symbolic(al) [1]783, [6]303
literalism [3]153; *see also* letter(s) (written character[s]), and spirit
literality, carnal [3]731
Literary World [1]clxiii, clxiiin, [2]214
literati, French [4]185
literature [2]1024n
book-society [5]866; classical [4]343; comic [2]780; English [3]484, [5]848; German comic [2]780; Greek [1]182; Hebrew [6]67; historic [1]423; restoration of [2]12; reviewing spirit of [2]999; Roman [4]336
Lithica [1]776n, [2]582n
lithographer [4]534, 534n
lithography [4]534n
lithomancy [1]775
lithotomy [2]611
litigiousness [2]530
"little" [5]862
little [5]99n
little-goes [5]502, 502n
Littlehampton [1]494, [2]133, [5]403
liturgists [5]505
"liturgy" [6]86
liturgy/liturgies [1]260, 261, 281, 319, 332, 806, [2]531, 651, 1141, [4]658, 665, [5]127, 504, 504n, 522, 526, 530, 574, 659, 667
Baxter's objections to [1]242; C of E [1]320, 358, 520, [3]369, [5]471, 484; compilers of [5]519; imperfections of [6]43; incomparable [5]507; Moravian [3]494; only test needed [1]311; reform of [3]167; reformation of [5]521; revision of [1]331; scriptural [1]343; superiority of our [5]510; transcendent [1]328

livelihood
difficulty of [5]323; honourable [5]367
liver [3]125–6, [4]432, [5]462
role of [2]367–8; schirrous [5]252, 559
Liverpool [1]32, 500, [2]873, [3]628n, 638, [4]29, 532n
Athenaeum Library [1]221n; L. Theatre [2]169
Liverpool, Earl of *see* Jenkinson, Robert Banks
living, the [5]482
exemplary [5]135
livings [2]912
good [1]310
Livingston, Arthur (1883–1944) *see* Milton *Sonnet 2* tr Livingston
Livingstone, James, 1st Earl of Newburgh (d 1670) [4]83 ("Newborough")
Livius Andronicus (fl 3rd century BC) [2]776, 776n
Livy (Titus Livius) (59 BC–AD 17) [1]cvii, 221, [2]470n, 776n, 969n, [4]99, 311n, [5]533n, 576
Livy tr B. O. Foster [5]562, 562n q, tr F. G. Moore [3]652
lizard(s) [2]545, 545n, [4]502
flying [4]499
Lloyd, Charles (1748–1828) [6]20, 20n
Lloyd, Charles (1775–1839) [2]861n, [3]881, [5]165, [6]20n
letter to [1]412n q
Nugae Canorae MT [3]712–14, presentation copy [3]712
Lloyd, Robert (1733–64) [1]lxxxviii, 38
loach [4]802
load-stone *see* lodestone
loaf/loaves [3]741, [5]374
and fishes [1]815, 815n, [2]453, 1086, 1159, [4]67, [5]62–3
lobsters [4]96
locability [3]399
locality/localities [2]639, [5]644
of sensations [1]518
loch [4]802
Lock, Mr [1]697
Locke, John (1632–1704) [1]cxxiii, 198n, 255n, 256, 256n, [2]31, 538n, 558, 610, 788, 867, 869, 1203, [3]177n, 243n, 266n, 602n, 764, 877, 877n, [4]12, 27n, 75, 105–6, 105n, 107, 110, 111, 112, 115, 116, 174, 175n, [6]69n, 81 ("Lock")
C's projected book [1]756, 756n; debts to Aristotle and Descartes [5]732, 732n; and Descartes [4]25, 25n; heartless sobriety [1]621, 621n; on ideas [5]17, 17n, 828, 828n; influence of [4]109; innate ideas [2]543; low-church [2]26, 26n; piety of [4]27; system of [4]113; theory of knowledge [2]341
An Essay Concerning Human Understanding [2]543n, 867n, [3]388n, 877n, [4]25–6 ("Lock"), 26n q, 106, 106n, 239n, [5]432, ed Fraser [3]559n–60n q; *Letter Concerning Toleration* [1]256n, [2]26n; *Letters for Toleration* [1]256n; *Reasonableness of Christianity* [2]26n; *Two Treatises of Government* [4]12n
Lockhart, Charlotte Sophia (née Scott) (1799–1837), letter to [1]513n q
Lockhart, John Gibson (1794–1854) [2]979, 979n
and Asgill project [1]lxv; letter to [2]904n
Lockian(s) [2]1013, 1013n, [4]239
Lockianism [4]107
"locust" [5]105, 105n
locust(s) [2]511, 646n, [5]117, [6]166
lodestone [1]775, 776n
first [6]251 ("load-stone")
lodge(s) [1]340
lodger [3]185, 185n
Lodore [4]692, 692n
Lodwick, Francis (1619–94) *Essay towards a Universal Alphabet* [3]828n
Loeb, C. W. [1]119
Loeb, J. A. [1]119
Loewe, M. (fl 1822) *A Treatise on the Phenomena of Animal Magnetism* MT [3]715–17
Lofft, Capell (1751–1824) *see* Milton *Paradise Lost* ed Lofft
"lofty" [1]61
log(s) [3]157, [4]453, [5]471
Logan, John (1748–88) [1]38
logic [1]348, 632, 639, 770, [3]163, 201, 256–62, 516, 934n, [4]145, 292, 734, [5]9, 133, 153, 177, 204, 274, 324, 420, 775, [6]25, 171–6, 298
aberration from [5]562; accuracy of [5]624; aesthetic [4]708; of Aristotle [5]803; arrangement of thoughts [3]950; bad [1]396, [5]339; best [5]155; Bruno on [5]812; of Bull and Waterland [6]74; canon(s) of [4]426, [5]664; canonic [5]324; cement of [4]679; of chemist [4]317; common [4]156; conceptual [5]449, 599, 627; consequential [3]763; contempt of [5]428; crazy [3]455; criterional [5]324; cunning [2]550; dichotomic [5]459–60; of dichotomy [2]1193, [3]363; discursive [3]1091; dry [1]325; dry leaves [1]325; empir-

ical [4]454; eristic [6]80; exhaustive [5]744; fair [4]452; false [3]199, 1051; fiction of [2]1002; field [5]161; form(s) of [3]18, [6]285; formal [5]744; French [5]836; of Fuller [2]803; gifts of [2]1156; Greek l. in Donne [2]318; higher [4]454; ideal [3]451; of ideas [5]796; illogical [5]186; inductive [4]15; Inquisitor's [1]252; judicial [3]364; logical intellect [3]746; logico-psychological division [3]967; love of [4]624; manuals of [1]298; mere [5]176; and metaphysics [4]454, 454n; misapplied [5]592; mockery of [4]858; need for [4]426, 426n; neglected by German philosophers [2]994, 1002; neglected by medical profession [2]362, 362n; organic [5]324; original [4]291; perversion of [5]774; of philosophers [5]673; Platonic [4]160, [6]315; Plotinian [5]755; polar [1]347, 563n, [3]361n, *see also* polarity; possibles of [3]395; presumptuous [2]460, [5]190; propaedeutic [3]935, 935n; queer [5]369; region of [5]126; and rhetoric [5]615; rhetorical [5]663; role of mind in [3]275; root of [5]729; rules of [5]369; science of understanding [3]558; searching [3]919; simple [6]174; Socinian [2]800; sound [5]340; Steffens's [5]286; strange [1]441; suspicious [4]451; syllogistic [3]257n; systematic [5]502; of Jeremy Taylor [5]555; technical [5]242; of thought [1]221; transcendental [4]156, 157, 157n, [5]81, 324; trichotomy in [1]347–8; of trichotomy [5]459; twist of [4]414; unguarded [5]70; Unitarian [5]7; uses of [5]269; versatility of [5]597; whimsical [1]459, [6]112; *see also* pentad, logical

logician(s) [2]140, [3]451, [5]153, 470, 545, 560, 646, 675

acute [5]564; elder [3]139; New England [3]817; old [3]257; Plato as [4]127; principles of [4]454; Scholastic [1]354

logodaedaly [2]38, [3]476, 589

"logolatry" [6]143, 143n

logolatry [4]426n

logomachist [5]63

logomachy [1]551, [2]29, 591, [3]589, 911, [4]136, 369, [5]21

pedantic [5]716

logos/logoi [1]484, 484n, [2]430, 430n, 433, 464, *881n*, [3]11, 11n, [4]94, 94n, 111n, 313, 313n, [5]95, 716–17, 828

l. alogos [3]141; *l. anthropinos* [3]746; *l. epistemonikos* [1]595; *l. Kyrion* [1]447, 448; *logos* and *logoi* [2]429, 429n; *l. poietikoi* [1]174n; *l. psilanthropos* [5]752, 752n; *l.* and *rhema(ta)* [1]669n, [5]770, 770n, 778n; *l. spermatikos* [1]174; *see also* word(s)

Logos/Logos [1]432, 484, 484n, 661, 661n, [2]137, 208n, 264, 423, 427, 434n, 462, 487, 582, 582n, 659, 659n, 735, *881n*, [2]1010n, [3]16n, 23n, 24, 59–60, 91, 106n–7n, 151n, 460, 460n, 521, 524, 524n, 662, 913, 913n, 919, 944, [4]200, 200n, 324, 406, 407n, 444, 492, 644, [5]15–16, 19, 19n, 31, 56, 97, 190, 439, 553n, 614, 614n, 766, 777, 781, [6]32n, 89, 143, 303, 306, 306n

adequate idea of divine beings [1]573; allegory of [2]429n; Calvin on [1]477; coeternal [1]679, [5]400; defined [3]23; divine [5]657; divinity of [2]843; doctrine of [5]27n; as energy [1]624; filiation of [1]564, [3]857; gnostic doctrine [3]612; idea [3]92; incarnation of [1]574, [5]680; influence on body [1]620; Intelligence [1]653, 653n; intelligential imagination [2]713; Jehovah [1]785; St John on [2]478–9; Love uniting with [1]661; personeity of [2]457; Philo on [2]458, [5]741; pleroma of [1]640; practical reason [2]182; product of [4]14; revealed [6]83; substantial Idea [3]545; supreme Idea [1]694; symbol of the Deity [1]564; *theanthropos* [2]824, [4]407n; in Trinity [1]690; understanding [2]715, 729n; union with [6]70; as Word [1]583; working of [1]200. *See also* Jehovah-Word; Jesus Christ; Word

Lohenstein, Daniel Caspar von (1635–83) [2]782–3

Eitelkeit des Glückens und des Hofes [2]783n

Loire [2]769–70

Lollards [5]143n

"Lollius" [4]808, 808n–9n

Lollius Urbicus (3rd century) [4]809n

Lolme, Jean Louis de (c 1740–1806) [4]12, 15

La Constitution de l'Angleterre [4]12n, tr as *The Constitution of England* [4]12n

Lolos, Anastasios *see* Pseudo-Methodius *Apocalypse* ed Lolos

Lombard, Peter (c 1100–60) [2]11–12, [3]366, 366n, [5]790, 790n, 792–3

Sententiae [3]366n

London [1]lxxix, lxxx, lxxxi, lxxxiii, lxxxvi, xciii, xcvin, xcvii, cx, clxxi, 32, 76, 89n, 90n, 155, 156, 197, 230, 290, 334, 346, 350, 431, 761, [2]6n, 140, 816, 868, 942, 979n, 981n, [3]308, 333, 333n, 636, 694, 824, 1081, [4]32, 72, 171, 287, 289, 505n,

London—*continued*
538n, 548–9, 549n, 578, 724, [5]46n, 132, 138, 142, 234, 299, 471, 619, 866, [6]206n
Admiralty [4]534, 534n, Court of [3]500, 500n–1n; African Association [1]528n; African Institution [4]8; Anti-Slavery Society [1]31, [4]151n; Athenaeum [4]105; Baptist Missionary Society [2]801; Barclay's brewery [5]250, 250n; Battersea [2]1184; Bedlam [1]804, [5]185; Berners St [6]156, 158; Billingsgate [1]859n; Birdcage Walk [3]976, 976n; Blackfriars' Bridge [5]299; Blandford Place [5]392; British and Foreign Bible Society [1]440n, [2]261, 261n, 1184, [3]309n; British Institution [2]235n, 1195n, [4]821n; British Library [1]cvii, cli, clxxiv, [2]796, 883n, 1048, [4]143, 341, [5]850, acquisition of marginalia [1]clxin, clxiv–clxv, clxvn, clxvii, clxviii, clxx, acquisition of mss by C [1]clxxii, clxxiii, Ashley Collection [1]clxi, clxvn, clxxiii, auctioneers' catalogues in [1]clvii, clxin, marginalia in [1]9, 24, 28, 31, 104, 113n, 121, 203, 222, 231, 365, 373, 476, 508, 511, 526, 535, 553, 712n, 738, 802, [2]19, 20, 32, 90, 94, 133, 139, 176, 210, 339, 353, 359, 373, 415, 435, 478, 503, 519, 533, 558, 596, 600, 616, 623, 626, 627, 638, 639, 647, 691, 696, 784, 805, 806, 808, 822, 845, 880, 907, 911, 926, 958, 959, 988, 998, 1050, 1064, 1072, 1089, 1095, 1115, 1131, 1184, 1191, 1203, [3]3, 10, 75, 106, 114, 134, 140, 170, 196, 220, 230, 239, 241, 250, 252, 256, 263, 269, 304, 314, 316, 336, 367, 371, 415, 537, 640, 655, 712, 718, 782, 805, 810, 839, 846, 848, 864, 874, 906, 915, 918, 932, 954, 974, 983, 995, 1013, 1019, 1049, 1064, 1078, 1083, [4]3, 5, 7, 8, 9, 40, 122, 154, 207, 233, 242, 310, 313, 329, 344, 360, 391, 398, 402, 447, 463, 465, 469, 485, 487, 504, 541, 578, 593, 603, 617, 681, 686, 778, [5]3, 46, 48, 87, 96, 101, 194, 255, 268, 307, 334, 352, 361, 382, 392, 401, 403, 432, 463, 478, 499, 669, 686, 688, 691, 824, 830, 851, [6]3, 44, 50, 54, 73, 95, 125, 136, 147, 169, 171, 216, 225, 285, Ottery Collection [1]clxvn, clxxii, clxxiii, [2]830, Poole mss [2]967, transcript(s) of marginalia in [1]240, 279, 743, [2]650, 1118, [3]415, 719, [4]334, [5]853, W. H. P. Coleridge collection [1]clxvn, clxvii; British Museum [1]ciii, 121, [2]1116, 1169, [5]501, [6]57, *see also* London: British Library; Camden Chapel [4]3; Change-Alley [3]501; Charterhouse [1]183n, [2]821n, [3]704, 704n; Cheam [2]912; Chelsea [1]500, [3]630; Christ's Hospital [1]lxxivn, civ, 42n, 129 ("Blue-coat School"), 354n, 513n, 637n, [2]4, 351, 354n, 981n, 1188, [3]146n, 163n, [4]11, 12n, 175, [5]127n; Church Missionary Society [3]309, 309n; Clare Market [1]183, 183n; Clifford's Inn [2]351; Cornhill [4]658n; Court of Chancery [3]500n–1n; Court of King's Bench [1]727n, [2]1140, 1140n, [3]501n, [4]633; Covent Garden Theatre [2]169, 413n, [3]484n, [5]861, 862n; Crown and Anchor [3]146; Curry's (bookseller) [6]265; Cuthell and Martin's (bookseller) [2]973n, [4]343n; Dr Williams's Library [1]cxlviiin, cli, [2]1169, [3]366, [4]279, [5]501, marginalia in [2]180, [4]261, 270, 373, [5]241, transcript(s) of marginalia in [3]707, [4]105; Drury Lane Theatre [1]50, [4]598n, 658n, 770n, [5]861, 862n, [6]270; East India House [1]xc, 724n, *see also* East India Company; Essex Street Chapel [3]146, 146n; Euston Square [2]179, 180, 194; Exeter Exchange [4]488, 488n, [5]832, 832n; Fleet Prison [6]208n; Gallery of British Artists [2]180; Gravel Pit Chapel [5]657n; Gresham College [1]872; Grosvenor Square [4]542; Grub Street [1]182; Hackney [3]738n; Hammersmith [1]xciv, [2]242n, 243n, 526, [4]96; Hampstead [1]cxxxv, cxxxviii, 413, [3]308, 843; Hampstead Heath [2]1112n; High Holborn [1]688, 688n; Highgate *see* Highgate; Holborn [1]765, [2]912, [3]974, [4]343n; Hood's (bookseller) [1]xcvin; Humane Society [2]1083, 1083n; Hurst, Chance, and Co (publisher) [1]28n, [2]1190n; Inner Temple [5]478; Islington [2]767; Jewish Historical Society [2]1189; Keats House, marginalia in [6]246; Kentish Town [4]101n; King's Bench prison [5]394; King's College [1]cxxxviiin, clx, [2]373, 955n, [4]11; Lackington, James (bookseller) [3]887, 887n, [4]631, 631n; Lambeth [2]260, 937, [4]301n, [5]537, 537n, [6]152; Law Society [1]279; Lincoln's Inn [1]cxxxv, [2]142, [5]533; Lincoln's Inn Fields [1]cxxxviii, cxxxviiin, 183n; L. Bridge [2]182n; L. Hospital [1]282n; Mechanics' Institution [2]981n; Missionary Society [1]33; Longman's (publisher) [4]343n, [5]502n; Maggs Bros (bookseller) [1]488, [2]794; Medical and Chirurgical Society [3]126n; Meux's brewery [5]250, 250n; Mile

End [4]542; National Gallery [2]180, 1195n; Newgate [3]146, 501, [4]241n, 636, [5]145n; Old Bailey [3]722, [4]633, [5]513, 513n, [6]134, 134n; Pall Mall [2]180; Paternoster Row [4]85; Percy Society [2]214; Pickering and Co (publisher) [2]245; Prayer-book and Homily Society [4]681; Red Cross St Library [1]ciii, [2]519; Regent's Park [1]cxxxv, cxxxviii; Roake and Varty (publisher) [2]210; Robinsons' (publisher) [3]887, 887n; Rodd, Thomas [1]clxvii; Rolandi's Circulating Library [6]156, 158, 159; Roxburghe Club [1]clxxiiin, [2]702, *702n*, sale cvii; Royal Academy [2]180, 235n, 1066n, [3]899n, 900n; Royal College of Surgeons [1]228, 296n, [2]824n, [4]5, [5]252n; Royal Institution [1]lxxxiv, lxxxv, 99n, [2]117, [3]400, [4]392n, 503n, 836–7, 836n, 837n, [5]255n, see also *Quarterly Journal of Science, Literature, and the Arts*; Royal Society of Literature [1]cxxxix, cxli, cli, clxxi, 31, 432n, 738, 795n, [2]907, [3]92n, 191n, see also *Transactions of the Royal Society of Literature*; Royal Society [1]615n, [2]883n, 1140, 1140n, [4]85n, 526n, 837n, [5]638, see also *Philosophical Transactions*; St Augustine's [4]179; St George's Church [3]602, 602n, [5]78, 78n–9n; St George's Hospital [5]184; St Giles in the Fields [2]567, 567n, [4]663, 663n; St James's [5]60; St James's Park [3]976n; St Lawrence Jewry [3]665n; St Luke's [4]650; St Mark's College [2]650; St Marylebone [5]78n–9n; St Pancras [4]3; St Paul's Cathedral [2]1179n, [3]166, 587n, 721, 792; St Thomas's Hospital [1]clixn, clx, [2]827n, 1183n, [5]175n; Salutation and Cat [5]531, 531n; Savoy Chapel [2]816; Seven Dials [2]567n; Shakespeare Gallery [2]1195n; Sion College Library [1]ciii, [2]926, 1095, 1169, [3]486, [5]501, marginalia in [1]850, [5]221; Smithfield Market [2]282, [3]186, [4]96; Society for Diffusing Information on the Subject of Capital Punishment and Prison Discipline *On the Effects of Capital Punishment as Applied to Forgery and Theft* [4]241n; Society for Missions in Africa [3]309n; Society of United Theological Booksellers [4]672, 673; Soho [1]xciv; Sotheby's [1]clxiii, clxiv, clxvii, clxix, 760, [6]257, sale catalogue(s) [1]clxvi, 475, [2]964; South Audley Street [1]160n; Southgate, Henry [1]clxi; Southwark [5]250n; Spring Gardens [1]519n, [2]196n; Strand [3]146n; Swedenborg Society [1]659n, [3]432n, marginalia in [5]441, 462; Taylor and Hessey (publisher) [2]133, 289n, 814n, 1169, [3]537, [5]686n; Temple [1]124, 124n, [4]72; Tottenham Court Road [5]250n; Tower [2]939n, [5]13; Tower Hamlets [5]317n; Tower Hill [2]932n, [5]316, 317n; Twinings [5]680; Union Fire Office [4]658, 658n; Unitarian Society [3]673, 673n; University College [1]513n, 738, [2]954n, 981n, 1188, [4]41n, marginalia in [3]321, [4]615, [6]131, transcript of marginalia in [5]854; University of [1]738, [2]352, 830, 954, *954n–5n*, 979n, 980n, 1184; Victoria and Albert Museum [2]888n, marginalia in [1]52, 716, [2]7, [4]161, [6]34; Vauxhall [2]196, *196n*; Wapping [2]567, 567n; Wentworth House [6]246; Westminster [2]937, [4]634; Westminster Bridge [2]182; Westminster Cathedral [2]1102n; Westminster, College of [2]937; Westminster Hall [5]832, 832n; Westminster Library [1]lxxxvii, ciii, 269n, [4]677; Westminster School [2]3, 4, 54n, 66, 821n, 979

London Apprentice [3]702

London Encyclopaedia [3]984 q

London Journal [3]163n

London Magazine [1]xcix, xcixn, cxvi, 365, [2]140, 1048, 1116, 1169, [3]719

London Prodigal [3]702n

London Review [1]500

The London Stage 1660–1800 ed Hogan [5]23n

Londonderry [5]281, 281n

Long, George (1780–1868) [5]478

Long, Kingsmill (fl 1625) *see* J. Barclay *Argenis* tr Long

Longaville (*Love's Labour's Lost*) [4]696

longevity [1]782, [2]1185, [3]360, [4]201n, 491

Longinus (legend) [1]683

Longinus, Cassius (c 213–73) [1]8n, 371n, 397n, [2]355, 355n, 687n, 1067, [5]748

Peri hypsous (*De sublimitate*) ed Weiske [1]8 q, 8n, tr Fyfe as *On the Sublime* [2]355n q

longitude [1]769, [5]814

Longman and Co *see* London: Longman's

Longman, Thomas Norton (1771–1842) [1]cv, [2]243n, 845

Long-Wellesley, William Pole Tylney (1788–1857) [2]211, 211n

Lonsdale, Earl of *see* Lowther, James

Lonsdale, Roger *see* T. Gray *Poems* ed Lonsdale

"look out" [4]411

looking-glass(es) [2]1011, 1019, [3]20, 382, 393, 740, 740n, 858, [5]405; *see also* mirror(s)
loop-holes [3]896
loquentes [5]787, 787n
lord(s) [5]278
  and lordship [1]667; and tenant [1]383; two [6]144
"Lord" [2]469, 469n, [5]514, 514n, 618–19, 618n, 621n, [6]77, 77n, 143, 178, 178n
Lord, the [3]738, [5]11n, 14, 157, 415, 622, [6]68
  character of [5]535; Day of [3]433, [4]244n, see also *Dies Messiae*; divinity of [1]358; of Lords [5]658; one [5]34; return of [4]252; Servant of [1]435; applied to Son [5]59; Word of [3]689[4]2
Lord's Day [1]334, [2]1153. *See also* Sabbath(s); Sunday
Lord's Prayer [1]311, 325, 326, 561–2 q, 729, [2]837, 903, 903n, 1179n, [3]417n, 432, 453n, 760, 823, [4]175, 625, [5]95 q, 95n, 129, 520, 520n, 522–3, 523n, 524, 606, 606n q, 630, 630n q
  German [1]607n, 670
Lord's Supper [1]333, 349, 703, [2]38, 452, 683, [3]440, [4]483–4, 484n, [5]398, 398n, 399, 566, 566n, 669–85
  rejected by Quakers [1]821; *see also* Eucharist
lordliness [2]219
"lore" [4]730n, [5]347
lore of life [5]347
Loretto [1]47–8, 48n
Los Angeles CA
  University of California, Clark Library, marginalia in [4]69
Losh, James (d 1834) [1]xcviii
loss [4]158–9
lost, the [1]609
Lost List see G. Whalley
"lot" [6]212
Lot (Bible) [2]836, [6]105
Lothian, John Maule (b 1896) *see* Shakespeare *Twelfth Night* ed Lothian and Craik
lots [5]152
lottery/lotteries [3]207, 207n, 789, 789n, [5]502n
Louis XI (in Scott) [4]612, 612n, 613
Louis XI, King of France (1423–83) [2]99, [5]44, 45
Louis XIV, King of France (1638–1715) [1]335n, 540, [2]79, [4]73 ("King of France"), 75 ("Grand Monarque")
  wars of [5]276
Louis XVI, King of France (1754–93) [6]120
  death of [1]278; murder of [2]43n, [6]258
Louis XVII, King of France (1785–95) [3]160n
Louis XVIII, King of France (1755–1824) [3]160, 160n, [5]279
Louis Philippe, King of France (1773–1855) [1]32, 32n
louse/lice [1]168n, [2]887, [3]824, [4]309, 634, [5]841
  l.-disease [2]615, 615n, 887, 887n
lousiness [5]834
"love" [2]527, 527n, [4]654n
love [1]605, 627, 637, 680, 754, 754n, 789, 789n, 878, [2]95, 198, 402, 636–7, 882, 1162, [3]18, 64, 151, 195, 266, 466, 558, 566, 611, 699, 776, [4]224, 238, 400, 410, 429, 463, 480, 612, 810, 829, 830–1, 834, 835, 851, 856, [5]26, 27, 93, 99, 100, 159, 201, 208, 304, 578, 590, 642, 644, 648, [6]309
  absolute [3]460; in action [2]250; animal [2]1053; attachment of [5]367; in B&F [1]393; Böhme on [1]604, 614, 680; of boys [1]42n; brotherly [2]476; carnal and spiritual [1]12; Christian [2]329, [5]433; C's analysis of [3]265n–6n; conjugal [2]262, [6]157; l.-creed [2]225; unto death [6]105; debile [1]301; defect of [4]366; denial of [5]476; De Wette on [2]192–3; divine [1]601, 731, [2]37, [5]404n; earthly [5]821; an element [3]265; as emulation [1]525; of enemies [5]132; energic [4]258; eternal [5]424; exclusive [2]197, [3]497, [5]130; faith as [1]814; as fire [5]707; at first sight [2]812; and fondness [4]814; free act of [5]457; freest [2]261; French misuse of word [2]527, 527n, [3]1003, 1003n; and friendship *see* friendship; God as [1]645, [5]122–3; God is [2]249; of God [3]671, [4]597, 652–3, [5]471; God's [1]790, [4]589; of good [3]9, 459; highest [1]754, [4]597; infinite [5]585; light of [5]466; its own logic [3]778; l.-longing [4]285; and lust [1]393, 393n, 601n, [2]73, 73n, 527, 658, 938n, 1113, [3]265–6, [5]292, 292n, [6]325–6, 326n; and madness [1]804; between males [1]*42n*; melting-pot of [1]123; between men [4]467; misnamed [4]653; mystery of [3]591; negative folly [4]366; of neighbour [5]562; neighbourly [1]184; is as its object [2]192; omnipotence of [3]391; Platonic [2]694–5; principle of [3]76–7; reigning [5]419; and republics [5]275, 275n; respiration of [1]694; ruling [5]419n; sacrifice of [5]523; and salvation [2]27; signs of [1]11; l.-songs [2]779; spirit of [4]431, 432;

state of [4]625; synonym of Holy Spirit [2]305; true [4]292, 335, 335n; of truth [3]9; with desire of union [2]249; unselfish [4]852, [5]420; and will [3]264–5, 264n; and wisdom [5]469, 469n; of wisdom [4]615; wisdom of [1]805, [4]112, [5]228; without l. [6]322; woeful [2]596; woman-like [4]801

Lovejoy, Arthur Oncken (1873–1963) *Essays in the History of Ideas* [3]737

Lovel, William (in Scott) [4]585, 586, 586n

Lovell, Robert (?1770–96) [2]55n

"lovely" [5]834, 834n, 840, 842, 843, 844, 845, 846

lover(s) [2]646, [4]451, [5]821
  espoused [5]819; fountain of [5]845; supposed [5]236

Lovibond, Edward (1724–75) [1]38

loving-kindness [2]1167

Lowe, Edward Clarke (1823–1912) [5]48

lower and higher [1]719

Lowes, John Livingston (1867–1945) [1]civ, [2]245
  The Road to Xanadu [1]lxxvii, clii, cliv, clxxi, 226, 431n, 828, 851, [2]158, 165n, 508n, 587, 985

lowest and highest [5]445

Loweswater [3]974, 980

Lowth, Robert (1710–87) [4]284
  De sacra poesi Hebraeorum [2]413n, [3]32n; *A Short Introduction to English Grammar* [4]284n

Lowther, James, 1st Earl of Lonsdale (1736–1802) [2]529, 529n

Lowther, William, 2nd Earl of Lonsdale (1757–1844) [2]529n

loyalist(s) [1]223, 393, [4]42

loyalty [1]396, [3]250, [4]23, 480, 789, [5]521
  court-l. [2]219; romantic [1]398

Loyola, Ignatius, St (c 1495–1556) [5]121, 121n

lubber [4]534

Lubdhaca (myth) [2]584

Luc, Jean André de (1727–1817) [3]938, 939, 940, 941, 947, 948, 948n, 950, 952
  "Analysis of the Galvanic Pile" MT [3]947–9; 950; *Bacon tel qu'il est* [3]950n; *Lettres sur l'histoire physique de la terre* [3]948n; *Précis de la philosophie de Bacon* [3]950n

Lucan (Marcus Annaeus Lucanus) (39–65) [1]38, [2]126n, [3]175
  tr Rowe [1]38
  Pharsalia [2]126, 126n, [3]220, 220n

Lucas, Edward Verrall (1868–1938) *Life of Charles Lamb* [1]clxiin q, [3]140; *see also* C. and M. Lamb *Letters*, *Works* ed Lucas

luce [4]691–2, 755, 782

Luce, Arthur Aston (1882–1977) *see* Berkeley *Works* ed Luce and Jessop

Lucian (c 120–80) [1]454n, [2]774, [4]466, 466n, 627, 627n, 660, 660n, [5]232, 232n, 561
  "Alexander seu pseudomantis" [3]642; *De morte Peregrini* [4]660n; *How to Write History* [5]561n

Lucifer [1]571, 580, 599, 605, 640, 646, 656, 733, [2]301, [3]92, 92n, 417, [5]421; *see also* Devil

Lucifer (*Paradise Lost*) [4]727n

Lucilius, Gaius (c 180–102 BC) [2]231n, 756, 756n, 757, 757n, 758n, 760

Lucina (in B&F) [1]397

luck [2]247, 247n

Lucretius (Titus Lucretius Carus) (c 99–55 BC) [1]38, 390n, 851n, [2]240, 867n, [3]335, 529, 650–2, [4]336n, 727, [6]75, 75n, 312, 314
  tr Creech [1]38, 51, 82; tr Dryden [1]390n
  De rerum natura [4]727n q, [5]233n, 811n, [6]75n, 289n, tr Rouse, rev M. F. Smith [3]651 q

Lucy, Sir Thomas (1532–1600) [4]755, 782

Lud [6]206, 206n

ludicrous, the [2]159

Ludlow, Edmund (c 1616–92) [1]223, 223n, [3]801, 801n
  Memoirs [3]801n, [6]185n q

luein [1]61

lues [2]364n, 806, [4]630, 630n

Luke, St (1st century) [2]36, 438, 440, 442, 456, 470, 492, 493, 701, 706, 1159, [3]446, 607, 691, [4]474, 474n, 480, 480n, 646n, [5]635, 651, 667
  and Acts of the Apostles [1]459, 511, [3]9; *see also* Bible: NT: GOSPEL(S); Luke

Lull, Raymond (c 1235–c 1315) [5]813, 813n

lullaby [2]1081

lumen [1]688n
  l. and *lux* [1]687, 687n–8n, 712, [3]746, 746n, [5]797n; *l. fatuum* [5]96; *l. siccum* [3]557, 557n, 724, *see also* light, dry

luminary [2]818

luminosity [3]128, 944–5

"lump" [3]455

lump(s) [5]552
  of sugar [4]16

lunacy [2]682, [4]501n
  in B&F [1]393; of understanding [2]482

lunar caustic [3]129

lunatic(s) [2]1109, 1109n, [3]927

lungs [1]868, [2]858, 859, [3]125–6, 853, 1002, 1036, [4]183, 385, [5]462

Lusatia [1]553, 558
lust [1]393, 393n, 560, [2]742n, 1053–5, 1113, [3]605, 735, 806, 808, 1068, [4]341, 693, [5]130, 476, 584, 588
of blasphemy [1]6; of fruition [5]309; hypocrite [6]322; and love *see* love; loveless [6]325–6; of plunder [4]735
"Luster's Tables" [1]lxxxix–xc
"lustrous" [2]87
Lustspiele [1]400
lusus naturae [1]180, 180n, 368
lute [5]591
Eolian [1]609, 609n; *see also* harp
Luther, Martin (1483–1546) [1]lxx, cxxviii, cxliv, 93n, 198n, 274, 283n, 284, 417n, 473, 509n, 531, 805, 805n, [2]30, 64, 64n, 260, 279, 299, 304, 304n, 459n, 592, 702, 716, 883, 1097, 1097n, 1139n, 1167, 1175, 1192n, [3]20, 77n, 142, 142n, 231, 309, 310n, 367, 426, 426n, 493n, 515, 515n, 582, 682, 696, 877, 877n, 922, 984, 1068, [4]42, 191, 192, 192n, 231, 269, 643, 644, [5]5, 76, 76n, 202, 325, 398n, 467n, 497, 497n, 589, 595, 603, 603n, 604n, 643, 661, 667, 667n, 802–3, [6]83, 116, 117n, 192, 260, 263, 298, 298n
age of [2]1146; anti-lutheran gloom [3]625; on Apollos [2]563, 706, 706n; as black swan [3]756; on canon [1]493n; on Christ as Word [2]205; C's admiration for [3]719; commentary on Gal [4]631, 631n; and consubstantiation [1]297, 297n, 862, 862n, 863, [2]280, 671, 671n; and Erasmus [3]774–5; error of [1]863; on Eucharist [6]20–1, 21n; on Fathers [2]272; fineness of [3]753; on free will [2]676, 677, 1099, [3]736–7, 737; as great model [1]813; on Heb [1]467; impetuous [2]496, 496n–7n; irreverence of [3]77; Irving and [3]3, 426n, 431, 431n, 434; on justification [3]31, 31n; love of St Paul [3]745; Pauline [1]460; Pauline spirit [2]501; postils of [3]752, 752n, 781; on prayer [1]674; on predestination [1]835; redivivus [3]434; retrograde [6]20; on Rev [2]490, 490n; on Sabbath [1]268; on salvation [5]466; on sin [1]714; solifidian [2]298, 298n, 299; spirit of [1]843; table-talk [5]76n; translation of Bible [2]417, 417n, 474, *474n*; a translator [3]726; vision of Devil [3]198n, 212n, 305n
Colloquia mensalia ("Table Talk") tr H. Bell [1]lxxxix–xc, ci, cxxxviiin, 282, 282n, 460, 460n, 795n, 810, 810n, 819, [2]716n q, 773–4, 774 q, 774n, 1033, 1038n; MT [3]718–80; [5]608, 608n; *Contra Henricum Regem Anglicum* [3]760n q; *De servo arbitrio* [2]1099; *Des theuren Mannes Gottes, D. Martin Luthers sämtliche . . . Schrifften und Wercke* ed Boerner [3]723n, 781; *Greater Catechism* [1]268n; *Luthers Samptliche Schriften* ed Walch [3]781; "Samptliche Schrifften"† [3]781; *Table Talk* see *Colloquia Mensalia*; *Works* ed Pelikan and H. T. Lehmann [6]83n q
Lutheran(s) [1]198n, 307n, 674, 736n, 810, [2]809n, [3]232n, 234, 260, [4]43, 629, 631, 659, 672, [5]11, 393, 394, 395, 469, 613
doctrine of ubiquity [2]670; persecutions of [6]108; *see also* divines, Lutheran
Lutheranism [4]658
lux [1]688n
l. lucifica [3]28, [4]540, [6]296; *l.* and *lumen* see *lumen*; *l. phaenomenon* [6]226, 227
luxury [2]98
Lyall, Robert (1790–1831) [3]941
lycanthropy [5]679, 679n
Lycas (in Virgil) [6]205
Lyceum *see* Athens
Lycophron (b c 320 BC)
Alexandra [2]505n; *Cassandra* [2]155, 155n, 505, 505n
Lycurgus (c 390–c 325 BC) [2]89n, 891
Lycurgus of Sparta (c 600 BC) [1]705, [2]1138, 1138n, [3]698, 698n, 738, [4]650, 650n
Lycus (river) [1]465
Lydgate, John (?1370–?1451) *Troy-book* [4]808–9
Lyer Laid Open [2]111
lying [1]332, [2]522, 947, [6]100
Lyly, John (c 1554–1606) [1]62
lymph [3]612, [4]493–4, [5]233
Lynam, Robert (1796–1845) *see* P. Skelton *Complete Works* ed Lynam
Lynceus (myth) [2]1031, 1031n
Lyndhurst, Baron *see* Copley, John Singleton
"Lyndsay, David" *see* Dodds, Mary Diana
Lynman *see* Lynam
lynx [2]1031, 1031n
Lyon, George Francis (1795–1832) *Private Journal* [2]834n, 1108, 1108n
lyric(s) [2]762, 876, [4]731, 837, 864
Greek [2]413; impassioned [4]104; Italian [4]290; and stoic [2]65
Lysias, Claudius (c 458–c 380 BC) [2]456, 456n
Lyttelton, George, 1st Baron Lyttelton (1709–73) [1]38
The History of the Life of King Henry the Second MT [3]784–8
Lyward, George A. [2]215

"M." ^{4}768
Maass, Johann Gebhard Ehrenreich (1766–1823) ^{2}542n, ^{4}106n, 108n
  Versuch über die Einbildungskraft ^{3}75; MT 789–93
"Mac" ^{3}795
Macarius (c 300–c 390) ^{2}1041
Macartney, James (1770–1843) ^{3}940, 941
Macbeth (*Macbeth*) ^{4}774, 775, 787–9, 864, ^{6}114
Macbeth, Lady (*Macbeth*) ^{4}732n, 771, 772, 772n, 776, 789, 791
Maccabaeus, Judas (d 160 BC) ^{2}149n, 416, ^{4}477, ^{5}520
Maccabees ^{2}156n, 157, 157n, 377, 411, 417n, 430, 430n, 1075, ^{3}103–4, 420, 420n, 606–7, 607n, ^{4}246, 246n; *see also* Bible: Apocrypha: OT: 1 and 2 Macc
Macdiarmid, John (1779–1808) ^{1}cxxxviiin
  Lives of British Statesmen, &c. MT ^{3}794–803
MacDonnell, Eneas (1783–1858) ^{1}857n
Mace, Daniel (d 1753) *see* Bible: NT: Greek: ed Mace
Macedonia ^{1}464, ^{5}515n
  Macedonian empire ^{3}923
Macedonians ^{2}751, 751n
Macgregor, Peter Balderston (fl 1884) ^{3}827
Machiavelli, Niccolò (1469–1527) ^{3}166, 251, 251n, 877n, ^{5}40
Machin, George Ian Thom *The Catholic Question in English Politics, 1820 to 1830* ^{2}474n q
"machine(s)" ^{2}130, 130n, ^{5}175
machine(s) ^{2}545, 619, ^{3}853, ^{4}159, ^{5}431
  analogy of ^{1}114; animal as ^{4}211–12, 212n; for cogitation ^{5}790; electric ^{5}349; happy ^{4}444; passive ^{5}156
machinery
  accidents in ^{1}868; of poem ^{5}117; poetic ^{4}478; without power ^{4}173; of Providence ^{4}629
MacIvor, Fergus (in Scott) ^{4}579, 580, 581
Mackall, Leonard L. (1879–1937) ^{6}156, 158, 159
Mackarness, John Fielder, Bishop of Oxford (1820–89) ^{1}816
MacKenna, Stephen (1872–1934) *see* Plotinus *Enneads*, *Our Tutelary Spirit* tr MacKenna
mackerel ^{4}267
Mackereth, John (fl 1723) ^{3}977
Mackintosh, Sir James (1765–1832) ^{2}353, 845, 847, 850, ^{3}236, 795n, ^{5}533, *533n–4n*
  C's attack on ^{2}760n
  A Discourse on the Study of the Law of Nature and Nations ^{2}851, ^{5}534n; *Vindiciae Gallicae* ^{3}991n
Maclaine, Archibald (1722–1804) *see* Mosheim *An Ecclesiastical History* tr Maclaine
Macklin, Charles (c 1697–1797) *Love à la Mode* ^{2}529n
MacMahon, Thomas O'Brien (fl 1789) ^{3}1065
Macpherson, James (1736–96) *The Poems of Ossian*† ^{3}804
MacQuirk, Edward (fl 1769) ^{3}224
Macrobius, Ambrosius Theodosius (5th century) ^{2}1172n
  Saturnalia ^{2}755–6q
macrocosm ^{5}406n
  and microcosm ^{5}715
macula/maculae ^{2}155, 827, 1159, ^{3}869
Madagascar ^{3}1080
Madai ^{5}337
mad-doctor ^{3}173
"made" ^{2}273, 273n, 750, ^{3}915
Madeira ^{2}92
madhouse(s) ^{4}164, ^{5}476
madman/madmen ^{2}771, ^{3}249n, ^{5}185, 471, 625, ^{6}262
  impurities of ^{5}563; malignity of ^{1}869; mystified ^{5}123; raving ^{1}272
madness ^{1}370, 496, 804, ^{2}1109, ^{3}475, ^{4}191n, 501n, 544, 821, 825, ^{5}296n, 428, 428n, 820, ^{6}125
  cranny of ^{1}621n; definition of ^{6}288; false ^{4}822; Hamlet's ^{4}856; pious ^{3}699; three sorts ^{6}287
Madrid ^{3}1065, ^{4}532, 532n, ^{5}70
Maecaenas, Gaius Cilnius (c 70–8 BC) ^{2}1018n, ^{4}694–5
Maeonides (myth) ^{6}218
Maevius (1st century BC) ^{1}98, ^{3}412n, ^{5}831
magazine(s) ^{1}158, 164, ^{2}64, ^{3}418
  penny ^{2}980
Magdalo ^{2}256
Magdeburg ^{5}298, 298n
Magee, William (1766–1831) ^{1}262, 262n
  Discourses on the Scriptural Doctrines of Atonement and Sacrifice ^{1}262n
maggot(s) ^{2}569, ^{4}39, 762–3, 847
  mental ^{1}168n; of wit ^{1}168, 168n
Maggs Bros *see* London
Magi (Bible) ^{2}258, ^{4}54, 55, ^{5}226, 233
Magi, Egyptian ^{6}105
"magic" ^{6}97n
magic ^{1}671, ^{2}452, 727, ^{3}708, 920n, ^{4}145, ^{5}423, ^{6}120
  celestial ^{5}648; Eucharist as ^{5}684; natural ^{2}144, ^{5}64; somnial ^{1}808

"magical" [6]97
magician(s) [3]105n, [6]105n, 112
 Egyptian [1]419, [2]1105, 1107, 1107n; priests as [5]577
magistracy
 spiritual [2]697; supreme [5]321; temporal [1]256
magistrate(s) [1]248n, 311, 313, 323, 339, [2]108, 377, [3]367–8, 368n, 471, 586, 768, [6]155
 chief [3]228; *de jure magistratus* [1]281; duty of [1]248; fallible [6]154; first [4]48; licensing [5]316, 317n; Roman [2]1173; use of sword by [1]293
Magna Carta [1]294, [5]44
magna mater [3]448
magnet(s) [1]563, [2]311, 335, 1110, [3]80–1, 379, 682, [4]498, 527, [5]266, 294, [6]120
 first [6]251n; major [5]267; power of [2]1186; tripolar [2]556, 556n
magnetiser(s) [3]210, 389, 391, 395, 396, 398, 868, 872, 1039, 1039n, [5]141, 404
magnetism [1]177, 578, 582, 775, [2]546, 853, 853n, 854n, 855n, 1007, 1008n, 1009n, 1010n, [3]123, 123n, 210, 211, 256, 364, 395, 949, 997n, 998, 1002, 1011, 1060, [4]225, 494n, 527, [5]245, 246n, 258, 265, 266, 435, 451, 764, [6]227, 233
 animal *see* animal magnetism; of the Earth [5]267; in life [3]125; magnetic efflux [3]43; negative [1]775; potenziated [3]842; ultimate principle of [5]776; vital [2]1008
magnetist(s) [4]271, 272, [5]141, 723, 723n
 empirical [5]191
"magnetopathia" [3]374, 374n
magnifying [5]291
 glass *see* glass, magnifying
"magnisonant" [6]251, 251n
magnitude(s) [4]522, [5]291, 734
 physical [5]382; sensation of [5]409
magnolia [5]278
Magog (Bible) [3]70, [5]337
magpie [1]111, [3]1020
mahogany [4]235, [5]542
Mahomet/Mohammed/Muhammad (c 570–c 632) [2]1025, 1025n, 1086, 1086n, 1114n, [3]673, 673n, 674, [4]357n, [5]519, 834
 and mountain [2]304; *see also* Mehmed II
Mahometan(s)/Mohametan(s) [1]304, [2]739n, [3]699, 700, [4]85, 644
Mahometanism [1]288, [2]1114, [3]924n, 927
Mahon, Charles James Patrick (1800–91) [1]859n
Mahony, Mr [2]163, 164n
Mai, Angelo (1782–1854) [2]923, 923n
Maia *see* Maya
Maiades (myth) [5]227
maid [1]657
 servant m. [3]666
"Maid, Moorish" (SH) [1]lxxxvii
"maiden" [3]976, 981
mail, coat of [5]563
Maimonides, Moses (1135–1204) [3]563, 1085, 1085n, 1089, 1090, [4]247, 247n, [5]786–7 q
Mair, M. L. (née Wordsworth) (fl 1833) [4]29
Maitland, Charles *see* Maitland, John
Maitland, James, 8th Earl of Lauderdale (1759–1839) [4]634
Maitland, John, 1st Duke and 2nd Earl of Lauderdale (1616–82) [1]350, 351n, 353n, [3]539, 539n ("Charles")
Maître Pierre (in Scott) [4]612, 612n
majestic, the [2]1070
"majesty" [1]865, 865n
majesty [1]483, [2]949, 949n, 1201, [3]800, 800n, [4]841
 of style [1]765
major(s) in syllogism *see* syllogism
majority [1]319, 341, [2]949, [3]240, 800n, [5]632, 639, [6]11
 act of [2]940; and minority [1]834, 875
"makes" [3]193, [4]172
Malachi (Bible) [2]150, 894, [3]41
Malachias/Malachy, St (1094–1148) [5]662, 662n
Malaprop, Mrs (in Sheridan) [3]370n
malaria [1]48n, [2]364, [3]601, 601n, [4]149n
Malay [1]540, [5]253n, 337, 353
 as degenerous race [1]540
Malayans [3]356n
Malcolm III, King of Scotland (c 1031–93) [1]383, [6]94, 94n
Malcolm (*Macbeth*) [4]726, 726n–7n
Malcolm, Sir John (1769–1833) *History of Persia* [2]597, 597n, 1114n
malcontents [2]384, [5]510
male(s) [1]654, [2]1017
 and female *see* female; love between [1]42n; solitary [5]248; m.-virgin [1]658; *see also* man
Malebranche, Nicolas (1638–1715) [2]623, 623n, [4]78
 caricature of [2]1030
Malesherbes, Chrétien Guillaume de Lamoignon de (1721–94) [3]207
malice [2]239, 315, [3]575
malignancy [5]146

malignity [1]869, [4]862
of madmen [1]869
Mallet, David (1705–65) [1]38
"Life" by Anderson MT [1]75
Excursion [1]75; *see also* F. Bacon, *Works*; H. St John *Works* ed Mallet
Malone, Edmond (1741–1812) [1]221n, [4]696n, 698n, 720n, 723n, 731n, 740n, 760n, 766n, 783n, 806n, 848n, 852n
Malta [1]lxxxii, lxxxiin, lxxxvi, xcv, cx, 90n, 210, 543, 560n, 697, 769, [2]372, 417, 695n, 738, 795, 889n, 978n, 1064, 1204n, [3]129, 294n, 500, 503, 765n, 884n, 974, [4]32, 35, 85n, 290n, 329, 338, 574, 575, [5]359, 824, 831–2, 831n, 835n, 840, 841
Knights of [2]978n; loss of books en route to [1]52; noise [2]979n; San Antonio [5]831, 831n; *see also* Valetta
Maltese [2]978, 978n
Malthus, Thomas Robert (1766–1834) [2]845, [4]619
An Essay on the Principle of Population [1]lxxxi, [2]849, 849n, 850; MT [3]805–9; 810; *The Grounds of an Opinion on the Policy of Restricting the Importation of Foreign Corn* MT [3]810; [5]852
Malthusianism [5]323n
Malus, Etienne Louis (1775–1812) [3]942
Mameluke [2]742n
Mamertus (in B&F) [1]394
mammal(s) [2]860–1
mammalia [2]176, 368, [4]501
mammock [3]161, 161n
Mammon (Bible) [2]899, 979, [3]5
worshipper of [2]320
mammonolatry [1]257n, 307
mammoth [1]61, *61n–2n*, [3]452, [4]532n
Mamre [6]107n
"man" [5]495–6, [6]302
man/men [2]566, 920, 1026, [3]985, [4]266, 548, [5]21, 278, 287n, 388, 435, 460, 483, 709, 766
action on [3]494; and animal *see* animal; on his back [4]450; m.-beast [1]626; beheaded [5]65; best of [5]820; better [5]229; better before wiser [3]879, 958; body and soul in [2]310, 311, 572; born for trouble [1]425; and brute(s) [4]91–8, 167, 394; classes of [4]24; common [5]407; contains mystery [3]24; contrivances of [5]297; corrupt [1]634, 812; creation of [1]636, [3]60, [6]138; definition of [5]405n–6n; development of [2]1005; dignity/dignities of [4]98, [5]475–6; distinctive interest [5]135; and dog [4]93; domestic [5]380; duty to a [5]304; dwarf [2]346, 346n; dying [5]495; educated [5]481; enlightened [4]605; entire [5]500; Fall of *see* Fall; fallen [5]98, 394; fallible [2]30; fear of [2]269; five races [5]253; fleshy [5]703; frail [4]862; free [5]277; free will [5]394; freedom of [4]444; as full stop [1]133; as generic being [4]422; gentlest [1]350; giant [5]406; m.-gins [2]980; and God *see* God; God's favourite [3]621; in God's image [4]531; good [4]137, [5]315; good-hearted [5]464; high-church [5]661; an historic being [3]729; history before birth [1]750; honest [6]10; human in [5]93; immortality of [1]675, [3]317; incarnating [5]524; inner [1]786, [5]467, 514; intellective faculty [5]455; interior [5]723; just [6]138–9, 139n, 141; kindness of [4]212; language proper to [1]538; learned [2]338; not made to live alone [3]906; lives on oxen [3]324; lower nature of [1]457; m.-kind [5]248; mean thing [3]426, 581; meaning of [3]520; measure of creation [3]1036; mental activity in [4]390; m.-milliner [5]88; moral [1]288, [5]771; moral being of [4]446; mortal [5]233; must ascend [3]581; natural [2]1187, [3]433, 526; natural mind of [3]424, 426, 431; and nature [2]347, [3]558, [5]336; nature in [3]478; nature of [3]403, 914, [5]598, 600; necessity of [3]674–5; new [3]876, 878; old Indian [2]987; Old M. [5]678; Old M. of the Mountains [5]143, 143n; *peculia* of [4]421; pen-m. *see* penman; perfect [6]70; personality of [4]93; philosopheme of [2]389; pious [5]455; poor thing [3]546; practical [5]789; primacy of [4]501; private [5]322; Prometheus [1]706; proud [6]49; redemption of [3]447; regenerate [1]713, [2]690, [3]13; regenerated [3]518, [6]300; relations of [5]393; reverence of [2]344; rich [5]587, 686; rights of [2]511, [4]23; self-conscious [5]723; self-love of [4]522; sensual [5]516; separate essences [2]610–11; separate principles in [4]430; sexless [5]407; and society [5]37; Son of *see* Son; speculative [1]288; spirit in [1]430; spirit of [6]302; spiritual [2]938, [3]527, [5]703, [6]310; and stone [5]204; thoughts of [3]326; threefold [4]412, 412n; m.-traps [5]315; turn of life in [6]125; two genera of [4]135; unit in dyad [2]1186; unity of [3]716; universal [2]159; utterable [2]141; whole [1]702, [2]297, 427, 1177, [3]558, [5]801; wise [3]607; and woman/women [1]779, [3]1003, [4]335, 615, 689, 828, [5]130, [6]156, *see also*

man/men—*continued*
female, and male; woman in [3]906n. *See also homo;* human being; humanity; male(s); masculine
Manasseh [2]833
Manasseh/Menasseh Ben Joseph, Ben Israel (1604–57) *Spes Israelis* [1]cvi, 121
Manasses, Prayer of *see* Bible: Apocrypha: OT: Prayer of Manasses
manatee [4]533
Manby, Richard (fl 1733–69) [6]72
Manchester
John Rylands Library [1]761, marginalia in [1]742
Manchester, Duchess of (fiction) [4]650
Manchester, Earl of *see* Montagu, Edward
mancipia [1]35, 35n
Mandeville, Bernard de (1670–1733)
The Fable of the Bees [1]clxv, [2]636, 636n; MT [3]811–12; [4]623, 623n, [5]39n, ed Kaye [3]811
Mandeville, Sir John (d c 1372) [1]771–2, 772n
The Voiage of Sir John Mandevil [1]772n
mandrake [1]776, *776n*, [3]182
manducation [1]657, [5]550, 555n
mane [1]628, 628n
manes [1]431, 431n
Manes (Manichaeus) (c 215–75) [2]721, 721n, 731n, [5]625, 625n
manganese [3]1020n, [5]261, 262n
mango [4]88
manhood [4]816, [5]9n, 169
mania [2]454, 720, [3]986
maniac [6]102
Manichaean(s)
asceticism [3]625n; morals [3]625; system [5]625n
Manichaeanism/Manichaeism [1]619, 619n, [2]721, *721n*
Manichaeus *see* Manes
manifestation(s) [1]595, [2]584, [5]210, 360, 459, 459n, 464, 466, 542, 607
act of [5]719; dyad of [1]653; mode of [5]611; order of [2]575, [3]24; partial [2]993
manifold [3]247–8, 248n, 249, 790
manifoldness [3]841
Man-in-the-Moon [2]190
manioc [2]298, 298n
manipulation, theletic [6]103
manipulator [4]682
"mankind" [5]233
mankind [2]263, [4]850, [5]37, 281
accuser of [6]98; common sense of [4]863, [5]743; corrupt state of [5]277; divided into two parts [5]770; division of [4]138; first race of [3]105; general experience of [4]717; history of [1]719n; hopelessness of [5]745; idea of [5]487; moral interest of [5]124; one species [1]539; races of [1]779; redemption of [5]55
Manley, Mary de la Rivière (1663–1724) [2]767
Manley, Sir Roger (c 1626–88) [2]767
manliness [2]694, [4]794
manna [3]471n
manner and matter [2]108, [4]405, 632
manner(s) [1]496, [3]171
English [3]173; in Fielding's time [2]694; Greek [3]173; kingly [4]800; loose [1]356; methodistical [3]601; and morals [3]679; refinement of [2]672–3; reformation of [4]660; of 1650 [3]907; state of [1]151
mannerism [2]54, [4]162
Manners, John, Marquis of Granby (1721–70) [3]223
Männlein [5]248
Manoa [5]105
Mansfield, Lord *see* Murray, William
mansion-house [2]655
Manso, Giovanni Battista (c 1560–1645) [3]413n
Mant, Richard, Bishop of Down and Connor (1776–1848) [3]309, 309n, [5]189, 495, 495n; *see also* Bible: *The Holy Bible, with Notes* ed Mant and D'Oyly
mantle [6]216
Manton, Thomas (1620–77) [4]182
Mantua [2]763–4
Mantuan *see* Virgil
manualists [2]172
Manuel I, Comnenus, Byzantine Emperor (c 1120–80) [2]660 ("Immanuel")
manufactories [2]1192
manufacture [2]1192n
French [5]309
manufacturers, prejudice against [6]216
manufacturing [6]44
manure [2]349, [3]324, [5]256
manuscripts [4]767
Manwaring, Roger, Bishop of St David's (1590–1653) [2]1103
"many" *see* "menie"
many, the [2]82, [4]678, [5]189
and few [5]770; and one [2]884, [3]60, 328, [5]459; in one [2]1030
map(s) [2]629, 830, [3]567
in Bible [1]440, *440n*; cordiform [2]17n; county [2]820; old and new [4]601; of philosophy [5]692; play [2]74
Mapledurham [5]48

Mapletoft, John (fl 1750) [4]69
marah [2]509n
Marah (river) [2]509, 509n
marasmus [1]524, [4]77
marble [3]21, [4]450, 460, [5]844, 860
Marburg, Colloquy of [3]761n
Marcellus (*Hamlet*) [4]839, 840, 844–5
Marcellus, Bishop of Ancyra (fl 330–43) [2]735
  Apologia [1]312n
Marcellus, Marcus Claudius (42–23 BC) [1]109n
Marcion (c 100–c 165) [2]*32n–3n*, 438, *438n*, 439, 439n, 721n, [6]58
Marcionites [2]32, 32n, 683
Marcosians [4]258
Marcus, Adalbert Friedrich (1753–1816) [3]114, 115, 123n, [4]164, 369n; see also *Jahrbücher der Medicin* ed Marcus and F. W. J. Schelling
Marcus Aurelius Antoninus *see* Aurelius
mare(s) [3]920n
  blind [3]341–2, [6]170, 170n
Margaret of Lancaster *see* Beaufort, Margaret
Margaret, Queen of England (Margaret of Anjou) (1429–82) [2]122
Margaret, Queen of Scots (1489–1541) [2]9
margin(s) [1]531, [5]644
marginale [2]367, 367n
marginalia intentionalia [1]lxxiii
Maria (in B&F) [4]693n
Maria Theresa, Empress of Austria (1717–80) [5]275n
Mariamne (Bible) [4]748
Marienhausen [2]982
Marine (in B&F) [1]401
Marine Dictionary [2]587
mariner [3]204–5, 401, 720
Mariner, William (1791–1853) [4]165 ("Marianer")
Marini *see* Marino
Marino, Giambattista (1569–1625) [2]102 ("Marini"), 117
Marion's Isle [2]74
Maris (fl 325) [5]626
Marius [1]878 q
Marius, Gaius (157–86 BC) [3]447, [5]536
mark(s) [3]791, [5]632
  of Christian [5]491; C's *see* Coleridge, S. T. I (3) signs; contra-distinguishing [5]599; conventional [5]650; of cross [2]1158; distinctive [5]569; distinguishing [5]730; of the Messiah *see* Messiah; and proofs [5]565; scientific [5]244
Mark, St (1st century) [2]36, 440, 442, 1078, [3]36, 446, [4]472, 473n, 474, 646n, 526, 667. *See also* Bible: NT: GOSPEL(S); Mark
Mark Antony *see* Antony
market [1]123
  intercourse of [5]481
Markland, Jeremiah (1693–1776) [5]128n
  Remarks on the Epistles of Cicero to Brutus and of Brutus to Cicero [5]128n
Markwick, William (1739–1815) [6]147
Marlborough, Duchess of *see* Churchill, Sarah
Marlborough, Duke of *see* Churchill, John; Spencer, George
Marlowe, Christopher (1564–93) [1]62
  Tamburlane [3]186n
Marmontel, Jean François (1723–99)
  Moral Tales [2]161, 161n
marom [3]32n
Marot, Clément (c 1497–1544) [2]769–70
marriage(s) [1]266, 349, 704, 751, 752n, 754, 754n ("union"), 938n, [2]703, 914, 914n, [3]493n, 736, 776–8, 807–8, 933, [4]335 ("conjugal state"), [5]38, 295, 323, 550, 566, [6]263
  Christian [3]497, [5]636; of clergy [3]785n; of cousins [2]91, [3]778, 778n; with deceased wife's sister [3]778, 778n; dogmas concerning [2]26; feast [5]796; laws of [5]647; left-hand [5]634; mixed [4]257, 257n; Moravian [3]493–4, 494n, 496; morganatic [5]634n; prohibited [5]393, 393n; of Protestant and RC [1]274; ring in [1]323; as sacrament [1]472, 472n, [5]398n; second [4]485; in Spenser's *Epithalamion* [1]80; spiritual [3]266; as symbol [2]742n
marrow
  m.-bones [5]295, and cleavers [1]183, 183n; of divinity [1]819
Marrs, Edwin W., Jr *see* Lamb, C. and M. A. *Letters* ed Marrs
Mars (myth) [1]219, [2]7, 208, 581, [3]681, [4]835n
Mars (planet) [1]622, 625n, 626, [2]557, [5]339
Marseilles [3]1085
marsh(es) [2]363
Marsh [2]77
Marsh, Herbert, Bishop of Llandaff (1757–1839) [2]53n, 913, *913n–14n*, [3]594n, [4]22, 22n, 23, 24, [5]540, 540n
  The Authenticity of the New Testament [4]59n; *A Dissertation on the . . . Canonical Gospels* [4]469; *see also* Michaelis *Introduction to the New Testament* tr Marsh

Marsh, James (1794–1842) [2]21
Marsh, Jeremiah (1667–1734) [2]77
Marshall, Edward (1815–99) [2]245
Marshall, G. (fl 1810) [3]942
Marshall, John (?1784–1837) *Royal Navy Biography* [4]534n
Marshall, Louisa A. (fl 1809) [2]590
Marshall, Stephen (?1594–1655) [6]186
marsh-land [4]22
Marshman, Joshua (1768–1837) [3]673n
Marston, John (1576–1634) [2]16
Antonio's Revenge [3]177n
Marston Moor [2]1196n, 1197n, 1199, [4]590
Marsyas (myth) [2]135, 135n
marten [1]399n
Marten/Martin, Harry (1602–80) [1]278, [2]43n, 949, 971n, [5]144, 145n, [6]258, 258n
Martha (Bible) [2]314
M.'s Creed [5]618n
Martial (Marcus Valerius Martialis) (c 40–c 104) [1]182n, [2]678n q, [3]175
Epigrams [4]584 q, 584n q
Martin, St, of Tours (c 316–97) [6]318, 318n
Martin V (Odonne Colonna), Pope (1368–1431) [1]502, [2]507n
"Martin, Betty", (all) my eye and [3]438, 438n, 842, 842n, [5]296n
Martin del Barco *see* Barco
Martin, John (1789–1854) [1]802
Martinus (in B&F) [1]394n
Martres, Mr (fl 1810) [3]943
martyr(s) [1]731, 809, [2]476, 717, 717n, [3]27, 317, 368n, 442, 443, 586, 798, 921, 926, [4]181, 629, [5]618, [6]100, 260
of C of E [3]561, [4]643; intercession of [2]673; Protestant [4]643n; Scottish [2]1175; seven [3]595; Spanish [5]821; m.-worshippers [2]970
martyrdom [1]332, [2]712, 712n, 716, 717n, 718, 719, 725, 725n, 728, 740, 1138, [3]57, [6]141
Marullus (*Julius Caesar*) [4]732, 732n, 733n, 805
Marut (myth) [3]92 ("Murat"), 92n
Marvell, Andrew (1621–78) [2]49, [5]42, [6]333
On Paradise Lost [2]77, 77n; *The Rehearsal Transpros'd* [1]402n
marvellous, the [2]808, 1060
love of [3]1069
Marx, Karl Friedrich Heinrich (1796–1877)
On the Origin of the Doctrine of Contagion, review of MT [2]364
Mary (fiction) [2]658
Mary (servant) [4]538, 538n
Mary, Virgin (Bible) [1]44, 48n, 506, 506n, 519, 519n, 668, 675, 743, [2]63, 270–1, 323, 329, 477, 661–2, 724, 749, 915, 916, 921, [3]14n, 36, 37, 55, 155, 430, 435, 440, 457, 606, 611, 729, 730, 730n, [4]51, 52–3, 58, 253, 256, 297, 478, [5]371, 472, 523–4, 547, 622, 622n, 628 ("Mother"), 628n, [6]91, 109
Jovinian's heresy concerning [2]667; miracles of [1]48; pregnancy of [2]273; recollections of [4]476–7; virginity of [2]272, 275, 276, 711, [4]250–1, 251n
Mary Magdalene, St (Bible) [2]1077–8, [3]665, 666
Mary I, Queen of England (1516–58) [1]318, 835, [2]69, 663, 813, 938n, [3]803n, [4]643n, [5]505, 506
Marian persecutions [3]368n; reign of [2]813
Mary II, Queen of England (1662–94) [1]733, 866n, [3]140–1, 144n, 152, 152n, 161, 665
Mary of Guise (1515–60), death of [3]819, 819n
Mary, Queen of Scots (1542–87) [1]301n, [2]508, 509n, [3]144n, 483, 819, [6]145
Mascal(l), Leonard (d 1589) [4]745n
masculine, the [1]551, 662; *see also* man
mask(s) [3]220, 223, 917, 1083, [4]787n
devil's [1]593; handsome [3]136; m.-figure [1]54
Mason, John Monck (1726–1809) [4]812n
Mason, W. (fl 1820) *see* Bunyan *Pilgrim's Progress* ed Mason
Mason, W. Wallis (fl 1810) [3]939
Mason, William (1725–97) [2]72–3
Life and Letters of Gray [2]867n; *see also* T. Gray *Works* ed Mason
Masons [3]679n; *see also* Freemasons
masor [2]577n
Masora(h)/Masoreth/Massora(h) [1]415, [2]381, 381n, [4]246, 246n
Masorites [2]314
Masrekah [1]418
mass (ceremony) [1]530, 838
popish [5]395
mass (physical) [1]299, 653, [5]287, 357, 430, 431
globous [1]623; of population [3]63
massacre [2]401, 908, [6]14
massacring [5]276
Massey, Dudley (fl 1946) [2]158
Massinger, Arthur (d c 1606) [2]78n
Massinger, Philip (1583–1640) [1]43, 43n, 362, 365, 377, 377n, [2]127, 761, 778, [3]192, [4]736, [6]205
and B&F [1]398; blank verse of [1]217; in C's

lectures [1]cxxxix; comic metre of [1]384; dedications [2]78; a democrat [1]380; praise of his metre [1]390; and Shakespeare [1]43, 43n, [2]778n; superior to B&F [1]390; a Whig [1]389
The Bondman [2]78n; *A New Way to Pay Old Debts* [2]78n; *The Plays* ed W. Gifford [2]78n; MT [3]813–15; [6]206n; *A Very Woman* [6]206n
mass-light [1]572
master(s) [3]889, [4]827
common [5]642; m.-impulse [2]160; m.-minds [6]66; m.-truth [2]280
materia [1]547, 547n, [4]328, [5]786
m. medica [3]116, 843; *m. prima* [1]570, 622, [2]618, [5]159
material(s)
erroneously identified with God [1]620; heterogeneous [5]431; m. substance defined [3]277–8
materialisation [1]652
materialism [1]105, 125, [3]243n, 867, 966n, [4]171n, 262, 351, 412, 430n, [5]175n, [6]170
bold [3]324; corpuscular [5]826; crass [1]120, 120n, [2]558, [3]873; Eschenmayer's [2]538; grossest [5]296; in India [2]341
materialist(s) [1]137, 495, 676, [2]340, 801, 802, 1155, [3]524, 560, 911, [4]239, 266–7, [5]692, 716, 720n, [6]306
materiality
of God [5]493; system of [1]597
materiel [5]599
mates [3]193
mathematician(s) [1]213, [2]616, 1133, [3]90n, 318, 339, 680, 1014
disputes of [1]106–8; Greek [3]726; mere [4]159
mathematics [1]285, 346–7, 615, 616n, 793n, [2]642, 979n, [3]118n, 163, 349, 966n, 1051, [4]109, [5]244, 297, 311, 324, 329, 744
C's neglect of [4]503; principle of [3]1050; Hobbes's ignorance of [5]811; importance of [1]615–16; mathematical figures [3]670; metaphoric use of [1]178; and metaphysics [3]959, 959n; Proclus on [4]154–60; mathematical system of phenomena [3]283; theorems of [4]13
Mather, Alexander (1733–1800) [5]168, 169
Mather, Cotton (1663–1728) [6]104, 105n
Magnalia Christi Americana [1]lxxi, lxxin–lxxiin, xciii, clxvii, [2]1174, 1174n; MT [3]816–26; [4]307n
Mather, Increase (1639–1723) [3]821, [6]104
mathesis [4]157
Mathews, Charles (1776–1835) [3]485n
Mathewson, Mrs (fl 1916) [4]199
Mathias, Peter *The Brewing Industry in England 1700–1830* [5]250n
Mathias, Thomas James (?1754–1835) [2]847
The Pursuits of Literature [2]850; *see also* T. Gray *Works* ed Mathias
Mathiolus, Petrus Andreas (Pietro Andrea Mattioli) (1500–77) [5]836
Matonabbee (d 1782) [2]986–7, *987n*
matrimony/Matrimony [3]440n, [5]398, 398n, 566n. *See also* marriage; *BCP*: "Solemnization of Matrimony"
matrix [1]668, [5]451; *see also* mother (matrix)
matron, shiftless [5]504
matter(s) [1]596, 609, 619, [2]665, 1012, [3]43n, 67, 84, 130, 275–6, 287–8, 288–9, 296, 324, 944, 1056, [4]444, 444n, 523, [5]3, 3n, 32, 357, [6]132
of bodies [4]159; and body *see* body; without body [5]165n; chaotic [4]141; coarse or fine [3]325; and cogitation [6]238; constituent powers [3]292; not necessarily corpuscular [3]202; dead [4]322; defined [1]70n, [3]118, 118n, 277–8, 851, 851n; in Descartes [1]524; divisibility of [2]1186, [3]118, [5]734; essence of [3]286–7; of fact [1]388, [2]1053; first [2]1144, [3]915; fixed [1]152; and form *see* form; formless [3]22; forms of [2]457; ground of [3]1024; homogeneous with spirit [1]598; imaginable [6]87; impenetrability of [3]279–80, 280n; inanimate [5]728; indifferent [1]321; Kant's definitions [3]277; Kant's theory of [3]343, 343n; of law [3]54; and manner *see* manner; metaphysical treatment of [3]291; and mind [4]452; a mode of spirit [1]70; negative [4]316; in Newton [3]286; organised [1]537, [5]545; passive [5]231; phantom [1]691; phenomenality of [2]890; in Plato [5]752; Plato on [1]114; points of [3]282; and powers [3]199, 295, 297; as product [3]138–9; qualities of [1]537; quantitative [5]557; radiant [5]451; related to light [2]1007n; and soul [4]127; in Spinoza [1]105, 105n; and spirit [1]70, 70n, 114n, 792, [2]890–1, [3]130, 276, 492, 1086, [5]418, 673, [6]114n, 114n; as substance [3]298; see also *hyle*
Matthew, St (1st century) [2]36, 276, 437, 440, 442, 453, 631, 893, 1078, [4]472, [5]516
pseudo-Matthew [1]491n. *See also* Bible: NT: GOSPEL(S); Matt

Matthews, Henry Bathurst H. (d 1827) [4]534n
Matthews/Mathews, Lieutenant [4]534, 534n
Matthiae, August Heinrich (1769–1835) [2]54n
 A Copious Greek Grammar tr E. V. Blomfield [2]142, 1090n; MT [3]827–36; see also *Hymn to Ceres* ed Matthiae
Matthiae, C. F. (fl 1777) [2]1091n
Matthisson, Friedrich von (1761–1831) [1]828
 Gedichte Copy A [1]lxxx; MT [3]837; *Copy B* MT [3]838
maudlinism [1]736
Mauduyt de la Varenne, Pierre Jean Claude (?1732–92) [3]1067n
Maulay/Mauley, Peter de (c 1378–1415) [5]97
Maule, Thomas (1645–1724) [3]826
 Truth Held Forth and Maintained [3]826n
Maurice, Frederick Dennison (1805–72) [1]xcviii
Maurice, Thomas (1754–1824) *The History of Hindostan* [1]400n, [2]339
mausoleum [4]810
Mawkish, Mr (fiction) [4]262
mawkishness [1]642
maxim(s) [2]809, [3]166, 317, 539n, 596, 596n, 959, 970, 970n, [4]844, 846, [5]37, 73, 73n, 86, 86n, 135
 common [5]560; of experience [5]425; and law [3]254; of policy [1]471; political [3]483; and principles [3]163, 163n; public [5]396; questionable [1]517; *regula maxima* [3]163
maximum [5]350, [6]132
Maximus Confessor, St (c 580–662) [1]162, 192, [3]136, [5]24
 Ambigua [3]134; *Scholia* [3]134
Maxwell, Henry Constable [5]818
Maxwell, James Coutts *see* Shakespeare *Titus Andronicus* ed Maxwell
Maxwell, S. (fl 1823)
 The Battle of the Bridge; or, Pisa Defended MT [3]839–40, presentation copy [3]839
"may" and "can" [3]679
May [5]306, [6]207
May (in Scott) [4]589
May, John [5]490
May, Thomas [4]237
May, Thomas (1595–1650) *see* J. Barclay *Argenis* tr Le Grys and May
Maya/Maia (myth) [2]340, [6]8, 8n
Maycock, J. D. (fl 1810) [3]938
Mayhew *see* Mayow, John
Mayo, Henry (fl 1643) [3]486
Mayow, John (1643–79) [3]1011 ("Mayhew"), 1011n
 Tractatus quinque medico-physici [3]1011n
Mays, James Carthew Carden [2]1116, [3]893n
 coeditor [5]691
 "Coleridge's Borrowings from the Jesus College Library, 1791–94" [3]283n, 977n
Mazarin, Jules, Cardinal (1602–61) [1]335, 335n
maze(s) [3]223, 1008
 fancy's [2]16
McAlpin, Sergeant (in Scott) [4]590
McC., E. R. [4]237
McClelland, John (d 1650) [2]1169, 1179, 1180
McCrie, Thomas (1772–1835) [5]506n
 The Life of John Knox [5]505n
M'Donnell, Eneas *see* MacDonnell
McEnery, John I. *see* Cyril of Alexandria *Epistles* tr McEnery
McFarland, Thomas *Coleridge and the Pantheist Tradition* [1]5n, 139n, [3]75, [5]335n
Mcgarry, Daniel D. *see* John of Salisbury *Metalogicon* tr Mcgarry
M'Quirk *see* MacQuirk
"me" [5]94
me on/onta [1]114, 691, [2]425, 802, [3]520, [4]127, 136, 407n, 444, 444n, 531, [5]95, 752, [6]302
meadow-land [5]589
mean
 between extremes [5]420; golden [5]521
meaning(s) [1]159, 377, 731, [2]883, 1192, [3]12, 35, 261, 345, 418, 522, 600, [4]427, 523, 702, 723, [5]37, 681, [6]286, 305
 absolute [2]316; arbitrarily fixed [3]130; arbitrary [3]741; affixed by Christ [5]650; confusion of [3]277; density of [1]464; diluted [6]211; direct [4]747; diverse [1]813; double [1]466, 685, [3]50, [4]521, 761, [5]592, *see also* equivocation; evangelical [5]580; of Evangelists [3]58; of existence [3]349; fixed [3]130; inward [5]729; literal [2]230; literal and symbolic [2]286; low [1]766; and metre [3]652; moral [1]673; obvious [3]19; one word one m. [1]495; plain [5]591; positive [6]79; primary [3]35; real [3]31; of Scripture [2]531; in Steffens [5]368; sublime [3]1088; substantial [3]84; substratum of [5]173; Swedenborg's [5]410; too deep [4]734; translator's notion of [1]455; of words [2]249, [3]1018; writer's [2]569

meanness [2]1066
means [3]29, [5]123, 367
and end(s) *see* end(s); faculty of [3]424
measure(s) [3]1090, [4]303, 367, [5]81, 749
of infinity [5]482; passive [1]274; of spiritual entities [5]452; of truth [6]78
measurement [5]599
meat [4]273
cold [2]999; and drink [5]362, 372; strong [1]312, [3]758, [5]620
mechane [1]557n
mechanic(s) [3]296, 301–2, 920
celestial [3]325, 325n
mechanics' institutes [2]979n, 981n
mechanique [1]793, 793n, [5]743, 743n
mechanism [2]788–9, 853, [3]199, 696
of cause and effect [2]802; Newtonian [3]325n; of thinking [5]552; worship of [3]77; *see also* philosophy, mechanic
mechanist [3]853
Meckel, Johann Friedrich, the Younger (1781–1833) [2]1026, 1026n
System der vergleichenden Anatomie [2]1026n; MT [3]841–2
Medabberin [5]786, 787, 787n
medal [5]191, 658, 658n
Mede, Joseph (1586–1638) [3]922, 922n, 923, 924, 924n, 925, [6]16, 166
Clavis Apocalyptica [3]922n, [6]166n; *Works* [6]16n q, 166n q
Medea (myth) [1]537n
Medes [5]337
media
gradative [1]550; higher [5]752
Media [1]440 ("Medea"), [2]417, 418
Median empire [3]923
mediation [4]156
mediator(s) [1]288, [2]495, 583, [3]106–7, 328, [5]182, 626
Christ as [4]547–8, [5]483; divine [1]507; one only [2]63; words as [3]424–5
"Medical Treatises" MT [3]843–4
Medici, Catherine de', Queen of France (1519–89) [2]410n–11n, 1198n
Medici, Cosimo de', the Elder (1389–1464) [4]144
Medici, Giovanni de' *see* Leo X
Medici, Lorenzo de' (1449–92) [4]290
Medici(s), the [5]275, 275n
medicine(s) [1]714, 786, [3]64, 67, 114–31, 397, [5]583, 675, 812
defined [4]320, [5]137; empirical [3]365; excremental [3]728n; injudicious [5]171; my m. not everyone's food [1]13; quack m. [2]1088
Medico-Chirurgical Society of Edinburgh *Transactions*† [3]845
mediety [5]297
mediocres, patrician [2]76
meditation(s) [1]158, 878, [2]296, 1025, [3]563, [5]90, 110, 168, 176, 781, 795
grove of [3]564; self-m. [5]229
Mediterranean [1]lxxix, lxxxi, lxxxiii, cix, cxiii, 167n, 441n, 542, 761, [2]131, 236n, 874, 978n, [3]1044n, [4]533n, [5]337, 382, 836n
"medium" [4]95
medium [1]281, [3]444, 518, 559
Christ is m. [3]568; divine [4]855; fine [4]604; Gospel m. [1]814; unforgeable [5]687; universal [5]451
Medlicot, Sir John (fl 1674) [1]350
Medo-Persia [3]419
meekness [2]1140, [3]550, [5]539, 648
spirit of [3]587; Wesleyan [5]148
Meercraft (in Jonson) [3]191, 191n
"meet with" [5]487
Meetingers [5]736
meeting-house(s) [1]265, 349, [6]259
mega biblion mega kakon [1]299
Megara [4]463
megatherium/megatherion [1]61, *62n*, [4]532, 532n
Megiddo [3]470n
Mehmed II (1432–81) [5]832 ("Mahomet")
Mehujael (Bible) [2]576
Meiners, Christoph (1747–1810) [3]243n
Lebensbeschreibungen berühmter Männer [3]308n, 794n, [4]144n
meiosis [2]498
Me-ites [5]148
Mela, Pomponius (fl c 43) *De situ orbis* [1]cxiv
melancholy [4]191n, 762, [5]163, 529n, 823, [6]125
Melanchthon ("Melancthon") (Philipp Schwarzerd) (1497–1560) [1]477n, 835, [2]528, 528n, 765–6 q, 1097, 1097n, [3]718, 727, 742, 742n, 748, 749, 749n, 750, 756, 773, 877, 877n, [4]231, 643, 670n, [5]643, 661
creed of [6]60; de-augustinised Luther [5]76, 76n; humane [4]670; on philosophy [5]802–3; race of [1]531, [2]1139n
Melbourne
Baillieu Library, University of Melbourne, marginalia in [5]389; State Library of Victoria, marginalia in [4]25
Melchior (legend) [4]55n

Melchisedech (Bible) [1]709
Meleager (in Spenser) [1]59
Melgarejo, Ruy Diaz (in Barco) [3]1077
Melissus of Samos (5th century BC) [2]340n, [5]708–10
Melito, Bishop of Sardis (115–85) [2]375n, [4]253, 253n
Mellin, August Wilhelm von, Count (1754–1835) [3]939
Melmoth, William ("Thomas Fitzosborne") (1710–99) *see* Pliny *Letters* tr Melmoth, rev Hutchinson
melody [3]861n, [4]313, 313n, 498
melting-pot [1]123
Melvill, Henry (1798–1871) [5]78
Melvill, Mr [6]132
Melville, Andrew (1545–1622) [2]1169
Melville, Viscount *see* Dundas, Henry
Melzar (Bible) [1]843n
membrane [1]671
memento(s) [2]1062
 arbitrary [5]546
memini [1]419n
Memnon (in B&F) [1]366
Memnon, statue of [1]572n
memoir(s) [1]699
 family [2]1106; historical [4]605
memorabilia [1]448, [4]470, 478, 646, [5]526n, 560n
 of Jesus [4]68
memoria technica [1]509, 509n–10n, [2]853n
memorial(s) [3]142, [4]478
 of the prophets [5]526, 526n
"memory" [5]25
memory [1]158, [2]629, 629n–30n, 860, [3]85, 792, 740, [4]13, 13n, 92, 221, 272, 451, 537, 846, [5]26, 126, 174, 473, 780–1, 825, [6]102
 artefact of [3]127; associative [4]606; deliquium of [3]461, 461n; disburthened/unloaded by writing [3]668, 687; habit of [3]265; historical [5]414; hylozoic [4]31, 31n; laws of [2]609; loss of [2]388, [5]820; plastic [3]377; relation to judgment [1]108; suspension of [5]820; technical [1]770, *770n–1n*; testimony of [3]661; volatilised [4]412; weak [4]589; weakening of [1]109
Memrumus (myth) [2]576
Menander (c 343–291 BC) [2]775n, [4]147
Menardus (Nicolas Hugues Ménard) (1585–1644) [1]492
Menasseh Ben Israel *see* Manasseh
Menasses *see* Bible: Apocrypha: OT: Prayer of Manasses
Mence, Samuel (c 1781–1860), letter(s) to [2]521 q, [3]878n, [6]184
Mendelssohn, Moses (1729–86) [1]297, 425n, [3]75, 88n, 331, 656, 675, 675n, 699, 699n, 700 q, 705, 790n, 955, 955n, 957, 969, [4]227, 228, 265n, [5]582, 582n
 Kant's argument against [3]297, 297n, 298; on knowledge [3]366; translator of Mishnah [1]513n
 Jerusalem [1]lxxx, [3]331n; MT 846–7; 848; *Morgenstunden* [3]331n, 366n, 846; MT 848–61; *Philosophische Schriften*† [1]clxvi, [3]862
mendicants [5]645
Mendip Hills [2]691
Mendoza, Isaac (in Sheridan) [2]1103n
Mendoza, Pedro Gonzalez de (1428–95) [5]104, 105, 106
Menecrates (b c 340 BC) [4]147
Menexenus [2]1069n
"menial" [2]955
menials [5]280
"menie" [2]955, 955n
Menippus (1st half of 3rd century BC) [2]758n
mens [4]144, 144n, 400, [5]202, 493
 m. conciliatrix [5]469; *see also* mind(s)
Menschheit [4]653, 653n
menschlich [2]1051, 1051n
"mense" [4]285, 285n
menstruum [3]709
mente sub una [5]602, 602n
mention [1]61, 61n
mentiri [1]61, 61n
Menzini, Benedetto (1646–1704) *Poesie* MT [3]863
Mephibosheth (Bible) [2]836
mephitis [4]509
Mercantile Gazette [2]1121n
Mercerus, Josias (fl 1594) [1]118
merchant [3]204, [6]216
mercurial sublimate [4]622
Mercurio Peruano [4]201n, [5]105
mercury [1]546, 547, 547n, 548, 549, 549n, 572, 629, 629n, 772, 779, 780, 784, [3]125–6, 126, 325, [4]622n, [5]255, 259, 260, 263
 Böhme on [1]630, 631, 634; *see also* quicksilver
Mercury (myth) [1]692, [2]575, 576n, 583, [5]227; *see also* Hermes
Mercury (planet) [1]12, [2]557, [5]263n

Mercury [2]118
Mercutio (*Romeo and Juliet*) [4]829–30, 832
mercy/mercies [1]601, 731, [2]1180, [3]61, [4]429, 663, [5]31, 32
arbitrary [5]420; divine [2]165, 560, [5]66, 171; free [1]528; of God [1]470, [2]295, [3]63, 307, 671, [5]178, 587; ineffable [1]609; m.-justice [3]307; stupendous [6]105
"merder" [3]894, 894n
Meredith, James Creed *see* Kant *Critique of Judgment* tr Meredith
Merian, Maria Sibylla (1647–1717) [3]1073n
Merian, Matthew (1593–1650) [5]46, 46n, [6]266
Merione (in B&F) [1]370
"merit" [5]182
merit(s) [1]3–4, 173, [2]674, 707, 1041, 1162, [3]232n, 456, 604, [4]24, 620, 622, 628, 628n, 629, 766, 855, [5]596
of Christ [5]587, 678; positive [4]234
meritmongers [4]280
Merlin (legend) [2]410, 410n, [3]105, 105n, [6]160
Merlin, John *see* Milner, John
mermaid(s) [2]1112n, [4]169, 169n, 606n, 738, 761–2, 767
Meroz (Bible) [2]835
Merrick, Mr, Jr (fl 1810) [3]940
Merrilies, Meg (in Scott) [4]594, 594n, 598, 598n, 607
merry-andrew [3]495, 495n
Mersey (river) [3]628
Mersey, Viscount *see* Bigham, Charles
Mersius, Joannes (Johannes van Meurs) (1579–1639) [4]343
Mervyn, Arthur (in Scott) [4]580 ("Melvyn")
Meshach (Bible) [2]570, 570n, [3]70, [4]50n
Mesmer, Friedrich/Franz Anton (1734–1815) [1]455n, 581n, [2]402, 402n, 548n, [3]364, 364n, 372n, 396n, 864, [5]136, 136n, 183, 183n, [6]104, 120–1, 170, 170n
followers of [3]396n; materialism of [3]867, 867n, 873; students of [3]374–5
Mesmerismus ed Wolfart [3]378n; MT 864–73, tr Hackforth [3]868–9 q
mesmerism [2]704, [3]94n, 353n, 364n, 864–73, 1038–9, 1039n, 1067n, [4]325n, 496n, 513–14, 536n, 544n, 592n, 682n, [5]136n, 183n, 191n, 391n, 467n, 517n, 723n, 726n, 759n, [6]99n, 100, 103, 103n
and females [2]700, 700n; *see also* animal magnetism
mesmerist(s) [3]364, 396, 871, [4]497n, [5]141, 183n, 184n
mesothesis [2]58, 316, [3]6, 6n, 15–16, 15n, [4]167–9
mesotheton [4]314, 314n
mess, boast at [3]681
messenger(s) [2]429, [3]450, [5]34, [6]117
of God to man [5]63
"Messiah(s)" [4]48
Messiah(s) [1]435n, 436, 438, 438n, 441, 673, 733, [2]144n, 150n, 153, 284, 430, 462n, 465, 483, 494, 505, 563, 754, 798–9, 922, 1075, 1075n, 1076, 1173, [3]6n, 32, 34n, 102–3, 102n, 103n, 455, 457, 465, 469, 469n, 472, 477, 481, 731n, 733, 775, 988n, [4]44n, 49, 50, 51, 52, 54, 57, 59, 60–1, 62, 298, 471, 476, 477, 483, 726, [5]33, 635, [6]32, 68, 141
characteristics of [3]668n; concept of [4]62n; day(s) of [1]863, [4]244, 244n, [5]606–7, 606n, see also *Dies Messiae*; descending [3]443; false [3]922n; in humiliation [1]427; idea of [3]925, 925n; Jesus Christ as [2]483, [4]471, 476, [5]635; Jewish fancies about [3]34; Jewish prejudices respecting [2]483–4; of the Jews [3]738; m.-king [3]452, 453; Marks of the [1]282, [2]444–5, 445n, [3]668, 668n, [4]245, 245n, 470, 470n, 475; meaning of [2]485; messianic psalms [1]706, 708; Michael a name for [3]594, 594n; monarchy of [4]246; new [2]754; prophecies of [4]471; as redeemer [2]456; suffering [5]606; titles of [1]438
Messiahship [2]485, [4]646, [5]635
Messier, Charles (1730–1817) [4]517–18
Messina [2]647, 978n, [5]846, 846n
Church of the Sacrae Letterae [5]846
Messinese [2]978
metabasis [5]796
m. eis allo genos [2]263, 657, 1154, [3]128, 158, 211, 362, 362n, 362–3, 394, [5]70, 70n, 285, 456, 632, 855, 855n
metal(s) [1]597, 663, 780, [2]824–5, 854, 854n, 855, 856, 856n, [3]125, 286, 324, 481, 580, 951, 995, 998n, 1001, 1005, 1022n, 1025, 1025n, 1029, 1029n, 1030, 1033, 1033n, 1057, 1058–9, 1061, 1062, 1063, [4]320, 324, 384, 513, 526–7, 526n, [5]244, 246, 260, 261, 263, 264, 341–2, 347, 358, 438, [6]116, 227–8
cohesive [5]262; definition of [5]247, 247n; elective attraction of [5]294; element of [1]571; etherial [1]569; noble [3]1000; oxi-

metal(s)—*continued*
dated [1]663; plates of [2]1107, 1107n; precious [5]248, 262; sovereign [5]540; tropical [1]596; volatile [5]248
metalleity [3]1024, [4]315, 315n
metallity [5]341
character of [3]1004
metalloids [3]1030n, 1031
"metallology" [1]639, 639n
metallon [1]572, [3]1024–5, [4]315, 315n
metamorphosis [5]260, [6]326
progressive [2]1026
metanoēsis [5]583
metanoia [2]787 ("*metanoounta*"), 787n, [3]477, 598, 598n, 734, 734n, [4]621n, 855, [5]172, 172n, 424, 424n, 559, 559n, 582, 650, 650n
metaphor(s) [1]236, 338–9, 345n, 713, [2]559, 659, 756, 832, 1021, 1043, 1053n, 1124, 1132, 1168, 1187n, [3]249, 465, 470, 541, 565, 611n, 622, 673, 1018, 1029, 1086, 1093, [4]218, 234n, 284, 375, 385, 458, 498, 511, 635, 635n, 701, 763, 769, [5]19, 166, 176, 504n, 751, [6]21, 109
alchemistic [1]668; and analogy *see* analogy; arbitrary [3]1003; in Bible [1]200; bold [3]1004; in character [3]757; chemical [3]709; common [4]737; crude [2]200; defined [2]657–8, 657n; in De Wette [2]206; doctrine explained away into [1]283; for elucidation [2]1161; end of [5]673; entangling [5]269; geometrical [1]178, [3]273n; of glory [3]29, 29n; of grammarians [3]830; Hebrew [6]119; incongruous [5]111; indeterminate [5]504; inward [2]643; from known to unknown [5]672, 672n; mathematical [5]290; mere [5]550; metaphorise [1]644; more than [1]568; in OT [5]672; of St Paul [3]311; practical [5]5n; preachers' [3]69; repulsive [5]677; self-complimentary [6]118; are sorry logic [3]758; Spinoza's [3]855; substantiated [4]234; and symbol [1]524, 862, [2]280, [3]531, 531n, [5]550n, [6]315, 315n; taste in [4]635; of time [4]123; too bold [3]29; as transfer [3]835, 835n; tricksy companions [5]130, 130n; turned into miracle [2]836; unguarded [5]767; vegetable [2]689; visual [3]676
Metaphrastes, Simeon (fl c 960) *Menologion* [2]699, 699n
metaphysic [3]1091
metaphysician(s) [1]495, 566, [2]316, [3]322, 339, 844, [5]615
Cabiric [5]153; crass [2]734; exposes ignorance [5]244; German [5]372; mere [5]367; profound [5]474; Spanish [4]95; before Spinoza [5]203
"metaphysics" [5]*180n,* 615n
metaphysics [1]577, [2]405, 677, [3]295, [4]143, [5]96, 153, 153n, 469, 555, 812, [6]116
abstract [4]325–6, 326n; Baxter's [1]355; contempt of [5]428; decried [5]74; defined [1]819, 819n; English m. weak [2]1136; German [5]309; and logic [3]967; and mathematics [3]959, 959n; meaning of [3]877–8, 877n; metaphysical subjects [3]913; neglect of [4]106; no light of faith without [1]820; nomenclature of [3]130; prior to logic [4]454; profoundest truth of [5]425; without psychology [1]281, 298; system of [5]201, 714
"metapothecary" [5]202n
metapothecary/metapothecaries [5]201
Metastasio, Pietro (1698–1782)
Isacco [6]324n; *Opere* MT [6]320–9
metastasis [2]672, [3]436, 436n, [5]136, 141
metatheses [4]432
metempsychosis [1]134–5, [2]344, 348–9, 348n
meteor(s) [2]508, [4]397, [6]152
m. stones [3]949, [5]340
meteorites [3]949n, [5]338, 339–40, [6]135n
meteorologists [2]887
meteorology [3]935, [5]246
Meteyard, Eliza (1816–79) *Life of Josiah Wedgwood* [3]631, 638n q
method [1]286, [2]605, 609, 953n, [5]451, 529
beauty of [2]1016; child's [5]365; "Chloro-esteesian" [4]327; Schelling's [4]374–5
Methodism [2]496n, 695, [4]548, 619–74, [5]120–93
Arminian [5]133, 134n; Calvinistic [4]669–70, [5]185; form of fanaticism [1]30
Methodist(s) [2]714, [3]309n, 601, [5]527
Arminian [4]648; Calvinist(ic) [3]495, [4]647–8, [5]162n; Field-M. [1]270, 270n, [6]261; fierce [4]859, 859n; lives of [4]624; misrepresented [4]620; modern [3]528, 818, [6]312; pagan [4]160; story about [2]497; Wesleyan [1]341, 341n, [4]644, [5]81n, 154; Whitfieldite [4]644
Methodist Magazine [4]636, [5]154n
Methodius *see* Pseudo-Methodius
methodos [5]796
Methuen, Paul Cobb (1752–1816) [1]494, [4]183n
Methuen, Thomas Anthony (1781–1869) [1]clxvii, [2]252n, [6]73
Methuselah (Bible) [2]576 ("Methusael") [3]39n, [4]201 ("Methusalem"), 201n

metre(s) [2]128, 129, 133, 874, 874n–5n, [3]192, 194, 701, 839, 887, 903–4, 911, 914, 1070, [4]507n, 603–4, 603n, 708, 709, 710, 734, 740, 758n, 783, 784, 850, [5]118, 688–90, [6]212
Aristophanic [1]387, 387n; burlesque [2]768; classical [3]814; comic [1]383–4, 391; Donne's [2]216, 216–17, 221, 226, 229; effect of [3]897; in English verse [1]377; execrable [6]272; finger-m. [3]899, 899n; humoured [2]762; iambic [2]770; imitative [3]651–2; Italian [4]290; Jonson's [3]171; Massinger's [1]390, [3]813–15; philosophy of [1]376; Plautine [1]387, 387n; pleasing [4]288; of Psalms [2]413–14; regular [4]805; rhythmless [4]795; schemes of [2]761; Shakespeare's [4]759; slovenly [1]378; of *Titus Andronicus* [4]724, 724n, 795; unrealising [3]405; virtual [4]805. *See also* foot/feet (metrical); poetry; prosody; scansion; stanza; versification; *and particular metres by name*
metrists [4]162
Metrodorus (c 330–277 BC) [4]147
metron [4]604n
metropolis [3]478
Metternich, Klemens Wenzel Nepomuk Lothar von, Prince (1773–1859) [3]250n, [5]281, 281n
Metzger, Lore (d 1997), coeditor [1]20, 104, 535, [2]533, 1050, 1064, 1072, [3]75, 93, 196, 371, 640, 657, 715, 789, 846, 848, 864, 954, 995, 1013, 1049, [4]122, 207, 213, 215, 261, 264, 270, 279, [5]87, 199, 241, 255, 268, 307, 334, 352, 361, 824
meum and *tuum* [2]1071
Mexico [2]163n, [5]337, 337n
Meyer [5]142, 142n
Meyer, Abraham [1]697
mezzotint *see* engraving
miasma/miasmata [2]362, [4]149n
mica [5]246
Micaiah (Bible) [3]1087, [5]565
Micanzio, Fulgentio (fl 1646) [1]846, 846n
mice [2]1126, [5]388
Michael, St [2]973n, [3]417, 449n, 470, 473, 535, 535n, 594n, [6]317, 317n
popular notions of [3]200; "Genie Prince" [3]417; name for Messiah [3]594, 594n
Michael (*Paradise Lost*) [5]236n
Michaelis, Johann David (1717–91) [2]439n, 481n, [3]646, 646n, [4]337n
a Socinian [1]197
Introduction to the New Testament ed and tr H. Marsh [2]53n, 146n, 913n, [3]20n q, 594n q, 646n; *Mosaic Law* [2]145, 146, *146n*
Michal (Bible) [5]590n
Michelangelo (1475–1564) [2]235, 235n, [4]824, 824n
Mickle, William Julius (1734–89) [1]38
"micranthrope" [1]671, 671n
microcosm/microcosmos [1]671, [4]529, [5]448, 448n
and macrocosm *see* macrocosm
microphone [4]503, 503n
microscope [1]792, 792n, [2]612, [4]333, 394, [5]291, 409, 771, 771n
microscopic vision [3]692; solar [1]519, [2]285, 285n, [4]82, 82n, [5]344, 346n
Midas (myth) [2]869, 869n
Middelburg [3]204
middle ages [2]459, [4]259, [5]86, 740, [6]138n
Jews in [5]234
Middle East [1]441n
middle passage [3]1082
middle state [2]685
middle term *see* term
Middleham [2]845
Middlesex [2]6n, [4]848n
Middleton, Conyers (1683–1750) [1]317, 317n, [3]922, [6]57
Middletonian controversy [6]57
A Free Inquiry [1]317n; *Letter from Rome* [1]317n, [3]922n; *Letter to Dr. Waterland* [6]57n
Middleton, Erasmus (1739–1805) [3]514, 544, [6]295, 312
Middleton, Thomas Fanshaw, Bishop of Calcutta (1769–1822) [1]716, [3]11n
The Doctrine of the Greek Article [1]467n, 574n, [6]26n
Midrash
Midrashic books [3]684
midshipman [3]1080
midwife [1]755
might, right of [6]11
Migne, Jacques Paul (1800–75) see *Patrologiae cursus completus . . . series graeca, Patrologiae cursus completus . . . series latina* ed Migne
Mignon (in Goethe) [4]610, 610n, 611
migration(s) [4]257n, [6]147
Milan, Council of [5]632
miles [3]975
miles [5]619
milestones [4]115
Miletus [5]224, 694
Milgate, Wesley *see* Donne *The Satires* ed Milgate

militia [5]619
milk [3]128, 570, 758, [4]336, [5]620
from males [1]243, 244n; mixed with wine [2]365; pure [5]613
Milky Way [3]339–41, 340n, [4]508
mill(s) [3]341–2, [5]595, 729–30, 730n
mare in [6]170, 170n; sacks on the [3]895, 895n
Mill, David (1692–1756) [4]244
Mill, John (1645–1707) [1]492, 492n, [6]178
Mill, John Stuart (1806–73) [1]740n
Logic [3]16n
Millenarian(s) [3]478, [5]630, [6]165
m. dogma [4]244
Millenaries, Catholic [5]630
"Millenary Petition" [1]310n
millennium [2]712, 712n, [3]9, 9n, 309, 417, 441–2, 445, 452–3, 461n, 481, 521, 731, [4]244–5, 246, [5]606, 630
miller(s) [3]971
Miller, Frank Justus (1856–1938) *see* Ovid *Metamorphoses* tr Miller
Miller, John (1787–1858)
Sermons MT [3]874–80, presentation copy [3]874
Miller, Walter (1864–1949) *see* Xenophon *Cyropaedia* tr Miller
mille-unity [5]25
milliner [5]88
Mills, Thomas (fl 1813) [6]38
An Essay on the Utility of Bloodletting, in Fever [6]38n
Milne, Mrs (fl 1818) [1]xcviii, [4]826, 826n, 843, 870
Milner, Isaac (1750–1820) *see* Joseph Milner *Practical Sermons*, *Works* ed I. Milner
Milner, John, Bishop of Castabala (1752–1826) [1]855, 857, *857n*, 858, 858n, 859, [3]459
Strictures on the Poet Laureate's "Book of the Church" [1]855
Milner, Joseph (1744–97) [4]616, 616n, [5]162, 162n
History of the Church of Christ [4]616n; *Practical Sermons* ed I. Milner [4]616n; *Works* ed I. Milner [4]616n q
Milnes, Richard Monckton, Baron Houghton (1809–85) [4]189, [6]257
Milo [5]837
Milton, John (1608–74) [1]cvn, cxxxi, 223, 223n, 280, 280n, 366n, 401, 615n, 728, 845n, [2]116, 131, 133, 158, 213–14, 226, 656, 756n, 761, 816, 823n, 1092, 1131, [3]133, 177n, 303n, 342n, 403, 413, 438n, 485, 882n, 886, 990, [4]162, 172 q, 583n, 644, 731, 731n, 736, 841, 842, [5]86, 86n, 110, 493n, 502n, [6]192n q, 251
abuse of fire-arms [2]126; and his age [2]781; aim of [2]356; ambition of [2]972; in Anderson's *British Poets* [1]37; blank verse of [1]218; blindness of [1]810n, [2]492n; borrowed from Virgil [2]971; and Butler [2]763, 763n; and Cowley [2]254, 654, 654n; diction of [1]25n; as divine bard [2]947; double epithets in [2]1119n; editions of [3]883; on excommunication [6]58; and Fathers [2]684, 684n; grandeur of [3]412; Hayley's life of [6]199n, *see also* Hayley; and Herbert [2]1033; on Job [2]413, 413n; juvenile [3]899, 899n; last years of [3]324; "Life" by Anderson MT [1]69–70; metres of [4]603–4, 687; "Milton Gallery" [3]900n; misled [2]1200; musician [2]65–6; pause in [4]162–3; platonising spirit [2]974n; poetry belongs to whole world [3]883; prose of [2]1062–3, style [5]533, works [3]881–4; recommended to HC [1]42; republican [3]178; Russel's copy of [1]xcvin; a serpent [2]946; and Shakespeare [2]218; sonnet(s) [2]66, 66n, 1122, 1122n; Spinozism of [3]138; sublimity [1]180; submission to ancients [1]71; and Swift [5]477; and Jeremy Taylor [5]521n, 524n; use of sources [2]973–4; versification of [5]689; versions of [4]289
Ad Carolum Deodatum MT [3]904–5; *Ad Salsillum* MT [3]905; *L'Allegro* MT [3]893–4; *Answer to Eikon Basilike* [1]336–7, 337n; *Areopagitica* [2]1200n; *A Complete Collection of the Historical, Political, and Miscellaneous Works* ed T. Birch [1]lxiii, lxxxvi, 280n, 320n, [2]55n, 413n; MT [3]881–4; *Comus* MT [1]72; [2]98, 98n q, 974n; MT [3]896–9; *De idea Platonica* MT [1]73; *Defensio secunda pro populo Anglicano* [2]970n, tr Wrangham as *Second Defence of the People of England* [6]218; *Doctrine and Discipline of Divorce* [3]883n; *Eikonoclastes* [2]971n q; *Lycidas* [2]498n q, 812, 812n, [3]413n; MT [3]888–93; [4]708 q, 708n; *Mansus* [3]413n; "Of Education" [2]1092n; *Of Reformation Touching Church-Discipline in England* [1]141n q, [2]684n–5n q, [6]58; "Of That Sort of Dramatic Poem Which Is Called Tragedy" MT [1]71–2; *Of True Religion* [4]246n q; *On Shakespear* [2]234 q, 234n q; *On the Morning of Christ's Nativity* MT [3]899–900; *On the New Forcers of Conscience* [1]320

q, 320n q; *On the University Carrier* MT [3]901–2; *Paradise Lost* [1]10n q, 69; MT [1]70; 70n–1n q; 221, 401n q, 600, 600n, 601 q, 601n, 676n q, 739, [2]125, 125n q, 127n q, 164, 458, 458n, 484, 511 q, 511n, 570n, 654n, 656n, 789, 789n q, 1080n q, 1170 q, [3]14, 60n q, 138n q, 175, 175n, 177n, 395 q, 395n q, 402, 403 q, 408, 411, 412, 413n q, 476 q, 476n q, 494n, 560 q, 560n, 767, 767n q, 890, 896, 1065, 1065n, 1093, 1093n, [4]353n q, 441n, 458 q, 458n q, 479n, 603, 644, 644n, 727n, 799 q, 799n, 841n, 842n, [5]236, 236n q, 353 q, 353n q, 477, [6]98 q, 98n q, 117, 117n q, 218 q, S. Barrow's commentary [3]165n, ed Bentley [3]890n, commendatory verses [2]77, compared to Rev [3]453, cost of [1]69n, epic [2]968, ed Lofft [3]890n, ed T. Newton [1]clxii, [3]885, 890n, 892, 895, mythos [3]473, origins of [2]966, profane [2]947, pun in [2]239, small payment for [1]69; *Paradise Regained* [1]25, 25n q, 46 q, 46n q; MT 71; [2]66n, 88, 337, 337n–8n q, 734, 734n q, 896n, 968, 969n q, [4]479, 479n; *The Passion* MT [3]900–1; *Il Penseroso* MT [3]895–6; *Poemata* [2]812n; *Poems* [6]334; *Poems* (1823) [4]603n; *Poems upon Several Occasions* ed T. Warton MT [3]886–905; *Poetical Works* ed Tonson [3]883n; *Pro populo Anglicano defensio* [2]972n, 1200n, [3]151n; *Reason of Church Government* [2]55n q, 413n q, 505n, 896n, 967, [3]179n q; *Samson Agonistes* [2]505n, [4]168, 632, 632n; *Sonnet XI* MT [1]72; *Sonnet 2* tr Livingston [3]902; *Sonnets* MT [3]902–3; *To Cyriack Skinner* [1]69n q; *To the Lord General Cromwell* [1]73, 73n; *To the Lord General Fairfax* [1]69n q; *Translation of Psalm VII* MT [3]903; *Translation of Psalm VIII* MT [3]903–4; *Translation of Psalm LXXXII* MT [3]904; *Treatise of Civil Power in Ecclesiastical Causes* [6]58n q; *Works* (1738) ed T. Birch [1]337n, [2]505n q, 685n, 1092n q, [6]58n q; *Works* (1753) [3]883n; *Works* (1933) [6]219n q

Miltoniad [2]1120

Miltonism [2]1120n

Milward, Richard (1609–80) *see* Selden *Table-Talk* ed Milward

Mimas [3]648

Mimnermus (fl 632–629 BC) [4]147

mince-meat [5]711

"mind" [1]656, [5]174, 175, 200, 202, 202n

mind(s) [1]171, 688, [2]250, 891, 999–1000, 1000n, 1109, 1141, 1155, [3]18, 29, 151, 715, [4]144, 448, 695, [5]204, 825

no abstraction [4]228; act of [5]459; active powers of [1]808; activity of [1]280, [2]639; as agent [3]275; aggregate of [1]180; of all men [5]594; Aristotle on [2]552; association cannot explain m. [2]961; believing [3]445, [4]605; body and *see* body; conciliatory [5]469n; confusion of [1]826; and conscience [3]588–9; constitution of [4]130; craves excitement [2]999; creative [1]565, [5]620; defined [3]277–8, 559; development of [2]601; as directive power [4]450; discerning [1]820; discontinuous [1]164, 174; discursions of [2]656; distraction of [3]867; divine [1]573, [3]88; effeminated [6]324; not an Eolian Harp [3]248; eternal [5]159, 372, 751, 753; ether as [6]8, 8n; expanding [3]671; as eye [1]674; eye of *see* eye; facts of [4]647; faculties of [4]731; feeling m. [5]477; fineness of [1]327; of the flesh *see* flesh; as focus [3]116; m.-forms [5]357; free power of [2]160; front of [4]845; German [4]325; giant [3]179; of God [3]151; great [1]795, [5]362; growth of [2]637; have a m. to [1]157; healthful [5]483; human [1]508, [3]849, 893, [5]61, 775, [6]20, 114, 115; improvement of [2]98; indolence of [6]124; infinite [3]679, [5]14, 18; instinct to aim high [2]42; and language [5]481; law(s) of [4]123, [5]372; and life [2]1000, 1000n, [5]443; little [1]795; living [4]489; Locke's model [5]432n; make of [1]758, 758n; manly [3]722; and matter *see* matter; mechanism of [2]640; mighty [2]781; mood of [2]636; of nation [5]299–300; natural [3]424, 426, 431; negative subjectivity of [4]542; objective [5]710; omnipotence of [3]237; omniscient [3]853; opulence of [5]487; original [2]788; passive [2]639; passiveness of [6]102; Petvin on [4]105–16; philosophic [5]753; philosophising [2]609; powerful [4]173; pre-inquisition into [5]81; presence of [4]760; produces form [4]217; products of [3]276; public [1]336, 343; pure intelligence [1]557n; rank of [5]452; reflecting [4]579, [5]66; related to being and spirit [2]248; sanity of [5]98; science of [1]566; self-knowing [5]741; self-possessing [4]113; self-subsisting [4]125; sensual [3]42; giving shake to [5]72; singleness of [5]783; slavery to eye [3]138, 138n; soft [3]501; sole reality [5]707; of the spirit [2]1151; spiritual [3]755; as subject-object [4]125; substantial [5]400; supreme [1]694, [2]568, 882, [4]27, [5]19, 27, 728, *see also* God; tense [5]789; *terra incognita* of [4]801; tran-

mind(s)—*continued*
sitional [5]805; two sorts of [5]269; unarmed [1]804; universal [4]826; unsensualised [1]222, 222n; weak [5]406; Wesley's [5]129. See also *mens; nous/Nous*
minding [3]526
mind's eye *see* eye
"mine" [2]18
mine(s) [2]746, [3]191, 883
adit of [5]81, 82n; salt [5]351
Minell, Jan (1625–83) [6]213n
miner [4]595n
mineral(s) [3]325n, [4]315
mineralogist [2]338, [5]481
mineralogy [5]167
Minerva (myth) [2]8, 575, 583, 583n, [4]648; *see also* Athena
mingere [1]768n
minim(s) [3]865, 1065, [4]408
"minimifidian(ism)" [1]512, 512n–13n, [3]557, 557n
minimifidian(s) [3]612, 612n
minion [2]929, [3]797
"minionism" [2]944, 944n, [4]766n
minister(s) (church) [1]307, 308, 529, 530, [2]937, 1096, 1141, [3]48, 734, 744, [5]163, 530
boring [3]29; of C of E [2]297, 352, [5]145, 471; dissenting [1]265, [6]47, 145, 259; ejected [1]333, 352, 359; first [6]19; godly [1]319; of the Gospel [2]294, [6]23; holy [1]353; learned [6]259; London [2]1198; vain [1]328; *see also* clergy
ministers (parliamentary) [4]20, [5]40
ministration, separate [5]658
ministry (church) [1]527, 532, [3]6n, 605, [5]167, 509
Minkwitz, John von (fl early 16th century) [3]757
Minnesinger [5]325, 325n
"minor(s)" [1]245
minor(s) in syllogism *see* syllogism
minoration [1]767
Minorca [2]93
minority, illustrious [5]770
Minos (myth) [5]44
Minotaur (myth) [1]51
mint [5]167
minuets [3]175
minus, plus and [4]358
minutiae [1]394, 397, 764, 797n, [2]346
mira [6]109
Mirabeau, Honoré Gabriel Riqueti, Comte de (1749–91) [2]510n
mirabilia [2]924
miracle(s) [1]134, 244, 273n, 282–3, 454, 462, 462n, [2]30, 257, 283, 452, 663, 699, 704, 708, 725, 728, 737, 742–3, 746, 747, 752, 835, 839, 922, 1014–16, 1056, 1058–9, 1060n, 1085–6, 1085n, 1111, 1153, 1154, 1173, [3]5–6, 35, 180, 305, 308n, 320, 425, 451, 598, 598n, 660–1, 660n, 662, 676, 698, *708n–9n*, 726, 763n, 987–8, 988–9, 989n, 1069, [4]40n, 44, 44n, 65, 67, 132, 132n, 145, 269, 301, 475, 476, 627, 641, 642, 645, 656, 668, 673, [5]12, 32n, 50–1, 52, 53, 60, 71, 151n, 172, 212, 383n, 513n, 516, 519, 529, 536, 565, 605, 645 ("miraculous"), 656–7, 678, 766, 767, 823, 823n, [6]106n, 119, 119n, 139
age of [4]260; of Apostles [3]8; beginning of [4]66; Böhme on [1]683; at Cana [2]204, 262; of Christian dispensation [5]62–4; of Christianity [1]201; C's "Definition" of [1]lxxxvn; continued [5]814; credibility of [2]202; daemoniacal [4]673; definition of [2]896n–7n, [5]32, 53, 53n, 63–6, 765, [6]134–5, 135n; disputes about [1]317, 317n; Eichhorn on [2]435; gift of [1]327; of gift of tongues [4]248, 248n, 250; gifts of healing as [3]734; Gospel m. [5]822; greatest [2]315; highest sense of [2]493; imaginary [5]65; and imposture [3]708; of Incarnation [1]507; inconveniences of [3]721; of Jesus Christ [2]288, 289, 453–4, 462, 1005, 1086, 1159, [3]709; Kant's opinion of [2]185, 185n; of loaves and fishes [1]815, 815n, [2]453, 1086, 1159, [4]67, [5]62–3; as means of introducing religion [2]342; metaphor turned into [2]836; miraculous and marvellous [2]1060; mode of [6]109; as modes of thinking [2]462; moral [3]696; of Moses [2]161, 398; most momentous [4]256; most stupendous [5]644; of NT [2]194, [5]140; plain [5]125; Puritan [3]821; raising of Lazarus [2]262, 262n; role of [2]663; sensuous [5]644; and sign [2]653; spiritual [2]1045; standing [5]51; status of [4]260n; m.-stories [5]677; superfluous [4]45; thumping [3]726; true [5]190, [6]118–19; true and false [5]383–4, 383n, 384n; vindication of [2]161; of the Virgin [1]48
mirage [5]299
miranda [6]109
Miranda (*Tempest*) [4]765, 795, 831
Miriam (Bible) [2]838, 838n
"Mirone, M. de" *see* Saumery, Pierre Lambert de

mirror(s) [1]149, 149n–50n, [2]249, 1110, [3]12, 381, 382, 393n, 660, 773, 857, 866, 872, 967, [4]787, [5]243, [6]240
Claude Lorraine [4]337, 337n; concave [5]244; of faith [2]423; flash in [1]619; of idea [3]20; inward [1]238n; metallic [2]206; in NT [1]237, 237n; polished [5]112; of soul [1]671; of symbols [3]62. *See also* glass(es); looking-glass(es)
mirth [3]553
Mirza (in *Spectator*), "Vision" of [3]759, 992
misalliances [4]257
"misanthropy" [2]1173, 1173n
misanthropy [4]819, [5]475
miscarriage [5]468
miscellany [2]431, 1016
mischief, love of [3]225
Mischna, Hebraice et Latine ed Surenhusius [1]513n
"miscreant" [2]656, 656n
miscreant [1]212
"misepiscopy" [2]1173, 1173n
miser [1]184
miserable, the [2]1187
misery [2]176, 1187, [3]809, [4]9, [5]270
eternal [2]263, 567, [5]601; general [2]129; utter [5]593
miseteon [1]397, [4]693; *see also* hateful
m. and *phoberon* [1]371, 371n
miseton [1]371n, [2]687, [4]620
misgrowths, tolerable [1]516
mish-mash/mischmasch [2]1015
Mishnah [1]513n
misinterpretation [2]798, 896, [3]734, [4]306, [6]59, 91
mislaying [4]278
misnomer [3]50
"miso-fanatic" [5]124, 124n
misology [3]493
miso-romanists [6]33
"misosophy" [2]1147, 1147n
misprint(s) [1]391, [2]1036
missing [1]600
mission(s) [3]309–10, [5]105n–6n, 416n
of Apostles [2]455, [3]6, 6n–7n; Christ's [5]63; divine [5]62; public [4]480; of the Seventy [3]734
missionary/missionaries [1]305, 305n, 528, 528n, [2]703, 720, 720n, [3]6, 7, 8, 27, 673, [4]651, [5]105, [6]246
accounts of [5]416; Apostolic [3]8; Catholic [1]811; society/societies [3]309n, [4]633
Mississippi (river) [2]980, [4]532n
Missouri (river) [2]980
mist(s) [3]736, [4]360, 434, 504, [5]371
luminous [1]558; painted [2]1065
mistake [5]562, [6]6
mister [3]889
mistletoe [3]884
mistranslation(s) [2]56, [3]466, 722, [5]845, [6]76, 119
mistress [4]451, 718
"misty-magnific" [5]534
Mitchell, Brian Redman *Abstract of British Historical Statistics* [2]622n
Mitchell, James (c 1621–43) [2]1176
Mitchell, Samuel L. (fl 1815) [1]205
mite(s) [4]16, [5]409
Mitford, John (1781–1859) [1]240, 277n
Mithras (myth) [2]573
mitre [5]638, 660
Mitscherlich, Christoph Wilhelm (1760–1854) see *Hymn to Ceres* ed Mitscherlich
mittelst [1]21–2
mixed race *see* race, mixed
mixty maxty [2]999
Mizraim (Bible) [2]577, 577n
Mnaseas (3rd century BC) [2]583n
Mnemon (myth) [3]1075
mnemonic(s) [1]770, *770n–1n*, [4]13
Bruno on [5]812
mnemosynon [1]863
mnestheti [1]419n
Moab (Bible) [1]421, 421n, [3]70, 419, [6]219
Moabites [1]442, 442n, 873, 874
mob(s) [2]453, 521, [3]164, 1038n, [4]804, 848, [6]52
appeals to [6]329; Shakespeare's contempt for [1]389; written for [4]729
mob-cap [4]848
mobility [1]614, [5]344
"mobled" [4]848–9, 848n
Mocha [4]29
mock-axioms [5]561
mockery, treacherous [2]283
mock-heroic [1]382, [2]499
mocking-bird [4]76
mock-logic [5]753
mock-modesty [2]527
"mode" [2]281, 789
mode(s) [4]355, 416, 437, [5]97, 542
model(s) [3]894, 900
directive [5]510; for mankind [2]206; of private prayer [5]512
moderates [3]166n
moderation [2]827, 1198
Modern Language Notes [2]17n
Modern Language Review [6]156, 158

modesty [1]330, [3]494, [4]489n, 654, 659, 665, 771
of elephants [4]489
Modiano, Raimonda, coeditor [2]533, 596, 600, 616, 623, 627, 639, 852, 988, 998, 1050, 1064, 1072, [3]75, 93, 115, 196, 236, 239, 241, 250, 252, 256, 263, 269, 304, 314, 316, 321, 338, 371, 789, 841, 846, 848, 864, 954, 995, 1013, 1049, [4]40, 122, 207, 213, 215, 261, 264, 270, 279, 313, 345, 360, 373, 393, 398, 402, 447, 463, 487, 504, 541, [5]87, 241, 255, 268, 307, 334, 352, 361, 691, 824, [6]125, 225
modifiability [1]597
modification(s) [1]595, 611, 614, [3]790, 855, 860, 861, [5]435, 443
modus [5]6
m. intuendi [5]734; *m. subsistendi* [5]20
möglich [2]202
Mogul [1]706
Mohammed *see* Mahomet
moisture [3]67
mola(s) [1]776, [5]468, 468n
mole (animal) [2]247, [3]172, 172n
m.-hill [3]920
mole (blemish) [5]416
Molière (Jean Baptiste Poquelin) (1622–73) [3]701n, [4]78
Tartuffe [1]402n
molluscae/molluscs [2]368, [3]1037, [5]257, 360
Molly the Maid (fiction) [5]83
Moloch (Bible) [1]449, 518, [3]699, 699n, [4]514
Molther, Philipp Heinrich (1714–80) [5]148
molybdoena [5]261
moment, distinguishable [5]385
monachor [4]190
monad(s)/monas [1]563n, 586n, 599, 599n, 643, 689, 689n, [2]425, 425n, 628n, [3]281, 282–3, 298, 328, 361–2, 362n, 865, 1052, 1054–5, [4]208–9, 413, [5]230–1, 410, 542, 733
monadology [3]283
monarch(s) [4]807, [5]38, 40, 530
Coronation oath of [1]864–5; French and Spanish [2]1101
monarchianism [1]249n
monarchist [3]883
monarchy/monarchies [2]950, [3]149, 419, 468, 573, 799, 803, [4]16, 79, [5]39, 39n, 42, 275n, 279, 659, 829
antiquity of [2]414; arbitrary [2]358; in England [2]68–9; feudal [2]57; limited [5]537; Messianic [4]246; papal [5]634
monastery/monasteries [1]522, [2]716, 733n, 982–4, [6]17 (“monastic”)
in Ireland [1]214; monastic life [3]310
monasticism [2]728n
Monck, Anne (née Clarges), Duchess of Albemarle (d 1670) [4]74
Monck, George, 1st Duke of Albemarle (1608–70) [1]255, 333, 333n, [2]817–18, 818n, [4]72
money/monies [2]160, 620–1, [3]5, 191, [4]862, [5]537, 686–7
m.-changers [2]486, [4]66; love of [1]184; paper [2]311n, 953, 953n, [5]276n; relative value of [2]64; represents labour [5]380; substance of [5]276; *see also* bullion
Money, William (fl 1815) [1]cxlin
mongers [3]988
Mongolia [2]528, 528n
Mongolian(s) [1]540, [3]356n, [5]253, 253n
mongrels [5]118
Monica, St (c 331–87) [2]823
monk(s) [1]870, [2]764, 770, [3]427n, 645, 754, 774
Carthusiasn [5]496; Egyptian [2]1041; m.-moral [5]605; red-hot [6]72; sullen [6]234; 13th-century [5]693n
monkery, popish [2]916
monkey(s) [2]263, [4]169
Monkhouse, John (1782–1866) [2]1118n
monkshood [6]103n
Monlucius *see* Montluc
Monmouth, Duke of *see* Scott, James
mono-dramatist [6]114
monogenes [2]798, 798n, 880, [3]16, 24
monogenesis [5]252n
monologue, dramatic [6]142
“mononomian” [5]588, 588n
monopoly [1]724, 724n, 763, 797, [2]674, [5]162
monotheism [1]587, [2]583n, 1106, [3]328, 328n, 649, [4]226
Arian [1]587
monotheist, Moses a [2]389
mons a non movendo [3]1037–8, 1038n, [5]99n
monster(s) [1]295, 368, [4]241, 732, 774
influence on B&F [1]398; moral [1]212, [4]75, 772; in Shakespeare [1]393; *see also* sea-monster
“monstrous” [5]250
monstrous, the [1]60
Montacute/Montagu, Catherine de (née de Grandison), Countess of Salisbury (d 1349 or 1354) [2]826n
Montagu, Basil (1770–1851) [1]xciii, xcvii,

cxi, 156n, 173n, 527, 761, [2]180, 1131, [3]10, 59, 191 ("Montagus")
owner of annotated books [2]808; supplier of books to C [2]804; *see also* F. Bacon *Works* ed Montagu
Montagu, Charles, 1st Earl of Halifax (1661–1715) [1]37, [2]79
Montagu, Edward, 1st Earl of Sandwich (1625–72) [4]72
Montagu, Edward, 2nd Earl of Manchester (1602–71) [1]255
Montagu, Elizabeth (née Robinson) (1720–1800) *Letters* [4]170
Montagu, Laura (née Rush) (d 1806) [2]968n, [3]59 ("Mrs Basil"), 191n ("Montagus")
Montagu, Richard, Bishop of Chichester and Norwich (1577–1641) [1]359, 359n, [2]260, 260n, 1100, 1103 ("Mountague")
Montague, old (*Romeo and Juliet*) [4]828
Montaigne, Michel Eyquem de (1533–92) [1]763, 763n, 796
Essays [1]lviii, 108 q, 108n–9n, [5]810, 810n
"Montalte, Louis de" *see* Pascal, Blaise
Montanists [2]712n, 713n
monte di pieta [4]628
Montesinos (*Don Quixote*) [3]207n
Montesquieu, Charles de Secondat, Baron de la Brède et de (1689–1755) [1]213
De l'esprit des lois [2]345 q
Montgolfier, Jacques Etienne (1745–99) [2]321n
Montgolfier, Joseph Michel (1740–1810) [2]321n
Montgomery [1]272
month, apocalyptic [6]294
Monthly Magazine [1]91n, 828, [2]351, [4]291n–2n, [5]191
Monthly Repository [3]673n
Monthly Review [1]91n, [3]209n
Montluc, Jean de, Bishop of Valence and Die (d 1579) [5]549n ("Monlicius")
Montrose, Marquis of *see* Graham, James
mood(s) [3]63, [4]795
dreamy [2]45; genial [2]119; Luther's [3]724; of mind [2]636
moods (of verb) [4]509
moon(s) [1]763, 797, [2]557, 887, 1160, [3]865–6, [4]73, 400, 501n, 513, [5]357, 359, 386, 426–7, [6]250
eclipsed [1]705; faces in [3]920; formation of [4]201–2, 202n, 517, 517n, [5]358; made of green cheese [4]16; of Jupiter [5]249; man in [5]712; motion of [5]351n; mountains of [4]508; news from [4]501, 502; Pythagorean [5]232; setting [2]87; and weather [5]359
"moonery" [5]296, 296n
moonshine [1]103, [2]440, 480, [5]295, 813
dial read by [2]561
Moor(s) [2]401, [4]861, 861n, [5]106n, 821, 831, 844
Moore, Edward (1712–57) [1]38
The Gamester [4]826, 826n
Moore, Frank Gardner (b 1865) *see* Livy tr Moore
Moore, Henry (fl 1667) [4]74
Moore, John (1729–1802) *Zeluco* [3]180, 180n
Moore, Sir John (1761–1809) [2]794
Moore, Thomas (1779–1852) [2]133, 900, 900n, [3]952, 952n
Life of Byron [5]866; *see also* Byron *Letters and Journals* ed Moore
Moore, William (fl 1810) [3]940, 941, 942
Moorman, Mary Caroline (née Trevelyan) (b 1905)
William Wordsworth, a Biography [1]37, 717 q, 760, [2]529n, [3]698n; *see also* WW *Letters; . . . the Middle Years* ed de Selincourt, rev Moorman
moral(s) [2]764, 926, [3]23, 253, 806, 810, [4]192, 663, 811, [5]41, 208, 229
change [2]692; Christian [2]320; common [5]226; history of [5]41; of Jacobean period [1]398; of Jesus [5]766; m. law *see* law; law of [1]166; Manichaean [3]625; and manners [3]679; party in [3]883; of people at large [5]512; m. philosophy *see* philosophy; principle in [1]874; prudential [2]1167; public [5]145, 315; science of [5]578; state of [5]415; Stoic [4]157; strict [4]657; sublime [6]264; m. worth [3]677
morale [5]176
moralising [4]238
moralism [5]163
moralist(s) [3]63, [4]310
Johnson as [2]76, 76n; national [2]72; shallow [2]184
morality [1]283, 815, [2]849, [3]31, 264, 722, [4]73, 109, 111, 220, 624, 640, [5]135, 369, 771, 866
affected [1]395; calculation of consequences as [1]223, 223n; Christian [5]67; code of [5]323; common [1]513; fragmentary [2]319; generalising [4]238; of the Gospel [1]429; ground of [4]78; Jesuit [3]768; Kantian [3]959; and law [2]529–30; lax [2]84;

morality—*continued*
motive to [3]737; outward [3]497; pagan [2]291; of a people [2]928; postulates of [5]457; practical [3]642; prudence substituted for [2]291; pure [5]618; relative [2]322; relaxed [2]700; and religion [5]822; religious [5]535; rule of [3]37; shallow [2]429; subversion of [4]626; system(s) of [4]280, 667
Morality (in Bunyan) [4]651n
Moravia [5]128
Moravian(s) [1]736, 736n, [2]496n, 717, 717n, [3]492–8, [4]281, 631, 640n, [5]81n, 124, 126, 127, 130, 130n, 131, 133, 148, 151, 153, 153n, 154, 156, 157, 181n
doctrine of [5]150; sexual practices of [5]151n. *See also* church(es): Moravian; Zinzendorf
morbus pediculosus [2]887n
mordaunt [2]496, [3]918
Mordecai (Bible) [1]844n, [2]894
More, Hannah (1745–1833) [1]736, *736n*, [3]507, 602, 602n, [4]549n
Coelebs in Search of a Wife [1]736n; *Strictures on the Modern System of Female Education* [1]736n
More, Henry ("Alazonomastix Philalethes") (1614–87) [1]lxxxix, cxliv, 353n, 358, 358n, 685n, [2]294n, 547n, 788n, 954n, [3]38, 38n, 920, 1067, 1074–5 q, [4]93, 389, 389n, [5]80, 81n, 82n
wronged by RS [3]1075
Antidote against Atheism [5]383, 383n; *Collection of Several Philosophical Writings* [4]93n; *Enchiridion ethicum* [1]clxv, [4]93, 93n; *Enchiridion metaphysicum* [4]93n; *Enthusiasmus triumphatus* [2]452n; *Explanation of the Grand Mystery of Godliness* [3]39n, [6]265; *Immortality of the Soul* [1]152n; *Observations upon "Anthroposophia Theomagica", and "Anima Magica Abscondita" by Alazonomastix Philalethes* [1]358n; MT [3]906–8; 915; *Philosophical Poems* [1]xcn, clin, [2]715n; MT [3]909–14; 919n; *Platonick Song of the Soul* [2]715, 715n, 909, 1076 q; *Psychodia Platonica* [3]906; *The Second Lash of Alazonomastix* [3]358n, 906; MT 915–17; *Song of the Soul* see *Platonick Song of the Soul*; *The Theological Works* [1]358n; MT [3]918–29
More, Sir Thomas (1478–1535) [1]213, 833, [2]528, [3]794, 795–6, [4]678, 678n, [5]392
Utopia [1]833, [2]766, tr G. Burnet [1]833n; *Works* ed Rastell [1]833n
Morea [4]184
Morell, Thomas (1703–84) [6]213; see also *Gradus ad Parnassum* ed Morell
Morgan family (John and Mary Morgan, and Charlotte Brent) [1]xcvin, xcvii, [2]668, 753, 1118n, [3]368n, 930n, [4]719n, [6]156, 158
letter to [2]686 q; marginalia addressed to [4]686, 721
Morgan, John James (d 1820) [1]xciv, xcvi, [2]587n, 1121, 1121n, [4]403, 403n, 684, 699n
annotator [1]373, [2]339; letter(s) to [1]cxi q, cxin, 240, [2]650n; marginalia associated with [1]37, 52; monogram [1]53; owner of annotated books [1]cxxii, 52, [2]526, [4]686, 721; relationship with C [1]*53*; supplier of books to C [1]cvi
Morgan, Mary (née Brent) (b 1782) [1]xcvi, 53, [2]242n, 1120n, 1121, 1121n, [3]682n, [4]403, 403n, 686, 692, 692n, 699n, 705n
"Morganwg, Iolo" *see* Williams, Edward
Moriah [2]836
Morians [1]708
Morley, Edith Julia (1875–1964) [2]180
The Life and Times of Henry Crabb Robinson [1]clxixn; *see also* H. C. Robinson *Blake, Coleridge, Wordsworth*, and *Henry Crabb Robinson on Books and Their Writers* ed Morley
Morley, George, Bishop of Winchester (1597–1684) [1]254, 255, 328
Mornay, Philippe de (1549–1623) [2]770n–1n
morning [1]515
Morning Chronicle [4]836n, [6]45, 45n
Morning Light [5]473
Morning Post [1]92n, 93n, 162n, [2]70n, 529n, 685, 820n, 846, 846n, 1121n, [3]882n, [4]18, [6]45, 45n
Morning Watch ed Tudor [2]46
Mornington, Earl of *see* Wellesley, William
moroc [4]87n
Morose (in Jonson) [3]180, 181, 182
morphe [2]1090, [5]470
m. amorphous [1]548
Morris, Brian Robert *see* Shakespeare *Taming of the Shrew* ed Morris
Morse, Samuel Finley Breese (1791–1872) *Academies of Arts* [4]6
Morshead, Sir Owen Frederick (1893–1977) [1]clxxiiin
mortality [3]317, 769
Morton, John, Archbishop of Canterbury (c 1420–1500) [1]291

Morton, John Maddison (1811–91) [2]75
Morton, Thomas (fl 1813) *An Essay on the Trinity* [2]359
Mosaic code *see* Moses
Moschus of Syracuse (fl c 150 BC) [2]55, 55n, [4]147
tr F. Fawkes [1]38
Moscow [2]1091n
Möser, Justus (1720–94) [1]5, 6n, [3]967
Brief an den Vikar in Savoyen [1]6n
Moses (Bible) [1]419, 419n, 420, 423, 456, 463n, 468, 475, 624, 669, 683, 705, 783, 785, 788n, 794, 794n, 807, 850n, [2]144, 144n, 145n, 150, 284, 285, 286, 287, 292, 378, 384n, 392, 394, 396, 396n, 399, 414, 419, 440, 467, 470, 480, 489, 679, 743, 786, 799, 807, 838, 838n, 893–4, 895n, 901, 1041, 1053, 1153, [3]33, 40, 40n, 53, 60, 105, 106, 109, 113, 113n, 446, 489, 519, 658–9, 738, 740, 767, 771, [4]47, 48, 173, 246n, 251, 296, 683, [5]54, 62, 64n, 364, 416, 417, 430, 465, 470, 567, 591, 591n, 635, 656, 775, [6]92, 105n, 110, 112, 144, 301
account of Deluge by [3]480; as author [2]397–8; author of Deut [1]422; not author of Gen [1]616; author of parts of Gen [1]783; beauty of [3]569; a better teacher [5]348; body of [3]535, 535n, 594n, [6]317, 317n; Books of [6]5; and burning bush [2]402; character of [3]698; Mosaic code [2]145–6, 501, [4]64; contemporaries of [2]385; cosmogony [2]346; Mosaic darkness [3]139, 1024; Mosaic dispensation [3]427; M.-face [3]735; far-sighted statesman [1]424; Mosaic law(s)/law(s) of [2]278, 383, 470, 471, 485, 495, 1106, [3]21, 53–5, 101, 112, 112n, 437n, 468, 737–41, [4]252, 651, [5]54, 504n, 535, 623, 624, 635; likeness to Christ [2]145; in love [2]384, 384n; miracles of [2]161, [3]987; negotiation with Pharoah [2]387; ordinances of [5]393; Mosaic records [3]355–6, 356n; religion of [4]625; rites of [5]641; rod of [1]822; time of [3]473; vast mind of [2]147; veil of [2]138, 138n; zealous monotheist [2]389
Moses, Anne [5]499
Moses, John [5]499
Moses, Matthew [5]499
Mosheim, Johann Lorenz von (1694–1755) [2]698, [3]138n, 671 q, 671n
Ecclesiastical History tr Maclaine [3]73n, [5]127n q
moss(es) [3]342, [4]278
moss-rose [2]95, 1013, 1013n, [5]363
"motes" [5]233, 233n
moth [2]568, 568n
mother (matrix) [1]628, 635, 637, 641, 647, 651, 652, 661–2, 664–5, 666, 692; *see also* matrix
mother(s) (parent) [3]329n, [4]335, 654, 829, [5]367
and babe [1]289; and child [2]658, 922; Church [5]510, 510n; Church as [5]543; eternal [1]652; of famous men [4]477; and father *see* father; Great [3]448n; Holy [2]1201; immaculate [1]506; informs against child [1]501; m.-marks [3]131n, 392; maternal impressions [3]392n; pride of [2]70; m.-spots [1]229n; m.-tongue [3]318, [4]282; m.-waters [4]488
motion(s) [1]868, [2]789, 807, 889, 1008, [3]273, 274–5, 275n, 281–2, [3]299–300, 301–2, [4]92, 389, 430, 445, 460, [5]267, 430, 457, 704, 708, 711, 720, [6]151, 170
formative [1]525; influx of [3]249; line of [2]865; mechanic [5]615; muscular [5]6; picturesque [5]825; progressive [5]712; thousandfold [5]133
motive(s) [1]361, [2]1005, 1106, 1180, [3]54, 63–4, 63n, 602n, [4]606, [5]177, 605, 828, [6]56
of abhorrence [4]728; chain of [3]423; Christian [6]55; defined [4]436; m.-hunting [4]862; m.-mongering [4]855; m.-mongers [3]602; m.-seeking [4]440; selfish [4]551
motivity [5]267
motivo [6]6, 6n
motors, supersensual [1]525
motory [1]626, 626n
Motte, Mellish Irving (1801–81) [2]20
motto [2]338, 809, [3]189
m.-manist [1]lxvi
mottophilist [1]lxvi
mould(s) [1]683, 683n, [4]322
of man [1]151
moulder [2]1148
mouldings [5]272
Moulin, Pierre du (1601–84) [1]335
Moultrie, John (1799–1874) [1]cln
Mount, Jehovah on [2]489
Mount of Piety [4]628n
Mount, Sermon on the *see* Jesus Christ: Sermon on the Mount
Mountague, Richard *see* Montagu, Richard
mountain(s) [2]372, 691, 1070, [3]334, 478, 644, 859, 1038n, [4]278, 526, [5]249, 348, 456, [6]249
dark [1]822; m. districts [2]1017; formation of

mountain(s)—*continued*
[1]664; m.-goat [4]535; highest [5]386, 387, 387n; and molehill [2]498; of moon [5]232; Old Man of the [5]143, 143n; origin of [5]340; m.-rats [5]686; in Sicily [5]359
mountebank(s) [3]1014, [4]26, 646–7
mouse [1]325, [2]933, [3]334
blind [2]498; m.-trap [3]177n
mouth [1]608, 657
ecstatic [5]84
mouton [5]280
mover
first [3]347n; prime [4]815, [5]457n
Mowbray (*Richard II*) [4]796, 797, 799
moxa [1]786
Moxon, Edward (1801–58) [1]clxii, clxiin, [3]507
Sonnets [1]clxv
Moxon, Emma (née Isola) (d 1891) [1]clxii
Moyer, Samuel (d c 1683) [4]74
Moyles, R. G. *The Test of "Paradise Lost"* [3]890n
Mozambique [3]1081
Mozart, Constanze (née Weber) (1763–1842) [2]65n
mud [5]295
warm [5]811
Mudworth [3]104
Muggleton, Lodowick (1609–98) [3]991n
mugwort [1]786n
Muir, Kenneth (b 1907) *see* Shakespeare *Macbeth*, *King Lear* ed Muir
Muirhead, John Henry (1855–1940) *Coleridge as Philosopher* [1]555
mulatto(es) [1]383, [6]326, 326n
mule(s) [2]662, [3]47, 383, 676, 1044, 1044n, [4]811, [5]387, 652
Müller [2]759
Müller (probably Friedrich, 1749–1825) [1]828
Müller, Johannes von (1752–1809) *Geschichte der Schweizer* [4]226, 226n q
multeitas [1]622
"multeity" [1]152, 152n–3n, 304n
multeity [1]595, 622n, 679, 737, [2]58, 334, 792, 1186–7, [3]1024, [4]381, *381n–2n*, 454, 491, [5]231, [6]227
and unity [5]266; in unity [1]595
multiformity [4]783
multiplication [3]807, [5]487
multiplication table [2]281
multiplicity and unity [2]884
multiscience [2]999n
"multisciolous" [2]999, 999n
multitude [1]788, [5]32
"multivocal" [2]1150, 1150n
multivocal [2]758
Mumbo-Jumbo [5]83, 83n
mummery/mummeries [1]702, 719, 863, [2]737, 1097, 1158
mumpsimus [1]260, 260n, [2]827, 935, 935n, [3]26, 26n, 257, 257n, 438, 439n
Munby, Alan Noel Latimer (1913–74) "The Sales of William Pickering's Publications" [1]clxiin
mundus [2]684, 684n, [5]456n
m. sensibilis [3]278, 285, 285n
Mundy [3]1073n
Mungo (in Bickerstaffe) [2]428, 428n
Munich [2]1086n
Münster [4]28, 28n, [5]501, 501n
Congress of [3]993; convocation at [3]759 ("Muntzer")
Munster, Earl of *see* Fitzclarence, George Augustus Frederick
muo [1]472, 472n
Muratorius (Lodovico Antonio Muratori) (1672–1750) *Annali d'Italia* [2]472, [3]251n
murder [1]166, 342–3, 822, 877, [3]824, 1081, [4]237–41, 662, [5]103
licence for [2]908; pulpit [3]819; of Servetus [4]670
murderer(s) [2]970
first [6]325
murdering [5]276
Murdockson, Meg (in Scott) [4]589, 589n
muriatic acid *see* acid(s)
muriatic acid gas *see* gas(es)
Murphy, Arthur (1727–1805) [4]581
The Citizen [4]581n
Murray, Charles (1754–1821) [6]270
Murray, Sir George (d 1846) [6]28n
Murray, Sir John (1718–77) [5]316, 316n
Murray, John (1778–1843) [1]122, 131, 542, 802, 855, [2]86, 794, 840n, 977, 979n, 1178n, 1189, [3]514, [6]296
and Asgill project [1]lxv; debt to [3]1049, 1049n; and *Faust* project [1]cvii; letter(s) to [1]511 q, 831, [2]804 q, 824n q, [5]239; supplier of books to C [3]537
Murray, John (d 1820) [3]941, 942
Murray, Lindley (1745–1826) [5]502, 502n
Murray, William, 1st Earl of Mansfield (1705–93) [3]501, 501n
"murthero-maniacal" [4]238, 238n
Murthwaite, Mr [3]978
Musaeus (5th–6th century) [4]147
tr F. Fawkes [1]38

muscles [2]539, 1003, [4]149, 542, [5]260
of motion [6]126
Muscogulges [1]226
Muscovites [3]820
Muse(s) (myth) [4]610, 610n, [5]859
fountain of the [5]528n; Historic [2]831
Musenalmanach ed Bürger [4]466n
museum [1]763, 797, [2]1181, [3]629
Museum der Alterthum-Wissenschaft ed F. A. Wolf and Buttmann [1]584n
mushroom(s) [4]665, [5]495, [6]64
music [1]735, [3]496, 945, 993, [4]53, 168, 679, 844, 860, [5]294–5, 296
appropriate [3]651; Chinese [4]511; musical glasses [3]43, 43n; Greek [4]511; of the heart [1]325; Italian [2]978n; luminous [4]313n; musical notes [3]815; potentiality of [5]591; between sense and sensuality [2]65; in sonnet [3]902–3; words and [2]413
musician [3]248, [5]728
musk [1]228, [2]1066, [3]125–6, 126n, 586
musketeers [3]165
Muslims, conversion of [2]740n
Musophilus (in S. Daniel) [2]15
Mussolini, Cesare (fl 1794–1800) *Italian Exercises* MT [3]930–1
"must" [5]705
mustard seed [4]668
muster [5]380, 380n
m.-roll [5]639
mutes [4]165
mutilation [5]544
mutton [2]1006n, [4]695, 695n, [5]249
leg of [1]336
Mycone [5]836
"myriad-minded" [4]697n, 766n
myrionous [2]11, [4]766n
myriotheism [2]924
Myrmidons [4]812
myrtle [3]889
Mysore [2]339, [4]85n
mystae/mystai [2]575, 824, [5]123, 123n, [6]7
mysterion [1]471–2, 471n, 472n, 490n
"mystery" [1]490, 490n, [4]407, 407n, [5]398, 398n, 566, 795
mystery/mysteries [1]201, 237, 471, 782, [2]249, 508, 658, 659, 676, 735, 1038, 1150, 1187n, [3]24, 49, 61, 102, 467, 560, 878, [4]267, 269, 305, 346, 407, 453, 492, 512–13, 528, 636, 665, [5]26, 27, 32, 56, 60, 135, 152, 201, 297, 594, 615, 628, 658, 767, 842
abysmal [1]693; mysterious acts [3]757; adorable [2]263; ancient [5]295; aweful [1]568; Cabiric [6]5; Christian [2]671, [4]46n; of Christianity [1]313, [5]82; of darkness [1]518, [2]891; of Devil [2]1109n; Eleusinian [1]237n ("rites"), 472, 598n, 639, 639n, 665, 665n, *see also* Samothracian *below*; of evil [5]424; explaining away [5]546; of faith [2]1151; fundamental [1]464; heavenly [2]564; heralds of [5]535, 535n; higher [1]312; highest [1]543; of human nature [3]266; of an I AM [5]616; indispensable to morality [3]31; ineffable [1]605; love of [1]746; of love [3]591; of m. [3]12; m. in [4]436; m.-solving [3]328; prevailing indifference to [2]1175; of regeneration [3]427; sacred [3]709; Samothracian [1]472, 659, 660n, [2]573–85, [3]399n, 473, 682, 683n, [4]37n, 424n, 594n, 595n, [5]153n, [6]5n, *see also* Cabiri, Samothrace; Scriptural [1]358; spiritual [5]599, 673; sublime [2]1062; supreme [4]257; of theism [3]86; of Trinity [1]782, [5]59; of tri-unity [2]741; union of [3]311–12
"mystic" [1]472
mystic(s) [1]341, 561n, [3]564n, 682, [4]226, 259, 259n, 654, [5]123, 153n, [6]318
attainments of [5]796; Christian [5]796; Persian [2]597
mysticism [1]472n, 509, 560n, 669n, [2]615n, [3]82, 560–1, [4]226n, 443, [5]285, 291n, 516n, 743n, 794–5, 795n
medieval [5]795n; uncouth [4]443
myth [1]587, [2]1106, [3]1066, [5]248n
of Adam's rib [1]684; and allegory [1]812n; of Cain and Abel [2]177, 177n; Greek [5]528n; mythic history [3]105; mythical poesy [1]432; of serpent [1]684–5; of Shem, Ham, Japheth [2]177, 177n
mythologist [2]579
mythology/mythologies [2]582, 1012, [3]474, [4]504, 507, [5]594, 644
Egyptian [3]92n; Greek [1]472, [2]344, [3]92n, 473, [5]347n; Greek and Roman [1]543; heathen and Christian [1]543n; national [4]594n; pagan [2]234; Persian [3]92n
mythos/*mythus* [2]585, [3]436, [4]192, [5]336, 603
of Fall [3]473; Greek [2]584–5; Platonic [5]166
mythosophisch [4]504, 504n

n [2]1089–90, 1089n–90n
Naaman (Bible) [1]832n
Nabi [2]373; *see also* prophets
nadir [2]327, [4]167, [5]41
naevus [1]228, 229n
Nahrungsmittel [3]128, 128n

naiad [3]231
nail(s) [1]617, 764, 797, [2]822, [4]461
nain see *ayin*
"name" [1]471, 471n, [4]186, 186n
name(s) [2]673, 961, [3]13, 43, 135–6, 135n, 715–16, 976
abstract [5]757; appellative [2]674, 674n; of Christ [1]428, [5]637; C's "Samuel" [3]165, 165n; cosmogonical [2]577; double [5]402n; forgotten [5]467; of God *see* God, name of; holy [5]31n; humour in [2]1126; incommunicable [3]30; Jehovah Word as [3]102; meaning in scripture [1]713; new-naming [2]1002; and *nomen* [1]787; and *numen*, [2]915, 915n; and power [5]11, 11n, 31, 31n, 653, 653n; proper [3]517, [4]421, [5]173, [6]299; question of [5]508; in science [3]1043; symbolic(al) [3]422, [5]698; tender [2]636; see also *nomen*
napellus [6]103, 103n
Naphtali (Bible) [2]834
Naples [2]417, [4]86n, 191, 339, 343, [5]39n, 276n, 279, 834
Phlegraean Fields [1]449, 449n
Napoleon I, Emperor of France (Napoleon Bonaparte/Buonaparte) (1769–1821) [1]60n, 292n, 419n, 656, 656n, 771n, 850n, [2]159, 400, 846, 846n, 848, [3]132, 160, 160n, 188, 188n, 785, 785n, 851, 852n, 884, 920, [4]62, 171, 735, 817, [5]309n, 312, 312n, 379n
paltry Corsican [1]715; unification of Europe [2]619n
Codice di Napoleone MT [3]932–3
Narasingha (myth) [2]346
Narcissus (myth) [1]149
narcotic(s) [3]397, 750, [4]323–4, 323n, 325, [5]529, [6]103
narration(s) [4]499, 780, 840, 863, [5]14, 689
enigmatic [1]423; historical [5]560; inartificial [4]472; in RS's sphere [4]171; verity of [5]513
narrative(s) [4]475, 478, [5]630
associated with heroic ages [1]422, 423; in dialogue [3]813; epic [4]848; historical [3]422; motley [5]153; unconnected [4]471
narrators
original [1]456; veracity of [5]513
narrow-mindedness [1]821
Naseby [4]590, 590n
Battle of [2]948n, 1196n
nashku bar [1]427
naso-ductility [1]332
Nassau, Duke of *see* Friedrich Wilhelm
Nasse, Christian Friedrich (1778–1851) see *Archiv für den thierischen Magnetismus* ed Eschenmayer, Kieser, and Nasse
Natal [4]334
Nathan (Bible) [3]606
Nathan (in Lessing) [3]217, 699, 699n
Nathan ben Kalymos, Isaac (fl early 15th century) [2]314n
Nathanael/Nathaniel (Bible) [2]37, 37n, [4]682, 682n, [6]170, 170n
nation(s) [1]865, [2]899, 1192, [3]50, 53, 152, 478, 755, 801, [4]819, [5]40, 282, 638, 644, [6]11
authority of [6]23; constitution of [3]112; *corpus politicum* [6]60; corrupt [2]818; desire of [3]738; dominated by commerce [5]428; European [5]101; French [5]273; Gentile [3]34; Grand [4]193; Hebrew [2]421; idea of [3]157–8, 158n; idolatrous [6]141; Jewish [1]695, [3]465, [4]637; king represents [2]114; mind of [5]299–300; nationalist [3]165; origin of [4]257n; and people [2]943; power and right of [1]864–5; power of [1]728; not a property [1]424; teach all n. [2]154; will of [1]338, 866
national debt *see* debt
nationality
antipathies of [2]163; loss of [2]147
"nationalty" [6]22, 22n
nationalty [1]739n, [2]72, 80, 80n, 294, 937, [3]51, 51n
natives [1]383, [3]883
Nativity [3]30n, [5]662
natura [3]520n, [6]302n
n. gemina [5]444; *n. naturans* [1]537n, [2]602, 602n, [5]715; *n. naturata* [1]537n; *n. naturans* and *n. naturata* [4]324, 324n, [5]203, 203n, 512n, 826n
"natural" [4]779
natural, the [4]599
natural history [1]426, 536, [2]165, [5]289
natural philosophy [1]774, [2]727, [6]99; see also *Naturphilosophie*
natural religion *see* religion
naturalism [3]205, [4]499
naturalist(s) [1]495, 539, [2]824, [3]612, 1080, [4]161, 530, [5]133, 253, 517, 716, [6]132
English [4]499; German [2]860, [3]1043; inferior [6]96; philosophic [4]492; philosophising [1]654; sentimental [3]1080
"nature" [1]113, 180, [2]1150, [3]64, 424n, 520n, [4]110, 110n, 512, [5]175, 613, [6]302n
nature [2]176, 632, 863n, [3]334, 721n, 841, 985, [5]7, 162, 213, [6]51
absolute [5]356n; not absolute [4]381–2,

381n, 382n; active powers in [5]451; acts of [1]612; all reason above it [3]746; and art [2]1052; ascent of [1]299; beauty in [5]363; blindly wise [1]653; Böhme on [1]604; book of [1]747, [3]919; Browne and [1]763; as bullion [3]984; HC as child of [1]42; compass of *see* compass of nature; construction of [5]715n; continuity of production in [1]536–7; contradicted [5]272; converted [1]656; convulsed [4]824; copy of [1]384; corrupt [2]1109, [3]878, 879, [5]604; corrupted [5]588; corruption of [5]594; course of [6]118, 134; cube of [1]663; definition of [1]113, [3]943–4, [6]134; of deity [5]718; depravation of [2]1164; descent of [4]524–5; descriptions of [6]162; desires against [1]42, 42n; detachment from [3]417, 919, [4]524n; divine [1]434, 564, 690, 691, [2]671, [3]709–10, 944, [5]27, 716; dynamic [4]324; efficient causes in [5]701; effort of [5]310; encroachments of [3]137; evil [3]447, [5]616; external [4]385; facts in [3]60; facts of [5]782, 795; faith of [2]547; fidelity to [4]779; flashes of [4]808; forms of [1]558; fulfilment of [3]482; geneic [2]431; genial [5]681; and God *see* God, and nature; godhead in [3]59; gossiping with [5]319; ground of [5]814; happy [5]512; high road of [4]731; hint of [2]983; horror of vacuum in [4]288, 288n; human *see* human nature; of "I" [5]172; idea of [5]450; imperfect world of [2]1021; impersonal absolute [6]5; infant of [1]776; inorganic [5]453; natural instinct [3]99; and intelligence [4]451; as language [3]279; language of [1]602, 607, 628, 630, [5]467; law(s) of [2]202, 633, 1144, [4]379, [5]383; life of [5]336, 715; light as heart of [1]623; light of [2]786–7; no light of [2]298; Lord of [1]597; and man *see* man, and nature; in man [3]478, [5]600; of man [1]812; march of [3]417; material [4]668; mere [5]590; natural in [5]93; n.-man [2]388, 388n; need for negative principle [1]667; negative unity in [5]452; neither first nor last in [3]423, 424; objective [5]415, [6]132; observer of [2]164; Oken's theory of [2]1007n; opposite of deity [5]453; opposites of [6]228; organic [2]995n; phaenomena of [6]314; philosophy of [3]299, see also *Naturphilosophie*; poles of [3]1021n, [4]395–6; power in [1]589; in power of will [2]825; powers of [2]347; pre-impregnated [1]602; prophecies of [3]704; prostituted [3]907; reactions in [4]149; real [2]1019; natural reason [3]509; representation of [3]301; revolves [1]643; rights of [4]23; romance of [2]1119; Schelling's concept of [4]373–90, [6]236–7; scheme of [3]920; science of [3]299; sensual [5]474; and Shakespeare [4]817; solution of [1]661; as sphere [5]600; and spirit [2]1014–15, 1019–20; spirit of [4]420; not a state [2]675; subject to reason [5]318; substantive [3]1004; supersensual [5]474; suspension of laws of [5]65; sympathies of [4]809, 810; terror of [1]284; theory of [4]448; of things [1]573; torn asunder from [4]729; truth of [4]787; truth to [4]784; ultimates of [5]790; unity of [1]639, [2]634; voice of [6]328; wild [5]390; a will [3]525; and will [5]784, [6]309; in will [1]812; wisdom of [2]345; words of [3]522; and world [4]362; worship of [2]583

nature-philosophers [3]909; see also *Naturphilosoph/Naturphilosophen*

Naturgeist [4]420n

natürlich [3]81

Naturphilosoph/Naturphilosophen [1]696, 696n, [2]539, *539n*, 554n, 860n, 995n, 1156n, [3]127n, 393, 393n, 518n, 842, 842n, 949, 996n, 997n, 1017n, 1021n, 1037, [4]274n, 319, 319n, 366n, 371n, 387n, 395, 395n, 420n, 424, 424n, 523, [5]94n, 228n, 297, 349n, 358n, 428n, 445n, [6]300n

C's objections to [4]316n; error(s) of [2]853–7, 853n, 1002, [5]357; superior airs of [4]372; vanity of [3]1017; *see also* nature-philosophers

Naturphilosophie/Nature-philosophy [1]547n, 556, 584n, 588n, 602n, 696n, [2]533, *539n*, 853n, 863n, 1000, 1000n, 1007n, 1066, [3]61n, 123, 139n, 292n, 317n, 327n, 598n, 715, 867, 873, 943, 944n, 949n, 950n, 951n, 995–1012, 1019–48, 1050n, 1051n, [4]275n, 315n, 327n, 328n, 345, 350, 356, 360n, 373–90, 381n, 391–7, 394n, 420, 420n, 421n, 423–4, 487n, 504, 523n–4n, [5]241, 243, 243n, 258n, 261n, 264n, 265n, 327, 334n, 356n, 715, 715n, 719, 743, 809, [6]225, 230, 236, 238

C's attitude [1]clii; foundered [2]1024; fundamental falsity of [3]1055; poetic [2]863; *see also* polarity

Nauck, August (1822–92) *Tragicorum graecorum fragmenta* [5]866n

navy [5]194, 396

British [2]620

Navy List [4]534n

Naylor, James (1617–60) [4]182

Nazarenes [2]437, 437n, [4]248, 249, 250, 251

Nazareth [1]48n, [4]54–5
Nazarite(s) [2]833, [3]52
Nazianzen *see* Gregory of Nazianzus
ne plus ultra [1]356
ne quid nimis [3]225
Neaera *see* Nerissa
Neal, Daniel (1678–1743) *History of the Puritans* ed E. Parsons [4]170, 171, 177
near-sightedness [5]268
"'neath" [4]151, 151n
neatness [4]278
Nebrio [5]836
Nebuchadnezzar, King of Babylon ("Nebuchadrezzar") (604–561 BC) [2]570n, 574n, 849, 893–4, [3]419n, 462, 465, 478–9, [6]217
nebulae [2]557
"necessary" [5]567
necessary, conditional [5]276
necessitarian(s) [2]614, 801, [3]63n, [4]280
 modern [3]737, 737n; n. debates [3]602n
necessitarianism [2]801
necessity [2]249, 261, 603, 665, [3]81, 137, 737, 969, [4]107, 109, 436, 638, [5]10, 614, 828
 blank [5]615; and compulsion [2]641; eternal [5]424; formal [5]455; and freedom *see* freedom; and liberty [1]827; moral [5]273; physical [3]806; political [5]273; of reason [3]332; slave of [1]172; subjective [1]537; two classes of [5]208
Necho II, Pharoah (fl 609–594 BC) [3]470n
neck, crick in [5]295
necromancers [3]212
necrosis [4]77
nectar [2]167
Ned (in Brooke) [1]730
needful, the [4]604
needle, magnetic [3]1062, [5]266–7
needlepoint [5]444
negation(s) [1]238, 563, 574, 685, 685n, [2]170, 170n, 218, 306, 425, 559, 559n, 995, 996, [3]85, 357, 363, 1053, [4]443, 444n, [5]29, 202, 204, 459, 729, 751
 bodily [1]393; darkness of [5]595; of denial [2]644; of motion [4]430; and position [5]815; and privation [2]671, 671n; of space [3]357; of will [6]300
negative(s) [1]594, [4]301, 706, [5]159, 557
 and affirmative [5]413; double [5]131; needed in nature [1]667; and positive [1]161, 238, 395–6, 562, 594, 640, 645, 650, 662–3, [3]43, 139, 1060, [4]171, 385, 429–30, 542, [5]157, 277, 347, 347n, 348, 448, 452, 559, 648, 752, 797, [6]79, 228, 231; two [2]796
negativity of evil [2]199
negligence [5]383
negro(es) [2]801, [3]355, [4]201, 861, [5]187, [6]326, 326n
 African [5]352; cargo of [4]96; as degenerous race [1]540; quasi-Negroes [3]658; state of [3]1082
Nehemiah (Bible) [1]844n, [2]377, 383n, 894, [5]807, 807n
neighbour(s) [2]322, 888
 good [4]595; love of [5]471, 562; violated [1]874
Neigung [3]963
Neithe (myth) [3]92 ("Nëith"), 92n
Nelson, Horatio (1758–1805) [1]176, 177n
Nelson, John (1707–74) [5]163, 164
Nemesius of Emesa (fl 390) [1]58
 Cyril of Jerusalem and Nemesius of Emesa ed Telfer [3]934; *De natura hominis* ed Valla [3]934; MT [3]934–5
Nennius (fl 769) [2]1170n
neo-Kantians [2]594, 623n
neologism [5]481
"neologist(s)" [1]305, 306n
neologist(s) [3]3n
 neologic divines [4]41n; German [2]736, 736n, [3]420, 420n; neological school [2]481n
neology [2]442
"neoplatonic" [1]296n
neoplatonic(s) [4]421n
 doctrine [3]755n; emanation theory [3]949n; errors [5]761
"neoplatonism" [1]296n
neoplatonism [1]115n, 298n–9n, 656n, 719n, [5]82n
"neoplatonist" [1]296n
neoplatonist(s) [1]lxx, 296, 586n, 645n, [2]726, 726n, 889n, [3]909n, [4]259n, [5]12, 226, 740n, 743, 746
 interpretation of Plato [1]573n
neopythagoreans, maxims of [3]539n
nepenthe [3]553
nepios [1]245, 245n
nepotism [5]49
Neptune (dog) [4]73
Neptune (myth) [1]639, [3]413, [5]7, [6]202
Neptunism [3]60n
Neptunists [1]664n
Nerissa (*Merchant of Venice*) [4]780 ("Neaera"), 780n
Nero (Nero Claudius Caesar) (37–68) [1]482, 486n, 753, 832n, [2]126n, 509n, 515n, 706,

949, [3]7n, 505, 922, 922n, 929n, [4]627n, [5]85n, 202, 636, 829, 829n
Nerva, Marcus Cocceius (c 32–98) [2]692
nerve(s) [1]671, [3]84, 325, 372n, 380, 380n, 382, 384, 1036, 1037, [4]109n, 164, 389, 448, [5]137, 165, 260, 280, 289–90, [6]66
abdominal [5]136; animal matter of [1]666; auditory [4]638; n.-ether [4]493–4, 494n; excited state of [2]403; excitement of [5]444; factual [5]168; nervous fevers [4]149; ganglia [2]859, 860; generate heat [1]623–4, 624n; hardihood [2]700; and heart [1]577; n.-knots [5]260; olfactory [5]293; optic [4]83; principles of [1]590; of sensation [6]126; sphere of [3]380, 380n; sympathetic [3]381, 381n; weakness of [1]813
nervous system(s) [1]671, [2]402, 704, 728, 768, [3]21, 126, [4]263, 500, [5]171, 180, 183, 759, [6]103, 120
Nesbitt, Fanny (fl 1793) [2]95–6, *95n*
nest [3]129, 1074
Nestor (*Troilus and Cressida*) [4]810
Nestorians [2]659
Nestorius (d c 451) [2]661, [3]369, 369n
net [4]835, [5]588
Nether Stowey [1]lxxix, lxxxiv, lxxxv, cv, cvi, cviii, cxi, [2]97, 170, 797, 820n, 1110, 1191, [4]312, 837, 837n, [5]382, [6]266
Stowey Book Society [1]lxxxv, cv
Netherlands [2]163, 163n, [3]978
nettles [3]819
Neumegen, Leopold (d 1875) [2]1189
"neuropathology" [6]100, 100n
neurosphere [3]383n, 384, 387n, 389, 390, 390n
Neuser, Adam (d 1576) [3]683n
Neville, Charles, 6th Earl of Westmorland (1543–1601) [3]144n
Neville, Richard, 16th Earl of Warwick and Salisbury (1428–71) [2]101
Neville, Richard Griffin, 3rd Baron Braybrooke (1783–1853) *see* Pepys *Memoirs* ed Braybrooke
Nevis [1]90n
"new birth" [5]125, 125n
new birth [3]60, [4]636, [5]129, 191, 466, 608
New Cambridge Bibliography of English Literature [1]clin
New Church *see* Swedenborg: New Church
New England [2]522, 1174, [3]816–26, 884
New English Bible *see* Bible: *NEB*
New Evangelical Magazine [3]309n
New France [3]884
New Haven CT
Yale University, Beinecke Library, marginalia in [1]clxiii, clxix, clxxiv, 88, 409, [2]213, 1105, [3]503, 715, [5]486
New Holland [2]74, 74n, [3]1074; *see also* Australia
New Jerusalem [2]199, [3]432, 432n, 510, 521, 983
New Jerusalem Church *see* Swedenborg: New Church
A New Method of Learning with Facility the Greek Tongue [3]828, 828n
A New System of Practical Domestic Economy [2]616n
New York City [1]xci, clxv–clxvi, [2]525, 593, 791, [4]105, 207
Bartlett and Welford (booksellers) [1]clxii, [2]593, 791, 842; Columbia College [4]6; Columbia University Library, marginalia in [1]clxvi, [3]93; Dibdin Club [1]clxiiin; New York Public Library (Berg Collection) [1]clxxiv, [2]967, marginalia in [1]clxi, clxvi, clxviii, 116, 414, 760, 816, [2]573, 1032, [3]841, [4]18, 203, [5]108, 222, transcripts of marginalia in [1]414, Rare Book Room, marginalia in [3]132, transcript of marginalia in [3]132; Parke-Bernet [1]118, 715, [2]525, 963, [3]804, [5]479, [6]265; Pierpont Morgan Library [1]501, [2]166n, marginalia in [1]155, 718, 870, [5]818, 866; Scribner and Welford (booksellers) [1]clxv, clxvi
New Zealand [2]73
Newark [2]357
new-birthites [4]640
Newborough, Lord *see* Livingstone, James
new-broom [2]980
new-broomers [2]979
Newburgh, Earl of *see* Livingstone, James
Newcastle [2]1197n
Newcastle, Duke of *see* Cavendish, William
Newcome, William, Archbishop of Armagh (1729–1800)
Attempt Towards Revising Our English Translation of the Greek Scriptures [2]482n; *Historical View of the English Biblical Translations* [2]482n
Newcomen, Matthew (?1610–69) [1]259
Newes from Turkie [2]111
Newgate *see* London
Newgate Calendar [4]241, 241n, 658, 658n
Newlands [1]cx
new-light men [2]788

Newman, John Henry, Cardinal (1801–90) [1]306n
new-naming [5]350
Newport, Treaty of [1]290n, 353n, [3]801n
news [5]51
newspaper(s) [1]164, [2]118, 459, [3]227, 418, 987, [4]185, [5]644
Newton, Alfred Edward (1864–1940) [4]237
Newton, Sir Isaac (1642–1727) [1]107 q, 153n, 177n, 182n, 184, 184n, 198n, 569n, [2]788, 869, 889, [3]133, 324, 426, 426n, 946n, [4]187, 271n, 305, 313n, 365, 377, 581, 581n, [5]327, 382n, 452 ("Newtonian"), 564n, 825n, [6]52
  attacked [2]787n; and calculus [1]4, 5n; on colour [3]1018n, [4]209n; discoveries of [5]564; error(s) of [1]108, [3]286, 286n; on gravity [3]139n, [5]351n; on Greek article [1]489–90 q; inferior to Shakespeare [3]342, 342n; last years of [3]324; and Leibniz [1]74n; on light [3]944; Newtonian mechanism [3]325n; optics [2]610, 613, [3]1013–14, 1014n, 1018; polarity in [1]660; Newtonian scheme [5]560; a Socinian [1]197, 197n; Newtonian system [2]668, 668n, [4]20; Newtonian theory [3]61n; a male-virgin [1]658
  Observations on the Prophecies of Holy Writ [2]382, 382n; *Principia mathematica* [1]739, [3]285 q, 1010n, [4]304, [5]382; *Works* ed Horsley [2]382n
Newton, John (1725–1807) [4]650
Newton, Thomas, Bishop of Bristol (1704–82) *see* Milton *Paradise Lost* ed Newton
Newton, Thomas (d 1843) [1]615, 615n
  Illustrations of Sir Isaac Newton's Method of Reasoning [1]615n; *Treatise on Conic Sections* [1]615n
Newtonians [1]862, [5]720
New-York Mirror [4]161
nexus [4]317
ngang see *ayin*
Niagara [1]810, [4]408
nibble [1]325
Nic. Sr. *see* Nick, Old
Nicaea/Nice, Council of [2]32n, 442, 726n, 730n, 731n, 732n, 740, 741n, 1149, [3]235n, 692n, 761–2, 761n–2n, [5]50n, 558, 578, 620n, 626
  Nicene doctrine [2]33–4, 33n; *see also* Creed, Nicene
Nicaria [5]837
Nice (in Thrace), Synod of [2]732n, [3]145n, [5]633n
Nicephorus (legend) [2]724n
Nicetas Acominatus (Choniates) (d c 1220) [2]660
Nicholas I, Emperor of Russia (1796–1855) [1]32, 32n
Nicholas Senior *see* Nick, Old
Nichols, John (1745–1826) [2]805; *see also* Hogarth *Genuine Works* ed Nichols and Steevens
Nicholson, William (1753–1815) ed *A Journal of Natural Philosophy, Chemistry, and the Arts* [1]lxxviiin; MT [3]936–53; 1033n q, [5]82, 82n, 344, 346n, 771n
Nicholson's Journal see Nicholson, William
nichtig [5]370
nichts [6]243, 244
nick-names [4]842
nick-naming [6]243
Nick, Old ("Nic") [1]32n, 484 ("Nicholas"), 484n, 873, 873n, [3]926, 926n, 955, 955n, 963, 973, [5]83, 83n
Niclaes, Hendrik (c 1502–c 1580) [2]327n, [3]926, 926n, 927
Nicodemus (Bible) [1]202n, [2]256, 319, 321, 1085n, 1087–8, [3]427, 664–5, [4]641, [5]157, 192, 193, 583n
Nicolai, Christoph Friedrich (1733–1811) [1]3, [3]207, 656, 657, 657n, 706, [5]582n
  misunderstood Kant [3]248n
  ed *Briefe, die neueste Litteratur betreffend* [1]297, 297n; *Ueber meine gelehrte Bildung* MT [3]965–73
Nicolaitans [2]505, 506, [5]624, [6]59
Nicolas (Bible) [2]506n
Nicolas, Henry (1502–80) [3]927, 928
Nicole, Pierre ("Guillaume Wendrock") (1625–95) *see* Pascal *Les provinciales* ed Wendrock, Cordero, and Brunetti
Nicoll, Allardyce (1894–1976) *see* Homer: *Chapman's Homer* ed Nicoll
Nicolson, Joseph (fl 1762), and Richard Burn
  The History and Antiquities of the Counties of Westmorland and Cumberland Copy A [1]lxxxiii; MT [3]974–9; *Copy B* MT [3]980–2
Nicolson, William, Bishop of Carlisle (1655–1727) [2]815–16, 816n, [3]978
  Historical Library [2]816n
Nicomedia [5]626
Nicostratus [4]147
Nidecker, Heinrich Albert (b 1894) [1]clin, clii
Niebuhr, Barthold Georg (1776–1831) *History of Rome* [2]781n

Nieto, David (1654–1728) [1]113, 113n
night(s) [1]119, 515, 576, [5]264
  Attic [5]531, 531n; Böhme on [1]606; handmaid to day [1]685; of the senses [5]795
nightingale(s) [1]47, 47n, [3]516n, [4]529–30, [5]770n
  Spartan's comment on [3]389n
nightmare ("night-mair") [1]370, [3]215, 215n, 216, [5]83, 554
  happy [2]167
nightshade [2]168, 168n, [3]879, [5]565, [6]174
nihil ad rem [1]874
nihil in intellectu quod non prius in sensu [1]354, [4]174–5, 174n
"nihili-nauci-pili-flocci-al" [1]329
"nihiliscience" [6]243, 243n
nihilists [5]95
nihility [1]246, [4]706
Nile [1]710n, 746, 779, [2]239, 416, [5]64, 841, [6]196
  Battle of [1]177n; nondescript [1]811
nimis [2]451
Nimrod (Bible) [1]656, 656n
  land of [1]443, 444, 444n
nincompoop [5]598
nine [1]691n, [2]556, [4]37, 37n
  n.-pin [3]362, 362n
Nineveh [6]117
Nio [5]836
Niobe (myth) [6]105
Nisbet, John (?1627–85) [2]1181n ("Nisbit")
Nisibis [2]742
nisus [5]431
  n. formativus [1]550n, [4]432, 432n, [5]473n; spiritual [5]589
nitor [1]606
nitrarch [1]570
nitre [1]572–3, [3]125–6
nitric gas *see* gas(es)
nitric oxide *see* oxide(s)
nitrogen [1]571n, 573, 594, 596, 597, 614, 628, 663, 666, 737, 780, [2]546, 546n, 852, 852n, 853n, 854–5, 854n, 855–6, [3]43, 44, 45, 129, 443, 951, 951n, 952, 997n, 1002, 1020, 1021n, 1022, 1026, 1027, 1027n, 1057, 1057n, 1060, [4]315, 315n, 387, 396n, [5]246, 246n, 247, 247n, 257, 258, 259, 260, 260n, 264, 264n, 356, 397, 438, [6]132–3, 227
  in animal life [3]68, 68n; and hydrogen [1]650; superoxygenised hydrocarburet [1]641, 641n
nitrous gas *see* gas(es)
nitrous oxide *see* oxide(s)
nitrous vapour [3]1027
nits [4]309
no man's land [5]70
no one [5]33
Noachidae *see* Noah, sons of
Noah (Bible) [1]112n, 539, 685, 782–3, [2]177n, 387, 574n, 577, 579, 580, 581, 582, 584, [3]356n, 480, 481, 593, 594n, 644, 757, 782, [4]257, [5]388, [6]119
  sons of/Noachidae [1]539, 539n, [2]397n, [3]356, [4]257n, 583, [5]337n, [6]5n
nobility [2]1142, [4]138, [5]272–3, 283
  natural [1]788n; prostration of [1]833
noble(s) [1]290, [5]520
  Jewish [2]411; poor [5]634
Noble, George (fl 1805) [2]1204n
Noble, Samuel (1779–1853) *An Appeal in behalf of the Views of the Eternal World and State* MT [3]983–94
nobleman/noblemen [1]55, [3]693, [4]240
  French [4]240
nobleness, innate [2]926
nodes [2]942, [4]521
no doing [4]625
Noel, Gerard T. (1782–1851) [4]3
noeron and *noeton* [2]425, 426n
noetic [3]16, 16n, 451
  transcendental [5]81
Noke, Captain (fiction) [1]50, 50n
Nokes, John (fiction) [3]367
nolens volens [6]134
Noll, Old [3]188, 188n
nomad [3]21
no-meaningness [5]365
nomen [1]787, 787n, [4]186n, [5]31
  and *numen* [1]428n, 438, 438n, [3]135–6, 136n, 576, 576n, [5]11n, 31n; *see also* name
nomenclature [3]1042–3, [5]450, 481
  chemical [1]177, 570n, 573; French [1]570
nominalism [3]136n, 347n
  and realism [3]135, 135n, [4]422
nominalist(s) [4]422n
  and realist(s) [2]43, 430, 430n, 882, [3]135
nominative, the [3]15
non liquet [5]141
non vere ens [1]565n
non-coherent, the [5]356
Nonconformist(s) [1]270, 283n, 346, 357, [4]307, 307n, [5]146
Nonconformists' Memorial [4]182–3 q
non-descript [3]9, [4]268
non-ens [2]992
non-entity [2]1010, [3]363, [4]235, [5]638

Nonius Marcellus (?4th century) [2]757n
Nonnus (fl c 400) [2]579n, 582, 584
  Dionysiaca tr Rouse [2]578, 579, 579n, 584n
non-resistance [1]820
nonsense [1]719, [2]17, 540, 572, 992, [3]345, 485, 685, 1059, [4]106, 408, 625, [5]111, 296n, 542, 556, 654, [6]51, 288
  blasphemy of [6]75; of Fathers [5]638; heretical [6]64; mischievous [6]21
non-subscribers [1]338
Nootka [3]1074
Norfolk [1]763, 797
Norfolk, Duke of *see* Howard, Bernard Edward
Norman(s) [3]786, [4]15, 594, [5]44
Norna (in Scott) [4]598, 598n, 606–7
North [1]596, [4]738n, [5]265
  barren [6]251; cold [2]17; frozen [4]525; ideal [5]435; pure [5]266; *see also* compass of nature
North America [3]493n, [5]299, [6]35
North American Review [2]952n
North British Review [2]794, [5]108
North, Frederick, 2nd Earl of Guilford (1732–92) [3]222
North Pole [1]399n
North, Sir Thomas (?1535–?1601) *see* Plutarch *Lives* ed and tr North
Northampton [4]287
Northcote, Henry Stafford (1792–1851) [6]189
Northcote, James (1746–1831) [1]58n, [2]235, 235n
Northcote, Sir Stafford Henry (1762–1851) [6]189
Northumberland [3]975
  witch-finders in [6]104
Northumberland, Earl of *see* Percy, Henry
North-West Passage [1]204n
Norton, Charles Eliot (1827–1908) [2]215
Norton, Thomas (1532–84)
  see T. Sackville and Norton; Calvin *Institution of the Christian Religion* tr Norton
Norway [3]1062, [5]312
Norwegians, as generous/Iapetic race [1]540
Norwich [4]283
Norwich, Oscar I. *Maps of Africa* [4]601n
nosce te ipsum [1]734, 734n, [3]919
nose(s) [3]1035, [4]509, 630, 630n, [5]544, 712
  Bardolph's [3]182; Böhme's counsellor [1]578
Nose, Karl Wilhelm (1753–1835) [3]939
nosology [3]397, [4]183
Nostradamus (Michel de Nostredame) (1502–66) [2]410, *410n–11n*, 517, 517n, [3]105, 105n, [4]72
  Centuries [2]411n
nostrils [1]332
Nosworthy, J. M. *see* Shakespeare *Cymbeline* ed Nosworthy
"not", omitted [1]lixn
notary [5]10, 10n, 13
not-being [1]573, [2]989
note(s) [1]cxxxn, 440
  abuse of [2]122; explanatory [2]399; or mark [5]565; on a n. [1]459
Notes and Queries [1]cxxvii q, cxxviiin, cxlin, 162n, 761, [2]214, 1064
not-god [1]691
Nothgottes [2]982
nothing(s) [1]231, 238, 238n, 689–91, [2]887–8, 988, 989–90, 990n, 991–2, 993, [3]116, 120, 121, 122, 296, 345, 729–30, 1053, 1054, 1055, 1056, 1060, 1091, [5]95, 99n, [6]243
  creation out of *see* creation, *ex nihilo*; and something [1]173, [5]460, [6]245
nothingising [5]97
Notice des tableaux exposés au Musée d'Anvers MT [3]993–4
"notion" [1]62, 62n, [6]171–2
notion(s) [2]359, 626, 729, 1148, 1162, [3]253, 524, 857, [4]401, [5]63, 161, 369, 615, 701, 752, 825, [6]87
  abstract [1]372, [5]610; and being [5]764; chimerical [2]393; clear [5]557; and conception(s) *see* conception(s); false [3]788, 829, [5]131; and feelings [6]126; Greek [4]62; and ideas *see* ideas; kinds of [6]172; metaphysical [5]548; old [5]285; only words [1]561; play of [5]701; popular [2]1146, [5]170; primary [2]989, 991; not punishable [2]107; scientific [6]174; of size [1]774; and spirit [5]550; thought composed of [2]626
notional, the [3]606, [5]674
"notionalise" [3]429, 430n
notionalist [5]699
not-thing [1]691
Nottingham [1]293, 336n, [2]60, 1191
Nottinghamshire [1]336n
Noto [4]235, 235n
Notus [6]200–1
noumenon/noumena (*noumenon/noumena*) [1]787n, [2]915, 915n, [3]202, 313, 1022, [4]107, 107n, 125n, 186n, [5]5, 5n, 175, 580, 594
  homo n. [3]265, 265n; name [1]787; and phenomenon/phenomena [1]201, 524, 839,

[2]431, 672, 802, 1144, 1144n, [3]313, 394, 394n, 431, 737n, [4]308, 308n, 436, 648, 648n, 702, [5]4–5, 5n, 17, 17n, 31, 175n, 542, 548, 592, 614–15, 614n, 672, 672n, 680, 712–13, 826, 826n, [6]8; world of [1]201; see also *corpus noumenon*
noun(s) [3]15, 19, 450, 830, 830n, 835, 1004, [4]166
 formation of participle from [4]14, 14n; substantive [3]11, 279; *see also* substantive
nous/Nous [1]163, 164n, 479n, 557, 557n, [2]249, 332, 424, 425, 430, 430n, 881n, [3]16, 16n, [4]113, 154–5, 155n, 186n, 196, [5]234, 702, 721, 742n, 752
 esemplastic [1]595; pure reason [2]713; reason [2]715, 729n; *see also* mind(s)
Nova Scotia [3]884
Novalis *see* Hardenberg
Novatian (3rd century) [1]470, 470n, [5]586, [6]92
novel(s) [2]1084, [3]94, 180, 484, 634, [4]781, 826, [5]119
 confined to unities [2]76; defect in [4]594; enchanting [1]722; French [2]782; founded on facts [5]226; and history [2]448; love in [6]322; new race of [4]76
novelists, old [4]610
Novell, Archibald (fl 1685) *see* Thévenot *Travels . . . into the Levant* tr Novell
Novellae [4]666, 666n
Novello, Vincent (1781–1861) [2]65n
novelty [3]403, 1054, [4]728, [5]455, 523
 seeming [5]99
November [1]764, 797
Nowell, Alexander (?1507–1602) [2]69
nucleus [1]580, 785, [5]338
 dark [1]785
nudity [6]157, 205
nugacities [2]925n
"nugifying" [2]925, 925n
nuisance [2]108
nullifidian [2]1171
nullity [1]749, [2]247
"null-punct" [1]691, 691n
Numa Pompilius (8th–7th century BC) [1]315, 705, [3]738, 739n, [4]650, 650n, [5]487
"number" [5]697–8
number(s) [1]574, 599, 689, 690–1, 690n, [2]1136–7, 1186, [3]904, 904n, 1024, [5]487
 above number [2]1137; of the beast *see* six hundred and sixty-six; cabbala of [6]294; doctrine of [4]511n; excess of [4]303; Greek [4]36n; and idea(s) [5]230, 698, 698n; infinite [3]89n–90n, 90, [5]720; nature of [3]966; numeration [3]126; odd [1]564n; perfection of [4]201; of Pythagoras [2]429, [4]115, 115n, [5]541n; self-moving [5]233; substantial [1]691
numbering [4]113
numen/numina [1]428, 428n, 523, 787n, [2]915, 915n, [3]1022, [4]186n, 648
 and *nomen* see *nomen;* original [1]119
numerus numerans/numeri numerantes [1]691, [5]233
Numidia [3]419
"Numps" [3]188, 188n
Nun (Bible) [2]145n
nun(s) [1]504–5, [2]92, 93, [3]774, [4]195
nunnery/nunneries [1]505, 522, [3]906, [5]821
Nuremberg [2]755n, [3]985, [6]122
nurse(s) [3]748, [4]489
nursery-tale [2]1106, [4]815, 818
nut, double [2]389
nutmegs [3]884
nutrition [3]67
nutting [2]980
Nye, Philip (?1596–1672) [4]182
Nye, Stephen (?1648–1719) [5]28, 29, 33, 34
 A Brief History of the Unitarians Called Also Socinians [5]28–9 q
Nym (in Shakespeare) [3]174, 187, 187n–8n
Nysian Plain [2]1091, 1091n
Nysten, Pierre Hubert (1771–1818) [4]164

"O. A." (Amelia Opie) [1]90
"O. P. Q." *see* Wilks, John
oak(s) [2]312, 1200, [3]102, 697, 1020, [4]525, 827, 830, [5]681, 701, 720
 faith as [1]287
oasis [2]1018
Oates, J. C. T. [1]xcvn
Oates, Titus (1649–1705) [3]166n, [6]145, 145n
oath(s) [1]250–1, 270–2, 275, [3]149, 158, 164, 164n, 183n, 801, [4]367, [6]262, 263, 264
 of Allegiance [1]166n, [3]154n, 164, [5]675; Coronation [1]294, 864–5, 866, *866n*, [3]143, 144n, 152n, 154n, 164, [4]19, 20n, [5]44; Covenant [4]307; Etcetera [1]232, [5]544, 544n; extorted [3]160–1; Highgate [3]164; immorality of [1]342; of obedience [5]538, 538n; of Succession [5]392
oats [2]648
ob [1]420, [2]56, 1108, 1108n, [3]771, 771n
"obedience" [3]515n, [6]297, 297n
obedience [2]945, [3]54, 518–19, 749, [5]73, [6]301
 due to law [1]875; oath of *see* oath(s); pas-

obedience—*continued*
sive [1]289, [2]766, [3]142, 147, 148, 159; perfect [5]822; pretence to [2]19; refusal of [1]319, 321; spirit of [5]123
Oberon (*Huon of Bordeaux*) [4]827n
obeying, two ways [1]807
"object" [2]992, *992n*
object(s) [2]991–2, [3]12, [4]125, 126, 415, [5]15, 81
impressions from [5]382; nature of [3]43; necessarily finite [4]414; outward [4]820, 838; of spiritual intuition [5]408; stream of [4]542; and subject [1]602, 618, 646–8, 648n, [2]615n, 991–2, [3]264, [4]220, 251, 416–17, 448, 450, 451, 454, 542–3, [5]159, 201, 410n, 649, 718–19, [6]170, 238, 241–2; supersensual [1]682; supersensuous [3]560, [5]751, 792; and thought [3]83; of the understanding [5]599; unsouled [5]175
objections, silly [4]674
objective, the [2]627, 631, 881, 887, 1175, [3]13, 74, 520n
and subjective [1]283, 517, 517n, [2]887, 989, [3]150, 151, 216, 275, 618, 618n, 919, 989, 1007, 1036, [4]389, 448, [5]49, 123, 165, 175, 203, 289, 355, 355n, 372, 443, 465, 628, 743, 775, 776, 790, [6]76, 76n, 89n, 302n; subjectively [3]276
objectively-subjective, the [3]74
objectivity [3]270, 829, [4]450, 543, [5]175, 410, 789
and subjectivity [3]1068, [4]845; true [5]795
oblations [2]670
"obligate" [3]107, 109, 109n
obligation(s) [1]874, [2]1193, [3]267, 489, [5]578
Christian [5]398; civil [1]833; and compulsion *see* compulsion; imperfect [2]618; moral [3]154, [4]652–3; perpetual [2]38; universal [2]811
oblivion [1]631, [4]159
obscenity [2]947n, [5]811
obscure, the [2]962, [4]520, 520n
obscurity/obscurities [2]423, 630, [3]1058, [4]713, [5]173–4, 862 ("obscure")
Fichte's [2]625; mystical [4]427
observances [4]625, 731, 829, 829n, 846
royal [1]450
observation(s) [2]1025, [3]1006, [5]110, 168, [6]52, 96
general [2]972; judicious [1]765; original [4]194
Observations on the Universe see Dalberg
observer [5]431
obstacle [4]458
obstinacy [5]476
obtunding [2]831
obtuseness [2]478, [4]600, 602, [5]753
Occam/Ockham, William of (c 1285–c 1349) [1]286, 301, [2]183, 183n, 661, 681, [3]135n, 136n, 347, 347n, [5]7n, 549, 549n, 637n, 800, 800n, 804n, 805, 805n, 806, 806n, 812
O.'s Razor [3]345n
Occamists [5]478
occasion [4]211
occasionalism [4]354n
occidentise [1]578, 579
ocean [2]995, 995n, [3]77, 100, [5]338
great [5]225; northern [5]267; of papers [3]987; subterraneous [4]491
Ocellus Lucanus (c 500–400 BC) [5]692, 692n
O'Connell, Daniel (1775–1847) [1]859n, 860, [2]900, 900n
O'Connor, Roger (1762–1834) [1]860, 860n
octave [3]910
Octavia (d 11 BC) [2]878
Octavian, Emperor, Romance of [3]1069 ("Octouian"), 1070 q
Octavius, Gaius *see* Augustus
octosyllabics [2]768n
oddity/oddities [1]763, 764, 796, 797n, [2]54
ode(s) [2]1051
of Horace [2]240; of Pindar [4]117–21; Pindaric [1]428, 428n; Sappho's [2]1067; Spenser's *Epithalamion* [1]80; war [6]119
Odes and Addresses see T. Hood and J. H. Reynolds
Odin (myth) [4]489–90
odorifique [6]235
odour(s) [5]340, 599, [6]230, 230n
Odysseus *see* Ulysses
Oecolampadius, Joannes (1482–1531) [3]724, 761, 761n, [5]549, 549n
Oeder, Professor (fl 1746) [3]215
Oedipus (myth) [2]584–5 ("Oidipus")
Oersted, Hans Christian (1777–1851) [1]clii, [2]539n, [3]104, 104n
Ansicht der chemischen Naturgesetze [3]104n; MT 995–1012
Oetinger, Friedrich Christoph (1702–82) [4]491
"off" [3]833
offence, rock of [3]1001
office, delegation of [5]536
officer(s) [1]339
civil [1]308; life of [5]379

offspring [5]465
Ogden, C. K. [4]69, [6]131
ogdoa [4]37n
O'Gorman, the [1]859, 859n
oil [1]551, [2]1186, [3]324, [4]169
 boiling [2]459; o.-instillator [1]812; olive [2]296; and water [1]574
ointment(s) [2]749
 narcotic [6]99
Oken, Lorenz (1779–1851) [1]556, 563n, [2]67, 539n, *1007n*, [3]114, 117, 1074n, [5]347n, 699n, 786, 786n
 notation of [1]690n
 Erste Ideen zur Theorie des Lichts [2]1007n; MT [3]1013–18; [5]851, [6]3; *Lehrbuch der Naturgeschichte* [1]570n, 642n, [2]545n, 1007n; MT [3]1019–48; *Lehrbuch der Naturphilosophie* MT [3]1049–63, tr A. Tulk as *Elements of Physiophilosophy* [3]1049
Okenisms [2]1007, 1007n, [3]1042, 1052, 1061
olam [1]434n
old age [1]273, 819
Old Bailey *see* London
old clothesman [4]52
old man [2]472
Old Nick *see* Nick, Old
Old Noll *see* Noll, Old
Old Sarum [3]800, 800n
Oldenburg, Henry (?1615–77) [3]887, 1091n, [5]200
olive
 branches [1]445; leaf [3]644; tree [1]782, [3]455, 480
Oliver (*As You Like It*) [4]784, 817, 817n
Oliver, Harold James *see* Shakespeare *Merry Wives*, *Timon of Athens* ed Oliver
Oliver, John (fl 1750–85) [5]168
Olivers, Thomas (1725–99) [5]168, 170, 191
olla podrida [1]212, 604
Olney [2]1156n
Olympiad [5]694n
Olympus [2]901
Omalius d'Halloy, Jean Baptiste Julien d' (1783–1875) [3]939
omega [2]67n
 alpha and *see* alpha
omen [3]987
omichein [1]768n
omikron [2]67n
omissions [5]575
omneitas [1]651, 651n
omneity [1]602, 651n, 749, [5]357, [6]235
omnia in singulis [2]488
omniana [1]772
Omniana see R. Southey *Omniana*
"omnifidience" [6]120, 120n
"omnify" [5]508, 508n
omnipotence [1]627, 862, [2]152, 278, 652, 676, [3]27, 505, [4]429, [5]155, 158, 466
omnipresence [1]524, [2]419, 568, 668, 671, 671n, [3]495n, [4]126, 298, 299, [5]155, 360, 493, 706
omnipresent, the [5]482
omni-radiance [5]792
omniscience [2]152, 652, [5]65, 158, 160, [6]243
omniscient, the [1]320, [5]369, 482
 o. mind [3]853
omnium gatherum [1]499
on dit [1]447, 454
on, me see *me on/onta*
on/onta [1]460, *461n*, 785, 785n, [2]249, 305, 726, 726n, [3]913, [4]406, 406n, 531, [5]97, [6]85, 85n, 87, 91, 114, 141
On the Soul of the World and Nature [6]6n
onbreathing [5]184
one [2]1186, [4]36, 113, 269, 364
 and all see *hen kai pan*; and many *see* many; many in [2]1030; not a number [5]699, 699n; and the one [5]231; origin of [1]651; and two [5]541–2. *See also* individual; unit; unity
One, the [1]561, [2]996–7, 1186, [4]421, 421n, [5]97n, 708, [6]20
 absolute [3]17; eternal [3]29; imperturbable [3]12; indecomponible [3]915; supreme [5]482
oneiromancy [5]726
oneiroscopy [5]726
Oneirosoph/Oneirosophen [4]504, 504n
oneness [1]561, [2]250, [4]113
one-pairists [5]252
one-sidedness [3]132
"one-side-mindedness" [1]808, 808n–9n
Onesimus (2nd century) [4]253n
onion, epicurean [1]652, 652n
Onkelos (1st century) [3]1092
"onlook" [2]607n
only-begetter [2]882
onomatopoeia [4]186
ontology [3]202
ontos on/onta [2]135, 135n, [5]615, 680, 707
onus probandi [2]43
opacity [3]1058–9, [4]42
open-heartedness [1]347
openness [4]9
opera [2]196
 comic [4]169; o. house [3]894
operation, internal [5]652

operatives [3]358
Ophelia (*Hamlet*) [1]394, [4]743, 851, 852, 856, 857, 858, 859
ophites [1]776n
Ophites [2]717
opiate(s) [1]765, 797, [5]419
Opie, Amelia (née Alderson) (1769–1853) [1]90, *90n*; *see also* Aepio
Father and Daughter [1]90n; *Poems* [1]90n
Opie, Iona (née Archibald) see *Classic Fairy Tales*, *Oxford Dictionary of Nursery Rhymes* ed Opie and Opie
Opie, John (1761–1807) [1]90n
Opie, Peter Mason (1918–82) see *Classic Fairy Tales*, *Oxford Dictionary of Nursery Rhymes* ed Opie and Opie
opinion(s) [2]28, 42, 667, [4]80, 141, 475
erroneous [5]166; general [6]286; individual [1]330; opposite [2]529; public [3]679, [6]46; and truth [5]641
opinionism [2]1016
Opitz, Martin (1597–1639) [5]47, 47n
Teutsche Gedichte [1]clxv, [5]47n; *Umständliche Nachricht* [5]47n
opium [1]228, 714n, [2]859, [3]126, 366, 371, 399, 747n, [4]10n, 84, 85, 273, 318n, 324, 324n, 465n, 533n
as aphrodisiac [1]777; and *bhang* [4]84–5; C's addiction [1]714n, [3]747n, [4]10n, 465n; o.-eaters [5]584, 584n; effects of [3]371, 399; first action [4]183; and irritability [3]126, [4]273; and nerves [2]859; *see also* laudanum
opposite(s) [1]331, [2]316, 854–5, 855n, [3]262, 916, 1003n, 1026n, [4]451, 834, [5]231, 621
all of one [5]715; balancing of [5]717; both desirable [5]321; and contrary *see* contrary; correspondent [5]372; reconciliation of [1]368n; sporting with [4]851; union of [1]662
opposition(s) [4]673, [5]557
oppression [1]13
oppressors [5]281
optic(s) [3]393n, [4]209n, [6]132
Newtonian [2]610, 613, [5]452n; cylinder [3]716, 716n
opticians [2]610
optimism [1]514
opulence [1]378, [2]219, 220
Opuscula mythologia, physica et ethica ed Gale [2]665n, [3]648
oracle(s) [1]420n, 439, 440, 665, [2]30, 77, 77n, 288, 405–6, [3]21, 110, 462, 1088, [4]194, 514–15, 627n, 706–7, [5]517n, 640, [6]100
ancient [6]99n; of Apollo [2]727, 733; Chaldaic [5]237, 238, 238n; of Daniel [2]410–11; divine [2]343, [3]24; gypsy [2]785; Hebrew [2]371, [3]33, 452; of the OT [2]409; of the Sibyl [6]5; sublime [1]436
Die Orakel des Propheten Mica ed Grosschopf [2]371
orange (botany) [3]85, 355
o.-sucking(s) [2]59, [3]713; tree *see* tree(s)
orange (colour) [4]167
Orange, Prince of *see* William III
orangutan(s) [3]811 ("ouran outang"), [4]98
orations
funeral [2]749; premeditated [2]455
orator(s) [4]26, 604, [5]487, 528
art of [4]742; pagan [1]315
oratory/oratories [1]522, 580, [5]324, 581n
orb, silent [5]157
Orbilius (in Horace) [2]76
orbit [5]232, 431
orchard [5]593
o.-robbing [2]980
ordeals [2]459
order [3]791, 1025, [4]141, 158n, [5]642
animal [4]155; Christian [1]349; conservation of [2]300; divine [5]410; learned [5]79, [6]23; of manifestation [2]575; and passion [4]168; relation of [5]443; temporal [5]639; world of [2]583
order(s)
mendicant [3]427; monastic [5]121, 121n
"ordered" [3]664
Orders [3]440n, [5]398n, 566n
ordinance(s) [1]805, [3]878, [5]123
ordination [1]246, 349, 353, 532, 532n, [2]472, 1096, [3]720, 768, [5]163, 537, 566
ordo ordinans [4]155, 226, 226n
Ordonio (*Remorse*) [6]49, 49n
ordonnance [4]367, [5]529
ore(s) [1]663, [3]1061
Orellana (river) [2]980
orexis [1]146n
organ(s) [1]132, 132n, 299, 536, 634, 737, [3]559, 559n, 1034, [4]149–50, 385, [5]297
actions of [5]168; affections of [5]559; appropriate [6]51; bodily [5]172; body as [1]132; organic body [1]735; diseased [5]420; organic forms [2]1036; higher [5]752; hydraulic [3]248n; of insight [5]755; male and female [4]432; medial [3]551–2; of science [4]503; of sense [6]126, 132; thinking [5]552; of thought [5]481; of truth [3]641; vital [5]546
organic, the, and dynamic [4]321–2
organicism [2]539n

organisation [1]132, 132n, 537, 550, [2]891, [3]600, 870, [4]93, 322, 375, [5]460, 730
animal [6]103; bodily [5]795; excitant of [6]226; and mechanism [1]132n; result of [5]826
organised, the, and inorganic [1]662
organism(s) [1]135, [2]544, 549, [5]460, 715, 827
bodily [5]418; finite [3]119; material [3]14; particular [1]662; of religion [1]517; simplest [4]165; universal [6]235; vital, defined [1]550–1
organismus/*organismus* [2]145, 566, [3]14, 43, 393, 749, [4]373–5, 385, 492n, [5]304, 398, 568
auditual [1]577; perfect [6]103; spiritual [5]175; total [1]662; unity of integers [2]365
organist [1]737
of light [3]559
organon [5]826, 826n
organon, infallible [5]714
orgasm(s) [1]518n, [2]1053
orgies [3]495
Oriel College *see* Oxford
Orient [2]1022, [4]226n
"oriental" [4]40, 40n
orientiren [4]218
orientise [1]578, 579
Origen (c 185–c 254) [1]491, 745, [2]33n, 306, 327 q, 375n, 377, 501, 502, 714n, 720–1, 721n, 722 q, 1177n, [3]440, 446n, 533, 612, 728, 728n, [4]472, 643, [5]572, 591, 594 q, 594n, 629, 637, 638n, 748, 748n, 766n, [6]91, 319
not annotated by C [1]lxiii; misunderstood [5]573; on prayer [2]723, 723n; scheme of education [2]722; works of [5]638
Contra Celsum [2]317, 317n, [3]612n, [4]472n; *Hexapla* [2]270n; *On the Spirits* [5]748; *Peri archon* [2]721n; *That the King is the Only Maker* [5]748–9
origin [5]201, 573n–4n, 656, 659
original, the [5]29
and copy *see* copy
original sin [1]269, 302, 302n, 324, 358, 507, 790, [2]247, 315, 583n, 668, 675, 723, 809n, 1170, 1192n, [3]18n, 266, 515, 515n, 517, 596, 596n, 730, 879, 879n, [4]434n, 656, [5]157, 158n, 497n, 498n, 528, 591–2, 591n, 593–4, 596–9, 599–600, 600n, 610n, 611, 613, 614–15, 615n, 616, 617, 650, 655, [6]139, 297n, 298n, 299
dogma of [5]608; of Platonism [3]915; refutation of [5]590; in woman [3]730
originality [2]628, [3]451
of Heraclitus [5]715
origination [5]26, 201
form of [5]626; problem of [5]455, 456–7
Orion [4]515, 516
Orkney Islands [4]604
Orlando (*As You Like It*) [3]406
Orléans [2]769–70
Orléans, Louis Philippe Joseph, Duc d' (1747–93) [2]510, 510n, [4]634
Ormathwaite, Baron *see* Walsh, John Benn
Ormond, Duke of *see* Butler, James
ornament(s) [2]617, 1139, [4]158
ornature, poetic [2]513
ornithology, Parnassian [4]76
Orontes (in Virgil) [6]205
Orontes (ship) [4]534n
Oroondates (in Calprenède) [5]821, 821n
Orosius, Paulus (fl 417) [3]693–4 q
Seven Books of History against the Pagans tr Raymond [2]336n
Orpheus (myth) [1]775, 776, 776n, [2]239, 973n, 981n, [4]147, 489–90, [6]8, 211n
Orphic hymns *see* hymns, Orphic
orrery [4]13, 13n
Orrery, Earl of *see* Boyle, Charles
Orsini, Gian Napoleone Giordano (1903–76) *Coleridge and German Idealism* [2]594, 595, 639
Orsino (*Twelfth Night*) [4]704
orthodoxist(s) [1]477, 560, [2]924
"orthodoxy" [3]144
orthodoxy [2]806, [3]416, 541, [4]304, 630, [6]80
improving [1]358; of Nonconformists [1]346
orthography [6]27
Orumi [6]279
Osbaldistone, Frank (in Scott) [4]586, 586–7, 587n
oscillation(s) [1]641, [3]835, [5]358, 750, 798
osmium [2]825, 825n, [5]261
Osrick (*Hamlet*) [4]859
Ossa [4]188, [5]483, 483n
Ossian *see* Macpherson, James
ostentation [4]100, 814
ostrich [1]cxviin, cxxi, 482, [4]629
Ostrogoths [5]195n
O'Sullivan, Samuel (1790–1851)
The Agency of Divine Providence Manifested MT [3]1078–9, presentation copy to C [3]1078
Otfried/Otfrid von Weissenburg (c 800–c 870) [1]151, 151n
Othello (*Othello*) [3]407, [4]748, 865, 866
blackamoor tradition [4]861, 861n; not jealous [4]867; role of [4]42

other ^{2}825
 and better *see* better
otherness ^{3}107n; *see also* alterity
Otho, Marcus Salvius (32–69) ^{1}486, 486n, ^{3}929, 929n
ottava rima ^{1}117n, 217, 217n, ^{2}795n
otter ^{1}778
Otter, William (1768–1840) ^{2}373
Ottery Collection *see* London: British Library
Ottery St Mary ^{1}cxi, 59, 59n, 750
Otto I, the Great, Holy Roman Emperor (936–73) ^{5}127
Otway, Thomas (1652–85) ^{1}37, ^{2}83, 126, ^{4}822, 822n
 Venice Preserv'd ^{4}823n q
oudeis ^{2}766, 766n, ^{5}33, 33n
"ought", and "shall" ^{3}749
Oulton ^{6}216
oun ^{1}458–9, 459n
ounce *see* ownce
ouranos ^{1}670, 670n
"ourishness" ^{4}827, 827n
ouroboros ^{5}614n
ousia ^{1}614, ^{2}726, 731, 731n, 734, 734n, 852, ^{3}202, 232, 428, 952, 952n, 1055, 1056, ^{4}451, 626, 626n, 627, 718, 763, 786, 786n, ^{6}87, 87n; *see also* being
outbreathing(s) ^{1}687, ^{5}231
outcasts ^{5}106
outcry ^{5}181
"outerance" ^{1}637, *637n–8n*
outerance ^{1}525, 525n, ^{3}12n
Outis ^{3}817–18, 817n
outlawry ^{2}401
outline(s) ^{2}456, 993, 1115, ^{3}42, 730, 978, ^{4}827, ^{5}133, 409, 704, 815
 dissolving ^{3}736; vague ^{5}581
"outness" ^{4}222, 222n
outness ^{1}638n, ^{3}424, 829
outshadowing ^{3}24
outvote ^{3}249, 249n
outward ^{3}454
 fugitive ^{1}637; and inward ^{1}813
outwardness ^{1}670
 sense of ^{3}260
oven, artificial ^{6}149
over-all ^{5}504
overflow ^{4}842, ^{5}520
overflowing ^{1}564, 564n, ^{5}487, 487n
overgrowths ^{5}528
overlaying ^{4}278
overlord ^{3}104
"overly" ^{2}1197, 1197n
overseer ^{5}537
oversight ^{4}64
Ovid (Publius Ovidius Naso) (43 BC–AD 17) ^{1}399, ^{2}762, 973n, ^{3}391n, ^{4}201, 336n
 Amores ^{5}529n; *Art of Love* ^{1}544, 544n; *Fasti* ^{3}735n; *Heroides* tr Showerman ^{3}834n q; *Metamorphoses* ^{1}281 q, 281n q, 558 q, 558n, 669n, ^{2}869n, 971 q, 971n q, ^{5}117n, 745n, tr F. J. Miller ^{3}650–1 q; *Remedia amoris* ^{3}111 q, 111n
ovum ^{5}504, 504n–5n
Owen, John (1616–83) ^{1}346–7, 346n, 351, 351n
 Works ^{1}346n
Owen, Warwick Jack Burgoyne *see* WW *Prose Works* ed Owen and Smyser
Owen, William Fitzwilliam (1774–1857) *Narrative of Voyages to Explore the Shores of Africa, Arabia, and Madagascar* MT ^{3}1080–2
owl ^{3}453, ^{6}148
ownce ^{5}387
ox/oxen ^{1}327, 877, ^{3}324, 381, 1077, ^{4}322, ^{5}101
oxalkalarch ^{1}570
oxazotocarbons ^{3}1005
Oxenstierna, Axel Gustafsson, Count (1583–1654) ^{2}60
Oxford ^{1}500, 809n, ^{2}15n, ^{3}107, 816–17, 922
 Blackwell's (bookseller) ^{1}cxxxviiin, ^{2}259, 590, 796, sale catalogue (1945) ^{1}clxx, ^{2}796, (1948) ^{2}796; Bodleian Library, marginalia in ^{2}259, ^{6}270; Christ Church ^{3}703, 703n; O. Churchmen ^{1}531; Emmanuel College ^{2}351; Hebdomadal Council ^{2}265n; Keble College, marginalia in ^{1}clxi, 503; Manchester College, marginalia in ^{5}199; St Mary Magdalen ^{2}259; Merton College ^{3}827; Oriel College ^{1}7, 41, 500, ^{2}818, ^{4}107n, ^{6}147; O. Movement ^{3}922n; O. University ^{2}821, 956–7, 956n–7n, 978, ^{3}488; Talboys ^{3}107, 107n; Trinity College ^{2}24; Worcester College ^{1}clxixn
Oxford, Earl of *see* Harley, Robert
Oxford and Cambridge Review ^{1}354n
Oxford Book of Christian Names ed Withycombe ^{3}165n
Oxford Book of Medieval English Verse ed Sisam and Sisam ^{4}282
Oxford Classical Dictionary ed N. G. L. Hammond and Scullard ^{2}134n, 340n
Oxford Companion to Music ed Scholes ^{5}295n

Oxford Dictionary of English Proverbs ed F. P. Wilson [5]595n
Oxford Dictionary of Nursery Rhymes ed I. A. and P. Opie [5]224n, 609n q
Oxford Dictionary of the Christian Church ed Cross [1]416, [2]274n q, 415n, 480n, 714n, 721n, 726n, 894n, [3]369n, 1083n, [4]307n q, 347n q, [5]5n q, 14n q, 513n, 596n
Oxford English Dictionary [1]clxiii, 58n, 60n, 124n, 141n, 152n, 153n, 161n, 169n, 223n, 246, 254n, 258n, 296n, 297n, 306n, 344n, 346n, 351n, 399n, 403n, 410n, 423n, 505n, 512n–13n, 519n, 527n, 536n, 537n, 550n, 574n, 579n, 591 q, 596n, 613n, 620n, 626n, 643n, 671n, 696n, 710n, 725n, 736n, 740n, 769n q, 772n, 776n, 778n–9n, 780n, 788n, 808n, 814n, 862n, [2]18n, 22n, 26n, 35n q, 36n, 37n, 38n, 52n, 73n, 108n, 121n, 130n, 136n, 137n, 170n, 192n, 220n, 223n, 227n, 263n, 265n, 279n, 298n, 300n, 332n, 340n, 387n q, 426n, 496n, 527n q, 529n, 547n, 558, 614n, 672n, 674n, 681n, 725n, 739n, 786n, 799, 802, 823n, 827n, 835n, 886n, 898n, 907n, 916n, 924n, 925n, 927n, 930n, 931n, 935n, 944n, 946n, 955n, 980n, 990n, 1029n, 1036n, 1042n, 1064n, 1065n, 1124n, 1147n, 1150n, 1173n, 1174n, 1197n, [3]4n, 16n, 136n, 160n, 172n, 177n, 183n, 188n, 216n, 257n, 355n, 357n, 376n, 377n, 420n, 452n, 472n, 501n, 519n, 591n, 601n, 633n, 692n, 716n, 721n, 821n, 833n, 897n, 919n, 976n, 981n, 1057n, 1066n, [4]14n, 77n, 89n, 96n, 110n, 156n, 181n, 253n, 263n, 280n, 284n q, 285n q, 291n, 299n, 320n, 326n, 384n, 448n, 464n, 503n, 509n, 542n, 579n, 603n, 627n, 630n, 658n q, 692n, 705n, 723n, 745n, 768n, 769n, 787n, 788n, 801n, 807n, 811n, 827n, 845n, 848n q, 849n, [5]13n, 15n q, 27n, 70n q, 71n, 73n q, 76n, 83n, 91n, 97n q, 110n q, 112n, 127n q, 168n, 228n q, 242n, 247n, 251n q, 280n, 296n q, 347n, 360n q, 365n q, 386n, 388, 395n, 428n, 445n, 484n, 492n, 502n q, 506n, 508n, 548n, 566n, 615n, 689n, 738n, 769n, 770n, 778n q, 857n, [6]5n, 20n, 37n, 71n, 78n, 100n, 103n, 110n, 120n, 135n, 143n, 212n, 236n, 238n, 251n, 252n q, 301n
  word not in [1]152n, 381n, 504n, 507n, 517n, 569n, 579n, 580n, 594n, 602n, 630n, 638n, 652n, 653n, 660n, 667n, 675n, 694n, 696n, 819n, 872n, [2]6n, 22n, 39n, 59n, 63n, 69n, 73n, 85n, 92n, 137n, 141n, 200n, 223n, 250n, 321n, 340n, 344n, 388n, 431n, 499n, 516n, 569n, 578n, 582n, 723n, 798, 819n, 859n, 882n, 890n, 891n, 999n, 1026n, 1028n, 1042, 1053n, 1137n, 1147n, 1175n, 1181n, 1186n, [3]90n, 91n, 138n, 183n, 209n, 289n, 307n, 323n, 327n, 341n, 356n, 374n, 383n, 418n, 434n, 560n, 852n, 935n, 949n, 955n, 1088n, [4]20n, 42n, 83n, 145n, 168n, 182n, 194n, 234n, 238n, 243n, 301n, 314n, 380n, 389n, 396n, 400n, 466n, 581n, 603n, 663n, 682n, 730n, [5]76n, 133n, 147n, 155n, 159n, 198n, 265n, 271n, 297n, 301n, 335n, 372n, 418n, 530n, 588n, 589n, 712n, 734n, 827n, 835n, [6]26n, 100n, 123n, 243n
oxidation [3]1000, 1059, [5]342, 343, [6]227–8, 231
oxide(s) ("oxyd") [1]663, [3]127, [5]438
  nitric [1]617n, [3]1004; nitrous [3]375, *375n–6n*, 399, 399n, 1027, [4]169, 183, 183n, [5]169
Oxlee, John (1779–1854)
  The Christian Doctrines of the Trinity and Incarnation MT [3]1083–93, presentation copy to C [3]1083
Oxonian [1]212
oxycarbonazotes [3]1005
oxydrates [3]1005
"oxygen" [5]346
oxygen [1]63n, 548, 552, 589, 594, 597, 598, 599, 611, 613, 614, 617, 635, 636, 641, 643, 662, 663, 666, 667, 737, 775, 780, 785, [2]69, 534n, 546, 546n, 572, 852, 852n, 853n, 854–5, 854n, 855, 855n, [3]43, 44, 45, 61, 61n, 67, 129, 443, 951, 952, 997, 998, 999, 1001, 1004, 1007, 1017, 1020, 1021, 1021n, 1022, 1026, 1027, 1027n, 1057, 1057n, 1058, 1060, [4]13, 16, 315, 315n, 319, 324, 385, 387, 388n, 392, 428, 492, 526, [5]246, 247, 247n, 255, 259, 261, 266, 335, 335n, 342, 343, 344, 346, 438, 548, 548n, [6]116, 132, 227, 228–9, 231
  associated with male [1]654; in blood [2]857, [4]390; dynamic [5]265; role in animal life [3]68; role in vegetation [3]68; solar origin of [4]387–8, 388n; in water [2]1144, 1144n; renamed zoote [1]570, 572
oxymel [1]642, 642n, [5]231

oxymorons [2]569n
oxymuriate [4]539
oxymuriatic acid *see* acid(s)
oxymuriatic gas *see* gas(es)
oyster(s) [3]324, 391, 391n, [4]30, 93, [5]176
shell [3]944, 945, 945n; o.-woman [4]599
oystracism [5]191

pacation [1]359
Pacchiaretti see *Pajarete*
Pace, Richard (c 1482–1536) *De fructu* [1]260n
Pacific Ocean [1]536n, 537, [4]202, 489, [5]116, 307n
packing-engine [2]227
Paddyism [1]204
paean [1]592
paedo-baptist(s) [1]245, [5]651, [6]41, 258
paeon(s) [1]377, [2]124, 124n, 129, [3]814
primus [1]384
Pafford, John Henry Pyle *see* Shakespeare *Winter's Tale* ed Pafford
pagan(s) [2]497, [3]309, [4]145, 160, 160n, 666
christened [2]655
Pagan (in Bunyan) [1]814
Paganini, Niccolo (1782–1840) [2]537n
paganism(s) [1]315, [2]255, 304, [3]470, 473, 473n, 874, [4]43, 145, 811, [5]709, [6]61, 108, 167
converts from [5]522; father of [3]446; heroes of [4]146; overthrow of [3]475
Page, Sir Francis (c 1661–1741) [1]727
Paget/Pagit, Eusebius (?1547–1617) [1]476
Pahvahdam [2]342
"pain" [2]1163, 1163n
pain(s) [2]173, 251, 251n, 255, 326, 603, [3]120, 399, 909, 910, [4]270n, 277, 652, [5]95, 181, 210, 419, 713, 766, [6]126
cowardice of [4]10; intellectual [2]959; intolerable [5]584; local [5]560; may be a blessing [2]199; and pleasure [2]162, 191, 563, 639, [3]272, 975, [4]134, 209, 276, [5]370, [6]243
Paine, Thomas ("Payne") (1737–1809) [1]462n, [3]222, 539n, 698, 1068, [4]623, [5]119, 119n
Age of Reason [3]698n, [5]119n; *Rights of Man* [3]222n, [4]342n
painter(s) [2]1110, [5]581–2
Italian [1]627
painting(s) [3]993–4, [4]168, 419, 421, 766, 811n
Aders's [2]179–80
Pajarete ("Pacchiaretti") [1]lxiii, lxxxi, [2]132, *132n*, [4]32
Pakington, Lady Dorothy (d 1679) [2]409n
Paladon (in R. Southey) [4]461n
palate [1]607, 655
Palermo [1]502, 522, [2]978n, [3]786, 786n
Palestine [1]421n, 440, [2]374, 376, 380, 394, 421, 451, 470, 513, 515n, 739, 1017, [3]6, 20, [4]68, 248, 257, 471, 481, [5]181n, 645
Christian(s) of [2]700, [6]139; churches of [2]436–7, 709, 710n; heretics in [5]623
Paley, William (1743–1805) [1]244n, 462n, *511n–12n*, 812n, [2]81, 663n, 896n, 1060, [3]308, 308n, 666n, 708n–9n, 722, 763n, [4]16 q, 260n, 337n, 626, 626n, 652, [5]65, 384n, 513n, 667 ("Paleyan")
anti-Paleyan [3]666; and Grotius/"Grotio-Paleyan" *see* Grotius; heartless sobriety [1]621, 621n; on miracles [1]683; moral doctrine [1]223n; school of [1]462, 462n, [2]324, [5]384; shallow morality [2]429; a Socinian [1]511n
Horae Paulinae [1]511, 511n, [4]337, 337n; *Natural Theology* [1]511n, [2]324n, 788n, [4]638–9, 639n, [5]730, 730n; *Principles of Moral and Political Philosophy* [1]172, 172n, 511n, [2]429n; *Reasons for Contentment* [1]511n; *View of the Evidences of Christianity* [1]511n, [5]51n, 65n q
Paleyan(s) [2]450
Paleyanism [2]291
Paleyo-Grotian *see* Grotius
Palgrave, Francis Cohen (1788–1861) [5]79, 79n
The Rise and Progress of the English Commonwealth [5]79n
Palingenius (Pier Angelo Manzoli de la Stellata) (c 1500–c 1543)
Zodiacus vitae tr Googe [2]870, 870n q
palinodia [3]145
palladium [2]825, 825n, [5]261
Pallas [2]7, [3]648, [6]157; *see also* Athena/Athene
Palli (myth) [2]584
palliation [3]787
pallium [1]857n
Palmer, Kenneth *see* Shakespeare *Troilus and Cressida* ed Palmer
Palmerin de Oliva [3]1066
palpability [1]604n
and power [1]604
palsy [5]11, [6]55
of superstition [5]188
Pamela (in Sidney) [2]971n
Pamphagus [4]630, 630n

pamphlet(s) [4]675
political [2]411
"Pamphlets—Divinity" [1]203, [4]3–4
"Pamphlets—Miscellaneous" [4]5–6
"Pamphlets on the Reform Bill" [4]7
"Pamphlets on the Slave Trade" [1]31, [4]8
pan [1]848, 848n, [2]344, [5]455, 455n, [6]5
panacea(s) [2]387, [3]709n
Panchatantra [2]772n
Pandects [4]666, 666n
Pandora (myth) [1]58, [2]86, 1063
panegyric [2]321, 353
paneidolon [4]337, 337n
panhylists [5]716
panorama [5]756
panourgia [4]196, 196n
panourgoi [4]192, 192n
panpharmacon [3]709, 709n
Pantagruel (in Rabelais) [4]78n, 190, 193, 194, 195, 196, 630n
pantheism [1]238n, 242n, 556n, 600n, 602, 603n, 619, 679, 681, [2]200, 344, 583, 883, 883n, 995n, 1007n, 1107, [3]23n, 137n, 901, 1050, [4]420n, 423, 523, [5]251n, 406, 456, 470, 482, 716n, 769, 769n, [6]116
as atheism [3]136–7, 1083–4, 1091, [6]75–6; Böhme and [1]600, 652, 677; of Bruno [5]810; erroneous [1]114; Greek [2]695; Indian [1]646; intellectual [1]120, 120n; and John [2]462–3; Manichean [1]627; Oken's [3]1055; Phoenician [6]5; and physiology [3]1042; Schelling's [2]554n; Socinianism as [1]198n; Spinozistic [2]623n
pantheist(s) [1]619, [2]199n, 292, 575, [3]698, [5]118n
Pantheon [5]39
Indian [1]400; *see also* Rome
Pantheos [5]227
pantisocracy [1]cxiii, [2]847n
pantomime [1]150, 150n, [4]610
ancient [4]787
Panurge (in Rabelais) [4]78, 78n, 192, 192n, 193, 194, 195, 196, 630n
Panyasis/Panyassis (5th century BC) [4]147
papacy [1]473, [2]290, [3]458, 760n, [4]43, 548, [5]143n, 195, 195n, 507, 660, 662
blighting influence [2]982; good effects of [6]14; Lambeth [5]537
paper(s) [3]741
bad [3]887, 887n; C's complaints [2]519–20, 519n, 520n; in C's German books [1]lxxii, 520; German [1]487, 487n, 519, 519n; money [5]686–7; ocean of [3]987; scarcity of [1]lxxi
Papers of the Bibliographical Society of America [1]89n
Papias (2nd century) [2]400n, 501, 502, 712, [5]629, 643
papist(s) [1]274, 309, 311, [2]27, 30, 220, 813, 1104, [3]148, 694, 759, 823, 1078, [4]22, 180–1, 632, [5]5, 14, 526, 562, 617, 639, [6]118, 154–5, 263
benighted [2]64; comments of [6]166; error of [5]394; Irish [2]59, [6]13; persecutions of [6]108; and RCs [2]935, 935n; a sect [1]315; *see also* church(es): RC
papistry [2]1158, [5]144
ascetic [5]163; pitch-stains of [1]316
"papoduly" [2]38, 38n
papoduly [1]257n
"Papophobists" [2]935, 935n
Pappen, Catherine (née von Axen) [5]97, 97n
papyrologiophagous [1]88
para [3]834, 834n
parable(s) [1]448, 512, [2]207, 444, 447, 559, [3]422, 595, 622, [5]420, 582, [6]118
of labourer [1]201; mythological [1]587; of Temptation [4]60
parabolai [1]447
Paracelsus (Theophrastus Bombastus von Hohenheim) (1493–1541) [1]296, 296n, 569n, 685n, 719n, 750, 791–2, [2]13n, 788n, 804, 824–5, 824n, [3]682, 683n, 817n, [4]424, 424n, [5]809
Böhme and [1]634, *634n*, 668; Paracelsian term [3]722n
Omnia opera [1]296n, [2]824, 824n, [6]334
paraclete [3]460, 460n, 674, [4]300
paradise [1]394, 654, 655, 768, [2]1022, 1052–3, 1074n
fruits of [3]463; man has no guts in [1]655, 657; *see also* Eden
paradox(es) [2]869n, [3]301, 342, 1061, [4]380, [5]792
of Gorgias [5]719n, 720–1; p.-monger [3]1050; Stoic [5]612; useless [4]420; Zeno's [5]712n
paradoxist [5]686
paradoxy [3]661
Paraeus, David (1548–1622) [2]505n
paragraphs, musical [5]689
Paraguay [5]104, 254
parakolouthein [1]477n
parallax [2]884
parallelepiped [3]1066n
parallelism(s) [6]139
rule of [1]470, [3]32, 32n; verbal [2]974n, [3]888
parallelismus [2]427

parallelogram(s) [1]601, [4]863
paralogism(s) [1]785, 868, [2]677, 1154, [3]1086
paralysis [4]638
of Christianity [5]515
paramour [4]816
paraphalakarinismos [3]59, 59n
paraphrase(s) [2]495, [3]27, [4]642, 656, [6]151
Ciceronian [5]789
parasites [3]447
parasol [2]599
parastesismos [3]67
Paraswama (myth) [2]346n
parchment [1]872, [2]409
parent(s) [1]662, [2]273, 404, [4]466, [5]74, 751
affection of [3]401, [5]476n; alienated [2]659; and child [2]200; last will of [5]651; love of [1]729; pious [5]821; wicked [1]266
parenthesis/parentheses [2]233, 455, [4]722, 735
in Matt [6]217; in St Paul [1]459; philo-parenthesist [3]138, 138n
pariahs [2]347
Paris (city) [2]511, 808, 1198n, [3]116, 160n, 1067, [4]171, 192, [5]373, 576
P. line [3]384, 384n; Massacres of [1]858n; Palais Royal [5]832, 832n; Sorbonne [1]814; University of [1]486
Paris (myth) [5]522n
judgment of [6]157, 157n
Paris/Parris, Samuel (1653–1719/20) [3]824
Parisatis (legend) [5]75, 75n
parish/parishes [5]144, 174
parishioner [1]352
poor [1]530
Park, John James (1795–1833) [3]500
Conservative Reform MT [4]9–10; *The Dogmas of the Constitution* MT [4]11–17
Park, Mungo (1771–1806) [1]528, 528n
The Journal of a Mission to the Interior of Africa [1]528n; *Travels in the Interior Districts of Africa* [1]528n
Parke-Bernet *see* New York
Parker [5]48
Parker, Edmund [1]701
Parker, John William (1792–1870) [5]48
Parker, Matthew, Archbishop of Canterbury (1504–75) [1]287n, [3]795, 795n
Parkinson, James (1755–1824) [3]937
Parkinson, Richard (1748–1815) [3]940
parliament(s)/Parliament [1]290, 343, 865, [2]43, 61, 62–3, 210, 211, 908, 946, 949n, 970, 1103, 1194, 1198, [3]152, 157, 164, [4]8, 20, 81, 659, 678, [5]544, 640, 644, [6]324
Act(s)/Bill(s) [2]941, 1180, [3]143, 149, 489, [4]667, [5]315, 632, 639, [6]29: Alien B. [5]143, 143n; Catholic Emancipation A. [1]865n, [2]935, 935n, [3]154, 154n, [4]20n; Catholic Emancipation B. [2]211 ("Relief"), 211n, 511n, [3]144n, [4]18, 20, 24 ("Relief"), 24n; Corn B. [3]810, *see also* corn laws; Corporation A. [1]809n; Deceased Wife's Sister's Marriage A. [5]393n; Exclusion B. [3]141n, 143, 144n; A. of Indemnity [4]79; A. of Indulgence [1]230; Nonconformists Relief A. [1]321n; B. of pains and penalties [3]797, 797n; Reform B. [2]210–11, [3]140, 141n, 154, 154n, 159, 788n, [4]7, 9, 11, 11n, 79n, [6]44–53; RC Peers B. [3]489n; Septennial A. [1]359n; A. of Settlement [1]866n, [4]19n; A. of Supremacy [3]539n; Test A. [1]711n, 809n, [2]48, 48n, [3]141n, [4]20, 20n; Toleration A. [1]321n, [2]717n; A. of Uniformity [1]230, 283n, 321n, 343, 353n, [2]89n, 651n, 1043n, 1198n, [3]801n, [4]630n, [5]146; A. of Union [5]659n; *see also* poor: p.-laws
being in arms against [5]146; under Charles I [2]114, 114n; as Church [1]318; customs of [4]12; English [4]307n; House of Commons [1]122, [2]68, 115, 933, [3]222, 797, 800, [4]8, 12–13 ("Lower House"), 13n, 14, 23, 80, 634, [5]124n, 147, 659n, [6]28n, 48, 52; House of Lords [1]355, 740n, [3]221, 797, 799, [4]13, 79, 96n; Houses of [1]275, 309, 527, 864, [2]357, 945, 1139, [3]884, [4]97n, [6]264; interference of [4]75; Irish [5]659; laws of [4]12; Long [2]932n, 1102n; members of [1]355, [2]120; omnipotent [3]796; powers [2]949; Puritan [2]61; Republican [2]109; reform of [3]788; role in English history [1]834; rules of [4]12; Short [2]931n, 1102n; weather-cock [5]519
Parliamentarians [1]803, [2]269, [4]590
Parliamentary Debates MT [4]18–24
Parma [1]831
Parma, Duke of (Alessandro Farnese) (d 1592) [4]199
Parmenides of Elea (b c 510 BC) [1]187, [2]340n, 425n, [5]705–7
Parmigianino, Girolamo Francesco Maria Mazzola (1503–40) [3]899 ("Parmeggiano"), 899n
Parnassus [1]801, [2]134, [6]281, 281n
Parnell, Thomas (1679–1718) [1]38, 156n
Parnell, William (d 1821) *An Historical Apology for the Irish Catholics* [1]lxxxiv, [2]48, 966; MT [4]25–6
Paro [5]836

parody/parodies [1]366n, 370, [4]192
paronomasia [1]684
paroxysm [1]455
Parr, Samuel (1747–1825) [2]76, 353, 845, 847, 848
 A Spital Sermon [2]850; MT [4]27–8
Parret (river) [2]820, 820n
parricides [2]661
parrot [1]111, [2]820, 820n, [3]955, 963, [4]319, [5]753
parrotry [4]660
Parry, Charles Henry (1779–1860) [1]204n
Parry, Frederick (fl 1799) [1]204n
Parry, Sir William Edward (1790–1855) *Narrative of the Attempt to Reach the North Pole* [1]204, 204n, [2]834n, 1108n, [3]989, 989n
pars pro toto [1]524, 601
parson [5]278
 claims of [6]23; in Hogarth [3]189
Parsons, Abraham (d 1785) *Travels in Asia and Africa* ed Berjew MT [4]29–31; 489–90 ("Parson")
Parsons, Edward (1762–1833) *see* Neal *History of the Puritans* ed Parsons
Parsons, Robert (1546–1610) [2]771
part(s) [3]44
 and whole(s) [1]234, 292, 524, 524n, 549, 601, 603, 862, [2]159, 631, 1055, [3]213, 678, 841, [4]157, [5]267, 316 ("entireness"), 528, 550, 698, 794
"parthenolatry/parthenolatries" [1]519, 519n
parthenolatry [1]257n, [2]916, 916n
Parthia
 Parthian empire [2]653
partiality, shameless [1]727
partibility [4]425
participium [3]546
participle(s) [3]450, [4]166, [5]114, 114n
 formed from noun [4]14, 14n; as substantives [2]128, 128n
particle(s) [2]962, 1205, [3]202, 292, 343, 915
 component [5]827; elementary [3]328; Greek [6]139; of human body [1]737; ultimate [2]890; use of [5]487; vibrating [6]173
particular(s) [1]679, [4]362, [5]459, [6]132
 and universal [2]279, [5]756, 758; views of [5]453
particularisation(s) [3]517, [5]438, [6]299
particularism [1]639, 639n, [2]674, 674n
particularity [2]855, [3]746
"particulative" [1]595, 596n
partisan(s) [1]224, 331, [3]147, [5]70, 541
 conscientious [5]696; furious [1]318
partisanship [1]808
partnership, secret [1]518
parturience [1]601
parturition [2]273
party/parties [1]520, [2]1197, [3]166, 695, [5]124, [6]10
 anti-prelatic [2]260, [5]521, 640; Cavalier [5]146; Episcopalian [1]332; Evangelical [5]521; high-church [2]1135, [5]578; hostile [3]147; jaundice of [1]291; madness of [2]732, [3]233n; p.-malice [2]315; Milton's [3]883; parliamentary [5]640; p.-passion(s) [1]234, [3]803; p.-spirit [1]213, [3]146, [4]827; Pontificial [5]521; prelatic(al) [1]318, 803; Presbyterian [1]318, 333; Reformed [5]521; revolutionary [2]118; Romish [1]332, 843; royal [1]803; royalist [1]182, [5]507
partyman [3]143
Parvati (myth) [4]30n
Pascal, Blaise ("Louis de Montalte") (1623–62) [4]32, 78, [5]178, 178n
 paradox of [2]227n
 Les provinciales tr Wendrock, Cordero, and Brunetti [1]lxiiin, lxxxi; MT [4]32–4
pasce oves [5]634, 634n
"pasch" [3]913, 913n
paschein [3]83, 83n, 720, 720n
"pasigraphy" [5]228, 228n
Pasini, Giuseppe Luca (1687–1770) *Vocabolario italiano-latino* MT [4]35–8
Pasley, Sir Charles William (1780–1861) [5]196 ("Paisley"), 196n
"pass" [3]913, 913n
passage
 blind [3]740; crowded [3]1010
Passavant, Johann Carl (1790–1857) *Untersuchung über den Lebens Magnetismus und das Hellesehen* [2]551n
passio [5]26
passion(s) [1]157, 169, 178, 280, [2]639, 689, 922, [3]63, 222, 227, 381, 720, 806, 813, [4]103, 268, 598, 679, 718, 731, 734, 735, 781, 809, 820, 835, 857, [5]25n, 363, 784, [6]28
 and action *see* action; blind [2]315; connate [5]613; corporeal [5]614; creates beauty [4]292; deep [4]834; deification of [4]429; disappointed [4]860; drudge of [5]622; evil [6]46; of factionary [6]59; gestures of [3]382; insight into [4]828; and metre [1]377; momentary [2]639; moody [4]361; need images [4]278; and order [4]168; parasite plants [4]278; in poetry [4]162; power of [4]860; ruling [5]70, 161, 419; seat of [4]786; suffering

passion(s)—*continued*
[1]728; suppressed [4]842; truth in [1]49; unphilosophic [4]348; violent [3]384; working of [1]397; writing from [3]404; *see also* passivity
Passion, the [5]524
passionateness [2]636–7
passive, the [5]653, 724
passive obedience *see* obedience
passiveness [4]821
political [5]40
passivity [1]648, [3]79, 83, [5]25n
of the soul [5]236; *see also* passion
Passover [1]873, [2]387, 902n, [4]484
Passow, Franz (1786–1833) [1]7
past, the [3]163, 286, 307, [5]269, 302
consciousness of [5]414; and future *see* future; indefinite [5]321; knowledge concerning [5]415; value of [1]280
paste-board [2]1155
Pasteur, Louis (1822–95) [2]366n
pastor(s) [1]310, 322, 339, 356, [2]475, [3]875
Christian [2]295
pastoral, the [1]60, [2]55, 1051
emblem of [6]325
Patagonians [5]252
patchwork [2]421, [4]169
patent(s) [1]763, 797, [5]89
celestial [5]659
pater infantium, durus [5]586, 586n
patere [1]237n
paternity, divine [3]16
"path" [4]807, 807n
path [3]564, 601
pathemata [1]447
pathetic, the, and horrible [1]397
pathology [3]67, 871, [4]581
pathos/*pathos* [3]374n, [4]794, 806, 820, 825, 826, 834, [6]219
pati and *agere* see *agere*
patient(s) [2]402, [4]259, [5]171, 583
cataleptic [5]517; magnetic [5]141; *see also* agent and patient
patior [5]26n
Patmos [2]459, 460, [3]928, 929
Paton, Captain John (d 1684) [2]1171n
patriarch(s) [1]444, [2]743, 1198, [3]446, 456, 1089, [5]253, 537
of Protestantism [2]304
Patrician [5]646
Patricius (d 371) [2]823, [5]234, 238n
Patrick, St (probably c 390–c 460) [1]522, [5]51
Patrick, Simon, Bishop of Ely (1626–1707) [5]80
patriot(s) [2]929, 1143, [3]148, 796, 799, 799n, [5]681
under Charles I [2]929; Crown and Anchor p. [3]146; English p. of Restoration [3]153; German [5]278; mistaken [1]223
patriotism [4]798, 804, [5]104, 378, 379, 829
extinction of [5]644
Patripassians ("Patropassians") [2]33, 33n, 34n, 208
Patripassionists [5]210
Patrizi, Francesco (1529–97) *see* Zoroaster *Oracula* ed Patrizi
Patroclus (in Homer) [1]790
Patrologiae cursus completus . . . series graeca ed Migne [2]334n, 364n, 718n, 733n, [5]620n
Patrologiae cursus completus . . . series latina ed Migne [1]491n, 565n, 605n, [2]334n, 437n, 969n, [5]11n q, [6]115n
patron [1]394, [2]927, 1018n
patronage [1]309, [2]81, 235, [5]322
pattern(s) [2]489, [4]313
Patterson [4]617, [6]285
Patterson, Mr *see* Patteson, Henry
Patteson, Frances (fl 1911) [3]838
Patteson, Frances Duke (née Coleridge) (1796–1842) [5]97, 97n
Patteson, Henry (1757–1824) [1]697
Patteson, John (1790–1861) [5]97n
Pattison, William (1706–27) [1]38
Paul (fiction) [5]200
Paul, St, the Apostle (d c 65) [1]lxi, 166, 235, 236, 252, 253, 340, 437, 438, 438n, 491n, 504, 529, 588, 684, 687, 702n, 751, 785n q, 807, 824, 832, 877, [2]34, 35, 37, 58, 64, 184, 199, 208, 256, 264, 270, 271, 273, 280, 451, 456, 468, 472, 486, 489, 493, 495, 496, 564, 591n, 592, 661, 670, 670n, 684, 700, 701, 705, 705n, 706, 707, 709, 712, 717n, 735, 742n, 838, 839n, 913, 922, 938n, 949, 1085, 1162, 1177, 1178, [3]14n, 36, 49, 87, 142, 309, 422, 426n, 446, 542, 561n, 611, 611n, 669, 669n, 678, 691, 695, 725, 726, 738, 739, 743, 745, 751–2, 760, 772, 777, 1085, 1085n, 1090, [4]41, 69, 171, 226, 250, 252, 254–5, 296, 357, 420, 473, 474, 477, 477n, 484, 616, 624, 637, 646, 655, 656, [5]14 q, 15, 20, 34, 58, 96, 128n, 165–6 q, 384, 390–1, 466, 492n, 506, 513, 514n, 515, 515n, 518, 522, 525, 536, 545, 546 q, 574 q, 575, 579, 582, 587–8, 603, 625, 628, 634, 645n, 647, 649, 654, 656, 682, 778, 807, 807n, [6]23, 28n, 55, 68, 70, 72, 77,

85, 91, 101, 114, 117, 140n, 141, 292, 303
apostle to understanding [4]399; apostles and [2]469, 470–1, 475; in Arabia [3]21; auditor(s) of [3]446, [5]138, 668n; authorship of Epistles [5]128, 128n; authorship of Heb [2]563, [3]19; belief in ascension [3]925; on circumcision [5]623–4; concept of soul [3]44; conversion of [2]252, 252n, 337, 491n–2n, 492, [3]987, 987n, [5]125n, 172; differs from Paulus [4]45; difficulty of writings [2]501; disciple of [1]465; distinguishes body, soul, spirit [3]38–9; earnest prose [2]499; epilepsy [2]705–6; episcopacy [3]7n; epistles in harmony with John [1]463; epistles of *see* Bible: NT: EPISTLE(s); establishment of bishops [5]503; and *evangelium infantiae* [2]35; on faith [6]223; figure in [2]685; glorifies Plato [3]511; on *gnosis* [2]285; Heb ascribed to [2]400, 400n; and the Jews [2]567, [3]738, 745; journey to Rome [2]500; language of [5]76; on law [2]184, 278, [3]753; letters of [5]739; lived to doubt his own interpretations [3]731; and Luther [3]745; on meaning of "body" [2]924; metaphors of [1]200, 200n, [3]311; misunderstood [2]499–501; and Mosaic law [2]470–1; most difficult passage in [1]463; parentheses of [1]459; Pauline Christianity [2]469–70; Pauline sobriety [3]528, [6]311; as planting [5]395; on prayer [1]782; premises of [3]54; on redemption [2]657; on resurrection [1]127; at Rome [5]635–6, 635n; school of [2]437; silence of [2]275; not source of historical fact [2]452; source of Luke's gospel [2]451; spirit of [2]266; spiritual sage [2]919; style of [1]113, 113n, [2]454–5, 455n; theological system of [3]424; words of [4]40; writings of [1]734, 816, [3]74, 107, 926, [6]66–7; *see also* Saul of Tarsus
Paul the Hermit, St (c 230–c 343) [2]737–8
Paul III (Alessandro Farnese), Pope (1468–1549) [1]831, [2]781, [3]232n, [5]14, 14n
Paul IV (Gian Pietro Carafa), Pope (1476–1559) [3]232n
Paul V (Camillo Borghese), Pope (1552–1621) [1]843n
Paul of Samosata (fl 260–272) [2]726n, [3]691, 691n, [5]525, 667, 667n
Paulding, James Kirke (1778–1860) *The Lay of the Scottish Fiddle* [4]171
Paulin, Roger *Ludwig Tieck: A Literary Biography* [4]427n
Paulinity [5]128
Paulinus, St, Bishop of Trier (d 358) [2]729
Paulinus, St (Paulus Nolanus), Bishop of Nola (c 353–431), [3]540, [5]587, 587n, [6]318n
Paulists [3]458
Paullini, Christian Franz (1643–c 1712) *Disquisitio* [1]lxix, lxxxi, civ; MT [4]39
Pauloeides [1]459, 459n
Paulus, Heinrich Eberhard Gottlob (1761–1851) [1]305, 306n, [2]144, 144n, 194n–5n, 481n, 736n, [4]40, 227, 227n, [5]199, 204
C's differences from [4]46, 46n
Handbuch [4]41n; *Das Leben Jesu* [1]306n, [2]194n–5n q; MT [4]40–68; *see also* Spinoza *Opera* ed Paulus
Paulus Nolanus *see* Paulinus, St, Bishop of Nola
Paulus the Lawyer [5]595
pauper(s) [1]529n, [2]159, [5]278
Pausanias (fl 143–176) *Description of Greece* tr W. H. S. Jones [4]464n q
Pavillon, Gertrude (in Scott) [4]613
pawnbrokers [5]234
Pawson, John (1737–1806) [5]168, 174, 174n–5n
Payagoaes [5]104
Paybody, Mr [3]795n
pea-blossom [4]93
peace [2]847, [5]276–7, 642, 822
attribute of [5]854; of Christ [2]296; inward [3]551–2; love of [2]286, [5]510
peach [4]168, 168n
marble p. [4]780
peacock [3]812, 888
Peake's Commentary on the Bible ed M. Black and Rowley [1]416, 422n, 434n, 532n, [2]1029n
Peale, Rembrandt (1778–1860) *An Historical Disquisition on the Mammoth* [1]62n
Pearce, Zachary, Bishop of Rochester (1690–1774) [3]889
pearl(s) [2]219, [4]29–30, 30n, 91n, 93, 95, [5]191
Pearson, Edward (1756–1811) *Twelve Lectures* [2]153, 153n
Pearson, George (1751–1828) [3]942
Pearson, John, Bishop of Chester (1613–86) [2]294n, 880
An Exposition of the Creed [2]334, 334n, [3]539n, 612n, 733n; MT [4]69–70; [5]619n, 637, [6]63; see also *Critici sacri* ed Pearson and others
Pearson, Richard (1765–1836) [4]312
peasant(s) [5]282, [6]44
Scotch [4]657; wishes of [5]278

peasantry [5]512
pebble [5]682
peccability [3]49
peccadilloes [2]735
peculia [4]421, 421n
peculiarity/peculiarities [1]763, 796, [2]54
pedant(s) [1]528, [2]763, [4]609
pedantry [2]528n, 933, [3]905, [4]283
classical [1]220; of French [4]780; mathematical [5]424; witty [2]930
pederasty [1]lxxxi, 43n, [3]699, 699n, 893n
pedlar [5]366
"pedoeuvres" [1]862, 862n
Peel, Sir Robert, the Younger (1788–1850) [3]154, [4]21, [5]124, 124n, [6]47, 47n
language of [6]48
peer(s) [3]786, 786n, [4]13, 13n
peerage [3]800
peevishness [4]709
Pegasus (myth) [4]192
polemic [5]528, 528n
peiro [5]104, 104n
Peisistratus/Pisistratus (600–527 BC) [2]89n, 891, [5]224
Pelagian(s) [1]821, [2]247n, 1178, [3]308n, [4]596, 596n, [5]135, 135n, 394, 609, 610–11
Pelagianism [1]149, 814, *814n*, [3]308, [4]596n, [5]596, 597n, 610n
Pelagius (c 360–c 420) [2]809–10, 1099, [5]596
Peleus (myth) [4]289
Pelham MA [1]205
Pelikan, Jaroslav *see* Luther *Works* ed Pelikan and Lehmann
Pelion [4]188, [5]483, 483n
Pella [2]833, 833n
Pember, Robert (d 1560) [2]64
Pembroke, Countess of *see* Herbert, Mary
pen(s) [1]lxxi
C's use of [1]cxxix; steel [1]cxxix; tongue of dream [1]808
Penance [1]349, [3]440n, 759, [5]398n, 496, 566n, 651
RC doctrine [6]256
pencil(s) [1]lxxi, 487
C's use of [1]cxxix
pendentis [3]680
pendulum [3]834
penetrability [3]280
peninsula(s) [5]528
Peninsular War [2]163n, [5]104n, 195n
penitence [1]400, [2]560, [5]420, [6]325–6
penitent [5]494
dying [2]27, [5]589
penman/penmen [5]515, [6]98
apostolic [3]524, [6]306; inspired [1]560; sacred [2]561, [3]1086, [5]473; of Scripture [2]806
Penn, Granville (1761–1844) [2]164n ("Grenville")
Penn, William (1644–1718) [3]927
Some Fruits of Solitude [3]928n; *see also* G. Fox *Journal* ed Penn
Pennant, Thomas (1726–98) [6]147, 148
Pennsylvania [3]495n
Pennsylvania, University of *see* Philadelphia PA
Penrith [2]1118n, [4]675
Penrose, Thomas (1743–79) [1]38
pentad [1]563n, 643, [2]1202n, [3]361n, 399n, 416, 416n, 831n, 916n, 1012n, [4]166n, 323, [5]242n, 266, 266n, 444, 444n, 661, 663
of biography and history [2]51–2; of Christianity [2]290; of Church [1]806; of grammar [3]835n; logical [1]231, [3]6n, 15–17, 15n, [4]166–8; Noetic [5]631; philosophical [3]451; of races [1]539–40, [3]356n
pentameter [3]814
Italian [2]8
Pentateuch *see* Bible: OT: Pentateuch
pente [4]37
Pentecost [2]653, 653n, 701n, [4]248n, 260, 476, 476n, [5]535, 651n, 741n
people [1]220, 865, [2]899–900, 900n, [3]206n, [4]251, [5]40, 135, 147, 270, 311, [6]11
chosen [5]649; common [4]223; dispersion of [1]832; drest [2]999; English [1]401; fallen [5]41; morals of [5]512; and populace [3]799; and public [1]220; share in government [4]21; sovereign [2]511, 511n; sovereignty of [2]195, [3]157, [6]50–1, 51; unlearned [4]300
Peor-Apis (myth) [6]219
Pepin/Pippin the Short, King of the Franks (d 768) [5]104, 104n
Pepys, Samuel (1633–1703) [2]17n, [4]385n, 390n
Diary [2]196n q; *Memoirs* [2]1191; MT [4]71–83
Pepys, William Haseldine (1775–1856) [2]857, 857n–8n, 858n, [3]937, 1002n, 1033n
peras [5]104, 104n
perceiving and knowing *see* knowing
perception(s) [1]270, 679, [2]547, 547n, 603, 606, 607, 608–9, 679, 860, 1002n, [3]23, 45, 116, 128n, 391, 790, 791, 848, 858,

967, ^{4}93, 130, 346, 351, 414, 447–8, 452, 453, 460, 461–2, 864, ^{5}410, 793
absurd ^{3}644; act of ^{3}389; an art ^{3}94; condition of ^{3}381; confused ^{3}966, ^{4}366; defect of ^{5}459; defined ^{2}639; etymology of ^{2}610; form of ^{1}537; generalised ^{5}599; ground of reality in ^{5}443; and image ^{5}409; and imagination ^{4}217; immediate ^{4}155; instrument for ^{5}418; laws of ^{3}270; permanent in ^{3}244; positive ^{3}90; role of memory in ^{3}377; and sensation ^{3}399; spiritual ^{3}551
Perceval, John James, 3rd Earl of Egmont (c 1737–1822) ^{1}lxxxv q, 9
Perceval, Spencer (1762–1812) ^{1}9
percipi and *esse* see *esse*
percipiency ^{2}547, 547n
percipient ^{1}525, ^{4}269, ^{5}443, ^{6}8
and perceptum ^{5}410
Percival, Robert (1765–1826) *An Account of the Island of Ceylon* ^{1}777n; MT ^{4}84–9
Percy, Henry (1364–1403) *see* Hotspur
Percy, Henry, 8th Earl of Northumberland (1564–1632) ^{2}929
Percy, John ("John Fisher") (1569–1641) ^{2}24, ^{3}486
Percy Society *see* London
Percy, Thomas (1729–1811) *Reliques of Ancient English Poetry* ^{1}lxxx, cixn; MT ^{4}90; 815n
Percy, Thomas, 7th Earl of Northumberland (1528–72) ^{3}144n
perdition ^{5}8–9
Pereira, Gometius (b 1550) *Antoniana Margarita* ^{1}lxxi, xciii, clxvii; MT ^{4}91–8
Pererius, Benedictus (Benito Pereira) (1535–1610) ^{6}112
"perfect" ^{5}170
perfecter ^{4}648
perfection(s) ^{2}206–7, 1021, 1165, ^{3}358, 859, ^{4}136, 364–5, ^{5}154, 169, 170n, 173, 212, ^{6}316
of the Deity ^{2}183; divine ^{5}20; eternal ^{1}627; fullness of ^{5}457; ideal ^{2}205; modes of ^{5}18; monsters of ^{1}849; moral ^{3}263; progressive ^{5}419
Pergamos ^{3}422n, ^{6}168n
peri ^{4}595, 595n
peri ^{5}104, 104n
Peri hypsous see Longinus
"perichoresis" ^{5}704n
perichoresis ^{1}640, *640n*, ^{2}666, 882, ^{3}428n, 460, ^{4}400, 400n, 682, 682n
Pericles (c 500–429 BC) ^{2}1018n, 1069n
Periegesis ^{2}980, 981n
perihelion ^{3}323, 324
period(s)
long ^{6}144; long-breathed ^{5}534; musical ^{4}721
Periodical Accounts Relative to the Baptist Missionary Society ^{2}339
Peripatetics ^{1}185n, ^{3}916, 916n, ^{4}174, ^{5}805–6, ^{6}4; *see also* philosophy, peripatetic
periphery ^{3}349, 357
periphrasis ^{5}271, 546
perishing ^{3}63
perisson ^{1}564–5, 564n, 573
peritura ^{4}136
periwinkle ^{4}286
perjury ^{1}271, ^{3}183, ^{6}262
Perkins, Elisha (1741–99) ^{3}1067, 1067n
permanence ^{3}800, ^{5}273
permanent, the ^{1}395
Perpetua, St (d 203) ^{2}699, 699n
Perpetuus, St ^{2}699
Perron, Jacques Davy du, Cardinal (1556–1618) ^{5}576, 579
perruption ^{4}227
perruquier ^{5}669
persecution(s) ^{1}273, 807, ^{2}336, 827, 1081, ^{3}232, 582, 694, 734, 794, ^{4}20, 587, ^{5}37, 471
appetite for ^{2}1102; of Arminians ^{5}596; defence of ^{5}625; a duty ^{3}818; foulest ^{5}616; mania of ^{2}913; Neronian ^{5}85; religious ^{2}973, ^{5}143
persecutor(s) ^{1}281, ^{2}938, ^{5}544
Jewish ^{6}101; popish ^{2}813
Persephone (myth) ^{2}583n, 584n, 1091n; *see also* Proserpine
persequi ^{3}818
Perseus (myth) ^{4}192
perseverance ^{5}137, 137n
final ^{1}222; of saints ^{1}826–7
Persia ^{1}440, 764, 764n, 771, 797, 799, ^{2}401, 418, 433, 597, 739, 740, 865, 1012, ^{3}70, 419, 473, 474, 673, ^{5}830, ^{6}150, 270, 271, 272, 274, 281
captivity in ^{3}436; Persian empire ^{3}923; fables ^{3}1090; Genie Prince of ^{3}417; legends ^{2}919; mythology ^{3}92n; wisdom of ^{3}92
Persian (language) ^{6}150n
Persian(s) ^{2}419, 421, 742, 898, ^{4}513n, 529–30, 780, ^{5}156, 337, 353
as generous/Iapetic race ^{1}540; P. hyperbole ^{1}706; P. monarch ^{3}722

persiflage [1]139
Persius (Aulus Persius Flaccus) (34–62) [1]cvii, 38, [2]758, 760n
tr Dryden [1]38; style [2]760–1
Satirarum liber ed I. and M. Casaubon [1]cvii; MT [4]99–100
"person(s)" [1]681, 681n, [2]21, 250, 250n, 264, 264n, 789–90, [3]11, 11n, 53, 233n, [5]15, 308, 408, 408n, 627, 799n, [6]76, 87
person(s) [1]395, [2]1030, 1043, 1043n, [3]17, 233n, 558, 917, [4]262, 648, 816, [5]6, 7, 25, 59, 285, 411, 614
ad extra [1]785, 785n; bad translation [3]428; Church not p. [2]680; correlative [5]304; distinction of [5]25; divine [3]52; division of [5]535; and errors [3]368; flux of [5]273; of God [2]571; in grammar [6]26; Hebrew word [2]446; insulated [1]676; mistranslation of [2]726; moral [3]154; particular [4]24; and personeity [3]520, 520n, [6]302, 302n; plurality of [5]19; processional [3]77, 77n; quoad p. [5]616; sacred [2]936; Second [5]626; or self-knowing mind [5]741; of Son of God [3]14; subordination of [6]82; and thing(s) [1]35, 35n, 424, [2]321, [3]157–8, 720, 831, [4]341–2, 341n, [5]75n, 613, 613n, 649, [6]22, 28–9; three [5]6, 7, 16, 26; in Trinity [1]434, [2]*21n*, [5]24; will of [3]18
persona/personae [2]250, 250n, 726n, 731, 731n, [3]173, 428, 428n, 917
p. patiens [4]815
personal(s) [1]395
"personality" [1]681
personality/personalities [1]565, [3]266, 729, [4]93, 159, 226, [5]182
defined [2]659–60; derivation of [6]5; divine [2]1175; of evil spirits [5]86, 86n; of God [4]44, [5]86n; of the Godhead [3]1093; of Holy Ghost [2]751, 751n, 752n, [5]798; meaning "body" [2]924; and personeity [3]720; principle of [3]520, [6]302; royal [4]20; in Trinity [2]598; of Word [2]479
personation [3]182
personator [2]464
"personeity" [1]304, 304n
personeity [1]153, [2]419, 456, 457, [3]27, 428, [5]86, 86n, [6]82, 302
divine [3]944; of God [5]481; of Holy Ghost [2]751n, 752n; and person *see* person; and personality [3]720; primal [6]5
personification(s) [1]57, 397, 725, [2]482, 515, 798, [3]401, 404, 1022, [4]41, [5]117, 117n, [6]32
allegorical [1]432, 432n; of wisdom [2]433
personifying [5]764, 766
persönlich [5]308
Persönlichkeit [5]293
perspective(s) [2]267, [3]340, 341, 743, 748, [4]126, 160
different [5]371; false [2]824
persuasion [2]1160
Peru [2]163n, [3]1077, [4]201, 201n
Pesahim [2]513n
Pescheräh [5]252
Pestalozzi, Johann Heinrich (1746–1827) [5]311, 311n, 325
pestilence [5]274, 277
pet [4]278
petah [2]789, 789n
Petau, Denis *see* Petavius
Petavius, Dionysius (Denis Petau) (1583–1652) [1]478n, [2]666, 666n, [3]764, 928, [5]24, [6]292–3, 294, 294n
Dogmata theologica [3]762n, 764n
Peter (fiction) [5]20, 21, 23, 28, 200, 791, [6]299
Peter, St/Simon Barjona/Simon Peter (d c 64) [1]235n, 294, 309n, 449n, 451, 457, 458, 511, 512, 514–15, 843n, [2]38n, 256, 257, 276, 293, 470, 484, 498, 653, 653n, 670, 670n, 700, 703, 705, 705n, 706, 712, 713n, 717n, 722n, 834, 924n, 1045, 1080, 1096n, [3]6n–7n, 36, 40, 76n, 234, 234n, 309, 422, 446, 455, 466, 467, 467n, 480, 541–3, 594, 669n, 711, 725, 745, 1069, [4]472, 474, 474n, 641, [5]14, 60–1, 515, 526, 534, 539, 628, 634, 646 q, 667, [6]23
Apostle of the Circumcision [3]467, 467n; Bishop of Rome [3]458, [6]15, 15n; episcopacy of [3]7; epistles of [3]482; P's Creed [5]618n; "Rockman" [3]458, 458n; at Rome [3]6–7, [5]635–6, 635n; school of [2]437; shadow of [5]859, 859n; vision of [2]470
Peter Comestor (d c 1179) [2]11–12
Peter Lombard *see* Lombard
Peter Martyr (Pietro Martire Vermigli) (1500–62) [5]391
Peterloo Massacre [2]211n
Petersburg [3]383
petitio principii [3]359, 363, 504, 643, [4]422, [5]4, 508, 761, 776
petitio rei sub lite [5]33
petition(s) [5]530
unconditional [2]185
petra [3]458, 458n
Petracci, Pietro (fl 1608) *see* Petrarch *Il Petrarca* ed Petracci

Petrarch (Francesco Petrarca) (1304–74) [1]221n, [3]265, 265n, 882n
in C's lectures [1]cxxxix; ed Sotheby [1]xcv, xcvn, xcvin
Il Petrarca . . . Copy A ed Petracci MT [4]101; *Le Rime Copy B* MT [4]102–4; *Petrarch's Lyric Poems* tr and ed Durling [4]102–4; *Trionfo della fama* tr E. G. Williams [2]868 q, 868n
petrifaction(s) [5]310, 374
Petronius (latter half of 1st century) [2]758n, [3]174
Satyricon [1]67n q, [6]148n q
petros [3]458, 458n
petticoat(s) [3]586, 587n, [5]119
scarlet [5]662
Petty-Fitzmaurice, Henry, 3rd Marquis of Lansdowne (1780–1863) [2]954n, [6]47, 47n
pettytoes [5]224n
Petvin, John (b c 1690) [2]867n
Letters concerning Mind [1]lxxxix, clxiii; MT [4]105–16
Pevsner, Sir Nikolaus Bernhard (1902–83) [1]498 q
pewterer [3]181
Pfaff, Johann Friedrich (1765–1825) [5]246–7
Pfeiffer, Rudolph *History of Classical Scholarship* [2]36n
phaenomenon/phaenomena *see* phenomen/phenomenon/phenomena
Phaer/Phayer, Thomas (?1510–60) *see* Virgil *Aeneid* tr Phaer
Phaeton (myth) [1]399, [5]745n
phainetai [5]266, 266n
Phalakrinismos [3]59, 59n
Phalaris (c 570–554 BC) [2]570, [3]589n, [4]246n, [5]226
Phanocles (probably 3rd century BC) [1]145
Phantasie [5]795
phantasm(s) [1]451, 451n, [2]1076, [5]425, 483, 680
distinct [5]564; lifeless [1]120; subjective [5]755
phantasma [1]451n, [3]612
representative [5]734
phantasmagoria [4]193, [6]100, 100n–1n
phantast(s) [2]919, 919n, 1026n
"phantastery" [2]1026, 1026n
phantasy [5]734
phantom(s) [1]558, [2]1144, [3]520, 865, [5]201, 553, [6]66, 302
den of [1]646; eye-p. [6]244; material [5]18; matter as [1]691; numerical [5]7; unsubstantial [1]815
pharanx [1]26, 26n
Pharaoh [2]387, [5]62, 64, 64n
Pharaoh (Bible) [1]12, [2]292, 387, 1041
Pharisee(s) [1]353, 449, 451, 454, 703, [2]483, 495, 497, 567 ("Pharisaic"), 1075, 1076n, [3]6n, 56, [4]481, 628, 660
pharmacy [4]769
phasis [2]1142
Phavorinus, Varinus (d 1537) [5]546 q, 547, 547n
phenomen/phenomenon/phenomena [1]201, 524, 547, 547n, 787n, [2]802, 802n, 890n, [3]139, 199, 201, 202, 249, 357, 394, 394n, 454, 737, [4]61, 220, 220n, 413, [5]4–5 ("phainomena"), 32, 266, 405, 442
becomes law [4]379; defined [3]277–8, [5]615; external [4]674; *homo phaenomenon/phainomenon* [3]265, 265n, 312, 313; of material world [5]421; and noumenon/noumena *see* noumenon/noumena; in time [5]604; unusual [4]271
"phenomenal" [5]308
phenomenal and real [5]305
"phenomenically" [5]734, 734n
phenomenism [2]547n
Pherecrates (fl c 430–410 BC) [4]147
Pherecydes of Syros (fl 550 BC) [5]223
Pheres [4]595, 595n
Phidias/Pheidias (c 500–c 430 BC) [2]1018n
Philadelphia [3]422n
Philadelphia PA [3]495n, [6]168n
Athenaeum, marginalia in [2]179; Rosenbach Museum and Library, marginalia in [1]clxiii, [6]249; University of Pennsylvania Library, marginalia in [1]clxvi, 215
Philadelphians [1]297n
"philagathocaletheists" [5]470, 470n
"Philalethes, Alazonomastix" *see* More, Henry
"Philalethes, Eugenius" *see* Vaughan, Thomas
Philanax Anglicus [1]335
"philanthropic" [2]73, 73n
philanthropist(s) [2]980 ("felon-trappists"), 1143, [5]293
philanthropy [3]250, [4]533
philauty [2]980n
Philemon (c 361–c 263 BC) [2]724, 775n, [4]147
philheautists [2]980
Philip, St (1st century) [2]37n, [3]432, 432n, [5]535–6
Philip I, King of France (1052–1108) [3]785

Philip II, King of Macedon (382–336 BC) [1]42, 42n
Philip II, King of Spain (1527–98) [1]318, [3]1077
Philip III, King of Spain (1578–1621) [2]936n
Philip IV, King of Spain (1605–65) [2]936n
Philippa (13th century) [5]194
Philippe IV, King of France (1268–1314) [5]194
Philippi [1]464
Philippides (fl 311 BC) [4]147
Philippus (fl c 40) [4]147
Philips, Ambrose (1674–1749) [1]38, 60n
Philips, John (1676–1709) [1]37
Philistines [5]506
Phillips, Charles (?1787–1859) *Calumny Confuted* [1]100, [4]6
Phillpotts, Henry (1778–1869) [1]861
Philo Judaeus (c 30 BC–AD 45) [1]694n, [2]325, 798n, [3]533, 533n, [4]303, 426n, 440n, [5]27, [6]99–100, 100n, 137–8, 142, 143 q, 319, 319n
 on angels [1]468n, [2]429, 429n; and authorship of Wisd of Sol [2]429n, 430n, 431–2, [6]138–42, 138n, 144; on Logos [2]433, 433n–4n, 457–8, 798, [3]524, 524n, [5]27n, 741, [6]306, 306n; writings of [5]807, 807n, [6]32, 32n
 De confusione linguarum tr Colson and Whitaker [2]458 q; *De legum allegoria* tr Colson and Whitaker [2]432n q; *De migratione Abrahami* tr Colson and Whitaker [2]458 q; *De opificio mundi* [2]426n, 458n; *Opera* [2]429n; *Quaestiones in Genesin* [2]434n q; *Quis rerum divinarum heres* [6]100n; *Quod Deus immutabilis sit* [2]429n
Philo of Athens (159–80 BC) [5]728
Philo of Byblus/Byblos (64–161) [2]576n
Philo of Larisa (159–80 BC)
Philobiblion [2]97
"philochristianism" [4]269, 269n
"philo-despot" [2]927, 927n
philo-despotist [1]224
"philogynic" [2]73, 73n
philokalia [5]130, 130n
philokalos [3]1075, [5]130n
philologer [2]892
 and philosopher [4]111n
Philological Quarterly [2]985
philologist(s) [2]379, [5]735
 old [3]257; and philosopher [4]220, 220n
philology [4]111
 and philosophy [4]111, 111n, [5]752, 752n, 770
"philo-parenthesist(s)" [3]138, 138n
philo-parenthesist [1]lxvin
Philopatris [4]660n
"philopoesy" [5]271, 271n
"philopsophy" [2]1147, 1147n
Philo-Romanists [4]22
philosophe(s) [5]703 ("Philosophs"), 703n
philosopheme(s) [2]389, 389n, [5]719
philosopher(s) [1]686, [2]480, 727, 1080, [3]136, 531, [4]310, 448, [5]88, 168, 363, 476, 545
 Alexandrine [5]740; all [3]856; all English [4]235; is *always*, not *now* [2]848; ancient [4]648, [5]406–7; ancient and modern [4]107; Bacon as [4]159–60, 160n; and Bible [5]317–18; biform [5]95; Böhme as [1]558; born, not made [2]601; Browne as [1]762, 796; categoric [5]692; considerateness of [3]365; critical [2]615, 615n, [4]413; and divines [6]79; dynamic [5]545; eclectic [2]1002, [5]226, 743; elder [5]707, [6]6; elder German [4]523; and empirist [6]236; in fashion [2]999; French [1]623; function is to distinguish [4]492; genuine [2]186, [5]204; German [2]1016, 1028, [4]269, [5]95, 363; great [4]418; Greek [1]242, [2]695, 1012, [3]87, [4]128, [5]54, 481, 803; Greek and Roman [3]626; on happiness [6]316; mannered [5]301; mechanic [4]506; monk as [6]234; of nature see *Naturphilosoph/Naturphilosophen*; need mathematics [2]616; nominal [5]385; old [3]257, [5]704; original [5]201; pagan [4]651; and philologer [4]111n; and poet [2]135, [5]242, 858; post-Kantian [4]538, [5]90n, 743n; profoundest [4]654; as prophet [5]89; purpose of [3]715; religious [5]86; split by Schelling [4]461; P's Stone [1]750; superstition of [4]601; true [5]411; of the understanding [5]692, 692n
"philosopherists" [3]383, 383n
Philosophical Magazine ed Tilloch [3]936, 1032n, [4]82n, [5]346n
Philosophical Magazine and Journal [4]82, 82n, 505n, 532n, [5]344, 346n, 771n
Philosophical Transactions of the Royal Society [1]lxxvii, lxxxv, 570n, 639n, 792, [2]69n q, 858n, 885n, 967, [3]60n, 868n, 869n, 870n, 945n, 948n, 949n, 1002n, [4]263n, 312, 396n, 526n q, 737n, [5]232n, 255n, 261n, 291n, 504n, 505n, 734n
Philosophical Transactions of the Royal Society . . . Abridged† [4]88, 88n, 312
philosophics [3]484
philosophisers [5]416
philosophism [2]1064, 1064n
philosophist(s) [2]421, 1080, [3]913

"philosophy" [4]615, 615n, [5]744

philosophy/philosophies [1]562, 644, 647, [5]123, 208, 710

abstract [5]673; age of [1]719; of an age [3]235; Alexandrine [2]203, [4]158, 158n, 426n, [6]143; all follows the Greeks [3]534; all schools of [4]663; ancient [2]648, [5]702; ancient and modern [4]105–6; anti-creation [4]367, 367n; Aristotelian [3]1085, [5]329; birth of [5]468; C's [4]15; canon of [3]328; Chaldaic [5]233; and Christianity [2]343, [5]384–5; concerns of [5]94; critical [2]1203, [4]157–8, 445, [5]743n, 771, 790; crown of [1]585; defined [4]111, 112, [5]776; definition [5]469, 469n; derived from the Greeks [6]317; discursive [1]108n; divine [2]452; docimastic [3]1090; duty of [4]437; dynamic [1]177n–8n, [3]1020n, [5]714n, *see also* polarity; Eclectic [2]1015, [4]125; Eichhorn's lack of [2]500; elder [5]27; Epicurean [5]81n; experimental [4]28; exploded [3]565; fantastic [3]920; fashionable [4]125; of Fichte and Schelling [4]158, 158n; fundamental question of [5]698; genera of [5]692; genuine [5]552; German [2]1000, 1015, [3]791, [5]244; God the keystone [1]585; grammar of [5]95; Grand Turk of [6]234; Greek [3]76, 446, [4]426n, 533n, [5]82, [6]138n, 143; Greek pantheism [3]901; Heraclitic [5]715, 719; history of [1]lxix, 557, [2]52, 52n, [3]318, [5]222–38, 691–816; introductories to [5]92; of Kant *see* Kant; Leighton and [3]625; light of [4]162; limitations of [5]92n; and magic [4]145; map of [5]692; materialist [4]629n; and mathematics [3]1050, 1050n; mechanic [1]410, [2]853, 853n, 889, [5]421; Melanchthon's view of [5]803; mere [1]559; merely intelligential [6]108; modern [3]511; moral [3]134, 252–5, 263–8, 602n, [4]145; moral and religious [5]520; of morals [2]472; mystic [5]795, 796; natural *see* natural philosophy; of nature [3]299; nature-p. [4]420, 420n, see also *Naturphilosophie;* Neoplatonic [1]298n; new and newest [4]155; one [5]318; operatives in [3]358; patriarchal [6]113; peripatetic [2]956; pernicious [5]296; and philology *see* philology; philosophic and poetic genius [3]918; philosophic grammar *see* grammar; of physical dynamics [5]434; Platonic [4]157, [5]86, 547, 751, 752; and poetry [2]544, [3]675, 913, [4]512; polar [1]638, [3]378n, *see also* polarity; postulate of [3]345, [4]455–6; principle of all [1]561; propaedia of [5]82; proper objects of [5]752; Pythagorean [5]86; realism in [3]283; of reflection [4]217; reflective system [3]291; and religion [1]298, 598, [3]36, [4]398–401, [5]93; of religion [5]777; relation to metaphysics and psychology [1]281; religious [6]307; Roman [5]747n; under Romans [5]745n; assert same truth [5]320; Scholastic [3]85, [5]767–9, 801, 812; schools of [5]86; and science [3]908; science of ideas [2]500; sciential [5]430; sects in [5]157; shallow [2]126; should be translatable [2]993–4; Sophistic [4]157; speculative [4]127, [5]327, 733; as spiritual light [5]93; split by Schelling [4]461; Stoic [4]157, [5]86, 739; symbolic [5]699; system of [5]744; transcendental [1]633, [3]258, [4]122n, 374, 374n, [5]362n, 719, 719n; true [1]49, [3]740, [4]269, [5]201, [6]113; only two schools [2]1147; of universals [5]447; value of [5]88; vision of [5]745; vital [1]410; wild [5]170

Philostratus, Flavius (c 170–c 250) [1]454n, [2]704, 706, 708, [3]923, 923n, [4]292n

philoxenos [2]684, 684n

philtres [4]861

Phineus (myth) [6]218

Phipps, Augustus (1762–1822) [1]697 ("Phips")

Phipps, Sir William (1651–95) [3]816 ("Phips")

phiz [4]630

phlegm [4]762, [5]98

Dutch [2]827

phlegmatist [2]123

Phlegon (2nd century) [2]902

Phlegraean Fields *see* Naples

phlogiston [1]63, *63n*, 639, *639n*, [2]868n, [3]1031, [6]229, 229n

phlox [2]576n

Phlox (myth) [2]576

phoberon and *miseteon* see *miseteon*

Phocion (c 402–318 BC) [2]936, 936n–7n

Phocylides of Miletus (mid-6th century BC) [4]147

Phoebus (myth) [6]209; *see also* Apollo

Phoenicia [2]573, 580

Phoenician (language) [4]243, 243n

Phoenician(s) [1]678n, [2]394, 576, 576n, 577, 579, [5]337

phoenix [3]952, [4]418

phoronomy [3]274–5, 274n, 275n, 301–2

phos [1]465, 465n–6n, 685, 688n, [2]576n

Phos (myth) [2]576

"phosopyr" [5]335, 335n

phosopyr [5]344n

phosphate of lime [3]443, [4]274

Phosphor [3]92, 92n

phosphorescence [3]944–5, 945n, [4]537–8
phosphoric acid [1]783
phosphorus [1]572, 666, 737, [2]546, 546n, [3]44, 45, 129, [5]397, 438, [6]116
Photinus, Bishop of Sirmium (4th century) [2]743
Photius (c 820–91) [1]27n, 772n, 781, 781n
photopyr [5]344, 344n
photosynthesis [4]531n
phraseology, inconvenient [5]470
phrenology [2]1012n, [4]5
phronema sarkos [1]358, *358n–9n*, 430n, 504n, 682, 684, 693, [2]332, 1151n, [3]424, 526, 563, 746, 754, [4]168, 168n, [5]185, 185n, 668, 668n, [6]310, 310n; *see also* flesh, mind of the
phronesis [2]713, [3]16n
phrontistes [2]871, 871n
Phrygia [1]7, 465, [2]717n
phthiriasis [2]615n
phthonos [4]141, 141n
phthoric [5]438
phthorium [3]1032
phyllomania [3]451, 451n
phyllon [1]772
physician(s) [2]868, 1166, [3]116, 126, 397, 447, 843, [4]731, [5]171, 517
  compassionate [5]420; first [6]46; German [3]397; irreligious [1]781; wise [5]583
"physics" [5]715, 715n
physics [3]278, [4]379, [5]244, 331–2, 644
  atomic [4]271; distinction of [6]97; experimental [3]843; of Heraclitus [5]721; Heraclitus on [5]715; moral [5]176; More's scheme of [3]920; outdated [5]442n; Platonists' errors in [2]648; of Schelling [4]372; speculative [4]376–7, 377n; true system of [1]70, [3]1093n
"physiogeny" [4]326n
physiognomy [2]1012n
"physiogonist" [1]537, 537n
"physiogony" [1]537n, [5]445, 445n
physiogony [2]576, [3]919, [5]445
"physiographer" [1]537, 537n
"physiography" [4]326, 326n
physiography [3]355n, 919, [5]167
physiolatry [4]110, 110n
"physiologist" [4]421n
physiologist(s) [2]366, 857, [3]38, 612, 682, 841, [4]319, 421n, 499, [5]180, 789
"physiology" [4]420n
physiology [1]577, [3]871, 919, 935, 1042, [4]389n, 421, [5]167
  French [1]62n; humoural [3]565, [5]98; More's scheme of [3]920; of *Naturphilosophie* [3]715; physiological deities [2]575; principles of [3]67; transcendental [1]678
physionomy [1]410
physiophilosophy [1]696n
Physiosoph/Physiosophen [4]504, 504n
"physiosophic" [2]387, 387n, [3]598, 598n, [5]427, 427n–8n
"physiosophy" [2]539n, [5]427n–8n
physiotheism [1]678
physiotheist [1]598n, 678
physis [1]696n, [5]715
phytium [1]572
phyto- [4]326, 326n
phytochemistry [4]315, 323
"phytomet" [1]572
phytonomy [4]326
phytozöium [1]596, 596n
phytozoon [1]596n
"pia-fraudish" [2]1173, 1173n
piastre(s) [5]842–3, 843n, 846
Picart, Bernard (1663–1733) *Ceremonies and Religious Customs of the Various Nations of the Known World* [3]21n
Pickering and Co *see* London
Pickering, William (1796–1854) [1]clxi, clxiin, 240, [4]294, [6]257
pickling [3]44–5
picnic [3]445, 768, 768n
Pico della Mirandola, Giovanni (1463–94) [1]lxxx, 574n, 634n q, 756, [2]678, 678n, 889n, [3]308n, 794, 794n, [4]144, 144n, 614, 614n, [5]237, 237n
  Disputationes adversus astrologiam divinatricem [4]144n, 614n
Pictet, Marc Auguste (1752–1825) [3]942, [5]243
pictogram [1]684n
"picturative" [3]289, 289n
picture(s) [3]138, 194, 567, 790, 871
  allegorical [3]676; electrical [4]827, 827n; p. language [1]647, [2]346; miniature [5]825; moves [4]766; p.-word [3]949; poor men's books [2]*301n*; on a screen [4]826, 826n–7n
Picture of Cebes [1]155, 156; MT 182–5, 187–91
picturesque, the [1]72, 72n
pie (bird) [1]111
pie, mince [5]711
Pier Angelo Manzoli de la Stellata (c 1500–c 1543) [2]870n
Pierce, Thomas (1622–91) [1]257, 257n, 258
  The Restoration of the Blessed Charles [1]257n

Piers Plowman see Langland
Pietism [5]81n, 296
Pietists [5]81, 291n
piety/pieties [4]624, [5]155
household [5]138; natural [1]782, [3]431; Swedenborg's [5]446
pig(s) [2]983, [4]96, [5]101
of lead [1]782; p.-nature [4]645, 645n
pigeon(s) [2]580, [3]175, 884, [4]65, 65n, [5]226, 862
Mahomet's [2]1086, 1086n
pike [4]755
p.-staff [4]636
Pilate, Pontius (d c 36) [1]447, 454, 458, [2]485, 671, 918, 918n, [3]6n, [4]51n, [5]628, [6]33
Pilati di Tassulo, Carlo Antonio di (1733–1802) [4]68n
Di una riforma d'Italia [4]68, 68n
pilchards [1]cv, cvn
pile
electric [3]1010; galvanic [3]947–8, 948n, 950, 1033
pilgrim(s) [1]48n, 872, [3]148
progress of [1]814; p.'s progress of mind [2]601
Pilgrim Trust [1]clxxiii
pill(s) [4]622
blue [3]397; white [4]657
pillar(s) [2]678, [3]564, 1015
of faith [5]570, 570n; mock [5]39; of salt [6]105
pillory [4]667
pillow [3]751
"pillows" [3]900
pimples [3]37, 417
pin(s) [1]386, [5]713
p.-cushion [6]241; prick of [2]341, [5]236
Pindar (c 522–c 440 BC) [1]lxxxiv, cxxxi, 38, 519, [2]346, 354, 567n, 631, 892, [3]175, 902 ("Pindarus"), [4]631
English P. (T. Gray) [4]291; ed Heyne [1]576n; ed Schmied [1]576n; tr R. West [1]38; Theban republican [2]353
Carmina ed Heyne [2]1089; *Nemean Odes* tr Sandys [1]575–6, 575n–6n q, [2]89n q; *Odes of Pindar* tr Sandys [4]117; *Olympian Odes* [1]566 q, 566n q, [2]486n q, 632n, [3]637n q; *Periodos* ed Schmied MT [4]117–21; *Pythian* [2]346n q; *see also* ode(s), Pindaric
"Pindar, Peter" [1]519n
pine [1]442n
Piniero (in B&F) [1]393
pink [4]286
Pinney, Azariah (1775–1803) [1]89n
pioneer [1]434, [3]774
pioneering [4]624
pipe [2]123
pippin(s) [3]167
Pippin *see* Pepin
"pippy" [3]1066n
Piragybe [5]103
Piranesi, Giambattista (1720–78) [1]lxxxvii, [2]1118, *1118n*
pirate, American [1]212
Pirgo [5]836
Pisa [1]lxxxiii, [2]765n
Council of [2]505–7, *507n*, [5]633
Pisistratus *see* Peisistratus
Piso Caesoninus, Lucius Calpurnius (fl 58 BC) [5]747, 747n
piss [1]768, [4]756n, 785, 785n
pistol [3]946, [4]235
Pistol (in Shakespeare) [3]174, 187, 187n–8n
Pistorius, Hermann Andreas (1730–95) [2]959
pitch [4]186, 186n, [5]251
p.-stains [1]316
pith-ball [1]341
Pitman, J. R. (probably John Rogers Pitman, 1782–1861) [5]500n
Pitt, Christopher (1699–1748) *see* Virgil *Aeneid* tr Pitt
Pitt, John, 2nd Earl of Chatham (1756–1835) [5]316, 316n
Pitt, William, the Elder, 1st Earl of Chatham (1708–78) [1]724n, [3]224n
Pitt, William, the Younger (1759–1806) [1]92n, 162, 162n, 262n, 722, [2]48n, 71, 71n, 847n, 914n, [4]608, 608n
irresistible [3]148, 148n; "Pittism" in House of Commons [2]71, 71n; Pitt-dinners [2]73
Pittites [6]46
pity [1]731, [4]718, [5]590
stimulus of [1]244
più nel/nell' uno [2]792, [3]60
Pius IV (Giovanni Angelo de' Medici), Pope (1499–1565) [3]232n, [5]14n
Pius V (Antonio Ghislieri), Pope (1504–72) [2]1153
Pius VII (Barnaba Gregorio Chiaramonti), Pope (1740–1823) [3]785n
Pizzarro/Pizarro, Francisco (c 1478–1541) [2]163n
place [3]61, [4]108, 108n, 157, [5]156, 822
importance of [3]264; unity of [4]779, 826, 863–4
Place, Francis (1771–1854) *The Principles of Population* [2]754n

placebo [3]397n
placemen [4]23, [6]24
Placentino *see* Valla
Placidi, G. B. (fl 1732) *see* Dante *Divina Commedia* ed Placidi
plagiarism(s) [1]74, [3]539n, 703–4, 888n, [4]376n, 611n, 614n, 715 ("plagiary"), [5]261n, 343n, 694n, 732n
 from Burmese [3]1054; charges against C [1]cxlviii, clxixn, [4]837, 837n. *See also* borrowing(s); imitation
plague(s) [2]725, [4]149, [5]537
 in Egypt [2]387, [4]86n, [6]138, 141; of 1665 [2]1179, 1179n
plaice [1]371, [3]132
"plain" [5]151–2, 152n
plains [2]1017
planariae [2]276, 276n
planet(s) [1]623n, 625, 625n, [2]517, 556n, 557n, 885n, 887, [3]322–3, 344, 1035, 1058, [4]268, 394, [5]266, 338, 430
 bursten [5]340; density of [5]263; mass of [5]350; motion of [1]527; names of [4]513, 513n; nucleus of [1]663; origin of [2]885–6, 885n, [5]266n
planks [1]153
plant(s) [1]548, [2]860, 1008n, 1026, 1185, [3]748, 889, 1023, [4]225, 266, 492, 493, [5]250–1, 256, 256n, 271, 286, 286n, 287–9, 287n, 290–1, 292, 310, 565, 583, 816
 analogy of [2]933; aquatic [5]346n; and carbon [5]347; life of [4]317; and light [4]315–16; living [1]133; need water [3]127–8; notion of [6]174; parasite [4]278; physiography [4]326, 326n; spontaneity of [3]75–6; stamens of [5]294; water-p. [5]345–6
plantae [5]287
Plantagenets [2]64, 826, [3]166
plantain [4]88, 89n
plantations [4]827
planter(s) [1]200, [4]342
plassein [1]113n
"plastic" [1]113, 113n, 114, [5]444
plastisch [1]72n
Plata, Rio de la [2]981n
plate [5]581
Platea [5]832n
platinum [1]546, 546n, [2]825, 825n, [3]325, 1033, 1033n, [5]260, 261n
Platner, Ernst (1744–1818) [4]122–38
 genius of [4]125
 Philosophische Aphorismen [3]38, 38n, 377n; MT [4]122–38; 217n
Plato (c 427–347 BC) [1]lxiii, lxix, xcii, cxxiii, cxxxi, 194 q, 557, 568, 573, 615, 622n, 790, [2]86, 143, 154n, 343n, 349, 430, 569, 695, 695n, 720, 722n, 727, 865, 881n, 996, 996n, 1051, 1143n, [3]84, 93–4, 94n, 135n, 206, 532, 618, 622, 643n, 672, 766, 873, 909n, 915n, 966n, 968, [4]28, 105–6, 105n, 115n, 139, 158, 158n, 303, 444, 444n, 472, 653, 654, 654n, [5]44, 174, 545, 583, 642n, 691, 695, 699, 711n, 726, 729–33, 737, 740, 740n, 742, 744, 747, 750, 751n, 801–2, 811, [6]5, 133, 309
 Academy *see* Athens: Academus/Academy; and Aristotle *see* Aristotle; and Bacon [6]315; British (F. Bacon) [3]919n, 950n, [4]403n; calumny of [3]649; conception of [4]472, 472n; on creation [4]367, 367n; Platonic dialect [4]157; discipline of [6]137; on divinity as light [2]419, 424–6, *425n*; and Erasmus [2]703, 703n, [5]391, 517; fiction of [4]156; glorified by St Paul [3]511; on God [1]585, 585n, [2]996, [4]367n, [5]481–2, 482n; Gray's account [2]866–72; harmony in [1]575; and Heraclitus [5]716; ideas of [1]563n, [2]429, 552, 631–2, [4]511n, [5]229n, 230, 703; on light [2]424–6, 425n; and Locke [4]105–6; on love [4]335n; on mathematics [4]159, 159n; on matter [1]114–15; Milton's platonising spirit [2]974n; misinterpreted [1]73; mistranslated [2]247–8, 248n; mode of conveying truth [4]416; nail-parings of [1]617; philosophy of [1]410; and Plotinus [4]146, [5]751–3, 751n, 796; predisposes to Christian faith [3]619; pseudo-platonic [2]199; purpose of his writings [6]6; republic of [2]994; scholars of [5]735; not a self-thinker [4]127; semi-platonic notions [3]926; on serpent symbol [2]1069, 1069n; on the soul [4]126–7; spiritual children of [5]770; successors of [5]732, 743n; system of [5]749; Platonic theology [4]154; Platonic theory of sight [3]389; on time [4]367n; Platonic triad [3]460n, 913; world-soul [2]423–4; Platonic year [3]160, 160n
 Apology [5]726n; *Cratylus* [1]606, *669n*, [6]8n; *The Cratylus, Phaedo, Parmenides and Timaeus* tr T. Taylor MT [4]139–42; *Epinomis* [4]113; *Epistles* tr Bury [2]867n q; *Gorgias* [3]672; *Hippias Major* [2]868–70; *Laws* [2]996n q, [4]108, [5]482n, 751 ("De Legibus"); *Meno* [2]627n, 869n, [4]653n; *Parmenides* [2]869n, [4]211, 648n; *Phaedo* [2]695 ("*Phaedon*"), 872n, [4]139, tr Fowler [1]557n q; *Phaedrus* [2]425n, 869n, 889n,

981n, [4]653n, [5]391n q, 517n, 672n, 751, tr Hackforth [3]868–9 q; *Philebus* [1]573n, 575n; "The Philosopher" [6]7, 7n; *Politicus* [6]7; *Protagoras* [2]868, 868n, 870–2, tr Bury [2]871; *Republic* [2]419n–20n, 424n, 425n, 632n, [3]525n, [4]111n, 156n, 159n q, 648n, [5]751, [6]307n; *Sophist* [1]573n, [2]869n, 872n, [6]7; *Symposium* [4]112, [6]309n; *Theaetetus* [2]868n, 869n, 996n, [5]95n, tr Cornford [3]389n–90n q; *Timaeus* [1]115n, 573n, [2]569n, 703n, [4]108, 154, 367n, 648n, [5]692, 811n, [6]6, 6n; *Works* [2]1123n, tr F. Sydenham [2]865

Platonism [2]872, [3]766, 909–14, 1090, [4]139, 350n, [5]743n, 745, 800n, [6]6
- Alexandrian/Alexandrine [2]433, [6]139; Christian [3]740n; corruption of [5]743; esoteric doctrines [5]731n; and Jewish beliefs [2]421; original sin of [3]915; not in Plato [2]867, 867n; and Plotinism [5]81n, 82, 82n; present *supercilium* toward [2]648; pseudo-P. [3]920

Platonist(s) [1]665, [2]1147, [3]94n, 531, 622, [4]115, 158n, 160, 531n, [5]54, 95, 698n, 739–40, 741, [6]315
- Alexandrian [2]427; and Aristotelian(s) *see* Aristotelian(s); Cambridge [1]lxx, 358n, [3]909n, [5]80, 80n–1n, 82n, 85n, 553n; gross errors in physics [2]648; Jewish [2]458; Proclo-Plotinian [3]909; on three knowledges of God [1]793–4; Tuscan [3]308

platter [3]340, 341

plausible, the [3]260–1

Plautus, Titus Maccius (c 250–184 BC) [2]240, 775, 775n, [3]174, [4]336n
- metres [1]387, 387n
- *Casina* [3]505n; *Comoediae* [3]505n

play (not labour) [2]1065
- p.-room [4]820; p.-thought [5]597; on words [2]326, 427, [4]796, 842

play(s) (drama) [4]781
- blank verse [2]216; essence of [3]172; historic(al) [4]712, 797; love in [6]322; satyr p. [2]757, 757n

player(s) [4]251, 746
- addition of [4]723; *see also* actor(s)

pleader, official [6]186

"pleasant" [6]309, 309n

pleasure(s) [1]367, 825, [2]603, [3]532, 910, [4]136, 444, 548, 652, 679, 810, [5]95, 210, 822, [6]309
- associated with power [2]636; as a balance [4]183; carnal [5]630; cause of [4]766; intellectual [2]959; and pain *see* pain; real [4]729; sensual [2]160

plebs [3]152, 154, 154n, 158n, 799, 799n

Pleistocene age [1]61n, 62n

plenipotentiaries [2]39

plenitude [1]600, 609, 652, [2]553

Plenty, Goddess of [1]408

plenum [3]292, 865, 865n, 916, [5]719, 720n

pleonasm [5]71, 755, 793

pleonecta [3]132

pleroma [1]466, 466n, 679, 690, 690n, 691, [2]263, 291, 429, [3]16, 16n, 31, 31n, 66, 534, 534n, 617, 876, [6]316, 316n
- of the Word [1]640, 640n

plethora [1]524, [4]744–5, 745n

"pleurisy" [4]744–5, 745n

pleurisy [5]125

plexus solaris [6]103, 170

Plinlimmon [6]220

Pliny, the Elder (Gaius Plinius Secundus) (c 24–79) [3]1088, 1089n
- *Natural History* [4]630n

Pliny, the Younger (Gaius Plinius Caecilius Secundus) (c 62–113) [1]218n, 778, [2]272, 918, [3]694–5 q, [4]82n, 627, 627n, 648, [5]525n
- *Letters* [1]512, 757 q, [2]476, 476n, [4]648n–9n q, [5]525, tr Melmoth, rev W. M. L. Hutchinson [5]525n q, [6]254, 254n q

plodder [3]190

plot (of play) [4]375, 712, 852, 857, 861

Plot, Robert (1640–96) *Natural History of Staffordshire* [3]633, 633n

Plotinism [3]915, 1090
- postulate of [5]755

Plotinists [3]135n, [5]80, 755

Plotinus (205–70) [1]lviii, lxxxiii, cv, cxxiii, 115n, 296, 298, 298n, 580n, 691n, [2]727, [3]554, 909n, 915n, [4]158, 258, 259n, 426n, 444, 653n, [5]468, 740, 740n, 743, 743n, 744–5, 747n, 748, 752, 753, 754, 755, 758, 773, 776, 806, [6]100, 100n, 143, 146
- read by Böhme [1]656; conjurer [4]146; contemporaries of [5]747, 747n; followers of [2]1002, [5]796; on magic [2]727, 727n; on matter [1]582 q; pantheism of [5]769; and Plato *see* Plato; Proclo-plotinian Platonists [3]909; pupil of [6]143n; Plotinised Spinozism [3]123n; successors of [5]224, 763; system of [5]751, 757; Tennemann and [5]756; value of [5]744n; wizardry of [4]143
- *Enneads* [1]582n, [4]421n, [5]468n q, 544 q, 544n q, 754n q, tr MacKenna [3]755n q;

Plotinus—*continued*
... *operum philosophicorum omnium libri LIV* ed Ficino ^{2}727n, ^{3}755n; MT ^{4}143–6; *Our Tutelary Spirit* tr MacKenna ^{4}145, 145n q; *Plotinus* tr A. H. Armstrong ^{2}727n, ^{5}754n q; *see also* Porphyry *Life of Plotinus*

plough ^{2}648, 983

"ploutonomist(s)" ^{6}19–20, 20n

Plowman's Tale ^{6}22

Plume, Thomas (1630–1704) ^{2}911

Plumier, Charles (1646–1704) ^{3}638

Plumptre/Plumtre, Huntingdon (1602–60) ^{1}767n

plum-pudding ^{2}425, ^{4}668

plunder ^{4}735

plural, majestic ^{3}418

plurality ^{2}21, ^{4}451, 454, ^{5}24

of persons ^{3}1092, ^{5}19; and unity ^{5}721–2, ^{6}316; in unity ^{2}1020

plus and minus ^{4}358

Plutarch (c 46–c 120) ^{1}lviii, 757 q, ^{2}255, 255n, 355, 937n, ^{4}738n, 770n, ^{5}715n, 810, 810n

pseudo-Plutarch ^{1}639n, *see also* Aetius

De Pythiae oraculis tr Babbitt ^{6}5n q; *Isis and Osiris* ^{6}219; *Life of Homer* ^{2}386n; *Life of Solon* ^{2}1042n; *Lives* ^{5}248, ed and tr T. North ^{3}897, 897n, ^{4}761; *Moralia* ^{2}255n, 732 q, 732n q, ^{3}389 q, 389n q, 516 q, 516n q, 642, ^{5}84n, 770 q, 770n q, ^{6}299 q, 299n q, 324 q, 324n q; *On the Oracles at Delphi* ^{5}84n

Pluto (myth) ^{1}543, 793, ^{2}575, 583, 583n, ^{4}677, 677n, ^{5}7

"Plutonic" ^{6}207, 207n

Plutonism ^{3}60n

Plutonist(s) ^{1}664n

"plutonomist" ^{6}20n

Plymouth ^{2}95n, 650

pneuma/pneumata ^{1}175, 175n, 479, ^{3}39n, 594, 594n

and *psyche* ^{1}620. *See also* spirit(s)

pneumation ^{1}164n

poachers ^{2}980

pocket-picking ^{5}97

poem(s) ^{3}484, 634, 638, ^{4}476, 478, 479

approach to ^{4}828; didactic ^{2}968; drama as ^{1}376; dramatic ^{3}894, 922; epic ^{5}110; funereal ^{2}238; heroic ^{1}217, ^{2}738, 1120, *see also* epic; less precise than philosophy ^{3}675; metaphysical ^{2}224; most perfect ^{2}968; most precious ^{1}426; narrative ^{6}210; original ^{2}1120; Orphic ^{6}211n; and poet ^{4}161–2; political ^{2}155; not rhyme only ^{3}972; satirical ^{2}757; and vision ^{2}459; written in old age ^{2}458, 459

"poematic" ^{1}407

poena damni ^{5}601, 601n, 611

poesy/poesies ^{5}289, 749

generic term ^{4}864; German ^{5}309; Hebrew ^{3}32; and history ^{1}446; as making ^{5}749; Miltonic ^{4}604; mythical ^{1}432; nature's ^{5}813; of *Naturphilosophie* ^{2}863; of OT ^{4}47; symbolic ^{3}30

poet(s) ^{2}433, 480, ^{3}225, 704, ^{4}530, 781, 787

for all ages ^{4}861; Arabian ^{6}159; bad ^{4}759; Chapman an original ^{2}1120; character of ^{1}367; Christian ^{2}973; C a humble one ^{1}482; conversation of ^{1}91; defined ^{4}162n; divine ^{3}886; dramatic ^{3}173, ^{4}723, 731; duty of ^{4}151; ear of ^{3}891; editions of ^{4}768; Elizabethan ^{2}235; faults of elder ^{3}913; feeling of ^{5}858; first duty of ^{5}114; genius of ^{1}482; genuine ^{1}377, ^{2}406; German ^{4}269, ^{5}198, 688–9; greatest ^{4}748; Greek ^{2}865, ^{4}604, 768, ^{5}688; Hebrew ^{2}864; Herbert a true ^{2}1034; imaginative ^{5}813; inspired ^{2}406; invents visions ^{2}470; Italian ^{1}117n; Jewish ^{2}1106; laureate ^{1}55–6, 56n; logician and linguist ^{2}140–1; and mock p. ^{5}110; must have thought ^{2}219–20; Orphic ^{6}211; partial to rhyme ^{1}755; and philosopher *see* philosopher(s); philosophic ^{3}913; of philosophy ^{3}99, 99n; and plodder ^{3}190; poor ^{6}324; popular ^{2}15; and prophets ^{2}402; sense of term ^{4}161–2; solo ^{1}402; strict meaning of ^{4}76; tragic ^{1}150; and tree ^{1}612; ventriloquist ^{3}179; Virgil as ^{2}88; write of passions ^{1}49; *see also* genius(es), poetic

Poetae graeci veteres ^{1}xcv, ^{2}632n

Poetae minores graeci ^{1}cxxxn, 26; MT ^{4}147

poetaster ^{2}727

poetry ^{3}511, ^{4}678–9, 864, ^{5}526, 835, ^{6}161–2, 327–9

ancient ^{4}604; art of ^{3}897; classes of ^{3}886; C's definition of ^{1}368n; poetic decorum ^{3}1086; devotional ^{6}116; diction of *see* diction, poetic; discursive and sensuous ^{2}135; dramatic ^{4}162; English canon ^{1}37; epic ^{5}110; feeling for ^{1}367; poetic feeling ^{2}637; fictions of ^{1}29; flat ^{1}723; frippery ^{2}544; poetic genius ^{3}889; Hebrew ^{2}1052, 1052n, ^{3}472; identity of other knowledges ^{4}161; intentional ^{2}1052; interpretation of ^{1}482; Italian ^{3}909–10, ^{6}157; logic of ^{4}679n; lyric ^{2}762; metaphysical ^{2}224, 864; Milton's ^{3}883; modern Latin ^{2}240; necessarily ideal ^{1}368; object of ^{2}355–6;

and philosophy *see* philosophy; power of [3]893; and prose [2]406, 406n, [3]897; rules for [6]161–2; satiric [3]225; South African [1]31; spirit of [1]482; sublime [2]1123; symbolic [1]485, [3]472; poetic taste [3]400, 1088; thought and passion in [4]162; two modes of [1]72; and unpoetic subjects [1]401; use of [2]959; vices of modern English [2]240. *See also* metre(s); poesy/poesies
Poetry of the Anti-Jacobin [5]145n
Poins (*2 Henry IV*) [4]239n
point(s) [2]607, 887–8, 889, [3]276, 1011, 1034, 1057, [5]714
central [5]644; equatorial [5]203; of indifference [5]265; physical [3]1039, 1041; produced [5]733; of space [3]276, 277, 282; of view [5]469
pointer [2]1158n
C as [1]lix, 331, 331n
Poiret, Pierre (1646–1719) [5]813
More Specific Remarks on Sound Education [5]813 q
poison(s) [1]10, 590, 685, 713, 786, [2]366–7, 1206, [3]747, 750, 802, 1044, 1083, [4]149, 317–18, 494–5, 502, 834, [5]5n, 75, 75n, 188–9, 258, 259, 528n
p.-bag [4]177; p.-berries [3]879; deadly [5]552; defined [4]320, 321, [5]137; p.-fangs [4]501; subtle [5]135
poisoning [6]101
Poissy [5]549n
Poitiers [4]193
poker(s) [2]16, [3]860, [5]581
Poland [1]198n, [2]46, 909, 909n, 1188, [4]299, [5]47
oppressors of [5]281
polar bear [4]534
Polaris [1]399n
polarisch [2]858, 859
polarity/polarities [1]662–4, [2]859n, 1019n, [3]256n, 916n, 1051, 1052, 1052n
in the absolute [4]366n; of body [2]566; of body and soul [2]311; in Böhme [1]611–12, 623–4, 628, 643; C revises his scheme [1]660; in Deity [1]678; dynamic [1]568n, [2]1028, 1028n; error of *Naturphilosophie* [3]1055; grand principle of [3]1018; inexplicable [5]356; law of [1]643, 662, [3]292, [5]714n; in love [2]197; magnetic [4]498; in religion [3]21; scheme of [1]666; three-term [3]295, 295n. *See also* antithesis; compass of nature; logic, polar; *Naturphilosophie*; philosophy, dynamic; philosophy, polar; pole(s)
"polarly" [2]859n
pole(s) [1]589–90, 594, 597, 598–9, 780, [2]853, 854n, 1006–7, 1015, [3]746, 998, 998n, 1004, 1060, 1060n, 1062, 1063, [4]315–16, 315n, 323–4, [5]203, 279, 344, 776
aboriginal [3]1015; actual and potential [2]431; in blood [2]859; of the earth [4]527; extreme [1]399; of gravitation [1]597; identity of [6]230; of immortality [2]1186; of line [5]715; magnetic [2]1186; of nature [3]1021n, [4]395–6, 395n–6n; North and South [3]1029, 1031n; opposite [3]1003, [5]266–7; outward [6]226; positive [5]152, [6]228; positive and negative [1]539; in procreation [2]1001; real and ideal [4]168; South [5]248, 267; of will [3]350; polar zone [2]1112; *see also* polarity
Pole, Matthew *see* Poole
Pole, Reginald (1500–58) [2]71
Pole, William de la, 4th Earl and 1st Duke of Suffolk (1396–1450) [2]121–2
polemic [5]527
polemists [1]314
Policandre [5]837
police [3]436, [5]85, 102
policy [4]799, 811
Church [5]433; probable [5]641; short-sighted [1]359; tricky [2]936
polish [3]831, [5]358
Politian (Angelo Ambrogini) (1454–94) [1]756, [4]290
letters [2]476, 476n
political economy [2]88, 311, 952, [3]484, [5]93n
political science [4]14
politicians [3]164, [4]79
politics [2]616–22, 1199, [4]14
and Church [3]71–2; C's political religion [3]801; domination of [5]428; fulfils prophecy [3]71; Shakespeare's [4]804
polity, scheme of [3]112
pollard man [4]78
pollex/Pollex [4]37, 37n
Pollio, Gaius Asinius (76 BC–AD 4) [1]737, [2]755–6
pollution [3]62
Pollux (myth) [5]197, 197n
Polonius (*Hamlet*) [4]841, 844, 846, 852, 854, [5]611n
poltergeist(s) [5]122, 165
polyarchy [4]13, 15
Polybius (c 203–c 120 BC) [2]156, 950, [4]631
Polycarp, St (c 69–c 155) [1]186, 492, [2]501, 502, 719, 719n, [6]58, 63
Epistle to the Philippians [2]712
polygamy [2]6, 1017, 1160, [3]497, 699, [4]28n, [5]501n

polygenesis [5]252n
Polyhistor *see* Alexander Polyhistor
polymorph [5]406
Polynesia [2]74
Polynices (myth) [2]584
Polyphemus (myth) [3]817, 817n
polyphloisbon [1]269n
polypus/polyp/*polypi*/polyps [2]276, 276n, 366, [3]1037, 1041, 1042, [4]36, 165, 448, 529
polysyllables [2]121
polytheism [1]249n, 307n, 616, 645n, 659, [2]344, 345, 346, 389, 482, 665, [3]328, 328n, 493, 529n, 658, 692, [4]226, [5]12, [6]314n
  Greek and Roman [5]414; origin of [1]659n; Roman [1]472
Pomey, François Antoine (1618–73) [6]110n
Pomfret, John (1667–1702) [1]37
pomp [5]142
Pompeii [6]254n
Pompey (Gnaeus Pompeius Magnus) (106–48 BC) [3]405, 447, 905, [5]536, 843
Pomponazzi, Pietro (Pomponatius) (1462–1525) [5]805–6, 806n, 812
pond [2]220, [4]527
Pond, John (1767–1836) *see* Laplace *System of the World* tr Pond
ponderability [1]594
pondus [2]852, 852n
poneron/poneros [2]1179n, [3]774, [4]233, 233n–4n, [5]74, 85, *85n*
Ponocrates (in Rabelais) [4]196
Pontifex Maximus [3]234, 240, 240n
pontiff, Roman [6]14
pontificate [6]15
Pontine Marshes [4]149, 149n, [5]276, 276n
Pontoppidan, Erik (1698–1764) *History of Norway* [2]1112n, [4]606n
Pontus [1]778, [2]474, [5]634, 634n
poodle [5]293n
pool [3]581
Poole, Matthew ("Pole") (1624–79) *Synopsis criticorum* [2]46–7, [5]167, 167n
Poole, Thomas (1765–1837) [1]xciii, 9, 331n, 756n, [2]16n, 587n, 696, 953n, [3]368n
  death of [1]clx; C's letter(s) to [1]154 q, 161n–2n q, 163n q, 580n q, [3]101n q, 243n, 342, 342n q; HNC letter(s) to [1]lxxixn q, cix, cxxiv–cxxv q, cxxivn q, cxxxviiin q; library [2]967; memorandum for [5]383n; mss [2]967; owner of annotated books [1]lxxi, lxxvii, lxxviin, lxxxiv–lxxxv, 9, [2]48, 97, 245, 797, 903n, 966, 966–7, 1110, [4]25, 84, 199, [5]382, [6]266; reaction to *LR* [1]cxlii; supplier of books to C [1]xcvii, cv, cvi, [5]36; *see also* M. E. Sandford *Thomas Poole and His Friends*
poor, the
  education of [3]700; infirm [1]355; p.-laws [3]810, 810n, [6]22; maintenance of [6]22; p.-rates [6]22; rich and [5]417, 417n
Poor, Henry William (1844–1915) [2]1112, [4]338
pope(s) [1]315, 329, 352, 522, 846, [2]40, 304n, 697, 742n, 1153, [3]155, 234, 458, 723, 727, 760, 760n, 774, 818, [4]96, [5]143, 559, 632, 636, 639, 661
  authority of [2]1098, [3]234n; dislike of [1]805; p.'s eye [1]336, 336n; and hierarchy [6]22; as image or idol [1]523, 523n; infallibility of [2]1140, [3]233, [5]617; joint-stock company [3]153; at Lambeth [2]260; present [3]785; papal spirit [3]697; wicked [1]831–2
Pope, Alexander (1688–1744) [1]38, 50, 156n, 514, 727n, 872, [2]216, 375, 1090, 1090n, [3]174, 703, 920, [4]76, 466n, 712n, 747, 808, 843n, [5]768, [6]199, 199n
  and Denham [1]74; mean brute [2]768; pastorals [1]60n; wit of [2]17
  Collected Works tr Dusch [3]703–4; "Dignity, Use and Abuse of Glass Bottles" [1]390n; *Dunciad* [1]402n, [2]768 q; *Eloisa to Abelard* [3]403–4, [6]324n; *Epistle to Dr Arbuthnot* [1]74 q, 74n q; *Essay on Man* [1]174, 184n, 747n, [2]535 q, 536n q, 601n q, 869 q, [3]134, 134n q, 484n, 674 q, 674–7, 675n, [4]679, 679n; *The Fourth Satire of Dr. John Donne . . . Versifyed* [3]174n; *Inscriptio* [4]190 q, 190n q; *Memoirs of . . . Martin Scriblerus* ed Kerby-Miller [1]156, *156n*; *Poems* ed Butt [4]190n q, ed G. Tillotson [1]390n; *Rape of the Lock* [1]390 q, 390n, [2]1106, 1106n; *The Second Satire . . . Versifyed* [3]174n; *Works* [1]156n, [3]174n. *See also* Homer: *Homer, Iliad, Odyssey* tr Pope
Pope, Alexander (1763–1835) [6]270
popery [1]327, 805, 806, 865, [2]31, 652, 1158, [3]47, 166, 308, 455, 457, 780, 874, [5]532, 683, [6]108
  assumption of [1]313–14; dregs of [2]480; errors of [1]250; hankering for [2]127; versus p. [1]274; preparation for [4]549; relic of [1]530; relicts of [2]27; retenta of [1]286; securities against [4]19
popgun [3]805

Popish Plot [6]145n
poppy/poppies [4]318, 318n, 525, [5]533, 533n
populace [2]900, 900n, [5]38
and people *see* people; Shakespeare's contempt for [1]389
popularity [3]57, [4]610, 610n
population [2]848–9, [3]805–9
of East [5]262; increase of [1]349; increasing [5]323; tables of [2]6n; universal [1]865
populus [3]152, 799, 799n
Porcacchi da Castiglione Aretino, Tomaso (b c 1530) [1]116
porcelain [3]630, 631, 638
vase [3]480
porch [4]815
painted [2]154
Pordage, John (1607–81) [1]297, 297n, [3]705, 705n
Theologia mystica [1]297n, [3]705n
pore(s) [3]61, [4]271, 271n
porphyry [3]630, [4]517, 517n, [5]358, 844
Porphyry (c 232–c 305) [1]cxxiii, 691n, [2]411, 412, 412n, 1123, 1123n, [3]111, [5]224n, 226, 226n, 747, 747n, [6]7, 100, 100n
strange compound [2]727, 727n; unreliability [5]229, 229n; wizardry of [4]143
Against the Christians [3]573, 573n; *Life of Plotinus* [4]144–6, tr A. H. Armstrong [5]748
porpoise [4]533, 533n
porridge [3]126
Porson, Richard (1759–1808) [1]27n, 376, *376n–7n*, 387n
Greek types [1]26; *see also* Aeschylus ed Porson
Port Royal *see* Lancelot and Arnaud *Grammaire générale*
port wine [2]365
Porta, Giovanni Battista della (1543–1615) [6]99
porter (drink) [2]1113
porter (person) [2]489
Porter (*Macbeth*) [4]729, 772
Porteus, Beilby, Bishop of London (1731–1808) [4]549n
A Summary of the Evidences for the Truth and Divine Origin of the Christian Revelation [4]549n; *Works* [4]549n
Portia (*Merchant of Venice*) [4]765, 780
Portland, Duke of *see* Bentinck, William Henry Cavendish
portrait(s) [2]1195n, [3]20, [4]792, 792n–3n, [5]5
in boyhood [4]783; of Leighton [6]312; p.-painter [2]1195
Portsmouth [1]lxxxii, 76, 155, [2]964, 1102
Portugal [1]88, [2]163n, [3]133, [4]299, [5]279, 834, [6]13
Portuguese (language), dialects [3]830
Portuguese (people) [2]230n, [4]30, [5]103
colonisers [5]106
Portus, Aemilius (1550–c 1615) *see* Proclus *Platonic Theology* ed and tr Portus
Posen [2]1188
Posidippus (3rd century BC) [4]147
Posidonius (c 135–c 51 BC) [5]225
position(s) [3]1024, [4]316, 450, [5]157
abstract [5]186; contradictory [2]152; *de forma* [5]409; divine [3]116; general [5]325; and negation [5]815, 815n; self-evident [5]560
positive(s) [1]594, 640, [4]113
and certain *see* certain; and negative *see* negative; of right [4]171; sole [4]358
positiveness [2]1088, [3]849, [4]829, 830
of Jeremy Taylor [5]646
posse and *esse* see *esse*
"possession" [4]155, [5]514
possession (by spirits) [2]31, 739n, 1105, 1109, [4]145n, [6]119n
possession(s) (ownership) [1]356, [4]411, [5]278, 299, 304, 745
possibility/possibilities [3]331, 344–5, 346, 349, 858, [4]436, 437, [5]252, 424
eternal [1]669, [2]202; infinite [5]358; and reality [5]809
possible(s) [2]202
of logic [3]395; and real [4]224, [5]269, [6]173
posterity [2]947, [3]225, [5]208, 829, 829n
postils, Luther's [3]752, 752n
postpositions [3]830
postscriber [2]463
post-script [6]142
postulate(s) [2]197, [3]345, 959n, 1091, [4]125, 455–6
in dynamics [3]997; lazy [3]97; moral [4]216, [6]108; of morality [5]457; of reason [3]989; system grounded on [3]959
potash [1]570, [3]951, 951n, [4]319, 526, 526n, 539, [5]255, 255n, 261
potassium [1]572, [3]481, 950, 951, 951n, 1027n, 1033, 1033n, [4]319, 319n–20n, 526, 526n, 837n, [5]255n, 261, 338
p. chlorate [4]539n; p. oxymuriate [4]539n
potassyl [1]570
potato(es) [4]38, 317–18, [5]175
small [5]224, 224n
pot-companion [4]660

potence [3]1004
potencies [1]70
potentates, Catholic [2]934, 1139
potential [2]279, 658–9, 824, [3]545
and actual *see* actual; and real [1]604, 658–9
potentiality [1]232, 627, 691, [2]326, [3]22n, 858, 1024, [4]165, [5]360, 654, 763
actualised [5]424; antedated [3]1051–2; not in God [1]694; state of [6]113
Potenz [2]550
"potenziate" [1]344, 344n, [3]386n
potenziation [1]578, 578n, [3]46, [6]233
potenziren [3]386
pothos [1]146n, 600, 600n–1n, 653, 653n, [4]292
Pothos (myth) [4]463
Potiers [2]347
potions [6]99
pot-orator [3]666
potsherd [2]162
potter(s) [1]862, [5]202n
Staffordshire [5]395
Potter, George Reuben (1895–1954) *see* Donne *Sermons* ed Potter and E. M. Simpson
Potter, John, Archbishop of Canterbury (c 1674–1747) [5]134, 135
Archaeologia Graeca [1]42, 42n
Potter, Stephen (1900–69) *see* Coleridge, Sara (Mrs C) *Minnow* ed Potter
pottery/potteries [2]165, [3]627–39, 638
potting [3]44
Potts, Jonathan (fl 1794) [4]676n
Poulton, William (fl 1855–62) [2]840
pound sterling [2]425, 572
pound weight [2]425
Pouqueville, François Charles Hugues Laurent (1770–1838) [4]184 q
poverty [2]303, [3]806
abject [1]755; and indigence [2]97–8; voluntary [5]539
Povy, Thomas (1615–c 1702) [4]80
powder(s) [3]294
anti-friction [1]527, 527n; antimonial [6]39; sympathetic [6]97
Powell, Jane (?1761–1831) [6]270
Powell, Lawrence Fitzroy (1881–1975) *see* Boswell *Life of Johnson* ed Hill, rev Powell
Powells, family of (fiction) [1]xcixn
power(s) [1]547, 547n, 604, 656, 693, [2]620, 751n, 854n, 891, 996n, 1003, [3]13, 29, 83, 85, 86, 139, 150, 282, 324, 343, 585, 1029, [4]11, 131n, 413, 487, 817, 818, [5]7, 17, 142, 159, 169, 208, 244, 442, [6]75, 143
absolute [4]412; acoustic [5]294; as act [1]70, [2]636, [5]654; act of causing [5]443; active [3]129; adaptive [5]266; antagonist [5]689; appetite of [5]161; astringent [1]775; atoning [4]225; attractive [5]265, 588; and authority *see* authority; balance of [4]149; binding [1]345; bishop's [5]537; blind [5]614; in Böhme [1]563, 633, 638, 641; captiver of [5]451; central [5]266; centrific [4]324; centrifugal [5]776; chemical [4]494n, [6]226–7; comparative [1]808, [6]102; compass of *see* compass, of powers; compulsory [5]538; conception of [4]131; constituent [3]288, [4]150, [5]697; constructive [3]944, [5]750; contractive [5]262, 265, 346; corporific [3]949; creative [3]176; cross one another [3]1010–11; daemonial [1]455; delegated [3]149; of depth [3]139; differences [2]855n; dilative [5]265, 346; dilative and contractive [3]996; dimensions of [3]123, 123n; discord of [5]87; dispensing [2]43, [3]157; of distance [3]1015; divine [2]183; divining [1]163n; division of [2]115, [5]233; doctrine of [3]135–6, 135n; of dominion [5]614; efficient [3]736; elastic [5]277; elementary [1]568, 776, 780, [5]784n; its own end [1]656; evolution of [4]324n; excessive [4]15; executive [3]801, [5]537; exhibitable [5]666; existing [2]507; explosive [5]338; of faith [5]12; focal [5]244; and force(s) *see* force(s); four [1]598, 631, [3]1006n, [5]451; free act of [5]457; functional [4]316; germ of [2]201; gift of [5]654; in God [1]567, 568; of God [1]561; good [5]518; of governing [1]341–2; grounding [2]1009; higher [5]173; higher and lower [2]1019; human [2]747; and idea [1]706, [2]1134, 1148; ideal [2]853–4, 853n, [5]258, 346n, 781; idealising [4]78; not imageable [3]301; imaginative [1]280, [3]559, [5]813; incinerative [3]61; infinite [3]206; infusion of [5]536; innate [2]220; instrumental [5]453; intellectual [4]811; intrinsic cause [1]787; invisible [1]580; kingly [5]399; and knowledge [5]274; latent [2]368; legislative [6]53; of life [4]389; of the lifeless [5]421; living [4]442, [5]662, 681; love of [2]636; lust of [4]816; magical [1]671; magnetic [1]775, [2]1186, [5]266; man of [3]727; material [3]202; not material [3]199, 199n; and matter [3]295; mechanic [2]1148, [6]134; mental [5]798; miraculous [3]564; modifying [1]590, 633,

[2]825, 853n; of monarch [1]243, 243n; moral [4]408; moving [5]205; multiform [5]813; of muscles [2]1003–4; and name [5]11, 11n; of nature [4]396; omnipresent [2]201; one [1]177, [3]948n, [5]714; outward [5]304; paramount [5]258; of parliament [2]61, 949; penetrative [5]358; of people [1]732; plastic [1]113, [2]1028, [4]266, [5]858; pleasure associated with [2]636; plurality of [2]311; polar [3]1003; political [4]22, [5]41, [6]52; positive and negative [6]231; predominant [5]264; primal [5]707; primary [1]563; producing [5]265; and product(s) [3]947, [5]264n; product of [5]398; productive [4]165, [5]418, 418n; prudential [4]648; quantum of [2]278; realising [4]450; redeeming [5]189; representing [5]410n; reproductive [3]123; repulsive [5]265; retroitive [4]390; and right [6]51; Roman [2]513; royal [4]15; science of [3]325n; solar [1]626; in soul [3]297; space-filling [2]1013; space-penetrating [5]291; sphere of [3]283; spiritual [1]582, [5]423; spirituality of [5]550; and strength [3]378, 378n; substantiative [2]663; substantive [1]611, [3]997n, [5]266; superhuman [5]645; supreme [2]357, 1142; surface [1]594; and symbol [3]108; synthetic [1]623, 665; temporal [1]258, 360; three [2]1008, 1008n; three faculties [4]93; transfer of [3]386; transitive [5]775; two forces [3]1024–5; unlimited [3]671; unresisted [5]719; of vision [5]15; vital [2]1148, [4]321, [5]258, 342; vivific [5]452. See also *dynamis;* force(s); *vis*
pox [3]806
practice
  measure of [1]492; medical [5]320
The Practice of Christian Graces [2]409, *409n*
prae- see pre-
praecordia [3]612, 612n
Praed, Winthrop Mackworth (1802–39) [1]cln ("M. W. Praed")
praefectus [1]852
"praenunciations" [3]209, 209n
praesence [1]562
"praetereunce" [5]360
"praeterience" [5]360n
praeternatural, the [4]729, [5]164
"praeterscriptural" [3]66, 66n
pragmata [5]5
praise(s) [3]522, [4]736, [6]304
  act of [6]146
Praktische Anweisung zur Kenntniss der Hauptveränderungen und Mundarten der teutschen Sprache [6]287n
Prati, Gioacchino de' (1790–1863) [1]xcviii, clxi, [2]142, 892n, [3]308, [5]142, 142n, [6]18n
prawns [4]694
praxasthe [1]427n
  p. paideias [1]427
praxeis [1]447
Praxiteles (4th century BC) [2]416
prayer(s) [1]234n, 251, 281, 319, 429n, 516, 530, 713n, [2]185, 233, [3]155, 155n, 267–8, 499, 513, 572, 579, 580, 608, 615, 751, 754n, 879, 1069, [4]299, 335–6, 336n, 681–2, 682n, [5]93, 95, 151, 168, 483–4, 493, 562, 670, 820
  act of [6]146; afternoon [1]878; agony of [5]589; to angels [2]723; answers to [4]260; p.-book of Edward VI *see* Edward VI; to Christ [2]39, [3]692; common [1]260, 261, 262, 324; continued [1]320; for dead [1]781; defined [1]702; of Dissenters [1]325; domestic [5]512; efficacy of [3]754; encyclopaedia of [5]520; for enlightenment [1]453; p.-exercises [1]875; extemporary [1]264, [6]259; extempore [1]328, [5]530; form(s) of [1]178, [5]510, 520, 527, 530; gift of [5]529; habitual [2]162; houses of [5]129; indecent familiarities in [2]1175; Kant's opinion of [2]185, 185n; Lord's *see* Lord's Prayer; maledictory [5]681; and medical quackery [1]298; mode of [4]140; Moravian practice of [3]494n; "Nightly P." [1]713n; objections to [2]182–3; one set of [5]521; petitionary [1]782; Polycarp's [2]719–20; "pray always" [1]11; preaching [1]265, [6]259; Presbyterian's [3]227; private [5]512; Protestant views [1]674; and psalms [1]429; public [1]349, 355, [2]653, [5]530; public, private, domestic [1]260, 261; Puritan objections to [2]972; for redemption from body [2]1177; replies to [1]282; selection of [5]523; set form(s) of [5]509, 518–19, 522; RS on [2]63; theory of [5]494, 494n; three kinds [2]282–3; trembling [2]145
praying [3]770
pre-/*prae* [1]562, *562n*, 788, 788n, [3]11, 11n
preacher(s) [1]260, 396, 806, [2]295, 917, 1202, [3]27, 416, 450–1, 450n–1n, 727, 879, [4]471, [5]433, 631, 663
  Christian [2]291; duties of [3]568–9; first [1]353; itinerant [4]627; lay-p. [5]164; Luther as [3]743; Methodist [5]167n; modern [2]338; monkish [2]313; moral [2]655; object of [3]462; in pentad [2]290; poor [5]143n; professional [1]529; Solomon's Song p. [5]81,

preacher(s)—*continued*
81n; ultra-calvinistic [3]69; unlearned [1]824; Wesleyan [5]167
preaching(s) [1]349, [2]1157, 1157n, [3]686, 691, 732, 744, [5]14, 135, 162, [6]104
of apostles [4]475; apostolical [2]452; ardour of [3]435; efficacy of [2]1156; evangelical [4]619–74; field [5]161; with tongue only [5]390
preachments [1]325
precedence, importance of [3]264
"precedent" [2]823, 823n
precedent(s) [2]529, 751, [3]163
precept(s) [2]207, [5]560, 630
gospel [1]821, [3]696; moral [4]649; specific [1]877
precipice [1]394
precipitancy [1]418
precipitates [1]67n
precipitation [4]832
precision
philosophical [1]567; scientific [5]452
preconception [2]632
precondition [3]12
precursor [5]650
predestinarians [5]655n, 842
predestination [1]222, 346n, 825, 827, 835, [2]517, 1193, [3]101, 102n, 235, 818n, [4]438–9, 644, [5]68, 75, 75n, 76n, 156, 156n, 160n, 186, 278, 498n, 588n, 609n, 610n
Predeterminants [1]233
predetermination [5]707
predicabilia [4]458
predicates [4]157
co-ordinate [4]128
prediction(s) [2]155, 387, [3]71, 110, 417n, 449, 452, 453, 463, 472, [6]105; *see also* prophecy
predispositions [2]543, [5]738
predominance(s) [1]632, 633, 660–1
pre-existence [2]432, 432n, 487, [6]139
pre-experience [4]465
preferment [2]1100, [5]501
p.-hunter [1]50; lust of [6]43; road of [5]531
preformation [3]243
preformationists [3]243n
"pregenite" [2]723, 723n
pregnancy [2]273, [4]164
Mary's [2]270
prejudice(s) [1]142, 300, 673, [2]480–1, 744, 810, [3]138, 754, [4]51, 306, 583, [5]62, 476, 743, [6]109
aristocratic [4]138; drudge of [5]622; of education [4]239; factious [2]932; force of [5]415; gentile [2]709; innocent [6]102; invincible [5]649; power of [6]18; prevailing [5]85–6; Scottish [6]216; sectarian [1]280; university [2]817
prelacy [1]233, 338, [2]814, 1138, [3]803, [4]79
defined [5]147n; diocesan [1]275, [6]264; and episcopacy [2]61, 61n; overthrow of [5]640
prelate(s) [1]250, 807, [3]803n, [5]503, 508n, 640
English [5]508; Romish [5]539
prelatist(s) [1]318, 320, 873, [2]57, 1139, 1198, [5]510
premeditation [5]529
Premier, the [4]608
"premises" [5]736–7
premise(s) [2]1166, [5]138, 155, 156
improved [4]267; Locke's [4]116; mendicant [5]155; of St Paul [3]54; Jeremy Taylor's [5]622
prenotions [5]444
preparations [5]738
prepon [4]796
preposition(s) [3]834, [4]166
"preposterise" [1]602, 602n
preposterous [2]591n, [5]362
prepuce [5]830
prerogative [1]350, 833, [2]934
presbyter(s) [1]338, 339, [2]*1042n–3n*, 1095–7, [3]688, 720, 874, [5]503, 684
Presbyterian(s) [1]246, 256, 269, 311, 313, 320, 321n, 327, 333, 336, 531n, 674, 728, 728n, [2]260n, 651n, 946, 973, 1042n, 1149, 1198–9, [3]227, 483, [4]590–1, 591n, 609, 609n, [5]129n, 146, 503n, 508, 539
Baxter and [1]230; bigotry of [3]802; Dissenters [4]643n; evolution of [1]346; Scottish [3]141n, [4]307n; true [2]1199; weak [1]318
Presbyterianism [1]271, [2]936n, [4]79, 307n
presbyteros [5]503n
presbytery/presbyteries [2]1042, 1042n, [5]129n, 147n, 537
synodical [1]271, [6]261
prescience [2]152, [4]272, [5]186
divine [5]155, 160; God's [1]827
prescription(s) [2]1166, [5]529
presence
angel of [3]102; contingent and necessary [3]494, 495n; divine [2]147; effective [5]471; of God [5]493; immediate [6]170; necessary [4]298–9, [6]146; real *see* real presence; transcendent [1]562n
present [3]286, [4]356, [5]302
as a city [5]321; relation to past [1]280

presentation [4]217
sense of [4]273
presentiment(s) [3]205, [4]538–9, 581, 605, 834, 859, [5]723, 788
preservation [3]59n, 949n, [4]295, [5]206–7, 207n, 385, 385n
of material world [3]949
Preservative against Popery [3]231n, [5]620n
preserving [3]45
"president" [2]823, 823n
president [5]536
American [5]279; temporary [1]341
pre-Socratics [1]lxx
press [3]71, 679
anonymous [3]418–19, 419n; p.-error [4]521; logical [5]665
Preston [2]211n
Preston, John (1587–1628) [6]258
presumption [1]456, 827, [4]595
presuppositum [2]990n, 991, 1106, [5]159
Pretender(s), the *see* Stuart/Stewart, Charles Edward and James Francis Edward
pretension [2]216
"preterience" [5]360n
preternatural, the [3]661
Pretyman, George *see* Tomline, Sir George Pretyman
Preussische Jahrbücher [2]186n
Prévost, Pierre (1751–1839) [3]942
prey, birds of [1]425
Priam (in Virgil) [6]213
Priam (myth) [2]155n, [4]627n
Priapus (myth) [3]401
Price, Sir John, of Buckland [5]191
Price, Richard (1723–91) [3]602n, [4]644
and J. Priestley *A Free Discussion of the Doctrines of Materialism and Philosophical Necessity* [4]644n
prick [5]713
"prickle" [1]641
prickles [3]776, [5]608
pride [3]812, [4]709, 816, 818, [5]104, 151, 159, [6]256
of blood [4]583; of Enlightenment [2]480; female [1]392; of French [1]477; of man of science [3]365; national [2]145; spiritual [1]320, 695, [5]170
priest(s) [1]352, 423, 529, 530, [2]377, 460, 727, 827, 951, 1095–7, [3]212, 874, [5]88, 226, 578, 608
bigotted [6]145; Catholic [1]811; conclave of [1]341; and congregation [1]246; priestly despotism [3]819; duty of [3]232; high [2]485, [6]234; ignorant [2]721; Jewish [3]109; marriage of [3]785n; *pontifex maximus* [3]234, 240, 240n; popish [1]353; proud [5]814; reliance on [1]204; rogue [5]281; role of [1]846, 847; RC [1]826, [2]1152, [5]819; in Sicily [4]235; venerated [4]477; will of [1]847; p.-worship [1]824; as wretches [4]86; *see also* clergy
priestcraft [3]180
priestesses [5]517n
priesthood [5]578, 605
abolition of [1]832; Catholic [1]805; ignorant [5]805; in Ireland [2]936; Jewish [2]1153, [5]624
Priestleian(s) [2]801, [5]7
P. Unitarian [3]670, 671, *671n*; P. Unitarianism [3]305n
Priestley, Joseph (1733–1804) [1]lviii, 63n, 198n, 205, 316n, 671, 779, 779n, 867, [2]404n, 663n, 799, 801–2, 803, 857n, 858n, 1060, [3]602n, 671n, 692, 737, 738, 738n, [4]27n, 160, 160n, 171, 390, 390n, 629, 629n, 638, 639n, 644, [5]7n, 162, 162n, 622, 622n, 657, 657n, 825n, [6]71
freezing water [1]650; and phlogiston [1]639n; piety of [4]27; and Unitarians [2]27, 27n, [4]46, 46n
Disquisitions relating to Matter and Spirit [4]171n q, 629n; *Doctrine of Philosophical Necessity Illustrated* [4]629n; "Experiments on the Production of Air by the Freezing of Water" [1]650n; *Hartley's Theory of the Human Mind* [6]334; *History of the Corruptions of Christianity* [3]1092n, [5]622n; *Letters* [4]665n; *Memoirs* [1]650n; *see also* R. Price and Priestley *A Free Discussion*
Priestley, Richard (1771–1852) [1]lxxii, [2]519, 519n
prima materia [1]630
primate [5]258
"primitive" [2]260
primogeniture [4]213–14, 214n, 817, [5]56, 273
primrose [4]708
Primrose, James (d 1659) *De vulgi in medicina erroribus* [1]766, 766n
prince(s) [4]278
duty of [5]538
Prince Edward's Isles [2]74
Prince of Wales's Fort [2]985, 987n
Prince Regent
Danish [5]313; *see also* George IV
Prince, Samuel (d c 1864) [4]71
Princes Isle [5]832

Princeton, NJ
  Princeton University Library, marginalia in [1]clxiii, clxvi, 3, [2]99, 158, 526, [4]215, 264, transcript of marginalia in [5]854
Princeton University Library Chronicle [2]99
principia [4]175
principium essendi [5]15
principle(s) [1]321, 527–8, 835, [2]936, 945, 1008, [3]9, 65, 209n, 328, 354, 1090, [4]113, 258, 603, [5]269, 455, 737, 770
  absolute [5]788; may appear absurd [5]304; of action [5]650; active [5]405, 750; antecedent [2]466; anti-Christian [6]55; of beauty [3]259; of being and knowing [4]460, 460n; in Böhme [1]628–61 *passim*; of Catholic Relief Bill [4]24; centripetal [1]569; common [1]611; of compromise [3]141, 141n; conservation of [6]49; corrupt [1]356; and deeds [5]562; Epicurean [1]305; erroneous [3]787, [6]50; evil [3]305, [5]85, 86, [6]138; false [5]105; and female heart [4]689; first [2]716, [3]948, [5]123, 745, 757; of fluid [6]228; founding [4]371; French [4]160n; of the gaseous [6]228; general [1]825; of government [5]661; idea of [2]674; individualising [4]420; of interpretation [3]33; invisible [5]825; in law [3]501; law confused with [4]496; of legality [3]72; Locke's [4]116; of logic [4]454; logical [4]175n; in man [4]430; man of [2]940; manly [3]8; and maxims *see* maxims; meaning of [3]805; metallic [1]780; most mysterious [4]653; negative [5]277; and observation [6]96; opposite [3]162; patriotic [3]468; philosophic [5]15; of philosophy [1]561; of physiology [3]67; and product [4]387; of psychology [3]63; of reason [3]255; re-introitive [1]667; Romish [4]20; and rules [4]826; saving [1]11; of selfhood [4]425–6; selfish [1]680; seminal [1]356; septic [4]148, 148n; solid [3]1014; of soul [5]756; substantial [1]663; subversive [3]846; supernatural [5]600; of taste [3]401; and theory [1]531, [4]13; three [5]742; of toleration [2]934–5; in Tom Jones [2]693; tracking of [2]952–3; ultimate [5]776; universal [5]766, 800; unprincipled [3]166; vital [1]178, [2]1026, [3]44, 44n, [4]149–50, [5]420, [6]152; Whig [4]14
Pringle, Sir John (1707–82) *Observations on the Diseases of the Army* MT [4]148–50
Pringle, Thomas (1789–1834) [1]31, [4]151n
  letter to [2]964
  Afar in the Desert [1]31; *African Sketches* MT [4]151–3; *Ephemerides* [1]31; *Poetical Works* ed Ritchie [1]31; see also *Friendship's Offering* ed Pringle
print(s) [2]508
printer [3]772, [4]761
printing [1]766, [2]459, [6]63
Prior, George, Jr (fl 1810) [3]938
Prior, Matthew (1664–1721) [1]38, 117n
Prior, Thomas (c 1682–1751) *An Authentick Narrative of the Success of Tar-Water* [1]409
"Priscian" [5]111, 111n
Priscian (Priascianus Caesariensis) (fl 500) [2]54n, 59n, 881n
prism [4]313n, 337n
prison(s) [3]26, 26n, 501n
  breaking of [2]312; p.-house [3]27; reform [4]241n
prisoners [1]344, [5]396
privation(s) [2]218, 559n, [3]916, 916n, [4]443, [5]61, 202, [6]46
  and negation [2]671, 671n
privilege(s) [1]396, [2]933, [3]151
  committee of [2]949
Privy Council *see* Council, Privy
Proast, Jonas (c 1642–1710) [1]256n
probability/probabilities [1]775, [2]28, 695, 831, [3]364, [4]109, 480, 765, 780–2, [6]61, 145
  historic [6]324; philosophic [3]261; plethora of [5]104
"probable" [4]779
probable, the [3]260–1
probation [4]465, [5]424
probity [1]171
problem(s)
  names for [5]790; synoptic [5]607n
procedence [1]564
"proceeding" [2]732, 732n
proceeding [2]248–50, [3]139n, [5]799
proceleusmatics [1]377
process(es) [1]597, 602, 606, 680, [2]1161, [5]66, 410, 455, 583, 650
  of acquiring truth [1]303; cabbalistic [1]670; chemical [5]247; of Christian faith [3]697; fanciful [6]143; organific [5]430; organising [1]537; presumptuous [6]298; psychological [4]55; redemptive [3]919; spiritual [3]927; universal [1]558; vital [5]431
procession [1]564, [2]882, [3]13, 16, 16n, 79, 139, 139n, 460, [5]11, 576–7, 799
proclamation [2]946, [3]6, 489
Proclus (412–85) [1]cxxiii, 60n, 298, 298n, 580n, 645n, 690n, [2]432n, 433, 1123, 1123n, [3]909n, [4]141, 158, 421, 426n, 489–90, [5]234, 234n, 743, 743n, 747, 753, 759–61, [6]143, 143n
  read by Böhme [1]656; contemporaries of [5]747, 747n; Proclo-plotinian Platonists

^{3}909; and Schelling ^{4}426; wizardry of ^{4}143
Commentary on the Timaeus of Plato ^{4}141n; *Elements of Theology* tr E. R. Dodds ^{1}665n; *In Platonis theologiam* ^{1}568n, 656n, ed and tr Portus as *Platonic Theology* ^{4}156n, ^{5}748, 748n; *The Philosophical and Mathematical Commentaries . . . Theological Elements* tr T. Taylor ^{1}cvi, 60n, 298n, 665n, ^{2}1123n; MT ^{4}154–60
proconsuls ^{3}471
procrastination ^{2}560, ^{3}212, ^{4}855
procreation ^{1}753–4, ^{2}540–2, 1001, ^{3}1044
Procris (myth) ^{6}156, 157, 157n
Procrustes (myth) ^{5}592
Procter, Bryan Waller ("Barry Cornwall") (1787–1874) ^{1}365, ^{2}140
Dramatic Scenes and Other Poems ^{1}cxlin; MT ^{4}161–3; *Marcian Colonna*, presentation copy to C ^{4}161
prodigal ^{2}994, ^{3}720
P. Son ^{1}201–2
producent ^{4}267, ^{5}788
"product" (verb) ^{2}930, 930n
product(s) ^{1}152, ^{2}634, 1026, 1028, 1067, 1144, 1185, ^{3}14, 520, 1024, 1061, ^{4}125, 165, 267, 328, ^{5}715
absolute ^{5}788; coeternal ^{3}139; elementary ^{5}444; immediate ^{6}8; of mind ^{3}276; of opposites ^{5}714; and principle ^{4}387; and productivity ^{5}445, 451; rudimental ^{1}776; sensuous ^{3}947
production ^{2}641, ^{3}59, 531, ^{6}315
line of ^{1}651; projective ^{2}367; real ^{5}714; subjective ^{1}639
"productive" ^{4}452–3
productivity ^{1}626, ^{2}1009, 1026, ^{3}278, ^{4}328, 389, 500
and product ^{5}445; vital ^{5}444
profanation ^{1}782
profaneness ^{3}45
professio fidei ^{3}689–90
profession(s) ^{1}281, ^{4}28, 138, 731
choice of ^{5}367; Church as ^{2}321; civic ^{3}785; of faith ^{3}689–90; learned ^{2}530; liberal ^{6}14; medical ^{3}843; outward ^{1}813, ^{5}639; positive ^{5}432; of soldier ^{5}379, 380, 381; and trade ^{5}378, 378n, 381
professor(s) ^{2}999, ^{3}5, 5n, ^{5}362, 379, 385, 692
profit(s) ^{2}636, 807
profligacy ^{5}521
progenitors ^{3}596
prognostic(s) ^{3}452
prognosticate ^{3}472
prognostication(s) ^{3}110, 417, 417n
and prophecy ^{3}105, 110n
progress ^{1}356, ^{4}526
progressive faculties ^{3}317; by induction ^{4}160; of intellect ^{5}866; in science ^{5}447; in virtue ^{5}229
progression(s) ^{1}151, ^{3}266, 800, ^{4}159, 266, 494, ^{5}10, 177, 374, 561
conditions of ^{5}529; in knowledge ^{3}697; line of ^{1}651; object of soul ^{6}127; of the social state ^{6}53; spiritual ^{1}674; triple ^{5}444; of vital growth ^{1}468
progressiveness ^{1}142, ^{5}302
prohibition ^{5}507
projection ^{2}885, ^{3}1016, 1022, ^{5}134
separative ^{5}438; volcanic ^{5}338
prolepsis ^{1}691, 693, ^{2}320, ^{3}345, 889, ^{5}784
Prometheus (in Aeschylus) ^{4}845, 845n
Prometheus (myth) ^{1}543, ^{3}92, 92n
promiscuus ^{3}695
promise(s) ^{1}431, 439, 705, ^{3}609, ^{5}649, ^{6}262
to apostles ^{5}608; conditional ^{3}463, 464; deceiving ^{1}445; divine ^{3}521, ^{5}632; to Jews ^{3}464–5; of prophets ^{5}674; ray of ^{5}420; spirit of ^{1}438
prompter ^{4}723
pronoun(s) ^{3}890n
personal ^{1}437; relative ^{2}1195
pronunciation ^{3}889, ^{4}185
rapid ^{1}384
"proof" ^{2}362
proof(s) ^{2}609, 810, ^{4}364, ^{5}71, 72, 325, 341, 554, 754
a posteriori ^{5}729; absence of ^{5}415; apodictic ^{5}766; Cartesian ^{3}330, 330n; chasms in ^{2}607; differ in value ^{5}658; external ^{5}516; modes of ^{3}262; moral ^{5}703, 703n; negative ^{1}423; positive ^{4}301, ^{5}598; proper ^{5}565; purely intellectual ^{5}455; specific ^{5}383
propaedeutic ^{3}362n
propaedia ^{3}362
of philosophy ^{5}81–2
propagation ^{3}1016
propaideia ^{1}598, ^{3}918, 918n
propaideutikos ^{1}513, 513n
Propator ^{3}493, 493n
"proper" ^{5}428
Propertius, Sextus (c 48–c 15 BC) *Catulli Tibulli Propertii Opera* ^{1}lxxviii
property/properties ^{1}395, 739–40, ^{2}529, 529n, 899, ^{3}426, 835, 889, ^{5}6, 75n, 159, 282, 283, 304, 443, ^{6}23, 244
absolute ^{6}44; Church ^{1}359, ^{2}943; common

property/properties—*continued*
[2]124; defined [3]799; fetters of [6]325; God's right of [5]613; hereditary [5]273; landed [1]360, [5]577; nation is not a [1]424; national and circulating [1]356; and nationalty [6]22; occult [3]952; panic of [3]148, 148n; rights of [1]36; theory of [2]618; usufructuary [5]529; *see also* propriety/proprieties
prophecy/prophecies [2]46, 142–57, 402–5, 543–4, 785, [3]33, 34, 40, 55, 71, 102, 102n, 207, 208, 209, 305, 353, 417, 421, 425n, 457, 462, 463, 465, 477, 563, 580, 611, 662, 668, 920, 923, 1069, [4]476, 537, 581, 605, 788, [5]53, 60, 391, *391n*, 523, 656, 766, [6]166
criterion of science [3]426; of Daniel [3]419–21, [6]217; prophetic era [3]101; faculty of [1]111; fulfilment of [2]495, [4]44; interpretation of [1]434; of Isaiah [3]110; of Joel [2]653; and miracles [1]282; more sure word of [2]288, [3]422, 691; narrative [6]207; of OT [1]316, [3]462; power of [5]425; and prognostication [3]105, 110n; of Rev [3]694; Rev as prophetic drama [2]505; a rich mine [2]142; safe [2]1179; Scripture [5]57, [6]107; series of [5]765; spirit of [5]565; Sybilline [6]165; needs symbols [3]425; tendency to [5]517
prophesiers [5]391
prophet(s) [1]346, 442, 444, [2]373, 360, 377, 411–12, 419, 467, 894, 1107, 1111, [3]33, 105n, 106, 446, 456, 468, 482, 533, 731, 767, 987, 1088, [4]295, 472, 475, 477, [5]34, 59, 89, 391n, 414, 414n, 465, 517n, 529, 535, 570, 656, 677
commissioned [2]406; Daniel as [2]409; evangelical [1]734; false [3]642; great [2]799; Hebrew [1]543, [2]150, [3]563; for hire [5]624; Jewish [3]691, [4]656; memorials of [5]526, 526n; of OT [2]480; oriental [3]674; promised [3]738; promises of [5]674; as unaided men [1]438; writings of [4]638
prophetic, the [2]824
propheticality [3]188
Prophets (Books of OT) *see* Bible: OT: prophets
"propiority" [4]168, 168n
Propontis [5]833
proportion(s) [1]780, [3]1027, [4]169, 324, 691, [5]98
proposition(s) [4]127
identical [5]775; irrational [2]281; self-conscious [4]92; universal [2]1178
propriation [2]657
proprietage [3]51, 51n
proprietates [3]1091
proprietor(s) [1]356, [3]799, [5]304
propriety/proprieties [1]739, 739n, [2]514, 943, 945, 1175n, [3]17, 889, [5]512
in choice of words [4]799; dramatic [3]436, [6]140; *see also* property/properties
proprius [3]426, 426n
proproton [2]745, 745n
pros [2]598, 598n, [3]24, 24n
prosaism [1]487
prose
Attic [3]227n; Donne's [2]254; English [3]887; English p. classics [3]882; flat [3]899; flat poetry [1]723; and poetry *see* poetry; printed as blank verse [1]408; St Paul's [2]499; Shakespeare's [4]805; style *see* style; and verse [1]408
proselyte(s) [2]320
proselyter(s) [1]496, [2]459
proselytism [3]318, [4]21
Proserpine (myth) [1]639, 639n, 678, [2]575, 583, 583n; *see also* Persephone
prosody [3]815, [4]603n
in classical satires [2]757; English [1]858, [6]255n; Greek [2]579, 579n; Greek and Latin [1]858; *see also* metre(s)
prosperity of the wicked [5]61
Prospero (*Tempest*) [4]765, [5]130n
prostitutes [4]695n, 714n
prostitution [3]907, [5]678
Protagoras (c 490–c 420 BC) [2]868, 868n, 1123
protection [5]652
Protectorate *see* England
Protestant(s) [1]223n, 713, 804, [2]24, 30, 39, 40, 195, 220, 663, 664, 675, 701, 806, 813, 934, 1149, [3]148, 216, 235, 669, 883, [4]172, 180–1, 551n, [5]105, 140, 297–8, 394, 521, 561, 617, 636, 639, 661, 673, [6]292
agreement with RCs [2]702; ante-Lutheran [5]549; anti-episcopal [3]686; bibliolatry of [2]35, 37; C of E [5]151; common ground of [2]26; considers Scriptures primary [1]314; consistent [1]345; controversies [5]504; English [3]156; enlightened [5]177; error of [5]550; fashion in argument among [1]317; French [3]785, [4]172; in general [2]40; high-church [6]118; idol of [1]820; infra-p. [1]863; jealous [5]658; learned [4]43; low-church [6]118; marrying Papist [6]263; masters [4]259; missions of [5]105n–6n; objections to Council of Trent [3]232, 232n; persecution of [1]255n; persecution of heretics by

[2]666–7; prayer [2]723; on sacraments [5]675; Scriptural [5]662; sensuality [2]984; source of differences between [1]674; strict [2]916; strife among [6]20; what constitutes a [5]497; zealots [4]24
Protestantism [1]514, [2]480, 663, 826, 936n, 1036, [3]669, [4]595, [5]298
on Continent [1]733; defenders of [4]22; genius of [1]516; in Great Britain [5]144; history of [1]515–16; languid [1]234; modern [3]451; patriarchs of [2]304; regular [2]31; sets up infallibility of Bible [1]515; undervalued [4]269
protestation [4]860
Proteus (in Homer) [1]799
Protevangelium see *Proto-evangelium*
"prothesis" [2]990n
prothesis [1]348, 563, 649, [2]990, 990n, 991, 992, 993, 995n, 1186, [3]6, 416, 449, 450, 453, 916n, [4]166, 166n, [5]49, 444, [6]92
related to synthesis [1]651; system of [3]361; and thesis [4]257, [5]235
proto- [1]466, 466n
Proto-evangelium [1]452n, [2]444, 447, [4]470, 470n, 475; see also *Urevangelium*
proto-evangellion [2]921
protogenes [2]33, 722–3, 722n
protogonos [2]576n
Protogonus (myth) [2]576
proton pseudos [1]203, 340, *340n*, 617, 660, 678, 678n, [2]197, 990, 996, 1028, [3]233, 235, 294, 516, 1051, 1052, [4]22, [5]27, 95, 594, [6]298
Böhme's [1]617; Kant's [3]277
proto-parent [5]504
protos [1]340n
prototokos [2]722n, 732n, [5]29
prototype(s) [1]573, 582, [3]78, 78n
celestial [2]488; soul [2]553–4
protoxide [3]127, 1020
protozoa [4]448, 448n
Prout, William (1785–1850) *On Chemistry, Meteorology, and the Function of Digestion* [2]883n
Provençal (language) [4]291
Provence, Count of *see* Louis XVIII
proverb [1]425
English [4]235; Greek [5]495; homely [2]1156
providence(s)/Providence [1]163, 171, 514, 706, [2]161, 176, 288, 694, 929, [3]23, 53, 73, 313, 447, 454, 470, 471, 472, 675, 801, [4]260, 473, 589, 629, 650, [5]61, 75, 160, 529, 607, 644, 652
avenging [2]495; Divine [1]448, [5]632; especial [5]516; hand of [2]933; Judgment of [2]818; ordinary [5]536–7; personal [1]436; plan of [2]517; retributive [3]797; ruling [1]447; scheme of [2]279; universal [5]653
provision-loft [3]741
proximity [1]537
proxy/proxies [1]865, [2]826
"prozoote" [1]594, 594n
prozote [1]595
prudence [1]171–2, 172n, [2]291, 926, 928, 940, 1167, [3]4–5, 5n, 50n, 466, 474, 492–3, 497, 763, 777, [4]78, 162, 256, [6]91
Christian [1]263, 781, [3]585; holy [3]744, 750; selfish [4]653
prudentialist [1]812
Prudentius, Marcus Aurelius Clemens (348–c 410)
Prudentius tr H. J. Thomson [5]601–2 q; *Psychomachia* [2]433, 433n
Prujean, Francis [5]818
prunes [4]694, 694n
Prussia [2]622, [5]279, 312n, 634
King of [5]191
Prussian [5]280
prussic acid *see* acid(s)
Pryce, Mr (fl 1818), letter to [2]650 q, [3]966n q
Prynne, William (1600–69) [1]850, [2]932, 932n, 1102n, [4]176, [5]616, 616n
Przewalski's horse [2]528n
psalm(s) [2]89, 89n, 651n, 1051, [3]904, [5]512, 527, 667n
imprecatory [3]770. See also *BCP*; Bible: OT: Psalms
psalmist(s) [5]95, 484, 681
psalmody [5]147, 512
Psalter [6]17
Psellus, Michael (11th century) [5]234, 235
pseud-evangelia [3]40
pseudo-Athanasian Creed *see* Creed, pseudo-Athanasian
Pseudo-Athanasius [4]300, [5]8n, 11
pseudo-Catholic [1]863, [4]20
pseudo-Catholicism [1]516
Pseudo-Dionysius (fl c 500) [1]562, [5]662 ("Dennis"), 662n ("Areopagite")
Celestial Hierarchy [3]683 q, 685, 685n, 1083, 1083n
Pseudo-Matthew [1]491n
Pseudo-Methodius [5]402 ("Methodius")
Apocalypse des Ps-Methodios ed Lolos [5]402n
pseudo-mystics [3]358
pseudo-Pauline [1]201
pseudo-Plutarch [1]639n; *see also* Aetius

pseudos, proton see *proton pseudos*
"pseudosophy" [2]614, 614n
psilanthropic [2]442, [3]730, 730n
"psilanthropism" [4]253, 253n, [5]563, 563n, [6]71, 71n
psilanthropism [2]464, [5]626
  Priestleian [6]74
"psilanthropist(s)" [2]22, 22n, [4]46, 46n
psilanthropist(s) [3]738, [5]433, 667
  Priestleian [4]46, 46n
"psilanthropy" [4]46n
psilanthropy [2]1079n
"psilology" [2]1147, 1147n
"psilo-phaenomenonism" [2]547, 547n
psilos [2]547n
"psilosopher(s)" [4]627, 627n, [6]124n
psilosophers [2]853
"psilosophists" [5]201, 201n–2n, [6]124 ("psilophists"), 124n
psilosophists [1]621n, [4]97, 501n
"psilosophy" [3]199, 199n, [4]627, 627n, [5]202n, 309n, [6]124n
psilosophy [2]265, 265n, 853n, [3]511, [4]648
  Arian [2]265; French [5]309
psyche/psyche [1]125, 126n, 163, 164n, 175, 175n, [2]431, 431n, [3]39n, 44, 442–3, 520, 580, [4]267n, [5]591n–2n, [6]302
  and *pneuma* [1]620; *see also* soul(s)
Psyche (myth) [2]87, 87n, [3]911, 913, 1066n, [4]647n, [5]591
psychical, the [3]44
psychography [5]738, 738n
"psychological" [4]52, [5]148, 252
"psychologist" [4]181, 181n–2n
psychologist(s) [3]992, [4]92, 639
  Plato as [4]127
psychology [2]410, 533–57, 1059n, [3]253, 967, [4]156, 415, [5]167, 738, 738n, [6]242
  awaking from abject state [1]374; difficulties in [2]547; essay on [5]360; grounds of [3]101; higher [3]318; psychological insight [3]662; Kant and [4]143, 143n; laws of [3]204; without metaphysicist [1]281, 298; principles of [3]63; Schelling's contempt for [4]415; scientific [1]566; sexual [3]906n; shallow [4]106; sound [5]422
"psychooid" [3]935, 935n
psychosomatists [3]396
Ptolemy I, Lagi, King of Egypt (c 367–283 BC) [6]3, 4
Ptolemy II, Philadelphus, King of Egypt (309–246 BC) [2]381n, 416, 832n, 895n
Ptolemy IV, Philopator, King of Egypt (reigned 221–205 BC) [6]141, 141n
Ptolemy VI, Philometor, King of Egypt (c 186–145 BC) [2]417n
Ptolemy (Claudius Ptolemaeus) (c 90–168) [3]426
  Ptolemaic scheme [5]560; Ptolemaic system [3]201
Ptolomaeus Lagis *see* Ptolemy I
pub(s) [3]164n
public, the [2]80, [4]270
  dust in eyes of [4]670; and people [1]220; psilosophical [3]339; reading [2]76, 599, [4]607, 610, [5]174; religious [3]451; scientific [5]638; spirit [2]206; *see also* mind, public
Public Advertiser [3]220
publican [1]703
publications
  modern [1]766; of opinions [2]108
Publications of the Modern Language Association of America [2]169
public-houses [5]317n
publicist [5]283
Publicola, Publius Valerius [4]770, 770n
publisher, impatient [4]597
pudding(s) [2]1156, [3]751
  black [2]811; Yorkshire [5]110
puerilities [2]475
Pufendorf, Samuel von (1632–94) [6]71
puff [3]930, 930n
puffers [3]682
puffing up [5]492
"Pugh, Edward" *see* Hughson, David
Pugh, John (Johannis Pughe) [1]155
pugilist(s) [1]379, [5]13
Pulci, Luigi (1432–84) [2]795n, [4]290
Pull Court [4]69
pulley of devotion [1]325
"pulmonists" [5]147, 147n
pulpit [1]398
  p. murder [3]819; p. rebukes [3]819; style in [5]480
pulsation [4]520
pulse [1]525
pulverisation [6]227
pulverise [3]60, 60n, 61
"pulverivorous" [6]110, 110n
pun(s) [1]324, 610, *610n*, [2]334, 756n, 760n, 808n, [3]175n, 193, 754n, [4]756, 768, 800, 842n, [5]111, 226, 287, 292, 795
  allegory degenerates into [1]821; bad [2]239; commonplace [5]812; in S. Daniel [2]125; in Donne's sermons [2]254; droll [3]149; French [1]76; grave [3]47; Latin [2]756n; in Milton [2]125; origin of [3]1065; and "Punic" [2]886, 886n; pun-like [3]978;

sneaking affection for [1]354; system supported by [2]574; unconscious [3]976; *see also* words, play on
punch [1]369
Punch-and-Judy [2]537n
punctuality [3]276
punctuation [3]272, [5]533
true scheme of [5]502
punctum indifferens [3]15n
"pungency" [1]641
pungency [1]631
"pungent" [1]611
pungent, the [1]617, 618, 618n, 667
Punic and punning [2]886, 886n
Punic War, Second [1]177n
punishment(s) [2]108, 1138, [3]317, 740–1, [4]645, [5]61, 103, 470, 559, 593, 613, 614, 728
divine [2]800–1; eternal [5]819
punning [2]886n, 1152, [5]478n
punster(s) [1]354, [5]95
puppet(s) [1]369, 386, [3]179
p. show [2]508
Purchas, Samuel (1577–1626) [2]165n
Purchas His Pilgrimage [1]clxixn
purchase [5]66
"purchased" [2]1161
purgatory/Purgatory [1]512, 845, [2]26, 27, 135, 559n, 566n, 685, 685n, 809n, 1075n, 1152, [3]212, 212n, 216, 794, [4]86, 162, 177, 246, 589, [5]497, 558–9, 605, 821
purification [3]544
"purify" [3]61
Puritan(s) [1]233, 256, 286, 287n, 319, 327, 338, 339, 872–3, 875, 879, [2]57, 273, 274n, 338, 656, 813n, 935, 972, 1100, 1136, 1139, 1156, 1157, 1157n, 1173, [3]483, 818, 819, 821, 990, [4]73, 79, 173–4, 179, 182, 594, 609, 643, 657, 657n, 723, 723n, [5]146, 146n, 155n, 192, 507, 521n, 526, 596, 640
abuse of [4]78; Dissenters [4]643n; party [2]260; temper of [4]176; tenets of [1]222
"Puritan Tracts" *see* "Cromwellian Tracts"
Puritanism [1]804, [2]523, [3]820, [4]180, [5]123, 124
purity [1]657 ("pure"), 657n, 814, [3]137, [4]732
Desdemona's [4]865; of heart [5]618; of mind [4]654, 833; progressive [3]699
Purkis, Samuel (fl 1799–1809) [1]536n, [4]85, 85n
Purl, Anthony [4]91, 91n
purse(s) [3]373, [4]860
pursemen [2]979
purser, East Indian [4]30, 30n
Purver, Anthony (1702–77) [3]1065
pus [1]388, 388n, [3]60n, [5]233
Pusey, Edward Bouverie (1800–82) *see* Justin Martyr *Works* tr Pusey
Puseyism [2]1038n
pusillanimity [2]1024, 1024n, 1201
pustules [2]85
putrefaction [1]643, [3]1029, [5]127
putridity [2]545, [3]613, [5]467
Pütter (probably Johann Stephan Pütter, 1725–1807) [1]197
puture [3]981
Puységur, Armand Marie Jacques de Chastenet, Marquis de (1751–1825) [2]402, 402n, 548n, [3]396n
puzzle-peg [1]41, 43, [2]74n
Pygmalion (myth) [3]391, 391n, [5]310, 310n
pygmy/pygmies [2]346, 346n
Pyne, M. Taylor (1855–1921) [4]215
pyr [2]576n, [3]61, 61n
Pyr (myth) [2]576
pyramid(s) [1]793, [3]715, [5]844, 845
of science [1]177
Pyramus and Thisbe (myth) [2]782, 887
Pyrenees [4]341
pyroeides [2]425, *425n*
"pyrophose" [5]335, 335n
pyrophose [5]344, 344n
pyrrhics [2]128
Pyrrho/Pyrrhon of Elis (c 360–c 270 BC) [1]781n, [5]728–9
Pyrrhonists [5]814, 814n
Pyrrhus, King of Epirus (319–272 BC) [2]416
Pyrrhus (myth) [4]627n
Pythagoras (6th century BC) [1]187, 410n, 563n, 615, 719n, [2]343, 343n, 348, 430, 557, 607n, 708, 727, 1136, 1136n, 1137n, [3]206, 230n, 539n, 780, 968, [4]115, 147, 400n, 511, 511n, [5]223, 225–9, 230, 459 ("Pythagorean"), 573, 694n, 696–703, 696n, 733, [6]5
astronomy of [5]232; biographies of [5]224n; birth of [5]696n; and Christ [5]226; on colours [5]452, 452n; discipline of [6]137; intention of [5]541; maxim(s) of [1]767, [3]539n; numbers of [2]429; philosophy of [1]410; tetractys of [1]348, 348n; theosophy of [1]691; defines soul [5]233
Pythagorean(s) [1]196, 547n, 563n, 564, 564n, [2]425n, [4]115, 367n, [5]228, 228n, 230, 231, 232, 233, 694–703
P. band *see* band

Pythagoreanism [5]745
Pythagoreme [5]232
Pythagorites [5]233
Pytho [2]1108n
Pytho [5]391n
Python (myth) [5]117n
Pythoness(es) [1]420, 420n, [5]517n
Pythonists [5]391n
 Christianised [5]391

Q. Curtius *see* Curtius Rufus, Quintus
quack (doctor) [2]454, 824, [4]622, 657, [5]136
quackery [1]298, [2]192, 192n, 454, [3]128, 1018, [4]617, [5]296
quack-quack [2]177, 177n
quaintness [1]765, [2]296
Quaker(s) [1]176, 176n, 181n, 248, 248n, 270, 275, 275n, 276, 296, 529, 674n, 818, 821, [2]76, 76n, 85, 85n, 191, 328n, 653, 653n, 714n, 717, 717n, 755, 980n, [3]700, 700n, 809n, 823, 823n, 826, 826n, 927–8, *927n–8n*, 952n, 1065n, [4]20, 181n, 182, 216, 216n, 241n, 308n, 660, 671, [5]187, 509, 509n, 569, 577, 651, 651n, 671, 671n, [6]60, 60n
 changed names of days [2]810–11, 811n; church government of [1]341, 341n; error of [2]811; glory of [4]308; idolise words [3]809; lewd [5]812; and oaths [1]275, [6]263; peaceable [1]323; on prayer [1]674; shun speech [3]493; Society of Friends [2]811n; on witchcraft [3]823
Quakerism [5]569n, [6]60n
quale [5]270, 702
"qualify" [1]567
qualification, cautious [5]424
qualis [1]656, 656n
"quality" [1]655–6, 656n
quality/qualities [1]567, 600, 606, 618, 791–2, [2]996–7, 1137, [3]1004, 1006, [4]324–5, 355, [5]6, 443
 four [1]588; infinite [2]563; occult [4]98; and quantity [1]128, 563, 642, 791–2, [3]130, 260, [4]604, [5]428, 450, 702, [6]115; root of [6]301; q. tone [3]358
"quantity" [5]697
quantity/quantities [1]377, 563, [2]996–7, 997n, [3]274, 832, [4]355, 503
 and accent [5]690; antecedent of [5]230; impossible [5]794; intensive or extensive [3]272, 454; material [1]683; mathematical language of [1]178; and quality *see* quality; as symbol [1]563; unknown [5]580
Quantock Hills [2]691
quantum [4]24, 217, [5]270, 701
Quarles, Francis (1592–1644) [1]56, 771n, [2]1033, [5]100 q
 Drayton epitaph [1]56, 56n
 Emblems [1]clxv, 56n; *Peace, peace, my dear!* [1]56n
quarrels [3]670, 776
quarry [4]450, 620
Quarterly Journal of Foreign Medicine and Surgery MT [4]164–9
Quarterly Journal of Science, Literature, and Art [1]641n, [4]503n
Quarterly Review [1]lxxxvn q, cxliii, 147, 148n, 488–9, 489n, [2]86, 359, 482n, 755n, 794, 904n, 932n, 977, 979n, 980n, [3]239, 500, 991n q, [4]6, 76n; MT 170–88; 619, 620n q, 627, 651, 651n, 665n q, 671n, [5]102, 102n, 105n, [6]48, 48n
"quarters" [1]381, 382
quarto [1]157, 157n
quartz [1]571, 572, 666, [3]1022, [5]245–6, 344n, 438
"quasific" [5]155, 155n
quasi-tritheism [5]7, 7n
quaternion [1]579, 597, 649n
queen
 he-queen [2]63; of Sweden [5]414, 414n
Queen's University *see* Kingston ON
Queen's Ware [3]629, 635, 637, 638
Quell [1]656
"Quercetanus" *see* Duchesne, Joseph
querist [3]690
Querist [1]410n
question(s) [3]221, 225, [5]776
 "Curious Questions" [3]45; form of [5]455; philosophical [5]4
questionists [2]30
questuary [1]779
qui bene distinguit [4]421, 421n
quibble(s) [3]349, [5]21, 157
Quickly, Mistress (in Shakespeare) [4]589, 589n
quicksilver [1]546, 547, [2]1011, [3]1029, 1041, [5]15, 387; *see also* mercury
Quicunque vult [1]587n
quid pro quo [2]1008, 1008n, [3]817, [4]443, [5]455, 470, 719, [6]114
quidditas [5]789, 789n
quiddity/quiddities [2]917, [5]428
Quillinan, Dora (née Wordsworth) (1804–47) [1]762, [2]180
Quillinan, Edward (1791–1851) [1]761–2
Quimboraca, Dr (fiction) [3]365
Quince (*Midsummer Night's Dream*) [2]782
quinces [4]162

quincunx [1]764, 797, 765
quinquarticular controversy [2]913
quinquinity [5]242
quintessence [1]638
Quintilian (Marcus Fabius Quintilianus) (c 35–c 100) [1]cvii, [2]757, 758n, 761 q, 761n, 776, [3]175, [4]99, [6]138
Institutio oratoria [2]757n q, [4]736n q
Quinziano Stoa, Gianfrancesco, formerly Conti (1484–1557) [2]7n, 8n, 9
quires [1]381, 382
Quirinus (myth) [2]898, [3]681
quirks [2]917
"quit" [3]181, 181n
quitch [4]186
Quito [5]105
Quixote *see* Don Quixote
quod primum verum [5]560
quos Deus vult perdere [5]866
quota [1]683
quotation(s) [2]1071, [3]530, [5]189

"R." (R. Southey) [1]89
"R", C's mark [2]259, 261
"R. S. Y." (R. Southey) [1]89
rabbi(s) [2]495, [3]54, 446, 459, 461n, 1086, 1088, [4]244, 247, [5]606, 630
aphorisms of [4]475; celebrated [1]448; rabbinical figments [3]452; interpretations of [3]1085–6; rabbinical literature [3]1088; rabbinic romance [3]103; rabbinical tradition [1]513, [3]594, 1090; *see also* fable(s), rabbinical
rabbins [3]684
rabbit(s) [1]421, [3]1035, 1035n, [4]636, 636n, 788
rabble [2]521, [3]164
Rabelais, François (c 1490–c 1553/4) [1]486, 486n, 727, [2]38n q, 499, 499n, [3]365n, [4]78, 78n, 192, 192n, 630n
morality of [4]190; and Swift [4]189
Pantagruel [2]769; *Works* tr and ed Le Duchat and others MT [4]189–98
Rabelaisians [4]192
rabies [1]477, [5]679n; *see also* hydrophobia
Rabshakeh (Bible) [2]308
"race" [1]443
race(s) [3]355–6, 355n–6n, 1025, [4]149, 341, [6]131
antipathy of [1]383; Cainite [6]5; Caucasian [5]336; and climate [5]309; C's division of [1]539–41; degenerous [1]539–40; demoralisation of [5]271; dispersion of [5]337n; distinct [2]147; diversity of English and French [5]195; division(s) of [1]539n; emigrant [5]234; first [3]105; five [5]253; French scheme of [5]271; generous [1]539–40; Gothic [4]37n; Greco-Roman [4]37n; Hammonic [1]539–40; historic [1]539; human *see* human race; Japetic/Iapetic [1]539–40, [4]37n; of mankind [1]779, [2]176; mixed [1]539–40, [4]583, 583n, [5]337; Mosaic account of [5]336–7; origin(s) of [4]583n, [5]253, *336n–7n*, [6]5n; pentad of [1]539; primary [1]779; refined [2]421; reproduction of [5]295; Semitic [1]539–40; and species [2]176; speculations about [5]352n; tetrad of [1]539; theory of [1]541n; wicked [5]373
Racheo (in Boccaccio) [1]543–4, 544n
Racine, Jean (1639–99) [4]736
and Shakespeare [2]123, 123n
rack(s) [3]223, [5]396
Rackham, Harris (1868–1944) *see* Cicero *De finibus* tr Rackham
Radamanthus (myth) [5]44
Radcliffe, Ann (1764–1823) [4]607 ("Ratcliff"), 607n
The Italian [4]607n; *The Mysteries of Udolpho* [4]607n
radiance [1]524, [2]206
radical(s) [2]210, 688, [3]146, [4]151, [6]44n
radix [1]653
rage, epidemic [5]41
ragea [4]29
Rahab (Bible) [1]708
railers at religion [3]586
railing (invective) [3]626
rain(s) [1]596, 710, [2]326, 887, 1038, [3]832
rainbow [3]653, [4]222–3, [5]95, 431
Rainolds/Reynolds, John (1549–1607) [2]812, 813, 813n
Rajaniti [2]584–5, 585n
Ralegh/Raleigh, Sir Walter (c 1552–1618) [1]57n, [2]64, 129, 129n, 818, [3]178n, [5]387–8, 387n
The History of the World [1]lxxxv, clin, 645n q, [2]1086n; MT [4]199–202; [5]387n q
Rama (myth) [2]342, 346, 346n
Ramath-lehi [1]422, 423
Ramayana [2]346
Rambouillet, Charles (fl 1728) [4]32
ram-cats [2]1053
ramenta [3]1093
Rameses [2]830
Ramler, Karl Wilhelm (1725–98) [1]23 q, [3]656
Rammohun Roy (Rama Mohana Raya) (1774–1833) [3]673n
Ramoth-Gilead [6]109n

Ramsgate [1]xcix, cxv, 761, [2]142, 520n, 599n, 698, [3]539n, 886
Randolph, Thomas (1605–35) [1]254n
Drayton epitaph [1]56n
Poems MT [4]203–5
Randolph, Thomas Jefferson (1792–1875) *see* Jefferson *Memoirs* ed Randolph
rank(s) [2]617, [4]240, 723, 796, 814, 860, [5]634
of creatures [3]580; gradations of [5]381; high [4]729; men of [5]362; of mind [5]452; pressure of [2]159; reverence for [1]499; and schools [5]366; in society [2]319
Rankine, James (fl 1830) "Case in Which Hydatids Were Contained in the Synovial Sheaths . . . of the Hand" MT [2]367
Rann, Joseph (1733–1811) *see* Shakespeare *Dramatic Works* ed Rann
ransom [2]659, [3]311
redemption as [1]429; of the soul [1]429
rant [2]1064, [3]179
Ranters [1]296, [2]496n, 714, 714n, [5]509n
rape [1]393, [5]103
The Rape of Helen tr "C" [1]38
Raper, Matthew (fl 1787) *see* Grellmann *Dissertation* tr Raper
Raphael (myth) [4]650
Raphael (*Paradise Lost*) [3]402, 494, 560, 1093n
Raphael (Raffaello Santi/Sanzio) (1483–1520) [2]235, 235n, [3]969, [5]815, 815n
Rapin-Thoyras, Paul de (1661–1725) *The History of England*† tr N. Tindal [4]206
rapscallion [2]511
rapture(s) [4]183
divine [5]822; religious [5]517
rarefaction [5]292
rarities, cabinet of [1]763, 797
Rastell, William (c 1508–65) [1]833, 833n; *see also* T. More *Works* ed Rastell
rat(s)
r.-catchers [2]348; water-r. [5]411
ratio [2]654, [4]144, 144n, [5]781, 782
grounds of [2]64; *see also* reason(s)
ratiocination(s) [2]695, [3]221, [4]220
ratiocinative, the [5]461
rational, the and irrational [6]115
rationalist(s) [4]639, [5]759
rationality [2]1192; *see also* reason(s)
Ratzeburg [1]671, [2]369, [5]181
Ravaillac, François (1578–1610) [4]181, 181n
Ravana (myth) [2]342, 346
raven [2]574n, 580, 737, 737n, [3]1045
ravines [1]435
ravishing [5]276
ray(s) [2]206, 206n, [3]426, 616–17, 723, 790, [5]133, 290, 491, 758
convergent and divergent [1]12; of faith [2]1178; of heat [3]29n; of promise [5]419; reflected [4]258; solar [3]945; of sun [3]29
Ray, John (1627–1705) [1]243, 244n
The Wisdom of God Manifested [1]244n
Raymond, Irving Woodworth (b 1898) *see* Orosius *Seven Books of History* tr Raymond
Raymond of Sabunde (fl 1434) [5]798–800
Theologia naturalis [5]799 q
Raysor, Thomas Middleton (1895–1974) [1]clii, cliii q, cliv; *see also* S. T. Coleridge IX *Coleridge's Miscellaneous Criticism*, *Coleridge's Shakespearean Criticism* ed Raysor
razor [5]712
Occam's [5]7n
reaction(s) [3]1010–11, [5]410
mutual [1]185, [2]248; reciprocal [2]624, 624n
Read, Sir Herbert Edward (1893–1968) *Coleridge as Critic* [1]288n
reader(s) [2]221, [3]444, [5]70, 173–6, 658
attentive [1]633; belief of [4]597; classical [4]727; of C's period [1]221; common [1]440, [5]566; competent [5]866; contemptuous [1]557; educated [1]561; effect on [4]581; English [3]677, [4]499, [5]244, [6]137; his own Evangelist [4]482; every man a [4]610; excluded [3]483; first [1]468; general [5]504; good [4]604; Greek [6]139; of Herbert [2]1034; inspired [5]473; intelligent [2]840; intended [3]20; judicious [1]447; lay [2]1156, 1156n, 1157n; let into secret [4]800; philosophic [4]173; of poetry [6]329; public [1]358; and punctuation [5]502; of Swedenborg [5]455; thinking [3]990; thoughtful [1]601, [5]413; uncertain [1]821; unconscious expectation of [4]604; of weak minds [5]406; young [4]612; youthful [2]1193
reading [2]561, 1016, [3]438
aloud, of Scriptures [1]349; of Bible [1]804; careless [2]103; made easy [4]190; exclusive [2]1157; extensive [6]25; first [2]969; flat [6]210; how to read [2]220, 225–6; immense [5]663; increase of [5]484; mannered mode of [3]914; in meekness [1]558; moral effect [2]764n; obscure [5]528; as personal encounter for C [1]lxix; pleasure of [1]280; of prayers or sermons [5]510; public *see* public, reading; of reviews [2]64; of Scriptures [5]514; Jeremy Taylor's [5]619; tuneful [4]604

Reading [5]48, 619
re-agency [4]389
reagent(s) [4]316, 320, 322, 322n
"real" [5]397, 397n, 400n
real(s) [1]604
absolutely [5]372; and actual *see* actual; argument for the [2]605–6; must be possible [3]312; negation of [5]459; and possible *see* possible; and potential *see* potential; and symbolic [5]687n; three only [5]443; and unreal [2]1193, [5]720
real presence [1]297, 839, [3]439, 439n, 1078, 1078n, [5]5n, 393, 393n–4n, 671n, [6]21; *see also* Eucharist
realisation, absurd [5]610
realism [2]604
of abstracts [2]433; consequences of [3]283; dynamic [3]136, 136n; and idealism *see* idealism; Newtonian dogmatic [1]108; and nominalism *see* nominalism
realist(s) [3]135, [4]416, 422n, [5]718, 720, 720n
and nominalist(s) *see* nominalist(s)
Realitabilität [4]406, 406n
Realität [4]350, 350n, 403n, 404, 406
"reality" [5]175
reality/realities [1]565, [2]135, 607, 612, 629, 643, 994, 1186, [3]13, 23, 67, 135, 260, 270, 363, 849, 858, [4]122, 219, 403n, 404, 436, 437, 450, [5]61, 370, 382, 413, 707, 754, 755, 788, [6]173
cause of [5]372; conditional and unconditional [3]43; contains actual and potential [1]694; conviction of [5]772; degrees of [1]238; empiric [3]248; everyday [4]790; form of [3]331; gradation in [3]755; individual [5]186; infinite [5]358; intense [1]563; mode of [3]345; negative [4]781; objective [2]1160, [3]276, [5]415, 701, 720; outward [5]552; personal [1]659; potential [1]614; powerful [5]638; progressive [3]644; scintillations of [2]553; sense of [5]372; source of [5]459; spiritual [6]311; subjective [5]132; substance of [1]712; supersensual [5]781; supporting [4]216; supreme [1]179, [3]524, [6]306; and symbol [1]812n; and thoughts [1]808; transcendent [3]989, [5]798–9; two forms of [1]231; ultimate [5]443; universal [5]410; unqualified [3]358; utmost [5]442; will causative of [4]400
realness [2]167
re-ascent [5]439
"reason" [5]175, 640
reason(s) [1]171, 178, 237, 304, 432, 504, 712, [2]359, 405, 559, 622, 663, 768, 882, 938, 1010, 1011, 1016, 1018, 1155, [3]13, 16n, 25, 42n, 151, 518, 806, [4]144, 195, 398, 548, 616, 674, [5]76n, 124, 131, 159, 174, 297, 302, 425, 463, 475–7, 541, 592, 613, 677, 754, 756, 780–1, 789, 795, 800, [6]56
absolute [3]460, [6]115; abstract [4]158; act of [4]221; age of [5]119; allegory of [3]92; and appetites [4]445; aversion to [4]648; and belief [4]301–2; and Christian doctrine [3]606; not conscience [4]263; conviction of [2]1133; darkness in [6]28; deeper than [2]1028; defined [1]682, [3]557–8, 723, [5]191–2, 777; no degrees of [3]207; developed [5]653; De Wette's definition [2]189; dictate(s) of [1]877, [4]598; disapproving [1]723; discourse of [3]150, 150n, [4]543, [5]781; divine [2]1193; divine and human [4]136; dogmatic [5]813; energic [2]1175; Eternal [1]435, [5]604; and evidence [4]301; eye of [1]576; and faith *see* faith; formal [4]219; forms of [2]1024; and heart [2]614; highest sense [2]1010n; human [5]557, 830; as idea [5]729; ideal [5]797; ideal in [5]52; imaginative [1]595; immortal [5]177; imperatives in [3]357; implies virtue [1]869; ineffectual [2]160; intuitions of [3]1091; Kant's concept of [3]97; law of [1]819; legislative [5]749; light of [2]482, 1000, [3]661, [4]656, [5]68, 425; living [5]372; logical and practical [3]700; loss of [6]287; lost [1]622; mechanism of [3]77; mere [5]96–7; misdefined [2]360; moral [3]54, 958; natural [2]930, [3]509, 610, [5]28; necrosis of [4]77; *nous* [2]713, 715, 729n; object of [3]332; objectivity of [5]758; one and the same in all [3]558; overlaid [2]153; parity of [1]473; perfect [5]476; personal agent [5]764–5; point of [6]240; positive and negative [5]797; postulate(s) of [2]1106, [3]989; power(s) of [5]425, 805; power of ideas [4]93; practical [1]303, 685, [2]182, 192, 644, 1151, [4]220, 409, [5]750, 755; practical and speculative [2]678, [3]682; principle of [3]255; Procrustean bed of [4]669; proof of [4]652; proofs of human [1]111; pure [1]819, [2]297, 713, [3]49, [4]155, 155n, 157, 648, [5]457, 820, 822, [6]307; realities of [3]849; r. in r. [3]163; and reasoning [5]750, 756, 789n, [6]286; reasonless [5]310; and religion [1]576, [5]8, 484, 678, [6]73–4; in religion [1]752; resignation of [6]80; and revelation [2]1151, 1152; right [1]358, 878, [2]186, [3]482, [5]464; right r. of faith [1]123; rightly called [5]400; and scripture(s) [3]150, [5]664–5, [6]42; self-evident [5]656; self-sufficing [4]278;

reason(s)— *continued*
seminal [1]174n; in sense [3]163; source of ideas [3]423, [4]78; speculative [5]750; subjective and objective [3]150; substantial [3]23, [4]258; supernatural [2]1150, [4]588; Supreme [1]824, [2]162, 305, 423, 884, 898, [3]151, 696, [4]135, [5]97, 614, [6]74; telescope of [1]170; theanthropy of [5]730; theoretic [4]409; transcendental concept of [3]244–5, 245–6; tri-unity [2]680; truth(s) of [4]108–9, [5]599; unaided [5]82; and understanding [1]70, 122, 122n, 123, 239, 304, 304n, 497n, 515, 515n, 527, 651, 654–5, 682–3, 693, 819, 869, [2]108, 188, 277, 277n, 296, 332–3, 482, 641, 654, 663, 678, 679, 680, 715n, 1151–2, 1192n, [3]49, 104, 163, 246–7, 423, 435, 516, 526, 557–60, 620, 720, 746, 848, 848n, 875n, 908, 908n, 968, 968n, 1082, 1091, [4]78, 144, 154–5, 155n, 194, 213–14, 214n, 352–3, 360, 360n, 369, 369n, 370, 372, 454n, 543, 579n, [5]305, 484, 492–3, 602, 640, 640n, 692n, 699n, 729, 730–1, 738, 750, 752, 756, 766, 781, 797, 798, [6]28, 64, 64n, 87, 114, 114n, 299, 300, 310; universal [2]267, [3]104, 150, [4]263, 863, [5]8, 68, 484, 755, 756; of the universal [6]78; victorious [4]287; war with feeling [4]437; and wickedness [4]589–90; and will [1]171, 640, [2]261, 315, 543, [3]104, 424, 547, 558, 720, [4]443–4, 548, 784, 784n, [5]176, 500, 500n, 514, 611, 751, 755, 784, 784n, [6]73; in will [5]789; will in [1]818; will of [4]168; see also *Vernunft*
reasoners [1]281
German [5]325
reasoning(s) [2]1154, [3]1050, [5]50, 69, 122, 251, 460
art of [1]632; captious [3]200; chain of [5]622; false [5]385; German [3]372; human [5]155; lax [5]555; metaphysical [5]410; mode of [5]306; prime end of [5]459; prudential [4]791; in theology [5]803; and wit [2]71
Réaumur, René Antoine Ferchault de (1683–1757) [4]30n
re-baptisation [5]643
Rebarbara [3]779
Rebecca (in Scott) [4]593, 594
rebel(s) [2]970, [3]149
solus [5]281
rebellion [3]160, [5]143
rebirth [2]1185
rebukes, pulpit [3]819
rebus [5]226n
recantation [2]938
recapitulation [2]151
receptivity [1]655, [3]242, 749, [4]220
Rechtslehre [2]618
recipiency, doctrine of [5]474
recipient(s) [5]26
correlative [2]402; passive [5]654
reciprocity in love [1]754
recitative [4]604
recognition [3]792
recollection(s) [1]172, [3]661, [4]221 ("recollect"), 477, [5]467
partial [1]560
Recollects, monastery of [3]993, 993n
reconcilement with God [3]551
Recorder, Mr [2]107, [5]240
re-creation [3]60, [4]621, [5]190
recrements [1]657
recrimination [1]251
rectitude, original [5]162
rector [1]308, [2]72
red [2]608, [3]1017, 1018, [4]167, [6]171–2
Red Sea [2]394, 416, 513, 574n, [4]29, [6]119, 119n
redbreast [3]1045
redeemed, the [1]575, [4]435, [5]777
Redeemer [1]448, 702, 707, 712, 813, [2]37, 584, 618, 657–9, 1074, 1166, [3]33, [4]481, 596, 653, [5]9, 420, 524, 626; *see also* Jesus Christ
redemption [1]284, 297, 302, 358, 429, 507, 644, 813 ("redeem"), [2]40, 139, 139n, 267, 270, 327, 454, 489–90, 583n, 662, 676, 705, 716, 786, 923, 1062, 1161, 1166, 1187n, [3]14, 26, 27, 29, 33, 42, 55, 65, 70, 200, 311–13, 311n, 447, 465, 515, 517, 536, 544, 683, 741, 747, 748, 876, 919, [4]580, 596n, 620, 629, 634, 641, 646, 652, 662, 665, 672, [5]9, 25, 55, 152, 158n, 165, 433, 465, 497, 497n, 591, 592, 670n, 672, 766, [6]74, 217, 297n, 299
from body [2]1177–8; Christianity as [2]434; in C of E [2]265; commencement of [2]562; consequences of [2]657–8; in creation [2]293; creation first act of [3]22, 66; debtor and creditor scheme [2]263, [3]47; doctrine of [5]524; economy of [1]574; final end of [5]603; free gift [5]670; fruits of [6]43; Grotian theory of [1]198–202; metaphor of [2]657–8; necessity of [2]1187; *opus operans* of [5]583; perfected [3]417; plan of [5]167; prophecy of [3]102; as ransom [1]429; representation of [1]123; and salvation [1]232; scheme of [5]614; self [5]135; from without [2]247
re-descent [5]607

Redi, Francesco (1626–97) [4]290, 290n
Bacco in Toscana [4]290n
Reed, Henry (1808–54) *Memoir of Thomas Gray* [2]864, 867n
Reed, Isaac (1742–1807) *see* Shakespeare *Plays* (1803) and (1809) ed Reed
Reed, Mark Lafayette *Chronology of Wordsworth* [1]227n; *see also* WW *The Thirteen-Book Prelude* ed Reed
Rees, Abraham (1743–1825) *Cyclopaedia* [1]549n, [2]388n, 580n, [3]126n, 1066n, [4]670n, [5]669n; articles in: "Cabbala" [4]246n; "China" [5]366n, 407n; "Comet" [4]518n; "Creed" [4]301n; "Density" [5]263n; "Marriage" [5]634n; "Masora" [4]246n; "Moon" [5]232n; "Phthiriasis" [2]615n; "Rays of Heat" [3]29n
Reeve, Clara (1729–1807) *see* J. Barclay *The Phoenix* tr Reeve
Reeve, Henry (1780–1814) [3]937
Reeves, Jonathan (d 1787) [5]179
refinement [3]753, 831, 1087
refineries [4]494
reflection(s) [1]141–2, 146, 149, 299, [2]479, 609–10, 632, 1019, 1067, 1134, [3]20, 62, 91, 121, 212, 393, 393n, 581, 610, 660, 741, 1036, [4]125, 131, 277, [5]795, [6]242
cool [4]744; fact of [1]348; of "I AM" [2]596; lamp of [5]130; light of understanding [3]472; moral [2]687; period of [2]65; philosophy of [4]217; *primae viae* of [2]63; results in language [1]538; reflective system [3]291; as understanding [5]752; of volition [5]290
Reflector ed L. Hunt [1]366, 366n
reflexes [5]305
reflex-faculty [1]325
reform(s) [2]507, 814
of conduct [5]650; moral [1]290; of parliament [3]788; reform, to, and regenerate [1]513
reformation [5]190, [6]263
means of salvation [2]495; zeal for [1]843
Reformation, the (in Church) [1]315, 329n, 493n, 817, 831, [2]260, 298, 496n, 507n, 911, 935, 1097n, 1167, [3]31, 136n, 165n, 166, 489, 489n, 775n, 877n, 984, 1078, [4]191, [5]143, 145n, 328–9, 467n, 661, [6]16n
in England [1]422, 422n, 831–9, [2]1158, [3]515, [5]144n, [6]298; of English Church [1]271, [6]261; founders of [3]308; German [1]835; history of [4]670; imperfection of [2]806; pioneers of [2]1178n; Spanish [2]740; stream of [2]304; Swiss [2]304
Reformed, the [5]398, 673
"reformer" [4]14
reformer(s) [1]817, [2]806, 917, 1138, [3]153, 561, 764, [4]68n, 177, 660, [5]505, 566, 595, 661
arguments of [5]396; in the Church [2]1199; of Church [2]1138, [3]561, [5]128; earliest [5]202; early [5]182; English [5]399; first [1]358, 805, 810, [2]1157; flagitious [2]48; in reign of Edward VI [1]329; theological [1]835
refreshment [1]714
"refulgent" [5]112
re-fundence [1]694, 694n
Regan (*King Lear*) [1]393, [4]817, 818, 820
regenerate(d), the [3]512, 513
"regeneration" [1]263
regeneration [1]202, 358, 582, 625, [2]26, 27, 40, 265, 496, 558, 574n, 690, 801, 1022, [3]51, 60, 311, 427, 596, 741, 748, 752, [5]152, 172, 192, 192n, 229n, 608, 649–50, 665, [6]315
regicide(s) [1]289, [2]970n, 1197, [4]73, 181n, [5]143, 144
regiment(s) [5]377, 378
of books [5]120
Regiomontanus (Johannes Müller) (1436–76) [1]746
Regius, Henricus (1598–1679) [4]106n
Regnans in excelsis [5]143n
regress, infinite [3]347–8, 347n
regret(s) [2]237, [4]810
and remorse [3]206, 956, [4]434, 434n, 651–2, 651n, 855n
regula/regulae [1]377, 378, [5]13
r. fidei [1]312, 312n, 345, 345n, [3]689, 766, [4]175, 175n; *r. maxima(e)* [3]163, 596, [5]86, 425, 425n; *r. veritatis* [3]687
"regular" [1]378
regulator, state as [5]363
regulus [1]216, 216n
Rehberg, August Wilhelm (1757–1836)
Ueber das Verhältniss der Metaphysik zu der Religion [1]lxxxiii, clxvi; MT [4]207–12; *Untersuchungen über die Französische Revolution* MT [4]213–14
Rehoboam, King of Judah (Bible) [1]422, [2]383, 399, 894, 894n, 927
Reid, Thomas (1710–96) [1]75n, [6]131
Reignolds, Dr *see* Reynolds, Edward
Reignolds/Reynolds, John (d 1684) [1]254, 259
Reil, Johann Christian (1759–1813) [3]372, 372n, 380, [5]141, 141n; see also *Archiv für Physiologie*; Steffens *Beiträge* ed Reil

Reimarus, Hermann Samuel (1694–1768) [3]89–90, 670, [4]221n, 228
Abhandlungen von den vornehmsten Wahrheiten der natürlichen Religion [3]89n q; *Apologie . . . für die vernünftigen Verehrer Gottes* [3]667n; *Fragmente eines Ungenannten* (*Wolfenbüttel Fragments*) [1]350n, [3]660n, 667n, 670, 683
Reimarus, Johann Albert Heinrich (1729–1814) [3]641n
Ueber die Gründe der menschlichen Erkentniss und der natürlichen Religion [2]609, 609n; MT [4]215–31; 264
Reinecke Foss [1]cvi, cviii
Reineke Fuchs [2]771–3
Reinhard, Karl von (1769–1840) *see* Bürger *Sämmtliche Schriften* ed Reinhard
Reinhold, Karl Leonhard (1758–1823) [3]319, 319n, [6]234, 238
Briefe über die Kantische Philosophie [6]234n; *Versuch einer neueren Theorie des menschlichen Vorstellungsvermögens*† [4]232
"reintroitive" [1]667n
Reiske, Johann Jacob (1716–74) [3]656
Reith, George [5]669
Rejected Addresses see Smith, James and Horace
rekindling [5]176
Reland, Adrian (1676–1718) [2]575
relapse of nature [1]664
relation(s) [1]152–3, [2]359, 634, [3]23, 116, 202, 286, 328, 399, 517, 679, 841, 1024, [4]124, 126, 166, 269, 355, [5]230, 369, 788
degraded [5]463; effect of change in [3]744; essential [3]17; eternal [4]400; existence of [5]368; of finite beings [6]299; general [1]354; idle [5]487; interchangeable [5]548; intuitions of [5]409–10; memorable [5]414n, 560n; of order [5]443; outward [3]275; product of [5]370; simple [5]428; of space [3]301, 343; in Swedenborg [5]414, 414n, 415; terms of [5]22; universe of [2]1019
relationship, symbols of [1]418
"relative" [5]231
relative and absolute [5]356
relativeness [2]322
relic(s) [1]372, [2]917, 1158
of a higher state [5]467
relicts of things [3]705
religieux [3]427
"religio" [6]314
religio [3]509n, 529, [4]727n
"religion" [2]655, 655n, [4]175, 625, 625n
and *threskeia* [3]722
religion(s) [1]647, 878, [2]147, 165, 530, 768, 938, [3]250, 304–13, 511, 774, 883, [5]82n, 104, 145, 169, 327, 672
adds to reason [3]509; aids of [2]1034; arguments for [2]149; Arian [6]74; articles of *see* Articles of Religion; binding [5]598; body of [5]188; bonds of [3]620; made business [1]319; cause of [4]674; ceremonial [1]877; childhood and [2]536; of Christ [4]667; Christ the r. [3]662; Christian [2]917, [3]680, [4]207–8, 548, 646, [5]64, 505, 568, 766, [6]105–6; of Christians [4]479; common creed [4]663; consists of ideas [3]743; danger to [5]385; deepest form [5]271; distinguished from philosophy and history [3]36; doctrines of [5]803; enthusiasm in [3]494; essence of [1]283, [4]299; etymology [3]509n; evidences of [2]247, [5]598; filagree [5]860; first step [5]842; founded on past [2]574; founded on truth [2]194; fundamental truth [2]278; fuss about [1]270, [6]261; general [4]665; God in [4]226; grammar of [5]95; of heart [1]754, 754n; Hebrew [3]108; in higher classes [4]580; of ideas [2]295; without ideas [1]122; among Indians [2]986–7; instituted [3]21; internal [5]644; Jewish [2]421, [3]468, [4]625, [6]138n; laughing at [5]644; and law [1]281, [5]622; local [5]644; love of God [5]562; and madness [1]804; and miracles [1]282–3; motives in [2]807; natural [1]269, [3]36, 658, 670, [5]584, [6]261; necessarily revealed [3]365; necessity of [5]644, 809; object(s) of [4]595, [6]28; obliges [2]654; odious sense [3]483; old [1]315, [5]718; organism of [1]517; pagan [4]625, [6]74; persecution in [5]37; philosophic [5]822; and philosophy *see* philosophy; philosophy of [5]777; popular [1]472; positive [6]18, 73; pretended [6]74; proof of [2]342; proves miracles [2]1059; pseudo-Christian [6]74; purity of [1]679; railers at [3]586; rational [2]788, [6]267; and reason *see* reason; reformed [1]271, [6]261; revealed [2]452, 482, [5]61, 71; and revelation [5]71; Sabellian [6]74; *sansculotterie* of [6]81; Schleiermacher's view of [2]999n; and science [2]181–2, 186; science of moral world [2]544; sects in [5]157; sensuous element in [2]643; Socinian [6]74; sole foundation of [5]596; solves problem of discontinuity [1]598; speculative [2]986; sphere of [3]886; religious spirit [3]994; spiritual [2]651; and state [5]302; superseding

philosophy [1]299; superstructure of [4]652; symbols of [6]109; without symbols [3]425; systems of [4]667; and taste [5]130; total scheme [3]606; as a trade [1]29; true [4]625–6; truths of [2]1160, [3]513, [4]446; universal [4]357; unlawful [2]939; wounds under Henry VIII [1]357; yearning after [3]764
religionist(s) [1]729, [2]70
religiosity [4]440
religious, the [2]1080
Relly, James (c 1722–78) *The Believer's Treasury* [4]4; MT 233–6
rem credimus [2]281, 281n, [3]934n, [5]5, 5n, 554, 554n, 681n
remarkables [4]477
Rembrandt Harmensz van Rijn (1606–69) [1]lviii, [2]1118n, 1195, 1195n
remedy/remedies [5]136, 425
"remembrance" [5]673n
remembrance(s) [5]614
remembrancer [5]673, [6]262
remembrancing [5]397, 513
Remigius of Auxerre (c 841–c 908) [3]135n
reminiscence
doctrine of [5]751; patriotic [4]795
remission of sins *see* sins
Remnant, Peter *see* Leibniz *New Essays* tr and ed Remnant and Bennett
Remnant, William (fl 1798) [1]828
Remonstrants [1]199n
remorse [1]368, [3]605, 735, 909, [4]239, 436, 503
and regret *see* regret
remotenesses [1]764, 797n
"remuneration" [3]177, 177n
Renaissance [1]117n
Le Renard contrefait [2]771–2
renascence [1]602
Rendall, F. G. [2]179
rendering, false [5]31
Rennell, Thomas (1787–1824) [1]488
Rennes [4]193
rennet [5]613
Reno (river) [3]902
renovators [2]917, [5]505
rent [5]514
clause [4]11, 11n
"repentance" [4]855n
repentance [1]260, 400, 847, [2]27, 292, 309, 1176–9, [3]544–5, 598, 734, 987, [4]306, 623, 634, 639, 640, 640n, 651, 663, [5]163, 172n, 494, 559n, 582–3, 589, 605, 608, 648–9, 652, 654, [6]168, 264, 298n
acts of [5]497; Christian [1]202; deathbed [2]337, [5]585, 587n; fruits of [5]684; invitation to [5]674; saving [5]424; Jeremy Taylor on [1]334, [3]747, [5]491n, 678n
repetition [4]829, [5]18
report(s), parliamentary [5]644
reporter [6]98
representant and represented [5]687
"representation" [6]172
representation(s) [3]201, 244n, 319, 404–5, 405–6, 660, 791, 1021, [4]217n, 426, [5]60
of divinity [2]255; dramatic [4]779–81; faculty of [2]1013; forms of [4]156, 156n; geometric [3]301; partial [5]406; scenic [4]160; scheme of [3]802
representative(s) [1]339, 466, 865, [2]639, [3]800, 947, [4]798, 829, [5]300, 302, 550
adequate [1]123; of community [5]530; elementary [1]598; immediate [2]192; of people [1]341, [2]949; proper [5]409; of the realm [3]164; sensuous [5]699; of supreme reason [2]182–3; universal [2]165
reprieve, miserable [6]49
reprobate(s) [1]817, [3]479, [4]435
reprobation [1]222, [5]157, 158, 610n
reproduction [2]365, 366, 1026n, [3]59, 60, 123, 123n, 126, [4]70, [5]258, 784; *see also* generation
reproductivity [1]626, [5]258
reproof [5]634
reptile(s) [2]818, 860–1
republic(s) [1]807, 864, [2]950, 994, 1017, [4]145, 251, 701, [5]39, 275, 275n, 279
in England [4]675; Greek [5]644; unsuccessful in war [2]101
republican(s) [2]48, [3]178, 178n, 883, [4]79, 660, [5]146
described [1]224; English [2]1195; and philo-despotist [1]224; Roman [4]807; Theban [2]353
republicanism [4]14
repugnance [4]431
repulsion [1]82n, 177, 563, 589, 604, 631, 632, 641, 643, 660, 665, 666, 776, [2]788, 789n, 853, 853n, 854–5, 855n, 886, 996–7, 997n, 1186, [3]139, 280, 280n, 281–2, 292, 997n, 1008, 1021, 1021n, 1022, 1027, 1060, [4]396, [5]264n, 266, 342, 438, 715, [6]228
attraction and *see* attraction; centrality and *see* centrality; Descartes on [1]82; dilation and *see* dilation; effective [5]704; not primary force [1]648; repulsive force [3]998
repulsive, the [1]611, 612, 639
reputation [1]397, [4]113, 241, 584, 611
and fame *see* fame; pure [1]386

res [3]730, [5]428, 428n
r. ipsissima [5]544
research(es)
critical [5]298; historical [4]473; metaphysical [4]157; scientific [5]361
resentment [2]1158, [4]709, 842
reservoir [2]566
reshith [1]608n
residence-chamber [5]828
resignation [2]165, [4]625
resistance [1]692, [2]631, 632, [3]280, 756, [4]217
resistedness [5]719
resistee [1]692
Resolution (ship) [2]73
resolution in parliament [4]12
respect [5]9, 651
respiration [2]857, 857n–8n, [3]1002n, [4]385n
organs of [5]231; *see also* breathing
responsibility [1]827, [3]1083, 1091, [5]425
moral [1]496, [3]136
respublica [5]428
rest [5]342
resting-place [1]752, 754, [3]348
restiveness [5]652
restlessness [4]260
restoration, day of [1]873
Restoration, the [1]275, 318, 333n, 359, [2]260n, 273, 818n, 838, 928, 1102n, 1196n, 1197n, [3]540n, 561, 801, [4]657n, [5]145, 145n, 501, 501n, 532, 544n, 616, 661, [6]258, 263
churchmen of [3]163; disgraceful era [1]268, [6]260; fashionable arguments [1]313
Restorer [1]602
restraining [5]150
restraint [2]934, [5]103
resurrection [2]832
of body [2]184, 1036n, [3]442, 443, 520–1, [4]69–70, 247, [6]139, 302; of dead [1]125, 125n, [2]184, 446, 469, 656, 1075n, 1076, [4]645, [5]295–6, [6]106; general [2]268, 313–14, [3]444–5, [4]244, [6]115; r.-men [3]742, 742n; millenniary [6]303; Priestley on [4]171, 171n
Resurrection (of Jesus Christ) [1]127, 267, 456, 575, 863, 863n, 877, [2]267, 452, 469, 483, 923, 924, 1061, 1072, 1076–9, 1081, 1082, 1085n, 1086–8, 1173, [3]9n, 39, 40, 43n, 45, 56n, 442, 443, 483, 521, 597, 597n, 613, 663–4, 667, 691, [4]248n, 304, 637, 663, 669, [5]70, 71, 397, 535, 607, 618, [6]105, 139, 260, 303
"retiary" [5]597, 597n
retribution [2]1081, [4]663
"retrograde" [4]521
retrogression [4]159
"retroition" [1]667n
retroition [1]577, 577n,
"retroitive" [1]667n
retropulsion, meaning of [6]239, 239n
Reuchlin, Johann (1455–1522) [1]719n, [2]528, 528n, [3]308, 308n
reunion [5]542
revalescence [5]583
"revelation" [4]674
revelation(s)/Revelation [1]608, [2]189, 204, 360, 404–5, 421, 487, 644, 787, 919, 1150, 1151, 1187, [3]62, 352, 425n, 436, 446, 563, 661, 698, 1091, [4]45, 215–16, 479, [5]8, 81n, 82, 82n, 425, 465, 765–6, 803, 823
ab extra [5]155; *ab intra* [5]155; ambiguous [1]11; Bible as system of [3]365; book of [3]919; by Christ [5]578; in Christ [5]57; of Christ [4]667; Christian [4]646; confirming [3]987; defence of [1]747; direct light [3]472; esoteric [5]731; general or particular [5]463; necessity of [1]574; negative condition [2]663; objective [5]628; private [5]464; and reason [2]1151, 1152; rejection of [4]297; and religion [5]71; religious [5]385; revealed commentary [3]448; scheme of [2]561; species of [3]641; spirit of [3]710–11; subjective [5]628; unfolding [3]23
revenge [1]462, 751, [3]156
revenues of Church [1]356
reverence [4]480, [5]642, 650
excessive [5]54; of man [3]699; for professions [4]731; for rank [1]499; want of [5]476; of womanhood [4]335
reverie [2]922
review(s) [1]147, 147n–8n, 158, 164, 216, 216n, [2]598–9
anonymous [3]418–19, 419n; itch to be witty in [2]64; model of [3]365; r.-monger [4]188; r.-scribe [4]25; R. Southey's r. of Malthus [3]805, 806; reviewing spirit [2]999, 999n
Review of English Studies [1]cxxxviiin, 555, [4]76n
reviewer(s) [2]599, [3]280n
modern [2]763; R. Southey the king of [4]183; spirit of [3]280
revisions [4]472, 473
Revivals, Methodist [5]135, 135n
reviviscence [5]545
revolution(s) [1]423, [3]61, 478, 482n, [5]269, 581
American [3]133; English (1642) [3]802; English (1688) [1]281, 298, 333, [2]43, 291,

675, 836, 1152, 1167, [3]163, 167–8, 489, 489n, 757n, 984, 1078, [4]11, 19, 20, 79–80, 79n–80n, 81; French *see* French Revolution; Maccabaic [3]420; mental [5]123
Revolutionists [4]342
Revue de littérature comparée [1]clii, cliin
Revue germanique [1]cliin
reward(s) [3]740–1, [5]670
Reynard the Fox [2]772n, [5]46, 46n; see also *Reinecke Foss*
Reyneke voss de olde [5]46n
Reynolds, Edward, Bishop of Norwich (1599–1676) [4]182, [5]520, 520n
Reynolds, Frederic (1764–1841) [2]75
Reynolds, John (1549–1607) *see* Rainolds
Reynolds, John (fl 1620–40) *The Triumphes of Gods Revenge agaynst . . . Murther* [1]lxxxix, clxiii; MT [4]237–41
Reynolds, John (d 1684) *see* Reignolds
Reynolds, John Hamilton (1796–1852) *see* T. Hood and Reynolds *Odes and Addresses*
Reynolds, Sir Joshua (1723–92) [2]235n
rhapsode(s) [2]89, *89n*, 1129, 1130n
rhapsody [2]1120, 1130n, [3]449
Rhea (myth) [2]573
rhema/rhemata [6]303
and *logos* see *logos*
rhematic [2]881n
Rhenferd, Jacob (1654–1712) [1]cxxxin, 416, [2]830, [3]928, 929, 1084, [5]625n, 645
Dissertatio de fictis judaeorum haeresibus [2]833n, [5]623, 623n; *Opera philologica* [1]532, 533n, [2]270n, 437, 437n, 700, 700n, 710, 710n, 718, 718n, 833, 833n, [3]929n, 1084n; MT [4]242–60; [5]606n, 623n
rheonta [5]95
rhetores [2]36
rhetoric [2]253, [3]221, 222n, 227n, 547, [4]145, 625, [5]765
Donne's [2]292, 299, 318; ebullient [5]563; inducements of [5]649; and logic [5]615; modern [4]649; polemic [3]760; reduction of [6]285; of Sophists [2]776; trick of [2]933; Wesley's [5]189; wordy [6]140
rhetorician(s) [2]683, [3]447, [5]841
Browne as [1]788
rheumatism [3]1067, 1067n
Rhianus/Rhianos (2nd half of 3rd century BC) [4]147
Rhind, Mrs [3]483
Rhine [2]180, [3]961–2, [4]341–2
rhinoceroses [2]862, [5]811
Rhodes [4]504n, [5]84n, 832, 840, 841; *see also* leaper, Rhodian
Rhodian leap *see* leap, Rhodian
rhodium [2]825, 825n, [5]261
Rhodomannus, Laurentius (Lorenz Rhodoman) (1546–1606) [3]830
rhomboid [4]863
Rhone [6]195
rhyme(s) [1]755, [2]795, 795n, 1039–40, 1044, 1168, [3]224, 713, 889–90, 891, 899, 911, 1070, 1074, [4]755, 783, 796, 797, 853, [5]111, 689, 768, 860, [6]38, 39, 199, 202
in S. Daniel [1]44n–5n; force of [2]1040; French [3]972; necessities of [6]209; polysyllabic [2]121; in Spenserian stanza [1]117n; translations in [6]210; wasted [1]44
rhythm [3]896, [4]735, 791, 805
defined [4]604; Jonson's [3]171; Massinger's [3]813; and metre [4]604, [5]689, 689n
rib
Adam's [1]683–4; fifth [2]814, 814n
ribbon(s) [2]482, [3]340, 341
Ribera, Francesco de (1537–91) [3]1064
Ricardo, David (1772–1823) [2]616n, [6]20, 20n
Ricaut/Rycaut, Sir Paul (1628–1700) *State of the Turkish Empire* [3]183
rice-grounds [3]771
rich, the [4]100
Richard (fiction) [2]683
Richard II, King of England (1367–1400) [2]124, 407, 823, 823n
Richard III, King of England (1452–85) [2]826
Richard III (*Richard III*) [1]212, 212n, 393, 397
Richard, Bishop of Chichester *see* Curteys
Richard of St Victor (d 1173) [3]682, 682n, [5]783–4, 795, 795n, 797
Richardson, Jonathan (1665–1745), and Jonathan Richardson (1694–1771) *Explanatory Notes and Remarks on Milton's Paradise Lost* [3]890n
Richardson, Robert (fl 1810) [3]940
Richardson, Samuel (1689–1761) [2]764n
and Fielding [2]692–3
Clarissa Harlowe [2]693, [4]610, 610n; *Pamela* [2]693; *Sir Charles Grandison* [1]3
Richardson, William (1740–1820) "A Letter on the Alterations . . . in the Structure of Rocks" [3]937; MT 943–4
Richelieu, Armand Jean Duplessis, Duc de (1585–1642) [2]60
Richter (probably Jeremias Benjamin Richter, 1762–1807) [4]396
Richter, Johann Paul Friedrich ("Jean

Richter, Johann Paul Friedrich—*continued* Paul") (1763–1825) [1]752n, [2]768n, 1115, [5]181n
Jean Paul's Fata und Werke vor und in Nürnberg [4]279; *Jean Pauls Geist* MT [4]261–3; *Das Kampaner Thal* [4]215; MT 264–9, tr Gowa *The Campaner Thal* [4]264–9; *Museum* [2]180; MT [4]270–8; *Palingenesien* MT [4]279–80; *Vorschule der Aesthetik* [2]17n, 191n
Rickman, John (1771–1840) [2]696
riddle(s) [1]472, [2]219, 482, 1145, [3]871, [6]220
of fisherman [1]757; my ree [2]204; of world [2]601, 1018
ride and tie [3]456, 456n
ridicule [2]972, [5]98, 428
riding-habit [1]389
Ridley, Maurice Roy (b 1890) *see* Shakespeare *Antony and Cleopatra, Othello* ed Ridley
Ridley, Nicholas, Bishop of Rochester (c 1500–55) [1]809, 809n, [2]264, 264n
Ridolfi/Ridolfo, Robert di (1531–1612) [2]509n
Ridout, J. G. (fl 1803) [4]85, 85n
Riederer, Johann Bartholomäus (1720–71) [2]781
Nachrichten zur Kirchen-, Gelehrten- und Bücher-Geschichte [2]781n
rifacimento ("rifacciamento") [1]633, 633n, [2]377n, [3]926n
rifles [3]1081
Rigg, James Harrison (1821–1909) *Modern Anglican Theology* [2]333n q
Riggall, Edward (fl 1880) [1]clxvii
right(s) [2]562, [3]167, [4]21, 815, [5]162
anti-protestant [5]507; of Christendom [5]312; of citizens [3]818; civic [3]799; civil [2]1139; of creatures [2]162; determination of [2]43; divine [3]490, 677, [4]173, [5]544; of dominion [5]614; and duty/duties *see* duty/duties; of electing [5]300; elective [4]19; established by law [4]80; ground of [1]311; hereditary [2]118, [4]19; of judgment [5]614; of king and subject [1]290; law of [2]618n; of man [2]511, [4]23; morally considered [3]960; natural [6]10–11; of nature [4]23; and obligations [2]107; original [2]1098; positive and negative [1]395–6; without power [6]51; proprietary [5]159; public [5]40; religious [3]801; and wrong [2]124, [3]136, 1083, 1091, [5]596, 598, 614, 656
righteousness [2]591–2, 1165, [3]50, 455–6, 735, 735n, [4]640, [5]31, 492, [6]16, 43
of Christ [1]702, [2]1166, 1177; fruits of [1]11; garment of [1]815, 815n; imputed [1]470, 470n, [3]31, [4]657, 657n, [5]171; machines of [3]453; sun of [5]523; works of [4]620
rigid, the [2]1013
Riley, Arthur (fl 1855) [2]158
rill [2]591
Rimini, Council of [2]732, 732n, 744n, [3]145n, 232, 232n, 233n, 761, 761n, [5]627, 627n, 632–3, 633n
Rimius, Heinrich (fl 1750–59) [3]494n, 495
A Candid Narrative of the Rise and Progress of the . . . Moravians† [1]clxvii, [3]495n, 496 q, [4]281; *A Solemn Call on Count Zinzendorf*† [4]281; *see also* Zinzendorf *Sermons* ed Rimius
Rimmon (myth) [1]832n
ring
in church ritual [1]321; concentric [5]431; in marriage [1]323;
r.-dove [6]153
ringleaders [6]46
Rink, Friedrich Theodor (1770–1821) *see* Kant *Sammlung . . . kleiner Schriften* ed Rink
Rinonichi, Bartholomaeus de (Bartolommeo Albizzi) (d 1401) *Liber conformitatum* [2]765n
Rio de la Plata *see* Plata
rioters [6]44, 46
Rips, Count von (in Bürger) [1]829, 829n
Ritchie, Leitch (c 1800–65) *see* T. Pringle *Poetical Works* ed Ritchie
rite(s) [1]539, 711, 834, [3]494, [4]638, [5]651
bloody [5]647; Jewish [5]649; sacramental [5]658
Ritson, Joseph (1752–1803) [1]lxxi, [4]285, 285n, 731n, 804n
Ancient Songs [1]xcii; MT [4]282–8; *A Select Collection of English Songs* MT [4]289–93
Ritter, Johann Wilhelm (1776–1810) [3]127, 127n, 950, 951n
ritual [2]655
Jewish [5]523; Romish [1]517; sacramental [5]568
rivalry [2]637, [5]135
river(s) [2]566, 640, 801, [3]77, 230–1, 511, [4]94, 341, [5]385
from Eden [1]779; of fire [6]153; r.-horse [4]533
Rivet, André (1572–1651) [3]824
road(s) [3]975, [5]580
broad [5]158; excellent [2]88; made [5]387; middle [5]11; right [5]37; Roman [3]976, 981; safe [1]334; straightest [1]178; to truth [5]776; zodiacal [5]157
Roake and Varty *see* London

Roback [1]840
Robarts, Sarah [4]636, 636n
robber(s) [1]342, [2]509, 683, 708, [4]671, 735, [6]262
Robberds, John Warden (fl 1827–43) *Memoir of the Life and Writings of William Taylor* [1]90n
robbery/robberies [1]343, 395, [4]718
robe(s) [3]603
  Coan [6]157; of light [2]544
Robert, Duke of Normandy (?1054–1134) [3]786
Roberts, Daniel S. [6]290
Roberts, Lloyd (fl 1903) [1]761
Roberts, Samuel (1763–1848) [3]943
Roberts, Sarah [4]636
Robertson, Joseph (1726–1802) *see* A. Sidney *Works* ed Robertson
Robertson, William (1721–93) [1]cviii, [1]75n
robin [3]1045
Robinquet (fl 1821) "Observations on Aroma" [1]641n
Robins, Benjamin (1707–51) [2]754n
  New Principles of Geometry [2]754n
Robinson, Sir Christopher (1766–1833) *Reports of Cases* [3]500, 501n
Robinson, Frederick John, Viscount Goderich (1782–1859) [6]28
Robinson, George (1737–1801), and John (1753–1813) *see* London: Robinsons'
Robinson, Henry Crabb (1775–1867) [1]xcvii, clixn, 372n, [3]366, [4]105, 731n, 787n, [5]241
  collection of mss [1]cxlviiin; death [1]clxi; letter(s) to [3]265n q, 266n q; library of [1]cli; owner of annotated books [1]xcv, clix, 104n, 283n, [2]179, 180, 195n, 374n, 1115, [3]321, 707, 719, [4]261, 270, 279, 373, 403n, [5]199; reports C's lectures [1]212n; supplier of books to C [1]xcviii, cvi, 3, 7, [2]519, [3]855n, [4]227n
  Blake, Coleridge, Wordsworth, Lamb, etc. ed E. J. Morley [2]179; *Diary, Reminiscences and Correspondence* ed T. Sadler [2]595 q, 955n q; *Henry Crabb Robinson on Books and Their Writers* ed E. J. Morley [1]clixn q, clxn q, clxii q, clxiin, clxviiin q, 131 q, 145n q, 211, 242n q, 488, 717, 761, [2]76n, 179 q, 180, 181 q, 235n, 310n q, 374n, 519 q, 755n, 1038n, 1115, 1116, 1120n, [3]707, 842n, [4]105 q, 402 q, 261, [5]199, 241
Robinson, Jack (fiction) [3]438, 740n
Robinson, Mark P. [1]clxxiii
Robinson, Robert (1735–90) [4]300n
  "Memoirs of the Author" by G. Dyer [4]294
  History of Baptism [1]245n, 470n, [4]306, 306n; *Miscellaneous Works* [1]lxxxv, clxi; MT [4]294–309
Robinson, Walter [2]190n
Rochester, Earl of *see* Wilmot, John
Rochester Grammar School [2]978n
rock [3]235, 302
  of ages [3]611; in Bible [5]634–5; man of the [5]635; of offence [3]1001; opening [5]528; Peter as [3]234n; of separation [3]230
rockman (St Peter) [3]458, 458n, [5]634
rod [4]175
  Aaron's [1]457n, [5]52–3, 52n–3n; of gold [4]189, 189n; of Moses [1]822, [2]387, 387n
Rodd, Thomas (1796–1849) *see* London
Roderigo (in B&F) [1]399, 400
Roderigo (*Othello*) [4]746, 860–1, 866
Roe, Sir John (1581–c 1608) [2]231n
Roger of Ford (Roger the Cistercian) (fl 1170–80) [2]819, 819n
Rogers, Samuel (1763–1855) [1]542, 716, [2]180, 353
  Recollections of the Table Talk [2]133, [6]324n q
Roget, Peter Mark (1779–1869) *On Animal and Vegetable Physiology* [2]883n
roguery [5]822
Roland (in Scott) *see* R. Graeme
Rolandi's Circulating Library *see* London
roll(s) [1]439
  sacred [2]894
Rollins, Hyder Edward (1889–1958) *see* Keats *Letters* ed Rollins
Romaic (language) [4]185
Roman(s) [1]157, 431, [2]372, 410, 711, 1016, 1022, [3]149, [4]483, 780, [5]57, 307, 328–9, 337, 379, [6]27, 207–8
Roman Catholic(s) [1]711n, [2]24, 260n, 983, [3]308n, 764, [4]18–24, 41n, 86n, 551n, 628, [5]274n, 543n, 658
  agreement with Protestants [2]702; not catholic [3]310n; contradictory terms [4]246n; Romish delusions [3]467; and emancipation debate [2]696–7; errors of [2]707, 707n; hagiolatry of [2]35, 37; insufficiency of [4]24; in Ireland [1]214n; lay [1]865; missions of [5]105n–6n; and oath of allegiance [1]166n; own a foreign sovereign [1]256; and papists [2]935, 935n; pious [2]1162; on prayer [2]723; turn religion into superstition [1]516–17; not Roman before Luther [4]42–3; Scriptures withheld from [2]261; sophisms of [1]517. *See also* Catholic Emancipation; church(es): RC

Roman Catholicism [3]144n, [4]21; *see also* church(es): RC

romance(s) [1]284, [2]92, 167, 708, 718, 728, 738, 779, 783, 971, [3]207, 484, 595, 923, [4]75, 282, 362
  deistico-psychological [4]41; Greek [5]223; Miltonic [4]82; of nature [2]1119; parody of [4]192; philosophical [5]226; rabbinic [3]103; of Shakespeare [1]400

romancer(s) [2]470, [5]308

Romanism [1]305, 358, [2]523, 1041, 1177, [3]310, 451, 457, [4]678, [5]510n
  tenets of [1]314; *see also* church(es): RC

Romanist(s) [1]259, 297, 478, 512, 848, [2]29, 31, 35, 38, 40, 663, 667, 672, 697, 1106, [3]697, 738, [4]43, 177, 246, 246n, [5]4, 52, 555, 559, 572, 573, 661, 662, 671, 673, 675, 835, [6]256, 292
  ascetic [5]498; combat with [1]317; compared to Moravians [3]494; doctrinal [4]181; error of [5]550; essence of [5]497; how to confute [2]39; idolatry of [2]344; pseudo-Catholic [3]310; shield and sword of [5]576; *see also* church(es): RC

romantic, the [5]390
  loyalty [1]398

romanticism, German [2]863n

Rome [1]315n, 430, 471, 559, 770, 805, 831, 842, [2]235n, 276, 480, 500, 505n, 513, 515n, 522n, 570, 670, 670n, 678n, 706, 717n, 792, 809, 878, 918, 931n, 949, 1017–18, 1018n, 1066n, 1123, 1153, 1154, [3]418, 419, 448, 448n, 466, 541, 542, 694, 786, 794, 899n, 924, [4]149n, 427, 474n, 627, 650n, 807, 864n, [5]45, 85n, 276n, 282, 537n, 565, 652, 652n, 662, 689n, 693n, 747, 835, 835n, [6]14, 82, 198
  armies of [2]515; as Babylon [2]513; bishop(s) of [3]440n, [5]635, [6]15, 15n, *see also* pope(s); Capitol [3]769, 769n, [5]69; Church of *see* Church of Rome; Roman drama [2]776; Roman emperors *see* emperor(s); Roman empire *see* empire(s); fall of [2]504; history of [3]110; incapable of freedom [2]692; legal code of [2]1139; Roman monarch [3]722; New [2]670; Pantheon [1]201, [3]310, 310n; St Paul at [3]7n, [5]635–6, 635n; St Peter at [5]635–6, 635n; St Peter's [1]201, [2]1069, 1069n; power of [2]156, 156n, 157; primacy of [4]43; road to [2]917; Roman road *see* road; senate [2]950; symbol of [3]467; Vatican Library [2]923n; Vatican Museum [5]117n; yoke of [5]127

Romeo (*Romeo and Juliet*) [4]828, 829, 830, 831, 832, 835

Romist [5]135

romp [3]496

Romulus (in Virgil) [6]207

Ronconi, Giulio (fl 16th century) [2]8n, 10

Rondeletius (Guillaume Rondelet) (1507–66) [1]778

rondillo [3]175

rook [3]1045, 1045n

root(s) [1]426, [3]11, [4]318
  ax at [5]729; bitter [1]602; invisible [4]266; living [5]471

rope [1]869, [4]613
  of sand [3]296

Rosalind (*All's Well*) [1]cxviii

Rosaline (*Love's Labour's Lost*) [4]696 ("Rosamond"), 696n, 698, 783

Rosaline (*Romeo and Juliet*) [4]828–9, 831

rosary [5]444

Roscellinus (Roscellin) (d c 1125) [3]135n, [5]777

Roscoe, William (1753–1831) [1]*221n,* [3]884, 884n
  The Life and Pontificate of Leo the Tenth [1]217, 221, 627n

Roscommon, Earl of *see* Dillon, Wentworth

rose [2]625, [3]460, 704, 790, 1034, [4]529–30, [6]172
  r.-leaves [1]552; of shoe [3]899

Rose, Hugh James (1795–1832) *Prolusio* [4]6; MT 310–11

Rose, Samuel (1767–1804) [1]220n

Rosencrantz (*Hamlet*) [4]763 ("Ros."), 763n, 854

Rosenmüller, Johann Georg (1736–1815) [4]41, 41n
  Scholia in Novum Testamentum [3]3

Rosenroth, Christian Knorr von (1636–89) see *Kabbala denudata* tr Rosenroth

Rosetta [4]29

Rosetto [5]843

Rosicrucian [3]315, 315n

rosin [4]827

Ross, George Robert Thomson (fl 1911) *see* Descartes *Philosophical Works* tr Haldane and Ross

Ross, John (1777–1856) [1]204n
  A Voyage of Discovery [3]989n

Ross, John Duckett (fl 1810) [3]938, 942

roster [5]380, 380n

Rota, Bernardino (1508–75) [2]10

rote [5]174

Rothschild, Nathan Meyer (1777–1836)

[1]723, 723n, [5]775 ("Rothschield"), 775n, [6]20, 20n
Rotterdam [1]199n, [3]204, 774, 775
Roundhead(s) [2]512, 512n, [3]488, 489
"round" [5]212
roundness [5]202
rouse [1]786
Rouse, William Henry Denham (1863–1950) *see* Lucretius *De rerum natura* tr Rouse, rev M. F. Smith; Nonnus *Dionysiaca* tr Rouse
Rousseau, Jean Jacques (1712–78) [4]306–7, [5]703n
 opposed by Möser [1]6n; plan of education [6]126, 126n
 Emile [6]126n, tr Foxley [4]306n q, 307
Roussier, Pierre Joseph (1716–90) [4]511
Routh, Martin Joseph (1755–1854) *Reliquiae sacrae* [5]601n
routs [1]164
Row, Moll [1]750, 750n
Rowe, Nicholas (1674–1718) [1]38, [2]83, 240, 240n, [4]698, 869
 Tamerlane [3]186n; *see also* Lucan tr Rowe
Rowena (in Scott) [4]594
Rowley, Harold Henry (1890–1969) *Darius the Mede and the Four World Empires in the Book of Daniel* [3]573n; see also *Peake's Commentary on the Bible* ed M. Black and Rowley
Roxburgh, William (1751–1815) [3]939, 943
Roxburghe Club *see* London
Roxburghe, Duke of *see* Ker, John
Roxburghshire [4]574
Roy, Henry de *see* Regius
Royal Academy *see* London
Royal Institution *see* London
Royal Society *see* London
Royal Society of Literature *see* London
royalist(s) [2]114, 932, 950, 1103, [4]42
royalty [3]799
 Christ's [5]537
ruach [2]769, 769n, [3]1086, 1086n, [4]254, [6]116
rubbish [2]429, 816
Rubicon [4]807
ruby [3]600, 600n
rudeness [1]423, [4]599
Rudolphi, Carl Asmund (1771–1832) [3]380, 380n
Ruffhead, Owen (1723–69) [1]50
Rufinus (c 345–440) [1]236n, [2]721n q, [3]768n, [5]386, 619
 Commentarius in symbolum apostolorum [1]312n
Rügen [4]489–90, [5]197n
Ruhnken, David (1723–98) see *Hymn to Ceres* ed Ruhnken
ruin(s) [1]207n
Ruinart, Thierry (1657–1709) *Acta primorum martyrum sincera et selecta* [2]718n, 719, 719n, 728
Ruiz de Padron, D. Antonio José (1757–1823) *The Speech of Doctor . . . Ruiz de Padron* ed Felix and others [4]170
rule(s) [2]729, [3]91, [4]780, [5]38, 799
 a priori [3]259; alien [3]516, [6]298; arbitrary [1]223; carpenter's [5]714; of Christian [5]562; of distinction [3]696; and exception [5]632; of faith *see* faith; fixed [5]578; general [1]517, 724, [5]319, 587, [6]304; golden [5]540, C's [1]lxi q, [5]360, 360n; grounded [5]638; to judge feelings [1]751; and law [1]377; means to an end [4]863; of parliament [4]12; posthumous [3]160; and principle(s) [4]826; for reasoning [5]756; requires expounder [2]38; of truth [3]687; universal [5]589
rulers [3]72, 755
Rullion [2]1171n
rump [5]105
Runge, Ferdinand Friedrich (1795–1872) *Neueste phytochemische Entdeckungen* MT [4]313–28
Rupert, Prince (1619–82) [2]1196–7, *1196n*, 1199
Rupertus (Rupert of Deutz) (c 1075–1129) [3]460, [5]662, 662n
Ruscelli, Girolamo (d 1566) *Del modo di comporre in versi nella lingua italiana* MT [4]329–31
ruse de guerre [5]616
rush-lights [3]917
Rushworth, John (1612–90) [3]486
 Dialogues, concerning Traditions [2]25
Russel, Mr (fl 1814) [1]xcvin
Russell, Francis, 5th Duke of Bedford (1765–1805) [4]634
Russell, John, 4th Duke of Bedford (1710–71) [3]226
Russell, Lucy (née Harington), Countess of Bedford (d 1627) [2]233n, 236
Russell, William, Lord Russell (1639–83) [3]140
Russia [1]697, [2]909, 909n, [3]133, 757n, 1074, [5]315
 Russian Bible Society [6]246; Russian character [3]883–4, 884n; emperor of [5]191; Russian Greekists [3]756–7

Russian (language) [2]836
Russian(s) [2]620, [3]233
rust [1]666, [2]572, 816, [3]1004, [6]230
Rust, George, Bishop of Dromore (d 1670) [5]486, 531n, 681n
rustic [2]648
Rusticus, Quintus Junius (d c 168) [1]162
Rutland [3]104
"Ryalto" (William Taylor of Norwich) [1]90
Ryan, M. J. (fl 1927) "Coleridge and Anster" [1]100
Ryan, Mr (fl 1804) [3]974
Rydal
R. Mount [1]xcii, civ, clvi, clviii, clixn, clxviii, 760, 761, [2]180, [4]29, C's books at [1]cxi; Library [2]4, catalogue [1]cxii, cxiin, [2]102; Stepping Stones [1]226; R. Water/ Rydalmere [4]29
Rydale [1]clxviii
Ryder, Dudley, 1st Earl of Harrowby (1762–1847) [4]170, [6]48, 48n, 49, 49n
Ryland, John (1753–1825) [2]801n, 802n
Rylands Library *see* Manchester

s [2]1091–2, 1092n
"S." (R. Southey) [1]89
S., J. *Soliloquies Theologicall* [4]173–4
S., Mr [2]163–4, 164n
S., Susan [1]723
Saavedra Fajardo, Diego de (1584–1648) [3]736, 736n
The Royal Politician Represented in One Hundred Emblems [3]736n
Saba [2]384n
Sabaeans [5]237
Sabbatarians [1]876
Sabbath(s) [1]268–9, 268n–9n, 334n, 419, 419n, 718–21, 870–9, 873, [2]1175, [3]17, 471, [5]606
S.-breaking [4]662; of contemplation [5]795; of the Messiah [5]607; of mind [3]460. *See also* Lord's Day; Sunday
sabbatical year [2]785
Sabellian(s) [2]33n, 265n, [5]210, [6]87–8
Sabellianism [1]249, 249n, [2]32, 265, 735, [5]8n, 21, 22, 23, 543, 556, 556n, [6]78
Sabellius (fl 215) [1]249n, [2]666
sable [1]399, 399n
Sachs, Hans (1494–1576) [1]131, [2]755, 755n, [5]91, 91n
Gedichte Fabeln und gute Schwenk [2]755n; *Sehr herrliche schöne und wahrhafter Gedicht Fabeln und gute Schwenk* [6]334; *Die ungleichen Kinder Eva* [2]755n, 780, 780n
sacks [5]595
on the mill [3]895, 895n
Sackville, Charles, Lord Buckhurst, 6th Earl of Dorset (1638–1706) [1]37
Sackville, Richard, 3rd Earl of Dorset (1590–1624) [2]119n
Sackville, Thomas, Lord Buckhurst, 1st Earl of Dorset (1536–1608) [1]37, [3]702
and Thomas Norton *Ferrex and Porrex, or Gorboduc* [3]702, [4]848n
"sacrament" [3]440, [5]398n
sacrament(s) [1]246, 328, 445, 472n, [3]598, 607, 757, [5]546, 652, 675, 676, [6]264
in C of E [1]472n, [5]398n, 566, 566n, [6]21n; lesser [3]440n; means of grace [2]326; outward [1]821; quasi-sacramenta [1]349; in Scripture [1]277; seven [3]440, 440n; symbol [1]472, [5]648; as symbolic institutions [5]398. *See also* Baptism; Confirmation; Eucharist; Extreme Unction; Matrimony; Orders; Penance
Sacrament, the (Eucharist) [1]267, 705, 835, 846–7, [2]279, 281, 304n, [5]652, 657, 675, 676, [6]260; *see also* Eucharist
as medicine [1]714, [5]675; not confined to any day [1]877; preparation for [1]712–14; as symbol [1]704; *see also* Eucharist
"Sacramentarian" [5]5n, 671n
Sacramentarian(s) [1]509, 509n–10n, 524
"Sacramentary" [5]5n, 671n
Sacramentary/Sacramentaries [1]862, [5]5, 11, 397, 397n, 554, 554n, [6]21, 21n
doctrine of [1]713; Swiss [5]671
sacramentum [1]472, 472n, [5]675
"sacred" [6]18n
"sacrifice" [2]672
sacrifice(s) [1]438, 529, 530, [2]343, 659, 718, 785–6, 834, 897, 898, [3]38n, 311, 417, 513, 604
animal [4]252; to fashion of age [5]421; human [6]324; of love [5]523
sacrilege [1]356
Saddington, John (fl 1810) [3]938
Sadducees [1]773, [2]1075, [3]56, 478, [4]663, 663n
Sadducism [3]822, 822n
Sadler, James (1753–1828) [2]321n
Sadler, Thomas (c 1647–c 1685) [1]802
Sadler, Thomas (1822–91) *see* H. C. Robinson *Diary* ed Sadler
saeculum, hoc [5]606–7; see also *seculum*
safety [2]206, [5]302, 647

sage(s) [3]524
ancient [1]669; Ephesian [5]715; Greek [3]649, [6]306; holy [3]468; oriental [6]306
Sage, Isaac [5]36
sailor(s) [3]101, 102n, 1080, [5]481
Phoenician [6]5n
Sainsbury, William (fl 1809) *Disputatio medica inauguralis de apoplexia sanguinea* [4]183, 183n
"saint(s)" [4]746, 746n
saint(s) [1]297, 543, 817, [2]562, 652, 662, 663, 667, 674, 1015, [3]821, [5]665
communion of [2]673; of C of E [6]82; fellowship of [3]603; final perseverance [1]826; great [5]820; grim [2]806; invocation of [1]783, [3]444, [5]835; legends of [5]821; lives of [2]1058; modern [3]710; mystic [5]821; perseverance of [1]453; prayer to [2]723n; regenerate [1]730; reverence of [5]524n; ubiquity of [2]668; s.-worship [5]497. *For particular saints, search by name*
St Albans, Duke of *see* Beauclerk
St Albans, Viscount *see* Bacon, Francis
St Andrews [5]172n
St Asaph [4]665n
St Bartholomew's Act [5]144, 144n
St Bartholomew's Day [2]1198, 1198n, Massacre [3]803, 803n
St Christopher's [2]93
St Eustatius [5]187
St Germain, Synod of [1]478n
St Giles in the Fields *see* London
St Helena [4]534n
St Ives [2]211n
St John, Henry, 1st Viscount Bolingbroke (1678–1751) [1]184, 184n, 248n, [3]703
Letters on the Study and Use of History [3]484n; *Works* ed Mallet [1]184n
St Lawrence [4]681
St Lawrence (river) [2]980
St Leonard's [1]816
St Leonards, Baron *see* Sugden, Edward Burtenshaw
St Louis MO [6]251
Washington University, marginalia in [2]1117
St Luke's *see* London
St Paul's Cathedral *see* London
St Peter's *see* Rome
St Petersburg [1]213, 213n
St Privet [5]166
Saint, W. (fl 1810) [3]937
Sainte-Marie, Etienne (1777–1829) [4]164
Saintsbury, George Edward Bateman (1845–1933)
History of Criticism [2]413n q; *History of English Prosody* [1]57n q
saintship [5]524, 662
Salamanca [3]365
Salamis [5]181n, 224
Salem MA [3]824, 825n, 826, [6]105n
Salisbury [2]89, 1046n, [5]140n
Salisbury, Countess of *see* Montacute/Montagu, Catherine de
Salisbury, Richard Anthony (1781–1829) [3]937
Salisbury, William (d 1823) [3]939, 943
salitter [1]569–70, 569n, 571, 572, 572–3, 575, 588, 589, 608, 619, 620
saliva [5]260
Sallust (Gaius Sallustius Crispus) (86–34 BC) [3]185 q, 185n, [4]311n, 336n, [5]576
Sallust/Sallustius (fl 363) [5]12, 740, 740n
Concerning the Gods and the Universe [2]234, 234n, [5]12n
Salmasius, Claudius (Claude de Saumaise) (1588–1653) [1]119, 120n, [2]919, 946, 947, 972n, [3]795n, [5]39, 39n
Defensio regia, pro Carolo [5]39n; *Epistola ad Andream Colvium* [2]919n
salmon [1]88, [4]431, 802
Salmon, Mrs (d 1760) [4]780, 780n
Salmon, Robert (1763–1821) [3]938
salnitre [1]636
saloon [3]32
Salsillus *see* Salzilli
salt(s) [1]667, 779, 780, [3]44, 1005, [4]148n, 384, [5]351
alkaline [5]255; Böhme on [1]630; neutral [2]572; pillar of [2]836;
salting [3]44
saltus [2]37, 37n, [4]460, [5]310, 310n, 455, 455n, 456n
"salvation" [4]644, 644n
salvation [1]11, 232, 315, [2]27, 269, 352, 683, 707, 1085, 1096, 1150, 1161, 1176–9, [3]112, 310, 513, 550, 554, 566, 747, [4]295, 304, 596, 620, 623–4, 628, 628n, 648, [5]66, 129, 137, 178, 180, 188, 466, 492, 492n, [6]43
assurance of [3]875; blown to atoms [5]562; by Christ alone [1]786–7; made easy [5]641; economy of [5]570, 571n; by faith alone [2]1162; ground of [1]504; indispensable to [5]567–8; justification and [1]703; loss of [2]35, [5]664; of mankind [3]112; means of [4]634; negative of [5]189; pale of [5]628; ref-

salvation—*continued*
ormation as means of [2]495; sufficiency of Scripture to [5]576; by works [2]1177
salve [2]749
salve-ation [2]749
Salzburgische Litteraturzeitung [3]961–2
Salzilli, Giovanni (Salsillus) (fl 1637) [3]905
Samaria [2]830, [5]565
Samaritan(s) [2]408, [3]110, 659
S. text *see* Bible: OT: Samaritan text
sameness [3]834
and difference [4]603
Samian (Pythagoras) [5]699
Samian letter *see* letter, Samian
Sam-in-sattin-hose [5]525
Samlah (Bible) [1]418
Sammlung Deutscher Gedichte [1]clxviiin
Sammlung von Minnesingern [1]clxviiin
Sammlung vorzüglich schöner Gedichte MT [4]332
Samos [5]696, 837, 838, [6]199
Samosata [5]525n
Samothrace [1]665, [2]573, [3]399, [6]5
mysteries of *see* mysteries, Samothracian
Samouelle, George (fl 1819) *The Entomologist's Useful Compendium*† [4]333
Sampson (in Scott) [4]581
Samson (Bible) [1]422, 423, [2]342, [3]508n, [4]839, [6]220
Samuel (Bible) [1]110, 423, 424, [2]400, 400n, 1108, [3]108n
San Marino CA
Henry E. Huntington Library, marginalia in [1]clxiii–clxvii, clxx, clxxiv, 7, 100, 722, [2]966, 967, 1190n, [3]400, 816, 827, [4]105, 294, 338, [5]454
Sanchuniathon/Sanchoniatho (legend) [2]576, 576n, 578n
Sancroft, William, Archbishop of Canterbury (1617–93) [3]167, 167n
sanctification [2]659, [3]517n, 548, 550, 748, [4]624, 629, [5]152, 583, [6]302
true [5]670
Sanctifiore (in Reynolds) [4]241, 241n
sanction
implied [5]658; royal [5]632
sanctity [5]466
sanctum [2]516
sand(s) [2]899–900, 900n, 1186, [5]527
figures in [1]735; figures of [3]43; s.-grains [5]304; in pineal gland [2]548; s.-rope [3]296; s.-winds [3]129
sandals [4]651n
Sanders, C. [1]3
Sanders, Charles Richard (b 1904) *Coleridge and the Broad Church Movement* [2]332; *see also* T. and J. Carlyle *Collected Letters* ed Sanders
Sanders, Nicholas (c 1530–81) *Book of the English Schism* [1]839
Sanderson, Robert (1587–1663)
De juramenti promissorii obligatione [2]522, 522n; *De juramento* [2]941, 941n
Sanderson, Sir William (?1586–1676) *History of Charles I* [2]1102n
Sandes Library *see* Kendal
Sandford, Charles Waldgrave (b 1828) [2]967
Sandford, Daniel, Bishop of Edinburgh (1766–1830) [4]334
Remains [1]cii; MT [4]334–7
Sandford, John (1801–73) [2]967, [4]334
Sandford, Margaret E. (fl 1888) *Thomas Poole and His Friends* [1]9, 224n, [2]587n
Sandford St Martin [2]245
Sandiford, Rowland (fl 1728) [3]488
sandstone [5]245–6
Sandwich, Earl of *see* Montagu, Edward
Sandys, George (1578–1644) [1]55
Sandys, Sir John Edward (1844–1921) *see* Pindar *Nemean Odes, Odes* tr Sandys
sang-froid [5]767
Sanhedrim/Sanhedrin [1]458, [2]485, 494, 1173, [4]51 ("Synedrium"), 51n
sanies [3]60, 60n
sanity [5]98, 473
Sannazarius *see* Sannazaro
Sannazaro, Jacopo (Sannazarius) (1458–1530) [1]60, 60n
Arcadia [1]60, 60n; *Opera omnia* [1]37, 60n; MT [4]338–40
Sanscrit (language) [2]382 ("Sanscript"), 898, [3]1043, [4]509, 509n, [5]9, 119, 368
sansculotterie [6]81
sansculottes [6]81n
Santorini [5]836
sap [1]692, [2]1038
of faith [1]823
sapientia [5]202
"sapientise" [5]506, 506n
Sapor *see* Shapir II
sapphic (metre) [3]814
Sapphira (Bible) [5]645, 645n, [6]55, 55n
sapphire [1]420, [3]1034
Sappho (b c 612 BC) [2]55n, 354–5, 355n, 1067
tr Fawkes [1]38
Sapricius (legend) [2]724n

Saracen(s)/Sarazen(s) [2]739, 739n
Sarah (Bible) [1]473, [2]1137–8, [6]110, 119, 119n
Saravia, Hadrian à (1531–1613) [1]294, [2]1135, [3]795n
Sarbiewski, Maciej Kazimierz (Casimir) (1595–1640) *Carmina* [1]civ
sarcasm [4]715
"sarcomorphic" [2]1175, 1175n
sarcophagi [5]836
Sardi, Alesandro (1520–88) *Johannis Seldeni . . . liber de nummis* [6]265
Sardica, Council of [2]740, 740n
Sardis [3]422n, [6]168n
Sarepta [6]246
Sargeaunt, John (1857–1922) *see* Terence *Heauton timorumenos* tr Sargeaunt
"Sariola" (SC) [3]930
sarkia [1]163n
Sarmations [1]191
Sarpi, Paolo (1552–1623) [1]839, 840, 841, 842, 843, *843n*, 846
sarsaparilla [4]622
sarx [2]487, [4]420, [6]88
  s. egeneto [1]446, [2]271, 315, [3]14, 14n, 545, [6]65. *See also* flesh; *kata sarka*; *phronema sarkos*
Sassen, S. E. W. von [1]100
Satan [1]451, 600n, 774, [2]308, 315, 705, 896, *896n*, 1167, [3]57, 68, 92, 92n, 417n, 433, 442, 473, 481n, 513, 535, 546, 672n, 709, 742n, 851, [4]726, [5]85, 383, 421, 422n, [6]97–8, 97n–8n, 101, 102, 109, 118, 317
  accuser [3]746–7; cercoceronychous [5]82, 82n; genesis of [1]647; guilt of [5]784; in Job [3]436–7; and miracles [5]823; *kerkokeronycha S.* [1]351, 351n; personal [5]578; in Rev [1]483; tail-horn-hoofed [1]351, 351n; wonders of [6]119n; *see also* Devil
Satan
  (*Paradise Lost*) [3]175, 413n, 1065n, [4]727n, 841n, 842n, [5]236n, 353n; (*Paradise Regained*) [2]969
satellites [2]1142, [5]430
  of sun [1]626
satellitium [3]452, 452n
satire [2]687, [3]223, 225, [4]194, 195, 578, 623, 783, [5]415, 476
  derivation of [2]230, 230n–1n; in English verse [2]759–60; ironical [2]774; and irony [3]811; Roman [2]757–62, 757n, *758n*
satirist [3]225
satisfaction [4]183, [5]66, 618
Satterthwaite, James (c 1772–1827) [1]98, *98n–9n*
  Lines on the Portrait of a Lady MT [1]98
satura [2]230n
saturation [3]1003
Saturn (myth) [2]575, 578n
Saturn (planet) [1]12, 625n, 626, 626n, [2]556n, 557, [3]480, [4]73, 518n, 610
satyr [2]230, [6]326
  libidinous [3]185; s.-plays [2]757, 757n
Satz [4]127, 127n
saucer [4]517
Saul, King of Israel (Bible) [1]110, 798, [2]329, 917, 1108, [3]109
Saul of Tarsus (St Paul) [2]252, 256; *see also* Paul, St
Saumery, Pierre Lambert de ("M. de Mirone") (c 1690–c 1767) *Anecdotes vénitiennes* [1]698, 699n
Saurin, Jacques (1677–1730) [4]294
sausage(s) [2]366–7, [3]751
Saussure, Nicolas Théodore de (1767–1845) [3]939
Sautel, Pierre Just (1613–62) *Annus sacer poeticus* [3]1072
savage(s) [2]177, [3]402–3, 596, 806, [4]115, 748, [5]101, 102
  half-wise [6]322; s. state [2]206; wishes of [2]42
Savage, H. E. [1]722
Savage, Richard (c 1697–1743) [1]38
savagery [2]176, 414
"saved" [1]232
Savigny, Friedrich Carl von (1779–1861) [4]11, 341
  Of the Vocation of Our Age tr Hayward MT [4]341–2
Savile, Sir Henry (1549–1622) [5]42, 43
savine [1]772
Saviour [2]1166, 1179, [3]33, 741, [5]56, 620, [6]119
  crucified [5]491; love of [4]620; two-fold character of [4]260; *see also* Jesus Christ
Savonarola, Girolamo (1452–98) [3]794
"savoury" [5]124
Savoy [2]827n
  Conference [1]250n, 259, 283n, 332n, [2]522n, 970n; Declaration [1]283n, 321n
Saxon (language) [1]702, 845, [2]271, [4]282, 285, [6]286
Saxon(s) [3]46, 978, [4]594, [5]38, 279
Saxony [2]936n
Say and Sele ("Seal"), Lord *see* Fiennes, William

saying(s) [1]513
and unsaying [6]287
Scafell [2]691n, [6]249, 249n
scaffold [3]42
Scaglia, Caesar Alexandre (d 1641) [3]993–4, 993n
scale(s) [1]331, [2]683, [5]81
ascending [4]318, 318n; of being [3]1093n; of creation [3]580–1; intensities of [5]370; of understanding [5]427
Scaliger, Joseph Justus (1540–1609) [2]831–2, [3]928, 929n, 1069n
notes on NT [1]416
De emendatione temporum [3]929n; *Iambi gnomici* [2]832n
Scaliger, Julius Caesar (1484–1558) [1]8n, 221n, 533, 533n, [2]126n, 355
De subtilitate [1]clxv
scandal [2]1055, [5]575
Scanderoon [4]29
scansion [1]376 ("scanned"), [2]762; *see also* metre(s)
Scapula, Joannes (fl 1580) [1]472n, 496n, [2]1130n, [3]764n
Lexicon graeco-latinum [1]lxxxvi; MT [4]343
Scarborough, Yorkshire [1]90n
scarlet [3]388
s. fever [2]362
Scarlett, James Richard, Baron Abinger [2]117
Scarpa, Antonio (1747–1832) [4]164
scavenger [2]429
scazon [6]252
"scene" [5]861, 861n–2n
scene [4]852
scenery [1]375, [2]196, [3]406
theatrical [5]158n, 614
"scent" [6]212, 212n
scent [4]259
sceptic(s)/Sceptic(s) [1]174, 433, 781, [3]333, [4]130, 224, 668, 839n, [5]71, 75, 742n, 747, 747n, 750, 814, 814n
scepticism [1]283, 781n, [2]585, 710, [3]562, 966, [4]125, 125n, 219, 230n, [5]122, 141, 810–11, [6]217
confutation of [4]129; enlightened [3]56; in excess [2]746; habit of [2]475; restless [5]642; twitches of [6]104
sceptre [1]337, [2]143, 144n
Scharf, George (1788–1860) [1]cxv, cxvn
Schauen [3]209
Scheele, Carl Wilhelm (1742–86) [1]779, 779n, [3]1020, [5]346, 346n
Scheidius, Everardus (Everhard Scheid) (1742–94) *see* Lennep *Etymologicum linguae graecae* rev ed Scheid
Schein [3]249n, [4]128–9, 157, [5]359, 360, 360n, 772
Schelling, Friedrich Wilhelm Joseph von (1775–1854) [1]ci, cxxiii, cxxviii, clii, cliv, 131, 138, 556, 584n, [2]186, 187, 187n, 188n q, 193, 199, 389n, 539n, 594, 595, 615n, 623, 854n, 863n, [3]114, 127n, 842, 842n, 909n, 944n, 995, 997n, 1051n, [4]132, 158, 224, 274, 274n, 319n, 327n, 328n, [5]90n, 95, 203n, 266, 297, 308n, 320 q, 356, 427, 428n, 692n, 715, 715n, 719n, 743, 744, 744n, 753, 762, 773, 809, 809n
atheism of [2]554, 554n, [3]123; and Böhme [1]619, 620, [4]425, 427, 427n, 432, 432n–3n, 434; on breadth [3]1011; clear thinker [2]203; on colour [3]1018; conclusions of [4]221, 221n; dualism of [2]1007n; error(s) of [1]138, 602, 602n, [4]381, 381n, 382, [5]761 ("Schellingian"); fellow labourer [4]344–5; and Fichte [6]234, 234n, 242, 242n; defined "fluid" [1]548, 548n, [3]294; followers of [2]1002; Grand Turk of philosophy [6]234; great philosopher [4]418; on hardness [3]1009; and Jacobi [3]97, 97n, 99, 99n, [6]234, 234n; Jesuitical [2]188, [4]360; and Kant *see* Kant; on light [3]1016; mistakes [6]230; *Naturphilosophie* of [1]696, 696n, [3]715, 867, 867n; pantheism of [1]138n–9n, [2]554n; polarity in [1]660; and Proclus [4]421, 421n, 426, 426n; and Roman Catholicism [5]274, 274n; against S. [2]1030, 1030n; on solar system [5]339; and Spinoza [3]123, 123n, [6]238; Spinozism of [4]456, 456n; and Steffens [5]241; and Swedenborg [5]335n; system of [4]357, [5]806; theology of [3]82, 82n, 330
Abhandlungen zur Erläuterung des Idealismus der Wissenschaftslehre [4]221n, 344, 402; *Characteristick der alten Mysterien* [2]575n; *Darlegung* [3]114, [4]344, 425n; MT 344–59; *Darstellung* [4]361–2 q; *Denkmal* [1]lxix q, 585n, 619, 619n, [2]188n, [3]97n, 99n q, [4]344; MT 360–72; 398, 463, [5]762n; *Einleitung in die Philosophie der Mythologie* [4]463; *Einleitung zu . . . Naturphilosophie* [2]180, 1020n, [3]82n q, 286n, 291n, 292n, 294n q, [4]328n; MT 373–90; [6]226, 226n; *Erster Entwurf eines Systems der Naturphilosophie* [3]1016n, 1018n, [4]373, [5]264n, 266n, 762n; *Ideen zu einer Philosophie*

der Natur [3]289n, 1009n, 1016n, [4]224n q, 344; MT 391–7; [5]245n, 266n, tr E. E. Harris and Heath as *Ideas for a Philosophy of Nature* [4]391–7; ed *Jahrbücher der Medicin* see *Jahrbücher der Medicin* ed Marcus and Schelling; *Philosophie und Religion* [4]344, 360; MT 398–401; 463; *Philosophische Briefe* [2]641n, [4]344, 357, 357n, 402; *Philosophische Schriften* [1]lxxiv q, [2]642n, [3]330n, [4]221n, 344, 348n q, 357n, 383n, 391; MT 402–46; *Philosophische Untersuchungen über das Wesen der menschlichen Freyheit* [3]330, [4]344, 383n, 402; *Sämmtliche Werke* ed K. F. A. Schelling [4]221n, 224n q, 274n, 345–464 *passim*; *System des transcendentalen Idealismus* [1]lxix q, [2]554n, 623n q, [3]1011n, [4]122n q, 132n, 221n, 344, 352n, 391, 412n, 417, 417n; MT 447–62, tr Heath as *System of Transcendental Idealism* [4]447–62; *Über das Verhältniss der bildenen Künste zu der Natur* [4]344, 402; *Ueber das Wesen der menschlichen Freyheit* see *Philosophische Untersuchungen* ... above; *Ueber den Begriff der speculativen Physik* [1]548n q; *Ueber die Gottheiten von Samothrace* [1]617n, 639n, 653n, 665n, 692n, [2]573, 575n q, 583n, [3]399n, 683n, [4]360, 398; MT 463–4; 595n, [6]3, 5n; *Ueber die Möglichkeit einer Form der Philosophische Schriften* [4]344; *Vom Ich als Prinzip der Philosophie* [4]344, 357, 357n, 402; *Weltalter* [4]463; ed *Zeitschrift für spekulative Physik* see *Zeitschrift* ed Schelling

Schelling, Karl Eberhard (fl 1806) [3]114, 115, 119n, 122n, [6]104, 104n
- "Grundsätze zu einer künftigen Seelenlehre" [5]360, 360n; "Ideen und Erfahrungen über den thierischen Magnetismus" [6]121n

Schelling, Karl Friedrich August (fl 1856) *see* F. W. J. Schelling *Sämmtliche Werke* ed K. F. A. Schelling

Schellingians [3]119, 119n, [5]321, 360, 744
- error of [3]1051

Schellingites [4]155

schema [5]581

schematisms [2]999, [5]351

scheme(s)
- benignant [5]644; Grotio-Paleyian [3]763, [5]513n; Homoousian [5]626; Jewish [5]606; Kantian [5]701; Newtonian [5]560; secret [1]471; Jeremy Taylor's [5]614; theological [5]664

Schenk, Jakob (1508–46) [3]759 ("Jeckle")

Scheol *see* Sheol

Schernberg, Theodoricus (fl 1483–1502) *Apotheosis Johannis VIII Pontificis Romani* [2]773

Schiff, Gert *Johann Heinrich Füsslis Milton-Galerie* [3]900n

Schill, Johann Gottfried (fl 1823) [6]246 ("Golfried")

Schiller, Johann Christoph Friedrich von (1759–1805) [1]72n, 100, 632n, [6]156, 158
- *Musen-Almanach für das Jahr 1797* [4]466n; *Wallenstein* [4]787, 787n, 792, 792n

Schilter, Johann (1632–1705) *Thesaurus antiquitatum* [1]629n

Schindler, Valentin (d 1604) [2]1108n

"schism" [6]55n–6n

schism(s) [1]234, 321, 359, [2]1141, 1199, [3]69, [5]162, 166, 521
- in C of E [1]333; commands against [1]339; Methodist [4]644; misty [5]795; no sin [6]42

schismatic(s) [1]352–3, [2]1199, [6]55–6, 59

Schlegel, August Wilhelm von (1767–1845) [1]lxiii, 131, 148, 148n, [4]776, 794n, 826n, 836–7, 836n, 837n
- blunders of [3]702; Shakespeare lectures [3]657, 888; source for C [1]72n
- *Beyträge* [1]132; *Gedichte* MT [4]465–7; *Die Gemählde* [1]132; *Die Kunst der Griechen* [1]132; *Der rasende Roland* [1]132; *Die Sprachen* [1]132; *Ueber dramatische Kunst und Litteratur*† [4]468, 787n, tr J. Black as *A Course of Lectures* [4]776n; *Ueber Zeichnungen* [1]132; *Vorlesungen* [1]xcvi, clxvi, [3]702n, 888n; and K. W. Friedrich Schlegel *Elegien* [1]132, *Idyllen* [1]132, *Sonnette* [1]132. See also *Athenaeum* ed A. W. Schlegel, K. W. F. Schlegel, and Schleiermacher; Calderón *La Devoción de la Cruz* tr A. W. Schlegel; *Spanisches Theater* ed A. W. Schlegel

Schlegel, Karl Wilhelm Friedrich von (1772–1829) [1]131, 148n, [2]958, [5]89, 320 q
- conversion to Roman Catholicism [1]144–5, 145n
- *An die Deutschen* [1]132; *An Heliodora* [1]132; *Geschichte der alten und neuen Litteratur* [2]398n; *Gespräch über die Poesie* [1]132; *Ideen* [1]132; *Ueber die Philosophie* [1]132; *Ueber die Unverständlichkeit* [1]132. See also *Athenaeum* ed

Schlegel, Karl Wilhelm Friedrich von—*continued*
A. W. Schlegel, K. W. F. Schlegel, and Schleiermacher; Hardenberg *Novalis Schriften* ed Tieck and Schlegel
Schlegels, the [2]999n, [3]127n
Schleiermacher, Friedrich Daniel Ernst (1768–1834) [1]131, 148n, 584n, [2]481n, 568, 736n, 999, *999n*, 1048, [3]3n, 30n, 127n, 421n, [4]58, [5]128n
review of Kant [1]151; tr Plato [3]868; school of [2]205; sermons [4]469
A Critical Essay on the Gospel of St. Luke tr Thirlwall [1]clxx, [2]193n, [3]17n, [4]41n, 59n; MT 469–84; *Gelegentliche Gedanken über Universitäten in deutschem Sinn* [4]485; *Ueber den sogenannten ersten Brief des Paulos an den Timotheos* [2]193n, [4]41, 41n; MT 485–6; *Ueber die neue Liturgie* [4]485; *Ueber die . . . Synodalverfassung* [4]485; see also *Athenaeum* ed A. W. Schlegel, K. W. F. Schlegel, and Schleiermacher
schleppen [1]658
Schmid, Karl Christian Erhard (1761–1812) [3]319 ("Schmidt"), 319n
Wörterbuch zum leichtern Gebrauch der Kantischen Schriften [3]965, 965n
Schmid, Konrad Arnold (1716–89) [3]656
Schmidel, Ulrich (?1510–?1579) [5]105
Schmidt, J. A. (fl 1805) [3]114
Schmidt (probably Johann Andreas Schmid[t], d 1726) [3]644
Schmied, Erasmus (1570–1637) *see* Pindar *Periodos* ed Schmied
Schneider, Johann Gottlob (1750–1822) [1]7
Schoenbaum, S. (1927–96) *Shakespeare's Lives* [4]724n
scholar(s) [1]874, [2]727, [5]74, 167, 385, 533, 738
classical [3]891; critical [5]619; plain-minded [2]607; prepared [4]156
Scholastic(s) [3]949n, [5]767–9
Scholasticism [1]538n, [3]13, 365, [5]795n
decline of [5]801–2; distinctions of [3]519–20, 520n; Kantian [4]354
Scholes, Percy Alfred (1877–1958) see *Oxford Companion to Music* ed Scholes
Scholfield bequests [6]218
scholiasts [4]768
Scholz, Johann Martin Augustin (1794–1852) [3]1013
Solemnia natalitia regis [3]1013, [5]851, [6]334
Schomberg, Frederick Hermann, 1st Duke of Shomberg (1615–90) [3]162
Schönheit [5]363
school(s)/School(s) [1]804, [5]49, 597
Alexandrian/Alexandrine [4]421, [5]744, 745; Catholic [1]214, 214n; charity [1]498n; distinctions of [5]673; s. doctrine [1]845; emulation in [1]726; founders of [5]744; girls' boarding-s. [3]906; Greek [6]317; lessons [5]110; national [5]366; Peripatetic [5]733, 826, 826n; s.-philosophers [5]802; of philosophy [5]86, 692; public [2]978–80, 979n–80n; Pythagorean [2]1136, [5]232; Sceptic [5]742; theological [5]480
schoolboys [1]220, 234, [2]199, 582, [3]807, [4]737, 737n, 757, 783, [5]160, 296
schoolgirls [1]220, [5]313
schooling [1]356
Schoolman/Schoolmen [1]232n, 255, 286, 749, [2]260, 299n, 652, 1110, [3]30, 85, 85n, 135, 511, 604, 616, 722, 877n, 1068, 1078, 1078n, [4]160, 353, 354, 354n, 422n, 643n, 661, [5]407, 661, 792, 803–4, 803n, 805, 806, [6]116
and Aristotle [2]12, 12n; Christian [3]1085; defended [2]12–13; greatest of [5]790; object of [3]1085; style of [2]12
schoolmaster(s) [1]356, [2]980, [4]783, [5]74, 361, 378
Catholic [1]214; punsters [1]354
schooner, Dutch [2]889
Schöttgen, Johann Christian (1687–1751) [3]684
Schrader (possibly Johann Gottlieb Friedrich Schrader, 1763–1832) [5]256, 256n
Schreiber, K. W. (fl 1831) *see* Böhme *Sämmtliche Werke* ed Schreiber
Schrickx, Willem, coeditor [2]596, 600, 616, 623, 626, 627, 638, 639, 988, 998
Schröter, Johan (1745–1816) [4]515
Schubert, Gotthilf Heinrich von (1780–1860) [1]clii, [2]539n, [4]505 ("Schubart"), 505n, 517n, [5]349, 349n, 427, 428n, 726n
Allgemeine Naturgeschichte [1]cliin, clxvii; MT [4]487–503; 517n, [5]249n q; *Ansichten von der Nachtseite der Naturwissenschaft* [3]390 q; MT [4]504–40; *Handbuch der Naturgeschichte* [2]852, [4]487n; *Die Symbolik des Traumes* MT [4]541–4
Schugotengon [4]489–90
Schuller, Georg Hermann (1651–79) [5]203
Schulz/Schultz/Schulze, Christopher Johann (1739–1805) [3]319, 319n, [6]234
Erläuterung über des Herrn Kant Critik der reinen Venunft [6]234n
Schuster, K. G. (fl 1787) [3]612n

Schütz, Christian Gottfried (1747–1832) *see* Aeschylus ed Schütz
Schwabians ^{3}978
Schwager, Johann Moritz (1738–1804) ^{2}754
Schwärmer ^{5}395
Schwarz, Wolfgang *see* Kant *Logic* tr Hartman and Schwarz
Schwarzschild, Heinrich S. (1803–78) *De fungis capitis* ^{3}1013, ^{5}851
"science" ^{3}91, ^{4}363n
science(s) ^{1}144, ^{2}1139, ^{3}331, 936–53, 1006, 1019–48, 1049–63, ^{4}95, 262, 375, 406, ^{5}208, 277, ^{6}96
age of ^{1}719; certain knowledge ^{1}128; circle of ^{5}655–6; and common sense ^{5}480; defined ^{3}295; distinct knowledge ^{4}348; dualism in ^{3}432; dynamic ^{3}325n; embryo ^{4}503; experimental ^{2}824; and faith ^{1}128, ^{2}186; falsities of ^{3}920; fundamental ^{1}763, 796; of government ^{6}52; ground of ^{3}292; *in posse* ^{1}642; infancy of a ^{5}811; Leighton against ^{3}625; men of ^{5}450; modern ^{5}318, 564n; of morals ^{5}578; natural ^{2}824, ^{3}919, ^{5}803; of nature ^{3}299; noetic ^{3}16; of observation ^{4}15; organ of ^{4}503; and philosophy ^{3}908; physical ^{6}86; and poetry ^{4}679; pride of man of ^{3}365; progress in ^{5}447; prophetic ^{3}426; psychological ^{1}813; pyramid of ^{1}177; real ^{3}1051, ^{5}460; and religion ^{2}181–2, 186; of sciences ^{5}447; of self-knowledge ^{5}481; state of ^{5}638; subjectivity of ^{2}887; superior ^{5}721; triumph of ^{2}825; truth of ^{3}63; ultimate ^{5}88
scientia scientiarum ^{5}362
"scientific" ^{4}363, 363n
scintillations ^{2}553
sciography ^{4}160
"sciolism" ^{5}110, 110n
sciolism ^{2}999n, ^{3}132, 257, 257n
sciolist ^{2}999n, ^{5}110n
"scious(ly)" ^{4}542, 542n
Scipio, Publius Cornelius (237–183 BC) ^{1}176, 176n–7n, 315, ^{3}652
Scipios, the ^{1}315
scoffing ^{4}287
Scollock *see* Scoltock
Scoltock, Hannah (fl 1787) ^{2}649, 685 ("Scollock")
Scopas/Skopas (4th century BC) ^{4}463
scope, unbounded ^{6}199
scorn ^{1}560, ^{3}56, 479, ^{4}722, 819, ^{5}423
Pharisaic ^{5}148; witty ^{5}611
scorners ^{1}576
scorpion(s) ^{2}511
s.-locusts ^{2}515
Scot(s) ^{1}350–1, ^{2}216, ^{3}226, 226–7, 403, 801n, ^{4}83, 83n, 185n, ^{5}43
C's hostility to ^{1}57, 57n; C's prejudice against ^{4}577; C's scorn for ^{4}90, 90n; and English ^{4}765–6; minion-kissing ^{4}766; prejudice against manufacturers ^{6}216; Presbyterian ^{2}523; stupid ^{3}404; Thomson as redeemer of ^{1}74; list of worthy ^{1}75n
Scot/Scott, Reginald (?1538–99) *The Discoverie of Witchcraft* ^{1}282n, ^{4}76
Scotch (language) ^{1}75, ^{5}651; *see also* Scottish
Scotch (people) ^{4}185–6, ^{5}280, 834
as generous/Iapetic race ^{1}540; loyal conduct of ^{1}333; metaphysicians ^{3}877–8
Scotchery ^{4}577
Scotchman/Scotchmen/Scotsmen ^{2}216, 216n, ^{4}25, 90, 185, 577, 587
has no notion of a jest ^{3}175; S.'s heart ^{3}795
Scotist ^{1}524, ^{2}615n, ^{5}478
Scotland ^{1}74, 271, 350, 351n, ^{2}826, 1055, ^{3}141n, 147, ^{4}24n, 574, 657, ^{5}43, 68, 145, 179, 295n, 857n
Church of *see* Church, of Scotland; Highlands ^{2}311; history of ^{2}1169–81, ^{3}483; the itch in ^{2}363–4; martyrs in ^{2}1175; Presbyterian Church in ^{4}591; reformed religion in ^{6}261; reputation for probity ^{1}34n; second sight in ^{3}653, 653n; in 1650 ^{1}294–5; witch-finders in ^{6}104
Scotsmen *see* Scotchman
Scott, George ^{3}827
Scott, James (fl 1810) ^{3}936
Scott, James, Duke of Monmouth (1649–85) ^{2}767, ^{5}43
Scott, John (1638–94/5) *The Christian Life* MT ^{4}545–73
Scott, John (1730–83) ^{1}38
Scott, John, 1st Earl of Eldon (1751–1838) ^{3}489, 489n, 501, 501n
Scott, Peter ^{5}853
Scott, Robert (1811–87) ^{1}33, 33n; *see also* Liddell and Scott
Scott, Sir Walter (1771–1832) ^{1}211, 725, 828, ^{2}1204n, ^{3}420n, 484n, ^{4}76, 76n, 603n, ^{5}114
appeal to actual ^{2}140; author of *Waverley* ^{4}593n; on Byron ^{4}76, 76n; cosmolater ^{4}581; debt to C ^{4}614, 614n; favourite of higher classes ^{4}594; Galt second to ^{2}840; great defect of ^{4}582; as historian ^{4}609; imitates Goethe ^{4}610, 610n, 611; literary sins ^{4}611; "Northern Enchanter"

Scott, Sir Walter—*continued*
[3]484–5, 484n; novelist, not poet [4]76, 76n; omission of article [6]205; popularity [4]609–10, 610n; and Scots [1]75n; and Shakespeare [3]484–5
The Abbot [4]576; MT 597–601; *The Antiquary* [2]1203, [3]485n, [4]576; MT 585–6; *The Black Dwarf* [4]576; *The Bride of Lammermoor* [4]576; ed *A Collection of Scarce and Valuable Tracts* [5]143n, [6]185n; *The Fortunes of Nigel* [2]822, 826, 826n, 927n, [4]576; MT 608–9; *Guy Mannering* [3]484n, 716n, [4]576; MT 581–5; 594, 594n; *The Heart of Midlothian* [3]484n, [4]576; MT 588–90; *Historical Romances Copy B* [4]576, 578; MT 593–602; 603; *Ivanhoe* [4]576; MT 593–4; *Kenilworth* [2]819n q, [4]576; MT 601–2; *The Lady of the Lake* [4]581n, [5]114n; *A Legend of Montrose* [4]576; MT 590–2; *Minstrelsy of the Scottish Border* MT [4]574–5; 595n; *The Monastery* [4]80, 80n, 576; MT 594–7; 599, 599n; *Novels and Romances Copy C* [4]576, 578, 593; MT 603–14; *Novels and Tales Copy B* [1]801, [4]576; MT 578–92; 593, 603; *Old Mortality* [4]576, 578; MT 587–8; 594; *Peveril of the Peak* [4]576; MT 609–11; *The Pirate* [4]576; MT 604–7; *Quentin Durward* [4]576; MT 611–14; *Rob Roy* [4]576; MT 586–7; *Waverley* [2]826n q, [4]576; MT 578–81; 601; "Waverley Novels" *Copy A* MT [4]576–614
Scott, William (fl 1844) [6]12
Scott, William, Lord Stowell (1745–1836) [3]501, 501n
Scotticism [4]579, 601n, 613
Scottish (language) [4]802; *see also* Scotch
Scottish National Dictionary [4]16n
Scotus *see* Duns Scotus
Scougal, Henry (1650–78) *The Life of God in the Soul of Man* MT [4]615–16
scoundrel [1]699
scourge [1]436
scourgings [2]716, [5]544
screen [4]826, 826n–7n
scribblers [4]193
scribbling [4]276
scribe(s) [2]377, 438, 483, 495, [5]56
Scriblerus Club [1]*156n*
Scribner and Welford *see* New York
Scribner, R. W. *For the Sake of Simple Folk* [3]766n
Scrimgeour, John (fl 1590–1620) [2]1174
Scriptores de re rustica [6]335
scripture(s)/Scripture(s) [1]277, 311, 352, 517, 673, 729, 781, 836, [2]684n, 803, [3]60, 72, 416, 438, 466, 521, 686, [4]522, 630n, 670, [5]8, 10, 30, 53, 124, 125, 128, 129, 134, 155, 189, 407, 413, 463, 464, 466, 481, 482, 483, 506n, 556, 569, 652, 663, [6]14, 62, 113, 115, 116, 303
authority of [1]318, 323, 344–5, [4]260, 668–9, [5]503, 570, [6]96; blank in [3]739; s. bread [2]338; and Church [1]805–6, [2]289, 290, 295, [3]451; as charter of the Church [6]19; difficulties in [2]679, [5]584; divine authority of [3]561; division of [5]507; doctrine of [5]383; double sense of [1]718–19; s. evidence [1]268; faith reconciled with [2]558; harmony of [5]398; not in hearts of people [2]737; Hebrew [1]718, [2]314, [5]54, [6]319; ignorance of [1]225; infallibility of [1]520–1, [2]30, [5]13–14; injunctions of [6]264; inspiration of [5]519; inspired [5]564, 620, [6]307; interpretation of [1]259, 355, 673, 805, [2]38–9, 40, 722, 1106, 1152–3, [5]519, allegorical [2]482, Jewish [2]153, literal [6]74, right [5]61; language of [2]508, 531; letter of [3]67; literal sense of [5]494; meaning of [2]531; metastasis of [2]672; misuse of [5]52; most difficult passage in [3]604; origin of [2]423; penmen of [2]806; proofs from [5]542; Protestant position on [5]395; reading aloud [1]349; and reason *see* reason; recitation of [1]355; right appreciation of [3]724; rule of faith [3]533, [6]319; speak to humankind [5]385; role of spirit in [1]674; study of [5]562, 629; subsidiary [5]571; super-foetation of [1]519; superiority of [3]766; supremacy of [5]573; symbolical language of [1]706; and Talmudic tradition [3]1090; test of [6]306; text of [5]494, 659; and tradition [2]195, [5]522n, 567, 572–3, 572n, 574, 575, 576, 630, [6]79; true sense of [6]91; true test of [3]523; truly religious use [1]469; truth of [6]42; understanding of [5]569; uppermost [1]314; vindications of [2]148; in Welsh [6]17; words of [5]579; s. words as symbols [1]719; written word in pentad [2]290; *see also* Bible
scrofula *see* king's evil
scrouge [2]227, 227n
Scudamore, Charles (1779–1849) *A Chemical and Medical Report* MT [4]617–18; [6]285
Scudaret [5]832
Scullard, Howard Hayes (1903–83) see *Oxford Classical Dictionary* ed Hammond and Scullard
sculleries [2]1064

scull-pan [2]496
sculptor [3]21
sculpture [4]419n
scum [1]601
scybala [3]374
Scyra [5]837
Scythia [5]387n
Scythian expedition [3]479
Scythian(s) [3]479n, [5]337, 352, 364
sea(s) [1]675, [3]77, [4]487–8, 525–6, [5]455
s.-beach [1]375; s.-brides [4]738; s.-cows [2]862; daemon of [1]425; s.-gull [2]580; s.-horses [5]411n; s.-leopards [2]1112; s.-lions [2]1112; s.-monster(s) [1]425, 425n, [4]606n; s.-queens [4]738, 761–2; s.-snake [2]1112n, [4]605–6, 606n; s.-waves [4]810
Sea Serjeants Meeting [4]203
Seagrim, Molly (in Fielding) [3]94n
seal (impressed) [3]741, 758, [5]83, 83n, 649
God's [3]622, [6]315
seal(s) (animal) [2]862, [4]169,
and s.-oil [2]1113
sealing [3]17
"Search, Edward" *see* Tucker, Abraham
season, in and out of [3]751
seat
of God [3]431; Sara's [3]837, 837n
Seba, Albert (1665–1736) [3]1073n
"sebanthropism" [2]344, 344n
seceders [4]20
Secker, Thomas, Archbishop of Canterbury (1693–1768) [3]605n q, [5]190n q
seclusion [3]94
Second Coming *see* Jesus Christ: Second Coming
second sight *see* sight, second
secrecy [2]574, [4]145
secret [4]800
secretaries [3]447
secretion [2]1167
sect(s) [2]247, 717, [3]69, 492, 493, 642, 700, 927, [4]305, 308, 370, 660
conflicting [5]589; dissenting [5]509n; dominant [1]531; error of [5]157; fanatical [1]803; favoured [1]527; s.-founder [6]59; Galilean [4]627; of the Gnostics [5]625; heretical [5]181; imaginary [6]59; Italian [5]223; moral conduct of [1]225; new [5]736; plebeian [5]384; political [5]301; Protestant [3]70; Pythagoro-platonic [6]61; recent [4]643; spirit of [4]632
sectarian(s) [2]524, [5]519
sectarianism [3]68, 69
sectaries [1]256, 319, [3]721
secularisations, shameless [1]357
seculum [3]461, *461n*
s. futurum [4]244, 244n, 246, 246n, 247; *see also* saeculum
Secundus (probably the Bishop of Tigisi, fl early 4th century) [5]626
security/securities [2]1207, [5]686, 829
against popery [4]19
sedative [4]183
Sedgwick, James (1775–1851) *Hints to the Public and the Legislature, on . . . Evangelical Preaching* [1]xciii, clxvii, [2]874; MT [4]619–74
Sedgwick, William (c 1610–c 1669) *Justice upon the Armie Remonstrance* [2]110, 111; MT [4]675–6; [5]170n
sedition [2]470, [4]481
seduction [6]157
see saw [3]404
seed(s) [1]550, 791, [2]689–90, 933, [3]14, [4]318, 525, 528, [5]232–3, 233n, 251
of Christ [1]430, 470; corruptible [2]1184; and flower [2]61; fluid [1]549; s.-pearl [5]527
seeing [2]604, [3]128, 389, [4]355, 358, 405–6, 538, [5]265
active and passive [2]1025; creative [2]548; inward [1]631; subjective [3]770; within [2]1115
Seekers [5]509, 509n
seeking [5]171, 467
Seele [1]125
Seelenkräfte [1]3–4
Seely, Urcraft (fiction) [2]536
"seem" [5]360
seemliness [5]194
ecclesiastical [5]162
seer(s) [1]628, 705, [2]508, [3]426, [5]474
apostolic [1]473; gifted [1]661, [5]413; heavenly-minded [1]560; inside-s. *see* inside-seer(s); sublime [2]514
Séguin, Armand (c 1765–1835) [2]857n
Ségur, Alexandre Joseph Pierre, Vicomte de (1756–1805) *L'Education de l'amour* [1]90n
Sehnsucht [1]653, 653n
Seidler (fl 1746) [3]215
Seiler, Georg Friedrich (1733–1807) [1]480
Sein [4]403n, 404, [6]241 ("Seyn")
Seine [5]114
sëity [1]152n, 153
Sejanus (in Jonson) [3]184
Sejanus, Lucius Aelius (d 31) [3]178
Selborne [6]147
Selby-Bigge, Sir Lewis Amherst (1860–1951) *see* Hume *Enquiries* ed Selby-Bigge

Selden, John (1584–1654) [2]114, 114n, 928, [3]169, 309n, [4]243, 243n, [5]803
  History of Tythes [2]114n; *Seldeniana* [6]335; *Table Talk* [1]lxxxvn, cxlin, 269, 269n, [3]189, [4]243n, [5]803, 803n–4n q, [6]260, ed Milward MT [4]677–9
selection(s) [1]164, [3]59, [5]529
  and election [1]308
Seleucia, Council of [2]732n
Seleucus I (c 358–280 BC) [2]416
"self" [5]94
self/selves [1]163n–4n, 598, 691, [2]596, 801, 899, [4]112–13, 159, 162, 412, 412n, 413, 455–6, 495, [5]161, 177, 789
  absolute [1]647; animal [2]690; desert of [2]899; destroyed [3]645; distinct [1]153; dividual [3]563; empirical [3]720; fantastic [1]620; identified with touch [1]670; individual [4]855; individualising [4]348; light of God in all [1]629; past [3]494; primal [1]694; principle of [5]777; spiritual [2]690; transfigured [2]642; *see also* I
self-abasement [3]750
self-accusation [4]436
self-action [1]647
self-adulation [2]637
Self-Affirmant, Eternal [2]324
self-affirmation [1]152, 460, 618, [3]12, [5]790, [6]83, 238
  divine [1]610
self-applause [2]840
self-assertion [3]176
self-attribution [1]694
self-bewitched, the [6]99
self-center, the [5]425
self-circumscription [2]674
self-comparativeness [4]595
self-complacency [4]137, [5]174
self-comprehension [1]564, 793, [4]112
self-conceit [1]367, 370, 561, [2]999, [4]672, [5]476
self-condemnation [1]429
self-consciousness [1]647, [2]533, 534, 534n, 552, 603, 609–10, 638n, 1109, [3]25, 499, 588, [4]93, 220–1, 221n, 412n, 453, 457–8, [5]14, 27, 94, 94n, 177, 300–2
  act of [3]357; divine act of [1]573; universality of [5]816
self-constitution, act of [1]659
self-construction [1]679
self-contempt [4]596
self-contradiction [2]950, [3]428
self-defence [3]867, [5]312
self-delusion(s) [2]840, [5]161
self-denial [5]153
self-desertion [1]692
self-evidence [5]455
self-examination [1]813, [5]413
self-existence [2]666
self-finding [1]692, [3]264n; see also *Empfindung*
self-government, moral [1]322
selfhood [5]466
self-importance [5]162
self-inanition [1]601, 605
self-instructor [5]201
self-interest [2]636, [4]73, 77, 162
self-intuition [4]144
"selfish" [2]946, 946n
selfishness [1]680, 752, 754, [2]635, 840, 946, 946n, [3]499, 528, [4]792, 814, [5]379, [6]312
  enlightened [2]27; slothful [5]829
self-knowledge [1]696, 734, [4]348, [5]795, [6]238, 241
  science of [5]481
self-love [1]560, 560n, [2]596n, [3]252–3, 602, 602n, [4]73, 78, 522, 606, [5]423, 682
self-lust [1]560, [4]341
self-magnetising [1]674
self-magnetism [6]99
self-manifestation [1]681, [3]24
self-mechanism [1]679
self-murder [1]166, 166n, 180; *see also* suicide
selfness [2]840, 1019–20, [3]499
  principle of [2]250
self-oblivion [5]121
self-opinion [4]860, [5]476
self-origination [2]458, 790, [5]556
self-outrages [1]518
self-overrating [1]514–15
self-perception [2]547, [4]414
"self-ponence" [3]852, 852n
self-portrait [3]20
self-position [4]783
self-preservation [1]336
self-privation [1]685, 685n
self-production [1]lxi, [5]542
self-realisation [1]640, 694
  act of [1]696
self-redemption [5]135
self-representation [3]213, 213n
self-retention [1]665
self-righteousness [4]627–8
self-sanctifiedness [4]629
self-sublimation [2]1000
self-subsistence [2]458, [3]73, [5]443, 810
"self-subsistent" [5]4

self-subsistent(s) [1]355, [5]25–6, 25n
self-sufficiency [1]514, [5]148
self-torture [6]256
self-trumpeters [1]378
self-watchfulness [2]635
self-will [1]238, [4]495
self-willing [5]165
semainei [5]396
semeion [3]988, 988n
Semele (myth) [2]584n
semen [1]550, 640
semi-breve [1]346, 346n
semicolon(s) [2]160
as fish [1]133
semi-demi-quaver [1]346, 346n
semi-materialist [5]548
semina rerum [5]233, 233n
semi-possibles [2]387
Semites [4]243n
"semitic" [4]243, 243n
Semitic languages *see* languages, Semitic
Semler, Johann Salomo (1725–91) [2]146n, 481, 481n, [3]764, 764n, [4]337n, [5]540, 540n
"semperfuity" [3]91, 91n
sempiterni [2]137, 137n
senate [3]108, 149, 149n
Roman [2]949, 950, [3]112, [5]536; Jewish [1]458
senator(s) [3]21, 240, 240n, [4]79
senatorial functions [4]23
senatorship [5]124
Sendschreiben an ... Herrn ... Teller [1]clxvii
Seneca, Lucius Annaeus (c 4 BC–AD 65) [1]174, 174n, 315, 755 q, 818, [2]276, 693–4, 758n, 763, 776n, 918, [3]179, 574 q, 621 q, 622, 652–3, 653 q, [4]608, 695, [5]128n, 385
De Beneficiis tr Aubrey Smith [5]40–1 q; *Hercules furens* [3]701 q, 701n; *Moral Epistles* [4]111n; *Seneca* tr Corcoran [3]653
senescence [4]525
senility [4]844
senna [4]622
Sennert, Daniel (1572–1637) [1]533n
Opera† [4]680
seno [2]380, 380n
sensation(s) [1]171, 299, [2]547, 603, 606–7, 639, 640–1, 1008, 1133, 1167, [3]209–10, 394, 517, 720, 790, 1036
accumulated [5]168; awaken thoughts [1]163; blind [6]149; in dreams [5]726; feverous [6]311; intense [1]496; and knowledge [2]341; language of [1]647, [4]838; of light and colour [2]403; locality of [1]518; morbid [6]102; organic [5]559; and perception [3]399; as self-perception [4]414; and sense [3]850; simple [6]172; state of [5]122; vital [5]177
sensationalists [5]692
"sense" [1]683
sense(s) (bodily or psychic) [1]580n, [2]844, 1002, 1018, 1146, [3]424, 524, 610, 723, 1036, [4]144, 674, [5]65, 174, 242, 242n, 260, 492–3, 548, 599, 752, 798, 803, [6]80
affection of [5]720; bodily [5]407; common *see* common sense; compulsion of [1]282; concretes of [1]595; creed of [3]563; crude notion of [4]508; defined [3]559; enthralment to [3]89; evidence of [3]661; facts of [2]1160; five [6]307; forms of [2]729, [3]848, 968; good [4]243, 372, [5]372, 476; higher [5]297; images of [5]795; impressible [1]655; independence from [2]959; inductions of [3]957; influence of [4]616; inner [2]679, [3]852, [4]542; and intellect [4]156; interdependent with understanding [1]683, internal [5]413; interior [1]818; intuitions of [5]771; laws of [3]201; man of [5]73; moral [2]26, 1080, [4]479, 481, [5]61, 477, 496, [6]298; objects of [1]359, 673, [5]715; organ(s) of [3]371, [6]132; originate in spirit [1]582; outward [4]544, [5]517; of outwardness [3]260; powers of [1]580; prison of [5]514; proof of [5]553–4; of propriety [5]512; reason in [3]163; religious [5]61; and sensation [5]95; and senses [5]405, 405n, 828, [6]87; and sensibility [3]559, 990; and sensuality [2]65; shape for [3]45; torpor of [2]859; and understanding [5]305, 813; vividness of [2]1133; world of [1]574, [3]423, [4]136, [5]405, 519, 598
sense (meaning) [1]232, [5]370
Böhme's [1]611; Christian [5]512; divine [1]601; double [1]718, [4]260; efficient [5]519; literal [1]521, 606, 783, [2]1080, 1159, [3]44, 49, [4]642, 655, [5]413, 494, 504, 560, [6]108; and metre [1]377, [2]221; primary [1]354, 473; relative [5]614; representative [2]87, 87n; same word, same s. [3]558–9; scrouge of [2]227; sound [2]327; spiritual [1]431; true [3]31; truest [5]150; unique [5]408; and word [4]216
sensibility [1]577, 626, [2]1008, 1008n, 1026n, 1080, 1176, [3]81n, 123n, 126, 241, 357, 424, 559, 581, 753, 1036, [4]238, 273, 388–9, 389n, 390, 398, 500n, 814, [5]126, 258, 259, 260, 784
affection of [5]599; combined with imagination [2]173; common [5]186; corporeal [5]172; exquisite [5]821; of plants [4]316; poetic [2]1034; religious [2]429; as warmth [5]783

"sensible" and "sensuous" [3]303, 303n
sensivity [4]500–1
sensorium [3]678
"sensual" [3]242
sensual, the [5]674
 and sensuous [3]259
sensualists [2]1075
sensuality [2]65, 984, [3]468, 493, [4]75, 355, 537, 673
sensuous, the [2]425, 918, [5]175
 and sensible *see* sensible; and sensual *see* sensual
sensus [4]144, 144n
sentence(s)
 balanced [3]225; detached [3]690, [5]571; length of [3]221, 223; short [6]144; single [6]308; verbal [2]30
sententiaries [3]533, [6]319
sentience [1]299
sentiency, organic [6]132
sentiment(s) [2]1122, [3]226, [4]730, [5]788
 pointed [4]475; touching [1]580
separation [1]574, [2]630, [3]59, [5]27, 364n
 destructive [5]438; and distinction [5]19; not distinction only [4]366, 366n; rock of [3]230–1
Separatists [1]283, 283n, [2]839
separative, the [3]1000
sephiroth [3]531, 622, 1091, 1091n, [6]141, 141n, 315
Sepoy [2]382, 382n
septem [2]1092
Septemberisers/Septembrisers [2]509, 510n, [3]188n
Septembrists [2]510n
"septic" [4]148, 148n
Septuagint *see* Bible: OT: Septuagint
sepulchres [1]764, 797, [2]1073
seraphim [3]1089
Serapion, Bishop of Antioch (fl 190–203) [2]750n
Serapis (myth) [1]798
Serbonian bog [2]615n
serfs [5]283
sergeant(s)/serjeant(s) [5]378
 recruiting [5]143
Sergeant, John (1622–1707) [5]560, 561n
series [4]132, 313
 doctrine of [5]447; infinite [3]332, [5]457
seri-fluids [5]98
sermo [4]93
sermon(s) [1]359, [3]685, [4]662, [5]135
 commonplace [5]96; forms of [5]510; Methodist [5]811; S. on the Mount *see* Jesus Christ: Sermon on the Mount; ordination [2]472; read from a book [3]732; sentimental [2]1016; and service [6]21; show character of age [2]328; superior [2]1167; for Trinity Sunday [5]60; two hours long [1]873, 875
sermoni propiora [2]353, *353n–4n*, 760, 760n
sermonisers [5]787
Sermons or Homilies [1]712n; MT [4]681–3
serpent(s) [1]399, 457, [2]717, 915, 915n, 1052–3, 1053–4, 1112n, 1167, [3]105, 234, 234n, 473, 473n, [4]368, 431, 502n, 595, 603, [5]225, [6]110, 112
 in Rev [2]515; symbol [1]684–5, [2]1069, 1069n–70n, [4]502; winged [3]200
serpentine [1]776n
Serra Leoa *see* Sierra Leone
Serres, Etienne Renaud Augustin (1786–1868) [4]164
Serres, Marcel de (1783–1862) [3]938, 939
Serubabel/Zerubbabel (Bible) [2]149, 894, [6]140, 140n
serum [3]60n, 612
servant(s) [1]449n, 873, 876, 878, [2]693
 differs from slave [1]874; in Isa [1]435, 435n; s.-song [1]435n, 449n
Servetus, Michael (1511–53) [1]477, *477n–8n*, [2]666–7, 667n, [3]368, 368n, [4]670, 670n
 Christianismi restitutio [1]478n; *De Trinitatis erroribus* [1]478n
service(s)
 daily [1]530; divine [1]329, [4]625; to God [5]493
Servius, Maurus Honoratus (fl end 4th century) [3]892–3, 893n
sesame [3]877
Sestius *see* Sextius
set-down [1]528
Seth (Bible) [1]453, [2]280, 1185, [3]285, [5]594, 594n, [6]5n
 children of [1]421, 421n, [5]645, [6]219; descendants of [6]5
Sethians [2]717, [4]257
Sethites [6]5
setting [1]446
seven [3]1053, [4]37, 37n
Seven Champions [3]103, 103n
Seven Dials *see* London
Seven Years' War [3]628n, 639n
Seventy, the ("70") [1]309, 309n, 444, 444n, [2]722, 722n, [3]734, [4]472, 474, 474n, [5]128, 567
Severn (river) [2]820, 820n, [3]165

Severus, Lucius Septimius (146–211) [1]188
Seville [1]281n, 500, 840, 844n
Sewall, Frank (1837–1915) *see* Kant *Dreams* ed Sewall, tr Goerwitz; Swedenborg *Worship and Love of God* tr Stroh and Sewall
Seward, Thomas (1708–90) [1]373, 374, 375, 375n, 376, 381, 382, 385, 386, 387, 391, 394, 395, 396, 399, 406, 407n
sex [2]1092
sex(es) [1]654, 767, [2]1113, [3]329, 1034
 sexual appetite [3]401, 808; sexual desire [3]265; determination of [2]857; sexual drive [2]1113; equality of [2]6n; generalities of [1]394; German word [3]1047; opposite [3]1002–3; sexual opposites [1]623; sexual passion [2]190–1; relations between [3]906n; transexion of hares [1]779
sexmillennium [6]207
Sextius Niger (1st century BC) [1]778 ("Sestius")
Sextus *see also* Tarquinius Sextus
Sextus Empiricus (c 200–50) [1]781, 781n, [5]704, 741–2, 742, 742n, 747, 747n, 753, 753n, 812, 812n
 Hypotyposeis Pyrrhoneioi [5]704–5 q, tr Bury as *Outlines of Pyrrhonism* [5]705
Sextus of Chaeroneia (fl 120–33) [1]160n
Sextus/Sixtus Senensis (1520–69) *Bibliotheca Sancta* [1]493n
Seymour, Edward, 1st Duke of Somerset (c 1506–1552) [3]795
Shabbethai Ben Meir Hakohen, Rabbi (1621–62) [3]1093 ("Shabtai")
Shabtai *see* Shabbethai
shade and light [4]167
shadow(s) [1]135, 565, 646, [2]882, 1193, [3]119, 119–20, 121, 405, 525, 581, 705, 740, 769, 1018, 1087, [4]396, 505, [5]29, 32, 249, 546, 591, 638
 contains a god [1]558n; s.-fight [5]161; ghost and [2]166; of imagination [4]790; and light [5]452, 452n; Peter's [5]859, 859n; and substance [1]632, [6]307
shadowyness [1]561
Shadrach (Bible) [2]570, 570n, [4]50n
Shadwell, Thomas (c 1642–92) *Dramatick Works* [1]clxix
Shaftesbury, Earl of *see* Cooper, Anthony Ashley
Shafton, Sir Piercie (in Scott) [4]80, 80n, 597n
Shakespeare, William (1564–1616) [1]lxvii, xcii, xciv, cxxvi, cxxxi, cxxxviiin, cxl, cxln–cxlin, clii, clv, clxiv, 57n, 365, 366n, 375, 559, 615n, 728, [2]14, 17n, 83, 158, 761, 816, 816n, 1004, 1119, 1119n, [3]133, 403, 408, 757, 883, 884, 886, [4]162, 192, 192n, 585, [5]327, 493n, [6]205, 251, 323n
an actor [2]776; age of [3]172; anachronism in [3]174; in Anderson [1]37; anti-Shakespeareanism [1]369; aristocrat in politics [1]380, 389; attack on in *Eclectic Review* [2]359; attributed plays [3]702; and B&F [1]381, 390, 393, 397, 400–1, 405, 406, 407, 407n, [2]778, [4]715, 715n, 719, 798; blank verse of [1]217; blend of philosophic and poetic genius [3]918; censured by Milton [1]72; characteristic features of [4]783; chronology [4]828n; C's sigla for S's sonnets [1]82–7; comedies never transprosed [1]402; comedies of [2]82n, [3]894; comic characters of [3]182; and contemporaries [1]362, 401, [3]171, 171n, 179, 179n, 187, and S. Daniel [2]120; and Defoe [2]160; and Donne [2]218, 317; dramatic poems of [3]894; excellence of [4]827; an exception [1]401; family friend [4]862; female characters of [3]171; and T. Fuller [2]804, 808; fuses comic and tragic [1]366, 367; Gray's imitation of [5]117n; and Greek [1]73n; grossness of [1]394, [3]171, 171n; histories of [2]387; history plays [4]712; all ideal [1]401; imagination and fancy in [2]418; imitation of [1]367; incomparable [4]736; on "ingenuous" [1]258n; not irregular [2]1119, 1119n; and Jonson [2]778n, [3]176n, 182–3, 186–7, 187n; Jonson's epitaph to [1]62; kings of [6]114n; letters in [4]239; in *LR* [1]cxl; his loveliest character [4]702; *lusus naturae* [1]180n; and Massinger [2]778n; metres of [4]687; and Milton [2]218; myriad-minded [4]697n; on new words [3]177, 177n; opulence of [1]378; outweighs Newton [3]342, 342n; plots of [1]378; predecessors of [2]781; prose S. [2]75, 75n; pure diction of [1]25n; purity of [1]43n; and Racine [2]123, 123n; and W. Scott [3]484–5, [4]589, 591–2, 591n, 609; and "sightless" [5]856, 856n; and Sophocles [1]72, 72n; sublime moral in [6]264; and Jeremy Taylor [5]615; thefts from [1]370; discussed with Tieck [1]xcviii; titles of plays [4]689, 689n; tone of [2]773; and tragicomedy [1]72; uniqueness of [1]389; never unworthy [2]222; Venetian [1]506n; versification of [1]374, [5]689; wisdom for all

Shakespeare, William—*continued*
ages [1]398; wit in [1]67n, [2]774; S's women [1]397

All's Well MT [4]700–2, 755–6, 784–5, ed G. K. Hunter [4]684; *Antony and Cleopatra* [1]373, [3]897, 897n; MT [4]736–9, 760; 761–2; MT 767–8; 806, 806n; MT 807–8, ed M. R. Ridley [4]684; Arden Edition [4]684–868 *passim*; *As You Like It* [1]400, [2]778n, 889n, [3]406, 899; MT [4]696–700; 748–53; MT 783–4; 817, 817n, 850n, ed Latham [4]684; *Comedy of Errors* [4]600; *Coriolanus* [3]395 q, 395n q; MT [4]730–2; 747, 747n q; MT 760, 766–7, 803–4; 809, ed Brockbank [4]684; *Cymbeline* [4]193 q, 193n, 712; MT 739–41, 761–2; 809; MT 812–14, ed Nosworthy [4]684; *Dramatic Works Copy C* ed Rann (1786–[94]) [1]clin, clii, cliii, cliiin, [2]160n, [4]684; MT 764–77; *Dramatic Works Copy D* ed Ayscough (1807) [1]lxx, clii, [4]684; MT 778–868; *Hamlet* [1]749n q, [2]656 q, 656n, 776 q, 776n, [3]150n q, 248n q, 405, 406, 1077 q, 1077n, [4]543 q, 543n, 627 q, 627n q, 690 q, 690n q, 712, 736; MT 742–5, 762–3; 786, 787; MT 836–59; [5]588 q, 588n q, 611n q, 781 q, 781n, ed Jenkins [4]684; *1 Henry IV* [1]593 q, 593n q, [2]570n, 774, 922, 922n, [3]187, 187n q, [4]55n, 186, 186n q, 589n, 712; MT 713, 758, 802, ed A. R. Humphreys [4]684; *2 Henry IV* [2]774, [3]177n, 663 q, 663n, [4]239n q, 305–6 q, 306n, 589n, 712; MT 713–15, 759, 803; [5]309n, [6]288n q, ed A. R. Humphreys [4]684; *Henry V* [2]774, [4]589n; MT 715–17, 803, ed Walter [4]684; *Henry VI* [4]795; *1 Henry VI* MT [4]759; *Henry VIII* [4]797; *Julius Caesar* [2]522, 522n, 950n; MT [4]732–6; 804; MT 805–7; 809; *King John* [1]366, 366n–7n q, 375; MT [4]710–12, 756–7; 797, ed Honigmann [4]684; *King Lear* [2]217n q, 567n q, [3]184, 188 q, 188n, 192, 405, 406, [4]11 q, 12n q, 168, 712; MT 717–20; 732n, 736, 747; MT 768–9; 809; MT 814–25, ed Muir [4]684; *Love's Labour's Lost* [2]585n, [3]895n q, [4]509n, 609n; MT 696; 759; MT 782–3; 783n, [5]595n q, ed R. David [4]684; *Macbeth* [1]57, 57n, [2]160, 160n [3]188 q, 188n, 406, [4]77, 77n, 708, 712, 721n; MT 726–9; 732n, 736; MT 769–76, 786–94; 796, 837–8, 864n, [5]856n q, [6]206n q, ed Muir [4]684; *Measure for Measure* [1]390n, [2]870n, [3]171, 171n; MT [4]693–5, ed Lever [4]684; *Merchant of Venice* [4]718, 718n; MT 765–6; 815n, ed J. R. Brown [4]684; *Merry Wives of Windsor* [2]89n q, 118n q, 778, 778n, [4]77n, 589n; MT 691–3, 754–5, 781–2, ed H. J. Oliver [4]684; *Midsummer Night's Dream* [1]57, 57n, [2]508, 508n q, 558n, 782, 887n, [4]72, 77n; MT 688–91, 755, 783, ed H. F. Brooks [4]684; *Othello* [1]50, 50n, 739, [2]223 q, 223n, [3]177n, 184, [4]72n, 77, 77n, 168, 284n q, 736; MT 746–8, 777; 850n; MT 860–8; [5]596 q, 596n, ed M. R. Ridley [4]684–5; *Pericles* [3]893 q, [4]809, 869; *Plays* (1778) [3]897n; *Plays* ed I. Reed (1803) [4]684–868 *passim*; *Plays† Copy E* ed I. Reed (1809) [4]869; *Plays† Copy F* ed Steevens (1811) [4]870; *Richard II* [1]400, [2]396n, 397, 823, 823n, [3]155n, [4]583 q; MT 712–13, 794–802; *Richard III* [1]398, 402n, [3]119n q; MT [4]759–60; *Riverside Shakespeare* [4]684; *Romeo and Juliet* [4]77n, 335n, 731n; MT 742; 759; 826–36; 842 q, 842n q, 859n, [5]99q, 99n q, ed Gibbons [4]685; *Sonnet 20* [1]43, 43n q; *Sonnet 27* [5]856n q; *Sonnet 33* [2]120 q, 120n q; *Sonnet 43* [5]856n q; *Sonnet 107* [4]477 q, 477n; *Sonnet 116* [1]41; *Sonnets* [1]40–1; MT [1]41–3, 80–1; *81n*; MT 82–7; [2]222, [4]466–7, 467n; *Stockdale's Edition Copy B* [1]clii, 39, [4]684; MT 754–63; 808n; *Taming of the Shrew* [4]77; MT 700, ed Morris [4]685; *Tempest* [1]cxln, 57, 57n, [3]182n, 187, [4]611n; MT 687–8, 764–5, 779–81; 795 q, 795n, [5]130n q, ed Kermode [4]685; *Timon of Athens* MT [4]720–3; 760n; MT 761; 809, ed H. J. Oliver [4]685; *Titus Andronicus* [3]702; MT [4]724–5; 795, 809, 848, 848n, ed J. C. Maxwell [4]685; *Troilus and Cressida* [3]177n; MT [4]741, 808–12; [6]334, ed Palmer [4]685; *Twelfth Night* [1]400, [2]464n, 778n, 888n, 1006n, [4]77n; MT 702–6, 756, 785–6; 812 q, 812n q, ed Lothian and Craik [4]685; *Two Gentlemen of Verona* [1]374, [2]464n, [4]695; *Venus and Adonis* [4]782, 782n; *Winter's Tale* [3]187; MT [4]706–10, 786, ed Pafford [4]685; *Works Copy A* ed Theobald (1773) [1]cxxii, clii, 53, [4]684; MT 686–753; 755n

"shall" and "ought" [3]749

Shallow (*2 Henry IV*) [4]589, 589n, 692, 692n, 715n, 755

shame [1]137, 394, [3]494, 521–2, [4]639, 816, 817, 818
of cross [6]304; false [5]415

Shand, William (fl 1830) [1]33, 33n, [2]907

Shandy, Walter (in Sterne) [4]719, 719n
shape(s) [1]152, 152n, 682, [2]1115, [3]44, 45, [5]704, [6]299
distinguishable [5]265; and form *see* form; or image [5]409; of man [5]475; principle of [5]230
shapelessness [5]266
Shapir II, King of Persia (309–79) [2]739–40 ("Sapor"), 740n
sharp(s) [1]739
Sharp, Granville (1735–1813) [1]455n, [6]177
Remarks on the Uses of the Definite Article [1]467n, [3]11n, [6]26n
Sharp, R. L. [2]17n
Sharpe, James, Archbishop of St Andrews (1613–79) [3]539, 539n
sharper [1]699
sharpness [1]583, [4]131
Sharrock, Roger *see* Bunyan *Pilgrim's Progress* ed Sharrock
Shaster [2]1123
shavelings [1]329, 473
Shaver, Alice C. *see* Shaver, Chester Linn
Shaver, Chester Linn (1907–80) [1]cxiin
and Alice C. Shaver *Wordsworth's Library: A Catalogue* [1]cxii, cxiin, clvi, clxix, clxx, 9, 42n, 217, 476, 535, 801, 854, 867, [2]4, 11, 102, 117, 474n, 482n, 521, 577n, 647, 824n, 973n, 976, 1032, 1117, 1119n, 1164n, 1203, [3]178n, 400, 499, 503, 723n, 781, [5]377; *see also* WW *Letters . . . the Early Years* ed de Selincourt, rev Shaver
Shaw, Cuthbert (c 1738–71) [1]38
Shaw, George (1751–1813) [4]312
Shaw, Peter (1694–1763) *see* Boerhaave *New Method* tr Shaw and Chambers
Shaw, Thomas (1694–1751) *Travels . . . to Several Parts of Barbary and the Levant* [4]53, 53n
Shawcross, John (1871–1966) [1]82n, [2]1064; *see also* Coleridge, S. T. III *BL* (1907) ed Shawcross
Shearer, Edna Aston (fl 1901) [3]400
Sheba, Queen of (legend) [3]710
Shechinah see *Shekinah*
shed [5]89
Shedd, William Greenough Thayer (1820–94) [1]cxxxiii, [2]169, [3]93; *see also* Coleridge, S. T. IX *Collected Works* ed Shedd
Shee, Sir Martin Archer (1769–1850) [2]235, 235n ("William")
sheen [3]898
Sheen [2]823, 823n
sheep [1]259, 259n, 339, [2]603, [3]571, 828, 828n, [5]101, 538
bleating [2]67; of Christ [1]848; and goats [4]662n–3n; with the rot [1]571
sheepdogs [3]21
Sheffield, John, 3rd Earl of Mulgrave, 1st Duke of Buckingham and Normanby (1648–1721) [1]38, [4]779n
sheik [3]21
Shekinah ("Schechinah") [2]465, 465n, 486, 486n, [3]978, 978n, [5]535
Sheldon, Gilbert, Archbishop of Canterbury (1598–1677) [1]249, 249n–50n, 255, 255n, 270, 275, 275n, 323, 323n, 352, 803, 803n, 808, [3]156n, 878, [5]544, 544n, [6]261, 263
shell(s) [3]944, 945, 945n, [4]148n, 525, 741, [6]148
shell-fish [2]346, [4]694, [5]257
Shelvocke, George (fl 1690–1728) *Voyages* [1]clxix
Shem (Bible) [1]539, 541n, 686, [2]177, 177n, 384–5, 385n, [4]243n, 257, 583n, [5]336–7, 337n, 352, [6]5n
descendants of [4]243, 243n
Shenstone, William (1714–63) [1]38, 329n
The Schoolmistress [4]605 q, 605n q
Sheol/Scheol [1]431, [2]1074n, [6]63
shepherd(s) [3]30, [4]53, 476, [5]589, 634, [6]325n
Shepherd (in Skelton) [5]76n, 77
Shepherd, Richard Herne (1842–95) [2]97
Sheppard, F. (fl 1745) [2]32
Sherbo, Arthur *see* S. Johnson *Johnson on Shakespeare*, *Works* ed Sherbo
Sheridan, Richard Brinsley (1751–1816) [1]92, 92n, 716, [2]17, 75
The Critic [3]391n q; *The Duenna* [2]1103n; *Pizarro* [4]28n, 598n
Sherive, Christopher Hardy (d 1800) [1]89, 90, 90n
Sherlock, Thomas, Bishop of London (1678–1761) [5]3
Sherlock, William, Dean of St Paul's (?1641–1707) [1]409, 565, [2]265, 265n, 571, 748n, [3]164, [4]247, [5]27
Practical Discourse concerning Death [4]247n; *Practical Discourse concerning a Future Judgment* [4]247n; *Present State of the Socinian Controversy* [2]265n; *A Vindication of the . . . Trinity* [1]566n, [2]265n, 571n; MT [5]3–35
shew-bread [5]374
shield [3]156, [4]673, [5]522, 576
gold and silver [4]246–7, 247n

shift [5]504
shilling(s) [5]435, 554
Shilo (Bible) [4]44, 44n
Shimei (Bible) [3]768
shin [1]571, 571n
shine [3]746, 898
shiningness [1]606
ship(s) [1]846, [2]580, [3]720, [4]170, 550, [5]32, 387
 crews of [6]214; Dutch [2]579
shipwreck [5]36
Shirley, James (1596–1666) [1]365, 373
Shirley, Walter (1725–86) [2]964
Shirley, William (fl 1739–80) *King Pepin's Campaign* [5]104n
shoal [5]366
shoe(s) [2]1203, [3]471, 472n, [5]91, 91n, 833
 rose of [3]899
shoemaker(s) [1]565, 621, [2]754, 755, [3]930n, [5]90
shop(s) [2]999
 cheap [5]686
shopkeepers [2]90, [4]719
short-hand [5]49
shoterim [3]109n
shower(s) [3]1073
Showerman, Grant (1870–1935) *see* Ovid *Heroides* tr Showerman
Shrewsbury [1]519n, [4]107
shrine [1]872, [4]42
 cloudy [1]431
shuffler [2]50
shuffling [2]39, 39n
Shute, Thomas (fl 1810) [3]939
shuttle-cock [3]167, [5]134
Shylock (*Merchant of Venice*) [1]276, [4]815, [6]264
Sibari (in Metastasio) [6]323, 323n
sibbens/sivvens [2]363, 363n, 364n
Sibbs/Sibbes, Richard (1577–1635) [6]258
Siberia [2]528
Sibthorp, Robert (d 1662) [2]1101
Sibyl(s) [2]410, 411n, [3]901, [5]84, [6]5n
 Cumaean [6]164–5; oracles of [6]5
siccine [2]239n
Sichaeus (in Virgil) [6]210, 215
Sicily [1]800, 845, [2]93, 372, 417, 545n, 570n, 978n, 1092, [3]129, 294n, 383, 786n, 802n, [4]86, 235, 235n, 246n, 299, 338, [5]277, 277n, 359, 834, 846n, [6]13, 199
 C in [5]80; ladies in [3]171; Mount Etna *see* Etna
sick [4]644, [5]586, 586n
"Sick, Communion of" see *BCP*
sickbeds [5]510
sickness [2]829, 1166, [3]312, 746, 776, [4]609, [5]120, 652
 bodily [5]654; spiritual [4]260
Siddons, Sarah (née Kemble) (1755–1831) [4]632, 721n
Sidmouth, Viscount *see* Addington, Henry
Sidney/Sydney, Algernon (1622–83) [3]882, 882n, [5]38–9, 86, 86n
 Works ed J. Robertson [1]clin, [2]966; MT [5]36–45
Sidney, Sir Philip (1554–86) [2]116, 119n, 837, 873, 976, 976n, [3]221, 250, 251n, 884, 888, [4]239
 Arcadia [1]lxxxviii–lxxxix, cviii, cxxi, 60n, [2]117, 119n, 971n, tr Hirschberg MT [5]46–7
Sidonia [2]660n
Siegen, Ludwig von (1609–c 1680) [2]1196n
Sierra Leone [4]88, [5]102 ("Serra Leoa")
siesta [3]105
"Siesti" (STC) [2]1120n
sieve
 Mogul s. of duty [1]cxix
sigh [4]745
sight(s) [2]403, 604, [3]23, 42, 128, 390, 552, 716, [4]272, 298, 405–6, 601, [5]236, 297, 406, 766
 feeling in [6]131; gift of [2]612, [5]415; hard to see [3]194; objective [3]989; objects of [5]713; Platonic theory of [3]389; restoration to [2]492; second [3]653n–4n, [4]83, 83n, 592, 592n; symbolical [5]474; touch substitutes for [3]389
"sightless" [5]856
sigillative [2]552
sigla for Shakespeare's sonnets [1]82–7
sign(s) [1]561, [2]270, [3]5–6, 6n, 757n, 791, 1026
 arbitrary [1]631; Baptism as [5]650; of body [3]14; C's *see* Coleridge, S. T. I (1) signs; ceremonial [3]757; of Christ's mission [5]62, 63; of independence [4]23; intelligible [1]538; manual [5]537; of Messiah [2]483; Messianic [2]462; and miracle [2]653; outward [4]625; of redemption [2]1166; required by Jews [3]988; sacramental [3]477; significant [6]109; and signified [3]848; and symbol [5]550; visible [2]301; worship of [3]108
signature [3]45
 in Böhme [1]689
"significant" [6]109
signum sub rei nomine [5]5
Sigonio, Carlo (c 1524–84) *De consolatione* [2]36n
Silas (Bible) [5]514n

silence [3]522, 577, [4]838, [6]304
injunction of [2]1173
Silenus (myth) [3]530n
Silesians [5]279
silex [3]1031n, [5]256, 257n, 840
silica [3]997, [5]256, 257
silicon [3]1022
silk [5]577
shot [1]762, 796
silkworm(s) [1]750, [6]138
silloi [2]759, 759n
Siloam [6]108
silver [1]351, 546, 603, [3]286, [5]262, 276, 542
mines [3]1062; nitrate [3]129n; turned red [5]837
Silver Drops, or Serious Things see Blake, William (d 1694)
Simeon (Bible) [1]418, 418n, [2]279, 280
Simeon, St (legend) [2]740
Simeon Ben Jochai (2nd century) [5]807
simile(s) [1]345n, 685, 822, [3]455, 455n, 773, [4]114, 277, 278n, 443, 788, [5]269
defective [2]1142; forgiving [1]602; imperfect [2]933; indeterminate [5]504; inverted [6]203; limps [6]19; misapplied [6]328; no s. quadrates [2]552, 552n; none squares [2]17; in poetry [4]162; of tree [1]426; out-of-the-way [1]673; unhappy [4]505; unlucky [5]671
similitude(s) [1]566, 654, 685, [3]914
laws of [5]410; of the Messiah [3]668n; unfair [1]657
Simmias (3rd century BC) [4]147
Simmons/Simons, Samuel (fl 1660–75) [1]69
Simon (Bible) [1]481–2
Simon Stylites, St (c 390–459) [5]99, 99n
Simon Barjona *see* Peter, St
Simon, Sir John (1818–97) *see* J. H. Green *Spiritual Philosophy* ed Simon
Simon Maccabeus (c 200–136 BC) [6]142n
Simon Magus ("Simon the Magician") (1st century) [2]256, 706, 923, [3]922, 922n
Simon of Cyrene (Bible) [2]923
Simon Peter *see* Peter, St
Simon, Richard (1638–1712) [1]417n
Simonides of Amorgos (fl c 660 BC) [4]147
Simonides of Ceos (c 556–468 BC) [5]12, 12n
Simphorosa *see* Symphorosa
Simple (*Merry Wives of Windsor*) [4]589, 589n
simple-heartedness [1]619
simplex et nuda [2]295–6, 296n
simplicity [4]498, [5]65, 133, 820
comparative [5]452; holy [4]710n; sublime [5]248
Simplicius of Cilicia (fl 530) [5]708n, 711n, 733–4 q
Simpson, Evelyn Mary (née Spearing) (1885–1963) *see* Donne, John *Sermons* ed Potter and Simpson; Jonson *Ben Jonson* ed Herford, Simpson, and Simpson
Simpson, John (fl 1811) [3]942
Simpson, Mrs [3]810
Simpson, Mrs Patrick (fl 1618) [2]1172
Simpson, Patrick (d 1618) [2]1172–3
Simpson, Percy (1865–1962) *see* Jonson *Ben Jonson* ed Herford, Simpson and Simpson
Simpson, Thomas (1710–61) *A New Treatise on Fluxions* [1]153n
Simson, Robert (1687–1768) *see* Euclid *Elements* ed Simson
simultaneity [4]313
"simultenise" [4]314, 314n
"sin" [2]247, [5]175, 590–1
sin(s) [1]469, 470, 714, 769, [2]251, 318–19, 934, 1096, 1176–9, [3]14, 306–7, 590, 735, 746–7, 751, [4]9, 64, 133n, 503, 580, 645, 652, 816, [5]179, 497, 584, 613, 820
abhorrence of [4]634; abortion of [3]735; absolute evil [2]326; actual [5]648; author of [5]616; after Baptism [1]470; based in will [1]824; beginners in [3]510; being of [5]176; born in [5]648; of childhood [1]285; Christ without [3]305; Christ's death through [1]702; confession of [1]714; conquered [5]670; consequences of [2]560, [5]559; contagion of [1]507; and death [2]802; death of [3]743; debtor and creditor account of [3]26, 26n; defined [1]303; deliverance from [5]172; discovery of [1]819; disease [2]591, 591n; disease in will [1]201; dread of [1]827; evil will [2]563; forgiveness of [2]208, 657, [5]654; forsaking of [4]43–4, 44n; and guilt [3]18, [5]616; gulf of [5]601; habitual [5]584–5, 585n, 587–8; hatred of [2]26, 27, 1178, [4]133, [5]494, 589; hereditary [3]596, 596n, [5]614; against Holy Ghost [1]872, [6]168; and imagination [2]160; s. *in* and s. *of* man [3]18; and inconvenience [1]352; kinds of [3]579; literary [4]611; mortal [5]819, 821; most devilish form of [6]304; negative [4]234; oath may be a [1]342; offering [1]200; original *see* original sin; of Platonism [3]915; precipitation of [4]596; by proxy [3]28; punishment of [3]25–6; remission of [1]847, [2]497, [3]733–4, 734n, [5]608, 622, 629; secret [6]310; self-origination of [6]217; sense of [3]750–1; sinfulness of [2]1176; and sinner(s) [4]133, [5]610; small [5]496; unique

sin(s)—*continued*
[1]873; universal [5]594; venial and mortal [2]668–9; wilful [5]583; within us [1]819; of world [2]489–90
Sinai, Mount [1]421, 833, [2]144, 396, 465n, 901, [3]49, 53, 595, [4]47, [5]187, 858, [4]651n; *see also* anti-Sinai
"sincere" [6]289, 289n
sincerity [1]619, [5]172
Sinclair, Sir John (1754–1835) *Code of Health and Longevity* [4]201n
Sinclair, John D. *see* Dante *Divine Comedy* tr Sinclair
sinecure(s) [2]80–1, 80n
sinfulness, ground of all [5]784
Singer, George John (1786–1817) [3]938
singing [2]862
single-mindedness [1]808, [5]501, 516
singular and plural [5]340
singularity [4]454
sink-a-pace [4]756, 785
sinlessness [4]655
sinner(s) [3]513, 579, [4]621, 639, 657, [5]132, 163n, 179, 188, 420, 585, 678, 684
conscious [3]512; evil imagination of [2]160; humble [5]685; mortal [5]395; penitent [2]787; punishment of [3]671; and sin *see* sin; will of [5]599
"sinneth" [1]470
Sion *see* Zion
Sion College Library *see* London
Siph [2]584
siphon [1]659
Sirius (planet) [2]920n, [3]1015, [4]516, [5]610
Sirmium, Council of [2]334n, 732n, 743, 744
sirname/surname [5]63
Sirven, Pierre Paul (1709–77) [6]32
Sisam, Celia see *Oxford Book of Medieval English Verse* ed Sisam and Sisam
Sisam, Kenneth see *Oxford Book of Medieval English Verse* ed Sisam and Sisam
Sisanto Thermia [5]837
Sisera [1]822, 822n, [2]917
sister(s) [3]666, [4]597, [5]821
deceased wife's [5]393
"sit" [1]402
Sita (myth) [2]346, 346n
sitience [3]1024
sitting [2]1186
Siva (myth) [3]59n
six [4]37, 37n
six hundred and sixty-six ("666") [1]482n, 485–6, 486n, [3]929
Sixtus IV (Francesco della Rovere), Pope (1414–84) [1]281n
Skeat, Walter William (1835–1912) [2]759n
Skeffington, Sir Lumley (1771–1850) [4]607, 607n
skeleton(s) [1]783, [3]123, 211, 259, [5]133
of mammoth [1]61, [3]452; of wood [1]682
Skelton, John (c 1460–1529) [2]759
Colyn Cloute [2]759n; *Phyllyp Sparrow* [2]760n, [4]710–11, 711n; *Speke Parrot* [2]759n; *Why Come Ye Nat to Court?* [2]759n
Skelton, Philip (1707–87) [2]142, 152
"Life" by Burdy [5]48; MT 49; his ruling passion [5]70
Complete Works ed Lynam [2]152n, 1154; MT [5]48–77; 523n q
Skenderia [5]842
skene [3]28
Skepper, A. B. (fl 1806) [4]289
skia [1]431n
Skiddaw [1]cx, [2]691, 691n, [3]183, 183n, [5]371, [6]249, 249n
skillet [2]496
skimming [2]190
skin(s) [1]228, [4]149, [6]120
of Christianity [1]814, 815n; fair [2]85; four [2]409, 409n; secretion from [6]104
skindapsos [3]504, 505n
Skinner, Stephen (1623–67) *Etymologicon linguae anglicanae* [3]1067n, [6]149n
skip-jacks [2]217
skirmishing [5]70
Skopas *see* Scopas
Skrimshire, William, Jr (fl 1810) [3]936
skull [1]626, 764, [3]716, [5]825; *see also* scull-pan
skunk [3]586, 586n
sky-lark [1]483
sky-scrapers [3]66, 66n
slander(s) [2]664, 716, 743, 977, 978, [3]418, 586, [4]623, 671, [5]161
slanderer(s) [2]692, [3]66, [4]643, [5]422, 625, [6]101
slang [1]155, 156–7, 182, [3]534, 534n, 541, 680, [4]160, [5]70n, 111, 386n, 478n, [6]316, 316n
s.-fineries [5]861; technical [5]96
slaughter [1]157
s.-house [3]383, [4]481
slave(s) [1]245, [2]512, 659, 801, 899, [4]811, 861, [5]117, [6]35
s.-girl [1]5; among Greeks [5]323; of lamp [5]167, 167n; Methodist [5]187; penitent

[1]200; Roman [1]874; Russian [1]224; sentiment of [5]829; soul of [5]278; s.-trade [1]738, [2]387, 387n, 1017, [3]883n, [4]8, 96, 96n, 342n, [5]678; triumphant [2]908; of will [2]168
slavery [1]31–6, [2]907–9, 1017, 1113, [4]215, 264, [5]208, [6]28–9
abolition of [1]90n, [4]8; C's argument against [1]424n; of Jews in Egypt [3]658; of mind to eye [3]138, 138n; redemption from [1]200; well-regulated [6]36
slavishness [3]734
Slav(s) [1]540 ("Sclavic")
Slavonic (language) [5]239
sleep [2]410, 569, 624, 1007, [4]223, 781, [5]169, 725–6, 790
of animal magnetism [3]371; charmed [2]515; curative power of [3]374; dead s. [3]614, 614n; and death [2]1008–9; definition of [4]542–3; flying in [5]771; images in [5]122; magnetic [2]859; morbid [5]517; nature of [6]102; phantasms of [1]764, 797 ("phantoms"); proper [4]543–4; prophetic [4]503; state of [4]60; talking in [1]205, [5]366
sleeping [3]770
Slender (*Merry Wives of Windsor*) [4]589n ("Slander")
sling [5]204, 682
Slipslop, Mrs (in Fielding) [3]370, 370n
slit [2]557
Slop, Dr (in Sterne) [4]785, 785n
sloth [4]75
slough, popish [1]879
slowness [2]835
slumber [3]212, 217
slyness [2]840
smallclothes [4]190, 190n
smallpox [3]634, [4]149
Smart, Christopher (1722–71) [1]38
Smeathman, Henry (d 1786) "Of the Termites in Africa and Other Hot Climates" [4]88n
Smectymnuus [1]332n
Smedley, Edward (1788–1836) *Religio Clerici* [6]335
smell [1]578, 657, [3]383, 913, 1036, 1075, [4]273, [5]265, [6]235
language of [1]111; sense of [4]530, [5]292, 293; sickly [1]736
Smellie, William (1740–95) *see* Buffon *Natural History* ed Smellie
smelling [1]578
smile [2]37
malignant [3]225; would-be [4]360
smilings [3]525, 525n, [6]307, 307n
Smith, Adam (1723–90) [1]258n, [5]93, 93n
Smith, Aubrey *see* Seneca *De Beneficiis* tr Smith
Smith, Charles (1798–1891) *Seven Letters on National Religion* MT [5]78–9
Smith, David Nichol (1875–1962) *see* Swift *Tale of a Tub* ed Guthkelch and Smith
Smith, E. (fl 1814) [2]668n
Smith, Edmund (1672–1710) [1]37
Smith, Felix (fl 1776) [5]222
Smith, Harry Bache (1860–1936) [1]clxxiii
Smith, Herbert Weir *see* Aeschylus *Prometheus vinctus* tr Smith
Smith, James (1775–1839), and Horace Smith (1779–1849) *Rejected Addresses* [2]211n, [4]658n
Smith, Sir James Edward (1759–1828) [3]937
Smith, John (1618–52) [1]580n, [5]80, 84, 85
Select Discourses [1]cxl, 587n, 598n, 794n q; MT [5]80–6
Smith, John (fl 1821) [4]71
"Smith, John" *see* Wilson, John
Smith, John Raphael (1750–1812) [2]180
Smith, Joshua Toulmin (1816–69) [5]199
Smith, Logan Pearsall (1865–1946) *The Life and Letters of Sir Henry Wotton* [1]843n
Smith, M. F. *see* Lucretius *De rerum natura* tr Rouse, rev Smith
Smith, Norman Kemp *see* Kemp Smith, Norman
Smith, Philip (?1634–84) [3]821
Smith, Sydney (1771–1845) [2]914n, [4]627n, 630n
Smith, Sir Thomas (1513–77) [2]66, 68n
Smithfield *see* London
Smithson, James Louis Macie (1765–1829) [3]942
"smoke" [2]1124, 1124n
smoke [1]558, 737, [3]125, 946, [4]530
beacon of [3]539; columns of [1]621
Smollett, Tobias George (1721–71) [1]38, [1]75n
The Adventures of Ferdinand Count Fathom [3]180, 180n; *Roderick Random* [4]594n
"smooth" [3]952
smoothness [2]238
Smyrna [2]719n, [3]422n, [6]168n
Smyser, Jane Worthington *see* WW *Prose Works* ed Owen and Smyser
snail(s) [4]525, [5]360

snake(s) [3]769, 1044, [4]86–7, 430–1, 494–5, 501, 502, [5]614, 614n
s.-charmers [2]348; in hen's egg [1]436
sneer(s) [2]846, [3]223, 225, 226, [4]287–8, [5]161
coarse [5]565; of Hume [5]729; Miltonic [5]524; worthless [1]148
sneering [2]408
sneeringness [2]59
snore(s) [1]684
parenthetic [2]516
snort [1]332
Snout (*Midsummer Night's Dream*) [2]558n
snow [2]834, [5]340
red [3]989, 989n; s.-shoes [2]190
snow-drop [5]118
snowflake [2]472
"snuff" (verb) [2]832
snuff [3]355, [4]610
s.-box [5]712; s.-shops [6]212
snuffle [1]332
Snyder, Alice Dorothea (1887–1950) [1]555, [3]886
"American Comments on Coleridge a Century Ago" [1]cxxxiiin; "On Reading Coleridge" [1]cxxxiiin; *see also* Coleridge, S. T. IX *Coleridge on Logic and Learning* ed Snyder
Soame, John (d 1738) *Hampstead-Wells see* "Medical Treatises"
soap-film [2]1010
soaring [1]558
Soave, Francesco (1743–1806) *see* Virgil *Georgica . . . hexaglotta* tr Soave
sobriety/sobrieties [5]171
heartless [1]621; Pauline [6]311
society/societies [2]1148, 1206, 1206n, [3]808, 846, [4]241, [5]36–7
best [4]708; capabilities of [2]97; encroachments of [3]137; final cause of [5]37; fundamentals of [1]395; gradations of rank in [2]319; harmony of [1]877; learned [1]213; lower orders of [3]401; members of [4]22; new [5]38; order in [1]321; particular [1]355; peace of [2]530; professions essential to [5]381; religious [2]352; scientific [5]638; spiritual [5]418; state(s) of [6]28, 216; usages of [4]731
Society for Diffusing Information *see* London
Socini *see* Socinus, and Sozini, Lelio
Socinian(s) [1]*198n*, 256, 297, 313, 316n, 507, 674, [2]498, 531, 742n, 798, 798n, 799n, 992, 992n–3n, 1055, 1055n, [3]308n, 367, 524, 653, 673, 684, 698, [4]297, 297n, 301, 302, 302n, 483, 639, 641, 649, 656, 656n, 662, 663, 667, 672, [5]3, 6, 6n, 8, 12, 30, 56, 135, 139, 385, 553, 569, 597n, 598, 617, 618, 677, 842, [6]71, 77n, 146, 306
anti-S. [2]923; argument against [1]441, [2]798–9; battle array of [6]140; Chillingworth as [2]34; Church S. [2]655; in C of E [1]343; gloss of [5]651; infra-S. scheme [2]485, [3]434, 434n; S. logic [2]800; on miracles [3]708; modern [2]22, [3]692; on resurrection [1]127; sceptical [3]672n; stronghold of [2]798; and understanding [2]296; and Unitarians [4]670n
Socinianism [1]244, 244n, 249n, 334n, 358, 359, 514, 644n, [2]31, 35, 652, 695n, 1088n, [3]77, 305, 308, 367, 709n, 785, [4]297, 302, 641, 642, 643n, 665, 669, [5]35, 465, 516n, 553, 585, 585n, 597, 614, 621, 657, [6]63, 71, 77, 78, 81
and Calvinism [2]797–803; confuted by Böhme [1]644; consistent [6]75; and doctrine of John [2]462–3; modern [5]563, 563n; and Newton [1]197n; a puny heresy [6]178; relation to Arianism and Unitarianism [2]265; spirit of [1]359, [5]516; stronghold of [4]637; tendency to [2]39; Ultra-S. [5]162
Socinus, Faustus (Fausto Paulo Sozzini) (1539–1604) [1]198n, 334, [2]35, [4]643, 643n, 668, 670, 670n, [5]6n, 139n, 465, 465n
Sockburn [1]lxxix, 227n
"Socrates" [5]742
Socrates (469–399 BC) [1]16, 168, 168n, 181, 410, [2]65, 143, 343, 349, 416, 569, 811–12 q, 866, 866n, 868n, 870, 871–2, 871n, 872n, 1069n, [3]76, 368, 569, 672, 1088n, [4]139, 267, 310n, [5]65n, 227n, 360n, 391n, 722–8, [6]9, 125, 176, 222–3
and Christ [2]872n, [5]12; daemon of [5]723n; soul of [1]181; as a stone [1]396
Socrates Scholasticus (c 380–450) [3]232, 232n, 692n
The Ecclesiastical History [3]762n
Socus (myth) [5]227
soda [1]570, 737, [3]951, [4]274, [5]255, 255n, 261
caustic [3]951n
sodium [3]481, 950, 951, 951n, [4]837n, [5]255n, 261
s. hydroxide [3]951n
Sodom [1]418, [4]176
Sodomites [2]717
sodyl [1]570

Soemmering, Samuel Thomas von (1755–1830) [6]104
softlings [5]103
Sografi, Antonio Simone (1760–1825) [4]169n
Sohar/Zohar [3]684, [4]246n, [5]807, [6]141, 141n
Soho (near Birmingham) [3]637
soil(s) [5]256, 309
Sol [2]583, 583n; *see also* Apollo
Solander, Daniel Charles (1736–82) [2]861n
solar microscope *see* microscope
solar plexus [3]387, [5]136
solar system [2]394, 556n, 557, [3]201, 341, [5]225, 266, 339, 430n
soldier(s) [1]157, 293, 396, [3]388, 645, [4]616, [5]378, 380
  Austrian [5]276; in B&F [1]378; English as [2]100; Neapolitan [5]276; profession of [5]381
soldiery [5]323
sole(s) (fish) [1]371, [3]132 ("soals")
Solebay [4]72
solecism [1]725, [3]899
Solemn League and Covenant [1]270n, [2]523, [4]307n, [5]147n, [6]258, 261
"Solemnisation of Matrimony" see *BCP*
Solger, Karl Wilhelm Ferdinand (1780–1819) [2]186, [5]87, 93n, 95 ("Solgar")
  Erwin [1]clxvi, 131, [2]1069n, [4]352n; *Philosophische Gespräche* MT [5]87–95
solid(s) [1]177, 550, [3]129–30, [6]227
  species of [5]451
solidification [4]517
solidity [1]579
  matter as [3]280, 282
Solifidian(s) [2]497n, [5]408, 408n
solifidianism [1]814, *814n*, [2]298, 298n, [6]120
soliloquy [4]854
solitary [1]496
solitude [1]754, [3]608
soll [3]749
Solomon (10th century BC) [1]418n, 422n, 428, 430, 433, 788n, [2]147, 147n, 148, 276, 341, 399, 460, 460n, 836, 894, 894n, 1153, 1156, [3]109n, 553, 573, 606, 617, 622, 624, 697–8, 710, 767, 768, [5]682, 811, [6]113, 114n, 143, 144
  genuine works of [6]142; saying of [5]605 q; Scotch (James I) [2]1134; second [6]140n; Temple of [2]395
Solon (c 640–c 558 BC) [1]705, 877, 877n, [2]89n, 870, 870n, [3]698, 698n, 738, [4]147, [5]224
solstice, summer [3]324
"solve" [5]61
solvent(s) [5]529
  universal [2]387
soma [1]163, 164n, [2]487, [6]88
  s. hypostatikon [1]863; *s. psychikon* and *s. pneumatikon* [1]175n
somation [1]164n
somatology [2]1002
somatosphere [3]371–2, 372n, 383n, 387, 387n, 392
Somers Tracts *see* Sir W. Scott ed *A Collection of Scarce and Valuable Tracts*
somersault [3]88n
Somerset, Duke of *see* Seymour, Edward
Somerset, Earl of *see* Carr/Ker, Robert
Somersetshire [2]691, [4]236
Somerville, John Southey, 15th Lord Somerville (1765–1819) [3]937
Somerville, William (1675–1742) [1]38
something [2]991
  and nothing [5]460
somewhatness [5]370
somnambules [4]514, [6]170
somnambulism [3]47, 209–10, 386, 391, [4]513–14
  somnambulistic gifts [4]518; magnetic [5]467; manual [1]808
somnambulist(s) [3]117, 209, 353, 353n, 387, 388, 389, 390, 396, 1039, [4]272, 272n, 536, [6]170n
"somniloquise" [5]296
"somniloquist" [1]808, 808n
somniloquists [5]391
Somnus (in Homer) [1]799
somosphere *see* somatosphere
son(s)
  rebellious [2]659; youngest [4]719
Son [1]466n–7n, 507, 561, [2]992, 993n, [3]11–14, 16, 18, 66, 77, 106, 151, 428, [4]258, 300, 400, [5]20, 33, 58, 235, 653
  articulation of the Word [3]61; begotten [5]118; eternally begotten [2]723, 729, 732; only-begotten [5]58; co-eternal [1]435, 629, 694, [5]56; co-eternity of [2]731; divinity of [2]752; Eternal [5]58; and Father [5]16, 18; in Father [5]20; of God [1]432, 436, 484, 484n, 568, [2]281, [4]49–50, 50n, 57, 57n, [5]26, 55, 483, 614, 627, 635, 657, 772, [6]32–3, 65, 139n; of God and Man [4]260; gospel of [3]427; judgment committed to [5]31–2; as Logos [1]573; of Man [1]436, 441, [3]434, 447–8, [4]65, 260, [5]55, 182, 372, 523, 607, 645; the "Person" of the Father [3]53; *pleroma* of [3]31; redeemer [3]26; subordi-

Son—*continued*
nation of [5]9–10; and sun [1]170, 170n, 200, 200n, 438n, 564, 564n, 612, 612n, 648, 648n, 812, [2]35, 206, 206n, 271, 271n, 729, 729n, 884, 884n, 885, [3]723, 723n, [4]842. *See also* Jesus Christ; Trinity
Sonderung [5]364, 364n
Soner (probably Ernst Soner, 1572–1612) [3]671
song(s) [2]221
article on [4]656, 656n; drinking [1]369, 369n; English [4]289–93, old [4]282–8; heroic [1]422; old [4]714; spiritual [5]512
sonnets [1]716, [2]55, [3]891, 891n, 903, [4]102, [5]853–65
prefatory [2]1120
sonship, mysterious [5]634
soothsayers [5]391n, 517n
soothsayings [3]920
soph, junior [3]902
sophia/Sophia [1]478–9, 478n, 479n, [2]205, 305, 305n, 422, 423, 430, 430n, [3]151, 424, 460, 460n, 913, 988, 988n, [4]111n, [5]19, 19n, [6]108
s. santa [2]423, 423n; *see also* wisdom
sophism(s) [1]203, 253, 517, 868, [2]199, 602, 644, 734, 771, 800n, 1008, 1150, 1154, 1163, [3]179–80, 317, 362, 391, 529, 652, 803, 860, 934, [4]115, 265, 276, 277, 298, 364, [5]70, 392, 547, 553, 620, 632, 711, 712, 712n, 721, 742, 790, [6]155, 286, 292, 314
circular argument [2]253; *cum hoc ergo propter hoc* [1]693; gross [1]324; of horse's tail [3]158, 158n; impudent [1]204; inhuman [1]318; miserable [5]753; part for whole [2]115, 115n; tangle of [2]941; tangle of truth and [3]201
sophisma [1]253
sophist(s)/Sophist(s) [1]8, 522, [2]40, 870, 871n, 1138, [3]778, 988, [4]157 ("Sophistic"), [5]491, 720
rhetoric of [2]776
Sophistae [2]36
sophistes [2]870, 870n, 871n
sophistry [1]2, [2]204, 326, 404, 656, 989–90, 1088, 1133, 1140n, [3]135, 225, 342, 658, 670, 671, 958, [4]588, 661, [5]301, 543, 616, 647, 677
self-exposing [5]396; shallow [5]811; in Spinoza [5]211; unworthy [5]304
Sophocles (496–406 BC) [2]458, 458n, 1090, 1090n, [3]894, [4]631
Sophoclean drama [4]168; and Shakespeare [1]72, 72n
Antigone [5]866n; *Oedipus Rex* [2]691; *The Syrian Women* [1]27n
sophos [2]870, 870n, 871n
Sorbonne *see* Paris
s'orienter [4]219, 219n
Soritas (myth) [5]227
sorites [2]800
sorrow [4]609, [5]420
godly [4]634; sign of [1]324; stream of [3]555
sort [4]23
sortilege [1]782
sot(s) [5]190, 252
Sotades (3rd century BC) [4]147
Sotheby, William (1757–1833) [1]clxiii, clxvii, 212n, [2]356n, 873, [6]30
ed Petrarch [1]xcv, xcvn, xcvin; letter(s) to [1]cvin q, 716, [2]354n, 974n q, [6]31n; supplier of books to C [1]cvi; tr Virgil [1]cvi; *see also* Virgil *Georgica* tr Sotheby
Sotheby's *see* London
"soul" [1]125, 620, [2]534–5, 535n, 537, [6]115
soul(s) [2]891, 1109, [3]67, 324, 392, 429, 520, 715, [5]9, 61, 131, 156, 171, 285, 357, 369, 448, 448n, 460, 559, 715, 752, 825, 827
actions of [6]139; actuated by faith [5]466; not always alone [3]494; animal [1]111, [3]44, 424; archetypal [3]121n; ascent of [5]771; attribute of [5]751; birth in [4]653; and body *see* body; boorly [5]278; calumny of [2]1083; Christ acting on [6]296; in Christ's train [3]443; conception of [3]120; copy-s. [2]553–4; cravings of [4]647; creative [2]1028; s.-danger [1]277, [6]264; death of [5]609; defect in [5]614; defined [1]620, [3]277–8, 559, [5]447, by Pythagoras [5]233; and deity [1]181; disembodied [5]559; diverted [5]496–7; doctrine of [3]909–14; drawn inward [5]188; and dreams [4]268; education of [5]496; essence of [4]292; eulogy of [4]421; not analogous to eye [3]121; faculty in [5]141; faculty of [3]297; fallen [2]583; s.-father [2]219; fearing sin [2]1177–8; s.-filth [5]835; finding itself [2]1163; as a glow-worm [1]169; and God [5]84; of good-hearted man [4]238; growth of [4]159; habit of [4]157; Hebrew word for [2]446; hell of [3]215; highest function of [5]530; human [3]720, 855, [5]271; without I [3]393; immortal [5]181; immortality of [1]748, [2]987n, [5]82–3, 727–8; impenitent [3]25; incarnate [3]594; not indifference-point [3]379; individual [5]411; innocent [4]791; intellectual [5]473; knowledge of

[5]795; and life *see* life; life of [2]1004–5, 1151; lifting up of [1]320; as light [3]1087; living [1]126, 675, [2]496, [4]531; lofty [5]278; manifestation of [3]119; measure by loss [4]158; s.-mother [2]219; s.-murder [1]341, 341n, [2]935; object of [6]127; origin of [1]659; ovarium in [2]542; in every part [5]600; passion of [2]922; passive [5]189; passivity of [5]236; in St Paul [3]44; perishing of [3]63; Plato on [4]126–7; poles in [3]4–5; power of [1]344, [2]536n, 537, 539; prenatal history of [1]750, 750n; principle of [5]756; proper [4]650; prototype s. [2]553–4; purified [5]781; rational [1]111; reduced to spirit [1]574; regenerate [3]520, [6]302; regeneration in [5]665; remembers [3]122; right-principled [4]10; seat of [1]135, [5]280; seeing [5]751; self-flattering [4]855; separated [6]63; sin of [3]747; during sleep [5]725–6; s.-powers [3]382; and spirit [1]124, [2]1010, 1109, [3]39, 39n, 393, 518, 546, 594n, [4]420, 420n, [5]411, 421, [6]16, 116, 300; stillness of [1]509; *tabula rasa* [2]552; things outward to [5]828; total [6]126; may trust in Christ [4]596; universal [6]116; of universe [3]82; needs union with God [3]592; unreconciled [6]256; wicked [2]292; world *see* world-soul; see also *psyche*/psyche

"sound" [6]288–9

sound(s) [1]653, [2]732, [3]323, 386, 896, 1025, 1025n
 analogous [5]198; articulate [4]489; articulated [1]731; beauty of [3]891; blue [3]1024; discordant [5]111; divine [5]72; harmonious [5]689; and light [1]572, 572n; without meaning [3]12; mere [5]770; origin of [1]637–8; power of [6]226; propagation of [6]235; smelling a [6]86, 86n; smooth [3]952; verbal [5]777–8, 778n; vermicular motion of [3]390, 390n; s.-waves [3]945n, [4]313n

soup, stone [4]645

"sour" [1]611

sour, the [1]666
 harsh [1]613

source [1]821, [2]591, [5]133
 dark [1]678; and effluents [5]604

"sourness" [1]641

sourness [1]631, 633, 642

South [1]596, [5]248, 265, [6]308
 ideal [5]438; natives of [2]1113; S. pole [5]248; pure [5]266; *see also* compass of nature

South Africa [3]1074n, [4]151n, 535

South America [4]299, 532n, [5]105, 106
 horses in [2]528; Inquisition in [4]28, 28n

South, Robert (1634–1716) [5]17n, 63, [6]308n
 Sermons [3]528, 528n, [5]63n; *Tritheism Charged* [5]7n

South Sea Bubble [2]53

South Sea Islanders [5]416

South Sea Islands [2]176–7

Southam, Mrs Wallace [3]930

Southampton [3]803

Southampton, Earl of *see* Wriothesley, Thomas

Southcott, Joanna (c 1750–1814) [3]991n

Southerne, Thomas (1660–1746) [2]77
 The Fatal Marriage [4]826, 826n

Southey, Caroline Anne (née Bowles) (1786–1854) [1]clixn

Southey, Charles Cuthbert (1819–88) [1]lxvii, clxvii, clxviii, [5]120; *see also* RS *Life and Correspondence*, *Life of Wesley* 3rd ed, ed C. C. Southey

Southey, Edith (née Fricker) (1774–1837) [1]clixn

Southey, Edith May (1804–71) [1]cxii

Southey, Kate (b 1810) [5]120

Southey, Robert (1774–1843) [1]lxxixn, lxxxvi, civ, 89, 90, 90n, 91n, 95, 97n, 99n, 292n, 331n, 501, 716, 725, 805, [2]35n, 81, 164n, 351, 739n q, 794, 861n, 932, 932n, 1112n, [3]459n, [4]93n, 183n, 283n, 606, 606n, 627n, 737n, [5]96, 102, [6]17n, 95, 121, 121n, 251n
 and Anderson's *British Poets* [1]37; annotator [1]40, 91n, [3]805, 816, [6]161; arrival at Greta Hall [1]cx; baleful influence on HC [1]c; and beetles [3]1036; "Bibliotheca Britannica" project [2]1131; bibliomania [1]lxix; as biographer [5]121; and Blanco White [1]500, 522; and body of Christ [1]863; book-borrowing [2]804; book recommended to [3]930; Bristol lectures [1]830; on Bunyan [1]802; careless writer [5]196, 196n; character [2]64n; C's assistance to [2]849n; C's criticism of [2]932n; C's love for [1]808; compared with C [1]330–1; compliment to [2]84; death of [1]cxiii, clixn, clxi; dogmatic [5]111n; his English [5]111, 114, 114n; as greyhound [1]lix; as historian [2]929, [5]153–4; his intended history of monastic orders [5]121; Husseian spirit [2]62, *62n*; imitation of [2]93n; imitators [4]162–3; Jesuits and [1]699n; kindliness of [5]138; lent books by C [1]cxii; letter(s) from C to [1]94n, 149n q, 200n q, [2]696, 845 q, 1048 q, 1072, 1085n q, [3]165n q, 378n q, 837n q, 881 q, [4]639n q; letter(s) from

Southey, Robert—*continued*
HNC to [1]lixn–lxn q, clxviiin; letter to HNC [1]clixn q; letter to William Taylor [4]619; library [1]cxiii, 398n, 854, [2]804, 874, [3]504n, [6]103n, 147; library sale [1]clxvii–clxviii; admires Lucan [2]126n; "Mahomet" project [3]230n; marginalia addressed to [1]lxxxi, 41, 806, 810, [3]1068, [4]95, 665, 666, [5]145; marriage [2]365, 365n; and "metapothecary" [5]202n; misuse of participles [2]128, 128n; owner of annotated books [1]lxiiin, lxxi, lxxxi, xciii, c, cxxii, cxlin, clxviiin, 217, 222, 840, [2]4, 44, 753, 874, [3]492, [4]29, 32, 91, 619–20, [5]194, 818; parody of [4]658n; partisan for Stuarts [1]808, 808n; preserver of marginalia [1]xciii; pun by [2]756n; purchases from C's library [1]xcivn; quarrel with C [1]173n; reactionary [2]20; from republican to Tory [1]806n–7n; as reviewer [4]619, 620n, 651n, 665n, 671n, [5]102n; reviews MT [4]171–83; second marriage [1]clixn; service to morality [1]817; "smartness" of tone [2]54, 54n; sonnets [5]857; Southeyising [2]983, 983n; "Spectator" project [1]158n; supplier of books to C [1]cvi, [4]203, [5]143n; on Swedenborg [3]991; undergraduate [2]956n; unsoutheyian mood [3]1075; use of language [4]172n; use of "talented" [4]14n; on Thomas Taylor [4]160, 160n; on translation [4]289, 289n; and Wesley [5]150, 151, 151n, 154, 154n, 161, 179, 189; on WW [1]844

ed *Annual Anthology* II see *Annual Anthology*; *Battle of Blenheim* MT [1]92; *Book of the Church* [1]807n, 855, 856, [2]63n q, 83–4, 932n, [3]991n, [6]13n; *Catalogue of the Valuable Library of the Late Robert Southey* [1]clxviiin, 398n, [3]819n, [4]91, 281; *Common-Place Book* ed Warter [2]23; *Curse of Kehama* [4]461, 461n, [5]121, 121n; *Death of Wallace* MT [1]96; *Devil's Walk* [5]97n q; *The Doctor* ed Warter [1]cxiv; MT [5]96–100; *Dramatic Fragment* MT [1]98; *Eclogue: The Wedding* MT [1]94; *Epigram XI* MT [1]98; *History* MT [1]93; *History of Brazil* [1]clxvii, [4]28n; MT [5]101–7; *Inscription for an Apartment in Chepstow Castle* [5]144, 144n–5n; *Joan of Arc* [1]cxiii, clin, 100, [2]122n, 804, [3]61n; MT [5]108–19; *Life and Correspondence* ed C. C. Southey [1]331n, [4]737n; "Life of Bunyan" [1]cxiii, 488, [4]657n; *Life of Dr Bell* [4]619; *Life of Nelson* [1]cxiii; *Life of Wesley* [1]lxiii, lxiv, lxv, lxvii, xciii, ci–cii, cxiii, clxviii, 122, [2]496, 496n, [3]991n; MT [5]120–93; 518, 518n, [6]123, 123n q, 3rd ed, ed C. C. Southey [1]clxviii, [5]120; *Lives of the British Admirals* I [1]cxiv; MT [5]194–7; *The Mad Woman* [1]92n; *New Letters* ed Curry [1]lxxin, lxxiin q, xcivn q, cxin q, 53, 89, 97n, 98n, 772n, [2]359, 587n, 753, 845 q, 1204n, [3]805, 893n, [4]160n, [5]121n q; *Ode to Silence, alias Unanimity* MT [1]92; *Omniana* [1]cxiii, cxxxix, clxi, clxin, 158n, 772, 772n–3n, [2]452n, [3]817n, 909, 952n; MT 1064–77; [4]91, 93n, [6]149n, HNC's additions [1]cxxxiv, "Souls of Brutes" [4]95n; *On a Dull Fellow* MT [1]94; *Origin, Nature and Object of the New System of Education* [1]xcvi ("pamphlet on . . . education"); *Poems* [1]clxi, [5]145n; *Poetical Works* [5]145n; *St Juan Gualberto* MT [1]91; *Selection from the Letters* ed Warter [1]cxiv q, cxivn, cxliin; *Song of the Araucans* MT [1]99; *Sonnet V* MT [1]95; *Sonnet VI* MT [1]95; *Sonnet XIII* MT [1]96; *Sonnet XX* MT [1]96; *Thalaba* [1]376n, [3]92n; *To a Bee* MT [1]94; *To a Friend Expressing a Wish to Travel* MT [1]94; *Vezins and Regnier* MT [1]94; *Vindiciae ecclesiae anglicanae* [1]807n, 855, 859n q, [2]64n, [3]991n; *Vision of Judgment* [1]807n, [2]864; *Wat Tyler* [2]847n

Southeys, the [4]656n

Southgate, Henry *see* London

sovereign (monarch) [2]659, [3]478, [5]280, 675, 680

sovereign (money) [5]435

sovereignty [2]936, 946, [3]25, 26, 149, 157, [4]815
divided [4]341; of people [2]195, [3]157

Sozini, Lelio (1526–62) [4]643, 643n, 670

Sozomen, Salmaninius Hermias (5th century) [3]145, 145n

Sozzini, Fausto Paulo *see* Socinus

space(s) [1]563, [2]607, 1002n, 1013, [3]13, 241, 270, 322, 1011, [4]456, 456n, 503, [5]822, [6]233
abstract [6]158; construction in [6]115; continuity in [1]537; divisible [5]711; not divisible [5]712; empty [3]296; not empty [3]90; ethereal [5]225; finite [5]712; form of [5]430; idea of [3]916, 916n, [4]115; infinite [2]671, [5]460; infinite divisibility of [3]362; intuition of [2]563, [3]298; intuitive [2]611; Kant on [3]284, [4]217, [5]706; Leibniz on [3]290; material [6]144; matter in [3]275–6, 281–2, 287–9, 292; negation of [3]357; new world

of [4]263; as confused perception [3]966; form of perception [3]85; point of [3]282; properties of [3]79, 118; reality of [5]708, 710–12, 713, 720; relations of [3]301, 343; relations to [3]274–5; sensuous [3]303; symbolic import of [2]1145; three-dimensional [3]321–2, 333; and time [1]359, 537, 563, 577, 655, 682, [2]205, 293, 456, 539–40, 540n, 729, 1008, 1029, [3]13, 201, 242, 242n, 679, 737, 790, 835, 858, 966, [4]124–6, 132n, 156, 157, 166, 218, 223–4, 369, 413, 436, 440, 449, 458, [5]16, 141, 269, 297, 415, 468, 487, 594, 604, 614–15, 614n, 699, 712, 720, [6]158, 170, 207, 236; unity of [5]452; universal form [3]80; Zeno on [5]719–20

spade [2]983

Spain [1]477, 500, 840, 844, 845, 846, [2]401, 794, 936n, [3]7n, 133, 144n, 927n, 993, 1088n, [4]20, 199, 299, [5]104n, 195n, 222n, 507, 659, [6]13
 and Great Britain [3]696, 696n; history of [5]104; king of [5]39n, 639, 639n; Reformation in [2]740

Spalatin, Georg (1484–1545) [3]756

Spallanzani, Lazzaro (1729–99) [3]716

Spangenberg, August Gottlieb (1704–92) [5]152

Spanheim, Friedrich (1632–1701) [1]492

Spaniard(s) [2]740n, [3]160, [4]28n, 43, [5]101–7, 195
 cruelty of [2]163; deep and subtle [5]158; admiration of language [3]394; pride of [2]217

Spanisches Theater ed A. W. Schlegel [1]390n

Spanish (language) [1]113n, 814, [2]1092, [3]394, 830, [4]101n

Spanish match *see* Charles I

Spanish (people)
 character of [5]104; colonisers [5]106; S. readers [4]95; S. stage [1]389, 389n–90n

Spanzotti, Girolamo Vincenzo (1741–1812)
 Disordini morali e politici della Corte di Roma [4]68, 68n

spark(s) [1]621, [3]1032, [5]577

sparkles [1]170

Sparman, Andrew (Anders Sparrman) (1748–1820) *Voyage to the Cape of Good Hope* [4]87n

sparrow(s) [3]728–9, [4]711, 711n, [6]153

Sparrow, John (1615–?1665) [1]553, 554

Sparta [4]650n

Spartan [2]899, [3]389n, 516n, 965, [6]209

Spassky (fl 1819) [2]1115

"spatiuncles" [5]712, 712n

spatula [3]815

spear(s) [6]208
 of Longinus [1]683

Specchi [1]237n

Special, Mary (fl 1740–65) [5]184, 184n

"species" [5]604n

species
 of Epicurus [5]604, 604n; and genus *see* genus/genera; gradation of [5]388; and race [2]176

specific(s) [2]387, [4]395, [5]409
 gravity *see* gravity, specific

speck [5]296

spectacle(s) [2]1031, [3]438, [4]375, 375n, 461, [5]297, 306n
 s.-glasses [3]38

spectator [4]788

Spectator [1]157n, 158n, [2]700n, [3]154n, 759n, 992n, [5]99n, ed D. F. Bond [4]841n q, [5]829n q

spectre [4]580

spectrum/spectra [2]332, [3]29n, 116, 1018, [4]83, [5]759
 ocular [4]263, 263n, 581

"spectum" [4]840, 840n

speculation [3]95, [5]326
 habits of [5]385; virus of [5]766

speculators [5]385

Spedding, James (1808–81) *see* F. Bacon *Works* ed Spedding, Ellis, and Heath

Spee, Friedrich (1591–1635) *Trutz Nachtigal* MT [5]198

speech(es) [2]470, 470n, [3]38, [5]60
 figure(s) of [2]164, 564, [3]345, 431, [4]41, 162, [5]774, 841; harsh [5]494; long [4]712; organs of [1]111, 607; parts of [3]450, [4]166–7; unnatural [4]598

Speed, John (c 1552–1629)
 America [2]754n; *Asia* [2]754n; *History of Great Britaine* [2]754n; *Theatre of the Empire of Great Britain* [2]754n

Speedwell (ship) [1]155, 156, 761, 769n

Speirs, James (fl 1880) [1]clxvii, [5]440

spell(s) [3]576, [5]157

spelling [3]889, 890n, [5]111, 325, 325n

Spelman, Sir Henry (1562–1641) [3]977, 981

Spence, Joseph (1699–1768) *Polymetis* [6]110n

Spence, William (1783–1860) *see* Kirby and Spence *Introduction to Entomology*

Spencer *see also* Spenser

Spencer, George, Marquis of Blandford, 5th Duke of Marlborough (1766–1840) [2]702n

Spencer, George John, 2nd Earl Spencer (1758–1834) [2]702
Spencer, Henry le, Bishop of Norwich (d 1406) [6]22
Spengler, Lassar/Lazarus (1479–1534) [6]122
Spenser, Edmund ("Spencer") (c 1552–99) [1]cxxxviiin, cxxxixn, 59, 728, 801, [2]14, 55, 121, 127, 1090, 1090n, [3]703, 886, 909, [4]162, 167, 605, 605n, 736, [5]110, 669, 669n, [6]158
in Anderson [1]37; borrows from Italians [3]909; in C's lectures [1]cxxxix; on S. Daniel [2]128, 128n; and Greek [1]73, 73n; laureate [1]56n; Spenserian stanza [1]116, *116n–17n*, [3]910, 910n
Astrophel [2]119n; *Colin Clout* [2]119n, 128n; *Epithalamion* MT [1]77–80; *Faerie Queene* [1]40; MT [1]54; 54n q; MT 76–7; 221, [2]1120, 1120n, 1155n q; *The Ruins of Time* [3]15n, [4]167n–8n q
Spenser/Spencer, John (1559–1614) *see* R. Hooker *Works* ed Spenser
sperm [3]1044
Speusippus (c 407–339 BC) [1]615, 616n, [2]872, 872n, [3]766, 766n, [4]472, 472n, [5]731, 732, 732n, 735, 736, 736n
fragment from [5]742, 742n
"spew" [1]580n
sphere(s) [2]1067, [5]131, 245, 406
of free will [5]305; of freedom [5]302, 305; nature as [5]600; nervous [3]392; of power [3]283; sensitive [3]383, 384, 385–6, 387
spheroid [3]865, [5]344
Sphinx [1]182, 187
Sphinx, Athanasius (fiction) [2]888
spice [2]737
Spice Islands [3]884, [5]309
spiculae [6]152
spider(s) [3]848, 1079, [5]466, 729, [6]149
theological [5]540, 540n; s.-web [3]26
Spiller, Robert Ernest (b 1896) *see* J. F. Cooper *Gleanings in Europe* ed Spiller
Spinoza, Baruch (Benedictus de Spinoza) (1632–77) [1]lviii, lxx, cxxiii, cxxxi, clixn, 283, 417n, 620, [2]199, 623, 623n, 897, 995 q, [3]75, 142n, 332n q, 357, 649, 790, 790n, 855, 856, 860, 877n, 991, 1085n, 1088n, [4]209, 224–5, 224n, 226, 324n, 353, 411, 413, 585, 676, 676n, [5]71, 71n, 83, 202, 301, 369 ("Spinozan"), 446, 446n, 456, 482, 716n, 814–16, 830, 830n
an Adwitamist [2]340; in Argens [1]104–5; atheism of [1]239n, 646n, [3]296; not an atheist [5]203; attack upon [4]230n; and Cabbala [3]1091; *cogitatio* of [5]710; C's admiration [2]803n; C's exposition of [6]238n; Spinozistic consequences [3]362; definition of "body" [2]631, 631n; divine nature in [5]716; error of [1]602, [4]110n; on extension [4]227, 229–30; free of lust for fame [1]104; on God [6]172; great defect [5]210; Spinozistic imitators [3]909; Jacobi on [4]224–6; and Leibniz [2]172, 172n; letters [3]89n, 117–18, [4]403; misrepresented [3]78–9, 78n; misunderstood [3]854, 973, 973n, [4]226, 227–30; and pantheism [1]139n, 646n, [3]901; ed by Paulus [4]40; profound [5]204; pure soul [5]203; pure spirit [3]80n; and Schelling [6]238, 243, 243n, 244n; scheme of interpretation [2]412; skeleton of [3]123; against S. [2]1030, 1030n; and Spinozism [2]340n, [5]207–8; a sublime thought of [1]790; system of [1]566, 566n, [2]1107, [4]348n, [5]201; treated hardly [5]208; and world-God [2]1145
Chief Works tr Elwes [3]78n, [5]199; *Collected Works* I tr Curley [5]199; *Correspondence* tr A. Wolf [3]1091n–2n q, [5]199; *Ethics* tr Curley [1]105n, 283n q, 566n, [2]631n, 996, [3]78n q, 79n q, 83n, 855n q, 860n q, 901n, 919n, 949n q, [4]209n q, 224n, 227n q, 229n q, 353n q, 403, 413n q, 444n q, [5]83n, 203n, 231n q, 710n, [6]172n q, 223, 223n q, tr Elwes [1]790n q; *Opera* [1]lxviii, 104n–5n, 283n; *Opera posthuma* [3]118, [4]227n, 228, 228n; *Opera quae supersunt omnia* ed Paulus [2]195n, [3]1092n, [4]403n, 227n; MT [5]199–220; *Principia philosophiae* [1]104n; *Tractatus politicus* [5]301n q; *Tractatus theologico-politicus* [6]265, tr Elwes [1]104n, [2]374, 374n q
Spinozism ("Spinosism") [2]283, 344, 554n, 995, 1015, [3]296n, 649n, 698, 854, [4]110, 226, 348, 348n, [5]71n, 231, 708, [6]237
atheistic [3]123, 123n; Calvinism and Socinianism lead to [2]803; defined [1]113, 113n, 114; difference of gospel faith from [3]23; essence of [5]206; of Greeks [3]649; Milton's [3]138; peculiarity of [3]79; reformed [2]602; of Schelling's system [4]456, 456n; and Spinoza *see* Spinoza
Spinozists [1]239, 242, 743, *743n*, [2]292, [3]695n, 782, 853–4, [5]456, 729
spiral(s) [2]940, [3]269
"spirit"/"Spirit" [3]524, 594, 594n, [4]60, 94, [5]175, 443, 516n, 517, [6]116–17

spirit(s)/Spirit(s) [1]166, 178, 598, 661, [2]33, 166, 198, 631n, 1019–20, 1202, [3]18, 42, 46, 53, 67, 77, 139, 416, 424, 428, 450, 723, 769, [4]127, 136, 137, 398, 648, [5]3–4, 3n, 15, 52, 58, 201, 357, 410, 439, 514, 516, 556, 565, 569, 631, 663, 798–9, [6]307

accursed [2]1085; accusing [5]86n; act of the [5]649; agency of [1]12; of alms [5]587; analogy of [5]579; ancestral [5]534; angelic [5]424; apostasis of [2]562; apostolic [3]20; apparitions of [6]106; ardent [1]590, 590n; authority of [5]568; avenging [3]594; bad [2]513; beatitude of [3]60; and body *see* body; Böhme on [1]589–98, 689; called up [5]503; catholic [2]811; as cause [4]354; in chemistry [6]116; chivalrous [5]277; Christian [5]161; Christ's words are s. [3]439; in the Church [5]571; commercial [5]196n; communion with [5]661; creaturely [1]601, 602; defined [3]277–8; descent of [1]327, [4]260; and devils [2]1109; discerned and discerning [1]824; disembodied [3]39; divine [5]181, 424, [6]20; erroneous [5]471; evangelical [1]729; even frame of [1]344; evil [2]292, 1167, [3]28, 474–5, 876, [5]86, [6]159; eye of [4]616; fall of [2]326, [3]436, 904; fallen [1]601, 825, [2]1105–6, [5]603; fallen and unfallen [4]548; Father of [5]482; fault-finding [5]744; of fear [5]123; finite [1]238, 460, [5]424, 706; and flesh *see* flesh; gifts of the [5]529; of God [3]24, 546; greater reality than sense [1]673; happiness of [4]136; turns heart [5]156; heretical [5]470; holiness of [4]653; Holy *see* Holy Spirit; homogeneous with matter [1]598; husk of [2]1003; not imageable [3]301; immediate operations of [2]281; immortal [1]175, [4]695; infallible [1]823, [2]561, [5]607; infinite [5]455–6; inner strivings of [4]498; insect [3]671; inspiring [1]818; invisible [5]383; invocation of [2]825; as island [1]70; law(s) of [1]201, [3]454; life-making [2]496; light of [2]1151; of literature [2]999; living [6]106; man as finite [1]676; in man [1]430; in mankind [1]675; and matter *see* matter; monocratic [5]152; of Mosaic law [5]535; multeity of [4]491–2; and nature [2]1014–15; nature of [5]415, 423; and notion [3]606, [5]550; of obedience [5]123; omnipresent [5]553; operations of [5]471; not organised [1]114; organising [6]8; papal [3]697; made perfect [5]725, 728; personeity [3]520, [6]302; personifying [5]764; philosophical [1]610; of philosophy [5]201; plastic [1]114; in Plotinus [4]145, 145n; positive and negative [2]890; positive unity in [5]452; as principle of individuality [1]137; Protestant views of [1]674; public [5]40, 638; pure [4]303; Quaker use of [3]927–8; quenched [3]451; s.-raising [4]143; and reason [5]191; reason is [2]663; receiving of the [5]665; recipients of [5]529; redemption by [3]22; regenerated [3]741; related to being and mind [2]248; religious [3]994; rewards of [5]627; rum [2]610; scientific [5]379; self-subsistent [5]457; sense of [2]286, [3]1086–7; sensualised [3]493; seven [5]411, 411n; of Socinianism [5]516; and soul *see* soul; spiritual self [2]690; spiritual system [3]201; subtlety of [1]737; of supplication [5]512; in Swedenborg [5]404, 404n, 411; tenet of [5]569; testimony of [1]302; things of the [5]583, 593; touch of [3]563; of truth [5]572, 642; truths of [1]872; tyrannous [5]271; undisciplined [1]684; unific [5]452; use of word in scripture [3]550; vindictive [5]161; way of [5]157; will of [2]279; wind [2]246; s.-world [3]432, 986; world of [3]352, [5]424, 465; see also *pneuma*/*pneumata*

"spiritual" [5]604

spiritualisation [5]630

spiritualist(s) [3]396, 925, [4]267

spirituality [3]922, [4]420, [5]137, 172, [6]58

of Christian motives [6]55; of man [5]433

Spitaller [5]180

Spitzbergen [1]204n

spleen [2]269, 367, 813, [5]462, 476

excision of [5]568

splendour [1]794

"splittery" [5]76, 76n

spondee(s) [2]874, [3]904, [4]687, [5]690, [6]252, 255

missing [4]844

sponges [5]837

spontaneity [2]249, 403, 641, [3]75–6, 76n, 81, 81n, [4]691, [5]205

and freedom [2]604–5, 611

spontaneous, the and voluntary [3]519, [5]298–9, [6]301

spontaneous combustion [5]252n

sport [2]239

sportsman [3]1080

spots on the sun [6]43

Spottiswoode, John (1565–1637) [1]850

The History of the Church of Scotland† [2]1095, [5]221

Sprague, Arthur Colby (b 1895) *see* S. Daniel *Poems* ed Sprague

Sprat, Thomas (1635–1713) [1]37
spring (mechanism) [5]208, 431
spring (season) [4]836n, [5]349
spring(s) (water) [2]220, 591, 1024n, [3]386, [5]133, 351, 351n
Spring Gardens *see* London
spring-guns [2]980
springiness [5]277n
"sprinkled" [1]776
sprinkling [5]651
spruce beer [3]45
spuriousness [1]491
Spurzheim, Johann Caspar (1776–1832) [2]1012n, [3]716n, [4]5, [5]422, 422n; *see also* Gall and Spurzheim
spy/spies [1]844, [2]1080, [5]143, 280n, [6]98
squab-pie [2]999
"square" [5]212
square(s) [1]601, [3]80, 85, 455, 1007, [4]115, [5]617
 round [4]588, [5]450; symbol [1]649, 649n
Square, Mr (in Fielding) [3]94, 94n
squatters [6]36, 37
squeak [1]325
squibs [4]13
squint [5]609
squinting [3]572
squire [5]609
stable-boy [5]366
Stackhouse, Thomas (fl 1825–35) *Copies of Drawings* [5]376
Stadtholder [3]796
Staël, Anne Louise Germaine (née Necker), Baronne de (1766–1817) [1]131, 148n
 De l'Allemagne [4]170
staff [3]615, 615n
Stafford, Mr (d c 1528) [5]390
Staffordshire [1]284, 862, [3]631, 632, 639, [5]395
stag [2]1185, [4]535, [5]476, [6]151
stage (coach) [2]194, [3]751
stage (theatre) [1]398
 Spanish [1]389
Stagyrite *see* Aristotle
Stahl, Georg Ernst (1660–1734) [1]63n, 550n, [2]868, 868n–9n, 1031, 1031n, [5]331–2, 811, 811n
 Theoria medica vera [2]1031n
stain from fruit [4]529
stair(s) [3]741, [5]72
staircase [2]609
stallion [3]193
stamens [5]294
stammering [2]1092n, [3]830
Stancarist(s) [2]292
Stancaro, Francesco (1501–74) [2]292n
Stanchio [5]838
Standard [1]436, 436n
standing [1]267, [6]260
Stanemore [3]981
Stanford CA
 Stanford University Library, marginalia in [1]clxvii, 840
Stangate Creek [1]lxxxiii
Stanhope, George (1660–1728) [1]155
Staniforth, Sampson (1720–99) [5]170
Stanley, Charlotte Margaret (née Hornby), Countess of Derby (d 1817) [2]169
Stanley, Edward George Geoffrey Smith, 14th Earl of Derby (1799–1869) [2]909, 909n, [6]49, 49n
Stanley, James, Bishop of Ely (?1465–1515) [2]70
Stanley, Thomas (1625–78) [1]cxviii, [5]222
 The History of Philosophy [1]clxi, 174n, 185n, 584n, 639n q, 661n, [2]172n, 1042, 1042n q, [3]539n q; MT [5]222–38; 714n; *see also* Aeschylus ed Stanley
Stanway [1]494
Stanyhurst, Richard (1547–1618) [3]1070 ("Stanihurst")
stanza
 octave and ennead [3]910; Spenserian *see* Spenser; *see also* metre(s)
stapelia [4]497
staple [2]291, 466, [4]310, [5]754, 754n
 s.-ring [1]539, 539n, [3]26, 26n
Stapleton, Thomas (1535–98) [2]680, 681, [5]551, 551n
star(s) [1]642, [2]143, 144n, 582, 932, [3]340, 341, 471, [4]162, 522, [5]426–7, 661, 709, 795
 of Bethlehem [3]653, 653n; in Cassiopeia [3]540, 540n; central [4]516; course of [1]180; double [3]73, 73n; Idalian [2]95; longitude of [1]769; lucky [6]146; morning [1]575; Pole [1]399n; in Rev [2]508, 510
Star Chamber [2]932, 1102n, [4]178, 308n, [5]521, 521n, 616, 616n
starch [1]596
stare [2]993
Starke, Mariana (?1762–1838) *Travels on the Continent*† [1]clxvi, [5]239
starlings [6]151
starting-post [5]10
starving [5]276
stasis/*stasis* [1]678, [2]675n, [3]436, 436n, 606, 606n

state(s) [2]51–2, 495, 1075, [3]53, 471, [4]313, [5]41, 279, 321, 363, 644
  aim of [5]302; best [3]645; cataleptic [5]517; s.-censor [3]110; church and *see* church(es), and s.; common [5]280; concept of [5]310–11; constituent [1]865; corrupt [5]159; ecclesiastic [5]537; formation of [5]299; freest [5]280; future [1]283, 445, [2]261, 695, 1075, 1081, [3]613, 678, [4]369, [5]495, 606; German [5]314; and government [3]787–8; Greek [3]108n; happiness of [5]361–2; idea of [5]269, 364–5, 371; interests of [3]679; Jewish [1]436, 832, [2]38, [3]50, 53–4, 106–13, [4]251, [5]522n, 535, 551, 624, [6]60; men made for [3]677–8; under Mosaic law [3]741; obedience to [6]51; organismus [5]304–5; perfect [3]678; permanence of [5]273; s.-pharisee [4]25; pillar of [4]737; primeval [3]105; principles of s. organisation [2]616; prosperous, Donne's definition of [2]311; purpose of [1]739; and person [2]58; as regulator [5]363; savage [2]206; skeleton [5]323; social [6]53; spiritual [5]606; s.-symbolique [2]1107; transitional [4]794, [5]606, 630, [6]230; true [5]282; tyrannical [3]645; voice of [5]322; s.-wisdom [2]936; work of [5]315
stateship [5]279
statesman/statesmen [2]51–2, 926, [3]154, 468, 844
  British [3]794–803; enlightened [6]6; Moses as [1]424; wicked [3]803; wonderful [2]927
statistics [2]97, 616
statists [3]251
Statius, Publius Papinius (c 45–96) [2]134, 134n, 431n, [5]110
  Achilleid [2]134n; *Sylvae* [3]227n; *Thebaid* [1]558 q, 558n q
"statue" [4]734
statue(s) [4]409, 450, 648, 649n, [6]105, 328
  of Aesculapius [5]384; of gold [4]811; of Janus [5]611; of Jupiter [5]658; Pygmalion's [5]310
statuesque, the [1]72, 72n
stature [5]169
statute(s) [1]753, 756, [2]210–11, 705, 750, 789, [3]21, 154, 233, 391
  s.-book [2]269, 454
Staughton, Dr (fl mid-17th century) [6]258
Stavorinus, John Splinter (1739–88) [2]73n
  Voyages to the East-Indies tr Wilcocke [2]527n
Stay, Benedetto (1714–1801) [1]569n
stealing [5]732
steam [5]557, [6]230
  s.-engine [4]173
steamboat [3]946, 947n, [5]862n
Stedman, John Gabriel (1744–97) *Narrative of a Five Years' Expedition* [2]296n, 827n
steeds, ethereal [5]745
steel [3]1067n, [5]294, 506
Steele, Sir Richard (1672–1729) [2]17n
  and Defoe [6]163
Steele, William (d 1680) *Mr Recorder's Speech* [2]111; MT [5]240
steeple(s) [5]321
  nodding [5]846
Steevens, George (1736–1800) [4]692n, 699n, 714n, 716n, 723n, 732n, 758, 760n, 766n, 802, 812n, 813, 826n, 848, 848n. *See also* Hogarth *Genuine Works* ed Nichols and Steevens; Shakespeare *Plays* ed Steevens
Steffens, Heinrich (1773–1845) [1]ci, cii, 131, 145n, 556, 648, [2]539n, 594, 854n, 1031, 1031n, [3]114, 115, 128, 842, 842n, 944n, 951, 951n, 1036n, 1061, [4]274, 274n, 319n, [6]228
  C's spiritual brother [5]280; C's wish to be his pupil [5]359; on colour [3]1018; contributions to *Zeitschrift* [6]225; elegant scheme of [3]1020; followers of [2]1002; and Kant [5]242, 243; on light [3]1016, 1016n; misconceived [3]119n–20n; his mistakes [6]230; Oken echoes [3]1031; perspicuous [6]226; polarity in [1]660; his prose style [5]271n, 287n, 314n; and Werner [1]664n
  Anthropologie MT [5]241–54; *Beyträge zur innern Naturgeschichte der Erde* [1]570n, [3]998n q, 1027n, [5]241, 245n; MT 255–67; *Beiträge zur psychischen Heilkunde* ed Reil [5]284 q; *Caricaturen des Heiligsten* [2]180; MT [5]268–306; *Die gegenwärtige Zeit* MT [5]307–33; *Geognostisch-geologische Aufsätze* [3]950n, 1031n, 1061n; MT [5]334–51; *Grundzüge der philosophischen Naturwissenschaft* [1]648n, [2]546n, 854n q, 856n, [3]518n, 997n q, 1016n, 1018n, 1020n q, 1025n, 1031n, [5]241, 255, 265n, 267n q; MT 352–60; [6]300n; *Turnziel: Sendschreiben an den Herrn Professor Kaysler und die Turnfreunde* [5]271n; "Ueber die Bedeutung der Farben in der Natur" [3]1018n; "Ueber die Geburt der Psyche" [5]284 q; *Ueber die Idee der Universitäten* MT [5]361–72; *Schriften* [3]1018n
Steinmetz, Adam (d 1832) [1]231

Stella (in Swift) [4]466, 466n
Stellatus, Marcellus Palingenius (fl 1528) *Zodiacus vitae* [2]763
"stem" [1]443
stem [2]61, 689, [5]189, 265
stenography [5]49
Stephanus, Henricus *see* Estienne, Henri
Stephen, St (d c 35) [2]286, 717n, 901, [5]295 ("Stephanus"), 295n, 296, 297n, 298, 299, [6]146
Stephens, Roger [1]231
Stepping Stones *see* Rydal
sterben [1]157n
stereotype [4]336–7, 337n
"sterilifidianism" [1]814, 814n
sterility [3]809
Sterling, Edward (1773–1847) [1]211
Sterling, John (1806–44) [1]cxxiv, cl, 211, [4]69, [5]373
letter to [1]481 q; supplier of books to C [1]xcviii
Arthur Coningsby MT [5]373–5
Sterne, Laurence (1713–68) [1]718, [2]17n, [4]779, [5]85
Tristram Shandy [2]121, [4]98n, 785n, [5]86n
Sterne, Richard (c 1596–1683) [2]409n
Sternhold, Thomas (1500–49) [3]904, 904n, [5]178, 178n
with John Hopkins, and others *The Whole Book of Psalms Collected into English Metre* [1]701
Stetigkeit [3]119, 119n
steward [5]587
Stewart *see also* Stuart
Stewart, Dugald (1753–1828) [1]75n, 621, 621n
Dissertation First† [5]376
Stewart/Stuart, Henry, Lord Darnley (1545–67) [1]301n, [3]483
Stewart, Robert, 2nd Marquis of Londonderry and Viscount Castlereagh (1769–1822) [4]21, [5]312, 312n
Stewart, Sir William (1774–1827) *Outlines of a Plan for the General Reform of the British Land Forces* MT [5]377–81
stews [3]193
Stibbs, Edward (fl 1880) [1]clxv–clxvi
stick [5]552
Stieglitz, Johann (1767–1840) [6]104, 120n
Ueber den thierischen Magnetismus [6]104n
stifle-damp [2]69n
stifle-stuff [5]258
stigma/stigmata [3]27, 1076
"Stilling", Dr *see* Jung
Stillingfleet, Edward (1635–99) [1]19n, 312n, 353, 353n, [2]31, 264, 265n, 294n, 348n, [3]309n, 459, 459n, 877, 877n, [4]336, 336n, [5]576, 576n, [6]117 q, 118 q
Origines sacrae [1]lxxxiv, lxxxv, 19 q, 353n, [2]26, 26n, [3]459n, 877n, 967; MT [5]382–8; *A Rational Account of the Grounds of the Protestant Religion* [5]576n; *Works* [5]577n
stimulability [3]596
stimulant(s) [1]777, [3]397, 397–8, 596, [4]183
disgusting [3]171
stimulus/stimuli [3]398, [5]172, 588
of death [3]612; sensuous [4]409
sting [5]588
Stirling [2]1171n
Stirling, Earl of *see* Alexander, William
Stirling, James Hutchison (1820–1909) [1]638n
stitch in side [1]129, [4]744–5
Stoa *see* Athens
"stoage" [5]388, 388n
Stobaeus, Ioannes (Ioannes Stovaios) (1580–1646) [5]702
Stobaeus, Johannes (5th century) [1]174n, 185n, [5]225n
Eclogarum physicarum [5]742n q; *Physica* [5]716–17 q
Stobert, Henry (fl 1822) *Chinzica* [3]839
stock [5]471
Stockdale, John (c 1749–1814) [1]373, [3]170, [4]778, 808; *see also* Shakespeare *Stockdale's Edition*
stock-exchange [3]602, [4]548
Stockholm [3]333, 334n, 351, 351n, 352, 985, [5]197
stocking [5]274
Stoddart, John (1773–1856) [2]1204n, *1204n*
Stoddart, Sarah *see* Hazlitt, Sarah
Stoffe [4]324, 324n; *see also* stuff(s)
stoic(s)/Stoic(s) [1]166, 166n, 174, 174n, 175, 180, [2]291, 595, 792–3, 793n, 1186, [3]346, 346n, 531, 556, 622, 642, 776, [4]157, 663, [5]83, 83n, 612n, [6]316
doctrine [1]167; genuine [1]174; hypocrisy [3]317; and lyricus [2]65; and stoicus below Platonic [1]179; on suicide [1]167n
stoicism [3]645, [4]654n, [5]86n
error of [1]172–3; history of [1]174
stoicus *see* stoic(s)/Stoic(s)
Stoker, William (1773–1848)
Pathological Observations, review of MT [2]367–8

Stokes, Mr (in Banim) [1]213, 214
Stolberg, Friedrich Leopold von, Count (1750–1819) [1]828, [4]489–90
"*Kirchengeschichte*" [4]489–90
stomach [4]432, [5]726, [6]102, 120
pit of [3]389; of understanding [3]347
stone(s) [1]396, [2]322, [3]129, 464, 550, 749, 946, [4]9, 380, 526, 628, [5]203–4, 310, 471, 613, 656, 682
cairn of [2]705; dwelling of [1]426; fit of the [1]184; graven [1]783; laying [3]837; of Malta [5]840; meteoric [3]949; of offence [1]649, 649n; precious [1]446, 448, 603, [5]262; thinking [3]80–1; twinned [4]741, 813–14
Stone, Christopher (fl 1922) [3]811
Stone, Reynolds (1909–79) [2]905n
stool [4]453
stop, full [1]133
storge [5]476, 476n
storm [1]612, [2]862
of disquiet [1]425
story/stories
horrific [1]627; marvellous [2]831; old [4]717; repetitions of [6]262
Story, George (1738–1818) [5]170, 171
Stothard, Thomas (1755–1834) [1]802
Stow, John (c 1525–1605)
Anneles of England [2]755n; *Summarie of Englyshe Chronicles* [2]755n
stowage [5]388n
Stowe, Calvin Ellis (1802–86) [3]107, 107n; *see also* Jahn *History* tr Stowe
Stowell, Lord *see* Scott, William
Stowey *see* Nether Stowey
strabismus [5]501
Strachan/Strahan, Archibald (d 1652) [2]1171n
Strada, Famiano (1572–1649) *Prolusiones* [2]973, 973n–4n
Strafford, Earl of *see* Wentworth, Thomas
Strahlenberg (probably Philipp Johan Tabbert von Stralenberg, 1676–1747) [4]489–90
strait-waistcoat [4]22, [5]453
Strand *see* London
strangenesses [1]763, 796
Strap, Hugh (in Smollett) [4]594, 594n
Strasbourg [2]548, 548n, [3]396, [5]404
Stratford [4]724, 755, 782
straw(s) [3]156, 310, 759, 877
animals of [4]97; chopped [1]234, [5]811; epistle of [3]724, 725n; man of [3]290; s.-men [4]106
"strays" [3]898
stream(s) [1]821, [2]591, 702, [5]133, 385
of error [4]9; of genius [5]528; of sorrow [3]555
street-walker [4]759, 803
strength(s) [2]419, [3]1008, [4]131n, 811, [5]169
masculine [4]649; and power [3]378, 378n
"strenuous" [3]177, 177n
striving [1]604, 646, [5]425
Stroh, Alfred Henry *see* Swedenborg *Worship and Love of God* tr Stroh and Sewall
Strong, George Templeton (1820–75) [1]clxi, clxiii, clxiiin, [2]213, 214, [4]105, 237, [6]249
stronghold [1]394, [3]976
strontian [1]570
strontianyl [1]570
Strozzi, Giovanni Battista (1504–71) [6]34
structure [1]536
strumpet(s) [1]393, 397, [4]548
Strymon (river) [1]464
Strype, John (1643–1737) [3]707
The History of the Life [of] . . . Edmund Grindal [2]1139n; MT [5]389–91; *Memorials of . . . Thomas Cranmer* [1]839, 839n; MT [5]392–400
Stuart(s) [1]728n, 808, [2]667, 929, 929n, 1041, 1136, 1175, 1201, [3]229, 540, 920, [5]662
age of [2]940; family timidity [2]521; S. Papers [1]357, 357n, 359; reign of [2]663; worthless [2]933n. *See also* Charles I; Charles II; James I; James II
Stuart/Stewart, Charles Edward (the Young Pretender) (1720–88) [5]316n
Stuart, Daniel (1766–1846) [1]lxxxiv, xcvi, xcvii, [2]845, [3]107, 107n, 755n
letter(s) to [1]373, [2]696 q, 753 q, [3]152n; owner of annotated books [3]881, 882; supplier of books to C [2]849n, [3]805
Stuart/Stewart, James Francis Edward (the Old Pretender) (1688–1766) [3]228, [6]32
Stuart, Ludovick, 2nd Duke of Lennox (1574–1624) [2]1125, 1127–8
Stuart-Wortley-Mackenzie, James Archibald, 1st Baron Wharncliffe (1776–1845) [6]48, 48n, 49, 49n
Stube [4]613, 613n
student(s) [2]955–7, [4]404–5, [5]167–8, 737
Studies in the History and Philosophy of Science [2]853n
study/studies [5]367
unprejudiced [5]466
studying [4]404
stuff(s) [3]44, 194, 194n, 486, 486n, 952, 1010, 1058, [4]316, 521, [5]344
elementary [1]537; meaning [3]129; see also *Stoffe*

stupidity [1]370, [4]647, [5]541, 822
stupor [4]137
Sturgeon, C. A. [1]155
Stutfield, Charles Bradshaw (fl 1822–53) [3]262, 262n
sty/stie [3]720
Calvin's [5]588
style [3]227, [5]396, 866
Asgill's [3]159; assertional [3]1061; Browne's [1]762, 796; Bunyan's [1]803; Ciceronian [2]763; Jeremy Collier's [1]155–61, 166–8, 177, 181n, 182–4; Defoe's [2]167, [6]163; dramatic [4]737; ease in [2]58–9; elevation of [4]838; epic [4]737; epistolary [4]239; figurative [2]15, [5]528; free and easy [1]177; Joseph Hall a corrupter of [1]845; Ibbetson's [4]82; "Junius"'s [3]220–9; laxities of [4]723; Leighton's [3]525, [6]307; monotony of [5]566; mythical [5]519; ornament of [5]765; periodic [2]167; Philo's [6]138, 144; prose [1]155, [3]220–2, 223, 882n, [5]533–4; purity of [2]411, [4]151; Shakespeare's [4]701; vague [5]534n; valiancy of [4]736; of Wisd of Sol [6]138; writer's [5]325; *see also* English (language)
Style, E. (fiction) [3]368
Styles, John (1782–1849) *Strictures on Two Critiques in the Edinburgh Review* [4]630n
Stymphalides (myth) [4]198
Styx (myth) [4]645n, [5]522n
Suard, Jean Baptiste Antoine (1734–1817) *see* F. M. von Grimm *Correspondance littéraire* ed Suard
Suarez, Francisco de (1548–1617) [1]civ
subauditur(s) [4]629, 723
"subemphatic" [2]124, 124n
"sub-existence" [4]301, 301n
subfiction [2]445n, [4]433n; *see also* suffiction
subintelligitur(s) [3]834, [5]774
subjacence [1]11
subject(s) [1]309, 648, 875, [2]891, 991–2, [3]28, 345, 393, 909n, [4]251, 433n, [5]4, 83, 304, 708
absolute [3]151; civil [1]339; co-operant [5]653; division of [2]318; duties of [1]833; liberty of [4]80; material s. [5]737; s.-matter [5]737; mystery in [4]494; no s. [3]346; oath of allegiance [3]164; and object *see* object; s.-object [3]559, [4]125; organised [5]431; rebellious [2]659; rights of [3]360, 755–6; unconscious [5]495; universal [3]347; unpoetic [1]401
"subjective" [2]627, [3]520n
subjective, the [2]631, 881, 887, 1175, [3]13, 74
C's s. phase [1]648; and objective *see* objective; seeing and hearing [3]770
subjectivism [4]421n
subjectivity [4]454
absolute [3]12, [6]74; Kantian [5]718; negative [4]542; in Swedenborg [5]416; universal [5]743
Sublapsarians [5]610, 610n
sublime, the [2]355, 1067, 1070, [3]401–2, 404, 408, 409, 410, 729, [5]390, 487n
and beautiful *see* beautiful; defined [2]1068–9, 1069n; false [5]487; *see also* Longinus *On the Sublime*
sublimity [1]430, 435, 765, [2]314, [3]453, [4]157, [6]219
of Aurelius [1]180; super-superlative [3]341–2; wild [4]607
submission [1]523
subordination [1]299, 395, [3]762, [5]9, 304
filial [3]588, [5]54; harmonious [2]65
subpedital [3]472n
subpeditry [3]472
"subposed" [4]234, 234n
subposition [2]605; *see also* supposition
subpositum [2]444
subscription [2]531, 531n
subsistence [3]18n
and existence [5]429, 429n
subsistency [3]11, 11n, 17, 17n, 23n
"substance" [1]145, 145n, 469n, [5]3–4, 3n, [6]87
substance(s) [1]524–5, 563, 579, 614, 683, 780, [2]306, 561, 618, 655, 843, 882, 891, [3]11n, 21, 83, 138, 233, 233n, 296, 297, 560n, 581, 606, 606n, 723, 757, 901, 901n, 916, 1006, [4]210, 211, 223, 250, 346, 433n, [5]17, 17n, 18, 175n, 208, 210, 210n, 213, 409, [6]123
substance and accident(s) *see* accident(s); and attribute(s) [5]448; cerebral [5]247; comminuted [3]1023; common notion of [6]241; of deity [5]718; discerptible [1]868; and form *see* form; God not [2]324; of guilt [4]235; idea of [2]625; imagined [5]450; imperishable [1]815; indecomponible [3]46; living [1]673, [4]314, [6]126; material [3]277–8, 298, [6]132; meaning of [2]671, [3]950, 950n; one [1]177, [3]362, [4]230, [5]83, 83n; phantom of [6]244; Plato on [4]127; and powers [3]297, [5]346; practical [4]634; self-subsistence [5]443; and shadow [1]632,

[6]307; simple [5]445; simplest [5]446; Spinoza's [3]855; spiritual [1]525; all subjective [5]175; substantiative power [2]663; superficial [5]753; universal [4]123
substans/substantia [1]469n, [2]726n, 731, [4]433, [5]453, 453n, 627
s. una et unica [5]83; *s. unica* [3]362, [5]446, 457, [6]244n
substantial, the [5]738
substantiality [2]663
"substantiate" [2]332
substantiation [5]63
substantive [2]960
compound [6]289. *See also* noun(s); verb(s), substantive
substration [6]233
substratum [1]469, 469n, [2]216, [3]1021, [4]223, [5]580
subsumption [5]455
subtlety/subtleties [4]502, [5]158, 541, 558, 790, [6]235
of Duns Scotus [5]790, 790n; useless [6]302
subtraction [5]487
succession [1]446, [3]88
apostolic *see* apostle(s); Oath of *see* oath(s); Protestant [4]24n; Romish doctrine of [1]515; to throne [4]19n
successive, the [1]619
"successry" [1]392
succumbence [5]805
Suckling, Sir John (1609–41) [1]37
marked passages [1]53
Sudbury [6]45, 45n
suds [4]636, 637
Suermeros [5]394
Suetonius (Gaius Suetonius Tranquillus) (75–160) [2]918, [3]57n, 174–5
Suez [4]29
suffering(s) [1]344, [2]160, [4]277, 285, 647, 820, [5]61, 236
of Jesus Christ [3]26, [5]535; passion as [1]728; of pleasure and pain [2]639; salutary effects of [1]734; vicarious [3]28
sufficiency [4]23–4
"sufficient" [2]1145, 1145n
sufficta [2]445
"suffiction(s)" [2]886, 886n, [4]13, 13n, [5]825, 825n
suffiction [2]605, [4]234n
and supposition [3]1026; *see also* subfiction
Suffolk, Duke of *see* Pole, William de la
suffrage [4]23
universal [6]52
sugar [1]596, 596n, [3]44, [4]16, [5]552, [6]152
of lead [1]596, 596n, [5]552; lumps of [5]351
Sugden, Edward Burtenshaw, Baron St Leonards (1781–1875) [5]478
Suicerus, Johann Caspar (1620–84) *Thesaurus ecclesiasticus* MT [5]401–2
suicide [1]166n, 167n, 180, [2]725, [3]747, [4]776
defensibility [2]236
Suidas (2nd half 10th century) [2]581, [4]191
sul [1]637
Sulla, Lucius Cornelius (138–78 BC) [2]615n, [3]447 ("Sylla")
sullenness [4]818, [5]396
Sully, Maximilien de Béthune, Duc de (1560–1641) [4]172
sulphur [1]547, 547n, 551, 552, 571, 629, 629n, 630, 670, 737, 779, 780, [2]546, 546n, [3]44, 1029, 1031, [4]315, [5]263, 438, [5]397
"sulphureous" [1]551
sulphuric acid [4]395
Sulpicius Severus (c 363–c 420) [6]318n
Sultana, Donald *Samuel Taylor Coleridge in Malta and Italy* [5]387n
Sulzer, Johann Georg (1720–79) [2]774, [6]135, 135n
sum [2]629, [4]122–3
summer [5]349
summit [1]752, 752n, 754
summum bonum [4]136n, [5]724
sumpsimus [2]935, 935n
sumption [5]550
sun [2]379–80, 380n
sun(s) [1]12, 561, 571, 623, 625, 625n, 763, 797, [2]250, 379–80, 380n, 393, 517, 557, 583, 591, 677, 829n, [3]29n, 150, 323, 340, 341, 472, 473, 866, 1058, [4]268, 326, 394, 487n, 513, 762–3, 846, 847, [5]133, 225, 226, 263–4, 266, 292, 349, 357, 359, 383, 426–7, 429–30, 452, 569, 653, 703, 715
analogy for Trinity [1]564; s.-beam [2]1186; chariot of [5]745; through cloud [3]17; dark nucleus of [1]785; distance from [5]264; earthy [1]593; effluent of [5]467; feminine in German [1]654; formation of solar system [5]339; glory of [3]616–17; gone backward [2]828–9; image of [1]774, [5]60; images of in dew-drops [1]815, 815n; intelligible [6]296, 296n; mock [5]298; oriental solar deity [2]580; origin of planets [2]885–6; oxygen from [4]387–8, 388n; rays of [3]29, [5]311,

sun(s)—*continued*
[6]144; of redemption [4]634; of righteousness [1]815n, [3]723, [5]523; rise of [5]156; rising [3]581; satellites of [1]626, [2]1142; size of [1]774n; solar disk [3]460; and Son *see* Son; spiritual [3]741; standing still [2]897, [6]119; symbol of God [1]687–8, *687n–8n*; system of [3]379; wives of [3]1035; *see also* solar system
Sunday [1]269, [2]1153
observation of [6]261; Trinity [5]60. *See also* Lord's Day; Sabbath(s)
Sunday Times [2]926
sunflower [2]580, 580n–1n, [4]286
sunienai [1]587n
sunrise [2]393, [5]371
sunset [2]45, 998n, 1070
sunshine [1]674, 808, [3]312, 466, 697, [5]751
picture [1]280
sunspots [1]630, 630n, [3]869, 869n–70n, [4]816n, [6]43
superannuation [2]1140, [4]846
"superbiloquies" [5]372, 372n
supercilium [2]648
supererogation [2]707, [3]455, 455n, [4]628, 628n
superficies [3]139, [5]230, 265, 453, 520
super-foetation [1]519, [5]778, 778n
"superfused" [1]776, 776n
super-humanity [5]618
superinduction [1]604
superintendents [2]1138
superior(s) and inferior(s) [2]319
superiority [2]1080, [4]759
intellectual [2]1156
superlative [5]566
supernatural [2]145, 1119n, [3]81, 205, 205n, 311, 320, 351, 662, 721n, 987, 991, [4]581n, 599, 653–4, [6]262, 294
act [3]708; light [3]439; reason is s. [2]1150
supernaturalist(s) [2]609, [4]599
super-numeral [1]689, 689n
supersensual [1]396, [2]425–6, [4]441, [5]809
"supersistent" [3]518, 518n
"superstition" [1]682, 774, [2]347, 1175, [3]85, [4]579, 579n
superstition(s) [1]163, 264, 330, 473, 509, 516–17, [2]314, 418, 663, 725, 1036, 1158, 1196, [3]76–7, 76n, 216, 483, 517, 517n, 529, 600, 645, 692, 771, 774, 823, [4]27, 145, 241, 307, 581, 601, 601n, 681, 727, 729, 770, 786, 801, 819, 834, [5]135, 142, 144, 189, 510, 516, 551, 561, 755, [6]14, 99, 167, 259, 263, 300, 300n, 314
baits of [1]745; carnal [3]34; Catholic [5]106; among Christians [4]299–300; crazy [1]393; debasing [1]397; defined [3]42; no degrees in [3]207; of the East [5]226; and enthusiasm [2]198, 198n; evil [1]275; fanaticism a form of [3]318; fever of [1]270, [6]261; hourly [1]223; in Irving [3]42; Judaic [6]261; keeping up [1]836; of letter [1]779; letter for spirit [3]724; of Methodists [4]658; palsy of [5]188; popish [1]254; popular [2]1106, [4]775; progress of [2]749; of property [6]44; Romish [1]705, 862; Sabbatical [1]874; in use of scriptures [1]469
superstructure [5]561
of chaff [5]596; fanciful [6]141; of religion [4]652
supplicant [5]483
supplication, spirit of [5]512
support(s)
flattering [1]344; spiritual [5]680
supporter [5]542
supposita [2]445
"supposition" [5]825n, [6]80n
supposition [2]444, 445n, 605, 886, 886n, [4]13, 234, 234n, 433n
impossible [6]80, 80n; rational [5]406; and suffiction [3]1026; *see also* subposition
"suppositum" [1]469n
suppositum [5]172, [6]116
suppression [4]842
suppressor [1]653
supra-humanity [5]621
Supralapsarian(s) [5]610, 610n, 613
supremacy, papal [5]497
Surenhusius, Guilielmus (Willem Surenhuys) (1666–1729) see *Mischna* ed Surenhusius
surface(s) [2]606, 606n, 607, 863, 863n, 1115, 1123, [3]138, 1036, [5]734, [6]233
expanding [4]412; s. powers [1]641; production of [6]232–3; s. sphere [1]579
surgeon(s) [2]771, [3]116, [4]28, [5]184
Italian [1]627
Surinam [3]1073n
S. toad [2]296, 296n
surplice [1]286, 286n–7n, 321–2, 321n, 343
surprise [4]489
Surrey [2]6n, [3]193
Surrey, Earl of *see* Howard, Henry
suscipient [2]402
Sussex, Duke of *see* Augustus Frederick

"sussorption" [3]1073, 1073n
sustainer [1]525
sustenance [1]525
 bodily [5]674
sustentation [4]9, [4]9n
Swabia [4]290n ("Swabian period")
swain, dying [5]821
swallow(s) [1]483, [2]938, [3]581
 migration of [6]147; nest of [6]148–9
swamp(s) [3]1076, [4]149n, [5]292
swan(s) [3]955, [5]69
 black [2]861, 861n; dying [5]745; Luther as black s. [3]756, 765, 765n, 769
Swandewit (myth) [4]489–90
swarm of thoughts [4]720
swarmers [5]395
Swartz, Christian Friedrich (1725–98) [1]431n
swearing [1]319, [5]146
Sweden [2]60, 936n, [3]133, [5]312
 Queen of [5]414, 414n
Swedenborg, Emanuel ("Swedenberg") (1688–1772) [1]lxiii, lxx, 558n, 560n, 606n, 659, *659n–60n*, 681n, 687n, 719n, [2]13n, 615n, [3]203, 333, *333n–4n*, 351, 351n, 352, 353, 732, 983–92, [5]150, 301, 334, 334n–5n, [6]99
 and Böhme [1]696, 696n; Swedenborgian Church *see* New Church *below*; desiderata in [5]411; frequent problem in [5]418; genius of [5]421; on God [1]681, 681n; hells of [5]559, 559n–60n; on Lord's Prayer [3]432; misrepresents opponents [5]468–9; New Church [1]687, 687n, [3]432n, 991, [5]403, 406, 433, 463; sanity of [5]473; and Schelling [5]335n; veracity of [5]407, 407n
 Apocalypse Explained [3]38, 38n; *An Appendix to the Treatise on the White Horse* tr C. A. Tulk [5]432; *Arcana coelestia* [2]136, 136n; *Conjugal Love* [5]403; *De arcanis coelestibus* [5]432; *De coelo et ejus mirabilibus, et de inferno* [3]986n; MT [5]403–25, tr D. H. Harley as *Heaven and its Wonders and Hell* [5]403; *De cultu et amore Dei* MT [5]426–31, tr Stroh and Sewall as *The Worship and Love of God* [5]426; *De equo albo* MT [5]432–9, tr Gorman, rev Acton and B. S. Willmott as *Concerning the White Horse in the Apocalypse* [5]432; *Divine Providence* [6]335; *The Nature of the Intercourse between the Soul and the Body*† [5]440; *Oeconomia regni animalis* [3]334n; MT [5]441–53, tr Clissold as *The Economy of the Animal Kingdom* [5]441; *Opera philosophica et mineralia* [3]334n; *Prodromus philosophiae* [3]334n; MT [5]454–61, tr J. J. G. Wilkinson as *Outlines of a Philosophical Argument* [5]454; *Regnum animale* [3]334n; MT [5]462, tr J. J. G. Wilkinson as *The Animal Kingdom* [5]462; *True Christian Religion* [1]606n, 659n, 695, [3]432n q, 732n, [5]335n, 403; MT 463–72; *The Wisdom of Angels*† [1]clxvii, [5]469n; MT 473–4
Swedenborgian(s)
 literal [5]414; pervading error of [3]989
Swedenborgianism of ancients [5]710, 710n
Swedes, as generous/Iapetic race [1]540
sweet, the [1]595, 604, 613
sweet-hearting [5]821
sweetmeats [1]731
sweetness [1]611, 632, 633, 642
"swerve" [3]18
Swift, Jonathan (1667–1745) [1]38, 156n, 718, 722, [2]82 q, 774, [3]177, 1043, [4]190n
 and Asgill [1]126n; and Defoe [2]158; genius of [4]189; Houyhnhnms of [2]347n; and Milton [5]477; Sabellian tendencies [5]556
 Battle of the Books [3]589n; *Gulliver's Travels* [1]318n, [2]202, 687, [5]475–7; *Journal to Stella* [4]466n; *Mechanical Operation of the Spirit* [2]768; *On Poetry* [5]442 q, 442n; *Remarks upon a Book* [3]177n; "Sermon on the Trinity" [5]556n; *Tale of a Tub* [2]688, [3]395n q, [5]476, ed Guthkelch and D. N. Smith [4]190n q; *Works* MT [5]475–7
swimming [5]837
Swinburne, Thomas (b c 1799) [5]478
 A Letter to . . . Robert Peel MT [5]478; 852
swine [3]453, [4]782
 Gadarene [6]102, 102n
Swiss [5]279
Switzerland [3]864, [5]311n
 Protestant [5]145
sword [1]331, [3]696, [4]761, [5]83, 576
 decision of [5]640; temporal [1]339
"swound" [5]861, 861n
Sybil *see* Sibyl
sycamore [5]838
sycophant [2]1141, [4]643, [6]101, 101n
Sydenham, Floyer (1710–87) *see* Plato *Works* tr Sydenham
Sydenham, Sir Philip [3]488
Sydenham, Thomas (1624–89) *Opera universa* [2]868, 868n
Sylla *see* Sulla

syllables [1]670, [2]574n
in Böhme [1]591; German [1]608; times of [1]377
syllabub [2]1065, 1065n
syllepsis [5]10
syllogism(s) [1]770, 770n, [3]94n–5n, 244–5, 257n, 284, 363, 675, 934, [4]115, 147, 235, [5]555, 649, 656, 737, 825, [6]285–6
legitimate [5]577; logical [6]174–5, 174n; major and minor in [1]128; papistic [5]395; Protestant [5]395
sylva [2]431, *431n*, [3]248, 248n, 249n
Sylvester, Charles (fl 1810) [3]938
Sylvester, Matthew (c 1636–1708) [1]230, 240, [2]1198, [4]73, [6]257
Elisha's Cry after Elijah's God [1]240; *see also* R. Baxter *Reliquiae* ed Sylvester
"symbol" [1]345n, [4]42, 42n, [5]490, 490n
symbol(s) [1]lxi–lxii, 138n, 345n, 472, 485, 670, 704, 719, [2]580, 689, 1053n, 1062, 1062n, 1069, 1079, 1106, 1201, [3]29n, 54, 425n, 429n, 433, 442, 600n, 758n, 927, 999, 1021n, [4]42, 258, 415n, 426, 502, 625–6, [5]357, 415, 591, 648, 674
acts as [1]634; air as [5]719; algebraic [1]633; and allegory *see* allegory; symbolical Apocalypse [3]477; apocalyptic [3]468; baptismal [1]312; boar as [2]983; bodily [4]413; of brotherhood [1]418; Christ's life as [2]279–80; circle for self-defining consciousness [1]690n; C's *see* Coleridge, S. T. I (1) his signs or logical symbols; C's doctrine of [5]413n, 550n; corporeal [3]997, 998; defined [5]698, 698n; degraded into metaphor [1]862; desiderata of [1]687; doctrine of [5]718; symbolic drama [3]417n; earthly [1]563; Eucharist as [1]469; in Eucharist [1]524; of feeling [2]222; of finites [5]457; fire as [3]1024; of God [3]108; grounded in prophecy [3]425; Hammonic the symbolic race [1]540; horse as [2]347; and idea [5]780; of ideas [5]692; symbolic(al) images [3]1089, [5]494; imponderable [3]998; symbolic import [3]732; symbolic institutions [5]398; literal meaning as [2]286; Jesus as [1]821; symbolic(al) language [2]712; language of Scripture [1]706; and literal [2]267, [6]303; literal interpretation of [3]443; literal s. of spiritual [5]413; Logos as [1]564; marriage as [1]751, [2]742n; mediating [4]78; and metaphor *see* metaphor; mirror of [3]62; symbolic money [5]687n; symbolical names [3]422; numerical [1]563n; outward [3]722; symbolic poesy/poetry [1]485, [3]30, 472; present ideas [2]410; quantity as [1]563; and radix [1]653; and reality [1]812n; of religion [6]109; in Rev [2]517; Rome as [3]467; *salitter* as [1]572; science of [3]600; in Scripture [1]719, 719n; of serpent [1]684; symbolical sights [5]474; and sign [3]757; and sign or figure [5]550; of space [2]1145; of tetrad [5]228; symbolic time [3]471; of unity [4]14; of universal process [1]558; symbolic(al) use [1]817–18, [3]723; visible [1]580; visions all symbolical [3]1088; visual [5]85
"Symbola Pythagorae" [3]539n
symbolic, the [2]1146, [4]798
and real [5]687n
symbolism in Ezek [2]487–8
symbolon [1]345, 345n, [2]1082n
s. fidei [1]236n, 312n
symbolum [3]445, 445n, 691n, 766, 766n, 768, 768n, [5]646, [6]62, 62n
s. fidei [5]13, 620; *s. portae* [5]642
Syme, James (1799–1870) "Quarterly Report of the Edinburgh Surgical Hospital" MT [2]365–6
symmetry [3]342, [4]82
Symmons/Symons, Caroline (1789–1803) [6]218
Symons, Arthur (1865–1945) [6]334
sympathists [4]845
sympathy/sympathies [1]397, 751, 752, [2]136, 159 ("sympathise"), 197, 1034, [3]318, 408, 409, 410, 492, 494, 601, 611, [4]792, [5]71, 134, 418, 504
anticipated [2]328; blind [1]850; confident [5]416; craving for [2]1176, [4]814; in education [1]726; hounding scent of [4]259; with mankind [1]836; of monstrosity [4]820; of nature [4]809, 810; painful [2]173; of sect [1]496
symphilosophy [1]136
Symphorosa (legend) [2]718
symphysikos [2]798, 798n
Sympson, John (b c 1710) [1]384, 398
symptoms [5]562
synagogue(s) [1]339, [2]377, 654, [3]20, 34, 768, [4]471, 474, 638, [5]128, 535
usage of [5]522
synaphe [4]155, 155n
syncretism [1]306, 306n
syncretists [2]193, 193n
"synenergema" [5]654, 654n
Synesius (c 370–413) [2]666, 666n
synetoisi phonounta [2]486
syngenesia [3]1074, 1074n
synocha [4]149

synod [3]418, [5]503. *For Church synods see place-names (e.g. Dort)*
synonym(s)/synonime(s) [1]560, [2]993, [3]18, 76, 187
lazy [4]626; superlative [5]484
synopsis [3]20, 451, [5]51
syntax [2]714, 881n
mismanagement of [2]127
syntaxist [4]723
synthesis/syntheses [1]348, 563, 597, 651, [2]629, 990, [3]6, 16, 18, 138, 344, 416, 450, 453, 851, 966, [4]111, 315, 384n, [5]49, 264, 444, 460, 533, 715, 715n, [6]132
absolute [4]460; of attraction and repulsion [1]571; of body and spirit [3]130; God as [2]247, 249; of intuitions [3]244–6, 247; love as [3]266; of opposites [1]568; wonderful [5]451
syntheta [1]780
synthetic, the [3]331
syntheton [2]311
syphilis [3]822, 822n, [4]164, 622, 622n, 630n
Syracuse [1]lxxxiii, cv, clxvi, [2]900, 900n, [4]86n, 209
Syria [1]721, 832, 832n, [2]418, 809
Syriac (language) [2]12n, 449, 661, 683, 706, 739, [4]258, [5]337, [6]140
Syrians [2]739n
as generous/Iapetic race [1]540
Syro-Chaldaic (language) [1]470, [2]382, 437, 446, 561, 574n, 653, [3]37, 1069, [4]243, 243n, 248n, [5]170, 396, 607
Syro-Macedonians [3]103–4
Sysiphus (myth) [2]878
system(s) [5]468
Alexandrine [6]143; arterio-muscular [1]624; bad [1]314; Brunonian [3]871; cerebro-nervous [5]258; Christian [5]560; of Christianity [5]568; circulating [5]292; C's [3]66; C's s. of divinity [3]436; commercial [5]276; corrupt [2]506; Fichte's [2]618; glandulovenous [5]258; harmonious [1]410; of Heraclitus [5]715, 717–18; Hutchinsonian [2]787; of ideal intuition [5]755; irritable [4]389, [5]259, 260; Irving's [3]418; Kantian [5]757, 813; Kant's [3]242, 253, [5]714, 743n; Manichaean [5]625n; mechanic [3]199, [5]208; Mesmer's [3]865; musculo-arterial [5]258; of natural history [1]536; Neoplatonic [5]743; nervous *see* nervous system; Newtonian [4]20; organic [5]258; philosophic [5]721; Plato's [5]732, [6]6; poetico-metaphysical [2]716; polar [1]642; must have postulates [3]959; of prothetic [3]361; pseudo-Pauline [1]201; Ptolemaic [3]201; of rational pathology [3]67; reflective [3]291; reproductive [5]259; rigid [5]683; Schubert's [4]499; Seneca incapable of [1]174; sensible [5]259; solar [5]225, 266, 339, 430, 430n; Spinoza's [5]815; spiritual [3]201; Steffens's [5]356; supposed [3]67; Swedenborg's [3]991, [5]405, 410, 412–13, 464, 469; Jeremy Taylor's [5]596; tetradic [3]1006; and theory [5]201; three coherent [1]679; true [5]622
systematisers [1]536
systematists [3]611

"T" [4]768, 768n
tabernacle [2]486, [3]41, 109n
"Tabernaclers" [4]663, 663n
table(s) [3]332, [4]235, 452, [5]774
astronomical [4]814; categoric [5]702; chronological [5]692; communion [1]322; of the law [2]19, 19n
tablet(s) [4]475
of the heart [3]54
Tablet of Cebes [3]992, 992n
tabula rasa [2]542, 552
Tacitus, P. Cornelius (c 55–c 120) [1]221, [2]68, 918, [3]174, 251, 251n, [4]311n, 627, 627n, 666, [5]576, [6]254n
Annals [2]109n, [5]85n; *Germania* [4]666n
tack, literal [2]87
"tact" [2]136, 136n
tact [1]27n, [2]563, [3]472, 890, [4]844
of genius [2]167; moral [1]393, 849; want of [3]469
tadpole [3]1073
Tahiti [1]536n
tail [1]626
of horse *see* horse
tailor(s) [2]754, 754n, [3]664, [4]80, 80n, [5]361 ("taylors"), 680
German [5]866 ("Taylor")
tailoring [2]165
Tait's Magazine [1]cviin
Talboys *see* Oxford
tale(s)
idle [2]274; legendary [1]345; Oriental [2]772; traditionary [3]595
talent(s) [1]136, 367, 367n, [2]617, [4]79, 622, 622n, 719, 816, [5]162, 366, 367, 661
academic [2]979; ennobled [6]57; genial [3]1019; and genius *see* genius; metaphysical [2]203; natural and cultivated [1]4; practical [5]319
"talented" [4]14, 14n

Talfourd, Sir Thomas Noon (1795–1854) [1]clxii
Taliesin (fl c 550) [2]1170n, 1170n
talisman(s) [1]336, 397, 419
talk [1]397
animated [1]383; interpocular [2]63
Talkative (in Bunyan) [1]803
talkativeness [4]773
"tall" and "short" [5]720
Talleyrand-Périgord, Charles Maurice de (1754–1838) [3]851, 852n
Talmud [1]513, 532, [2]377, 377n, 513, [3]707, [4]475, 475n
Alphabet of Ben-Sira [2]513n; *The Babylonian Talmud: Aboda Zara* tr Epstein [1]533n q; *Pesahim* [2]513n; *Testament of Solomon* [2]513n
Talmudist(s) [3]111, 449, 1089
Talus (in Spenser) [2]1155, 1155n
Tamburlane *see* Timur
Tamyris (myth) [6]218
Tangara (myth) [4]489–90
Tangatanga (myth) [4]489–90
tanks [2]1024n
Tannery, Paul (1843–1904) *see* Descartes *Oeuvres* ed C. Adam and Tannery
tan-pit [2]982
Tansley, Peter (fl 1810) [3]939
tantara [2]940
Tao [4]489–90
tapestry [5]395
tapeworm(s) [4]431–2, 432n, [5]468n
tapioca [2]298n
tap-room [3]666
tap-root [3]697, [5]189
tar(s) (sailor[s]) [6]214
Taran, Leonardo *Parmenides* [5]706n q
tarantula [5]66
Tardy de Montravel, A. A. (fl 1785) [3]377
target [3]601
Targums [1]421n
Tarquin(s) [1]610n, [4]189n, [5]41
Tarquinius (Lucius Tarquinius Priscus), King of Rome (reigned 616–578 BC) [5]45
Tarquinius (Lucius Tarquinius Superbus), King of Rome (reigned 534–510 BC) [5]533, 533n
Tarquinius Sextus (d ?496 BC) [5]533n
tarring [2]460, 460n
Tarsus [2]919, 919n
Tartar (language) [4]243, 243n
Tartar(s) [2]1017, [4]489–90
Tartary
Tartarian fury [4]82; Great Cham of [3]779
Tasker, Randolph Vincent Greenwood (b 1895) *see* Bible: NT: Greek: ed Tasker
task-work [3]741
Tasso, Torquato (1544–95) [1]117n, [2]10, 968, [4]605n, [6]328
taste [1]220, 321, 327, 367, 578, 580, [3]400–13, [4]408, 479, 481, [5]555, 599, 866
classical [2]979, 1034, [4]243; devotional [5]512; exquisite [3]1075; fine [3]701; finest [1]377; French [5]835, 835n; genial [2]1174; genius forms [2]781; an hydrate [1]579; moral [3]1076; poetic [3]1088, [5]858; in religion [5]130; vulgar [3]184
tasting [5]265
Tate, Nahum (1652–1715) [1]475, [5]178, 178n; *see also* Brady and Tate
Tatham, Mr (fl 1859) [1]clxviii
Tatian (Tatianus) (c 120–73) [2]440–1, 441n, [5]624
Diatessaron [2]439n, 443, 443n, 446
Tatler [1]763n, [3]586, 586n
tatterdemalions [5]139
Taube [4]65, 65n
Tauler, Johann (c 1300–61) [2]755n, [4]259, [5]795, 795n
Taurus [5]387, 387n, [6]280–1, 281n
"tautogeneity" [6]123, 123n
tautogeneity [3]997
tautology [1]325, [3]1051, [5]793
in words only [1]325
Taverner, Francis (fl 1662) [5]598n
Tavistock [1]59, 59n
taxation [1]178n, [6]52
tax(es) [1]359 ("taxing"), 530, [2]1101, [3]152, [6]60
church [2]1150n; C of E [5]532, 532n; t.-gatherer [1]530; t.-payers [2]80
Tayler, John James (1797–1869) [1]clxviiin
Taylor, Sir Henry (1800–86) [1]lxxiv, clxviiin
Taylor, Isaac (1787–1865) [1]lxxvi
Elements of Thought† [5]479; *Natural History of Enthusiasm* [1]cxvi; MT [5]480–5
Taylor, Jeremy (1613–67) [1]lxx, lxxxviii, cxxviii, 156n, 280, 280n, 351, 805, 805n, 845n, [2]273n, 294n, 355n, 522n, 558, 651n, 804, 816, 987n, 1041n, 1101n, 1131, [3]376n, 438n, 459, 459n, 511, 511n, 735n, 764, 778, 882, 882n, 921, 921n, [4]238n, 301n, 336, [5]5n, 80–1, 81n, 486, [6]258
Carlist [2]260, *260n*; character of [5]616; dearest Jeremy [5]547; errors of [5]599; father a barber [5]669, 669n; Gassendist [5]615; ground of errors [5]640; as himself

[5]527, 589; no metaphysician [5]615; mother of [5]669; on original sin [1]269, [3]515n, 879, 879n, [5]157, 157n–8n, 498, [6]298, 298n; Pelagian [5]610–11; prose style [5]502n, 533; recommended to Lamb [1]lxxxviii; on repentance [2]1176–7, 1178, [3]747, [5]163, 163n, [6]261; RC qualities [5]497, 497n; self-contradicting [5]509n; slippery [5]685; two-edged arguments [1]317
An Answer to a Letter [from] . . . the Lord Bishop of Rochester [3]515, 515n–16n q, [5]498n; MT 611–16; [6]298n q; *An Apology for Authorized and Set Forms of Liturgy* MT [5]504–30; *A Course of Sermons* [1]lxxx; MT [5]486–7; 625n q; *Deus justificatus* [1]302n, [3]879n, [5]498n, 596n; MT 608–11; 655n; *A Discourse of Confirmation* [1]532, 532n; MT [5]658–67; *Discourse of the Real Presence* [5]5n, 5n q, 396n, 397n, 525n q; MT 541–58; "A Dissuasive from Popery" [5]528, 528n q; MT 558–82; 563n q; *Doctrine and Practice of Repentance* [5]486; *Ductor dubitantium* [3]778n, [5]505n, 562, 562n; *Episcopacy Asserted* [5]503, 684n q; *Epistle Dedicatory* MT [5]502–3; *Golden Grove* [5]512n; *Great Exemplar* [5]598n; *Liberty of Prophesying* [5]501, 501n, 503, 503n, 528, 573n, 575, 575n q, 596; MT 616–58; *Of the Sacred Order and Offices of Episcopacy* [5]503; MT 531–40; "Of the Worship of Images" [1]519n; *Polemicall Discourses* [1]lxvn, lxxxviii, lxxxix, xc, xci, ci, cxlvii, clv, [2]507n, 1176n–7n q, [3]459n, 515n–16n q, 738n, 765n, 879n; MT [5]499–688; *The Rule and Exercises of Holy Living . . . Holy Dying Copy A* MT [5]488–9; 500, 512n; *Copy B* MT [5]490–8; 500, 512n; *Unum necessarium* [1]269, 269n, 334, 334n, [2]1176–7, 1177n, 1192n, [3]738n, 879n, [5]163n, 559n q; MT 582–608; *Whole Works* ed Heber [1]532n, [5]500, 500n, 669n; *The Worthy Communicant* [3]758n q; MT [5]669–85
Taylor, John (1781–1864) [4]469, [5]686n
An Essay on Money [5]852; MT 686–7
Taylor, John, of Birmingham (fl 1775) [3]638, 638n
Taylor, Thomas (1758–1835) [2]1123n, [4]139, 156, 156n, 160, 160n, [5]12n
tr Plato [1]lxiii, xcii. *See also* Plato *Cratylus, Phaedo . . .* ; Proclus *The Philosophical and Mathematical Commentaries . . . Theological Elements* tr Taylor
Taylor, W. (fl 1832) [1]34
Taylor, William, of Norwich (1765–1836) [1]ciii, 88, 89, 90, *90n–1n*, 828, [2]35n, 369, 1048, [4]283, 283n
Historic Survey of German Poetry [1]91n
Taylor, William F. (fl 1889) [1]clin
Critical Annotations of Samuel Taylor Coleridge [1]cli
tea [4]38, 109n, 619, [5]680
t.-cup [3]920; green [1]765, 797n; gunpowder [1]797; t.-pot [5]351; t.-spoon [5]860
teacher(s) [2]636, [5]433, 463
gifted [5]618; incomparable [1]354; inspired [2]463; invisible [5]642
teaching [3]622
inward [5]642; spiritual [5]569
tear(s) [2]45, [3]894, [4]267, 267n
Tearsheet, Doll (*2 Henry IV*) [4]713–14, 714n, 759, 803
teat, male [1]243
technites [2]576, 576n, 578n
Technites (in Fénelon) [2]576
technology [5]90
Techo, Nicolás del (1611–85) [5]104 q
teens [4]38
teeth [1]327n, 607, [4]164
Tegnér, Esaias (1782–1846) *Die Frithiofs-Sage* tr Helvig MT [5]688–90
Teitan [1]485, 486, [3]929n, [6]166, 166n
tekna Theou [1]484
Telauges (fl 5th century BC) [1]181
teleios [5]132, 169–70
Telemachus (myth) [1]220n
teleology [1]653
telescope(s) [1]170n, [2]867, 1046, 1164n, [3]73–4, 73n, 716n, [4]508, [5]291, 297, 418, 825
of reason [1]170; of the soul [1]671
Telfer, William (b 1886) *see* Nemesius *Cyril of Jerusalem and Nemesius of Emesa* ed Telfer
Telford, Thomas (1757–1834) [2]182n
Tell, William (legend) [2]201n
Teller, Wilhelm Abraham (1734–1804) *Beantwortung* [2]796
tellurian [1]785, 785n
tellurium [5]261
telos [3]834, 834n
Temani [1]418
"temper" [3]634
temper [4]278, [5]99
predominant [5]285
temperament [1]496, [4]762, 810, [5]98, 99, 284–5

temperance [1]286, [2]926
  of judgment [2]809
temperature [4]383
  organ of [6]104; sense of [3]716
tempest [2]220
templarity [2]465
temple/Temple [1]428, 428n, 430, [2]408, 416n, 455, 495, 832, 883, 920, 1153, [3]21, 112, 112n, 417, 448n, 468, 550, 707, 924, [4]58, 251n, 252
  building of [1]437; Christian [3]691; defiled [2]416n; Delphic [6]5; destruction of [1]832, [2]36n, 514, [3]20, 53, 448, 448n, [4]251, 251n, [5]128, 522n, 624, 667; dry rot in [5]516; t. ecstasies at Corinth [5]517; t.-going [4]625; Greek [1]328; Jesus presented in [4]477; killing in [5]229; t.-library [2]377; meaning of [2]486; money-changers in [4]66; new [5]535; plundered [2]377; rebuilding [2]746; in Rev [2]515–16; Samaritan [2]416, 416n; of Solomon [2]395; templarity of [2]465; walls of [1]250
Temple, Laura Sophia (b 1763) [2]1121, 1121n
Temple, Sir William (1628–99) [3]589n
"temporal" [1]497, 497n
temporal [1]806
  and chronical [1]497
temporality/temporalities [1]358, [4]218
temptation(s) [1]326, 342, [2]1106, 1176, 1177, 1179, [3]27, 49, 306, 436, 579, 709, 735, [4]9, 241, 588, 788, 817, [5]385
  besetting [5]634; of Christ *see* Jesus Christ, temptation of; parable of [4]60; tyrannous [5]678
tempter [3]49, [4]770, [6]98
temptibility [3]605
"ten" [5]701
ten [4]38, 38n, [6]294
  t. days [3]923; Pythagorean [2]557, 557n
Ten Commandments [1]311, [2]893, [3]50, 53, 496–7, 1087n, [4]175, 621, [5]12, 132, 406n
  First C. [5]406, 406n; Second C. [5]406, 406n, 657; Third C. [3]576; *see also* Decalogue
tenant and lord [1]383
tenderness [5]562
tendon [1]671
Teneriffe [5]387, 387n
tenet(s)
  abstract [4]580; characteristic [5]157; Egyptian [2]918; favourite [5]11; unimageable [5]406; Wesley's [5]162
Tennant, Smithson (1761–1815) [2]825n ("Smythson"), [3]1033, 1033n, [5]261, 261n
Tennemann, Wilhelm Gottlieb (1761–1819) [1]lviii, cxviii, cxxviii, 781n, [3]347n, [5]691
  desirability of selections from [5]691–2; not a true Kantian [5]*692n*; perturbations of [5]752–3, 752n; hostility to Schelling [5]744; "Tinny Man" [2]558, [5]801
  Geschichte der Philosophie [1]ci, cliv, 563n q, 584n, [2]172n, 869n, [3]682n, 728n, 766n, 923n; MT [5]691–816
Tennyson, Alfred, Lord Tennyson (1809–92)
  The Gardener's Daughter [5]857n; *Poems, Chiefly Lyrical* MT [5]817
Tennyson, Charles *see* Turner, Charles Tennyson
Tennyson, Hallam (1852–1928) [5]853
Tennyson Research Bulletin [5]853
tense(s) [3]784, [4]509
tension(s) [3]1015, 1016, 1059
  of ether [3]1015n; vivific [1]664
tent [3]28n, 41
Tenterden, Baron *see* Abbott, Charles
tenure [3]977, [4]284
Terence (Publius Terentius Afer) (c 190–159 BC) [1]218n, [2]240, [3]587n, [4]336n
  Andria [3]225n q; *Heauton timorumenos* tr Sargeaunt [3]923, 923n q
Teresa of Avila, St (1515–82) [1]cxliv, 63n, 517–18, 518n
  Crashaw poems on [1]48 q, 48n–9n
  Works [1]xciii; MT [5]818–23
term(s) [2]999, [3]565, 834, 1024
  absolute [2]278, [5]631; abstract [1]432; of abuse [5]768; abusive [1]876; adopted [6]306; ancient [4]136; antithetical [2]1193; appropriate [5]803; carelessness in [2]1152; change of [5]21; colloquial [5]480–1; common [4]107; confusion of [4]538; definition of [6]79; deprived of meaning [3]345; discussion of [3]589; dispute in [5]789; distinct [1]561; distinction of [1]632; equivalent [5]58; equivocal [2]1160, [5]856; explained by contraries [5]400; general [2]537, [3]791, 871, [4]144, 369, 426, 435, [5]63, 131, 366; generic [2]801, [3]261, 856, [4]228, [6]143; importance of [2]674; improper [5]397; lax [3]1087, [4]106; metaphorical [2]559; middle [3]910, [5]459; new [5]481, 579; no t. [3]346; nosological [3]397; positive [6]288; in pottery [3]633; precise [2]730; proper [5]155; of relation [5]22; relative [4]451; representative [3]54; scholastic [2]665; of theological schools [5]480; and things [1]496; traditional [3]524–5; undefined [5]408; use of [3]257

terminology
lax [4]17, 17n; philosophical [5]428
terminus [1]852n
ternary [1]565, 584
terra-cotta [3]630
terrestrial and celestial [1]138
terrible, the [1]397
and hated [1]371n
terriculum [1]805, [3]877
terrier [3]716, 716n, [5]274
terriery [3]716
terriform, the [5]451
terror(s) [1]483, [2]145, [3]584–5, 747, [4]145, 774, 776
imaginative [4]838; ingenerate in man [1]284; joyous [4]727; unmanly [1]369
Terror, The [1]292n, [2]511n
Terrorist(s) [2]509, 509n–10n, 510, [5]270
Terry, Daniel (c 1780–1827) [3]484, 484n
tertium [4]94
t. aliquid [1]594n, [2]572, [4]430, [5]761
Tertullian (Quintus Septimius Florens Tertullianus) (c 160–c 220) [1]245, 312n, 468n, 478n, 491n, [2]33 q, 34, 34n, 272n, 292, 404n, 438n, 459, 683, 683n, 685 q, 699, 720 q, 725n, 726n, 1029n, [3]7n, 310n, 459, 459n, 479, 486, 489, 489n–90n, 612, 687, 690–1, 695, 696, 697, 697n, 766n, [4]473, 473n, 513, 514, [5]384 q, 402, 571, 619, 620, 629, [6]72, 86n, 91, 93
Adversus Marcionem [2]33n, 439n; *Adversus Praxean* [2]33n, 34n, ed and tr E. Evans [6]90 q; *Apologeticus* [2]918n, [3]490n, [4]514n, tr T. R. Glover as *Apology* [6]89 q; *De carne Christi* [3]612n, ed and tr E. Evans as *Tertullian's Treatise on the Incarnation* [3]612n; *De testimonio animae* [3]479n
test
negative [2]136; of religious faith [1]249
The Testament of Solomon see Talmud
testicles [1]767, 767n, 773, 773n, 777–8
testimony [3]661, 919, 989, [4]640
apostolical [2]494; double [3]20; fallibility [2]1154; independent [5]141; posthumous [2]1173; role of [2]359–60
Tetens, Johann Nicolaus (1737–1807) [2]594
Philosophische Versuche [1]lx; MT [5]824–9
tetractys [1]562–3, *563n*, 579, 579n, 591, 594, 641n, 642, 643n, 649n, 652n, [2]557n, 745, 880, 880n, 991, [3]13n, 15n, 18, 361n, 416, 416n, [4]258, 258n, 400n, 511n, [5]459, 459n, 631n, 799, 799n, [6]71
material [1]611; noetic [3]16–17; Pythagorean [1]348, 348n, [5]235n, 542n; as triad [1]690; and trias [6]92, 93; in trias [6]73, 73n; *see also* tetrad
tetrad [1]348, 690, 690n, [2]726n, 854n, [3]1006, [5]631n
noetic [1]231, 231n; Pythagorean [5]227, 227n; of races [1]539; symbols of [5]228; *see also* tetractys
Tetrarch [5]539
"tetraxy" [4]400–1, 400n
tettaros [4]37
Teutonic (dialect) [4]37; *see also* Gothic (language)
text(s)
alterations to [2]216–17; in Bible [2]1152; and context [1]316; in contradiction [3]588; corrupt [4]711; discourses on [1]234; gloss slipt into [4]735; improvers of [2]482; interpolated [4]639; interpretation of [6]20; mere theme [2]338; t.-mode [5]15; one at a time [2]800; paronomastic [5]634; perverted [3]55; words and sense of [5]618; wresting of [3]443
textualists [4]357
texture [5]559
th [2]1091–2, 1092n
voiced and unvoiced [3]828, 828n
Thackeray, Henry St John (?1869–1930) *see* Josephus *Contra Apionem* tr Thackeray
Thales (b c 624 BC) [4]533n, [5]223–4, 693, 722, [6]133
Thames [2]520, 820
thankfulness [5]420
thanksgiving(s) [4]625, [5]512
Tharbis (Bible) [2]384n
thaumaturge [3]662
thaw [5]267
the *see* article, definite
Theane *see* Theano
Theano (6th century BC) [5]702 ("Theane")
theanthropos [4]407, 407n
theanthroposophy [1]696n
theanthropy [5]730, 730n
theates [5]21
theatre(s) [1]30, [3]405–6, 1011, [5]861
attendance at [2]84; large [4]712; tradition of [4]861
Theba [2]580
Theban(s) [2]558n, 567
band [1]42, 42n
Thebes [1]572, 572n, 757, [2]567n, [4]864n
Thecla (legend) [3]772 ("Tecla"), 772n
theft [1]877, [2]107, 899
theilen [3]94, 95n

theion [1]561, 561n, 585, 616, [3]76, 330, 658, 913, [5]85, 709, 710, 822
and *theos* [1]120n, 619n, 649n, [3]328, 330
theism [4]28, 368, [5]87, 456
Christian [2]1107, [4]585; mysteries of [3]86
theist(s) [2]205, [4]28, 719, [5]456, 718
Greek [3]649
"thelectic" [6]103, 103n
thelema [5]75
Thelusson, Peter (1737–97) [1]740, 740n
Thelwall, John (1764–1834) [4]306n, 837n, 864n
as annotator [1]716; letter(s) to [1]ciii q, civ q, 255n, 717 q, [2]94 q, [4]466n, [5]119n; supplier of books to C [1]civ; see also *Champion* ed Thelwall
Thelwall, Susan ("Stella") (née Vellum) (d 1816) [1]lxxviii, 716–17, [4]466n
themes [1]234, [2]220, 917
Thénard, Louis Jacques (1777–1857) [3]942, 1032n
Theobald, Lewis (1688–1744) [1]381, 382, 382n, 383, 385, 386, 387, 392, [3]176; *see also* Shakespeare *Works* ed Theobald
theocracy [2]146, 1172, [3]430, 470, 472, 819
Jewish [5]641; of Methodists [4]657; in Scotland [2]1172
Theocritus (c 300–260 BC) [2]55, 55n, 1051, [3]891–2, [4]147, [6]196 q, 196n q
tr Fawkes [1]38
Idylls [3]814 q, 814n q, [4]101n q
"Theoderit" (R. Southey) [1]89
theodicies [3]505
Theodor (in De Wette) [2]179–209
Theodore (in B&F) [1]366
"Theodore" (Dorothy Wordsworth) [4]287
Theodoret of Cyrrhus (c 393–458) [2]246n, 752, [3]147, [6]182
Historia ecclesiastica [4]627n
Theodoric, King of the Ostrogoths (c 455–526) [5]195, 195n, 309
theodota [1]687
Theodotion of Ephesus (2nd century) [4]255
Theodotus [1]162
Theognis (6th century BC) [4]147, 631
Theognis (fl 325) [5]626
theogony, Hesiodic [1]645
theologian(s) [1]282, [2]294, 452, 1141, [3]451, 464, [4]247, 670
ante-scholastic [4]108; C of E [2]260; dogma of [3]949; German [4]337; mystical [3]682; papal [5]632; philosophico-psychological [4]52; RC [5]542; sentimental [2]205; Spanish [5]158; systematic [5]15, 662; wretched [2]616
theologists, modern [2]663
theology [1]562, 644, [2]659, [3]67
apologising [2]1167; Brahmin [3]59; Calvinistic [5]75; Christian [5]9; common [5]457; desideratum in [2]267; dogmatic [3]1091; dualism in [3]432; errors in [5]640; evangelical [1]802, 802n; fashionable [2]343; hermeneutic [4]55; Kant's [3]956; metaphysical [5]469; Moravian [5]157, 157n; mystic [5]231; natural [2]324, [3]670; Platonic [4]157n; prevailing [2]882; of Schelling [4]372; Scholastic [3]626, [5]704n; speculative [1]664, [2]200; student of [5]803; Swedenborgian [3]991; symbolic [5]700; systematic [1]327; systems of [5]540; theocratic [2]246; tyro in [4]669; Wesley's [5]174
Theonas (fl 325) [5]626
Theophilactus/Theophylact (11th century) [3]460
Theophilus (Bible) [2]444n, [4]54
Theophilus, Patriarch of Alexandria (d 412) [5]573
Theophrastus (c 372–c 287 BC) [1]lxxviiin, [2]1147n, [6]3, 4
Theophronius, Bishop of Tyana (fl 341) [2]736
"theophysy" [1]660, 660n, [6]5, 5n
Theopompus (c 378–c 300 BC) [2]386n
theorein [1]632n, [5]413n
theorem(s) [3]276, [4]109, [5]413, [6]87
mathematical [4]13
theoria [1]58, 58n
Theorianus (fl 1170) [2]660
Theoricus [3]1070
theorist(s) [3]807, [4]239, 239n, [5]416, 596
"theory" [4]12, 12n
theory [1]58, 58n, [2]388, 388n, 421, [3]397, 565, [5]301, 304, 356, 598
definition of [4]12, 12n, 13; empirical [5]451; and fact *see* fact; false [3]755, [5]596; general [3]364; of government [4]12; and idea [4]13; imperfect [1]256; and law [4]13; in love with [3]38; polar [3]951; and principle [4]13; RC [5]571; and system [5]201; true or false [3]935
theos [1]179n, 561, 561n, [2]430n, [3]11, 11n, 17, 428, 913, [5]21, 22, 22n, 85, 709, 822
and *theion* see *theion*; without article [2]423; *see also* God
theosopher(s) [1]557, 559, [5]153, 153n
Brahmin [6]8
theosophist [5]714n
theosophy [1]410, 562, 570, 719n, [2]727n, [3]1091, [4]143, 145
Böhme's [1]632, 694; error of [1]584–5; of Pythagoras [1]691

Theotiscan (language) [2]188, 188n, [4]282, 282n, 290n
"therefore" [1]441, 459, [2]328, [3]724, 769, [4]91, 91n
Theresa, St *see* Teresa, St
Theresa (in *The Age*) [1]28, 28n
Thermopylae [3]108n
Thersites (*Troilus and Cressida*) [4]810, 811, 812, 812n
Theseus (myth) [1]374, [5]836
thesis [1]348, 563, 597, [2]989n, 990, 991, 992, 993, 1186, [3]6, 18, 137, 416, 449, 450, 451, 453, [6]92
  analytic [5]455; and antithesis [1]597, [2]171n; and prothesis [4]257
Thessalonians [2]494
Thessalonica [2]495
Thessaly [5]529n
theta [2]68, [3]828n
Thetis (myth) [4]167, [5]522n
  son of [3]15
theurgi [4]594, 595n
theurgy [3]920, [4]143, [5]762, 762n
Thévenot, Jean de (1633–67) *Travels . . . into the Levant* tr Novell MT [5]830–46
thickness [5]825
thief [1]308, [4]661
thimble(s) [4]767, [5]83
"thing" [1]238, [3]355, 730
thing(s) [1]547, 547n, [2]633, [3]23, 42, 87, 331–2, 855, [4]225, 423, 442, [5]6, 7, 18, 95, 210, 442
  and accidents [2]282; all generated [1]643; Church not a [2]680; creation of a [3]850; effects of [3]705; essence of [3]75; God's thoughts are [1]815; and idea *see* idea; infinite [5]7; itself [5]32, 544; in itself [1]524, [2]995, [3]249, 249n, 850, [4]413, [5]201, 580, see also *Ding an sich*; knowledge of [2]612, [6]172; and law [2]1144; and nothings [1]238; and person *see* person; and power [3]1029; really present [2]609; reductions of [5]273; and terms [1]496, [2]1193; and think [2]572, 572n, 991, [3]730, 730n; and thought(s) [1]179, 565, 647, [2]627, 654, 1134, 1144, [3]88, 326, 326n, 355, 643, 643n, 829, 848–9, 858, [4]168, [5]273, 755n, 775; truth of [1]775; vices turned into [3]135
"think" [5]774
think, to
  defined [3]730; and "thing" [2]572, 991n; *see also* thing
thinker(s) [2]824, [4]111
  original [2]999; systematic [2]12
thinking(s) [4]355, [5]649, 755
  fearless [2]832; forms of [4]218; highest form of [3]15; and knowing [5]772; laws of [5]159; legitimate [3]91; pure [5]466; schemes of [5]742; subjective [1]648, [5]708; thinging [1]815n; and thought [5]828; *see also* thought
thinness and thought [3]388, 388n
third, synthetic [5]231
Thirlby, Styan (?1686–1753) [4]696
Thirlmere [3]974 ("Thyrlmere"), [6]121, 121n
Thirlwall, Connop (1797–1875) *see* Schleiermacher *A Critical Essay* tr Thirlwall
thirst [3]401–2, 412
Thirty-Nine Articles *see* Articles of Religion
Thirty Years' War [2]918, [3]754n, [5]104, 104n
Thisbe (myth) *see* Pyramus and Thisbe
Thom, John Hamilton (1808–94) *see* Blanco White *Life* ed Thom
Thomas, St, Apostle (1st century) [2]37, 37n, 1078, [3]21, 21n, 667, [5]63, 63n, 555, [6]107
Thomas à Becket *see* Becket
Thomas à Kempis *see* Kempis
Thomas Aquinas *see* Aquinas
Thomist(s) [1]524, [5]791–2
Thompson, George (1796–1889) *Travels and Adventures in Southern Africa* [1]31
Thompson, William (c 1712–c 1766) [1]38
Thomson, Henry John *see* Prudentius *Prudentius* tr Thomson
Thomson, James (1700–48) [1]38, 57n, 615n
  "Life" by Anderson MT [1]74; and Mallet [1]75
  Castle of Indolence [3]248n, [5]489 q, 489n q; *Seasons* [1]75, [3]677, 976 q, 976n q
Thomson, Thomas (1773–1852) [3]940, 941, [5]847
  A System of Chemistry† [5]847
Thor (myth) [4]489–90, [5]730
thorn(s) [3]879
  crown of [5]608; in the flesh [2]705–6, [3]747, 772, 772n
Thornton, Henry (1760–1815) *Enquiry into the Nature and Effects of the Paper Credit of Great Britain* [1]39
thorough-break [5]181
thought(s) [1]105, 690, [2]605, 629, 844, 999–1000, [3]83, 95, 545, [4]130, 211, 679, 734, 787, [5]122, 125, 168, 210n, 214, 453, 473, 649, 813
  absolute [3]85; and act [5]93; and action(s) [1]702, [3]84; aggregate [4]228; as antecedent

thought(s)—*continued*
[5]66; arrangement of [3]950; asthmatic [5]534; basis of [2]170; bustle of [3]562; busy [3]563; commonplace [4]276, [5]99; composed of notions [2]626; confusion of [5]290; decisiveness of [5]686; defined [4]436; not divisible [5]712; empty [3]363; t.-experiment [3]997, 997n; father to [5]309; and feelings [1]763, 796; form of [5]347; God knows [5]368; God's [3]78, 88, [5]130; haemorrhage from [4]183; heterogeneous with space [4]218; imperfection of [1]326; infancy to youth of [3]1087; infinite [2]563, [4]112n; influence of [5]6; as integrals [5]304; and language [5]416; logic of [1]221; men of [5]770; of men [3]326; modes of [3]298; monopoly for [1]763, 797; necessity of [5]774; and object [3]83; objects of [4]140; order of [1]348, 574, [2]1144, [3]11; organ of [5]481; originality of [3]221; premature communication of [5]326; in poetry [4]162; poverty of [5]487; quantum of [4]217; and realities [1]808; recollectible [4]111; scattered [5]789; scheme of [3]295; and sensations [1]163; severe [2]65; speculative [5]813; sublimest [1]568; substance of [1]638; swarm of [4]720; and theorem(s) [6]87; and thing(s) *see* thing(s); and thinness [3]388, 388n; and a thought [2]627; train of [1]146, 575, [4]762; unconnected [2]341; unity of [3]77; and word(s) [2]458, [6]305; *see also* thinking
thoughtage [5]718
thoughtfulness [3]35
Thrace [1]464, [2]732n, 981n, [3]145, [5]633n, 833, [6]208
thraldom [3]977
Thraso (in Terence) [3]587, 587n
Thrasymenus [3]470
thread [3]813
gold [4]810
threat(s) [1]431, [6]118
to Adam [3]66; Christian [6]168
three [4]37, 37n, 201
acts in consciousness [1]566; Böhme's t. divisions [1]561, 561n; origin of [1]651
threskeia [2]655, 655n, [3]722, [4]625, 625n, 626, [5]644
throat [1]607
t.-cutting [1]157
throe, barren [1]604
throne [3]431, 443, 904, [5]530, 661
Christ's [5]607; David's [5]635; English [4]19n; of honour [5]421
thrush [1]483, [3]884
Thucydides (c 460–c 400 BC) [1]439, 439n, 771, [2]470n, 831, [4]311n, 631
History of the Peloponnesian War [2]574n
thumb [5]266
thumbers [3]183
thumper [1]505, [2]752, [3]817
thunder [1]370, [3]105
son of [3]753, [5]402, 402n
thunderstorm(s) [3]125, [6]153
Thurloe, John (1616–68) [5]146, 146n
Collection of the State Papers of John Thurloe ed T. Birch [5]146n
Thurn and Taxis [3]961–2
Thury, Louis Etienne François Héricart-Ferrand, Vicomte de (1776–1854) [3]936, 937
Thyatira [3]422n, [6]168n
Thyer, Robert (1709–81) *see* S. Butler *Genuine Remains* ed Thyer
Tiber ("Tyber") [2]513, [3]7n, 467, [6]198–9, 199n
Tiberias [2]256
Tiberias (lake) [3]667
Tiberius (Tiberius Claudius Nero) (42 BC–AD 37) [1]486n, [2]108n, 918, 918n, [3]177, 178, 179, 1079, 1079n, [4]480, [5]132, 132n, 371, 514, 514n, 539, 829, 829n
Tibet [2]1023
Tibullus, Albius (c 55–19 BC) [4]339, 339n
tr Grainger [1]38
Catulli &c [1]lxxviii
Tickell, Thomas (1685–1740) [1]38
ticket(s) [2]1080
silver [5]23, 23n
tidings, glad [1]446
Tieck, Christian Friedrich (1776–1851) [4]427, 427n
Tieck, Johann Ludwig (1773–1853) [1]131, 854, [2]794, 958, [3]127n, 378, 378n, 868, 868n, [4]427, 427n, 538 ("Tiek"), 538n, [5]87, 142, 142n, 848
letter(s) to [1]554 q, 572n q, 637n, [3]1014n; supplier of books to C [1]xcviii; and "Glycine's Song" [1]91n
The Old Man of the Mountain tr J. C. Hare [5]143n; MT 848; *Phantasien* [1]131; *Phantasus*† [5]848, 849; *see also* Hardenberg *Novalis Schriften* ed Tieck
Tiedemann, Dietrich (1748–1803) *System der stoischen Philosophie* [1]174, 174n
Tiefenthal [2]982
Tieftrunk, Johann Heinrich (1759–1837) [3]319, 319n, 330, 330n, 331, 331n, 332; *see also* Kant *Vermischte Schriften* ed Tieftrunk

Tien [5]407n
Tierra del Fuego [4]527–8, [5]252
Tierney, George (1761–1830) [1]92, 92n
tiger(s) [1]167, 825, [4]525, 534, [5]293, 304, 304n, 368, 387
tiger-lilies [3]760
Tigranes (in B&F) [1]380, 381
Tillemont, Louis Sébastien le Nain de (1637–98) [2]698
tiller(s) [3]779, [5]361
Tillet, Mathieu (c 1720–91) [3]128
Tilloch, Alexander (1759–1825) [4]82n; see also *Philosophical Magazine* ed Tilloch
Tillotson, Geoffrey (1905–69) *see* Pope *Poems* ed Tillotson
Tillotson, John, Archbishop of Canterbury (1630–94) [2]558, [3]459, 459n, 665, 665n, [4]301n, [5]384n, 543, 543n, 553, 585, 597
school of [5]384
Discourse against Transubstantiation [1]313, 313n, [5]543n; *Preservative against Popery* [5]6n; *Works* [5]585n q, ed T. Birch [4]301n q
tilting [3]757
Timaeus Locrus (c 400 BC) [2]665, 665n, [5]692, 692n, [6]6, 6n
timber [4]450
time(s) [1]563, 564, 653, [2]607, 685, 728, 741, 889, 1002n, [3]13, 62, 328, [4]201, 459, [5]156, 176n, 177, 211, 593
before t. [2]729; beginning of [3]348; begins perpetually [3]89; begotten in [5]627; birth of [2]578; and clock [6]173; commencement of [2]34; continuity in [1]537; creation in [6]315; in Deity [4]421; empirical [4]222; endless [3]89; eternal in [5]32; and eternity *see* eternity; excess of [4]303; form of [1]605; genius of [2]972; immanent in eternity [3]77; inch of [1]279, 286n; infinite [3]87–9; innate [5]814; law of association [4]221–2; mere [6]158; metaphors of [4]123; in metre [2]216; noumena not in [2]802; order of [6]166; phantom [3]85; predicabilia of [4]458; priority in [4]355, 355n; result of Fall [3]22; sense of [4]543; signs of [5]531; spirit of [2]788; states above and below [2]559; succession in [1]619; symbolic [3]471; total [1]377; transit t. [4]322; unity of [4]779, 826, 863–4, 864n; violation of [4]798; in visions [3]563–4; when t. was [3]49; without t. [2]569, 569n; world of [5]57; *see also* space, and time
timeless, the [1]685, 685n, [5]186n
The Times [1]356n, 738, [2]190n, [3]188n q, [5]317n, [6]45n
The Times Literary Supplement [2]158, 840, 966, [3]886, [4]139
timidity [6]322
Timkowsky, Romanus de (Roman Fedorovich Timkovskii) (1785–1820) [1]7
Timocles (fl 325 BC) [4]147
Timon of Phlius (c 325–c 235 BC) [2]759n, [6]6
Timothy, St (1st century) [2]661, [6]101
Timpler, Clement (fl 1604–17) *Metaphysicae systema* [1]clxvi
Timur/Tamburlane (d 1405) [3]186, 186n, [4]817 ("Tamurlane")
tin [1]546, [3]951, [4]692, 692n, [5]255, [6]245
Tindal, Matthew (1655–1733) [1]833, [2]786, 791, [5]76n
Tindal, Nicholas (1687–1774) *see* Rapin-Thoyras *History of England* tr Tindal
Tindal, William (1756–1804) *The History and Antiquities of the Abbey and Borough of Evesham*† [1]clxi, [5]850
tinder-spark [1]303
Tine [5]836
ting tang [2]1115
Tingis [4]81
tinker(s) [1]804, [2]558n, [4]650
king of [3]1076
tinman [2]558, 558n
tint, pastoral [4]708
tintinnabulation [2]1089n, 1090
tipplers [4]466
Tippoo Sahib (1751–99) [4]85, 85n
Tirant lo Blanch [4]654, 654n
Tiresias (myth) [6]218
Tischendorf, Constantin (1815–74) [1]490n
tit for tat [1]293
tit, Tom *see* tomtit
Titan(s) [1]485, [2]345, 584n, [3]473, 929
titanium [5]255, 261
tithe(s) [1]360, 360n, [2]294, 295, 899–900, [5]79, 577, 659, [6]22, 23, 60
in Ireland [5]659, 659n
Tithonus (myth) [2]580
Titian (Tiziano Vecellio) (c 1488–1576) [2]235
titivillitium [3]504, 504n–5n
title(s) [2]1196
printed [5]284; take-in [1]492, 493n; t.-words [5]72
Titling, Tim (fiction) [3]438
Tituba [3]825
titulus [2]577, 577n
"Titus" [2]67, [3]828
Titus, St (1st century) [6]57

Titus Flavius Sabinus Vespasianus (39–81) [1]315, 486, 486n, 832, 832n, [2]515, [4]251n, [6]60
Titus, Silius (c 1623–1704) [3]169
Tityrus (in Virgil) [6]221, 221n
Tiverton [2]95n
tlemi [3]12n
tmesis [3]192
to be *see* be
toad(s) [1]215n, 216n, 747, 778, [3]1079
  Surinam [6]290, 290n
"tobacco *hoc*" [3]830, 830n
Tobayares [5]103
Tobias (Apocrypha) [5]520
Tobin, James Webbe (1767–1814) [1]lxxxvii, 89, *89n–90n*, 98, 98n, 762n, [3]974
  letter(s) to [1]lxxix q, cix; owner of annotated books [1]lxxx, 226; supplier of books to C [1]xcvii
  Epigrams MT [1]98
Tobin, John (1770–1804) [1]89n
tocsin [4]638
Todd, Henry John (1763–1845) [6]184
Todd, John (fl 1825) [1]861
toddy [5]418
  t.-punch [2]310
to-dip [3]15
Todtentanz see *Danse des morts*
toes [4]38
Toft/Tofts, Mary (?1701–63) [3]1035n, [4]636n
toga [3]21
Togarmah (Bible) [3]70
tohu bohu [1]604, 604n, 669, [2]769n
Tokyo
  University of Tokyo Library [1]clxv
Toland, John (1670–1722) [1]248n
Toledo, Council of [5]633
tolerance [2]471, [3]98, 98n, 367–70, [4]671
  definition of [3]846n; ultra-t. [3]70; *see also* toleration
"toleration" [4]176
toleration [1]300, 313, 321n, 341, 341n, 358, [2]48, 530, 651, [3]85, 157n, 785, 846, 1071, [4]175, 308, [5]596, 617
  dishonest [2]194; of the immoral [1]150; of James I [2]934, 936; Lessing's position on [1]350n; principle(s) of [2]934–5, [5]616; religious [1]256, *321*, 321n, [2]813, [5]124, 501n; sermon against [5]625; universal [1]313; unlimited [1]256; *see also* tolerance
Tollet, George (1725–79) [4]745n, 848
Tom Thumb's Pretty Song Book [5]609n
tombs
  of the Ancients [1]237; Etruscan [1]237n
tombstone [1]764, 797
  proposal for C's [2]993
Tomkins [1]38
Tomline, Sir George Pretyman, Bishop of Lincoln (1750–1827) [1]262, 262n, [2]913–14, 914n, [4]301n, [5]202, 202n
  A Refutation of Calvinism [1]262n
tomtit [2]580, *580n–1n*, [3]727
tone [5]396
  Böhme on [1]604, 614; individual [2]813; manly [2]827; quality t. [3]358; Schelling's [6]238
Tonga Islands [4]165
Tonge, Jane (fl 1820) [5]817, 817n
tongue(s) [1]317n, 606, 607, [4]165
  bitter [1]613; Böhme's "counsellor" [1]578; t.-bully [1]378, [3]186; favour the t. [3]577, 577n; foreign [5]814; gift of [2]653n, 701, 701n, 703, [3]1069, 1069n, [4]248n, [5]666; preaching with [5]390; speaking with [2]1045, 1045n
Tonnelier, Mr. (fl 1810) [3]936
Tonson, Jacob (1656–1736) *see* Milton *Poetical Works* ed Tonson
Tooke, Andrew (1673–1732) *Pantheon* [1]civ, [3]735n, [6]110, 110n
Tooke, John Horne (1736–1812) [3]222, 222n, 800n, [4]166n, 167n, 284, [5]711n, 732, 732n–3n, 755n, [6]25n
  Diversions of Purley [1]lxxx, 606n, [2]380n, 653, 653n, [3]730n, 977n, [4]38n, 284n, [5]732n
tool(s) [5]476
  t.-house [5]89; shop of [6]103
Toolemak [2]1108n
Tooley, R. V. *Collectors' Guide to Maps of the African Continent and Southern Africa* [4]601n q
"too-muchness" [1]725, 725n
toothache [3]1067n, [6]125
topaz [5]834
Tophana [5]834
Tophet [1]448, [2]559, 559n, [3]38
Toplady, Augustus Montague (1740–78) [4]624
Torah [1]533n
torch [1]376
Torino (Turin) [4]35
torment(s) [3]25
  eternal [5]157; everlasting [2]559, 569, [3]66
Tornga (myth) [2]1108n
Toronto
  Victoria College Library (Coleridge Col-

lection) [1]xcii, cxli, clxvii, clxxi, clxxiii, clxxiv, 90n, 851, 855, [2]787n, 824n, 1101n, [4]100n, 151, 161, [5]47n, 202n, marginalia in [1]clxvi, 20, 211, 697, 777n, 828, 851, 856, [2]3, 86, 140, 352, 649, 792, 852, 976, 977, 1188, [3]837, 863, 993, [4]9, 32, 35, 71, 84, 99, 199, 213, 332, [5]78, 198, 373, [6]3, 25, 32, 94, 130, 161, 177, 251, 256, 295, 320, ms note in [2]980n q, transcript(s) of marginalia in [1]26, 197, 222, 227, 414, 545, 555, 831, 840, 856, 861, 867, [2]19, 25, 42, 48, 107, 112, 113, 158, 357, 361, 504, 519, 526, 533, 558, 627, 647, 691, 815, 828, 837, 954, 1169, 1191, [3]75, 101, 196, 241, 316, 484, 514, 784, 789, 794, 837, 843, 943, 954, 1064, 1080, [4]25, 71, 91, 143, 148, 164, 170, 294, 313, 402, 447, 469, 487, 620, 675, 681, [5]46, 120, 240, 246, 403, 454, 486, 499, 669, [6]10, 95, 154

torpedo [6]103

torpor [4]544

Torquay [1]clxxi, [2]132

Torres Vedras [2]940n

Torrey, Henry Augustus Pierson (1837–1902) *The Philosophy of Descartes* [2]169

Torricelli, Evangelista (1608–47) [5]644n

tortoise [3]444, [5]712, 712n

torture(s) [4]134, 238, 652, [5]106
  t.-monger [5]396

Tory/Tories [1]295, [2]210, 519–20, 688, [3]162, 162n, 799, [4]14, [6]44n
  B&F as [1]389; hatred of [4]20; unvacillating [6]47; and Whig(s) [1]122, 733, [4]42, 42n

Toryism [1]808, 808n, [4]14

Toscanus, Joannes Matthaeus (fl 1575) [2]764

Tostatus (Alfonso Tostado Ribera de Madrigal), Bishop of Avila (1400–54) [3]1068

total [1]740

"totalism" [1]638, 639n

totality [5]487, [6]242–4
  negative [2]674

totus in illo [1]763, 797

totus in omni parte [2]671, 671n

touch [1]112n, 670, 671, [2]548, 548n, [4]272, 273, 674, [5]191, 265, 554, 554n
  double [2]538n, [3]868, 868n, [5]192, 192n; feeling organised [1]579; language of [1]112; of mind [1]580n; sense of [2]136n, [3]216, 1036, 1036n; single [2]548; substitute for sight [3]389

Touchefaucet (in Rabelais) [4]191, 192

touching [5]184
  mighty [1]580

Touchstone (*As You Like It*) [1]cxviii

Toulon [6]147

tour(s) [3]397, [4]471

tourney-court [1]739

Tours [4]193

Tourte, Professor (fl 1810) [3]938

toutoukosmou [1]675

Towgood, Michaijah (1700–92) *Essay towards Attaining a True Idea of the Character and Reign of King Charles the First, and the Causes of the Civil War*† [1]488 ("Richard Towgood's *History*") [2]532

town, country [4]783

Townsend, George (1788–1857) *Accusations of History* [1]861

Townshend, Chauncey Hare (1798–1868) [4]117

Townshend, Thomas (d c 1680) [4]72

toys of despair [5]588

traces [2]539

tracks [3]976

tractors [3]1067, 1067n

"Tracts" [5]851–2. *See also* "Civil War Tracts"; "Cromwellian Tracts"; "English Tracts"; "Medical Treatises"; "Pamphlets—Divinity"; "Pamphlets—Miscellaneous"; "Pamphlets on the Reform Bill"; "Pamphlets on the Slave Trade"

trade [1]29, 515, [2]619, 620, [3]633
  balance of [1]123, 123n; fluctuations of [6]22; and profession *see* profession; science of [6]19–20; sphere of [6]44; *see also* commerce

tradesman/tradesmen [2]1088, [6]216

tradition(s) [1]539, [2]919, [3]102, 458, 686, 687, 689, 689n, 772, [4]250, 472, 477, 479, 504, 810, [5]297–8, 417, 573, 620, 630, 710
  apostolic(al) [1]879, [5]574, 576; catacombs of [4]810; of Church [2]445, 502, [4]256; in Church of Rome [1]345; condemned [5]567; dreams of [3]919; ecclesiastical [5]571, 572, 572n; improbable [5]524; Irenaean [6]63; mere [1]329; oral [3]726; pretended [2]39; rabbinical [1]513, [3]594, 1090, [5]645; and Scripture *see* Scripture; unwritten [2]38; vagabond [3]606; of vulgar [3]466

traduction [2]756

trafficking, indiscreet [5]663

tragedians
  Greek [3]701, [5]774; politics of [1]380

tragedy/tragedies [1]71–2, [3]404–5, 406, 408, [4]168, 409, 712, 736n, 838, 848, 863
of B&F [1]379, 393, [4]717, 719; B&F incapable of [1]367; derivation of [3]894, 894n; French [2]123n; Greek [1]71–2, [2]687, [3]894, [4]864, [5]866n; prose [4]169; Roman [2]775–6, 776n; Tom Thumb [6]202
tragic, the [4]787, 816
and comic [4]693
tragi-comedy [1]400
Trahern/Traherne, John Montgomery (1788–1860) [3]492
Traill, Henry Duff (1842–1900) *Life of Coleridge* [2]739n
Traill, Thomas Stewart (1781–1862) [3]936, 937, 942
traitor [2]950, [3]160
perjured [2]818
Trajan (Marcus Ulpius Trajanus) (c 53–117) [2]692, [4]627, 627n, [5]525n, 622, [6]99
trance(s) [1]576, [2]705, 1099, [3]614, 614n, 733
mesmeric [5]404n
tranquillity
genial [1]509; voluptuous [4]183
trans- [2]250n, 672n, 882n
Transactions of the Cambridge Bibliographical Society [3]283n, 977n
Transactions of the Royal Society of Literature [1]cxlin, clin, [3]499, 909
transcendency/transcendencies [3]13, [5]744, 751
"transcendent" [4]372, 372n, [5]138, 138n
transcendent(s) [3]29, 524n, [5]159, 508, 813, [6]78
idea of God [2]183; t. substratum [3]1021
transcendental analysis, science of [2]673
transcendental idealism *see* idealism
transcendentalism, American [2]21
"trans-conceive" [2]882, 882n
"trans-created" [3]519, 519n, [6]301, 301n
transcribers [5]637
transcription by Moses [2]392
"transcriptural" [1]736, 736n
"transdate" [5]297, 297n–8n
transexion [1]779
transfers, pantheistic [1]609
transfiguration [3]602
Transfiguration (of Jesus Christ) *see* Jesus Christ, Transfiguration of
transfusion [3]382
transgression [1]790, [5]73, 406
transgressor(s) [1]433, [2]659
"trans-imaginate" [3]90, 90n
"transimagine" [2]882, 882n
"transinfusion" [2]250, 250n
transition(s) [1]253n, 442, [2]852, [3]128n, 158n, 227, 732
abrupt [2]455, [3]629, [6]99; lyrical [3]713; slender [6]212; from something to nothing [1]173; strange [2]269; valid [5]776
transitive of forms [5]451
translation(s) [1]167, 455, 702, [2]136, 1120, [3]107, 466, [4]287, [5]866, [6]77, 77n, 137, 205
bad [2]718; of Bible [3]722; of characters [2]381; coinages a sign of [2]426; erroneous [1]666; error in [6]172; false [2]711; no faultless [2]1155; flat [2]756; free [6]138; of *homoousios* [5]627; from life [1]127–8; literal [2]346, 561, 714; marginal [3]19; Miltonic [2]974; mistranslation [2]655; pun-like [3]978; rhyme [6]210; signs of [2]426–7; Syriac [6]140; zeal for [6]17
translator(s) [1]444, 455, [2]446, 473, [3]107, [5]515
inspired [5]473; Luther as [3]726
translocation [2]672, [3]55, 55n
translucency [3]460, [5]491
transmentation [3]477, [5]172n
transmigration [2]348
transmutation [1]817, [2]607
of elements [2]281–2
transparency [1]594, 710, 710n, [2]922, [3]61, 61n, 1058–9, [5]751, [6]227–8
"transparent" [5]244, [6]228–9
transplantation [2]690
transport(s) [5]821
transportation [2]460, 899, [4]15, [5]103
transposition [4]734
transprosing [1]402
transrealisation [4]426
"transsensual" [2]802, 802n
"transteverine" [3]7, 7n
transubstantiate [3]50
transubstantiation [1]297n, 313, 313n, 471, 508, 509n, 523–5, 523n, 809n, 824, 861, [2]283, 304n, 719n, 1038, 1038n, [3]155–6, 156n, 189n, 232n, 439, 439n, 748, 780, 1068n, [4]177, 305, [5]4–5, 5n, 393, 393n, 397, 398n, 497, 541–58, 580, 585, 585n, 655, 674, 835, [6]21n, 105
controversy over [6]20; no-meaning [2]670; spiritual [2]281; *see also* Eucharist
Transubstantiationist [5]11 ("Trans—")
Transylvania [4]670n
trapp [4]517, 517n
trash [2]1004, [5]274, 298, 299
Jesuitical [5]302; mawkish [4]538; unnatural [1]405

Trasimene, Lake [3]470n
travail, woman in [1]817n
travel(s) [5]167
  books of [3]809; modern [2]980; Swedenborg's relations of [5]413
traveller(s) [1]227, [2]6, 655, [3]401, [4]743, 780
  American [4]532; sentimental [3]1081
Travers, Walter (?1548–1635) [2]1133, 1159–60, 1161, [4]179
travesty [1]167, [5]386
treachery [2]45, [4]689, [5]616
treason(s) [1]333, [2]1173, [4]181, 815, [5]143, 641n
  in the blood [5]596; high [1]395, [6]98
treasure(s)
  allegory of [1]559; of knowledge [5]59
treasury [3]741
treatise, experimental [1]826
treaty/treaties [3]801
  of Dover [1]353n; of Newport [1]290n, 353n, [3]801n
Trebisond [6]279
Tredennick, Hugh *see* Aristotle *Metaphysics* tr Tredennick
Tredie (myth) [4]489–90
tree(s) [1]662, 764, 774, 797, [2]879, 879n, [3]25n, 249, 249n, 332, 455, 581, 896, [4]273, 278, 827, [5]278
  apple [3]167, 373; figure of [3]1093; forbidden [3]105; fruit-t. [5]861; golden [3]395; hypocrite as a [1]426; imitated by poet [1]612; of knowledge [2]1052–3; lemon [5]831, 832, 843, 861; of life [1]692, [2]1053; locust [5]105; magnetised [3]373, 373n, 396, [4]325–6, 325n; oak [2]897, 897n, [5]681; olive [1]782, [3]455, 480; orange [5]843; orange or lemon [5]831, 832, 842, 861; perception of [3]967; prodigious [5]838; rooting up a [1]314; sawed into planks [1]153; transanimated [4]682n; upas [2]507, *507n*, 827, 827n; yew [5]226
trefoil [1]782
Tregellius (Samuel Prideaux Tregelles) (1813–75) [1]490n
treis [4]37, 37n
Trench, Richard Chevenix (1807–86) [2]558
Trenchard, John (1662–1723), and Thomas Gordon *Cato's Letters* [3]163, 163n
Trent, Council of [1]257, 493n, 843n, 862, 862n, [2]283, 415n, 677, 781, 1149, [3]230, 231, 231n, *232n*, 234, [5]5n, 14n, 521, 521n–2n, 639, 639n
Trent (river) [2]820, 820n, [3]628
trepidatiunculae [5]574
Tressilian (in Scott) [4]601–2
Trevenen, Emily (fl 1829–52) [1]861
Treviranus, Gottfried Reinhold (1776–1837) [5]142n
  Biologie [5]142n
Treviranus, Ludolph Christian (1779–1864) [5]142, 142n
triad(s) [1]348, 561, 562, 582, 643, [2]574, 843, [3]416, 416n, 1054–5, [4]489–90, [5]22, 201, 459n, 542
  Christian [3]59; first form [3]1052, 1052n; of grammar [3]835n; Platonic [3]913; in Pythagoras [1]691; subordinate [5]235; supreme [2]575, 575n; tetractys in [6]71; three [5]235–6, 235n–6n; zöo-dynamic [5]258, 258n; *see also* trias
tri-angelism [3]42, 42n
triangle(s) [1]674, [3]967, [4]113, 113n, 127–8, 640, [5]69, 371, 656, [6]175–6
  equilateral [2]425; square [5]711; symbol [1]649, 649n
trias [2]745, 745n, [4]258, [6]73, 93; *see also* triad
tribe(s) [3]108n, 464, 1025, [4]38, 257
  Canaanite [2]831; feudal [6]14; Hebrew [1]423; nomad [1]431; ten [2]1153; twelve [2]832
tribrach [1]671, 858
tribunes [3]240, 240n
tributaries [3]152
tribute [3]152
  t.-money [6]60
trichotomy [1]231, 231n, 347–8, 348n, [2]1193n
  Kant's [1]230; logic of [3]363, [5]459
trick(s) [4]375, 815, [5]517
  of hand [2]1005; optical [6]100
trickery [3]661
tricking [5]546
"tricksy" [5]130, 130n, 140, 140n
"tricky" [2]936
Tridentine *see* faith, Tridentine
Trieb [3]963; *see also* impulse(s)
trifle(s) [1]321, 330, [2]480
trilogy [4]864
trimming [1]259
Trimurti (myth) [3]59n, [4]489–90
Tring [1]816
Trinitarian(s) [2]531, [4]301, 302, 302n, [5]408, [6]263
  and Arians [1]274; C's T. position [2]24; medium [1]566
Trinitarianism [3]524n, [5]408n, 621, [6]75–6, 307n
  archaspistes of [6]93; Christian [6]141n
trinitas [2]33n
"Trinity" [3]328n–9n, [5]579

Trinity [1]242, 358, 434, 507, 561, 563n, 573, 586–7, 690n, 836, [2]200, 246n, 266n, 270, 305, 574, 583n, 597–8, 725n, 732, 741, 789–90, 797–9, 843, 992, 1046, 1055n, 1175, [3]11–14, 16, 17, 42n, 52n, 73–4, 78n, 135n, 146, 232, 233n, 369n, 460n, 514–15, 525, 534, 659–60, 684, 762n, 763, 857, 1054–5, 1083–93, [4]200n, 258n, 665, 665n, 670, 670n, [5]3–35, 55, 97n, 152, 210, 210n, 408, 542, 626, 766, 842, [6]54–72, 132, 145, 297, 297n, 307, 316
arguments against [2]844; Basilides's view [2]713; being, mind, spirit [2]248; birth of [1]649; Böhme on [1]565, 649, 672; Brahmin [3]59; Browne's a trefoil [1]782; bulwark against atheism [3]137; Calvin on [1]478; not peculiar to Christianity [2]360; C's schema of [1]479n; controversy [5]6n; described [1]564–5; doctrine of [2]205, [5]556, 556n, 557, 771, [6]26, 60; eclectic [2]426; economic [1]249n; faith in [6]146; form of idea of God [2]1145; fundamental article [5]57; generation of [1]689–91, 694, *694n*; ground of [3]66; among heathens [1]617; higher and lower [2]582–3, 583n; idea of [3]428, 761–2; infernal [3]473; and light symbol [1]687–8; medium [4]226; mystery/mysteries of [5]59, 524, 655, 830–1; *nous, logos, sophia* [2]430; perfection of reason [2]20; persons of [1]681, [6]178; pictures of [5]658; Platonic [4]303; "proceeding" in [2]248–50; proof of [5]783; as prophecy [3]102; rejected [3]308n; Scripture [4]300; sense and import [2]198; Skelton's discourses on [5]64; strange [5]614; sun as analogue [1]564; tenet of [5]770; as tetractys [2]745n, [3]18; tetrad of [2]726; true doctrine of [3]1091; true idea of [1]679; wisdom in [2]423. *See also* God; Holy Ghost; Son; Tri-unity
tripersonality [5]23, 26
triplet (in verse) [6]199
triplex see *animal triplex*
triplicity [4]412
Triploe Heath [1]293
Trismegistus [3]1038, 1038n
tritheism [2]265, 265n, 725n, [3]17, 42, 42n, [5]7n, 8n, 14, 21, 22, 23, 24, 28, 408n, 543, 626, [6]85, 144
tritheist(s) [2]748
defined [2]748n
Tritschler, Johann Christoph Salomon (d 1841) [3]389, 389n
triumph [3]1065
tri-une/triune [1]574, 642, 649, [3]13, 877, [4]201
Tri-unitarian [2]21
"Tri-unity" [3]328n–9n, [5]579
Tri-unity [1]348, 564, 588, 694, [2]33, 265, 680, 741, 748n, 797, 1145n, [3]328, 369, 369n, 611, 877n, [4]300, [5]6, 6n, 25, 783. *See also* God; Trinity
trivial, the [1]60
Troas [3]7n
trochaic [4]290
trochee(s) [2]874, 1039, 1040, [3]814, 904, [5]690, [6]255
"trocheised" [1]403, 403n
Troilus (*Troilus and Cressida*) [4]810
Trojan(s) [4]810, [6]215
T. War [3]648n, [5]522n; *see also* Troy
Trommsdorff, Johann Bartolomäus (1770–1837) [3]938, 940
tropics [3]1062, [5]248, 263
Trosse, Susanna (fl 1711) [2]1032
troubadours [2]779, 779n
troubles [3]584–5
trout [4]431, 802
trouveurs [2]779, 779n
Troy [2]573, [4]627n, 864n, [6]199, 211, 213
Trojan shore [6]197; *see also* Trojan(s)
true, the [2]930, [3]460, [5]740
truffle-dog [5]293
truism(s) [1]673, [2]613, 634, [3]685, 859, 1051, [4]238, 380, 625, 667–8, 736, [5]10, 55, 65, 409, 656, 855, 857
barren [1]732; fruitless [4]405; ridiculous [5]363
trumpet(s) [3]388, 452, [4]503n
dolorous [5]89; of Luther [2]883; of Resurrection [5]296; silver [1]182
trumpeter [4]548
trunk [3]181, 181n
trunk (of tree) [3]11, [4]43, 78, [5]471
Trussell, John (fl 1620–42) *A Continuation of the Collection of the History of England* [2]117
trust [1]739, [5]9
act of [2]1166
"truth" [6]301
truth(s) [1]468, 528, 731, [2]1012, 1051, 1133, 1141, 1192n, [3]13, 21, 36, 54, 173, 558, 610, [4]107, 115, 268, 817, [5]6, 71, 131, 304, 476, 516, 539, 555, 672
absolute [3]104, 231–2; acquirements of [5]825; and act [3]233; all-truths-including [6]71; all unique [5]32; assent to [6]307; and

beauty [5]859; and being [3]24; Being of [1]824; chain of [5]568; champion for [1]745; of charity [5]564; as Christ [3]23; Christian [1]179, [5]384; of Christian system [5]560; conversion to the [1]645; correspondent to [4]109; costume of [3]69; and delusion [1]134; despised [5]229; divine [2]1151; of a dogma [4]265; economising [5]520; effective [5]672–3; end of an historian [4]180; enduring [1]712; and error *see* error; essential [2]682, [6]19; eternal [3]49, [5]297; everlasting [1]446; and evidence [5]96; exclusive [4]587; between extremes [2]1178; and fact *see* fact; faculty of [2]188; and falsehood *see* falsehood; and fancy [5]406; foundation of religion [2]194; fragments of [4]259; fundamental [5]10, 27; general [1]13, [4]195, 731, 822; generalised [4]846; geometrical [5]370; glorious [5]208; God of [1]675, [3]661, [5]484; gospel [4]623; great [5]477; growth of [5]561; and half-t. [2]266, 328; heavenly [1]170; hidden [4]416; historic [4]55, [5]645; home [4]856; image in [5]409; imageless [1]774; immediate [4]78; important [5]189, 518; inconceivable [5]771; injured [1]184; inspired [5]515; interest of [3]347; intuition of [6]79; investigation of [3]222; involution of [3]357; law of [2]919; law of a thing [3]23; and lie [5]564; as light [6]78; light of [5]466; literal [4]47; living [5]409; love of [1]677, [3]9, 451, [4]111; management of [3]459; metaphor of [2]643; metaphysical [3]54, [4]110; moral [4]637; most momentous [3]877; must be whole t. [3]33; necessary [2]745, [3]967, [4]93, 130; objective [5]745; and opinion [5]641; organ of [3]641; partial [2]969; as parts of whole [2]1055; philosophic [1]583, [5]411; physical [1]763, 796; physiological [1]577; pioneering [5]92; poetic [5]835; powerful [5]561; t.-powers [2]295, 297, 1151, [3]163, 163n; practical [2]218, [5]90; primary [5]560; profoundest [5]231, 425; real [1]775; of reason [2]189, [3]56, [4]108–9; reception of [5]463; of religion [2]1160; revealed [3]446, [4]589, [5]61, 716; reverse of [1]661; revolutionary [2]343; road to [5]776; same [4]258–9, [5]320; saving [1]802, [2]63; of science [3]63; of Scripture [5]675, [6]42–3; searcher(s) after [4]297, 405; self-evident [2]1175, [3]809, [6]286; sense of [3]463, [5]483; sign of [5]632; speculative [5]166; spirit of [1]468, 824, 872, [2]561, [3]72, 587, 920, [5]572, 642; spiritual [1]504, 648, [2]295, 298, 1150, [3]96, 743, 762, [5]15, 421, [6]82; store-house of [5]803; subjective [5]49; sublime [5]55; substantive [6]78; supersensuous [5]752; transcendent [3]516, [6]298–9; transcendental [5]155; two senses of [3]518–19; ultimate [4]265; undemonstrable [5]425; universal [3]558, [5]599; ventriloquist [3]65; and veracity [3]9, 9n; very [5]449; vision of [4]157; voice of [2]614; what is t.? [3]849; whole [3]65, 77, 295n, 989; wild [2]634; is wisdom [3]151; *see also* verity/verities

tryers, committee of [2]439

Trypho (in Justin Martyr) [2]440, 440n, [6]145, 146

tsar/czar [3]756–7

Tschirnhaus, Ehrenfried Walther von (1651–1708) [5]203n

tub [4]497n

conventicle [1]872, 873

Tubal (Bible) [3]70

Tubal-Cain (Bible) [2]576

Tübingen [2]533

Tuch [2]1042, 1042n

Tucker, Abraham ("Edward Search") (1705–74) *Light of Nature Pursued* [2]786n–7n, [3]38, 38n

Tuckney, Anthony (1599–1670) [1]259

Tudesque (language) [4]290, 290n

Tudor, John (d 1862) [1]lxxiii, cxxii, clxi, 451n, [2]46, [5]139n; see also *Morning Watch* ed Tudor

Tudors [1]356, [2]826

Tuell, Anne Kimball (b 1876) *John Sterling* [4]69

Tuke, Sir Samuel (d 1674) *Adventures of Five Hours* [4]77, 77n

Tulk, Alfred (d 1891) *see* Oken *Elements of Physiophilosophy* tr Tulk

Tulk, Charles Augustus (1786–1849) [1]clxi, 687n, 696n, [3]432n, [5]403, 462

letter(s) to [1]288n, 556, 578n, 582n, 598n q, 613n q, 632n, 660n q, 664n, 681n, [2]1164n q, 1168 q, 1182 q, [3]286n, 1006n q, [4]420n, [5]469n, [6]230n; marginalia addressed to [6]95; note by [6]100n; owner of annotated books [5]80, 454; supplier of books to C [1]xcviii, 659n, [5]80, 463, 473; *see also* Swedenborg *An Appendix to the Treatise on the White Horse* tr Tulk

Tullian [1]829, 829n

Tullus Hostilius (7th century BC) [5]562, 562n

Tully *see* Cicero

tune [1]609, 735, [2]1003, [3]43, 496, [4]251, 827, 858, [5]25

tungsten [5]261

Tupi (language) ^{5}104
turban ^{3}110
turbidness ^{5}50
turbulence ^{1}678
turd(s) ^{3}870, 870n, 894n
turf-cover ^{2}216
Turk(s) ^{3}159, 820, ^{4}299, ^{5}10, 833, 834, 837, 842
  Grand ^{6}234; in Rhodes ^{5}841
Turkey ^{1}698, ^{2}73, 367, ^{4}84, 85, ^{5}279, 830, 837
Turner, Charles Tennyson (1808–79) ^{5}817, 853
  Collected Sonnets Old and New ^{5}853; *Sonnet V* "To the Lark" MT ^{5}854–5; *Sonnet VI* MT ^{5}855; *Sonnet IX* MT ^{5}856; *Sonnet X* MT ^{5}856–7; *Sonnet XI* MT ^{5}857; *Sonnet XII* MT ^{5}857–8; *Sonnet XIII* MT ^{5}858–9; *Sonnet XIV* "Autumn" MT ^{5}859; *Sonnet XV* MT ^{5}859–60; *Sonnet XVI* MT ^{5}860; *Sonnet XVII* MT ^{5}860–1; *Sonnet XVIII* MT ^{5}861; *Sonnet XIX* "Evening" MT ^{5}861; *Sonnet XX* MT ^{5}862; *Sonnet XXI* "On Startling Some Pigeons" MT ^{5}862; *Sonnet XXII* MT ^{5}862; *Sonnets and Fugitive Pieces* MT ^{5}853–65
Turner, Elizabeth (d 1685) ^{4}73
Turner, George (fl 1733) *A Brief and Distinct Account of the Mineral Waters of Piedmont* ^{3}843
Turner, Sir James (1615–?86) ^{2}1171n
Turner, Matthew (d c 1788) ^{3}639
Turner, R. K. ^{1}380n
Turner, Sharon (1768–1847) *A Vindication of the Genius of the Antient British Poems* ^{2}1170n, ^{6}17n
Turnham Green ^{3}630
turnip(s) ^{2}360, ^{3}807, ^{4}318, ^{6}153
turnkey ^{2}537
turpentine ^{3}377
turquoises ^{3}898
turtle ^{1}421, ^{3}175
"turtle-footed" ^{3}175, 175n
Turton, William (1762–1835) *see* Linnaeus *General System* tr Turton
Tuscany ^{5}39n, 275, 275n
  Tuscan Platonists ^{3}308, 308n
Tutchin, John (?1661–1707) ^{2}767–8
tutites ^{2}59
tutor(s) ^{3}447, ^{5}32
Twells, Leonard (1683–1742) *Vindiciae Apocalypseos* ^{6}164
twenty ^{4}38
Twesten, August Detlev Christian (1789–1876) *Commentatio critica de Hesiodi carmine* ^{2}86
twilight ^{1}515, 576, ^{2}65, ^{3}849, ^{5}130, 298
  dawn ^{1}705; dreamy ^{4}528
Twinings *see* London
twins, connate ^{1}666
Twisse, William (c 1578–1646) ^{1}351, 351n
twist in the brains ^{1}762, 796
two ^{4}36
  origin of ^{1}651
Twyman, Michael *Lithography 1800–1850* ^{4}534n
Tybalt (*Romeo and Juliet*) ^{4}830
Tydalmere ^{3}974
tympanum ^{1}638
Tyndale, William (c 1494–1536) ^{2}684n; *see also* Bible: Tyndale
type(s) ^{2}151, ^{3}469 ("typical"), 755, 775, ^{5}32, 57
  and anti-t. ^{5}59; of the Cross ^{5}31; in OT ^{5}676; particular ^{5}715; or symbol ^{2}286, ^{5}591
types (in printing) ^{1}766, ^{3}773
Typhon (myth) ^{6}219
typhus ^{4}149, 164, ^{6}38, 39
typography, blunders in ^{4}338
tyrannicide ^{4}181n, 807
tyrannicidium ^{5}70
tyranny/tyrannies ^{1}272, 322, 473, 803, ^{2}622, 622n, 846, ^{5}39n, 144, 145, ^{6}262
  alternate ^{1}651; paternal ^{4}307, 307n
tyrant(s) ^{1}397, ^{2}622, 1111, ^{3}178, 420, ^{5}38, ^{6}262
  Assyrian ^{2}570; in B&F ^{1}393; may be killed ^{2}771; mean ^{2}818; resistance to ^{3}180; rich ^{2}529; Thirty ^{1}181
Tyre ^{1}708, ^{6}199
  Council of ^{2}735
Tyrian(s) ^{1}876, ^{3}109, 109n, ^{6}210, 210n, 212
tyring-room ^{4}717
Tyrtaeus (fl c 685–668 BC) ^{4}147
Tyrus (Bible) ^{3}479
Tyrwhitt, Thomas (1730–86) ^{3}1070, ^{4}705n, 739n, 746n, 756n, 786n, 812, 860
Tyschen, Thomas Christian ("Tychson") (1758–1834) ^{2}188n, ^{4}282n, ^{6}17n
Tytler, James (1745–1804) ^{2}321n
Tzetzes, John (12th century) ^{5}226

ubi ^{4}108
ubiquity ^{2}568, 670, ^{5}493
Udal/Udall, John (?1560–92) ^{4}179, 180n
ugliness ^{1}747 ("ugly"), 747n

Ullswater [3]974 ("Ulswater")
Ulphilas/Wulfila, Bishop (4th century) [6]17, 17n
Ulrich, Johann August Heinrich (1746–1813) [4]207, 207n
Institutiones logicae et metaphysicae [4]207n
"ultrafidianism" [1]513n, [3]557n
ultrafidianism [1]746n
ulträisms [5]301
ultra-liberals [5]106
ultra-royalism [4]798
ultra-royalists [5]661
ultra-Socinian [6]77
ultra-Socinianism [5]162
ultra-tolerance [3]70
Ulysses/Odysseus (myth) [1]220n, [2]928, 936, 936n, [3]625
(in Homer) [2]928n, [3]817, 817n; knot of [3]468, 468n–9n; (in *Troilus and Cressida*) [4]810
"umbered" [4]740–1, 740n–1n, 813–14
umbra [1]431, 431n
umbrella [2]599, 599n
unbelief [3]466, 509, 572, 851, [4]683, [5]63, 620
credit of [4]581; heart of [5]516; subjective [5]771
unbeliever [1]514, [4]592, [5]71, 178, 654
unbrother-hood [2]77
uncharitableness [1]695, [2]35
unchastity [4]465
Uncle Toby (in Sterne) [4]98n
"unclean" [1]417, 417n
unconnected, the [1]158n
"unconscious" [5]723
"unction" [3]541, 541n
unction [1]817, [2]707, [5]495
of the spirit [3]721; spiritual [1]445; *see also* Extreme Unction
unctus [3]479
undergoer [4]285
underselling [5]686
undersheriff [2]949
under-song [3]906n
under-soph [2]917
"understand" [2]332
understanding(s) [1]158, 638, [2]332, 359, 1018, 1133, 1146, [3]12, 16n, 63, 91, 202, 242, 260, 332, 359, 518, 526, 723, 1087, [4]154, 375, 398, 415, 502, 589, [5]25, 26, 174, 242n, 405n, 425, 442, 463, 473, 476, 492, 668, 780–1, 795, 799
acquiescence of [5]11; act of [3]791; adaptive faculty [2]689, [3]581; allegory of [3]92; amoral [1]869; anthropomorphism of [5]730; categorical [4]93; and climate [2]418; common [1]462; conceptions in [2]295, 1148, conceptions of [3]49; [5]776, 795; conceptive faculty [5]803; conventional [1]863; convictions of the [1]675; convinced [6]11; defined [1]655, [2]277, 1018n, [3]423–4, 424–5, 557, [4]196, 370, 371, [5]599; derangement of [6]287; discursive [1]587, 595, [2]656; diversity of [5]66; enlightened [4]360; erring [5]298; errors of [1]823, [4]181, [6]28; factory of [2]295; faculty of words [3]423; and faith [5]564; finite [5]185, 191; fleshly [3]563; forms of [3]357, 1091, [4]174; heart as [2]680; human [2]171, 609n, [5]68, 156, 730, 842, [6]80, 306; imperfect [3]748; individual [5]484; in insects [2]861, 861n; instinctive [4]542; intellectual [3]746; interdependent with sense [1]683; laws of [3]721; too literal [1]470; as *Logos* [2]715, 729n; lunacy of [2]482; made human by ideas [3]524; medial faculty [3]423–4; mere conviction of [5]561–2; as mind of the flesh [1]504; misapplication of [2]844; as moonshine [2]480, 480n; nature of [2]844; notions of [2]729; St Paul speaks to [4]399; *phronema sarkos* [3]754; *phronesis* [2]713; products of [3]991, [5]750; pure [4]108; rational [3]150; and reason *see* reason; reason in [3]163; reflected light of [3]472; and sense [4]144; sensual [5]96; sensuous [1]693, [2]1151; shrewd [4]78; sin acts through u. [1]819; sphere of logic [5]627; and spirit [5]583; stomach of [3]347; subjective [5]790; symbolic use of [5]796; Wesley's [5]126; see also *Verstand*
undertaker [2]449
under-tint [3]906n
Undine (in La Motte-Fouqué) [4]595, 595n
"undivulsed" [1]653, 653n
uneducated [4]775
Unendlichkeit [5]315, 317
unenglishisms [6]205
unfold [1]140n
"unfolded" [1]644
unfriend [3]147
ungeachtet [1]21–2
"unicism" [3]77, 77n
"unicist(s)" [2]799, 799n
unicists [2]800
unicity [2]799n, 884, [3]77n, [5]26
unicorns [1]770
"Unidentified" MT [5]866–7
unificence [3]60
uniformity [1]332, [5]147

unigenous, the [3]1000
"unintroitive" [1]667n, [4]787, 787n–8n
union/Union
of churches [5]548; of deity and humanity [3]27; hypostatic(al) [3]611, [5]657; with Ireland [4]591, [5]659; of opposites [1]662; point of [2]147; with Scotland [4]591; transcendent [5]182
"uni-personalists" [2]22, 22n
unique(s) [2]816, [5]26
unit [2]1186, [3]126, 157
Unitarian(s) [1]235n, 316n, 435n, 500, 512, [2]247n, 261, 499n, 662, 742n, 786, 787, [3]49n, 524, 737, 738, 762n, [4]41, 160n, 297n, 299, 620, 629n, 643n, [5]3, 4, 7n, 28, 433n, 465n, 514n, 667, 783, [6]77n, 80, 87–8, 297n, 306
not Christians [2]36; church [3]146n; C as [1]566; on death of Christ [2]362; as demi-semi-quaver of Christianity [1]346; doctrine of [2]32; English [2]205, [4]46, 429, 429n; modern [1]359n, [2]27, 316, [3]515, 515n, [6]132, 297, 297n; U.-necessitarian [3]137n; perversion [1]461; philosophic [5]6–7; Priestleian [3]670, 671; reject *evangelium infantiae* [2]35; reject gospels of infancy [1]507; reject redemption [2]263; scoff of [3]1092; Society [5]657
Unitarianism [2]20, 695n, 1088, 1088n, [3]77, 671, 671n, 766n, [4]669n, [5]162n, 167, 563n, [6]74
blundering term [2]21–2; not Christianity [3]367n; modern [5]514, 657; Priestleian [3]305n; relation to Arianism and Socinianism [2]265; spirit of [1]359n; untenable [4]45
United States [4]97n; *see also* America
"uniting" [3]561
unitrine [1]587, 587n
unity/unities [1]617, 689, [2]1186–7, [3]12, 43, 66, 102, 129, 150, 834, 841, 1024, [4]169, [5]16, 302, 459, 568
absolute [5]743n; of absolute [5]357; accidental [6]8; antecedent [6]8; bond of [5]433; breach of [5]23; of church [5]147; of consciousness [3]243; of deity [3]660; and distinctity [2]300, [3]52; divine [5]408; dramatic [4]779, 779n–80n, 826, 863–4, 863n; federal [6]14; in God [2]1186; of God [5]54, 54n; of the Godhead [5]626; essential to imagination [4]382; of impression [4]773; in infinity [1]667; of interdependents [4]12; love of [5]510; and multeity [5]266; multeity in [1]595; and multiplicity [2]884; negative [2]748n, [5]452; applied to novel [2]76; original [2]554n, 1019n; and plurality [2]1020, [5]721–2, [6]316; polar [1]563; positive [2]198; quinquinity in [5]242; source of [5]771; spiritual [5]229; symbol of [4]14; of thought [3]77; of thought and act [5]93; tripersonality in [5]26
universal(s) [1]368, [3]545, [4]395, 492, [5]99, 99n, 302, 369, 409, 580
abstract [5]274, 792; in Defoe [2]165; and particular *see* particular; particularised [5]357
universalisation [5]438
universalisms [5]365, 365n
universality [3]244–5, [4]107, [6]64
want of [5]398
universative [1]595, 596n
universe [1]562, [3]341, 435, 504, 860, [4]268, [5]7, 357, 385, 405, 426–31
causes of [5]455; creation of [5]680; evils of [5]592; existence of [1]574; former of [5]482; and God [3]82; harmony of [4]511; idea of [4]141, 142; Kant's system of [3]342–4; life of [6]8; material [4]303; origination [5]456; of relations [2]1019; soul of [3]82
university/universities [1]478, [2]955–7, 978, 979n–80n, [3]971, [5]324
of Germany [3]318; idea of [5]365; Jewish [3]467; medical [4]96; as paradise [2]320; prejudice [2]817; wit [3]907
University College *see* London
unlearned, the [5]507, 675
unnaturalness [4]784
"unpossessedness" [4]787, 787n
unreal, the [5]175
and real *see* real
unrealities [5]708
unregenerate, the [3]737
"unriddle" [1]747, 747n
"unsearchable" [6]54
unseemliness [2]300
unser [1]608, 608n
unsheathing [2]135
unteachableness [5]476
unthinkingness [4]88, [5]117
unum necessarium [5]564
unusual, the [2]1060
unutterable, the [1]575
unweit [1]21–2
Unzer (probably Johann August Unzer, 1727–99) [4]275
upas tree *see* tree(s)
"uppropment" [1]507, 507n
Uppsala [3]333n
uprightness, German [2]204

"up-swing" [2]1181, 1181n
Ur [5]347
Urania (myth) [5]227
uranium [5]261
Uranus [1]12, [2]556, 556n, 577, 578n, 579, [4]326
Urbino [4]808, 809n
Urevangelium [1]452n, [2]270n, 435, 444, 447, 447n, 448n, 460, 461, 467, [4]469–70, 470n, 472n; see also *Proto-evangelium*
uric acid [3]1031, 1031n
Uriel (myth) [4]650
urine [3]1075
Urmensch [6]141n
urns [1]763, 790, 797
Ursa Major [1]399n
Ursache [5]210
Ursina (in Reynolds) [4]240, 241, 241n
Urtheil [4]127, 127n, 222
urtheilen [3]94, 95n
use and abuse [1]517, 517n
useful, the [6]309
Usher *see* Ussher
Usoüs (myth) [2]576
Ussher/Usher, James, Archbishop of Armagh (1581–1656) [1]291, 311, [2]711n, 913, [3]803, 803n, [4]172, 172n, [5]508, 508n–9n
  The Original of Bishops [3]803n, [4]172n, 509n
Usthazadius/Usthazanes, St (d 341) [2]740
usurpation(s) [3]734, [5]561
  papal [4]43; papistic [2]1041
usurper [1]295, [4]789
usury [2]310–11
Utarans [2]347
uterus [5]468n
  uterine life [2]535
utile [4]720
Utilitarian(s) [2]80
Utilitarianism [1]740, 740n, [2]251n
utility [2]601, 1012, [3]808, [5]493
Utopia [1]833, [2]766, 766n, [3]622, [4]190, 190n, [5]301n, 366
Utrecht [4]106n
"utter" [1]637
utterance [2]690, [3]12n, 29
Uzziah (Bible) [2]838, 838n

vacuity [3]916
vacuum [4]288, 397, [5]231, 644n, 720, 720n
vagrant [6]99
vain, the [1]184
Valancey (possibly Charles Vallancey, 1721–1812) [2]575
Valckenaer, Lodewijk Kasper (1715–85)
  Diatribe de Aristobulo Judaeo [2]339, [3]1013, [5]851; MT [6]3–9
"valdisonant" [2]582, 582n
Valens, Bishop of Mursa (4th century) [2]751
Valentinian I (321–75) [2]732n, 747
Valentinian II (371–92) [1]109n
Valentinians [2]715–17
Valentinus (fl c 136–160) [2]464, 464n, 714–17, 721n ("Valentinian")
Valerius Maximus (20 BC–AD 50) [3]540
Valese, Nicolas Fabrice (fl early 16th century) [2]770
Valesius [5]748–9
valet, Swiss [5]866
Valetta/Valletta [1]697 ("La Valette"), [2]978n ("Vallette"), [5]832
Valhalla [3]1072
valiance [4]789
valiancy of style [4]736
validity, objective [5]776
Valla, Giorgio (Placentinus) (1447–1500) *see* Nemesius *De natura hominis* ed Valla
valleys [2]372
  of vision [3]564
Valpy, Abraham John (1787–1854) [1]458n
value(s)
  derivative [3]459; spiritual [4]28n
vampire/vampyre [5]102
Van der Geest, Cornelius (1577–1638) [2]1195n
Van Diemen's Land [2]74, [4]15 ("Daemon's"), 15n
Van Dyck, Sir Anthony (1599–1641) [1]lviii, [2]1195, 1195n, [3]993–4, 993n, [6]158 ("Vandyk"), 158n
Van Marum, Martinus (1750–1830) [4]392, 392n
Vane, Henry ("Harry") (1613–62) [6]10
  A Healing Question Propounded and Resolved [2]111; MT [6]10–11
Vanini, Lucilio (1584–1619) [4]719
Vanists [5]509n
vanity/vanities [2]636–7, 915, 919, 999, [3]222, 812, 1018, [4]41, 260, [5]142, 170, 476, [6]302
  gratification of [5]379; of vanities [5]811
Vanston, William Justus Keough (1881–1957) [3]804
"vapour(s)" [3]187, 187n

vapour(s) [1]822, [3]805, [4]53, [5]165, 557
dank [5]292; gaudy [5]483
Vargas, Alphonsus/Alfonso de, Archbishop of Toledo (c1307–66) [3]366n
Vargas, Count de (fl 1810) [3]940
variation [4]500
variety/varieties [4]729
all sorts of [1]772; anomalous [1]368; law of [3]520; relief from [2]121
Varius Rufus (fl 20 BC) *Thyestes* [2]776, 776n
varnish [3]831
Varro, Marcus Terentius (116–27 BC) [2]54n, 575, 575n q, 583, 583n, 758n, 775n
Antiquitates rerum divinarum et humanarum [2]575n; *De lingua latina* [2]575n, 583n; *De re rustica* [2]575n
Varty, J. (fl 1810) [3]938
Vasari, Giorgio (1511–74)
Lives of the Painters ed E. H. Blashfield, E. W. Blashfield, and A. A. Hopkins [1]*627n*; *Vies des peintres* [1]627n
vase(s) [3]631
porcelain [3]480
vassals [3]693
vast, the [5]484
Vaughan, Robert (1795–1868) *The Life and Opinions of John de Wycliffe* [3]142n, [5]143n; MT [6]12–24
Vaughan, Thomas ("Eugenius Philalethes") (1621–66) [3]906, 907
Anima magica abscondita [3]906; *Anthroposophia theomagica* [3]906; *The Man-Mouse Taken in a Trap* [3]906; *The Second Wash* [3]906
"vaulting" [3]193, 193n
Vauquelin, Louis Nicolas (1763–1829) [1]641, 641n, [3]938, 939, 942, 943, [5]261, 261n
vaurien [2]1029, 1029n, [6]66
Vauxhall *see* London
Ve (myth) [4]489–90
Vega, Andreas de (1498–1549) *De justificatione doctrina universa* [2]677, 677n
Vega Carpio, Lope Félix de (1562–1635) [1]390n
vegetable(s) [1]596, 663, [2]689, 1013n, [3]128, 580
acids *see* acid(s), vegetable; and animal [4]493; decaying [6]231; elements of [1]570; food of [3]68; forms [1]764, 797n; life [3]125; odours [1]666; power [3]324; realm [5]259
vegetality [1]589, 596n
vegetation [2]1013n, [3]580, [5]257, 286–7, 348, 350
spiritual [3]697
"vegetive" [2]1008, 1008n
vegetivity [2]1008n
vehicle, occasional [5]451
veil [3]447, [4]477n, [5]130
Christ under [1]468; Epicurean [2]251; of Moses [2]138, 138n
vein(s) [3]123, 123n, [5]289–90, 789
Velia [2]53
velocity [2]889–90, [3]271–2, 273, 299–300, 302, [5]451
"velosity" [2]889–90, 890n
veneration [3]787
Venetian(s) [1]842, [4]746, 780
vengeance, spirits of [2]515
venialists [3]501
Venice [1]113n, 842, 843n, 846n, [2]586, [3]1068, [4]35, 240, 864n, [5]279, 846
Venetian divines [1]846
venison [2]636, [3]394
venom [5]521
green [1]786
ventriloquism [2]56, [3]179, [4]612n, [5]301 ("ventriloquised")
ventriloquist [1]370n, 420, [2]1108, 1108n, [3]65, [5]530
poet as [1]402
Venus (myth) [1]219, 544, [2]10, 96, 214, 580, 583, 583n, 739, [3]92n, [4]835n, [6]157, 211n. *See also* Aphrodite; Idalaea
Temple of *see* Corinth; Idumaea
Venus (planet) [1]12, 625n, 626, [2]557, 739, [3]92n, [5]225, 263, 263n
evening star [2]95; phases of [5]825
Venus de Medici [4]865
veracity [1]357, 357n, [2]360, 1192, 1192n, [3]9, [5]65, 168, 619, 681
Baxter's [1]306; God's [5]617, 618; and lie [5]820; Swedenborg's [5]413, 414n, 464, 474; and truth [3]9, 9n; and verity [1]306, 306n, [5]52, 513
verb(s) [3]15, 450, [4]166
active [5]774; determinant [4]322; Greek [6]26; Greek and Latin [6]25; impersonal [2]324; Italian [4]330; contains noun [3]835; v. substantive [3]11, 11n, 12n, 15n, 279, 279n, 449, 835, [4]166, [5]95, 170, 396, [6]8, 9n, *see also* infinitive; transitive [2]992
verbiage [1]528, [2]203, [3]806, 807, [5]447
verbosity [3]103
verbum [2]881n
v. sat [5]169
vere mortuus est [2]334–5, [3]56, 613
vere non ens [1]565n
Vergerio, Pietro Paolo (Vergerius) (1498–1565) [2]765

Verhältnisse [5]370
"verily" [5]399n
veriness [3]591
verity/verities [1]357, 357n, [3]848
eternal [3]11, [5]704; logical and real [5]743; metaphysical [1]783, [5]467; spiritual [3]42, [5]169, 599, 795; Swedenborg's [5]413; and veracity *see* veracity; *see also* truth(s)
vermes [5]287, 360; *see also* worms
vermöge [1]21–2
Vermont, University of *see* Burlington VT
Vernon, Diana (in Scott) [4]58, 587n
Vernon, Sir Frederick (in Scott) [4]587
Vernon, Mrs (fl 1859) [2]245
Vernunft [1]654, 655n, 682, [2]1016, [4]214, 214n, 372, 372n, [5]752
etymology of [2]188, 188n; and *Verstand* [1]869, [5]782; *see also* reason(s)
Die Vernunft fordert die Säkularisirungen [3]961
Die Vernunft fordert die Säkularisirungen nicht [3]961
Vernunft-gesetze [2]622, 622n
Vernunftglaube [4]446, 446n, [5]701, 701n, 718, 766
Veronensis *see* Emili, Paulo
Veronica, St (legend) [1]41, 41n
verse(s) [4]168, 679
after-dinner [2]758; blank *see* blank verse; copies of [2]917; v.-disguising [2]227; ferruminator of [4]291; intercurrent [4]795; Italian [4]290, 290n; Jonson's [3]192; Latin [1]770, [2]812; and prose [3]192; near prose [5]223
versification [1]374, 400, [2]123, 124, [3]402, 404, 702, 1074, 1076
Fletcher's [1]407; Italian [4]329; Lloyd's [3]714; Massinger's [3]813–15; *see also* metre(s)
version
erroneous [2]570; literal [1]467; or perversion [1]461
versöhnen [2]271, 271n, [3]46, 46n
Verstand [1]654, 655n, 682, 682n, [3]92, 260, [4]214, 214n, 370–1, 375, [5]242, 243, 752
and *Vernunft* see *Vernunft*; *see also* understanding
Verstandeswesen [2]480, 480n
Versuch einer ausführlichen Erörterung [3]961
"vertiginate" [5]27, 27n
Vesey, Francis (?1721–1804) *Reports of Cases* [3]500, 500n–1n
Vespasian (Titus Flavius Vespasianus) (9–79) [1]486n, 832, 832n, [2]515, 515n, [3]448, 448n, 928, 929
Vespucci, Amerigo (1451–1512) [5]102
vessel(s) [2]1024, [3]679, [5]266, 474
of Deity [2]135; splitting of [4]429–30
Vesta (myth) [1]639, 639n
Vesuvius [6]254n
vetches [4]531, 531n, [5]256
veto, royal [4]17
vibration(s) [2]960, 1080, [3]323, 944, 945, 945n
vibratiuncles [2]960
vicar [2]72, [3]214
Christ's [1]315
vice(s) [1]212, [2]19, 348, 640, 1163n, [3]134–5, 190, 510, 579, [4]238, 655, 660, 819, 860, [6]168
of Christians [5]416; of citizens [1]224; and crime [1]43; cruel [1]319; detestable [3]226; habits of [4]662; mouthing [1]369; primary act of [1]172; and virtue [3]317, 808, [2]319, [4]548–9, 626, [5]615, [6]139; *see also* evil(s)
vice-corpus [5]554
vice-gerent [3]455
vice-ghostship [1]873
viceroy [2]511
Vico, Giambattista (1668–1744) [1]lxx, [3]142, 142n, [6]18
not annotated by C [1]lxiii
Scienza nuova [1]lxcviii, [2]892, 892n, 1092n, [3]142n, [6]18n; *Vita* [6]18n
Victor of Marseilles, St (d c 290) [2]728
Victoria College *see* Toronto
Victorians [5]128n
Victorina (in Reynolds) [4]240
victory [5]651
temporary [2]42
Victualians [5]197n
videre [3]128
videri [3]130
Vienna [2]1086n, [3]103, [4]164, 836
Congress of [3]250n; Treaty of [5]312n
Vigilantius (fl c 400) [2]667
Vile (myth) [4]489–90
village [5]60
villain(s) [1]699, [2]687, 687n, 693, 980, [4]241, 629, 771
intellectual superiority of [1]212, 212n; professed [1]368; v.-trappists [2]980
villainy/villainies [1]212, [4]759
Villani, Giovanni (c 1275–1348) *Historie Fiorentine* [1]501–2 q
villanus [2]980, 980n
Villermé, Louis René (1782–1863) [4]164
Villiers, George, 1st Duke of Buckingham (1592–1628) [2]59, 927, 927n, 940, 942,

Villiers, George, 1st Duke of Buckingham—*continued*
942n–3n, 1101, 1103, [3]213, 796, 796n, 797, [4]608, 608n
minion [2]929, 929n, 944
Villiers, George, 2nd Duke of Buckingham (1628–87) [1]353n, [2]59
Vimiera [2]940n
Vincent, Miss (fiction) [5]622, 622n
Vincent, William (1739–1815) *The Greek Verb Analysed* [1]lxxx, [2]54n q; MT [6]25–7
"Vincentian Canon" [1]520n, [2]177n
Vincentius [1]258n
Vincentius Lerinensis (Vincent of Lérins), St (d c 450) [5]539
"Vindex" *The Conduct of the British Government* MT [6]28–9
vindicator [1]806
vindictiveness [1]320
vine(s) [1]246, 246n, [3]678n, [5]396, 396n, 580
vinegar [1]546, [4]745
Vines, Richard (?1600–56) [1]246
Viola (*Twelfth Night*) [4]704
violence, weapons of [1]418
violet (colour) [4]167
violets [3]1075, [4]708, [5]702
violin [2]537, 537n, [3]248
viper(s) [3]223, 1044, [5]506, 506n
vires representativae [5]410
Virgil (Publius Virgilius Maro) ("Mantuan") (70–19 BC) [1]38, 110n, 218n, 374, [2]55, 240, 762, 968, 973n, [3]401, 410, 411, 413, 767, 892, [4]336n, [5]110, 690, [6]30, 138, 328
and Christianity [2]971n, 972; tr Dryden [1]38; good ear [2]88; pronunciation of name [2]66, 66n; source for Milton [2]971–2
Aeneid [1]38, 109 q, 109n, 128 q, 128n q, 636n q, 683, [2]135 q, 135n q, 411n, 930 q, 930n, 971n, [3]153n q, 770, [4]171 q, 171n q, 607 q, 607n q, 608 q, [5]109, 109n, 544 q, 544n q, 832n, [6]110 q, 110n q, 148 q, tr Beresford [6]208, 208n, tr Dryden [6]148 q, 148n, 198–9, 198n–9n, 208, tr Fairclough [1]683n q, [3]650–1 q, 892 q, 893, [4]556 q, 608 q, [6]148n q, 197–215 q *passim*, tr Phaer [2]1125n, tr C. Pitt [1]38, tr WW [6]30; MT 197–215; *Bucolics* [1]384–5, tr Wrangham [6]218; *Culex* [3]413n q; *Eclogue IV* [2]411n; *Eclogues* [1]736n, [2]1000 q, 1000n q, [3]411n, 455 q, 455n, 530, 530n, [5]831n, tr Fairclough [6]221, 221n q; *Georgica ... hexaglotta* tr Guzman, J. H. Voss, Sotheby, Soave, and Delille MT [6]30–1, tr as *Georgics* [1]cvi, clxiii, 384–5, 471n, [3]409, 920n, [5]483n, tr Dryden [4]780n, [6]212n
virgin(s)
v. birth [3]36, [4]255–6; of chastity [1]669; icy-chaste [1]397; V. Mary *see* Mary; NT word [2]270; proud [1]600; vestal [2]834
virginity [2]335
of Adam [1]657–8; article of [5]628
Virgo [1]399n
virtualism [5]398n
virtue(s) [1]171–2, 184, 751, [2]618, 926, 940, 1163n, [3]120, 135, 135n, 316–17, 401, 497, 532, [4]137, 212, 238, 268, 551, 653, 816, 819, [5]40, 497, 592
ascetic [5]86; beauty of [2]1178; conversions to [1]369; early forms of [2]928; essence of [5]277; fashionable [2]545, [3]250; habit of [2]603; heroic [4]421; idea of [2]632, [3]317; implies reason [1]869; kinds of [4]137–8; manly [4]335; masculine [2]1197; mighty [5]497; negative [2]926; pagan morality as [2]291; perfect [5]208; permanency of [2]569; practice of [2]530; of private life [6]94; progress in [5]229; related to wickedness [2]84; saving [1]821; scale of [5]820; spiritual [5]414; as talisman [1]397; true [1]790; and vice *see* vice; will fountain of [2]247
Virtuosa, Lady (fiction) [5]83
virtuoso/virtuosi [5]83n
speculative [2]432
"virus" [4]148, 148n
virus [3]399, [4]816
of speculation [5]766
vis
v. flammea [5]783; *v. fluidifica* [6]227; *v. inertiae* [1]661, [3]44, *see also* inertia; *v. interna* [4]225; *v. motrix* [4]450; *v. plastica* [5]473; *v. productiva* [5]418; *v. representativa* [3]328; *v. scientifica* [4]648; *v. vitae* [2]348, 1000, [3]374, 398, [4]385, [6]8; *v. vivificans* [5]715; *see also* power(s)
viscera [5]559
Vishnu ("Veeshnoo"/"Vischnu") (myth) [1]400, [2]342, 346, 346n, [3]59n, [5]822
visibility [3]45, [5]443
visible, the [4]430, 430n
Visigoths [5]195n
vision(s) [1]437, 561, [2]314, 410, 1146, [3]443, 563–4, 604, 772, [4]477, [5]15, 371, 496, 517, 818
acuteness of [3]692; Apocalypse as [2]458–9; apocalyptic [3]472; beatific [1]657; in Bible [1]437; Böhme's [1]604, 639; distinct [4]601; Ezekiel's [2]410; inner [2]402–3; as instru-

ment [2]402; inward [5]627, 726; laws of [5]269; mental [5]32; of Peter [2]470; and poem [2]459; poetic [6]325; prophetic [4]787; single [6]131; symbolical [3]1088, [5]413; true [5]823n
visionary/visionaries [3]705, [4]654, [6]106
 Böhme as [1]558
visitation [4]635
visual, the, and conceptual [3]373
visualities [4]493
vita vivificans [6]296
vital principle *see* principle(s), vital
Vitalians [5]196–7, 197n
Vitalis, Mr (fl 1810) [3]942
vitalism [2]539n
vitality [1]537, [3]28; *see also* life
Vitellius, Aulus (15–69) [1]486, 486n, [3]929, 929n
Vitruvius (Marcus Vitruvius Pollio) (1st century BC) [4]160
 On Architecture [4]160n
Vitus, St (d c 303) [2]739n, [5]197, 197n
 Dance [2]739, 739n
Vives, Ludovicus (Juan Luis) (1492–1540)
 On the Causes of the Corruption of the Arts [5]804–5 q
Viviani, Domenico (1772–1840) [3]938
vividness [4]415
 of impressions [4]409
vivisection [4]96, 96n, [5]102 ("viva sectio"), 102n, 149n
vocable, barbarous [4]14
vocation [3]548
vocative [3]832
Voetius, Gisbertus (1589–1676) [4]106, 106n
Vogel, Mr (fl 1810) [3]940
voice [2]515
 from heaven [4]298; and metrical effect [6]201; small [5]187
void [1]601, [5]430, 698–700, 708n
volatilisers [3]41
volatility [2]856, [5]438
volcano(es) [2]515, [3]433, 949, [4]490–1, 510, 510n, 528, [5]338 ("volcanic")
 lunar [5]340
volenti nulla fit injuria [1]307, 307n
Volesus [1]176
Volga [3]1047
volition(s) [1]577, [2]247, [3]359, 868, 868n, [4]542, [5]25, 126, 133, 176, 183, 184, [6]223
 of acquiescence [5]126; earnestness of [3]867; fresh [1]401; instinctive [6]51; languor of [1]516; reflection of [5]290; suspension of [6]102; *see also* will(s)
Volk [3]206
Volkslieder [2]1048
Volksmärchen [3]103, 103n
Voltaire, François Marie Arouet de (1694–1778) [1]144n, [2]480n, 705, 705n, 768n, 973, [3]786, [4]623, [5]640, 640n, 703n, [6]32
 influence [2]480
 Les systèmes [3]972; *A Treatise on Toleration* tr D. Williams MT [6]32–3; *Zaïre* [6]324n
voltaism [4]319
voluntary, the, and spontaneous [3]519
voluntas [3]359
volunteer(s) [3]9, [5]381
voluptuary/voluptuaries [4]79, [5]517
vomiting [6]121–2
vonvornig [3]965, 965n
Voragine, Jacobus de (c 1230–98) [2]699, 699n
 Golden Legend [2]699n, [5]662, 662n
Voraussetzung [4]378–9, 378n
Vores, Thomas (fl 1859) [2]245
vornehm [2]421, 421n, 1080, 1080n, 1083, [3]358, 358n, [5]88, 88n, 718, 718n
Vorstellkraft [2]1013
Vorstellung/Vorstellungen [3]791, [4]211, 217, 435, [6]172
vortices [4]13, 13n
Voss, Gerhard Jan (Vossius) (1577–1649) [1]492, [2]579n, [3]733n, 762n
 Poeticarum institutionum libri tres [1]lxxxi; MT [6]34
Voss, Johann Heinrich (1751–1826) *see* Virgil *Georgica . . . hexaglotta* tr Voss and others
vote(s) of legislature [6]52
voters [4]96
Voulté, Jean (d 1642) [2]769–70 q ("Vouté")
Vouté *see* Voulté
vow(s) [1]272, [5]130
 by compulsion [6]262; constrained [2]984; oaths not [1]342
vowel(s) [1]770n, [3]827, [5]434, 435
 priority of [3]24, 24n–5n
voyage(s) [2]1024, [5]167
voyagers, philosophic [5]416
Vulcan (in Aeschylus) [4]845, 846n
Vulcan (myth) [1]799, [2]576n, 583, 583n, [3]649, [4]835, 835n, [5]227; *see also* Hephaestus
vulgar [1]254, [2]1158, [5]385
 ignorant [1]290; traditions of [3]466
vulgarism(s) [3]110, 534, 813, [4]579, 611, 796, [6]316

vulgarity [5]611
exquisite [6]203. *See also* coarseness; grossness
Vulgate *see* Bible
vulture(s) [1]483, [2]771, [5]292
vulva [2]772, 772n

Wachstumsmittel [3]128, 128n
Wackenroder, Wilhelm Heinrich (1773–98) [1]131
Waddesworth *see* Wadsworth
Wade, Josiah (1761–1842) [1]xciv, clx, clxi, [2]5, 967, 1121n, 1203, [4]295, [5]830, 844n
letters to [1]cxxiv; owner of annotated books [4]294; supplier of books to C [1]xcvii
Wade, Launcelot (c 1796–c 1830) [2]967, [4]306n
his executor [2]5; letter to [6]38
Wadsworth, James ("Waddesworth") (c 1572–1623) [1]840, 844, 844n, 847, 848
Wadsworth, James (1604–56) [1]844n
wages [3]741, [5]670, [6]22
of sin [2]326
waggery [4]817
Wahn [1]124, 124n
Wahn-Sinn [4]358
während [1]22
waistcoat [1]388–9, 389n
straight [5]603
Waistell, Charles (fl 1810) [3]939, 940
waiter, German [5]866
Wake, William, Archbishop of Canterbury (1657–1737) [1]491n, 492
Genuine Epistles of the Apostolic Fathers [1]488
Wakefield [2]127
Wakefield, Edward Gibbon (1796–1862) *A Letter from Sydney* ed R. Gouger MT [6]35–7
Wakefield, Gilbert (1756–1801) *Evidences of Christianity* [5]51n
Walch, Johann Georg (1693–1775) *see* Luther *Luthers Samptliche Schriften* ed Walch
Walcheren [5]316n
Walden, Baron Howard de *see* Howard, Theophilus
Wales [2]874, [5]179
ecclesiastical history of [6]17; North W. [4]783. *See also* Welsh (language); Welsh (people)
Wales, William (c 1734–98) [1]615, *615n*, [2]74n, 981n, 985
Walford, D. *see* Kant *Selected Pre-Critical Writings* ed Kerferd and Walford
Walker, Adam (?1731–1821) [4]13, 13n
Walker, Anthony (c 1622–92) [6]184, 185, 185n, 186
A True Account of the Author of a Book Entituled Eikon Basilike [2]523, 523n q, *425n*, [6]185n
Walker, David (d c 1840) [4]575, 575n
Walker, John (1674–1747) [4]180
An Attempt towards Recovering an Account of the Number and Sufferings of the Clergy of the Church of England [1]357, 357n, [4]180, 180n q
Walker, John (1732–1807) *A Dictionary of the English Language* MT [6]38–40
Walker, Mrs M. [3]990
walking [2]1186
wall(s) [1]273, [2]887, 887n, [3]472
Wall, William (1647–1728) *Conference between Two Men* [1]cxvi, cxvin; MT [6]41–3
Waller, Alfred Rayney (1867–1922) *see* B&F *Dramatic Works* ed Glover and Waller
Waller, Edmund (1606–87) [1]37
Go, Lovely Rose [1]81n; *To Mr. George Sandys* MT [1]81; *To Van Dyck* MT [1]81
Wallis, John (1616–1703) [1]259, [3]1070
Wallop, Richard (1616–97) [3]166, 166n
Walpole, Horace, 4th Earl of Orford (1717–97) [1]cix, [2]865
Walpole, Sir Robert (1676–1745) [1]162, 162n
Walsh, John Benn, Baron Ormathwaite (1798–1881)
On the Present Balance of Parties [4]7; MT [6]44–9; *Popular Opinions on Parliamentary Reform* [4]7; MT [6]50–3
Walsh, Thomas (fl 1752) [5]180, 180n–1n
Walsh, William (1663–1708) [1]37
Walsingham, Sir Francis (c 1532–90) [4]173
Walter, John Henry *see* Shakespeare *Henry V* ed Walter
Walter, Professor *see* Walther, Johann Gottlieb
Waltham MA
Brandeis University (Hofheimer Collection), marginalia in [5]490, [6]28
Waltharius [2]525
Walther (in De Wette) [2]198
Walther, Johann Gottlieb (1734–1818) [4]164 ("Walter")
Walther, Philipp Franz (1782–1849) [3]114

Walton, Izaak (1593–1683) [2]242, 914n, 1131, 1135, 1135n
on Donne [2]328, 328n
"The Life of Mr. George Herbert" [2]1032; MT 1046; *Compleat Angler* [1]lxxxviii, xc; *An Elegie upon Dr. Donne* MT [2]240–2; *Life and Death of Dr. Donne* [2]242n, 245
waltzing [2]191
"wane" [2]275, 275n
"want" [3]172, 172n
want(s) [5]363
wantonness [1]386, [2]1178, [4]801, 816
infidel [1]6
Wapping *see* London
war(s) [1]58, 442, [4]80, [5]195, 196, 274, 276–7, 640, 678, 752, [6]28
w.-chief [1]483; Christians in [1]711; civil *see* civil war(s); continental [6]16; costs of [2]622; of 1812 [1]32n; in heaven [3]472–3; Jewish [3]475; Napoleonic [5]379n; national [5]276; necessary [2]847; w.-ode [2]897; senseless [3]645; w.-trumpets [4]503
warbler [5]424
Warburton, William (1698–1779) [2]72, 142, [3]553, 695, 896n, 898, [4]690, 690n, 692, 694, 696, 701, 702, 703, 706, 707n, 710, 711, 712, 712n, 714, 715, 716n, 719, 720, 721, 723, 723n, 726, 733, 733n, 736, 737, 740, 740n, 742, 744, 747, 748, 762, 763n, 766n, 802, 843n, 847, [5]591
The Alliance between Church and State [1]360, 360n; *The Divine Legation of Moses* [2]828, 828n, [3]437, 437n, 553n, 649, 649n, 695n, [5]591n q; *Julian* [2]746, 746n, [4]627n; *Works* [5]591n q
ward(s) [1]245
Ward, Charles A. (fl 1891–95) [1]cxxvii
Ward, Edward (1667–1731) [1]182, 182n, [3]680, 680n
Ward, George (fl ?1764–81) [1]553
Ward, John (c 1679–1758) [2]3
Ward, Samuel (d 1643) [2]913
Ward, Seth, Bishop of Exeter (1617–89) [1]353, 353n, [4]76
Ward, Thomas (fl 1793–1827) [1]lxxviin, [2]967, [4]85n
Warden, Henry (in Scott) [4]598, 598n
Wardour, Sir Arthur (in Scott) [4]586, 586n
Wardour, Isabella (in Scott) [4]586, 586n
Wardrop, James (1782–1869) *History of James Mitchell* [2]359
Ware, Great Bed of [2]888
ware(s), Romish [5]663
"warely" [5]399, 399n
Waring, E. J. (fl 1843) [2]36
warming-plate [4]491
warmth [1]633, [2]854, 854n, 855, 860, [3]29, 1003, 1007, [4]448, 492, [5]168, 266, 450, 783, [6]230
of brooding [5]326; w.-sense [3]868; w.-stuff [3]46; theory of [6]226–7, 226n; *see also* heat
warning [5]634
warp [5]707
warriors [1]850
Warsaw [2]909n
wart(s) [3]717, [5]416
on heart [3]377
Warter, John Wood (1806–78) *see* R. Southey *Common-Place Book*, *The Doctor*, *A Selection from the Letters* ed Warter
Warton, Joseph (1722–1800) [1]38, [3]897, 897n
Observations on the Faerie Queene of Spenser [4]815n
Warton, Thomas (1728–90) [1]38
History of English Poetry [2]870n q, 1170n; *see also* Milton *Poems upon Several Occasions* ed Warton
Warwick, Earl of *see* Neville, Richard
Warwick, Sir Philip (1609–83) [1]280n
Warwickshire [4]724
Washer, John [1]365
washerwomen [4]636
Washington DC
Folger Shakespeare Library, marginalia in [1]39, [4]764; Library of Congress [1]clxvi
Washington, George (1732–99) [1]850n, [2]952n
wasps [2]983
wassail [3]896
wastcoateër [1]388–9
Wastdale [3]975, 980
Wastwater [3]974
watch(es) [2]788, 1036, 1036n, [3]790, [4]93, 826, [5]730, 730n
and watchmaker [2]324, 324n, [5]456n
watchmaker(s) [2]324n, [4]28, [5]456n
watchman [3]779
watch-word [1]472
water(s) [1]635, 776, [2]1037–8, 1038n, [3]61, 61n, 67, 85, 127, 293, 386, 402, 594–5, 952, 997, 997n, 1005, 1006, 1006n, 1007, 1022, 1028, 1029, 1051, 1057, 1063, [4]235, 273, 319–20, 320n, 395, 395n, 433, [5]155, 265, 338, 346, 347, 386, 451, 557, [6]228–9, 230
antitype of [3]594, 594n; in Baptism [1]323,

water(s)—*continued*
[3]597–8, 597n, [5]664, 675; bitter [2]508, 509, 509n; Böhme on [1]591, 593, 622, 654; brandy and [5]418; at Cana [2]204; chemical analysis [4]13n; composition of [2]1144, 1144n; concrete galvanism [1]579; constitution of [3]1006; dangerous [2]327; defined [1]597; dirty [5]649, 649n; w.-drinker [4]660; drop of [3]9; and electricity [1]650; first [4]533n; flush of [1]418; freezing of [5]246; fresh [4]488; frozen [4]430; w.-gas [5]557, [6]230; Heraclitus on [5]714; holy [2]1158, [5]652; hot [5]351, 351n; hyperoxygenation of [3]1032; w.-insects [3]352, 352n; w.-machines [2]545; mineral [4]617–18; mother of earth [1]662–3; nurse of growth [4]428; oxide of [1]650; and plants [3]127–8; w.-plants [5]346; in polar system [1]663; w.-pourer [1]812; primary [1]594; pun on Aquinas [3]193; quality of [1]568; w.-scenery [5]560; sea [5]351; w.-shaft [3]564; shapeless [5]266; in siphon [1]659; as species [5]557; w.-spirit [1]648; of the Spirit [1]464; spirit of the [1]654; w.-spout(s) [3]564n, 1073, [4]29; stagnant [2]364; standing [3]555; sweet [1]596, 597, 611, 612, 614, 614n, 617; Thales on [5]693, 693n, 722; w.-tints [3]898; walking on [2]189–90, 189n–90n; as w. [1]597; in w. [1]579, 579n, 622, 622n, see also *hydor en hydati*; w.-weeds [3]581; words for [1]607; in Xenophanes [5]707

Waterland, Daniel (1683–1740) [1]312n, 478n, 565, [2]265, 265n, 294n, 730, [3]369, 524, 877, 877n, [5]7, 7n, 8n, 12, 12n, 16, 16n–17n, 20, 22, 28, 64, 64n, 97, 174, 174n, 626, 627, 307
a prime favourite [6]69
Critical History of the Athanasian Creed [3]369n, [5]8n; *The Importance of the Doctrine of the Holy Trinity* [1]565n–6n, 800, [3]762n, [5]7n; MT [6]54–72; *A Second Vindication of Christ's Divinity* [2]665n q, 666n q, [5]75n; *A Vindication of Christ's Divinity* [1]clxvii, 358, 358n, 565n, [2]584, 584n, 730n, [3]369n, 877n, [5]7n, 579, 579n q, 626n, 730n, [6]71n; MT 73–93

Waterloo [1]715, [3]160n, [5]91n

Waterloo ON, University of [2]615n

Wathen, Samuel (d 1787) [5]190

Watkins, J. [2]1095

Watson, H. F. [2]985

Watson, John (1799–1827) [2]158, [3]262, 262n
supplier of books to C [3]886; transcriber of marginalia [3]514, [6]318; transcript of "Essay on Faith" [1]lxxiii

"Watson List" *see* Watson, Lucy Eleanor

Watson, Lucy Eleanor (née Gillman) (c 1838–1929) [1]488, 816
owner of annotated books [2]843, [3]983
Coleridge at Highgate [1]xcix, xcixn, cxvn, clvi, clxn, 414, [4]334; "Watson List" [1]clvi, 231, 488, [2]259, 1094

Watson, Richard, Bishop of Llandaff (1737–1816) [3]539, 539n
on miracles [1]683; school of [1]462
Apology for Christianity [1]462n; *Apology for the Bible* [1]462n, [3]539, 539n, [5]513n

Watson, Robert (fl 1854) [3]886

Watson, Seth Benjamin (1810–85) [4]778

Watts, Alaric Alexander (1797–1864) [2]616n
Poetical Sketches MT [6]94

Watts, Isaac (1674–1748) [1]38, [2]558, 1170 q, [4]466n
Horae Lyricae [2]1170n

Waugh, John [2]521

wave(s) [2]220, 995, 995n, [4]235, 267, 520, 829, [5]385, 455

wax [1]442n, [2]372, [3]741, [5]83, 83n
figure [4]780; religion as [2]205

"way" [1]813, 821, [6]205, 205n–6n

way
middle [1]281; up or down [4]383n

"we" [4]236, 762

we [2]1011, [3]444, 890n, 909, 909n, 912
and they [2]948; royal [3]240

weakness(es) [4]799, 860, [5]83, 822
human [1]565; inward [1]496; root of [2]1178

"weal" [5]428

weal [5]61, 189
common [5]642; public [5]643

wealth [1]185, 723, [3]585, 994, [4]79, [5]135, 299, 587
of a community [3]152; hereditary [5]273; trade-gained [2]311

weapon(s) [1]418
w.-salve [6]97

Weare, G. E. (fl 1905) [2]586

"weary" [1]613, 613n

weather [5]359
w.-cock [5]519; w.-glass [3]456, 456n; hot [5]271

web [3]26, [5]540

Webber, Daniel Webb (c 1757–1847) [4]19, 20, 20n

Weber, Henry William (1783–1818) [3]1070

"Webster" [4]20, 20n

Webster, Daniel (1782–1852) *An Address* [4]6, [6]335
Webster, John (c 1578–c 1632) *The White Divil* [2]217n
Webster, John (1610–82) [3]771
The Displaying of Supposed Witchcraft [1]420, 420n q, [2]1107n, 1109, [3]771n, 526n; MT [6]95–124
Webster's Dictionary [1]124n ("Webster")
Wechselwirkung [2]624, 624n
wedding-garment [1]815, 815n
Wedgwood [3]631
Wedgwood, Cicely Veronica (b 1910)
The King's War [2]948n; *The Trial of Charles I* [2]522n, 948n q
Wedgwood, Godfrey (1833–1905) [3]630n
Wedgwood, John (1766–1844) [3]639
Wedgwood, Josiah, the Elder (1730–95) [3]627–39
Wedgwood, Josiah, the Younger (1769–1843) [1]clxi, [3]627
letter(s) to [1]756n, 766n, [3]243n, [5]732n
Wedgwood, Mary (née Stringer) (d 1768) [3]632
Wedgwood, Sarah (née Wedgwood) ("Sara") (1734–1815) [3]629, 639
Wedgwood, Thomas (1685–1739) [3]632
Wedgwood, Thomas (1771–1805) [1]89n, 777n, [2]601n, [3]632, [4]84
Wedgwoods, the [2]848n, [4]787n, [5]533n
letter(s) to [1]cvn q, 354n, 409, [2]170, [4]25n
Wednesdays [3]933
week(s)
apocalyptic [6]294; days of [2]810–11, 811n; Creative [3]944; Great [5]606; Sacred [5]607
Weekly Dispatch [1]807n
wegen [1]23
weight(s) [1]51, [2]855, [3]1090, [5]81, 438, 599
Weimar, Duke of *see* Karl August
Weinholdt *see* Wienholt
Weird Sisters (*Macbeth*) [4]786, 787
Weishaupt, Adam (1748–1830)
Anschauung und Erscheinungen [1]clxvi; *Apologie des Misvergnügens und Uebels* MT [6]125–7; *Pythagoras*† [6]128; *Regierungskunst* [1]clxvi; *Ueber den Kantischen Anschauungen*† [6]129; *Ueber Wahrheit und sittliche Vollkommenheit* [1]lxviii; MT [6]130
Weiske, Benjamin (1748–1809) *see* Longinus *Peri hypsous* (*De sublimitate*) ed Weiske
Weismann, Christian Eberhard (1677–1747) [1]114
Weldon, H. W. (fl 1810) [3]937
Welford, Charles (fl 1848) [1]clxii
well [1]769
miracle of [2]752
well-being [5]724
moral [5]302
Weller, Jacob (1602–64) [3]830
Wellesley, Arthur, 1st Duke of Wellington (1769–1852) [1]850n, [2]100n, 211n, 940, 940n, 955n, [3]154, [5]91, 91n, 104, 104n, [6]46, 47, 47n, 48
Wellesley, William Pole Tylney Long, 4th Earl of Mornington (1788–1857) *A View of the Court of Chancery* [3]500
Wellhausen, Julius (1844–1918) [1]417n, [2]389n
Wellington, Duke of *see* Wellesley, Arthur
Wells, William Charles (1757–1817) *Two Essays* MT [6]131–3
Welsh (language) [2]574n, 1170n, [4]782, 782n, [6]17, 161
Welsh (people) [3]169, [5]280
as mixed race [1]540
Welshmen [4]16
wen [3]182
"Wendrock, Guillaume" *see* Nicole, Pierre
Wendross [5]390n
Wentworth House *see* London: Hampstead: Wentworth House
Wentworth, Thomas, 1st Earl of Strafford (1593–1641) [2]60, 60n, [3]795, 797, 798
Earl of Strafford's Letters ed Knowler [2]60n
Werkheiligkeit [5]497
Werlhof (probably Paul Gottlieb Werlhof, 1699–1767) [1]197
Werner, Abraham Gottlob (1750–1817) [1]664, *664n*, [3]60n, 481n, [5]257
Wesen [6]241
Wesley, Charles (1707–88) [1]341n, [5]125, 139n, 153, 156n
Wesley, Emilia (1691–?1770) [5]165
Wesley, John (1703–91) [1]341, 341n, 820n, [2]*496n–7n*, 1077, [3]528n, [4]619, 631, 643, 644n, 649, 658, 669, [5]65n, 120–93, 139n
Arminianism of [6]311; doctrine of selfishness [6]312; egotism [5]133n, 161n; a logician [5]153; Luther and [2]496; his mind [5]129; monocratic spirit [5]152; tenets of [4]622, [5]162
Journal [2]1058, 1058n, [4]631n q; *Sermons on Several Occasions* [3]528, 528n q, [6]311n
Wesley, Samuel (1662–1735) [5]164

Wesley, Samuel (1691–1739) [5]137, 139, 139n, 165
Wesley, Susannah (1669/70–1742) [5]164
Wesleyan Methodist Magazine [5]154n q
Wesleyans [4]648
Wesleys [5]162
 family of liars [5]165
West [1]596, [5]265, 266
 W. Asia [2]372; declining [2]17; golden [6]251; ideal [5]438; *see also* compass of nature
West, Benjamin (1738–1820) [4]780, 780n
West Indies [1]cxxxiv, 33, 33n, 383, 536n, [2]91, 801, [3]493n, [4]342, [5]117, 187, [6]28n
West, Mr (fl 1815) [1]cvi, 871, 871n
West, Richard (1716–42) *see* Pindar tr West
Western, Sophia (in Fielding) [2]693
Westminster *see* London
Westminster Assembly [1]283n, [3]803n, [4]172n, 173n, 307n, [5]147n, 508, 508n, 509, 509n, 520n, 530, 530n, 540n, [6]258, 259n
Westminster Confession [4]307, 307n, 657n
Westminster divines [3]803n
Westmorland [1]777n, [2]529n, [3]974–82, [4]29, 737, [5]234, [6]121n, 152, 249, 249n
Westmorland, Earl of *see* Neville, Charles
Westmorland Gazette [6]290
Weston-super-Mare [2]586
Westphal, Joachim Christian (fl 1797) *Neue Ideen zur Begränzung der einzelnen Gebiete des Naturrechts* [3]961, 962
Westwood, Thomas (fl 1829) [1]clxiin
Wetstein, Johann Jakob (Wetstenius) (1693–1754) [1]416, 483
Weymouth [6]29n
whale(s) [1]425, 427, 427n, 431, [2]862, 1112, [3]770–1, 771n, 1047, [4]525, 534, 636, [6]72, 119, 220
Whalley, George (1915–83) [4]402
 "Bristol Library Borrowings" [1]50n, 120n, 409, 830, [2]172n, 413n, 804, 985; *Coleridge and Sara Hutchinson and the Asra Poems* [1]762n; *Lost List* [1]30, 130, 154, 205, 228, 240, 700, 701, 717, 830, 854, [2]5, 11, 14, 25, 44, 46, 48, 97, 142, 357, 361, 1094
Whalley, Peter (1722–91) *see* B&F *Dramatic Works*; Jonson *Dramatic Works* ed Whalley
Wharey, James Blanton (1872–1946) *see* Bunyan *Pilgrim's Progress* ed Wharey
Wharncliffe, Baron *see* Stuart-Wortley-Mackenzie, James Archibald
Wharton, Henry (1664–95) *see* Laud *History*; *Second Volume* ed Wharton
Whately, Richard, Archbishop of Dublin (1787–1863) [1]500
wheat [1]595
 animality in [1]595; gluten of [3]68n
Wheatstone, Charles (1802–75) [4]503n
wheel [1]603, 603n, 609n, 628, 635, 651, 667, [2]1069, [4]450, [5]342
wheel-animal [3]1040, 1041n
Wheeler, Benjamin (1733–83) *Theological Lectures* pref J. H. Horne [1]cxlin; MT [6]134–5
Wheeler, [?J./I.] (fl 1825; probably John Wheeler, following) [6]335
Wheeler, John (1798–1862) [2]21
Wheeler, Kathleen, coeditor [3]236, 239, 241, 250, 252, 256, 263, [3]269, 304, 314, 316, 321, 338
"whereas" [3]910
whereness [2]887
whetstone [4]120, 120n
Whewell, William (1794–1866) *On Astronomy* [2]883n
Whieldon, Thomas (fl 1754–69) [3]635
Whig(s) [1]359, 732, [2]688, 980n, 1150n, [3]*141n*, 165, 166n, 228, 799n, [4]14, 21, 78, [6]32, 44n, 45
 G. Burnet [1]836; defined [3]799; history of whiggery [3]141, 141n; Machiavellian [3]166; Massinger as [1]389; W.-patriotism [2]1150; principle [4]14; and Tory *see* Tory
Whiggism [3]157, [4]14
whim(s) [1]124, 763, [3]964
 Judaical [1]872
whimmy [3]1088
whimsy/whimsies [1]519, [3]553, [5]166, 810
whim-wham [1]124n
whirl-breeze [5]306
whirlpool [2]614, 615n
whirlwind [5]187
whispers, wicked [3]466
"Whistlecraft, Robert and William" *see* Frere, John Hookham
Whiston, William (1667–1752) [1]492, [5]692, 693n, [6]109n, 217; *see also* Josephus *Jewish War* tr Whiston, *Works* ed Whiston
Whistons [5]692
Whitaker, Edward William (1752–1818) [6]166, 166n
 General and Connected View of the Prophecies [6]166n; *Commentary on the Revelation of St John* [6]166n
Whitaker, George Herbert (1846/7–1936)

see Philo Judaeus *De confusione, De legum allegoria, De migratione* tr Colson and Whitaker
Whitaker, John (1735–1808)
Mary Queen of Scots Vindicated [6]145n; *The Origin of Arianism Disclosed* MT [6]136–46
Whitaker, William (1548–95) [3]309, 309n
De authoritate scripturae [3]309n
Whitall, William Van R. [1]760
Whitbread, Samuel (1758–1815) [3]884, 884n
Whitby, Daniel (1638–1726) [6]55, 56, 57, 88, 89
A Paraphrase and Commentary on the New Testament [6]55 q, 56n; *A Treatise of Traditions* [6]70–1 q
"white" [2]960, 962
white [1]837, [3]1059, [4]98, 187, [5]654
white (archery) [4]310
White, Edward (fl 1818–27) [1]xc, [3]718, 719
White, Gilbert (1720–93) [3]352 ("Albinus"), 352n
Natural History of Selborne [1]xciii, civ, cxxii, clxviii; *Works, in Natural History* [3]352n; MT [6]147–53
White, Henry Kirke (1785–1806) [2]126n
White, Joseph (1745–1814) [4]649, 649n
Diatessaron [4]649, 649n
White, Joseph Blanco *see* Blanco White, Joseph
White Lady of Avenel (in Scott) [4]595, 595n, 596
Whitefield/Whitfield, George (1714–70) [1]270n, 820n, [3]528, 528n, [4]644n, 649, 658, 669, [5]65n, 123, 135n, 139, 154, 155, 157, 158, 179, 185n, [6]311
Whitehall *see* London
Whitehead, Paul (1710–74) [1]38, [2]769 ("Withead")
The Customs of the Times [2]769; *State-Dunces* [2]769
Whitehead, William (1715–85) [1]38
A Charge to the Poets [2]769, 769n
Whitelocke, John (1757–1833) [5]316, 316n
whiteness [1]386
Whiter, Walter (1758–1832) [1]608, 608n
Etymologicum Magnum [1]608n
whiterness [5]831
Whitfield, Thomas (fl 1602–42) *A Discourse of Liberty of Conscience* [2]111; MT [6]154–5
Whitgift, John, Archbishop of Canterbury (c 1530–1604) [2]813, 813n, 1134, [3]795, 795n, [5]155, 155n
Whitsunday [1]327, [2]246, 246n
Whitsuntide [6]260
Whittaker, Richard *see* Bible: NT: Greek: ed Whittaker
whittle [4]761
Whitwell, Anthony (fl 1769) [2]102
Whitwell, H. [2]102
Whitwell, R. [2]102
whiz-mist [2]646
whole(s) [1]152–3, [3]233, [4]353, [5]406, 418
life of [3]1042; and parts *see* part(s); perfect [3]910; unity of [5]302; visual [2]1070
Whole Duty of Man [2]409, 409n
whore(s) [1]772, [2]219
in Rev [1]817n
whoredom [5]146
whoremonger [4]660
"whose" [1]723, 725, [3]831, 887
"wicked" [1]817
wicked, the [4]435
annihilation of [5]584; prosperity of [5]61; state of [3]62
wickedness [2]168, [4]549, 589–90, 643, 777, 817–18
of Christians [5]415–16; not for comedy [2]83, 84; frenzy of [2]345; personification of [1]397; *see also* evil(s)
Wicket Gate (in Bunyan) [1]814
Widmerpoole, Joseph (fl 1642–8) [2]1195
widow(s) [1]387, [3]688
brother's [5]393
widrige [4]187, 187n
Wieland, Christoph Martin (1733–1813) [2]190, 190n
Comische Erzählungen MT [6]156–7; *Idris* [6]156; MT 158; *Neueste Gedichte* [6]158; MT 159–60
Wienholt, Arnold ("Weinholdt") (1749–1804) [3]397, 872, 872n, 1039n, [4]270, 273, [5]183, 183n, [6]121, 121n
Heilkraft des thierischen Magnetismus [4]270n
wife/wives [1]387, 662, [3]496, 666
community of [3]419; ideal of [2]166, 166n–7n; innocent [2]273; killed [4]748; of officers [5]380; one [5]634; of one man [4]485, 485n–6n; Peter's [2]473–5, 703, 703n; plurality of [2]938; poor [1]878; pregnant [4]96–7; selfish [4]594; sterile [4]432, 432n; of sun [3]1035
Wilamowitz-Moellendorff, Ulrich von (1848–1931) [1]25n ("Wilomowitz")
Wilberforce, William (1759–1833) [1]31, 322n, [3]309n, 507, 602, [4]96, 96n
Wilbraham, Mr (fl 1756) [2]529n

Wilcocke, Samuel Hull (fl 1797–1807) *see* Stavorinus *Voyages* tr Wilcocke
Wild, Charles Norris (fl 1879) [1]clxiv
Wilde, Allington (fl 1731–70) [1]701
wilderness [1]424, 471, [3]464, 471
Christ in [3]106–7, 107n; sandy [2]1018; symbol [1]817
Wildman, J. B. (fl 1832) [1]34, 35n, 36
Wilford, Francis (d 1822) [2]584, 585, 585n
wilfulness [4]784, [5]11
Wilhelm I, King of Prussia, 1st German Emperor (1797–1888) [3]217n
Wilkes, John (1727–97) [6]156, 156n–7n
Wilkes, John (fl 1810–29) see *Encyclopaedia Londinensis* ed Wilkes
Wilkie, William (1721–72) [1]38
Epigoniad [3]484, 484n
Wilkinson, C. H. [1]clxixn
Wilkinson, James John Garth (1812–99) *see* Swedenborg *The Animal Kingdom, Outlines of a Philosophical Argument* tr Wilkinson
Wilkinson, Thomas (1751–1836)
letter to [3]928n q; supplier of books to C [1]cv
Wilks, John, Jr ("O. P. Q.") (d 1846) [6]45, 45n
"will" [2]801, [5]25, 75n, 175, 603
will(s) [1]504, 688, [2]631, 768, 882, 922, 1014, 1155, 1166, 1192, [3]13, 18n, 24, 29, 86, 266, 518, 682, 709n, 715, 723, 806, 855, 860, 1087, [4]224, 398, 451, 452, 616, 629, 674, 695, 810, [5]6, 21, 22, 181, 205, 405n, 425, 453, 592, 681, 702, 792, [6]126
absolute [1]640, 696, [2]198, 287, 297, 726, 1137, [3]13, 18, 104, 151, 350, 428, 460, 736, [4]784, [5]372, 410, 755, 756, 791; non-absolute [3]1024; abysmal [1]630, [2]423; accompanies being [2]249; act of [1]344, [4]221, 598, [6]97; active [5]842; adhesion of the [1]823; as agent [4]272–3; allegory of [3]92; in animals [3]1041, 1041n; apostate [1]604; and appetence [3]18; arbitrium [3]709; attributed to God [3]358–9; auxiliaries of [3]312; averse [5]11; basis of [2]170; of body politic [2]1142; Böhme on [1]656, 677; Calvinist conception of [2]801; causative [4]400, [5]235, 410; chaos of [5]165; and choice *see* choice; C's ms on [1]693; to command nature [2]825; concentrated [2]922; concentred [2]41; concentric [5]208; concomitance of [1]263; conformed [3]54; corrupt [1]125, 812, [2]1109, [4]606; corruption in [6]28; corruption of [4]665, 672; creative [3]333, 1021; of creator [4]414; defect of [2]1160; denial of [3]737; devilish [1]827; in devils [1]640; distinctions in [3]359, 359n; divine [1]658, 659, [2]152, 192, 1193, [3]558, [4]426, 663, [5]435, 607, 792, [6]134; double [1]731n, [3]46, 46n, 235n; energetic [4]816; energy of [3]307, [4]625; *ens superens* [2]676; equals I AM [2]930; essence of [1]693–4; essential being [3]50; eternal [1]460, [6]5; evil [1]731, [2]562n, 563, [3]18, *see also* evil(s); evil in [2]1106, [3]305; and faith [1]287, [2]277, 297; and fate [4]794; of Father [3]60, 517, [5]58; fealty in [2]1151; of flesh [3]879, [4]168; follows nature [3]525; free *see* free will; free parts of [5]678; freedom of [1]10, [5]424, 822; of God [1]124, 659, [2]293, [4]341, [5]75, 466; not God [1]694; good and evil [2]278–9; ground of sin [1]824; guilt is in and of [1]605; habit of [2]1176; harlot [3]735; highest [2]640; history begins in a [4]269; holy [1]410, 824, [3]30, 206, 332–3, 333n, [4]444; idea of [2]324, [3]12, 12n; identity of [6]238; imperishableness of [5]425; impure [3]1039; independent of [4]641; individual [1]450, [2]267, [3]104, [4]233, [5]127, 189, 410, 777; individual and universal [2]332; indolence of [1]516; infinite [2]563, [3]90; and intellect [1]702, [5]216; in intellect [4]862; intelligent [1]355; intelligential [4]460; Jacobi on [3]75; in justification [3]749; Kant on [2]192, [3]358; last [5]651; life of [2]315; living [5]156; and love [3]264–5, 264n; man's [2]275, [5]394, 466, 470–1; in metaphysics [3]959; mirage of [5]299; moral [2]220, 345, 682, [4]787; multeity of [4]491–2; mysterious [1]201; a mystery [5]594; of the nation [1]338, 866; natural [2]495; and nature [5]784, [6]309; negation of [6]300; negative of [5]358; nucleus of life [1]580; obedience of [5]618; obscure [5]190; opposite [4]514; origin in [4]662, 662n; origin of evil [2]199; origin of vices [3]135; Paley on [4]638; not perfected [1]627; perversion of [5]11; polluted fountain [2]247; power of [4]274, 450, [6]103–4; presupposing [5]443; primal [4]423; principle of [1]178; principle of identity [2]250; pure act [2]251, [5]66; pure action [5]594; purifying of [5]480; radical [5]73; rational [4]542; realised [2]198; and reason *see* reason; in reason [1]818; redemption in [3]26; reformation in [4]621–2; regenerate [1]820; relation to touch [1]580; remanence of [5]603; responsible [3]877, 989; revelation of [1]597; secondary [2]543; self-realisation of [5]235; self-subsistent [2]615n; single [4]423; sinless [3]27; of sinner [5]599; slave of [2]168; of spirits [3]60; as spiritual entity [5]604, 604n; spiritual part [5]176; spiritual power [2]1109;

state of [5]497; as subjectivity [6]74; as substance [5]210; substance of ontology [3]202; substitute for reason [4]398; super-essential [1]689; supernatural [3]311; supreme [1]435, [2]305, 882, [6]83; suspension of [4]781; timeless [3]596; twofold [3]48; universal [4]263, 348, 444, 445; unregenerate [5]588; unwilling [1]813; w.-wantonness [4]78; wicked [5]410; and wish [3]513, [4]621, 621n, 855; w.-work [2]1180; w.-worship [2]220, [3]310, [5]142, 142n, 505, 505n, 510. *See also* arbitrement; volition(s)
Willan, Robert (1757–1812) [1]228
Willet, William (d 1778) [3]636
William I ("the Conqueror"), King of England (1027–87) [3]166, 785n ("of Normandy"), 786, [5]38, [6]249
William III, King of England, Prince of Orange (1650–1702), [1]183n, 713, 732–3, 733n, 866, 866n, [2]294, 827, 827n, [3]140–1, 141n, 144n, 146, 146n, 152, 152n, 153, 161, 167n, 168, 182, 665, [6]81
William IV, King of England (1765–1837) [3]154, 154n, [4]74n
William Albert Victor, Duke of Clarence (1864–92) [3]627
William of Moerbeke (c 1215–56) [2]12n
William of Normandy *see* William I
William of Occam *see* Occam
William of Orange *see* William III
Williams, Abigail (fl 1667) [4]73
Williams, Charles Hampden (fl 1830) [1]33, 33n
Williams, David (1738–1816) *see* Voltaire *A Treatise on Toleration* tr Williams
Williams, E. G. *see* Petrarch *Trionfo della fama* tr Williams
Williams, Edward ("Iolo Morganwg") (1746–1826) *Poems, Lyric and Pastoral* MT [6]161–2
Williams, Edward (1750–1813) [1]291, [3]517n, 562, 880n, [5]202, 202n, [6]299
A Defence of Modern Calvinism [2]677, 677n, [3]309, 309n, 562n, 737, [5]202, 202n; *An Essay on the Equity of Divine Government* [3]63n, 138n, 737, [5]202, 202n
Williams, George (fl 1810) [3]938
Williams, John, Archbishop of York (1582–1650) [2]925, 926, 1102n
Williams, John Hartwell Bonnell (fl 1816–32) [1]215
owner of annotated books [2]691; supplier of books to C [1]xcviii
Williams, Louisa [2]691
Williams, William Proctor *see* Gathorne-Hardy and Williams *A Bibliography of . . . Jeremy Taylor*
Williamson, Sir Joseph (1633–1701) [3]978
Willich, Anthony Florian Madinger (fl 1799–1809) *Elements of Critical Philosophy* [6]335
Williram/Willeram of Ebersberg (1048–85) [1]629, 629n
Willis, Francis (1718–1807) [3]149, 149n
Willkühr [2]603, [4]410
Willmott, B. S. *see* Swedenborg *Concerning the White Horse* rev Willmott
Willmott, Robert Aris (1809–63) *Conversations at Cambridge* [2]221n q
will-o'-the-wisp [2]447, [5]130 ("Will a Wisps")
Willson, D. Harris *King James VI and I* [5]834n
Wilmot, John, 2nd Earl of Rochester (1647–80) [1]37
Wilson, Adam (fl 1812) [4]30n
Wilson, Alexander (1714–86) [3]869, 870n
Wilson, Frank Percy (1889–1963) see *Oxford Dictionary of English Proverbs* ed Wilson
Wilson, John (c 1591–1667) [2]1174 ("Smith"), 1174n
Wilson, John (fl 1880) [1]clxiv–clxv, [2]958, 1116
Wilson, Matthew ("Edward Knott") (1582–1634) [2]24
Mercy and Truth [2]25, 25n
Wilson, Mr (fl 1810) [3]944
Wilson, Tom (fl 1812) [1]xcv
Wilson, Walter (1781–1847) [4]171
The History and Antiquity of Dissenting Churches [4]170, 171; *Memoirs of the Life and Times of Daniel De Foe* [2]158; MT [6]163; *see also* R. Leighton *Selections* ed Wilson
Wilson, William (fl 1859–69) *see* Clement of Alexandria *Writings* tr Wilson
Wilton [2]119n
Wiltshire [2]211n, [6]44
Winchester [2]945
Winchester College [2]820n, 979, [3]897, 897n
Winckelmann, Johann Joachim (1717–68) [4]419
Gedancken über die Nachahmung der griechischen Wercke in der Mahlerey und Bildhauer-Kunst [4]419n
wind(s) [1]612, [2]220, 246, 248, [3]946, 1086, 1087, 1087n, [4]29, 267, 273, 288, [5]251, 615
Windermere [2]220n, [3]974

Windham, William (1750–1810) [1]514n
winding sheet(s) [1]764, 797, [3]373
windmills [3]976
window(s) [3]212, 760, [5]472
 w. tax [1]530, *530n*
Windsor [3]501
 Windsor Castle [4]652; Royal Library [1]clxxiii
wine(s) [2]617, [3]360, [4]32n, 433, 529, [6]39
 bread and *see* bread; at Cana [2]204; love of [1]184; medical use [2]365; and Noah [1]112; w.-skin [2]135
wing(s) [3]93–4
 of angels [5]407; of army [3]652, 652n
winnowing [1]468
Winstanley, Denys Arthur (1877–1947) *Unreformed Cambridge* [2]957n q
winter [1]823, [5]349
 sadness of [4]836; w.-storm [2]862
Winterl, Jakob Joseph (1732–1809) [3]12
wires [3]45, [4]827
Wirkliches [4]418
Wirklichkeit [4]350, 350n, 403n, 404
Wisbech
 Wisbech Museum and Literary Institute, marginalia in [4]117
"wisdom"/"Wisdom" [5]19n, 202, 202n
wisdom/Wisdom [1]432, 478, 573, 657, [2]33, 305, 305n, 422, 423, 433, 583n, 930, 1140, [3]13, 87, 151, 163, 460, 564, 988, 988n, [4]111, 113, 224, 429, 449, 732, 819, [5]29, 40, 96, 159, 541, 681, [6]84, 157
 beginning of [3]583; collective [5]530; defect of love [4]366; defined [4]112; dictate of [5]766; divine [1]675, [2]560, [3]22, [5]830; essential [1]584; free act of [5]457; God's [2]207, 433, [3]79, 671, [4]410, 426, [5]592; human [1]256, [5]829; infinite [3]267; w. literature [1]433n; and love [5]469, 469n; of love [4]615; love of [5]228; lover(s) of [4]220, [5]362; of nature [2]345; of St Paul [5]518; perfect [2]261; Persian [3]92; personification of [2]433; of species [6]149; spirit of [1]398; supreme [3]857; traditional [3]524, [6]306; w.-mongers [3]988; see also *sophia*
wise, the [2]159
 w. man [1]184, [2]793; possess ideas [2]159
Wise, Thomas James (1859–1937) [1]clii, clxi, 279
 owner of annotated books [3]983
 Ashley Library: A Catalogue [2]650, 926; *Bibliography of Coleridge* [1]clii
wish(es) [2]405
 emancipation from [2]774; hidden [5]299; pious [6]146; Steffens's [5]309; unchristian [5]562; and will *see* will
wishing [1]702, [3]267, 513
wissen [4]405, 405n
Wissenschaft [4]363n, 380n
wissenschaftlich [4]363, 363n
Wissenschaftslehre [2]623, [4]158, 357, 357n, 458
wissentlich [2]626, 626n
Wissowatius (Andreas Wiszowaty) (1608–78) [3]657n, 672, 706, 706n, [5]6, 6n
wit [1]140, 144, [2]17n, 54, 218, 233, 236, 933, 1126, [3]225, 701, 972, 1047, [4]76, 243, 360, 589, 679, 779, 827, 830, 832, 858, [5]58, 175, 528, 541, [6]163
 after-w. [2]846; HC's [2]64, 71; Donne's [2]309; and fancy [1]67n; Fielding's [2]688; forced [4]356; French [2]1022; Frenchman's [3]884; T. Fuller's [2]808, 824, 834, 835; and humour *see* humour; itch of [3]280n; itch to be witty [2]64; maggots of [1]168, 168n; moral [1]174; pedantic [2]930; pilfered [1]221; Romish [1]831; Shakespeare's [2]774; two kinds of [1]67; university w. [3]907; and wisdom [2]931, 933
witch(es) [1]369–70, 420, 420n, [2]56, 1108, 1008n, [3]190n, 825, 826, [4]146, 499, 786, [5]383n, 598, [6]95–124
 belief in [1]282; W. of Endor *see* Endor; w.-fidianism [6]104; w.-monger [6]97; at Ottery St Mary [1]750n; w.-phobia [6]112; w.-trials [1]55n, [3]190
witchcraft [1]282n, 807n, [2]55–6, 985, [3]771, 771n, 817, 920, [4]145–6, 145n, [5]529n
 diseases mistaken for [3]822; Quaker accounts of [3]823
witcheries [1]558
 nerve-deranging [5]759
Wither, George (1588–1667) *Emblems* [1]56n
Witherby, H. F. (b 1873) and others *Handbook of British Birds* [1]47n
Withering, William (1741–99) *An Arrangement of British Plants* [1]lxxxvii, 777n, [2]168n
withholding [4]141, [5]150
"within" and "without" [5]716
Withycombe, E. G. see *Oxford Book of Christian Names* ed Withycombe
witness(es) [1]314, 456, [3]312, 726
 ear-w. [3]207; eye and ear [1]309; of miracle [3]708; pomp of [1]273, [6]262; three [3]477; two [1]445, 445n, [2]517, 707, 707n, [3]475–6, 477, 924–5, [5]402, *402n*

Wits, Herman (1636–1708) [4]244
Wittemberg [3]744, 778
witticisms, Seneca's [1]174
Witzel/Witzell, Georg (1501–73) [3]754
wizard(s) [3]1050n, [4]146
wizardry [4]143
Woden (myth) [2]979
Wodenoth/Woodnoth, Arthur (?1590–?1650) [2]1046
woe [5]61
and weal [5]189
wolf [1]825, [2]603, [4]92, 94, 731n, [5]586
in alchemy [1]215; of temporal power [1]258
Wolf (in Scott) [4]598n, 599, 600
Wolf, Abraham (1876–1948) *see* Spinoza *Correspondence* tr Wolf
Wolf, Friedrich August (1759–1824) [2]1129
Prolegomena ad Homerum [2]397n–8n, 892, 892n; see also *Museum der Alterthum-Wissenschaft* ed Wolf and Buttmann
Wolf, Johann Christoph (1683–1739) [3]353–4, [4]209
Curae philologicae et criticae [3]929n; MT [6]164–8
Wolfart, Karl Christian (1778–1832) [3]378, 378n, 396n, 873, 1049, [4]270, [5]183, 183n, 191
credulous [3]868; "Woolfart" [3]867
Darstellung einer lebensmagnetischen Kur [4]270n; *Erläuterungen zum Mesmerismus* [3]864, 867n, [4]270n; *Jahrbücher für den Lebens-Magnetismus* MT [6]169–70; *see also* Mesmer *Mesmerismus* ed Wolfart
Wolfenbüttel [6]21, 21n
Wolfenbüttel Fragments *see* Reimarus *Fragmente*
Wolff, Christian, Baron (1679–1754) [1]lxxxvi, [2]1016, *1016n*, [3]89n, 853, 853n, 954
Logic [2]1016n; MT [6]171–6; *Psychologia rationalis* [3]377 q, 377n, [4]217 q, 217n
wolfsbane [6]103n
Wolfson, Harry *Philosophy of Spinoza* [3]854n q
Wollaston, William (1659–1724) [1]546n, [2]520, 520n, 825n
Wollaston, William Hyde (1766–1828) [1]lxxii, [3]940, 941, [4]337, 337n, [5]261, 261n, 331–2, 734 ("Woolastin"), 811, 812n
"On the Finite Extent of the Atmosphere" [5]734, 734n
Wolsey, Thomas, Cardinal (c 1475–1530) [1]318n
woman/women [2]276, 1197, [3]577, 577n, 665, [5]36, 182, 594, 647
accomplished [2]968; best [2]234; birth of Christ from [5]55; cease to be things [2]321; character of [4]851n; in Church [5]667n; clairvoyance in [4]592; as clog [1]658; clothed with the sun [3]469–70, 471–2; in comedy [2]82, 83; counterpart of man [3]1003; creation of [1]683–4; debauching of [2]636; debt to Christianity [2]321; defective [4]23; degraded [4]693; excellent [2]878; extroitive natures of [4]689; fancy-vexed [3]772; favours of [3]681; have no generative emission [1]773; giving birth [3]867; good [4]777; Greek treatment of [2]1071; of high birth [4]599; Indian [2]987; with issue of blood [4]637, 637n; kills husband [2]772; lady's [4]747; language of [5]819; and love [4]801; love of [1]184; lovely [1]268, [5]834; man in [3]906n; their nature [4]731; old [2]432, 727, [3]586, [4]38; peasants [4]86; prefer beauty in lovers [6]156; Rabbit W. [3]1035, 1035n; rage of neatness [4]278; satire on [2]764; of Scyra [5]837; sense of beauty [4]82; Shakespeare on [4]866; in Shakespeare and B&F [1]397; sneers towards [4]866; soul of [2]1201; swallowed up [6]262; taken in adultery [5]575, 575n; in travail [1]817n; weak [1]398; on wedding night [3]730; whims of [1]381; witch [1]420; womanhood [2]1201; wooing of [6]322. *See also* female; feminine; lady/ladies
womanhood, reverence of [4]335
womb [1]601, [4]760
Wombwell, George (1778–1850) [2]905n
wonder(s) [1]61, 111, 370, 621, 747, [2]628, 808, [4]35, [5]32, [6]109n
w.-stories [3]351, 352
wonderment [1]60, [5]644
wont [5]442
wood(s) [1]662, [3]157, 649, [4]170, 450, [5]306
citron [4]81–2 ("citrine"), 82n; dead [5]467; rotten [3]1015; splitting noise [1]442n–3n, [2]372
Wood, Anthony à (1632–95) *Athenae Oxonienses* [4]724n
Wood, James (1760–1839) "New Theory of the Diurnal Motion of the Earth" [3]938; MT 949
woodbine [4]278
woodcock [6]153
Woodfall, Henry Sampson (1739–1805) [3]220
Woodnot *see* Wodenoth

Woodring, Carl Ray *Politics in the Poetry of Coleridge* [1]92n
wool [4]731
Woolf, Stuart *see* P. Levi *Se questa e un huomo* tr Woolf
Woolman, John (1720–72) *Journal* [2]755n
Woolston, Thomas (1670–1747) [1]248n, [6]108, 108n
Woolwich, Royal Military Academy [2]978n
woorali [2]827n
woorara [2]827, 827n
"word" [6]307, 307n
"Word" [3]524, 524n, [5]19n
word(s)/Word(s) [1]420, 435, 437, 438, 464, 484, 484n, 565, 591, 601, 609, 627, 629, 661, 705, 712, 824, [2]33, 279, 479, 489, 575, 583n, 992, 1010n, 1152, 1160, [3]12, 14n, 16, 23n, 29, 42, 66, 77, 102n, 106, 139, 151, 450, 536, 545, 720, 726, [4]94, 258, [5]58, 97n, 161, 201, 235, 369, 372, 397, 534, 546, 556, 663, [6]32, 306
abuse of [3]257, 257n, [4]625; of accommodation [2]293; as acts [4]442n; adequate [5]627; almighty [2]723; ambiguous [2]1150, [4]398; arbitrary [3]741; are but w. [1]395; articulation of [3]61; assurances of [5]554; authority of [5]568; barbarous [5]789; become flesh [3]17, 610, 876; black [3]496; Böhme's [1]561; books of the [5]434; w.-catcher [5]63; choice of [4]799, [6]286, *see also* diction; Christ as [2]205, [3]416; of Christ [3]439, [5]580; circulating [5]687; classes of [2]962n; coeternal [1]729, [5]483, 620, 679; are communicable man [2]141; and conceptions [3]848–9; confusion of [2]1164; in creation [2]419; creative [6]303; decreed [5]717; definition of [4]320; delegates of [5]553; determinate [2]43; dictated [5]473; different meaning [2]1065; dislocation of [5]113; dispute about [2]591, *see also* logomachy; Divine [5]569; divinity of the [5]433; duped by [3]871; enginery of [1]325; equivalent to name [1]706; equivocal use of [5]363; exhortative [5]583; eternal [3]723, [4]496, [5]466; eternally begotten [3]49; faculty of [3]423; of the Father [5]56; filial [3]369; filiation of [3]730; fix conceptions [5]599; fixed meaning [4]673; follies of [4]783; general or abstract [2]482; generalised [1]811; God in [1]652, [5]272; of God [1]329, [2]560, [3]13, 24, 762, [5]505; of gospels [5]516; idea of [3]101; ideal origin of [1]634; and idea(s) *see* idea(s); without ideas [2]732; idolised by Quakers [3]809; ignorance of [1]533; inadequacy of [3]743, 762; incarnate [1]302, [2]270, 423, [6]105; indwelling [3]689; informing [3]28; inspired [5]506; internal subjective [2]1148; interpretation of [5]651; interprets world [3]62; invention of [3]177; Jehovah-W. *see* Jehovah; and law [5]453; lax [3]788; liable to objections [2]30; and life [6]64; light [3]59–60; living [1]606, 606n, [5]684; of the Lord [3]689; loss of [5]428; Luther's use of [3]725; and meaning [1]731; meaning(s) of [2]1192, [3]600, 1018; without meaning [3]787, [5]770, 771; mediation of [1]446; mediators [3]424–5; mental [3]83; miracle by [5]814; misappropriation of [1]551; misuse of [2]296, [5]470; multiplied [3]889; new [5]579; new-minted [3]1043; newly-compounded [2]426; obsolete [4]768; old [3]633; one sense of [3]558–9; one w. one meaning [1]495; only-begotten [2]799; only person of Deity [6]76; in pentad [2]290; personality of [2]1175; plain [1]711; play on [2]326, 427, [4]796, 842, *see also* pun(s); polysyllabic [4]509; popular use of [5]174; poverty of [1]621; power of [5]425; products of understanding [3]991; prophetic [5]59–60; propriety of [4]151; ray from [3]426; as Reason [1]458; redemption by [3]14, 22; refer to thoughts [3]829; right and wrong senses [4]418; scholastic [3]365; of Scripture [5]515; self-subsistent [5]799; and sense [4]216, [5]618; sequency of [1]621; significance to Jews [2]429; simple [4]451; single [2]294; that are spirit [5]272; Spirit of the [5]778; w.-splitters [4]105; spontaneous rise of [2]403; sublime thought [1]568; suffering of [2]209; supposed modern [2]407; supreme reason [2]305; and syllables [2]1039–40; symbolical use of [3]425; and thought(s) [2]458, [6]305; undefined [5]370; untranslatable [4]358; use of [3]742, [5]547; vagueness in [5]481; visible [5]675; visual language [3]597; weight of [4]795; and w./W. [1]583, [2]*881n*, [3]521, 521n, 522–3, 908, 908n, [5]569, 569n, 630, 631, 684, [6]303, 303n, 305; written [2]1201–2, [3]762, [5]630, 684. *See also* God; *logos/logoi*; *Logos*/Logos
Wordsworth, Christopher (1774–1846) [2]522n, 524n, 914n, [3]11n
Six Letters to Granville Sharp [1]lxxxi, 455n, 467n, [6]26n; MT 177–83; "*Who Wrote EIKON BASILIKE ?*" *Considered* [2]521, 523n, [3]798n, 878, 878n; MT [6]184–6
Wordsworth, Dora *see* Quillinan

Wordsworth, Dorothy (1771–1855) [1]xciii, 227, 259n, [2]1121, [3]210, 210n, 400, 837, 837n, [4]29, 73n, 87n, 90, 287, 287n, 545, [5]824, [6]197
C's letter to [3]990n; JW letter to [1]76; letter(s) from [1]lxxxv–lxxxvi q, xcv q, cx q
Journal [1]42n, 76, 227n q, [3]837n; *Letters see* WW *Letters*
Wordsworth, Gordon Graham (1860–1935) [3]980
transcriber of marginalia [1]227
Wordsworth, H. B. (fl 1905) [4]90 ("H. B. W.")
Wordsworth, John (1772–1805) [1]724n
death of [1]lxxxiii, [5]824, 824n, 825n
Letters ed Ketcham [1]76 q, 160n
Wordsworth, John (1803–75) [1]37, 76, 724n, [2]695n, 889n
Wordsworth, Jonathan [1]clxixn
Wordsworth, Mary (née Hutchinson) (1770–1859) [1]259n, [2]1120n, 1121, [3]837, 837n, [5]824, [6]147, 197
amanuensis [6]194; burnt C's letters [1]760; death of [1]cxiv; owner of annotated books [1]760
Wordsworth, Richard, owner of annotated books [4]29
Wordsworth Trust [4]282, 289
Wordsworth, William (1770–1850) [1]cv, 227, 259n, 372n, [2]351, 848n, 861n, 879n, 983n, [3]179n, 837, 837n, [4]29, 73n, 161n, 162n, 176, 343, 545, 603n, 737n, 836, [5]99, 824, [6]177
active in reason and spirit [1]lxx; and Anderson's *British Poets* [1]37; annotated *TT* [1]clxviiin–clxixn; annotator [1]lxxxi, lxxxvi, 39–41, 41n, 52, 53, 81n; appeals to ideal [2]140; and Bartram's *Travels* [1]226; and G. Beaumont [1]160, 160n; blank verse of [1]218; book sent to [5]101; and Bowles [1]717; on Byron [4]76, 76n; and Chapman's Homer [2]1118, 1118n; and Chaucer [1]40, [4]291n; tr Chiabrera [2]23; cipher for [1]173n; C predicts his fame [1]41; and C's *Poems* (1797) [1]lxxxin; critique of [1]cxlviii, 368n; cured by C [3]210, 210n; death of [1]cxiv, clxi; deficiencies of [3]265n; epigraph in Anster *Poems* [1]100; estrangement from C [1]650n; in Germany [1]697; handwriting [1]lxxv; Hazlitt on style of [1]223n; holiday with C [4]48, 48n; initialled marginalia [1]372, 372n; introduced "ghyll" [1]423n; letter(s) from [1]lxxxiv, 828; letter(s) to [2]1066n q, [6]189; library [1]cxxiiin, 476, 725n, 854, [2]4, 11, 116–17, 132, 134n, 804, [3]504n, [5]377, [6]335; library catalogue see below *Catalogue* and Shaver; library sale [1]clxviii–clxix; on love [2]197n; mss [2]132n; on Murray [2]840n; name pronounced Wadsworth [1]848; owner of annotated books [1]lxxi, lxxx, lxxxi, xcii, cix, cxlin, clixn, clxxiv, 76, 226, 698, [2]102, 245, [3]499, 980, [4]90, 139, 282, 289, [5]475; philosophical poet [1]218n; Piranesi folios sent to [1]lxxxvii; pleased by Bloomfield [2]755n; poet [4]161, 161n; portrait by E. Aders [2]180; on public [1]220; quarrel with C [1]xciii, xcv, 173n, [2]45n, [3]863n; reactionary [2]20; reconciliation with C [1]372n; regenerator of language [6]210; religion of [3]698n; Rhine tour [2]180, 808; his school [2]4; on Shakespeare's sonnets [1]40–1; sonnets [5]857; *Spectator* project [1]158n; on Spenser [1]40; treatment of books [1]cvii; trip in 1828 [4]40; worshippers of [1]257n
Beauty and Moonlight [1]91n; "Benjamin the Waggoner" MS I MT [6]187–8; *Benjamin the Waggoner* ed Betz [6]187; *The Blind Highland Boy* [2]165n; *The Borderers* [2]563n; *The Brothers* [2]55; *Catalogue of the . . . Library of . . . William Wordsworth* [1]476, [2]521, 1032, 1117; *Convention of Cintra* [2]359; *Descriptive Sketches* [6]205; "Essay, Supplementary to the Preface" [2]102, [4]836n; *Essays upon Epitaphs* [2]23; *Evening Walk* [1]423n; *The Excursion* [1]558 q, 558n, 764n q, MT [6]189–93; *Gypsies* [5]112n; *The Idiot Boy* [2]404n; *Letters of William and Dorothy Wordsworth; the Early Years* ed de Selincourt, rev C. L. Shaver [1]220n, 226, [5]825n q; *Letters of William and Dorothy Wordsworth; the Later Years* ed de Selincourt, rev A. G. Hill [1]331n, [2]15n q; *Letters of William and Dorothy Wordsworth; the Middle Years* ed de Selincourt, rev Moorman [1]xciii q, cx q, cxn, 372n, 488, 766n, [2]133, 359, 753, 781n, 1118n, 1121n, 1122n, 1191, 1195n, 1203, 1204n, [3]400, [4]87n; *Lyrical Ballads* [1]91n, 99n, [2]356n, 983, 1121; *Michael* [2]55; *My Heart Leaps Up* [2]535 q, 535n; tr *La naissance de l'amour* [1]90n; *Ode: Intimations of Immortality* [1]593 q, 593n, [2]432n, 601n q, 715n, [3]909; *Ode to Duty* [2]614n q; *Poems* (1815) [4]836n; *Poems in Two Volumes* [2]222n; *Poetical Works* ed de Selincourt and Darbishire [1]37 q, 40, 76 q, 90n, 91n, 558n,

Wordsworth, William—*continued*
658n, 746n, ^{2}23, 98n, 102, 165n, 222n, 433n, 535n, 601n, 614n, ^{4}291n, ^{5}112n, ^{6}197; "The Prelude" MS B MT ^{6}194–6; *Prelude* ^{1}lxiii, lxxxiv, 218n, 764n q; *Prose* (1837), corrections ^{1}clxxii–clxxiii; *The Prose Works* ed W. J. B. Owen and Smyser ^{1}423n, ^{2}23, 102, 940n, 959n q, 1069n, ^{4}836n; *The Recluse* ^{1}175n; *She was a Phantom* ^{2}222, 222n; *Stanzas Written in Thomson's "Castle of Indolence"* ^{1}cv; "The Sublime and the Beautiful" ^{2}1069n; *The Thirteen-Book Prelude* ed M. L. Reed ^{6}194; *Tintern Abbey* ^{1}218n, 746n q, 764n, ^{2}98, 98n; "Translation of Virgil *Aeneid*" MT ^{6}197–215, ed Graver as *Translations of Chaucer and Virgil* ^{6}197 ("Graver"); *We Are Seven* ^{1}90n; *White Doe of Rylstone* ^{2}563n q; *Yarrow Visited* ^{1}37

Wordsworth, William (1810–83) ^{1}760

Wordsworth, William (b 1836) ^{1}760

Wordsworths ^{1}lxxix, lxxx, lxxxiii, lxxxvi, lxxxvii, xcii, xcivn, cix, 542, 766n, 796, ^{2}1191, ^{3}400, 657, ^{6}290, 291
Blomfield and ^{1}526; at Coleorton ^{2}245; C's estrangement from ^{1}xciv, cxiii; family offended ^{2}1120n; hexameters in letter to ^{1}671n–2n; letter to ^{2}131; move to Grasmere ^{1}cxi; project of sharing Greta Hall ^{1}cx

work(s) ^{2}29, 1161, 1162–3, ^{5}498n
covenant of ^{5}623; w.-days ^{3}471, 472, 581, ^{5}607, of meditation ^{5}795; doctrine of ^{2}703, ^{3}455, ^{5}497, 670; entireness of ^{5}316; and faith *see* faith; good ^{1}10–11, ^{2}655, 716, ^{5}135, 408n; greatest ^{4}403; w.-holiness ^{5}604, 604n; inspired ^{5}572; of the law ^{5}492; meaning of ^{2}501; merit of ^{3}604; purpose of ^{5}571; of righteousness ^{4}620; salvation by ^{2}1177

working(s) ^{3}564
powers of ^{5}654; spiritual ^{3}517, 517n, ^{6}299–300, 299n

workmen ^{6}22

world ^{1}602, ^{2}1021, 1106, ^{3}328, 348, 1042, ^{5}99, 142, 207, 721
aggregate of states ^{3}72; allness of ^{2}206; attributes of ^{6}75; Berkeley's analogy ^{4}114–15, 114n–15n; causative ^{5}615; Christian ^{4}642, ^{5}50; civilised ^{1}132, ^{5}51; to come ^{2}998; construction of ^{3}295–6; corporeal ^{4}448; cosmos ^{4}162; creation of ^{4}200, ^{5}607; destiny of ^{4}51; dispensations in ^{5}61; end of ^{2}38, ^{3}41, 60, 602, ^{5}624; eternity of ^{5}457; external ^{3}357, ^{5}370; final cause of ^{4}137; in flames ^{5}528; Gentile ^{5}415; and God *see* God; w.-God ^{2}1145, ^{4}409, ^{5}83, 83n; without God ^{2}788; governor of ^{5}457; ground of ^{5}730; happiness of ^{4}135; harmonious ^{2}629; heart of ^{3}601; intelligible ^{5}592; interpreted ^{3}62; invisible ^{4}141; law of ^{2}1175; Maker of ^{5}717; man of the ^{5}35; material ^{5}418, 421; moral ^{2}544; and nature ^{4}362; origin of ^{5}761; other ^{2}998, 998n–9n; outward ^{5}368; of phenomena ^{4}226; preservation of ^{3}949; problem of ^{2}995; redemption of ^{3}876; riddle of ^{2}601, 1018; of the senses ^{5}606; sensible ^{3}278n, 285, 285n, ^{5}592; soul of ^{1}180; Spinoza's view of ^{5}208; spirit w. ^{5}471; of spirits ^{5}424; spiritual ^{1}682, ^{2}313, ^{5}407, 410, 415, 452, 467, 473, 560n; w.-stuff ^{2}1002; symbol of ^{1}817; of time ^{5}57; ungodly ^{4}763; visible ^{1}179, ^{5}372, 633; wilderness ^{3}471; worldly ^{2}684

worldling ^{1}664, ^{2}926, ^{5}189

worldly-orthodox, the ^{5}229

Worldly-Wiseman, Mr (in Bunyan) ^{4}651n

world-soul ^{2}423–4, ^{5}713–14, 715n, 733n, 830n; see also *anima mundi*

worm(s) ^{2}569, 660, ^{3}324, 325, 377, 1037, ^{4}432n, 525, ^{5}177, 202, 287n
intestinal ^{1}460n; *see also* vermes

wormwood ^{5}155

"worship" ^{4}298–9

worship ^{3}495n, 1079, ^{4}625, ^{5}60, 505n
acceptable ^{5}483; ceremonial ^{3}722; of creature ^{2}743; forms of ^{1}204; Jewish ^{2}1153; of mechanism ^{3}77; public ^{1}324, ^{5}518; of relics ^{2}1158; three species of ^{5}510; true ^{1}846

Worship, William Taylor (fl 1818–32), letter to ^{1}xcix q

worth, inherent ^{3}459

Wotton Bassett ^{4}79n

Wotton, Sir Henry (1568–1639) ^{1}842–3, *843n*, ^{3}231n

wounds ^{3}438

Wrangham, Francis (1769–1842) ^{1}clx, 90, *90n*, 99n, ^{2}702n, ^{3}421n
letter to ^{6}216 q
Humble Contributions to a British Plutarch ^{6}216; *Life of Dr Richard Bentley* ^{1}377n, ^{3}731n, ^{4}6; MT ^{6}216–17; *Poems* ^{1}90n; *Scraps* MT ^{6}218–21; *Thirteen Practical Sermons* ^{1}90n, ^{6}335. See also *The British Plutarch*; Milton *Second De-*

fence ed Wrangham; Virgil *Bucolics* tr Wrangham
Wrangler(s) [3]821, 821n
wrath [3]61, 156
divine [2]160; of God [1]604–5, 608, 667–8
Wratislaw II, King of Bohemia (d 1092) [5]127
wriggling, itchy [1]394
Wright, Dr [3]101
Wright, Thomas (1711–86) [3]339
Wright, William (c 1794–1856) *Biblical Hermeneutics* [1]480–1
Wright, Wilmer Cave (?1866–1951) *see* Julian *Works* tr Wright
Wriothesley, Thomas, 4th Earl of Southampton (1607–67) [2]928, [3]803n
writ
holy [5]470; inspired [1]560
writer(s)
before Christ [4]649; duty of [2]781; elder [1]280, [5]229, 492; excellent [6]305; French [6]27; German [5]341; Greek and Latin [4]100; Hebrew [2]480; inspired [1]785, 805, 818, [2]375; medical [6]287; mystical [5]123; sacred [1]520, [2]286, 564; will of [1]401
Writer, Clement (fl 1627–58) [1]244
writing(s)
apostolic [3]685, 694, [5]520; controversial [5]526; disburthens/unloads memory [3]668, 687; for, not with, the age [5]89; French [2]238; inspired [2]1153, [6]65; manual somnambulism [1]808; modern [5]566; preservation of [5]516
wrong, private and public [2]941
Wroth, Lady Mary (fl 1621) [2]1127
Wyatt, Sir Matthew Digby (1820–77) [6]156
Wyatt, Sir Thomas (1503–42) [1]37
Wycherley, William (c 1640–1716) [2]83, [4]833n
Wycliffe, John (c 1329–84) [1]lxx, 858, [2]64, 64n, 507n, [3]142, 142n, [5]143 ("Wickliff"), 143n, [6]12–24
Wyndham, Henry Saxe (1867–1940) [6]246
Wynell, John (fl 1660–70) [2]362
Wynn, Charles Watkin Williams (1775–1850) [1]lxxiin, [5]124, 124n
letter to [5]121n q

Xavier, Francis, St (1506–52) [5]121, 121n
Xenocrates (c 395–314 BC) [5]733, 734
Xenophanes of Colophon (c 560–478 BC) [2]340n, 759n, [4]133, [5]703, 703n, 704, 704n, 707, 708–9
Xenophon (c 435–c 354 BC) [1]482n, [2]582, 831, [3]183, 622, [4]310, 310n, 311n, 631, [5]724n, 725n
Cyropaedia tr W. Miller [5]725–6 q; *Memoirs of Socrates* tr S. Fielding MT [6]222–3; *Memorabilia* [2]868n, 871n
Xerxes I, King of Persia (reigned 486–465 BC) [3]907
Ximenes (Francisco Jimenez de Cisneros) (1436–1517) [3]1068
xusmata [5]233n

Y [3]230, 230n
Yah [3]24n
Yahoo(s) [2]938, [5]477
Yahooism [5]476
Yahweh [1]417n, [3]28
Yajna (myth) [2]339
Yalden, Thomas (1670–1736) [1]38
Yale University *see* New Haven CT
Yarmouth [4]18n
Yates, Frances A. (1900–81) *The Art of Memory* [1]770n
yawn [1]370
year(s)
as days [5]349; measure of [4]201; Platonic [3]160, 160n; thousand [5]606
yearning(s) [1]600n, 653, 653n, 665n, [2]186, [3]399, 764, [4]463
yeast [6]39
Yeats, William Butler (1865–1939) [1]lxxv, 553
yellow [3]1017, 1018, [4]167
Yemen [5]308
yeomanry [1]290
yew [1]684, 777, [5]226
Yogacashta (myth) [2]584
yoke [4]699
York (city) [2]89, 1197n, 1199, [3]158, [4]630n
Convocation at [2]1150n; Cathedral [3]1042
York (county) [4]3, 96
York (people) [5]280
York, Duke of (later James II) [6]308n; *see also* Frederick Augustus
Yorke, Charles Philip (1764–1834) [4]18
Yorke, Philip, 1st Earl of Hardwicke (1690–1764) [3]500–2
Yorkshire [1]519n, 848, [4]633, [6]249
A Yorkshire Tragedy [3]702
"you" [3]809, [4]761
Young, Charles Mayne (1777–1856) [4]42, 42n

Young, Edward (1683–1765) [1]38, [2]17n, 761, [4]632
  "Life" by Anderson MT [1]50–1
  Complaint, or Night Thoughts [1]51, [3]886, 886n; *Love of Fame* [2]884n q; *Night Thoughts* see *Complaint*; *Revenge* [1]50, 50n; *Works* [1]50n
Young, H. S. (fl 1893) [2]873, 874
Young, Thomas (1773–1829) [3]936, 937, 939, 945n, [4]209n
  A Course of Lectures on Natural Philosophy† [6]224; *Syllabus* [1]39
Young, William [4]99
Young-Helmholtz Theory [4]209n
youth [1]657, [2]1088, [4]836n, 846
  unmarried [5]323
Yverdon [5]311n

Zacharias, father of John the Baptist (Bible) [4]481n
Zacharias, son of Barachias (Bible) [2]450
Zacheus (Bible) [2]256
Zagreus (myth) [2]584n
Zamolxis (legend) [5]364
Zangani, Cornelia, Countess [5]251, 252
zanyism [4]190
zeal [2]1197, [3]67, 492, 608, 1078, [4]251, [5]162
  excess of [5]651; inconsiderate [2]664; sabbatical [1]879; superiority of [1]515; warmth of [5]716
zealot(s), Protestant [4]24
Zelotae/Zealots [2]509, *509n*, 511, 515, 517, 833n, [3]147, [6]33, 33n
zealotry [5]529
Zebedee (Bible), sons of [2]447
zebra [4]535
Zechariah (Bible) [2]149n, 513, [3]112, 730
Zeitschrift für spekulative Physik ed F. W. J. Schelling [2]533, [4]274n, [5]245n, 762n; MT [6]225–45
Zelle *see* Celle
zenith [2]326, [4]167, [5]41
Zeno, St, Bishop of Verona (d 371) [2]666, 666n
Zeno of Citium (335–263 BC) [1]174n, [2]154n, 595, [4]158, 158n, 654, 654n, [5]225
Zeno of Elea (c 490–c 430 BC) [1]768, [2]340, 340n, 869n, [5]710–12, 719–20, 719n, 721, 733
zer [3]897
Zerah (Bible) [1]418
zero [1]562, 651, 651n, 689, [3]1050, 1051
  positive [1]562, 665, 665n, [2]1137n, [5]699, 699n, 701n
Zertrennlichkeit [4]425
Zerubbabel *see* Serubabel
zest [1]156
Zetlanders [4]606
"Zeus" [6]8, 8n
Zeus (in Aeschylus) [4]845n, 846n
Zeus (myth) [1]617, 617n, 675n, [2]583n, 584n, [3]473n, 729n, [4]118, [5]347n, 614, [6]7; *see also* Jupiter
Zigeuner [6]150n
zig-zag [5]726
Zimmermann, Eberhardt August Wilhelm von (1743–1815) *Geographische Geschichte des Menschen* [2]1048
Zimmern, Helen (1846–1934) [1]cli, clxvn, [2]1064
zinc [3]951
zingani/zingari [6]150, 150n
Zinzendorf, Nikolaus Ludwig, Count (1700–60) [1]736n, [3]493–4, 493n, 496, 497 q, [4]259, 259n, [5]128, 129, 130, 152, 153, 153n, 156, 156n, 166, 181, [6]83
  irreverence of [3]77, 77n
  Hymns [3]494n; *Maxims* ed Gambold [3]494n; *Sermons and Discourses* ed Rimius [3]494n; *Theologischer und dahin einschlagender Bedencken* [2]422, 423n, [6]83n; *see also* Moravian(s)
Zion/Sion [1]708, 708n, [3]478, 564
zodiac [5]157n
zoe [1]125, 126n
zohar [1]645n
Zohara (in Koran) [3]92n
"zoics" [3]278, 278n
zöium [1]572
zokar [1]419n
zoologists [3]1066
zoology [2]268, [4]448
zoomagnetism [1]581n, [2]458, 492, 492n–3n, 700n, 1011, [3]94, [5]136, 141, 411, 411n, [6]100
  as animal magnetism [2]41, 41n; *see also* animal magnetism
zoomagnetists [3]598, [5]136, 726, 786
zoometallic [1]577n
zoometallon [1]572
zoophyte(s) [1]578, 578n, 596n, [4]493, 525
"zooseptic" [4]149
"zoosophy" [5]347
zoosphere [3]383
zoote [1]572
Zoroaster (c 630–c 553 BC) [2]433, [5]222, 235, 237
  Oracula ed Patrizi [1]661n
Zoroastrian(s) [2]740n

Zoroastrianism [2]344n, 721n
"zote" [5]247, 247n
Zuinglius *see* Zwingli
Zulus [3]1081
Zumaque [5]105
Zündstoff [4]396, 396n
Zürich [2]304n
zürnen [4]285
zusammenhangen [4]520n
Zweckbegriff [2]631, 632n
Zwerg [4]594, 595n
Zwick, Henry Augustus (fl 1823) *Calmuc Tartary* MT [6]246
Zwingler, Theodorus (1533–88) [2]1083n
Theatrum vitae humanae [2]1082–3, 1083n
Zwingli, Huldreich/Ulrich (Ulricus Zuinglius) (1484–1531) [1]509n, 805, 805n, [2]304, *304n*, 668, [3]439, 439n, 515, 515n, 724, 759, 760, 760n, 761, 761n, [4]643, [5]398n, 671 ("Zwinglius"), 671n, [6]298, 298n
Zwinglian(s) [3]232n
Zwinglianism [5]398n